Direct Social Work Practice
Theory and Skills
Seventh Edition

Dean H. Hepworth
Professor Emeritus, University of Utah
Arizona State University

Ronald H. Rooney
University of Minnesota

Glenda Dewberry Rooney
Augsburg College

Kimberly Strom-Gottfried
University of North Carolina at Chapel Hill

Jo Ann Larsen
Private Practice, Salt Lake City

THOMSON

BROOKS/COLE

Australia • Canada • Mexico • Singapore • Spain • United Kingdom • United States

THOMSON

BROOKS/COLE

Direct Social Work Practice: Theory and Skills, Seventh Edition

Dean H. Hepworth, Ronald H. Rooney,
Glenda Dewberry Rooney, Kimberly
Strom-Gottfried, Jo Ann Larsen

Executive Editor: *Lisa Gebo*

Assistant Editor: *Alma Dea Michelena*

Editorial Assistant: *Sheila Walsh*

Technology Project Manager: *Barry Connolly*

Marketing Manager: *Caroline Concilla*

Marketing Assistant: *Rebecca Weisman*

Marketing Communications Manager: *Tami Strang*

Project Manager, Editorial Production: *Mary Noel*

Art Director: *Vernon Boes*

Print Buyer: *Barbara Britton*

Permissions Editor: *Sarah Harkrader*

Production Service: *Linda DeMasi, Stratford Publishing Services, Inc.*

Copy Editor: *Jill Hobbs*

Cover Designer: *Bill Stanton*

Compositor: *Integra Software Services Pvt. Ltd.,*

Printer: *Transcontinental/Louiseville*

Printed in Canada

1 2 3 4 5 6 7 09 08 07 06 05

For more information about our products, contact us at:
Thomson Learning Academic Resource Center
1-800-423-0563

For permission to use material from this text or product, submit a request online at **http://www.thomsonrights.com**. Any additional questions about permissions can be submitted by email to **thomsonrights@thomson.com**.

Library of Congress Control Number: 2005923883

Student Edition: ISBN 0-534-64458-9

Instructor's Edition: ISBN 0-495-00855-9

Thomson Higher Education
10 Davis Drive
Belmont, CA 94002-3098
USA

Asia (including India)
Thomson Learning
5 Shenton Way
#01–01 UIC Building
Singapore 068808

Australia/New Zealand
Thomson Learning Australia
102 Dodds Street
Southbank, Victoria 3006
Australia

Canada
Thomson Nelson
1120 Birchmount Road
Toronto, Ontario M1K 5G4
Canada

UK/Europe/Middle East/Africa
Thomson Learning
High Holborn House
50/51 Bedford Row
London WC1R 4LR
United Kingdom

Brief Contents

Contents

CHAPTER 3
OVERVIEW OF THE HELPING PROCESS   33

CHAPTER 4
OPERATIONALIZING THE CARDINAL SOCIAL WORK VALUES   54

CHAPTER 9
ASSESSMENT: INTRAPERSONAL AND ENVIRONMENTAL FACTORS   206

CHAPTER 11
FORMING AND ASSESSING SOCIAL WORK GROUPS   283

CHAPTER 17
ADDITIVE EMPATHY, INTERPRETATION, AND CONFRONTATION   521

CHAPTER 18
MANAGING BARRIERS TO CHANGE   542

Preface

Welcome to the seventh edition of *Direct Social Work Practice*. With this edition, Ron welcomes Glenda and Kim as full co-authors in the ongoing quest to provide students with the theory and empirically guided tools they need to begin direct social work practice.

Goals for the Seventh Edition

The prior six editions of *Direct Social Work Practice* have explicitly guided and modeled for social work students ways to implement practice skills. In this seventh edition, we integrate strengths-based and solution-focused interventions more extensively into a problem-solving framework.

With each new edition, we always seek to update the theory and knowledge base of the book. The text has reflected models and theories current in their day. Instructors familiar with prior editions will notice that, in streamlining and focusing the seventh edition, we have eliminated a chapter on problem-solving interventions

The book continues to emphasize diversity in direct practice through extensive examples, dialogues, and references.

We place direct practice skills in a current social and policy context as we consider social work's special niche. This emphasis flows from our commitment to work with clients in the context of their environments.

In addition, we incorporate technology into the learning of direct practice skills. Each chapter includes Internet resources as well as guides for use of InfoTrac College Edition®, an Internet retrieval service that you are entitled to receive free of charge for 4 months as a purchaser of this book. We also explore the dynamics of operating groups through technology in Chapter 16.

Theoretical Orientation

Direct Social Work Practice, seventh edition, addresses human problems from an ecological systems framework. We believe that direct social work practitioners assist clients in addressing such problems in the context of individual, couple, family, group, and environmental interventions. Those interventions are derived from the particular mission and values of the profession, drawing on the best available evidence to support their efficacy. We present a systematic–eclectic perspective requiring social work practitioners to draw from a variety of models, theories, and techniques to match the unique wants and needs of their clients. In selecting strategies for treatment, we are drawn to those approaches that are empirically grounded and fit social work values oriented to strengths and empowerment. Hence, the book is strongly influenced by task-centered, crisis intervention, cognitive-behavioral, and solution-focused approaches. We also include interventions on modifying environments as we take a multidimensional view toward assessment and intervention.

Structural Organization

The book has four parts. Part 1 introduces the reader to the social work profession and direct practice, and provides an overview of the helping process. Chapter 1 begins with a new example involving an immigrant teenager and her family. It introduces evidence-based approaches as a current influence on social work practice. Chapter 2 presents roles and the domain of the field. In the seventh edition, it now includes the supervisor role among systems and maintenance roles. Chapter 3 provides an overview of the helping process and highlights the greater emphasis on the solution-focused approach in this edition.

Part 1 concludes with Chapter 4, which presents the cardinal values of social work, including the emphasis on competence and integrity, and the operationalization of those values in ethical practice.

Part 2 presents the beginning phase of the helping process. It opens with Chapter 5, which focuses on relationship-building skills. Those skills include new emphases on communicating with clients regarding their rights to informed consent and confidentiality. Chapter 6 presents theories and skills related to eliciting concerns, exploring problems in depth, and providing direction and focus to sessions. Chapter 7 addresses barriers to communication. The revised list of these barriers includes a subset of concerns that are more likely to occur in situations of power imbalance. The title of Chapter 8 has changed to reflect its focus on the *process* of assessment and on problem and strengths exploration. It includes material on culturally competent and solution-focused assessments, as well as assessments with children. Chapter 9 covers the assessment of intrapersonal and environmental systems. It includes sample cases in the section on how to write assessments, provides a special section on mental status exams, and addresses the criteria in the DSM-IV TR, adding content on assessing affective and thought disorders.

Chapter 10 focuses on family assessment. It includes content on socioeconomic stressors as well as an array of instruments to assist in assessing family strengths and stressors. Chapter 11 addresses the formation of social work groups. The seventh edition adds materials on co-leadership, culturally specific groups, and practice in rural areas to this chapter. Chapter 12 presents practical new information on goal setting and recording in ways that are both efficient and client focused.

Part 3 presents the middle phase (goal attainment) of the helping process. It begins with Chapter 13, which describes change-oriented strategies, including updated material on task-centered, crisis intervention, and cognitive restructuring approaches. A new figure explains crisis intervention theory, and a culturally responsive case example highlights cognitive restructuring with an African American adolescent. The chapter also includes a presentation of the solution-focused approach to practice.

In Chapter 14, the focus shifts to modifying environments, developing resources, and empowering clients. This chapter includes new case examples presented within a current sociopolitical context for practice and addresses cultural competence at the agency level. Chapter 15 presents methods for enhancing family relationships and includes several new case examples. Chapter 16 describes theories and skills that are applicable to work with groups, including more examples of culturally specific groups, a discussion of group composition, a consideration of ethical practice with task –groups, and materials on single-session groups. Chapter 17 offers coverage of additive empathy, interpretation, and confrontation with new examples and references. Chapter 18 focuses on dealing with obstacles to change and likewise includes new references and case examples.

Part 4 deals with the terminal phase of the helping process. Chapter 19 incorporates material on evaluation and elaborates on termination to address group dropouts and terminations associated with client or social worker death.

Alternative Chapter Order

The seventh edition of this book has been structured around phases of practice at systems levels ranging from individual, to family, to group, to macro practice. Some instructors prefer to teach all content about a particular mode of practice in one block. In particular, those instructors whose courses emphasize individual contacts may choose to present chapters in a different order than we have organized them (see Table 1). They may teach content in Chapters 5–9, skip ahead to Chapters 12 and 13, and then delve into Chapters 17 and 18. Similarly, family content can be grouped by using Chapters 10 and 15 together, and

Table 1 Organization of chapters by mode of practice

MODE OF PRACTICE				
Across levels	Chapters 1–4	Chapter 19		
Individual		Chapters 5–9	Chapters 12 and 13	Chapters 17 and 18
Family		Chapters 10 and 15		
Group		Chapters 11 and 16		
Macro		Chapter 14		

groups by using Chapters 11 and 16 together. We have presented the chapters in the book in the current order because we think that presentation of intervention by phases fits a systems perspective better than beginning with a choice of intervention mode.

Acknowledgments

We would like to thank the following colleagues for their help in providing useful comments and suggestions. We have been supported by members of our writers' groups, including Terry Lum, Nancy Rodenborg, Karen Robards, Michael Chovanec, Ned Brooks, Joanne Caye, Susan Parish, Marci Thomas, Mary Altpeter, and George Gottfried. We also wish to thank Diane Wyant, Nikki Mowbray, Melissa Carmack, Anne-Marie Kupier, and Tara Tieso for their careful work in preparing the manuscript, including proofreading, preparing references, and indexing.. We also owe a debt of gratitude to our students—the users of this text—for their suggestions, examples, and encouragement.

We are very grateful to the reviewers of this edition, whose constructive criticisms and suggestions have been extremely helpful. They are Annecy Baez, New York University; Carolyn S. Carter, Juniata College; Nick Caruso, Arizona State University; A. Elizabeth Cauble, Kansas State University; Rebecca Chaisson, Tulane University; Mimi V. Chapman, University of North Carolina-Chapel Hill; Carolyn Dillon, Boston University; Sally Mathiesen, San Diego State University; Paula T. Morelli, University of Hawaii-Honolulu; Margaret M. Robinson, University of Georgia; Deborah Rougas, University of West Florida; Dorothy Stratton, Ashland University

Finally, this edition could not have been developed without the support, challenge, and inspiration of our friends and families, including George Gottfried, Chris Rooney, Lola Dewberry, Lou and Lesa DuBerry, Pat Rooney, Janet Williams and PHS '64, Finally, we want to express special appreciation for the enthusiasm, expertise, and patience of Lisa Gebo and her team at Brooks Cole.

About the Authors

Dean H. Hepworth is Professor Emeritus at the School of Social Work, Arizona State University, Tempe Arizona, and the University of Utah. Dean has extensive practice experience in individual psychotherapy, and marriage and family therapy. Dean was the lead author and active in the production of the first four editions, and he is the co-author of *Improving Therapeutic Communication*. He is now retired and lives in Phoenix, Arizona.

Ronald H. Rooney is Professor, School of Social Work, University of Minnesota, Twin Cities. Ron revised the 5th edition and 6th edition, with the assistance of the contributors. Ron's practice background is primarily in public and private child welfare, including work with involuntary clients, about which he does training and consultation. Ron is the author of *Strategies for Work with Involuntary Clients*.

Glenda Dewberry Rooney is a Professor at Augsburg College, Department of Social Work, Minneapolis, Minnesota. She teaches undergraduate and graduate direct practice courses, HBSE, ethics, child welfare, social work administrations and research. Glenda is involved with community agencies concerned with children, youth, and families as a trainer, advocate, and clinical and management consultant. Her collaboration with community agencies, including community based research projects has resulted in innovative approaches to client services. As an advocate she has been a catalyst for increasing the awareness of public officials, the media, and the community regarding the status of children of color in the child welfare system.

Kim Strom-Gottfried is Professor, School of Social Work, University of North Carolina at Chapel Hill. Kim revised and edited four chapters of this edition (chapters 4, 8, 9, and 20). Kim has extensive experience in direct service, administration, and planning in mental health. She provides training and consultation and research related to private practice, ethics, and managed care. Kim is the editor of *Social Work Practice: Cases, Activities and Exercises.*

Jo Ann Larsen is in private practice in Salt Lake City, Utah, and was formerly a faculty member at the School of Social Work, University of Utah. Jo Ann was active in the preparation of the first four editions of the book. Jo Ann has extensive experience in psychotherapy with individuals, families, and groups. Jo Ann is the author of four books on women's issues.

PART 1

Introduction

Part 1 of this book provides you with a background of concepts, values, historical perspectives, and information about systems. This information will, in turn, prepare you to learn the specific direct practice skills described in Part 2.

Chapter 1 introduces you to the social work profession; explains its mission, purposes, and values; and describes how systems perspectives can guide you in conceptualizing your work.

Chapter 2 elaborates on the roles played by social workers, including the distinctions made between clinical and direct social work practice, and presents a philosophy of direct practice.

Chapter 3 offers an overview of the helping process, including exploration, implementation, and termination.

Finally, Chapter 4 introduces the cardinal values and ethical concerns underlying social work.

The Challenges of Social Work

CHAPTER OVERVIEW

Chapter 1 introduces the mission of social work and the purposes of social work services, illustrates the roles played by social workers within the organizational context for such services, and identifies the value perspectives that guide social workers. Social workers attempt to understand the interactions of individuals and families with their environment by looking at those interactions through the lenses of ecology and systems. Some of the systems concepts useful to that understanding are illuminated in Chapter 1.

CASE EXAMPLE

Ayan, 15, is a Somalian refugee who lives with her aunt and uncle in a large city in the north central United States.[1] She has been referred to a school social worker, Jane Kringle, because her attendance at school has been sporadic recently. Upon talking to Ayan, the school social worker discovers that Ayan's aunt also considers her to be difficult in their home, ignoring family rules and disrespecting her uncle. For example, she has dated non-Somali boys against his wishes and has stopped wearing the traditional clothes preferred by Somalian women.

When Jane met with Ayan, she began by asking her how things were going for her in school. Jane then explained her own role in working with students—namely, interacting with those students who seek her assistance and those who are referred by parents and teachers. In Ayan's situation, Jane clarified that part of her role was to explore attendance problems and help students meet school attendance requirements. However, Jane also emphasized that she wanted to learn how Ayan viewed the situation and to assist her with her own concerns if possible.

Many social workers practice in settings such as schools in which they perform dual roles, protecting both the community at large and vulnerable persons as well as playing supportive roles (Trotter, 1999). No matter where they are employed, however, social workers are influenced by the social work value of self-determination. For this reason, in addition to exploring school attendance issues with Ayan and her aunt and uncle's concerns, the social worker explored Ayan's own concerns.

Ayan acknowledged that her attendance in class had been sporadic. Likewise, she agreed that relations were tense in her household. For her part, she insisted that adult immigrants from Somalia did not understand what it was like to be a teenager in an American high school. Although Ayan's name meant "lucky" in Somali, she did not feel lucky now. In fact, she felt very sad because her mother remained in a refugee camp in Africa and she suspected that her aunt and uncle were not doing all they could to help her mother immigrate.

Jane did not know whether Ayan's view of her aunt and uncle was accurate, but she nevertheless offered to explore the issue of her mother's immigration circumstances with Ayan's aunt and uncle. In addition, Jane asked Ayan about her willingness to address attendance issues and other household conflicts.

This case example highlights several aspects of social work practice. As a profession, we are committed to the pursuit of social justice for poor, disadvantaged, disenfranchised, and oppressed people (Finn & Jacobson, 2003; Pelton, 2003; Van Wormer, 2002; Carniol, 1992). In this case, in addition to seeing Ayan as being a troubled teen, Jane Kringle saw her as experiencing challenges caused by being detached from her biological mother and living as an immigrant. Of course, social workers are not the only helping professionals who provide direct services to clients in need. We have a special interest in helping empower members of oppressed groups (Parsons, 2002).

In fact, social workers work in quite diverse settings—governmental agencies, schools, health care centers, family and child welfare agencies, mental health centers, business and industry, correctional settings, and private practice. Social workers work with people of all ages, races, ethnic groups, socioeconomic levels, religions, sexual orientations, and abilities (see Table 1-1). Social workers themselves variously describe their work as rewarding, frustrating, satisfying, discouraging, stressful, and, most of all, challenging.

In the case example, Ayan did not seek assistance. Instead, she was *referred* by school staff because of her poor attendance. Meanwhile, her aunt and uncle acknowledged problems in living with Ayan in the home and requested assistance. Those who *apply* for services are most clearly *voluntary clients*. Many potential clients, including Ayan, become more voluntary if their own concerns are explicitly addressed. Social workers practice with clients whose level of voluntarism ranges from *applicants* who seek a service to *legally mandated clients* who receive services under the threat of a court order. Many potential clients fall between these two extremes, as they are neither legally coerced nor seeking a service (Trotter, 1999). These potential clients who experience nonlegal pressures from family members, teachers, and referral sources are known as *nonvoluntary clients*.

Table 1-1 Groups of people served by social workers

- Persons who are homeless
- Families who have problems of child neglect or sexual, physical, or spousal abuse
- Couples who have serious marital conflicts
- Families, including single-parent families, who have difficulties such as runaways, delinquency, or violence
- Persons with AIDS and their families
- Individuals and families who have law violations
- Unwed, pregnant teenagers
- Gay, lesbian, bisexual, or transgender persons with personal or family difficulties
- Individuals or families whose lives are disrupted by physical or mental illness or disability
- Persons who abuse substances such as drugs or alcohol and their families
- Foster parents, and children whose parents are deceased or who have been unable to safely care for them
- Immigrants and persons from oppressed groups who lack essential resources
- Persons with several physical or developmental disabilities and their families
- Aging persons seeking to live alone safely and those who are no longer able to care for themselves adequately
- Migrants and transients who lack essential resources
- Persons who are entering or returning to the job market after a period of public assistance
- Children (and their families) who have school-related difficulties
- Persons who experience high stresses related to traumatic events or to major life transitions such as retirement, the death of loved ones, children who leave home, or coming out (for gay, lesbian, and bisexual persons)
- Victims and perpetrators of domestic violence (though usually not served together)
- Victims of natural disasters

With each type of client (voluntary, legally mandated, and nonvoluntary), social work assessments include three facets:

1. Exploration of multiple concerns expressed by potential clients

2. Circumstances that might involve legally mandated intervention or concerns about health or safety

3. Other potential problems that emerge from the assessment

Such assessments also include strengths and potential resources. For example, the fact that Ayan is doing well in school, her ability to communicate her concerns clearly, and her willingness to acknowledge difficulties in the household are considered potential strengths.

THE MISSION OF SOCIAL WORK

The perspectives taken by social workers in their professional roles will influence how Ayan's concerns are conceptualized and addressed. According to the National Association of Social Workers (NASW), "the primary mission of the social work profession is to enhance human well-being and help meet the basic human needs of all people with particular attention to the needs and empowerment of people who are vulnerable, oppressed, and living in poverty" (NASW, 1999, p. 1). Similarly, the Council on Social Work Education (CSWE), the organization that accredits undergraduate and master's degree social work programs, describes the purpose of the social work profession as being "to enhance human well-being and alleviate poverty, oppression and other forms of social injustice" (CSWE, 2002, p. 6). Meanwhile, the International Federation of Social Workers defines the purpose of social work as including the promotion of social change and the empowerment and liberation of people to enhance well-being (IFSW, 2000, p 1). Recent reviews of the definition of the mission of social work maintain the focus on marginalized peoples and empowerment, but add an emphasis on global and cultural sensitivity (Bidgood, Holosko, & Taylor, 2003).

In this book, we will delineate the core elements that lie at the heart of social work wherever it is practiced. These core elements can be classified into four dimensions:

1. Purposes of the profession

2. Values and ethics

3. Knowledge base of direct practice

4. Methods and processes employed

Chapter 1 considers the first three dimensions. The fourth dimension is discussed in Chapter 3, where it helps to draw the "big picture" of the helping process and sets the stage for the remainder of the book.

PURPOSES OF SOCIAL WORK

Social work practitioners help clients move toward specific objectives. The means of accomplishing those objectives, however, varies based on the unique circumstances of each client. Even so, all social workers share common goals that constitute the purpose and objectives of the profession. These goals unify the profession and help members avoid developing too-narrow perspectives that are limited to particular practice settings.

To best serve their clients, social workers must be willing to assume responsibilities and engage in actions that expand upon the functions of specific social agencies and their designated individual roles as staff members. For example, the social worker who met with Ayan assessed issues and concerns with her that went beyond the educational mission of the public school setting.

CSWE describes the social work profession as receiving its sanction from public and private auspices, as the primary profession in the provision of social services, and as practiced in a wide range of settings (CSWE, 2002, p. 6). CSWE describes social work as having six purposes.

1. Social work should "enhance human well-being and alleviate poverty, oppression and other forms of social injustice" (CSWE, 2002, p. 6) The social worker's commitment to assist Ayan in seeking information about and possibly

providing assistance to her mother in the quest for immigration is consistent with this purpose.

2. Social work should "enhance the social functioning of individuals, families, groups, organizations, and communities by involving them in accomplishing goals, developing resources, and preventing and alleviating distress" (CSWE, 2002, p. 6). This purpose suggests that the social worker might assist Ayan in enhancing the functioning of her family living unit. For example, the client system might evolve from including solely Ayan to include her aunt and uncle and possibly the whole family unit. Ayan might also be connected to a recreational program or other resource designed to meet new needs as they are expressed. Social workers perform preventive, restorative, and remedial functions in pursuit of this purpose.

- *Prevention* involves the timely provision of services to vulnerable persons, promoting social functioning before problems develop. It includes programs and activities such as family planning, well-baby clinics, parent education, premarital and pre-retirement counseling, and marital enrichment programs.

- *Restoration* seeks to restore functioning that has been impaired by physical or mental difficulties. Included in this group of clients are persons with varying degrees of paralysis caused by severe spinal injury, individuals afflicted with chronic mental illness, persons with developmental disabilities, persons with deficient educational backgrounds, and individuals with many other types of disability.

- *Remediation* entails the elimination or amelioration of existing social problems. Clients in need of remedial services form the largest group served by social workers and include all the groups listed in Table 1-1 as well as many others. Many potential clients in this category are similar to Ayan in that they have been referred by others such as family members, neighbors, and doctors who have perceived a need; others may be legally mandated to receive services (Rooney, 1992) rather than seeking out the services on their own.

Enhancing social functioning involves addressing common human needs that must be adequately met to enable individuals to achieve a reasonable degree of fulfillment and to function as productive and contributing members of society. Essential resources and opportunities must be available to meet these human needs, and social workers are vitally involved in utilization and development of those resources. Indeed, Rosenfeld (1983) defines the domain of social work practice as consisting of incongruities or discrepancies between needs and resources that systems and social institutions have not managed adequately. Social workers aim "to match resources with needs to increase the 'goodness of fit' between them, largely by harnessing potential provider systems to perform this function" (p. 187). Tapping into these resources generally involves enhancing transactions between people and their social or physical environments. To further clarify the transactions between individual needs and environmental resources, social workers consider certain basic needs and the loci of resources that correspond to those needs.

These interactions are graphically demonstrated in Table 1-2, which shows how people depend on the environment for the fulfillment of their basic needs. Thus, social work practice is directed to the interface between people and their environments.

Problems that arise at this interface are not exclusively caused by environmental deficiencies, of course. Many clients have an impaired ability to utilize the available resources. Practitioners, therefore, often must focus their efforts on helping clients develop the interpersonal skills required to reduce the mismatch between their own needs and the available environmental resources (see Table 1-2).

3. Social work focuses on the "planning, formulation and implementation of social policies, services, resources, and programs needed to meet basic human needs and support the development of human capacities" (CSWE, 1995, p. 135). This purpose suggests that although some social workers provide direct services to clients, others act indirectly to influence the environments supporting clients, thereby developing and maintaining the social infrastructure that assists clients in meeting their needs.

Table 1-2 Human needs and related loci of resources

HUMAN NEEDS	LOCI OF RESOURCES
Positive self-concept: Identity Self-esteem Self-confidence	Nurturance, acceptance, love, and positive feedback provided by significant others (parents, relatives, teachers, peer group)
Emotional: Feeling needed and valued by others Companionship Sense of belonging	Parents, marital partner, friends, siblings, cultural reference groups, and social networks
Personal fulfillment: Education Recreation Accomplishment Aesthetic satisfaction Religion	Educational, recreational, religious, employment, and other social institutions
Physical needs: Food, clothing, housing Health care Safety Protection	Economic, legal, and health care institutions; formal social welfare systems; law enforcement; and disaster relief organizations

4. Social work seeks to "formulate and implement social policies, services and programs that meet basic human needs and support the development of human capacities" (CSWE, 2002, p. 6).

5. Social workers "pursue policies, services and resources through advocacy and social or political actions that promote social and economic justice" (CSWE, 2002, p. 6). Both the fourth and fifth purposes demonstrate social workers' commitment to implement policies and services that pursue the three goals of meeting human needs, developing capacities, and promoting social and economic justice. They are also reflected in the second value in the social work Code of Ethics: "Social workers challenge social injustice" (NASW, 1999). This value encourages social workers to pursue social change on behalf of vulnerable or oppressed people who are subject to poverty, discrimination, and other forms of injustice. The focus of efforts

geared toward populations at risk should increase the power of these individuals to influence their own lives.

The CSWE's curriculum policy statement also requires that social work education programs "[u]nderstand the forms and mechanisms of oppression and discrimination and apply strategies of advocacy and social change that advance social and economic justice" (CSWE, 2002, p. 9). If resources and opportunities are to be available to all members of society, then laws, governmental policies, and social programs must assure equal access of citizens to those resources and opportunities. Social workers promote social justice by advocating for clients who have been denied services, resources, or goods to which they are entitled. They also work to develop new resources to meet emerging needs.

Unfortunately, social work clients are often disempowered because of their membership in devalued and oppressed groups. Achieving social justice requires working on many levels to restore power and efficacy to members of such disempowered groups (Parsons, 2002). Social workers must also actively combat racism, sexism, and other forms of discrimination that threaten to block their clients' access to resources.

This purpose also means that social work efforts must target populations deemed to be "at risk." To ensure that this purpose is met, social work educational programs "must prepare social workers to practice without discrimination, with respect and with knowledge and skills related to clients' age, class, color, culture, disability, ethnicity, family structure, gender, marital status, national origin, race, religion, sex, and sexual orientation" (CSWE, 2002, p. 7).

In promoting social and economic justice for at-risk populations, social workers in direct practice join with other social workers and groups to promote social action and legislation that redress wrongs resulting from unfair decisions and dysfunctional policies and practices. Moreover, they advocate for programs and resources that will increase opportunities and enhance the welfare of disadvantaged people. In particular, they speak out on behalf of people who are unable to advocate effectively for themselves, such as persons with developmental disabilities or severe mental illness.

The objective of promoting social and economic justice merits a renewed commitment by social workers given the conservative trends in the political climate over the past three decades (Specht & Courtney, 1994). Providers of social services and their clientele have suffered major setbacks in recent years, as the United States has sought to cope with the terrorist attacks of September 11, 2001, the movement from a strong to a declining economy, the shift from budget surpluses to budget deficits, tax cuts geared toward the upper income tiers, and losses of domestic jobs to overseas workers. In an even earlier era, the radical restructuring of the government's approaches to poverty of women and children in the form of Pub. L. No. 104–193, the Personal Responsibility and Work Opportunity Reconciliation Act of 1996, "ended welfare as we know it" (Hagen, 1998). Specifically, work requirements for women were increased even though no guarantee of child care support was provided. In addition, educational assistance was decreased. In another blow, the specific circumstances of women who tend to work in the part-time, low-wage, low-benefit services sector were not addressed. In essence, the law increased the accountability demanded from recipients of aid without requiring comparable accountability from state and federal governments regarding the types of employment attained and income levels of those women (Hagen, 1998). Recognizing these discrepancies, social workers need to advocate for the welfare of low-income families and children and monitor whether services and supports are actually sufficient to reduce poverty and improve the welfare of children.[2]

Some have argued that today's social workers espouse social justice but no longer prioritize strategies to achieve it—that as a profession we have aimed more at protecting social work roles than at transforming social services delivery (Jacobson, 2001). Others have expressed the opinion that the fighting spirit of social work advocacy at multiple levels has never been more necessary than in the current era of uncaring economic forces and resurrected punitiveness (Van Wormer, 2002). We agree with Van Wormer. Reflecting this view, this book places the teaching and practice of direct practice skills in a context of an environment that is often hostile to clients.

6. Social work focuses on "[t]he development and testing of professional knowledge and skills related to [the prior five] purposes" (CSWE, 1995, p. 140). Members of the social work profession try to expand the knowledge base for assisting clients by providing services that are efficient, ethical, and effective. Social work is now feeling the influence of evidence-based treatment, which strives to base treatment on the best available information (Thyer, 2002). This purpose suggests that social workers should seek out practice-related research findings to inform their choice of practice alternatives and should share those findings with clients.

This purpose is also reflected in the sixth value in the NASW Code of Ethics: "Social workers practice within their areas of competence and develop and enhance their professional expertise" (NASW, 1996). This value commits individual social work practitioners to continually increase their professional knowledge and skills and to "aspire to contribute to the knowledge base of the profession."

SOCIAL WORK VALUES

All professions have value preferences that give purpose and direction to their practitioners. Indeed, the purpose and objectives of social work and other professions emanate from their respective value systems. Professional values, however, are not separate from societal values. Rather, professions espouse selected societal values. Society, in turn, sanctions the activities of professions through supportive legislation, funding, delegation of responsibility for certain societal functions, and mechanisms for ensuring that those functions are adequately discharged. Because a profession is linked to certain societal values, it tends to serve as society's conscience with respect to those particular values.

Values represent strongly held beliefs about how the world should be, about how people should normally behave, and about what the preferred conditions of life are. Broad societal values in the United States are reflected in the Declaration of Independence, the Constitution, and the laws of the land, which declare and ensure certain rights of the people. In addition, societal values are reflected in governmental entities and programs designed to safeguard the rights of people and to promote the common good. Interpretations of values and rights, however, are not always uniform. Consider, for example, the heated national debate over the right of women to have abortions; the controversy over the rights of gays, lesbians, and bisexuals to enjoy the benefits of marriage; and conflicts between advocates of gun control and those espousing individual rights.

The values of the social work profession also reflect strongly held beliefs about the rights of people to free choice and opportunity. They recognize the preferred conditions of life that enhance people's welfare, ways that members of the profession should view and treat people, preferred goals for people, and ways in which those goals should be reached. We next consider five values and purposes that guide social work education. Chapter 4 will examine these values and describe others that are contained in the NASW Code of Ethics. These five values are italicized, and the content that follows each is our commentary.

1. *Social workers' professional relationships are built on regard for individual worth and dignity, and are advanced by mutual participation, acceptance, confidentiality, honesty, and responsible handling of conflict* (CSWE, 1995, p. 139). This value is also reflected in several parts of the Code of Ethics. The first value of the code is simple: "Social workers' primary goal is to serve" (NASW, 1999, p. 5). That is, service to others is elevated above self-interest and social workers should use their knowledge, values, and skills to help people in need and to address social problems. The second value states that they serve others in a fashion such that "social workers respect the inherent dignity and

worth of the person." Every person is unique and has inherent worth; therefore, social workers' interactions with people as they pursue and utilize resources should enhance their dignity and individuality, enlarge their competence, and increase their problem-solving and coping abilities.

People who receive social work services are often overwhelmed by their difficult circumstances and have exhausted their coping resources. Many feel stressed by a multitude of problems. In addition to helping clients reduce their stress level, practitioners aid clients in many other ways: They help them view their difficulties from a fresh perspective, consider various remedial alternatives, foster awareness of strengths, mobilize both active and latent coping resources, enhance self-awareness, and teach problem-solving strategies and interpersonal skills.

Social workers perform these functions while recognizing "the central importance of human relationships" (NASW, 1999, p. 5). This principle suggests that social workers engage clients as partners in purposeful efforts to promote, restore, maintain, and enhance the clients' well-being. This value is reflected in yet another Code of Ethics principle: "Social workers behave in a trustworthy manner" (p. 6). This principle suggests that social workers practice consistently with the profession's mission, values, and ethical standards, and that they promote ethical practices in the organizations with which they are affiliated (p. 6).

2. *Social workers respect the individual's right to make independent decisions and to participate actively in the helping process* (CSWE, 1995, p. 139). People have a right to freedom as long as they do not infringe on the rights of others. Therefore, transactions with people who are seeking and utilizing resources should enhance their independence and self-determination. Too often in the past, social workers and other helping professionals have focused on "deficit, disease and dysfunction" (Cowger, 1992). The attention currently devoted to empowerment and strengths behooves social workers to assist clients in increasing their personal potential and political power such that clients can improve their life

situation (Finn & Jacobson, 2003; Parsons, 2002; Saleebey, 1997). Consistent with this value, this book incorporates an empowerment and strength-oriented perspective for working with clients. Chapter 13 focuses on skills designed to enhance clients' empowerment and capacity for independent action.

3. *Social workers are committed to assisting client systems to obtain needed resources.* People should have access to the resources they need to meet life's challenges and difficulties as well as access to opportunities to realize their potentialities throughout their lives. Our commitment to client self-determination and empowerment is hollow if clients lack access to the resources necessary to achieve their goals (Hartman, 1993). Because people such as Ayan from the case example often know little about available resources, practitioners must act as brokers by referring people to resource systems such as public legal services, health care agencies, child welfare divisions, mental health centers, centers for elderly persons, and family counseling agencies. Some individual clients or families may require goods and services from many different providers and may lack the language facility, physical or mental capacity, experience, or skills needed to avail themselves of essential goods and services. Practitioners then may assume the role of case manager; that is, they may not only provide direct services but also assume responsibility for linking the client to diverse resources and ensuring that the client receives needed services in a timely fashion. The broker and case manager roles are discussed in Chapters 2 and 14.

Clients sometimes need resource systems that are not available. In these cases, practitioners must act as program developers by creating and organizing new resource systems. Examples of such efforts include the following: working with citizens and public officials to arrange transportation to health care agencies for the elderly, persons with disabilities, and indigent people; developing neighborhood organizations to campaign for better educational and recreational programs; organizing tenants to assert their rights to landlords and housing authorities for improved

housing and sanitation; and organizing support groups, skill development groups, and self-help groups to assist people in coping with difficult problems of living.

Social workers also frequently pursue this goal by facilitating access to resources. They perform the role of facilitator or enabler in carrying out the following functions: enhancing communication among family members; coordinating efforts of teachers, school counselors, and social workers in assisting troubled students; helping groups provide maximal support to their members; opening channels of communication between coworkers; including patients or inmates in the governance of institutions; facilitating teamwork among members of different disciplines in hospitals and mental health centers; and providing for consumer input into agency policy-making boards. Later chapters in this book deal specifically with this objective.

4. *Social workers strive to make social institutions more humane and responsive to human needs.* Although direct practitioners work primarily in providing direct service, they also have a responsibility to work toward improving clients' quality of life by promoting policies and legislation that enhance physical and social environments. The problems of individuals, families, groups, and neighborhoods can often be prevented or at least ameliorated by implementing laws and policies that prohibit contamination of the physical environment and enrich both physical and social environments. Therefore, direct social workers should not limit themselves to remedial activities but rather should seek out environmental causes of problems and sponsor or support efforts aimed at improving their clients' environments. Chapters 14 and 18 discuss this topic at greater length.

Social workers also demonstrate this value when they assume the role of expediter or troubleshooter by scrutinizing the policies and procedures of their own and other organizations to determine whether their clients have ready access to resources and whether services are delivered in ways that enhance their clients' dignity. Complex application procedures, needless delays in providing resources and services, discriminatory policies, inaccessible agency sites, inconvenient service delivery hours, dehumanizing procedures or staff behaviors—these and other factors may deter clients from utilizing resources or subject them to demeaning experiences.

Systematically obtaining input from consumers is one method of monitoring an organization's responsiveness to clients. Advocacy actions in conjunction with and on behalf of clients are sometimes required to secure the services and resources to which clients are entitled (as discussed in more detail in Chapters 14 and 18). Social workers may support this value by performing the roles of coordinator, mediator, or disseminator of information. For example, as a case manager, a social worker may coordinate the medical, educational, mental health, and rehabilitative services provided to a given family by multiple resource systems. A mediator may be required to resolve conflicts between agencies, minority and majority groups, and neighborhood groups. The social worker may disseminate information regarding legislation or new funding sources that could potentially affect the relationships between public and private agencies by strengthening interactions between these resource systems.

Social workers must also collaborate with key organizations to facilitate mutual awareness of changes in policies and procedures that affect ongoing relationships and the availability of resources.

5. *Social workers demonstrate respect for and acceptance of the unique characteristics of diverse populations.* Social workers perform their services with populations that are characterized by great diversity, including "groups distinguished by race, ethnicity, culture, class, gender, sexual orientation, religion, physical or mental ability, age, and national origin" (CSWE, 1995, p. 140). Similarly, NASW's Code of Ethics requires social workers to understand cultures, recognize strengths in cultures, have a knowledge base of their clients' cultures, and deliver services that are sensitive to those cultures (NASW, 1999, 1.05). This value suggests that social workers must be informed about and respectful of differences. They must educate themselves over time as a part

of lifelong learning—unfortunately, there is no "how-to" manual that will guide the practitioner in understanding all aspects of diversity. To demonstrate this value, the practitioner must continually update his or her knowledge about the strengths and resources associated with individuals from such groups to increase the sensitivity and effectiveness of the services provided to those clients.

An increasing number of social workers are themselves members of these diverse populations. They face the challenge of working effectively with both clients and agency staff from the majority culture as well as persons from their own group.

Values and Ethics

Turning the five values described above into reality should be the mutual responsibility of individual citizens and of society. Society should foster conditions and provide opportunities for citizens to participate in policy-making processes. Citizens, in turn, should fulfill their responsibilities to society by actively participating in those processes.

Considered individually, these five values and the profession's mission are not unique to social work. Their unique combination, however, differentiates social work from other professions. Considered in their entirety, these ingredients make it clear that social work's identity derives from its connection with the institution of social welfare. According to Gilbert (1977), social welfare represents a special helping mechanism devised to aid those who suffer from the variety of ills found in industrial society: "Whenever other major institutions, be they familial, religious, economic, or educational in nature, fall short in their helping and resource providing functions, social welfare spans the gap" (p. 402).

These five values represent the prized ideals of the profession and, as such, are stated at high levels of abstraction. As Siporin (1975) and Levy (1973) have noted, however, different levels of professional values exist. At an intermediate level, values pertain to various segments of society—for example, characteristics of a strong community.

At a third level, values are more operational, referring to preferred behaviors.

For example, the ideal social work practitioner is a warm, caring, open, and responsible person who safeguards the confidentiality of information disclosed by clients. Because you, the reader, have chosen to enter the field of social work, most of your personal values probably coincide with the cardinal values espoused by the majority of social work practitioners. By contrast, at the intermediate and third levels of values, your views may not always be in harmony with the specific value positions taken by the majority of social workers.

Self-determination refers to the right of people to exercise freedom of choice when making decisions. Issues such as those described above may pose value dilemmas for individual practitioners because of conflicts between personal and professional values. In addition, conflicts between two professional values or principles are common. Public positions taken by the profession that emanate from its values also sometimes stand in opposition to the attitudes of a large segment of society. For example, professional support for universal health coverage has not been endorsed by the U.S. Congress (Webber, 1995).

We suggest that social workers should be sufficiently flexible to listen to many differing value positions on most moral and political issues. Different value positions do not necessarily reflect divergence among social workers on the five core values of the social work profession. Rather, they reflect the existence of many means of achieving given ends. Indeed, rigid assumptions about preferred means to an end often crumble when put to the test of hard experience. Consistent with our preference for flexibility, we reaffirm our commitment to the value that social workers, whatever their beliefs, should assert them in a forum of professional organizations such as NASW. We maintain further that social workers should accord colleagues who differ on certain value positions the same respect, dignity, and right to self-determination that would be accorded clients. Differences on issues may be frankly expressed. Those issues can be clarified and cohesiveness among professionals can be fostered by debate conducted in a climate of openness and mutual respect.

Conflicts between personal and/or professional values and the personal values of a client or group sometimes arise. Not infrequently, students (and even seasoned practitioners) experience conflicts over value-laden, problematic situations such as incest, infidelity, rape, child neglect or abuse, spousal abuse, and criminal behavior. Because direct practitioners encounter these and other problems typically viewed by the public as appalling, and because personal values inevitably shape the social worker's attitudes, perceptions, feelings, and responses to clients, it is vital that you remain flexible and nonjudgmental in your work. It is equally vital that you be aware of your own values, recognize how they fit with the profession's values, and assess how they may affect clients whose values differ from your own or whose behavior offends you.

Because values are critical determinants of behavior in interactions with clients and other professional persons, we have devoted Chapter 4 to practice situations involving potential value dilemmas, including exercises to assist you in expanding your awareness of your personal values. Chapter 4 also deals at length with the relationship-enhancing dimension of respect and contains exercises to assist you in responding respectfully to value-laden situations that may potentially be painful for both you and your clients.

Social Work's Code of Ethics

An essential attribute of legitimate professions is a code of ethics consisting of principles that define expectations of each profession's members. A code of ethics specifies rules of conduct to which members must adhere so as to remain in good standing within a professional organization. It thus defines expected responsibilities and behaviors as well as prescribed behaviors. Central to the purposes of a code of ethics is its function as a formalized expression of accountability of (1) the profession to the society that gives it sanction, (2) constituent practitioners to consumers who utilize their services, and (3) practitioners to their profession. By promoting accountability, a code of ethics serves additional vital purposes, including the following:

1. It safeguards the reputation of a professional by providing explicit criteria that can be employed to regulate the behavior of members.
2. It furthers competent and responsible practice by its members.
3. It protects the public from exploitation by unscrupulous or incompetent practitioners.

Most states now have licensing boards that certify social workers for practice and review allegations of unethical conduct (Land, 1988; DeAngelis, 2000). Similarly, local and state chapters of the NASW establish committees of inquiry to investigate alleged violations of the profession's Code of Ethics, and national committees provide consultation to local committees and consider appeals of decisions made by local chapters. We have blended the values in the code of ethics above in our presentation of the five values stated by CSWE.

KNOWLEDGE BASE OF SOCIAL WORK PRACTICE

One of the core elements of social work practice is the knowledge base that underlies it. Although much of this knowledge base is borrowed from other disciplines in the social and behavioral sciences, it is organized in unique ways in social work practice. Other basic concepts are unique to social work.

The profession's universe of knowledge can be organized into the following five categories, which are regarded as core curriculum areas by the CSWE.

1. *Human behavior and the social environment.* Knowledge about "human bio-psycho-social development, including theories about the range of social systems in which individuals live (families, groups, organizations, and communities)" (CSWE, 1995, pp. 139–140) is required to function effectively as a social worker. Such knowledge, including that of human growth and

development with particular emphasis on the life tasks encountered by individuals during different developmental stages, is essential to practitioners. To assess and work with human problems, practitioners must be aware of the needs and resources associated with each developmental theme. They must also become aware of how these needs are identified and met in different cultures.

Knowledge of ecological systems theory, which we discuss later in this chapter, is also essential, as is knowledge about the forces that motivate behavior in groups and organizations. As part of its mission of enhancing the social functioning of people, social work pays special attention to the factors that contribute to developmental difficulties. Understanding the effects of these factors, which commonly involve inadequate physical and emotional resources, is essential to planning and implementing effective preventive and remedial programs. Social work's focus on the person in a situation is reflected in "the ways in which systems promote or deter people in the maintaining or achieving of optimal health and well-being" (CSWE, 1995, p. 141).

2. *Social welfare policy and services.* Content in this curriculum area "must be presented about the political and organizational processes used to influence policy, the process of policy formulation, and the frameworks for analyzing social policies in light of principles of social and economic justice" (CSWE, 1995, p. 141).

Social work's emphasis on knowledge concerned with social policy most sharply differentiates its curricula from the curricula of related disciplines. This broad body of knowledge embodies the complex factors involved in the formulation of social policies that shape and guide planning of human service systems at all levels of government as well as in the private sector. To practice in full accordance with the mission and ethics of the profession, social workers have a responsibility to participate in developing and utilizing social policies that enhance the social functioning of individuals, families, groups, and communities. Their study of social welfare policy and services must occur in the context of the profession's commitment to social and economic justice. In particular, social work must address the consequences of oppressed conditions (Longres, 1991). Knowledge of inequities in the distribution of opportunities, resources, goods, and services in the United States, and the effects of these inequities on minority and disadvantaged groups, are essential to social work practitioners (Brill, 1990).

3. *Social work practice methods.* These methods "focus on strengths, capacities and resources of client systems in relation to their broader environments" (CSWE EPAS, IV F, 1996). Further, social workers must be able to identify issues, problems, resources, and assets. That is, the social work practitioner must identify, analyze, and implement empirically based interventions to achieve client goals while simultaneously promoting social and economic justice (CSWE EPAS, IV F, 1996).

To do so, social workers need knowledge and practice skills that enable them to enhance the social functioning of clients. Knowledge of and skills in practice methods vary according to the level of client system served by practitioners. These levels have been designated as *micro, mezzo,* and *macro*.

Effective practice requires knowledge related to all three levels of practice. Nevertheless, schools of social work commonly offer "concentrations" in either micro or macro practice and require less preparation in the other methods. Curricula vary, of course. Some schools have generalist practice curricula, which require students to achieve balanced preparation in all three levels of practice. Undergraduate programs and the first year of graduate programs typically feature generalist practice curricula, which aim to prepare students for working with all levels of client systems.

The practice methods that correspond to the three levels of practice are as follows:

• *Micro-level practice.* At this level, the population served by practitioners includes a variety of client systems, including individuals, couples, and families. Practice at the micro level is designated as direct (or clinical) practice because

practitioners deliver services directly to clients in face-to-face contact. Direct practice, however, is by no means limited to such face-to-face contact, as we discuss in Chapter 2.

• *Mezzo-level practice.* The second level is defined as "interpersonal relations that are less intimate than those associated with family life; more meaningful than among organizational and institutional representatives; [including] relationships between individuals in a self-help or therapy group, among peers at school or work or among neighbors" (Sheafor, Horejsi, & Horejsi, 1994, pp. 9–10). Mezzo events are "the interface where the individual and those most immediate and important to him/her meet" (Zastrow & Kirst-Ashman, 1990, p. 11). Mezzo intervention is hence designed to change the systems that directly affect clients, such as the family, peer group, or classroom.

• *Macro-level practice.* Still further removed from face-to-face delivery of services, macro practice involves the processes of social planning and community organization. On this level, social workers serve as professional change agents who assist community action systems composed of individuals, groups, or organizations to deal with social problems. For example, social workers may work with citizen groups or with private, public, or governmental organizations. Activities of practitioners at this level include the following: (1) development of and work with community groups and organizations; (2) program planning and development; and (3) implementation, administration, and evaluation of programs (Meenaghan, 1987).

Administration entails playing a leadership role in human service organizations that seek to effectively deliver services in accordance with the values and laws of society. It includes the processes involved in policy formulation and subsequent translation of that policy into operational goals, program design and implementation, funding and resource allocation, management of internal and interorganizational operation, personnel direction and supervision, organizational representation and public relations, community education, monitoring, evaluation, and innovation to improve organizational productivity (Sarri, 1987, pp. 29–30). Direct practitioners are necessarily involved to some degree in administrative activities, as we discuss in Chapter 2. In addition, many direct practitioners who hold master's degrees become supervisors or administrators later in their professional careers. Knowledge of administration, therefore, is vital to direct practitioners at the master's degree level, and courses in administration are frequently part of the required master's degree curriculum in social work. Although many direct practitioners engage in little or no macro-level practice, those who work in rural areas where practitioners are few and specialists in social planning are not available may work in concert with concerned citizens and community leaders in planning and developing resources to prevent or combat social problems.

4. *Research.* Social work students study research so as to have "a scientific, analytic and ethical approach to building knowledge for practice" (CSWE EPAS, IV G, 1996). Research is used to support the assessment and identification of high-quality services; to improve practice, policy, and service delivery; and to evaluate the social workers' own practice (CSWE EPAS, IV G, 1996). In addition, the movement toward evidence-based practice requires practitioners to have skills in finding and assessing evidence for interventions (Thyer, 2002).

5. *Field practicum.* The field practicum is designed to support the integration of empirical and practice-based knowledge and promote professional competence (CSWE EPAS, IV H, 1996). Graduates of social work programs consistently report that their experiences in the field practicum are integral to their learning how to practice as responsible professionals. Your learning of content in your classroom courses and from this book will be greatly enhanced if you have the opportunity to apply your knowledge, values, and skills in the field and receive modeling and appropriate feedback from your field instructor.

PRACTICING COMPETENTLY: AN ETHICAL REQUIREMENT

According to the profession's Code of Ethics, "social workers practice within their areas of competence and develop and enhance their professional expertise" (NASW, 1996, p. 4). Consequently, attaining and maintaining competence in practice is an ethical requirement of social workers. To meet this requirement, aspiring social workers must achieve proficiency in a broad range of activities. The rationale for this requirement is compelling because much is at stake for consumers of social work services.

Clients have a right to expect competent services from professional social workers. Some have argued that to assure this competence, social workers should be prepared to deliver empirically supported interventions (Myers & Thyer, 1997). Where available, then, social workers should be guided by synthesized knowledge from empirical research. Of course, sometimes the conditions under which research was conducted do not match the situation in which you find yourself in an agency (Lambert & Ogles, 2004). Also, knowledge is less well developed in some newer areas of practice. In such circumstances, social workers should be aware of and guided by expert consensus (Rosen & Proctor, 2001). You are ethically responsible as a social worker for being aware of evidence of effectiveness. While it is not possible to have expertise in the entire range of concerns dealt with by social workers, you and the agencies that support your practicum or employment can be expected to be knowledgeable about the principal concerns of your client group and social problem and aware of the preferred practice for that group and problem based on the best available data (Thyer & Wodarski, 2004; Thyer, 2002).

Evolving Theory and Competence

Possessing skills alone does not ensure competence—after all, without an underlying knowledge base, a social worker practitioner would simply be a technician. To analyze problems, persons, and situations; to plan remedial interventions; and to implement appropriate techniques requires an adequate grasp of practice theory and knowledge about human behavior in the social environment.

The social work practitioner uses his or her skills to understand the systems and contexts in which problems take place. Direct practice theory takes place within a complex domain that has expanded rapidly in recent years. This expansion has supplied much needed vigor, albeit not without troublesome growing pains. Much of the new theory has not extended the margins of preexisting theory but rather has replaced the older theory. Incorporating new theory, therefore, has posed some challenging dilemmas for schools of social work.

Trend toward Integrating Practice Models

Because humans experience a broad array of problems, no single approach or practice model is sufficiently comprehensive to adequately address them all. Moreover, the techniques associated with one practice model may be applied equally effectively by social workers who espouse other models. Indeed, although some social workers identify largely with one practice model, few limit themselves to the interventions and techniques from that model. In fact, research suggests that more than half of current practitioners of psychotherapy integrate two or more approaches in their work (Lambert, Bergin, & Garfield, 2004, p. 7). Single-model practitioners do a disservice to themselves and their clients when they attempt to fit all clients and problems into their chosen model. Practitioners should select interventions and techniques that best fit certain types of problems and clients (Berlin & Marsh, 1993).

Practice theories vary widely in their worldviews, targets of intervention, specifications of techniques, methods of assessment, length of intervention, and other important dimensions. Some interventions are more relevant to and cost-effective for certain problems than are others. Except for a limited number of problems, no single theory has proven to be more effective than other practice theories, although some interventions have proven to be effective and others ineffective in treating certain problems. Practitioners and agencies should consult evidence of effectiveness related to problems and concerns prominently addressed in the organization (Thyer & Wodarski, 2004).

The proliferation of theories in the social sciences, social work, and allied disciplines has ushered in a new era that offers practitioners specific interventions proven effective for specific problem situations. Achieving this promised success presents a formidable challenge, however, because available knowledge is often fragmented. To integrate the many theories and interventions, a generic framework is essential. Fortunately, such a unifying framework—known as the ecological systems model—is available (Germain, 1979, 1981; Meyer, 1983; Pincus & Minahan, 1973; Siporin, 1980).

Ecological Systems Model

Adaptations of this model, originating in biology, make a close conceptual fit with the "person-in-environment" perspective that dominated social work until the mid-1970s. Although that perspective recognized the influence of environmental factors on human functioning, internal factors had received an inordinate emphasis in assessing human problems. In addition, a perception of the environment as constraining the individual did not sufficiently acknowledge the individual's ability to affect the environment.

This heavy emphasis, which resulted from the prominence and wide acceptance of Freud's theories in the 1920s and 1930s, reached its zenith in the 1940s and 1950s. With the emergence of ego psychology, systems theory, theories of family therapy, expanded awareness of the importance of ethnocultural factors, and emphasis on ecological factors in the 1960s and 1970s, increasing importance was accorded to environmental factors and to understanding the ways in which people interact with their environments.

Systems models were first created in the natural sciences. Meanwhile, ecological theory developed from the environmental movement in biology. Ecological systems theory in social work adapted concepts from both systems and ecological theories.

Two concepts of ecological theory that are especially relevant to social workers are habitat and niche. *Habitat* refers to the places where organisms live and, in the case of humans, consists of the physical and social settings within particular cultural contexts. When habitats are rich in the resources required for growth and development, people tend to thrive. When habitats are deficient in vital resources, physical, social, and emotional development and ongoing functioning may be adversely affected. For example, a substantial body of research indicates that supportive social networks of friends, relatives, neighbors, work and church associates, and pets mitigate the damaging effects of painful life stresses. By contrast, people with deficient social networks may respond to life stresses by becoming severely depressed, resorting to abuse of drugs or alcohol, engaging in violent behavior, or coping in other dysfunctional ways.

Niche refers to the statuses or roles occupied by members of the community. One of the tasks in the course of human maturation is to find one's niche in society, which is essential to achieving self-respect and a stable sense of identity. Being able to locate one's niche, however, presumes that opportunities congruent with human needs exist in society. That presumption may not be valid for members of society who lack equal opportunities because of race, ethnicity, gender, poverty, age, disability, sexual identity, or other factors.

An objective of social work, as noted earlier, is to promote social justice so as to expand opportunities for people to create appropriate niches for themselves. Ecological systems theory posits that individuals constantly engage in transactions with other humans and with other systems in the environment, and that these individuals and systems reciprocally influence each other.

Each system is unique, varying in its characteristics and ways of interacting (e.g., no two individuals, families, groups, or neighborhoods are the same). As a consequence, people do not merely react to environmental forces. Rather, they act on their environments, thereby shaping the responses of other people, groups, institutions, and even the physical environment. For example, people make choices about where to live, whether to upgrade

or to neglect their living arrangements, and whether to initiate or support policies that combat urban decay, safeguard the quality of air and water, and provide adequate housing for the elderly poor.

Adequate assessments of human problems and plans of interventions, therefore, must consider how people and environmental systems influence one another. The importance of considering this reciprocal interaction when formulating assessments has been reflected in changing views of certain human problems over the past decade. Disability, for example, is now defined in psychosocial terms rather than in medical or economic terms. As Roth (1987) has clarified, "What is significant can be revealed only by the ecological framework in which the disabled person exists, by the interactions through which society engages a disability, by the attitudes others hold, and by the architecture, means of transportation, and social organization constructed by the able bodied" (p. 434). Disability is thus minimized by maximizing the goodness of fit between the needs of people with physical or mental limitations and the environmental resources that correspond to their special needs (e.g., rehabilitation programs, special physical accommodations, education, and social support systems).

It is clear from the ecological systems perspective that the satisfaction of human needs and mastery of developmental tasks require adequate resources in the environment and positive transactions between people and their environments. For example, effective learning by a student requires adequate schools, competent teachers, parental support, adequate perception and intellectual ability, motivation to learn, and positive relationships between teachers and students. Any gaps in the environmental resources, limitations of individuals who need or utilize these resources, or dysfunctional transactions between individuals and environmental systems threaten to block the fulfillment of human needs and lead to stress or impaired functioning. To reduce or remove this stress requires coping efforts aimed at gratifying the needs—that is, achieving adaptive fit between person and environment. People, however, often do not have access to adequate resources or may lack effective coping methods. Social work involves helping such people meet their needs by linking them with or developing essential resources. It could also include enhancing clients' capacities to utilize resources or cope with environmental forces.

Assessment from an ecological systems perspective obviously requires knowledge of the diverse systems involved in interactions between people and their environments:

- Subsystems of the individual (biophysical, cognitive, emotional, behavioral, motivational).
- Interpersonal systems (parent–child, marital, family, kin, friends, neighbors, cultural reference groups, spiritual belief systems, and other members of social networks).
- Organizations, institutions, and communities.
- The physical environment (housing, neighborhood environment, buildings, other artificial creations, water, and weather and climate).

These systems and their interactions are considered in Chapters 8–11.

A major advantage of the ecological systems model is its broad scope. Typical human problems involving health care, family relations, inadequate income, mental health difficulties, conflicts with law enforcement agencies, unemployment, educational difficulties, and so on can all be subsumed under this model, enabling the practitioner to analyze the complex variables involved in such problems.

Assessing the sources of problems and determining the focuses of interventions are the first steps in applying the ecological systems model.

Pincus and Minahan have adapted systems models to social work practice, suggesting that a *client system* includes those persons who are requesting a change, sanction it, are expected to benefit from it, and contract to receive it (Pincus & Minahan, 1973; Compton & Galaway, 2005). Potential clients who request a change are described as *applicants*. Many clients reach social workers not through their own choice but rather through referral from others. *Referrals* are persons who do not seek services on their own, but do so at the behest of other professionals and family members. Meanwhile, *contacted persons* are approached through an outreach effort (Compton & Galaway, 2005). Some referred and contacted individuals may not experience pressure from that contact. As noted earlier, some individuals do experience pressure and social workers should consider them to be "potential clients" and to be aware of the route that brought them to the social worker and their response to that contact.

The next step is to determine what should be done vis-à-vis the pertinent systems involved in the problem situation. In this step, the practitioner surveys the broad spectrum of available practice theories and interventions. To be maximally effective, interventions must be directed to all systems that are critical in a given problem system.

The *target system* refers to the focus of change efforts. With a voluntary client, it will typically encompass the concerns that brought the individual to seek services. With nonvoluntary clients, it may include illegal or dangerous behaviors that the person does not acknowledge. The *client system* consists of those persons who request or are expected to benefit from services. Note that this definition includes both applicants or voluntary clients and nonvoluntary clients.

When a client desires assistance on a personal problem, the target and client systems overlap. Frequently, however, clients request assistance with a problem outside themselves. In such instances, that problem becomes the center of a target system. For example, when Ayan requests assistance in finding out about her mother's immigration status, that problem becomes the focus of the target system. Even when the target system and the client system overlap, it is important to focus on the *problem* that is the overlap rather than on the entire person as the target. Focusing on a person as the target system objectifies that individual and diminishes the respect for individuality to which each person is entitled.

The *action system* refers to those formal and informal resources and persons that the social worker needs to cooperate with to accomplish a purpose. It often includes family, friends, and other resources as well as more formal resources.

For example, the action system for the immigration problem would include Ayan's aunt and uncle as well as federal and international agencies that deal with immigration. The *agency system* is a special subset of an action system that includes the practitioners and formal service systems involved in work on the target problems (Compton & Galaway, 2005).

Social systems also vary in the degree to which they are open and closed to new information or feedback. Closed systems have relatively rigid *boundaries* that prevent the input or export of information. Open systems have relatively permeable boundaries permitting a more free exchange. Families may vary from being predominantly closed to new information to being excessively open. In fact, all families and human systems exhibit a tension between trying to maintain stability and boundaries in some areas while seeking and responding to change in others. Systems theorists also suggest that change in one part of a system often affects other parts of the system. For example, work with Ayan around her expressed concern about her mother may cause her to feel more comfortable in the home of her aunt and uncle and more willing to obey family rules.

The principle of *equifinality* suggests that the same outcome can be achieved even with different starting points. For example, your classmates have come from different places both geographically and in terms of life experience. Despite their different origins, they have all ended up in the same program of study. The principle of *multifinality* suggests that beginning from the same starting points may end in different outcomes. Just as you and your classmates are engaged in the same course of study, you are likely to end in diverse settings and locales for your own practice experience.

Nonlinear Applications of Systems Theory

Traditional systems theory suggests that systems or organizations are characterized by order, rationality, and stability (Warren, Franklin, & Streeter, 1998). Hence, the emphasis in such stable systems is on concepts such as boundaries, homeostasis, and equilibrium. In addition to ordered circumstances,

systems theory can be useful for consideration of nonlinear systems. Systems in the process of change can be very sensitive to initial events and feedback to those events. For example, a nonlinear change would be the circumstance in which an adolescent's voice changes by 1 decibel of loudness resulting in a change of 10 decibels in an adult (Warren et al., 1998). Minor incidents in the past can reverberate throughout a system. Some have suggested that this proliferation supports the notion that family systems can make significant changes as a result of a key intervention that reverberates and is reinforced in a system.

Such nonlinear circumstances emphasize the concept of multifinality—that is, the same initial conditions can lead to quite varied outcomes. Among the implications of multifinality are the possibility of considering chaos not as a lack of order but rather as an opportunity for flexibility and change.

Limitations of Systems Theories

While systems models often provide useful concepts for describing person–situation interactions, they may have limitations in suggesting specific intervention prescriptions (Whittaker & Tracy, 1989). Similarly, Wakefield (1996a, 1996b) has argued that systems concepts do not add much to domain-specific knowledge. Others claim that, however faulty or inadequate, systems theory provides useful metaphors for conceptualizing the relations between complex organizations.

Perhaps we should not place such high expectations on the theory (Gitterman, 1996). We take the view that systems theory provides useful metaphors for conceptualizing the varied levels of phenomena social workers must recognize. By themselves, those metaphors are insufficient to guide practice. Concepts such as equifinality and multifinality cannot be rigidly applied in all human and social systems.

Systematic Eclecticism

To make judicious choices and to implement chosen interventions skillfully requires knowledge of numerous practice theories and techniques and a rigorous approach to selecting those that are most appropriate for a given client (Turner, 1996). Systematic eclecticism (Beutler & Clarkin, 1990; Fischer, 1978; Siporin, 1979) is one rigorous approach to practice. A systematic eclectic practitioner does not adhere to a single theory exclusively. Instead, he or she selects those models and theories that best match a given problem situation and gives the highest priority to those techniques that have been empirically demonstrated to be effective and efficient.

Systematic eclecticism requires the practitioner to keep abreast of emerging theories and research findings. In our judgment, this approach to practice holds the highest promise of being effective with a broad range of clients and problems. The theoretical base of this book, therefore, is systematic eclecticism practiced under the umbrella of ecological systems theory. The systematic eclecticism approach to practice would be fairly straightforward if clear guidelines for selecting theories and interventions were available. Unfortunately, the state of the art in social work has not yet reached that level of sophistication. However, significant progress was made in the early 1990s (Beutler & Clarkin, 1990; Burman & Allen-Meares, 1991) and pertinent criteria have been identified (as discussed in Chapter 13).

Seven general criteria also exist to guide social workers in deciding which theories and interventions to study in depth.

1. The extent to which a given theory has been supported by empirical research is an important criterion. Theories with research-proven tenets and established efficacy are preferred over theories that have not been subjected to rigorous empirical testing. A number of writers have stressed the importance of basing direct practice on empirical research. Other writers caution that these adherents of empirically based practice have taken an extreme position that discounts the importance of other approaches to expanding knowledge (Witkin, 1998). We believe that a variety of approaches to knowledge can be useful. Nevertheless, empirically supported interventions are preferable and should be sought first.

2. When two interventions have both been proven effective, the intervention that produces results with the less expenditure of time, money, and effort is more efficient and, therefore, preferable.

3. Interventions and techniques subsumed under the theory should be specifically delineated. For example, theories that are largely composed of abstractions fail to tell practitioners how to implement theory in actual practice situations and have limited value. Psychoanalytic theory has been criticized for that reason. Behavior modification, by contrast, is characterized by a high degree of specificity with which its procedures are delineated.

4. Ethical and value implications of interventions play a role in social work practice. Social workers should avoid interventions that subject the client to emotional trauma or humiliation, that violate confidentiality, or that otherwise conflict with the profession's code of ethics. Assessing whether the information source highlights health and strengths versus pathology is important because of social work's value emphasizing strengths. A similar value leads to a preference for methods that emphasize collaborative work with clients versus practitioner manipulation. Hence, how power is viewed in the approach and the roles played by the social worker and the client or consumer are important criteria (Laird, 1993).

5. The social worker must have knowledge and skill with respect to given interventions. It is vital that the social worker be well grounded in the rationale for an intervention, indications and contraindications for employing it, cautions to be observed, guidelines for appropriate timing, and specific procedures for implementing it. Interventions are best learned under careful supervision, and social workers have an ethical responsibility not to apply them in a haphazard manner or to subject clients to the risk of trial-and-error learning.

6. The intervention should lend itself to ethnocultural sensitivity or appropriateness. That is,

models may include some assumptions that can match or be congruent with cultural beliefs while other assumptions may be inconsistent.

7. The context of agency, environment, client, and community variables (among others) must be considered when adapting theories and procedures originally developed outside the social work field. This does not preclude using knowledge and techniques developed elsewhere; indeed, social work has benefited greatly by borrowing from other fields. Rather, it demands that those procedures and techniques be carefully studied for their efficacy within social work practice as well.

Because this book takes a systematic eclecticism approach to direct practice, we have drawn from and integrated numerous behavioral theories and models of practice gleaned from social work and other helping professions. These theories and models include the task-centered system, cognitive therapy, behavior modification, client-centered therapy, ego psychology, role theory, social learning theory, decision theory, crisis intervention, existential theory, solution-focused brief treatment, motivational interviewing, and several models of family therapy. We refer to these theories and models throughout the book, and you will study some of them in depth during your professional education.

Summary

This chapter introduced social work as a profession marked by a specific mission and well-established values. As social workers and their clients operate in many different kinds and levels of environments, ecological and systems concepts are useful metaphors for conceptualizing what social workers and clients must deal with. Chapter 2 will delve deeper into specifying direct practice and the roles that social workers play.

Internet Resources

See our companion website for hot links to some helpful URLs. Note that URLs are subject to change. We will endeavor to update the links on the companion website as much as possible.

Social workers and their clients increasingly make use of the Internet to gather information to form solutions to problems. Each chapter will include Internet sites you can use to further your knowledge.

You may also choose to use InfoTrac College Edition with the free 4-month subscription you received upon purchasing this book. Enter the URL as follows: *http://www.infotrac-college.com*. You will be asked to provide the password that was included with your purchase. After providing identifying information, you can then enter key

words or subjects for a review of articles available on this subject. For example, if you enter the key word "empowerment," you can access a useful article such as Boehm, A., & Staples, L. (2002). The functions of the social worker in empowering: The voices of consumers and professionals. *Social Work 47* (4).

Outside of the InfoTrac College Edition, you can browse several sources that you should find useful by accessing one of the following sites.

For opportunities to chat with social workers, review job listings, and find other social work links: *http://www.socialworker.com/*.

Internet Exercise

The following Internet-based exercise will enrich your classroom learning. Assume that you are a social work field student in a hospital setting and are assigned to work with a Hmong client for the first time. Your client is scheduled to undergo a blood transfusion, and you have heard that this procedure might be a problem for some individuals. You can find a useful resource to assist you in answering your questions about blood transfusions at *http://www.hmongnet.org/faq/blood.html/*. Discuss with your classmates and your instructor your conclusions about how you would approach work with this client related to the blood transfusion.

Related Online Content

Visit the *Direct Social Work Practice* companion website at *http://socialwork. wadsworth.com/hepworth7* for additional learning tools such as glossary terms, chapter outlines, InfoTrac College Edition keywords, relevant web links, and chapter practice quizzes. Also, be sure to check out the Direct Practice Virtual Reader, where the authors have personally selected articles relevant to this chapter using InfoMarks.

Notes

1. This disguised case example was provided by Hassan Ugas, an MSW candidate at the University of Minnesota, with consultation from Dr. Karen Schwartz, Carleton College, Ottawa, Canada.
2. For an account of one state's efforts to support the goal of work while maintaining adequate support for families, see Hage (2004).

CHAPTER 2

Direct Practice: Domain, Philosophy, and Roles

CHAPTER OVERVIEW

This chapter presents a context and philosophy for direct practice, including definitions of direct and clinical practice, and descriptions of the varied roles played by direct social work practitioners.

DOMAIN

Prior to 1970, social work practice was defined by methodologies or by fields of practice. Social workers were thus variously identified as caseworkers, group workers, community organizers, child welfare workers, psychiatric social workers, school social workers, medical social workers, and so on. The terms *direct practice* and *clinical practice* are relatively new in social work nomenclature.

The profession was unified in 1955 by the creation of the National Association of Social Workers (NASW) and, with the inauguration of the journal *Social Work*, the gradual transformation from more narrow views of practice to the current broader view was under way. This transformation accelerated during the 1960s and 1970s, when social unrest in the United States prompted challenges and criticisms of all institutions, including social work. Persons of color, organized groups of poor people, and other oppressed groups accused the profession of being irrelevant given their pressing needs. These accusations were often justified, because many social workers were engaged in narrowly focused and therapeutically oriented activities that did not

address the social problems of concern to oppressed groups (Specht & Courtney, 1994).[1]

Casework had been the predominant social work method during this period. Casework comprised activities in widely varying settings, aimed at assisting individuals, couples, or families to cope more effectively with problems that impaired social functioning. At the same time group work had evolved as a practice method, and group workers were practicing in settlement houses and neighborhoods, on the streets with youth gangs, in hospitals and correctional institutions, and in other settings. Although the units targeted by group workers were larger, their objectives still did not address broad social problems. It was clear that urgent needs for broadly defined social services could not be met through the narrowly defined remedial (therapeutic) efforts of the casework and group work methods.

The efforts of Gordon (1965) and Bartlett (1970) to formulate a framework (i.e., common base) for social work practice composed of purpose, values, sanction, knowledge, and common skills resulted in a broadened perspective of social work. Because this new perspective was not oriented to methods of practice, a new generic term was created to describe it: *social work practice*.

Generalist Practice

The Council on Social Work Education (CSWE) responded to the evolution of the social work practice framework by adopting a curriculum policy statement stipulating that to meet accreditation standards, social work educational programs must have a curriculum containing foundation courses that embody the common knowledge base of social work practice. Both undergraduate (BSW) and graduate (MSW) programs embody such foundation courses and thus prepare students for generalist practice. BSW curricula, however, are designed primarily to prepare generalist social workers and avoid specialization in practice methods. The rationale for generalist programs, as discussed in Chapter 1, is that practitioners should view problems holistically and be prepared to plan interventions aimed at multiple levels of systems related to client concerns. Similarly, client goals and needs should suggest appropriate interventions, rather than interventions inspiring the selection of compatible goals. Client systems range from micro systems (individuals, couples, families, and groups) to mezzo to macro systems (organizations, institutions, communities, regions, and nations).

Connecting client systems to resource systems that can provide needed goods and services is a paramount function of BSW social workers. Many BSW programs, in fact, prepare students to assume the role of case manager, a role that focuses on linking clients to resource systems. We alluded to this role in Chapter 1 and discuss it briefly later in this chapter and more extensively in Chapter 14.

The first year (foundation year) of MSW programs also prepares graduate students for generalist practice. Although a few MSW programs prepare students for "advanced generalist practice," the vast majority of second-year curricula in the MSW programs permit students to select specializations or "concentrations" within methods of practice or within fields of practice (e.g., substance abuse, aging, child welfare, work with families, health care, or mental health) (Raymond, Teare, & Atherton, 1996). Methods of practice typically are denoted as *micro* or *macro*, the former referring to direct practice and the latter denoting social policy, community organization, and planning to bring about social and economic justice. MSW students thus are prepared for both generalist and specialized practice.

Both similarities in orientation and differences in function between BSW and MSW social workers and the importance of having practitioners at both levels are highlighted in the following case example. Note that similarities and differences exist on a continuum such that some MSW social workers perform some of the tasks otherwise ascribed to the BSW practitioner, and vice versa. Similarly, differences in their tasks may arise based on geographic region, field of practice, and availability of MSW-trained practitioners.

CASE EXAMPLE

Arthur and Marlene are unmarried adults, each of whom has developmental disabilities. They have two sons. Arthur and Marlene came to the attention of child protection services because Roger, the older of their sons who also has a developmental disability, told his teacher that his younger brother, Roy, 13, who does not have a developmental disability, and Roy's friends had sexually molested Roger. Roy admitted to the offense when interviewed, as did his friends. Roy stated that he learned the behavior from a neighbor who had been sexually abusing him since age 7.

The family participated in an assessment conducted by Christine, a BSW social worker employed by the county's child protection agency. Roger was placed in residential care, and Roy was charged with sexual assault. Meanwhile, the neighbor boy was charged with three counts of first-degree sexual assault and was incarcerated pending a hearing. Christine then met with Arthur and Marlene to conduct a strengths-based and risk assessment. This assessment revealed that Arthur and Marlene had coped well with parenting on many fronts, including maintaining their children in good school performance, and supporting their hobbies and avocations. Some concern was raised about their capacities to protect their children from danger in this instance. As a result of the collaborative assessment conducted by Christine, a plan was developed with the goal of Marlene and Arthur's resumption of care for their children.

Christine acted as the case manager, coordinating the efforts of several persons who were assisting Marlene, Arthur, and their children in pursuit of their goal of restoration of custody. Christine played dual roles (Trotter, 1999, p. 49) in this case: (1) ensuring social control designed to protect the public and vulnerable persons and (2) providing assistance to the family (i.e., a helping role). Sometimes those roles can be played simultaneously, sometimes they can be played in sequence, and sometimes only one of the two roles can be filled by the caseworker. In this instance, Christine initially carried out her assessment with her actions largely being guided by her role of protecting the public and vulnerable persons. After she came to agreement with Arthur and Marlene about the plan for regaining custody of their sons, Christine became more free to play a helping role. This plan included a referral to Debra, an MSW practitioner with special expertise in work with children with sexual behavior difficulties. Debra was able to work with Roy, Roger, and their parents and make a recommendation to the child welfare agency and court about when and under what conditions living together as a family would again be safe.

As this example indicates, frequently MSW direct practitioners provide more in-depth individual and family services than fits the caseloads, responsibilities, and training of BSW practitioners. They can coordinate their services to better serve families.

Direct Practice

Direct practice includes work with individuals, couples, families, and groups. Direct social work practitioners perform many roles besides delivering face-to-face service; they work in collaboration with other professionals, organizations, and institutions, and they act as advocates with landlords, agency administrators, policy-making boards, and legislatures, among others. The term *clinical practice* is often used interchangeably with *direct practice*, but the terms may have different meanings for different people. Clinical social work practice has been defined as "the provision of mental health services for the diagnosis, treatment and prevention of mental, behavioral and emotional disorders in individuals, families and groups" (Clinical Social Work Federation, 1997).

Proponents of the term *clinical practice* have emphasized that clinical social work entails liberating, supporting, and enhancing people's adaptive capacities and increasing the responsiveness of physical and social environments to people's needs. Swenson suggests that "clinical social workers work with clients to bring about social psychological change and to increase access to social and economic resources (Swenson, 1995, p. 503). Similarly, the Clinical Social Work Federation states that clinical social workers "share with all social work practitioners a goal of enhancement and maintenance of the physical, psychological and social functioning of individuals, families and groups" (Clinical Social Work Federation, 1997). Some persons think that the term *clinical practice* connotes psychotherapy done in mental health or independent practice settings, an elitist form of practice and perhaps a narrow psychiatric perspective (Waldfogel & Rosenblatt, 1983). Similarly, the term suggests a focus on disease and pathology rather than health and strengths.

In this book, we will use the terms *direct practice* and *clinical practice* to refer to practice done in any of the diverse settings in which micro-level services are delivered. Services delivered by direct practitioners may be addressed to most of the troubling situations encountered by people and may be delivered in any of the diverse settings listed at the beginning of Chapter 1.

Direct practice encompasses a full range of roles, including acting as a psychotherapist. Central to assisting people with difficulties is knowledge of and skill in assisting people in deciding how best to work on their concerns. That assistance requires knowledge and skills in assessing human problems and in locating, developing, or utilizing appropriate resource systems. Skills in engaging clients, mutually planning relevant goals, and defining the roles of the participants are also integral parts of the helping process. Likewise, the practitioner must possess knowledge of interventions and skills in implementing them. A more extensive review of the helping process is contained in Chapter 3, and this entire book is devoted to explicating the theory and skills related to direct practice with clients.

PHILOSOPHY OF DIRECT PRACTICE

1. The problems experienced by social work clients stem from lack of resources, knowledge, and skills (societal, systemic, and personal sources), either alone or in combination.

2. Because social work clients are often subject to poverty, racism, sexism, heterosexism, discrimination, and lack of resources, social workers negotiate systems and advocate for change to ensure that their clients obtain access to their rights, resources, and treatment with dignity. They also attempt to modify or develop resource systems to make them more responsive to client needs.

3. People are capable of making their own choices and decisions. Although controlled to some extent by their environment, they are able to direct their environment more than they realize. Social workers aim to assist in the empowerment of their clients by helping them gain (1) the ability to make decisions and (2) access to critical resources that affect their lives and increase their ability to change those environmental influences that adversely affect them individually and as members of groups.

4. Because social service systems are often funded on the basis of individual dysfunctions, social workers play an educational function in sensitizing service delivery systems to more systemic problem-solving approaches that emphasize health, strengths, and natural support systems.

5. Frequently, social workers deal with persons who are reluctant to receive services through referrals pressured by others or under the threat of legal sanctions. While people have a right to their own values and beliefs, sometimes their behaviors violate the rights of others, and the social worker assists these clients in facing these aspects of their difficulties. Because reluctant or involuntary clients are often not seeking a helping relationship but rather wishing to escape one, negotiation is frequently required.

6. Some clients apply for services because they wish to experience change through a social worker's assistance. Such clients are often helped by having an accepting relationship, with appropriate self-disclosure, which will allow them to seek greater self-awareness and to live more fully in the reality of the moment.

7. All clients, whether voluntary or involuntary, are entitled to be treated with respect and dignity, and to have their choices facilitated.

8. Client behavior is goal directed, although these goals are often not readily discernible. Clients are, however, capable of learning new skills, knowledge, and approaches to resolving their difficulties. Social workers are responsible for helping clients discover their strengths and affirming their capacity for growth and change.

9. While clients' current problems are often influenced by past relationships and concerns, and although limited focus on the past is sometimes beneficial, most difficulties can be alleviated by focusing on present choices and by mobilizing strengths and coping patterns.

Figure 2-1 Principles of a Philosophy of Direct Practice

Direct practitioners of social work must be knowledgeable and skilled in interviewing and in assessing and intervening in problematic interactions involving individuals, couples, families, and groups. Knowledge of group processes and skills in leading groups are also essential, as are skills in forming natural helping networks, functioning as a member of an interdisciplinary team, and negotiating within and between systems. The negotiating function requires skills in mediating conflicts, advocating for services, and obtaining resources, all of which embody high levels of interpersonal skills.

Some have questioned whether engaging in psychotherapy is appropriate for a profession whose mission focuses on social justice (Specht & Courtney, 1994). Others have countered that a social justice mission is not necessarily inconsistent with use of psychotherapy as one tool in pursuit of this goal (Wakefield, 1996a, 1996b). According to Swenson (1998), clinical work that draws on client strengths, that is mindful of social positions and power relationships, and that attempts to counter oppression is consistent with a social justice perspective. In our opinion, these debates are moot. Many of today's practitioners in social work and other helping professions practice psychotherapy that draws on additional theory bases such as behavioral and family systems models. Clinical practice in a managed care environment focuses on specific problems, strengths, and resources; is highly structured and goal oriented; and develops tangible objectives for each session intended to achieve the overall treatment goals (Franklin, 2002).

A PHILOSOPHY OF DIRECT PRACTICE

As a profession evolves, its knowledge base expands and practitioners gain experience in applying abstract values and knowledge to specific practice situations. Instrumental values gradually evolve as part of this transformation; as they are adopted, they become principles or guidelines to practice. Such principles express preferred beliefs about the nature and causes of human problems. They also describe perspectives about people's capacity to deal with problems, desirable goals, and valued qualities in helping relationships. Finally, those principles include beliefs about vital elements of the helping process, the roles of the practitioner and the client, characteristics of effective group leaders, and the nature of the human growth process.

Over many years, we have evolved a philosophy of practice from a synthesis of principles gained from sources too diverse to acknowledge, including our own value preferences. We thus offer as our philosophy of direct practice the principles outlined in Figure 2-1.

ROLES OF DIRECT PRACTITIONERS

During recent years, increasing attention has been devoted to the various roles that direct practitioners perform in discharging their responsibilities. In Chapter 1, we referred to a number of these roles. In this section, we summarize these and other roles and refer to sections of the book where we

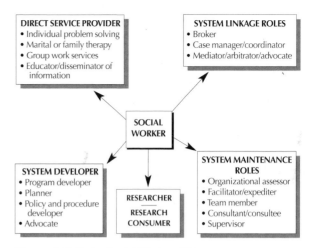

Figure 2-2 Roles Social Workers Play

discuss certain roles at greater length. We have categorized the roles based in part on a schema presented by Lister (1987) (see Figure 2-2).

Direct Provision of Services

Roles subsumed under this category include those in which social workers meet face to face with clients or consumer groups in providing services:

- *Individual casework or counseling.*

- *Marital and family therapy* (may include sessions with individuals, conjoint sessions, and group sessions).

- *Group work services* (may include support groups, therapy groups, self-help groups, task groups, and skill development groups).

- *Educator/disseminator of information.* The social worker may provide essential information in individual, conjoint, or group sessions or may make educational presentations to consumer groups or to the public. For example, practitioners may conduct educational sessions dealing with parenting skills, marital enrichment, stress management, or various aspects of mental health or health care (Dore, 1993).

These roles are primary in the work of most direct service social workers. Because this book is aimed at preparing social workers to provide such direct services, we will not elaborate further on these roles in this section.

System Linkage Roles

Because clients may need resources not provided by a given social agency and lack knowledge of or the ability to utilize other available resources, social workers often perform roles in linking people to other resources.

Broker

To perform the role of broker (i.e., an intermediary who assists in connecting people with resources), social workers must have a thorough knowledge of community resources so that they can make appropriate referrals. Familiarity with the policies of resource systems and working relationships with key contact persons are essential to making successful referrals. In the earlier case example, Christine, the BSW-trained social worker, brokered services for Marlene, Arthur, and their children, including the referral to Debra, the MSW-trained sexual behaviors counselor. Before some people are able to avail themselves of resources, they may require the practitioner's assistance in overcoming fears and misconceptions about those services.

Social workers also have responsibilities in developing simple and effective referral mechanisms and ways of monitoring whether clients actually follow through on referrals. Chapter 3 presents guidelines to assist you in gaining skills in referring clients to needed resources.

Case Manager/Coordinator

Some clients lack the ability, skills, knowledge, or resources to follow through on referrals to other systems. In such instances, the social worker may serve as case manager, a person who assumes primary responsibility for assessing the needs of a client and arranging and coordinating the delivery of essential goods and services provided by other resources. Case managers also work directly with clients to ensure that the needed goods and services are provided in a timely manner.

Case managers must maintain close contact with clients (sometimes even providing direct casework services) and with other service providers to ensure that plans for service delivery are in place and are delivered as planned. It is noteworthy that in the case manager role, practitioners function at the interface between the client and the environment more so than in any other role. Because of recent dramatic increases in the numbers of people needing case management services (e.g., homeless individuals, elderly clients, and persons with serious and persistent mental illness), numerous articles have appeared in the literature focusing on the clients who need such services, issues related to case management, and various functions of case managers. Because we discuss these topics at some length in Chapter 14, we defer discussion of them to that chapter.

Mediator/Arbitrator

Occasionally breakdowns occur between clients and service providers so that clients do not receive the needed services to which they are entitled. For example, clients may be seeking a resource to which they believe they are entitled by their health insurance. In other cases, participants in workfare programs may find themselves sanctioned for failure to meet program expectations (Withorn, 1998).

Service may be denied for several reasons. Perhaps clients did not adequately represent their eligibility for services, or strains that sometimes develop between clients and service providers may precipitate withdrawals of requests for services by clients or withholding of services by providers.

In such instances, practitioners may serve as mediators with the goal of eliminating obstacles to service delivery. *Mediation* is a process that "provides a neutral forum in which disputants are encouraged to find a mutually satisfactory resolution to their problems" (Chandler, 1985, p. 346). When serving as a mediator, you must carefully listen to and draw out facts and feelings from both parties to determine the cause of the breakdown. It is important not to take sides with either party until you are confident that you have accurate and complete information. When you have determined the nature of the breakdown, you can plan appropriate remedial action aimed at removing barriers, clarifying possible misunderstandings, and working through negative feelings that have impeded service delivery. The communication skills used in this process are delineated in subsequent chapters of this book.

In recent years, knowledge of mediation skills has evolved to a high level of sophistication. Today, a growing number of practitioners are working independently or in tandem with attorneys to mediate conflicts between divorcing partners regarding child custody, visitation rights, and property settlements. These same skills can be used to mediate personnel disputes, labor management conflicts, and victim–offender situations (Umbreit, 1993).

Client Advocate

Social workers have assumed the role of advocate for a client or group of clients since the inception of the profession. The obligation to assume this role has been reaffirmed most recently in the NASW Code of Ethics, which includes advocacy among the activities performed by social workers in pursuit of the professional mission (NASW, 1996, p. 2).

With respect to linking clients with resources, advocacy is the process of working with and/or on behalf of clients to obtain services and resources that would not otherwise be provided. We discuss circumstances under which this might occur and appropriate remedial measures at length in Chapter 19. We also discuss skills involved in advocacy (including social action for groups of clients) in Chapter 14.

System Maintenance and Enhancement

As staff members of social agencies, social workers bear responsibility for evaluating structures, policies, and functional relationships within agencies that impair effectiveness in service delivery.

Organizational Analyst

Discharging the role of organizational analyst entails pinpointing factors in agency structure, policy, and procedures that have a negative impact on service delivery. Knowledge of organizational and administrative theory is essential to performing this role effectively. We focus on this role in

Chapter 14 in more depth. You will also learn more about organizational dynamics in courses concerned with organizational theory.

Facilitator/Expediter

After pinpointing factors that impede service delivery, social workers have a responsibility to plan and implement ways of enhancing service delivery. This may involve providing relevant input to agency boards and administrators, recommending staff meetings to address problems, working collaboratively with other staff members to bring pressure to bear on resistant administrators, encouraging and participating in essential in-service training sessions, and other similar activities.

Team Member

In many agency and institutional settings (e.g., mental health, health care, rehabilitation, and education settings), practitioners function as members of clinical teams that collaborate in assessing clients' problems and delivering services (Sands, 1989; Sands, Stafford, & McClelland, 1990). Such teams commonly consist of a psychiatrist or physician, psychologist, a social worker, a nurse, and perhaps a rehabilitation counselor, occupational therapist, educator, or recreational therapist, depending on the setting. Members of the team have varying types of expertise that are tapped in formulating assessments and planning and implementing therapeutic interventions. As team members, social work practitioners often contribute knowledge related to family dynamics and engage in therapeutic work with family members.

Sometimes such teams are dominated by members from more powerful professions (Bell, 2001). Dane and Simon (1991) note that social workers in such host settings, in which the mission and decision making may be dominated by non-social workers, often experience a discrepancy between their professional mission and the values of the employing institution. They can act, however, to sensitize team members to strengths and advocate for a more holistic approach while exercising their knowledge of resources and expertise in linking clients with resources. Social workers also are expected to apply their knowledge of community resources in planning for the discharge of patients and facilitating their reentry into the community following periods of hospitalization. In so doing, social workers bring their systems and strengths perspectives to teams that are sometimes more deficit focused.

Social workers are also increasingly involved in collaborative work across systems such as schools and child welfare, which require the ability to work within several systems simultaneously (Bailey-Dempsey & Reid, 1995). As team members, social workers also often serve as case managers in coordinating discharge planning for patients (Dane & Simon, 1991; Kadushin & Kulys, 1993).

Consultant/Consultee

Consultation is a process whereby an expert enables a consultee to deliver services more effectively to a client by increasing, developing, modifying, or freeing the consultee's knowledge, skills, attitudes, or behavior with respect to the problem at hand (Kadushin, 1977). Although social workers both provide and receive consultation, there has been a trend for MSW social workers to serve less as consumers of consultation and more as providers. BSW social workers may provide consultation regarding the availability of specific community resources. More often, however, they are consumers of consultation when they need information about how to work effectively in problem solving that encompasses complex situations and behaviors. Social workers assume the consultee role when they need expert knowledge from doctors and nurses, psychiatrists, psychologists, and other social workers who possess high levels of expertise related to certain types of problems (e.g., substance abuse, child maltreatment, sexual problems).

Social workers serve as consultants to members of other professions and to other social workers in need of their special expertise, including when they fill the role of supervisor. For example, they may provide consultation to school personnel who need assistance in understanding and coping with problem students; to health care providers who seek assistance in understanding a patient's

family or ethnic and cultural factors; to court staff regarding matters that bear on child custody decisions and decisions about parole and probation; and in many other similar situations.

Supervisor

Relations between consultants and consultees in social work frequently occur within the supervisory relationship. Supervisors play a critical role in the support of quality direct practice work performed by social work practitioners. Supervisors are responsible for orienting staff to how they can learn through supervision, lines of authority, requirements, and policies of the setting (Munson, 2002, p. 38). Social work supervisors frequently utilize case presentations made by staff social workers as a key mechanism in learning. Such presentations should be organized around questions to be answered. Supervisors assist staff in linking assessment with intervention plans and evaluation. Special responsibilities include helping supervisees identify when client advocacy is needed, identifying and resolving ethical conflicts, and monitoring issues of race, ethnicity, lifestyle, and vulnerability as they affect the client–social worker interaction. In addition, supervisors often take the lead in securing resources for staff and facilitating linkages with other organizations.

Researcher/Research Consumer

Practitioners face responsibilities in both public and private settings to select interventions that can be evaluated, to evaluate the effectiveness of their interventions, and to systematically monitor the progress of their clients. Implementing these processes requires practitioners to conduct and make use of research.

Actual research conducted by direct practitioners sometimes involves single-subject (i.e., single-system) designs. This type of research design enables practitioners to obtain measures of the extent (frequency and severity) of problem behaviors before they implement interventions aimed at eliminating or reducing the problem behaviors or increasing the frequency of currently insufficient behaviors (e.g., doing homework, engaging in prosocial behaviors, setting realistic and consistent limits with children, sending positive messages, abstaining from drinking). These measures provide a baseline against which the results of the interventions can be assessed by applying the same measures periodically during the course of the interventions, at termination, and at follow-up (Reid, 1994). Perhaps more frequently, practitioners use some form of Goal Attainment Scaling that calls for rating goal achievement on a scale with points designated in advance (Corcoran & Vandiver, 1996).

Unless practitioners employ such designs to evaluate their practice, they place too much reliance on clinical judgment. Assessing progress through repeated measures, by contrast, enables both client and practitioner to discern small changes that might otherwise be underestimated or to determine that interventions are not producing the desired changes and a different approach is indicated.

System Development

Direct practitioners sometimes have opportunities to improve or to expand agency services based on assessment of unmet client needs, gaps in service, needs for preventive services, or research indicating that more promising results might be achieved by interventions other than those currently employed.

Program Developer

As noted earlier, practitioners often have opportunities to develop services in response to emerging needs of clients. Such services may include educational programs (e.g., for immigrants or unwed pregnant teenagers), support groups (e.g., for rape victims, adult children of alcoholics, and victims of incest), and skill development programs (e.g., stress management, parenting, and assertiveness training groups).

Planner

In small communities and rural areas that lack access to community planners, direct practitioners may need to assume a planning role, usually in concert with community leaders. In this role, the practitioner works both formally and informally with influential people to plan programs that respond to unmet and emerging needs. Such needs could include child care programs, transportation for elderly and disabled persons, and recreational and health care programs, to name just a few.

Policy and Procedure Developer

Participation of direct practitioners in formulating policies and procedures typically is limited to the agencies in which they provide direct services to clients. Their degree of participation in such activities is largely determined by the style of administration with a given agency. Able administrators generally solicit and invite input from professional staff about how the agency can more effectively respond to the consumers of its services. Because practitioners serve on the "front lines," they are strategically positioned to evaluate clients' needs and to assess how policies and procedures serve—or fail to serve—the best interests of clients. For these reasons, social workers should become actively involved in decision-making processes related to policies and procedure.

In rural areas and small communities, direct practitioners often participate in policy development concerned with the needs of a broad community rather than the needs of a circumscribed target group. In such instances, social workers must draw from knowledge and skills gained in courses in social welfare policy and services and community planning.

Advocate

Just as social workers may advocate for an individual client, so they may also join client groups, other social workers, and allied professionals in advocating for legislation and social policies aimed at providing needed resources and enhancing social justice. We discuss skills in advocacy and social action in Chapter 14.

Summary

Direct social work practice is characterized by performance of multiple roles. Those roles are carried out at several system levels, depending on the level of the concerns addressed. Knowledge and skills related to some of these roles are taught in segments of the curriculum that lie outside direct practice courses. To do justice in one volume to the knowledge and skills entailed in all these roles is impossible; consequently, we have limited our focus primarily to the roles involved in providing direct service.

Internet Resources

See our companion website for hot links to some helpful URLs. Note that URLs are subject to change. We will endeavor to update the links on the companion website as much as possible.

Using InfoTrac College Edition, you can search keywords such as "mediation," "program planning," and "consulting." Additional resources on clinical social work are available at *http://www. cswf.org/.* Through the InfoTrac College Edition, you can access an article describing the mediation role by van Wormer (2003).

Related Online Content

Visit the *Direct Social Work Practice* companion website at *http://socialwork. wadsworth.com/hepworth7* for additional learning tools such as glossary terms, chapter outlines, InfoTrac College Edition keywords, relevant web links, and chapter practice quizzes. Also, be sure to check out the Direct Practice Virtual Reader, where the authors have personally selected articles relevant to this chapter using InfoMarks.

Notes

1. Some argue that currently social workers are more likely to espouse social justice than to prioritize strategies to achieve it. They assert that the profession appears to aim more at protecting social work roles than transforming social service delivery (Jacobson, 2001).

CHAPTER 3

Overview of the Helping Process

CHAPTER OVERVIEW

This chapter provides an overview of the three phases of the helping process: exploration, implementation, and termination. The helping process focuses on problem solving with social work clients in a variety of settings, including those found along a continuum of voluntarism. Hence, the process is presented with the larger systems context in mind. In addition, we present the structure and ingredients of interviews that will be examined in more detail in Chapters 5 and 6.

COMMON ELEMENTS AMONG DIVERSE THEORISTS AND SOCIAL WORKERS

Direct social workers working with individuals, couples, families, groups, and other systems draw on contrasting theories of human behavior, use different models of practice, implement diverse interventions, and serve widely varying clients. Despite these varied factors, such social workers share a common goal: to assist clients in coping more effectively with problems of living and improving the quality of their lives. People are impelled by either internal or external sources to secure social work services because current solutions are not working in their lives. Helping approaches differ in the extent to which they are problem versus goal focused. We take the position that it is important for direct social workers to take

seriously the problems compelling clients to seek services as well as to work creatively with them toward achieving solutions that improve upon the initial problematic situation.

Whether a potential client perceives a need or seeks help is a critical issue in planning how services may be offered. Their reaction to those internal or external sources plays a part in their motivation for and reaction to the prospects for contact with a social worker. As described in Chapter 1, some potential clients are *applicants* who request services of a social worker to deal with these internal or external problems (Alcabes & Jones, 1985). Often a need for help has been identified by external sources such as teachers, doctors, employers, or family members. Such persons might be best considered *referrals* because they did not apply for service (Compton & Galaway, 2005). Persons who are referred vary in the extent to which they perceive that referral as a source of pressure or simply as a source of potential assistance. As introduced in Chapter 1, others are at least initially *involuntary clients* who respond to perceived requirements to seek help as a result of pressure from other persons or legal sources (Reid, 1978). Individuals who initiate their contact as applicants, referrals, or involuntary clients are all potential clients if they can negotiate a contract addressed to some of their concerns.

However potential clients begin their contact, they face a situation of disequilibrium in which they can potentially enhance their problem-solving ability by developing new resources or employing untapped resources in ways that reduce tension and achieve mastery over problems. Whatever their approach to assisting clients, most direct social workers employ a process aimed at reducing client concerns. That is, social workers try to assist clients in assessing the concerns that they perceive or that their environment presses upon them, making decisions about fruitful ways to identify and prioritize those concerns. Next, the social worker and client jointly identify potential approaches to reduce those concerns and make decisions about which courses of action to pursue. Involuntary clients face situations in which some of these concerns are not of their choice and some of the approaches to reducing those concerns may be mandated by other parties.

Even in these circumstances, clients have the power to make at least constrained choices regarding how they address these concerns or additional concerns beyond those that they have been mandated to address. After these strategic approaches have been identified and selected, they are implemented. Working together, the client and the social worker then assess the success of their efforts and revise their plans as necessary. Social workers use a variety of communication skills to implement the problem-solving process given the many different systems involved in clients' concerns.

The first portion of this chapter gives an overview of the helping process and its three distinct phases; subsequent parts of the book are organized to correspond to these phases. The latter part of this chapter focuses on the structure and processes involved in interviewing—a critical aspect of dealing with clients. Later chapters deal with the structure, processes, and skills involved in modifying the processes of families and groups.

THE HELPING PROCESS

The helping process consists of three major phases:

>Phase I: Exploration, engagement, assessment, and planning
>
>Phase II: Implementation and goal attainment
>
>Phase III: Termination

Each of these phases has distinct objectives, and the helping process generally proceeds successively through them. The three phases, however, are not sharply demarcated by the activities and skills employed. Indeed, the activities and skills employed in the three phases differ more in terms of their frequency and intensity than in the kind used. The processes of exploration and assessment, for example, are central during Phase I, but these processes continue in somewhat diminished significance during subsequent phases of the helping process.

Phase I: Exploration, Engagement, Assessment, and Planning

The first phase lays the groundwork for subsequent implementation of interventions and strategies aimed at resolving clients' problems and promoting problem-solving skills. It represents a key step in helping relationships of any duration and setting—from crisis intervention and discharge planning to long-term and institutional care. Processes involved and tasks to be accomplished during Phase I include the following:

1. Exploring clients' problems by eliciting comprehensive data about the person(s), the problem, and environmental factors, including forces influencing the referral for contact

2. Establishing rapport and enhancing motivation

3. Formulating a multidimensional assessment of the problem, identifying systems that play a significant role in the difficulties, and identifying relevant resources that can be tapped or must be developed

4. Mutually negotiating goals to be accomplished in remedying or alleviating problem and formulating a contract

5. Making referrals

We briefly discuss each of these five processes in the following sections and refer to portions of the book that include extensive discussions of these processes.

Exploring clients' problems by eliciting comprehensive data about the person(s), the problem, and environmental factors, including forces influencing the referral for contact. Contact begins with an initial exploration of the circumstances that have led the potential client to meet with the social worker. Social workers should not assume that potential clients are applicants at this point, because self-referred persons are the minority of clients served in many settings; even those who self-refer often do so at the suggestion or pressure of others (Cingolani, 1984).

Potential clients may be anxious about the prospect of seeking help and lack knowledge about what to expect. For many, the social worker will have information from an intake form or referral source about the circumstances that have brought them into contact. These many possibilities can be explored by asking questions such as the following:

- "I have read your intake form. Can you tell me what brings you here, in your own words?"

- "How can we help you?"

- "I see that you were referred by your employer. How do you feel about that?"

These questions should elicit a beginning elaboration of the concern or pressures that the potential client sees as relating to his or her contact. The social worker can begin to determine to what extent the motivation for contact was initiated by the potential client and to what extent the motivation represents a response to external forces.

The social worker should also give a clear, brief description of his or her own view of the purpose of this first contact and encourage an exploration of how the social worker can be helpful.

Establishing rapport and enhancing motivation. Effective communication in the helping relationship is crucial. Unless the social worker succeeds in engaging the client, the client may be reluctant to reveal vital information and feelings and, even worse, may not return after the initial session.

Engaging clients successfully means establishing rapport, which reduces the level of threat and gains the trust of clients, who recognize that the social worker intends to be helpful. One condition of rapport is that clients perceive a social worker as understanding and genuinely interested in their well-being. To create such a positive perception among clients who differ in significant

ways from the social worker (including race or ethnicity), the social worker must attend to relevant cultural factors and vary interviewing techniques accordingly (interviewing is discussed later in this chapter and throughout the book). Further, when potential clients have been referred by others, these individuals will need to be reassured that their wishes are important and that they do not have to necessarily work on the concerns seen by the referral source.

Potential clients who are not applicants or genuinely self-referred frequently have misgivings about the helping process. They do not perceive themselves as having a problem and often attribute the source of difficulties to another person or to untoward circumstances.

Such clients confront social workers with several challenging tasks:

- Neutralizing negative feelings

- Attempting to help potential clients understand problems identified by others and assessing the advantages and disadvantages of dealing with those concerns

- Creating an incentive to work on acknowledged problems

Skillful social workers often succeed in tapping into the motivation of such involuntary clients, thus affirming the principle from systems theory that motivation is substantially influenced by the interaction between clients and social workers.

In other instances, clients may freely acknowledge problems and do not lack incentive for change but assume a passive role, expecting social workers to magically work out their difficulties for them. Social workers must avoid taking on the impossible role that some clients would ascribe to them. Instead, they should voice a belief in clients' abilities to work as partners in searching for remedial courses of action and mobilize clients' energies in implementing the tasks essential to successful problem resolution.

One very useful strategy is to acknowledge the client's problem and explicitly recognize the client's motivation to actively work toward its solution. Potential clients do not lack motivation; rather, they sometimes lack motivation to work on the problems and goals perceived by others. In addition, motivation relates to a person's past experience, which leads him or her to expect that behaviors will be successful or will fail in attempting to reach goals. Hence, individuals with limited expectations for success often appear to lack motivation. As a consequence, social workers must often attempt to increase motivation by assisting clients to discover that their actions can be effective in reaching their goals (Gold, 1990).

Social workers, therefore, must be able to tap into client motivation and assist those individuals who readily acknowledge a problem but are reluctant to expend the required effort or bear the discomfort involved in effecting essential change. A major task in this process is to provide information to the potential client about what to expect from the helping process. This socialization effort includes identifying the kinds of concerns with which the social worker and agency can help, client rights including confidentiality and circumstances in which it might be abridged, and information about what behavior to expect from the social worker and client (Videka-Sherman, 1988).

The task for clients in groups is twofold: They must develop trust in the social worker, and they must develop trust in the other group members. If group members vary in race, ethnicity, or social class, the group leader must be sensitive to such cultural determinants of behaviors. He or she must assume a facilitative role in breaking down related barriers to rapport not only between the social worker and individual group members, but also among group members.

Developing group norms and mutual expectations together assists in the creation of a group cohesiveness that helps groups become successful. Establishing rapport requires that social workers demonstrate a nonjudgmental attitude, acceptance, respect for clients' right of self-determination, and respect for clients' worth and dignity, uniqueness and individuality, and problem-solving capacities (discussed at length in Chapter 4). Finally, social workers foster rapport when they relate to clients with empathy and authenticity. Both skills are considered in later chapters of this book.

Formulating a multidimensional assessment of the problem, identifying systems that play a significant role in the difficulties, and identifying relevant resources that can be tapped or must be developed. Social workers must simultaneously establish rapport with their clients and explore their problems. These activities reinforce each other, as astute exploration yields both information and a sense of trust and confidence in the social worker.

A social worker who demonstrates empathy is able to foster rapport and show the client that the social worker understands what he or she is expressing. This, in turn, encourages more openness on the client's part and expands his or her expression of feelings. The greater willingness to share deepens the social worker's understanding of the client's situation and the role that emotions play in both their difficulties and their capabilities. Thus the social worker's communication skills serve multiple functions: They facilitate relationship building, they encourage information sharing, and they establish rapport.

Problem exploration is a critical process, because comprehensive information must be gathered before all of the dimensions of a problem and their interaction can be understood. Exploration begins by attending to the emotional states and immediate concerns manifested by the client. Gradually, the social worker broadens the exploration to encompass relevant systems (individual, interpersonal, and environmental) and explores the most critical aspects of the problem in depth. During this discovery process, the social worker is also alert to and highlights client strengths, realizing that these strengths represent a vital resource to be tapped later during the goal attainment phase.

Skills that are employed in the exploratory process with individuals, couples, families, and groups are delineated later in this chapter and at length in subsequent chapters. To explore problematic situations thoroughly, social workers must also be knowledgeable about the various systems commonly involved in human difficulties, topics considered at length in Chapters 8–11.

Problem exploration skills are used during the assessment process that begins with the first contact with clients and continues throughout the helping relationship. During interviews, social workers weigh the significance of clients' behavior, thoughts, beliefs, emotions, and, of course, information revealed. These moment-by-moment assessments guide social workers in deciding which aspects of problems to explore in depth, when to explore emotions more deeply, and so on. In addition to this ongoing process of assessment, social workers must formulate a working assessment from which flow the goals and contract upon which Phase II of the problem-solving process is based. An adequate assessment includes analysis of the problem, the person(s), and the ecological context.

Because there are many possible areas that can be explored but limited time available to explore them, focus in assessment is critical. Retaining such a focus is promoted by conducting the assessment in layers. At the first layer, you must focus your attention on issues of client safety, legal mandates, and the client's wishes for service. The rationale for this threefold set of priorities is that client wishes should take precedence in circumstances in which legal mandates do not impinge on choices or in which no dangers to self or others exist.

When you analyze the problem, you can identify which factors are contributing to difficulties—for example, inadequate resources; decisions about a crucial aspect of one's life; difficulties in individual, interpersonal, or societal systems; or interactions between any of the preceding factors. Analysis of the problem also involves making judgments about the duration and severity of a problem as well as the extent to which the problem is susceptible to change, given the client's potential coping capacity. In considering the nature and severity of problems, social workers must weigh these factors against their own competencies and the types of services provided by the agency. If the problems call for services that are beyond the agency's function, such as prescribing medication or rendering speech therapy, referral to another professional or agency may be indicated.

Analysis of the individual system includes assessment of the client's wants and needs, coping capacity, strengths and limitations, and motivation to work on the problem(s). In evaluating the first two dimensions, the social worker must assess such factors as flexibility, judgment, emotional characteristics, degree of responsibility, capacity to tolerate stress, ability to reason critically, and interpersonal skills. These factors, which are critical in selecting appropriate and attainable goals, are discussed at length in Chapter 9.

Assessment of ecological factors entails consideration of the adequacy or deficiency, success or failure, and strengths or weaknesses of salient systems in the environment that bear on the client's problem. Ecological assessment aims to identify systems that must be strengthened, mobilized, or developed to satisfy the client's unmet needs. Systems that often affect clients' needs include couple, family, and social support systems (e.g., kin, friends, neighbors, coworkers, peer groups, and ethnic reference groups); spiritual belief systems; child care, health care, and employment systems; various institutions; and the physical environment.

Cultural factors are also vital in ecological assessment, because personal and social needs and the means of satisfying them vary widely from culture to culture. Moreover, the resources that can be tapped to meet clients' needs vary according to cultural contexts. Some cultures include indigenous helping persons, such as folk healers, religious leaders, and relatives from extended family units who have been invested with authority to assist members of that culture in times of crisis. These persons can often provide valuable assistance to social workers and their clients.

Assessment of the client's situational context also requires analyzing the circumstances as well as the actions and reactions of participants in the problematic interaction. Knowledge of the circumstances and specific behaviors of participants before, during, and after troubling events is crucial to understanding the forces that shape and maintain problematic behavior. Assessment, therefore, requires that social workers elicit detailed information about actual transactions between people.

Whether making assessments of individuals per se or assessments of individuals as subsets of couples, families, or groups, it is important to assess the functioning of these larger systems. These systems have unique properties, including power distribution, role definitions, rules, norms, channels of communication, and repetitive interactional patterns. Such systems also boast both strengths and problems that strongly shape the behavior of constituent members. It follows that individual difficulties tend to be related to systemic difficulties, so interventions must therefore be directed to both the system and the individual.

Assessments of systems are based on a variety of data-gathering procedures. With couples and families, social workers may or may not conduct individual interviews, depending on their theoretical biases, practice styles, agency practices, and impressions gained during preliminary contacts with family members. If exploration and assessment are implemented exclusively in conjoint sessions, these processes are similar to those employed in individual interviews except that the interaction between the participants assumes major significance. Whereas information gleaned through individual interviews is limited to reports and descriptions by clients, requiring the social worker to make inferences about the actual interaction within the relevant systems, social workers can view interactions directly in conjoint interviews and group sessions. In such cases, the social worker should be alert to strengths and difficulties in communication and interaction and to the properties of the system (see Chapters 10 and 11). As a consequence, assessment focuses heavily on the styles of communication employed by individual participants, interactional patterns among members, and the impact of individual members on processes that occur in the system. These factors are weighed when selecting interventions intended to enhance functioning at these different levels of the larger systems.

Finally, a working assessment involves synthesizing all relevant information gathered as part of the exploration process. To enhance the validity of such assessments, social workers should involve clients in the process by soliciting their perceptions and assisting them in gathering data about their perceived difficulties and hopes. Social workers can share their impressions with their clients, for example, and then invite affirmation or disconfirmation of those impressions. It is also beneficial to highlight their strengths and to identify other relevant resource systems that can be tapped or need to be developed to resolve the difficulties. When social workers and their clients reach agreement about the nature of the problems involved, they are ready to enter the process of negotiating goals, assuming that clients are adequately motivated to advance to Phase II of the helping process.

Mutually negotiating goals to be accomplished in remedying or alleviating the problem and formulating a contract. If the social worker and the individual client, couple, family, or group have reached agreement concerning the nature of the difficulties and the systems that are involved, the participants are ready to negotiate individual and/or group goals. This mutual process aims to identify what needs to be changed and what related actions need to be taken to resolve or ameliorate the problematic situation. We briefly discuss the process of goal selection in this chapter and at length in Chapter 13. If agreement is not reached about the appropriateness of services or clients choose not to continue, then services may be terminated. In some situations, then, services are finished when the assessment is completed.

In the case of involuntary clients, some may continue the social work contact under pressure even if agreement is not reached about the appropriateness of services or if problems are not acknowledged. After goals have been negotiated, participants undertake the final task of Phase I: formulating a contract. The contract (see Chapter 12), which is also mutually negotiated, consists of a formal agreement or understanding between the social worker and the client that specifies the goals to be accomplished, relevant strategies to be implemented, roles and responsibilities of participants, practical arrangements, and other factors. When the client system is a couple, family, or group, the contract also specifies group goals that tend to accelerate group movement and to facilitate accomplishment of group goals.

Mutually formulating a contract is a vital process because it demystifies the helping process and clarifies for clients what they may realistically expect from the social worker and what is expected of them; what they will mutually be seeking to accomplish and in what ways; and what the problem-solving process entails. Contracting with voluntary clients is relatively straightforward; it specifies what the client desires to accomplish through social work contact. Contracting with involuntary clients contains another layer of legally mandated problems or concerns in addition to the clients' expressed wishes.

The solution-focused approach takes the position that goals are central when working with clients (De Jong & Berg, 2002). Those goals, however, may not be directly related to rectifying or eliminating the concern that initially prompted the contact. The solution may be reached without working from a problem viewpoint. For example, a child referred for setting fires might work toward a goal of becoming safe, trustworthy, and reliable in striking matches under adult supervision. By focusing on goals as perceived by clients, an empowering momentum may be created that draws out hidden strengths and resources. We also take the position that empowering clients to discover and make best use of available resources is desirable. Sometimes, focusing on problems can be counterproductive. However, in funding and agency environments that are problem focused both in terms of philosophy and funding streams, ignoring problem conceptions is not wise.

In summary, we are influenced by solution-focused methods to support client ownership of goals and methods for seeking them (De Jong, 2001). We differ from the solution-focused method, however, in that we do not assume that all clients have within them the solutions to all of their concerns. Expert information about solutions that have worked for clients in similar situations can often prove valuable (Reid, 2000). Rather than assuming that "the client always knows" or "the social worker always knows," we take the position that the social worker's task is to facilitate a situation in which both client and worker share their information while constructing plans for problem resolution (Reid, 2000).We explore the solution-focused method more in Chapter 13.

Making referrals. Exploration of clients' problems often reveals that resources or services beyond those provided by the agency are needed to remedy or ameliorate presenting difficulties. This is especially true of clients who have multiple unmet needs. In such instances, referrals to other resources and service providers may be necessary. Unfortunately, clients may lack the knowledge or skills needed to avail themselves of these badly needed resources. Social workers may assume the role of case manager in such instances (e.g., for persons with severe and persistent mental illness, individuals with developmental and physical disabilities, foster children, and infirm elderly clients). Linking clients to other resource systems requires careful handling if clients are to follow through in seeking and obtaining essential resources.

Phase II: Implementation and Goal Attainment

After mutually formulating a contract, the social worker and client(s) enter the heart of the problem-solving process—the implementation and goal attainment phase, also known as the action-oriented or change-oriented phase. Phase II involves translating the plans formulated jointly by the social worker and individual clients, couples, families, or groups into actions. In short, the participants combine their efforts in working toward the goal assigned the highest priority. This process begins by dissecting the goal into general tasks that identify general strategies to be employed in pursuit of the goal. These general tasks are then subdivided into specific tasks that designate what the client and social worker plan to do between one session and the next (Epstein, 1988; Reid, 1992; Robinson, 1930; Taft, 1937).[1] Tasks may relate to the individual's personal functioning or to his or her interaction with others present in the client's environment, or they may involve interaction with other resource systems, such as schools, hospitals, or law enforcement agencies. The processes of negotiating goals and tasks are discussed in detail in Chapter 12.

After formulating goals with clients, social workers select and implement interventions designed to assist clients in accomplishing those goals and subsidiary tasks. Interventions should directly relate to the problems that were identified and the goals that were mutually negotiated with clients and derived from accurate assessment. Helping efforts often fail when social workers employ global interventions without considering clients' views of their problems and ignore the uniqueness of each client's problems.

Enhancing Self-Efficacy

Research findings (Bandura & Locke, 2003; Washington & Moxley, 2003; Lane, Daugherty, & Nyman, 1998) have strongly indicated that the helping process is greatly enhanced when clients experience an increased sense of self-efficacy as part of this process. *Self-efficacy* refers to an expectation or belief that one can successfully accomplish tasks or perform behaviors associated with specified goals. Note that the concept overlaps with notions of individual empowerment.

The most powerful means for enhancing self-efficacy is to assist clients in actually performing certain behaviors prerequisite to accomplishing their goals. Another potent technique is to make clients aware of their strengths and to recognize incremental progress of clients toward goal attainment.

Family and group members also represent potent resources for enhancing self-efficacy. Social workers can develop and tap these resources by assisting families and groups to accomplish tasks that involve perceiving and accrediting the strengths and progress of group and family members. We consider other sources of self-efficacy and relevant techniques in Chapter 13.

Monitoring Progress

As work toward goal attainment proceeds, it is important to monitor progress on a regular basis. The reasons for this are fourfold:

1. *To evaluate the effectiveness of change strategies and interventions.* Social workers are increasingly required to document the efficacy of services to satisfy third-party payers with a managed care system. In addition, social workers owe it to their clients to select interventions based on the best available evidence

(Thyer, 2002). If an approach or intervention is not producing desired effects, social workers should determine the reasons for this failure or consider negotiating a different approach.

2. *To guide clients' efforts toward goal attainment.* Evaluating progress toward goals enhances continuity of focus and efforts and promotes efficient use of time (Corcoran & Vandiver, 1996).

3. *To keep abreast of clients' reactions to progress or lack of progress.* When they believe they are not progressing, clients tend to become discouraged and may lose confidence in the helping process. By evaluating progress periodically, social workers will be alerted to negative client reactions that might otherwise undermine the helping process.

4. *To concentrate on goal attainment and evaluate progress.* These efforts will tend to sustain clients' motivation to work on their problems.

Methods of evaluating progress range from eliciting subjective opinions to using various types of measurement instruments. Single-subject research is convenient, involves little or no expense, appeals to most clients, and can be employed with minimal research expertise. In addition, social workers can now access a variety of standardized outcome measurement instruments that are often useful. Chapter 12 includes more extensive discussion of single-subject research and outcome measurement.

Barriers to Goal Accomplishment

As clients strive to accomplish goals and related tasks, their progress is rarely smooth and uneventful. Instead, clients typically encounter obstacles and experience anxiety, uncertainties, fears, and other undesirable reactions as they struggle to solve problems. Furthermore, family or group members or other significant persons may undermine the client's efforts to change by opposing such changes, by ridiculing the client for seeing a social worker, by making derisive comments about the social worker, or by otherwise making change even more difficult for the client. (For this reason, it is vital to involve significant others in the problem-solving process whenever feasible.) Because of the challenges posed by these barriers to change, social workers must be mindful of their clients' struggles and skillful in assisting them to surmount these obstacles.

Barriers to goal accomplishment are frequently encountered in work with families and groups. Such barriers include personality factors that limit participation of certain group members, problematic behaviors of group members, or processes within the group that impede progress. They also encompass impediments in the family's environment.

Still other barriers may involve organizational opposition to change within systems whose resources are essential to goal accomplishment. Denial of resources or services (e.g., health care, rehabilitation services, and public assistance) by organizations, or policies and procedures that unduly restrict clients' access to resources, may require the social worker to assume the role of mediator or advocate. Chapter 14 highlights ways of overcoming this type of organizational opposition.

Relational Reactions

As social workers and clients work together in solving problems, emotional reactions on the part of either party toward the other party may impair the effectiveness of the working partnership and pose an obstacle to goal accomplishment. Clients, for example, may have unrealistic expectations or may misperceive the intent of the social worker. Consequently, clients may experience disappointment, discouragement, hurt, anger, rejection, longing for closeness, or many other emotional reactions that may seriously impede progress toward goals.

Couple partners, parents, and group members may also experience relational reactions to other members of these larger client systems, resulting in problematic interactional patterns within these systems. Not uncommonly, these reactions reflect maladaptive attitudes and beliefs learned from relationships with parents or significant others. In many other instances, however, the social worker or members of clients' systems may unknowingly behave in ways that trigger unfavorable relational reactions by individuals or family or group members. In either event, it is critical to explore and resolve these harmful relational reactions. Otherwise, clients' efforts may be diverted from working toward goal accomplishment or—even worse—clients may prematurely withdraw from the helping process.

Social workers are susceptible to relational reactions as well. Social workers who relate in an authentic manner provide clients with experience that is transferable to the real world of the client's social environment. They communicate that they are human beings who are not immune to making blunders and experiencing emotions and desires as part of their relationships with clients. It is vital that social workers be aware of their unfavorable reactions to clients and understand how to manage them. Otherwise, they may be working on their own problems rather than the client's issues, placing the helping process in severe jeopardy. Chapter 17 offers advice to assist social workers in coping with potential relational reactions residing with the client(s), the social worker, or both.

Enhancing Clients' Self-Awareness

As clients interact in a novel relationship with a social worker and risk trying out new interpersonal behaviors in their couple, family, or group contacts, they commonly experience emotions that may be pleasing, frightening, confusing, and even overwhelming. Although managing such emotional reactions may require a temporary detour from goal attainment activities, these efforts frequently represent rich opportunities for growth in self-awareness. Self-awareness is the first step to self-realization. Many voluntary clients wish to understand themselves more fully, and they can benefit from becoming more aware of feelings that have previously been buried or denied expression.

Social workers can facilitate the process of self-discovery by employing additive empathic responses during the goal attainment phase. Additive empathic responses focus on deeper feelings than do reciprocal empathic responses (referred to earlier in the discussion of Phase I). This technique can be appropriately applied in both individual and conjoint interviews as well as in group sessions. Additive empathy (discussed at length in Chapter 17) is particularly beneficial in assisting clients get in touch with their emotions and express those feelings clearly to their significant others.

Another technique used to foster self-awareness is confrontation (a major topic of Chapter 17). This technique helps clients become aware of growth-defeating discrepancies in perceptions, feelings, communications, behavior, values, and attitudes, and then examine these discrepancies in relation to stated goals. Confrontation is also used in circumstances when clients act to violate laws or threaten their own safety or the safety of others. Confrontation must be offered in the context of goodwill, and it requires high skill.

Use of Self

As helping relationships grow stronger during the implementation and goal attainment phase, social workers increasingly use themselves as tools to facilitate growth and accomplishment. Relating spontaneously and appropriately disclosing one's feelings, views, and experiences ensure that clients have an encounter with an open and authentic human being. Modeling authentic behavior encourages clients to reciprocate by risking authentic behavior themselves, thereby achieving significant growth in self-realization and in interpersonal relations.

Indeed, when *group leaders* model authentic behavior in groups, members often follow suit by exhibiting similar behavior. Social workers who relate in an authentic manner provide their clients with experience that is transferable to the clients' real-world social relationships. A contrived, detached, and sterile "professional" relationship, by contrast, lacks transferability to other relationships. Obviously, these issues should be covered in the training process for social workers.

Assertiveness involves dealing tactfully but firmly with problematic behaviors that impinge on the helping relationship or impede progress toward goal attainment. For example, when clients' actions contradict with their goals or are potentially harmful to themselves or others, the social worker must deal with these situations. Further, social workers must sometimes relate assertively to larger client systems—for example, to focus on behavior of group members that hinders the accomplishment of goals. Using oneself to relate authentically and assertively is a major focus of Chapter 5.

Phase III: Termination

The terminal phase of the helping process involves three major aspects:

1. Assessing when client goals have been satisfactorily attained
2. Helping the client develop strategies that maintain change and continue growth following the termination
3. Successfully terminating the helping relationship

Deciding when to terminate is relatively straightforward when time limits are specified in advance as part of the initial contact, as is done with the task-centered approach and other brief treatment strategies. Decisions about when to terminate are also simple when individual or group goals are clear-cut (e.g., to get a job, obtain a prosthetic device, arrange for nursing care, secure tutoring for a child, implement a specific group activity, or hold a public meeting).

In other instances, goals involve growth or changes that have no limits; thus judgments must be made by the social worker and client in tandem about when a satisfactory degree of change has been achieved. Examples of such goals include increasing self-esteem, communicating more effectively, becoming more outgoing in social situations, and resolving conflicts more effectively. In these cases, the ambiguity of termination can be reduced by developing specific, operational indicators of goal achievement, as discussed in Chapter 12. Today, however, many decisions about termination and extension involve third parties, as contracts for service and payers such as managed care may regulate the length and conditions of service (Corcoran & Vandiver, 1996).

Successfully Terminating Helping Relationships

Social workers and clients often respond positively to termination, reflecting pride and accomplishment on the part of both parties (Fortune, Pearlingi, &Rochelle, 1992). Clients who were required or otherwise pressured to see the social worker may experience a sense of relief at getting rid of the pressure or freeing themselves from the strictures of outside scrutiny. In contrast, because voluntary clients share personal problems and are accompanied through rough emotional terrain by a caring social worker, they often feel close to the social worker. Consequently, termination tends to produce mixed feelings for these types of clients. They are likely to feel strong gratitude to the social worker, but are also likely to experience a sense of relief over no longer having to go through the discomfort associated with exploring problems and making changes (not to mention the relief from paying fees).

Although clients are usually optimistic about the prospects of confronting future challenges independently, they sometimes experience a sense of loss over terminating the working relationship. Moreover, uncertainty about their ability to cope independently may be mixed with their optimism.

When they have been engaged in the helping process for a lengthy period of time, clients may develop a strong attachment to a social worker, especially if the social worker has fostered dependency in their relationship. For such individuals, termination involves a painful process of letting go of a relationship that has satisfied significant emotional needs. Moreover, these clients often experience apprehension about facing the future without the reassuring strength represented by the social worker. Group members may experience similar painful reactions as they face the loss of supportive relationships with the social worker and group members as well as a valued resource that has assisted them to cope with their problems.

To effect termination with individuals or groups and minimize psychological stress requires both perceptiveness to emotional reactions and skills in helping clients to work through such reactions. This subject is discussed in detail in Chapter 19.

Planning Change Maintenance Strategies

Social workers have voiced concern over the need to develop strategies that maintain clients' changes and continue their growth after formal social work service is terminated (Rzepnicki, 1991). These concerns have been prompted by findings that after termination many clients relapse or regress to their previous level of functioning. Consequently, more attention is now being paid to strategies for maintaining change. Planning for follow-up sessions not only makes it possible to evaluate the durability of results, but also facilitates the termination process by indicating the social worker's continuing interest in clients, a matter we discuss in Chapter 19.

THE INTERVIEWING PROCESS: STRUCTURE AND SKILLS

Direct social workers employ interviewing as the primary vehicle of influence, although administrators and social planners also rely heavily on interviewing skills to accomplish their objectives. Interviews vary according to purpose, types of setting, characteristics, and number of participants. For example, they may involve interaction between a social worker and individuals, couples, and family units. Interviews are conducted in offices, homes, hospitals, prisons, automobiles, and other diverse settings. Despite the numerous variables that affect interviews, certain factors are common to all effective interviews. This section identifies and discusses these essential factors and highlights relevant skills.

Physical Conditions

Interviews sometimes occur in office or interview settings over which the social worker has some control. Interviews that take place in a client's home, of course, are more subject to the client's preferences. The physical climate in which an interview is conducted partly determines the attitudes, feelings, and degree of cooperation and responsiveness of people during interviews. The following conditions are conducive to productive interviews:

1. Adequate ventilation and light
2. Comfortable room temperature
3. Ample space (to avoid a sense of being confined or crowded)
4. Attractive furnishings and décor
5. Chairs that adequately support the back
6. Privacy appropriate to the cultural beliefs of the client
7. Freedom from distraction
8. Open space between participants

The first five items obviously are concerned with providing a pleasant and comfortable environment and need no elaboration.

Privacy is vital, of course, because people are likely to be guarded in revealing personal information and expressing feelings if other people can see or hear them. Likewise, interviewers sometimes have difficulty in concentrating or expressing themselves when others can hear them. Settings vary in the extent to which social workers can control these conditions. For example, in some circumstances families may prefer to have trusted family members, friends, or spiritual leaders present to consider resolution of some issues (Burford & Pennell, 1996). In some settings, it may be impossible to ensure complete privacy. Even when interviewing a patient in a hospital bed, however, privacy can be maximized by closing doors, drawing curtains that separate beds, and requesting that nursing staff avoid nonessential interruptions. Privacy during home interviews may be even more difficult to arrange, but people will often take measures to reduce unnecessary intrusions or distractions if interviewers stress that privacy enhances the productivity of sessions. Social workers in public social service settings often work in cubicle offices. To ensure privacy, they can conduct client interviews in special interview rooms.

Because interviews sometimes involve intense emotional involvement by participants, freedom from distraction is a critical requirement. Telephone calls, knocks on the door, and external noises can impair concentration and disrupt important dialogue. Moreover, clients are unlikely to feel important and valued if social workers permit avoidable intrusions. Other sources of distraction include crying, attention seeking, and restless behavior of clients' infants or children. Small children, of course, cannot be expected to sit quietly for more than short periods of time. For this reason, the social worker should encourage parents to make arrangements for the care of children during interviews (except when it is important to observe interaction between parents and their children). Because requiring such arrangements can create a barrier to service utilization, many social workers and agencies maintain a supply of toys for such occasions.

Having a desk between an interviewer and interviewee(s) emphasizes the authority of the social worker. For some Asian clients, emphasizing the authority or position of the social worker may be a useful way to indicate that he or she occupies a formal, appropriate position. With many other clients, a desk between social worker and client creates a barrier that is not conducive to open communication. If safety of the social worker is an issue, then a desk barrier can be useful. In some instances, an interviewer may believe that maximizing the social worker's authority through a desk barrier will promote his or her service objectives.

In most circumstances, however, social workers strive to foster a sense of equality. Hence, they arrange their desks so that they can rotate their chairs to a position where there is open space between them and their clients. Others prefer to leave their desks entirely and use other chairs in the room when interviewing.

Structure of Interviews

Interviews in social work have a purpose, structure, direction, and focus. The purpose is to exchange information systematically with a view toward illuminating and solving problems, promoting growth, or planning strategies or actions aimed at improving the quality of life for people. The structure of interviews varies somewhat from setting to setting, from client to client, and from one phase of the helping process to another.

Indeed, skillful interviewers adapt flexibly both to different contexts and to the ebb and flow of each individual session.

Each interview is unique. Nevertheless, effective interviews conform to a general structure, share certain properties, and reflect use of certain basic skills by interviewers. In considering these basic factors, we begin by focusing on the structure and processes involved in initial interviews.

Establishing Rapport

Before starting to explore clients' difficulties, it is important to establish rapport. Rapport with clients fosters open and free communication, which is the hallmark of effective interviews. Achieving rapport enables clients to gain trust in the helpful intent and goodwill of the social worker, such that they will be willing to risk revealing personal and sometimes painful feelings and information. Some clients readily achieve trust and confidence in a social worker, particularly when they have the capacity to form relationships easily. Voluntary clients often ask, "Who am I and why am I in this situation?"; involuntary clients have less reason to be initially trusting and ask, "Who are you and when will you leave?" (Rooney, 1992).

Establishing rapport begins by greeting the client(s) warmly and introducing yourself. If the client system is a family, you should introduce yourself to each family member. In making introductions and addressing clients, it is important to extend the courtesy of asking clients how they prefer to be addressed; doing so conveys your respect and desire to use the title they prefer. Although some clients prefer the informality involved in using first names, social workers should be discreet in using first-name introductions with all clients because of their diverse ethnic and social backgrounds. For example, some adult African Americans and members of other groups may interpret being addressed by their first names as indicative of a lack of respect (Edwards, 1982; McNeely & Badami, 1984).

With many clients, social workers must surmount formidable barriers before establishing rapport. Bear in mind that the majority of clients have had little or no experience with social work agencies and enter initial interviews or group sessions with uncertainty and apprehension. Many did not seek help initially; they may view having to seek assistance with their problems as evidence of failure, weakness, or inadequacy. Moreover, revealing personal problems is embarrassing and even humiliating for some people, especially those who have difficulty confiding in others.

Cultural factors and language differences compound potential barriers to rapport even further. For example, some Asian Americans who retain strong ties to cultural traditions have been conditioned not to discuss personal or family problems with outsiders. Revealing problems to others may be perceived as a reflection of personal inadequacy and as a stigma upon the entire family. The resultant fear of shame may impede the development of rapport with clients from this ethnic group (Kumabe, Nishida, & Hepworth, 1985; Lum, 1996; Tsui & Schultz, 1985). Some African Americans, Native Americans, and Latinos may also experience difficulty in developing rapport because of distrust that derives from a history of being exploited or discriminated against by other ethnic groups (Longres, 1991; Proctor & Davis, 1994).

Clients' difficulties in communicating openly tend to be exacerbated when their problems involve allegations of socially unacceptable behavior, such as child abuse, moral infractions, or criminal behavior. In groups, the pain is further compounded by having to expose one's difficulties to other group members, especially in early sessions when the reactions of other members represent the threat of the unknown.

One means of fostering rapport with clients is to employ a "warm-up" period. This is particularly important with some ethnic minority clients for whom such openings are the cultural norm, including Native Americans, persons with strong roots in the cultures of Asia and the Pacific Basin, and Latinos. Aguilar (1972), for example, has stressed the importance of warm-up periods in work with Mexican Americans. Many Native Hawaiians and Samoans also expect to begin new contacts with outside persons by engaging in "talk story," which involves warm, informal, and light personal conversation similar to that described by Aguilar. To plunge into discussion of serious problems without a period of talk story would be regarded by members of these cultural groups as rude and intrusive. Social workers who neglect to engage in a warm-up period are likely to encounter passive-resistant behavior from members of these cultural groups. A warm-up period and a generally slower tempo are also critically important with Native Americans (Hull, 1982). Palmer and Pablo (1978) suggest that social workers who are most successful with Native Americans are low-key, nondirective individuals.

Warm-up periods are also important in establishing rapport with adolescents, many of whom are in a stage of emancipating themselves from adults. Consequently, they may be wary of social workers. This is especially true of individuals who are delinquent or are otherwise openly rebelling against authority. Moreover, adolescents who have had little or no experience with social workers have an extremely limited grasp of their roles. Many adolescents, at least initially, are involuntary clients and perceive social workers as adversaries, fearing that their role is to punish or to exercise power over them.

With the majority of clients, a brief warm-up period is usually sufficient. When the preceding barriers do not apply, introductions and a brief discussion of a timely topic (unusual weather, a widely discussed local or national event, or a topic of known interest to the client) will adequately foster a climate conducive to exploring clients' concerns.

Most clients, in fact, expect to immediately plunge into discussion of their problems, and their anxiety level may grow if social workers delay getting to the business at hand (Ivanoff, Blythe, & Tripodi, 1994). This is particularly true with involuntary clients who did not seek the contact. With these clients, rapport often develops rapidly if social workers respond sensitively to their feelings and skillfully give direction to the process of exploration by sharing the circumstances of the referral, thereby defusing the threat sensed by such clients.

Respect for clients is critical to establishing rapport. In both this chapter and Chapter 1, we stressed the importance of respecting clients' dignity and worth, uniqueness, capacities to solve problems, and other factors. An additional aspect of showing respect is demonstrating common courtesy. Being punctual, attending to the client's comfort, listening attentively, remembering the client's name, and assisting a client who has limited mobility convey the message that the social worker values the client and esteems his or her dignity and worth. Courtesy should never be taken lightly.

Verbal and nonverbal messages from social workers that convey understanding and acceptance of clients' feelings and views also facilitate the development of rapport. This does not mean agreeing with or condoning clients' views or problems, but rather apprehending and affirming clients' rights to have their own views, attitudes, and feelings.

Attentiveness to feelings that clients manifest both verbally and nonverbally and empathic responses to these feelings convey understanding in a form that clients can readily discern. Empathic responses clearly convey the message, "I am with you. I understand what you are saying and experiencing." The "workhorse" of successful helping persons, empathic responding, is important not only in Phase I of the helping process but in subsequent phases as well. Mastery of this vital skill (discussed extensively in Chapter 5) requires consistent and sustained practice.

Authenticity, or genuineness, is yet another social worker quality that facilitates rapport. Being authentic during Phase I of the helping process means relating as a genuine person rather than assuming a contrived and sterile professional role. Authentic behavior by social workers also models openness, which encourages clients to reciprocate by lowering their defenses and relating more openly (Doster & Nesbitt, 1979).

Encounters with authentic social workers also provide clients with a relationship experience that more closely approximates relationships in the real world than do relationships with people who conceal their real selves behind a professional facade. A moderate level of authenticity or genuineness during early interviews fosters openness most effectively (Giannandrea & Murphy, 1973; Mann & Murphy, 1975; Simonson, 1976). At this level, the social worker is spontaneous and relates openly by being nondefensive and congruent. In other words, the social worker's behavior and responses match her or his inner experiencing.

Being authentic also permits the constructive use of humor. Relating with a moderate level of authenticity, however, precludes a high level of self-disclosure. Rather, the focus is on the client, and the social worker reveals personal information or shares personal experiences judiciously. During the change-oriented phase of the helping process, however, social workers sometimes engage in self-disclosure when they believe that doing so may facilitate the growth of clients. Self-disclosure is discussed at length in Chapter 5.

Rapport is also enhanced by not employing certain types of responses that block communication. To avoid hindering communication, social workers must be knowledgeable about such types of responses and must eliminate them from their communication repertoires. Toward this end, Chapter 7 identifies various types of responses and interviewing patterns that inhibit communication and describes strategies for eliminating them.

Beginning social workers often fear that they will forget something, fail to observe something crucial in the interview that will lead to dire consequences, freeze up or become tongue-tied, or talk endlessly to reduce their anxiety (Epstein, 1985). Practice interviews such as those presented in subsequent chapters will assist in reducing this fear. It also helps to be aware that referred clients need to know the circumstances of the referral and clarify choices, rights, and expectations before they are likely to establish rapport with the social worker.

Starting Where the Client Is

Social work researchers have suggested that *motivational congruence*—that is, the fit between client motivation and what the social worker attempts to provide—is a major factor in explaining more successful findings in studies of social work effectiveness (Reid & Hanrahan, 1982). Starting with client motivation aids social workers in establishing and sustaining rapport and in maintaining psychological contact with clients.

If, for example, a client appears to be in emotional distress at the beginning of the initial interview, the social worker might focus attention on the client's distress before proceeding to explore the client's problematic situation. An example of an appropriate focusing response would be, "I can sense you're having a difficult time. Could you share with me what you're experiencing right now?" Discussion of the client's emotions and related factors tends to reduce the distress, which might otherwise impede the process of exploration. Moreover, responding sensitively to clients' emotions fosters rapport—clients begin to regard social workers as concerned, perceptive, and understanding persons.

Novice social workers sometimes have difficulty in starting where the client is because they worry that they will not present quickly and clearly the services of the agency, thus neglecting or delaying exploration of client concerns. Practice will allow them to relax and recognize that they can meet the expectations of their supervisors and others by focusing on client concerns while sharing content about the circumstances of referrals and their agency's services.

Starting where the client is has critical significance when you are working with involuntary clients. Because these clients are often compelled by external sources to see social workers, they frequently enter initial interviews with negative, hostile feelings. Social workers, therefore, should begin by eliciting these feelings and focusing on them until they have subsided. By responding empathically to negative feelings and conveying understanding and acceptance of them, skillful social workers often succeed in neutralizing these feelings, which enhances clients' receptivity to exploring their problem situations. For example, social workers can often reduce negative feelings by clarifying the choices available to the involuntary client. If social workers fail to deal with their clients' negativism, they are likely to encounter persistent oppositional responses. These responses are frequently labeled as resistance, opposition to change, and lack of motivation. It is useful to reframe these responses by choosing not to interpret them with deficit labels, but rather replacing them with expectations that these attitudes and behaviors are normal when something an individual values is threatened (Rooney, 1992).

Language also poses a barrier with many ethnic minority and immigrant clients who may have a limited grasp of the English language, which could cause difficulty in understanding even commonplace expressions. With ethnic minority clients and clients with limited educational levels, social workers must slow down the pace of communication and be especially sensitive to nonverbal indications that clients are confused. To avoid embarrassment, ethnic minority clients sometimes indicate that they understand messages when, in fact, they are perplexed.

Using Interpreters

When ethnic minority and immigrant clients have virtually no command of the English language, effective communication requires the use of an interpreter of the same ethnicity as the client, so that the social worker and client bridge both cultural value differences and language differences. To work effectively together, however, both the social worker and the interpreter must possess special skills. For their part, interpreters must be carefully selected and trained to understand the importance of the interview and their role in the process, as well as to interpret cultural nuances to the social worker. In this way, skilled interpreters assist social workers by translating far more than verbal content—they also convey nonverbal communication, cultural attitudes and beliefs, subtle expressions, emotional reactions, and expectations of clients.

To achieve rapport, of course, the social worker must also convey empathy and establish an emotional connection with the ethnic minority client. The interpreter thus "must have the capacity to act exactly as the interviewer acts—express the same feelings, use the same intonations to the extent possible in another language, and through verbal and nonverbal means convey what the interviewer expresses on several levels" (Freed, 1988, p. 316).

The social worker should explain the interpreter's role to the client and ensure the client of neutrality and confidentiality on the part of both the social worker and the interpreter. Obviously, these factors should also be covered in the training process for interpreters. In addition, successful transcultural work through an interpreter requires that the social worker be acquainted with the history and culture of the client's and the interpreter's country of origin.

Social workers must also adapt to the slower pace of interviews when an interpreter is involved. When social workers and interpreters are skilled in collaborating in interviews, effective working relationships can evolve, and many clients experience the process as beneficial and therapeutic. As implied in this brief discussion, interviewing through an interpreter is a complex process requiring careful preparation of interviewers and interpreters.

The Exploration Process

When clients indicate that they are ready to discuss their problematic situations, it is appropriate to begin the process of exploring their concerns. Messages like the following are typically employed to initiate the exploration process:

- "Could you tell me about your situation?"
- "I'm interested in hearing about what brought you here."
- "Tell me about the difficulties you've been having, and we can think about them together."

The client will generally respond by beginning to relate his or her concerns. The social worker's role at this point is to draw out the client, to respond in ways that convey understanding, and to seek elaboration of information needed to gain a clear picture of factors involved in the client's difficulties.

Some clients spontaneously provide rich information with little prompting. Others—especially referred and involuntary clients—may hesitate, struggle with their emotions, or have difficulty finding the right words to express themselves. Because referred clients may perceive that they were forced into the interview as the result of others' concerns, they may respond by recounting those external pressures. The social worker can assist in this process by sharing his or her information about the circumstances of the referral.

To facilitate the process of exploration, social workers employ a multitude of skills, often blending two or more in a single response. One such skill, *furthering responses,* encourages clients to continue verbalizing their concerns. Furthering responses, which include minimal prompts (both verbal and nonverbal) and accent responses, convey attention, interest, and an expectation that the client will continue verbalizing. They are discussed in depth in Chapter 6.

Other responses facilitate communication (and rapport) by providing immediate feedback that assures clients that social workers have not only heard but also understood their messages. *Paraphrasing* provides feedback indicating that the social worker has grasped the content of the client's message. In using paraphrasing, the interviewer rephrases (with different words) what the client has expressed. *Empathic responding,* by contrast, shows that the social worker is aware of the emotions the client has experienced or is currently experiencing. Both paraphrasing and empathic responding, which are discussed in Chapters 5 and 6, are especially crucial with clients who have limited language facility, including ethnic minority, immigrant, and developmentally disabled clients. When language barriers exist, social workers should be careful not to assume that they correctly understand the client or that the client understands the social worker.

With ethnic clients who have been culturally conditioned not to discuss personal or family problems with outsiders, social workers need to make special efforts to grasp their intended meanings. Many of these clients are not accustomed to participating in interviews and tend not to state their concerns openly. Rather, they may send covert (hidden) messages and expect social workers to discern their problems by reading between the lines. Social workers need to use feedback extensively to determine whether their perceptions of the clients' intended meanings are on target.

Using feedback to ascertain that the social worker has understood the client's intended meaning, and vice versa, can avoid unnecessary misunderstandings. In addition, clients generally appreciate a social worker's efforts to reach shared understanding, and they interpret patience and persistence in seeking to understand as evidence that the social worker respects and values them. It is not the ethnic minority client's responsibility, however, to educate the social worker.[2] Conversely, what the social worker thinks he or she knows about the minority client's culture may actually be an inappropriate stereotype, because individuals and families vary on a continuum of assimilation and acculturation with majority culture norms (Congress, 1994). Based on a common Latino value, for example, the social worker might say, "Can you call on other family members for assistance?"

Exploring Expectations

Before exploring problems, it is important to determine clients' expectations, which vary considerably and are influenced by socioeconomic level, cultural background, level of sophistication, and previous experience with helping professionals. In fact, socialization that includes clarifying expectations about the roles of clients and social workers has been found to be associated with more successful outcomes, especially with involuntary clients (Rooney, 1992; Videka-Sherman, 1988).

In some instances, clients' expectations diverge markedly from what social workers can realistically provide. Unless social workers are aware of and deal successfully with such unrealistic expectations, clients may be keenly disappointed and disinclined to continue beyond the initial interview. In other instances, referred clients may have mistaken impressions about whether they can choose to work on concerns as they see them as opposed to the views of referral sources such as family members. By exploring these expectations, social workers create an opportunity to clarify the nature of the helping process and to work through clients' feelings of disappointment. Being aware of clients' expectations also helps social workers select their approaches and interventions based on their clients' needs and expectations, a matter discussed at greater length in Chapter 5.

Eliciting Essential Information

During the exploration process, the social worker assesses the significance of information revealed as the client discusses problems and interacts with the social worker, group members, or significant others. Indeed, judgments about the meaning and significance of fragments of information guide social workers in deciding issues such as which aspects of a problem are salient and warrant further exploration, how ready a client is to explore certain facets of a problem more deeply, which patterned behaviors of the client or system interfere with effective functioning, and when and when not to draw out intense emotions.

The direction of problem exploration proceeds from general to specific. Clients' initial accounts of their problems are typically general in nature ("We fight over everything," "I don't seem to be able to make friends," "We just don't know how to cope with Scott. He won't do anything we ask," or "Child protection says I don't care for my children"). Clients' concerns typically have many facets, however, and accurate understanding requires careful assessment of each one. Whereas open-ended responses may be effective in launching problem explorations, other types of responses are used to probe for the detailed information needed to identify and unravel the various factors and systems that contribute to and maintain the problem. Responses that seek concreteness are employed to elicit such detailed information. Many types of such responses exist, each of which is considered at length in Chapter 6. Another type of response needed to elicit detailed factual information is the closed-ended question (also discussed in Chapter 6).

Focusing in Depth

In addition to possessing discrete skills needed to elicit detailed information, social workers must be able to maintain the focus on problems until they have elicited comprehensive information. Adequate assessment of problems is not possible until a social worker possesses sufficient information concerning the various forces (involving individual, interpersonal, and environmental systems)

that interact to produce the problems. Focusing skills (discussed at length in Chapter 6) blend the various skills identified thus far with summarizing responses.

During the course of exploration, social workers should elicit information relevant to numerous questions, the answers to which are crucial in understanding which factors bear on the clients' problems, including ecological factors. These questions (discussed in Chapter 8) serve as guideposts to social workers and provide direction to interviews.

Employing Outlines

In addition to answering questions that are relevant to virtually all interviews, social workers may need to collect information that answers questions pertinent to specific practice settings. Outlines that list essential questions to be answered for a given situation or problem can prove extremely helpful to beginning social workers. It is important, however, to maintain flexibility in the interview and to focus on the client, not the outline. Chapter 6 provides examples of outlines and suggestions for using them.

Assessing Emotional Functioning

During the process of exploration, social workers must be keenly sensitive to clients' moment-to-moment emotional reactions and to the part that emotional patterns (e.g., inadequate anger control, depression, and widely fluctuating moods) play in their difficulties. Emotional reactions during the interview (e.g., crying, intense anxiety, anger, and hurt feelings) often impede problem exploration and require detours aimed at assisting clients to regain their equanimity. Note that the anxiety and anger exhibited by involuntary clients may be influenced by the circumstances of the involuntary contact as much as by more enduring emotional patterns.

Emotional patterns that powerfully influence behavior in other contexts may also be problems in and of themselves that warrant careful exploration. Depression, for example, is a prevalent problem in our society but generally responds well to proper treatment. When clients exhibit symptoms of depression, the depth of the depression and risk of suicide should be carefully explored. Empathic communication is a major skill employed to explore these types of emotional patterns. Factors to be considered, instruments that assess depression and suicidal risk, and relevant skills are discussed in Chapter 9.

Exploring Cognitive Functioning

Because thought patterns, beliefs, and attitudes are powerful determinants of behavior, it is important to explore clients' opinions and interpretations of those circumstances and events deemed salient to their difficulties. Often, careful exploration reveals that misinformation, distorted meaning attributions, mistaken beliefs, and dysfunctional patterns of thought (such as rigid, dogmatic thinking) play major roles in clients' difficulties.

Messages commonly employed to explore clients' thinking include the following:

- "How did you come to that conclusion?"
- "What meaning do you make of . . .?"
- "How do you explain what happened?"
- "What are your views (or beliefs) about that?"

Assessment of cognitive functioning and other relevant assessment skills are discussed further in Chapter 9.

Exploring Substance Abuse, Violence, and Sexual Abuse

Because of the prevalence and magnitude of problems associated with substance abuse (including alcohol), violence, and sexual abuse in our society, the possibility that these problems contribute to or represent the primary source of clients' difficulties should be routinely explored. Because of the significance of these problematic behaviors, we devote a major portion of Chapter 9 to their assessment.

Negotiating Goals and a Contract

When social workers and clients believe that they have adequately explored the problems prompting the initial contact, they are ready to enter the process of planning. By this point (if not sooner), it should be apparent whether other resources or services are needed. If other resources are needed or are more appropriate, then the social worker may initiate the process of referring the client elsewhere. If the client's problems match the function of the agency and the client expresses a willingness to continue with the helping process, then it is appropriate to begin negotiating a contract. When involuntary clients are unwilling to participate further in the helping process, their options should be clarified at this point. For example, they can choose to return to court, choose not to comply and risk the legal consequences of this tactic, choose to comply minimally, or choose to work with the social worker on problems as they see them in addition to legal mandates (Rooney, 1992).

In a problem-solving approach, goals specify the end results that will be attained if the problem-solving efforts succeed. Generally, after collaborating in the exploration process, social workers and clients share common views about which results or changes are desirable or essential. In some instances, however, social workers may recognize the importance of accomplishing certain goals that clients have overlooked, and vice versa. Social workers introduce the process of goal negotiation by explaining the rationale for formulating those goals. If stated in explicit terms, goals will give direction to the problem-solving process and serve as progress guideposts and as outcome criteria for the helping efforts. To employ goals effectively, social workers need skills in persuading clients to participate in selecting attainable goals, in formulating general task plans for reaching these goals, and in developing specific task plans to guide the social worker's and client's efforts between sessions.

When resolving the problematic situation requires satisfying more than one goal (the usual case), social workers should assist clients in assigning priorities to those goals so that the first efforts can be directed to the most burdensome aspects of the problem. Stimulating clients to elaborate goals enhances their commitment to actively participate in the problem-solving process by ensuring that goals are of maximal relevance to them. Techniques such as the "miracle question" from the solution-focused approach can be employed to engage clients in elaborating their vision of goals (De Jong & Berg, 2002). Even involuntary clients can often choose the order in which goals are addressed or participate in the process of making that choice. Essential elements of the goal selection process and the contracting process are discussed in depth in Chapter 12.

Ending Interviews

Both initial interviews and the contracting process conclude with a discussion of "housekeeping" arrangements and an agreement about the next steps to be taken. During this final portion of the interview process, social workers should describe the length and frequency of sessions, who will participate in them, the means of accomplishing goals, the duration of the helping period, fees, the date and time of the next appointment, pertinent agency policies and procedures, and other relevant matters. When you have completed these interview processes, or when the time allocated for the interview has elapsed, it is appropriate to conclude the interview. Messages appropriate for ending interviews include the following:

- "I see our time for today is nearly at an end. Let's stop here, and we'll begin next time by reviewing our experience in carrying out the tasks we discussed."

- "Our time is running out, and there are still some areas we need to explore. Let's arrange another session when we can finish our exploration and think about where you'd like to go from there."

- "We have just a few minutes left. Let's summarize what we accomplished today and what you and I are going to work on before our next session."

Goal Attainment

During Phase II of the helping process, interviewing skills are used to help clients accomplish their goals. Much of the focus during this phase is on identifying and carrying out actions or tasks that clients must implement to accomplish their goals. Not surprisingly, preparing clients to carry out these actions is crucial to successful implementation. Fortunately, effective strategies of preparation are available (see Chapter 13).

As clients undertake the challenging process of making changes in their lives, it is important that they maintain focus on a few high-priority goals until they have made sufficient progress to warrant shifting to other goals. Otherwise, they may jump from one concern to another, dissipating their energies without achieving significant progress. The burden, therefore, falls on the social worker to provide structure for and direction to the client. Toward this end, skills in maintaining focus during single sessions and continuity between sessions are critical (see Chapter 6).

As noted earlier, obstacles to goal attainment commonly arise during the helping process. Individual barriers typically include fears associated with change as well as behavior and thought patterns that are highly resistant to change efforts because they serve a protective function (usually at great psychological cost to the individual). With couples and families, barriers may include entrenched interactional patterns that resist change because they perpetuate power or dependence, maintain safe psychological distance, or foster independence (at the cost of intimacy). In groups, barriers may involve dysfunctional processes that persist despite repeated efforts by leaders to replace these patterns with others that are conducive to group goals and to group maturation.

Additive empathy is used with individuals, couples, and groups as a means to recognize and to resolve emotional barriers that block growth and progress. Confrontation is a high-risk skill used to assist clients in recognizing and resolving resistant patterns of thought and behavior. Because of the sophistication required to use these techniques effectively, we have devoted Chapter 17 to them and have provided relevant skill development exercises. Additional techniques for managing barriers to change (including relational reactions) are discussed in Chapter 18.

Summary

This chapter examined the three phases of the helping process from a global perspective and briefly considered the structure and processes involved in interviewing. The inside cover of the book summarizes the constituent parts of the helping process and demonstrates their interrelationships with various interviewing processes. The remaining parts of the book focus in detail on the three phases of the helping process and on the interviewing skills and interventions employed during each phase.

Internet Resources

See our companion website for hot links to some helpful URLs. Note that URLs are subject to change. We will endeavor to update the links on the companion website as much as possible.

Three useful books that can orient you toward use of the Internet and World Wide Web are Vernon and Lynch (2000), Kardas (1999), and Grant and Grobman (1998).

A useful site for many social work sources is SWAN: Social Work Access Network (*http://www. sc.edu/swan/*). You can also explore social work from an international perspective by accessing the website for the International Federation of Social Workers (*http://www.ifsw.org/*), which includes an international definition of social work practice and a policy statement on peace and social justice. You can also find a useful source on prevention at http://www.uky.edu/RGS/Prevention Research. Using InfoTrac College Edition, you can access an article by Reisch (2002) on social justice.

Related Online Content

Visit the *Direct Social Work Practice* companion website at *http://socialwork. wadsworth.com/hepworth7* for additional learning tools such as glossary terms, chapter outlines, InfoTrac College Edition keywords, relevant web links, and chapter practice quizzes. Also, be sure to check out the Direct Practice Virtual Reader, where the authors have personally selected articles relevant to this chapter using InfoMarks.

Notes

1. The idea of specific phases and their accompanying tasks in structuring casework was originally developed by Jessie Taft and Virginia Robinson and the Functional School. This concept was later extended by Reid (1992) and Epstein (1988) in the task-centered approach.
2. Lila George, Research Director, Leech Lake Tribe (personal communication, 1993).

Operationalizing the Cardinal Social Work Values

CHAPTER OVERVIEW

As we noted in Chapter 1, social work practice is guided by knowledge, skills, and values. Chapter 4 addresses the last of those three areas. It introduces the cardinal values of the profession and the ethical obligations that arise from those values. Because, in practice, values can clash and ethical principles may conflict with each other, the chapter also describes some of these dilemmas and offers guidance about resolving them. As you read this chapter, you will have opportunities to place yourself in complex situations that challenge you to analyze your personal values and to assess their compatibility with social work values.

THE INTERACTION BETWEEN PERSONAL AND PROFESSIONAL VALUES

Values are "preferred conceptions," or beliefs about how things ought to be. All of us have values: our beliefs about what things are important or proper that then guide our actions and decisions. The profession of social work has values, too. They indicate what is important to social workers and guide the practice of the profession. Social workers must be attuned to their personal values and be aware of when those values mesh or clash with those espoused by the profession as a whole. Beyond this, social workers must recognize that

their clients also have personal values that shape their beliefs and behaviors, and these may conflict with the social worker's own values or with those of the profession. Further, the larger society has values that are articulated through policies and laws. These can also conflict with social workers' own beliefs, their clients' values, or the profession's values.

Self-awareness is the first step in sorting out these potential areas of conflict. The following sections describe the core values of the profession, provide opportunities to become aware of personal values, and describe the difficulties that can occur when social workers impose their own beliefs on clients.

THE CARDINAL VALUES OF SOCIAL WORK

The Code of Ethics developed by the National Association of Social Workers (NASW, 1999) and the professional literature articulate the core values of the profession and the ethical principles that represent those values. They can be summarized as follows:

- All human beings deserve access to the resources they need to deal with life's problems and to develop their potentialities. The value of service is embodied in this principle, in that social workers are expected to elevate service to others above their own self-interest. In particular, the profession's values place a premium on working for social justice. Social workers' "change efforts are focused primarily on issues of poverty, unemployment, discrimination, and other forms of social injustice. These activities seek to promote sensitivity to and knowledge about oppression and cultural and ethnic diversity. Social workers strive to ensure access to needed information, services, and resources; equality of opportunity; and meaningful participation in decision making for all people" (NASW, 1999, p. 5).

- The value that social workers place on the dignity and worth of the person is demonstrated through respect for the inherent dignity of the persons with whom they work and in efforts to examine prejudicial attitudes that may diminish their ability to embrace each client's individuality.

- Social workers view interpersonal relationships as essential for well-being and as "an important vehicle for change" (NASW, 1999, p. 5). The value placed on human relationships affects the way social workers relate to their clients and the efforts that social workers make to improve the quality of the relationships in their clients' lives.

- The value of integrity means that professional social workers behave in a trustworthy manner. They treat their clients and colleagues in a fair and respectful fashion; they are honest and promote responsible and ethical practices in others.

- The value of competence requires that social workers practice only within their areas of ability and continually develop and enhance their professional expertise. As professionals, social workers must take responsibility for assuring that their competence is not diminished by personal problems, by substance abuse, or by other difficulties. Similarly, they should take action to address incompetent, unethical, or impaired practice by other professionals.

What do these values mean? What difficulties can arise in putting them into practice? How can they conflict with social workers', clients', and society's values? The following sections describe these values and situations in which conflicts can

occur. Skill-building exercises at the end of the chapter will assist you in identifying and working through value conflicts.

1. *All human beings deserve access to the resources they need to deal with life's problems and to develop to their fullest potential.* A historic and defining feature of social work is the profession's focus on individual well-being in a social context. Attending to the environmental forces that create, contribute to, and address problems in living is a fundamental part of social work theory and practice (NASW, 1999, p. 1).

Implementing this value means believing that people have the right to resources. It also means that as a social worker you are committed to helping secure those resources for your clients and to developing policies and implementing programs to fill unmet needs. While this value seems an easy choice to embrace, sometimes specific cases can bring out conflicting beliefs and personal biases that challenge the social worker in upholding it. To enhance your awareness of situations in which you might experience such difficulties, imagine yourself in interviews with the clients in each of the following scenarios. Take note of your feelings and of possible discomfort or conflict. Next, contemplate how your response is or is not consistent with the social work value in question. If the client has not requested a resource but the need for one is apparent, consider what resource might be developed and how you might go about developing it.

Situation 1 You are a practitioner in a public assistance agency that has limited, special funds available to assist clients to purchase essential eyeglasses, dentures, hearing aids, and other prosthetic items. Your client, Mr. Y, lives in a large apartment complex for single persons and is disabled by a chronic psychiatric disorder. He requests special aid in purchasing new glasses. He says he accidentally dropped his old glasses and they were stepped on by a passerby. However, you know from talking to his landlord and his previous worker that, due to his confusion, Mr. Y regularly loses his glasses and has received emergency funds for glasses several times in the last year alone.

Situation 2 During a home visit to a large, impoverished family in the central city, you observe Eddy, a teenage boy, drawing pictures of animals. The quality of the drawings reveals an exceptional talent. When you compliment him, Eddy appears shy, but his faint smile expresses his delight over your approval. Eddy's mother then complains that he spends most of his free hours drawing, which she thinks is a waste of time. At her remarks, Eddy's smile dissolves in hurt and discouragement.

Situation 3 During a routine visit to an elderly couple who are recipients of public assistance, you discover that the roof on their home leaks. Your clients have had small repairs on several occasions, but the roof is old and worn out. They have gathered bids for re-roofing, and the lowest bid was more than $3,500. They ask whether your agency can assist them with funding. State policies permit expenditures for such repairs under exceptional circumstances, but much red tape is involved, including securing special approval from the county director of social services, the county advisory board, and the state director of social services.

Situation 4 Mr. M sustained a severe heart attack 3 months ago. His medical report indicates that he must limit his future physical activities to light work. Mr. M has given up and is asking you to pursue worker's compensation and other resources that would help support his family. You are concerned that while Mr. M might be entitled to these supports, they may reduce his motivation to pursue rehabilitation and work that he can reasonably do given his physical condition.

The preceding vignettes depict situations in which clients need resources or opportunities to develop their skills or potential or to ensure their safety and quality of life. Possible obstacles to responding positively to these needs, according to the sequence of the vignettes, are as follows:

1. Judgmental attitude by the worker
2. Failure to recognize an ability that might be developed, or reluctance to pursue it because it is not related to a goal for work

3. Failure to offer options because of the work involved or the pressure of other responsibilities
4. Skepticism that services will be effective in helping the client and judgments that they may have unintended effects

As you read the vignettes, you may have experienced some of these reactions or additional ones. This discomfort is not uncommon, but such reactions indicate a need for expanded self-examination and additional experience to embrace the social work value in challenging situations. The next section describes some strategies for addressing these types of conflicting reactions.

2. Social workers respect the inherent dignity and worth of the person. Social workers recognize the central importance of human relationships (NASW, 1999, p. 5). These values means that social workers believe that all people have intrinsic value, whatever their past or present behavior, beliefs, lifestyle, or social status, and that understanding these qualities is essential in involving clients as partners in change. These values embody several related concepts, sometimes referred to as "unconditional positive regard," "nonpossessive warmth," "acceptance," and "affirmation."

These values also recognize that respect is an essential element of the helping relationship. Before people will risk sharing personal problems and expressing deep emotions, they must first feel fully accepted and experience the goodwill and helpful intent of their service providers. This may be especially difficult when individuals who present for services feel ashamed or inadequate in requesting assistance. When clients are seeking services involuntarily, or when they have violated social norms by engaging in interpersonal violence, criminal behavior, or moral infractions, they will be especially alert to perceived judgments or condemnation on the part of the social worker. Your role is not to judge whether clients are to blame for their problems or to determine whether they are good or bad, evil or worthy, guilty or innocent. Rather, your role is to seek to understand your clients and their difficulties and to assist them in searching for solutions to their problems.

Intertwined with acceptance and nonjudgmental attitude is the equally important value stating that every person is unique and that social workers should affirm the individuality of those whom they serve. People are, of course, endowed with widely differing physical and mental characteristics; moreover, their life experiences are infinitely diverse. Consequently, people differ in terms of their appearance, beliefs, physiological functioning, interests, talents, motivation, goals, values, emotional and behavioral patterns, and many other factors. To affirm the uniqueness of another person, you must be committed to entering that individual's world, endeavoring to understand how that person experiences life. Only by attempting to walk in his or her shoes can you gain a full appreciation of the rich and complex individuality of another person.

Affirming each client's individuality, of course, goes far beyond gaining an appreciation of that person's perspectives on life. You must be able to convey awareness of what your client is experiencing moment by moment and affirm the validity of that experience. This affirmation does not mean agreeing with or condoning all of that person's views and feelings. Part of your role as a social worker entails helping people disentangle their confusing, conflicting thoughts and feelings; align their distorted perceptions with reality; mobilize their particular strengths, and differentiate their irrational reactions from reality. To fulfill this role, you must retain your own separateness and individuality. Otherwise, you may over-identify with clients, thereby losing your ability to provide fresh input. Affirming the experiences of another person, then, means validating those experiences, thus fostering that person's sense of personal identity and self-esteem.

Opportunities for affirming individuality and sense of self-worth are lost when unexamined prejudices and stereotypes (either positive or negative) blind social workers to the uniqueness of each individual client. Labels—such as "gang banger," "sorority girl," "old people," or "mental patient"— perpetuate damaging stereotypes because they obscure the individual characteristics of the people assigned to those labels. Working from these preconceptions, professionals may fail to effectively engage with clients; they may overlook needs or capacities and, as a result, their assessments, goals, and interventions will be distorted.

The consequences of such practice are troubling. Imagine an elderly client whose reversible health problems (associated with inadequate nutrition or need for medication) are dismissed as merely symptomatic of advanced age. Also consider the developmentally disabled client who is interested in learning about sexuality and contraceptives, but whose social worker fails to address those issues, considering them irrelevant for members of this population. Perhaps the sorority member will fail to disclose symptoms of an eating disorder or suicidal ideation to the social worker who presumes she "has everything going for her." What about the terminally ill patient who is more concerned about allowing her lesbian partner to make her end-of-life decisions than she is about her illness and impending death? Clearly, avoiding assumptions and prejudices is central to effective social work practice.

Sometimes, the ability to embrace these first two sets of values comes with increased experience and exposure to a range of clients. Seasoned practitioners have learned that acceptance comes through understanding the life experience of others, not by criticizing or judging their actions. As you work with clients, then, you should try to view them as persons in distress and avoid perceiving them based on labels, such as "lazy," "irresponsible," "delinquent," "dysfunctional," or "promiscuous." As you learn more about your clients, you will find that many of them have suffered various forms of deprivation and have themselves been victims of abusive, rejecting, or exploitative behavior, which resulted in their diminished sense of self-worth. Remember also that your clients have abilities and assets that may not be apparent to you. Consistent respect and acceptance on your part are vital in helping them gain the self-esteem and mobilize capacities that are essential to change and to well-being.

However, withholding judgments does not mean that you must condone or approve of illegal, immoral, abusive, exploitative, or irresponsible behavior. Like other persons, social workers have their own values and moral codes and are offended by child neglect, rape, exploitation, and other such behaviors. Moreover, social work as a profession and social workers as individuals have responsibilities to assist people to live according to the laws of society.

In doing so, the social worker, without blaming, must assist clients in taking responsibility for the part they play in their difficulties. Indeed, change is possible in many instances only when clients gain awareness of the effects of their decisions and seek to modify their behavior accordingly. The difference between "blaming" and "defining ownership of responsibilities" lies in the fact that the former tends to be punitive, whereas the latter flows from the social worker's positive intentions to be helpful and to assist clients in change.

As a practitioner, you will inevitably confront the challenge of maintaining your own values (except those that hinder relating effectively to people) without imposing them on your clients. A first step toward resolving this issue is addressing your own judgmental tendencies. Yet another challenge is to develop composure, so that you don't reveal embarrassment or dismay when people discuss problems associated with socially unacceptable behavior.

The value clarification exercises that follow will help you to identify your own particular areas of vulnerability. In each situation, imagine yourself in an interview or group session with the client(s). If appropriate, you can role-play the situation with a fellow student, changing roles so that you can benefit by playing the client's role as well. As you imagine or role-play the situation, be aware of your feelings, attitudes, and behavior. After each situation, contemplate or discuss the following questions:

1. What feelings and attitudes did you experience? Were they based on what actually occurred or did they emanate from preconceived beliefs about such situations or individuals?

2. Were you comfortable or uneasy with the client? How did your classmate perceive your attitudes toward the "client"? What cues alerted him or her to your values and reactions?

3. Did any of the situations disturb you more than others? What values were reflected in your feelings, attitudes, and behavior?

4. What assumptions did you make about the needs of the client(s) in each vignette?

5. What actions would you take (or what information would you seek) to move beyond stereotypes in understanding your client(s)?

Situation 5 Your client is a 35-year-old married male who was sentenced by the court to a secure mental health facility following his arrest for peering in the windows of a women's dormitory at your college. He appears uncomfortable and blushes as you introduce yourself.

Situation 6 You are assigned to do a home study for a family interested in adoption. When you arrive at the home for the first interview, you realize that the couple interested in the adoption consists of two gay males.

Situation 7 You are a child protective worker, and your client is a 36-year-old stepfather whose 13-year-old stepdaughter ran away from home after he had sexual intercourse with her on several occasions during the past 2 months. In your first meeting, he states that he "doesn't know what the big deal is . . . it's not like we're related or anything."

Situation 8 Your 68-year-old client has been receiving chemotherapy for terminal cancer at your hospital for the past month. Appearing drawn and dramatically more emaciated than she was last month, the client reports that she has been increasingly suffering with pain and believes her best course of action is to take an overdose of sleeping pills.

Situation 9 You are a probation officer. The judge has ordered you to complete a pre-sentencing investigation of a woman who was arrested for befriending elderly individuals and persons with mental retardation, and then stealing their monthly disability checks.

Situation 10 You have been working for 8 weeks with an 8-year-old boy who has experienced behavioral difficulties at school. During play therapy he demonstrates with toys how he has set fire to or cut up several cats and dogs in his neighborhood.

Situation 11 Your client, Mrs. O, was admitted to a domestic violence shelter following an attack by her husband, in which she sustained a broken collarbone and arm injuries. This occasion is the eighth time she has contacted the shelter. Each previous time she has returned home or allowed her husband to move back into the home with her.

Situation 12 A low-income family with whom you have been working recently received a substantial check as part of a settlement with their former landlord. During a visit in which you plan to help the family budget the funds to pay their past due bills, you find the settlement money is gone—spent on a large television and lost in gambling at a local casino.

Situation 13 You are an African American outreach worker. One Caucasian client has expressed appreciation for the help you have provided, yet tells you repeatedly that she is "afraid, living in this area with so many coloreds."

Situation 14 You are working with a high school senior, the eldest girl in a large family from a strict religious background. Your client wants desperately to attend college but has been told by her parents that she is needed to care for her younger siblings and assist in her family's ministry.

If you experienced discomfort or negative feelings as you read or role-played any of the preceding situations, your reactions were not unusual. Most people are repulsed or angered by some of the problematic behaviors embodied in the situations described. It can be challenging to look beyond appalling behaviors to see clients as individuals in distress. However, by focusing selectively on the person rather than on the behavior, you can gradually overcome the inclination to label people negatively and learn to see them in full perspective.

How does this acceptance play out in practice? Acceptance is conveyed by listening attentively; by responding sensitively to the client's feelings; by using facial expressions, voice intonations, and gestures that convey interest and concern; and by extending courtesies and attending to the client's comfort. These skills are discussed and demonstrated in Chapter 6 and in exercises at the end of this chapter.

If you are unable to be open and accepting of people whose behavior runs counter to your values, your effectiveness in helping them will be diminished, because it is difficult—if not impossible—to conceal negative feelings toward others. Even if you can mask your negative feelings toward certain clients, you are likely to be unsuccessful in helping them, as clients can quickly detect insincerity. To expand your capacity for openness and acceptance, it may be helpful to view association with others whose beliefs, lifestyles, and behaviors differ strikingly from your own as an opportunity to enrich yourself as you experience their uniqueness. Truly open people relish such opportunities, viewing differences as refreshing and stimulating and seeing these interactions as a chance to better understand the forces that motivate people. By prizing the opportunity to relate to all types of people and by seeking to understand them, you will gain a deeper appreciation of the diversity and complexity of human beings. In so doing, you will be less likely to pass judgment and will achieve personal growth in the process. You might also find it helpful to talk with other social workers who have been in the field for some time. How do they manage value conflicts? Are they still able to treat clients with respect, even while disdaining their actions?

3. *The value of integrity means that social worker professionals behave in a trustworthy manner.* As an ethical principle, integrity means that social workers act honestly, encourage ethical practices in their agencies, and take responsibility for their own ethical conduct (Reamer, 1998a). In the real world, it means that social workers present themselves and their credentials accurately, avoid other forms of misrepresentation (e.g., in billing practices or in presentation of research findings), and do not participate in fraud and deception. Integrity also refers to the ways that social workers treat their colleagues. Professionals are expected to treat one another with respect, avoid involving clients or

others in professional disputes, and be forthright in their dealings with fellow professionals. These expectations are important not only for our individual trustworthiness, but also because each of us serves as a representative of the larger profession and we should act in ways that do not dishonor it.

This may seem to be a relatively straightforward expectation. However, challenges can arise when pressures from other colleagues or employing organizations create ethical dilemmas. In those cases, the challenge is not what is right, but rather how to do it. Following are two examples of such dilemmas involving the principle of integrity. What strategies might you pursue to resolve these dilemmas and act with honesty and professionalism? Later sections of this chapter will provide further guidance regarding ethical decision making.

Situation 15 Your agency recently received a large federal grant to implement a "Return to Work" program as part of welfare reform. Although the evaluation protocol is very clear about what constitutes "work," the agency is pressuring you and your coworkers (none of whom are social workers) to count clients' volunteer efforts and other nonpaying jobs as "work" in an effort to ensure that this valuable program will continue. The agency maintains that paying jobs are difficult to find, so clients who are actively working—even in noncompensated jobs—"fit the spirit, if not the letter of the law."

Situation 16 Your supervisor wants to assess your effectiveness in conducting family sessions. Because he fears that if clients know they are being taped, their behaviors will change and his findings will be distorted, he has told you to tape these sessions without their knowledge. The supervisor feels that because he discusses your cases with you anyway, the taping without explicit client permission should be acceptable.

4. *The value of competence requires that social workers practice only within their scope of knowledge and ability and that they enhance and develop their professional expertise.* As with the value of integrity, this principle places the burden for self-awareness and self-regulation on the social worker. An expectation of practice as a professional is that the individual will take responsibility for knowing his or her own limits

and seek out the knowledge and experience needed to develop further expertise throughout the span of his or her career. This principle means that social workers will decline cases where they lack sufficient expertise, and that they will seek out supervision for continuous self-examination and professional development. The NASW Code of Ethics also includes cultural competence among its expectations for social workers, requiring an understanding of various cultures, their strengths, the effects of oppression, and the provision of culturally sensitive services (NASW, 1999).

Self-regulation also requires the social worker to be alert to events or problems that affect his or her professional competence. For example, is a health or mental health problem hindering the social worker's service to clients? Are personal reactions to the client (such as anger or sexual attraction) impairing the social worker's judgment in a particular case?

Developing and maintaining competence is a career-long responsibility, yet it can be challenging to uphold (Hargrove, 1986). Consider the following scenarios:

Situation 17 You are a new employee at a small, financially strapped counseling center. The director of your agency just received a contract to do outreach, assessments, and case management for frail elders. Although you took a human behavior course as a social work student, you have never studied or worked with older adults, especially those at risk. The director has asked you to lead this new program and has emphasized how important the new funding is for the agency's survival.

Situation 18 For the past few weeks, you've found yourself attracted to one of your clients, thinking about him or her often and wondering what the client is doing at different times of the day. You wonder if this attraction could affect your objectivity on the case, but are reluctant to discuss the situation with your supervisor because it might affect his or her evaluation of you later this year.

What is competence? Do social workers ever feel totally competent? What is impairment? And how can we tell when it applies to us and our practice? Self-evaluation requires self-knowledge and introspection. Measuring one's competence requires seeking input from colleagues and supervisors. Professional development requires actively seeking out opportunities to hone existing skills and develop new ones, whether through reading, continuing education, course work, or case conferences. When you do not have the skills, abilities, or capacity demanded by a client's situation, a referral is necessary, which may mean elevating the client's needs above your own.

In this section's presentation of the social work profession's cardinal values, numerous situations and cases have highlighted the potential for value conflicts. Self-awareness, openness to new persons and events, and increasing practice experience are all crucial elements in overcoming value conflicts. But what if you've done these things and values still conflict? Social workers occasionally encounter situations in which they cannot conform to the profession's values or in which a client's behaviors or goals evoke such negative reactions that a positive helping relationship cannot be established. For example, practitioners who have personal experience with child abuse or who are intensely opposed to abortions may find it difficult to accept a pedophile as a client or to offer help to a person experiencing an unintended pregnancy. In such instances, it is important to acknowledge these feelings and to explore them through supervision or therapy. It may be feasible to help the worker overcome these difficulties to be more fully available as a helping person. If this is not possible, however, or if the situation is exceptional, the social worker and his or her supervisor should explore the possibility of transferring the case to another practitioner who can accept both the client and the goals. In such circumstances, it is vital to clarify for clients that the reason for the transfer is not personal rejection of them but rather recognition that they deserve the best service possible and that the particular social worker cannot provide that service because of value conflicts. This type of explanation conveys goodwill and safeguards clients' self-esteem. When

a transfer is not possible, the social worker is responsible for being up front with the client about his or her difficulties while committing to carrying out ethical and professional responsibilities. When practitioners frequently encounter difficulties in accepting clients, they owe it to themselves and to future clients to seriously consider whether they have chosen the appropriate profession.

ETHICS

Codes of ethics are the embodiment of a profession's values. They set forth principles and standards for behavior of members of that profession. In social work, the primary Code of Ethics is promulgated by the NASW. It addresses a range of responsibilities that social workers have as professionals, to their clients, to their colleagues, to their employers, to their profession, and to society as a whole. This section addresses four primary areas of ethical responsibility for social workers: self-determination, informed consent, maintenance of client–social worker boundaries, and confidentiality. First, however, it discusses how ethics are related to legal responsibilities and malpractice risks. The section concludes by summarizing the resources and processes available for resolving ethical dilemmas.

The Intersection of Laws and Ethics

The practice of social work is governed by a vast array of policies, laws, and regulations. Whether established by court cases, the U. S. Congress or state legislatures, licensure boards, or regulatory agencies, these rules affect social workers' decisions and actions. For example, state mandatory reporting laws require social workers to report cases where child abuse is suspected. The Health Insurance Portability and Accountability Act (HIPAA) regulates the storage and sharing of patient records (U. S. Department of Health and Human Services, 2003). Some states' health department rules may require social workers to divulge the names of HIV-positive clients to public health authorities; in other states, rules may forbid the sharing of patient's names or HIV status. Licensure board regulations may forbid social work practice by persons with felony convictions. Federal court cases may extend evidential privilege to communications with social workers (Reamer, 1999). Federal laws may prohibit the provision of certain benefits to undocumented immigrants.

Good social work requires practitioners to be aware of the laws and regulations that govern the profession and apply to their area of practice. But knowing the laws is not enough. Consider the following case.

CASE EXAMPLE

Alice is a 38-year-old woman who has presented for treatment, wracked with guilt as the result of a brief extramarital affair. In her third session, she discloses that she is HIV-positive, but is unwilling to tell her husband of her status because then the affair would be revealed and she fears losing him and her two young daughters. You are concerned about the danger to her husband's health, and press her to tell him or to allow you to do so. Alice responds that if you do, you will be breaking your promise of confidentiality and violating her privacy. She implies that she would sue you or report you to your licensing board and to your profession's ethics committee.

This case neatly captures the clash of ethics, laws, and regulations and illustrates the stakes for workers who make the "wrong" decision. In a scenario such as this one, the social worker just wants a clear answer from a lawyer or supervisor who will tell him or her exactly what to do. Unfortunately, matters are not that simple. Good practice requires knowledge of both the applicable ethical principles and the relevant laws. Even with this knowledge, dilemmas may persist. In this case example, the ethical principles of self-determination and confidentiality are pitted against the principle to protect others from harm, which itself is derived from a court case (Cohen & Cohen, 1999; Reamer, 1995). The particular state or setting where the case takes place may have laws or regulations that govern the social worker's actions. Finally, the threat of civil litigation for malpractice looms

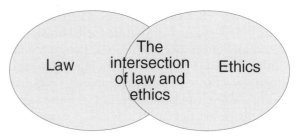

Figure 4-1 The Relationship of Law and Ethics

large, even when the social worker's actions are thoughtful, careful, ethical, and legal.

When you think about the intersection of laws and ethics, it may be helpful to think of a Venn diagram, in which two ovals overlap (see Figure 4-1). In the center are areas common to both ethics and laws; within each oval are items that are exclusive to laws and ethics, respectively. Some standards contained in the NASW Code of Ethics are not addressed by laws and regulations (such as the prohibition of sexual relationships with supervisees or standards on treating colleagues with respect). Similarly, some areas of the law are not covered by the Code of Ethics. For example, it is illegal to drive while intoxicated, but the Code of Ethics lacks a standard related to that act. Where the two realms intersect, there can be areas of agreement as well as areas of discord. As the Code of Ethics notes,

> Social workers' primary responsibility is to promote the well-being of clients. In general, clients' interests are primary. However, social workers' responsibility to the larger society or specific legal obligations may on limited occasions supersede the loyalty owed clients and clients should be so advised. (NASW, 1999, p. 7)

Also,

> Instances may arise when social workers' ethical obligations conflict with agency policies or relevant laws or regulations. When such conflicts occur, social workers must make a responsible effort to resolve the conflict in a manner that is consistent with the values, principles, and standards expressed in this Code. If a reasonable resolution of the conflict does not appear possible, social workers should seek proper consultation before making a decision. (NASW, 1999, pp. 3–4)

The processes for ethical decision making are addressed later in this chapter. For now, though, it is important to acknowledge that social workers must know both the law and ethical principles to practice effectively. Workers must also recognize that sometimes conflicts will occur between and among ethical and legal imperatives. Thoughtful examination, consultation, and skillful application of the principles will serve as guides when conflicts and dilemmas arise.

Key Ethical Principles

The NASW Code of Ethics contains 155 standards, addressing a variety of ethical issues (such as conflicts of interest, competence, or confidentiality) for social workers in a range of roles (such as supervisor, teacher, direct practitioner or administrator). In this section, we examine four key areas of immediate relevance to direct practitioners: self-determination, informed consent, professional boundaries and confidentiality.

Self-Determination

Biestek (1957) has defined self-determination as "the practical recognition of the right and need of clients to freedom in making their own choices and decisions" (p. 103). Self-determination is central to the social worker's ethical responsibility to clients:

> Social workers respect and promote the right of clients to self-determination and assist clients in their efforts to identify and clarify their goals. Social workers may limit clients' right to self-determination when, in their professional judgment, clients' actions or potential actions pose a serious, foreseeable, and imminent risk to themselves or others. (NASW, 1999, p. 7)

This value also embodies the beliefs that clients have the capacity to grow and change and to develop solutions to their difficulties, as well as the right and capacity to exercise free choice responsibly. These values are magnified when practitioners adopt a strengths-oriented perspective, looking for positive qualities and undeveloped potential rather than pointing out limitations and past mistakes (Cowger, 1994; Saleeby, 1997). Such a positive perspective engenders hope and courage on the client's part and nurtures self-esteem. These

factors, in turn, enhance the client's motivation, which is indispensable to achieving a successful outcome.

The extent to which you affirm the client's right to self-determination rests in large measure on your perceptions of the helping role and of the helping process. If you consider your major role to be that of providing solutions or dispensing advice freely, you may foster dependency, demean clients by failing to recognize and affirm their strengths, and relegate them to a position of passive cooperation (or passive resistance, a frequent response under such circumstances).[1] Such domineering behavior is counterproductive. Not only does it discourage open communication, but, equally important, it denies clients the opportunity to gain strength and self-respect as they actively wrestle with their difficulties. Fostering dependency generally leaves people weaker rather than stronger and is a disservice to clients.

The type of relationship that affirms self-determination and supports growth is a partnership wherein the practitioner and the client (whether an individual, a couple, or a group) are joined in a mutual effort to search for solutions to problems or to promote growth. As enablers of change, social workers facilitate clients in their quest to view their problems realistically, to consider various solutions and their consequences, to implement change-oriented strategies, to understand themselves and others more fully, to gain awareness of previously unrecognized strengths and opportunities for growth, and to tackle obstacles to change and growth. As helpful as these steps are, however, ultimately the responsibility for pursuing these options rests with the client.

Just as fostering self-determination enhances client autonomy, exhibiting paternalism (i.e., preventing self-determination based on a judgment of the client's own good) infringes on autonomy. Linzer (1999) refers to paternalism as "the overriding of a person's wishes or actions through coercion, deception or nondisclosure of information, or for the welfare of others" (p. 137). A similar concept is paternalistic beneficence, wherein the social worker implements protective interventions to enhance the client's quality of life, sometimes despite the client's objections (Abramson, 1985; Murdach, 1996).

Under what conditions might it be acceptable for a social worker to override a client's autonomy? Paternalism may be acceptable when a client is young or mentally incompetent, when an irreversible act such as suicide can be prevented, or when the interference with the client's decisions or actions ensures other freedoms or liberties, such as preventing a serious crime (Abramson, 1985; Reamer, 1989). Murdach suggests three gradations of beneficent actions, which vary in their level of intrusiveness depending on the degree of risk and the client's decision-making capacity. Yet, even under these circumstances, social workers must weigh the basis for their decisions against the potential outcomes of their actions. For example, if a psychiatric patient refuses medication, some would argue that the client lacks competence to make such a decision, and that forcing him or her to take the medication would be "for the client's own good." Yet diagnosis or placement is not a sufficient basis for overriding the client's autonomy. For this reason, states have developed elaborate administrative and judicial processes that must be traversed before a person can be involuntarily hospitalized or medicated.

Even when clients have reduced capacity for exercising self-determination, social workers should act to ensure that they exercise their capacities to the fullest feasible extent. For example, self-determination can be extended to individuals who are terminally ill by educating them about their options and encouraging them to articulate their desires through advance directives, which provide instructions to health care personnel regarding which medical interventions are acceptable. These directives become operative when the patient's condition precludes decision-making capacity. Advance directives can take the form of living wills or authorizing an individual to act with durable power of attorney. The latter procedure is broader in scope and more powerful than a living will. The person designated to have durable power of attorney or medical power of attorney is authorized to make decisions as if he or she were the patient when grave illness or accident has obliterated the patient's autonomy.

Operationalizing clients' rights to self-determination sometimes can pose perplexing challenges. Adding to the complexity is the reality that in certain instances, higher-order principles such as safety supersede the right to self-determination. To challenge your thinking about how you might affirm the value of self-determination in practical situations, we have provided exercises that consist of problematic situations actually encountered by the authors or colleagues. As you read each scenario, analyze the alternative courses of action that are available and think of the laws, policies, and resources that you might consult as part of your decision making. Consider how you would work with the client to maximize self-determination, taking care also to promote his or her best interests.

Situation 1 In your work for the state welfare department, you oversee the care of numerous group home residents whose services are paid for by the state. Two of your clients, both in their twenties, reside in the same home and have told you that they are eager to get married. The administrator of the home strenuously protests that "the two are retarded" and, if they marry, might produce a child they could not properly care for. Further, she has stressed that she has no private room for a couple and that if the two marry, they will have to leave the group home.

Situation 2 A 15-year-old runaway, who is 4 months pregnant, has contacted you several times in regard to planning for her child. During her last visit, she confided that she is habituated to heroin. You have expressed your concern that the drug may damage her unborn child, but she does not seem worried, nor does she want to give up use of the drug. You also know that she obtains money for heroin through prostitution and is living on the street.

Situation 3 While making a visit to Mr. and Mrs. F, an elderly couple living in their home on their own savings, you discover that they have hired several home health aides who have stolen from them and provided such poor care that their health and nutrition are endangered. When you discuss with them your concern about the adequacy of their care, they firmly state that they can handle their own problems and "do not want to be put in a nursing home!"

Situation 4 As a rehabilitation worker, you have arranged for a young woman to receive training as a beautician in a local technical college, a vocation in which she expressed intense interest. Although initially enthusiastic, she now tells you that she wants to discontinue the program and go into nursing. According to your client, her supervisor at the college is highly critical of her work and the other trainees tease her and talk about her behind her back. You are torn about what to do, because you know that your client tends to antagonize other people with her quick and barbed remarks. You wonder if, rather than change programs, your client needs to learn more appropriate ways of communicating and relating to her supervisor and coworkers.

Situation 5 A middle-aged woman with cancer was so debilitated by her latest round of chemotherapy that she has decided to refuse further treatment. Her physician states that her age, general health, and stage of her cancer all argue for continuing her treatments, given the likelihood of a successful outcome. Her family is upset at seeing your client in pain and supports her decision.

Providing Informed Consent

Six principles in the NASW Code of Ethics address facets of informed consent. At its essence, informed consent requires that social workers "use clear and understandable language to inform clients of the purpose of the services, risks related to the services, limits to services because of the requirements of a third-party payer, relevant costs, reasonable alternatives, clients' right to refuse or withdraw consent, and the time frame covered by the consent. Social workers should provide clients with an opportunity to ask questions" (NASW, 1999, pp. 7–8). The Code of Ethics also indicates that clients should be informed when their services are being provided by a student.

Some workers view informed consent as a formality to be disposed of at the first interview or as a legalistic form to have clients sign and then file away. In fact, informed consent should be an active and

ongoing part of the helping process. Given the tension and uncertainty that can accompany a first session, clients may not realize the significance of the information they are provided. In addition, new issues may emerge that require discussion of the client's risks, benefits, and options (Strom-Gottfried, 1998b). Therefore, it makes sense to revisit the parameters of service and invite questions throughout the helping process. Having a "fact sheet" that describes relevant policies and answers commonly asked questions can also help clients by giving them something to refer to between meetings, should questions arise (Houston-Vega, Nuehring, & Daguio, 1997).

To facilitate informed consent for persons with hearing, literacy, or language difficulties, social workers should utilize interpreters, translators, and multiple communication methods as appropriate. When clients are temporarily or permanently incapable of providing informed consent, "social workers should protect clients' interests by seeking permission from an appropriate third party, informing clients consistent with the client's level of understanding" and "seek to ensure that the third party acts in a manner consistent with the client's wishes and interests" (NASW, 1999, p. 8). Even clients who are receiving services involuntarily are entitled to know the nature of the services they will be receiving and to understand their right to refuse service.

Preserving Professional Boundaries

Boundaries refer to clear lines of difference that are maintained between the social worker and the client in an effort to preserve the working relationship. They are intended to help prevent conflicts of interest, in which the social worker makes the client's interests the primary focus and avoids situations in which his or her professional practice is compromised. In part, boundaries help clarify that the client–social worker relationship is not a social one. Also, even though it may involve a high degree of trust and client self-disclosure, the relationship is not an intimate one, such as might be experienced with a friend, partner, or family member. When clients can trust that boundaries exist and will be maintained by the social worker, they are more able to focus on the issues for which they are seeking help. They can freely share of themselves and trust that the social worker's reactions and statements—whether of support, confrontation, or empathy—are artifacts of the working relationship, not social or sexual overtures or personal reactions such as might arise when friends disagree.

Sometimes social workers and other helping professionals have a difficult time with the notion of boundaries, perceiving that they establish a hierarchical relationship in which the client is deemed "less worthy" than the social worker. Some professionals may also feel that establishing such boundaries is a cold and clinical move, treating the client as an object instead of a fellow human deserving of warmth and compassion (Lazarus, 1994). Our viewpoint is that the two positions are not mutually exclusive. Social workers can have relationships with clients that are characterized by collaborative problem solving and mutuality, and they can react to clients authentically without blurring the boundaries of their relationship or obscuring the purpose of their work.

The NASW Code of Ethics addresses boundaries through six provisions:

1. "Social workers should not take unfair advantage of any professional relationship or exploit others to further their personal, religious, political, or business interests" (NASW, 1999, p. 9).

2. "Social workers should not engage in dual or multiple relationships with clients or former clients in which there is a risk of exploitation or potential harm to the client. In instances when dual or multiple relationships are unavoidable, social workers should take steps to protect clients and are responsible for setting clear, appropriate, and culturally sensitive boundaries. (Dual or multiple relationships occur when social workers relate to clients in more than one relationship, whether pro-fessional, social, or business. Dual or multiple relationships can occur simultaneously or consecutively.)" (NASW, 1999, pp. 9–10).

3. "Social workers should not engage in physical contact with clients when there is a possibility of psychological harm to the client as a result

of the contact (such as cradling or caressing clients) . . ." (NASW, 1999, p. 13).

4. "Social workers should under no circumstances engage in sexual activities or sexual contact with current clients, whether such contact is consensual or forced" (NASW, 1999, p. 13).

5. "Social workers should not engage in sexual activities or sexual contact with clients' relatives or other individuals with whom clients maintain a close personal relationship when there is a risk of exploitation or potential harm to the client. Sexual activity or sexual contact with clients' relatives or other individuals with whom clients maintain a personal relationship has the potential to be harmful to the client and may make it difficult for the social worker and client to maintain appropriate professional boundaries. Social workers—not their clients, their clients' relatives, or other individuals with whom the client maintains a personal relationship—assume the full burden for setting clear, appropriate, and culturally sensitive boundaries" (NASW, 1999, p. 13).

6. "Social workers should not engage in sexual activities or sexual contact with former clients because of the potential for harm to the client" (NASW, 1999, p. 13).

Although these standards of practice may seem self-evident, they represent an area fraught with difficulty within the profession. Research on ethics complaints indicates that in NASW-adjudicated cases, boundary violations accounted for more than half of all cases in which violations occurred (Strom-Gottfried, 1999a). Similarly, in research on the frequency of malpractice claims against social workers for the period 1961–1990, Reamer (1995) found that sexual violations were the second most common area of claim, and the most expensive in terms of money paid out. Most social workers cannot imagine developing sexual relationships with their clients; yet, this outcome is often the culmination of a "slippery slope" of boundary problems that may include excessive self-disclosure on the part of the worker, the exchange of personal gifts, socializing or meeting for meals outside the office, and arranging for the client to perform office and household chores or other favors (Borys & Pope, 1989; Epstein, Simon, & Kay, 1992; Gabbard, 1996; Gartrell, 1992).

It is not uncommon to experience feelings of sexual attraction for clients. When such feelings arise, however, it is crucial to raise them with faculty or supervisors so they can be acknowledged and examined. Such discussion normalizes and neutralizes these feelings and decreases the likelihood that the worker will act on the attraction (Pope, Keith-Spiegel, & Tabachnick, 1986). These issues will be observed further in the Chapter 19 discussion on relational reactions.

Other boundary issues can be both subtle and complex. For example, you may meet a neighbor in the agency waiting room or run into a client while doing your grocery shopping. You may decide to buy a car and find that the salesperson is a former client. You may visit a relative in the hospital and discover that her roommate is a current or former client. Friends in need of social work services may ask to be assigned to your caseload, because you already know them so well. A client may ask you to attend a "family" event, such as a graduation or wedding. You may resonate with a particular client and think what a great friend he or she could be. The possibilities are endless, and addressing them involves other ethical principles, such as maintaining confidentiality and avoiding conflicts of interest. The key is to be alert to dual relationships, to discuss troubling situations with colleagues and a supervisor, and to take care that the primacy of the helping relationship is preserved in questionable boundary situations (Brownlee, 1996; Erickson, 2001; Reamer, 2001). It is incumbent on the social worker to ensure that clients are not taken advantage of and that their services are not obscured or affected detrimentally when boundaries must be crossed.

Safeguarding Confidentiality

From a practical standpoint, confidentiality is a *sine qua non* of the helping process: Without the assurance of confidentiality, it is unlikely that clients would risk disclosing private aspects of their lives that, if revealed, could cause shame or damage to their reputations. This is especially true when clients' problems involve marital infidelity, deviant sexual practices, illicit activities, child abuse, and the like. Implied in confidentiality is an assurance that the practitioner will never reveal such personal matters to others.

Social workers are bound by the NASW Code of Ethics to safeguard their clients' confidentiality. Numerous standards operationalize this principle, but in essence, social workers are expected to respect clients' privacy, to gather information only for the purpose of providing effective services, and to disclose information only with clients' consent. Disclosure of information without clients' permission should be done only for compelling reasons, and even under these circumstances, there are limits on what information can be shared and with whom. These exceptions to confidentially will be addressed later in this section.

An unjustified breach of confidentiality is a violation of justice and is tantamount to theft of a secret with which one has been entrusted (Biestek, 1957). Maintaining strict confidentiality requires a strong commitment and constant vigilance, because clients sometimes reveal information that is shocking, humorous, bizarre, or titillating. To fulfill your responsibility in maintaining confidentiality, you must guard against disclosing information in inappropriate situations. Examples include discussing details of your work with family and friends, having gossip sessions with colleagues, dictating within the listening range of others, discussing client situations within earshot of other staff, and making remarks about clients in elevators or other public places.

The emergence of technology that permits the electronic collection, transfer, and storage of information raises new complexities for maintaining client privacy (Gelman, Pollack, & Weiner, 1999). When you leave a voice mail for a client, are you certain that only the client will receive the message? When a colleague sends you a fax on a case, can you be sure that others will not see that information before you retrieve the document? As authors such as Davidson and Davidson (1996) have noted, these technological advances have emerged at the same time that insurance companies and others who fund services are demanding increasingly more detailed information about cases before they will approve reimbursement for services. As a result, clients should be well informed about the limits of confidentiality and the potential risks of information shared for insurance claims (Corcoran & Winslade, 1994).

Beyond ethical standards, the Health Insurance Portability and Accountability Act of 1996 (HIPAA) established federal standards to protect the privacy of personal health information. HIPAA regulations affect pharmacies, health care settings, and insurance plans as well as individual health and mental health providers. The rules affect identifiable client information in all forms, including paper records, electronic data and communications, and verbal communications. There are several important provisions for social workers in HIPAA (HIPAA Medical Privacy Rule, 2003; Protecting the Privacy of Patients' Health Information, 2003).

- Psychotherapy notes" have a particular protection under HIPAA. The release of those notes requires special, separate authorization. Psychotherapy notes must be kept separately in client files, and meet other criteria to be protected.

- Clients should be provided access to their records, and have the opportunity to seek corrections if they identify errors or mistakes. However, under HIPAA, client access to psychotherapy notes is restricted.

- Clients must be given information on the organization's privacy policies and they must sign a form or otherwise indicate that they have received the information.

- Client records or data should be protected from non-medical uses, such as marketing, unless the client gives specific permission otherwise.

- Clients should understand their rights to request other reasonable efforts to protect confidentiality, such as requesting to be contacted only at certain times or numbers.

- Organizations and the individuals who work in them (in clinical, clerical, administrative and other roles) must take care to ensure that security standards are in place and that they are reinforced though staff development and agency policies.

- When state laws are more stringent than the provisions in HIPPA (when they offer greater protections for clients) those laws take precedence over HIPAA.

- HIPAA recognizes the validity of professional standards, such as those contained in the NASW Code of Ethics, and in some cases, those provisions may be more stringent than HIPAA's.

What Are the Limits on Confidentiality?

While social workers are expected to safeguard the information they collect in the course of their professional duties, there are several situations in which helping professionals are allowed or compelled to share case information. These include: when seeking supervision or consultation, when the client waives confidentiality, when the client presents a danger to self or others, for reporting suspicions of child or elder maltreatment, and when presented with a subpoena or court order.

Supervision and Consultation

The right to confidentiality is not absolute, because case situations are frequently discussed with supervisors and consultants and may be presented at staff conferences. Disclosing information in these instances, however, is for the purpose of enhancing service to clients, who will generally consent to these uses when their purposes are clarified. The client has a right to be informed that such disclosures may occur, and practitioners seeking supervision have a responsibility to conceal the identity of the client to the fullest extent possible and to reveal no more personal information than is absolutely necessary.

Other personnel such as administrators, volunteers, clerical staff, consultants, board members, researchers, legal counsel, and outside persons who may review records for purposes of quality assurance, peer review, or accreditation may have access to files or case information. This access to information should be for the purposes of better serving the client, and these individuals should sign binding agreements not to misuse confidential information. Further, it is essential that social workers promote policies and norms that protect confidentiality and assure that case information is treated carefully and respectfully.

Client Waivers of Confidentiality

Social workers are often asked by other professionals or agencies to provide confidential information about the nature of their client's difficulties or the services provided. Sometimes, these requests can be made with such authority that the recipient is caught off guard, inadvertently acknowledging a particular person as a client or providing the information requested about the case. In these instances, it is important that such data be provided only with the written, informed consent of clients, which releases the practitioner and agency from liability in disclosing the requested information. Even when informed consent is obtained, however, it is important to reveal information selectively based on the essential needs of the other party.

In some exceptional circumstances, information can be revealed without informed consent, such as a bona fide emergency in which a client's life appears to be at stake or when the social worker is legally compelled, as in the reporting of child abuse. In other instances, it is prudent to obtain supervisory and legal input before disclosing confidential information without the client's written consent for release of information.

A final example of the client's waiver of confidentiality occurs if the client files a malpractice claim against the social worker. Such an action would "terminate the patient or client privilege" (Dickson, 1998, p. 48), freeing the practitioner to share publicly such information as is necessary to mount a defense against the lawsuit.

Danger to Self or Others

In certain instances, the client's right to confidentiality may be less compelling than the rights of other people who could be severely harmed or damaged by actions planned by the client and confided to the practitioner. For example, if the client plans to commit kidnapping, injury, or murder, the practitioner is obligated to disclose these intentions to the intended victim and to law enforcement officials so that timely preventive action can be taken. Indeed, if practitioners fail to make appropriate disclosures under these circumstances, they may be liable to civil prosecution for negligence. The fundamental case in this area is the Tarasoff case (Reamer, 1994). In it, a young man seeing a psychologist at a university health service threatened his girlfriend, Tatiana Tarasoff. The therapist notified university police; after interviewing the young man, they determined that he did not pose a danger to his girlfriend. Some weeks later the young man murdered Tarasoff, and her family filed a lawsuit alleging that she should have been warned. Ultimately, the court ruled that mental health professionals have an obligation to protect their clients' intended victims.

This court decision has led to varying interpretations in subsequent cases and in resulting state laws, but two principles have consistently resulted from it (Dickson, 1998; Houston-Vega, Nuehring, & Daguio, 1997): If the worker perceives a foreseeable and imminent threat to an identifiable potential victim, the social worker should (1) act to warn that victim or (2) take other precautions (such as notifying police or placing the client in a secure facility) to protect others from harm.

Another application of the duty to protect personal safety involves intervening to prevent a client's suicide. Typically, lawsuits that cite a breach of confidentiality undertaken to protect suicidal clients have not been successful (VandeCreek, Knapp, & Herzog, 1988). Conversely, "liability for wrongful death can be established if appropriate and sufficient action to prevent suicide is not taken (Houston-Vega, Nuehring, & Daguio, 1997, p. 105). Knowing when the risk is sufficient to warrant breaking a client's confidence is both a clinical decision and an ethical matter. Chapter 8 offers guidelines to use for determining the risk of lethality in suicidal threats or in client aggression.

Suspicion of Child or Elder Abuse

The rights of others also take precedence over the client's right to confidentiality in instances of child abuse or neglect. In fact, all 50 states now have statutes making it mandatory for professionals to report suspected or known child abuse. Moreover, statutes governing the mandatory reporting of child abuse may contain criminal clauses related to the failure to report. Note that practitioners are protected from both civil and criminal liability for a breach of confidentiality resulting from the legal mandate to report (Butz, 1985). Some states have established similar provisions for reporting the suspected abuse of the elderly or other vulnerable adults (Corey, Corey, & Callanan, 2003; Dickson, 1998).

Although afforded immunity from prosecution for reporting, practitioners must still confront the difficult challenge of preserving the helping relationship after having breached the client's confidentiality.[2] One way of managing this tension is through informed consent. As noted earlier, clients should know at the outset of service what the "ground rules" for service are and what limits exist on what the social worker can hold as confidential. When clients understand that the social worker must report suspected child abuse, such a report may not be as damaging to the social worker–client relationship. Similarly, the Code of Ethics states, "Social workers should inform clients, to the extent possible, about the disclosure of confidential information and the potential consequences, when feasible before the disclosure is made" (NASW, 1999, p. 10). With informed consent, and careful processing of the decision to file a child abuse report, feelings of betrayal can be diminished and the helping relationship preserved.

The decision to comply with mandated reporting requirements may not always be straightforward, however. As Long (1986) reports, "On Indian reservations and in small rural towns it is often impossible to prevent community awareness of abuse victims, abuse perpetrators, and abuse informants. Despite the best efforts of health care professionals involved, abuse perpetrators may learn of an informant through informal channels or through tribal court procedures" (p. 133). Further, the sense of loyalty to one's clan members may take precedence over the commitment to protect an informant and the need to protect an abused child. Consequently, tribal sanctions may be more severe in relation to the informant than to the abuser. Definitions of abuse also differ from culture to culture, and within certain subcultures even severe abuse (according to common standards) may not be considered a problem by the victim or other family members.

Subcultural differences are by no means limited to members of ethnic minority groups. Long provides additional documentation indicating how closely knit Anglo health care practitioners discounted reports of child abuse perpetrated by a colleague and hindered effective intervention (Long, 1986). Clearly, professional and social class loyalties have shielded abusers and hampered efforts to protect abused children. In part, mandated reporting measures have emerged in response to professionals' reluctance to break confidentiality in such cases.

Subpoenas and Privileged Communication

Yet another constraint on the client's right to confidentiality is the fact that this right does not necessarily extend into courts of law. Unless social workers are practicing in a state that recognizes the concept of privileged communication, they may be compelled by courts to reveal confidential information and to produce confidential records. "Privileged communication" refers to communications made within a "legally protected relationship," which "cannot be introduced into court without the consent of the person making the communication," typically the patient or client (Dickson, 1998, p. 32).

Determining the presence and applicability of privilege can be complicated, however. As Dickson notes, "Privilege laws can vary with the profession of the individual receiving the communication, the material communicated, the purpose of the communication, whether the proceeding is criminal or civil, and whether the professional is employed by the state or is in private practice, among other factors" (1998, p. 33). At the federal level, the U. S. Supreme Court in *Jaffee v. Redmond* upheld client communications as privileged and specifically extended "that privilege to licensed social workers" (Social Workers and Psychotherapist-Patient Privilege: *Jaffee v. Redmond* Revisited, 2005).

Despite the apparent clarity that this ruling brings to the federal courts, the ambiguity and variability on the state level mean that social workers must understand their state laws and regulations and assure that clients are fully informed about the limits to confidentiality should records be subpoenaed or testimony required. Bernstein (1977) suggests that practitioners explain to clients that they may be "subpoenaed in court, records in hand, and forced under penalty of contempt to testify under oath, as to what was said between the parties and what was recorded concerning such exchanges" (p. 264).[3] Bernstein further recommends that clients sign a document verifying their understanding of this possibility and that the document be kept in the client's case file.

Laws recognizing privileged communication are created for the protection of the client; thus the privilege belongs to the client and not to the professional (Schwartz, 1989). In other words, if the practitioner were called to take the witness stand, the attorney for the client could invoke the privilege to prohibit the practitioner's testimony (Bernstein, 1977). Conversely, the client's attorney could waive this privilege, in which case the practitioner would be obligated to disclose information as requested by the court.

Another important factor regarding privileged communication is that the client's right is not absolute (Levick, 1981). If, in a court's judgment, disclosure of confidential information would produce benefits that outweigh the injury that might be incurred by revealing that information, the presiding judge may waive the privilege. Occasionally, the privilege is waived in instances of legitimate criminal investigations, because the need for information is deemed more compelling than the need to safeguard confidentiality (Schwartz, 1989). In the final analysis, then, courts make decisions on privilege-related issues on a case-by-case basis.

Because subpoenas, whether for records or testimony, are orders of the court, social workers cannot ignore them. Of course, subpoenas may sometimes be issued for irrelevant or immaterial information. Therefore, social workers should be wary about submitting privileged materials. Careful review of the subpoena, consultation with the client, and consultation with a supervisor and agency attorney can help you determine how to respond. The following sources provide helpful information for social workers contending with subpoenas: Austin,

Moline, and Williams (1990); Dickson (1998); Houston-Vega, Nuehring, & Daguio (1997); and Polowy and Gilbertson (1997).

Confidentiality in Various Types of Recording

Accreditation standards, funding sources, state and federal laws—all may dictate how agencies maintain record-keeping systems. Because case records can be subpoenaed and because clients and other personnel have access to them, it is essential that practitioners develop and implement policies and practices that provide maximal confidentiality. To this end, social workers should adhere to the following guidelines:

1. Record no more than is essential to the functions of the agency. Identify observed facts and distinguish them from opinions. Use descriptive terms rather than professional jargon, and avoid using psychiatric and medical diagnoses that have not been verified.

2. Omit details of clients' intimate lives from case records; describe intimate problems in general terms. Do not include verbatim or process recordings in case files.

3. Maintain and update records to assure their accuracy, relevancy, timeliness, and completeness.

4. Employ private and soundproof dictation facilities.

5. Keep case records in locked files, and issue keys only to those personnel who require frequent access to the files. Take similar privacy precautions to protect electronically stored data.

6. Do not remove case files from the agency except under extraordinary circumstances and with special authorization.

7. Do not leave case files on desks where others might gain access to them or keep case information on computer screens where it may be observed by others.

8. Take precautions, whenever possible, to ensure that information transmitted through the use of computers, electronic mail, facsimile machines, voice mail, answering machines, and other technology is secure; that it is sent

to the correct party; and that identifying information is not conveyed.

9. Use in-service training sessions to stress confidentiality and to monitor adherence to agency policies and practices instituted to safeguard clients' confidentiality.

10. Inform clients of the agency's authority to gather information, the conditions under which that information may be disclosed, the principal uses of the information, and the effects, if any, of limiting what is shared with the agency.

11. Establish procedures to inform clients of the existence of their records, including special measures (if necessary) for disclosure of medical and psychological records and a review of requests to amend or correct the records (Schrier, 1980).

The NASW Code of Ethics reflects most of these provisions, stating that "social workers should provide clients with reasonable access to records concerning the clients" (NASW, 1999, p. 12). It further notes that the social worker should provide "assistance in interpreting the records and consultation with the client" (p. 12) in situations where the worker is concerned about misunderstandings or harm arising from seeing the records. Access to records should be limited "only in exceptional circumstances when there is compelling evidence that such access would cause serious harm to the client" (p. 12). In our opinion, the trend toward greater client access to records has enhanced the rights of clients by avoiding misuse of records and has compelled practitioners to be more prudent, rigorous, and scientific in keeping case records.

Social workers sometimes record live interviews or group sessions so that they can analyze interactional patterns or group process at a later time as well as scrutinize their own performance with a view toward improving their skills and techniques. Recording is also used extensively for instructional sessions between students and practicum instructors. Yet another use of recordings is to provide firsthand feedback to clients by having them listen to or view their actual behavior in live sessions.

Before recording sessions for any of the preceding purposes, social workers should obtain written consent from clients on a form that explicitly specifies how the recording will be used, who will listen to or view the recording, and when it will be erased. A recording should never be made without the client's knowledge and consent. Clients vary widely in their receptivity to having sessions recorded; if they indicate reluctance, their wishes should be respected. The chances of gaining their consent are enhanced by discussing the matter openly and honestly, taking care to explain the client's right to decline. If approached properly, the majority of clients will consent to taping. Indeed, it has been our experience that students are more uncomfortable with taping than are clients.

Social workers who tape sessions assume a heavy burden of responsibility in safeguarding confidentiality, because live sessions can prove extremely revealing. Such recordings should be guarded to ensure that copies cannot be made and that unauthorized persons do not have access to them. When they have served their designated purpose, tapes should be promptly erased. Failure to heed these guidelines may constitute a breach of professional ethics.

Understanding and Resolving Ethical Dilemmas

Social workers sometimes experience quandaries in deciding which of two values or ethical principles should take precedence when a conflict exists. In the foregoing discussions of self-determination and confidentiality, for example, we cited examples of how these rights of clients and ethical obligations of social workers are sometimes superseded by higher-order values (e.g., the right to life, safety, and well-being). Thus, clients' right to confidentiality takes second place when they confide that they have physically or sexually abused a child or when they reveal imminent and serious plans for harmful acts that would jeopardize the health or safety of other persons. Moreover, you may find that certain policies or practices of your employing agency seem detrimental to clients. You may be conflicted about your ethical obligations to advocate for changes, because doing so may jeopardize your employment or pose a threat to your relationships with certain staff members.

Situations such as these present social workers with agonizingly difficult choices. Reamer (1989) has developed general guidelines that can assist you in making these decisions. Here we present our versions of some of these guidelines and illustrate instances of their application.

1. *The right to life, health, well-being, and necessities of life takes precedence over rights to confidentiality and opportunities for additive "goods" such as wealth, education, and recreation.* We have previously alluded to the application of this principle in instances of child abuse or threats of harm to another person. In such circumstances, the rights of both children and adults to health and well-being take precedence over clients' rights to confidentiality.

2. *An individual's basic right to well-being takes precedence over another person's right to privacy, freedom, or self-determination.* As stated in the language of the courts (which have consistently upheld this principle), "The protective privilege ends where the public peril begins" (Reamer, 1994, p. 31). The rights and needs of infants and children to receive medical treatments thus supersede parents' rights to withhold medical treatment because of their religious beliefs.

3. *A person's right to self-determination takes precedence over his or her right to basic well-being.* This principle maintains that people are entitled to act in ways that may appear contrary to their best interests, provided they are competent to make an informed and voluntary decision with consideration of relevant knowledge, and as long as the consequences of their decisions do not threaten the well-being of others. For example, if an adult chooses to live under a highway overpass, we may find that lifestyle unwise or unhealthy, but we have no power to abridge that choice. This principle affirms the cherished value of freedom to choose and protects the rights of people to make mistakes and to fail. As noted earlier, this principle must yield when an individual's decision might result in either his or her death or in severe and impeding damage to his or her physical or mental health.

4. *A person's rights to well-being may override laws, policies, and arrangements of organizations.* Ordinarily, social workers are obligated to comply with the laws, policies, and procedures of social work agencies, other organizations, and voluntary associations. When a policy is unjust or otherwise harms the well-being of clients or social workers, however, violation of the laws, policies, or procedures may be justified. Examples of this principle include policies or practices that discriminate against or exploit certain persons or groups. An agency, for example, cannot screen clients to select only those who are most healthy or well-to-do (a practice known as "creaming" or "cherry-picking") and then refuse services to those individuals in dire conditions. In situations such as these, the well-being of affected groups takes precedence over compliance with the laws, policies, and arrangements at issue.

Ethical social work includes advocacy for changes in laws and policies that are discriminatory, unfair, or unethical. For example, in regard to the ethical challenges posed by managed care, Sunley (1997) suggests engaging in both "case advocacy" and "cause advocacy" to help both individual clients and groups of clients who may be disadvantaged by particular policies or practices. Resources such as Frey (1990) and Brager and Holloway (1983) provide helpful guidance for acting as an effective agent of change within troubled systems.

Although Reamer's guidelines serve as a valuable resource in resolving value dilemmas, applying them to the myriad situations that social workers encounter inevitably involves uncertainties and ambiguities, a reality that practitioners must accept. What should you do when you find yourself confronted with an ethical dilemma? Corey, Corey, and Callanan (2003) suggest taking eight steps:

1. Identify the problem or dilemma, gathering as much information about the situation from as many perspectives as possible.

2. Identify the potential issues involved, determining the core principles and the competing issues.

3. Review the relevant codes of ethics.

4. Review the applicable laws and regulations.

5. Consult with colleagues, supervisors, or legal experts.

6. Consider the possible and probable courses of action.

7. Examine the consequences of various options.

8. Decide on a particular course of action, weighing the information you have and the impact of your other choices.

These procedures need not be followed in the order listed. Nevertheless, completing each of these tasks is important for conducting a thorough and thoughtful examination of the issues and options in play in your ethical dilemma. Beyond these steps, you should be sure to document carefully the input and considerations taken into account at each phase of the decision-making process.

Summary

This chapter introduced the ethics and values that support the social work profession. It provided guidelines for supporting self-determination, respecting confidentiality, obtaining informed consent, maintaining boundaries, and resolving ethical dilemmas. In Chapter 5, we will move toward putting these professional values into action as you learn beginning skills for effective communication with and on behalf of clients.

Internet Resources

See our companion website for hot links to some helpful URLs. Note that URLs are subject to change. We will endeavor to update the links on the companion website as much as possible.

Visit *http://www.naswdc.org/pubs/code/* to review the full text of the NASW Code of Ethics and *http://www.ifsw.org/Publications/4.4pub.html#standards/* to find the Code of Ethics for the International Federation of Social Workers. The following site will also provide the codes of ethics of other professions: *http://www.iit.edu/ department/csep/*. What similarities and differences do you find? How might these play out in an interdisciplinary team confronted by ethical dilemmas?

For more information on HIPAA, visit: *http://www.hhs.gov/ocr/hipaa*.

Using InfoTrac College Edition, you can search using the keywords "social work ethics," "self-determination," "privileged communication," and "beneficence" to read and/or download useful articles related to social work values and ethics.

Related Online Content

Visit the *Direct Social Work Practice* companion website at *http://socialwork. wadsworth.com/hepworth7* for additional learning tools such as glossary terms, chapter outlines, InfoTrac College Edition keywords, relevant web links, and chapter practice quizzes. Also, be sure to check out the Direct Practice Virtual Reader, where the authors have personally selected articles relevant to this chapter using InfoMarks.

Skill Development Exercises in Managing Ethical Dilemmas

The following exercises will give you practice in applying ethics concepts and ethical decision making to specific practice situations. These situations include some of the most difficult ones that we and our colleagues have encountered in practice. Note that the appropriate response or course of action is rarely cut and dried. After reading each situation, consider the following questions:

1. What conflicting principles and feelings are in play in the case?

2. What are the pros and cons of the various courses of action?

3. What guidelines are applicable in resolving this dilemma?

4. What resources could you consult to help you decide on an ethical course of action?

Situation 1 A male client confided in an individual marital therapy session several weeks ago that he is gay, although his wife does not know it. The client's wife, whom you have also seen conjointly with him, calls you today troubled over the lack of progress in solving marital problems and asks you point-blank whether you think her husband could be gay.

Situation 2 You are forming a youth group in a state correctional facility. From past experience, you know that youths sometimes make references in the group to previous offenses that they have committed without being apprehended. You also know that they may talk about plans to escape from the institution or about indiscretions or mis-demeanors they (or others) may have committed or plan to commit within the institution, such as smoking marijuana or stealing institutional sup-plies or property from peers or staff. Are you required to share all of the information you learn in the group? How can you encourage trust and sharing if there are limits to confidentiality?

Situation 3 In conducting an intake interview with a client in a family agency, you observe that both of her young children are withdrawn. One of the children is also badly bruised; the other, an infant, appears malnourished. Throughout the interview, the client seems defensive and suspi-cious and appears ambivalent about having come for the interview. At one point, she states that she feels overwhelmed with her parenting respon-sibilities and is having difficulty in coping with her children. She also alludes to her fear that she may hurt them but then abruptly changes the subject. As you encourage her to return to the discussion of her problems with the children, your client says that she has changed her mind about wanting help, takes her children in hand, and hastily leaves the office.

Situation 4 You have seen a husband and wife and their adolescent daughter twice regarding rela-tionship problems between the parents and the girl. The parents are both extremely negative and blam-ing in their attitudes toward their daughter, stating that their troubles would disappear if she would just "shape up." Today, during an individual interview with the girl, she breaks into tears and tells you that she is pregnant and plans to "go somewhere" with her boyfriend this weekend to get an abortion. She pleads with you not to tell her parents; she feels they would be extremely angry if they knew.

Situation 5 In a mental health agency, you have been working with a male client who has a history, when angered, of becoming violent and physically abusive. He has been under extreme psychological pressure lately because of problems relating to a recent separation from his wife. In an interview today, he is extremely angry, clenching his fists as he tells you that he has heard that his wife has initiated divorce proceedings and plans to move to another state. "If this is true," he loudly protests, "she is doing it to take the kids away from me, and I'll kill her rather than let her do that."

Situation 6 Some of your clients in your private practice rely on their health insurance to pay for their counseling. One client is addressing sensitive issues and is very concerned about anyone else knowing about his situation, especially his employer. Recent experiences have increased the severity of his condi-tion, and you must share this development with the care manager at the insurance company to get fur-ther treatment sessions approved. You have concerns about sharing the information with his insurer, especially via its voice mail system. The insurance company representative replies that this practice is organizational policy and, if you cannot abide by it, you are unlikely to get approval for continuing treat-ment and unlikely to receive further referrals from the insurer.

Situation 7 You and your spouse are advertis-ing for a housekeeper to clean your home once a week. One of the applicants is a former client. In her letter she states that she needs the work very badly and hopes you won't discriminate against her just because she saw you for service in the past.

Situation 8 You are a social work student beginning your first field placement. At orien-tation, your supervisor informs you that you should not tell clients that you are a student. She acknowledges that the school wants you to inform clients of your status as a social worker in training, but states that it is her opinion and agency policy that the clients not be told. She believes it under-mines their confidence in the services they are getting and creates problems when the agency tries to collect fees for its services.

Situation 9 You are a social worker in a high school that has strict rules about student health and safety. Specifically, the rules state that you cannot tell students about contraceptives or safe sex practices, even if asked, nor can you refer them to someone who is likely to tell them of such options. You are instructed to refer students with such problems or questions only to their parents or their family physician.

Skill Development Exercises in Operationalizing Cardinal Values

To assist you in developing skill in operationalizing the cardinal values in specific practice situations, we have provided a number of exercises with modeled responses. As you read each one, note which values are germane to the situation and whether one of the six threats to acceptance and respect is involved in the client's messages. To refresh your memory, the values are as follows:

1. Social workers value service to others and a commitment to social justice in helping clients get deserved and needed resources.

2. Social workers value the inherent dignity and worth of others.

3. Social workers value the primacy of human relationships

4. Social workers behave with integrity.

5. Social workers are responsible for practicing with competence.

Next, assume you are the client's service provider and formulate a response that implements the relevant social work value. After completing each exercise, compare your response with the modeled response that follows the exercises. Bearing in mind that the modeled response is only one of many possible acceptable responses, analyze it and compare it with your own. By carefully completing these exercises, you will improve your competence in putting values into action in the varied and challenging situations encountered in direct social work practice.

Client Statements

1. *Group member* [*in first group session*]: Before I really open up and talk about myself, I need to be sure what I say isn't blabbed around to other people. [*Turning to social worker.*] How can I be sure that won't happen?

2. *Adolescent in correctional institution* [*after social worker introduces self*]: So you want to help me, huh? I'll tell you how you can help. You can get me out of this damn place—that's how!

3. *Female client, age 21* [*to mental health practitioner*]: Yeah, I know that kicking the habit was a victory of sorts. But I look at my life and I wonder what's there to live for. I've turned my family against me. I've sold my body to more rotten guys than I can count— just to get a fix. I've had three STDs. What do I have to offer anyone? I feel like my life has been one big cesspool.

4. *Teenage male* [*in a group session in a correctional setting*]: [*Takes off shoes and sprawls in his chair. His feet give off a foul odor; other members hold noses and make derisive comments. He responds defensively.*] Hey, get off my back, you creeps. What's the big deal about taking off my shoes?

5. *Female* [*initial interview in family counseling center*]: Before I talk about my marital problems, I need to let you know I'm a Seventh Day Adventist. Do you know anything about my church? I'm asking because a lot of our marital problems involve my religion.

6. *Female client* [*sixth interview*]: Maybe it sounds crazy, but I've been thinking this last week that you're not really interested in me as a person. I have the feeling I'm just someone for you to analyze or to write about.

7. *Teenage female* [*caught with contraband in her possession by a supervisor-counselor in a residential treatment center*]: Please don't report this, Mrs. Wilson. I've been doing better lately, and I've learned my lesson. You won't need to worry about me. I won't mess with drugs anymore.

8. *Client* [*observing social worker taking notes during initial interview*]: I'm dying to know what you're writing down about me. Maybe you think I'm a nut. Can I take a copy of your notes with me when we're done?

9. *Male parolee, age 27, who has a reputation as a con artist* [*in mandatory weekly visit to his parole officer*]: Man, you've really got it made. Your office is really fine. But then you deserve what you've got. You've probably got a terrific wife and kids, too. Is that their picture over there?

10. *Female client, age 34* [*in third interview*]: I'm really uptight right now. I've got this tight feeling I get in my chest when I'm nervous. [*Pause.*] Well, I guess I'll have to tell you if I expect to get anything out of this.

[*Hesitant.*] You know the marital problems we've talked about? Well, Jack doesn't know this, but I'm a lesbian. [*Blushes.*] I've tried—I've really tried, but Jack doesn't turn me on. I can't even tolerate sex unless I'm thinking about other women. Jack thinks something's wrong with him, but it's not his fault. [*Chin quivers.*]

11. **Black male probationer** [*to white therapist*]: You're so damn smug. You say you want to help me, but I don't buy that crap. You don't know the first thing about black people. Man, I grew up where it's an accomplishment just to survive. What do you know about life in my world?

Modeled Responses

1. "Ginny raises a good point that concerns all of you. So that you can feel more comfortable about sharing personal feelings and experiences with the group, we need an understanding that each of you will keep what is shared in the strictest confidence. I can assure you that I'll keep information confidential myself, but I am interested in hearing from the rest of you regarding the question that Ginny is asking."

2. "I guess that's what I'd want if I were in your situation. As a matter of fact, that's what I want for you, too. But we both know the review board won't release you until they feel you're prepared to make it on the outside. I can't get you out, but with your cooperation I can help you to make changes that will get you ready for release."

3. "I can hear that you're down on yourself. Even though you've done a lot that you feel bad about, I'm impressed at what it's taken to get and stay clean. That's a giant step in the right direction. How can we keep your misgivings about the past from sabotaging the path you're on now?"

4. "I think we need to look as a group at how we can give Jim some helpful feedback rather than making fun of him. Let's talk about what just happened. Maybe you could begin, Jim, by sharing with the group what you're feeling just now."

5. "I have to confess I know just a little bit about your religion, which may make you wonder if I can appreciate your problems. I can assure you I'll do my best to understand if you're willing to help me with that. The most important thing, though, is your comfort about it. How do you feel about sharing your problems with me under these circumstances?"

6. "That sounds like a painful feeling—that I'm not personally concerned with you as an individual. I'd like to explore that with you further because that's not at all how I feel about you. Can we talk a bit about how I've come across to you and how you've reached that conclusion?"

7. "I'm sorry you're still involved with drugs, Joy, because of the difficulties it's caused you. I don't like to see you get into trouble but I have no choice. I have to report this. If I didn't, I'd be breaking a rule myself by not reporting you. That wouldn't help you in the long run. Frankly, I'm going to keep worrying about you until I'm satisfied you're really sticking to the rules."

8. [*Chuckling.*] "It's not nutty at all to wonder what I'm thinking and writing. I'm writing down what we talk about. What you tell me is important, and notes help to refresh my memory. You're welcome to look at my notes if you like. Actually, I would be interested in hearing a little more about your concerns regarding what I might think of you."

9. "As a matter of fact it is, and I think they're pretty terrific. But we're here to talk about you, Rex. I'd like to hear how your job interview went."

10. "Keeping this secret has been very painful for you. I gather you've been afraid I'd condemn you, but I'm pleased you brought it up so that we can work on it together. It took some real courage on your part, and I respect you for that."

11. "I'd be phony if I said I understood all about being black and living in your neighborhood . . . and I'm sorry if it seems I'm being smug. I am interested in you, and I'd like to understand more about your life."

Notes

1. After goals have been mutually identified and roles in helping the relationship clarified, practitioners need not hesitate to offer advice, because their expertise and input will give impetus and direction to the change efforts. Our point is that giving advice should not be the primary means of assisting clients.

2. Butz (1985) discusses related issues at length and makes a number of recommendations. To do justice to his discussion, however, would exceed space limitations. Instead, we refer you to his article.

3. Privileged communication is a legal right that protects clients from having a confidence revealed publicly from the witness stand during legal proceedings. Statutes that recognize privileged communication exempt certain professions from being legally compelled to reveal content disclosed in the context of a confidential relationship.

PART 2

Exploring, Assessing, and Planning

Part 2 of this book deals with processes and skills involved in the first phase of the helping process. Chapter 5 begins this exploration by setting the context and developing skills for building effective working relationships with clients, one of the two major objectives of initial interviews. Chapter 6 shifts the focus to skills required to accomplish the second major objective: to thoroughly explore clients' difficulties.

Chapter 7 identifies verbal and nonverbal patterns of communication that impede the development of effective working relationships.

Chapters 8 and 9 focus specifically on the process of assessment. Chapter 8 deals with explaining the process, sources of information, delineation of clients' problems, and questions to be addressed during the process. Chapter 9 highlights the many dimensions of ecological assessment, delineating the intrapersonal, interpersonal, cultural, and environmental systems and noting how they reciprocally interact to produce and maintain problems.

Chapter 10 narrows the focus to family systems. It discusses various types of family structures and considers the dimensions of family systems that must be addressed in assessing family functioning, including the cultural context of families.

In Chapter 11, the focus changes to groups. Here the discussion hones in on purposes of groups, selection of group members, arrangements to be made, and ways to begin group process. It then points out various factors to be considered in assessing the functioning of groups.

Part 2 concludes with Chapter 12, which deals with negotiating goals and contracts with both voluntary and involuntary clients. Included in this chapter are theory, skills, and guidelines that address these processes, which lay the foundation for the process of goal attainment.

CHAPTER 5

Building Blocks of Communication: Communicating with Empathy and Authenticity

CHAPTER OVERVIEW

All social work relationships occur in a context. Chapter 5 explores how you can develop micro direct practice skills and apply them in a context to help your clients. Interviews follow a structure that reflects predictable elements of contact between a potential client, a social worker, and the setting that the social worker represents. In other words, interviews have beginnings that focus on settling into roles, reviewing legal and ethical limits and boundaries, and attempting to establish rapport. From this point, the social worker engages the client in assessing what has brought the client into contact with the setting or agency. Based on this joint exploration, the social worker and the client then discuss creating a contract or agreement about what they will attempt to do together to address the client's concerns and developing goals to guide the social worker's practice in the case. If contact will last beyond one session, the session ends with the development of tasks or concrete plans about what the social worker and the client will do prior to the next session to advance their common work. This interview structure is held together with practice skills that are designed to help the social worker connect with clients by communicating empathically, assertively, and authentically.

ROLES OF THE PARTICIPANTS

Clients often have little understanding of the helping process and may have expectations that differ from those of the social worker. Unfortunately, these discrepant expectations may impair the helping process. The findings of two classic research studies (Aronson & Overall, 1966; Mayer & Timms, 1969) revealed that unacknowledged discrepancies in expectations produced dissatisfactions and higher rates of discontinuance from therapy of lower-class clients as compared with middle-class clients. The potency of using a "role induction interview" to increase the likelihood that clients will continue contact with the social worker beyond the initial interview has been demonstrated by Hoehn-Saric and colleagues (1964). In their study, clients prepared by role induction continued contact at a higher rate and fared better in treatment than control clients who received no special preparation. Kooden (1994) has described how a gay male therapist can serve as a model for socialization of gay adolescents through self-disclosure. Finally, texts on work with involuntary clients emphasize the importance of clarifying the practitioner's and client's roles in developing a working relationship (Rooney, 1992; Trotter, 1999).

The following guidelines will assist you to achieve similar positive results in role clarification.

1. *Determine your clients' expectations.* The varied expectations that clients bring to initial sessions

include lectures, magical solutions, advice giving, changing other family members, and so on. With clients who are members of ethnic minority groups and inexperienced with professional helping relationships, sensitively exploring expectations and modifying the social worker's role when necessary are critical.

Clients sometimes explicitly state their expectations without prompting from a social worker. For example, after reciting the difficulties created by her son, a mother declared, "We were hoping you could talk with him and help him understand how much he is hurting us." Notice that the mother's "hope" involved a request for specific action by the social worker. When clients express their expectations spontaneously in this way, you have the opportunity to deal with unrealistic goals. Frequently, however, clients do not openly express their expectations, and you will need to elicit them. It is important not to probe too far into expectations until you have established rapport, however, because the client's request often turns out to be a most intimate revelation.

For this reason, seeking disclosure too soon may put a client on the defensive. The social worker should therefore try to weave exploration of the client's expectations into the natural flow of the session sometime after the client has had ample opportunity to report his or her difficulties and to discern the sensitive understanding and goodwill of the social worker.

If voluntary clients have not spontaneously revealed their requests and the timing appears right, you can elicit their requests by asking a question similar to one of the following:

• "How do you hope (or wish) I (or the agency) can assist (or help) you?"

• "When you thought about coming here, what were your ideas about the kind of help you wanted?"

For potential clients who were referred or mandated to receive service, such requests may be elicited in the following way:

• "We have explored the reasons why you were referred/required to seek our service. But I would

like to know what *you* hope to gain from this process."

2. *Briefly explain the nature of the helping process, and define the client–social worker relationship as partners seeking a solution to the client's difficulties.* Clients often hope that social workers will give them advice that they can implement immediately, thereby quickly remedying their problems. They will give up these unrealistic expectations with less disappointment in favor of a more realistic understanding if you clarify how you can actually be of help and why it would be less useful to approach their problems with this kind of "magic potion" strategy. It is very important to convey your intention to help clients find the best possible solution and to clarify that offering advice prematurely would likely be a disservice to them. In the absence of such an explanation, clients may erroneously conclude that you are unwilling to meet their expectations because you are not concerned about them. Indeed, Mayer and Timms (1969) found that clients who were dissatisfied with the service they received for interpersonal problems reasoned that the counselor's failure to give concrete advice stemmed from a lack of interest and desire to help. Taking the time to explore expectations and to clarify how you can help thus prevents clients from drawing unwarranted negative conclusions that may result in premature discontinuance of the contact.

Note that we are not arguing against the value of giving advice to clients. Rather, our point is that to be effective, advice must be based on adequate knowledge of the dynamics of a problem and of the participants in it. This level of understanding is unlikely to be achieved in an initial session.

You can assist many clients to modify their unrealistic expectations and clarify your respective roles by delivering a message similar to the following:

• "I can sense the urgency you feel in wanting to solve your problems. I wish I could give advice that would lead to an easy solution. You've probably already had plenty of advice, because most people offer advice freely. It has been my experience, though, that what works for one person (couple or family) may not work at all for another."

- "As I see it, our task is to work together in considering a number of options so that you can decide which solution best fits you and your situation. In the long run, that's what will work best for you. But finding the right solution takes some time and a lot of thought."

The preceding role clarification embodies the following essential elements mentioned earlier: (1) acknowledging and empathizing with the client's unrealistic expectation and sense of urgency; (2) expressing the social worker's helpful intent; (3) explaining why the client's unrealistic expectation cannot be fulfilled; and (4) as part of the social worker's expertise, clarifying the helping process and defining a working partnership that places responsibility on the client for actively participating and ultimately making choices as to the courses of action to be taken.

When couples seek help for relationship problems, they commonly view the partner as the source of difficulties and have the unrealistic expectation that the couples counselor will influence the partner to shape up. Because this expectation is so pervasive, we often elicit partners' expectations early in the initial session (individual or conjoint) and clarify the social worker's helping role, thereby setting the stage for more productive use of the exploration to follow. Clarifying the helping process early in the session tends to diminish the partners' tendency toward mutual blaming and competition. Moreover, partners are less likely to respond defensively when the social worker refuses to be drawn into the "blame game" and focuses instead on assisting each person to become aware of his or her part in the difficulties. The following excerpt of an actual session typifies our approach to role clarification with couples.

Social worker: How much understanding do you have about how couples counseling works?

First partner: Not very much, really. We just know we need help because we're fighting all the time. [*Second partner in agreement.*]

Social worker: Perhaps it would be helpful if I took just a few minutes to explain how I work with couples. Would that be agreeable with you?

Both partners [*nod affirmatively*]: Yes, we'd like that.

Social worker: Okay, then, I'll explain it as best I can and give you a chance to ask any questions. It's important that all three of us have the same understanding about what we're going to be doing. [*Partners nod in understanding.*] As I see it, my role is to help each of you to better understand yourself and your partner. Marital problems usually are caused by the fact that the needs of one or both partners aren't being met adequately. Lots of factors can block the meeting of important needs; when they do, problems in relationships develop. My job is to help each of you to understand your partner's needs better and to be more aware of your own needs so that you can express them clearly to your partner. To do so, you have to communicate in such a way that you really understand each other better. So another part of my job is to help you to communicate more effectively.

Second partner: Good! We need that. Our communication is really bad. We can't seem to talk without getting into a fight.

Social worker: Well, we'll need to work on that. Part of my job will be to help you see what's going wrong in your communication and to help you get back on track by learning new ways of communicating. In some ways, that means I'll function much as a teacher at times.

First partner: That's okay. If it will help, I'm willing to learn.

Social worker: That willingness will be a real asset. Another thing that's important to understand is that I can't help by assigning blame to either of you. It's been my experience that most partners in a relationship believe that the other person is causing the difficulties, and many of their struggles involve blaming each other. Usually it isn't one person or the other who's at fault. Both partners contribute to the difficulties, and my task is to assist each of you in seeing the part you play in them. It's important that you understand this.

Otherwise, you might think I'm siding with your partner when I focus on your part. I won't be taking sides, but if you think I am, please let me know. Otherwise, you're likely to resent me, and I won't even be aware of it. To work effectively together, we'll have to be open with one another. I'll be open with you, but I have to expect the same of you. [*Pause.*]

Further clarification of the roles of the participants will occur later in the session as the participants negotiate goals and formulate a contract.

Implied in the preceding excerpt is another aspect of the client's role—to be open in sharing feelings, thoughts, and events. By explaining the rationale for openness and by expressing your intent to communicate openly, you enhance clients' receptiveness to this factor. To focus on this aspect of the client's role, consider making the following points:

Social worker: For you to receive the greatest benefit, you need to be as open as possible with me. That means not holding back troubling feelings, thoughts, or events that are important. I can understand you and your difficulties only if you're open and honest with me. Only you know what you think and feel; I can know only as much as you share with me.

Sometimes it's painful to share certain thoughts and feelings, but often those are the very feelings that trouble us the most. If you do hold back, remind yourself that you may be letting yourself down. If you're finding it difficult to share certain things, let me know. Discussing what's happening inside you—why it's difficult—may make it easier to discuss those painful things.

I'll be open and honest with you, too. If you have any questions or would like to know more about me, please ask. I'll be frank with you. I may not answer every question, but I'll explain why if I don't.

To enhance clients' participation in the helping process, it is also important to emphasize that they can accelerate their progress by working on their difficulties between appointments. Some clients mistakenly believe that change will result largely from what occurs in sessions. In actuality, the content of sessions is far less significant than how clients apply the information gained from them. The following message clarifies this aspect of a client's responsibility:

Social worker: We'll want to make progress toward your goals as rapidly as possible. One way you can accelerate your progress is by working hard between our sessions. That means carrying out tasks you've agreed to, applying what we talk about in your daily life, and making mental notes or actually writing down thoughts, feelings, and events that relate to your problems so we can consider them in your next session. Actually, what you do between sessions is more important in accomplishing your goals than the session itself. We'll be together only a brief time each week. The rest of the week you have opportunities to apply what we talk about and plan together.

Yet another aspect of the client's role involves keeping appointments. This factor is obvious, but discussing it emphasizes clients' responsibilities and prepares them to cope constructively with obstacles that may cause them to fail or to cancel appointments. The following message clarifies this aspect of the client's role:

Social worker: As we work together, it will be critical for you to keep your appointments. Unforeseen things such as illness happen occasionally, of course, and we can change appointments if such problems arise. At other times, however, you may find yourself feeling discouraged or doubting whether coming here really helps. You may also feel upset over something I've said or done and find yourself not wanting to see me. I won't knowingly say or do anything to offend you, but you may have some troubling feelings toward me anyway. The important thing is that you not miss your appointment, because when you're discouraged or upset we need to talk about it. I know that may not be easy, but it will help you to work out your problematic feelings. If you miss your appointment, you may find it even harder to return.

A final task for the social worker is to emphasize that difficulties are inherent in the process of making changes. Clarifying this reality further prepares clients for the mixed feelings that they will inevitably experience. When these difficulties are highlighted early in the helping process, clients can conceive of such feelings and experiences as natural obstacles that must be surmounted, rather than yield to them or feel defeated. An explanation about these predictable difficulties similar to the following clarifies the vicissitudes of the change process:

Social worker: We've talked about goals you want to achieve. Accomplishing them won't be easy. Making changes is seldom possible without a difficult and sometimes painful struggle. People usually have ups and downs as they seek to make changes. If you understand this, you won't become so discouraged and feel like throwing in the towel. I don't mean to paint a grim picture. In fact, I feel very upbeat about the prospects of your attaining your goals. At the same time, it won't be easy, and I don't want to mislead you. The important thing is that you share your feelings so that we can keep on top of them.

Over the years, numerous clients have reported retrospectively that they appreciated receiving these kinds of explanations during the initial session. When the going became rough and they began to waver in pursuing their goals, they recalled that such discouragement was natural and, rather than discontinuing the contact, mustered up the determination to persevere.

In addition to clarifying the client's role, it is vital to clarify your own role. Stress that you will be a partner in helping clients to understand their difficulties more fully. Because you have an outside vantage point, you may be able to help them see their difficulties from a new perspective and to consider solutions that they may have overlooked. We recommend that you clarify further that, although you will be an active partner in considering possible remedial actions, the final decisions rest with the clients themselves. You will help them to weigh alternatives, but your desire is to see clients develop their strengths and exercise their capacities for independent action to the fullest extent possible. In addition, emphasize that you plan to assist clients in focusing on their strengths and any incremental growth they achieve. Stress that although you will actively perform this function in the initial stage of the helping process, at the same time you will be encouraging your clients to learn to recognize their own strengths and grow independently.

Another aspect of the helping role that you should clarify for clients is your intention to assist them in anticipating obstacles they will encounter in striving to attain their goals and your willingness to help them formulate strategies to surmount these obstacles. Clarifying this facet of your role further reinforces the reality that change is difficult but you will be with and behind your clients at all times, offering support and direction. You might share that each family faces its own unique situation and has its own set of values, noting that it will be your job to get to know these values and situations from the clients' point of view. Only then will you attempt to help the clients plan what makes sense for them to do.

Some special hurdles must be overcome to develop productive working relationships between social workers and potential clients in mandated settings, because the mandated client did not seek the contact and often perceives it as being contrary to his or her interests. In the following dialogue, notice how the social worker begins to develop expectations about a collaborative relationship.

Client: I didn't like the earlier workers because they came into my house telling me what I can and can't do. One thing I don't like is someone telling me what I can do with my kids and what I can't.

Social worker: It sounds like you had a negative experience with earlier workers.

Client: Yeah, I did. I did not like it at all because they were telling me what I should do.

Social worker: I'm going to take a different approach with you because I don't feel that I know it all; you know best about the situation occurring in your own family and in your own life. I will want you to tell me about the problems you are concerned about and how we can best resolve those together.

Client: Okay.

Social worker: My job will be to develop a case plan with you. I won't be the one to say, "This is what you need to do." I want you to have input in that decision and to say, "Well, I feel I can do this." I will be willing to share ideas with you as we decide what to work on and how to do it. I will need to include any court-mandated requirements, such as our need to be meeting together, in the agreement. However, I want you to have a lot of say in determining what we work on and how.

The social worker interprets the client's comment about previous workers as pertinent to exploring what their own working relationship might be like. She describes her own role and clarifies what the client can do in a clear and tangible way to work on goals important to her.

COMMUNICATING ABOUT INFORMED CONSENT, CONFIDENTIALITY, AND AGENCY POLICIES

The encounter between the social worker and the client exists within a context of limits and possibilities and rights. In this regard, the social worker must share the rights and limits to communication discussed in Chapter 4: discuss confidentiality and its limits, obtain informed consent, and share agency policies and legal limits. Consider how the social worker in the preceding example might approach this task:

Social worker: What you say to me is private in most circumstances. I will share what we have discussed with my supervisor. In certain circumstances, however, I might have to share what we have discussed with others. For example, if you threatened to seriously harm another person, I would have a duty to warn that would mean that I could not keep that information private. For example, if your children were in danger, I am a mandated reporter and I would have to share that information. Similarly, if you were to seriously consider harming yourself, I would have to share

that information. If a judge were to subpoena my records, he or she could gain access to a general summary of what we have done together. Do you have any questions about this?

It is important that this section of the initial interview be presented in language that the client readily understands so that the discussion embodies the spirit of informed consent. The exact content of this discussion will vary with the setting in which you work. It is important that you carry out this duty in a genuine fashion, rather than presenting it as a ritualistic sharing of written forms that has the appearance of obtaining informed consent but ignores its intent. In hurried agency practice, sometimes this principle is violated. Discuss with your supervisor what information needs to be shared with clients and how that is done in ways that are useful to those clients.

FACILITATIVE CONDITIONS

The social worker uses communication skills as building blocks to help develop a productive working relationship with clients. This chapter focuses on two of the three skills embodied in what have been called the *facilitative conditions* or *core conditions* in helping relationships. These conditions or skills were originally denoted by Carl Rogers (1957) as *empathy, unconditional positive regard,* and *congruence.* Other terms have since evolved, and we shall refer to the conditions as *empathy, respect* or *nonpossessive warmth,* and *authenticity* or *genuineness.* Because we addressed nonpossessive warmth or respect at length in Chapter 4, we limit our focus here to empathy and authenticity.

Research (primarily in psychology) has documented that these three facilitative conditions are associated with positive outcomes. One important study by a social worker (Nugent, 1992) further found that these conditions were effective in facilitating positive helping relationships. For these reasons, it is vital that social workers master these skills. While they are particularly useful in treatment situations with voluntary clients, we will also describe ways that the facilitative conditions can serve as building blocks in both involuntary relationships and other situations such as discharge planning that do not have therapy as the primary focus (Bennett, Legon, & Zilberfein, 1989).

EMPATHIC COMMUNICATION

Empathic communication involves the ability of the social worker to perceive accurately and sensitively the inner feelings of the client and to communicate his or her understanding of these feelings in language attuned to the client's experiencing of the moment. The first dimension of empathy, empathic recognition, is a precondition of the second dimension, demonstrating through accurate reflection of feelings that the social worker comprehends the client's inner experiencing.

Empathic communication plays a vital role in nurturing and sustaining the helping relationship and in providing the vehicle through which the social worker becomes emotionally significant and influential in the client's life. In mandated circumstances in which involuntary clients are not seeking a helping relationship, conveying empathic understanding reduces the level of threat perceived by the client and mitigates his or her defensiveness, conveys interest and helpful intent, and creates an atmosphere conducive to behavior change. In addition, many clients live in environments that constrict resources and opportunities. Social worker empathy with the social and economic context of problems is an important adjunct to empathy with personal experiencing (Keefe, 1978).

In responding to clients' feelings, social workers must avoid being misled by the conventional facades used to conceal emotions. As a consequence, the empathic communicator responds to the feelings that underlie such flippant messages as "Oh, no, it doesn't really matter" or "I don't care what he does!" These messages often mask disappointment or hurt, as do messages such as "I don't need anyone" when the client is experiencing painful loneliness, or "I don't let anyone hurt me" when the client is finding rejection hard to bear. To enter the client's private world of practical experience, the social worker must also avoid making personal interpretations and judgments of the client's private logic and feelings that, in superficial contacts, might appear weak, foolish, or undesirable.

Being empathically attuned involves not only grasping the client's immediately evident feelings, but also, in a mutually shared, exploratory process, identifying the client's underlying emotions and discovering the meaning and personal significance of the client's feelings and behavior. In getting in touch with these camouflaged feelings and meanings, the social worker must tune in not only to verbal messages but also to more subtle cues, including facial expressions, tone of voice, tempo of speech, and postural cues and gestures that amplify and sometimes contradict verbal meanings. Such nonverbal cues as blushing, crying, pausing, stammering, changing voice intonation, clenching jaws or fists, pursing the lips, lowering the head, or shifting the posture often reveal the presence of distressing feelings and thoughts.

Empathic communication involves "stepping into the shoes of another," in the sense that the social worker attempts to perceive the client's world and experiences. When the client feels pressure from an involuntary referral, the empathic social worker understands and is aware of that pressure and how it feels. At the same time, the social worker must remain outside of the client's world and avoid being overwhelmed by his or her fears, anger, joys, and hurts, even as the social worker deeply senses the meaning and significance of these feelings for the client. "Being with" the client means that the social worker focuses intensely on the client's affective state without losing perspective or taking on the emotions experienced by the client.

A person who experiences feelings in common with another person and is similarly affected by whatever the other person is experiencing usually responds sympathetically rather than empathically. Sympathetic responding, which depends on achieving emotional and intellectual accord, involves supporting and condoning the other person's feelings (e.g., "I'd feel the same way if I were in your position" or "I think you're right"). In contrast, empathic responding involves understanding the other person's feelings and circumstances without taking that person's side (e.g., "I sense you're feeling . . ." or "You seem to be saying . . .").

When social workers support their clients' feelings, the clients may feel no need to examine their behavior or circumstances and may not engage in the process of self-exploration that is so vital to growth and change. Instead, clients tend to look to the social worker to change the behavior of other persons who play significant roles in their problems. Retaining separateness and objectivity thus is a critical dimension in the helping process. Clearly, when social workers assume their clients' feelings and positions, they lose not only the vital perspective that comes from being an outsider but also the ability to be helpful.

Of course, being empathic entails more than just recognizing clients' feelings. Social workers must also respond verbally and nonverbally in ways that affirm their understanding of clients' inner experiencing. It is not unusual for a person to experience empathic feelings for another individual without conveying those feelings in any way to the second party. Exhibiting high-level empathy requires skill in verbally and nonverbally demonstrating understanding. A common mistake made by social workers is to tell clients, "I understand how you feel." Rather than producing a sense of being understood, such a response often creates doubts in the client's mind about the social worker's perceptiveness, because any specific demonstration of understanding is lacking. Indeed, use of this response may mean that the social worker has not explored the client's feelings sufficiently to fully grasp the significance of the problematic situation.

To convey unmistakably the message, "I am with you; I understand," the social worker must respond empathically. Use of this skill creates an atmosphere of acceptance and understanding in which the client is more likely to risk sharing deeper and more personal feelings. Later in this chapter, we present theory and exercises for developing skill in empathic responding. Initially, we provide a list of affective words and phrases intended to expand your vocabulary so that you can meet the challenge of responding to the wide range of emotions experienced by clients. We also provide exercises to help you to refine your ability to perceive the feelings of others—a prerequisite to the mastery of empathic communication. To assist you to discern levels of empathy, we include a rating scale for empathic responding, accompanied by examples of social worker responses and exercises. These exercises will help you to gain mastery of empathic communication at an effective working level.

DEVELOPING PERCEPTIVENESS TO FEELINGS

Feelings or emotions exert a powerful influence on behavior and often play a central role in the problems of clients. Applicants or voluntary clients often enter into the helping relationship with openness and hope that they will explore both their concerns and their related feelings. Conversely, involuntary clients experience strong feelings but have not actively sought out a helping relationship for dealing with them (Cingolani, 1984). Hence, use of the skills sometimes takes a slightly different course with these clients, as one of the social worker's goals is to express empathy with the *situation* the involuntary client experiences and the feelings related to them.

To respond to the broad spectrum of emotions and feeling states presented by clients, the social worker must be fully aware of the diversity of human emotion. Further, the social worker needs a rich vocabulary of words and expressions that not only reflect clients' feelings accurately but also capture the intensity of those feelings. For example, dozens of descriptive feeling words may be used to express anger, including *furious, aggravated, vexed, provoked, put out, irritated,* and *impatient*—all of which express different shades and intensities of this feeling.

When used judiciously, such words serve to give sharp and exact focus to clients' feelings. Possessing and utilizing a rich vocabulary of affective words and phrases that accurately reflect these feelings is a skill that often is not developed by even experienced social workers. It is important to realize that high-level empathic responding takes place in two phases: (1) a thinking process and (2) a responding process. A deficient vocabulary for describing feelings limits social workers' ability to conceptualize and hence to reflect the full intensity and range of feelings experienced by clients.

It has been our experience that beginning social workers typically have a limited range of feeling words from which to draw in conveying empathy. Although literally hundreds of words may be used to capture feelings, learners often limit themselves to, and use to excess, a few terms, such as *upset* or *frustrated*, losing much of the richness of client messages in the process.

The accompanying lists illustrate the wide range of expressions available for social workers' use in responding to clients' feelings. Note, however, that using feeling words in a discriminating fashion is not merely important in empathic responding but is indispensable in relating authentically as well. Becoming a competent professional requires passing through a maturing process whereby social workers develop not only the capacity to deeply share the inner experiencing of others, but also a way to express their own personal feelings constructively.

Note that different expressions may be used in the various subcultures with which you work. For example, your choice of a meaningful affective word for happiness may differ for an adolescent and for an elder.

AFFECTIVE WORDS AND PHRASES

Competence/Strength

convinced you can	confident
sense of mastery	powerful
potent	courageous
resolute	determined
strong	influential
brave	impressive
forceful	inspired
successful	secure
in charge	in control
well equipped	committed

Competence/Strength (continued)

sense of accomplishment	daring
feeling one's oats	effective
sure	sense of conviction
trust in yourself	self-reliant
sharp	able
adequate	firm
capable	on top of it
can cope	important
up to it	ready
equal to it	skillful

Happiness/Satisfaction

elated	superb
ecstatic	on cloud nine
on top of the world	organized
fantastic	splendid
exhilarated	jubilant
terrific	euphoric
delighted	marvelous
excited	enthusiastic
thrilled	great
super	in high spirits
joyful	cheerful
elevated	happy
lighthearted	wonderful
glowing	jolly
neat	glad
fine	pleased
good	contented
hopeful	mellow
satisfied	gratified
fulfilled	tranquil
serene	calm
at ease	awesome

Caring/Love

adore	loving
infatuated	enamored
cherish	idolize
worship	attached to
devoted to	tenderness toward
affection for	hold dear

Caring/Love (continued)

prize	caring
fond of	regard
respect	admire
concern for	taken with
turned on	trust
close	esteem
hit it off	value
warm toward	friendly
like	positive toward
accept	

Depression/Discouragement

anguished	in despair
dreadful	miserable
dejected	disheartened
rotten	awful
horrible	terrible
hopeless	gloomy
dismal	bleak
depressed	despondent
grieved	grim
brokenhearted	forlorn
distressed	downcast
sorrowful	demoralized
pessimistic	tearful
weepy	down in the dumps
deflated	blue
lost	melancholy
in the doldrums	lousy
kaput	unhappy
down	low
bad	blah
disappointed	sad
below par	

Inadequacy/Helplessness

utterly	worthless
good for nothing	washed up
powerless	helpless
impotent	crippled
inferior	emasculated
useless	finished
like a failure	impaired

Inadequacy/Helplessness (continued)

inadequate	whipped
defeated	stupid
incompetent	puny
inept	clumsy
overwhelmed	ineffective
like a klutz	lacking
awkward	deficient
unable	incapable
small	insignificant
like a wimp	unimportant
over the hill	incomplete
immobilized	like a puppet
at the mercy of	inhibited
insecure	lacking confidence
unsure of self	uncertain
weak	inefficient
unfit	

Anxiety/Tension

terrified	frightened
intimidated	horrified
desperate	panicky
terror-stricken	paralyzed
frantic	stunned
shocked	threatened
afraid	scared
stage fright	dread
vulnerable	fearful
apprehensive	jumpy
shaky	distrustful
butterflies	awkward
defensive	uptight
tied in knots	rattled
tense	fidgety
jittery	on edge
nervous	anxious
unsure	hesitant
timid	shy
worried	uneasy
bashful	embarrassed
ill at ease	doubtful
uncomfortable	self-conscious
insecure	alarmed
restless	

Confusion/Troubledness

bewildered	puzzled
tormented by	baffled
perplexed	overwhelmed
trapped	confounded
in a dilemma	befuddled
in a quandary	at loose ends
going around in circles	mixed-up
disorganized	in a fog
troubled	adrift
lost	disconcerted
frustrated	floored
flustered	in a bind
torn	ambivalent
disturbed	conflicted
stumped	feeling pulled apart
mixed feelings about	uncertain
unsure	uncomfortable
bothered	uneasy
undecided	

Rejection/Offensive

crushed	destroyed
ruined	pained
wounded	devastated
tortured	cast off
betrayed	discarded
knifed in the back	hurt
belittled	abused
depreciated	criticized
censured	discredited
disparaged	laughed at
maligned	mistreated
ridiculed	devalued
scorned	mocked
scoffed at	used
exploited	debased
slammed	slandered
impugned	cheapened
mistreated	put down
slighted	neglected
overlooked	minimized
let down	disappointed
unappreciated	taken for granted

Rejection/Offensive (continued)

taken lightly	underestimated
degraded	discounted
shot down	

Anger/Resentment

furious	enraged
livid	seething
could chew nails	fighting mad
burned up	hateful
bitter	galled
vengeful	resentful
indignant	irritated
hostile	pissed off
have hackles up	had it with
upset with	bent out of shape
agitated	annoyed
got dander up	bristle
dismayed	uptight
disgusted	bugged
turned off	put out
miffed	ruffled
irked	perturbed
ticked off	teed off
chagrined	griped
cross	impatient
infuriated	violent

Loneliness

all alone in the universe	isolated
abandoned	totally alone
forsaken	forlorn
lonely	alienated
estranged	rejected
remote	alone
apart from others	shut out
left out	excluded
lonesome	distant
aloof	cut off

Guilt/Embarrassment

sick at heart	unforgivable
humiliated	disgraced
degraded	horrible
mortified	exposed
branded	could crawl in a hole

Guilt/Embarrassment (continued)

like two cents	ashamed
guilty	remorseful
crummy	really rotten
lost face	demeaned
foolish	ridiculous
silly	stupid
egg on face	regretful
wrong	embarrassed
at fault	in error
responsible for	goofed
lament	blew it

Use of the Lists of Affective Words and Phrases

The lists of affective words and phrases may be used with the exercises at the end of the chapter to formulate responses that capture the nature of feelings expressed by clients. Note that involuntary clients are more likely to initially experience the emotions of anger, resentment, guilt, embarrassment, rejection, confusion, tension, inadequacy, helplessness, depression, and discouragement. In Chapter 7, we will explore barriers to effective communication. One of those barriers can be the social worker's inability to achieve empathy with such involuntary clients, as the social worker may believe that they have brought on these negative feelings as a result of their own irresponsible actions. That is, some social workers feel that perhaps involuntary clients deserve these feelings because they have not fully accepted responsibility for their part in the difficulties they have experienced. As noted in Chapter 4, the social work value of acceptance of worth suggests that we can empathize with feelings of despair and powerlessness *even if* clients have not yet taken responsibility for the consequences of their actions.

After you have initially responded to "feeling messages," check the lists to determine whether some other words and phrases might more accurately capture the client's feelings. Also, scan the lists to see whether the client's message involves feelings in addition to those you identified. The lists may similarly assist you in checking out the accuracy of your reflective responses as you review taped sessions.

The lists of affective words and phrases are offered here for the purpose of helping you communicate more empathically with your clients. However, words can have different connotations within the same language based on age, region, ethnic group, and social class. We suggest that you sit down with your coworkers and colleagues and compile your own more specialized list of feeling words for specific groups that you routinely encounter. Issues may also arise when you try to use an unfamiliar slang vernacular, thus defeating the purpose of empathizing. However, making the effort to clarify words that accurately describe what the client is feeling often conveys your genuine interest.

Acquisition of a broader emotional vocabulary is a step toward expressing greater empathy for clients. It allows you to more effectively convey your understanding and compassion for what they are experiencing. Because many clients want to change their situations as well as their feelings about it, conveying empathy is the first step toward helping them work on those concerns.

Although the lists of affective words and phrases presented in this chapter are not exhaustive, they encompass many of the feelings and emotions frequently encountered in the helping process. Feeling words are subsumed under 11 categories, running the gamut of emotions from intense anguish and pain (e.g., *grieved, terrified, bewildered, enraged,* and *powerless*) to positive feeling states (e.g., *joy, elation, ecstasy, bliss,* and *pride in accomplishment*). Given our emphasis on clients' strengths, we have taken care to include a grouping of terms to assist social workers in capturing clients' feelings related to growth, strengths, and competence.

Feeling words in each category are roughly graduated by intensity, with words conveying strong intensity grouped toward the beginning of each category and words of moderate to mild intensity appearing toward the end. In responding to client messages, the social worker should choose feeling words that accurately match the intensity of the feelings the client is experiencing.

To illustrate, picture an African American client in a drug aftercare program who has returned to work as a meter reader. He reports that when he knocked on the door in a largely white suburb intending to read the meter, the elderly white woman would not let him in, despite his wearing his picture identification name tag on his uniform: "I was so low down and depressed. What can you do? I am doing my thing to keep straight, and I can't even do my job because I'm black." Such a response appropriately calls for an intense response by the social worker: "Sounds like you felt demeaned and humiliated that you couldn't do your job because of this woman's fear of black people. You felt discriminated against, disrespected, yet you did not let these humiliating feelings carry you back to drug use—you kept your head on course, keeping straight, and not being stopped by other people's perceptions."

In addition to using words that accurately reflect the intensity of the client's feelings, it is important to respond with a tone of voice and nonverbal gestures and expressions that similarly reflect the intensity of feelings conveyed by the verbal response. The proper intensity of affect may also be conveyed by using appropriate qualifying words— for example, "You feel (somewhat) (quite) (very) (extremely) discouraged by your low performance on the entrance test."

Clients' messages may also contain multiple feelings. Consider the following client message: "I don't know what to do about my teenage daughter. I know that she's on drugs, but she shuts me out and won't talk to me. All she wants is to be out with her friends, to be left alone. There are times when I think she really dislikes me." Feeling words that would capture the various facets of this message include *confused, bewildered, alarmed, troubled, overwhelmed, lost, desperate, worried, frightened, alienated, rejected*, and *hurt*. A response that included all of these feeling words would be extremely lengthy and overwhelming to the client. However, a well-rounded empathic response should embody at least several of the surface feelings, such as *worried* and *confused*, and be delivered with appropriate timing. The social worker might also bring deeper-level feelings into focus, as explained in the following paragraphs.

Notice in the preceding client message that many feelings were implied but not explicitly stated. Some of these emotions would likely be just beyond the client's level of awareness but could easily be recognized if they were drawn to the client's attention. For example, the client might emphatically confirm a social worker response that sensitively identifies the hurt, rejection, and even anger inherent in the client's message. Without the social worker's assistance, the client might not develop full awareness of those deeper-level feelings.

In responding to client messages, you must be able to distinguish between readily apparent feelings and probable deeper feelings. In the early phase of the helping process, the social worker's objectives of developing a working relationship and creating a climate of understanding are best accomplished by using a reciprocal level of empathy—that is, by focusing on the client's immediately evident feelings. As the client perceives your genuine effort and commitment to understand his or her situation, that experience of being "empathically received" gradually yields a low-threat environment that obviates the need for self-protection.

Note that clients from oppressed groups, such as the African American client in the earlier example, may rightly feel better understood by the social worker yet continue to feel disillusioned by an alien environment. It is important to acknowledge those feelings about the environment. Cingolani (1984) writes of the "negotiated relationship" with such clients as a substitute for the "helping relationship." Even in negotiated relationships, however, increased trust is essential. That trust may be gained by actions taken outside the session that indicate that the social worker is trustworthy and has the client's best interest at heart, as well as by verbal conveyance of empathy during the session. Similarly, Ivanoff, Blythe, and Tripodi suggest that too much emphasis on empathy can feel manipulative to involuntary clients (1994, p. 21). With voluntary clients, the resultant climate of trust sets the stage for self-exploration, a prerequisite to self-understanding, which in turn facilitates behavior change. This positive ambience prepares the way for the use of "additive" or "expanded" levels of empathy to reach for underlying feelings as well as to uncover hidden meanings and goals of behavior.

Conversely, attempting to explore underlying feelings during the early phase of the helping process is counterproductive. Uncovering feelings beyond the client's awareness before a working relationship is firmly established tends to mobilize opposition and may precipitate premature termination of the contact. Involuntary clients in a negotiated relationship may never desire such uncovering of deeper feelings and may find exploration of them to be intrusive (Ivanoff, Blythe, and Tripodi, 1994, p. 21).

Exercises in Identifying Surface and Underlying Feelings

In the following exercise, identify both the apparent surface feelings and the probable underlying feelings embodied in the client's message. Remember that most of the feelings in the messages are merely implied, as clients often do not use feeling words. As you complete the exercise, read each message and write down the feelings involved. Next, scan the lists of affective words and phrases to see whether you might improve your response. After you have responded to all four messages, check the feeling words and phrases you identified with those given at the end of the chapter. If the feelings you identified were similar in meaning to those identified in the answers, consider your responses to be accurate. If they were not, review the client messages for clues about the client's feelings that you overlooked.

Client Statements

1. *Elderly client:* I know my children have busy lives. It is hard for them to have time to call me.

   Apparent feelings:

   Probable deeper feelings:

2. *Client:* I don't know if my husband loves me. He says he cares, but he doesn't pay much attention to me, particularly when we're with other people. Sometimes he even seems ashamed of me.

   Apparent feelings:

   Probable deeper feelings:

3. *Client:* When I was a teenager, I thought that when I was married and had my own children,

I would never yell at them like my mother yelled at me. Yet, here I am doing the same things with Sonny. [*Tearful.*]

   Apparent feelings:

   Probable deeper feelings:

4. *African American client in child welfare system:* The system is against people like me. People think that we drink, beat our kids, lay up on welfare, and take drugs.

   Apparent feelings:

   Probable deeper feelings:

Exercises at the end of this chapter for formulating reciprocal empathic responses will also assist you in increasing your perceptiveness to feelings.

ACCURATELY CONVEYING EMPATHY

Empathic responding is a fundamental, yet complex skill that requires systematic practice and extensive effort to achieve competency. Skill in empathic communication has no limit or ceiling; rather, this skill is always in the process of "becoming." In listening to their taped sessions, even highly skilled professionals discover feelings they overlooked. Many social workers, however, do not fully utilize or selectively employ empathic responding. They fail to grasp the versatility of this skill and its potency in influencing clients and fostering growth in moment-by-moment transactions.

In fact, some social workers dismiss the need for training in empathic responding, mistakenly believing themselves to already be empathic in their contacts with clients. Research findings indicate that beginning social work students relate at empathic levels considerably lower than the levels necessary to work effectively with clients (Fischer, 1978; Larsen, 1975).

These findings are not totally unexpected, of course, because comparatively few people are inherently helpful in the sense of relating naturally with high levels of empathy or any of the other core conditions. Although people achieve varying degrees of empathy, respect, and genuineness through their life experiences, attaining high levels of these skills requires rigorous training. Research scales that operationalize empathy conditions have been developed and validated in extensive research studies (Truax & Carkhuff, 1967). These scales, which specify levels of empathy along a continuum ranging from high- to low-level skills, represented a major breakthrough not only in operationalizing essential social worker skills but also in establishing a relationship between these skills and successful outcomes in practice.

The empathic communication scale has proved particularly helpful to social work educators in assessing pre- and post-levels of empathy of trainees in laboratory classes (Larsen & Hepworth, 1978; Wells, 1975). The scale has been further employed to help students distinguish between high- and low-level empathic responses and has been used by peers and instructors in group training to assess levels of students' responses. Students then receive guidance in reformulating low-level responses to bring them to higher levels.

The Carkhuff (1969) empathy scale, which consists of nine levels, has been widely used in training and research, and similar versions of this scale can be found in the literature. Although we have found nine-point scales valuable as training aids, they have proven somewhat confusing to students, who often have difficulty in making such fine distinctions between levels. For this reason, we have adapted the nine-level scale described by Hammond, Hepworth, and Smith (1977) by collapsing it to the five-level scale presented later in this section.

On this empathic communication scale, level 1 responses are generally made by social workers who are preoccupied with their own—rather than their clients'—frame of reference; for this reason, they completely fail to match the clients' feelings. At this low level of responding, social workers' responses are usually characterized by the ineffective communication styles identified in Chapter 7. Responses at level 2 convey an effort to understand but remain partially inaccurate or incomplete.

At level 3, the midpoint, social workers' responses essentially match the affect of their clients' surface feelings and expressions. This midpoint, widely referred to as "interchangeable" or "reciprocal"

responding in the literature, is considered the "minimally facilitative level" at which an effective and viable process of helping can take place.

Above the midpoint, social workers' responses add noticeably to the surface feelings. At the highest level, they add significantly to the clients' expressions. At these higher levels of empathic responding, social workers accurately respond to clients' full range of feelings at their exact intensity and are "with" clients in their deepest moments. Level 4 and 5 empathic responses, which require the social worker to infer underlying feelings, involve mild to moderate interpretations.

Empathic Communication Scale

African American male [*to child welfare worker*]: I don't trust you people. You do everything you can to keep me from getting back my son. I have done everything I am supposed to do, and you people always come up with something else.

Level 1: Low Level of Empathic Responding

At level 1, the social worker communicates little or no awareness or understanding of even the most conspicuous of the client's feelings; the social worker's responses are irrelevant and often abrasive, hindering rather than facilitating communication. Operating from a personal frame of reference, the social worker changes the subject, argues, gives advice prematurely, lectures, or uses other ineffective styles that block communication, often diverting clients from their problems and fragmenting the helping process. Furthermore, the social worker's nonverbal responses are not appropriate to the mood and content of the client's statement.

When social workers relate at this low level, clients often become confused or defensive. They may react by discussing superficialities, arguing, disagreeing, changing the subject, or withdrawing into silence. Thus, the client's energies are diverted from exploration and/or work on problems.

Level 1 Responses
- "Just carry out the case plan and you are likely to succeed." (*Giving advice.*)

- "Just think what would have happened if you had devoted more energy in the last year to carrying out your case plan: You would have been further along." (*Persuading with logical argument; negatively evaluating client's actions.*)

- "How did you get along with your last social worker?" (*Changing the subject.*)

- "Don't you think it will all work out in time?" (*Leading question, untimely reassurance.*)

- "Why, that's kind of an exaggeration. If you just work along with me, before you know it things will be better." (*Reassuring, consoling, giving advice.*)

- "I don't think you have a very positive attitude. If you had just taken responsibility for your own actions and completed your case plan, you wouldn't have gotten yourself into this situation." (*Judging and blaming client.*)

The preceding examples illustrate ineffective styles of communication used at this low level. Notice that messages reflect the social worker's own formulations concerning the client's problem; they do not capture the client's inner experiencing. Such responses stymie clients, blocking their flow of thought and producing negative feelings toward the social worker.

The final response above could have actually been rated on a negative scale of empathic responding. That is, not only is the response not empathic, but it is actively attacking and judgmental. Instead of conveying empathy, it conveys antipathy. Social workers' frustration with clients who endanger others is understandable. Statements like the one above, however, greatly hinder further efforts to work with them in a collaborative fashion.

Level 2: Moderately Low Level of Empathic Responding

At level 2, the social worker responds to the surface message of the client but erroneously omits feelings or factual aspects of the message. The social worker may also inappropriately qualify feelings (e.g., "somewhat," "a little bit," "kind of") or may inaccurately interpret feelings (e.g., "angry" for "hurt," "tense" for "scared"). Responses may also emanate from the social worker's own conceptual formulations, which may be diagnostically accurate but not empathically attuned to the client's expressions.

Although level 2 responses are only partially accurate, they do convey an effort to understand and, for this reason, do not completely block the client's communication or work on problems.

Level 2 Responses

- "You'll just have to be patient. I can see you're upset." The word *upset* defines the client's feelings only vaguely, whereas feeling words such as *angry*, *furious*, and *discounted* more accurately reflect the client's inner experiencing.

- "You feel angry because your case plan has not been more successful to date. Maybe you are expecting too much too soon; there is a lot of time yet." The listener begins to accurately capture the client's feelings but then moves to an evaluative interpretation ("you expect too much too soon") and inappropriate reassurance.

- "You aren't pleased with your progress so far?" This response focuses on external, factual circumstances to the exclusion of the client's feelings or perceptions regarding the event in question.

- "You feel like things aren't going too well." This response contains no reference to the client's immediately apparent feelings. Beginning social workers often use the lead-in phrase "You feel like . . ." without noticing that, in employing it, they have not captured the client's feelings.

- "You're disappointed because you haven't gotten your son back?" This response, although partially accurate, fails to capture the client's anger and distrust of the system, wondering whether any of his efforts are likely to succeed.

- "I can see you are angry and disappointed because your efforts haven't been more successful so far, but I think you may be expecting the system to work too quickly." Although the message has a strong beginning, the empathic nature of the response is negated by the listener's explanation of the reason for the client's difficulties. This response represents a form of taking sides—that is, justifying the actions of the child welfare system by suggesting that too much is expected of it.

The preceding responses illustrate many of the common errors made by social workers in responding empathically to client messages. Although some part of the messages may be accurate or helpful, all the responses in some way ignore or subtract from what the client is experiencing.

Level 3: Interchangeable or Reciprocal Level of Empathic Responding

The social worker's verbal and nonverbal responses at level 3 convey understanding and are essentially interchangeable with the client's obvious expressions, accurately reflecting factual aspects of the client's messages and surface feelings or state of being. Reciprocal responses do not appreciably add affect or reach beyond the surface feelings, nor do they subtract from the feeling and tone expressed.

Acknowledging the factual content of the client's message, although desirable, is not required; if included, this aspect of the message must be accurate. Level 3 responses facilitate further exploratory and problem-focused responses by the client. The beginning social worker does well in achieving skill in reciprocal empathic responding, which is an effective working level.

Level 3 Responses

- "You're really angry about the slow progress in your case and are wondering whether your efforts are likely to succeed."

- "I can tell you feel very let down and are asking yourself, 'Will I ever get my son back?' "

Essentially interchangeable, these responses express accurately the immediately apparent emotions in the client's message. The content of the responses is also accurate, but deeper feelings and meanings are not added. The second response also illustrates a technique for conveying empathy that involves changing the reflection from the third to the first person, and speaking as if the social worker were the client.

Level 4: Moderately High Level of Empathic Responding

Responses at level 4 are somewhat additive, accurately identifying the client's implicit underlying feelings and/or aspects of the problem. The social worker's response illuminates subtle or veiled facets of the client's message, enabling the client to get in touch with somewhat deeper feelings and unexplored meanings and purposes of behavior. Level 4 responses thus are aimed at enhancing self-awareness.

Level 4 Responses

- "You feel very frustrated with the lack of progress in getting your son back. You wonder whether there is any hope in working with a new worker and this system, which you feel hasn't been helping you."

This response not only conveys immediately apparent feelings and content but also is noticeably additive in reflecting the client's deeper feelings of suspicion of institutional racism.

Level 5: High Level of Empathic Responding

Reflecting each emotional nuance, and using voice and intensity of expressions finely attuned to the client's moment-by-moment experiencing, the social worker accurately responds to the full range and intensity of both surface and underlying feelings and meanings at level 5. The social worker may connect current feelings and experiencing to previously expressed experiences or feelings, or may accurately identify implicit patterns, themes, or purposes. Responses may also identify implicit goals embodied in the client's message, which point out a promising direction for personal growth and pave the way for action. Responding empathically at this high level facilitates the client's exploration of feelings and problems in much greater breadth and depth than responding at lower levels.

Level 5 Responses

- "Not succeeding in getting custody of your son by now has angered and frustrated you very much. I'm sensing that you're unsure of whether any efforts will succeed and maybe are thinking, 'The system is stacked against me.' You want to be able to trust that your efforts are likely to succeed and that I and this child welfare system will do all we can to assist you."

Significantly additive, this response goes well beyond the surface feelings in reflecting the client's keen disappointment and his underlying fear that he may never regain custody of his son.

In addition, the latter part of the response includes an action or goal statement that paves the way for further exploration of the problem.

Client suspicions of institutional racism and the lack of responsiveness of the system are not alleviated exclusively or even primarily by empathic statements, however well formed. The key to engaging client motivation would be demonstrating that the social worker and agency will respond in a reliable, trustworthy fashion.

Exercises in Discriminating Levels of Empathic Responding

The following exercises ask you to rate responses for their level of empathy and are designed to assist you in refining your ability to determine the helpfulness of responses. These exercises will prepare you for subsequent practice in formulating your own empathic messages. Three client statements are given, followed by several possible responses. Using the empathic scale, rate each response. Rating messages will be less difficult if, using the list of affective words and phrases, you first identify the feelings contained in the client's message. After you have rated each response, compare your rating with those given at the end of the chapter. Referring to the rating scale, analyze the responses you rated inaccurately, trying to pinpoint the reason for the authors' ratings.

Client Statements

1. *Single woman, age 80 [to social worker concerning her request to move to an independent living complex provided for ambulatory elderly persons]:* Goodness, the more I think of moving, the more scared I get. I have neighbors here who look after me, and I won't know a soul there. I'm afraid I'll be all alone.

Level Responses
1. "It's pretty scary to you, leaving your neighbors and familiar surroundings. But there will be a lot of friendly people there and things to do. Besides, they fix one hot meal for you every day."

2. "Don't worry, you'll make friends in no time, and you'll wish you'd moved sooner."

3. "Did you sign those application papers I left with you a few days ago?"

4. "Just thinking about moving worries you because you'll be leaving your own neighborhood and friends. Even though your life would be much easier, you're unsure you'll be better off in other ways."

5. "So I gather in some ways you'd rather stay right where you are rather than gamble on a change."

6. "Lots of other people in the new apartments were just as scared as you before they moved, but I don't know a single one who's sorry now."

7. "It sounds as though you have some pretty mixed feelings about moving. Part of you wants to go because you could live more comfortably, but another part of you is afraid you'll feel alone and lost and wants to cling to people you know care about you."

8. "Are you saying we just ought to forget the whole thing?"

2. *Male, age 16 [in weekly visit to social work probation officer]:* I don't see the sense in having to come here every lousy week. I haven't been in any trouble now since I went to court a month ago. You should know by now you can trust me.

Level Responses
1. "A month isn't very long, you know. And how can I be sure you're staying out of trouble?"

2. "I gather you'd rather not have to see me. I can understand that, but the judge ordered it and you'd be in trouble with him if you didn't meet the conditions of your probation."

3. "Has it been a month since you went to court? I didn't think that it had been that long."

4. "You'd prefer not coming here and feel you've earned my trust."

5. "Having to come here each week gripes you, and I gather you're irritated with me for encouraging you to follow the judge's order."

6. "Look, you got yourself into this mess so don't complain to me if you don't like it. Maybe you'd like to talk the judge into changing his mind."

7. "It irritates you to have to come here each week. You'd like to get me off your back."

8. "You're confused about why you have to come here and wish you didn't have to."

3. *Group member* [*in hesitant, quiet voice*]: It's really hard for me to say what I want to say in this group. When I do start to talk, I get tongue-tied, and my heart starts beating faster and faster. I feel like some of you are critical of me.

Level Responses
(By Group Members or Group Leader)

1. "Yeah, I feel that same way sometimes, too."

2. "It is frightening to you to try to share your feelings with the group. Sounds like you find yourself at a loss for words and wonder what others are thinking of you."

3. "I know you're timid, but I think it's important that you make more of an effort to talk in the group, just like you're doing now. It's actually one of the responsibilities of being a group member."

4. "You get scared when you try to talk in the group."

5. "I sense that you're probably feeling pretty tense and tied up inside right now as you talk about the fear you've had in expressing yourself."

6. "Although you've been frightened of exposing yourself, I gather there's a part of you that wants to overcome that fear and become more actively involved with the rest of the group."

7. "What makes you think we're critical of you? You come across as a bit self-conscious, but that's no big deal."

8. "You remind me of the way I felt the first time I was in a group. I was so scared, I just looked at the floor most of the time."

9. "I wonder if we've done anything that came across as being critical of you."

RESPONDING WITH RECIPROCAL EMPATHY

Reciprocal or interchangeable empathic responding (level 3) is a basic skill used throughout the helping process to acknowledge client messages and to encourage exploration of problems. In the initial phase, empathic responding serves a vital purpose in individual, conjoint, and group sessions: It facilitates the development of a working relationship and fosters the climate of understanding necessary to promote communication and self-disclosure. In this way, it sets the stage for deeper exploration of feelings during subsequent phases of the helping process.

Note that the benefits of making additive empathic responses at levels 4 and 5 are not contingent on the frequency of their usage. In fact, making one such response in a first or second interview may be helpful and appropriate. More frequent attempts presume a depth of relationship that has not yet developed. Additive empathic responses exceed the level of feelings and meanings expressed by clients and are thus reserved, in large part, for the later phases of the helping process.

Because reciprocal responding is an essential skill used frequently to meet the objectives of the first phase of the helping process, we recommend that you first aim to achieve beginning mastery of responding at level 3. Extended practice of this skill should significantly increase your effectiveness in establishing viable helping relationships, interviewing, and gathering data. This remainder of this chapter provides guidelines and practice exercises that will help you in mastering reciprocal responding. Although responding at additive levels represents an extension of the skill of reciprocal responding, the former is an advanced skill that can be used in a variety of ways to achieve specific objectives. For this reason, it has been grouped with other change-oriented or "action" skills presented in Part 3 of the book.

Constructing Reciprocal Responses

To reach level 3 on the empathic scale, you must be able to formulate responses that accurately capture the content and the surface feelings in the client message. It is also important to frame the message so that you do not merely restate the client's message.

The following paradigm, which identifies the elements of an empathic or reflective message, has proven useful for conceptualizing and mastering the skill of empathic responding:

You feel   about   because   .
                              Accurately
                              identifies
                              or describes
                              feelings

The response focuses exclusively on the client's message and does not reflect the social worker's conceptualizations.

The following excerpt from a session involving a social worker and a 17-year-old female illustrates the use of the preceding paradigm in constructing an empathic response:

Client: I can't talk to my father without feeling scared and crying. I'd like to be able to express myself and to disagree with him, but I just can't.

Social worker: It sounds as though you just feel panicky when you try to talk to your father. I gather you're discouraged because you'd like to feel comfortable with your dad and able to talk openly with him without falling apart.

Many times, client messages contain conflicting or contrasting emotions, such as the following: "I like taking drugs, but sometimes I worry about what they might do to me." In such cases, each contrasting feeling should be highlighted:

• You feel _____, yet you also feel _____.
• I sense that you feel torn because while you find taking drugs enjoyable, you have

nagging thoughts that they might be harmful to you.[1]

Remember that to respond empathically at a reciprocal level, you must use language that your clients will readily understand. Abstract, intellectualized language and professional jargon create barriers to communication and should be avoided. It is also important to vary the language you use in responding. Many professionals tend to respond with stereotyped, repetitive speech patterns, commonly using a limited variety of communication leads to begin their empathic responses. Such leads as "You feel . . ." and "I hear you saying . . ." repeated over and over not only distract the client but also seem phony and contrived. This kind of stereotyped responding draws more attention to the social worker's technique than to his or her message.

The list of varied introductory phrases will help you expand your repertoire of possible responses. We encourage you to read the list aloud several times and to review it frequently while practicing the empathic communication training exercises in this chapter and in Chapter 17, which covers additive empathic responding. The reciprocal empathic response format ("You feel   because   ") is merely a training aid to assist you in focusing on the affect and content of client messages. The leads list will help you respond more naturally.

Exercises designed to help you to develop level 3 reciprocal empathic responses appear at the end of the chapter. Included in the exercises are a variety of client statements taken from actual work with individuals, groups, couples, and families in diverse settings.

In addition to completing the skill development exercises, we recommend that you record the number of empathic responses you employ in sessions over several weeks to determine the extent to which you are applying this skill. We also suggest that either you or a knowledgeable associate rate your responses and determine the mean level of empathic responding for each session. If you find (as most beginning social workers do) that you are underutilizing empathic responses or responding at low levels, you may wish to set a goal to improve your skill.

Leads for Empathic Responses

Could it be that . . .

I wonder if . . .

What I guess I'm hearing is . . .

Correct me if I'm wrong, but I'm sensing . . .

Perhaps you're feeling . . .

Sometimes you think . . .

Maybe this is a long shot, but . . .

I'm not certain I understand; you're feeling . . .

As I hear it, you . . .

Is that the way you feel?

Let me see if I'm with you; you . . .

The message I'm getting is that . . .

If I'm hearing you correctly . . .

So, you're feeling . . .

You feel . . .

It sounds as though you are saying . . .

I hear you saying . . .

So, from where you sit . . .

I sense that you're feeling . . .

Your message seems to be . . .

I gather you're feeling . . .

If I'm catching what you say . . .

What you're saying comes across to me as . . .

You're feeling . . .

I'm not sure if I'm with you but . . .

You appear to be feeling . . .

It appears you feel . . .

Maybe you feel . . .

Do you feel . . .

I'm not sure that I'm with you; do you mean . . .

It seems that you . . .

Is that what you mean?

What I think I'm hearing is . . .

I get the impression that . . .

As I get it, you felt that . . .

To me it's almost like you are saying . . .

So, as you see it . . .

I'm picking up that you . . .

I wonder if you're saying . . .

So, it seems to you . . .

Right now you're feeling . . .

You must have felt . . .

Listening to you, it seems as if . . .

You convey a sense of . . .

As I think about what you say, it occurs to me you're feeling . . .

From what you say, I gather you're feeling . . .

Employing Empathic Responding

In early sessions with the client, empathic responding should be used frequently as a method of developing rapport and "staying in touch" with the client. Responses should be couched in a tentative manner to allow for inaccuracies in the social worker's perception. Checking out the accuracy of responses with appropriate lead-in phrases such as "Let me see if I understand . . ." or "Did I hear you right?" is helpful in communicating a desire to understand and a willingness to correct misperceptions.

In initially using empathic responses, learners are often leery of the flood of emotions that sometimes occurs as the client, experiencing none of the usual barriers to communication, releases feelings that may have been pent up for months or years. It is important to understand that empathic responses have not "caused" such feelings but rather have facilitated their expression, thus clearing the way for the client to explore and to consider such feelings more rationally and objectively.

You may worry, as do many beginning social workers, about whether you will "damage" the client or disrupt the helping relationship if your empathic responses do not always accurately reflect the client's feelings. Perhaps even more important than accuracy, however, is the "commitment" to understand conveyed by your genuine efforts to perceive the client's experience. If you consistently demonstrate your goodwill and intent to help through attentive verbal and nonverbal responding, an occasional lack of understanding or faulty timing will not damage the client–social worker relationship. In fact, your efforts to clarify the client's message will usually enhance rather than detract from the helping process, particularly if you respond to corrective feedback in an open, nondefensive, and empathic manner.

Multiple Uses of Empathic Communication

Earlier in the chapter, we referred to the versatility of empathic communication. In this section, we delineate a number of ways in which you can employ reciprocal empathic responding.

Establishing Relationships with Clients in Initial Sessions

As discussed previously, the use of empathic responding actively demonstrates the social worker's keen awareness of clients' feelings and creates an atmosphere in which clients feel safe enough to risk exploring their personal thoughts and feelings. Numerous researchers have established that when social workers relate empathically, clients are more likely to continue contact than when little empathy is conveyed.

To employ empathy with maximal effectiveness in transcultural relationships, social workers must be sensitive to cultural factors. The importance of understanding cultural factors was documented almost 40 years ago by Mayer and Timms (1969), who studied clashes of perspectives between clients and social workers. Based on their findings, they concluded, "It seems that social workers start where the client is psychodynamically but they are insufficiently empathic in regard to cultural components" (p. 38).

Although empathic communication is important in bridging cultural gaps, it can be used to excess with many Asian Americans and Native Americans. Many members of these groups tend to be lower in emotional expressiveness than other client groups, and they may react with discomfort and confusion if a social worker relies too heavily on empathic communication. Nevertheless, it is important to "read between the lines" and to sensitively respond to troubling emotions that these clients do not usually express directly. Like other clients, they are likely to appreciate a social worker's sensitive awareness to the painful emotions associated with their difficulties.

We must reemphasize the importance of assuming a more directive, active, and structured stance with some Asian Americans. As Tsui and Schultz (1985) have clarified, "A purely empathetic, passive, nondirective approach serves only to confuse and alienate the [Asian] client" (p. 568). The same can be said of many Native American clients, based on their levels of acculturation.

Staying in Touch with Clients

Reciprocal empathic responding operationalizes the social work principle of "starting where the client is"

and keeps social workers attuned to their clients' current feelings. Although he or she inevitably employs many other skills and techniques, the social worker constantly returns to empathic responding to keep in touch with the client. In that sense, empathic communication is a fundamental intervention and a prerequisite to the use of other interventions. Gendlin (1974) uses the analogy of driving a car to illuminate the vital role of empathy in keeping in touch with clients. Driving involves much more than watching the road. A driver does many things, including steering, braking, signaling, and watching signs. One may glance at the scenery, visit with others, and think private thoughts, but watching the road must be accorded the highest priority.

When visibility becomes limited or hazards appear, all other activities must cease and the driver must attend exclusively to observing the road and potentially dangerous conditions. Just as some drivers fail to pay proper attention to their surroundings and become involved in accidents, so some social workers also fail to attend sufficiently to cultural differences and changes in clients' moods and reactions, mistakenly assuming they know their clients' frame of mind. As a consequence, social workers may fail to discern important feelings, and their clients may perceive them as disinterested or insensitive and subsequently disengage from the helping process.

Accurately Assessing Client Problems

The levels of empathy offered by social workers are likely to correlate with their clients' levels of self-exploration. That is, high-level empathic responding should increase clients' exploration of self and problems. As the social worker moves "with" clients by frequently using empathic responses in initial sessions, clients will begin to lay out their problems and to reveal events and relevant data. Figuratively speaking, clients then take social workers where they need to go by providing information crucial to making an accurate assessment. Such an approach contrasts sharply with sessions that emphasize history-taking and in which social workers, following their own agendas rather than the clients', spend unnecessary time asking hit-or-miss questions and gathering extraneous information.

Responding to Clients' Nonverbal Messages

Through their facial features, gestures, and body postures, clients often hint at feelings that they do not express verbally. In the course of a session, for instance, a client may become pensive, or he or she may show puzzlement, pain, or discomfort. In such instances, the social worker may convey understanding of the client's feeling state and verbalize the feeling explicitly through a reflective response that attends to the emotion suggested in the client's nonverbal expressions. For instance, in response to a client who has been sitting dejectedly with her head down for several minutes after having reported some bad grades, a social worker might say, "At this moment you seem to be feeling very sad and discouraged, perhaps even defeated." In group or conjoint sessions, the social worker might reflect the nonverbal messages of several, or all, of the members. For example, the social worker might say, "I sense some restlessness today, and we're having a hard time staying on our topic. I'm wondering if you're saying, 'We're not sure we want to deal with this problem today.' Am I reading the group correctly?"

Empathic responses that accurately tune into clients' nonverbal experiencing will usually prompt clients to begin exploring feelings they have been experiencing. Making explicit the nonverbal messages of clients is an important skill discussed in Chapters 6, 8 and 10 of this book.

Making Confrontations More Palatable

Confrontation is employed in the change-oriented phase to expand clients' awareness and to motivate them to action. It is most appropriate when clients are contemplating actions that are unlawful or that are dangerous to themselves or others. Confrontation is also appropriate when such actions conflict with the goals and values a client has chosen for himself or herself.

Of course, even well-timed confrontations may meet with varying degrees of receptiveness. Both concerns for the client's welfare and prudence dictate that the social worker determine the impact of a potential confrontation upon the client and implement a process for making such an intervention more palatable. This may be accomplished by employing empathic responses attuned to the client's reaction immediately following a confrontation. As social workers listen attentively and sensitively to their clients' expressions, the clients' defensiveness may abate. Indeed, clients often begin to process new information and think through and test the validity of their ideas, embracing those that fit and rejecting others that seem inapplicable. Guidelines for this important skill are presented in Chapter 17.

Blending confrontation and empathic responses is a particularly potent technique for managing group processes when the social worker must deal with a controversial issue or distractive behavior that is interfering with the work of the group.

Handling Obstacles Presented by Clients

Client opposition to what is happening in a session is sometimes healthy. What is often interpreted as unconscious resistance may, in fact, be a negative reaction to poor interviewing and intervention techniques used by the social worker or to client confusion, misunderstanding, or even inertia. For these reasons, it is important to carefully monitor clients' reactions and to deal directly and sensitively with their related feelings. Clients' verbal or nonverbal actions may comment indirectly on what is occurring in the helping process. For instance, a client may look at her watch and ask how long the session will last, shift her body position away from the social worker, begin tapping a foot, or stare out the window. When it appears that the client is disengaging from the session in this way, an empathic response that reflects the client's verbal and/or nonverbal message may effectively initiate discussion of what is occurring.

Social workers sometimes practice with highly verbal clients who talk rapidly and jump quickly from one topic to another. Overly verbal clients present a particular challenge to beginning social workers, who must often overcome the misconception that interrupting clients is rude. Because of this misconception, novice interviewers sometimes spend most of an initial session listening passively to highly verbal clients without providing any form or direction to the helping process. They may also allow clients to talk incessantly because they mistakenly view this as constructive work on problems. Quite the contrary, excess verbosity often keeps the session on a superficial level and interferes with problem identification and exploration. It may also indicate a more serious affective mental health problem.

It is important that social workers provide structure and direction to each session, thereby conveying an expectation that specific topics will be considered in depth. Much more will be said about this in later chapters. For now, we simply underscore the necessity of using empathic responses with highly verbal clients as a preliminary strategy to slow the process and to provide some depth to the discussion.

For example, a social worker might interject or intervene with "I'd like to interrupt to check whether I'm understanding what you mean. As I get it, you're feeling . . ." or "Before you talk about that topic, I would like to make sure I'm with you. You seem to be saying . . ." or "Could we hold off discussing that for just a minute? I'd like to be sure I understand what you mean. Would you expand on the point you were just making?"

Managing Anger and Patterns of Violence

During individual or group sessions, clients (especially those who were not self-referred and may be involuntary clients) often experience surges of intense and conflicting feelings, such as anger, hurt, or disappointment. In such instances, empathic responding is a key tool for assisting them to work through those feelings. As empathic responses facilitate expanded expression of these feelings, clients engage in a process of venting, clarifying, and experiencing different feelings. Over time, they may achieve a mellowing of emotions and a more rational and thoughtful state of being.

When it is employed to focus sharply on clients' feelings, empathic responding efficiently manages and modifies strong emotions that represent obstacles to progress. As the social worker successfully handles such moments and clients experience increased self-awareness and cathartic benefits, the helping relationship is strengthened.

Empathic responding is particularly helpful in dealing with hostile clients and is indispensable when clients become angry with the social worker, as illustrated in the following client statement: "What you're doing to help me with my problems doesn't seem to be doing me any good. I don't know why I keep coming." At such moments, the social worker must resist the temptation to react defensively, because such a response will further antagonize the client and exacerbate the situation. Responding by challenging the client's perception, for instance, would damage the helping relationship. The social worker's responses should represent a genuine effort to understand the client's experiencing and feelings and to engage the client in fully exploring those feelings.

Involuntary clients sometimes become frustrated with the seemingly slow pace of progress toward goals and may feel that policies and individuals in the system are acting to thwart them. Empathizing with this anger is necessary before the social worker and client can collaborate productively and figure out how to make the system work toward client goals (Rooney & Chovanec, 2004).

Keeping this idea in mind, consider the impact of the following reciprocal empathic response: "You're very disappointed that things aren't better, and are irritated with me, feeling that I should have been more helpful to you." This response accurately and nondefensively acknowledges the client's frustration with the situation and with the social worker. By itself, it would not be sufficient to calm the client's ire and to free the client to consider the problem more fully and rationally.

Carefully following the client's feelings and remaining sensitively attuned to the client's experiencing by employing empathic responses for several minutes usually assists both the social worker and the client to understand more clearly the strong feelings that prompted the client's outburst and to adequately assess the source of those feelings. Attending to the emotions expressed does not mean that the content is discounted. The social worker might, for example, follow the empathic response above by saying, "I'd like to explore more fully with you which parts of our work have not felt worthwhile to you."

When faced with angry clients in group and conjoint sessions, it is critical that the social worker empathically not only reflect the negative feelings and positions of the clients who are displaying the anger, but also reach for and reflect the feelings or observations of members who may be experiencing the situation differently. Utilizing empathic responses in this manner assists the social worker in gathering information that will elucidate the problem, helping angry members air and examine their feelings, and bringing out other points of view for the group's consideration. In addition, employing empathic responding at such moments encourages a more rational discussion of the issues involved in the problem and thus sets the stage for possible problem solving.

The principles just discussed also apply to clients who are prone to violent behavior. Such clients often come to the attention of social workers because they have abused their children and/or spouses. People who engage in violence often do so because they have underlying feelings of helplessness and frustration and because they lack skills and experience in coping with troubling situations in more constructive ways. Some have short fuses and weak emotional controls, and many come from backgrounds in which they vicariously learned violence as a mechanism of coping. Using empathy to defuse their intense anger and to tune into their frustrations is an important first step in working with such clients (Lane, 1986). Other clients may have difficulties with anger and express this emotion only when under the influence of alcohol or other substances. Helping them experience and ventilate anger when sober and in control is a major approach employed to assist such clients to learn constructive ways of coping with anger (Potter-Efron & Potter-Efron, 1992).

Utilizing Empathic Responses to Facilitate Group Discussions

Social workers may facilitate discussion of specific issues in conjoint or group sessions by first identifying a particular topic and then using empathic (or paraphrasing) responses to reflect the observations of various group members in relation to that topic. The social worker may also actively seek responses from members who have not contributed and then employ empathic responses (or paraphrases) to acknowledge their observations. Utilized frequently in this manner, empathic responding encourages (and reinforces) clients' participation in group discussions.

Teaching Clients to Respond Empathically

Clients often experience difficulties in their relationships because their styles of communication include many barriers that prevent them from accurately hearing messages or conveying understanding to others. An important task for the social worker involves teaching clients to respond empathically. This task is accomplished in part by modeling, which is generally recognized as a potent technique for promoting client change and growth. People who distort or ignore others' messages (e.g., in marital, family, and other close relationships) may benefit vicariously by observing the social worker listen effectively and respond empathically. Moreover, clients who are hard to reach or who have difficulties in expressing themselves may gradually learn to recognize their own emotions and to express themselves more fully as a result of the social worker's empathic responding.

Teaching empathic communication skills to clients also can entail assuming an educational role. Several approaches to assisting mates (married or otherwise) who are having serious conflicts rely on teaching both parties to gain and express empathy for each other. A similar approach has been employed in Parent Effectiveness Training (Gordon, 1970). Another approach, which seeks to increase empathy for children among parents at risk for child abuse, has successfully employed a cognitive component designed to assist these parents in assigning less negative meanings to behaviors that might otherwise be perceived by the parents as deliberately provocative (Whiteman, Fanshel, & Grundy, 1987).

Social workers' roles as educators require them to intervene actively at opportune moments to enable their clients to respond empathically, particularly when they have ignored, discounted, or attacked the contributions of others in a session.

With respect to this role, we suggest that social workers consider taking the following actions:

1. Teach clients the paradigm for empathic responding introduced in this chapter. If appropriate, ask them to engage briefly in a paired practice exercise similar to the one recommended for beginning social workers at the end of the chapter. Utilizing topics neutral to the relationship, have each person carefully listen to the other party for several minutes, and then reverse roles. Afterward, evaluate with participants the impact of the exercise on them.

2. Introduce clients to the list of affective words and phrases and to the leads list provided in this chapter. If appropriate, you may wish to have clients assume tasks during the week to broaden their feeling vocabulary similar to the tasks recommended for beginning social workers.

3. Intervene in sessions when clients ignore or fail to validate messages—a situation that occurs frequently during direct social work with couples, families, and groups. At those moments, interrupt the process in a facilitative fashion to ask the sender to repeat the message and the receiver to paraphrase or capture the essence of the former's message with fresh words, as illustrated in the following example:

16-year-old daughter: I don't like going to school. The teachers are a bunch of dweebs, and most of the kids laugh and make fun of me.

Mother: But you've got to go. If you'd just buckle down and study, school wouldn't be half so hard for you. I think . . .

Social worker [*interrupting and speaking to mother*]: I can see that you have some real concerns about Janet's not going to school, but for a moment, I'm going to ask you to get in touch with what she just said to you by repeating it back to her.

Mother [*looking at social worker*]: She said she doesn't like school.

Social worker: That's close, but turn and talk to Janet. See if you can identify what she's feeling.

Mother [*turning to daughter*]: I guess it's pretty painful for you to go to school. And you don't like

your teachers and you feel shut out and ridiculed by the kids.

Janet [*tearfully*]: Yeah, that's it . . . it's really hard.

Notice that the mother did not respond empathically to her daughter's feelings until the social worker intervened and coached her. This example illustrates the importance of persevering in teaching clients to "hear" the messages of others, a point we cannot overemphasize. Clients often have considerable trouble mastering listening skills because habitual dysfunctional responses are difficult to discard. This is true even when clients are highly motivated to communicate more effectively and when social workers actively intervene to assist them.

4. Give positive feedback when you observe clients listening to each other or, as in the preceding example, when they respond to your coaching. In the example, the social worker might have praised the mother as follows: "I liked the way you responded, because your message accurately reflected what your daughter was experiencing. I think she felt you really understood what she was trying to say." It is also helpful to ask participants to discuss what they experienced during the exchange and to highlight positive feelings and observations.

AUTHENTICITY

Although many theorists agree that empathy and respect are vital to developing effective working relationships, they do not agree about the amount of openness or self-disclosure practitioners should offer. *Self-disclosure* refers to the sharing with the client of opinions, thoughts, feelings, reactions to the client, and personal experiences of the practitioner (Deal, 1999). Decisions about whether or when to self-disclose must be guided by a perception of benefit to the client, not the practitioner's need to share. As one client said, "My case worker wanted to tell me all about his week end and his girlfriend and so on. And I said, 'TMI: too much information. I don't need to know this, and I don't want to know this.' I don't want to share this kind of information with him and don't want to know it from him." Clearly, this client did not perceive the benefit of this kind of personal sharing. Deal reports that although beginning practitioners frequently report engaging in self-disclosure, they seem less clear about the conditions under which it was appropriate to do so.

With respect to empirical evidence, numerous research studies cited by Truax and Mitchell (1971) and Gurman (1977) indicated that empathy, respect, and genuineness are correlated with positive outcomes. Critical analyses of these studies and conflicting findings from other research studies, however, have led experts to question these early findings and to conclude that "a more complex association exists between outcome and therapist 'skills' than originally hypothesized" (Parloff, Waskow, & Wolfe, 1978, p. 251).

Nevertheless, authenticity (also called genuineness) and the other facilitative conditions are still viewed as central to the helping process. *Authenticity* is defined as the sharing of self by relating in a natural, sincere, spontaneous, open, and genuine manner. Being authentic, or genuine, involves relating personally so that expressions are spontaneous rather than contrived. In addition, it means that social workers' verbalizations are congruent with their actual feelings and thoughts. Authentic social workers relate as real people, expressing their feelings and assuming responsibility for them rather than denying the feelings or blaming the client for causing them. Authenticity also involves being nondefensive and human enough to admit one's errors to clients. Realizing that they expect clients to lower their defenses and to relate openly (thereby increasing their vulnerability), social workers themselves must model humanness and openness and avoid hiding behind a mask of "professionalism."

Relating authentically does not mean that social workers indiscriminately disclose their feelings. Indeed, authentic expressions can be abrasive and destructive. Yalom and Lieberman (1971), for example, found in a study of encounter groups that attacks or rejections of group members by leaders or other members produced many psychological casualties. Social workers should thus relate authentically only when doing so is likely to further the therapeutic objectives. This qualification provides considerable latitude and is merely intended to constrain social workers from (1) relating abrasively (even though they may be expressing genuine feelings) and (2) meeting their own needs by focusing on their personal experiences and feelings rather than those of the client.

With respect to the first constraint, social workers must avoid misconstruing authenticity as granting free license to do whatever they wish, especially with respect to expressing hostility. The second constraint reiterates the importance of social workers' responding to clients' needs rather than their own. Moreover, when social workers share their feelings or experiences for a therapeutic purpose, they should immediately shift the focus back on the clients. Keep in mind that the purpose of relating authentically—whether with individuals, families, or groups—is to facilitate growth of clients, not to demonstrate one's own honesty or authenticity.

Types of Self-Disclosure

The aspect of authenticity denoted as self-disclosure has been variously defined by different authors (Chelune, 1979). For our discussion here, we define self-disclosure as the conscious and intentional revelation of information about oneself through both verbal expressions and nonverbal behaviors (e.g., smiling, grimacing, or shaking one's head in disbelief). Viewed from a therapeutic perspective, self-disclosure encourages clients to reciprocate with trust and openness.

Danish, D'Augelli, and Hauer (1980) have identified two types of self-disclosure, *self-involving statements* and *personal self-disclosing*. The former type includes messages that express the social worker's personal reaction to the client during the course of a session. Examples of self-involving statements follow:

- "I'm impressed with the progress you've made this past week. You applied what we discussed last week and have made another step toward learning to control angry feelings."

- "I want to share my reaction to what you just said. I found myself feeling sad for you because you put yourself down unmercifully. I see you so differently from how you see yourself and find myself wishing I could somehow spare you the torment you inflict on yourself."

- "You know, as I think about the losses you've experienced this past year, I marvel you've done as well as you have. I'm not at all sure I'd have held together as well as you have."

Personal self-disclosure messages, by contrast, center on struggles or problems the social worker is currently experiencing or has experienced that are similar to the client's problems. The following are examples of this type of self-disclosure:

- [*To couple*] "As you talk about your problems with your children, it reminds me of similar difficulties I had with mine when they were that same age." (The social worker goes on to relate his experience.)
  [*To individual client*] "I think all of us struggle with that same fear to some degree. Earlier this week I . . ." (The social worker goes on to relate events in which she experienced similar fears.)

Research findings comparing the effects of different types of self-disclosure have been mixed. Given the inconclusive findings, social workers should use personal self-disclosure judiciously. They should also recognize cultural variations that may suggest that some relatively low-level self-disclosure may be necessary early in the helping process. Logic suggests that self-disclosures of current problems may undermine the confidence of clients, who may well wonder how social workers can presume to help others when they haven't successfully resolved their own problems. Moreover, focusing on the social worker's problems diverts attention from the client, who may conclude that the social worker prefers to focus on his or her own problems. Self-involving disclosures, by contrast, appear to be of low risk and are relevant to the helping process.

Timing and Intensity of Self-Disclosure

Yet another aspect of self-disclosure focuses on the timing and level of intensity of the social worker's sharing, ranging from superficial to highly personal statements. Social workers should avoid sharing personal feelings and experiences until they have established rapport and

trust with their clients and the clients have, in turn, demonstrated readiness to engage on a more personal level. The danger in premature self-disclosure is that such responses can threaten clients and lead to emotional retreat at the very time when it is vital to reduce threat and defensiveness.

The danger is especially great with clients from other cultures who are unaccustomed to relating on an intense personal basis. Greater formality with less self-disclosure may be useful in cross-cultural transactions between Caucasian social workers and clients of color. With respect to Asian American clients, however, Tsui and Schultz (1985) indicate that self-disclosure by social workers may facilitate the development of rapport: Personal disclosure and an appropriate level of emotional expressiveness are often the most effective ways to put Asian clients at ease. Considering the generally low level of emotional expressiveness in Asian families, the therapist is, in effect, acting as a role model for the client, thereby showing the client how the appropriate expression of emotion facilitates the treatment process (Tsui and Schultz, 1985, p. 568). Asian American families, of course, are not homogenous, as their members differ in terms of their level of acculturation and familiarity with values such as self-disclosure.

As clients experience trust, social workers can appropriately relate with increased openness and spontaneity, assuming that their authentic responses are relevant to their clients' needs and do not shift the focus from the client for more than brief periods. Even when trust is strong, social workers should exercise only moderate self-disclosure—beyond a certain level, even authentic responses no longer facilitate the helping process (Truax & Carkhuff, 1964).

A Paradigm for Responding Authentically

Beginning social workers (and clients) may learn the skill of relating authentically more readily if they have a paradigm for formulating effective messages.

This paradigm includes the four elements of an authentic message:

(1) "I" ( )	About	Because
(2) Specific feeling or wants	(3) Neutral description of event	(4) Impact of situation upon sender or others

The following example (Larsen, 1980), involving a social work student intern's response to a message from an institutionalized youth, illustrates the use of this paradigm. The student describes the situation: "Don and I had a tough go of it last week. I entered the living unit only to find that he was angry with me for some reason, and he proceeded to abuse me verbally all night long. This week, Don approached me to apologize."

Don: I'm really sorry about what happened the other night. I didn't mean nothing by it. You probably don't want nothing more to do with me.

Student: Well, you know, Don, I'm sorry it happened, too. I was really hurt and puzzled that night because I didn't understand where all your anger was coming from. You wouldn't talk to me about it, so I felt frustrated and I didn't quite know what to do or make of it. One of my real fears that night was that this was going to get in the way of our getting to know each other. I really didn't want to see that happen.

Note that the student uses all of the elements of the paradigm: identifying specific feelings (hurt, puzzlement, frustration, fear); describing the events that occurred in a neutral, nonblaming manner; and identifying the impact she feared these events might have upon the client–social worker relationship.

As you consider the paradigm, note that we are not recommending that you use it in a mechanistic and undeviating "I-feel-this-way-about . . ." response pattern. Rather, we suggest that you learn and combine the elements of the paradigm in a variety of ways as you practice constructing authentic messages. Later, as you incorporate authentic relating into your natural conversational repertoire, you will no longer need to refer to the paradigm.

Note that this paradigm is also applicable in teaching clients to respond authentically. We suggest that you present the paradigm to clients and guide them through several practice messages, assisting them to include all of the elements of the paradigm in their responses. For example:

Specific "I" Feelings	Description of Event	Impact
I get frustrated	when you keep reading the paper while I'm speaking	because I feel discounted and very unimportant to you.

It is important to stress with clients the need to use conversational language when they express authentic messages. Also emphasize, however, that they should talk about their own feelings and opinions. Otherwise, they may slip into accusatory forms of communication as they vary their messages.

Guidelines for Responding Authentically

As you practice authentic responding and teach clients to respond authentically in their encounters with others, we suggest you keep in mind the following guidelines related to the four elements of an authentic message.

1. *Personalize messages by using the pronoun "I."* When attempting to respond authentically, both social workers and clients commonly make the mistake of starting their statements with "You." This introduction tends to focus a response on the other person rather than on the sender's experiencing. In contrast, beginning messages with "I" encourages senders to own responsibility for their feelings and to personalize their statements.

Efforts by social workers to employ "I" statements when responding can profoundly affect the quality of group processes, increasing both the specificity of communications and the frequency with which their clients use "I" statements. As a general rule, groups (including couples and families) are likely to follow a social worker's communication style.

Just as groups tend to follow suit when social workers frequently use "I" messages, they may also imitate counterproductive behaviors of the social worker. That includes communicating in broad generalities, focusing on issues external to the individual, or relating to the group in an interrogative or confrontational manner. For this reason, the behavior of some social workers may not necessarily be a good model for clients to emulate in real life.

Social workers must be careful to model the skills they wish clients to acquire. They should master relating authentically to the extent that they automatically personalize their messages and constructively share their inner experiencing with clients. To facilitate personalizing messages, social workers can negotiate an agreement with individuals or groups specifying that clients will endeavor to incorporate the use of "I" statements in their conversational repertories. Thereafter, it is critical to intervene consistently to assist clients to personalize their messages when they have not done so.

2. *Share feelings that lie at varying depths.* Social workers must reach for those feelings that underlie their immediate experiencing. Doing so is particularly vital when social workers experience strong negative feelings (e.g., dislike, anger, repulsion, disgust, boredom) toward a client, because an examination of the deeper aspects of feelings often discloses more positive feelings toward the client. Expressing these feelings preserves the client's self-esteem, whereas expressing superficial negative feelings often poses a threat to the client, creating defensiveness and anger.

For example, in expressing anger (and perhaps disgust) toward a client who is chronically late for appointments, the social worker may first connect his feelings of anger to feeling inconvenienced. In reaching for his deeper feelings, however, the social worker may discover that the annoyance derives from disappointment that the client is not fully committed to the helping process. At an even deeper level may lie hurt in not being more important to the client. Further introspection may also uncover a concern that the client is exhibiting similar behavior in other areas of life that could adversely affect his or her relationships with others.

The social worker may discover multiple (and sometimes conflicting) feelings that may be beneficially shared with the client, as illustrated in the following message:

Social worker [*To mother*]: I've been experiencing some feelings in the session I want to share with you because it may shed some light on what others may experience with you. I was wanting to tell you that it appears you often come to Robert's [the client's son] rescue in the session, and that sometimes you seem to protect him from the consequences of his own actions, but I held back and began to feel a slight knotting in my stomach. Then it hit me that I was afraid you'd be hurt and offended and that it might have a negative effect on our relationship. As I think about it just now, I'm aware that sometimes I feel I'm walking on eggshells with you. I don't like that because it puts distance between us. Another reason I don't like it is because I think I'm underestimating your ability to handle constructive feedback. I think you're stronger than you come across at times. [*Slight pause.*] Could you share what you're feeling just now about what I said?

Like prospective social workers, clients are prone to focus on one aspect of their experiencing to the exclusion of deeper and more complex emotions. Clients often have difficulty, in fact, pinpointing any feelings they are experiencing. In either case, social workers should persevere to help clients broaden their awareness of their emotions and to express them openly, as illustrated in the following exchange:

Social worker: When you told your wife you didn't want to take her to a movie and she said you were a "bump on a log"—that you never seemed to want to do anything with her—what feelings did you experience?[2]

Husband: I decided that if that's what she thought of me, that's what I'd be.

Social worker: Can you get in touch with what you were feeling? You told me a little bit about what you thought, but what's happening inside? Try to use feeling words to describe what you're experiencing.

Husband: [*pause*]: I felt that if she was going to get on my back . . .

Social worker [*gently interrupting*]: Can you use a feeling word like "bad," or "hurt," or "put down"? What did you feel?

Husband: Okay. I felt annoyed.

Social worker: So you experienced a sense of irritation. Good. I'm pleased you could get in touch with that feeling. Now see if you can get to an even more basic feeling. Remember, as we've talked about before, anger is usually a surface feeling that camouflages other feelings. What was under your annoyance?

Husband: Uh, I'd say frustrated. I just didn't want to sit there and listen to her harp at me. She never quits.

Social worker: I would like to check out something with you. Right now, as you're talking about this, it seems you're experiencing a real sense of discouragement and perhaps even hopelessness about things ever changing. It's as though you've given up. Maybe that's part of what you were feeling Saturday.

Husband: Yeah, I just turn myself off. There doesn't seem to be anything I can do to make her happy.

Social worker: I'm glad that you can recognize the sense of despair you're feeling. I also appreciate your hanging in there with me for a minute to get in touch with some of your feelings. You seem to be a person whose feelings run deep, and sometimes expressing them may come hard for you. I'm wondering how you view yourself in that regard.

In the preceding excerpt, the social worker engaged in extensive coaching to assist the client in discovering his underlying feelings. Deeper than the feelings of annoyance and frustration the client identified lay the more basic emotions related to feeling hurt and being unimportant to his wife. By providing other spontaneous "training sessions," the social worker can help this client to identify his feelings more readily, to find the feeling words to express them, and to begin formulating "I" statements.

3. *Describe the situation or targeted behavior in neutral or descriptive terms.* In their messages, clients often omit references or make only vague references to the situations that prompted their responses. Moreover, they may convey their messages in a blaming manner, engendering defensiveness that overshadows other aspects of their self-disclosure. In either event, self-disclosure is minimal and respondents do not receive information that could otherwise be of considerable value.

Consider, for example, the low yield of information in the following messages:

- "You're a neat person."
- "You should be more conscientious."
- "You're progressing well in your work."
- "You have a bad attitude."

All of these messages lack supporting information that respondents need to identify specific aspects of their behavior that is competent and warrants recognition or is substandard. Social workers should assist parents, spouses, or others to provide higher-yield feedback by including behavioral references. Examples of such messages follow (they involve a parent talking to a 6-year-old girl):

- "I've really appreciated all that you've done tonight by yourself. You picked up your toys, washed your hands before dinner, and ate dinner without dawdling. I'm so pleased."
- "I'm very disappointed with your behavior right now. You didn't change your clothes when you came home from school; you didn't feed the dog; and you haven't started your homework."

Note in the last example that the parent sent an "I" message and owned the feelings of disappointment rather than attacking the child for being undependable.

When responding authentically, social workers should carefully describe specific events that prompted their responses, particularly when they wish to draw clients' attention to some aspect of their behavior or to a situation of which they may not be fully aware. The following social worker's message illustrates this point:

Social worker: I need to share something with you that concerns me. Just a moment ago, I gave you feedback regarding the positive way I thought you handled a situation with your husband. [*Refers to specific behaviors manifested by client.*] When I did that, you seemed to discount my response by [*mentions specific behaviors*]. Actually, this is not the first time I have seen this happen. It appears to me that it is difficult for you to give yourself credit for the positive things you do and the progress you are making. This, in fact, may be one of the reasons that you get so discouraged at times. I wonder how you view your behavior in this regard.

Social workers constantly need to assess the specificity of their responses to ensure that they give clients the benefit of behaviorally specific feedback and provide positive modeling experiences for them. It is also vital to coach clients in giving specific feedback whenever they make sweeping generalizations and do not document the relationship between their responses and specific situations.

4. *Identify the specific impact of the problem situation or behavior on others.* Authentic messages often stop short of identifying the specific effects of the situation on the sender or on others, even though such information would be very appropriate and helpful. This element of an "I" message also increases the likelihood that the receiver will adjust or make changes, particularly if the sender demonstrates that the receiver's behavior is having a tangible effect on him or her.

Consider a social worker's authentic response to a male member of an adult group:

Social worker: "Sometimes I sense some impatience on your part to move on to other topics. [*Describes situation that just occurred, documenting specific messages and behavior.*] At times I find myself torn between responding to your urging us "to get on with it" or staying with a discussion that seems beneficial to the group. It may be that others in the group are experiencing similar mixed feelings and some of the pressure I feel."

Here the social worker first clarifies the tangible effects of the client's behavior on himself and then suggests that others may experience the behavior similarly. Given the social worker's approach, others in the group may be willing to give feedback as well. The client is then free to draw his own conclusions about the cause-and-effect relationship between his behaviors and the reactions of others and to decide whether he wishes to alter his way of relating in the group.

Social workers can identify how specific client behaviors negatively impact not only the social worker but also the clients themselves (e.g., "I'm concerned about [*specific behavior*] because it keeps you from achieving your goal"). Further, they may document how a client's behavior affects others (e.g., his wife) or the relationship between the client and another person (e.g., "It appears that your behavior creates distance between you and your son").

Clients often have difficulty in clarifying the impact of others' behavior on themselves. For example, a mother's message to her child, "I want you to play someplace else," establishes no reason for the request, nor does it specify the negative impact of the behavior on her. If the mother responds in an authentic manner, however, she clearly identifies the tangible effect of her child's behavior: "I'm having a hard time getting through the hallway because I keep stumbling over toys and having to go around you. I've almost fallen several times, and others might, too. I'm worried that someone might get hurt, so I'm asking you to move your toys to your room."

The preceding illustration underscores the point that when clients clarify how a situation affects them, their requests do not appear arbitrary and are more persuasive; hence, others are likely to make appropriate accommodations. We suspect that an important reason why many clients have not changed certain self-defeating behaviors before entering the helping process is that others have previously attacked or pressured them to change, rather than authentically and unabrasively imparting information that highlights how the clients' behavior strikes them. Others may have also attempted to prescribe behavioral changes that appear to be self-serving (e.g., "Come on, stop that sulking") instead of relating their feelings (e.g., "I'm concerned that you're down and unhappy; I'd like to help but I'm not sure how"). Such statements do not strike a responsive chord in clients, who may equate making changes with putting themselves under the control of others (by following their directives), thereby losing their autonomy.

In the following exchange, note how the social worker assists Carolyn, a group member, to personalize her statements and to clarify her reaction to the behavior of another member who has remained consistently silent throughout the first two sessions:

Carolyn: We've talked about needing to add new guidelines for the group as we go along. I think we ought to have a guideline that everyone should talk in the group. [*Observe that Carolyn has not personalized her message but has proposed a solution to meet a need she has not identified.*]

Social worker [*to Carolyn*]: The group may want to consider this guideline, but for a minute, can you get in touch with what you're experiencing and put it in the form of an "I" statement?

Carolyn: Well, all right. Janet hasn't talked at all for two solid weeks, and it's beginning to really irritate me.

Social worker: I'm wondering what else you may be experiencing besides irritation? [*Assists Carolyn to identify her feelings besides mild anger.*]

Carolyn: I guess I'm a little uneasy because I don't know where Janet stands. Maybe I'm afraid she's sitting in judgment of us—I mean, me. And I guess I feel cheated because I'd like to get to know her better, and right now I feel shut out by her.

Social worker: That response helps us to begin to get to the heart of the matter. Would you now express yourself directly to Janet? Tell her what you are experiencing and, particularly, how her silence is affecting you.

Carolyn [*to Janet*]: I did wonder what you thought about me since I really opened up last week. And

I do want to get to know you better. But, underneath all this, I'm concerned about you. You seem unhappy and alone, and that makes me uncomfortable—I don't like to think of your feeling that way. Frankly, I'd like to know how you feel about being in this group, and if you're uneasy about it, as you seem to be, I'd like to help you feel better somehow.

In the preceding example, the social worker assisted Carolyn to experience a broader range of feelings and to identify her reaction to Janet's silence. In response to the social worker's intervention, Carolyn also expressed more positive feelings than were evident in her initial message—a not infrequent occurrence when social workers encourage clients to explore deeper-level emotions.

Engaging one member in identifying specific reactions to the behavior of others provides a learning experience for the entire group, and members often expand their conversational repertoires to incorporate such facilitative responding. In fact, the extent to which social workers assist clients to acquire specific skills is correlated with the extent to which clients acquire those same skills.

Cues for Authentic Responding

The impetus for social workers to respond authentically may emanate from (1) clients' messages that request self-disclosure or (2) social workers' decisions to share perceptions and reactions they believe will be helpful. Next, we consider authentic responding that emanates from these two sources.

Authentic Responding Stimulated by Clients' Messages

Requests from Clients for Personal Information. Clients often confront students and social workers with questions aimed at soliciting personal information, such as "How old are you?", "Do you have any children?", "What is your religion?", "Are you married?" and "Are you a student?" It is natural for clients to be curious and to ask questions about a social worker in whom they are confiding, especially when their well-being and future are at stake.

Self-disclosing responses may or may not be appropriate, depending on the social worker's assessment of the client's motivation for asking a particular question. When questions appear to be prompted by a natural desire for information, such responses are often very appropriate. Seemingly innocuous questions, however, may camouflage deep concerns or troubling feelings. In such instances, providing an immediate answer may not be advisable because doing so may close the door to exploring and resolving clients' concerns and feelings (Strean, 1997). Clients are then left to struggle with their feelings alone, which may seriously impair progress or cause premature termination of the social work contact.

To illustrate, consider the following exchange from an initial session involving a 23-year-old student social worker and a 43-year-old woman who requested help in dealing with her marital problems:

Client: Are you married?

Student social worker: No, but I'm engaged. Why do you ask?

Client: Oh, I don't know. I just wondered.

Given the context of an older adult with a much younger student, the client's question was likely motivated by a concern that the student might lack life experience essential to understanding her marital difficulties or the competence needed to assist her in resolving them. In this instance, immediate authentic disclosure by the student was inappropriate because it did not facilitate exploration of the feelings underlying the client's inquiry.

Conversely, such an exchange may yield information vital to the helping process if the social worker avoids premature self-disclosure. It is sometimes very difficult to distinguish whether the questions of clients are motivated by a natural desire for information or by hidden concerns or feelings. As a rule of thumb, when you have questions about clients' motivation for making personal inquiries, *precede disclosures of views or feelings with either open-ended or empathic responses.* Responding in this manner significantly increases the probability that clients will reveal their underlying concerns. Notice what happens when the social worker utilizes an empathic response before responding authentically:

Client: Are you married?

Student social worker: I gather you're wondering if I can understand and help you with your difficulties in light of the fact that I'm much younger than you.

Client: Well, I guess I was thinking that. I hope it doesn't offend you.

Student social worker: To the contrary—I appreciate your frankness. It's natural that you want to have confidence in your counselor. I know there's a lot at stake for you. Tell me more about your concerns.

Here the student responded to the probable concern of the client and struck pay dirt. Such astuteness tends to foster confidence in clients and greatly facilitates the establishment of a therapeutic partnership. The fact that the student "leans into" the situation by inviting further exploration rather than skirting the issue may also be read by the client as an indicator of the student's own confidence in his or her ability to help. After fully exploring the client's concerns, the student can respond with an authentic response identifying personal qualifications:

Student social worker: I do want you to know that I believe I can be helpful to you. I have studied marriage counseling at some length, and I have counseled other clients whose difficulties were similar to your own. I also consult with my supervisor regularly.

Of course, the final judgment of my competence will rest with you. It will be important for us to discuss any feelings you may still have at the end of the interview as you make a decision about returning for future sessions.

Questions That Solicit the Social Worker's Perceptions. Clients may also pose questions that solicit the social worker's opinions, views, or feelings. Typical questions include "How do I compare to your other clients?", "Do you think I need help?", "Am I crazy?", and "Do you think there's any hope for me?" Such questions can pose a challenge for social workers, who must consider the motivation behind the question and judge whether to disclose their views or feelings immediately or to employ either an empathic or an open-ended response.

When social workers do disclose their perceptions, however, their responses must be congruent with their inner experiencing. In response to the question "Do you think there's any hope for me?" the social worker may congruently respond with a message that blends elements of empathy and authenticity:

Social worker: Your question tells me you're probably afraid that you're beyond help. Although you do have some difficult problems, I'm optimistic that if we work hard together things can improve. You've shown a number of strengths that should help you make changes, including [*reviews strengths*]. Of course, a lot will depend on whether you're willing to commit to making changes you think would improve your situation and to invest the time and effort necessary to achieve your goals. In that respect, you're in control of the situation and whether things change for the better. That fact is something that many people find encouraging to know.

It is not necessary to answer all questions of clients in the service of authenticity. If you feel uncomfortable about answering a personal question or deem it inadvisable to do so, you should feel free to decline answering. When doing so, it is important to explain your reason for not answering directly, again utilizing an authentic response. If a teenage client, for example, asks whether the social worker had sexual relations before she married, the social worker may respond as follows:

Social worker: I would rather not reveal that information to you, because it is a very private part of my life. Asking me took some risk on your part. I have an idea that your question probably has to do with a struggle you're having, although I could be wrong. I would appreciate your sharing your thoughts about what sparked your question.

The social worker should then utilize empathic responding and open-ended questions to explore the client's reaction and motivation for asking her question.

Authentic Responding Initiated by Social Workers

Authentic responding initiated by social workers may take several forms, which are considered next.

Disclosing Past Experiences. As previously indicated, self-disclosure should be sparingly used, brief, relevant to the client's concerns, and well timed. In relating to a particular client's struggle, a social worker might indicate, "I remember I felt very much like that when I was struggling with . . ." Social workers may also cite personal perceptions or experiences as reference points for clients—for example, "I think that is very normal behavior for a child. For instance, my five-year-old . . ." A fundamental guideline that applies to such situations is that social workers should be certain they are focusing on themselves to meet the therapeutic needs of their clients.

Sharing Perceptions, Ideas, Reactions, and Formulations. A key role of the social worker in the change-oriented phase of the helping process is to act as a "candid feedback system" by revealing personal thoughts and perceptions relevant to client problems (Hammond et al., 1977). Such responding is intended to further the change process in one or more of the following ways:

1. To heighten clients' awareness of dynamics that may play an important part in problems

2. To offer a different perspective regarding issues and events

3. To aid clients in conceptualizing the purposes of their behavior and feelings

4. To enlighten clients on how they affect others (including the social worker)

5. To bring clients' attention to cognitive and behavioral patterns (both functional and dysfunctional) that operate at either an individual or a group level

6. To share the social worker's here-and-now affective and physical reactions to clients' behavior or to processes that occur in the helping relationship

7. To share positive feedback concerning clients' strengths and growth

After responding authentically to achieve any of these purposes, it is vital to invite clients to express their own views and draw their own conclusions. *Owning* perceptions rather than using under-the-table methods to influence clients to adopt particular views or to change in ways deemed desirable by the social worker (e.g., "Don't you think you ought to consider . . .") relieves clients of the need to behave deviously or to defend themselves from the tyranny of views with which they do not agree.

Sharing perceptions with clients does involve some risk. In particular, clients may misinterpret the social worker's motives and feel criticized, put down, or rebuked. Clarifying the social worker's helpful intent before responding diminishes this risk somewhat. Nevertheless, it is critical to watch for clients' reactions that may indicate a response has struck an exposed nerve.

To avoid damaging the relationship (or to repair it), the social worker should be empathically attuned to the client's reaction to candid feedback, shifting the focus back to the client to determine the impact of the self-disclosure. If the client appears to have been emotionally wounded by the social worker's authentic response, the social worker can use empathic skills to elicit troubled feelings and to guide subsequent responses aimed at restoring the relationship's equilibrium. Expressions of concern and clarification of the goodwill intended by the social worker are also usually facilitative:

Social worker: I can see that what I shared with you hit you pretty hard—and that you're feeling put down right now. [*Client nods but avoids eye contact.*] I feel bad about that, because the last thing I'd want is to hurt you. Please tell me what you're feeling.

Openly (and Tactfully) Sharing Reactions When Put on the Spot. Clients sometimes create situations that put social workers under considerable pressure to respond to messages that bear directly on the relationship, such as when they accuse a social worker of being uninterested, unfeeling, irritated, displeased, critical, inappropriate, or incompetent. Clients may also ask pointed questions (sometimes

before the relationship has been firmly established) that require immediate responses.

The first statement of one female client in an initial interview, for example, was "I'm gay. Does that make any difference to you?" In the opening moments of another session, a pregnant client asked the social worker, "How do you feel about abortion?" Over the years, students have reported numerous such situations that sorely tested their ability to respond facilitatively. In one instance, a male member of a group asked a female student leader for her photograph. In another case, an adolescent boy kept taking his shoes off and putting his feet (which smelled very bad) on the social worker's desk. In reflecting on your practice experience, you can undoubtedly cite instances in which the behavior of clients caused you to squirm or produced butterflies in your stomach.

Experiencing Discomfort in Sessions. Sometimes intense discomfort may indicate that something in the session is going awry and needs to be addressed. It is important to reflect on your discomfort, seeking to identify events that seem to be causing or exacerbating it (e.g., "I'm feeling very uneasy because I don't know how to respond when my client says things like 'You seem to be too busy to see me' or 'I'm not sure I'm worth your trouble' "). After privately exploring the reason for the discomfort, the social worker might respond as follows:

Social worker: I'd like to share some impressions about several things you've said in the last two sessions. [*Identifies client's statements.*] I sense you're feeling pretty unimportant—as though you don't count for much—and that perhaps you're imposing on me just by being here. I want you to know that I'm pleased you had the courage to seek help in the face of all the opposition from your family. It's also important to me that you know that I want to be helpful to you. I am concerned, however, that you feel you're imposing on me. Could you share more of those feelings with me?

Notice how the social worker specifically identifies the self-defeating thoughts and feelings and blends elements of empathy and authenticity in the response.

Other situations that put social workers on the spot include clients' angry attacks, as we discuss later in this chapter. Social workers must learn to respond authentically in such scenarios. Consider a situation in which an adolescent attacks a social worker in an initial interview, protesting, "I don't want to be here. You social workers are all losers." In such instances, social workers should share their reactions, as illustrated in the following response:

Social worker: It sounds as though you're really ticked off about having to see me and that your previous experiences with social workers have been bummers. I respect your feelings and don't want to pressure you to work with me. I am concerned and uncomfortable, however, because you apparently have lumped all social workers together and that makes me a loser in your eyes. If you close your mind to the possibility that we might accomplish something together, then the chances are pretty slim I can be helpful. I want you to know that I am interested in you and that I would like to know what you're up against.

Intertwining empathic and authentic responses in this manner often defuses clients' anger and encourages them to think more rationally about a situation.

Sharing Feelings When Clients' Behavior Is Unreasonable or Distressing. Although social workers should be able to take most client behaviors in stride, sometimes they may experience justifiable feelings of frustration, anger, or even hurt. In one case, a client acquired a social worker's home phone number from another source and began calling frequently about daily crisis situations, although discussions of these events could easily have waited until the next session. In another instance, a tipsy client called the social worker in the middle of the night "just to talk." In yet another case, an adolescent client let the air out of a social worker's automobile tires.

In such situations, social workers should share their feelings with clients—*if they believe they can do so constructively.* In the following recorded case example, note that the student social worker interweaves authentic and empathic responses in confronting a Latino youth in a correctional institution who had

maintained he was innocent of hiding drugs that staff had found in his room. Believing the youth's story, the student went to bat for him, only to find out later that the client had lied. Somewhat uneasy at her first real confrontation, the student tries to formulate an authentic response. In an interesting twist, the youth helps her to be "up-front" with him:

Student social worker: There's something I wanted to talk to you about, Randy . . . [*Stops to search for the right words.*]

Randy: Well, come out with it, then. Just lay it on me.

Student social worker: Well, remember last week when you got that incident report? You know, I really believed you were innocent. I was ready to go to the hearing and tell staff I was sure you were innocent and that the charge should be dropped. I guess I'm feeling kind of bad because when I talked to you, you told me you were innocent, and, well, that's not exactly the way it turned out.

Randy: You mean I lied to you. Go ahead and say it.

Student social worker: Well, yes, I guess I felt kind of hurt because I was hoping that maybe you had more trust in me than that.

Randy: Well, Susan, let me tell you something. Where I come from, that's not lying—that's what we call survival. Personally, I don't consider myself a liar. I just do what I need to do to get by. That's an old trick, but it just didn't work.

Student social worker: I hear you, Randy. I guess you're saying we're from two different worlds, and maybe we both define the same thing in different ways. I guess that with me being Anglo, you can't really expect me to understand what life has been like for you.

Several minutes later in the session, after the student has further explored the client's feelings, the following interchange occurs:

Student social worker: Randy, I want you to know a couple of things. The first thing is that when social workers work with clients, they must honor what they call confidentiality, so I can't share what we talk about without your permission in most cases. An exception to this relates to rule or law violations. I can't keep that confidential. The second thing is that I don't expect you to share everything with me. I know there are certain things you don't want to tell me, so rather than lying about something that I ask you about, maybe you can just tell me you don't want to tell me. Would you consider that?

Randy: Yeah, that's okay. [*Pause.*] Listen, Susan, I don't want you to go around thinking I'm a liar now. I'll tell you this, and you can take it for what it's worth, but this is the truth. That's the first time I've ever lied to you. But you may not believe that.

Student social worker: I do believe you, Randy. [*He seems a little relieved and there is a silence.*]

Randy: Well, Susan, that's a deal, then. I won't lie to you again, but if there's something I don't want to say, I'll tell you I don't want to say it.

Student social worker: Sounds good to me. [*Both start walking away.*] You know, Randy, I really want to see you get through this program and get out as fast as you can. I know it's hard starting over because of the incident with the drugs, but I think we can get you through. [*This seemed to have more impact on Randy than anything the social worker had said to him in a long time. The pleasure was visible on his face, and he broke into a big smile.*]

Noteworthy in this exchange is that the social worker relied almost exclusively on the skills of authenticity and empathy to bring the incident to a positive conclusion. Ignoring her feelings would have impaired the student's ability to relate facilitatively to the client and would have been destructive to the relationship. In contrast, focusing on the situation proved beneficial for both.

Sharing Feelings When Clients Give Positive Feedback. Social workers sometimes have difficulty responding receptively to clients' positive feedback about their own attributes and/or performance. We suggest that social workers model the same receptivity to positive feedback that they ask clients to demonstrate in their own lives, as illustrated in the following exchange:

Client: I don't know what I would have done without you. I'm just not sure I would have made it if you hadn't been there when I needed you. You've made such a difference in my life.

Social worker: I can sense your appreciation. I'm touched by your gratitude and pleased you are feeling so much more capable of coping with your situation. I want you to know, too, that even though I was there to help, your efforts have been the deciding factor in your growth.

Positive Feedback: A Form of Authentic Responding

Because positive feedback plays such a vital role in the change process, we have allocated a separate section in our attempt to do justice to this topic. Social workers often employ (or should employ) this skill in supplying information to clients about positive attributes or specific areas in which they demonstrate strengths, effective coping mechanisms, and incremental growth. In so doing, social workers enhance their clients' motivation to change and foster hope for the future.

Many opportune moments occur in the helping process when social workers experience warm or positive feelings toward clients because of the latter's actions or progress. When appropriate, social workers should share such feelings spontaneously with clients, as illustrated in the following messages:

- "I'm pleased that you have what I consider exceptional ability to 'self-observe' your own behavior and to analyze the part you play in relationships. I think this strength will serve you well in solving the problems you've identified."

- "I've been touched several times in the group when I've noticed that, despite your grief over the loss of your husband, you've reached out to other members who needed support."

- [*To newly formed group*]: "In contrast to our first session, I've noticed that this week we haven't had trouble getting down to business and staying on task. I've been pleased as I've watched you develop group guidelines for the past 20 minutes with minimal assistance from me. I had the thought, 'This group is really moving.' "

The first two messages acknowledge strengths of individuals. The third lauds a behavioral change the social worker has observed in a group process. Both types of messages sharply focus clients' attention on specific behaviors that facilitate the change process, ultimately increasing the frequency of such behaviors. When sent consistently, positive messages also have the long-range effect of helping clients who have low self-esteem to develop a more positive self-image. When positive feedback is employed to document the cause-and-effect relationship between their efforts and positive outcomes, clients also experience a sense of satisfaction, accomplishment, and control over their situation.

Positive feedback can have the additional effect of increasing clients' confidence in their own coping ability. We have occasionally had experiences with clients who were on the verge of falling apart when they came to a session but left feeling able to manage their problems for a while longer. We attribute their increased ability to function in part to authentic responses that documented and highlighted areas in which they were coping and successfully managing problems.

Taped sessions of students and social workers often reveal relatively few authentic responses that underscore clients' strengths or incremental growth. This lack of positive feedback is unfortunate because, in our experience, clients' rates of change often correlate with the extent to which social workers focus on these two vital areas. If social workers consistently focus on their clients' assets and the subtle positive changes that often occur in early sessions, clients will typically invest more effort in the change process. As the rate of change accelerates, social workers can in turn focus more extensively on clients' successes, identifying and reinforcing their strengths and functional coping behaviors.

Social workers face several challenges in accrediting clients' strengths and growth, including improving their own ability to recognize and express fleeting positive feelings when clients manifest strengths or progress. Social workers must also learn to document events so that they can provide information about specific positive behaviors. Another challenge and responsibility is to teach clients to give positive feedback to one another, strategies that we discuss in Chapter 15.

To increase your ability to discern client strengths, we recommend that you and your clients construct a profile of their resources. This task may be completed with individuals, couples, families, or groups, and preferably occurs early in the helping process. In individual sessions, the social worker should ask the client to identify and list all the strengths she or he can think of. The social worker also shares observations of the client's strengths, adding them to the list, which is kept for ongoing review to add further strengths as they are discovered.

With families, couples, or groups, social workers may follow a similar procedure in assessing the strengths of individual members, but they should ask other group members to share their perceptions of strengths with each member. The social worker might also ask couples, families, or groups to identify the strengths and incremental growth of the group per se periodically throughout the helping process. After clients have identified their personal strengths or the strengths of the group, the social worker should elicit observations regarding their reactions to the experience. Often they may mutually conclude that clients have many more strengths than they have realized. The social worker should also explore any discomfort experienced by clients as they identify strengths, with the goal of having them acknowledge more comfortably their positive attributes and personal resources.

We further suggest that you carefully observe processes early on in sessions. Note the subtle manifestations of strengths and positive behavioral changes, systematically recording these in your progress records. Record not only the strengths and incremental growth of clients, but also whether you (or group members) focused on those changes. Keep in mind that changes often occur very subtly within a single session. For instance, clients may begin to discuss problems more openly during a later part of a session, tentatively commit to work on problems they had refused to tackle earlier, show growing trust in the social worker by confiding high-risk information about themselves, or own responsibility for the first time regarding their part in their problems. Groups and families may likewise experience growth within short periods of time. It is vital to keep your antenna finely tuned to such changes so that you do not overlook clients' progress.

RELATING ASSERTIVELY TO CLIENTS

Another aspect of relating authentically entails relating assertively to clients when a situation warrants such behavior. There are myriad reasons for relating assertively. To inspire confidence and influence clients to follow their lead, social workers must relate in a manner that projects competence. This is especially important in the initial phase of the helping process. Clients often covertly test or check out social workers to determine whether they can understand their problems and appear competent to help them.

In conjoint or group sessions, clients may question whether the social worker is strong enough to protect them from destructive interactional processes that may occur in sessions. Indeed, family or group members generally will not fully share, risk, or commit to the helping process until they have answered this question affirmatively through consistent observation of assertive actions by the social worker.

If social workers are relaxed and demonstrate through decisive behavior that they are fully capable of handling clients' problems and of providing the necessary protection and structure to control potentially chaotic or volatile processes, clients will typically relax, muster hope, and begin to work on problems. If the social worker appears incapable of curtailing or circumventing dysfunctional processes that render clients vulnerable, clients will have justifiable doubts about whether they should be willing to place themselves in jeopardy and, consequently, may disengage from the helping process.

Skill in relating assertively is also prerequisite to initiating confrontation, a major technique that social workers employ to surmount opposition to change. But social workers must employ confrontation with sensitivity and finesse, because the risk of alienating clients by using this technique is high. All forms of assertiveness, in fact, must be conveyed in a context of goodwill and empathic regard for clients' feelings and self-esteem.

In this section, we identify guidelines that can help you to intervene assertively with clients.

Making Requests and Giving Directives

To assist clients to relate more easily and work constructively to solve their problems, social workers frequently must make requests of them. Some of these requests may involve relating in new ways during sessions. For example, social workers may ask clients to do any of the following:

1. Speak directly to each other rather than through the social worker.
2. Give feedback to others in the session.
3. Respond by checking out the meanings of others' messages, take a listening stance, or personalize messages.
4. Change the arrangement of chairs.
5. Role-play.
6. Make requests of others.
7. Take responsibility for responding in specified ways during sessions.
8. Agree to carry out defined tasks during the week.
9. Identify strengths or incremental growth for themselves or others in the group or family.

When making requests, it is important to express them firmly and decisively and to deliver them with assertive nonverbal behavior. Social workers often err by couching their requests in tentative language, thus conveying doubt to clients about whether they must comply with the requests. The contrast between messages delivered in tentative language and those phrased in firm language can be observed in the exchanges given in Table 5-1.

Table 5-1 Tentative versus firm requests

TENTATIVE REQUESTS	FIRM REQUESTS
Would you mind if I interrupted . . .	I would like to pause for a moment . . .
Is it okay if we role-play?	I'd like you to role-play with me for a moment.
Excuse me, but don't you think you are getting off track?	I think we are getting off track. I'd like to return to the subject we were discussing just a minute ago.
Could we talk about something Kathy just said?	Let's go back to something Kathy just said. I think it is very important.

Many times social workers' requests of clients are actually *directives*, as are those under the column "Firm Requests" in Table 5-1. In essence, directives are declarative statements that place the burden on clients to object if they are uncomfortable, as the following message illustrates:

Social worker: Before you answer that question, please turn your chair toward your wife. [*Social worker leans over and helps client to adjust chair. Social worker speaks to wife.*] Will you please turn your chair, also, so that you can speak directly to your husband? Thank you. It's important that you be in full contact with each other while we talk.

If the social worker had given these clients a choice (e.g., "Would you like to change your chairs?"), they might not have responded affirmatively. We suggest that when you want clients to behave differently in sessions, you simply state what you would like them to do. If clients verbally object to directives or manifest nonverbal behavior that may indicate that they have reservations about complying with a request, it is vital to respond empathically and to explore the basis of their opposition. Such exploration often resolves fears or misgivings, freeing clients to engage in requested behavior.

Maintaining Focus and Managing Interruptions

Maintaining focus is a vital task that takes considerable skill and assertiveness on the social worker's part. It is often essential to intervene verbally to focus or refocus processes when interruptions or distractions occur. Sometimes, social workers may also respond assertively on a nonverbal level to prevent members from interrupting important processes that may need to be brought to positive conclusion, as illustrated in the following excerpt from a family session:

Kim, age 14 [*in tears, talking angrily to her mother*]: You hardly ever listen. At home, you just always yell at us and go to your bedroom.

Mrs. R: I thought I was doing better than that . . .

Mr. R [*interrupting his wife to speak to social worker*]: I think it's hard for my wife because . . .

Social worker [*holds up hand to father in a "halt" position, while continuing to maintain eye contact with mother and daughter; speaks to Kim*]: I would like to stay with your statement for a moment. Kim, please tell your mother what you're experiencing right now.

Interrupting Dysfunctional Processes

Unseasoned social workers often permit dysfunctional processes to continue for long periods either because they lack knowledge of how to intervene or because they think they should wait until clients have completed a series of exchanges. In such instances, social workers fail to fulfill one of their major responsibilities—that is, to *guide and direct* processes and to influence participants to interact in more facilitative ways. Remember that clients often seek help because they cannot manage their destructive interactional processes. Thus, permitting them to engage at length in their usual patterns of arguing, cajoling, threatening, blaming, criticizing, and labeling each other merely exacerbates their problems. The social worker should intervene in such circumstances, teaching the clients more facilitative behaviors and guiding them to implement such behaviors in subsequent interactions.

If you decide to interrupt ongoing processes, do so decisively so that clients will listen to you or heed your directive. If you intervene nonassertively, your potential to influence clients (particularly aggressive clients) will suffer, because being able to interrupt a discussion successfully demonstrates your power or influence in the relationship (Parlee, 1979). If you permit clients to ignore or to circumvent your interventions to arrest dysfunctional processes, you yield control and assume a "cone-down" position in relationship to the client.

With respect to interrupting or intervening in processes, we advocate using assertive—not aggressive—behavior. You must be sensitive to the vested interests of clients, because even though you may regard certain processes as unproductive or destructive, clients may not. The timing of interruptions is therefore vital. If it is not critical to draw clients' attention to what is happening immediately, you can wait for a natural pause. If such a pause does not occur shortly, you should interrupt. You should *not* delay interrupting destructive interactional processes, however, as illustrated in the following excerpt:

Wife [*to social worker*]: I feel the children need to mind me, but every time I ask them to do something, he [*husband*] says they don't have to do it. I think we're just ruining our kids, and it's mostly his fault.

Husband: Oh—well—that shows how dumb you are.

Social worker: I'm going to interrupt you because finding fault with each other will only lead to mutual resentment.

In this exchange, the social worker intervenes to refocus the discussion after just two dysfunctional responses on the clients' part. If participants do not disengage immediately, the social worker will need to use body movements that interfere with communication pathways or, in extreme instances, an exclamation such as "Time out!" to interrupt behavior. When social workers have demonstrated their intent to intervene quickly and decisively, clients will usually comply immediately when asked to disengage.

"Leaning Into" Clients' Anger

We cannot overstate the importance of openly addressing clients' anger and complaints. It is not unusual to feel defensive and threatened when such anger arises. Many social workers, especially those who are working with involuntary clients who are alleged to have harmed others, are inclined to retaliate, conveying the message, "You have no right to your anger. You have brought this on yourself. Do it my way or suffer the consequences." Responding assertively to a client's anger does not mean that you become a doormat, accepting that anger passively and submissively. Unless social workers can handle themselves assertively and competently in the face of such anger, they will lose the respect of most clients and thus their ability to help them. Further, clients may use their anger to influence and intimidate social workers just as they have done with others.

To help you respond assertively in managing clients' anger, we offer the following suggestions:

- Respond empathically to reflect clients' anger and, if possible, other underlying feelings (e.g., "I sense you're angry at me for _____ and perhaps disappointed about _____").

- Continue to explore the situation and the feelings of participants until you understand the nature of the events that inspired the angry feelings. During this exploration, you may find that the anger toward you dissipates and that clients begin to focus on themselves, assuming appropriate responsibility for their part in the situation at hand. The "real problem," as often happens, may not directly involve you.

- As you explore clients' anger, authentically express your feelings and reactions if it appears appropriate (e.g., "I didn't know you felt that way . . . I want to hear how I might have contributed to this situation. There may be some adjustments I'll want to make in my style of relating . . . I'm pleased that you shared your feelings with me.").

- Apply a problem-solving approach (if appropriate) so that all concerned make adjustments to avoid similar occurrences or situations in the future.

- If a particular client expresses anger frequently and in a dysfunctional manner, you may also focus on the client's style of expressing anger, identify problems that this communicative approach may cause him or her in relationships with others, and negotiate a goal of modifying this response pattern.

- In addition to empathizing with client anger, you can model assertive setting of personal limits and boundaries. For example, you might say, "I think that I have a good idea about how you are feeling about this situation and what you would like to be different about it. But I can't readily talk with you when you are so upset. Do you have a way of calming yourself down, or should we plan to meet again when you feel more in control of your emotions?" Alternatively, you might say, "I have pledged to do my part to listen to and respond to the issues you have raised. I am not willing to continue to be verbally abused, however."

Saying No and Setting Limits

Many tasks that social workers perform on behalf of their clients are quite appropriate. For example, negotiating for clients and conferring with other parties and potential resources to supplement and facilitate client action are tasks that are rightly handled by social workers (Epstein, 1992, p. 208). In contracting with clients, however, social workers must occasionally decline requests or set limits. This step is sometimes difficult for beginning social workers to take, as they typically want to demonstrate their willingness to help others. Commitment to helping others is a desirable quality, but it must be tempered with judgment as to when acceding to clients' requests is in the best interests of both social worker and client.

Some clients may have had past experiences that led them to believe that social workers will do most of the work required out of sessions. However, clients are often more likely to experience empowerment by increasing the scope of their actions than by having social workers perform tasks on their behalf that they can learn to do for themselves. Consequently, if social workers unthinkingly agree to take on responsibilities that clients can perform now or could perform in the future, they may reinforce passive client behavior.

Setting limits has special implications when social workers work with involuntary clients. Cingolani (1984) has noted that social workers engage in negotiated relationships with such clients. In negotiated relationships, social workers assume the roles of compromiser, mediator, and enforcer in addition to the more comfortable role of counselor. For example, when an involuntary client requests a "break" related to performance of a court order, the social worker must be clear about the client's choices and consequences of making those choices. He or she must also clarify what the client should expect from the social worker.

Rory [*member of domestic violence group*]: I don't think that it is fair that you report that I didn't meet for eight of the ten group sessions. I could not get off work for some of those sessions. I did all I could do.

Social worker: You did attend seven of the sessions, Rory, and made efforts to attend others. However, the contract you signed, which was presented in court, stated that you must complete eight sessions to be certified as completing the group. I do not have the power to change that court order. Should you decide to comply with the court order, I am willing to speak with your employer to urge him to work with you to arrange your schedule so that you can meet the court order.

In his response, the social worker made it clear that he would not evade the court order. At the same time, he assured Rory that if he chose to comply with the court order, the social worker would be willing to act as a mediator to assist him with difficulties in scheduling with the employer.

Being tactfully assertive is no easier for social workers with excessive needs to please others than it is for clients. These social workers have difficulty declining requests or setting limits when doing so is in the best interests of clients. Moreover, such social workers may benefit by setting tasks for themselves related to increasing their assertiveness. Participating in an assertiveness training group and delving into the popular literature on assertiveness may be highly beneficial as well.

Following are a few of the many situations in which you may need to decline requests of clients:

1. When clients invite you to participate with them socially

2. When clients ask you to grant them preferential status (e.g., set lower fees than are specified by policy)

3. When clients request physical intimacy

4. When clients ask you to intercede in a situation they should handle themselves

5. When clients request a special appointment after having broken a regular appointment for an invalid reason

6. When clients ask to borrow money

7. When clients request that you conceal information about violations of probation, parole, or institutional policy

8. When spouses request that you withhold information from their partners

9. When clients disclose plans to commit crimes or acts of violence against others

10. When clients ask you to report false information to an employer or other party

In addition to declining requests, you may need to set limits with clients in situations such as the following:

1. When clients make excessive telephone calls to you at home or the office

2. When clients cancel appointments without giving advance notice

3. When clients express emotions in abusive or violent ways

4. When clients habitually seek to go beyond designated ending points of sessions

5. When clients consistently fail to abide by contracts (e.g., not paying fees or missing numerous appointments)

6. When clients make sexual overtures toward you or other staff members

7. When clients come to sessions while intoxicated

Part of maturing professionally means learning to decline requests, set limits, and feel comfortable in so doing. As you gain experience, you will realize that you help clients as much by ensuring that they have reasonable expectations as you do by providing a concrete action for them. Modeled responses for refusing requests and for saying no to clients are found in the answers to the exercises designed to assist social workers to relate authentically and assertively.

Of course, social workers must also assert themselves effectively with other social workers and with members of other professions. Lacking experience and sometimes confidence, beginning social workers tend to be in awe of physicians, lawyers, psychologists, and more experienced social workers. Consequently, they may relate passively or may acquiesce in plans or demands that appear unsound or unreasonable. Although it is critical to remain open to the ideas of other professionals, beginning social workers should nevertheless risk expressing their own views and asserting their own rights. Otherwise, they may know more about a given client than other professionals but fail to contribute valuable information in joint case planning.

Beginning social workers should also set limits and assert their rights by refusing to accept unreasonable referrals and inappropriate assignments. Likewise, assertiveness may be required when other professionals deny resources to which clients are entitled, refer to clients with demeaning labels, or engage in unethical conduct. In fact, being assertive is critical when you act as a client advocate, a role discussed at length in Chapter 14.

Summary

This chapter prepared the way for you to communicate with clients and other persons on behalf of clients with appropriate empathy, assertiveness, and self-disclosure. Chapter 6 will build on these skills by developing your abilities in listening, focusing, and exploring. First, however, you should practice your new skills by completing the exercises in this chapter.

Internet Resources

See our companion website for hot links to some helpful URLs. Note that URLs are subject to change. We will endeavor to update the links on the companion website as much as possible.

You can enter keywords such as "empathy," "authenticity," "assertiveness" and "self-disclosure" in InfoTrac College Edition to find articles such as Carlozzi, Bull, Stein, Ray, and Barnes (2002) and Mitchell (1998).

Related Online Content

Visit the *Direct Social Work Practice* companion website at *http://socialwork. wadsworth.com/hepworth7* for additional learning tools such as glossary terms, chapter outlines, InfoTrac College Edition keywords, relevant web links, and chapter practice quizzes. Also, be sure to check out the Direct Practice Virtual Reader, where the authors have personally selected articles relevant to this chapter using InfoMarks.

Exercises in Responding Authentically and Assertively

The following exercises will assist you in gaining skill in responding authentically and assertively. Read each situation and client message, and then formulate a written response as though you were the social worker in the situation presented. Compare your written responses with the modeled responses, keeping in mind that these models represent just a few of the many possible responses that would be appropriate.

You will find additional exercises that require authentic and assertive responding in Chapter 17 (in the confrontation exercises) and in Chapter 18 (in the exercises concerned with managing relational reactions and resistance).

Statements and Situations

1. *Marital partner* [*in third conjoint marital therapy session*]: It must be really nice being a marriage counselor—knowing just what to do and not having problems like ours.

2. *Female client, age 23* [*in first session*]: Some of my problems are related to my church's stand on birth control. Tell me, are you a Catholic?

3. *Client* [*fifth session*]: You look like you're having trouble staying awake. [*Social worker is drowsy from having taken an antihistamine for an allergy.*]

4. *Adult group member* [*to social worker in second session; group members have been struggling to determine the agenda for the session*]: I wish you'd tell us what we should talk about. Isn't that a group leader's function? We're just spinning our wheels.

5. *Male client* [*sixth session*]: Say, my wife and I are having a party next Wednesday. We'd like to have you and your wife come.

6. *Client* [*calls 3 hours before scheduled appointment*]: I've had the flu the past couple of days, but I feel like I'm getting over it. Do you think I should come today?

7. *Client* [*scheduled time for ending appointment has arrived, and social worker has already moved to end session; in previous sessions, client has tended to stay beyond designated ending time*]: What we were talking about reminded me of something I wanted to discuss today but forgot. I'd like to discuss it briefly, if you don't mind.

8. *Client* [*has just completed behavioral rehearsal involving talking with employer and played role beyond expectations of social worker*].

9. *Female client* [*tenth interview*]: I've really felt irritated with you during the week. When I brought up taking the correspondence course in art, all you could talk about was

how some correspondence courses are ripoffs and that I could take courses at a college for less money. I knew that, but I've checked into this correspondence course, and it's well worth the money. You put me down, and I've resented it.

10. *Client* [*seventh session*]: You seem uptight today. Is something bothering you? [*Social worker has been under strain associated with recent death of a parent and assisting surviving parent, who has been distraught.*]

11. *Client* [*as the final session of successful therapy draws to a close*]: I really want to thank you for your help. You'll never know just how much help you've been. I felt like a sinking ship before I saw you. Now I feel I've got my head screwed on straight.

12. *Male delinquent on probation, age 15* [*first session*]: Before I tell you much, I need to know what happens to the information. Who else learns about me?

13. *Social worker* [*forgot to enter an appointment in daily schedule and, as a result, failed to keep a scheduled appointment with a client; realizing this the next day, she telephones her client*]

Modeled Responses

1. [*Smiling.*] "Well, I must admit it's helpful. But I want you to know that marriage is no picnic for marriage counselors either. We have our rough spots, too. I have to work like everyone else to keep my marriage alive and growing."

2. "I gather you're wondering what my stand is and whether I can understand and accept your feelings. I've worked with many Catholics and have been able to understand their problems. Would it trouble you if I weren't Catholic?"

3. "You're very observant. I have been struggling with drowsiness these past few minutes, and I apologize for that. I had to take an antihistamine before lunch, and a side effect of the drug is wanting to sleep. I want you to know my drowsiness has nothing to do with you. If I move around a little, the drowsiness passes."

4. "I can sense your frustration and your desire to firm up an agenda. If I made the decision, though, it might not fit for many of you and

I'd be taking over the group's prerogative. Perhaps it would be helpful if the group followed the decision-by-consensus approach we discussed in our first session."

5. "Thank you for the invitation. I'm flattered that you'd ask me. Although a part of me would like to come because it sounds like fun, I must decline your invitation. If I were to socialize with you while you're seeing me professionally, it would conflict with my role, and I couldn't be as helpful to you. I hope you can understand my not accepting."

6. "I appreciate your calling to let me know. I think it would be better to change our appointment until you're sure you've recovered. Quite frankly, I don't want to risk being exposed to the flu, which I hope you can understand. I have a time open on the day after tomorrow. I'll set it aside for you, if you'd like, in the event you're fully recovered by then."

7. "I'm sorry I don't have the time to discuss the matter today. Let's save it for next week, and I'll make a note that you wanted to explore this issue. We'll have to stop here today because I'm scheduled for another appointment."

8. "I want to share with you how impressed I was with how you asserted yourself and came across so positively. If you'd been with your boss, he'd have been impressed, too."

9. "I'm glad you shared those feelings with me. I can see I owe you an apology. You're right, I didn't explore whether you'd checked into the program, and I made some unwarranted assumptions. I guess I was overly concerned about your not being ripped off because I know others who have been by taking correspondence courses. But I can see I goofed because you had already looked into the course."

10. "Thank you for asking. Yes, I have been under some strain this past week. My mother died suddenly, which was a shock, and my father is taking it very hard. It's created a lot of pressure for me, but I think I can keep it from spilling over into our session. If I'm not able to focus on you, I will stop the session. Or if you don't feel that I'm fully with you, please let me know. I don't want to shortchange you."

11. "Thank you very much. As we finish, I want you to know how much I've enjoyed working with you. You've worked hard, and that's the primary reason you've made so much progress. I'm very interested in you and want to hear how your new job works out. Please keep in touch."

12. "Your question is a good one. I'd wonder the same thing if I were in your situation. I keep the information confidential as much as I can. We keep a file on you, of course, but I'm selective about what I put in it, and you have the right to check the file if you wish. I do meet with a supervisor, too, and we discuss how I can be of greatest help to clients. So I might share certain information with her, but she keeps it confidential. If you report violations of the law or the conditions of your probation, I can't assure you I'll keep that information confidential. I'm responsible to the court, and part of my responsibility is to see that you meet the conditions of your parole. I have to make reports to the judge about that. Could you share with me your specific concerns about confidentiality?"

13. "Mr. M, I'm very embarrassed to be calling you, because I realized just a few minutes ago I blew it yesterday. I forgot to enter my appointment with you in my schedule book last week and completely forgot about it. I hope you can accept my apology. I want you to know it had nothing to do with you."

Skill Development Exercises in Empathic Communication

The following exercises, which include a wide variety of actual client messages, will assist you in gaining mastery of reciprocal empathic responding (level 3). Read the client message and compose on paper an empathic response that captures the client's surface feelings. You may wish to use the paradigm, "You feel _____ about (or because) _____," in organizing your response before phrasing it in typical conversation language. Strive to make your responses fresh, varied, and spontaneous. To expand your repertoire of responses, we strongly encourage you to continue using the lists of affective words and phrases.

After formulating your response, compare it with the modeled response provided at the end of the exercises. Analyze the differences, paying particular attention to the various forms of responding and the elements that enhance the effectiveness of your own responses and the modeled responses.

Because this exercise includes 27 different client statements, we recommend that you not attempt to complete the entire exercise in one sitting, but rather work through it in several sessions. Consistent practice and careful scrutiny of your responses are essential in gaining mastery of this vital skill.

Client Statements

1. *Father of developmentally disabled child, age 14* [*who is becoming difficult to manage*]: We just don't know what to do with Henry. We've always wanted to take care of him, but we've reached the point where we're not sure it's doing any good for him or for us. Henry has grown so strong—we just can't restrain him anymore. He hit my wife last week when she wouldn't take him to the 7–11 late at night—I was out of town—and she's still bruised. She's afraid of him now, and I have to admit I'm getting that way, too.

2. *Latino* [*living in urban barrio*]: Our children do better in school if they teach Spanish, not just English. We're afraid our children are behind because they don't understand English so good. And we don't know how to help them. Our people have been trying to get a bilingual program, but the school board pays no attention to us.

3. *Female client, age 31:* Since my husband left town with another woman, I get lonely and depressed a lot of the time. I find myself wondering whether something is wrong with me or whether men just can't be trusted.

4. *Mother* [*to child welfare protective services worker on doorstep during initial home visit*]: Who'd want to make trouble for me by accusing me of not taking care of my kids? [*Tearfully.*] Maybe I'm not the best mother in the world, but I try. There are a lot of kids around here that aren't cared for as well as mine.

5. *Male ninth-grade student* [*to school social worker*]: I feel like I'm a real loser. In sports I've always had two left feet. When they

choose up sides, I'm always the last one chosen. A couple of times they've actually got into a fight over who doesn't have to choose me.

6. *Member of abused women's group:* That last month I was living in mortal fear of Art. He'd get that hateful look in his eyes, and I'd know he was going to let me have it. The last time I was afraid he was going to kill me—and he might have, if his brother hadn't dropped in. I'm afraid to go back to him. But what do I do? I can't stay here much longer!

7. *Male, age 34* [*to marital therapist*]: Just once I'd like to show my wife I can accomplish something without her prodding me. That's why I haven't told her I'm coming to see you. If she knew it, she'd try to take charge and call all the shots.

8. *African American man* [*in a group session*]: All I want is to be accepted as a person. When I get hired, I want it to be for what I'm capable of doing—not just because of my skin color. That's as phony and degrading as not being hired because of my skin color. I just want to be accepted for who I am.

9. *Client in a state prison* [*to rehabilitation worker*]: They treat you like an animal in here— herd you around like a damn cow. I know I've got to do my time, but sometimes I feel like I can't stand it any longer—like something's building up in me that's going to explode.

10. *Client* [*to mental health worker*]: I don't have any pleasant memories of my childhood. It seems like just so much empty space. I can remember my father watching television and staring at me with a blank look—as though I didn't exist.

11. *Patient in hospital* [*to medical social worker*]: I know Dr. Brown is a skilled surgeon, and he tells me not to worry—that there's very little risk in this surgery. I know I should feel reassured, but to tell you the truth, I'm just plain panic-stricken.

12. *Female member, age 29* [*in marital therapy group*]: I'd like to know what it's like with the rest of you. Hugh and I get into nasty fights because I feel he doesn't help me when I really need help. He tells me there's no way

he's going to do women's work! That really irritates me. I start feeling like I'm just supposed to be his slave.

13. *Male college student, age 21:* Francine says she's going to call me, but she never does— I have to do all the calling, or I probably wouldn't hear from her at all. It seems so one-sided. If I didn't need her so much I'd ask her what kind of game she's playing. I wonder if she isn't pretty selfish.

14. *White student, age 14* [*to school social worker*]: To be really honest, I don't like the black kids in our school. They pretty much stay to themselves, and they aren't friendly to whites. I don't know what to expect or how to act around them. I'm antsy when they're around and—well, to be honest—I'm scared I'll do something they won't like and they'll jump me.

15. *Single female, age 27* [*to mental health worker*]: I've been taking this class on the joys of womanhood. Last time the subject was how to catch a man. I can see I've been doing a lot of things wrong. But I won't lower myself to playing games with men. If that's what it takes, I guess I'll always be single.

16. *Married male, age 29* [*to marital therapist*]: Sexually, I'm unfulfilled in my marriage. At times I've even had thoughts of trying sex with men. That idea kind of intrigues me. My wife and I can talk about sex all right, but it doesn't get better.

17. *Married female, age 32* [*to family social worker*]: I love my husband and children, and I don't know what I'd do without them. Yet on days like last Thursday, I feel I could just climb the walls. I want to run away from all of them and never come back.

18. *Married blind female* [*to other blind group members*]: You know, it really offends me when people praise me or make a fuss over me for doing something routine that anyone else could do. It makes me feel like I'm on exhibition. I want to be recognized for being competent—not for being blind.

19. *Male teacher* [*to mental health social worker*]: I have this thing about not being able to accept compliments. A friend told me about how much of a positive impact I've had on several students over the years. I couldn't

accept that and feel good. My thought was, "You must be mistaken. I've never had that kind of effect on anyone."

20. *Lesbian, age 26* [*to private social worker*]: The girls at the office were talking about lesbians the other day and about how repulsive the very thought of lesbianism was to them. How do you think I felt?

21. *Male member of alcoholics group:* I don't feel like I belong in this group. The rest of you seem to have better educations and better jobs. Hell, I only finished junior high, and I'm just a welder.

22. *Male, age 30* [*to private social worker*]: Sometimes I can't believe how pissed off I get over little things. When I lose a chess game, I go into orbit. First, I'm furious with myself for blundering. It's not like me to make rank blunders. I guess I feel humiliated, because I immediately want to start another game and get even with the other guy.

23. *Male client, age 72* [*to medical social worker*]: Since I had my heart attack, I've just had this feeling of foreboding—like my life's over, for all practical purposes. I feel like I'm just an invalid—of no use to myself or anyone else.

24. *Child, age 15, in foster care* [*to child welfare worker*]: I've had it with them [*the foster parents*]. They want me to work all the time—like I'm a slave or something. If you don't get me out of here, I'm going to run.

25. *Family member, age 13* [*in initial family group session*]: Yeah, I can tell you what I'd like to be different in our family. I'd like to feel that we care about each other, but it's not that way. Every time I go in the house, Mom nags me, and Dad doesn't say anything—he doesn't seem to care. Sometimes I feel there's no point in going home.

26. *Married woman* [*in initial interview with marital therapist*]: I think this is just a complete waste of time. I didn't want to come and wouldn't be here if my husband hadn't forced me. He's the one who should be here—not me.

27. *Married woman* [*in YWCA adult women's group*]: This past week I've felt really good about how things are going—like I've finally got my act together. I've handled my emotions better, and for the first time in a long time, I've felt like an intelligent human being.

Modeled Responses

1. "So you're really in a difficult situation. You've wanted to keep Henry at home, but in light of his recent aggressiveness and his increasing strength, you're becoming really frightened and wonder if other arrangements wouldn't be better for both you and him."

2. "I can see you're worried about how your children are doing in school and believe they need a bilingual program."

3. "It's been a real blow—your husband leaving you for another woman—and you've just felt so alone. And you find yourself dwelling on the painful question, 'Is something wrong with me, or is it that you just can't trust men?' "

4. "This is very upsetting for you. You seem to be saying that it's not fair being turned in when you believe you take care of your children. Please understand I'm not accusing you of neglecting your children. But I do have to investigate complaints. It may be that I'll be able to turn in a positive report. I hope so. But I do need to talk with you further. May I come in?"

5. "I gather you feel you really got shortchanged as far as athletic talents are concerned. It's humiliating to you to feel so left out and be the last guy chosen."

6. "It sounds as though you lived in terror that last month and literally feared for your life. You were wise to remove yourself when you did. A number of other women in the group have had similar experiences and are facing the same dilemma about what to do now. As group members, each of us can be helpful to other group members in thinking through what's the best course of action. In the meantime, you have a safe place to stay and some time to plan."

7. "Sounds like you get pretty annoyed, thinking about your wife's prodding and trying to take charge. I gather it's important right now that you prove to her and to yourself you can do something on your own."

8. "I gather you're fed up with having people relate to you because of your race instead of being accepted as an individual—as yourself."

9. "If I understand you, you feel degraded by the way you're treated—as though you're less than a human being. And that really gets to you—sometimes you find yourself seething with resentment that threatens to boil over."

10. "From what you say, I get a picture of you just feeling so all alone as you were growing up—as though you didn't feel very important to anyone, especially your father."

11. "So intellectually, you tell yourself not to worry, that you're in good hands. Still, on another level you have to admit you're terrified of that operation. [*Brief pause.*] Your fear is pretty natural, though. Most people who are honest with themselves experience fear. I'd be interested in hearing more about your fears."

12. "So the two of you get into some real struggles over differences in your views about what is reasonable of you to expect from Hugh. You seem to be saying you very much resent his refusal to pitch in—that it's not fair to have to carry the burden alone. Hugh, I'd be interested in hearing your views. Then we can hear how other members deal with this kind of situation."

13. "Sounds like part of you is saying that you have a right to expect more from Francine— that you don't feel good about always having to be the one to take the initiative. You also seem to feel you'd like to confront her with what she's doing, but you're uneasy about doing that because you don't want to risk losing her."

14. "So, you're uncomfortable around your black classmates and just don't know how to read them. I gather you kind of walk on eggshells when they're around for fear you'll blow it and they'll climb all over you."

15. "There is a lot of conflicting advice around these days about how men and women should relate to one another, and it is hard to figure out what to believe. You know you don't want to play games, yet that is what the class is telling you to do if you don't want to be single."

16. "Things don't get better despite your talks, and you get pretty discouraged. Sometimes you find yourself wondering if you'd get sexual fulfillment with men, and that appeals to you in some ways."

17. "So even though you care deeply for your family, there are days when you just feel so overwhelmed you'd like to buy a one-way ticket out of all the responsibility."

18. "Are you saying that you feel singled out and demeaned when people flatter you for doing things anyone could do? It ticks you off, and you wish people would recognize you for being competent—not being blind."

19. "In a way, you seem to be saying that you don't feel comfortable with compliments because you feel you don't really deserve them. It's like you feel you don't do anything worthy of a compliment."

20. "You must have felt extremely uncomfortable and resentful believing that they would condemn you if they knew. It must have been most painful for you."

21. "Ted, you seem to feel uncomfortable, as if you don't fit in with the other group members. I gather you're worried the rest of the members are more educated than you are and you're concerned they won't accept you."

22. "When you lose, lots of feelings surge through you: anger and disappointment with yourself for losing, loss of face, and an urgency to prove you can beat the other guy."

23. "So things look pretty grim to you right now—as though you have nothing to look forward to and are just washed up. And you're apprehensive that things might get worse rather than better."

24. "You sound pretty mad right now, and I can sense you feel there has to be a change. I'd like to hear more about exactly what has been happening."

25. "Am I getting it right—that you feel picked on by Mom and ignored by Dad? You'd like to feel that they really care about you. You'd also like family members to show for each other."

26. "You're feeling pretty angry with your husband for forcing you to come. I gather that you resent having to be here now and just don't see the need for it."

27. "That sounds great. You seem delighted with your progress—like you're really getting on top of things. And most of all you're liking yourself again."

Answers to Exercise in Identifying Surface and Underlying Feelings

1. *Apparent feelings:* unimportant, neglected, disappointed, hurt. *Probable deeper feelings:* rejected, abandoned, forsaken, deprived, lonely, depressed.

2. *Apparent feelings:* unloved, insecure, confused, embarrassed, left out or excluded. *Probable deeper feelings:* hurt, resentful, unvalued, rejected, taken for granted, degraded, doubting own desirability.

3. *Apparent feelings:* chagrined, disappointed in self, discouraged, letting children down, perplexed. *Probable deeper feelings:* guilty, inadequate, crummy, sense of failure, out of control, fear of damaging children.

4. *Apparent feelings:* frustrated, angry, bitter; probable deeper feelings: depressed, discouraged, hopeless.

Answers to Exercises to Discriminate Levels of Empathic Responding

CLIENT STATEMENT	
Client 1	
Response	*Level*
1.	2
2.	1
3.	1
4.	3
5.	2
6.	2
7.	4
8.	1

CLIENT STATEMENT			
Client 2		*Client 3*	
Response	*Level*	*Response*	*Level*
1.	1	1.	1
2.	3	2.	4
3.	1	3.	2
4.	2	4.	2
5.	4	5.	5
6.	1	6.	1
7.	3	7.	2
8.	2	8.	2

Notes

1. Such highlighting of opposing feelings is a key technique for assisting clients in assessing their readiness for change in the motivational interviewing method (Miller and Rollnick, 2002).

2. In categorizing her husband as a "bump on a log," the wife makes a sweeping generalization that fits her husband's behavior into a mold. Although the social worker chose to keep the focus momentarily on the husband, it is important that he helps the couple to avoid labeling each other. Strategies for intervening when clients use labels are delineated in a later chapter.

CHAPTER 6

Verbal Following, Exploring, and Focusing Skills

CHAPTER OVERVIEW

Chapter 6 introduces verbal following skills and their uses in exploring client concerns and focusing. These skills are the building blocks for social workers' efforts to communicate empathically with clients. In addition to being helpful in work with clients in micro practice, such skills are useful at the meso level in work on behalf of clients, through advocacy, and in work with colleagues and other professionals.

MAINTAINING PSYCHOLOGICAL CONTACT WITH CLIENTS AND EXPLORING THEIR PROBLEMS

Verbal following involves the use of and, sometimes, blending of discrete skills that enable social workers to maintain psychological contact on a moment-by-moment basis with clients and to covey accurate understanding of their messages. Moreover, verbal following behavior takes into account two performance variables that are essential to satisfaction and continuance on the part of the client:

1. *Stimulus-response congruence*. The extent to which social workers' responses provide feedback to clients that their messages are accurately received.

2. *Content relevance*. The extent to which the content of social workers' responses is perceived by clients as relevant to their substantive concerns.

These variables were first conceptualized by Rosen (1972), who detailed empirical and theoretical support about how they related to client continuance. They received further validation as critical social worker behavioral responses in a study conducted by Duehn and Proctor (1977). Analyzing worker–client transactions, these authors found that social workers responded incongruently to clients' messages much more frequently with clients who terminated treatment prematurely than with clients who continued treatment. (Incongruent messages fail to provide immediate feedback to clients indicating that their messages have been received.) Further, social workers gave a lower proportion of responses that matched the content expectations of "discontinuers" than they did with "continuers." Duehn and Proctor concluded that responses that are relevant and that accurately attend to client messages gradually increase moment-by-moment client satisfaction with interactions in the interview. Conversely, continued use of questions and other responses that are not associated with previous client messages and that do not relate to the client's substantive concerns contribute to consistent client dissatisfaction. When client content expectations are not fulfilled, clients often prematurely discontinue treatment. In contrast, effective use of attending behaviors should enhance motivational congruence, or the fit between client motivation and social worker goals, a factor that is associated with better outcomes in social work effectiveness studies (Reid & Hanrahan, 1982). Employing responses that directly relate to client messages and concerns thus enhances client satisfaction, fosters continuance, and greatly contributes to the establishment of a viable working relationship.

Studies of how social work students learn the practice skills described in this book suggest that the skills can be taught and demonstrated successfully in simulated interviews (Sowers-Hoag & Thyer, 1985). However, generalization to field practice has not been conclusively demonstrated. For example, one study found that students in the field demonstrated increased skills in facilitation of empathy but not questioning or clarification skills (Carrillo, Gallant, & Thyer, 1995). Another study found that students in the field were more inclined to ask closed-ended questions and give advice than had been the emphasis in their training program (Kopp & Butterfield, 1985). A recent study found that while most of the practice skills of second-year students were not significantly more advanced than those of first-year students, the second-year students were better able to focus on tasks and goals compared with first-year students (Deal & Brintzenhofeszok, 2004).

Tsui and Schultz (1985) have emphasized the importance of explaining the relevance of questions to Asian Americans seen for mental health problems. In such cases, the social worker must explicitly educate the client about the purpose of questions regarding clinical history, previous treatment information, family background, and psychosocial stressors. The linkage of these issues to their current symptoms is not clear to many Asians or, indeed, to other clients. Many Asian clients conceive of mental distress as the result of physiological disorder or character flaws. This issue must be dealt with sensitively before any sensible therapeutic work can occur (Tsui & Schultz, 1985, pp. 567–568). Similarly, clients who are members of historically oppressed groups may perceive questions as interrogations not designed to help them with their own concerns, so the rationale for such questions must be explained.

In addition to enabling social workers to maintain close psychological contact with clients, verbal following skills serve two other important functions in the helping process. First, they yield rich personal information, allowing social workers to explore clients' problems in depth. Second, they enable social workers to focus selectively on components of the clients' experiences and on dynamics in the helping process that facilitate positive client change.

The following pages introduce a variety of skills for verbally following and exploring clients' problems. Some of these skills are easily mastered. Others require more effort to acquire. The exercises in the body of the chapter will assist you in acquiring proficiency in these important skills. Although empathic responding is the most vital skill for verbally following clients' messages, we have not included it in this chapter because it was discussed in detail in Chapter 5. Later, however, we discuss the blending of empathic responses with other verbal following skills to bolster your ability in focusing on and fully exploring relevant client problems.

VERBAL FOLLOWING SKILLS

The discrete skills highlighted in this chapter include seven types of responses:

1. Furthering
2. Paraphrasing
3. Closed-ended responses
4. Open-ended responses
5. Seeking concreteness
6. Providing and maintaining focus
7. Summarizing

FURTHERING RESPONSES

Furthering responses indicate social workers are listening attentively and encourage the client to verbalize. They are of two types: minimal prompts or accent responses.

Minimal Prompts

Minimal prompts signal the social worker's attentiveness and encourage the client to continue verbalizing. They can be either nonverbal or verbal.

Nonverbal minimal prompts consist of nodding the head, using facial expressions, or employing gestures that convey receptivity, interest, and commitment to understanding. They implicitly convey the message, "I am with you; please continue."

Verbal minimal prompts consist of brief messages that convey interest and encourage or request expanded verbalizations along the lines of the previous expressions by the client. These messages include "Yes," "I see," "But?", "Mm-mmm" (the so-called empathic grunt), "Tell me more," "And then what happened?", "And?", "Please go on," "Tell me more, please," and other similar brief messages that affirm the appropriateness of what the client has been saying and prompt him or her to continue.

Accent Responses

Accent responses (Hackney & Cormier, 1979) involve repeating, in a questioning tone of voice or with emphasis, a word or a short phrase. Suppose a client says, "I've really had it with the way my supervisor at work is treating me." The social worker might reply, "Had it?" This short response is intended to prompt further elaboration by the client.

PARAPHRASING RESPONSES

Paraphrasing involves using fresh words to restate the client's message concisely. Responses that paraphrase are more apt to focus on the cognitive aspects of client messages (i.e., emphasize situations, ideas, objects, or persons) than on the client's affective state, although reference may be made to obvious feelings. Four examples of paraphrasing follow.

EXAMPLE 1

Elder client: I don't want to get into a living situation in which I will not be able to make choices on my own.

Social worker: So independence is a very important issue for you.

EXAMPLE 2

Client: I went to the doctor today for a final checkup, and she said that I was doing fine.

Social worker: She gave you a clean bill of health, then.

EXAMPLE 3

Client: I just don't know what to think about the way my girlfriend treats me. Sometimes she seems so warm—like she really likes me—and at other times she acts really cold.

Social worker: Her hot and cold behavior really confuses you.

EXAMPLE 4

Managed care utilization reviewer: We don't think that your patient's condition justifies the level of service that you recommend.

Social worker: So you feel that my documentation does not justify the need that I have recommended according to the approval guidelines you are working from.

Note that in Example 4, paraphrasing is used as part of the communication with a person whose opinion is important because it relates to delivering client services, the health insurance care manager (Strom-Gottfried, 1998a). When employed sparingly, paraphrasing may be interspersed with other facilitative responses to prompt client expression. Used to excess, however, paraphrasing produces a mimicking effect.

Paraphrasing is helpful when social workers want to bring focus to an idea or a situation for client consideration. In contrast, this technique is inappropriate when clients are preoccupied with feelings. In such cases, social workers need to relate with empathic responses that accurately capture clients' affect and assist them to reflect on and sort through their feelings. Sometimes social workers may choose to direct the discussion away from feelings for therapeutic purposes. For instance, a social worker might believe that a chronically depressed client who habitually expresses discouragement and disillusionment would benefit by focusing less on feelings and more on actions to alleviate the distress. When the social worker chooses to deemphasize feelings, paraphrases that reflect content are helpful and appropriate.

Exercises in Paraphrasing

In the following exercises, formulate written responses that paraphrase the messages of clients and other persons. Remember, paraphrases usually reflect the cognitive aspects of messages rather than feelings. Modeled responses for these exercises appear at the end of the chapter. Note, however, that paraphrasing a client's or other person's comments does not mean that you agree with or condone those thoughts.

Client/Colleague Statements

1. *Client:* I can't talk to people. I just completely freeze up in a group.
2. *Wife:* I think that in the last few weeks I've been able to listen much more often to my husband and children.
3. *Client:* Whenever I get into an argument with my mother, I always end up losing. I guess I'm still afraid of her.
4. *Husband:* I just can't decide what to do. If I go ahead with the divorce, I'll probably lose custody of the kids—and I won't be able to see them very much. If I don't, though, I'll have to put up with the same old thing. I don't think my wife is going to change.
5. *Elder client:* It wasn't so difficult to adjust to this place because the people who run it are helpful and friendly and I am able to make contacts easily—I've always been a people person.
6. *Mother* [*speaking about daughter*]: When it comes right down to it, I think I'm to blame for a lot of her problems.
7. *Mother* [*participating in welfare-to-work program*]: I don't know how they can expect me to be a good mother and make school appointments, supervise my kids, and put in all these work hours.
8. *Member of treatment team:* I just don't see how putting more services into this family

makes sense. The mother is not motivated, and the kids are better off away from her. This family has been messed up forever.

9. *Terminally ill cancer patient:* Some days I am really angry because I'm only 46 years old and there are so many more things I wanted to do. Other days, I feel kind of defeated, like this is what I get for smoking two packs of cigarettes a day for 25 years.

CLOSED- AND OPEN-ENDED RESPONSES

Generally used to elicit specific information, *closed-ended questions* define a topic and restrict the client's response to a few words or a simple yes or no answer. Typical examples of closed-ended questions follow:

- "When did you obtain your divorce?"
- "Do you have any sexual difficulties in your marriage?"
- "When did you last have a physical examination?"
- "Is your health insurance Medicare?"

Although closed-ended questions restrict the client and elicit limited information, in many instances these responses are both appropriate and helpful. Later in this chapter, we discuss how and when to use this type of response effectively.

In contrast to closed-ended responses, which circumscribe client messages, *open-ended questions* and statements invite expanded expression and leave the client free to express what seems most relevant and important. For example:

Social worker: You've mentioned your daughter. Tell me how she enters into your problem.

Client: I don't know what to do. Sometimes I think she is just pushing me so that she can go live with her father. When I ask her to help around the house, she won't, and says that she doesn't owe me anything. When I try to insist on her helping, it just ends up in an ugly scene without anything being accomplished. It makes me feel so helpless.

In this example, the social worker's open-ended question prompted the client to expand on the details of the problems with her daughter, including a description of her daughter's behavior, her own efforts to cope, and her present sense of defeat. The information contained in the message is typical of the richness of data obtained through open-ended responding.

In other circumstances, such as in the prior example of a telephone conversation with a managed care utilization reviewer, the social worker can use an open-ended question to attempt to explore common ground that can lead to a mutually beneficial resolution.

Social worker [*to managed care utilization reviewer*]: Can you clarify for me how appropriate coverage is determined for situations such as the one I have described?

Some open-ended responses are unstructured, leaving the topic to the client's choosing (e.g., "Tell me what you would like to discuss today" or "What else can you tell me about the problems that you're experiencing?"). Other open-ended responses are structured in that the social worker defines the topic to be discussed but leaves the client free to respond in any way that he or she wishes (e.g., "You've mentioned feeling ashamed about the incident that occurred between you and your son. I'd be interested in hearing more about that."). Still other open-ended responses fall along a continuum between structured and unstructured, because they give the client leeway to answer with a few words or to elaborate with more information (e.g., "How willing are you to do this?").

Social workers may formulate open-ended responses either by asking a question or by giving a polite command. Suppose a terminally ill cancer patient said, "The doctor thinks I could live about six or seven months now. It could be less; it could be more. It's just an educated guess, he told me." The social worker could respond by asking, "How are you feeling about that prognosis?" or "Would you tell me how you are feeling about that prognosis?" Polite commands have the same effect as direct questions in requesting information but are less forceful and involve greater finesse. Similar in nature are embedded questions that do not take the form of a question but embody a request for information.

Examples of embedded questions include "I'm curious about . . . ," "I'm wondering if . . . ," and "I'm interested in knowing . . .". Open-ended questions often start with what or how. Why questions are often unproductive because they may ask for reasons, motives, or causes that are either obvious, obscure, or unknown to the client. Asking how ("How did that happen?") rather than why ("Why did that happen?") often elicits far richer information regarding client behavior and patterns.

Exercises in Identifying Closed- and Open-Ended Responses

The following exercises will assist you to differentiate between closed- and open-ended messages. Identify each statement with either a C for a closed-ended question or O for an open-ended question. Turn to the end of the chapter to check your answers.

1. "Did your mother ask you to see me because of the problem you had with the principal?"

2. "When John says that to you, what do you experience inside?"

3. "You said you're feeling fed up and you're just not sure that pursuing a reconciliation is worth your trouble. Could you elaborate?"

4. "When is your court date?"

Now read the following client messages and respond by writing open-ended responses to them. Avoid using *why* questions. Examples of open-ended responses to these messages appear at the end of the chapter.

Client Statements

1. *Client:* Whenever I'm in a group with Ralph, I find myself saying something that will let him know that I am smart, too.

2. *Client:* I always have had my parents telephone for me about appointments and other things I might mess up.

3. *Teenager* [*speaking of a previous probation counselor*]: He sure let me down. And I really trusted him. He knows a lot about me because I spilled my guts.

4. *Group nursing home administrator:* I think that we are going to have to move Gladys to another, more suitable kind of living arrangement. We aren't able to provide the kind of care that she needs.

The next sections of the book explain how you can blend open-ended and empathic responses to keep a discussion focused on a specific topic. In preparation for that, respond to the next two client messages by formulating an empathic response followed by an open-ended question that encourages the client to elaborate on the same topic.

5. *Unwed teenage girl seeking abortion* [*brought in by her mother, who wishes to discuss birth alternatives*]: I feel like you are all tied up with my mother, trying to talk me out of what I have decided to do.

6. *Client:* Life is such a hassle, and it doesn't seem to have any meaning or make sense. I just don't know whether I want to try figuring it out any longer.

The difference between closed-ended and open-ended responses may seem obvious to you, particularly if you completed the preceding exercises. It has been our experience, however, that beginning—and even seasoned—social workers have difficulty in actual sessions in determining whether their responses are open- or closed-ended, in observing the differential effect of these two types of responses in yielding rich and relevant data, and in deciding which of the two types of responses is appropriate at a given moment. We recommend, therefore, that as you converse with your associates, you practice drawing them out by employing open-ended responses and noting how they respond. We also recommend that you use the form provided at the end of the chapter to assess both the frequency and the appropriateness of your closed- and open-ended responses in several taped client sessions.

Discriminant Use of Closed- and Open-Ended Responses

Beginning social workers typically ask an excessive number of closed-ended questions, many of which block communication or are inefficient or irrelevant to the helping process. When this occurs, the session tends to take on the flavor of an interrogation, with the social worker bombarding the client with questions and taking responsibility for maintaining verbalization. Notice what happens in the following excerpt from a recording of a social worker interviewing an institutionalized youth.

Social worker: I met your mother yesterday. Did she come all the way from Colorado to see you?

Client: Yeah.

Social worker: It seems to me that she must really care about you to take the bus and make the trip up here to see you. Don't you think so?

Client: I suppose so.

Social worker: Did the visit with her go all right?

Client: Fine. We had a good time.

Social worker: You had said you were going to talk to her about a possible home visit. Did you do that?

Client: Yes.

When closed-ended responses are used to elicit information in lieu of open-ended responses, as in the preceding example, many more discrete interchanges will occur. However, the client's responses will be brief and the information yield will be markedly lower.

Open-ended responses often elicit the same data as closed-ended questions but draw out much more information and elaboration of the problem from the client. The following two examples contrast open-ended and closed-ended responses that address the same topic with a given client. To appreciate the differences in the richness of information yielded by these contrasting responses, compare the likely client responses elicited by such questions to the closed-ended questions used above.

EXAMPLE 1

Closed-ended: "Did she come all the way from Colorado to see you?"

Open-ended: "Tell me about your visit with your mother."

EXAMPLE 2

Closed-ended: "Did you talk with her about a possible home visit?"

Open-ended: "How did your mother respond when you talked about a possible home visit?"

Occasionally, beginning social workers use closed-ended questions to explore feelings, but responses from clients typically involve minimal self-disclosure, as might be expected. Rather than encourage expanded expression of feelings, closed-ended questions limit responses, as illustrated in the following example:

Social worker: Did you feel rejected when she turned down your invitation?

Client: Yeah.

Social worker: Have there been other times when you've felt rejected that way?

Client: Oh, yeah. Lots of times.

Social worker: When was the first time?

Client: Gee, that's hard to say.

Here, the social worker was leading the client here rather than finding out how she perceived the situation. Had the social worker employed empathic and open-ended responses to explore the feelings and thoughts associated with being rejected, the client would likely have revealed much more.

Because open-ended responses elicit more information than closed-ended ones, frequent use of the former technique increases the efficiency of data gathering. In fact, the richness of information revealed by the client is directly proportional to the frequency with which open-ended responses are employed. Frequent use of open-ended responses also fosters a smoothly flowing session; consistently asking closed-ended questions, by contrast, may result in a fragmented, discontinuous process.

Closed-ended questions are used chiefly to elicit essential factual information. Skillful social workers use closed-ended questions sparingly, because clients usually reveal extensive factual information spontaneously as they unfold their stories, aided by the social worker's open-ended and furthering responses. Although they are typically employed little during the first part of a session, closed questions are used more extensively later to elicit data that may have been omitted by clients, such as names and ages of children, place of employment, date of marriage, medical facts, and data regarding family or origin.

In obtaining this kind of factual data, the social worker can unobtrusively weave into the discussion closed-ended questions that directly pertain to the topic. For example, a client may relate certain marital problems that have existed for many years, and the social worker might ask parenthetically, "And you've been married for how many years?" Similarly, a parent may explain that a child began to be truant from school when the parent started to work 6 months ago, to which the social worker might respond, "I see. Incidentally, what type of work do you do?" It is vital, of course, to shift the focus back to the problem. If necessary, the social worker can easily maintain focus by using an open-ended response to pick up the thread of the discussion. For example, the social worker might comment, "You mentioned that Ernie began missing school when you started to work. I'd like to hear more about what was happening in your family at that time."

Because open-ended responses generally yield rich information, they are used throughout initial sessions. They are used most heavily, however, in the first portion of sessions to open up lines of communication and to invite clients to reveal problematic aspects of their lives. The following open-ended polite command is a typical opening message: "Could you tell me what you wish to discuss, and we can think about it together." Such responses convey interest in clients as well as respect for clients' abilities to relate their problems in their own way; as a consequence, they also contribute to the development of a working relationship.

As clients disclose certain problem areas, open-ended responses are extensively employed to elicit additional relevant information. Clients, for example, may reveal difficulties at work or in relationships with other family members. Open-ended responses like the following will elicit clarifying information:

- "Tell me more about your problems at work."
- "I'd like to hear more about the circumstances when you were mugged coming home with the groceries."

Open-ended responses can be used to enhance communication with collaterals, colleagues, and other professionals. For example, Strom-Gottfried suggests using effective communication skills in negotiation and communication between care providers and utilization reviewers. When a client has not been approved for a kind of service that the social worker has recommended, the social worker can attempt to join with the reviewer in identifying goals that both parties would embrace and request information in an open-ended fashion.

> "I appreciate your concern that she gets the best available services and that her condition does not get worse. We are concerned with safety, as we know you are. Could you tell me more about how this protocol can help us assure her safety?" (Strom-Gottfried, 1998a, p. 398).

It may sometimes be necessary to employ closed-ended questions extensively to draw out information if the client is unresponsive and withholds information or has limited conceptual and mental abilities. However, in the former case, it is vital to explore the client's immediate feelings about being in the session, which often are negative and impede verbal expression. Focusing on and resolving negative feelings (discussed at length in Chapter 12) may pave the way to using open-ended responses to good advantage. Using closed-ended messages as a major interviewing tool early in sessions may be appropriate with some children, but the use of open-ended responses should be consistently tested as the relationship develops.

When you incorporate open-ended responses into your repertoire, you will experience a dramatic positive change in your interviewing style and confidence level. To assist you to develop skill in blending and balancing open-ended and closed-ended responses, we have provided a recording form to help you examine your own interviewing style (see Figure 6-1). Using this form, analyze

SOCIAL WORKER'S RESPONSE	OPEN-ENDED RESPONSES	CLOSED-ENDED RESPONSES
1.		
2.		
3.		
4.		
5.		
6.		
7.		

Directions: Record your discrete open- and closed-ended responses and place a check in the appropriate column. Agency time constraints will dictate how often you can practice it.

Figure 6-1 Recording Form for Open- and Closed-Ended Responding Seeking Concreteness

several recorded individual, conjoint, or group sessions over a period of time to determine changes you are making in employing these two types of responses. The recording form will assist you in determining the extent to which you have used open- and closed-ended responses.

In addition, you may wish to review your work for the following purposes:

1. To determine when relevant data are missing and whether the information might have been more appropriately obtained through an open- or closed-ended response

2. To determine when your use of closed-ended questions was irrelevant or ineffective, or distracted from the data-gathering process

3. To practice formulating open-ended responses you might use instead of closed-ended responses to increase client participation and elicit richer data

SEEKING CONCRETENESS

People (including clients and beginning social workers) are inclined to think and talk in generalities and to use words that lack precision when speaking of their experiences. To communicate one's feelings and experiences so that they are fully understood, however, a person must be able to respond concretely—that is, with specificity. Responding concretely means using words that describe in explicit terms specific experiences, behaviors, and feelings. As an example, in the following message, an intern supervisor expresses his experiencing in vague and general terms: "I thought you had a good interview." Alternatively, he might have described his experience in more precise language: "During your interview, I was impressed with the way you blended open-ended with closed-ended questions in a relaxed fashion."

To test your comprehension of the concept of concreteness, assess which of the following messages give descriptive information concerning what a client experiences:

1. "I have had a couple of accidents that would not have happened if I had full control of my

hands. The results weren't that serious, but they could be."

2. "I'm uneasy right now because I don't know what to expect from counseling, and I'm afraid you might think that I really don't need it."

3. "You are a good girl, Susie."

4. "People don't seem to care whether other people have problems."

5. "My previous experience with social workers was lousy."

6. "I really wonder if I'll be able to keep from crying and to find the words to tell my husband that it's all over—that I want a divorce."

7. "You did a good job."

You could probably readily identify which messages contained language that increased the specificity of the information conveyed by the client.

In developing competency as a social worker, one of your challenges is to consistently recognize clients' messages expressed in abstract and general terms and to assist them to reveal highly specific information related to feelings and experiences. Such information will assist you to make accurate assessments and, in turn, to plan interventions accordingly. A second challenge is to help clients learn how to respond more concretely in their relationships with others—a task you will not be able to accomplish unless you are able to model the dimension of concreteness yourself. A third challenge is to describe your own experience in language that is precise and descriptive. It is not enough to recognize concrete messages; in addition, you must familiarize yourself with and practice responding concretely to the extent that it becomes a natural style of speaking and relating to others.

The remainder of our discussion on the skill of seeking concreteness is devoted to assisting you in meeting these three challenges.

Types of Responses That Facilitate Specificity of Expression by Clients

Social workers who fail to move beyond general and abstract messages often have little grasp of the specificity and meaning of a client's problem.

Eliciting highly specific information that minimizes errors or misinterpretations, however, represents a formidable challenge. Clients typically present impressions, views, conclusions, and opinions that, despite efforts to be objective, are inevitably biased and distorted to some extent. As previously mentioned, clients are also prone to speak in generalities and to respond with imprecise language. As a consequence, their messages may be interpreted differently by different people.

To help you to conceptualize the various ways you may assist clients to respond more concretely, the following sections examine different facets of responses that seek concreteness:

1. Checking out perceptions
2. Clarifying the meaning of vague or unfamiliar terms
3. Exploring the basis of conclusions drawn by clients
4. Assisting clients to personalize their statements
5. Eliciting specific feelings
6. Focusing on the here and now, rather than on the distant past
7. Eliciting details related to clients' experiences
8. Eliciting details related to interactional behavior

In addition to discussing these aspects, this section includes 10 skill development exercises, which are designed to bring your comprehension of concreteness from the general and abstract to the specific and concrete.

Checking Out Perceptions

Responses that assist social workers to clarify and "check out" whether they have accurately heard clients' messages (e.g., "Do you mean . . ." or "Are you saying . . .") are vital in building rapport with clients and in communicating the desire to understand their problems. Such responses also minimize misperceptions or projections in the helping process. Clients benefit from social workers' efforts to understand, because clarifying responses assist clients in sharpening and reformulating their thinking about their own feelings and other concerns, thereby encouraging self-awareness and growth.

Sometimes, perception checking becomes necessary because clients' messages are incomplete, ambiguous, or complex. Occasionally, social workers may encounter clients who repetitively communicate in highly abstract or metaphorical styles, or clients whose thinking is scattered and whose messages just do not "track" or make sense. In such instances, social workers must spend an inordinate amount of time sorting through clients' messages and clarifying perceptions.

At other times, the need for clarification arises not because the client has conveyed confusing, faulty, or incomplete messages, but rather because the social worker has not fully attended to the client's message or comprehended its meaning. Fully attending throughout each moment of a session requires intense concentration. Of course, it is impossible to fully focus on and comprehend the essence of every message delivered in group and family meetings, where myriad transactions occur and competing communications bid for the social worker's attention.

It is important that you develop skill in using clarifying responses to elicit ongoing feedback regarding your perceptions and to acknowledge freely your need for clarification when you are confused or uncertain. Rather than reflecting personal or professional inadequacy, your efforts to accurately grasp the client's meaning and feelings will most likely be perceived as signs of your genuineness and your commitment to understand.

To check your perceptions, try asking simple questions that seek clarification or combining your request for clarification with a paraphrase or empathic response that reflects your perception of the client's message (e.g., "I think you were saying _____. Is that right?"). Examples of clarifying messages include the following:

- "You seem to be really irritated, not only because he didn't respond when you asked him to help, but because he seemed to be deliberately trying to hurt you. Is that accurate?"

- "I'm not sure I'm following you. Let me see if I understand the order of the events you described . . ."

- "Would you expand on what you are saying so that I can be sure that I understand what you mean?"

- "Could you go over that again, and perhaps give an illustration that might help me to understand?"

- "I'm confused. Let me try to restate what I think you're saying."

- "As a group, you seem to be divided in your approach to this matter. I'd like to summarize what I'm hearing, and I would then appreciate some input regarding whether I understand the various positions that have been expressed."

In addition to clarifying their own perceptions, social workers need to assist clients in conjoint or group sessions to clarify their perceptions of the messages of others who are present. This may be accomplished in any of the following ways:

- *By modeling* clarifying responses, which occurs naturally as social workers seek to check out their own perceptions of clients' messages.

- *By directing* clients to ask for clarification. Consider, for example, the following response by a social worker in a conjoint session: "You [*mother*] had a confused look on your face, and I'm not sure that you understood your daughter's point. Would you repeat back to her what you heard and then ask her if you understood correctly?"

- *By teaching* clients how to clarify perceptions and by reinforcing their efforts to "check out" the messages of others, as illustrated in the following responses:

    [*To group*]: "One of the reasons families have communication problems is that members don't hear accurately what others are trying to say and, therefore, they often respond or react on the basis of incorrect or inadequate information. I would like to encourage all of you to

frequently use what I call 'checking out' responses, such as 'I'm not sure what you meant. Were you saying . . . ?', to clarify statements of others. As we go along, I'll point out instances in which I notice any of you using this kind of response."

[*To family*]: "I'm wondering if you all noticed Jim 'checking' out what his dad said. . . . As you may recall, we talked about the importance of these kinds of responses earlier. [*To father*] I'm wondering, Bob, what you experienced when Jim did that?"

Clarifying the Meaning of Vague or Unfamiliar Terms

In expressing themselves, clients often employ terms that have multiple meanings or use terms in idiosyncratic ways. For example, in the message, "My husband is cruel to me," the word *cruel* may have different meanings to the social worker and the client. If the social worker does not identify what this term means to a particular client, he or she cannot be certain whether the client is referring to physical abuse, criticism, nagging, withholding affections, or something else. The precise meaning can be clarified by employing one of the following responses:

- "In what way is he cruel?"

- "I'm not sure what you mean by 'cruel.' Could you clarify that for me?"

- "I can tell that is painful for you. Could you give me some examples of times he has been cruel?"

Many other words also lack precision, so it is important to avoid assuming that the client means the same thing you mean when you employ a given term. For example, *oversexed, codependent, irresponsible, selfish,* and *careless* conjure up meanings that vary according to the reference points of different persons. Exact meanings are best determined by asking for clarification or for examples of events in which the behavior alluded to actually occurred.

Exploring the Basis of Conclusions Drawn by Clients

Clients often present views or conclusions as though they are established facts. For example, the messages "I'm losing my mind" and "My partner doesn't love me anymore" include views or conclusions that the client has drawn. To accurately assess the client's difficulties, the social worker must elicit the information on which these views or conclusions are based. This information helps the social worker assess the thinking patterns of the client, which are powerful determinants of emotions and behavior. For example, a person who believes he or she is no longer loved will behave as though this belief represents reality. The social worker's role, of course, is to reveal distortions and to challenge erroneous conclusions in a facilitative manner.

The following responses would elicit clarification of the information that serves as the basis of the views and conclusions embodied in the messages cited earlier:

- "How do you mean, losing your mind?"

- "How have you concluded that you're losing your mind?"

- "What leads you to believe your partner no longer loves you?"

Note that entire groups may hold in common fixed beliefs that may not be helpful to them in attempting to better their situations. In such instances, the social worker faces the challenging task of assisting members to reflect upon and to analyze their views. For example, the social worker may need to help group members to assess conclusions or distortions like the following:

- "We can't do anything about our problems. We are helpless and others are in control of our lives."

- "People in authority are out to get us."

- "Someone else is responsible for our problems."

- "They (members of another race, religion, group, etc.) are no good."

In Chapter 13 we discuss the social worker's role in challenging distortions and erroneous conclusions and identify relevant techniques that may be used for this purpose.

Assisting Clients to Personalize Their Statements

The relative concreteness of a specific client message is related in part to the focus or subject of that message. Client messages fall into several different classes of topic focus (Cormier & Cormier, 1979), each of which emphasizes different information and leads into very different areas of discussion:

- *Focus on self,* indicated by the subject "I" (e.g., "I'm disappointed that I wasn't able to keep the appointment")

- *Focus on others,* indicated by subjects such as "they," "people," "someone," or names of specific persons (e.g., "they haven't fulfilled their part of the bargain")

- *Focus on the group or mutual relationship between self and others,* indicated by the subject "we" (e.g., "We would like to do that")

- *Focus on content,* indicated by such subjects as events, institutions, situations, ideas (e.g., "School wasn't easy for me")

Clients are more prone to focus on others or on content, or to speak of themselves as a part of a group rather than to personalize their statements by using "I" or other self-referent pronouns. This tendency is illustrated in the following messages: "Things just don't seem to be going right for me," "They don't like me," and "It's not easy for people to talk about their problems." In the last example, the client means that it is not easy for *her* to talk about *her* problems, yet she uses the term *people,* thereby generalizing the problem and obscuring her personal struggle.

In assisting clients to personalize statements, social workers have a three-part task:

1. Social workers must model, teach, and coach clients to use self-referent pronouns (*I, me*) in talking about their concerns and their own emotional response to those concerns. For example, in response to a vague client message that focuses on content rather than self ("Everything at home seems to be deteriorating"), the social worker might gently ask the client to reframe the message by starting the response with "I" and giving specific information about what she is experiencing. It is also helpful to teach clients the difference between messages that focus on self ("I think . . .," "I feel . . .," "I want . . .") and messages that are *other-related* ("It . . .," "Someone . . .").

2. Social workers must teach the difference between self-referent messages and subject-related messages (i.e., those dealing with objects, things, ideas, or situations). Although teaching clients to use self-referent pronouns when talking about their concerns is a substantive task, clients derive major benefits from it. Indeed, not owning or taking responsibility for feelings and speaking about problems in generalities and abstractions are among the most prevalent causes of problems in communicating.

3. Social workers must focus frequently on the client and use the client's name or the pronoun *you*. Beginning social workers are apt to attend to client talk about other people, distant situations, the group at large, various escapades, or other events or content that give little information about self and the relationship between self and situations or people. In the following illustration, the social worker's response focuses on the situation rather than on the client:

Client: My kids want to shut me up in a nursing home.

Social worker: What makes you think that?

In contrast, the following message personalizes the client's concern and explicitly identifies the feelings she is experiencing:

Social worker: You worry that your children might be considering a nursing home for you. You want to be part of any decision about what would be a safe environment for you.

A social worker may employ various techniques to assist clients to personalize messages. In the preceding example, the social worker utilized an empathic response. In this instance, this skill is invaluable to the social worker in helping the client to focus on self. Recall that personalizing feelings is an inherent aspect of the paradigm for responding empathetically ("You feel _____ about/because _____"). Thus, clients can make statements that omit self-referent pronouns, and by utilizing empathic responding, social workers may assist clients to "own" their feelings.

Eliciting Specific Feelings

Even when clients personalize their messages and express their feelings, social workers often need to elicit additional information to clarify what they are experiencing, because certain "feeling words" denote general feeling states rather than specific feelings. For example, in the message, "I'm really *upset* that I didn't get a raise," the word "upset" helps to clarify the client's general frame of mind but fails to specify the precise feeling. In this instance, "upset" may refer to feeling disappointed, discouraged, unappreciated, devalued, angry, resentful, or even incompetent or inadequate due to the failure to receive a raise. Until the social worker has elicited additional information, he or she cannot be sure of how the client actually experiences being "upset."

Other feeling words that lack specificity include *frustrated, uneasy, uncomfortable, troubled,* and *bothered*. When clients employ such words, you can pinpoint their feelings by using responses such as the following:

- "How do you mean, 'upset'?"
- "I'd like to understand more about that feeling. Could you clarify what you mean by 'frustrated'?"
- "Can you say more about in what way you feel bothered?"

Focusing on the Here and Now

Yet another aspect of concreteness embodies responses that shift the focus from the past to the present, the here and now. Messages that relate to the immediate present are high in concreteness, whereas those that center on the past are low in concreteness. Some clients (and social workers) are prone to discuss past feelings and events. Unfortunately, precious opportunities for promoting growth and understanding may slip through the fingers of social workers who fail to focus on emotions and experiences that unfold in the immediacy of the interview. Focusing on feelings as they occur will enable you to observe reactions and behavior firsthand, eliminating any bias and error caused by reporting feelings and experiences after the fact. Furthermore, the helpfulness of your feedback is greatly enhanced when this feedback relates to the client's immediate experience.

The following exchange demonstrates how to achieve concreteness in such situations:

Client [*choking up*]: When she told me it was all over, that she was in love with another man—well, I just felt—it's happened again. I felt totally alone, like there just wasn't anyone.

Social worker: That must have been terribly painful. [*Client nods; tears well up.*] I wonder if you're not having the same feeling just now—at this moment. [*Client nods agreement.*]

Not only do such instances provide direct access to the client's inner experience, but they also may produce lasting benefits as the client shares deep and painful emotions in the context of a warm, accepting, and supportive relationship. Here-and-now experiencing that involves emotions toward the social worker (e.g., anger, hurt, disappointment, affectional desires, fears) is known as *relational immediacy*. Skills pertinent to relational immediacy warrant separate consideration and are dealt with in Chapter 18.

Focusing on here-and-now experiencing with groups, couples, and families (a topic discussed at length in Chapter 15) is a particularly potent technique for assisting members of these systems to clear the air of pent-up feelings. Moreover, interventions that focus on the immediacy of feelings bring buried issues to the surface, paving the way for the social worker to assist members of these systems to clearly identify and explore their difficulties and (if appropriate) to engage in problem solving.

Eliciting Details Related to Clients' Experiences

As previously mentioned, one reason why concrete responses are essential is that clients often offer up vague statements regarding their experiences—for example, "Some people in this group don't want to change bad enough to put forth any

effort." Compare this with the following concrete statement, in which the client assumes ownership of the problem and fills in details that clarify its nature:

Client: I'm concerned because I want to do something to work on my problems in this group, but when I do try to talk about them, you, John, make some sarcastic remark. It seems that then several of you [*gives names*] just laugh about it and someone changes the subject. I really feel ignored then and just go off into my own world.

Aside from assisting clients to personalize their messages and to "own" their feelings and problems, social workers must ask questions that elicit illuminating information concerning the client's experiencing, such as that illustrated in the preceding message. Questions that start with "how" or "what" are often helpful in assisting the client to give concrete data. For example, to the client message, "Some people in this group don't want to change bad enough to put forth any effort," the social worker might respond, "What have you seen happening in the group that leads you to this conclusion?"

Eliciting Details Related to Interactional Behavior

Concrete responses are also vital in accurately assessing interactional behavior. Such responses pinpoint what actually occurs in interactional events—that is, what circumstances preceded the events, what the participants said and did, what specific thoughts and feelings the client experienced, and what consequences followed the event. In other words, the social worker elicits details of what happened, rather than settling for clients' views and conclusions.

An example of a concrete response to a client message follows:

High school student: My teacher really lost it yesterday. She totally dissed me, and I hadn't done one thing to deserve it.

Social worker: That must have been very disappointing. Can you lay out for me the sequence of events—what led up to this situation, and what each of you said and did? To understand better what went wrong, I'd like to get the details as though I had been there and observed what happened.

In such cases, it is important to keep clients on topic by continuing to assist them to relate the events in question, using responses such as "Then what happened?", "What did you do next?", or "Then who said what?" If dysfunctional patterns become evident after exploring numerous events, social workers have a responsibility to share their observations with clients, to assist them to evaluate the effects of the patterned behavior, and to assess their motivation to change it.

Specificity of Expression by Social Workers

Seeking concreteness applies to the communication of both clients and social workers. In this role, you will frequently explain, clarify, give feedback, and share personal feelings and views with clients. As a social worker who has recently begun a formal professional educational program, you may be prone to speak with the vagueness and generality that characterize much of the communication of the lay public. When such vagueness occurs, clients and others may understandably misinterpret, draw erroneous conclusions, or experience confusion about the meaning of your messages.

Consider the lack of specificity in the following messages actually delivered by social workers:

- "You seem to have a lot of pent-up hostility."
- "You really handled yourself well in the group today."
- "I think a lot of your difficulties stem from your self-image."

Vague terms such as *hostility, handled yourself well,* and *self-image* may leave the client in a quandary as to what the social worker actually means. Moreover, in this style of communication, conclusions are presented without supporting information. As a result, the client must either accept them at face value, reject them as invalid, or speculate on the

basis of the conclusions. Fortunately, some clients are sufficiently perceptive, inquisitive, and assertive to request greater specificity—but many others are not.

Contrast the preceding messages with how the social worker responds to the same situations with messages that have a high degree of specificity:

- "I've noticed that you've become easily angered and frustrated several times as we've talked about ways you might work out child custody arrangements with your wife. This appears to be a very painful area for you. I would like to know just what you have been feeling."
- "I noticed that you responded several times in the group tonight, and I thought you offered some very helpful insight to Marjorie when you said. . . . I also noticed you seemed to be more at ease than in previous sessions."
- "We've talked about your tendency to feel inferior to other members of your family and to discount your own feelings and opinions in your contacts with them. I think that observation applies to the problem you're having with your sister that you just described. You've said you didn't want to go on the trip with her and her husband because they fight all the time, yet you feel you have to go because she is putting pressure on you. As in other instances, you appear to be drawing the conclusion that how you feel about the matter isn't important."

When social workers speak with specificity, clarify meanings, personalize statements, and document the sources of their conclusions, clients are much less likely to misinterpret or project their own feelings or thoughts. Clients like to be clear about what is expected of them and how they are perceived, as well as how and why social workers think and feel as they do about matters discussed in their sessions. Clients also learn vicariously to speak with greater specificity as social workers model sending concrete messages.

Both beginning and experienced social workers face the additional challenge of avoiding inappropriate use of jargon. Unfortunately, jargon has pervaded professional discourse and runs rampant in social work literature and case records. Its use confuses, rather than clarifies, meanings for clients. The careless use of jargon with colleagues also fosters stereotypical thinking and is therefore antithetical to the cardinal value of individualizing the client. Furthermore, labels tend to conjure up images of clients that vary from one social worker to another, thereby injecting a significant source of error into communication. Consider the lack of specificity in the following messages that are rich in jargon:

- "Mrs. N manifests strong passive-aggressive tendencies."
- "Sean displayed adequate impulse control in the group and tested the leader's authority in a positive manner."
- "Hal needs assistance in gaining greater self-control."
- "The client shows some borderline characteristics."
- "The group members were able to respond to appropriate limits."
- "Ruth appears to be emotionally immature for an eighth-grader."

To accurately convey information about clients to your colleagues, you must explicitly describe their behavior and document the sources of your conclusions. For example, with the vague message, "Ruth appears to be emotionally immature for an eighth-grader," consider how much more accurately another social worker would perceive your client if you conveyed information in the form of a concrete response: "The teacher says Ruth is quiet and stays to herself in school. She doesn't answer any questions in class unless directly called upon, and she often doesn't complete her assignments. She spends considerable time daydreaming or playing with objects." By describing behavior in this way, you avoid biasing your colleague's perceptions of clients by conveying either vague impressions or erroneous conclusions.

It has been our experience that mastery of the skill of communicating with specificity is gained only through extended and determined effort. The task becomes more complicated if you are not aware that your communication is vague. We recommend that you carefully and consistently monitor your recorded sessions and your everyday conversations with a view toward identifying instances in which you did or did not communicate with specificity. This kind of monitoring will enable you to set relevant goals for yourself and to chart your progress. We also recommend that you enlist your practicum instructor to provide feedback about your performance level on this vital skill.

Exercises in Seeking Concreteness

In the following exercises, you should formulate written responses that will elicit concrete data regarding clients' problems. You may wish to combine your responses with either an empathic response or a paraphrase. Reviewing the eight guidelines for seeking concreteness (on page 141) as you complete the exercise will assist you in developing effective responses and help you to clearly conceptualize the various dimensions of this skill as well. After you have finished the exercises, compare your responses with the modeled responses.

Client Statements

1. *Adolescent* [*speaking of his recent recommitment to a correctional institution*]: It really seems weird to be back here.
2. *Client:* You can't depend on friends; they'll stab you in the back every time.
3. *Client:* He's got a terrible temper—that's the way he is, and he'll never change.
4. *Client:* My supervisor is so insensitive, you can't believe it. All she thinks about are reports and deadlines.
5. *Client:* I was upset after I left your office last week. I felt you really didn't understand what I was saying and didn't care how I felt.
6. *Client:* My dad's 58 years old now, but I swear he still hasn't grown up. He always has a chip on his shoulder.
7. *Elder client:* My rheumatoid arthritis has affected my hands a lot. It gets to be kind of tricky when I'm handling pots and pans in the kitchen.

8. *Client:* I just have this uneasy feeling about going to the doctor. I guess I've really got a hang-up about it.

9. *African American student* [*to African American social worker*]: You ask why I don't talk to my teacher about why I'm late for school. I'll tell you why. Because she's white, that's why. She's got it in for us blacks, and there's just no point talking to her. That's just the way it is.

10. *Client:* John doesn't give a damn about me. I could kick the bucket, and he wouldn't lose a wink of sleep.

Modeled Responses

1. "Can you tell me how it feels weird to you?"

2. "I gather you feel that your friends have let you down in the past. Could you give me a recent example in which this has happened?"

3. "Could you tell me more about what happens when he loses his temper with you?" or "You sound like you don't have much hope that he'll ever get control of his temper. How have you concluded he will never change?" [*A social worker might explore each aspect of the message separately.*]

4. "Could you give me some examples of how she is insensitive to you?"

5. "Sounds like you've been feeling hurt and disappointed over my reaction last week. I can sense you're struggling with those same feelings right now. Could you tell me what you're feeling at this moment?"

6. "It sounds as if you feel that your dad's way of communicating with you is unusual for someone his age. Could you recall some recent examples of times you've had difficulties with how he communicates with you?"

7. "It sounds as if the arthritis pain is aggravating and blocking what you normally do. When you say that handling the pots and pans is kind of tricky, can you tell me about recent examples of what has happened when you are cooking?"

8. "Think of going to the doctor just now. Let your feelings flow naturally. [*Pause.*] What goes on inside you—your thoughts and feelings?"

9. "So you see it as pretty hopeless. You feel pretty strongly about Ms. Wright. I'd be interested in hearing what's happened that has led you to the conclusion she's got it in for blacks."

10. "So you feel as if you're nothing in his eyes. I'm wondering how you've reached that conclusion?"

FOCUSING: A COMPLEX SKILL

Skills in focusing are critical to your practice for several reasons. Because your time with clients is limited, it is critical to make the best use of each session by honing in on key topics. You are also responsible for guiding the helping process and avoiding wandering. Helping relationships should be characterized by sharp focus and continuity, unlike normal social relations. As social workers, we perform a valuable role by assisting clients to focus on their problems in greater depth and to maintain focus until they accomplish desired changes.

In addition, families and groups sometimes experience interactional difficulties that prevent them from focusing effectively on their problems. To enhance family and group functioning, social workers must be able to refocus the discussion whenever dysfunctional interactional processes cause families and groups to prematurely drift away from the topic at hand.

To assist you in learning how to focus effectively, we consider the three functions of focusing skills:

1. Selecting topics for exploration

2. Exploring topics in depth

3. Maintaining focus and keeping on topic

Knowledge of these functions will enable you to focus sharply on relevant topics and elicit sufficient data to formulate an accurate problem assessment—a prerequisite for competent practice.

Selecting Topics for Exploration

Areas relevant for exploration vary from situation to situation. However, clients who have contact with social workers in the same setting, such as in nursing homes, group homes, or child welfare agencies, may share many common concerns.

Before meeting with clients whose concerns differ from client populations with which you are familiar, you can prepare yourself to conduct an effective exploration by developing (in consultation with your practicum instructor or field supervisor) a list of relevant and promising problem areas to be explored. This preparation will help you avoid a mistake commonly made by some beginning social workers—namely, focusing on areas irrelevant to clients' problems and eliciting reams of information of questionable utility.

In your initial interview with an institutionalized youth, for example, you could more effectively select questions and responses if you knew in advance that you might explore the following areas:

1. Client's own perceptions of the concerns at hand
2. Client's perceived strengths and resources
3. Reasons for being institutionalized and brief history of past problems related to legal authority and to use of drugs and alcohol
4. Details regarding the client's relationships with individual family members, both as concerns and sources of support
5. Brief family history
6. School adjustment, including information about grades, problem subjects, areas of interest, and relationships with various teachers
7. Adjustment to institutional life, including relationships with peers and supervisors
8. Peer relationships outside the institution
9. Life goals and more short-term goals
10. Reaction to previous experiences with helpers
11. Attitude toward engaging in a working relationship to address concerns

Because the institutionalized youth is an involuntary client, part of this exploration would include the youth's understanding of which parts of his work are non-negotiable requirements, and which parts could be negotiated or free choices (Rooney, 1992).

Similarly, if you plan to interview a self-referred middle-aged woman whose major complaint is depression, the following topical areas could assist you in conducting an initial interview:

1. Concerns as she sees them, including the nature of depressive symptoms such as sleep patterns and appetite changes
2. Client's perceived strengths and resources
3. Health status, date of last physical examination, and medications being taken
4. Onset and duration of depression, previous depressive or manic episodes
5. Life events associated with onset of depression (especially losses)
6. Possible suicidal thoughts, intentions, or plans
7. Problematic thought patterns (e.g., self-devaluation, self-recrimination, guilt, worthlessness, helplessness, hopelessness)
8. Previous coping efforts, previous treatment
9. Quality of interpersonal relationships (e.g., interpersonal skills and deficiencies, conflicts and supports in marital and parent–child relationships)
10. Reactions of significant others to her depression
11. Support systems (adequacy and availability)
12. Daily activities
13. Sense of mastery versus feelings of inadequacy
14. Family history of depression or manic behavior

Because she is self-referred, this client is likely to be more voluntary than the institutionalized youth. You should therefore pay more attention to identifying the specific concerns that have led her to seek help.

As noted previously, problem areas vary, and outlines of probable topical areas likewise vary accordingly. Thus, a list of areas for exploration in an initial session with a couple seeking marriage counseling or with a group of alcoholics will include a number of items that differ from those in the first list (i.e., the areas identified for the institutionalized youth). Note, however, that items 1, 2, and 8–11 would likely be included in all exploratory interviews with individual clients and would be equally applicable to preparatory interviews with prospective group members.

In using an outline, you should avoid following it rigidly or using it as a crutch; otherwise, you could potentially destroy the spontaneity of sessions and block clients from relating their stories in their own way. Instead, encourage your clients to discuss their problems freely while you play a facilitative role in exploring in greater depth any problems that emerge. In particular, you must use outlines flexibly—reordering the sequence of topics; modifying, adding, or deleting topics; or abandoning the outline altogether if using it hinders communication.

Of course, you cannot always anticipate fruitful topical areas. After all, although clients from the same population may share many commonalities, their problems inevitably have unique aspects. For this reason, it is important to review tapes of sessions with your practicum instructor or a field supervisor for the purpose of identifying other topical areas you should explore in future sessions.

Exploring Topics in Depth

A major facet of focusing is centering discussions on relevant topics to assure that exploration moves from generality and superficiality to greater depth and meaning. Social workers must have the skills needed to explore problems thoroughly, because their success in the helping process depends on their ability to obtain clear and accurate definitions of problems.

Selectively attending to specific topics is challenging for beginning social workers, who often wander in individual or group sessions, repeatedly skipping across the surface of vital areas of content and feelings, and eliciting largely superficial and sometimes distorted information. This tendency is illustrated in the following excerpt from a first session with an adolescent in a school setting:

Social worker: Tell me about your family.

Client: My father is ill and my mother is dead, so we live with my sister.

Social worker: How are things with you and your sister?

Client: Good. We get along fine. She treats me pretty good.

Social worker: How about your father?

Client: We get along pretty well. We have our problems, but most of the time things are okay. I don't really see him very much.

Social worker: Tell me about school. How are you getting along here?

Client: Well, I don't like it very well, but my grades are good enough to get me by.

Social worker: I notice you're new to our school this year. How did you do in the last school you attended?

By focusing superficially on the topics of family and school, this social worker misses opportunities to explore potential problem areas in the depth necessary to illuminate the client's situation. Not surprisingly, this exploration yielded little information of value, in large part because the social worker failed to employ responses that focused in depth on topical areas. In the next sections, we further delineate the skills that will considerably enhance a social worker's ability to maintain focus on specific areas.

Open-Ended Responses

Social workers may employ open-ended responses throughout individual, conjoint, and group sessions to focus unobtrusively on desired topics. Earlier we noted that some open-ended responses leave clients free to choose their own topics, whereas others focus on a topic but encourage clients to respond freely to that topic. The following examples, taken from an initial session with a mother of eight children who has depression, illustrate how social workers can employ open-ended responses to define topical areas that may yield a rich trove of information vital to grasping the dynamics of the client's problems.[1]

- "What have you thought that you might like to accomplish in our work together?"

- "You've discussed many topics in the last few minutes. Could you pick the most important one and tell me more about it?"

- "You've mentioned that your oldest son doesn't come home after school as he did before and help you with the younger children. I would like to hear more about that."

- "Several times as you've mentioned your concern that your husband may leave you, your voice has trembled. I wonder if you could share what you are feeling."

- "You've indicated that your partner doesn't help you enough with the children. You also seem to be saying that you feel overwhelmed and inadequate in managing the children by yourself. Tell me what happens as you try to manage your children."

- "You indicate that you have more problems with your 14-year-old daughter than with the other children. Tell me more about Janet and your problems with her."

In the preceding examples, the social worker's open-ended questions and responses progressively moved the exploration from the general to the specific. Note also that each response or question defined a new topic for exploration.

To encourage in-depth exploration of the topics defined in this way, the social worker must blend open-ended questions with other facilitative verbal following responses that focus on and elicit expanded client expressions. After having defined a topical area by employing an open-ended response, for instance, the social worker might deepen the exploration by weaving other open-ended responses into the discussion. If the open-ended responses shift the focus to another area, however, the exploration suffers a setback. Note in the following exchange how the social worker's second open-ended response shifts the focus away from the client's message, which involves expression of intense feelings:

Social worker: You've said you're worried about retiring. I'd appreciate your sharing more about your concern. [*Open-ended response.*]

Client: I can't imagine not going to work every day. I feel at loose ends already, and I haven't even quit work. I'm afraid I just won't know what to do with myself.

Social worker: How do you imagine spending your time after retiring? [*Open-ended response.*]

Even though open-ended responses may draw out new information about clients' problems, they may not facilitate the helping process if they prematurely lead the client in a different direction. If social workers utilize open-ended or other types of responses that frequently change the topic, they will obtain information that is disjointed and fragmented. As a result, assessments will suffer from large gaps in the social worker's knowledge concerning clients' problems. As social workers formulate open-ended responses, they must be acutely aware of the direction that responses will take.

Seeking Concreteness

Earlier we discussed and illustrated the various facets of seeking concreteness. Because seeking concreteness enables social workers to move from the general to the specific and to explore topics in depth, it is a key focusing technique. We illustrate this ability in an excerpt from a session involving a client with a serious and persistent mental illness:

Client: I just don't have energy to do anything. This medicine really knocks me out.

Social worker: It sounds as if the side effects of your medication are of concern. Can you tell me specifically what those side effects have been?

By focusing in depth on topical areas, social workers are able to discern—and to assist clients to discern—problematic thoughts, behavior, and interaction. Subsequent sections consider how social workers can effectively focus on topical areas in exploratory sessions by blending concreteness with other focusing skills. In actuality, the majority of responses that social workers typically employ to establish and maintain focus are blends of various types of discrete responses.

Empathic Responding

Empathic responding serves a critical function by enabling social workers to focus in depth on troubling feelings, as illustrated in the next example:

Client: I can't imagine not going to work every day. I feel at loose ends already, and I haven't even quit work. I'm afraid I just won't know what to do with myself.

Social worker: You seem to be saying, "Even now, I'm apprehensive about retiring. I'm giving up something that has been very important to me, and I don't seem to have anything to replace it." I gather that feeling at loose ends, as you do, you worry that when you retire, you'll feel useless.

Client: I guess that's a large part of my problem. Sometimes I feel useless now. I just didn't take time over the years to develop any hobbies or to pursue any interests. I guess I don't think that I can do anything else.

Social worker: It sounds as if part of you feels hopeless about the future, as if you have done everything you can do. And yet I wonder if another part of you might think that it isn't too late to look into some new interests.

Client: I do dread moping around home with time on my hands. I can just see it now. My wife will want to keep me busy doing things around the house for her all the time. I've never liked to do that kind of thing. I suppose it is never too late to look into other interests. I have always wanted to write some things for fun, not just for work. You know, the memory goes at my age, but I have thought about just writing down some of the family stories.

Note how the client's problem continued to unfold as the social worker utilized empathic responding, revealing rich information in the process. The social worker also raises the possibility of new solutions, not just dwelling in the feelings of uselessness.

Blending Open-Ended, Empathic, and Concrete Responses to Maintain Focus

After employing open-ended responses to focus on a selected topic, social workers should use other responses to maintain focus on that topic. In the following excerpt, observe how the social worker employs both open-ended and empathic responses to explore problems in depth, thereby enabling the client to move to the heart of her struggle. Notice also the richness of the client's responses elicited by the blended messages.

Social worker: As you were speaking about your son, I sensed some pain and reluctance on your part to talk about him. I'd like to understand more about what you're feeling. Could you share with me what you are experiencing right now? [*Blended empathic and open-ended response that seeks concreteness.*]

Client: I guess I haven't felt too good about coming this morning. I almost called and canceled. I feel I should be able to handle these problems with Jim [*son*] myself. Coming here is like having to admit I'm no longer capable of coping with him.

Social worker: So you've had reservations about coming [*paraphrase*]—you feel you're admitting defeat and that perhaps you've failed or that you're inadequate—and that hurts. [*Empathic response.*]

Client: Well, yes, although I know that I need some help. It's just hard to admit it, I think. My biggest problem in this regard, however, is my husband. He feels much more strongly than I do that we should manage this problem ourselves, and he really disapproves of my coming in.

Social worker: So even though it's painful for you, you're convinced you need some assistance with Jim, but you're torn about coming here because of your husband's attitude. I'd be interested in hearing more about that. [*Blended empathic and open-ended response.*]

In the preceding example, the social worker initiated discussion of the client's here-and-now experiences through a blended open-ended and empathic response, following it with other empathic and blended responses to explore the client's feelings further. With the last response, the social worker narrowed the focus to a potential obstacle to the helping process (the husband's attitude toward therapy), which could also be explored in a similar manner.

Open-ended and empathic responses may also be blended to facilitate and encourage discussion from group members about a defined topic. For instance, after using an open-ended response to solicit group feedback regarding a specified topic ("I'm wondering how you feel about . . ."), the social worker can employ empathic or other facilitative responses to acknowledge the contribution of members who respond to the invitation to comment.

By utilizing open-ended responses, the social worker can successively reach for comments of individual members who have not contributed ("What do you think about _____, Ray?").

In the next example, the social worker blends empathic and concrete responses to facilitate in-depth exploration. Notice how these blended responses yield behavioral referents of the problem. The empathic messages convey the social worker's sensitive awareness and concern for the client's distress. The open-ended and concrete responses focus on details of a recent event and yield valuable clues that the client's rejections by women may be associated with insensitive and inappropriate social behavior. Awareness of this behavior is a prelude to formulating relevant goals. Goals formulated in this way are highly relevant to the client.

Single male client, age 20: There has to be something wrong with me, or women wouldn't treat me like a leper. Sometimes I feel like I'm doomed to be alone the rest of my life. I'm not even sure why I came to see you. I think I'm beyond help.

Social worker: You sound like you've given up on yourself—as though you're utterly hopeless. At the same, it seems like part of you still clings to hope and wants to try. [*Empathic response.*]

Client: What else can I do? I can't go on like this, but I don't know how many more times I can get knocked down and get back up.

Social worker: I sense you feel deeply hurt and discouraged at those times. Could you give me a recent example of when you felt you were being knocked down? [*Blended empathic and concrete response.*]

Client: Well, a guy I work with got me a blind date for a dance. I took her, and it was a total disaster. I know I'm no Prince Charming, but you'd think she could at least let me take her home. After we got to the dance, she ignored me the whole night and danced with other guys. Then, to add insult to injury, she went home with one of them and didn't even have the decency to tell me. There I was, wondering what had happened to her.

Social worker: Besides feeling rejected, you must have been mad as blazes. When did you first feel you weren't hitting it off with her? [*Blended empathic and concrete response.*]

Client: I guess it was when she lit up a cigarette while we were driving to the dance. I kidded her about how she was asking for lung cancer.

Social worker: I see. What was it about her reaction, then, that led you to believe you might not be in her good graces? [*Concrete response.*]

Client: Well, she didn't say anything. She just smoked her cigarette. I guess I really knew then that she was upset at me.

Social worker: As you look back at it now, what do you think you might have said to repair things at that point? [*Stimulating reflection about problem solving.*]

In the next example, observe how the social worker blends empathic and concrete responses to elicit details of interaction in an initial conjoint session. Such blending is a potent technique for eliciting specific and abundant information that bears directly on clients' problems. Responses that seek concreteness elicit details. In contrast, empathic responses enable social workers to stay attuned to clients' moment-by-moment experiencing, thereby focusing on feelings that may present obstacles to the exploration.

Social worker: You mentioned having difficulties communicating. I'd like you to give me an example of a time when you felt you weren't communicating effectively, and let's go through it step by step to see if we can understand more clearly what is happening.

Wife: Well, weekends are an example. Usually I want to go out and do something fun with the kids, but John just wants to stay home. He starts criticizing me for wanting to go, go, go.

Social worker: Could you give me a specific example? [*Seeking concreteness.*]

Wife: Okay. Last Saturday I wanted all of us to go out to eat and then to a movie, but John wanted to stay home and watch TV.

Social worker: Before we get into what John did, let's stay with you for a moment. There you are, really wanting to go to a movie—tell me exactly what you did. [*Seeking concreteness.*]

Wife: I think I said, "John, let's take the kids out to dinner and a movie."

Social worker: Okay. That's what you said. How did you say it? [*Seeking concreteness.*]

Wife: I expected him to say no, so I might not have said it the way I just did.

Social worker: Turn to John, and say it the way you may have said it then. [*Seeking concreteness.*]

Wife: Okay. [*Turning to husband.*] Couldn't we go out to a movie?

Social worker: There seems to be some doubt in your voice as to whether John wants to go out. [*Focusing observation.*]

Wife [*interrupting*]: I knew he wouldn't want to.

Social worker: So you assumed he wouldn't want to go. It's as though you already knew the answer. [*To husband.*] Does the way your wife asked the question check out with the way you remembered it? [*Husband nods.*]

Social worker: After your wife asked you about going to the movie, what did you do? [*Seeking concreteness.*]

Husband: I said, nope! I wanted to stay home and relax Saturday, and I felt we could do things at home.

Social worker: So your answer was short. Apparently you didn't give her information about why you didn't want to go but just said no. Is that right? [*Focusing observation.*]

Husband: That's right. I didn't think she wanted to go anyway—the way she asked.

Social worker: What were you experiencing when you said no? [*Seeking concreteness.*]

Husband: I guess I was just really tired. I have a lot of pressures from work, and I just need some time to relax. She doesn't understand that.

Social worker: You're saying, then, "I just needed some time to get away from it all," but I take it

you had your doubts as to whether she could appreciate your feelings. [*Husband nods.*] [*Turning to wife.*] Now, after your husband said no, what did you do? [*Blended empathic and concrete response.*]

Wife: I think that I started talking to him about the way he just sits around the house.

Social worker: I sense that you felt hurt and somewhat discounted because John didn't respond the way you would have liked. [*Empathic response.*]

Wife [*nods*]: I didn't think he even cared what I wanted to do.

Social worker: Is it fair to conclude, then, that the way in which you handled your feelings was to criticize John rather than to say, "This is what is happening to me?" [*Wife nods.*] [*Seeking concreteness.*]

Social worker [*to husband*]: Back, then, to our example. What did you do when your wife criticized you? [*Seeking concreteness.*]

Husband: I guess I criticized her back. I told her she needed to stay home once in a while and get some work done.

In this series of exchanges, the social worker asked questions that enabled the couple to describe the sequence of their interaction in a way that elicited key details and provided insight into unspoken assumptions and messages.

Managing Obstacles to Focusing

Occasionally you may find that your efforts to focus selectively and to explore topical areas in depth do not yield pertinent information. Although you have a responsibility in such instances to assess the effectiveness of your own interviewing style, you should also analyze clients' styles of communicating to determine to what extent their behaviors are interfering with your focusing efforts. Many clients seek help because they have—but are not aware of—patterns of communications or behaviors that create difficulties in relationships. In addition, involuntary clients who do not yet perceive the relationship as helping may be inclined to avoid focusing. The following list highlights common types of client communications that may challenge your efforts to focus in individual, family, and group sessions:

- Responding with "I don't know"
- Changing the subject or avoiding sensitive areas
- Rambling from topic to topic
- Intellectualizing or using abstract or general terms
- Diverting focus from the present to the past
- Responding to questions with questions
- Interrupting excessively
- Failing to express opinions when asked
- Producing excessive verbal output
- Using humor or sarcasm to evade topics or issues
- Verbally dominating the discussion

You can easily see how individuals who did not seek help from a social worker and want to avoid focusing might use these kinds of methods to protect their privacy. With such involuntary clients, such behaviors are likely to indicate a low level of trust and a skepticism that contact with a social worker can be helpful. You can counter repetitive behaviors and communications that divert the focus from exploring problems by tactfully drawing them to clients' attention and by assisting clients to adopt behaviors that are compatible with practice objectives. In groups, social workers must assist group members to modify behaviors that repeatedly disrupt effective focusing and communication; otherwise, the groups will not move to the phase of group development in which most of the work related to solving problems is accomplished.

Social workers may use many different techniques for managing and modifying client obstacles. These techniques include asking clients to communicate or behave differently; teaching, modeling for, and coaching clients to assume more effective communication styles; reinforcing facilitative responses; and selectively attending to functional behaviors.

Intervening to Help Clients Focus or Refocus

Communications that occur in group or conjoint sessions are not only complex, but may also be distractive or irrelevant. Consequently, the social worker's task of assisting members to explore the defined topics fully, rather than meander from subject to subject, is a challenging one. Related techniques that social workers can employ include highlighting or clarifying issues and bringing clients' attention to a comment or matter that has been overlooked. In such instances, the objective is not necessarily to explore the topic (although an exploration may subsequently occur), but rather to stress or elucidate important content. The social worker focuses clients' attention on communications and/or events that occurred earlier in the session or immediately preceded the social worker's focusing response. This technique is used in the following messages:

- [*To son in session with parents*]: "Ray, you made an important point a moment ago that I'm not sure your parents heard. Would you please repeat your comment?"

- [*To individual*]: "I would like to return to a remark made several moments ago when you said _____. I didn't want to interrupt then. I think perhaps the remark was important enough that we should return to it now."

- [*To family*]: "Something happened just a minute ago as we were talking. [*Describes event.*] We were involved in another discussion then, but I made a mental note of it because of how deeply it seemed to affect all of you at the time. I think we should consider what happened for just a moment."

- [*To group member*]: "John, as you were talking a moment ago, I wasn't sure what you meant by _____. Could you clarify that for me and for others in the group?"

- [*To group*]: "A few minutes ago, we were engrossed in a discussion about _____, yet we have moved away from that discussion to one that doesn't really seem to relate to our purpose for being here. I'm concerned about leaving the other subject hanging because you were working hard to find some solutions and appeared to be close to a breakthrough."

Because of the complexity of communications in group and family sessions, some inefficiency in the focusing process is inescapable. Nevertheless, the social worker can sharpen the group's efforts to focus and encourage more efficient use of its time by teaching effective focusing behavior. We suggest that social workers actually explain the focusing role of the group and identify desirable focusing behaviors, such as attending, active listening, and asking open-ended questions. During this discussion, it is important to emphasize that by utilizing these skills, members will facilitate exploration of problems.

Social workers can encourage greater use of these skills by giving positive feedback to group or family members when they have adequately focused on a problem, thus reinforcing their efforts. Although group members usually experience some difficulty in learning how to focus, they should be able to delve deeply into problems by the third or fourth session, given sufficient guidance and education by social workers. Such efforts by social workers tend to accelerate movement of groups toward maturity, a phase in which members achieve maximum therapeutic benefits. A characteristic of a group in this phase, in fact, is that members explore issues in considerable depth rather than skim the surface of many topics.

SUMMARIZING RESPONSES

The technique of summarization embodies four distinct and yet related facets:

1. Highlighting key aspects of discussions of specific problems before changing the focus of the discussion

2. Making connections between relevant aspects of lengthy client messages

3. Reviewing major focal points of a session and tasks that clients plan to work on before the next session

4. Recapitulating the highlights of a previous session and reviewing clients' progress on tasks during the week for the purpose of providing focus and continuity between sessions

Although employed at different times and in different ways, each of these facets of summarization serves the common purpose of tying together functionally related elements that occur at different points in the helping process. They are considered in detail in the following sections.

Highlighting Key Aspects of Problems

During the phase of an initial session in which problems are explored in moderate depth, summarization can be effectively employed to tie together and highlight essential aspects of a problem before proceeding to explore additional problems. For example, the social worker might describe how the problem appears to be produced by the interplay of several factors, including external pressures, overt behavioral patterns, unfulfilled needs and wants, and covert thoughts and feelings. Connecting these key elements assists clients in gaining a more accurate and complete perspective of their problems.

Employed in this fashion, summarization involves fitting pieces of the problem together to form a coherent whole. Seeing the problem in a fresh and more accurate perspective often proves beneficial, because it expands clients' awareness and can generate hope and enthusiasm for tackling a problem that has hitherto seemed insurmountable.

Summarization that highlights problems is generally employed at a natural point in the session when the social worker believes that relevant aspects of the problem have been adequately explored and clients appear satisfied in having had the opportunity to express their concerns. The following example illustrates this type of summarization. In this case, the client, an 80-year-old widow, has been referred to a Services to Seniors program for exploration of alternative living arrangements because of her failing health, isolation, and recent falls. As the two have worked together to explore alternative living arrangements, the pair have identified several characteristics that would be important for the client in an improved living situation. Highlighting the salient factors, the social worker summarizes the results to this point:

Social worker: It sounds as if you are looking for a situation in which there is social interaction but your privacy is also important to you: You want to maintain your independence.

Summarizing responses of this type serve as a prelude to the process of formulating goals, as goals flow naturally from problem formulations. Moreover, highlighting various dimensions of the problem facilitates the subsequent identifications of subgoals and tasks that must be accomplished to achieve the overall goal. In the preceding example, to explore an improved living situation, the social worker would help the client analyze the specific form of privacy (whether living alone or with someone else) and the type of social interaction (how much and what kind of contact with others) she desires.

Summarizing salient aspects of problems is a valuable technique in sessions with groups, couples, and families. It enables the social worker to stop at timely moments and highlight the difficulties experienced by each participant. In a family session with a pregnant adolescent and her mother, for example, the social worker might make the following statements:

- [*To pregnant adolescent*]: "You feel as if deciding what to do about this baby is your decision—it's your body and you have decided that an abortion is the best solution for you. You know that you have the legal right to make this decision and want to be supported in making it. You feel as if your mother wants to help but can't tell you what decision to make."

- [*To mother*]: "As you spoke, you seemed saddened and very anxious about this decision your daughter is making. You are saying, 'I care about my daughter, but I don't think she is mature enough to make this decision on her own.' As you have noted, women in your family have had a hard time conceiving, and you wish that she would consider other options besides abortion. So you feel a responsibility to your daughter, but also to this unborn baby and the family history of conceiving children."

Such responses synthesize in concise and neutral language the needs, concerns, and problems of each participant for all other members of the session to hear. This type of summarization underscores the fact that all participants are struggling with and have responsibility for problems that are occurring, thus counteracting the tendency of families to view one person as the exclusive cause of family problems.

Summarizing Lengthy Messages

Clients' messages range from one word or one sentence to lengthy and sometimes rambling monologues. Although the meaning and significance of brief messages are often readily discernible, lengthy messages challenge the social worker to encapsulate and tie together diverse and complex elements. Linking the elements together often highlights and expands the significance and meaning of the client's message. For this reason, such messages represent one form of additive empathy, a skill discussed in Chapter 17.

Because lengthy client messages typically include emotions, thoughts, and descriptive content, you will need to determine how these dimensions relate to the focal point of the discussion. To illustrate, consider the following message of a mildly brain-damaged and socially withdrawn 16-year-old female—an only child who is extremely dependent on her overprotective but subtly rejecting mother:

Client: Mother tells me she loves me, but I find that hard to believe. Nothing I do ever pleases her; she yells at me when I refuse to wash my hair alone. But I can't do it right without her help. "When are you going to grow up?" she'll say. And she goes out with her friends and leaves me alone in that old house. She knows how scared I get when I have to stay home alone. But she says, "Nancy, I can't just baby-sit you all the time. I've got to do something for myself. Why don't you make some friends or watch TV or play your guitar? You've just got to quit pitying yourself all the time." Does that sound like someone who loves you? I get so mad at her when she yells at me, it's all I can do to keep from killing her.

Embodied in the client's message are the following elements:

1. Wanting to be loved by her mother, yet feeling insecure and rejected at times
2. Feeling inadequate about performing certain tasks, such as washing her hair
3. Feeling extremely dependent upon her mother for certain services and companionship
4. Feeling afraid when her mother leaves her alone
5. Feeling hurt (implied) and resentful when her mother criticizes her or leaves her alone
6. Feeling intense anger and wanting to lash out when her mother yells at her

The following summarizing response ties these elements together:

Social worker: So you find your feelings toward your mother pulling you in different directions. You want her to love you, but you feel unloved and resent it when she criticizes you or leaves you alone. And you feel really torn because you depend on her in so many ways. Yet at times, you feel so angry you want to hurt her back for yelling at you. You'd like to have a smoother relationship without the strain.

In conjoint interviews or group sessions, summarization can also be used effectively to highlight and to tie together key elements and dynamics embodied in transactions, as illustrated in the following transaction and summarizing responses of a social worker:

Wife [*to husband*]: You're just never home when I need you. I need your help making decisions about the children. We've got this big activity coming up with Susan this weekend. And where are you going to be? [*Said with animation and sarcasm.*] Boating—of course!

Husband [*bristling and defensive*]: You're damned right! You make it sound like a crime. I suppose you expect me not to go boating just because you can't make a decision. Once a year I get to do something I really enjoy, and you bitch about it. Why shouldn't you make decisions? I didn't marry you to make

your decisions for you. Making decisions about the children is your job. Why don't you learn to stand on your own two feet for a change?

Social worker: Let's stop here and think about what each of you is saying. [*To wife.*] You're feeling overwhelmed in coping with the children alone. I gather the bottom line for you is that your husband is very important to you, and you want to work together as a team in dealing with matters related to the children. [*Wife nods in agreement as husband listens attentively.*] [*To husband.*] And I gather you're reading your wife's message as an attempt to pass the buck to you. You also sounded as though you felt attacked and read her message as an attempt to deny you an opportunity to enjoy yourself. [*He vigorously nods affirmatively.*] [*To both.*] Each of you seems to be feeling a lack of caring and understanding by the other, but these needs get buried under your criticism and attempts to defend yourselves. Let's explore further what each of you is needing from the other.

Here the social worker's summarization employs additive empathy to identify the needs that underlie the negative and destructive messages exchanged by the spouses. Going beyond the negative surface feelings, the social worker summarizes implied messages and needs. The exploration of these underlying feelings may lead to increased understanding and to positive feelings rather than mutual recriminations.

Occasionally, client messages may ramble to the extent that they contain numerous unrelated elements that cannot all be tied together. In such instances, your task is to extract and focus on those elements of the message that are most relevant to the thrust of the session at that point. When employed in this manner, summarization provides focus and direction to the session and averts aimless wandering. With clients whose thinking is loose or who ramble to avoid having to focus on unpleasant matters, you may need to interrupt to assure some semblance of focus and continuity. Otherwise, the interview will be disjointed and unproductive. Skills in maintaining focus and continuity are discussed later in this chapter and in Chapter 13.

Reviewing Focal Points of a Session

During the course of an individual, conjoint, or group session, it is common to focus on more than one problem and to discuss numerous factors associated with each problem. Toward the end of the first or second session, depending on the length of the initial exploration, summarization is employed to review key problems that have been discussed and to highlight themes and patterns related to these problems. Summarizing themes and patterns expands each client's awareness of dysfunctional patterns and his or her role in the difficulties identified (assuming the client affirms the validity of the summarization). In this way, use of this skill opens up promising avenues for growth and change.

In fact, through summarizing responses, social workers can review problematic themes and patterns that have emerged in their sessions and test clients' readiness to consider goals aimed at modifying these problematic patterns. The following is an example of such a message:

Social worker: As we explored the stresses that appear to precede your periods of depression, the theme of your discounting yourself by trying so hard to meet unreasonable demands of your family members struck me as very significant, and you seemed to agree. As we begin to consider goals, I wonder what you think about working toward the goal of giving your own needs higher priority and learning to say "No!" and feeling good about it when others make demands that conflict with your needs?

Providing Focus and Continuity

The social worker can also use summarization at the beginning of an individual, group, or conjoint session to review work that clients have accomplished in the last session(s) and to set the stage for work in the present session. At the same time, the social worker may decide to identify a promising topic for discussion or to refresh clients' minds concerning work they wish to accomplish in that session. In addition, summarization can be employed periodically to synthesize salient points at the conclusion of a discussion or used at the end of the session to review the major focal points. In so doing, the social worker will need to place what was accomplished in the session within the broad perspective of the clients' goals. The social worker tries to consider how the salient content and movement manifested in each session fit into the larger whole. Only then are the social worker and clients likely to maintain a sense of direction and avoid needless delays caused by wandering and detours—problems that commonly occur when continuity within or between sessions is weak.

Used as a "wrap-up" when the allotted time for a session is nearly gone, summarization assists the social worker to draw a session to a natural conclusion. In addition to highlighting and linking together the key points of the session, the social worker reviews clients' plans for performing tasks before the next session. When the session ends with such a summarization, all participants should be clear about where they have been and where they are going in relation to the goals toward which their mutual efforts are directed.

ANALYZING YOUR VERBAL FOLLOWING SKILLS

After taking frequency counts over a period of time of some of the major verbal following skills (empathy, concreteness, open-ended and closed-ended responses), you are ready to assess the extent to which you employ, blend, and balance these skills in relation to each other. On the form for recording verbal following (Figure 6-2), categorize each of your responses from a recorded session. As you analyze your relative use and blending of responses alone or with your practicum instructor, determine whether certain types of responses were used either too frequently or too sparingly. Think of steps that you might take to correct any imbalances in your utilization of skills for future sessions.

CLIENT MESSAGE	OPEN-ENDED RESPONSES	CLOSED-ENDED RESPONSES	EMPATHIC RESPONSES	LEVEL OF EMPATHY	CONCRETE RESPONSES	SUMMARIZING RESPONSES	OTHER TYPES OF RESPONSES
1.							
2.							
3.							
4.							
5.							
6.							
7.							

Directions: Categorize each of your responses from a recorded session. Where responses involve more than one category (blended responses), record them as a single response, but also check each category embodied in the response. Excluding the responses checked as "Other Type of Responses," analyze whether certain types of responses were utilized too frequently or too sparingly. Define tasks for yourself to correct imbalances in future sessions. Retain a copy of the form so that you can monitor your progress in mastering verbal following skills over an extended period of time.

Figure 6-2 Recording Form for Verbal Following Skills

Summary

This chapter has helped you learn how to explore, paraphrase, and appropriately use closed- and open-ended responses as a means of better focusing, following and summarizing in your social work practice. These skills may be applied both with clients and with other persons and colleagues, on behalf of clients. In Chapter 7 we will explore some common difficulties experienced by beginning social workers and some ways to overcome them.

Internet Resources

See our companion website for hot links to some helpful URLs. Note that URLs are subject to change. We will endeavor to update the links on the companion website as much as possible. You can use InfoTrac College Edition to find useful articles about empowerment-based practice, including Rose (2000) and Ackerson and Harrison (2000).

For information and associated sites linked with education organizations, visit websites such as that of the Council on Social Work Education (CSWE; *http://www.cswe.org*) and the Canadian Association of Schools of Social Work (*http://www.cassw-access.ca*).

Related Online Content

Visit the *Direct Social Work Practice* companion website at *http://socialwork.wadsworth.com/hepworth7* for additional learning tools such as glossary terms, chapter outlines, InfoTrac College Edition keywords, relevant web links, and chapter practice quizzes. Also, be sure to check out the Direct Practice Virtual Reader, where the authors have personally selected articles relevant to this chapter using InfoMarks.

Modeled Responses to Exercise in Paraphrasing

1. "You just get so uptight in a group you don't function."
2. "So you've made some real progress in tuning in to your husband and children."

3. "Because your fears really block you when you argue with your mother, you consistently come out on the short side."
4. "You're really torn and wonder if not seeing the children very often is too high a price to pay for a divorce. You seem pretty clear, though, that if you stay with her, there won't be any improvement."
5. "So people's helpfulness here and your own skills in meeting people have helped your adjustment here."
6. "So you see yourself as having contributed to many of her problems."
7. "It sounds as if you feel overloaded with conflicting parenting and work responsibilities."
8. "It sounds as if your experience causes you to doubt whether more services would be helpful. Could you tell me about your feeling that the mother is not motivated?"
9. "So sometimes you feel cheated by life and at other times that your illness is a consequence for your smoking history."

Answers to Exercise in Identifying Closed and Open-Ended Responses

Statement	Response
1	C
2	O
3	O
4	C

Modeled Open-Ended Responses

1. "Could you tell me more about your wanting to impress Ralph?"
2. "What are you afraid you'd do wrong?"
3. "Given your experience with that probation officer, how would you like your relationship with me to be?"
4. "So you feel that your facility cannot provide what Gladys needs. Can you describe the kind of care you believe she needs?"
5. "So you don't trust that I want to try to help you make what you feel will be the best decision.

Can you tell me what I have done that has caused you to think that your mother and I are allies?"

6. "You sound as if you are at a pretty hopeless point right now. When you say you don't know if you want to keep trying to figure it out, can you tell me more about what you are thinking about doing?"

Notes

1. Note that several of these messages could also be categorized as seeking concreteness. Messages that seek concreteness and open-ended messages are not mutually exclusive; indeed, they often overlap to a considerable extent.

CHAPTER 7

Eliminating Counterproductive Communication Patterns

CHAPTER OVERVIEW

Chapter 7 explores communication difficulties that often arise in the practice of beginning (and many experienced) social workers and suggest some positive alternatives to these defective patterns. By becoming alert to these difficulties, beginning social workers can focus their attention on communicating in a positive fashion. In addition to applications in direct practice, the chapter provides numerous communication examples related to both meso and macro practice.

IMPACTS OF COUNTERPRODUCTIVE COMMUNICATION PATTERNS

As a beginning social worker, you bring to your practice a desire to be helpful and a commitment to improve your own skills. That desire and commitment will not directly translate into flawless skills that ensure that all clients solve their problems and appreciate your abilities. Instead, you will inevitably make mistakes that cause you to wonder whether you will ever find complete success, at least without great effort. But take heart: Even the most successful social workers were once beginners, and learning from your mistakes is an integral part of your education. This chapter is geared toward helping you recognize and overcome nonverbal and verbal communication patterns that may inhibit the helping process.

The communication repertoires of aspiring social workers usually include halting beginning practice of new skills and some response patterns that inhibit the free flow of information and negatively affect helping relationships. Such responses impede progress each time they occur, eliciting, for example, defensiveness, hostility, or silence. Consistent use of such responses can block growth, precipitate premature terminations of contact, or cause deterioration in clients' functioning. Nugent and Halvorson (1995) have demonstrated how differently worded active-listening responses may lead to different short-term client affective outcomes.

ELIMINATING NONVERBAL BARRIERS TO EFFECTIVE COMMUNICATION

Nonverbal behaviors strongly influence interactions between people. The importance of this medium of communication is underscored by the fact that counselors' nonverbal interview behavior contributes significantly to ratings of counselor effectiveness. Nonverbal cues, which serve to confirm or to deny messages conveyed verbally, are in large part beyond the conscious awareness of participants. In fact, they may produce "leakage" by transmitting information that the sender did not intend to communicate to the receiver. Facial expressions—a blush, a sneer, or a look of shock or dismay, for example—convey much more about the social worker's attitude toward the client than what is said aloud. In fact, if there is a discrepancy between the social worker's verbal and nonverbal communication, the client is more likely to discredit the verbal message. Over time, people learn through myriad transactions with others that nonverbal cues more accurately indicate feelings than do spoken words.

Physical Attending

Beginning social workers are often relatively unaware of their nonverbal behaviors, and they may not have learned to consciously use these behaviors to advantage in conveying caring, understanding, and respect. Therefore, mastering physical attending—a basic skill critical to the helping process—is one of the social worker's first learning tasks. Physical attentiveness to another person is communicated by receptive behaviors, such as facing the client squarely, leaning forward, maintaining eye contact, and remaining relaxed.

Attending also requires social workers to be fully present—that is, to keep in moment-to-moment contact with the client through disciplined attention. Attending in a fully present, relaxed fashion is not to be expected with beginning social workers, who are typically anxious about what to do next, how to help, and how to avoid hurting clients. Such skill is more likely to evolve with greater experience after novice social workers have engaged in considerable observation of expert social workers, role-playing, and beginning interviews with clients.

Cultural Nuances of Nonverbal Cues

To consciously use nonverbal behaviors to full advantage in transcultural relationships, social workers must be aware that different cultural groups ascribe different meanings to certain nonverbal behaviors. Eye-to-eye contact, for example, is expected behavior among members of mainstream American culture. In fact, people who avoid eye-to-eye contact may be viewed as untrustworthy or evasive. Conversely, members of some Native American tribes regard direct gazing as an intrusion on privacy. It is important to observe and investigate the norms for gazing before employing eye-to-eye contact with members of some tribes (Gross, 1995).[1]

It is hazardous to make generalizations across ethnic groups, however. A recent study reported that Filipino students were more similar to white students than to Chinese students in relation to many attitudes, perceptions, and beliefs. Meanwhile, the same study showed that women were more similar to one another across ethnic groups than they were to men within their own group (Agbayani-Siewart, 2004).

With this proviso in mind, social workers should consider the possibility that Asian clients might view helping professionals as authorities who can solve their problems (often presented as physical symptoms) by providing advice. Because of this respect for authority, the Asian client may speak little unless spoken to by the social worker; the social worker, in turn, may mistakenly perceive the client's behavior as passive, silent, and ingratiating. Consequently, "long gaps of silence may occur as the client waits patiently for the therapist to structure the interview, take charge, and thus provide the solution" (Tsui & Schultz, 1985, p. 565). Such gaps in communication engender anxiety in both parties that may undermine the development of rapport and defeat the helping process. Further, failure to correctly interpret the client's nonverbal behavior may lead the social worker to conclude erroneously that the client has flat affect (i.e., little emotionality). Given these potential hazards, social workers should consider being more active with Asian clients, including placing greater emphasis on clarifying role expectations.

Other Nonverbal Behaviors

Barriers that prevent the social worker from staying in psychological contact with the client can be caused by preoccupation with judgments or evaluations about the client or by inner pressures to find immediate solutions to the client's problems. Likewise, reduced focus on the client can result from being preoccupied with oneself while practicing new skills. Extraneous noise, a ringing phone, an inadequate interviewing room, or a lack of privacy can also interfere with the social worker's being psychologically present.

The social worker may convey a lack of concern for the client by displaying any of numerous undesirable behaviors and revealing postural cues. For example, staring vacantly, looking out the window, frequently glancing at the clock, yawning, and fidgeting suggest a lack of attention; trembling hands or rigid posture may communicate anger or anxiety. These and a host of other behavioral cues that convey messages such as inattention or disrespect are readily perceived by most clients, many of whom are highly sensitive to criticism or rejection in any form. Quite frankly, voluntary clients with sufficient resources and self-esteem are not likely to accept social worker behavior that they consider disrespectful, nor should they. This leaves the social worker with just those involuntary clients with fewer choices, fewer resources, and lower self-esteem, who may believe that they have little recourse other than accepting such behavior.

Taking Inventory of Nonverbal Patterns of Responding

To assist you in taking inventory of your own styles of responding to clients, Table 7-1 identifies recommended and not recommended nonverbal behaviors. You will probably find that you have a mixed repertoire of nonverbal responses, some of which have the potential to enhance helping relationships and foster client progress. Other, less desirable behaviors of the beginning social worker may include nervousness that may block your clients from freely disclosing information and otherwise retard the flow of the helping process. You thus have a threefold task: (1) to assess your repetitive nonverbal behaviors; (2) to eliminate nonverbal styles that hinder effective communication; and (3) to sustain and perhaps increase desirable nonverbal behaviors.

At the end of this chapter, you will find a checklist intended for use in training or supervision to obtain feedback on nonverbal aspects of attending. Given the opportunity to review a videotape of your performance in actual or simulated interviews and/or to receive behaviorally specific feedback from supervisors and peers, you should be able to adequately master physical aspects of attending in a relatively brief time.

Table 7-1 Inventory of practitioner's nonverbal communication

RECOMMENDED	NOT RECOMMENDED
Facial Expressions	
Direct eye contact (except when culturally proscribed)	Avoidance of eye contact
Warmth and concern reflected in facial expression	Staring of fixating on person or object
Eyes at same level as client's	Lifting eyebrow critically
Appropriately varied and animated facial expressions	Eye level higher or lower than client's
Mouth relaxed; occasional smiles	Nodding head excessively
	Yawning
	Frozen on rigid facial expressions
	Inappropriate slight smile
	Pursing or biting lips
Posture	
Arms and hands moderately expressive; appropriate gestures	Rigid body position; arms tightly folded
Body leaning slightly forward; attentive but relaxed	Body turned at an angle to client
	Fidgeting with hands
	Squirming or rocking in chair
	Slouching or placing feet on desk
	Hand or fingers over mouth
	Pointing finger for emphasis

(*continued*)

Table 7-1 *cont'd*

RECOMMENDED	NOT RECOMMENDED
Voice	
Clearly audible but not loud	Mumbling or speaking inaudibly
Warmth in tone of voice	Monotonic voice
Voice modulated to reflect nuances of feeling and emotional tone of client messages	Halting speech
Moderate speech tempo	Frequent grammatical errors
	Prolonged silences
	Excessively animated speech
	Slow, rapid, or staccato speech
	Nervous laughter
	Consistent clearing of throat
	Speaking loudly
Physical Proximity	
Three to five feet between chairs	Excessive closeness or distance
	Talking across desk or other barrier

A review of your taped performance may reveal that you are already demonstrating some of the desirable physical attending behaviors listed in Table 7-1. You may also possess personal nonverbal mannerisms that are particularly helpful in establishing relationships with others, such as a friendly grin or a relaxed, easy manner. As you take inventory of your nonverbal behaviors, elicit feedback from others regarding these behaviors. When appropriate, increase the frequency of recommended behaviors that you have identified. In particular, try to cultivate the quality of warmth, which we discussed in Chapter 3.

As you review videotapes of your sessions, pay particular attention to your nonverbal responses at those moments when you experienced pressure or tension; this assessment will assist you in determining whether your responses were counterproductive. All beginning interviewers experience moments of discomfort in their first contacts with clients, and nonverbal behaviors serve as an index of their comfort level. To enhance your self-awareness of your own behavioral patterns, develop a list of the verbal and nonverbal behaviors you display when you are under pressure. When you review your videotaped sessions, you may notice that under pressure you respond with humor, fidget, change voice inflection, assume a rigid body posture, or manifest other nervous mannerisms. Making

an effort to become aware of and to eliminate obvious signs of anxiety is an important step in achieving mastery of your nonverbal responding.

ELIMINATING VERBAL BARRIERS TO COMMUNICATION

Many types of ineffective verbal responses dissuade clients from exploring problems and sharing freely with the social worker. To understand why, we refer to reactance theory, which suggests that clients will act to protect valued freedoms (Brehm & Brehm, 1981). Such freedoms can include the freedom to have one's own opinions and the inclination to action. When such valued freedoms are threatened, clients will often withdraw, argue, or move to a superficial topic.

The following list identifies common verbal barriers that usually have an immediate negative effect on communications, thereby inhibiting clients from revealing pertinent information and working on problems:

1. Reassuring, sympathizing, consoling, or excusing

2. Advising and giving suggestions or solutions prematurely

3. Using sarcasm or employing humor that is distracting or makes light of clients' problems

4. Judging, criticizing, or placing blame

5. Trying to convince the client about the right point of view through logical arguments, lecturing, instructing, or arguing

6. Analyzing, diagnosing, or making glib or dogmatic interpretations

7. Threatening, warning, or counterattacking

The first three behaviors are mistakes that beginning practitioners commonly make across a variety of populations and settings, often reflecting the social worker's' nervousness and an abounding desire to be immediately helpful. Numbers 3–7 are also common, but are more likely to occur when the social worker is working with "captive clients"—a situation in which there is a power differential and the client cannot readily escape. An underlying theme of these behaviors can be the social worker reflecting a sense of superiority over persons whose behaviors or problem solving has been harmful to themselves or to others.

Reassuring, Sympathizing, Consoling, or Excusing

- "You'll feel better tomorrow."
- "Don't worry, things will work out."
- "You probably didn't do anything to aggravate the situation."
- "I really feel sorry for you."

When used selectively and with justification, well-timed reassurance can engender much needed hope and support.[2] By glibly reassuring clients that "things will work out," "everybody has problems," or "things aren't as bleak as they seem," however, social workers avoid exploring clients' feelings of despair, anger, hopelessness, or helplessness. Situations faced by clients are often grim, with no immediate relief at hand. Rather than gloss over clients' feelings and seek to avoid discomfort, social workers must undertake to explore those distressing feelings and to assist clients in acknowledging painful realities. Beginning social workers need to convey that they hear and understand their clients'

difficulties as they experience them. They will also want to convey hope while exploring prospects for change—albeit at the appropriate time in the dialogue.

Reassuring clients prematurely or without a genuine basis for hope often serves the purposes of social workers more than the purposes of clients and, in fact, may represent efforts by social workers to dissuade clients from revealing their troubling feelings. That is, reassurance may serve to restore the comfort level and equilibrium of social workers rather than to help clients. Instead of fostering hope, these glib statements convey a lack of understanding of clients' feelings and raise doubts about the authenticity of social workers. Clients may, in turn, react with thoughts such as "It's easy for you to say that, but you don't know how very frightened I really am," or "You're just saying that so I'll feel better." In addition, responses that excuse clients (e.g., "You're not to blame") or sympathize with their position (e.g., "I can see exactly why you feel that way; I think I would probably have done the same thing") often have the effect of unwittingly reinforcing inappropriate behavior or reducing clients' anxiety and motivation to work on problems.

Advising and Giving Suggestions or Solutions Prematurely

- "I suggest that you move to a new place because you have had so many difficulties here."
- "I think you need to try a new approach with your daughter. Let me suggest that . . ."
- "I think it would be best for you to try using time-out . . ."
- "Because your partner is such a loser, why don't you try to create some new relationships with other people?"

Little is known about the actual provision of advice in terms of its frequency or the circumstances in which it occurs (Jayaratne, Croxton, & Mattison, 1997). Clients often seek advice, and appropriately timed advice can be an important helping tool. Conversely, untimely advice may elicit opposition. Even when clients solicit advice in early phases of the helping process, they often react negatively when they receive it because the recommended solutions, which are invariably based on superficial information, often do not address their real needs. Further, because clients are frequently burdened and preoccupied with little-understood conflicts, feelings, and pressures, they are not ready to take action on their problems at this point. For these reasons, after offering premature advice, social workers may observe clients replying with responses such as "Yes, but I've already tried that," or "That won't work." In fact, these responses can serve as feedback clues that you may have slipped into the habit of giving premature advice.

While many clients seek advice from social workers because they see the practitioners as expert problem solvers, those social workers can (wrongly) seek to expedite problem solving by quickly comparing the current situation to other similar ones encountered in the past and recommending a solution that has worked for other clients. In such cases, social workers may feel pressure to provide quick answers or solutions for clients who unrealistically expect magical answers and instant relief from problems that have plagued them for long periods of time. Beginning social workers may also experience inner pressure to dispense solutions to clients' problems, mistakenly believing that their new role demands that they, like physicians, prescribe a treatment regimen. They thus run the risk of giving advice before they have conducted a thorough exploration of clients' problems. In reality, instead of dispensing wisdom, a major role of social workers is to create and shape processes with clients in which they engage in mutual discovery of problems and solutions—work that will take time and concentrated effort.

Beginning social workers who are working with nonvoluntary clients may feel justified in "strongly suggesting" their opinions because of the poor choices or problem solving they may presume landed these clients in their current predicament. As suggested in Chapter 4, social work practice does not have a place for judging clients: We may have to evaluate clients' performance and capabilities in certain circumstances, but that is not the same as judging them as people. Assisting clients through

modeling and reinforcement of pro-social behavior is not the same as judging clients and imposing social workers' own opinions (Trotter, 1999).

The timing and form of recommendations are all-important in the helping process. Advice should be offered sparingly, and only after thoroughly exploring the problem and the client's ideas about possible solutions. At that point, the social worker may serve as a consultant, tentatively sharing ideas about solutions to supplement those developed by the client. Clients who try to pressure social workers to dispense knowledge prematurely are merely depriving themselves of the opportunity to develop effective solutions to these problems. In such circumstances, social workers should stress clients' roles in helping to discover and tailor solutions to fit their unique problems.

Clients may expect to receive early advice if social workers have not appropriately clarified roles and expectations about how mutual participation in generating possible solutions will further the growth and self-confidence of clients. Assuming a position of superiority and quickly providing solutions for problems without encouraging clients to think through the possible courses of action fosters dependency and stifles creative thinking. Freely dispensing advice also minimizes or ignores clients' strengths and potentials, and many clients tend to respond with inner resentment to such high-handed treatment. In addition, clients who have not been actively involved in planning their own courses of action may, in turn, lack motivation to implement the advice given by social workers. Moreover, when advice does not remedy a problem—as it often doesn't—clients may blame social workers and disown any responsibility for an unfavorable outcome.

We do not mean to suggest that social workers should never give advice. Our point is that premature advice as well as advice shared in a judgmental tone should be avoided. As Chapter 10 explains, mutual exploration of possible solutions to client concerns should take advantage of the social worker's knowledge about resources and options (Reid, 2000). Indeed, failure to explore and present evidence about which solutions are most likely to be successful raises ethical concerns about the social worker's competence.

Using Sarcasm or Employing Humor Inappropriately

- "Did you get up on the wrong side of the bed?"
- "It seems to me that we've been through all this before."
- "You really fell for that line."
- "You think you have a problem."

Humor can be helpful, bringing relief and sometimes perspective to work that might otherwise be tense and tedious. Pollio (1995) has suggested ways to determine appropriate use of humor. Similarly, van Wormer and Boes (1997) have described ways that humor permits social workers to continue to operate in the face of trauma. Using plays on words or noting a sense of the preposterous or incongruous can help social workers and clients face difficult situations. Situations can be put into perspective, with both social workers and clients appreciating incongruous outcomes. Humor can also allow clients to express emotions in safe, less emotionally charged ways (Dewayne, 1978). Kane (1995) describes the way humor in group work can facilitate work with persons afflicted with HIV. In group work, Caplan (1995) has described how facilitation of humor can create a necessary safety and comfort level in work with men who batter.

Excessive use of humor, however, can be distracting, keeping the content of the session on a superficial level and interfering with mutual objectives. Sarcasm often emanates from unrecognized hostility that tends to provoke counter-hostility in clients. Similarly, making a comment such as "you really win the prize for worst week" when a client recounts a series of crises and unfortunate incidents runs the risk of conveying that the difficulties are not taken seriously. A better response would be to empathize with the difficulties of the week and compliment the client on persisting to cope despite them.

Judging, Criticizing, or Placing Blame

- "You're wrong about that."
- "Running away from home was a bad mistake."

- "One of your problems is that you're not willing to consider another point of view."
- "You're not thinking straight."

Responses that evaluate and show disapproval can be detrimental to clients and to the helping process. Clients usually respond defensively and sometimes counterattack when they perceive criticism from social workers; some may simply cut off any meaningful communication with social workers. When they are intimidated by a social worker's greater expertise, some clients also accept negative evaluations as accurate reflections of their poor judgment or lack of worth or value. In making such negative judgments about clients, social workers violate the basic social work values of nonjudgmental attitude and acceptance.

Such responses are unlikely to be tolerated by voluntary, noncaptive clients with adequate self-esteem or enough power in the situation to have alternatives. Such clients are likely to "fire" you, speak to your supervisor, or put you on notice if you act in such seemingly disrespectful ways. Others may shut down, perceiving you as having some power over them.

Involuntary clients often face what they believe to be dangerous consequences for not getting along with the social worker. Hence, some clients with substantial self-control and self-esteem may put up with such browbeating without comment. Others may respond in kind with attacks of their own that then appear in case records as evidence of client resistance.

If the social worker is concerned about danger to the client or to others, or about violations of the law, then he or she may ask a question to raise the client's awareness of consequences and alternatives. For example, the social worker might ask, "How do you look now at the consequences of running away from home?" or "How would this appear from your partner's point of view?"

Trying to Convince Clients about the Right Point of View through Logic, Lecturing, Instructing, or Arguing

- "Let's look at the facts about drugs."
- "You have to take some responsibility for your life, you know."

- "Running away from home will only get you in more difficulty."
- "That attitude won't get you anywhere."

Clients sometimes consider courses of action that social workers view as unsafe, illegal, or contrary to the client's goals. However, attempting to convince clients through arguing, instructing, and similar behavior often provokes a kind of boomerang effect—that is, clients are not only not convinced of the merits of the social worker's argument, but may also be more inclined to hold onto their beliefs than before. According to reactance theory, clients will attempt to defend their valued freedoms when these privileges are threatened (Brehm & Brehm, 1981). For some clients (especially adolescents, for whom independent thinking is associated with a particular developmental stage), deferring to or agreeing with social workers is tantamount to giving up their individuality or freedom.

In vigorously attempting to persuade clients to adopt another point of view, social workers often create power struggles, thereby perpetuating dynamics that have previously occurred in clients' personal relationships. By arguing, social workers ignore their clients' feelings and views, focusing instead on the social worker "being right"; this tactic may engender feelings of resentment, alienation, or hostility in clients. Such efforts are both unethical and ineffective.

Persuasion in the sense of helping clients to obtain accurate information with which to make informed decisions can be an ethical intervention. When clients contemplate actions that run contrary to their own goals, or will endanger themselves or others, then an effort to persuade can be an ethical intervention. Such efforts should not focus on the one "pet" solution of the social worker, however, but rather should assist the client in examining the advantages and disadvantages of several options, including those with which the social worker may disagree (Rooney, 1992). Hence, the effort is not to convince, but rather to assist clients in making informed decisions. For example, the social worker might ask whether the client is interested in exploring some factual information about

drugs. Similarly, the social worker might ask the client to think about the benefits of running away from home and then to consider the potential drawbacks of that action.

Analyzing, Diagnosing, or Making Glib or Dramatic Interpretations

- "You're behaving that way because you're angry with your partner."
- "Your attitude may have kept you from giving their ideas a fair hearing."
- "You're acting in a passive-aggressive way."
- "You're really hostile today."

When used sparingly and timed appropriately, interpretation of the dynamics of behavior can be a potent change-oriented skill (see Chapter 18). However, even accurate interpretations that focus on purposes or meanings of behavior substantially beyond clients' levels of conscious awareness tend to inspire client opposition and are doomed to failure.

When stated dogmatically (e.g., "I know what's wrong with you," or "how you feel," or "what your real motives are"), interpretations also present a threat to clients, causing them to feel exposed or trapped. When a glib interpretation is thrust upon them, clients often expend their energies disconfirming the interpretation, explaining themselves, or making angry rebuttals rather than working on the problem at hand.

Using social work jargon such as *fixation, transference, resistance, reinforcement, repression, passivity, neuroticism,* and a host of other terms to describe the behavior of clients in their presence is also destructive to the helping process. Indeed, it may confuse or bewilder clients and provoke opposition to change. These terms also oversimplify complex phenomena and psychic mechanisms and stereotype clients, thereby obliterating their uniqueness. In addition, these sweeping generalizations provide no operational definitions of clients' problems, nor do they suggest avenues for behavior modification. If clients accept social workers' restricted definitions of their problems, then they may define themselves in the same terms as those used by social workers (e.g., "I am a passive person" or "I have a schizoid personality"). This type of stereotypic labeling often causes clients to view themselves as "sick" and their situations as hopeless, providing them with a ready excuse for not working on their problems.

Threatening, Warning, or Counterattacking

- "You better . . . or else!"
- "If you don't . . . you'll be sorry."
- "If you know what's good for you, you'll . . ."

Sometimes clients consider actions that would endanger themselves or others or are illegal. In such instances, alerting clients to the potential consequences of those actions is an ethical and appropriate intervention. Conversely, making threats of the sort described above often produces a kind of oppositional behavior that exacerbates an already strained situation.

Even the most well-intentioned social workers may occasionally bristle or respond defensively under the pressure of verbal abuse, accusatory or blaming responses, or challenges to their integrity, competence, motives, or authority. Social workers conducting group sessions with adolescents, for instance, can testify that the provocative behavior of this client population may defeat even the most herculean efforts to respond appropriately.

Whatever the dynamics behind clients' provocative behavior, responding defensively is counterproductive, as it may duplicate the destructive pattern of responses that clients have typically elicited and experienced from others. To achieve competence, therefore, you must learn to master your own natural defensive reactions and evolve effective ways of dealing with negative feelings.

Empathic communication, for example, produces a cathartic release of negative feelings, defusing a strained situation and permitting a more rational emotional exploration of factors that underlie clients' feelings. For example, to reply to a client, "You have difficult decisions to make, and are caught between alternatives that you don't consider very attractive; I wish you well in making a decision

that you can live with in the future" can convey support and respect for the right to choose.

The negative effects of certain types of responses are not always immediately apparent because clients may not overtly demonstrate negative reactions at the time or because the retarding effect on the helping process cannot be observed in a single transaction. To assess the effect of responses, then, the social worker must determine the frequency with which he or she issues detrimental responses and evaluate the overall impact of those responses on the helping process. Frequent use of some types of responses by the social worker indicates the presence of counterproductive patterns of communication such as the following (note that this list is a continuation of the list of problematic social worker behaviors on pages 166–167):

8. Stacking questions
9. Asking leading questions
10. Interrupting inappropriately or excessively
11. Dominating the interaction
12. Fostering safe social interaction
13. Responding infrequently
14. Parroting or overusing certain phrases or clichés
15. Dwelling on the remote past
16. Going on fishing expeditions

Individual responses that fall within these patterns may or may not be ineffective when employed occasionally. When they are employed extensively in lieu of using varied response patterns, however, they inhibit the natural flow of a session and limit the richness of information revealed. The sections that follow expand on each of these verbal barriers and detrimental social worker responses.

Stacking Questions

In exploring problems, social workers should use facilitative questions that assist clients to reveal detailed information about specific problem areas. Asking multiple questions at the same time, or *stacking,* diffuses the focus and confuses clients.

Consider the vast amount of ground covered in the following messages:

- "When you don't feel you have control of situations, what goes on inside of you? What do you think about? What do you do?"

- "Have you thought about where you are going to live? Is that one of your biggest concerns, or is there another that takes priority?"

Stacking questions is a problem frequently encountered by beginning social work practitioners, who may feel an urgent need to help clients by providing many options all at one time. Adequately answering even one of the foregoing questions would require a client to give an extended response. Rather than focus on one question, however, clients often respond superficially and nonspecifically to the social worker's multiple inquiries, omitting important information in the process. Stacked questions thus have "low yield" and are unproductive and inefficient in gathering relevant information. Slowing down and asking one question at a time is preferable. If you have asked stacked questions (and all social workers have at many points), and the client hesitates in response, you can correct for the problem by repeating your preferred question.

Asking Leading Questions

Leading questions have hidden agendas designed to induce clients to agree with a particular view or to adopt a solution that social workers deem to be in clients' best interests. For example:

- "Do you think you've really tried to get along with your partner?"

- "You don't really mean that, do you?"

- "Aren't you too young to move out on your own?"

- "Don't you think that arguing with your mother will provoke her to come down on you as she has done in the past?"

In actuality, these types of questions often obscure legitimate concerns that social workers should discuss with clients. Social workers may conceal their feelings and opinions about such matters, however, and present them obliquely in the form of solutions (e.g., "Don't you think

you ought to . . .") in the hope that leading questions will guide clients to desired conclusions. It is an error, however, to assume that clients will not see through such maneuvers. Indeed, clients often discern the social worker's motives and inwardly resist having views or directives imposed on them under the guise of leading questions. Nevertheless, to avoid conflict or controversy with social workers, they may express feeble agreement or simply divert the discussion to another topic.

By contrast, when social workers authentically assume responsibility for concerns they wish clients to consider, they enhance the likelihood that clients will respond receptively to their questions. In addition, they can raise questions that are not slanted to imply the "correct" answer from the social worker's viewpoint. For example, "How have you attempted to reach agreement with your partner?" does not contain the hint about the "right" answer found in the first question given above. Similarly, the last question could be rephrased as follows: "I am not clear how you see arguing with your mother as likely to be more successful than it has proved in the past."

Interrupting Inappropriately or Excessively

Beginning social workers often worry excessively about covering all items on their own and their agency's agenda ("What will I tell my supervisor?"). To maintain focus on relevant problem areas, social workers must sometimes interrupt clients. To be effective, however, these interruptions must be purposeful, well timed, and smoothly executed. Interruptions may damage the helping process when they are abrupt or divert clients from exploring pertinent problem areas. Frequent untimely interruptions tend to annoy clients, stifle spontaneous expression, and hinder exploration of problems. Identifying and prioritizing key questions in advance with an outline can assist in avoiding this pattern.

Dominating the Interaction

At times, social workers may dominate the interaction by talking too much or by asking too many closed-ended questions, thus seizing the initiative for guiding discussions rather than placing this responsibility with clients. Other domineering behaviors by social workers include repeatedly offering advice, pressuring clients to improve, presenting lengthy arguments to convince clients, frequently interrupting, and so on. Some social workers are also prone to behave as though they are all-knowing, failing to convey respect for clients' points of view or capacities to solve problems. Such dogmatic and authoritarian behavior discourages clients from expressing themselves and fosters a one-up, one-down relationship in which clients feel at a great disadvantage and resent the social worker's supercilious demeanor.

Social workers should monitor the relative distribution of participation by all participants (including themselves) who are involved in individual, family, or group sessions. Although clients naturally vary in their levels of verbal participation and assertiveness, all group members should have equal opportunity to share information, concerns, and views in the helping process. Social workers have a responsibility to ensure that this opportunity is available to them.

As a general guideline, clients should consume more "speaking time" than social workers in the helping process, although during initial sessions with many Asian American clients, social workers must be more directive than they are with non-Asian clients, as discussed earlier. Sometimes social workers defeat practice objectives in group or conjoint sessions by dominating the interaction through such behaviors as speaking for members, focusing more on some members than on others, or giving speeches.

Even social workers who are not particularly verbal may dominate sessions that include reserved or nonassertive clients as a means of alleviating their own discomfort with silence and passivity. Although it is natural to be more active with reticent or withdrawn clients than with those who are more verbal, social workers must avoid seeming overbearing.

Using facilitative responses that draw clients out is an effective method of minimizing silence and passivity. When a review of one of your taped sessions reveals that you have monopolized the interaction, it is important that you explore the reasons for your behavior. Identify the specific responses that were authoritarian or domineering

and the events that preceded those responses. Also, examine the clients' style of relating for clues regarding your own reactions, and analyze the feelings you were experiencing at the time. Based on your review and assessment of your performance, you should then plan a strategy for modifying your own style of relating by substituting facilitative responses for ineffective ones. You may also need to focus on and explore the passive or nonassertive behavior of clients with the objective of contracting with them to increase their participation in the helping process.

Fostering Safe Social Interaction

Channeling or keeping discussions focused on safe topics that exclude feelings and minimize self-disclosures is inimical to the helping process. Social chit-chat about the weather, news, hobbies, mutual interests or acquaintances, and the like tends to foster a social rather than a therapeutic relationship. In contrast to the lighter and more diffuse communication characteristic of a social relationship, helpful, growth-producing relationships feature sharp focus and high specificity.

In general, safe social interaction in the helping process should be avoided. Two exceptions to this rule exist, however:

- Discussion of safe topics may be utilized to assist children or adolescents to lower their defenses and risk increasing openness, thereby assisting social workers to cultivate a quasi-friend role with such clients.

- A brief discussion of conventional topics may be appropriate and helpful as part of the getting-acquainted or warm-up period of initial sessions or during early portions of subsequent sessions. A warm-up period is particularly important when you are engaging clients from ethnic groups for which such informal openings are the cultural norm, as discussed in Chapter 3.

Even when you try to avoid inappropriate social interaction, however, some clients may resist your attempts to move the discussion to a topic that is relevant to the problems they are experiencing and to the purposes of the helping process. Techniques for managing such situations are found in Chapter 18 of the book. For now, simply note that it is appropriate for the social worker to bring up the agreed-upon agenda within a few minutes of the beginning of the session.

Responding Infrequently

Monitoring the frequency of your responses in individual, conjoint, or group sessions is an important task. As a social worker, you have an ethical responsibility to utilize fully the limited contact time you have with clients in pursuing your practice objectives and promoting your clients' general well-being. Relatively inactive social workers, however, usually ignore fruitful moments that could be explored to promote clients' growth, and they may allow the focus of a session to stray to inappropriate or unproductive content. To be maximally helpful, social workers must structure the helping process by developing contracts with clients that specify the respective responsibilities of both sets of participants. For their part, they engage clients in identifying and exploring problems, formulating goals, and delineating tasks to alleviate clients' difficulties.

Inactive social workers contribute to counterproductive processes and failures in problem solving. One deleterious effect, for example, is that clients lose confidence in social workers when they fail to intervene by helping clients with situations that are destructive to themselves or to others. In particular, clients' confidence is eroded if social workers fail to intervene when clients communicate destructively in conjoint or group sessions.

Although social workers' activity per se is important, the quality of their moment-by-moment responses is critical. Social workers significantly diminish their effectiveness by neglecting to utilize or by underutilizing facilitative responses.

Parroting or Overusing Certain Phrases or Clichés

Parroting a message irritates clients, who may issue a sharp rebuke to the social worker: "Well, yes, I just said that." Rather than merely repeating clients' words, social workers should use fresh language that captures the essence of clients' messages and places them in sharper perspective. In addition,

social workers should refrain from punctuating their communications with superfluous phrases. The distracting effect of such phrases can be observed in the following message:

Social worker: You know, a lot of people wouldn't come in for help. It tells me, you know, that you realize that you have a problem, you know, and want to work on it. Do you know what I mean?

Frequent use of such phrases as "you know," "Okay?" ("Let's work on this task, okay?"), "and stuff" ("We went to town, and stuff") or "that's neat" can annoy some clients (and social workers, for that matter). If used in excess, the same may be said of some of the faddish clichés that have permeated today's language—for example, "awesome," "sweet," "cool," "tight," or "dude."

Another mistake social workers sometimes make is trying to "overrelate" to youthful clients by using adolescent jargon to excess. Adolescents tend to perceive such communication as phony and the social worker as inauthentic, which hinders the development of a working relationship.

Dwelling on the Remote Past

Social workers' verbal responses may focus on the past, the present, or the future. Helping professionals differ regarding the amount of emphasis they believe should be accorded to gathering historical facts about clients. Focusing largely on the present is vital, however, because clients can change only their present circumstances, behaviors, and feelings. Permitting individuals, groups, couples, or families to dwell on the past may reinforce diversionary tactics they have employed to avoid dealing with painful aspects of their present difficulties and with the need for change.

Messages about the past may reveal feelings the client is currently experiencing related to the past. For example:

Client [*with trembling voice*]: He used to make me so angry.

Social worker: There was a time when he really infuriated you. As you think about the past, even now it seems to stir up some of the anger and hurt you felt.

As in this excerpt, changing a client's statement from past to present tense often yields rich information about clients' present feelings and problems. The same may be said of bringing future-oriented statements of clients to the present (e.g., "How do you feel now about the future event you're describing?"). As you see, it is not only possible but also often productive to shift the focus to the present experiencing of clients, even when historical facts are being elicited, in an effort to illuminate client problems.

Going on Fishing Expeditions

A danger that beginning (and many experienced) social workers face is pursuing content that is tangentially related to client concerns, issues of client and family safety, or legal mandates. Such content may relate to pet theories of social workers or agencies and be puzzling to clients. This kind of confusion may arise if the connection of these theories to the concerns that have brought clients into contact with the social worker is not clear. A wise precaution, therefore, would be to avoid taking clients into tangential areas if you cannot readily justify the rationale for that exploration. If the social worker feels that the exploration of new areas is relevant, then an explanation of its purpose is warranted.

GAUGING THE EFFECTIVENESS OF YOUR RESPONSES

The preceding discussion should assist you in identifying ineffective patterns of communication you may have been employing. Because most learners ask too many closed-ended questions, change the subject frequently, and recommend solutions before completing a thorough exploration of clients' problems, you should particularly watch for these patterns. In addition, you will need to monitor your interviewing style for idiosyncratic counterproductive patterns of responding.

The manual that is provided for instructors who use this book contains classroom exercises designed to assist students in recognizing and eliminating ineffective responses. Because identifying ineffective styles of interviewing requires selective focusing on the frequency and patterning of responses, you will also find it helpful to analyze extended segments of taped sessions using the form "Assessing Verbal Barriers to Communication," which is found at the end of this chapter.

One way of gauging the effectiveness of your responses is to carefully observe clients' reactions immediately following your responses. Because multiple clients are involved in group and family sessions, you will often receive varied verbal and nonverbal cues regarding the relative effectiveness of your responses when engaging clients in these systems.

As you assess your messages, keep in mind that a response is probably helpful if clients react in one of the following ways:

- They continue to explore the problem or stay on the topic.
- They express pent-up emotions related to the problematic situation.
- They engage in deeper self-exploration and self-experiencing.
- They volunteer more personally relevant material spontaneously.
- They affirm the validity of your response either verbally or nonverbally.

By contrast, a response may be too confrontational, poorly timed, or off target if clients react in one of the following ways:

- They reject your response either verbally or nonverbally.
- They change the subject.
- They ignore the message.
- They appear mixed up or confused.
- They become more superficial, more impersonal, more emotionally detached, or more defensive.
- They argue or express anger rather than examine the relevance of the feelings involved.

In analyzing social worker–client interactions, keep in mind that the participants mutually influence each other. Thus, a response by either person in an individual interview affects the expressions of the other person. In group and conjoint sessions, the communications of each person, including the social worker, affect the responses of all other participants. In a group situation, however, the influence of messages on the subsequent responses of other participants is sometimes difficult to detect because of the complexity of the communications.

Beginning interviewers often reinforce unproductive client responses by responding indiscriminately or haphazardly or by letting positive responses that support practice objectives or reflect growth pass without comment. It is important that you, as a beginning social worker, monitor and review your moment-by-moment transactions with clients with a view toward not allowing ineffective or destructive communication to be perpetuated by yourself and your clients.

Although beginning social workers may experience ineffective patterns of communication in individual interviews, they are even more likely to encounter recurring problematic communications in groups or in conjoint sessions with spouses or family members. In fact, orchestrating an effective conjoint interview or group meeting often presents a stiff challenge to even advanced social workers because of clients' rampant use of ineffective communications, which may provoke intense anger, defensiveness, and confusion among family or group members.

In summary, your task is twofold: You must monitor, analyze, and eliminate your own ineffective responses while simultaneously observing, managing, and modifying ineffective responses by your clients. That's a rather tall order. Although modifying dysfunctional communications among clients requires advanced skill, you can eliminate your own barriers to effective communication in a relatively short time. You will make even faster progress if you also eliminate ineffective styles of responding and test out your new communication skills in your private life. Unfortunately, many social workers compartmentalize and limit their helping skills to their work with clients but continue to use ineffective communication styles with their professional colleagues, friends, and families.

Social workers who have not fully integrated the helping skills into their private lives typically do not relate as effectively to their clients as do social workers who have fully implemented and assimilated those skills as a part of their general style of relating. We are convinced that to adequately master these essential skills and to fully tap into their potential for assisting clients, social workers must promote their own interpersonal competence and personality integration, thereby modeling for their clients the self-actualized or fully functioning person. Pursuing this personal goal prepares social workers for one of their major roles: teaching new skills of communicating and relating to their clients.

THE CHALLENGE OF LEARNING NEW SKILLS

Because of the unique nature of the helping process, establishing and maintaining a therapeutic relationship requires highly disciplined efforts on the social worker's part. Moment by moment, transaction by transaction, the social worker must sharply focus on the needs and problems of his or her clients. The success of each transaction is measured in terms of the social worker's adroitness in consciously applying specific skills to move the process toward the therapeutic objectives.

Interestingly, one of the major threats to learning new skills emanates from students' fear that in relinquishing their old styles of relating they are giving up an intangible, irreplaceable part of themselves. Similarly, students who have previously engaged in social work practice may experience fear related to the fact that they have developed methods or styles of relating that have influenced and "moved" clients in the past; abandoning these response patterns may mean surrendering a hard-won feeling of competency. These fears are often exacerbated when instruction and supervision in the classroom and practicum primarily strive to eliminate errors and ineffective interventions and responses rather than to develop new skills or enhance positive responses or interventions with clients. In such circumstances, students may receive considerable feedback about their errors but inadequate input regarding their effective responses or styles of relating. Consequently, they may feel

ASSESSING VERBAL BARRIERS TO COMMUNICATION				
Directions: In reviewing each 15-minute sample of taped interviews, tally your use of ineffective responses by placing marks in appropriate cells.				
15-Minute Taped Samples	*1*	*2*	*3*	*4*
1. Reassuring, sympathizing, consoling, or excusing				
2. Advising and giving suggestions or solutions prematurely				
3. Using sarcasm or employing humor that is distracting or makes light of clients' problems				
4. Judging, criticizing, or placing blame				
5. Trying to convince the client about the right point of view through logical arguments, lecturing, instructing, or arguing				
6. Analyzing, diagnosing, or making glib or dogmatic interpretations				
7. Threatening, warning, or counterattacking				
8. Stacking questions				
9. Asking leading questions				
10. Interrupting inappropriately or excessively				
11. Dominating the interaction				
12. Fostering safe social interaction				
13. Responding infrequently				
14. Parroting or overusing certain phrases or clichés				
15. Dwelling on the remote past				
16. Going on fishing expeditions				
Other responses that impede communication. List:				

ASSESSING PHYSICAL ATTENDING BEHAVIORS	
	Comments
1. Direct eye contact 0 1 2 3 4	
2. Warmth and concern reflected in facial expression 0 1 2 3 4	
3. Eyes at same level as client's 0 1 2 3 4	
4. Appropriately varied and animated facial expressions 0 1 2 3 4	
5. Arms and hands moderately expressive; appropriate gestures 0 1 2 3 4	
6. Body leaning slightly forward; attentive but relaxed 0 1 2 3 4	
7. Voice clearly audible but not loud 0 1 2 3 4	
8. Warmth in tone of voice 0 1 2 3 4	
9. Voice modulated to reflect nuances of feeling and emotional tone of client messages 0 1 2 3 4	
10. Moderate speech tempo 0 1 2 3 4	
11. Absence of distracting behaviors (fidgeting, yawning, gazing out window, looking at watch) 0 1 2 3 4	
12. Other 0 1 2 3 4	

Rating Scale:
0 = Poor, needs marked improvement.
1 = Weak, needs substantial improvement.
2 = Minimally acceptable, room for growth.
3 = Generally high level with a few lapses.
4 = Consistently high level.

vulnerable and stripped of their defenses (just as clients do) and experience more keenly the loss of something familiar.

As a beginning social worker, you must learn to openly and nondefensively receive constructive feedback about your ineffective or even destructive styles of relating or intervening. At the same time, you must take responsibility for eliciting positive feedback from educators and peers regarding your positive moment-by-moment responses. Remember that supervision time is limited and that the responsibility for utilizing that time effectively and for acquiring competency necessarily rests equally with you and your practicum instructor. It is also vital that you take steps to monitor your own growth systematically by reviewing audio- and videotapes, by counting your desirable and undesirable responses in client sessions, and by comparing your responses with the guidelines for constructing effective messages found in this book. Perhaps the single most important requirement for you in furthering your competency is to assume responsibility for advancing your own skill level by consistently monitoring your responses and practicing proven skills

Most of the skills delineated in this book are not easy to master. In fact, competent social workers will spend years perfecting their ability to sensitively and fully attune themselves to the inner experiencing of their clients; in furthering their capacity to share their own experiencing in an authentic, helpful manner; and in developing a keen sense of timing in employing these and other skills.

In the months ahead, as you forge new patterns of responding and test your newly developed skills, you will inevitably experience growing pains—that is, a sense of disequilibrium as you struggle to respond in new ways and, at the same time, to relate warmly, naturally, and attentively to your clients. Sometimes, you may feel that your responses are mechanistic and experience a keen sense of transparency: "The client will know that I'm not being real." If you work intensively to master specific skills, however, your awkwardness will gradually diminish, and you will eventually incorporate these skills naturally into your repertoire.

Summary

Chapter 7 outlined a series of nonverbal and verbal barriers to effective communication that are often experienced by beginning social workers. As you become alert to these potential obstacles and more skilled in applying more productive alternatives, you will become more confident in your progress. Chapter 8 asks you to apply your communication skills to one of the most important tasks you will face: conducting a multisystemic assessment.

Internet Resources

See our companion website for hot links to some helpful URLs. Note that URLs are subject to change. We will endeavor to update the links on the companion website as much as possible. For additional information about computer use in social services networks and links to other useful sites, you can access *http://ww2.uta.edu/cussn/*.

Related Online Content

Visit the *Direct Social Work Practice* companion website at *http://socialwork. wadsworth.com/hepworth7* for additional learning tools such as glossary terms, chapter outlines, InfoTrac College Edition keywords, relevant web links, and chapter practice quizzes. Also, be sure to check out the Direct Practice Virtual Reader, where the authors have personally selected articles relevant to this chapter using InfoMarks.

Notes

1. It is important not to set up artificial dichotomies that do not represent actual behaviors. Emma Gross (1995) argues, for example, that too frequently writers have inappropriately generalized across Native American cultures.
2. Reassurance is best directed to clients' capabilities. Appropriate reassurance can be effectively conveyed through the skill of positive feedback, as described in Chapter 5.

CHAPTER  8

Assessment: Exploring and Understanding Problems and Strengths

CHAPTER OVERVIEW

Assessment involves gathering information and formulating it into a coherent picture of the client and his or her circumstances. Because assessments involve social workers' inferences about the nature and causes of clients' difficulties, they serve as the basis for the rest of social workers' interactions with their clients—the goals they set, the interventions they enact, and the progress they evaluate. Chapter 8 focuses on the fundamentals of assessment and strategies used in assessing the problem and client strengths. Chapter 9 describes the characteristics that are taken into account when examining and portraying an individual's functioning and his or her relations with others and with the surrounding environment. Chapter 10 describes the methods and concepts employed when assessing family functioning and interactions.

This chapter begins by reviewing the complexity of assessment and drawing distinctions between assessment and diagnosis. Next, it examines the ways to attend to client strengths and assets, the sources of data that may inform the social worker's assessment, questions to bear in mind while conducting an assessment, and the various elements of problem analysis.

THE MULTIDIMENSIONALITY OF ASSESSMENT

Human problems—even those that appear to be simple at first glance—often involve a complex interplay of many factors. Rarely do sources of problems reside solely within an individual or within that individual's environment. Rather, *reciprocal interaction* occurs between a person and the external world. The person acts upon and responds to the external world, and the quality of those actions affects the external world's reactions (and vice versa). For example, a parent may complain about having poor communication with an adolescent child, attributing the difficulty to the fact that the teenager is sullen and refuses to talk about most things. The adolescent, in turn, may complain that it is pointless to talk with the parent because the latter consistently pries, lectures, or criticizes. Each participant's complaint about the other may be accurate, but each unwittingly behaves in ways that have produced and now maintain their dysfunctional interaction. Thus, the behavior of neither person is the sole cause of the breakdown in communication in a simple cause-and-effect (linear) fashion. Rather, their reciprocal interaction produces the difficulty; the behavior of each is both cause and effect, depending on one's vantage point.

The multidimensionality of human problems is also a consequence of the fact that human beings are social creatures who depend on both other human beings and complex social institutions to meet their needs. Meeting basic needs such as food, housing, clothing, and medical care requires adequate economic means and the availability of goods and services. Meeting educational, social, and recreational needs requires interaction with societal institutions. Meeting needs to feel close to and loved by others, to have companionship, to experience a sense of belonging, and to experience sexual gratification requires satisfactory social relationships within one's intimate relationships, family, social network, and community. Likewise, the extent to which people experience self-esteem depends on certain individual psychological factors and the quality of feedback from other people.

In conducting an assessment, a social worker needs extensive knowledge about the client and the numerous systems (e.g., economic, legal, educational, medical, religious, social, interpersonal) that impinge upon the client system. Assessing the functioning of an individual entails evaluating various aspects of that person's functioning. For example, the social worker may need to consider dynamic interactions among the individual's biophysical, cognitive, emotional, cultural, behavioral, and motivational subsystems and the relationships of those interactions to the client's problems. For a couple or family client system, assessment will entail paying attention to communication and interactional patterns as well as to each member of the system. Not every system and subsystem plays a significant role in the problems experienced by a given client system. However, overlooking relevant systems will result in an assessment that is incomplete at best and irrelevant or erroneous at worst. Interventions based on incomplete or inaccurate assessments, therefore, may be ineffective, misdirected, or even harmful.

In summary, the client's needs and the helping agency's purpose and resources will influence your choices and priorities during the assessment. You must be sure to attend to the client's immediate concern, or presenting problem; identify any legal or safety issues that may alter your priorities; be attuned to the many ways that strengths and resources may appear in the case; and consider all of the sources of information you may call upon to arrive at your assessment. You must also recognize the many facets to be taken into account in a multidimensional assessment, as well as the reciprocal nature of interactions, which requires an assessment that goes beyond mere cause and effect. Finally, you must be alert to your own history, values, biases and behaviors that might interject subjectivity into your interactions with clients and in the assessment that results.

DEFINING ASSESSMENT: PROCESS AND PRODUCT

The word *assessment* can be defined in several ways. For example, it refers to a process occurring between practitioner and client, in which information is gathered, analyzed, and synthesized to provide a concise picture of the client and his or her needs and strengths. In settings in which social work is the primary profession, the social worker often makes the assessment independently or consults with colleagues or a member of another discipline. Typically, formal assessments may be completed in one or two sessions. These assessments also represent opportunities to determine whether the agency or individual social worker is best suited to address the client's needs and wants. The social worker may identify the client's eligibility for services (for example, based on his or her insurance coverage or other admission criteria) and make a referral to other resources if either the program or the social worker is not appropriate to meet the client's needs.

In settings in which social work is not the only or not the primary profession (often called *secondary* or *host settings*), the social worker may be a member of a clinical team (e.g., in mental health, schools, medical, and correctional settings), and the process of assessment may be the joint effort of a psychiatrist, social worker, psychologist, nurse, teacher, and perhaps members of other disciplines. In such settings, the social worker typically compiles a social history and contributes knowledge related to interpersonal and family dynamics. The assessment process may take longer due to the time required for all of the team members to complete their individual assessments and to reach a collective assessment during a group meeting.

The focus of the assessment is also influenced by the auspices in which it takes place and the theoretical orientation from which the social worker practices. While some data are common to all interviews, the focus of a particular interview and assessment formulation may vary according to the social worker's mission, theoretical framework, or other factors. For example, a social worker who is investigating an allegation of child endangerment will ask questions and draw conclusions related to the level of risk or potential for violence in the case. A social worker whose expertise lies in cognitive-behavioral theory will structure the assessment to address the effects of misconceptions or cognitive distortions on the client's feelings and actions. A clinician in a correctional setting will use different concepts and standards to categorize offenders and to determine risks and needs (Beyer & Balster, 2001). This does not mean that in either case, the worker addresses *only* those issues, but rather that the questions asked and the conclusions drawn will be influenced by the social worker's mission, theory, and other factors.

Social workers engage in the process of assessment beginning with their initial contact with the client and lasting until the relationship's termination, which may occur weeks, months, or even years later. Thus, assessment is a fluid and dynamic process that involves receiving, analyzing, and synthesizing new information as it emerges during the entire course of a given case. In the first session, the social worker generally elicits abundant information; he or she must then assess that information's meaning and significance as the client–social worker interaction unfolds. This moment-by-moment assessment guides the social worker in deciding which information is salient and merits deeper exploration and which is less relevant to understanding the individual and the presenting problem. After gathering sufficient information to illuminate the situation, the social worker analyzes it and, in collaboration with the client, integrates the data into a tentative formulation of the problem. Many potential clients do not proceed with the social worker beyond this point. If their concerns can be best handled through a referral to other resources, if they do not meet eligibility criteria, or if they choose not to continue the relationship, contact often stops here.

Should the social worker and the client continue the contact, assessment continues as well, although it

is not a central focus of the work. Clients often disclose new information as problem solving progresses, casting the original evaluation in a new light. Sometimes this new perspective emerges as the natural result of coming to know the client better. In other cases, clients may withhold vital information until they are certain that the social worker is trustworthy and capable of helping them. As a result, preliminary assessments often prove inaccurate and must be discarded or drastically revised.

Note that the term *assessment* also refers to the written products that result from the process of understanding the client. As a product, assessment involves an actual formulation or statement *at a given time* regarding the nature of clients' problems and other related factors. A formal assessment requires analysis and synthesis of relevant data into a working definition of the problem that identifies associated factors and clarifies how they interact to produce and maintain the problem. Because assessments must constantly be updated and revised, it is helpful to think of an assessment as *a complex working hypothesis based on the most current data available.*

Written assessments range from comprehensive psychosocial reports to brief analyses about very specific issues, such as the client's mental status, substance use, or suicidal risk. They may summarize progress on a case or provide a comprehensive overview of the client to facilitate his or her transfer to another resource or termination of the client–social worker contact.

The scope and focus of the written product and of the assessment itself will vary depending on three factors: the *role* of the social worker, the *setting* in which he or she works, and the *needs* presented by the client. For example, a school social worker's assessment of an elementary school student may focus on the history and pattern of disruptive behaviors in the classroom, as well as on the classroom environment itself. A social worker in a family services agency seeing the same child may focus more broadly on the child's developmental history and his or her family's dynamics, as well as on the troubling classroom behavior. In another example, a hospital social worker whose focus is discharge planning may evaluate a client's readiness to leave the hospital after heart surgery and determine the services and information needed to make the return home successful. A social worker in a community health or mental health agency may assess the impact of the disease and the surgery on the client's emotional well-being and on his or her marital relationship. A social worker in a vocational setting may focus the assessment on the client's readiness to return to work and the job accommodations needed to facilitate that transition.

While the social worker's setting will lead to focused assessment on particular issues pertinent to that setting, certain priorities in assessment influence all social work settings. Without prioritization, workers run the risk of conducting unbalanced, inefficient, or misdirected evaluations. Initially, three issues should be assessed in all situations:

1. *What does the client see as his or her primary problems or concerns?* Sometimes referred to as "starting where the client is," this question highlights social work's emphasis on client self-determination and commitment to assisting clients (where legal, ethical, and possible) to reach their own goals. Practically speaking, sharing concerns helps alleviate the client of some of the burdens and apprehensions that brought him or her to the interview.

2. *What (if any) current or impending legal mandates must the client and social worker consider?* If the client is mandated to receive services or faces other legal concerns, this factor may shape the nature of the assessment and the way the client presents himself or herself. Therefore, it is important to "get this issue on the table" at the outset. For example, an adult protection worker must assess the risk of abuse, neglect, or other danger to an elderly client, whether or not the client shares those concerns.

3. *What (if any) potentially serious health or safety concerns might require the social worker's and client's attention?* Social workers must be alert to health problems and other conditions that may place clients at risk. These issues may

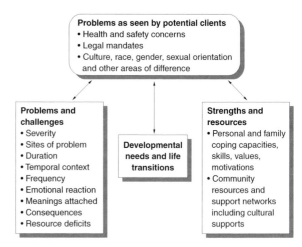

Figure 8-1 Overview: Areas for Attention in Assessing Strengths and Problems

be central to the client's presenting problem, or they may indicate a danger that requires immediate intervention by the worker. While the profession places high value on client self-determination, social workers must act—even if it means overruling the client's wishes—in situations that present "serious, foreseeable, and imminent harm" (NASW, 1999, p. 7).

After addressing these three fundamental questions, the social worker goes on to explore the client's functioning, interactions with his or her environment, problems and challenges, strengths and resources, developmental needs and life transitions, and key systems related to the case. The remainder of this chapter and Chapter 9 further delineate how each of these areas is assessed (see Figure 8-1).

ASSESSMENT AND DIAGNOSIS

It is important at this point to clarify the difference between diagnoses and assessments. *Diagnoses* are labels or terms that may be applied to an individual or his or her situation. A diagnosis provides a shorthand categorization based on specifically defined criteria. It can reflect a medical condition (e.g., "end-stage renal disease," "diabetes"), mental disorder (e.g., "depression," "agoraphobia"), or other classification (e.g., "mild retardation," "emotionally and behaviorally disturbed," "learning disabled"). Diagnostic labels serve many purposes. For example, they provide a language through which professionals and patients can communicate about a commonly understood constellation of symptoms. The use of accepted diagnostic terminology facilitates research on problems, identification of appropriate treatments or medications, and linkages among people with similar problems. For example, diagnosing a set of troubling behaviors as "bi-polar disorder" helps the client's physician and social worker identify necessary medication and therapeutic services. The diagnosis may comfort the client by helping "put a name to" the experiences he or she has been having. It may also help the client learn more about the disease, locate support groups, and stay abreast of developments in understanding the disorder.

But diagnoses have their difficulties, too. Although such labels provide an expedient way of describing complex problems, they never tell the whole story. Diagnoses can become self-fulfilling prophecies, wherein clients, their families, and their helpers begin to define the client only in terms of the diagnostic label. This distinction is captured in the difference between saying "Joe is a schizophrenic," "Joe has schizophrenia," or "Joe is a person with schizophrenia." While these labels carry a lot of power, they can sometimes be bestowed in error (the result of misdiagnosis or a diagnosis that changes over time), and they may obscure important information about the client's difficulties and capacities. Referring to a client as "mildly retarded," for example, may speak only to that individual's score on an IQ test—not to his or her level of daily functioning, interests, goals, joys, and challenges.

At this point, assessment steps in. Assessments describe the symptoms that support a particular diagnosis, but they go further to help us understand the client's history and background, the effect of the symptoms on the client, the available support and resources to manage the problem, and so on. In other words, diagnoses may result from assessments, but they tell only part of the story.

CULTURALLY COMPETENT ASSESSMENT

This book discusses many cultural factors related to various aspects of the helping process. In this section, we focus on general cultural factors that have relevance for the process of assessment. Here, we emphasize culture as it relates not only to racial or ethnic groups, but also to other groups (e.g., gay, lesbian, bisexual, transgendered, hearing impaired, elderly, and persons in recovery) that reflect distinct cultural attributes. Culturally competent assessment requires knowledge of cultural norms, acculturation, and language differences; the ability to differentiate between individual and culturally linked attributes; the initiative to seek out needed information so that evaluations are not biased and services are culturally appropriate; and an understanding of the ways that cultural differences may reveal themselves in the assessment process.

Cultures vary widely in their prescribed patterns of child-rearing, communication, family member roles, mate selection, and care of the aged—to name just a few areas of differentiation. For example, to whom would you address concerns in a Latino family about a child's truancy? What are normative dating patterns in the gay and lesbian communities? What are appropriate expectations for independence for a young adult with Down syndrome? How might Laotian parents view their child's educational aspirations?

Knowledge of your client's cultural norms is indispensable when the client's cultural background differs markedly from your own. Without such knowledge, you may make serious errors in assessing both individual and interpersonal systems, because patterns that are functional in one cultural context may prove problematic in another, and vice versa. Such errors in assessment may potentially lead to culturally insensitive interventions that may aggravate rather than diminish clients' problems. The necessary knowledge about cultural norms is not easy to obtain, however. It requires a baseline understanding of areas of difference and histories and risks of oppression experienced by different groups, self-examination for biases and prejudices, and ongoing conversation with clients and other key informants (Gilbert, 2003; Smith, 2004).

This last piece is important because of the considerable variations that occur within ethnic groups. Making overgeneralizations about members of these groups may obscure (rather than clarify) the meanings of individual behavior. For example, more than 400 different tribal groups of Native Americans live in the United States, and these groups speak more than 250 distinct languages (Edwards, 1983). Comparisons of Plains tribes with Native Americans of the Southwest have revealed sharply contrasting cultural patterns and patterns of individual behavior as well as marked differences in the incidence of certain social problems (May, Hymbaugh, Aase, & Samet, 1983). Similarly significant heterogeneity exists within every racial and cultural group.

Even where homogeneity exists in cultural subgroups, wide variations also exist among individuals. As a consequence, being knowledgeable about the cultural characteristics of a given group is necessary but not sufficient for understanding the behavior of individual members of the groups. The task confronting practitioners, therefore, is to differentiate between behavior that is culturally mediated and behavior that is a product of individual personality. In-depth knowledge about a given cultural group helps in making such distinctions. When in doubt, however, practitioners are advised to consult with well-informed and cooperative members of the culture in question.

In assessing the functioning of someone from an ethnic minority, it is important to consider the degree to which he or she experiences a goodness of fit with the culture in which he or she is situated. Ethnic minority clients are actually members of two cultures (or perhaps more, depending on the differences in the parents' families of origin), so their functioning must be considered in relationship to both their culture of origin and the majority culture. Clients from the same ethnic group may vary widely in the degree of their acculturation or their comfort with biculturalism due to several factors—for example, the number of generations

that have passed since the original emigration, the degree of socialization, and interactions with the majority culture. Consider these possibilities for distinguishing individual members of an ethnic minority:

1. The degree of commonality between the two cultures with regard to norms, values, beliefs, perceptions, and the like

2. The availability of cultural translators, mediators, and models

3. The amount and type (positive or negative) of feedback provided by each culture regarding attempts to produce normative behaviors

4. The conceptual style and problem-solving approach of the minority individual and his or her mesh with the prevalent or valued styles of the majority culture

5. The individual's degree of bilingualism

6. The degree of dissimilarity in physical appearance from the majority culture, such as skin color, facial features, and so forth (De Anda, 1984, p. 102)

Members of nondominant groups may experience psychological difficulties as a result of trying to identify with the dominant group while being treated in a prejudiced or racist manner by members of the group they aspire to join (Mayadas, Ramanathan, & Suarez., 1998–1999). Other difficulties may emerge from conflicting values between cultures. For example, Jamaicans and clients from other Caribbean countries are acculturated in their homelands, even though in the United States they may be categorized as African-Americans on the basis of skin tone or other features. Amish men or women who choose to leave the faith may find themselves caught between two worlds and accepted in neither (McGoldrick, Giordano, & Pearce, 1996). A lesbian whose religious faith condemns homosexuality may have difficulty reconciling her two worlds. These examples support the need for social workers to assess the biculturalism of clients, to sensitize themselves to various cultures, to encourage clients to maintain ties to their cultural roots, and to understand the complexities of interacting with other cultures.

Cultural self-awareness is likewise important for social workers themselves, as that knowledge will help them understand and serve their clients better (Gilbert, 2003).

Social workers should also consider the client's degree of bilingualism when conducting an assessment. In settings where multilingual services are unavailable, non–English-speaking clients may have great difficulty in formulating and explaining their problems. Even for clients who have a strong command of English, care providers "should be aware that the foundational thought structures through which the client processes the world will likely be in the primary language, with English language interpretations only a rough equivalent of the original. Subtle shifts in meaning can create confusion, frustration and even fear in the client or the client's family (Ratliff, 1996, pp. 170–171). An interpreter may be called in to bridge the language gap. Even when one is used, however, the social worker should recognize that interpretations may merely approximate what the client is attempting to convey. If an interpreter is not available, it is important to speak in simple terms and to proceed at a slower pace. Clients need ample time to process messages, and practitioners must exercise care in checking out whether clients have grasped the intended meaning of their messages and whether they have truly understood what the client is trying to express.

The use of interpreters is also an important issue to consider when working with deaf clients (Santos, 1995). The primary language used by many deaf people is American Sign Language (ASL), which is a unique and separate language from English, not merely a visual translation of English. Interpreters are often a necessity for deaf clients to communicate effectively with hearing social workers; at the same time, social workers should bear in mind that concepts may not be easily transferred from ASL to English. For this reason, they should take time to ensure that concepts are being accurately understood on both ends. Social workers working with deaf clients who use ASL should also apply the factors mentioned earlier for spoken language to make

sure that language differences do not become barriers to effective treatment.

Another issue for assessment is considering how the client's fluency in English may contribute to the presenting problem (e.g., the school is angry at the parents for not coming to teacher conferences when, in fact, the family didn't understand that they were required to do so). Language differences can block access to essential community resources (especially for clients isolated from their cultural reference groups) and limit access to information through newspapers, radio, and television. These obstacles, therefore, may produce social isolation and deprive people of information essential to locating and utilizing essential resources.

Clients from cultural groups that have endured a history of marginalization, oppression, and prejudice may approach helping agencies (and their representatives) with skepticism and even hostility. The possible reasons underlying this posture should be factored into the assessment process and findings. You can address anger and apprehensions by being genuine, trustworthy, and committed to the client's best interests (Harper & Lantz, 1996; Rooney, 1992). This interaction may be facilitated if the client and practitioner have some degree of cultural similarity. Of course, even when the social worker and client share a cultural background, they may differ in other important ways, such as values, education, socioeconomic status, and level of acculturation.

Cross-cultural contact also occurs between minority practitioners and clients from the majority culture. While the minority practitioner is usually more familiar with the majority culture than the majority practitioner is with minority cultures, clients often challenge the credibility of minority practitioners (Hardy, 1993; Proctor & Davis, 1994).

The client may ascribe credibility to a social worker because of his or her education, position, role, age, gender, and other factors emphasized in the client's culture—that is, because of factors over which a practitioner has little control. Credibility can also be achieved, however, when clients have favorable experiences with practitioners who foster respect, confidence, trust, and hope (Harper & Lantz, 1996); who address areas of difference in a straightforward manner; and who seek to learn about the client's culture by asking the client.

EMPHASIZING STRENGTHS IN ASSESSMENTS

Clients typically seek social work services for help with problems or difficulties. As a result, the assessment typically focuses on the problem—albeit sometimes with an overemphasis on client pathology and dysfunction at the expense of strengths, capacities, and achievements whose recognition might help provide a fuller understanding of the client. Research suggests that many social workers underestimate client strengths. While clients "presented themselves as proactive, autonomous, human beings . . . able to enhance their functioning and their competence," their workers viewed them as "reactive organisms with continuing problems, underlying weaknesses, and limited potentialities" (Maluccio, 1979, p. 399). Others (Presley, 1987; Toseland, 1987) found that clients who did not return after one session often terminated service "prematurely" for reasons other than dissatisfaction (e.g., because they felt they had benefited from the session and needed no further help). Presley thus concluded that "therapists may have a more fragile image of the client than appears warranted" (1987, p. 607).

Perhaps this negativism stems from a historical emphasis on client deficits (Saleeby, 1997), which viewed the professional's job as "fixing" the problem or person. It may also stem from eligibility requirements that require the client to look problem laden so as to qualify for (or continue to receive) services (Frager, 2000).That is, the funding for services, whether it comes through insurance reimbursement or government contracts, may be based on the client's difficulties and level of impairment. Emphasizing clients' strengths in a case report may cause utilization reviewers to question whether services are needed at all. In addition, some assessments are negative because they reflect troubling attitudes, values, or burnout on the part of the social worker, who may hold the client in contempt.

This tendency to focus on pathology has several important ramifications. First, to tap client strengths effectively, practitioners must be sensitive to them and skillful in utilizing them to accomplish case goals. Second, social workers who fail to account for strengths and selectively attend to pathology are ill equipped to determine the client's potential for growth and the steps needed to get there. Third, a large proportion of clients need help in enhancing their self-esteem. Troubled by self-doubts, feelings of inadequacy, and even feelings of worthlessness, their lack of self-confidence and self-respect underlies many dysfunctional cognitive, emotional, and behavioral patterns, including fears of failure, depression, social withdrawal, alcoholism, and hypersensitivity to criticism—to name just a few. To assist clients to view themselves more positively, social workers and their agencies must first view their clients more positively.

To emphasize strengths and empowerment in the assessment process, Cowger makes three suggestions to social workers:

1. Give preeminence to the *client's* understanding of the facts.
2. Discover what the client wants.
3. Assess personal and environmental strengths on multiple levels (1994, p. 265).

Cowger (1994) has developed a two-dimensional matrix framework for assessment that can assist social workers in attending to both needs and strengths. On the vertical axis, potential strengths and resources are depicted at one end and potential deficits, challenges, and obstacles are shown at the other end. The horizontal axis ranges from environmental (family and community) to individual factors. This framework provides a useful way to press us to move beyond the frequent preoccupation with personal deficits (*quadrant 4*), to include personal strengths and environmental strengths and obstacles (Cowger, 1992; see Figure 8-2). The case example demonstrates this framework in action.

Figure 8-2 Framework for Assessment

Source: Adapted from Charles D. Cowger, Assessment of Client Strengths. In D. Saleeby, *The strengths perspective in social work practice* (2nd ed.) (Figure 5.2, p. 69). Boston: Allyn & Bacon. Reprinted by permission of Allyn & Bacon.

CASE EXAMPLE

Tom is 20 years old, is Caucasian, and has been in the mental health system since he was 9 years old. He was raised by his mother and never knew his father. Tom had many problems during childhood and was placed in residential facilities on at least three occasions. His primary childhood diagnosis was conduct disorder, and he frequently got into fights during his adolescence. Records consistently indicate that Tom and his mother had a very stressful relationship. Tom's maternal grandparents were somewhat involved in his life, and he thinks highly of them. He reports feeling much love and support from them while he was growing up.

Tom was placed in a juvenile facility when he was 17 after hospitalization on a mental health unit, where he displayed psychotic behaviors and was occasionally violent. Just prior to turning 18, Tom entered the adult mental health system. At that time, he was transferred from a residential juvenile facility to the adult facility where he currently resides.

Tom is hoping to move into an apartment with his significant other (Sarah) in the near future. He currently has several diagnoses, including obsessive-compulsive disorder, bipolar disorder, anxiety disorder, and learning disorder. Although medication seems to control his troubling thoughts, he is easily frustrated and prone to verbal outbursts. Tom's overall IQ is 84, and he continues to attend special education classes at his high school, which he can continue to do until his twenty-second birthday. Tom has experienced considerable difficulty in maintaining part-time employment, even when the jobs included support from his school program. His level of independent living skills is assessed at well below the minimum needed to live independently. Tom has difficulty completing household tasks, including cooking and cleaning, without much assistance. In addition, he has difficulty in managing his money. Tom has learned to use public transportation, but he becomes easily aggravated when he must remember which bus to take and will sometimes take a cab home despite a lack of funds to pay the fare. Tom has consistently refused assistance in any of these areas, reporting that he does not need help.

Tom and Sarah met at a mental health facility and have known each other for about 6 months. Sarah has somewhat better independent living skills and reports that she will help Tom with cooking and taking the bus, among other things. Neither is currently employed, but both plan to get jobs to support themselves. They are now asking for assistance from staff in moving into an apartment together.

To assist in using the assessment framework, the information in the case example has been applied to the matrix in Figure 8-2. For example, *quadrant 4* (individual deficits, challenges, or obstacles) includes the behavioral consequences and difficulties related to Tom's multiple diagnoses. His difficulties with independent living skills and tendencies toward violence are concerns in relation to his living plans. Sarah may be in danger of domestic violence. In addition, without birth control, they may begin a pregnancy soon. Tom's low IQ may impede his learning the necessary independent living skills. The stressful relationship with his mother is of long standing. Finally, Tom is not open to obtaining help with these concerns, focusing instead on his desire to move in with Sarah.

Moving to *quadrant 3* (environmental factors, including family and community deficits, obstacles, and challenges), we note the stressful relationship between Tom and his mother and her probable lack of support for his plan. If he lives in the community, Tom's treatment will likely be primarily based on medication rather than mental health counseling. In addition, the mental health system is often lacking in resources to support independent living. Employment opportunities commensurate with Tom's skills may be limited as well.

When we move above the horizontal axis to consider potential strengths and resources, we become alerted to additional factors that are essential to the assessment. In *quadrant 1* (potential community resources and strengths), we note that Tom's grandparents have been a valuable source of support in the past and could possibly fill this role again. Sarah supports their joint plan. The high school can continue to support him in pursuing his education. Staff in his current facility and vocational services can assist Tom with acquiring more independent living skills. Finally, Tom's mother may be engaged in assisting Tom in making his plans succeed.

In *quadrant 2* (potential personal strengths and resources), we are struck by the fact that Tom has a clear goal to which he is highly committed. He has begun work on many independent living skills, is taking the bus, and is motivated to begin employment. Tom has developed a caring relationship with Sarah, and she is willing to commit to a more permanent relationship. His medication is assisting him in controlling psychotic thoughts.

This framework highlights two facts: A useful assessment is not limited to either deficits or strengths, and both the environmental and personal dimensions are important. Use of all four quadrants provides information that can help in pursuing the client's goals, while remaining mindful of obstacles and challenges.

The following list emphasizes strengths that may be overlooked or taken for granted during assessment. Cultivating your sensitivity to these strengths will help you be attuned to others as they emerge:

1. Facing problems and seeking help, rather than denying or otherwise avoiding confronting them
2. Risking by sharing problems with the social worker—a stranger
3. Persevering under difficult circumstances
4. Being resourceful and creative in making the most out of limited resources
5. Seeking to further knowledge, education, and skills
6. Expressing caring feelings to family members and friends
7. Asserting one's rights rather than submitting to injustice
8. Being responsible in work or financial obligations
9. Seeking to understand the needs and feelings of others
10. Having the capacity for introspection or for examining situations by considering different perspectives
11. Demonstrating the capacity for self-control
12. Being able to function effectively in stressful situations
13. Demonstrating the ability to consider alternative courses of actions and the needs of others when solving problems

SOURCES OF INFORMATION

Where do social workers get the information on which to base their assessment? Numerous sources can be used individually or in combination. The following are the most common:

1. Background sheets or other forms that clients complete
2. Interviews with clients (i.e., accounts of problems, history, views, thoughts, events, and the like)
3. Direct observation of nonverbal behavior

4. Direct observation of interaction between marital partners, family members, and group members

5. Collateral information from relatives, friends, physicians, teachers, employers, and other professionals

6. Tests or assessment instruments

7. Personal experiences of the practitioner based on direct interaction with clients

The *information obtained from client interviews* is usually the primary source of assessment information. The skills described in Chapters 5 and 6 for structuring and conducting effective interviews will help in establishing a trusting relationship and acquiring the information needed for assessment. It is important to respect clients' feelings and reports, to use empathy to convey understanding, to probe for depth, and to check with the client to ensure that your understanding is accurate. Interviews with child clients may be enhanced or facilitated by use of instruments (McConaughy & Achenbach, 1994; Schaffer, 1992). As with other information sources, verbal reports often need to be augmented because faulty recall, biases, mistrust, and limited self-awareness on the part of clients may not present a wholly accurate picture.

Direct observation of nonverbal behavior adds information about emotional states and reactions such as anger, hurt, embarrassment, and fear. To use these sources of data, the social worker must be attentive to nonverbal cues, such as tone of voice, tears, clenched fists, voice tremors, quivering hands, tightened jaws, pursed lips, variations of expression, and gestures; he or she must link these behaviors to the topic or theme during which they arise. The social worker may share these observations in the moment ("Your whole body deflated when you were telling me what she said") or note them to be included with other data.

Observations of interactions between spouses or partners, family members, and group members are also often enlightening. Social workers frequently are amazed at the striking differences between clients' reports of their relationships and the behaviors they actually demonstrate in those relationships. A social worker may observe a father

interacting with his daughter, impatiently telling her "I know you can do better"; in an earlier session, however, the father may have described his behavior to her as "encouraging." Direct observation may reveal that his words are encouraging while his tone and behaviors are not.

Observation can occur in natural settings (e.g., a child in the classroom, adults in a group setting, or a family as they answer a worker's question in session). Home visits are a particularly helpful forum for observation. One major benefit of in-home, family-based services is the opportunity to observe family difficulties firsthand rather than rely on secondhand accounts (Ronnau & Marlow, 1995). Observing clients' living conditions may reveal resources or problems that would otherwise not come to light.

Social workers can also employ *enactment* to observe interactions firsthand rather than rely on verbal report. With this technique, clients reenact an event during a session. Participants are instructed to recreate the situation exactly as it occurred, using the same words, gestures, and tones of voice as in the actual event. You might explain: "To understand what produced the difficulties in the event you just described, I'd like you to recreate the situation here in our session. By seeing what both of you do and say, and how you do it, I can get an accurate picture of what actually happens. I'd like you to replay the situation exactly as it happened. Use the same words, gestures, and tone of voice as you did originally. Now, where were you when it happened, and how did it start?" To counteract the temptation to create a favorable impression, the social worker can ask each participant about the extent to which the behaviors demonstrated in the enactment correspond with the behaviors that occurred in actual situations.

Enactment can also be used in contrived situations to see how a couple or family interact in situations that involve decision making, planning, role negotiation, child discipline, or similar activities. Social workers will need to exercise their creativity in designing situations likely to generate and clarify the types of interaction that the practitioner desires to observe. Another form of enactment involves the use of symbolic interactions—for example, through the use of dolls, games, or other forms of expressive or play therapy (Jordan & Hickerson, 2003).

Remember, however, that direct observation is subject to perceptual errors by the observer. Take care when drawing conclusions from your observations. Scrutinize how congruent your conclusions are with the information acquired from other sources. Despite the flaws, information from various forms of direct observation adds significantly to that gained from verbal reports.

Client self-monitoring is a potent source of information (Kopp, 1989). It produces a rich and quantifiable body of data and empowers the client by turning him or her into a collaborator in the assessment process. In self-monitoring, clients track symptoms on logs or in journals, write descriptions, and record feelings, behaviors, and thoughts associated with particular times, events, or difficulties. The first step in self-monitoring is to recognize the occurrence of the event (e.g., events that lead to anger outbursts, temper tantrums by children, episodes of drinking or overeating). Using self-anchored rating scales (Jordan & Franklin, 2003) or simple counting measures, clients and/or those around them can keep a record of the frequency or intensity of a behavior. How often was Joe late for school? How severe was Joan's pain in the morning, at noon, and in the evening? Which nights did Ralph have particular difficulty sleeping? Did this difficulty relate to events during the day, medications, stresses, or anything he ate or drank?

A major advantage of self-monitoring is that the process itself requires the monitor to focus attention on patterns. As a result, clients gain insights into their situations and the circumstances surrounding their successes or setbacks. As they discuss their recorded observations, they may "spontaneously operationalize goals and suggest ideas for change" (Kopp, 1989, p. 278). The process of recording also assists in evaluation, because progress can be tracked more precisely by examining data that show a reduction of problematic behaviors or feelings and an increase in desirable characteristics.

Another source for assessment data is *collateral contacts*—that is, information provided by relatives, friends, teachers, physicians, child care providers, and others who possess essential insights about relevant aspects of clients' lives. Of course, social workers must exercise discretion when deciding that such information is needed and in obtaining it. Clients can assist in this effort by suggesting collateral contacts who may provide useful information; their written consent (through agency "release of information" forms) is required prior to making contact with these sources.

In weighing the validity of information obtained from collateral sources, it is important to consider the nature of their relationship with the client and the ways in which that might influence these contacts' perspectives. For example, members of the immediate family may be emotionally involved or exhausted by the client's difficulties and unconsciously skew their reports accordingly. Individuals who have something to gain or to lose from pending case decisions (e.g., custody of a child, residential placement) may be less credible than individuals who are further removed from case situations. Conversely, individuals who have limited contact with the client (such as other service providers) may have narrowed or otherwise skewed views of the client's situation. As with other sources of information, input from collateral contacts must be critically viewed and weighed against other information in the case.

Another possible source of information consists of various *assessment instruments,* including psychological tests, screening instruments, and assessment tools. Some of these tests are administered by professionals, such as psychologists or educators, who have undergone special training in the administration and scoring of such assessment tools. In these cases, social workers might receive reports of the testing and incorporate the findings into their psychosocial assessments or treatment plans. Examples of these instruments include intelligence tests such as the WAIS or WISC (Lukas, 1993), tests of neurological functioning such as the Bender Gestalt, or projective tests such as the Rorschach or the TAT (Thematic Apperception Test).

Some instruments are designed for use by social workers and allied professionals. Examples include the WALMYR Assessment Scales, which can be used to measure depression, self-esteem, clinical stress, anxiety, alcohol involvement, peer relations, sexual attitudes, homophobia, marital satisfaction, sexual satisfaction, nonphysical abuse of partners, and a variety of other clinical phenomena.[1] Instruments such as the Beck Depression Inventory (Beck, Rush, Shaw & Emery, 1979) and the Beck Scale for Suicidal Ideation (Range & Knott, 1997) have well-established validity and reliability, can be effectively administered and scored by clinicians from a variety of professions, and can assist practitioners in evaluating the seriousness of a client's condition. Other instruments to measure alcohol or drug impairment may be conducted by the social worker, self-administered by the client, or computer-administered (Abbott & Wood, 2000).

Other tools may be helpful for identifying clients' strengths and needs, when used within the context of an assessment interview (VanHook, Berkman, & Dunkle, 1996). Examples include the Primary Care Evaluation of Mental Health Disorders (PRIME-MD), which helps with the identification of mental health problems (Spitzer et al., 1994), and the Older Americans Resources and Services Questionnaire (OARS), which provides information about the client's functioning across a variety of domains, including economic and social resources and activities of daily living (George & Fillenbaum, 1990). Other tools can be applied to a range of client populations to measure variables such as social functioning, well-being, mental functioning, and social networks (Wodarski & Thyer, 1998), and still others may be used in the evaluation of specific syndromes, such as eating disorders, conduct disorders, or anxiety.

Taking the use of instruments a step further, Nurius and Hudson (1988, 1993) have reported on the development of a computer-based evaluation tool that includes all of the WALMYR Assessment Scales and a Multi-Problem Screening Inventory (MPSI). The MPSI is a multidimensional self-report measure that helps practitioners to better assess and understand the severity or magnitude of client problems across 27 different areas of personal and social functioning. The completed instrument helps both the client and the social worker evaluate areas of difficulty and determine the relative severity of difficulties in the various life areas. In addition to providing for better accuracy and efficiency, these and other computerized instruments simplify the tracking of results over time and assist in gathering data for determining case progress.

Tests and screening instruments represent useful and expedient methods of quantifying data and behaviors. As a consequence, they can play an important role in assessments, case planning, and outcome evaluations. To use these tools effectively, however, practitioners must be well grounded in knowledge of test theory and in the characteristics of specific tests. Many tests, for example, have biases, low reliability, and poor validity; some are ill suited for certain clients and thus should be used with extreme caution. To avoid the danger of misusing these tools, social workers should thoroughly understand any instruments they are using or recommending, and seek consultation in the interpretation of tests administered by other professionals. Sources such as Corcoran and Fischer (1999), Thyer and Wodarski (1998 Wodarski and Thyer (1998), and Bloom, Fischer, and Orme (1999) can acquaint social workers with both available instruments and their proper use.

A final source of information for assessment is the social worker's *personal experience* based on direct interaction with clients. You will react in different ways to different clients, and these insights may prove useful in understanding how others respond to them. For example, you may view certain clients as being withdrawn, personable, dependent, caring, manipulative, seductive, assertive, overbearing, or determined. For instance, a client who reports that others take him for granted and place unreasonable demands upon him may appear to you to be self-deprecating and go to great lengths to please you. These experiences may provide you with clues about the nature of his complaint that others take advantage of him.

Some cautions are warranted with using this method. Clients may not behave with the social worker as they do with other people. Apprehension, involuntariness, and the desire to make a good impression may all skew the client's presentation of himself or herself. Also, initial impressions can be misleading and must be confirmed by additional contact with the client or other sources of information. All human beings' impressions are subjective and may be influenced by our own interpersonal patterns and perceptions. Before drawing even tentative conclusions, scrutinize your reactions to identify possible biases, distorted perceptions, or actions on your part that may have contributed to clients' behavior. For example, confrontational behavior on your part may spur a defensive response by the client. Perhaps the response reveals more about your actions than it represents the client's typical way of relating. Your perceptions of and reactions to clients may also be distorted by your own life experiences.

Self-awareness is indispensable to drawing valid conclusions from your interactions with clients and to creating assessments that give a thorough, accurate, and helpful representation of the client's history, strengths, and challenges.

QUESTIONS TO ANSWER IN PROBLEM ASSESSMENT

The following questions are not intended to be *asked* in the assessment, but instead are meant to be used by you as the social worker as a *checklist* to ensure that you have not overlooked a significant factor in your assessment of the problem.

1. What are the clients' concerns and problems as they perceive them?

2. Are any current or impending legal mandates relevant to the situation?

3. Do any serious health or safety issues need attention?

4. What are specific indications of the problem? How is it manifesting itself?

5. What persons and systems are involved in the problem(s)?

6. How do the participants and/or systems interact to produce and maintain the problem(s)?

7. What unmet needs and/or wants are involved?

8. What developmental stage or life transition is entailed in the problem(s)?

9. How severe is the problem, and how does it affect the participants?

10. What meanings do clients ascribe to the problem(s)?

11. Where do the problematic behaviors occur?

12. When do the problematic behaviors occur?

13. What is the frequency of the problematic behaviors?

14. What is the duration of the problem(s)?

15. What are the consequences of the problem?

16. Have other issues (e.g., alcohol or substance abuse, physical or sexual abuse) affected the functioning of the client or family members?

17. What are the clients' emotional reactions to the problem(s)?

18. How have the clients attempted to cope with the problem, and what are the required skills to resolve the problem?

19. What are the clients' skills, strengths, and resources?

20. How do ethnocultural, societal, and social class factors bear on the problem(s)?

21. What support systems exist or need to be created for the clients?

22. What external resources are needed by clients?

Questions 1–3 should serve as preliminary inquiries so that the social worker learns whether any prevailing issues may guide the direction of the interview. Questions 4–17 pertain to further specification of problems. They do not imply that a problem focus takes priority over explorations of strengths and resources (covered by questions 18–22). As suggested in the strengths matrix depicted in Figure 8-2, assessment of strengths, resources, and limitations or challenges is required for a full assessment.

Getting Started

After opening social amenities and an explanation of the direction and length of the interview, you should begin by exploring the client's concerns. Sometimes this question is a simple, open-ended inquiry: "Mrs. Smith, what brings you in to see me today?" This question allows the client the opportunity to express his or her concerns and helps give direction to the questions that will follow.

At this point, the worker must be attentive to other issues that may alter the direction of the interview, at least at the outset. If the client's request for service is nonvoluntary, and particularly if it results from a legal mandate (e.g., part of probation, the consequence of a child maltreatment complaint), then the nature of the mandate, referring information, and the client's perception of the referral will frame the early part of the first interview.

A further consideration at the first interview is whether any danger exists that the client might do harm to himself or herself or to others. Some referrals—for example, in emergency services—clearly involve the risk for harm, which should be discussed and evaluated at the outset. In other instances, the risk may be more subtle. For example, a client may open an interview by saying, "I'm at the end of my rope. . . . I can't take it any longer." The social worker should respond to this opening by probing further: "Can you tell me more . . .?" or "When you say you can't take it, what do you mean by that?" If further information raises the social worker's concerns about the danger for suicidal or aggressive behavior, more specific questioning should follow, geared toward assessing the lethality of the situation.

Whatever the client's presenting problem, if shared information gives rise to safety concerns, the social worker must redirect the interview to focus on the degree of danger. If the threats to safety are minor or manageable, the practitioner may resume the interview's focus on the issues that brought the client in for service. However, if the mini-assessment reveals serious or imminent risk to the client or others, the focus of the session must be on assuring safety rather than continuing the assessment.

Chapter 9 describes the process for conducting a suicide lethality assessment. Morrison (1995), Houston-Vega, Nuehring, & Daguio (1997), and Lukas (1993) offer additional guidelines for interviewing around issues of danger and assessing the degree of risk in various situations. Such texts can be useful resources for learning more about the topic.

Identifying the Problem, Its Expressions, and Other Critical Concerns

Your initial contacts with clients will concentrate on uncovering the sources of their problems and engaging them in planning appropriate remedial measures. People typically seek help because they have exhausted their coping efforts and/or lack resources required for satisfactory living. They have often found that, despite their most earnest efforts, their coping efforts are futile or seem to aggravate the problem.

Problem identification takes a somewhat different course when the client has been referred or mandated to receive service. Referred clients may approach services willingly, even if those services were prompted by the suggestion of a professional, friend, or family member. However, many referred clients acquiesce passively because someone else thinks that they "need help." Their initiation of contact does not necessarily imply willingness to accept services. Sometimes when clients are referred by others, the referral source (often a doctor, employer, family member, or school official) has a view of the problem and recommendations for a treatment plan. It is important to clarify with clients that they can choose to work on problems of concern to them, not necessarily the concerns identified by the referral source (Epstein, 1992).

Meanwhile, involuntary clients are at a later point on the continuum of voluntarism, reluctantly "seeking help" because of coercion from family members or some official power structure. Involuntary clients often do not perceive themselves as having problems or they portray pressure from the referral source as the problem. They may send the message: "I don't know why I should have to come. My wife (boss, parent) is the one with the problems. She's the one who should be here." When the source of motivation lies outside the client, it is more difficult to identify the parameters of the problem. After attempting to understand and reduce the client's negativism about being pressured to seek help, you should engage the client in an exploration of his or her life situation. The goals are to determine whether areas of dissatisfaction or interest on the client's part can be identified and used as a source of motivation. When and if the client acknowledges a problem, the boundaries of the problem will become clear, and the exploration can then proceed in a normal fashion.

Another variation on involuntariness may stem from the client's culturally derived attitudes toward help seeking. For example, the underutilization of (or "resistance" to) mental health services by Asian Americans may have its origins in several cultural themes. For example, an acceptance of "fate" may lead to "quiescence in the face of unpleasant life situations" (Yamashiro & Matsuoka, 1997, p. 178). A culture's tradition of arranged marriages may discourage the pursuit of formal assistance for problems that could reflect poorly on the suitability of a prospective spouse. Given the ways that religion and culture shape the perception of problems and therefore the methods chosen to address them, it is little wonder that Asian Americans and other cultural groups seek assistance first from "informal" helpers, such as spiritual leaders, community or clan leaders, or traditional healers. In light of this reluctance to seek help outside the family or culture, the social worker might encounter shame and apprehension during an initial interview. It is important to understand that this may not be the client's typical presentation of self, and that establishing rapport and trust may be slow and require both sensitivity and empathy. While the client may have appeared for services reluctantly, the strength required to take this step should be acknowledged.

When asked to describe their problems or concerns, clients often respond by giving a general account of their problems. The problem typically involves a deficiency of something needed (e.g., health care, adequate income or housing, companionship, harmonious family relationships, self-esteem) or an excess of something that is not desired (e.g., fear, guilt, temper outbursts, marital or parent–child conflict, or addiction). In either event, the difficulty often results in feelings of disequilibrium, tension, and apprehension. The emotions themselves are often a prominent part of the problem configuration, which is one reason why empathic communication is such a vital skill during the interview process.

This understanding of the *presenting problem* is significant because it reflects the client's immediate perceptions of the problem and is the impetus for seeking help. It is distinct from the *problem for work*. The issues that bring the client and the social worker together initially may not, in fact, be the issues that serve as the focus of goals and interventions later in the relationship. The problem for work may differ from the original or presenting problem for a number of reasons. As the helping process progresses, the development of greater information, insights, and trust may mean that factors are revealed that change the focus of work and goals for service. This does not mean, however, that you should disregard the problems that brought clients to you in the first place. The assessment process will reveal to you and the client whether the problem for work differs from the one that brought the client to your service.

The presenting problem is important because it suggests areas to be explored in assessment. If the difficulty described by parents involves their adolescent's truancy and rebellious behavior, for example, the exploration will include the family, school, and peer systems. As the exploration proceeds, it may also prove useful to explore the marital system if difficulty in the marital relationship appears to be negatively affecting the parent–child relationship. If learning difficulties appear to contribute to the truancy, the cognitive and perceptual subsystems of the adolescent may need to be assessed as part of the problem. The presenting problem thus identifies systems that are constituent parts of the problem and suggests the resources needed to ameliorate it.

The Interaction of Other People or Systems

The presenting problem and the exploration that follows usually identify key individuals, groups, or organizations that are participants in the client's difficulties. An accurate assessment must consider all of these elements and determine how they interact to produce difficulties. Furthermore, an effective plan of intervention should embody these same elements, even though it is not always feasible to involve everyone who is a participant in a given problematic situation.

To understand more fully how the client(s) and other involved systems interact to produce and maintain the problem, you must elicit specific information about the functioning and interaction of these various systems. Clients commonly engage in transactions with the following systems:

1. The family and extended family or kinship network

2. The social network (friends, neighbors, coworkers, religious leaders and associates, club members, and cultural groups)

3. Public institutions (educational, recreational, law enforcement and protection, mental health, social service, health care, employment, economic security, legal and judicial, and various governmental agencies)

4. Personal service providers (doctor, dentist, barber, or hairdresser, bartender, auto mechanic, landlord, banker)

5. Religious/spiritual belief system

Understanding how the interaction of these elements plays out in your client's particular situation requires detailed information about the behavior of all participants, including what they say and do before, during, and after problematic events. This specific information will help you and the client illuminate circumstances associated with the client's difficulties, the way that each person affects and is affected by others, and consequences of events that tend to perpetuate problematic behavior.

Bear in mind that human behavior is purposeful and can be understood by analyzing the forces that motivate people to behave as they do. Motivational forces consist of both external events (i.e., those that are visible to others) and covert forces (i.e., inner thoughts, beliefs, emotions, wishes, and images) as well as physiological and psychological states.

Certain circumstances or behaviors typically precede problematic behavior. One family member may say or do something that precipitates an angry, defensive, or hurt reaction by another. A child's outburst in the classroom may follow certain stimuli. A coworker's critical comment may be provoked by an episode of self-doubt and recrimination. Events that precede problematic behavior are referred to as antecedents. Antecedents often give valuable clues about the behavior of one participant that may provoke or offend another participant, thereby triggering a negative reaction, followed by a counter negative reaction, thus setting the problematic situation in motion.

In addition to finding out about the circumstances surrounding troubling episodes, it is important to learn about the consequences or outcomes associated with problematic behaviors. These results may shed light on factors that perpetuate or reinforce the dysfunctional behaviors.

Analyzing the antecedents of problematic behavior, describing the behavior in specific terms, and assessing the consequences or effects of the problematic behavior provide a powerful means of identifying factors that motivate dysfunctional behavior and are appropriate targets of interventions. This straightforward approach to analyzing the functional significance of behavior is termed the *ABC model* (A = antecedent, B = behavior, C = consequence). Although it is far less simple than it may seem, the ABC model provides a coherent and practical approach to understanding problems, the systems involved, and the roles they play.

Assessing Developmental Needs and Wants

As we noted earlier, clients' problems commonly involve unmet needs and wants that derive from a poor fit between these needs and resources in the environment. Determining unmet needs, then, is the first step in identifying which resources must be tapped or developed. If resources are available but clients have been unable to avail themselves of those resources, it is important to determine the barriers to resource utilization. Some people, for example, may suffer from loneliness not because of an absence of support systems but because their interpersonal behavior alienates others and leaves them isolated. Still other clients may *appear* to have emotional support available from family or others, but closer exploration may reveal that these potential resources are unresponsive to clients' needs. Reasons for the unresponsiveness typically involve reciprocal unsatisfactory transactions between the participants. The task in such instances is to assess the nature of the negative transactions and to attempt to modify them to the benefit of the participants.

Human *needs* include the universal necessities (adequate nutrition, clothing, housing, and health care). They are critical and must be at least partially met for human beings to survive and maintain sound physical and mental health and well-being. As we use the term, *wants* consist of strong desires that motivate behavior and that, when fulfilled, enhance satisfaction and well-being. Although fulfillment of wants is not essential to survival, some wants develop a compelling nature, rivaling needs in their intensity. For illustrative purposes, we provide the following list of examples of typical wants involved in presenting problems.

Typical Wants Involved in Presenting Problems

- To have less family conflict
- To feel valued by one's spouse or partner
- To be self-supporting
- To achieve greater companionship in marriage or relationship
- To gain more self-confidence
- To have more freedom
- To handle conflict more effectively
- To control one's temper
- To overcome depression
- To have more friends
- To be included in decision making
- To get discharged from an institution

- To make a difficult decision
- To master fear or anxiety
- To cope with children more effectively

In determining clients' unmet needs and wants, it is essential to consider the developmental stage of the individual client, couple, or family. For example, the psychological needs of an adolescent—for acceptance by peers, sufficient freedom to develop increasing independence, and development of a stable identity (including a sexual identity)—differ markedly from the typical needs of elderly persons—for health care, adequate income, social relationships, and meaningful activities. As with individuals, families go through developmental phases that include both tasks to be mastered and needs that must be met if the family is to provide a climate conducive to the development and well-being of its members.[2]

Although clients' presenting problems often reveal obvious needs and wants (e.g., "Our unemployment benefits have expired and we have no income"), sometimes the social worker must infer what is lacking. Presenting problems may reveal only what is troubling clients on the surface, and careful exploration and empathic "tuning in" are required to identify unmet needs and wants. A couple, for example, may initially complain that they disagree over virtually everything and fight constantly. From this information, one could safely conclude that the pair wants a more harmonious relationship. Exploring their feelings on a deeper level, however, may reveal that their ongoing disputes are actually a manifestation of unmet needs of both partners for expressions of love, caring, appreciation, or increased companionship.

The process of translating complaints and problems into needs and wants is often helpful to clients, who may have dwelled on difficulties or blamed others and have not thought in terms of their own specific needs and wants. The presenting problem of one client was that her husband was married to his job and spent little time with her. The social worker responded, "I gather then you're feeling left out of his life and want to feel important to him and valued by him." The client replied, "You know, I hadn't thought of it that way, but that's exactly what I've been feeling." The practitioner then encouraged her to express this need directly to her husband, which she did. He listened attentively and responded with genuine concern. The occasion was the first time she had expressed her needs directly. Previously, her messages had been complaints, and her husband's usual response had been defensive withdrawal.

Identifying needs and wants also serves as a prelude to the process of negotiating goals. Expressing goals in terms that address needs and wants enhances the motivation of clients to work toward goal attainment, as the payoff for goal-oriented efforts is readily apparent to them.

Of course, some desires are unrealistic when assessed against the capacity of the client and/ or opportunities in the social environment. Moreover, wanting to achieve a desired goal is not the same as being willing to expend the time and effort and to endure the discomfort required to attain that goal. These matters warrant extensive consideration and are central topics in Chapter 12.

Stresses Associated with Life Transitions

In addition to developmental stages that typically correspond to age ranges, individuals and families commonly must adapt to other major transitions that are less age specific. Your assessment should take into account whether the client's difficulties are related to such a transition and, if so, which aspects of the transition are sources of concern. Some transitions (e.g., geographical moves and immigrations, divorce, and untimely widowhood) can occur during virtually any stage of development. Many of these transitions can be traumatic and the adaptations required may temporarily overwhelm the coping capacities of individuals or families. Transitions that are involuntary or abrupt (a home is destroyed by fire) and separations (from a person, homeland, or familiar role) are highly stressful for most persons and often temporarily impair social functioning.

The person's history, concurrent strengths and resources, and past successful coping can all affect the adaptation to these transitions. The environment plays a crucial role as well. People with strong support networks (e.g., close relationships with family, kin, friends, and neighbors) generally have less difficulty in adapting to traumatic changes than do those who lack strong support systems. Assessments and interventions related to transitional periods, therefore, should consider the availability or lack of essential support systems.

The following are major transitions that may beset adults:

Role Changes

Work, career choices	Retirement
Health impairment	Separation and divorce
Parenthood	Institutionalization
Post-parenthood years	Single parenthood
Geographic moves and migrations	Death of a spouse or partner
Marriage or partnership commitment	

In addition to these transitions, other milestones affect specialized groups. For example, gay and lesbian persons have difficult decisions to make about to whom and under what conditions they will reveal their sexual identity (Cain, 1991a, 1991b); furthermore, they may need to create procedures and rituals for events (e.g., marriage, divorce, and end-of-life decisions) from which they are legally excluded because of their sexual orientation. A child whose parents are divorcing may experience a loss of friends and change of school along with the disruption of his or her family structure. The parents and siblings of individuals with severe illnesses or disabilities may experience repeated "losses" if joyous milestones such as graduations, dating, marriage, and parenthood are not available to their loved one. Retirement may not represent a time of release and relaxation if it is accompanied by poverty, poor health, or new responsibilities such as caring for ill family members or raising grandchildren (Gibson, 1999).

Clearly, life transitions can be differentially affected by individual circumstances, culture, socioeconomic status, and other factors. Social workers must be sensitive to these differences and take care not to make assumptions about the importance of a transitional event or developmental milestone.

Severity of the Problem

Assessment of the severity of problems is necessary to determine whether clients have the capacity to continue functioning in the community or whether hospitalization or other strong supportive or protective measures are needed. When functioning is temporarily impaired by extreme anxiety and loss of emotional control, such as when people experience acute post-traumatic stress disorder (Patten, Gatz, Jones, & Thomas, 1989), short-term hospitalization may be required. The acuteness of the situation will necessarily influence your appraisal of the client's stress, the frequency of sessions, and the speed at which you need to mobilize support systems.

Meanings That Clients Ascribe to Problems

The next element of assessment involves understanding and describing the client's perceptions and definitions of the problem. The meanings people attribute to events ("meaning attributions") are as important as the events themselves, because they influence the way people respond to their difficulties. For example, a parent might attribute his son's suicide attempt to his grounding the boy earlier in the week. The meaning in a job loss might entail feeling individual shame and failure versus seeing the layoff as a part of organizational downsizing. In both of the preceding meaning attributions, personal guilt might keep the client from seeking help from support systems that could otherwise assist the client in dealing with the problem. You, your clients, other participants in problems, and external observers thus may view problem situations in widely varying ways.

Determining these views is an important feature of assessment. Exploratory questions such as the following may help elicit the client's meaning attributions:

- "What do you make of his behavior?"
- "What were the reasons (for your parents grounding you)?"
- "What conclusions have you drawn about why your landlord evicted you?"
- "What are your views (as to why you didn't get a promotion)?"

Discovering meaning attributions is also vital because these beliefs about cause and effect can be powerful and may represent barriers to change. The following examples demonstrate distorted attributions (Hurvitz, 1975):

1. *Pseudoscientific explanations:* "My family has the gene for Alzheimer's disease. I know I'll get it, and there's nothing we can do about it."
2. *Psychological labeling:* "Mother is senile; she can't be given a choice in this matter."
3. *Fixed beliefs about others:* "She'll never change. She never has. I think we're wasting our time and money on counseling."
4. *Unchangeable factors:* "I've never been an affectionate person. It's just not in my character."
5. *Reference to "fixed" religious or philosophical principles, natural laws, or social forces:* "Sure, I already have as many children as I want. But I don't really have a choice. The church says that birth control is against God's will."
6. *Assertion based on presumed laws of human nature:* "All children tell lies at that age. It's just natural. I did when I was a kid."

Fortunately, many clients' attributions are not resistant to change. Some clients are open—even eager—to examine their role in problematic situations and want to modify their behavior. When obstacles such as those listed above are encountered, however, it is vital to explore and resolve them before attempting to negotiate change-oriented goals or to implement interventions. Figure 8-3 describes solution-focused questions that may assist in assessment.

Sites of Problematic Behaviors

Determining *where* problematic behavior occurs may provide clues about which factors trigger it. For example, children may throw tantrums in certain locations but not in others. As a result of repeated experiences, they soon learn to discriminate where certain behaviors are tolerated and where they are not. Adults may experience anxiety or depression in certain environmental contexts

---

SOLUTION-FOCUSED ASSESSMENT QUESTIONS

The theoretical orientation employed by the agency will shape the questions asked in the interview. Brief, solution-focused therapy is one model that is encountered in a variety of settings. This model is based on a number of assumptions—for example, that small changes can lead to larger differences, that focusing on the present can help the client tap into unused capacities and generate creative alternatives, and that paying attention to solutions is more relevant than focusing on problems. The solution-building questions that are central to this practice model can be used in other settings as well. Some examples follow:

1. *Seeking exceptions* involves asking questions to determine when the problem does not exist or does not occur. The answer may refer to different sites, times, or contexts. Exploration then asks the client to elaborate on what is different in those incidents and what other factors might cause it to be different.

2. *Scaling the problem* involves asking the client to estimate, on a scale of 1 to 10, the severity of the problem. The response can help in tracking changes over time, open up the opportunity to ask what accounts for the current level of difficulty or relief, and determine what it might take to move from the current level to a higher point on the scale.

3. *Scaling motivation* is similar to scaling problems or concerns. It involves asking the client to estimate

the degree to which he or she feels hopeful about resolution, or perhaps the degree to which he or she has given up hope. How would he or she rate his or her commitment to working on the problem?

4. The *miracle question* helps the practitioner to determine the client's priorities and to operationalize the areas for change. Essentially, the social worker asks, "If, while you were asleep, a miracle occurred and your problem was solved, how would things be different when you woke up?" This technique helps the client envision the positive results of the change process and elicits important information for structuring specific behavioral interventions (Jordan & Franklin, 2003).

As with other assessment tools, the key to successful use of these techniques lies in the sensitivity and timing with which they are employed. For example, asking the miracle question prematurely may lead the client to believe that you are not listening or are minimizing his or her distress. Typically, these questions may be prefaced by statements acknowledging the client's concern—for example, "I know your son's misbehavior has been troubling to you, but I wonder if there are times when he does follow your directions?" Sensitivity is also demonstrated through tone of voice, inflection, eye contact, and other nonverbal methods of attending that assure the client of your attention and regard.

Figure 8-3   Solution-Focused Assessment Questions

---

but not in others. One couple, for example, invariably experienced a breakdown in communication in the home of one spouse's parents. Some children have difficulty following directions at school but not at home, or vice versa. Determining where problematic behavior occurs will assist you in identifying areas that warrant further exploration and pinpoint factors associated with the behavior in question.

Identifying where problematic behavior *does not* occur is also valuable, because it provides clues about the features that might help in alleviating the problem and identify situations in which the client experiences relief from difficul-

ties. For example, a child may act out in certain classes at school but not in all of them. What is happening in the incident-free classes that might explain the absence of symptoms or difficulties there? How can it be replicated in other classes? A client in residential treatment may gain temporary respite from overwhelming anxiety by visiting a cherished aunt on weekends. In other instances, clients may gain permanent relief from intolerable stress by changing employment, discontinuing college, or moving out of relationships when tension or other unpleasant feeling states are experienced exclusively in these contexts.

Temporal Context of Problematic Behaviors

Determining *when* problematic behaviors occur often yields valuable clues about factors that play roles in clients' problems. The onset of a depressive episode, for example, may coincide with the time of year when a loved one died or when a divorce occurred. Family problems may occur when one parent returns from work or travel, at bedtime for the children, at mealtimes, or when children are (or should be) getting ready for school. Similarly, couples may experience severe conflict when one partner is working the midnight shift, after participation by either partner in activities that exclude the other, or when one or both drink at parties. These clues can shed light on the pattern of clients' difficulties, indicate areas for further exploration, and lead to helpful interventions.

Frequency of Problematic Behaviors

The frequency of problematic behavior provides an index to both the pervasiveness of a problem and its effects on the participants. As with the site and timing of symptoms, information on frequency helps you to assess the context in which problems arise and the pattern they follow in the client's life. Services for clients who experience their problems on a more or less ongoing basis may need to be more intensive than for clients whose symptoms are less frequent or intermittent. Determining the frequency of problematic behaviors thus helps to clarify the degree of difficulty and the extent to which it impairs the daily functioning of clients and their families.

Assessing the frequency of problematic behaviors also provides a baseline against which to measure behaviors targeted for change. Making subsequent comparisons of the frequency of the targeted behaviors enables you to evaluate the efficacy of your interventions, as discussed in Chapter 13.

Duration of the Problem

Another important dimension vital to assessing problems relates to the history of the problem—namely, *how long* it has existed. Knowing when the problem developed and under what circumstances assists in further evaluating the degree of the problem, unraveling psychosocial factors associated with the problem, determining the source of motivation to seek assistance, and planning appropriate interventions. Often significant changes in individuals' life situations, including even seemingly positive ones, may disrupt clients' equilibrium to the extent that they cannot adapt to changes. An unplanned pregnancy, loss of employment, job promotion, severe illness, birth of a first child, move to a new city, death of a loved one, divorce, retirement, severe disappointment—these and many other life events may cause severe stresses. Careful exploration of the duration of problems often discloses such antecedents to current difficulties.

Events that immediately precede decisions to seek help are particularly informative. Sometimes referred to as *precipitating events*, these antecedents often yield valuable clues about critical stresses that might otherwise be overlooked. Clients often report that their problems have existed longer than a year. Why they chose to ask for help at a particular time is not readily apparent, but uncovering this information may cast their problems in a somewhat different light. For example, a parent who complained about his teenage daughter's longstanding rebelliousness did not seek assistance until he became aware (1 week before calling the agency) that she was engaging in an intimate relationship with a woman 6 years her senior. The precipitating event is significant to the call for help and would not have been disclosed had the practitioner not sought to answer the critical question of why they were seeking help at this particular time.

In some instances, clients may not be fully aware of their reasons initiating the contact, and it may be necessary to explore what events or emotional experiences were occurring shortly before their decision to seek help. Determining the duration of problems is also vital in assessing clients' levels of functioning and in planning appropriate interventions. This exploration may reveal that a client's adjustment has been marginal for many years and that the immediate problem is simply an exacerbation of long-term multiple problems. In other instances, the onset of a problem may be acute, and clients may have functioned at an adequate or high level for many years. In the first instance, modest goals and long-term intermittent service may be indicated; in the second instance, short-term crisis intervention may suffice to restore clients to their previous level of functioning.

Other Issues Affecting Client Functioning

Numerous other circumstances and conditions can affect the problem that the client is presenting and his or her capacity to address it. For this reason, it is often wise to explore specifically the client's use of alcohol or other substances, exposure to abuse or violence, presence of health problems, depression or other mental health problems, and use of prescription medication.

Questions to probe into these areas should be a standard element of the initial interview. As such, they can be asked in a straightforward and nonjudgmental fashion. For example, opening questions might include the following:

- "Now, I'd like to know about some of your habits. First, in an average month, on how many days do you have at least one drink of alcohol?"
- "Have you ever used street drugs of any sort?"
- "Have you had any major illnesses in the past?"
- "Are you currently experiencing any health problems?"
- "What medications do you take?"
- "How do these medications work for you?"
- "Have you been in situations recently or in the past where you were harmed by someone or where you witnessed others being hurt?"

The answers you receive to these questions will determine which follow-up questions you ask. In some circumstances, you may ask for more specific information—for example, to determine the degree of impairment due to drug and alcohol use. At a minimum, you will want to learn how the client views these issues in light of the presenting problem. For example, you might ask these follow-up questions:

- "How has the difficulty sleeping affected your ability to care for your kids?"
- "What role do you see your alcohol use playing in this marital conflict?"
- "Did the change of medication occur at the same time these other difficulties began?"
- "I wonder if the run-in with the bullies has anything to do with you skipping school lately?"

Depending on the setting and purpose of the interview and on the information gathered, the social worker may focus the interview specifically on the client's medical history, abuse, substance use, or mental health. Further information on these assessments is included in Chapter 9. Lukas (1993) and Morrison (1995) also offer particularly good advice for conducting these kinds of specialized assessments.

Clients' Emotional Reactions to Problems

When people encounter problems in daily living, they typically experience emotional reactions to those problems. It is important to explore and assess these reactions for three major reasons.

First, people often gain relief simply by expressing troubling emotions related to their problems. Common reactions to problem situations are worry, concern, resentment, hurt, fear, and feeling overwhelmed, helpless, or hopeless. Being able to ventilate such emotions in the presence of an understanding and concerned person is a source of great comfort. Releasing pent-up feelings often has the effect of relieving oneself of a heavy burden. In fact, ventilating emotions may have a liberating effect for persons who tend to be out of touch with their emotions and have not acknowledged to themselves or others that they even have troubled feelings.

Second, because emotions strongly influence behavior, the emotional reactions of some people impel them to behave in ways that exacerbate or contribute to their difficulties. In some instances, in fact, people create new difficulties as a result of emotionally reactive behavior. In the heat of anger, a noncustodial parent may lash out at a child or former spouse. Burdened by financial concerns, an individual may become impatient and verbally abusive, behaving in ways that frighten, offend, or alienate employers, customers, or family members. An adult experiencing unremitting grief may cut himself or herself off from loved ones who "cannot stand" to see him or her cry. Powerful emotional reactions may thus be an integral part of the overall problem configuration.

Third, intense reactions often become primary problems, overshadowing the antecedent problematic situation. For example, some people develop severe depressive reactions associated with their life problems. A mother may become depressed over an unwed daughter's pregnancy; a man may react with anxiety to unemployment or retirement; and culturally dislocated persons may become depressed following relocation, even though they may have fled intolerable conditions in their homeland. Other individuals may react to problematic events by experiencing feelings of helplessness or panic that cause virtual paralysis. In such instances, interventions must address the overwhelming emotional reactions as well as the situation that triggered them.

Coping Efforts and Needed Skills

Perhaps surprisingly, the social worker can learn more about clients' difficulties by determining how they have attempted to cope with their problems. The coping methods that clients employ give valuable clues about their levels of stress and of functioning. Exploration may reveal that a client has few coping skills, but rather relies upon rigid patterns that are unhelpful or cause further problems. Some clients follow avoidance patterns—for example, immersing themselves in tasks or work, withdrawing, or numbing or fortifying themselves with drugs or alcohol. Other clients attempt to cope with interpersonal problems by resorting to aggressive, domineering behavior or by placating other participants or becoming submissive. Still other clients demonstrate flexible and effective coping patterns but collapse under unusually high levels of stress. By

contrast, other clients depend heavily on others to manage difficulties for them.

Likewise, approaches to problem solving vary among cultures. The stereotypical middle-class American strategy values an individually focused, analytical-cognitive approach (De Anda, 1984). Other cultures, however, embrace approaches based on group values about coping with problems. All cultures exert pressures on individuals to follow prescribed solutions for a given problem, and developing new or creative solutions may be discouraged or frowned upon. Deviating from cultural expectations for coping or problem solving may cause the client anxiety and/or guilt.

Exploring how clients have attempted to cope with problems sometimes reveals that they have struggled effectively with similar problems in the past but are no longer able to do so. In such instances, it is important to explore carefully what has changed. For example, a person may have been able to cope with the demands of one supervisor but not with a new one who is more critical and aloof or who is of a different generation, race, or gender than the client. The client's typical ability to cope may also be affected by changes in functioning. Severely depressed clients, for example, commonly overestimate the difficulty of their problems and under-estimate their coping abilities. Some clients are able to cope effectively in one setting but not in another. Thus, by exploring the different circumstances, meaning attributions, and emotional reactions of clients, you should be able to identify subtle differences that account for the varied effectiveness of your clients' coping patterns in different contexts.

Another aspect of assessment is the task of identifying the skills that clients need to ameliorate their difficulties. This information enables you to negotiate appropriate and feasible goals aimed at developing skills. To improve parent–child relationships, for example, clients may need to develop listening and negotiating skills. Socially inhibited clients may need to learn skills in approaching others, introducing themselves, and engaging in conversation. To enhance couples' relationships, partners often need to learn communication and conflict management skills. To cope effectively

ASSESSING CHILDREN

The assessment of children requires specialized skills as well as the thoughtful application of the techniques described in this book. For example, because children often present for service in relation to systems of which they are already a part (e.g., hospitals, schools, families), your assessment may be bounded by those systems. Similarly, children typically appear for service because someone else has identified a concern. This factor does not automatically mean that the child client will be resistant, but rather indicates that he or she may not perceive a problem or be motivated to address it.

In working with children, you may rely more than usual on certain data sources (e.g., collateral contacts or observations) and less than usual on other sources (e.g., the client's verbal reports). A trusting relationship with the child's primary caregivers will be vital to your access to the child and will dramatically affect the rapport you achieve with him or her. Depending on the child's level of development, he or she may have difficulty helping you construct the problem analysis or identify strengths or coping methods. Other data sources, such as parent interviews, may be needed to complete a satisfactory assessment.

Child assessments may also require new skills, such as the use of drawings, board games, dolls, or puppets as sources of information for the assessment. The way that the child approaches these activities can be as telling as the information they reveal (Webb, 1996). For example, are the child's interests and skills age-appropriate? What mood is reflected in the child's play, and is it frequently encountered? Do themes in the child's play relate to possible areas of distress? How often do those themes recur? How does the child relate to you and to adversity (the end of play or a "wrong move" in a game)? How well can the child focus on the task? The significance and meaning of your impressions from play should be evaluated on the basis of other sources of information.

A *developmental assessment* may be particularly relevant for understanding the child's history and current situation. With this type of assessment, a parent or other caregiver provides information about the circumstances of the child's delivery, birth, and infancy; achievement of developmental milestones; family atmosphere; interests; and significant life transitions (Jordan & Hickerson, 2003; Lukas, 1993; Webb, 1996). This information helps form impressions about the child's experiences and life events, especially as they may relate to his or her current functioning. As with other forms of assessment, you must organize and interpret what you discover from all sources so as to paint a meaningful picture of the child's history, strengths, and needs; this assessment will then serve as the basis of your goals and interventions.

---

with people who tend to exploit them, still other clients must acquire assertiveness skills.

Cultural, Societal, and Social Class Factors

As we noted in earlier, ethnocultural factors influence what kinds of problems people experience, how they feel about requesting assistance, how they communicate, how they perceive the role of the professional person, and how they view various approaches to solving problems. It is therefore vital that you be knowledgeable about these factors and competent in responding to them. Your assessment of clients' life situations, needs, and strengths must be viewed through the lens of cultural competence (Rooney & Bibus, 1995). What does this mean in practice? Some examples follow:

- A client immigrating from Mexico, Africa, or Eastern Europe may display psychological distress that is directly related to the migration or refugee experience. Beyond this consideration, a social worker who understands the ramifications of immigration may need to be sensitive to the special issues that may arise for refugees or others whose immigration was made under forced or dire circumstances (Mayadas et al., 1998–1999).

- An interview with an older person experiencing isolation should take into account that hearing difficulties, death or illness of peers, housing and economic status, and other factors may impede the client's ability to partake in social activities.

- Racial and ethnic stereotypes may lead to differences in the way that minority youth and majority youth are perceived when accused of juvenile crimes. Similarly, detrimental experiences with authority figures and institutional racism may affect the way that these clients interact with the social worker (Bridges & Steen, 1998).

- A young woman is persistently late for appointments, which her social worker interprets as a sign of resistance and poor organizational skills. In fact, the young woman must make child care arrangements and take three buses to reach the mental health clinic. Rather than indicating short-comings, her arrival at appointments (even late) is a sign of persistence and precise organization.

Chapter 9 addresses cultural factors as they apply to individual and environmental factors in greater detail.

External Resources Needed

When clients request services, you must determine (1) whether the services requested match the functions of the agency and (2) whether the staff possesses the skills required to provide high-quality service. If not, a referral is needed to assure that the client receives the highest quality of service to match the needs presented. Referrals may also be required to complement services within your agency or to obtain a specialized assessment that will be factored into your services (e.g., "Are the multiple medications that Mrs. Jones is taking causing her recent cognitive problems?"). In such instances, the practitioner performs a broker or case manager role, which requires knowledge of community resources (or at least knowledge of how to obtain relevant information). Fortunately, many large communities have community resource information centers that can prove highly valuable to both clients and professionals in locating needed resources. Remember that clients may benefit from help in a variety of areas—from financial assistance, transportation, and health care to child or elder care, recreation, and job training.

In certain instances, in addition to the public and private resources available in your community, you should consider two other major resources that may be less visible forms of assistance. The first is self-help groups, where members look to themselves for mutual aid and social support. In particular, the Internet has expanded the reach of such groups across geographic distances on a round-the-clock basis (Fingeld, 2000).

Natural support systems are a second underutilized resource that may be tapped to counter isolation and difficulties in coping. They include relatives, friends, neighbors, coworkers, and close associates from school, social groups, or one's faith community. Some therapists have developed innovative ways of tapping these support systems collectively through an intervention termed *network therapy*. These clinicians contend that much of the dysfunctional behavior labeled as mental illness actually derives from feelings of alienation from one's natural social network, which consists of all human relationships that are significant in a person's life, including natural support systems. In network therapy, these practitioners mobilize 40 to 50 significant people who are willing to come together in a period of crisis for one or more members of the network. The goal is to unite their efforts in tightening the social network of relationships for the purpose of offering support, reassurance, and solidarity to troubled members and other members of the social network. Mobilizing social networks is in keeping with the best traditions of social work.

In instances of cultural dislocation, natural support systems may be limited to the family, and practitioners may need to mobilize other potential resources in the community (Hulewat, 1996). Assisting refugees poses a particular challenge, because a cultural reference group may not be available in some communities. A language barrier may create another obstacle, and practitioners may need to search for interpreters and other interested parties who can assist these families in locating housing, gaining employment, learning the language, adapting to an alien culture, and developing social support systems.

In still other instances, people's environments may be virtually devoid of natural support systems. Consequently, environmental changes may be necessary to accomplish a better fit between needs and resources, a topic we consider at greater length in Chapter 9.

Summary

Chapter 8 introduced the knowledge and skills entailed in multidimensional assessment. A psychiatric diagnosis may be part of, but is not the same as, a social work assessment. The discussion in this chapter emphasized strengths and resources in assessments. A framework for prioritizing what must be done in assessment was presented, along with the components of the problem exploration. In Chapter 9, we consider the assessment of intrapersonal and environmental systems and the terms and concepts used to describe their functioning.

Internet Resources

See our companion website for hot links to some helpful URLs. Note that URLs are subject to change. We will endeavor to update the links on the companion website as much as possible.

The following sources provide tools and information on assessing individual needs across the lifespan: *www.childtrends.org; www.cyfernet.org; www. uncssp. org; http://www.archive.official-documents.co. uk/document/doh/facn/fw-00.htm;* www.healthandage.com.

Using InfoTrac College Edition, you can enter the keywords "social work assessment" to directly access useful articles such as Berkman, Chauncey, Holmes, Daniels, Bonander, Sampson, and Robinson (1999), Bisman (1999), and Cascio (1998).

Related Online Content

Visit the *Direct Social Work Practice* companion website at *http://socialwork. wadsworth.com/hepworth7* for additional learning tools such as glossary terms, chapter outlines, InfoTrac College Edition keywords, relevant web links, and chapter practice quizzes. Also, be sure to check out the Direct Practice Virtual Reader, where the authors have personally selected articles relevant to this chapter using InfoMarks.

Notes

1. For more information, consult Hudson, W. W. (1990). *WALMYR Assessment Scales, Scoring Manual.* WALMYR Publishing Company, P.O. Box 6229, Tallahassee, FL 32314-6229. (850) 656-2787. E-mail: scales@walmyr.com.
2. For resources on family development and norms across cultures, we suggest Congress (2002), Corcoran (2000); Lum (1996), and McGoldrick et al. (1996).

Assessment: Intrapersonal and Environmental Factors

CHAPTER OVERVIEW

Chapter 9 reviews two key aspects of a comprehensive assessment: those things going on within the client (physically, emotionally, cognitively) and those things going on within the client's environment (physical and social). The chapter introduces these areas for examination and helps you develop an understanding of the difficulties and the assets to consider in these systems. It also discusses how culture affects intrapersonal systems and offers guidance for understanding these effects when the social worker and client do not share common cultural backgrounds.

THE INTERACTION OF MULTIPLE SYSTEMS IN HUMAN PROBLEMS

Problems, strengths, and resources encountered in direct social work practice result from interactions among intrapersonal, interpersonal, and environmental systems. Difficulties are rarely confined to one of these systems, however, because a functional imbalance in one system typically contributes to an imbalance in others. For example, individual difficulties (e.g., feelings of worthlessness and depression) invariably influence how one relates to other people; interpersonal difficulties (e.g., job strain) likewise affect individual functioning. Similarly, environmental deficits (e.g., inadequate housing, hostile working conditions, or social isolation) affect individual and interpersonal functioning.

The reciprocal effects among the three major systems, of course, are not limited to the negative effects of functional imbalance and system deficits. Assets, strengths, and resources also have reciprocal *positive* effects. A supportive environment may partially compensate for intrapersonal difficulties; similarly, strong interpersonal relationships may provide positive experiences that more than offset an otherwise impoverished environment.

To adequately assess the many forces that interact to produce problems, you must be knowledgeable about the three major systems that are typically involved in problems. Recognizing this fact, we devote Chapters 9 and 10 to the complexities of these systems. This chapter deals with the intrapersonal (within the person) and environmental systems; Chapter 10 highlights interpersonal systems (between people), with particular emphasis on intimate partner and family systems.

Figure 9-1 depicts the range of elements to be considered in assessing individual and environmental functioning.

INTRAPERSONAL SYSTEMS

A comprehensive assessment of the individual considers a variety of elements, including biophysical, cognitive/perceptual, emotional, behavioral, cultural, and motivational factors. However, the social worker's assessment and written products may focus more sharply on some of these areas than others, depending on the nature of the

INTRAPERSONAL SYSTEMS

Biophysical Functioning

    Physical characteristics and presentation

    Physical health

Assessing Use and Abuse of Medications, Alcohol, and Drugs

    Alcohol use and abuse

    Use and abuse of other substances

    Dual diagnosis: comorbid addictive and mental disorders

Assessing Cognitive/Perceptual Functioning

    Intellectual functioning

    Judgment

    Reality testing

    Coherence

    Cognitive flexibility

    Values

    Misconceptions

    Self-concept

    Assessing thought disorders

Assessing Emotional Functioning

    Emotional control

    Range of emotions

    Appropriateness of affect

    Assessing affective disorders

        Bipolar disorder

        Major depressive disorder

        Suicidal risk

        Depression and suicidal risk with children and adolescents

Assessing Behavioral Functioning

Assessing Motivation

Assessing Environmental Systems

    Physical environment

    Social support systems

    Spirituality and affiliation with a faith community

Figure 9-1 Overview: Areas for Attention in Assessing Intrapersonal Functioning

client's difficulties, the reason for the assessment, and the setting in which the assessment is taking place. It is important to remember, however, that an assessment is just a "snapshot" of the client system's functioning at any given point in time. As we noted in Chapter 8, the social worker's beliefs and actions and the client's feelings about seeking help may distort the assessment at any given point. For all of these reasons, care and respect are required when collecting and synthesizing assessment information.

BIOPHYSICAL FUNCTIONING

Biophysical functioning encompasses physical characteristics, health factors, and genetic factors, as well as the use and abuse of drugs and alcohol.

Physical Characteristics and Presentation

The physical characteristics and appearance of clients may be either assets or liabilities. In Western society, physical attractiveness is highly valued, and unattractive people are typically considered disadvantaged in terms of their social desirability, employment opportunities, and marriageability, and perhaps even readjustment following institutionalization (Farina, Burns, Austad, Bugglin, & Fischer, 1986). It is thus important to be observant of distinguishing physical characteristics that may affect social functioning. Particular attributes that merit attention include body build, posture, facial features, gait, and any physical anomalies that may distort the self-image or pose a social liability.

Likewise, how clients present themselves is important. Clients who walk slowly, display stooped posture, talk slowly and without animation, lack spontaneity, and show minimal changes in facial expression may be depressed. Dress and grooming often reveal much about a person's morale, values, and standard of living.

The standard for assessing appearance is generally whether the dress is appropriate for the setting. Is the client barefoot in near-freezing weather or wearing a helmet and overcoat in the summer sun? Is the client dressed seductively or in pajamas, or "overdressed" for an appointment with the social worker? While attending to these questions, social workers should take care in the conclusions they reach. Westermeyer (1993) notes that the determination of "appropriateness" is greatly influenced by the interviewer's cultural background and values. A "disheveled" appearance may indicate poverty, carelessness, or the latest fashion. Being clothed in bright colors may indicate mania or simply an affiliation with a cultural group that favors that particular form of dress (Morrison, 1995; Othmer & Othmer, 1989).

Other important factors associated with appearance include hand tremors, facial tics, rigid or constantly shifting posture, and tense muscles of the face, hands, and arms. Sometimes these characteristics reflect the presence of an illness or physical problem. Such physical signs may also indicate a high degree of tension or anxiety, warranting exploration by the social worker. During the assessment, an effective social worker will determine whether the anxiety displayed is normative for the given situation or whether it is excessive and might reveal an area for further discussion.

Physical Health

Ill health can contribute to depression, sexual difficulties, irritability, low energy, restlessness, anxiety, poor concentration, and a host of other problems. It is therefore important for social workers to routinely consider their clients' state of health as they explore these individuals' situations. One of the first assessment activities is to determine if clients are under medical care and, if not, ask when they last had a medical examination. Social workers should rule out medical sources

of difficulties by referring clients for physical evaluations, when appropriate, before attributing problems solely to psychosocial factors. They should also be cautious and avoid drawing premature conclusions about the sources of problems when there is even a remote possibility that medical factors may be involved.

A variety of biophysical factors can affect cognitive, behavioral, and emotional functioning in individuals. For example, a history of child malnutrition has been linked to attention deficits, poor social skills, and emotional problems that may continue to affect children even after they become adequately nourished (Johnson, 1989). Nutritional deficits can also cause dementia in elderly people; however, some of this cognitive decline may be reversed if it is treated early enough (Naleppa, 1999). Encephalitis, which has been shown to cause brain damage, can lead to symptoms of attention deficit disorder (Johnson, 1989). Hormone levels also affect behavioral and emotional functioning—for example, high testosterone levels have been correlated with high levels of aggression (Rowe, Maughan, Worthman, Costello, & Angold, 2004).

Assessing the health of clients is especially important with groups known to underutilize medical care. They include people who live in poverty, ethnic minority groups, elderly people, immigrants (including refugees), foster children, unwed pregnant adolescents, homeless people, people with AIDS, and people who lack health insurance. These groups may experience a greater-than-average need for health care due to their health status. They may also be more vulnerable to disease due to poor nutrition, dangerous environmental conditions, and the lack of preventive services (Buss & Gillanders, 1997; Ensign, 1998; Jang, Lee, & Woo, 1998; Suarez & Siefert, 1998; Zechetmayr, 1997).

Along with the increased need for health care, members of particularly vulnerable groups may experience diminished access to care. In particular, access can be limited by three factors: affordability, availability, and acceptability (Julia, 1996).

Whether care is *affordable* depends on whether the client has health insurance coverage and whether he or she can pay for the services not covered by insurance. Approximately 44 million people in the United States lack basic health insurance. Even those who do have coverage may be unable or reluctant to pursue care, given the cost of medications, deductibles, and co-payments not covered by insurance. Concerns about costs may lead clients to delay basic care until the situation worsens to a dangerous level or to the point where even more expensive interventions are required. Individuals with extensive or chronic health problems, such as those with AIDS, may find that hospitalization and drug costs outstrip both their insurance coverage and their income, thereby affecting even those with considerable financial assets and high-paying jobs.

Availability refers not only to the location of health care services, but also the hours they are available, the transportation needed to reach them, and the adequacy of the facilities and personnel to meet the client's needs (Mokuau & Fong, 1994). If the nearest after-hours health care resource is a hospital emergency room, it may be the facility of choice for a desperate mother, even if the health concern (e.g., a child's ear infection) might be better addressed in another setting.

Acceptability refers to the extent to which the health services are compatible with the client's cultural values and traditions. Chapter 8 discussed the importance of understanding how culture may affect the client's interpretation of his or her problems. An important task in intrapersonal assessment involves determining clients' views about the causes of illness, physical aberrations, disabling conditions, and mental symptoms, because their expectations regarding diagnoses and treatment may differ sharply from those presented by Western health care professionals (Yamamoto, Silva, Justice, Chang, & Leong, 1993) and their rejection of these formulations may be misinterpreted as noncompliance or resistance (Al-Krenawi, 1998). For these reasons, all practitioners should be knowledgeable about the significance of folk healers and shamans for clients from an array of cultural groups (Canda, 1983).

Beyond differences in beliefs, differences arise related to clients' comfort in accepting care. New immigrants may have limited knowledge of Western medical care and of the complex health care provider systems in the United States, and they may be reticent to seek care because of concerns about their documentation and fears of deportation (Congress, 1994). The use of indigenous healers or bilingual and bicultural staff can enhance the acceptability of health care to these individuals.

A health assessment may also entail gathering information about illnesses in the client's family. A Genogram may be helpful in capturing this information. This tool, which is similar to a family tree, graphically depicts relationships within the family, dates of births and deaths, illnesses, and other significant life events. It reveals patterns across generations of which even the client may not have been aware (Andrews, 2001; McGoldrick, 1985). You may also find out about family history simply by asking the client. For example, you might ask, "Has anyone else in your family ever had an eating disorder?" or "Is there a history of substance abuse in your family?" This information helps in assessing the client's understanding of and experience with a problem. It may also identify the need for a referral for specialized information and counseling related to genetically linked disorders (Waltman, 1996).[1]

Beyond gathering information on the family history of disease, it is helpful to understand the family's understanding of and attitude toward illness and the way in which the family copes with and is affected by illness. The illness of a member—particularly of a parent—creates imbalance in a family system, often requiring adjustment in role performance by family members. Outside resources (e.g., financial aid, homemaking services, or visiting nursing service) may be required to assist families to maintain their equilibrium in such circumstances.

Cultural values and the family's way of life will also affect the course of a patient's illness and recovery. The family naturally influences decision making during each phase of a member's illness, beginning with the initial steps involved in seeking medical care, the response to the diagnosis, and the compliance or noncompliance with the treatment recommendations.

Assessing Use and Abuse of Medications, Alcohol, and Drugs

An accurate understanding of a client's biophysical functioning must include information on his or her use of both legal and illicit drugs. First, it is important to determine which prescribed and over-the-counter medications the client is taking, whether he or she is taking them as prescribed, and whether they are having the intended effect. Another reason for evaluating drug use is that even beneficial drugs can produce side effects that affect the functioning of various biopsychosocial systems. An array of common reactions such as drowsiness, changes in sexual functioning, muscle rigidity, disorientation, inertia, and stomach pains may result from inappropriate combinations of prescription drugs or as troubling side effects of single medications (Denison, 2003). Finally, questioning in this area is important because the client may report a variety of conditions, from confusion to sleeplessness, which may necessitate a referral for evaluation and medication.

Alcohol is another form of legal drug, but its abuse can severely impair health, disrupt or destroy family life, and create serious community problems. Conservatively estimated to afflict 9 to 10 million Americans, alcoholism can occur in any culture, although it may be more prevalent in some than in others. Alcoholism is also associated with high incidences of suicide, homicide, child abuse, and partner violence.

Like alcohol abuse, the misuse of illicit drugs may have detrimental consequences for both the user and his or her family, and it brings further problems due to its status as a banned or illegal substance. For example, users may engage in dangerous or illegal activities (such as prostitution or theft) to obtain their supply of drugs. In addition, variations in the purity of the drugs used or the methods of administration (i.e., sharing needles) may expose users to risks beyond those associated with the drug itself.

The following sections introduce the areas for concern related to alcohol and drug abuse and the strategies for effectively assessing their use and dependence.

Alcohol Use and Abuse

Alcoholism, although a part of human life for thousands of years, is still not fully understood by modern professionals. The disease model of alcoholism, which provides the most established and accepted view of alcoholism today, first entered the professional literature through the writings of Benjamin Rush, M.D., in the early 1800s. Although different perspectives and treatments have emerged in recent years, especially those dealing with the influences of family, biology, and genetics, no single, universally effective treatment for alcohol dependence exists (Goodwin & Gabrielli, 1997).

Alcoholism differs from heavy drinking in that the former condition causes distress and disruption in the life of the person with alcohol dependency, as well as in the lives of members of that person's social and support systems (Goodwin & Gabrielli, 1997). Alcoholism is marked by a preoccupation with making sure that the amount of alcohol necessary for intoxication remains accessible at all times, which may cause the person to surround himself or herself with heavy drinkers in an attempt to escape observation. As alcoholism advances, the signs tend to become more concealed, as the user hides bottles or other "evidence," drinks alone, and covers up drinking binges. Feelings of guilt and anxiety over the behavior begin to appear, which usually leads to more drinking in an effort to escape the negative feelings, which in turn leads to an intensification of the negative feelings. This cycle of guilt and escape continues and despondency sets in, until the person "falls to rock bottom" and seeks treatment (Goodwin & Gabrielli, 1997, pp. 143–144).

Women who drink have patterns more like nonaddicted women than like men who drink. They are more likely to abuse prescription drugs, to consume substances in isolation, and to have had the onset of abuse after a traumatic event such as incest or racial or domestic violence (Nelson-Zlupko, Kauffman, & Dore, 1995). In addition, these women typically come from families in which drugs and alcohol were used. Women are less likely than men to enter and complete treatment programs. Their obstacles to treatment often include social stigma associated with alcoholism and a lack of available transportation and child care while in treatment (Yaffe, Jenson, & Howard, 1995). Because guilt and shame tend to be high already among alcohol-abusing women, aggressive confrontation designed to break through denial tends to be counterproductive. Instead, treatment approaches that focus on strengths, including coping tools such as identifying those characteristics of the unhealthy environment that have triggered drug usage and familiarizing women with a context of oppression, are recommended for better serving the needs of this population (Nelson-Zlupko, Kauffman & Dore, 1995).

Another serious problem associated with alcohol abuse involves adverse effects on offspring produced by the mother's alcohol consumption during pregnancy.[2] The potential effects range from full-blown fetal alcohol syndrome (FAS) to fetal alcohol effects (FAE). FAS is found in infants of chronic alcoholic mothers who have four to six drinks per day; it is characterized by prenatal and postnatal growth retardation, mental retardation, central nervous system defects, and abnormalities in shape and size of the head and/or facial features (dysmorphology). The severity of FAE (found in mothers who are social drinkers) varies according to the amount of alcohol consumed, but the risks associated with two drinks daily include miscarriage, prenatal growth retardation, behavioral deficiencies, and various anomalies. With increased consumption, partial effects of FAS may develop. In addition, some newborns demonstrate withdrawal effects from alcohol such as irritability, tremulousness, alcohol on the breath, transient seizures, and jitteriness.

Because excessive alcohol consumption can cause potentially severe damage to developing fetuses, social workers should routinely question mothers about their use of alcohol during pregnancy, gathering a history of consumption of beer, wine, and liquor (focusing on frequency, quantity, and variability). Other questions for substance abuse assessment are included in Table 9-2 on page 213.[3]

Use and Abuse of Other Substances

People abuse many types of drugs. Because immediate care may be essential in instances of acute drug intoxication, and because abusers often attempt to conceal their use of drugs, it is important that practitioners recognize the signs of abuse of commonly used drugs. Table 9-1 categorizes the most commonly abused drugs and their indications. In addition to those signs of abuse of specific drugs, common general indications include the following:

- Changes in attendance at work or school
- Decrease in normal capabilities (e.g., work performance, efficiency, habits)
- Poor physical appearance, neglect of dress and personal hygiene
- Use of sunglasses to conceal dilated or constricted pupils and to compensate for eyes' reduced ability to adjust to sunlight
- Unusual efforts to cover arms and hide needle marks
- Association with known drug users
- Need to steal or engage in prostitution to raise cash to support a drug habit

In assessing the possibility of drug abuse, it is important to elicit information not only from the suspected abuser (who may not be a reliable reporter for a number of reasons) but also from people who are familiar with the habits and lifestyle of the individual. Likewise, the social worker should assess problems of drug abuse from a systems perspective. Explorations of family relationships, for example, often reveal that drug abusers feel alienated from other family members. Moreover, family members often unwittingly contribute to the problems of both alcoholics and drug abusers. Consequently, many professionals regard problems of drug abuse as manifestations of dysfunction within the family

Table 9-1 Indications of abuse of commonly used drugs

TYPE OF DRUG	TYPICAL INDICATIONS
1. Central nervous system depressants (alcohol, Quaalude, Doriden, and various barbiturates)	Intoxicated behavior with/without odor, staggering or stumbling, "nodding off" at work, slurred speech, dilated pupils, difficulty concentrating
2. Central nervous system stimulants (amphetamines, including methamphetamine or "speed")	Excessively active, irritable, argumentative, nervous, dilated pupils, long periods without eating or sleeping
3. Cocaine and crack (also CNS)	Energetic, euphoric, fixed and dilated pupils, possible tremors (euphoria quickly replaced by anxiety, irritability, and/or depression, sometimes accompanied by hallucinations and paranoid delusions)
4. Opioids (opium, heroin, morphine)	Scars on arms or backs of hands from injecting codeine drugs, fixed and constricted pupils, frequent scratching, loss of appetite (but frequently eat sweets); may have sniffles, red and watering eyes, and cough until another "fix," lethargic, drowsy, and alternate between dozing and awakening ("nodding")
5. Cannabinols (marijuana, hashish)	In early stages, may be euphoric and appear animated, speaking rapidly and loudly with bursts of laughter; pupils may be dilated and eyes bloodshot; may have distorted perceptions such as increased sense of taste or smell; increased appetite; in later stages, may be drowsy
6. Hallucinogens (LSD, STP, DOM, mescaline, DTM, DET)	Behavior and mood vary widely, may sit or recline quietly in trancelike state or appear fearful or even terrified; dilated pupils in some cases; may experience nausea, chills, flushes, irregular breathing, sweating, or trembling of hands; may experience changes in sense of sight, hearing, touch, smell, and time
7. Inhalants and volatile hydrocarbons (chloroform, nail polish remover, metallic paints, carbon tetrachloride, amyl nitrate, butyl, isobutyl, nitrous oxide, lighter fluid, fluoride-based sprays)	Reduced inhibitions, euphoria, dizziness, slurred speech, unsteady gait, giddiness, drowsiness, nystagmus (constant involuntary eye movement)
8. Anabolic and androgenic steroids	Increased muscle strength and reduced body mass; aggression, competitiveness, and combativeness

Source: Lowinson, Ruiz, Millman, and Langrod (1997).

system. Keep in mind that drug abusers both affect and are affected by the family system.

Dual Diagnosis: Addictive and Mental Disorders

Because alcohol and other drug abuse problems can occur concomitantly with a variety of health and mental health problems, accurate assessment is important for proper treatment planning. As Lehman (1996) suggests, several combinations of factors must be taken into account:

• The type and extent of the substance use disorder

• The type of mental disorder(s) and the related severity and duration

- The presence of related medical problems
- Comorbid disability or other social problems resulting from use, such as correctional system involvement, poverty, or homelessness

Depending on the combination of factors that affect them, clients may have particular difficulty seeking out and adhering to treatment programs. Furthermore, an understanding of the interaction of these factors may affect the social worker's preferred intervention. For example, some psychiatric problems may emerge as a result of substance use (e.g., paranoia or depression). Social problems such as joblessness or incarceration may limit the client's access to needed treatment for substance abuse. Problems such as personality disorders may impede the development of a trusting and effective treatment relationship. Lehman (1996) suggests that the consistent use of screening devices will help alleviate gaps in assessment and identify service priorities for both the social worker and the treatment team. Smyth (1996) advocates motivational interviewing and the application of "stages of change" as methods for encouraging client participation in treatment of both disorders.

Using Interviewing Skills to Assess Substance Use

Social workers are often involved with substance users before they have actually acknowledged a problem or sought help for it (Barber, 1995). It may be difficult to be nonjudgmental when the user denies that illicit or licit substances are a problem and attempts to conceal the abuse by blaming others, lying, arguing, distorting, attempting to intimidate, diverting the interview focus, or verbally attacking the social worker. Despite these aversive behaviors, the social worker needs to express empathy and sensitivity to the client's feelings, recognizing that such behaviors are often a subterfuge behind which lie embarrassment, hopelessness, shame, ambivalence, and anger.

When asking about alcohol use, be forthright in explaining why you are pursuing that line of questioning. Vague questions tend to support the client's evasions and yield unproductive responses. The questions listed in Table 9-2 should be asked in a direct and compassionate manner. They address the extent and effects of the client's substance use, and the impact on his or her environment.

Table 9-2 Interviewing for substance abuse potential

The first six questions will help guide the direction of your interview, the questions you ask, and your further assessment.

1. Do you—or did you ever—smoke cigarettes? For how long? How many per day?
2. Do you drink?
3. What do you drink? (Beer, wine, liquor?)
4. Do you take any prescription medications regularly? How do they make you feel?
5. Do you use any over-the-counter medications regularly? How do they make you feel?
6. Have you ever used any illegal drug?
7. When was the last time you had a drink/used?
8. How much did you have to drink/use?
9. When was the last time before that?
10. How much did you have?
11. Do you always drink/use approximately the same amount? If not, is the amount increasing or decreasing?
12. (If it is increasing) Does that concern you?

(continued)

Table 9-2 *Cont'd*

13. Do most of your friends drink/use?

14. Do (or did) your parents drink/use?

15. Have you ever been concerned that you might have a drinking/drug problem?

16. Has anyone else ever suggested to you that you have (or had) a drinking/drug problem?

17. How does drinking/using help you?

18. Do other people report that you become more careless, or angry, or out of control when you have been drinking/using?

19. Do you drink/use to "get away from your troubles?"

20. What troubles are you trying to get away from?

21. Are you aware of any way in which drinking/using is interfering with your work?

22. Are you having any difficulties or conflict with your spouse or partner because of drinking/using?

23. Are you having financial difficulties? Are they related in any way to your drinking/using?

24. Have you ever tried to stop drinking/using? How?

Source: From *Where to Start and What to Ask: An Assessment Handbook* by Susan Lukas. Copyright © 1993 by Susan Lukas. Used by permission of W. W. Norton & Company, Inc.

ASSESSING COGNITIVE/PERCEPTUAL FUNCTIONING

Assessing how clients perceive their worlds is critically important, because people's perceptions of others, themselves, and events largely determine how they feel and respond to life's experiences in general and to their problematic situations in particular. Recall from Chapter 8 that the meanings or interpretations of events—rather than the events themselves—motivate human beings to behave as they do. Every person's world of experience is unique. Perceptions of identical events or circumstances thus vary widely according to the complex interaction of belief systems, values, attitude, state of mind, and self-concept, all of which in turn are highly idiosyncratic. It follows, then, that to understand and to influence human behavior you must first be knowledgeable about how people think. Our thought patterns are influenced by intellectual functioning, judgment, reality testing, coherence, cognitive flexibility, values, beliefs, self-concept, cultural belief system, and the dynamic interaction among cognitions, emotions, and behaviors that influence social functioning.

In the following sections, we briefly consider each of these factors.

Intellectual Functioning

Understanding the intellectual capacity of clients is essential for a variety of reasons. Your assessment of the client's intellectual functioning will allow you to adjust your verbal expressions to a level that the client can readily comprehend, and it will help you in assessing strengths and difficulties, negotiating goals, and planning tasks commensurate with his or her capacities. In most instances, a rough estimate of level of intellectual functioning will suffice. In making this assessment, you may want to consider the client's ability to grasp abstract ideas, to express himself or herself, and to analyze or think logically. Additional criteria include level of educational achievement and vocabulary employed, although these factors must be considered in relationship to the client's previous educational opportunities, primary language, or learning difficulties, because normal or high intellectual capacity may be masked by these and other features.

When clients have marked intellectual limitations, your communications should include easily understood words and avoid abstract explanations. To avoid embarrassment, many people will pretend that they understand when, in fact, they do not. Therefore, you should make keen observations and actively seek feedback to determine whether the client has grasped your intended meaning. You can also assist the client by using multiple, concrete examples to convey complex ideas.

When a client's presentation is inconsistent with his or her known intellectual achievement, it may reveal an area for further investigation. For example, have the client's capacities been affected by illness, medications, a head injury, or the use of substances?

Judgment

Some people who have adequate or even keen intellect may nevertheless encounter severe difficulties in life because they suffer deficiencies in judgment. Clients with poor judgment may get themselves into one jam after another. Examples of deficiencies in judgment include consistently living beyond one's means, becoming involved in "get rich quick" schemes without carefully exploring the possible ramifications, quitting jobs impulsively, leaving small children unattended, moving in with a partner with little knowledge of that person, failing to safeguard or maintain personal property, and squandering resources.

Deficiencies in judgment generally come to light when you explore in detail clients' problems and the patterns surrounding them. You may find that a client acts with little forethought, fails to consider the probable consequences of his or her actions, or engages in wishful thinking that things will somehow magically work out. With other clients, dysfunctional coping patterns may lead predictably to unfavorable outcomes. Because they fail to learn from their past mistakes, these individuals appear to be driven by intense impulses that overpower consideration of the consequences of their actions. Impulse-driven clients may lash out at authority figures, write bad checks, misuse credit cards, or do other things that provide immediate gratification but ultimately lead to loss of jobs, arrest, or other adverse consequences.

Reality Testing

Reality testing is a critical index to a person's mental health. Strong functioning on this dimension means meeting the following criteria:

1. Being properly oriented to time, place, person, and situation
2. Reaching appropriate conclusions about cause-and-effect relationships
3. Perceiving external events and discerning the intentions of others with reasonable accuracy
4. Differentiating one's own thoughts and feelings from those of others

Clients who are markedly disoriented may be severely mentally disturbed, under the influence of drugs, or suffering from a pathological brain syndrome. Disorientation is usually easily identifiable, but when doubt exists, questions about the date, day of the week, current events that are common knowledge, and recent events in the client's life will usually clarify the matter. Clients who are disoriented typically respond inappropriately, sometimes giving bizarre answers. For example, in responding to a question about his daily activities, a recluse reported that he consulted with the White House about foreign policy.

Some clients who do not have thought disorders may still have poor reality testing, choosing to blame circumstances and events rather than take personal responsibility for their actions (Rooney, 1992). For example, one client who stole an automobile externalized responsibility for his behavior by blaming the owner for leaving the keys in the car. Some clients blame their employers for losing their jobs, even though they habitually missed work for invalid reasons. Still others attribute their difficulties to fate, claiming that it decreed them to be losers. Whatever the sources of these problems with reality testing, they serve as impediments to motivation and meaningful change. Conversely, when clients take appropriate responsibility for their actions, that ownership should be considered an area of strength.

Perceptual patterns that involve distortions of external events are fairly common among clients but may cause difficulties, particularly in interpersonal relationships. *Mild distortions* may be associated with stereotypical perceptions (e.g., "All cops are out to get teenagers" or "The only interest men have in me is sexual"). *Moderate distortions* often involve marked misinterpretations of the motives of others and may severely impair interpersonal relationships (e.g., "My boss told me I was doing a good job and that there is an opportunity to be promoted to a job in another department; he's only saying that to get rid of me" or "My wife says she wants to take an evening class, but I know what she really wants . . . to meet other men"). In instances of *extreme distortions*, individuals may have *delusions* or false beliefs—for example, that others plan to harm them. On rare occasions, people suffering delusions may take violent actions to protect themselves from their imagined persecutors.

Dysfunction in reality testing of psychotic proportions is involved when clients "hear" voices or other sounds (auditory hallucinations) or see things that are not there (visual hallucinations). These individuals lack the capacity to distinguish between thoughts and beliefs that emanate from themselves and those that originate from external sources. As a consequence, they may present a danger to themselves or others when acting in response to such commands. Social workers must be able to recognize such severe cognitive dysfunction and respond with referrals for medication, protection, and/or hospitalization.

Coherence

Social workers occasionally encounter clients who demonstrate major thought disorders, which are characterized by rambling and incoherent speech. For example, successive thoughts may be highly fragmented and disconnected from one another, a phenomenon referred to as *looseness of association* or *derailment* in the thought processes. As Morrison puts it, the practitioner "can understand the sequence of the words, but the direction they take seems to be governed not by logic but by rhymes, puns or other rules that might be apparent to the

patient but mean nothing to you" (1995, p. 113). Another form of derailment is *flight of ideas*, in which the client's response seems to "take off" based on a particular word or thought, unrelated to logical progression or the original point of the communication.

These difficulties in coherence may be indicative of mania or thought disorders such as schizophrenia. Incoherence, of course, may also be produced by acute drug intoxication, so practitioners should be careful to rule out this possibility.

Cognitive Flexibility

Receptiveness to new ideas and the ability to analyze many facets of problematic situations are conducive not only to effective problem solving but also to general adaptability. People with cognitive flexibility generally seek to grow, to understand the part they play in their difficulties, and to understand others; these individuals can also ask for assistance without perceiving such a request to be an admission of weakness or failure. Many people, however, are rigid and unyielding in their beliefs, and their inflexibility poses a major obstacle to progress in the helping process.

A common pattern of cognitive inflexibility is thinking in absolute terms (e.g., a person is good or evil, a success or a failure, responsible or irresponsible—there are no in-betweens). Clients who think this way are prone to criticize others who fail to measure up to their stringent standards. Because they are difficult to live with, many of these individuals appear at social agencies because of relationship problems, workplace conflict, or parent–child disputes. Improvement often requires helping them examine the destructive impact of their rigidity, broaden their perspectives of themselves and others, and "loosen up" in general.

Negative cognitive sets also include biases and stereotypes that impede relationship building or cooperation with members of certain groups (e.g., authority figures, ethnic groups, and the opposite sex) as individuals. Severely depressed clients often have another form of "tunnel vision," viewing themselves as helpless or worthless and the future as dismal and hopeless. When they are lost in the depths of illness, these clients may selectively attend to their own negative attributes, be unable to feel good about themselves, and have difficulty opening themselves to other options.

Values

Values are an integral part of the cognitive-perceptual subsystem, because they strongly influence human behavior and often play a key role in the problems presented for work. For this reason, you should seek to identify your clients' values, assess the role those values play in their difficulties, and consider ways in which clients' values can be deployed to create incentives for change. Your ethical responsibility to respect the client's right to maintain his or her values and to make choices consistent with them requires you to become aware of those values. Because values result from our cultural conditioning, understanding the client's cultural reference group is important, particularly if it differs from your own. For example, traditional Native American values—(1) harmony with nature versus mastery of nature, (2) orientation to the present versus orientation to the present and future, (3) orientation to "being" activity versus orientation to "doing" activity, and (4) primacy of family and group goals versus primacy of individual goals (DuBray, 1985)—would be significant both in assessing Native American clients and in crafting appropriate interventions for their problems. Understanding the individual *within* his or her culture is critical, however, because people adopt values on a continuum, with considerable diversity occurring among people within any given race, faith, culture, or community (Gross, 1995).

Value conflicts often lay at the heart of clients' difficulties—for example, when an individual is torn between a desire for independence on the one hand and loyalty to his or her family on the other hand. Value conflicts may also be central to difficulties between people. Parents and children may disagree about dress, behavior, or responsibilities. Partners may hold different beliefs about how chores should be divided, how finances should be handled, or how they should relate to each person's family of origin.

Being aware of clients' values also aids you in using those values to create incentives for changing

dysfunctional behavior—for example, when clients express strong values yet behave in direct opposition to those values. *Cognitive dissonance* may result when clients discover inconsistencies between their thoughts or values and behaviors. Examining these contradictions can help reveal that this behavior is inconsistent and self-defeating. As an example, suppose an adolescent who has protested that his parents should trust him agrees that being trusted is important to him. The practitioner then clarifies that the client's persistent lying to his parents defeats any possibility of his meriting their trust. Only by changing his behavior can he realistically expect them to trust him.

Examples of questions that will clarify clients' values follow:

- "You say you believe your parents are old-fashioned about sex. What are your beliefs?"
- "If you could be married to an ideal wife, what would she be like?"
- [*To a couple*]: "What are your beliefs about how couples should make decisions?"
- "So you feel you're not succeeding in life. To you, what does being successful involve?"

Misconceptions

Cognitive theory holds that beliefs are important mediators of both emotions and actions (Ellis, 1962; Lantz, 1996). It makes sense, then, that mistaken beliefs can be related to problems in functioning. Examples of common misconceptions and contrasting functional beliefs include: "The world is a dog-eat-dog place; no one really cares about anyone except themselves" versus "There are all kinds of people in the world, including those who are ruthless and those who are caring; I need to seek out the latter and strive to be a caring person myself"; or "All people in authority use their power to exploit and control others" versus "People in authority vary widely—some exploit and control others, while others are benevolent; I must reserve judgment, or I will indiscriminately resent all authority figures."

It is important to identify misconceptions and their sources so as to create a comprehensive assessment. Depending on how central misconceptions are to the client's problems, the goals for work that follow may involve modifying key misconceptions, thereby paving the way to behavioral change. As with other areas, client strengths may derive from the *absence* of misconceptions, and from the ability to accurately perceive and construe events and motivations.

Self-Concept

Convictions, beliefs, and ideas about the self have been generally recognized as one of the most crucial determinants of human behavior. Thus, it is a strength to have good self-esteem and to be realistically aware of one's positive attributes, accomplishments, and potentialities as well as one's limitations and deficiencies. A healthy person can accept limitations as a natural part of human fallibility without being distressed or discouraged. People with high self-esteem, in fact, can joke about their limitations and failings.

Many people, however, are tormented with feelings of worthlessness, inadequacy, and helplessness. These and similarly self-critical feelings pervade their functioning in diverse negative ways, including the following:

- Underachieving in life because of imagined deficiencies
- Passing up opportunities because of fears of failing
- Avoiding social relationships because of fears of being rejected
- Permitting oneself to be taken for granted and exploited by others
- Excessive drinking or drug use to fortify oneself because of feelings of inadequacy
- Devaluing or discrediting one's worthwhile achievements
- Failing to defend one's rights

Often clients will spontaneously discuss how they view themselves, or their description of patterns of difficulty may imply damaged self-concept. An open-ended query, such as "Tell me how you see yourself," will often elicit rich information. Because many people have not actually given much thought to the matter, they may hesitate or appear perplexed. An additional query, such as

"Just what comes into your head when you think about the sort of person you are?" is usually all that is needed to prompt the client to respond.

Instruments have also been developed to measure self-esteem. The Index of Self-Esteem, one of the WALMYR scales (Hudson, 1992), can be completed by clients in a matter of minutes. It is also easily scored and interpreted.

Cognitive or Thought Disorders

The *Diagnostic and Statistical Manual* (DSM-IV-TR) is an important tool for understanding and formulating psychiatric diagnoses (American Psychiatric Association, 2000). As you assess the client's cognitive functioning, you may note signs and symptoms of thought disorders and developmental delays. Three key disorders to be alert to are mental retardation, schizophrenia, and dementia.

Mental retardation is typically diagnosed in infancy or childhood. It is defined as lower-than-average intelligence and "significant limitations in adaptive functioning in at least two of the following skill areas: communication, self-care, home living, social/interpersonal skills, use of community resources, self-direction, functional academic skills, work, leisure, health and safety" (American Psychiatric Association, 2000, p. 41). General intellectual functioning is appraised using standardized tests, and other measurement instruments may be used to assess the client's adaptive functioning, or ability to meet common life demands. Four levels of mental retardation are distinguished: mild, moderate, severe, and profound.

Schizophrenia is a psychotic disorder that causes marked impairment in social, educational, and occupational functioning. Its onset typically occurs during adolescence or young adulthood, and development of the disorder may be abrupt or gradual. It is signified by a combination of *positive and negative symptoms*. In this context, these terms do not refer to whether something is good or bad, but rather to the presence or absence of normal functions. For example, positive symptoms of schizophrenia "include distortions in thought content (delusions), perception (hallucinations), language and thought processes (disorganized speech), and self-monitoring of behavior (grossly disorganized or catatonic behavior)" (American Psychiatric Association, 2000, p. 299). Negative symptoms include flattened affect, restricted speech, and *avolition*, or limited initiation of goal-directed behavior.

Dementia is characterized by "multiple cognitive deficits that include memory impairment and at least one of the following: *aphasia* (deterioration in language functioning), *apraxia* (difficulty with motor activities), *agnosia* (failure to recognize familiar objects), or *disturbance in executive functioning* (abstract thinking, and planning, sequencing, and ceasing complex activities)" (American Psychiatric Association, 2000, p. 148). These deficits must be of a sufficient severity to affect one's daily functioning to warrant a diagnosis of dementia.

MENTAL STATUS EXAMS

One specialized form of assessment is the *mental status exam*. This exam is intended to capture and describe features of the client's mental state. The terminology developed in conjunction with these instruments has greatly facilitated communication among professions for both clinical and research purposes. Certain features on the mental status exam are associated with particular conditions, such as intoxication, dementia, depression, or psychosis.

The mental status exam consists of the following items (Lukas, 1993; Gallo, Fulmer, Paveza, & Reichel, 2000), many of which are described elsewhere in this chapter:

Appearance
How does the client look and act?

Stated age, dress and clothing

Psychomotor movements, tics, facial expressions

Reality Testing
Judgment

Dangerous, impulsive behaviors

Insight
- To what extent the client understands his or her problem
- How the client describes the problem

Speech
Volume: slow, inaudible

Rate of speech: rapid, slow

Amount: poverty of speech

Emotions
Mood: how the client feels most of the time
- Anxious, depressed, overwhelmed, scared, tense, restless, euthymic, euphoric

Affect: how the client appears to be feeling at this time
- Variability (labile)
- Intensity (blunted, flat)

Thought
Content: What the client thinks about
- Delusions: unreal belief, distortion

  Delusions of grandeur: unusual or exaggerated power

  Delusions of persecution: unreal belief that someone is after the client

  Delusions of control: someone else is controlling the client's thoughts or actions

  Somatic delusions: unreal physical concerns
- Other thought issues

  Obsessions: unrelenting, unwanted thoughts

  Compulsions: repeated behaviors, often linked to an obsession

  Phobias: obsessive thoughts that arouse intense fears

  Thought broadcasting: belief that others can read the client's mind

  Ideas of reference: insignificant or unrelated events that have a secret meaning to the client
- Homicidal ideation: desire or intent to hurt others
- Suicidal ideation: range from thought, desire, intent, or plan to die
- Process: how the client thinks

  Circumstantiality: lack of goal direction

  Perseveration: repeated phrase, repeated topic

  Loose associations: move between topics without connections

  Tangentiality: barely talking about the topic

  Flight of ideas: rapid speech that is unconnected

Sensory Perceptions
Illusions
- Misperception of normal sensory events

(continued)

Hallucinations
- Experience of one of the senses: olfactory (smell), auditory (hearing), visual (sight), gustatory (taste), tactile (touch)

Mental Capacities

Orientation times four: oriented to time, person, place, and situation

General intellect: average or low intelligence

Memory: remote (past presidents), recent (what the client ate yesterday for breakfast), and immediate (remember three items)

Concentration: Distraction during interview, count backward by 3s

Attitude toward Interviewer

How the client behaves toward the interviewer: suspicious, arrogant, cooperative, afraid, reserved, entertaining, ability to trust and open up, forthcoming

SAMPLE MINI MENTAL STATUS REPORT

Mr. Stewart presents as unshaven, thin, with unkempt hair, and older than his stated age. No abnormal body movements or tics are noted. Mr. Stewart is alert and oriented times four. His thought content and processes appear normal (although there are no specific questions to address delusions, hallucinations, or intellect). He describes his mood as euthymic, and his affect is guarded. While he is inquisitive about the clinician's notes and he provides only brief answers, Mr. Stewart is cooperative. His judgment is impaired, as seen by his driving while intoxicated and missing work. Mr. Stewart's insight is very limited, as he has come for evaluation to appease his wife and does not see his drinking as heavy or problematic. He denies thoughts or plans of suicide or homicide.

Treatment of individuals with these diagnoses is specialized and varied, but may include use of medication as well as vocational, residential, and case management services. Understanding the features of these and other cognitive/thought disorders will assist you in better understanding clients, in planning appropriate treatment, and in understanding how your role with clients meshes with that of other service providers.

ASSESSING EMOTIONAL FUNCTIONING

Emotions are affected by cognitions and powerfully influence behavior. People who seek help often do so because they have experienced strong emotions or a sense that their emotions are out of control. Some clients, for example, are emotionally volatile and engage in violent behavior while in the heat of anger. Others are emotionally unstable, struggling to stay afloat in a turbulent sea of emotion. Some people become emotionally distraught as the result of stress associated with the death of a loved one, divorce, severe disappointment, or another blow to self-esteem. Still others are pulled in different directions by opposing feelings and seek help to resolve their emotional dilemmas. To

assist you in assessing emotional functioning, the following sections examine vital aspects of this dimension and the related terms and concepts.

Emotional Control

People vary widely in the degree of control they exercise over their emotions, ranging from *emotional constriction* to *emotional excesses*. Individuals who are experiencing constriction may appear unexpressive and withholding in relationships. Because they are out of touch with their emotions, they do not appear to permit themselves to feel joy, hurt, enthusiasm, and other emotions that might otherwise invest life with zest and meaning. These individuals may be comfortable intellectualizing but retreat from expressing or discussing feelings. They often favorably impress others with their intellectual styles, but sometimes have difficulties maintaining close relationships because their emotional detachment thwarts them from fulfilling the needs of others for intimacy and emotional stimulation.

People with emotional excesses may have a "short fuse," losing control and reacting intensely to even mild provocations. This behavior may involve anger and escalate to interpersonal violence. It can also include other emotions such as irritability, crying, panic, despondency, helplessness, or giddiness. The key in assessing whether the emotional response is excessive entails determining whether it is appropriate and proportionate to the stimulus.

Your assessment may stem from your personal observation of the client, feedback from collateral contacts, or the client's own report of his or her response to a situation. As always, your appraisal of the appropriateness of the response must factor in the client's culture and the nature of his or her relationships with you. Both may lead you to misjudge the client's normal emotional response and what is considered "appropriate" emotional regulation.

Cultures vary widely in their approved patterns of emotional expressiveness.[4] Nevertheless, emotional health in any culture shares one criterion: It means having control over the emotions to the extent that one is not overwhelmed by them. Emotionally healthy persons also enjoy the freedom of experiencing and expressing emotions appropriately. Likewise, it is a strength to be able to bear painful emotions without denying or masking feelings or being incapacitated by them. Emotionally healthy persons are able to discern the emotional states of others, empathize, and discuss painful emotions openly without feeling unduly uncomfortable—recognizing, of course, that a certain amount of discomfort is natural. Finally, it is a strength to be able to mutually share deeply personal feelings in intimate relationships.

Range of Emotions

Another aspect of emotional functioning involves the ability to experience and to express a wide range of emotions that befits the vast array of situations that humans encounter. Some individuals' emotional experiencing remains confined to a limited range, which often causes interpersonal difficulties. For example, if one partner has difficulty expressing tender emotions, the other partner may feel rejected, insecure, or deprived of deserved affection.

Some individuals are unable to feel joy or to express many pleasurable emotions, a dysfunction referred to *anhedonia*. Still others have been conditioned to block out their angry feelings, blame themselves, or placate others when friction develops in relationships. Because of this blocking of natural emotions, they may experience extreme tension or physiological symptoms such as asthma, colitis, and headaches when they face situations that normally would engender anger or sadness. Finally, some people, to protect themselves from unbearable emotions, develop psychic mechanisms early in life that block them from experiencing rejection, loneliness, and hurt. Often this blockage is reflected by a compensatory facade of toughness and indifference, combined with verbal expressions such as "I don't need anyone" and "No one can hurt me." Whatever its source, a blocked or limited range of emotions may affect the client's difficulties and thus represent a goal for work.

Emotionally healthy people experience the full gamut of human emotions within normal limits of intensity and duration. The capacity to experience joy, grief, exhilaration, disappointment, and the rest of the full spectrum of emotions is, therefore, a strength.

Appropriateness of Affect

Direct observation of clients' affect (emotionality) usually reveals valuable information about their emotional functioning. Some anxiety or mild apprehension is natural in initial sessions (especially for involuntary clients and those referred by others), as contrasted to intense apprehension and tension at one extreme or complete relaxation at the other. Healthy functioning involves spontaneously experiencing and expressing emotion appropriate to the context and the material being discussed. The ability to laugh, to cry, and to express hurt, discouragement, anger, and pleasure when these feelings match the mood of the session constitutes an area of strength. Such spontaneity indicates that clients are in touch with their emotions and can express them appropriately.

Inordinate apprehension—often demonstrated by muscle tension, constant fidgeting or shifts in posture, hand wringing, lip-biting, and similar behaviors—usually indicates that a client is fearful, suspicious, or exceptionally uncomfortable in unfamiliar interpersonal situations. Such extreme tension may be expected in involuntary situations. In other cases, it may be characteristic of a client's demeanor in other contexts.

Clients who appear completely relaxed and express themselves freely in a circumstance that would normally evoke apprehension or anxiety may reflect a denial of a problem and or a lack of motivation to engage in the problem-solving process. Further, a charming demeanor may reflect the client's skill in projecting a favorable image when it is advantageous to do so. In some situations, such as in sales or promotional work, this kind of charm may be an asset; in other circumstances, it may be a coping style developed to conceal the individual's self-centeredness and manipulation or exploitation of others.

Emotional blunting is what the term suggests: a muffled or apathetic response to material that would typically evoke a stronger response (e.g., happiness, despair, anger) For example, emotionally blunted clients may discuss, in a detached and matter-of-fact manner, traumatic life events or conditions such as the murder of one parent by another, deprivation, or physical and/or sexual abuse. Emotional blunting can be indicative of a severe mental disorder, a sign of drug misuse, or a side effect of medications, so it always warrants special attention.

Inappropriate affect can also appear in other forms, such as laughing when discussing a painful event (gallows laughter) or smiling constantly regardless of what is being discussed. Elation or euphoria that is incongruent with the individual's life situation, combined with constant and rapid shifts from one topic to another (flight of ideas), irritability, expansive ideas, and constant motion, also suggests mania.

In transcultural work, appropriateness of affect must be considered in light of cultural differences. According to Lum (1996), minority clients may feel uncomfortable with nonminority social workers but mask their emotions as a protective measure, or they may control painful emotions according to culturally prescribed behavior. Measures to assure appropriate interpretation of client affect include understanding the features of the client's culture, consulting others familiar with the culture or the client, and evaluating the client's current presentation with his or her demeanor in the past.

Affective Disorders

The DSM-IV-TR (American Psychiatric Association, 2000) contains extensive information on the criteria for diagnosing affective disorders (i.e., disorders of mood). Of particular importance for the direct social worker are *bipolar disorders* (known formerly as manic-depressive illness) and *unipolar/ major affective disorders* (such as severe depression). Treatment of clients with these diagnoses generally includes medication (often with concurrent cognitive or interpersonal psychotherapy). These diagnoses provide direction in treatment planning. Moreover, they can often be linked to suicidal ideation and other serious risk factors.

Bipolar Disorder

The dominant feature of bipolar disorder is the presence of manic episodes (mania) with intervening periods of depression. Among the symptoms of mania are "a distinct period of abnormally and persistently elevated, expansive or irritable mood . . ." (American Psychiatric Association, 2000, p. 362) and at least three of the following:

- Inflated self-esteem or grandiosity
- Decreased need for sleep
- More talkative than usual or pressure to keep talking
- Flight of ideas or subjective experience that thoughts are racing
- Distractibility
- Increase in goal-directed activity (either socially, at work or school, or sexually) or psychomotor agitation
- Excessive involvement in pleasurable activities with a high potential for painful consequences, such as unrestrained buying sprees, sexual indiscretions, or foolish business investments

Full-blown manic episodes require that symptoms be sufficiently severe to cause marked impairment in job performance or relationships, or to necessitate hospitalization to protect patients or others from harm.

If exploration seems to indicate a client has the disorder, immediate psychiatric consultation is needed for two reasons: (1) to determine whether hospitalization is needed and (2) to determine the need for medication. Bipolar disorder is biogenetic, and various compounds containing lithium carbonate may produce remarkable results in stabilizing and maintaining affected individuals. Close medical supervision is required, however, because commonly used medications for this disorder have a relatively narrow margin of safety.

Major Depressive Disorder

Major depressive disorder, in which affected individuals experience recurrent episodes of depressed mood, is far more common than bipolar disorder. Major depression differs from the "blues" in that *dysphoria* (painful emotions) and the absence of pleasure (anhedonia) are present. The painful emotions commonly are related to anxiety, mental anguish, an extreme sense of guilt (often over what appear to be relatively minor offenses), and restlessness (agitation).

To be assigned a diagnosis of major depressive episode, a person must have evidenced depressed mood and loss of interest or pleasure as well as at least five of the following nine symptoms for at least 2 weeks (American Psychiatric Association, 2000, pp. 375–376):

- Depressed mood for most of the day, nearly every day
- Markedly diminished interest or pleasure in all, or almost all, activities
- Significant weight loss or weight gain when not dieting or decrease or increase in appetite
- Insomnia or hypersomnia
- Psychomotor agitation or retardation
- Fatigue or loss of energy
- Feelings of worthlessness, or excessive or inappropriate guilt
- Diminished ability to think or concentrate, or indecisiveness
- Recurrent thoughts of death or suicidal ideation or attempts

A number of scales are available to assess the presence and degree of depression, including the Depression Scale in the WALMYR Scales (Hudson, 1992), the Beck Depression Inventory (Beck, Ward, Mendelson, Mock, & Erbaugh, 1961), and the Zung Self-Rating Depression Scale (Zung, 1965). All of these instruments are easy to complete, to score, and to interpret. They are also highly correlated with one another.

When assessment reveals that clients are moderately or severely depressed, psychiatric consultation is indicated to determine the need for medication and/or hospitalization. Antidepressant medications have proven to be effective in accelerating recovery from depression and work synergistically with cognitive or interpersonal psychotherapy.[5]

In assessing depression, it is important to identify which factors precipitated the depressive episode. Often an important loss or series of losses will have occurred, and clients may need assistance in working through grief associated with these losses and developing compensatory sources of companionship and support. While depression and mourning may share certain characteristics such as intense sadness and sleep and appetite disturbances, grief reactions generally do not include the diminished self-esteem and guilt often observed in depression. "That is, the people who have lost someone do not regard themselves less because of such a loss or if they do, it tends to be only for a brief time. And if the survivors of the deceased experience guilt, it is usually guilt associated with some specific aspect of the loss rather than a general, overall sense of culpability" (Worden, 1991, p. 30).

Suicidal Risk

When clients exhibit severe depressive symptoms or hopelessness, it is critical to evaluate suicidal risk so that precautionary measures can be taken when indicated. With adults, the following factors are associated with high risk of suicide:

- Feelings of despair and hopelessness
- Previous suicidal attempts
- Concrete, available, and lethal plans to commit suicide (when, where, and how)

- Family history of suicide
- Perseveration about suicide
- Lack of support systems
- Feelings of worthlessness
- Belief that others would be better off if the client were dead
- Advanced age (especially for white males)
- Substance abuse

When a client indicates, directly or indirectly, that he or she may be considering suicide, it is incumbent on the social worker to address those concerns through careful and direct questioning. The social worker may begin by stating, "You sound pretty hopeless right now; I wonder if you might also be thinking of harming yourself?" or "When you say 'They'll be sorry' when you're gone, I wonder if that means you're thinking of committing suicide?" An affirmative answer to these probes should be followed with a frank and calm discussion of the client's thoughts about suicide. Has the client considered how he or she might do it? When? What means would be used? Are those means accessible? In asking these questions, the social worker is trying to determine not only the lethality of the client's plans but also the specificity. If a client has a well-thought-out plan in mind, the risk of suicide is potentially greater.

An understanding of the client's history, especially with regard to the risk factors mentioned and previous suicide attempts, will also help the worker decide the degree of danger presented and the level of intervention required. In addition, the following scales can be used to evaluate suicidal risk: the Hopelessness Scale (Beck, Resnik, & Lettieri, 1974), the Scale for Suicide Ideation (Beck, Kovacs, & Weissman, 1979), and the Suicide Probability Scale (Cull & Gill, 1991).[6]

When the client's responses indicate a potentially lethal attempt, it is appropriate to mobilize client support systems and arrange for psychiatric evaluation and/or hospitalization if needed. Such steps provide a measure of security for the client who may feel unable to control his or her impulses or who may become overwhelmed with despair.

Depression and Suicidal Risk with Children and Adolescents

Children and adolescents may experience depression just as adults do, and suicide can be a risk with these groups. It is estimated that 500,000 young people between ages 15 and 24 attempt suicide each year and nearly 5,000 children and youth (age 5 to 24) kill themselves each year. In fact, suicide is the third leading cause of death for those in the 15-to 24-year-old age bracket (McIntosh, 2003).

Clearly, it is important to recognize the symptoms of depression in adolescents and the behavioral manifestations that may be reported by peers, siblings, parents, or teachers. Common symptoms of depression in adolescents include the following:

- Anhedonia
- Depressed mood
- Significant weight loss or gain
- Insomnia or hypersomnia
- Psychomotor agitation or retardation
- Fatigue or loss of energy
- Feelings of hopelessness, worthlessness, guilt, and self-reproach
- Indecisiveness or decreased ability to concentrate
- Suicide ideation, threats, or attempts
- Recurring thoughts of death

Childhood depression does not differ markedly from depression in adolescence; the behaviors manifested and the intensity of feelings are similar, once developmental differences are taken into consideration (Wenar, 1994). One major difference between childhood and adolescent depression appears when comparing prevalence rates between the sexes. The prevalence of depression is approximately the same in boys and girls in middle childhood, but beginning in adolescence twice as many females suffer from depression as males (Kauffman, 1997). Also, adolescent girls diagnosed with depression report more feelings of anxiety and inadequacy in middle childhood, whereas adolescent boys report more aggressive and antisocial feelings (Wenar, 1994).

Because parents, coaches, and friends often do not realize the child or adolescent is depressed, it is important to alert them to the following potentially troublesome symptoms (American Association of Suicidology, 2004; Gold, 1986):

- Deterioration in personal habits
- Decline in school achievement
- Marked increase in sadness, moodiness, and sudden tearful reactions
- Loss of appetite
- Use of drugs or alcohol
- Talk of death or dying (even in a joking manner)
- Withdrawal from friends and family
- Making final arrangements, such as giving away valued possessions
- Sudden or unexplained departure from past behaviors (from shy to thrill seeking or from outgoing to sullen and withdrawn)

Given the mood swings and tempestuousness typical of adolescence, these warning signs should be regarded as indications of serious depression only when they persist for 10 days or longer. If you observe several of these symptoms, psychiatric consultation is advisable.

Suicidal risk is highest when the adolescent, in addition to exhibiting the aforementioned symptoms of severe depression, shows feelings of hopelessness, has recently experienced a death of a loved one, has severe conflict with parents, has lost a close relationship with a key peer or a sweetheart, and lacks a support system. Brent and colleagues indicate that "interpersonal conflict, especially with parents, is one of the most commonly reported precipitants for completed and attempted suicides" (1993, p. 185). Other studies have indicated that moderate to heavy drinking or drug abuse is implicated in at least 50% of adolescent suicides (Fowler, Rich, & Young, 1986).

While completed suicides and suicide attempts are more common among adolescents (with adolescent males completing more suicides and adolescent females attempting more suicides), the number of younger children completing and attempting suicide is increasing (Kauffman, 1997).

Therefore, it is important to be cognizant of depressed behavior and signs of suicide ideation in children as well as adolescents. Warning signs of suicide ideation in younger children are similar to those discussed for adolescents, albeit translated to the appropriate developmental level.

When faced with a young client who is considering suicide, social workers should use the same lethality assessment questions discussed earlier for work with adults. In addition, assessment tools geared to evaluating suicide risk in children and adolescents are available, such as the Children's Depression Scale (Kovacs, 1992) and the Johns Hopkins Depression Scale (Joshi, Capozzoli, & Coyle, 1990). After the degree of lethality is determined, appropriate interventions can then be implemented, such as making a no-suicide agreement, teaching nonviolent ways to solve problems and get attention, and reestablishing or creating peer and adult support networks (Kauffman, 1997).

An additional technique for exploring and responding to suicidal ideation in young people is to ask "Who would find you?" This question helps uncover the "child's suicidal fantasies and actions, affects, concepts of death and family circumstances" (Pfeffer, 1986, p. 176) and aids in the assessment of interpersonal conflicts that may have precipitated the suicidal threat. The client's responses to probes such as "How would they find you?", "Would you still be alive?", and "How would they react?" will help the interviewer to weigh the level of suicidal risk and learn more about the feelings and needs leading to the consideration of suicide. These questions also facilitate the development of curative responses, such as examining how the client might meet the needs expressed (for love, forgiveness, acceptance) without resorting to self-injurious behaviors (Holman, 1997).

ASSESSING BEHAVIORAL FUNCTIONING

In direct social work practice, change efforts frequently target behavioral patterns that impair the client's social functioning. As you assess behavior, it is important to keep in mind that one person's behavior does not influence another person's behavior in simple linear fashion. Rather, a circular process takes place, in which the behavior of all participants *reciprocally* affects and shapes the behavior of other participants.

Because behavioral change is commonly the focus of social work interventions, you must be skillful in discerning and assessing both dysfunctional and functional patterns of behavior. In individual sessions, you can directly observe clients' social and communication patterns as well as some personal habits and traits. In conjoint interviews and group sessions, you can observe these behavioral patterns as well as the effects that these actions have on others.

In assessing behavior, it is helpful to think of problems as consisting of excesses or deficiencies on the part of clients. For excesses-related problems, interventions aim to *diminish* or *eliminate* the behaviors, such as temper outbursts, too much talking, arguing, competition, and consumptive

excesses (e.g., food, alcohol, sex, or shopping) For behavioral deficiencies, when assessment reveals the absence of needed skills, interventions aim to help clients *acquire* the skills and behaviors to function more effectively. For example, a client's behavioral repertoire may not include skills in expressing feelings directly, engaging in social conversation, listening to others, solving problems, managing finances, planning nutritional meals, being a responsive sexual partner, or handling conflict.

In addition to identifying dysfunctional behavioral patterns, it is important to be aware of those behaviors that are effective and represent strengths. To assist you in assessing both dysfunctional and functional patterns of behavior, Table 9-3 lists numerous patterns of individual behavior. The behavioral categories in Table 9-3 do not include dysfunctional patterns of interaction between two or more persons in couples, family, and group contexts, as these are addressed in later chapters in this book. Instead, the list focuses on

Table 9-3 Behavioral patterns

DIMENSIONS OF BEHAVIOR	DYSFUNCTIONAL PATTERNS	FUNCTIONAL PATTERNS (STRENGTHS)
Power/control	Autocratic, overbearing, aggressive, ruthless, demanding, domineering, controlling, passive submissive; excludes others from decision making	Democratic, cooperative, assertive; includes others in decision making, stands up for own rights
Nurturance/support	Self-centered, critical, rejecting, withholding, demeaning, distant, punitive, fault-finding, self-serving, insensitive to or unconcerned about others	Caring, approving, giving, empathic, encouraging, patient, generous, altruistic, warm, accepting, supportive, interested in others
Responsibility	Undependable, erratic; avoids responsibility, places pleasure before responsibility, externalizes responsibility for problems, neglects maintenance of personal property	Dependable, steady, consistent, reliable, follows through, accepts responsibility, owns part in problems, maintains personal property
Social skills	Abrasive, caustic, irritable, insensitive, aloof, reclusive, sarcastic, querulous, withdrawn, self-conscious, ingratiating, lacks social delicacy	Outgoing, poised, personable, verbally fluent, sociable, witty, courteous, engaging, cooperative, assertive, spontaneous, respectful to others, sensitive to feelings of others, has sense of propriety

Coping patterns	Rigid, impulsive, rebellious; avoids facing problems, uses alcohol or drugs when under stress, becomes panicky, lashes out at others, sulks	Flexible; faces problems, considers and weighs alternatives, anticipates consequences, maintains equilibrium, seeks growth, consults others for suggestions, negotiates and compromises
Personal habits	Disorganized, dilatory, devious, dishonest, compulsive, overly fastidious, impulsive, manifests poor personal hygiene, has consumption excesses, has irritating mannerisms	Planful, organized, flexible, clean, efficient, patient, self-disciplined, well groomed, honest, open, sincere, temperate, considerate, even dispositioned, punctual
Communication	Mumbles, complains excessively, nags, talks excessively, interrupts others, tunes others out, stammers, yells when angry, withholds views, defensive, monotonic, argumentative, taciturn, verbally abusive	Listens attentively, speaks fluently, expresses views, shares feelings, uses feedback, expresses self spontaneously, considers others' viewpoints, speaks audibly and within tolerable limits
Accomplishment	Unmotivated, aimless, nonproductive, easily discouraged, easily distracted, underachieving, lacks initiative, seldom completes endeavors, workaholic, slave to work	Ambitious, industrious, self-starting, independent, resourceful, persevering, successful in endeavors, seeks to advance or improve situations
Affectionate/sexual	Unaffectionate, reserved, distant, sexually inhibited, promiscuous, lacking sexual desire, engages in deviant sexual behavior	Warm, loving, affectionate, demonstrative, sexually responsive (appropriately)

those patterns that most frequently create interpersonal difficulties.

As you review Table 9-3, you may question whether some of the patterns are functional or dysfunctional. This determination, of course, depends on the situational context within which the behavior occurs. Aggressive behavior may serve a self-protective function in a prison environment but may be dysfunctional in family relationships or in most groups. Your evaluation, then, must take context into account, and consider the effect of the behavior on the client's environment and success in functioning.

Note that Table 9-3 includes many adjectives and verbs that are very general and are subject to different interpretations. In assessing behavior, it is vital to specify actual problem behaviors. For example, rather than assess a client's behavior as "abrasive," a social worker might describe the behaviors leading to that conclusion—the client constantly interrupts his fellow workers, insults

them by telling them they are misinformed, and boasts about his own knowledge and achievements. It is easier for you and the client to focus your change efforts when detrimental behavior is operationalized.

An adequate assessment of behavior, of course, goes beyond merely identifying dysfunctional behaviors. You must also determine the antecedents of behaviors—when, where, and how frequently they occur—and specify the consequences of the behaviors. Further, you should explore thoughts that precede, accompany, and follow the behavior, as well as the nature of and intensity of emotions associated with the behavior.

ASSESSING MOTIVATION

As introduced in Chapter 8, evaluating and enhancing client motivation are integral parts of the assessment process. When working with family members or groups, social workers are likely to encounter a range of motivation levels within a single client system. Clients who do not believe that they can influence their environments may demonstrate a kind of *learned helplessness*, a passive resignation that their lives are out of their hands. Others may be at different phases in their readiness to change. Prochaska and DiClemente (1986) suggest a five-stage model for change: *precontemplation, contemplation, determination, action,* and *maintenance.* The initial stage is characterized by a lack of awareness of the need for change. In the contemplation stage, the client recognizes his or her problem and the consequences that result. In the determination phase, the client is committed to action and works with the clinician to develop a plan for change. Action and maintenance implement the changes identified and take steps to avoid problem recurrence.

To assess motivation, the social worker needs to understand the person, his or her perception of the environment, and the process by which he or she has decided to seek help. Motivation, of course, is a dynamic force that is strongly influenced by ongoing interaction with the environment, including interaction with the social worker. *Motivational interviewing* is a specialized, person-centered method for addressing ambivalence and enhancing motivation (Moyers & Rollnick, 2002).

As Reid (1978) points out, motivation consists of two critical aspects. The first aspect is the *direction* of the motivation—that is, toward what goals is the client motivated? Clients are generally motivated to fulfill certain wants or needs. In evaluating the direction of motivation, the central issue is whether clients' wants are realistic and achievable. Some clients seek to accomplish goals that exceed their capacity (e.g., vocational goals that require aptitude well beyond that possessed by the client). Others express wants that require changes beyond the sphere of influence of the client or practitioner (e.g., "I want you to persuade my wife to drop her divorce action and to reconcile with me" or "I want you to get my kids back; they need me and are not happy in that foster home"). In such instances, you must tactfully assist clients

to recognize the unrealistic nature of their wants and direct them toward realistic goals that are relevant to their problematic situation (e.g., "Only the judge has the authority to return your children to you, but I'm very willing to assist you in making whatever changes are necessary to meet the conditions he has specified for the return of your children").

The second aspect concerns the *strength* of motivation. Clients often have "wants" but lack the willingness or skills needed to participate actively in planning and implementing remedial actions. Many clients have misconceptions about the helping role, assuming that the practitioner has "magical power" with which to solve difficulties. Other clients are willing to participate but mistakenly perceive their role as a passive one. Strengths in motivation are apparent when the client is committed to change, views the practitioner as a partner and facilitator, and assumes responsibility for mutually exploring his or her problems and for planning and implementing the remedial measures.

You can often determine the direction and strength of the client's motivation by carefully exploring the life events that precipitated the decision to seek service. When clients seek service shortly after critical events occur and request assistance in modifying behavior or circumstances associated with these events, their motivation is likely to be adequate in both direction and strength.

In contrast, when the decision to seek assistance resulted from a referral in the form of an ultimatum from a family member or employer, the client's motivation is likely to be weaker. When nonvoluntary clients lack motivation to work on the problems attributed to them by their referral sources, social workers should first clarify the choices available to them. Such a clarification focuses attention on the problems acknowledged by clients rather than those identified by other parties (Reid, 1978). Consequently, it is possible to find problems for which there *is* adequate motivation both in strength and direction if attention is devoted to those problems acknowledged by clients.

ASSESSING ENVIRONMENTAL SYSTEMS

After evaluating the history and pattern of the presenting problem and various facets of the client's individual functioning, the social worker must assess the client in the context of his or her environment. The environment was a central concern of pioneers in social work in the late 1800s and early 1900s, but receded into the background of social work theory by the 1920s, having been overshadowed by theories related to individual functioning—most notably, Freudian psychoanalysis. The trend of emphasizing the individual continued until the 1960s and 1970s, when it was supplemented by interactional and systems theory (including theories of family therapy). Although theoreticians did not exclude the environment from their formulations, they accorded it minor significance. The early 1970s witnessed a strong resurgence of interest in the environment. This development was greatly influenced by ecological and systems theories, as well as by the increased emphasis placed on the environment by prominent ego psychologists. Coinciding with this change, milieu treatments came into prominence in many residential and institutional settings.

The ecological perspective does not represent a swing of the pendulum from primary focus on the person to the other extreme of primary focus on the environment. Rather, assessment focuses on the *transactions* between the two, or the *goodness of fit* between the person and his or her environment. Problem-solving efforts may be directed toward assisting people to adapt to their environments (e.g., training them in interpersonal skills), altering environments to meet the needs of clients more adequately (e.g., enhancing both the attractiveness of a nursing home and the quality of its activities), or a combination of the two (e.g., enhancing the interpersonal skills of a withdrawn, chronically ill person and moving the person to a more stimulating environment). This part of assessment, then, goes beyond the evaluation of resources described in Chapter 8 to take a holistic view of the client's environment and examines the adequacy of various aspects of the environment to meet the client's needs. The issues of affordability, availability, and accessibility (introduced earlier in this chapter) provide a useful framework for examining transactions with the environment and targeting the nature of strengths and barriers in those transactions.

In assessing environments, you should give the highest priority to those aspects that are most salient to the client's individual situation. The adequacy of the environment depends on the client's life stage, physical and mental health, interests, aspirations, and other resources. For example, a family may not be concerned about living in a highly polluted area unless one of the children suffers from asthma that is exacerbated by the physical environment. Another family may not worry about the availability of day treatment programs for an adult child with mental retardation until a crisis (e.g., death of a parent or need to return to work) forces them to look outside the family for accessible, affordable services.

You should tailor your assessments of clients' environments to their varied life situations, weighing the individual's unique needs against the availability of essential resources and opportunities within their environments. In addition to noting the limitations or problems posed by inadequate physical or social environments, acknowledge the strengths at play in the client's life—the importance of a stable, accessible, affordable residence or the value of a support system that mobilizes in times of trouble.

The following list describes basic environmental needs; you can employ this list in evaluating the adequacy of your client's environments:

1. A physical environment that is adequate, is stable, and fosters the client's health and safety (this includes housing as well as surroundings that are free of toxins and other health risks)

2. Adequate social support systems (e.g., family, relatives, friends, neighbors, organized groups)

3. Affiliation with a meaningful and responsive faith community

4. Access to timely, appropriate, affordable health care (including physicians, dentists, medications, and nursing homes)

5. Access to safe, reliable, affordable child and elder care services

6. Access to recreational facilities

7. Transportation—to work, socialize, utilize resources, and exercise rights as a citizen

8. Adequate housing that provides ample space, sanitation, privacy, and safety from hazards and pollution (both air and noise)

9. Adequate police and fire protection and a reasonable degree of security

10. Safe and healthful work conditions

11. Adequate financial resources to purchase essential resources

12. Adequate nutritional intake

13. Predictable living arrangements with caring others (especially for children)

14. Opportunities for education and self-fulfillment

15. Access to legal assistance

16. Employment opportunities

We will address the first three areas—physical environment, social support systems, and faith community—in depth, in light of their particular importance for client functioning. This discussion may also help you to generalize some of the complexities of environmental assessment to the other 13 areas.

Physical Environment

Physical environment refers to the stability and adequacy of one's physical surroundings and whether the environment fosters or jeopardizes the client's health and safety. A safe environment is free of threats such as personal or property crimes. Assessing health and safety factors includes considering sanitation, space, and heat. Extended families may be crammed into small homes or apartments without adequate beds and bedding, homes may not be designed for running water or indoor toilets, or access to water may be broken or shut off. Inadequate heat or air conditioning can exacerbate existing health conditions and lead to danger during periods of bad weather. Further, families may take steps to heat their residences (such as with ovens or makeshift fires) that can

create further health dangers. Sanitation may be compromised by insect or rodent infestations or by owner or landlord negligence in conforming to building standards and maintaining plumbing. The home may be located in areas with exposure to toxic materials or poor air quality.

For an elderly client, an assessment of the physical environment should also look at the client's living situation and consider whether that situation meets the client's health and safety needs (Rauch, 1993). If an elderly client lives alone, does the home have adequate resources for the client to meet his or her functional needs? Can the client use bathroom and kitchen appliances to conduct his or her daily activities? Does clutter contribute to the client's confusion or risk (e.g., not being able to find bills or stumbling over stacked newspapers)? Is the home a safe environment for the client to be in, or do some aspects of the building (e.g., stairs or loose carpeting) pose a danger to less mobile clients? If the client resides in an institution, are there mementos of home and personal items that bring comfort to the individual?

Tools designed to assess functional ability provide objective information that can be used to screen for and address risk factors, as well as to evaluate progress at a later date. Instruments such as the Older American Resources and Services (OARS) questionnaire utilize information gathered from the client, from collateral contacts such as family members, and from interviewer impressions regarding different aspects of the client's life, including activities of daily living (ADLs) and the client's environment, with which to assess functioning (Van Hook et al., 1996).

When the environment poses dangers to clients or exacerbates other problems, steps must be taken to improve living conditions. Because of the geographic ties and the scarcity of adequate low-cost housing, moving to a better neighborhood or a safer home may not be feasible. Some groups, such as the elderly, may qualify for subsidized housing facilities, which provide both adequate housing and social opportunities. You may also help clients to access home improvement, heating assistance, and other programs to enhance their living conditions. When other parties are responsible for detrimental environmental conditions, social workers should assist clients in undertaking advocacy actions to address these problems or in organizing with other neighbors to lobby for change and develop "block watch" or other mutual aid services.

Social Support Systems

Embodied in the earlier list of resources are social systems that provide needed goods and services. Diverse social support systems either are part of the problem configuration or represent resources needed to improve the client's quality of life. To enable you to identify pertinent social systems, Figure 9-2 depicts interrelationships between individuals and families and other systems (Hartman, 1994).

Systems that are central in a person's life appear in the center of the diagram in Figure 9-2. These systems typically play key roles as both sources of

Figure 9-2 Diagram of Ecological Social Systems

difficulties and resources that may be tapped or modified in problem solving. Moving from the center to the periphery in the areas encompassed by the concentric circles are systems that are progressively farther removed from individuals and their families. There are exceptions, of course, such as when an individual feels closer to an intimate friend or a pastor than to family members. Moreover, if clients' situations require frequent contacts with institutions or organizations (e.g., child protective services, income maintenance programs, and judicial systems), those institutions will no longer occupy a peripheral position because of how dramatically they affect individuals and families at such times. The intensity of affiliation with extended family or kinship networks may vary by cultural group and reflect the effects of migration and cultural dislocation (Jilek, 1982; Kumabe et al., 1985; Mwanza, 1990; Ponce, 1980; Sotomayor, 1991; Sue, 1981). Reciprocal interactions thus change across time, and diagrams depicting these interactions should be viewed as snapshots that remain accurate only within limited time frames.

The challenge in diagramming clients' social networks is to include the salient boundaries of the clients' situation and to specify how the systems interact, fail to interact, or are needed to interact in response to clients' needs. One useful tool is the *eco-map*, which identifies and organizes relevant environmental factors outside of the individual or family context. Eco-maps are useful in clarifying the supports and stresses in the client's environment, revealing patterns such as social isolation, conflicts, or unresponsive social systems. They also show the direction in which resources flow (for example, if client gives but does not receive support).

The eco-map can be completed by the worker following discussion with the client or in tandem with the client (Strom-Gottfried, 1999b). In it, the client system (individual, couple, or family) are in the middle circle and the systems relevant to their lives appear in the surrounding circles. The nature of positive interactions, negative interactions, or needed resources can be depicted by using colored lines to connect the individual or other family members to pertinent systems, where

different colors represent positive, negative, or needed connections and interactions with those systems. If colored lines do not appeal to you, then you can use different types of lines—single, double, broken, wavy, dotted, or cross-hatched—to characterize the relationships and the flow of resources among the systems.

Social support systems (SSSs) are increasingly recognized as playing a crucial role in determining the level of social functioning. Theorists have long recognized the critical importance of a nurturing environment to healthy development of infants and children, but it is now clear that adults also have vital needs that can be met only through affiliation with supportive systems. What benefits accrue from involvement with SSSs?

1. Attachment, provided by close relationships that give a sense of security and sense of belonging

2. Social integration, provided by memberships in a network of people who share interests and values

3. The opportunity to nurture others, which provides incentive to endure in the face of adversity

4. Physical care when persons are unable to care for themselves due to illness, incapacity, or severe disability

5. Validation of personal worth (which promotes self-esteem), provided by family and colleagues

6. A sense of reliable alliance, provided primarily by kin

7. Guidance, child care, financial aid, and other assistance in coping with difficulties as well as crises

Consequently, the lack of adequate SSSs is a vulnerability and may represent a source of distress, whereas adequate SSSs reduce the effects of stressful situations and facilitate successful adaptation. Knowing what the SSSs are and what roles they play with clients is essential for assessment and may even be the focus of interventions that tap into the potential of dormant SSSs or mobilize new ones.

Members of certain groups may have particular need for enhanced SSSs, or may be especially vulnerable due to limited or blocked SSSs:

- The elderly (Berkman et al. 1999)

- Abused or neglected children (Brissette-Chapman, 1997)

- Teenage parents (Barth & Schinke, 1984; Brindis, Barth, & Loomis, 1987; De Anda & Becerra, 1984)

- Persons with AIDS (Indyk, Belville, Lachapelle, Gordon, & Dewart, 1993)

- Widows and widowers (Lieberman & Videka-Sherman, 1986)

- Persons with severe mental illness, and their families (Zipple & Spaniol, 1987; Rapp, 1998)

- The terminally ill (Arnowitz, Brunswick, & Kaplan, 1983)

- Persons with disabilities (Hill, Rotegard, & Bruininks, 1984; Mackelprang & Hepworth, 1987)

- Persons who experience geographical and/or cultural dislocation as refugees and immigrants (Hulewat, 1996)

The reasons for diminished social supports may vary by group, and each presents challenging opportunities to social workers when collaborating to develop natural support networks and to plan service delivery systems that respond to the individual's unique needs.

In some vulnerable groups, you may find that other, more experienced and sophisticated members of the group are willing to assist "newcomers" to find their way through the maze of bureaucratic structures. Indigenous nonprofessionals have also been employed as staff members to serve as client advocates, provide direct outreach, organize disenfranchised people for social action, and assume the role of advocate or interpreter (in both language and policy). For example, they may assist people to utilize resources within a given agency, intervene with other social systems to obtain timely responses, provide direct services (e.g., homemaking, babysitting, shopping, and escorting clients to various agencies), discuss problems in times of crisis, and render technical assistance (e.g., completing forms, writing letters, and establishing eligibility for services) (Congress, 1994; Harper & Lantz, 1996).

Within some cultures and geographic regions, the extended family may provide an extensive network of support and assistance in crisis situations. There may also be cultural variations in the person to whom one turns for assistance with life problems. In many Native American tribal groups, for example, members actively seek counsel from elders in coping with family problems. This wisdom is highly valued, and elderly members of the tribe are accorded much respect (Hull, 1982). Southeast Asian immigrants may seek assistance from clan leaders, shamans, or herbalists, depending on the nature of the difficulty. Similar examples of specialized supports abound in other cultures and communities.

To this point, we have highlighted the positive aspects of SSSs. It is also important to note that some SSSs may foster and sustain problems in functioning. For example, overprotective parents may stunt the development of competence, autonomy, and personal responsibility in their children. Street gangs and other antisocial peer groups may foster violence and criminality, even as they provide a sense of belonging and affiliation. Friends may ridicule a woman in her forties who wants to return to school, thereby undermining her confidence.

Social workers must be aware of the various social networks at play in a client's life, and assess the roles that those SSSs play in the client's difficulties or in the client's ability to overcome such problems. Sometimes, a negative support system can be counteracted by the development of prosocial or positive networks. At other times, the system itself may be the focus of intervention, as the social worker strives to make the members aware of their roles in the client's problems and progress.

As noted in Chapter 8, assessment of social supports involves examining their reciprocal interactions with the client and the client's perceptions of their importance. A number of instruments have been developed to assess SSSs: the Schedule for Social Interaction (Henderson, Duncan-Jones,

Byrne, & Scott, 1980), the Social Support Network Inventory (Flaherty, Gaviria, & Pathak, 1983), the Perceived Social Support Network Inventory (Oritt, Paul, & Behrman, 1985), and the Questionnaire on Resources and Stress (Clayton, Glidden & Kiphart, 1994). An instrument that is especially practical for social workers is the Social Network Grid (Tracy & Whittaker, 1990). This instrument yields the following information:

1. Key persons in clients' social networks
2. Areas of life in which the support occurs
3. Specified types of support provided by each person
4. The degree to which support persons are critical
5. Whether the support is reciprocal or unidirectional
6. The degree of personal closeness
7. The frequency of contacts
8. Length of the relationship

Completion of the grid, for which Tracy and Whittaker provide explicit instructions, yields rich information for both the practitioner and the client and helps provide direction for intervention.

Spirituality and Affiliation with a Faith Community

The issue of one's spirituality and its expression actually transcends the categories of individual functioning and environmental systems. Spirituality can shape beliefs and provide strength during times of adversity, and the link to a faith community can be a tangible source of resources and social support. While we have placed our discussion of this issue within the context of assessing environmental systems, we will address assessment of faith more broadly.

Canda differentiates between spirituality and religion, suggesting that *spirituality* is the totality of the human experience that cannot be broken into individual components, whereas *religion* is the socially sanctioned institution based on those spiritual practices and beliefs (1997). Sherwood also distinguishes between spirituality and religion,

wherein the former reflects the "human search for transcendence, meaning and connectedness beyond the self" and "religion refers to a more formal embodiment of spirituality into relatively specific belief systems, organizations and structures" (1998, p. 80). He cites a typology by Ressler wherein persons may fall into one of four categories: spiritual and nonreligious; religious and dispirited; dispirited and nonreligious; and spiritual and religious. A "spiritual assessment," then, may help the worker to better understand the client's belief system and resources.

Questions such as "What are your sources of strength and hope?", "How do you express your spirituality?", "Do you identify with a particular religion or faith?", and "Is your religious faith helpful to you?" can begin to elicit information as the foundation to seeking further understanding about the client's beliefs. Authors such as Sherwood (1998) and Ellor, Netting, and Thibault (1999) offer a variety of guides for gathering information about both clients' spiritual beliefs and religious affiliations.

Why is it important to understand the role of religion and spirituality in the lives of your clients? As Ratliff notes in discussing health care settings,

> Religious beliefs may dictate food choices, clothing styles, customs of birthing and dying, etiquette in the sick room, use of modern conveniences, invasive procedures, organ donation, reception, use of blood products, certain diagnostic tests, gynecological procedures, spiritual influences on or control of sickness and healing, the wearing of protective devices or tattoos, and the need for prayers and rituals performed by various religious specialists. (1996, p. 171)

At times, religious issues may be central to the presenting problems clients bring to service. For example, parents may disagree about the spiritual upbringing of their children; couples may be at odds over the proper roles of women and men; families may be in conflict about behaviors proscribed by certain religions, such as premarital sex, contraceptive use, alcohol use, divorce, or homosexuality (Meystedt, 1984).

As Thibault, Ellor, and Netting (1991), conceptualize it, spirituality involves three relevant areas: cognitive (the meaning given to past, current, and personal events), affective (one's inner life and sense of connectedness to a larger reality), and behavioral (the way in which beliefs are affirmed, such as through group worship or individual prayer). Thus, spiritual beliefs may affect the client's response to adversity, the coping methods employed, the sources of support available (e.g., the faith community may form a helpful social network), and the array of appropriate interventions available. Particularly when clients have experienced disaster or unimaginable traumas, the exploration of suffering, good and evil, shame and guilt, and forgiveness can be a central part of the change process. As Ellor et al. (1999) and others suggest, social workers must be aware of their own spiritual journey and understand the appropriate handling of spiritual content, depending on the setting, focus, and client population involved. Social workers are also advised to involve clergy or leaders of other faiths to work jointly in addressing the personal and spiritual crises faced by clients (Grame et al., 1999).

WRITTEN ASSESSMENTS

The assessment phase is a critical part of the helping process: It provides the foundation on which goals and interventions are based. It is also an ongoing part of the helping process, as appraisals are reconsidered and revised based on new information and understanding. As a written product, assessments may be done at intake, following a period of interviews and evaluations, and at the time of transfer or termination (a summary assessment). They may be brief and targeted (such as an assessment for referral), a detailed report for the court or another entity, or a comprehensive biopsychosocial assessment. Whichever form it takes, several standards must be followed to craft a sound document that clearly conveys accurate information and credible depictions of the client (Kagle, 2002).

1. *Remember your purpose and audience.* They will help you decide what should be included and maintain that focus. Know the standards and expectations that apply in your work setting, and understand the needs of those who will review your document.

2. *Be precise, accurate, and legible.* It is important that any data you include be accurate. Erroneous information can take on a life of its own if what you write is taken as fact by others. If you are unclear on a point or if you have gathered conflicting information, say so.

Document your sources of information and specify the basis for conclusions or criteria on which a decision was based (for example, to refer the client to another agency or to conclude that suicidal risk was slight).

Present essential information in a coherent manner. An assessment is intended to be a synthesis of information from a variety of sources, including observation, documents, collateral contacts, and client interviews. Organizing that material so that it paints a comprehensive picture of the client's situation, strengths, and challenges at that particular moment is not easy. Avoid going off on tangents or piling up excessive details that derail the clarity of your document. Keep details that illustrate your point, document your actions, or substantiate your conclusions.

3. *Use labels, subjective terminology, and jargon carefully.* In assessing the social functioning of individuals, social workers often make global judgments—for example, "At best, this person's level of functioning is marginal." Such a sweeping statement has limited usefulness, because it fails to specify areas in which the client's functioning is marginal and it emphasizes deficits. Instead of using labels ("Alice is a kleptomaniac"), use the client's own reports or substantiate your conclusion ("Alice reports a 3-year history of shoplifting on a weekly basis" or "Alice has been arrested five times for shoplifting and appears unable to resist the compulsion to steal small items on a regular basis"). You should be factual and descriptive, as opposed to relying on labels and subjective terms.

Take care to create a document that demonstrates respect for your client. Should he or she read it, would it be considered a fair characterization of the client's presentation of self, life circumstances, assets, and needs? For help in honing your skills and expanding your assessment vocabulary, consult resources such as Zuckerman (1997) and Kagle (1991).

This chapter ends with two examples of written assessments, incorporating the concepts described in this chapter. The first is written in a child protective services setting, the second in a family services agency.

REPORT DATE: 11/1/05

REFERRAL INFORMATION

Edgar Jones is a Caucasian, 23-year-old father of three children, ages 6, 3, and 10 months. The family was referred for assessment following a report last evening of child neglect, filed by a neighbor who saw the children playing in the street well after midnight. Police responding to the call found the children in good health and reasonably clean, but distressed and fearful, asking repeatedly for their father. The children were placed in emergency care overnight and officers eventually located Mr. Jones at his place of employment. According to Patrolman Rogers, Mr. Jones was "visibly upset" about the children's situation, but stated that he "had no choice" but to leave the 6-year-old in charge of the others, because he had no child care and could not afford to miss work (Mr. Jones loads trucks at United Parcel Service from 10 P.M. to 6 A.M.).

BACKGROUND INFORMATION

Mr. Jones married his wife Ella after she became pregnant during their junior year of high school. All three children are from that relationship. The couple had a fairly tumultuous early marriage. Mr. Jones acknowledges a problem with alcohol use and two convictions for breaking and entering when he was 19 and 20 years old. Mr. Jones attributes those crimes to "getting crazy and partying" and states that he has been sober with the help of AA since 1995. Mr. Jones has been employed at UPS for 2 years and is now in line for transfer to a day shift.

Mr. Jones reports that his wife "got messed up on crack" about a year ago and left the family in September of this year. Her current whereabouts are unknown. Mr. Jones seems annoyed but otherwise unperturbed by his wife's drug use or her disappearance. Since Mrs. Jones' departure, the children have stayed with a family friend while Mr. Jones is at work. However, that relationship soured a week ago. Since then, the children

have been left alone during his working hours. Mr. Jones reports taking precautions, such as assuring that they are asleep before he leaves for work, and locking the doors and any dangerous items, "so they can't get into trouble if they wake up before I get home."

During the day, the oldest child is enrolled in school. According to school personnel, the child attends school regularly and appears withdrawn, though well cared for. The two youngest children are cared for by Mr. Jones, who states that he sleeps during their nap times, and occasionally puts them in the playpen for safety while he sleeps or does errands. In their interactions with their father, the children seem somewhat tentative, though not fearful. They are clearly glad to see him, and he appears to be attentive to them and responsive to their needs. He states that "the kids were always Ella's deal" and that he is "figuring out what they need as I go along." He appears open to information and capable of implementing it, but at this point is grossly uninformed about the capacities and needs of young children such as his. He does appreciate the gravity of the current situation and is adamant in his contention that it will not happen again.

Mr. Jones appears to have few formal or informal supports to help him with the responsibilities in attending to the daily needs of his family. His primary activities are work and his recovery program, and his social contacts seem confined to those arenas. He has been estranged from his family of origin since the birth of his first child. He describes long-standing friends and acquaintances as "not too trustworthy," implying that they are involved with drug use.

PLAN

Work with Mr. Jones to develop alternative work or child care options and monitor weekly for the next 3 months. Provide client with written material on parenting and child development. Recommend parenting class (optional at this time) to better prepare Mr. Jones to address his children's developmental needs and their reactions to the abrupt loss of their mother. Support Mr. Jones in continuing his self-care and sobriety.

DATE OF SERVICE: 5/5/05

IDENTIFYING INFORMATION

Jack and Marie Smith presented for service, requesting assistance with recent marital difficulties having to do with Mr. Smith's retirement. This assessment is based on information gathered during the initial interview. The Smiths describe themselves as African American; he is 65, and she is 53. Mrs. Smith is employed as an esthetician; Mr. Smith is retired. The couple has two grown children, both of whom are married and live out of state.

ASSESSMENT INFORMATION

The couple presented as well groomed, polite, and apprehensive. Mrs. Smith reports that she initiated the contact following weeks of "almost constant bickering" and that her husband reluctantly agreed to attend. Mr. Smith retired 4 months ago from a local accounting firm. The retirement had been anticipated, but was precipitated by a merger in which senior employees were offered incentives to retire early. Both Mr. and Mrs. Smith agreed that the retirement was appropriate and timely.

Mrs. Smith continues to work. She states that her employment is "less for the money than the social aspect," as she values the time spent with her coworkers and customers.

Mrs. Smith states that since the date of his retirement, her husband had been "a drag on the system," "moping around the house," "not doing anything to help out," and "spending money like it is going out of style" on televised shopping stations, Internet purchases, and trips to a nearby casino. When asked, she states that they had a satisfying sexual relationship throughout the course of their marriage, but that over the last few months her husband has shown little interest in her and has rejected her attempts at all forms of physical intimacy. She states that she is "afraid this is what the rest of my life will be like" and wants to do what they can to change things now.

Mr. Smith acknowledges that retirement has brought a change from the structure and high pressure of his career. He defends the way he spends his days as relaxation he has earned after his lifetime of work. He maintains that because his wife is at work anyway, it "should be no concern of hers" what he does with his money. He reports that he enjoys the escape of the casino and that he spends only a pre-allotted amount of money when he goes there. With regard to their sexual relationship, Mr. Smith states that there have been "dry spells" at different points in their marriage and that this

period is another of those—one that he is clearly uncomfortable discussing.

During the session, the couple displayed a communication pattern that they say is relatively similar to that which they experience at home. Mrs. Smith sharply voices her discontent, and Mr. Smith offers a rejoinder and refuses to discuss the matter further. Mr. Smith states that because he is older, he is more "laid back" and refuses to waste time and energy on disagreements. He notes that this was his style in dealing with workplace conflicts and with difficulties with his children when they were younger. The Smiths agree that this pattern is frustrating and unconstructive, but state that it is how they have always dealt with conflict—each goes his or her own way, to work or friends—and the disagreement blows over; only the frequency of these disagreements is different now.

Both clients report that their health is good and that there are no prevailing financial difficulties or extramarital involvements, nor is there a history of violence or substance abuse.

CONCLUSION

This couple has enjoyed a relatively harmonious marriage of almost 30 years. They have successfully raised two children and maintained fruitful and financially rewarding careers. The core issue at this time appears to stem from Mr. Smith's retirement and the role changes that this change has necessitated. Mrs. Smith has continued with her usual activities but appears to have expectations for her husband that have not been well articulated or explored. It may also be that this transition has highlighted and exacerbated the age and developmental differences between the two partners. Mr. Smith appears to be somewhat at sea with his newfound freedom, enjoying the independence from his work-related constraints but experiencing some void in the meaningfulness of his activities. The couple appears to have a limited capacity to discuss difficulties, which is sorely tested by their current change in circumstances.

PLAN

Provide conjoint therapy to focus on communication and problem-solving skills, examination and discussion of mutual expectations, and development of common activities. Explore and address particular fears and other concerns as they arise.

Summary

This chapter discussed assessment of physical, cognitive/perceptual, emotional, and behavioral functioning, as well as motivation and cultural and environmental factors. Although each of these factors was presented as a discrete entity here, these factors are neither independent nor static. Rather, the various functions and factors interact dynamically over time and, from the initial contact, the practitioner is a part of that dynamic interaction. Each factor is therefore subject to change, and the social worker's task is not only to assess the dynamic interplay of these multiple factors but also to instigate changes that are feasible and consonant with clients' goals.

Assessment involves synthesizing relevant factors into a working hypothesis about the nature of problems and their contributory causes. You need not be concerned in every case with assessing all of the dimensions identified thus far. Indeed, an assessment should be a concise statement that embodies only the most pertinent factors.

This chapter's scope was limited to intrapersonal and environmental dimensions. It excluded conjoint, family, and group systems, not because they are unimportant components of people's social environments, but rather because they generally are the hub of people's social environments. To work effectively with interpersonal systems, however, requires an extensive body of knowledge about these systems. Therefore, we devote the next two chapters to assessing marital and family systems and growth-oriented groups.

Internet Resources

See our companion website for hot links to these URLs. Note that URLs are subject to change. We will endeavor to update the links on the companion website as much as possible.

You can access information about coexisting psychiatric disorders at *http://hstat.nlm.nih.gov/ hq/Hquest/db/local.tip.tip9/screen/TocDisplay/s/ 55531/action/Toc* and information on schizophrenia at *http://www.mhsource.com/schizophrenia/ schizfaq.html.*

The following websites are useful resources on suicide prevention and intervention:

http://www.suicidology.org/

http://www.suicideinfo.ca/csp/go.aspx?tabid=5

http://www.afsp.org/index-1.htm

http://www.nimh.nih.gov/SuicideResearch/ suichart.cfm

http://www.Angelfire.com/ga4/ suicideawareness/147. html

http://www.cdc.gov/programs/injury2.htm

http://www.unicef.org/pon96/insuicid.htm

The following websites are helpful sources for further information on substance abuse:

National Institute on Drug Abuse: *http://www. nida.nih.gov*

National Institute on Alcohol Abuse and Alcoholism: *http://www.niaaa.nih.gov*

American Society of Addiction Medicine's *Patient Placement Criteria,* second edition: *http://www.asam.org/*

Using InfoTrac College Edition, you can search using the keywords "dual diagnosis," "alcohol abuse assessment," "drug abuse assessment," "affective disorders," "suicide assessment," or "social support systems." You can also access the helpful article by Berg-Weger, Rubio, and Tebb (2000).

Related Online Content

Visit the *Direct Social Work Practice* companion website at *http://socialwork. wadsworth.com/hepworth7* for additional learning tools such as glossary terms, chapter outlines, InfoTrac College Edition keywords, relevant web links, and chapter practice quizzes. Also, be sure to check out the Direct Practice Virtual Reader, where the authors have personally selected articles relevant to this chapter using InfoMarks.

Notes

1. Bernhardt and Rauch (1993) offer an informative guide for social workers interested in learning more about the genetic basis for illnesses and about conducting genetic family histories.

2. See Steinmetz (1992) for an article about FAS, including photographs comparing a normal fetus with one damaged by excessive alcohol consumption by the mother. Detailed information about FAS and FAE has been presented in articles by Giunta and Streissguth (1988) and Anderson and Grant (1984). Anderson and Grant have discussed such treatment programs, and Giunta and Streissguth have discussed the needs of caregivers of children with FAS, as well as related family needs and community services and resources.

3. For a more comprehensive list of questions and a discussion of assessment for substance use, see Lukas (1993).

4. For example, individuals from Jewish, Greek, Lebanese, or Italian cultures may express emotions more freely, particularly within their families, than might those from Scandinavian, English, or east Indian cultures (McGoldrick, Giordano, & Pearce, 1996). Latinos also tend to be emotionally reactive, and vary in emotional expressiveness when they switch from speaking Spanish to English as (Queralt, 1984).

5. See Walsh and Bentley (2002) for further information on psychotropic medications, their effects, and side effects.

6. Range and Knott (1997) offer a comprehensive evaluation of these and 17 other suicide assessment instruments.

CHAPTER 10

Assessing Family Functioning in Diverse Family and Cultural Contexts

CHAPTER OVERVIEW

Chapter 10 focuses on family dimensions of the assessment phase of the helping process. It is intended to assist you in developing skills in family assessment. In practice with families we emphasize adopting both a "cultural variant" and a "family variant" perspective so that families are assessed within their own idiosyncratic context. Within this framework, *family* is defined as a social system in which each of its constituent parts and subsystems interact with one another in a predictable, organized fashion. Given that these parts are the sum of the whole, this chapter considers the family as a unit. Because families as social systems interact with, influence, and are influenced by other systems in the social environment, we discuss these factors as well.

THE EVOLUTION OF FAMILY SYSTEMS

Social work from its professional beginning has been concerned with the family as a unit and as a focus of intervention. Nichols and Schwartz (2004) trace social work's contributions to families back to the friendly visitors of the Charity Organization Societies. With a focus on the family as a unit, these family caseworkers met with families in their home. In effect, their work marked the beginning of outreach and home-based family services. The profession's focus on the person and the environment was anticipatory of "family's therapy's ecological approach, long before systems theory was introduced" (Nichols & Schwartz, 2004, p. 17). Conceptualizing the family as a treatment unit was clarified in Mary Richmond's classic 1917 text *Social Diagnosis*, which introduced the family system.

The family has the highest significance among the various systems of concern to social work. It consists of people who share both history and future and performs the essential functions of "meeting the social, educational and health care needs of its constituent members" (Hartman, 1981, p. 10). It is largely through the family that character is formed, vital roles are learned, and members are socialized for participation in the larger society. All families feature defined patterns of relating, decision making, and division of roles and labor, some of which may be culturally derived. Family configurations may consist of single or two parents, gay or lesbian families, blended or reconstituted families, and multigenerational systems (Crosson-Tower, 2004).

Irrespective of its form, the family performs certain functions and has certain responsibilities to and for its members. Constable and Lee characterize the family as "the basic informal welfare system in any society" (2004, p. 9). The manner in which family functions and responsibilities are implemented is influenced by such factors as cultural or racial preferences and socioeconomic status, rather than family configuration.

SOCIAL WORK PRACTICE WITH FAMILIES

Social workers practice with families in a variety of settings and with a range of problems. In some instances, their practice involves formally designated family interventions intended to affect family structure, relational patterns, and processes. In other cases, social workers' interaction with family members relates to a specific concern and agency function. For example, social workers in health and long-term care settings often focus on the health, safety, and independence issues of the elderly or infirm and work as a part of an interdisciplinary team. In child welfare settings, they may focus on the health and safety of children and provide services to preserve or reunify families. Practice also includes multisystems interventions that address situational, relationship, or environmental stressors between families and the systems in which they interact (Boyd-Franklin & Bry, 2000; Constable & Lee, 2004). In the social justice or relational justice practice framework, social work practice with families includes an assessment of the family system in the broader context of society—in particular, the influence of economics, politics, and power on family functioning (Constable & Lee, 2004; Finn & Jacobson, 2003; Boyd-Franklin & Bry, 2000).

The family therapy literature represents a rich, informative resource for work with families. Nevertheless, elements from that perspective must be used selectively when therapy is not the agency function, the concern of the family, or a family need (Kilpatrick & Holland, 2003; Nichols & Schwartz, 1998; Reid, 1985).

DEFINING FAMILY

Now more than ever, social workers come in contact with families for whom influences of culture, race, and lifestyle shape how family is defined, how families function, and what relational patterns they exhibit. Social workers also face the challenge of assessing families during the evolution of the "traditional family" into other more accommodating forms. "It is a phenomenon of our times that people have discovered so many ways to come together as family," observes Meyer (1990, p. 4). She asserts that many social workers (among others) have not fully recognized these new family forms as "permanent features of the American landscape" (p. 4). Applying a broader "lens" to define the family, Carter and McGoldrick (1999a) include extended kin, the community, and the cultural group as part of the family. Such broader definitions of family along with marked growth in diverse populations in the United States present challenges for social workers in assessing family functioning. Family membership is achieved in a variety of ways. For example, members may enter the family system through marriage or commitment or through birth or adoption. Membership in families is also achieved through informal arrangements that extend family relationships beyond the immediate household, such as connections to friends, intergenerational networks and communities (Hines & Boyd-Franklin, 1996; Hardy, 1997), or the "family of creation" (Weston, 1991).

Given the nature of modern families, how should social workers tackle this daunting task? Meyer (1990), in advocating for a less standardized view of what constitutes family, urges social workers to free themselves of their personal and professional biases that force families into preformed nuclear patterns, thus creating the illusion of clinical pathology. Rather, social workers can conceptualize the modern family as "two or more people who are joined together by bonds of sharing and intimacy." This flexible, "no-fault definition" will aid social workers in meeting clients on their own turf, in their own terms, within their own self-definition (Meyer, 1990, p. 16).

Because family needs and circumstances vary, assessing families through the lenses of their particular level of functioning, strengths, migratory status, and the life cycle are also important factors (Kilpatrick & Holland, 1999; Hernandez & McGoldrick, 1999). This approach allows for more collaborative practice with families in which strengths, cultural, racial, and lifestyles differences can be explored in the context of change and problem solving. McGoldrick (1998) reminds us that the trend toward greater multiculturalism in the United States requires social workers to become more inclusive in our understanding of emotional and social connectedness in our work with families. Collaborative practice as a framework has broad implications for families in general, yet guides social workers to reflect upon those indigenous patterns and perceptions that influence help-seeking behavior within diverse groups (Constable & Lee, 2004; Green, 1999; Laird, 1993; Hirayama, Hirayama, & Cetingok, 1993).[1]

FAMILY STRESSORS

Effective assessment of families requires a broad understanding of the social and cultural context in which they are expected to function. A majority of families served by social workers and other helping professionals frequently encounter a hostile or indifferent environment. This is especially true for those families who do not conform to traditional images by virtue of family form, race or culture, or sexual orientation. Stressors experienced by families include limited access to affordable health care, a shortage of day or after-school care, insufficient income, unsafe neighborhoods, and poor schools. Tensions between work and family—for example, inflexible workplace policies—also influence family functioning. Conflicts may arise for families who do not match the image of the traditional family—for example, the denial of comparable family benefits for domestic partners. The legal labyrinth that gay and lesbian families continue to face includes issues related to medical and child care, power of attorney, family benefits, and the civil rights of commitment.

Public Policy

Public policy is another source of stress for families. The "family values" movement during the 1992 presidential campaign and the emphasis on personal responsibility under the Clinton administration effectively changed the social contract in the United States. In contrast to the programs developed as part of Lyndon Johnson's Great Society movement, which were intended to rectify social inequities, social welfare policies of the 1990s took on a tone of "shame and blame." The focus on personal responsibility was carried forward under the George W. Bush administration's "compassionate conservatism," and programs in the new century that supported families appeared to be more symbolic than substantive. As politicians and the American public have struggled to reconcile feedback on the role of government and its responsibility to citizens with the roles and responsibilities of states, individuals, families, and communities, it is clear that the landscape of social welfare has changed. Perhaps the most pervasive sentiment behind these initiatives is the public attitude of not wanting someone to live off "my hard work and earnings." This sentiment focused on individuals and excluded environmental factors.

In addition to the changes in the social contract at the individual level, remedies to poverty and other social problems have been framed as political solutions. Unlike earlier social welfare initiatives, the programs developed under the new social contract are less consistent with the value base and social justice principles held by the social work profession.

Work and Family

Families in all socioeconomic strata experience stressors. Findings from a national survey conducted by the Search Institute (2002) suggested that a cross section of parents at all socioeconomic levels feel the need for community support and for work–family balance. The world of work and the state of the economy continue to be significant stressors for families (Ostroff and Atwater, 2003; Ehrenreich, 2001). Barbara Ehrenreich's *Nickled and Dimed* (2001) called attention to the plight of low-wage earners, some of whom were homeless because their earnings were insufficient to afford housing. Subsequently, the extent to which companies paid their workers a living wage, corporate profits, and employee benefits received national attention, as did the plight of farm laborers; for example, grocery store workers in California on strike seeking better wages and benefits. Farm workers were joined by thousands as they rode a bus across the nation to highlight their substandard work and living conditions.

All members of U.S. society are affected by these situations and benefit when they improve. In effect, we subsidize employers through Medicare and the Food Stamp programs by providing these benefits for those individuals who lack health care and are paid inadequate wages. Moreover, while retail giants may increase families' purchasing power, this trend comes at the expense of their own employees, whose low wages make lower prices possible.

According to Ostroff and Atwater (2003), gender—despite improvements in the labor market—remains a major determinant of earning power. Women, even at managerial levels, are paid less than their male peers as well as the employees whom they supervise.

The average American spends more time engaged in work activities than in family or leisure activities when one factors in staying late at work or bringing work home. Yet, the George W. Bush administration, with the support of segments of the business community, opposed legislation that would extend overtime benefits to millions of workers. Middle-income families face pressures despite their healthy level of income. For the most part, their income will prove insufficient in the event of a major emergency, and they typically have inadequate savings for retirement. Moreover, the net worth of households within an income range of $20,000 to $80,000 largely grew as a result of an increased valuation of their homes, rather than any increase in wages (Crenshaw, 2003). In October 2003, *The Washington Post* reported that while highly skilled workers were able to find jobs in such growth fields as health care, manufacturing jobs, which are often the most readily available to blue-collar workers, were being eliminated or outsourced abroad.

Changes in the state of the economy may affect some groups more than others. During the last recession, U.S. unemployment was highest in the Hispanic and African American communities.

For example, Hispanic American women, due to their concentration in low-wage, low-skilled jobs, are vulnerable when shifts in the economy result in high rates of unemployment (Solis & Corchado, 2002).

These stressors for families illustrate an observation made by Constable and Lee (2004), who asserted that families today may have less control over their functioning than their ancestors, for whom family interventions occurred only when they "demonstrated gross inadequacies" (p. 58). In general, stressors for families that influence their functioning stem from a variety of environmental factors, such as those created by public policy. Tensions between work and family— whether created by inadequate earnings, poor working conditions, or high workload demands— affect family functioning as well as the ability to carry out family roles and responsibilities. In working with families, be aware of the extent to which work (or lack of work), public policy, and other environmental factors support or burden family well-being and hinder access to resources (Zimmerman, 1995; Vosler, 1990). Also, you should be aware that extreme stress might occur in minority or culturally diverse families whose configuration, values, or beliefs clash with those of the dominant work culture.

Family Resilience

Every family, despite the stressors and strains it faces, has strengths, displays an enormous amount of resilience, and has resources that can help its members survive. Families continue to celebrate rites of passage that emphasize their continuity. For example, the Quinceanero marks an adolescent girl's entry into adulthood in Hispanic families. Numerous other rituals focusing on the possibilities of future generations are observed in immigrant, African American, Native American, and Southeast Asian communities, including religious, coming of age, spiritual, or naming ceremonies. Indeed, almost every family, irrespective of its culture, race, or class, has some way of marking and celebrating individual and family passages. The family system, even when it differs from the traditional configuration, has demonstrated a capacity to adapt to a vast range of environmental challenges. Signs of hope attesting to the resilience of families are evident in family celebrations and rituals, as well as family activism.

One sign that families are seeking to regain control of their time and relationships is the emergence of movements such as "Putting Families First." This grassroots movement, which was initiated by family social scientist William Doherty at the University of Minnesota, quickly gained national momentum. Other hopeful signs include the efforts of advocates who are diligently trying to force policy-makers to craft family friendly policies.

A SYSTEMS FRAMEWORK FOR ASSESSING FAMILY FUNCTIONING

A primary characteristic of any system is that all of its parts are engaged in transactions. There is interdependence between systems and their component parts. As a consequence, whatever affects that system—albeit internal or external—affects the whole to some extent. In general systems terms, the system as a whole is greater than the sum of its parts. Systems constantly exchange information with other systems. They manage inputs from other systems thorough boundary maintenance. When faced with such inputs, a system may seek to ensure stability or equilibrium, change, or remain in a steady state (Martin & O'Connor, 1989).

The systems framework is useful for assessing families in that the focus may be on the internal family system, yet the same framework can also include larger systems' influence on the family. For example, a complete family assessment should include both mezzo- and micro-level factors such as communication styles, culture, and family interactions and dynamics. Questions might also be raised about whether dynamics internal to the family system are precipitated by or maintained by macro-level factors, such as socioeconomic status; institutionalized discrimination or bigotry; the experience of refugee, migrant, or immigrant status; and the state of the overall economy.

As an example, consider the micro, mezzo, and macro dynamics in a family in which the father has recently lost his job and now works part-time as a handyman and part-time for a vendor who sells beverages during sports events. The mother in the family has a full-time job cleaning houses. Because of the drop in the father's income, she has taken a part-time job in the evenings, leaving an older child to care for the household. In your initial contact with the family, they describe conflict in their relationship as a primary concern. The mother also states that when the father is not working, he sits on the couch watching television and drinking beer, leaving her and the older child to do most of the work around the house. As a result, the mother and father have arguments about child care, household tasks, and finances. The older child, who was formerly a good student, is now having problems in school and has been reported to the school truancy officer for skipping classes. As you read the descriptions of the assessment instruments in Table 10-1, reflect upon which of these instruments might be used to assess this family.

Family Assessment Instruments

Several tools are available to aid the assessment process. These tools and their authors are summarized in Table 10-1.

In addition to the multidimensional assessment process outlined in Chapter 8, you may use these instruments to further your understanding of family dynamics, internal and external relationships, and stressors. In some instances, you will find it beneficial to combine assessment tools so that you can develop a more complete picture of the family. These tools also facilitate your engaging the family in the assessment process. An assessment of internal family functioning, including mapping family structure, family history, and showing relationships, is aided by completion of the Genogram (McGoldrick & Gerson, 1985). Similarly, the Ecomap enables you to focus on the social context of families and interactions between the family and the larger society (Hartman & Laird, 1983). The Social Support Network Map allows you to examine the structure and quality of the family's interconnected relationships and social supports

Table 10-1 Family assessment tools

TOOL	AUTHOR(s)
Clinical Assessment Package for Assessing Risks and Strengths (CASPARS)	Gilgun (1994, 2001)
Culturalgram	Congress (1994)
Ecomap	Hartman & Laird (1983)
Family Assessment Wheel	Mailick & Vigilante (1997)
Genogram	McGoldrick & Gerson (1985)
Integrative Model by Level of Need	Kilpatrick & Cleveland (1993)
Multisystems	Boyd-Franklin Bry (2000)
Social Support Network Map	Tracy & Whittaker (1990)

(Tracy & Whittaker, 1990). You will also find the Culturalgram (Congress, 1994) a useful tool for assessing family dimensions in the context of culture, because "the systems view limits important cultural considerations" (Green, 1999, p. 8). The Family Assessment Wheel allows you to examine the sociopolitical and cultural context of the family experience (Mailick & Vigilante, 1997). Hirayama, Hirayama, and Cetingok (1993) suggest both the Ecomap and the Genogram as useful tools in assisting refugees to understand patterns of social relationships and communication shifts associated with the tensions of relocation.

The family assessment model developed by Kilpatrick and Cleveland recognizes five levels of family need and functioning (Kilpatrick & Holland, 2003). A "Level 1" family's needs for example are related to basic survival, such as food, shelter and medical care. Assessments of families at this level would therefore focus on their strengths and basic resources need. In contrast, a "Level 3" family has succeeded in satisfying its basic needs, so the assessment would focus on relationships, boundaries, alliances, and communication skills.

The Multisystems approach developed by Nancy Boyd-Franklin (Boyd-Franklin & Bry, 2000) is derived from structural, behavioral family therapy. It is also applicable to social work practice with families, however. This approach recognizes that assessment and intervention goals involve families

as well as the systems external to the family that affect and serve as resources to families.

Strengths-Based and Risk Assessments

Strengths-based measures for families and children include the Family Functioning Style Scale (FSSS) and the Family Resources Scale (FRS). Both allow you to include strengths in your assessment of families and to consider a range of family functioning (i.e., capabilities).

Often social workers are called upon to assess risks in families—for instance, in cases involving child neglect and abuse, probation, and family violence. Risk assessment tools are standardized structured actuarial tools that specify indicators and scores in an attempt to predict the probability of future behaviors or maltreatment. Risks can be either enduring or transient. Assessment tools, however, tend to emphasize enduring risks, for which an intervention is warranted. Even in cases involving enduring risks, you should strive to conduct a balanced assessment, including micro, mezzo, and macro level strengths, protective factors, and resilience. In this way, risks are not overly emphasized at the expense of strengths and environmental factors.

The Clinical Assessment Package for Assessing Risks and Strengths (CASPARS) developed by Gilgun (1994, 2001) for families receiving mental health and child welfare services responds to this concern. Specifically, CASPARS measures both risks and protective factors related to family relationships, peer relationships, and sexuality. ROPES, a similar instrument cited in Jordan and Franklin (2003), considers family *resources, options, possibilities, exceptions,* and *solutions* (hence the instrument's name). New initiatives in child welfare—for example, alternative or differential response teams—are designed to balance families' risks and strengths, with interventions consisting of services for families instead of out-of-home placement.[2]

SYSTEMS CONCEPTS

Families, like other systems, are divided into subsystems such as parents, siblings, and kin who join together to perform various family functions. Members of the family system influence and are influenced by every other member, creating a system that has unique properties and that is governed by both implicit and explicit rules that specify roles, power structures, forms of communication, and ways of problem solving, decision making, and negotiating. Roles, power structure, and communication patterns are the dynamic processes of the system and its interrelated and interdependent constituent parts.[3]

Because the family is a unique system, using the systems framework will enable social workers to analyze and assess the content and processes of families as well as external influences. In the interest of addressing the importance of family assessment in which formal family therapy is neither requested nor delivered by the agency, we will illustrate family assessment concepts and their application through several case examples. The first takes place in a health care setting.[4]

CASE EXAMPLE

Carlos Diaz, 66, lives with his 16-year-old son John in a subsidized apartment on the second floor of a three-story building. Mr. Diaz is diabetic, is visually impaired but not legally blind, and has a history of heavy alcohol use, though he has abstained from alcohol for the last 7 years. Mr. Diaz's companion of 18 years, Ann Mercy, recently died of a massive stroke. She had provided emotional support, given Mr. Diaz his insulin injections, and managed the household. Mr. Diaz has difficulty walking, has fallen several times in the past year, and is now hesitant to leave his apartment. In addition to John, Mr. Diaz has eight children from an earlier marriage who live in nearby suburbs, though only one, Maria, calls him regularly. Mr. Diaz's physician considers his current living arrangement to be dangerous because of the need for Mr. Diaz to climb stairs; the doctor is also concerned about his capacity to administer his own insulin. A medical social worker convenes a family meeting with Mr. Diaz, John, his daughter Maria, and his stepdaughter Anita.

Application of Systems Concepts

Problems occur in a person or family and situation context. In this case example, the problems occur in part because of Mr. Diaz's living situation, his access to alternative living environments, and the availability of a continuum of care that might include in-home supports. Mr. Diaz's income and health insurance coverage will also influence the alternatives available to the family. Such systems factors should always be accorded prominence to avoid assumptions that problems are caused by factors internal to the family system. In this case, both internal and external factors impinge upon and disrupt family functioning and influence family dynamics When families experience a disruption, like that faced by the Diaz family, family dynamics are often directed toward restoring equilibrium.

Family Homeostasis

Homeostasis is a systems concept that describes the function of a system to maintain or preserve equilibrium or balance. When faced with a disruption, a system tends to try to regulate and maintain system cohesion. For example, it may try to maintain the status quo in response to family transitions in the life cycle or stressors associated with acculturation or environmental events. As systems, families develop mechanisms that serve to maintain balance (i.e., homeostasis) in their structure and operations. They may restrict the interactional repertoires of members to a limited range of familiar behaviors and develop mechanisms for restoring equilibrium whenever it is threatened (in much the same way that the thermostat of a heating system governs the temperature of a home).

The death of a family member (in this case, Ann Mercy) is one of the factors that has disrupted the Diaz family's equilibrium. In effect, previously established patterns and expectations—for example, Mr. Diaz's role as the head of the family and his ability to care for himself and John—have been called into question because of Mr. Diaz's physical condition. Atchey notes that "it is common for the elderly to feel a lower power as a result of social limitations imposed by others' perceptions of physical conditions as well as the limitations of the condition itself" (1991, p. 79). As observed in the Diaz case, intergenerational conflicts may also occur around issues of care taking, dependency, or a decline in health, especially with the loss of a spouse. Mr. Diaz may be seen as attempting to restore family equilibrium in the family system by asserting his independence and protecting his role. Minuchin (1974) speaks of this tendency of families to maintain preferred patterns as long as possible and to offer resistance to change beyond a certain range of specific behaviors:

> Alternative patterns are available within the system. But any deviation that goes beyond the system's threshold of tolerance elicits mechanisms, which reestablish the accustomed range. When situations of system disequilibrium arise, it is common for family members to feel that other members are not fulfilling their obligations. Calls for family loyalty and guilt producing maneuvers then appear. (p. 52)

When the medical social worker convenes the Diaz family, she recognizes that the previous state of equilibrium in Mr. Diaz's life and health care has been disrupted by the death of Ann Mercy. Maria is concerned about Mr. Diaz's capacity to care for himself and his son John. Ann Mercy's daughter, Anita (from a previous marriage), has taken Ann Mercy's possessions, including a washing machine, without Mr. Diaz's knowledge or approval and is an additional disruptive dynamic. Mr. Diaz fears that his children want to place him in a nursing home and to remove John from his care. He states

emphatically that he can administer his own insulin and can cook, clean, and vacuum, although he has not done these tasks. Mr. Diaz's wishes can be seen as an effort to protect his independence and restore as much of the family equilibrium as possible. Meanwhile, other family members (except John) and his doctor doubt his capacity to assume these duties. These dynamics, including those stemming from family rules about behavior, play a decisive role in the family's interactions.

FAMILY RULES

Family homeostasis is maintained to the extent that all members of the family adhere to a limited number of rules or implicit agreements that prescribe the rights, duties, and range of appropriate behaviors within the family. Rules are formulas for relationships or guides for conduct and interactions in the family. They represent a set of prescriptive behaviors that define relationships and organize the ways in which family members interact. Implicit rules (i.e., unwritten, covert laws governing behavior) are often beyond the participants' level of awareness; thus they must be inferred from observing family interactions and communications. Examples of implicit rules that dictate the behavior of members in relation to family issues include the following:

- "Father has the final word" (a rule observed in the Diaz family).
- "You know that your parents expect us for the holidays."
- "Children don't talk back to their parents."
- "Avoid saying what you really feel."
- "Elderly parents are cared for by their children."
- "In this house, we respect the privacy of other family members."

Families do, of course, formulate rules that are openly recognized and explicitly stated, such as the following:

- "That gangsta rap is not coming in this house."
- "We don't allow children to play violent video games."

- "Children are limited to two hours of TV per day."
- "There will be no swearing in this house."

In assessing family systems, you are most interested in the implicit rules that guide a family's actions. To the extent that these rules have a disruptive effect, Because these rules are unwritten, their impact on the lives of families often goes unrecognized, and members become caught in situations in which their behavior is dictated by forces of which they are unaware. By adhering to such "rules," family members often perpetuate and reinforce the very problematic behavior of which they complain.

Although rules govern the processes of families, they differ drastically from one culture to another and from one family to another. Examples of culturally based rules that govern family processes include the following:

- "Do not bring attention to yourself."
- "Respect your elders."
- "Avoid shaming your family at all costs."
- "Bring honor to your family."
- "The duty of children is to listen and obey."
- "Elders in the family possess wisdom."
- "Share what you have with your relatives."
- "A wife's duty is to her husband."
- "Always defer to authority."

These rules may differ significantly from the typical family rules in Western society, which tend to stress competitiveness, assertiveness, individualism, and limited obligations beyond the nuclear family. You will undoubtedly recognize some of these rules from your own family. Two of these rules appear to be influencing the Hispanic Diaz family: (1) Respect your elders and (2) the duty of children is to listen and obey. In this context, Mr. Diaz perceives the violation of these rules as a threat to his autonomy as the family decision maker and his role as head of the family. Reactions to these rules on the part of the various family members contribute to the family dynamics and impede attempts by the social worker to move the family toward consensus and problem solving.

Functional and Dysfunctional Rules

The implicit rules or "norms" found in a family system may be either functional or dysfunctional in a situational context. Examples of rules that may have consequences for families include the following:

- "Dad can express his needs and wants, but other members of the family can't express theirs unless they are consistent with those of Dad."
- "Be careful what you say around Mom. She might get upset."
- "Self-control is evidence of strength. Don't let people see your weaknesses."
- "Avoid serious discussions of family problems."
- "Don't take responsibility for your own behavior. Always put the blame on someone else."
- "Don't be different from other family members."
- "It is important to win all arguments."

If rules are functional, they enable the family to respond flexibly to environmental stress, to individual needs, and to the needs of the family unit. Functional rules provide the family with opportunities to explore solutions, thereby contributing to the development of capable, adaptive, and healthy family members within the family system. Rules that permit the system to respond flexibly are optimal. Examples of functional rules include the following:

- "In this family, everyone's ideas and feedback are important."
- "It is acceptable to be different; family members don't always have to agree or to like the same things."
- "It is desirable to talk about any feelings—disappointments, fears, hurts, anger, criticisms, joys, or achievements."
- "It is important to work out disagreements with other family members."
- "It is okay to admit mistakes and to apologize; other family members will understand and provide you with support."

As you observe family processes, keep in mind that all families have functional and facilitative rules as well as dysfunctional rules. Identifying both types of rules is critical to making a balanced assessment of family functioning. Generally, family systems operate according to a relatively small set of rules governing relationships and behavior. Your understanding of family rules will enhance your assessment of the situation. Because families are rule-governed, many behaviors or communications you observe are likely to be stylized or patterned. Be alert to repetitive sequences of behavior in all areas of family life; behaviors that are crucial to the operations of the family will appear over and over. As a result, you will have many opportunities to observe stylized behavior that is an integral part of the family's functioning. Because culture may play a decisive role in family rules, you should avoid assessing family rules using indices that may be relevant to native U.S. families. In fact, some racial and ethnic families may function optimally with rules that are opposite of those previously described.

In the Diaz family, the medical social worker observed that two rules, "Dad has the final say" and "respect your elders," posed difficulties for problem solving. Given an opportunity to contribute, others in the family suggested potential solutions and supported Mr. Diaz's independence. The role of the social worker in this case was to establish a climate in which members expressed their concerns without blaming other members or assuming defensiveness or polarized positions. For this turnaround to occur, the neutrality of the social worker was important.

Cautions about Assessing Rules

Perceptions of whether rules are dysfunctional warrant further words of caution. In this case example, the rules observed by Mr. Diaz formed the basis for norms stating that parents are to be obeyed and have status. His assertion of his parental status coupled with his limited capacity to care for himself and John, although in conflict with the views of his daughter, may be a cultural factor. Likewise, Anita's unwillingness to honor the family rules resulted in conflict. The basis for her behavior may have also stemmed from intergenerational tension (adult child–parent) or

tension between traditional norms, and the degree of acculturation of various family members (child reared in the United States and parent born in another country) (McAdoo, 1993, p. 11). A labeling of rules as dysfunctional by U.S. standards may, in fact, be biased when applied to certain racial or cultural groups. Rules should therefore be explored in the context of cultural expectations and the family's origins. Because it is almost impossible to be attentive to all the nuances of race and culture without making generalizations, asking the client about the role of culture or race may provide the "most direct and accurate information about cultural realities" (Caple, Salcido, & di Cecco, 1995, p. 162; McAdoo, 1993).

Violation of Rules

When rules are violated and new behaviors are introduced into its system, a family may employ habitual modes of restoring conditions to a previous state of equilibrium, thereby keeping the system "on track." These modes often take the form of feedback to members, filled with "shoulds," "oughts," and "don'ts" intended to modify or eliminate behaviors that deviate from the norm. Family members, through anger, depression, silence, guilt induction, or other such forms of behavior may also counteract irregularities in the system. To help you grasp the potency of a system in limiting or eliminating proscribed behaviors, note the pressure exerted by Mr. Diaz on his stepdaughter to adhere to the rule of "Dad has the final say":

Anita: I have taken Mom's things, including the washing machine, because they were hers. She bought them. I want things to remember her by, and she said I could have them.

Mr. Diaz: You have no right to come in here and take things that belonged to your mother and me. You show no respect for your stepfather.

Anita: You were often a burden to Mom with your drinking and providing for your insulin. It is clear that you can't take care of John and something has to be done. You are not my father.

Mr. Diaz: You cannot come into this house and decide how things will be done. [He turns away and stops speaking to Anita]

Anita: If you don't agree, I can go to court to get custody of John.

In the preceding scene, Anita and Mr. Diaz do not agree on the rule that "Dad has the final say" because Anita does not consider Mr. Diaz to be her father. If the family has a rule that anger may not be expressed overtly—for example, in a physically or verbally aggressive manner—family members may stop speaking and ignore an offending member until the latter offers an apology. The family's rule about anger is unclear, but it may be assumed that Anita has violated an implicit rule, which Mr. Diaz perceives as a sign of disrespect.

The previous examples of rules may remind you of incidents in your own nuclear or extended family in which your behavior was regulated, reinforced, or extinguished by the behaviors of other family members. As you contemplate your own experiences, perhaps you can begin to appreciate more fully the potent influence of the family in shaping the lives and behaviors of clients, even years after they have physically departed from their families of origin.

Flexibility of Rules

The opportunity to influence rules or to develop new rules varies widely from family to family. Optimally, families will have rules that permit the system to respond flexibly to change and to evolve new rules compatible with changing needs of family members. In contrast, rigid rules prevent members from modifying their behavior over time in response to changing circumstances and pressures, thus crystallizing relationships and stereotyping roles.

With respect to flexibility of rules, Becvar and Becvar (2000a) discuss the concepts of morphostasis and morphogenesis. *Morphostasis* describes a system's tendency toward stability, a state of dynamic equilibrium. *Morphogenesis* refers to the system-enhancing behavior that allows for growth, creativity, innovation, and change (p. 68). For a system to find and maintain balance, it must be able to remain stable in the context of change and to change in the context of stability (Becvar &

Becvar, 2000a). Optimally, system rules will allow for a change when it is necessary to meet individual and family needs. As you assess family systems, then, you must not only identify a family's rules and operations, but also determine the degree of flexibility (or rigidity) of the rules and of the system itself. This may be observed in part by assessing the degree of difficulty that a family experiences in adjusting and maintaining a dynamic state of balance in response to potential developments that occur during its life cycle, such as individual maturation, emancipation of adolescents, marriage, birth, retirement, aging, and death.

Pressures on families are also caused by ongoing developmental changes in children, who may press for redefinition of family rules or pursue interests and values alien to those embraced by the family. These pressures cause "disequilibrium within the family system, a sense of loss, and perhaps a feeling of strangeness until new transactional patterns restore family balance" (Goldenberg & Goldenberg, 1991, p. 40).

In addition to assessing the stresses on rules caused by developmental changes and internal events (inner forces), the social worker must assess the extent to which a family's rules allow the system to respond flexibly to dynamic societal stresses (outer forces), such as loss of a job, concerns about neighborhood safety, relocation of the family, occurrence of a natural disaster, or uprooting of the family experienced by immigrants or refugees. Complicating these dynamics even further for immigrant or refugee families are the vast contrasts between themselves and the Western culture. The process of immigration and cultural transition requires a large number of life changes over a short period of time— for example, material, economic, and educational changes; changes in roles; and the loss of extended family, support systems, and familiar environments (Green, 1999).

Responding successfully to inner and outer stresses requires constant transformation of the rules and behaviors of family members to accommodate ongoing changes while maintaining family continuity. Families often seek help because of an accumulation of events that have strained the coping ability of the entire family or of individual members. Even when these changes are for the better, they may overwhelm the coping mechanisms and resilience of individual members or an entire family system.

Most families have rules that do not allow the system to respond readily to dynamic inner and outer forces. Indeed, the "normal" family or optimally functioning family may actually be an atypical phenomenon. The Diaz family may fall in the midrange of this continuum, because they have both rigid and functional rules. The rule that "Dad has the final say" is a rigid rule with Mr. Diaz's biological children. However, the rule that "Taking care of family members is a primary obligation" is functional in that it has meant that both Maria and John, two of Mr. Diaz's biological children, wish to assist him in continuing to live independently and safely. Maria, for example, offers to help her father find a first-floor apartment near her and to join with John in learning how to administer his insulin.

CONTENT AND PROCESS LEVELS OF FAMILY INTERACTIONS

To make adequate family assessments and to identify important rules and behaviors, it is important for social workers to understand the concepts of *content* and *process* levels of interaction. Suppose that the following scenario occurs in your office in a family agency as you conduct an initial interview with Mr. and Mrs. Barkley. In response to your inquiry about the problems they are experiencing, Mr. Barkley glances at his wife and then indicates that she has been depressed and "sick" for some time, and that the couple has come to your agency seeking help for "her" problem. As you look at Mrs. Barkley, she nods her assent. You are concerned at this moment with what the couple is saying to you (the content of the discussion); at the same time, you are keenly interested in assessing the underlying intent or meaning of messages and in observing the manner in which the spouses are relating or behaving as they talk about their problems. In other words, you are observant of the process that occurs as the couple discusses

content. You make mental note of the facts that the husband—with tacit approval from the wife—speaks for his wife and that the problem as defined by both spouses resides with the wife. Both spouses disregard any impact of the problem on the husband, any possible part he might play in reinforcing or exacerbating his wife's depression or other problematic behavior, or any problems he might be experiencing. With respect to roles, the couple has presented the wife as the "problem person" and the husband as the social worker's "consultant." Several important interactional behaviors thus occurred at the process level in the opening gambit of the session, revealing information about the manner in which the spouses define their problem and how they relate, and pointing to promising avenues for exploration in assessing their problems.

Families' rules are often revealed at the process level, but may be ignored by you as you selectively attend to what clients are "saying." For this reason, using your observational skills to attend to what people are doing as they discuss problems is crucial to assessing and intervening effectively in family systems. Otherwise, in this case you could easily become caught up at the content level by continuing to explore the etiology of Mrs. Barkley's "depression." The husband maintains his role as information-giver and Mrs. Barkley is the passive, identified client, while all involved ignore the stylized behaviors of the couple that play a vital part in their problems. Family relationships form reciprocal repetitive patterns and have *circular* rather than *linear* motion. Carter and McGoldrick (1999b) caution social workers against cause–and-effect thinking, which asks why and looks for someone to blame. Instead, they suggest, "identifying patterns and tracing their flow" may prove useful, because family patterns "once established, are perpetuated by everyone involved in them, although not all have equal power or influence" (p. 437).

Before we leave this case, consider for a moment that cultural norms may dictate that Mr. Barkley act as the spokesperson for the family. He describes Mrs. Barkley as being restless and as having headaches and frightening dreams that prevent her from sleeping. While the content and process of their interaction is similar to the previous couple, in this situation the content level pertains to how depression is culturally described. The process level has a cultural component, in that Mr. Barkley serves as the spokesperson. Think about how you could draw Mrs. Barkley into the conversation, taking care to not alter the culturally derived status and role relationship between the couple. You might ask Mr. Barkley if it is permissible to direct exploratory questions to the wife, explaining that hearing from her will improve your understanding of their concerns. In this way, you show the couple that you respect their family structure and cultural norms. You might also inquire about how their own culture would deal with the situation as Mr. Barkley has described it, as well as what prompted the couple's decision to seek help.

Sequences of Interaction

To assess families adequately, paying attention to the sequences of interaction that occur between members is important. All families play out scenarios or a series of transactions in which they manifest redundancies in behavior and communication. These interactions may also be culturally based, as illustrated in the Barkley family example. Analysis of interactional sequences may reveal coping patterns that are utilized by individuals or by the entire family system. Observation of interactional sequences may yield a rich trove of information concerning communication styles, the behaviors of individuals, and the manner in which all family members reinforce counterproductive interactions.

To illustrate how this works, consider the following excerpt taken from the first minutes of a session with the Diaz family. In this example, Mr. Diaz, daughter Maria, son John, and stepdaughter Anita demonstrate the sequential behaviors that have a powerful impact on the family system. The medical social worker involved with this family has convened a family group conference to consider health and safety alternatives for Mr. Diaz.

Anita [*to social worker*]: Carlos can't maintain himself or John. John runs wild, with no appropriate adult supervision, and Carlos can't take care of himself now that Mother has died. [*Anita looks earnestly at the social worker while Mr. Diaz sits stolidly, arms folded, glowering straight ahead.*]

Maria [*to social worker*]: Dad is having trouble with John and hasn't taken care of himself all these years with Ann Mercy doing the cooking and cleaning and injecting his insulin. [*To Mr. Diaz.*] Dad, I respect you and want to help you in any way, but things just can't continue like they are.

Mr. Diaz [*to social worker*]: These children "no tienen respeto." They don't give me the respect they should give the father of this family. They want to put me in a nursing home and take John away from me.

Anita: Maybe that would be for the best, since you can't take care of yourself or John.

Maria [*to social worker*]: Dad is used to having his own way and we do respect him—at least I do—but he won't listen to how some things have to change.

Mr. Diaz: Maria, you have been a good daughter, and I am surprised at your behavior. I would think that you would stick by your father if anyone would.

John: Dad, you know I stick by you. And I can help with some things, too. I want to stay with you. We have been getting along okay, and I want to be a good son and take care of you.

Anita: John, you have been running in the streets, in trouble with the law, taking money from your father. You are no help to him, and he can't be a good parent to you.

Maria: John, I know you want to help, and you are close to your dad. But you have made a lot of problems for him, and I, too, wonder if you can take care of him or he can take care of you.

In this excerpt, the family plays out a discordant thematic interaction that, with slight variation, can be observed over and over in the family's transactions. Families may discuss an endless variety of topics or content issues, but their processes often exhibit a limited number of behaviors. It is as though the family is involved in a screenplay, and once the curtain is raised, all members participate in the scenario according to the family script. It is important to understand that this family script has no beginnings or endings; that is, anyone may initiate the scenario by enacting his or her "lines." The rest of the family members almost invariably follow their habitual styles of relating, editing their individual scripts slightly to fit different versions of the scene being acted out by the family. In these scenes, the subjects discussed will vary, but the roles taken by individual family members and the styles of communicating and behaving that perpetuate the scenario fluctuate very little.

In the preceding scenario, notice the sequencing of the transactions that took place:

1. Anita speaks forthrightly about her concerns about John and Mr. Diaz's capacity for parenting him because of Mr. Diaz's medical condition. Responding nonverbally (folding his arms and glowering), Mr. Diaz declines to participate openly (a patterned behavior when there is disagreement).

2. Maria affirms some of Anita's concerns but also speaks directly to her father, affirming her respect for him as father and head of the family.

3. Mr. Diaz asserts that his children "no tienen respeto" and that their motivation is to put him away.

4. Anita does not deny that a nursing home might be the best solution.

5. Maria reasserts her respect for her father, yet notes that some things must change.

6. Mr. Diaz addresses Maria and questions whether she is, in fact, showing proper respect for him as her father.

7. John joins the fray and tries to identify himself as a good son with "respeto," which adds another dimension to the transactions.

8. Anita puts John in his place by doubting whether he has acted as a good son or whether Mr. Diaz can be a good parent to him.

9. Maria supports John's desire to be a good son but agrees that there are persistent problems with Mr. Diaz and his care of John.

In observing this and other similar scenarios of the Diaz family, you can identify patterned behaviors and "rules" governing family sequenced interactions that may not be apparent when observing single transactions. For example:

- Anita, perhaps because she is a stepdaughter, does not acknowledge the family rule of "respeto" and challenges Mr. Diaz's wishes and capabilities.
- Maria does acknowledge Mr. Diaz's place in the family and tries to show appropriate respect while acknowledging that problems do exist.
- John attempts to forge a strong coalition with Mr. Diaz by identifying his wishes to maintain the current situation.
- Mr. Diaz addresses the social worker and Maria, ignoring Anita, who has violated a family rule.
- Anita and Mr. Diaz invariably disagree.
- Maria attempts to mediate, affirming Mr. Diaz's position and the rule, while acknowledging problems.

As the social worker in this situation, your first impulse might be to shout "Stop!" In reality, observing the interaction responses in family enables you to focus interventions strategically on the family's limited number of processes. By analyzing the rules and patterns involved in the interaction, the social worker had multiple entry points for intervening in the family processes to assist the family in coming to a decision. For example, there is the agreement between the stepsisters (Maria and Anita) that Mr. Diaz cannot continue to live his life as he has in the past and that change is required. Mr. Diaz's role is not altogether clear at this point, but he understands that he needs help in maintaining his independence and caring for himself and John. It is obvious, that *he* is the focus of the family's problem, rather than his physical condition. An alliance is formed between the parent–child subsystem consisting of Mr. Diaz and John, who are allied as the two males in the family and protective of each other, and between the two stepsisters. In working with the family, the social worker had two major tasks: 1) focusing members' attention on Mr. Diaz's needs related to his physical condition; 2) engaging members in discussion that facilitates problem solving around this issue. Even so, family rules and patterns are playing a part in the problem and its potential resolution, and therefore must be addressed.

Employing "Circular" Explanations of Behavior

To this point, we have discussed the interactions and dynamics of the Diaz family from a systems framework. We emphasized the repetitive interactional patterns and the reciprocal influence of all actors in the family system. In so doing, we applied the concept of *circular causality*, demonstrating that each member's behavior becomes a stimulus to all other involved members of the system.

The concept of circular behavior stands in contrast to a *linear explanation* of the causes of behavior. In a linear explanation, event A causes event B; event B causes event C; and so forth. To illustrate the difference between these two conceptual frameworks for viewing the causality of behavior, we turn once again to the Diaz family. Employing a linear explanation of behavior, one would say, "When Anita attacks Mr. Diaz, he defends himself." A circular explanation of behavior would take the following form: "When Anita attacks Mr. Diaz, he defends himself, and Maria acts to mediate, supporting both Mr. Diaz and Anita. The mediation is not accepted, and the charges and countercharges between Anita and Mr. Diaz continue, with John attempting to ally himself with his father."

Nichols and Schwartz (1998) underscore the point that *circular* and *linear* concepts of causality reflect contrasting approaches in assessing and intervening in family processes. The circular explanation is systemic and is systems oriented—not only because it offers a more adequate description of behavior, but also because it offers a greater number of alternatives for intervention. In the preceding example, if the social worker had operated from a linear orientation, she might have intervened to stop Anita from attacking Mr. Diaz. Instead, she employed a circular explanation of the causes of behavior, targeting the entire circular pattern for intervention. Examining the role of the external factors, such as the level of insurance coverage, also prompted the social worker to assist family members in exploring environmental constraints and environmental solutions that might affect the goal of Mr. Diaz continuing to live independently. By addressing both mezzo level and macro level factors, the resource assistance and family supports necessary to achieve this goal was clarified.

By emphasizing circular influences in your interviewing style in the assessment process, you may observe three types of differences that may be useful to explore:

- Differences between individuals (e.g., "Anita gets angry the most.")
- Differences between relationships (e.g., "What is the difference between the way Mr. Diaz treats Anita compared to how he treats Maria?")
- Differences between time periods (e.g., "How did she get along with Mr. Diaz last year as compared to now?")

By orienting the assessment to solicit information regarding differences, you should be able to elicit relevant data more efficiently than if you tried to obtain linear descriptions. Linear explanations focus on the action–reaction cycles—that is, assigning responsibility or blame to one or more members whose problematic behavior is conspicuous. If you are not attuned to the repetitive nature of linear interactions, you may sharply reduce your ability to help family members reframe their behaviors and move away from counterproductive patterned interactions.

Family members also tend to explain behavior using a linear orientation, often assigning arbitrary beginnings and endings to sequences of interaction in ways that define other members as villains and themselves as victims. Mr. Diaz, for instance, viewed himself as an innocent victim of Anita's disrespectful behavior. Further, he perceived her as the person who had upset the family system. In situations of this nature, a task is to counteract the linear perspective of one person as the initiator and the other person as the reactor. You can explain systems concepts emphasizing the role, responsibility, and reciprocity of all family members in maintaining and developing functional interactions and problem solving. In the interest of problem solving, you can also share your observations so that each member can reflect on his or her role in the situation. Your ultimate goal is to create a climate in which family members' thoughtful (rather than reactive) responses become the norm.

With the Diaz family, we applied the systems concepts of homeostasis, sequences and patterns of interaction, and linear and circular communications. Family rules and their influence on these transactions were also discussed as an integral part of the assessment process. In further assessing this family, you might utilize one of the family strengths assessment tools to explore potential resources, and the family's social support network, both of which might include viable alternatives that would support Mr. Diaz's desire to live independently and to care for John.

ASSESSING PROBLEMS USING THE SYSTEMS FRAMEWORK

The utilization of a systems perspective on family problems has implications for gathering relevant data in the assessment process. Many clients—even those designated as troubled by other family members—see themselves as victims of the actions of others or of external forces over which they have no control. When families initially seek help, they are often prepared to "complain" about those who are "causing" their problems. . . . Because of their selective perception of the "causes" of events, these individuals often do not offer information that assists social workers in formulating a clear picture of how these problems may be reinforced and exacerbated either by the identified client or by others in the family system. They may also omit details with regard to other systems that influence the problems that they are experiencing. As a consequence, it is important that you have a conceptual framework and accompanying skills with which to identify themes within the family's processes and to elicit relevant data about the family system. Otherwise, you may unwittingly adopt clients' definitions of "who has the problem,"

focus interventions on changing the behavior of these selected persons, and neglect the influence of other family members and events.

Although systemic patterns of interaction that restrict and mold clients' behavior are woven throughout the fabric of many family problems, you often do not have the opportunity of observing these interactions firsthand. Family members, for instance, may refuse service or be absent or unavailable. In the Diaz case, Anita lived in another city and was available only briefly. It was unclear whether she would be involved with the family beyond the family conference as a participant in problem solving. In some cases, a family member may describe problems that he or she is experiencing in relationships with family members or with significant others who are not present. In other situations, a family member may be reluctant to participate.

When you cannot directly observe interactional and problem-solving processes, you then face the important task of eliciting highly specific information from family members. This is best accomplished by carefully exploring a number of critical incidents that illustrate the problem, before, during, and after, the context in which the problem occurred, and its duration and frequency. Further, you will want to explore how the family has coped, the extent to which other systems are involved, their attempts to resolve the situation, as well as resources and strengths. In instances in which family relationships are identified as a concern, you will want to identify underlying family patterns, establish the sequences of discrete transactions, and elicit descriptive information about the behaviors and communications of all involved. Given that clients tend to summarize critical incidents ("the teacher called and said that Shondra was messing up in school"), possibly omitting critical details (her father was recently sentenced to prison for five years), it is helpful to explain to them that you are searching for each discrete event or transaction that occurred in any critical incident targeted for exploration.

We recommend that you ask family members to give a descriptive account of an event so that you see what happened as clearly as if you had been present. As members provide this descriptive information, you can also observe family relationships. In observing the interactions between family members, you can identify key interaction patterns and the nature of alignments among various subsystems of the family. In such explorations, it is not uncommon to discover that other persons (e.g., sibling, stepfather, grandparents) and systems play significant roles in contributing to or resolving the family's problem. Based on information gained through your exploration of family affiliative ties and rules, you will often need to redefine and expand the problem system to include more actors than were originally identified.

In assisting families to understand the need for an overall assessment of the family, it is helpful to explain that the family is a "system." You should stress that the entire family is affected by, and may even exacerbate, problems experienced by one member. Exploring with each family member the way in which they are affected by the problem can help them to understand the family systems framework. Parents of youth who are in trouble with juvenile courts, for example, are often at their wit's end and simply want the child out of their hair for a time. Often, they may say, "Take him. I can't do anything with him anymore; he doesn't listen to me. Maybe time away from home will change his attitude." Tears, guilt, and fears about what is happening to the child and the family may punctuate their tirade, despite their anger. Redefining the problem as a family issue invokes both relief and fears. Note, however, that this approach works only to the extent to which you are nonaccusatory and nonjudgmental, because parents or other family members often interpret the problem as a failure on their part.

DIMENSIONS OF FAMILY ASSESSMENT

In explicating the integral concepts of a systems framework for viewing family functioning in the Diaz family, we set the stage for the family assessment. Table 10-2 highlights the dimensions of assessment used as guidelines for exploring and organizing the massive amount of data you will

Table 10-2 Dimensions of family assessment

Family context

Family strengths

Boundaries and boundary maintenance

Family power structure

Family decision-making processes

Family goals

Family myths and cognitive patterns

Family roles

Communication styles of family members

Family life cycle

gather in working with family systems. These dimensions will assist you in assessing interactions and evaluating aspects of family operations—a critical preliminary step when planning interventions to assist a family in problem solving. Keep in mind that you can augment your assessment by appropriately using the assessment tools described in Table 10-1.

We recommend that in employing these dimensions to formulate assessments and plan interventions you utilize the following format.

1. *Identify the dimensions that are most relevant to your clients.* Although the dimensions apply to the processes of couples and families, some may not be pertinent given the presenting complaint and the nature of the help requested by the family. For example, a family may seek help because of stress caused by providing care for an elderly relative living in the home. Your initial exploration may reveal no major concerns in the relative's functioning (e.g., decision making) as a contributing factor to the family's problem. Thus, you would narrow the assessment to an exploration of the specific problem identified by the family—in this case, caregiver-related stress.

2. *Use the dimensions to guide your exploration of family behavior.* After the first session, review the dimensions and develop relevant questions to further your exploration in subsequent

sessions. For example, how do they handle or cope with problems? Explore family communication patterns.

3. *Use the dimensions as guidelines for organizing new data into themes and patterns.* Determine the family's or couple's rules or habitual ways of relating in relation to *each* relevant dimension. For example, ask about the family's rules in relation to decision making, roles and power structure, and family goals.

4. *Based on the relevant dimensions, develop a written profile of behaviors of individual members within the system.* For example, with respect to the dimension of communication, a family member may tend to paraphrase messages of others and personalize statements. The same person may be prone to interrupt and to talk excessively, thus monopolizing the session. Developing a profile of behaviors for each family member will provide a framework not only for assessing behaviors but also for planning interventions.

5. *Employ the dimensions to assess relevant behaviors of the entire family, developing a profile of salient functional and problematic behaviors that are manifested by the system itself.* For the dimension of communication, functional behaviors of a family may include listening responses and responses that acknowledge the contributions of others (e.g., "You did a good job"). In contrast, responses observed in the same family that may include labeling of members (e.g., You are dumb.") or frequent responses of anger directed toward other members are counterproductive.

Family Context

Factors involved in assessing family context include culture, race, socioeconomic class, family form, sexual orientation, and experiences of oppression and discrimination. Recall also the discussion of family stressors presented earlier in this chapter. The extent to which each of these factors influences family functioning or impinges on the family system is an essential part of the assessment process. Families learn to live in a context, often coping with situations that over time may disrupt the family system and diminish family well-being. The dimension of family context entails simply mapping family life and family functioning to external relational factors. The Ecomap can assist you and the family to identify stressors in this regard. In assessing family context with a newly arrived immigrant family, for example, you could use the Culturalgram or the Family Assessment Wheel to assess the family's relative functioning with its situation and to identify stressors associated with the loss of their cultural reference group (Congress, 1994; Mailick & Vigilante, 1997).

An assessment dimension of family context would also focus on the extent to which the family has access to basic resources, such as food, health care, housing, financial aid, or job training, and their ability to secure such resources (Kilpatrick & Holland, 1999; Vosler, 1990). Assisting families to meet their survival needs must take precedence, in fact, over interventions to change family dynamics or to teach communication or parenting skills (Kilpatrick & Holland, 1999). Often, families who lack basic resources are in a crisis, for example, a family who is homeless. Therefore, assessment and intervention strategies related to, for example, communication skills are simply not relevant to this family at this point in their life. This dimension may, however, become relevant when their dire need for basic sustenance is satisfied.

Family Form

Paramount to gathering data and assessing families is the task of accurately viewing the family within the context of its cultural milieu, sexual orientation, and family form. The social worker's challenge in deciding exactly who makes up the family is emphasized by McPhatter (1991), who observed that in exploring the structure of a family, the practitioner should not make assumptions about family composition and type based on traditional definitions of family. Family form has evolved from the post–World War II ideal of the two-parent, one-wage-earner unit. Also, in a majority of poor and minority families, women have almost always worked outside the home. The fact that the definition of "family" differs greatly from culture to culture adds even more complexity to the social worker's task of assessing family context.

Although the contexts of families may differ dramatically, the external systems of the dominant culture typically have considerable influence on family functioning. Carter and McGoldrick (1999a) note, for example, that gay and lesbian couples experience harassment, violence, and the denial of "key legal protections and entitlements" (p. 352). This lack of protection, along with the lack of roles and language for gay or lesbian families, are not only stressors, of course, but it should be noted that these families are "vulnerable to intrusion and invalidation" (Slater, 1995). Minorities who are gay or lesbian face additional difficulties of racial discrimination and may have access to fewer resources because of the stigma of their sexual orientation in their communities. Moreover, limited social support for gay and lesbian youth is available, and in many instances these young people experience both family and social isolation (Morrow, 1993).

It is vital, then, that social workers include the larger contextual issues (e.g., race, culture, class, gender, sexual orientation) and their influence in the assessment of families. In gathering contextual information you are able to develop a working knowledge of the family in its own reality. This knowledge will include culture, biculturalism, ethnic status, language, social class, customs, history, and sexual orientation—all factors that may affect families and the problems they experience. In engaging families to filter out the extent to which these factors are important, you can emphasize what Norton (1978) and McPhatter (1991) call a "dual perspective." This perspective involves "the conscious and systematic process of perceiving, understanding and comparing simultaneously the values and attitudes of the larger societal system with those of the client's immediate family and community system" and is a vital construct in assessing the social context of a family's presenting problems (McPhatter, 1991, pp. 14–15). In their elaboration on the context of diverse families, Kilpatrick and Holland (1999) maintain that the "dual perspective fosters problem resolution in

tune with distinct values and community customs" (pp. 40–41). This perspective recognizes that families are members of two systems, one of "which is dominant or sustaining and the other, the nurturing system. Attention to the influence of both systems is important" (pp. 40–41).

Utilizing the dual perspective helps to identify the points of conflict between the family and larger systems, such as in an assessment of same-sex couples. These couples live in the context of "homophobia" in the larger culture, defined operationally as the fear and hatred of same-sex intimacy and, love. As a consequence, these couples may risk job loss, freedom, access to benefits, custody of children, and the ability to jointly purchase homes if they are explicitly identified as a couple. A dual perspective is a necessity for assessing the rich variety of family cultures, because family behavior can be understood in the larger cultural context in which it is embedded. Such a perspective also will prevent you from relying on broad generalizations about particular groups, considering behavior patterns or lifestyles as indicators of dysfunction (Green, 1999; McAdoo, 1993), In utilizing a dual perspective, social workers can view the functionality of a family's behavior within the context of what is "normal" for that particular family's culture

Numerous authors have cautioned social workers about imposing their own cultural views on the families they serve. Such errors may cause social workers to intervene in ways that are actually disruptive to the family system. For instance, terms such as *enmeshment, fusion,* and *undifferentiated ego mass* may be inappropriate when describing the interdependence observed in some families (Flores & Carey, 2000; Berg & Jaya, 1993; Boyd-Franklin, 1989; Bernal & Flores-Ortiz, 1982). Similarly, although women have a shared history of discrimination, gender when combined with race or ethnicity may not be assumed to be the most important factor for women of color because their lives are also shaped by other realities of oppression (Brown & Root, 1990).

Contextual family factors may also be influenced by narrow definitions of family, personal bias, or oppression. A narrow perspective on family form, for example, presents difficulties for gay or lesbian families because their perspective of "family" means caring, committed, and intimate relationships over time (Native families may also be misunderstood. For instance, the effects of poverty, discrimination, culture, and a collective remembered history have shaped Native American attitudes toward child welfare, social workers, and other professionals. In many Native American families, the extended family structure has been important to economic, social, and spiritual survival. As a consequence, not understanding the practice of consulting about important decisions with the family and reliance on family input for a course of action can cause further alienation between you and the family (Horesji, Heavy Runner, & Pablo 1992). In failing to appreciate the family context emphasized in cultural factors, you may unintentionally assess dimensions in a way that has limited relevance to the family situation.

Diversity within Groups

Family context has a cultural component that may not only influence help-seeking behavior, but also determine how problems are defined. For example, because of perceptions of mental illness and such diseases' negative connotations for self and the family, Southeast Asian families may respond to assistance that focuses on the cognitive, rather than the emotional, aspects of family difficulties (Hirayama, Hirayama, & Cetingok, 1993). Moreover, the principle of self-determination may have a different meaning for some cultural or ethnic groups. Ewalt and Mokuau (1996), for example, suggest that the term may have greater meaning for interests and obligation to an entire group than in the notion of individualism and autonomy.

In working with families who are ethnically or racially diverse, Green (1999) suggests that a basic dimension of cultural competence is identifying what is salient about a client's culture and honestly addressing this factor (p. 37). As an exemplar, Green presents a case described by Rooney and Bibus (1996) and involving a Native American family (p. 43). In this case, Rooney and Bibus integrate the lenses of culture as a critical context in addressing difficulties with parental substance abuse. In utilizing the culturally defined definition

of family, other relatives and tribal members are viewed as resources for the children in the family while the parents receive treatment. Context in this case also takes into account the historical experience of Native Americans when children were systematically separated from their families and tribal connections.

To facilitate an assessment of context with diverse families, Lum (2004) and Chau (1990) have developed practice assessment dimensions in which psychosocial and socio-environmental factors affect clients—for example, oppression and powerlessness. Lum (2004) also identifies the spiritual dimension as being important. These dimensions may be integrated so that social workers are ethnically sensitive throughout the helping process.

It is not possible for you to understand the cultural nuances and their implications in every diverse family. Unfortunately, when you have acquired knowledge of various groups, you face an increased danger of stereotyping. As a social worker, you may feel caught between wanting to be sensitive and culturally competent, yet experiencing resentment when you are lectured about the importance of understanding racial and cultural differences. At the risk of adding to this tension, we feel that it is important to discuss aspects of culture and race that are important considerations in the overall assessment of family context.

First, recognize that members of various groups may differ considerably from profiles or descriptions of typical behaviors. This point is particularly important for members of minority groups.

Second, understand that there are vast differences in race, language, and culture within groups designated as racial or ethnic minorities (Green, 1999). Spanish-speaking people, for example, share some aspects of Hispanic or Latino heritage such as a similar language. At the same time, they belong to diverse cultures, social classes, and nationalities and therefore vary in many respects. McAdoo (1993); Hirayama, Hirayama, and Cetingok (1993); and Caple, Salcido, and di Cecco (1995) are among the writers who inform us that all group members do not necessarily embrace the normative values of a particular group. Accordingly, differences may be observed along intergenerational lines (as in the case of family rules in the Diaz family) and based on the evolving degree of acculturation. With respect to acculturation, children may adapt to new cultures at a much more rapid pace than their parents because of their exposure to the dominant culture through school, and perhaps because they have no or few years of contact with their culture of origin (Caple, Salcido, & di Cecco, 1995; Hirayama, Hirayama, & Cetingok, 1993).

Third, the values of cultural groups are not fixed but continually evolving. As a consequence, variations may occur within families and reflect their stage in the acculturation process.

Fourth, as a means to sort out cultural variations and nuances, McAdoo (1993) suggests using your acquired knowledge to formulate a hypothesis and then exploring the extent to which this information is relevant in a particular family's situation. The implications of these observations are critical and unique for each family system. Therefore, we must be able to individualize each family within its cultural context.

Immigrant and Refugee Status

As you assess the context of families from various cultural groups, you must be aware of the extent to which a family may struggle with efforts to maintain the values and norms of its country of origin while adapting selectively to aspects of American society. When working with such families, it is advisable to obtain information about the family's migration history and look for continuing stresses placed on the family by its efforts to accommodate two (and sometimes more) cultures. Depending on their country of origin, some immigrants and refugees will be more educated and less poor. Nevertheless, all ethnic minority groups in the United States who have migrated or come as refugees face issues related to acculturation. As McGoldrick, Giordano, and Pearce (1996) observe, family values and identity may be retained for several generations after the migration experience and continue to influence the family's outlook, life cycle, and development. Indeed, this experience often preempts the completion of family developmental

tasks, and it may require the reconstruction of social networks that have been diminished as a result of leaving the family's cultural reference group.

Rooney (1997) emphasized the dilemma that immigrant and refugee families face in a society that can be both welcoming and hostile. Employers, for example, see such individuals as a source of labor. Yet as the workforce has become more diverse, workplace policies have not kept pace with family concerns and may constrain an employee's ability to fulfill traditional role obligations. The pressure to conform may distract or delay the new worker's ability to find a place in the employment organization's culture, resulting in stress in the family system. Language is yet another source of conflict, as reflected in U.S. society's indifference to bilingualism and anti-pluralistic public policy. In the late 1990s, for example, several states passed legislation that made English their official language. In addition, societal expectations assume that immigrants and refugees will act, speak, and dress like the majority population. Tensions exist in the interactions between majority and immigrant groups, and between racial minority and immigrant groups (Rooney, 1997, p. 316). Most often, these tensions are related to jobs, resources, and language and are played out in schools and neighborhoods.

The essence of systems thinking is seeing patterns. Over time, social work practice with families has encouraged the use of a systems perspective that includes context—specifically, the reality of the family. In presenting this view, we urge consideration of both internal and external forces that influence the family system, shape family dynamics, and affect the family's status in relationship with the larger social environment. External issues such as racism, classism, poverty, work pressures, and homophobia may be referred to as "extra-familial obstacles" (Nichols & Schwartz, 1998, p. 135). While all families encounter obstacles in their transactions with the other social systems, these obstacles may disproportionately affect more-diverse families, add stressors, and affect the resources available to them. We hope that our discussion will increase your understanding of family context and the relevance of this dimension in the assessment process.

Family Strengths

All families have a range of individual member and group strengths that you should identify during the assessment process. However, because of the deeply entrenched focus on pathology in the helping professions, you must revise your perceptional sets to discern and highlight family strengths. In the process of seeking help, clients have been socialized to articulate their problems in exchange for services and often must do so to establish their eligibility for those services. Highlighting what is going right and what is working in families is difficult under these circumstances, and you may need to educate families to focus on their strengths. Assessing and accrediting the strengths inherent in the family system require deliberate and disciplined of all involved.

According to Jordan and Franklin (2003), the strengths perspective is more of a "philosophical stance than a set of defining assessment and practice skills" (p. 29). Even so, identifying and utilizing strengths is consistent with the values and principles of the social work profession. A focus on strengths does not preclude paying attention to problems or risks. Instead, strengths are recognized as important to resolving problems. Assessing strengths in families may be oriented toward the future—that is, highlighting goals, aspirations, hopes, and dreams beyond the current difficulties that the family is experiencing. Such an assessment also includes current functioning, and aspects of the family climate such as spirituality or religion, coping with adversity, adapting to changes, and resilience. Strengths may take the form of protective factors that are external to the family—for example, connections to a larger social network. The strengths perspective is based on the empowerment and humanistic notion that people can change and grow (Jordan & Franklin, 2003). In short, strengths are integral resources in the helping process.

In your assessment, you need to pay particular attention to the strengths of families from various cultural or racial groups, many of whom have been disadvantaged by historic discrimination or, in the case of political refugees, extreme losses. The hopefulness of refugees or immigrants may be affected by their circumstances. Although they may feel demoralized and powerless, they have demonstrated an amazing capacity to survive. Providing these families with an opportunity to tell their story will reinforce the notion of family strengths, even in the most difficult circumstances.

Assessment questions that explore family strengths and resources focus on the following topics:

- Family traditions or rituals
- Patterns of help-seeking behavior
- Information about how a problem would be handled in the particular family or its community
- Individuals or institutions that the family may turn to in times of difficulty
- Family capacities, adaptations, hopes, dreams, or aspirations

Although these questions are useful with all families, they may have particular relevance to minority groups as a means to identify and observe strengths. Also, as you work with families, you may develop strengths assessment questions that can be integrated into your practice.

Boundaries and Boundary Maintenance of Family Systems

Boundaries, a central concept in family systems theories, utilize abstract dividers between and among other systems, or subsystems within the family or between the family and the environment. These boundaries may change over time as the system experiences various developmental levels. For example, when a child begins school, the boundaries of the family systems willingly expand to permit interactions with the educational system. Conversely, entry into the family by a juvenile probation officer may be met with reactions, yet the family system by necessity must accommodate this intrusion.

In adapting Bertalanffy's general systems theory, Martin and O'Connor (1989) conclude that all systems are open and interdependent with their environment. Within this framework, no system is ever truly closed. It does, however, selectively respond, permit, screen, or reject inputs, in the form of information, people, or events, through the boundary maintenance function. Examining the family system's boundaries and boundary maintenance will allow you to assess the extent to which the family is an *included* system—specifically, to determine its connection to other kin, the community, and membership with other groups. The Social Support Network Map assessment tool can assist you in this regard.

External Family Boundary Maintenance

Because open systems are part of still larger systems, families necessarily engage in diverse transactions with the environment. At the same time, they differ widely in the degree to which they are open to transactions with other systems and in the flexibility of their boundaries. By "flexibility," we mean the extent to which outsiders are permitted or invited to enter the family system, members of the family are allowed to invest emotionally and engage in relationships outside the family, and information and materials are exchanged with the environment. Individuals are given the freedom to regulate their interactions external to the family as long as they do not adversely affect other family members or violate the family norms. Those who hold authority in families (e.g., the parental subsystem) perform the bounding functions in such a way that they create discrete family space that exists apart from the larger space of the neighborhood and community. This may also be observed in larger family systems such as a clan, in which family is defined in a much broader context.

A family system with thick boundaries is characterized by strict regulation that limits its transactions with the external environment and restricts incoming and outgoing people, objects, information, and ideas. Thick boundaries preserve territoriality, protect the family from undesired intrusions, safeguard privacy, and, in some instances, foster secrets. Authorities in such a family or clan maintain tight control of traffic at the system's perimeter, and the bounding function is rarely relinquished or shared

with outsiders or even with family members who have not been assigned the role of performing bounding functions. This form of boundary maintenance is not necessarily a reason for concern, except when there is evidence of harm to family members.

When assessing the bounding patterns of families, social workers must take into consideration the family's unique style, strengths, and needs. Families may have more flexible boundaries with extended family members, perhaps including well-defined obligations and responsibilities to one another. Conversely, those boundaries may appear less flexible when external influences intrude upon family traditions and values and are seen as a source of conflict or disruption to the family system. At still other times, the family may change to accommodate new inputs over the course of the life cycle or during transitions. Immigrant families, for example, are generally open to new information as they make the transition to a new society. Simultaneously, they may erect boundaries in an effort to screen out what they deem to be undesirable aspects of the new culture. An article in the September 4, 2003, edition of *The New York Times Sunday Magazine* illustrates this point. Entitled "For Schooling, a Reverse Emigration to Africa," it tells the story of immigrant Ghanaian parents who send their children back to Ghana so that their children can avoid negative elements in U.S. society.

In another case, immigrant parents participated in a series of focus groups. Dominant themes that emerged related to the extent that formal institutions are able to cross family boundaries. The immigrants were confused about interventions from child protective services, concerned that schools could teach certain content without seeking permission from parents. They were also concerned about the influences of the media and popular culture on their children that were inconsistent with their values and beliefs. Above all, they experienced a loss of respect, and a sense of powerlessness in their parental roles. As one parent indicated, "When I tell my child to do or not do something and he doesn't like it, he will tell me, 'I am going to call 911 and report you.'"[5]

Knowledge of the boundaries and boundary maintenance functions of the family should assist you in identifying the bounding patterns of families you encounter in practice. Bear in mind that the discussion here has emphasized prototypes that may guide you in assessing the bounding patterns of families. In actual practice, your assessment should consider each family's unique style of transacting with the environment and give credibility to the reality of their experience.

Internal Boundaries and Family Subsystems

Assessing the bounding patterns in blended families or families in which parents share custody may prove to be particularly difficult. Children caught in these situations often have to adapt to the expectations, rules, or norms of two households. For them, boundary ambiguity arises as they traverse between households and between parenting adults. Intergenerational or stepparent boundaries may be problematic and result in conflict. In the Diaz family, for example, the role of Anita (the stepdaughter) in the family's decision making about her brother John and stepfather was unclear. Completing family Genograms, in which you and the family pictorially diagram the family's history and constellation over several generations, can provide important data on bounding patterns when working with any type of family (Kilpatrick & Holland, 1999). In the Diaz family, the Genogram would portray relationships between family members; information about previous marriages, divorces, or deaths; and details about the family life cycle, including changes in the children's living arrangements. In summary, the Genogram provides a picture of where family members have been and who was involved, as well as which relational interactions they need to resolve.

Family Subsystems and Coalitions

All families develop networks of coexisting subsystems formed on the basis of gender, interest, generation, or functions that must be performed for the family's survival (Minuchin, 1974). Members of a family may simultaneously belong to numerous subsystems, entering into separate and reciprocal relationships with other members of the nuclear family, depending on the subsystems they share in common (e.g., husband/wife, mother/daughter, brother/sister, father/son), or with the extended family (e.g., grandmother/granddaughter, uncle/nephew, mother/son-in-law). Each subsystem can be thought of as a natural coalition between participating members. Of course, many of the coalitions or alliances that families form are situation related and temporary in nature. For example, a teenager may be able to enlist her mother's support in asking her father's permission for a special privilege. A grandmother living in a home may voice disagreement with her daughter and son-in-law regarding his disciplinary decisions, thus temporarily forming a coalition with the children. Such passing alliances are characteristic of temporary subsystems. We noticed this in the situational alliance between the Diaz stepsisters, as well as between John and Mr. Diaz.

Other subsystems—especially partners or spouses, parental, and sibling subsystems—are more enduring in nature. According to Minuchin (1974), the formation of stable, well-defined coalitions between members of these vital subsystems is critical to the well-being and health of the family. Unless there is a strong and enduring coalition between parents, for instance, conflict will reverberate throughout a family, and children may be co-opted into one faction or another as parents struggle for power and control. In general, the boundaries of these three subsystems must be clear and defined well enough to allow members sufficient differentiation to carry out functions without undue interference (Minuchin, 1974). At the same time, they must be permeable enough to allow contact and exchange of resources between members of the subsystem. Minuchin points out that the clarity of the subsystem boundaries has far more significance in determining family functioning than the composition of the family's subsystem. For instance, a parental subsystem that consists of a grandmother and an adult parent–child may function perfectly adequately.

The relative integrity of the boundaries of the spouse, parental, and sibling subsystems is determined by related rules of the family. A mother clearly defines the boundary of a parental subsystem, for instance, by telling her oldest child not to interfere when she is talking to a younger child about assigned chores that the child has left undone. The message, or "rule," then, is that children are not allowed to participate in the parenting role with other children. The mother, however, may delegate responsibility for parenting to an older child when she leaves the home. In this instance, the "rules" regarding who does the parenting and under what circumstances clearly delineate the boundaries of the parental and sibling subsystems.

Cultural and Family Variants

Culture and race play a critical role in many family subsystems. For example, traditionally many Native American tribes did not consider people to be functional adults until they reached their mid-fifties or became a grandparent. For this reason grandparents were assigned the child-rearing responsibilities. Thus the parenting subsystem included grandparents and grandchildren, rather than parents and their own children. Similar arrangements may be found in other minority-group families, whereby a variety of adults may perform the function of a parent, and in which there is a distribution of family roles and tasks (Carter & McGoldrick, 1999a; McAdoo, 1993; Boyd-Franklin, 1989).

The clarity of boundaries within a family is a useful parameter for evaluating family functioning. Minuchin (1974) conceives of all families as falling somewhere along a continuum of extremes in boundary functioning, where the opposite poles are disengagement (diffuse boundaries) and enmeshment (inappropriately rigid boundaries). Family closeness in an enmeshed family system is defined as everyone thinking and feeling alike. Membership in such families requires a major sacrifice of autonomy, thereby discouraging members from exploration, independent action, and problem solving. In contrast, members of disengaged families tolerate a wide range of individual variations by members but are apt to lack feelings of family solidarity, loyalty, and a sense of belonging.

Individuals in such families find it difficult to give or to get support from other family members. Family organization in such systems is unstable and chaotic, and it may become factionalized, with leadership shifting on a moment-to-moment basis. Family members often develop individual bounding patterns or become disengaged from the larger family. Yet, when a member of this kind of family experiences high-level stresses that significantly affect other members, this tension will typically activate the family's supportive systems. Otherwise, these systems tend not to respond even when a response is appropriate—for example, parents may not become concerned when an adolescent stays out all night. At the enmeshed end of the continuum, one member's behavior immediately affects others, reverberating throughout the family system. Parents accustomed to the adolescent staying at home will respond to any variations with excessive speed and intensity—becoming very angry, for instance, when the adolescent decides to go out and gets in trouble with the police.

Enmeshment and disengagement are not necessarily dysfunctional processes. Indeed, they may have little or no relevance for some cultural, racial, or socioeconomic groups. According to Minuchin (1974), every family experiences some enmeshment or disengagement between its subsystems as the family passes through various developmental phases. During a family's early developmental years, for instance, a caretaker and young children may represent an enmeshed subsystem. A cultural variant however, is that children may be attached to more than one caretaker. Adolescents gradually disengage from the parental–child subsystem, as they move toward independence and perhaps prepare to leave home. Of course, each of these notions has a cultural variant and may not be a relevant expectation in some cultures. For example, in some cultures, adolescents may be married, although they will live in their own family. In others, young adults live with their families until they are married. Therefore, fluid roles, bonding patterns, and rules as framed in Western society may not signal an enmeshed or disengaged style of relating. Social workers are advised to assess relationships in a cultural context, paying particular attention to culturally derived subsystems or coalitions between family members and patterns of relating. One last word of caution is in order. Social workers would be well advised to closely examine the notion of the "parentified child." This all-inclusive, generally negative term is used to describe a child who has responsibilities or performs roles believed to be beyond normative expectations. In some families, parents out of necessity may delegate responsibilities to a child. Morever, in many cultures, the notion of ages and stages of childhood is not observed and children perform a variety of functions that are critical to maintaining the family system. For some rural farming families and those at the lower end of the socioeconomic spectrum worldwide, children may participate in the division of labor in the household as a matter of survival. Obviously, when compared to Western culture's preferred perception of childhood, this may not be an ideal situation. Such cases warrant your attention if the role of the child exceeds the limits of safety, if a parent or other supervising adult is unavailable for a prolonged period of time, or if children are performing duties that affect their growth and well-being. Even so, you may assume an educational rather than a punitive role with parents, ensuring that they understand that the issue at hand is the health and safety of the child, rather the structural arrangements in the family system.

Relationships in Disengaged Families

In disengaged families, some members may form coalitions. In general, these alliances are apt to be fragile and short-lived, based on immediate gratification of the needs of the family member. Because of the transitory nature of such coalitions, members will abandon the relationship once their needs are satisfied or the alliance no longer serves their purposes. In such families, the relative lack of opportunity to sustain stable alliances typically proves detrimental to the growth needs of individuals. The resulting "disconnectedness" of this transactional family style leaves members isolated and alienated from one another. Disconnected

family members often form relationships and loyalties outside the family unit in an attempt to meet their needs.

In assessing the various structural arrangements of a family, attend to those alignments between family members and outsiders that tug at family loyalties and cause acute family stress. For example, a grandparent living outside the home may take the side of children in family disputes and provide a refuge for them, interfering with the ability of the parents and children to work out their difficulties. Of course, relationships between family members and grandparents or other relatives are not necessarily a disruptive force. These individuals may also perform vital supportive functions in families. Their involvement can at times be a significant connection for children, and they may be a primary resource for the transmission of family history, values, and beliefs.

Social workers and other professionals can unwittingly reinforce disengagement in families when they connect with one family member, rather than with the family system as a whole. This problem may be exacerbated in especially troubled families, in which there is a tendency to rescue a member (often a child) from dysfunctional family dynamics. In one case, a mother with a history of substance abuse complained—appropriately so—that the social worker routinely came to her home and picked up her daughter, and she had no idea what they were doing or what they discussed. The social worker's rationale for focusing on the daughter was that she had little hope of the mother changing, and that the daughter needed a positive influence in her life. The social worker could have seized on the mother's complaint as a means to engage her. In fact, the mother's complaint suggested that she wanted to be involved. The dynamic of "rescuing" is often associated with social workers in high-stress job situations, such as child protective services, substance abuse, and family violence programs. Highly stressed parents may also disengage by assigning their parental role to a social worker by telling the child, "If you don't go to school, I am going to call your social worker." In either case, it is advisable to assess these dynamics and work to reconnect members to the family system.

Family Power Structure

Aspects of power may be defined as psychological, economic, and social. The focus of the discussion here deals primarily with power as a dynamic process within the family system. Recall that in the systems framework the family as a system interacts with and is influenced by other systems. Thus, power may serve as an external factor that influences power as a dimension within the family. Zimmerman (1995) for example, points to "the differences in male and female power and the results of policies and programs that disadvantage women" (p. 207). Miller (1994) calls our attention to historical events that influence family structure, gender roles, and even courtship and marriage. Further, Miller asserts, "the family's construction of power is shaped in a context of neighborhood and community" (p. 224). The relevance of power is evident in political processes, occupational opportunities, social class, race and ethnicity, and policies that "differentially affect the fortunes of families" (Miller, 1994, p. 224). In analyzing the power of policies and political structures on family functioning, Lewis, Skyles, and Crosbie-Burnett (2000) point to the "allocation of goods and services that have differentially affected education, health, hunger, family structure and functioning, and life expectancy," especially among families of color and low-income families.

Families may experience a lack of power as a result of classism, bigotry, prejudice, discrimination, or historical oppression that has been institutionalized into the formal and informal fabric of society. Examples include social policies that define "family" as being limited to a nuclear family configuration, essentially excluding extended family and significant nonbiological kin. Lack of power can take the form of denial of basic resources or access to socioeconomic, health, and housing opportunities. Power also resides in the positions of the social worker, the politician, and the social welfare organization. Their ability to define family needs or functioning can determine what level of services a family may receive or whether they receive any services at all. In assessing power as it relates to families, we believe that the systems external to the family represent an important dimension. These external vestiges of power influence family functioning and well-being irrespective of power differentials in the family structure.

Elements of Power within the Family System

Having alerted you to some of the external issues related to power, we now turn to the process of exploring power within the family system. All families develop a power structure. Through this structure, the family system is able to maintain the behaviors of individuals with acceptable limits and to provide leadership to assure family maintenance. Parental subsystems, for example, use the power vested in their roles to socialize, establish rules, and shape the behaviors of their children.

One element of power relates to the capacity of dominant family members to impose their preferred interpretations or viewpoints on other members, in effect denying a meaning or reality other than their own (Kilpatrick & Holland, 1999, p. 29). This exercise of power has disruptive consequences for the family, because members feel pressured to experience, speak about, or react to events or situations in the manner prescribed by the dominant member. In addition, dominant family members may determine the boundaries of the family system in situations involving family violence or child abuse. In some families, culture, customs, or traditions are enforced even though some members may question their value. They may cooperate to avoid conflict, however, thereby allowing the family to maintain a perception of balance. When all members do not embrace this power structure, conflict can result. Power may also be leveraged in the form of scapegoating—a dynamic that focuses the attention and energy of the family on a particular member.

Power is a socially constructed dynamic that varies according to such factors as culture as well as preferences within the family system. In assessing power, you should listen to family members, allowing them to tell their stories so that you may better understand the nature of this dynamic in their family. In the family system, power may be held both covertly and openly. For instance, one individual may be formally acknowledged as the central figure in the family and thus have more power in family decision making. In traditional Western culture, at one point in time, this status was generally associated with the economic resources of the male. Even so, other, less visible members or subsystems held significant power in the family.

Distribution and Balance of Power

Families are often viewed as having a single, monolithic power structure, but this is not always true. In some modern families, one individual may be the primary decision maker in some situations; in other families, other members may participate equally. Although on a surface level the male may be the central family figure, you should explore the extent to which he is actually the central decision maker and avoid making a premature assessment. Keep in mind that power may shift depending on the situation or family structure. Today's families are more diverse in both form and structure, causing some traditional roles to become eroded and others to evolve in their stead. Other sources of power may emerge within the family as a result of family coalitions or subsystems. For example, a strong alliance may exist between a child and grandparents or between a parent and child. In addition, extended kin, clan, tribal, or family and friendships networks may hold power that becomes apparent during family decision making.

The extent to which children are able to influence decisions made by the parental subsystem or assume the decisive role illustrates their role in the family's power structure. Parental subsystems hold power, and they appropriately exert influence over children. Yet, on a situational basis, a parent may delegate parental authority to an older child. Situational shifts in power occur as the result of both inner and outer forces—for example, loss of employment, decline of a member's health, life-cycle changes, or opposition to family rules. In immigrant or refugee families where language is an issue, a child may interpret for parents. This form of power is temporary and must not be construed as the child holding power beyond the particular situation.

Notably, power can shift in divorce and remarriage. Adult factors associated with holding more power include custody of the children, level of education, or income. Sometimes custody may be distributed equally through joint custody. In the past, laws have generally given women more power in custody decisions, except in lesbian unions where societal discrimination takes precedence. Interpersonal alliances tend to change in remarriage and divorce, and grandparents may lose or gain power. In a single-parent family system, power shifts may produce conflict when the parent initiates a role of authority with an adolescent of the opposite gender. Finally, children in a divorce and remarriage situation may acquire more power than they previously held when both parents resided in the same household.

Multicultural Perspectives

Although almost all cultures tend to view males as central power figures, social workers are advised to refrain from making this generalization. Many cultures are male oriented, so that females may appear to lack power in the traditional sense. The preceding section explored the question of who holds power and under what circumstances. In such assessments, caution is advised when making assumptions, especially when dealing with racial or ethnic groups.

For instance, groups may differ in their gender-role definitions, expectations, and responsibilities, yet these roles may not be uniformly constructed as lacking in power. Women, grandparents, aunts or uncles, and other significant individuals included in the family system may have considerable power in the family. Elders, for example, have powerful roles in some Latino or Hispanic, Asian American, African American and immigrant families and communities. In some Latino families, the existence of male dominance and female subordination as a cultural ideal ignores the norm of "hembrismo" or "marianismo," which emphasizes the status of the mother (Hines, Garcia-Preto, McGoldrick, Almeida, & Weltman, 1992). The covert power held by women in some cultures, despite what may be observed as their subservient status, is referred to by Rotunno and McGoldrick (1982) as a paradox: What is observed as a cultural female script does not diminish the powerful role these women play in the family system. In assessing power in diverse families, you should explore family power in cultural context, which includes covert and overt factors as well as individual power.

Assessing Power

As the result of many complex factors, including industrialization, higher levels of female education, increased rates of female employment, the contributions of the feminist perspective, and the equal rights movement, families in Western society appear to be moving toward more egalitarian definitions of male and female roles. At the same time, many families continue to experience stress because of the difficulties in trying to resolve discrepancies between traditional and egalitarian definitions of male–female roles. As immigrant families enter the United States, they may face the same issues.

The balance or distribution of power can be disrupted when families encounter stressful situations (e.g., loss of a job, changes in health or mental health, a traumatic event), resulting in the realignment of the family's power base. In fact, the emotional impact of stressors and the tumultuous upheaval can lead family members to struggle for power and control. In a transitional situation, this tension may greatly contribute to a family's difficulties. In assessing family systems, therefore, you must determine not only how power has been distributed in the family in the past, but also whether changing conditions of the family are threatening the established power base. You must also assess the extent to which the family systems allow power to be flexibly reallocated, and how they permit roles to be adjusted to meet the demands of changing circumstances. Finally, you must assess how members view the relative vestment of power in the family: Even if power is distributed unequally, the family may be well satisfied with the arrangement. Thus, unless power dynamics play a significant role in family problems, it is not appropriate to attempt to make adjustments in this area.

A number of factors, then, are addressed when social workers and families assess the power base and the manner in which power is distributed: who holds the "balance of power"; who, if anyone, is the formally designated leader; to what extent power is covertly held by members who have aligned to form a power bloc; and to what extent covert power accrues to individual members who are manifesting extreme symptoms in the family. The role of a family's culture in determining the distribution of power is also considered.

Keep in mind that power in families may shift on a situational basis, and power can be distributed among many members on some level. Sometimes families' struggles over power may result in destructive coalitions that are evident in those families' processes. Also remember that all families must address power issues and allocate power in some manner. It is the functionality of the power structure in meeting individual psychological needs and promoting the health of the system that must be determined when assessing this dimension of family functioning. Assessment questions that address the functionality of the power structure include the following:

- Is the family's power structure stable, allowing the system to carry out its maintenance functions in an orderly manner, or does the power base shift as members compete for power?

- Does the power base reside within the executive subsystem or within covert coalitions in the family?

- Are members of the family satisfied with the relative distribution of power?

- Does the power structure allow the family to maintain its cultural heritage?

- How does culture influence the power structure in the family?

- To what extent have external conditions necessitated power adjustments in the family?

Family Decision-Making Processes

The family's style of decision making is closely tied to its power dimension. Families range from the extremes of leaderless groups in which no one has sufficient power to determine and direct activities or organize decision making, to families in which absolute power to make decisions is rigidly held by one member. Although effective deliberation and decision making are considered to be important in determining the well-being of the system, most families do not consciously select a modus operandi for making family decisions. Rather, the family's style of decision making usually evolves in its formative stages of development and is often patterned after decision-making approaches modeled by parents in the families or culture of origin. In some instances, persistent conflicts experienced by families can be traced back to the inability to resolve, at a covert level, incompatible expectations (emanating from role models they have experienced) regarding the distribution of power and the manner in which decisions should be made in the family. As children are added to the system, they may be pulled into the situation, as neither parent is fully successful in wresting power from the other.

Of course, approaches to decision making may change over the course of the family life cycle. Young children, for example, have fewer opportunities to fulfill the decider role. As they become adolescents and young adults, they may have more input into family decisions, though the parental subsystem retains the right of making the final decision. For some families, decision making may extend beyond the immediate family, reflecting the expectations of family tradition, race, or culture. In the traditional Hmong community, for example, decision making about health matters and the use of Western medicine requires the consultation and approval of esteemed individuals in the clan. Cultural norms also play a role in decision making. A Native American colleague who is a member of the Upper Sioux, Lakota Tribe, advised that decisions are made based on their influence on the future. Given the many variants of culture and the options for distribution of power that may exist in a family, decision making may shift on a situational basis and be influenced by other factors.

In the assessment of decision making in the family, the overall goal is to determine the extent to which decisions facilitate family well-being, disrupt the family system, or promote conflict. Prolonged or unresolved conflict may factionalize the family unit and prompt some members to disengage. To assess the decision-making processes found in families, it is important to understand the elements that are inherent in effective problem solving with family systems. We offer the following guidelines:

1. *Effective decision making requires open feedback and self-expression among family members.* This includes skills in compromise, agreeing to disagree, or taking turns to negotiate and resolve differences.

2. *Members should be able to say what they think and feel without fearing conflict* between themselves and others in the system.

3. *Without open feedback and self-expression, decision-making processes will be unresponsive to the needs of individual family members* that emerge as the system goes through transitional developmental phases that demand adaptation to internal and external stresses and crises.

4. *Effective decision making requires a philosophical or attitudinal set on the part of each family member that all members of the system "count"*—that is, the family must agree that each member's needs will be taken into consideration in decision making that will affect that member.

Satir (1967) identified four exhaustive solutions to what she calls the four "self-other" dilemmas in relationships that apply to decision-making processes in families:

- In the first position, the person discounts the wants of self ("I count myself out"). Operating from this position, people handle differences by submitting, agreeing, placating, apologizing, or in other ways discounting their own needs, regardless of how they really feel, when negotiating with others.

- In the second position, a person discounts the wants of the "other" ("I count you out"). In this position, individuals may behave by finding fault, blaming, and disagreeing with others, thus leaving no room for negotiating differences.

- In the third position, the person discounts the wants of both "self" and the "other" ("Let's count us both out"). Operating from this position, individuals may exclude both themselves and others by being irrelevant, changing the subject, leaving the situation, or behaving in other ways that make it impossible to negotiate differences openly with others.

- In the fourth position, the person takes into account the wants of other parties involved ("I count myself in but try to make room for others"). In this position, the individual openly and clearly negotiates differences with others and permits or invites others to do the same.

Satir (1967) describes the fourth position as the "only growth-producing" solution to negotiation of differences between self and others. This alternative allows individual members to flourish while remaining a part of the system, and it vitalizes and energizes the system itself. By contrast, the other three positions may promote individual survival at the expense of other members of the family and produce conflict, intrigue, and resentment in the system that divert energies from productive tasks and block the family's developmental progress. These positions can be viewed as interpersonal patterns or styles of individual family members that are consistently expressed in the family. In decision making (as well as other interpersonal events), individual family members and the family as a unit may "count in" some members and "count out" others. Before a family may become an optimally nurturing environment for individual growth, all members must be "counted in" in the sense that their needs are considered when the family makes important decisions affecting them. Members of the family are likely to contribute productively when they know that every member "counts" and that needs, rather than power, are at issue in the decision-making process.

In traditional patriarchal families, the issue of the wife's feeling "counted in" in the decision-making process (even if both spouses agree that the husband should have the final say) is of obvious importance. Further, although children should have considerably less power than parents in a family and often should not be vested with decision-making authority in problem-solving processes, they should have the opportunity, as appropriate to their age, to express themselves or to give feedback in relation to decisions that affect them. Examples of such decisions include activities in which the family engages, responsibilities assigned them in the home, and their personal leisure-time activities.

5. *Effective decision making requires members of a family system to think in terms of needs rather than solutions.* Members of families are often conditioned by life experiences to see problem solutions in terms of dichotomies: "Either we do things your way or mine; one of us has to lose." This narrow approach to problem solving centers on competing solutions, thereby preventing negotiation and compromise. "Do what I want, think what I think, feel what I feel"—in other words, "Do things my way"—is often the position taken by individual family members as they attempt to coerce or coax others to adopt their solutions to life's problems. In assuming this stance, they operate from the principle that love and total agreement go together. Needs include basic conditions (e.g., to be trusted, to be considered) that must be addressed if the family is to arrive at a satisfactory solution.

6. *Effective decision making requires family members to be able to generate alternatives.* This activity closely parallels group brainstorming, in which members generate options, no matter how far-fetched, without facing criticism or censorship. Individuals manifest this skill when they draw from a repertoire of ideas that are not merely variations on a single theme but rather different categories of solutions to a given problem. In the assessment process, then, one of your tasks may be to determine to what extent families identify alternatives in contrast to quarreling over competing solutions.

7. *Effective decision making requires family members to weigh alternatives.* Decisions may be made in families after gathering information, receiving input from members, and deliberating on the options. Alternatively, they may be made impulsively without gathering or weighing relevant information or without considering the needs of family members in relation to possible solutions.

8. *Effective decision making requires that the family organize itself so as to carry out decisions by assigning tasks to individual members.* Planning to implement a decision is just as important as making the

decision initially. Some systems are so disorganized and chaotic that members have great difficulty either making a decision or implementing it. In other systems, members lack motivation to carry out decisions because their input was not elicited or considered in the decision-making process. Thus, even when decisions have been made in the system, the process may break down at the point of implementation. Ascertaining the extent to which families can implement as well as make decisions is a key task in assessing family functioning.

9. *Effective decision making requires room for negotiation and adjustment of earlier decisions based on new information and emerging individual and family needs.* Some systems, of course, are much more responsive and flexible to change than others.

In assessing the family's decision-making style, you should elicit information and view the processes you observe in relation to the preceding guidelines. Bear in mind that you are looking for both functional and disruptive patterns in each of these areas. In addition, note that the decision-making skills described here represent optimal family functioning as perceived and encouraged in Western culture. These skills may not be observed or desirable in some families, and they may not be fully developed even in families with roots in Western culture.

Decision making, as a key to autonomous functioning of the family unit, is not an ideal in all families. Such skills may not be considered to be important in families from different ethnic backgrounds. Many cultural groups have no frame of reference for "joint decision making" and, in fact, espouse cultural values that stand in direct contradiction to the methods of decision making discussed here. Including family members in decision making and assuring that the needs of all are satisfied is a Western ideal advocated by helping professionals and social scientists. Although this book indicates that families need to learn decision-making skills, you must assess whether introducing these skills to family members will facilitate family functioning or disrupt the family by disturbing deeply engrained and culturally sanctioned patterns of behavior. Hence, collaboration with families in the assessment process is essential.

Consider the case of a young Somali woman who is currently living with her parents. She would like to move into her own apartment so that she is closer to the university where she attends classes. In assessing the resources available for this move, she described a family situation in which she and other family members were expected to contribute a portion of their earnings to family members still living in Somalia. The social worker who described this situation in case consultation believed that this expectation affected the well-being of the client. In her view, this arrangement prohibited the young woman from moving out and living independently. Examining this situation through the lens of Western values—namely, autonomy and independence—the social worker asserted the right of the young woman to manage her own money. Intervention in this situation by the social worker without consideration for the context of the family's cultural values and norms was potentially disruptive to this family system. This situation represents a clash of the values of two cultures. Such cases require social workers to work with clients in such a way that does not isolate them from the family system and their community. In this case, the social worker sought the advice and assistance of leaders in the Somali community.

Decision making as a family process is neither uniform nor universal. Indeed, similar to power, this dimension has considerable variations. Some styles may share common elements, however. In a study by McAdoo (1993), few differences distinguished the decision-making responses of African Americans and their white counterparts of similar socioeconomic status. The study results did reveal that African Americans of lower socioeconomic status who had fewer resources tended to be more cooperative than other groups in their relationships and decision-making patterns. Thus, McAdoo stresses the importance of recognizing family context in understanding decision-making and broader relational patterns. In particular, cooperation may be a value because it results in lower-income African Americans helping one another to "survive and thrive within the American community" (p. 119). This value or sense of obligation is clearly not specific to African Americans, as it is also evident in other ethnic or racial groups.

Family Goals

The family is a social group in which members typically cooperate and coordinate their efforts so as to achieve certain goals. While family members may talk to each other about goals, and children may express a preference, similar to decision making and power, family goals are generally established by the parental subsystem. Families may establish goals in one of two ways. First, they may adopt and have in common goals established by society—for example, socializing children, transferring major cultural patterns, and meeting certain personal, nurturing, and safety needs of family members. Second, partners may bring individual goals with them into the family, perhaps based on preferences of their family or culture of origin.

Goals that families espouse may be openly recognized or embraced by the family or they may be covert and beyond the family's awareness. "We want to put all the kids through college" and "It is important for children to remember the old ways" are examples of explicit goals. Covert or unrecognized goals also have a profound influence on a family system. In a competitive society, a covert goal may drive a family's striving toward being at the top of the social ladder, which in turn influences individual member behavior. At the same time, families who are new arrivals to Western society may want their children to maximize opportunities yet maintain connections with their traditional roots. The first goal related to opportunities is explicit; the other is unspoken, yet understood by family members.

When families are in crisis, the system's goals and their ordering often become more apparent, for at these times families may be forced to choose between competing goals and values. For example, a wide variety of responses would be observed if one were to study a number of families confronted with a sudden and drastic reduction in income. When faced with expenditures of its limited financial resources, a family may, for example, decide that maintaining an adequate diet for the children is a priority. In a study that examined definitions

of child neglect, the participants reported that when their funds were limited, they chose food and clothing for their children over, for example, a bed with a frame. As a result, the sleeping arrangement for a child may be a mattress on the floor. Their reasoning for such decisions and others had to do with their avoiding an intervention by child protection services, especially if their children went to school hungry or wore clothes that call attention to themselves (Rooney, Neathery, & Suzek, 1997).

Family goals may also conflict with societal and professional expectations in other ways. Consider the case of a single mother whose priority goal is to move her family to a better, safer neighborhood. To accomplish this goal, she holds down two jobs, one of which is the evening shift in a convenience store adjacent to the apartment building in which the family currently lives. Her 12-year-old child is delegated the responsibility of caring for the younger siblings, ages 6 and 8. This arrangement has generally worked, and the mother checks on the children during her break. One night, a neighbor reports to the authorities that the children are home alone, which results in an intervention from child protection services. The mother is devastated, angry, and confused. Her goal is reasonable and rational from her point of view. The manner in which she seeks to reach her goal, however, is perceived as irresponsible and problematic, because the children lack adult supervision. The mother's actions are understandable in light of her goals and aspirations for her family, especially when they are understood in the context in which they were developed.

In most families, members vary in regard to the goals each considers important and the value each attaches to common goals. Parents may have a goal of their children being well educated. As in any organization, a family functions best when there is a high degree of consensus concerning the majority of family goals. Provisions within the system to negotiate and to take into consideration the unique needs, aims, and wishes of individuals are also important. Because goals often are not expressed explicitly, differences among family members in relation to major goals and expectations may not be worked through, creating dissension and disappointment within the group. Further, because of pressures from the most powerful or influential members of the group, the family may give "lip service" to particular goals, although some or most of the members may not agree in principle with them.

While family goals may vary and may break down in times of crisis, family goals represent a strength that may be used as a resource in problem solving. Many patterns of interaction in families evolve in part to achieve goals. If you examine the family's interactions without considering the goals of the system, you may miss the meaning of patterns that you identify. To illustrate this and other points discussed throughout this section, consider the following case example of a covertly held goal around which family energies are extensively organized.

CASE EXAMPLE

In the White family, an overriding goal of the family was to "keep the house clean." This goal had been set and maintained by Mrs. White, who felt constant pressure to maintain a clean house so as to avoid criticism from her own mother and other relatives. The inability to maintain this goal and other factors caused Mrs. White to become depressed and disengaged from the family.

When Mrs. White was active in the family, she constantly pressured her daughters, ages 8 and 10, to keep the house clean and orderly. To her two older girls, ages 16 and 18, both of whom attended school and had part-time jobs, she gave permission to participate only minimally in housecleaning chores because "they're tired when they come home and need time to relax and study." Seeing the older girls often excused from housecleaning (even when they left messes), the two younger girls became extremely resentful and often complained to Mr. White about the situation. Their verbal attacks directed toward the older sisters included such accusations as "You don't act like you're members of the family" and "You don't care about anyone but yourself." Assuming the role of their absent mother, they monitored the older sisters, pointing out the messes they had created and ordered them to clean them up, which the older girls always refused to do. Feeling mistreated and misunderstood, the older sisters would defend themselves and counterattack by name-calling and threatening.

In an attempt to maintain peace, Mr. White consistently served as a mediator between the warring factions and often picked up or cleaned the house to avoid the inevitable disputes that might otherwise arise. In addition, whenever Mrs. White was intermittently engaged in the family, he felt compelled to mediate between her and their daughters because she usually found something out of order and would angrily blame one of the younger daughters for "not doing her job."

In this illustration, all members of the White family attempted to adhere to the mother's goal of keeping the house clean. Because the younger girls experienced more pressure than the older girls, however, more of their energies were invested in carrying out or persuading other members of the family to carry out this goal. The unequal distribution of power in the family had shaped the alliances that existed when this family initially sought help. It was only when the social worker in this case explored and clarified the family goal and rules associated with it that family members became able to recognize the extent to which their behaviors revolved around this goal.

In summary, we offer the following questions to assist you in assessing family goals for both strengths and difficulties:

- Are goals that guide the family group clear to all members?
- To what extent are members aware of the family's overriding goals?
- Is there a shared consensus among members regarding major goals and the priorities assigned to these goals?
- Has the family experienced conflict because of a lack of consensus regarding the primary goals of individual family members?
- Do goals held in common by the family meet the needs of individual members and promote the well-being of the group as a whole?
- To what extent are patterns of interaction related to covert goals espoused by the family?
- Do external pressures influence family goals?
- To what extent are family goals signs of strengths and hopes for the future?

To the extent that goals are clear, that consensus exists regarding major goals, and that goals serve the needs and interests of the individual members and of the group as a whole, families manifest key strengths on this dimension of family functioning. We reiterate what has been a recurring theme throughout this chapter—namely, that social workers must view the family's goals within the family's cultural context and avoid the hazard of assessing family goals against those deemed desirable in Western culture. Also, to avoid biased evaluations, it is important not to view a family as deficient simply because the means used to achieve its goals may not conform to the ideals and resources of the mainstream culture. Rather, it is important to determine the specific goals of the family and to assess them in their appropriate context, including family and cultural variants.

Family Myths and Cognitive Patterns

Earlier in this chapter, we emphasized how family rules pervade all aspects of family life. Rules have both a behavioral component and a cognitive component. That is, the behaviors manifested by family members flow from, and are inextricably related to, shared perceptions or myths about one another, the family unit, and the world at large. These shared perceptions may be congruent with the views of neutral outside observers or may be distortions of reality—in other words, ill-founded, self-deceptive, well-systematized beliefs uncritically held by members. Such distortions are often part of the beliefs or myths subscribed to by the family that help shape, maintain, and justify interactional patterns and relationships. The following case illustrates this point.

CASE EXAMPLE

Over the past four years, 10-year-old Jeffrey's interactions with his teachers have been consistently conflicted because of his open defiance of classroom rules, argumentative behavior, and physical skirmishes with other children. As a result of these problems, his parents have changed Jeffrey's enrollment from one school to another several times during the past three years. Both parents share the cognitive set that "The teachers do not try to understand Jeffrey." Given this perceptual set, they regard each school contact as a battleground in which they must argue, protest, protect their rights, and defend their son. Continually bombastic, they have alienated school personnel, pushing them to take extreme stands on issues that might otherwise be mutually negotiated if the parents were amenable. The parents' constant negative and angry comments at home regarding Jeffrey's teachers and his school reinforce Jeffrey's classroom behavior.

In the preceding case example, the behaviors and cognitive processes of the family are mutually reinforcing. The myth—"Jeffrey is okay"—determines the behavior, which predictably elicits negative responses from school personnel. In turn, the family's negative encounters with the school officials reinforce and confirm their perceptions that the world is dangerous and that school personnel are inattentive to their son's needs and cannot be trusted. Sometimes, systems are in fact unresponsive to your client's needs. They may have constructed myths and rely on them in their interactions with families or individuals. In either case you should assess the context of family relationships with these systems so as to obtain a complete picture of these transactions.

Social cognitions play a role in how individuals and families interpret and remember information, and how they categorize internal and external events. These thematically organized categories are referred to as "cognitive schema" (Berlin & Marsh, 1993, p. 5). In a general sense, schemas are generalizations that may be utilized to process information about attributes, guide perceptions, and influence memory. Imagine, for example, the cognitions that may be held about people with certain attributes, such as people or certain groups who receive financial assistance from the government. Other myths include perceptions that "certain groups are more capable." In addition, seeing a group of youth with certain physical attributes and who are dressed in a certain style may cue perceptions of them as being members of a violent gang. Stored memories derived from schemas can be an integral part of the shared experience of families who derive from a homogeneous group. For example, it may be difficult for African Americans who share a history of racial discrimination and oppression to distinguish when race is not a dynamic in social situations or in an encounter with the police.

Berlin and Marsh (1993) maintain that the cognitions associated with schemas may persist long after a particular event or episode has occurred. Not all schemas are problematic, of course. The important thing to remember is that a schema functions as a heuristic device that allows an individual to take a shortcut when processing information. When cognitions based on schemas are challenged, the result is cognitive dissonance; thus they are not easily replaced. Schemas can also function as both internal and external bounding patterns of the family.

Potentially damaging to development are the persistent beliefs or myths within a family that single out one member as being different or deviant from the group. When assigned labels such as "sick," "bad," "crazy," or "lazy," a family member may become the scapegoat for the family, carrying the blame for all of its problems. This pattern obscures the fact that other members also bear responsibility for difficult transactions and communications. In many families, members may carry permanent labels, such as "never-do-well," "intellectual one," "baby of the family," "strict parent," "family pet," "clown," "good child," or "geek." It should be noted that labels such as "talented," "handsome," and "ambitious" may also separate and estrange a member of the family from others and cause other members to resent the inordinate amount of attention, praise, and recognition accorded to that individual. Labels stereotype roles of family members, causing other members to relate to them on the basis of a presumed single characteristic and to overlook a wide range of attributes, attitudes, and strengths. This pattern only serves to limit the number of behavioral options available within the family.

Family Roles

Family roles may be thought of as being complementary and reciprocal, and family members as being differentiated into social roles within the family system. Role theory, when applied to the family system, suggests that each person in a family fulfills many roles that are integrated into the family's structure and that represent certain expected, permitted, or forbidden behaviors. According to Nichols and Schwartz (1998), family roles are not independent of each other. Rather, role behavior involves two or more persons engaging in reciprocal transactions. Roles within the family system may be assigned on the basis of legal or chronological status or cultural and societal scripts. In many families, role assignments are based on gender. At the same time, as with power and decision making, roles may be flexible and diffused throughout the family system.

Roles and role expectations are learned through the process of social interactions, and they can be based on status. Role status locates the individual in a particular social position. In contrast, the role that an individual fills in the family system has specific attitudes—that is, behaviors that are expected of people in that particular situation.

In sorting out roles in the family system, individual role behavior may be *enacted, prescribed,* or *perceived* (Longres, 1995). In the enacted role, a mother may, for example, engage in the actual behaviors expected of her position in the family. A prescribed role is influenced by the expectations that others hold for the individual; those expectations may be influenced by societal or cultural preferences. For example, a major premise of attachment theory is that bonding between a mother and a child is important. Yet, as we have learned from other cultures, children may bond and be attached to a range of adults in their lives. Perceived role behavior focuses on the expectations held by others about a person who is filling that role. For example, when interacting with a bank official, a male may always presumed to be the primary decision maker in the family and the head of the household.

Roles are both learned and accrued. The role of parent, for example, is both accrued and learned. Similarly, the various roles that exist between couples in a relationship are learned based on interactions over time. Satisfaction with the respective role behavior between individuals indicates a level of harmony in an interpersonal relationship. Janzen and Harris (1997) refer to "harmonized" interpersonal roles as independent–dependent relationships. In addition, roles may be either *complementary* or *symmetrical.* An example of a complementary independent–dependent role is the relationship that exists between parents and children in which the needs of both are fulfilled. In contrast, symmetrical relationships are equal, as in the case of a couple in which each partner shares family chores, decision making, and child-rearing duties. Roles for the most part are not static, but rather evolve as a result of interactions and negotiation. As a consequence, they often defy traditional stereotypical behaviors. In actuality, role relationships in most families operate along a continuum and may be characterized as complementary, quid pro quo, or symmetrical.

Life transitions and conflict often demand changes, flexibility, and modifications in role behavior. A family may experience role transition difficulties in making the necessary adjustments when an elderly relative comes to live in their home, for instance. The elderly parent may experience difficulties in adjusting to becoming dependent on adult children. Another significant change for some parents is adjusting to the void when children leave the home. Conflict in the family may occur when individuals become dissatisfied with their roles, when there is disagreement about roles, or when individuals holding certain roles become overburdened. Parents, for example, may disagree about discipline: One parent may overdiscipline children, while the other may have a more permissive style of parenting.

Interrole conflict occurs when individuals face competing and multiple role obligations, especially when two or more roles are incompatible. In exploring the concerns of employed women, Rooney (1997) found that women, whether single or married, experienced difficulties with their management of multiple roles. Excessive role demands as described by the women in this study amounted to feeling caught between juggling multiple roles—for example, wife or partner, mother, daughter, employee, and often caretaker for an elderly parent. Multiple role taking, compliance with gender-based roles, and time pressures were complicated by such factors as the separation of work and family, unresponsive workplace policies, and lack of time for self. The women in the study also reported feeling interpersonal conflict, diminished physical stamina, and concerns for their physical health, which has a detrimental effects on their job performance and on their lives.

Minority women experienced similarly arranged gender divisions of labor stressors. In addition, gender-based role division carried the adjoining weight of strong cultural norms explicit to gender role expectancies. For single mothers, the absence of another parent meant that they had to assume both the male and female roles in the family system. Also single, never-married women reported being expected to act as the primary caretakers for elderly individuals in the family. A point to consider with minority families is the fact that interrole conflict may occur in their transactions with the larger community—for example, a cultural expectation of caring for the elderly, or being responsible for family in a broader sense.

Intrarole tensions may emerge in the family when contradictions between role performances arise. Imagine a child who has broad responsibilities in the family, yet is expected to be obedient. Also reflect on the potential for conflict between two individuals who contribute to the economic interest of the family, yet are not equal participants in making decisions about how the family spends its money. The latter example may of course be complementary or quid pro quo. Nevertheless, if both individuals are not satisfied with the arrangement, tensions can occur.

Understanding the distribution of roles within the family, the way in which these roles are defined, and role conflict are important elements in the assessment of the role dimension. Because each culture or family configuration may have its own definitions of roles, social workers must also determine and assess the goodness of fit with the needs of family members. Assessment then must consider how well members are satisfied with respective roles and, if a member is dissatisfied, whether the family is amenable to modifying or changing determined roles.

Communication Styles of Family Members

One theme that cuts across many cultural groups is that of patterns discouraging the open expression of feelings. Although Western culture espouses the value that openness and honesty are the best, the reality is that most people have considerable difficulty in asserting themselves or in confronting others, particularly in ways that are facilitative. The Western society value of open and honest expression is not consistent across cultures, nor is it embraced across racial groups.

Problems experienced by families from diverse groups, then, may partially arise because of cultural norms about openness. In some instances, you may be able to assist clients to understand their cultural norms and make decisions about their communication patterns. Before attempting to make such a change, you must first determine whether the family's communication patterns and styles negatively affect members' relationships. If they do, then you may be able to move forward and elicit family members' willingness to change, weighing with them the cultural implications associated with making such a change. Whether or not family communication patterns are culturally influenced or otherwise determined, they may be faulty, causing significant problems for family members. You therefore must be prepared to assess the impact of a family's communication styles on the problems of its members. To do so, you must be aware of the complexities of communication and prepared to assess the function of members' communication styles across a number of dimensions.

Congruence and Clarity of Communication

Family members convey messages through both verbal and nonverbal channels and qualify those messages through other verbal and nonverbal messages. A task of social workers, therefore, is to assess the *congruency* of communications—that is, whether there is correspondence between the various verbal and nonverbal elements of messages. According to Satir (1967) and other communication theorists, messages may be qualified at any one of three communication levels:

1. *Verbal level.* When people explain the intent of their messages, they are speaking at a meta-communication level: "I was trying to see whether you agreed with me," or "I thought you were feeling bad, and I was trying to comfort you." Contradictory communications occur when two or more oppositional messages are sent in sequence via the same verbal channel: "I love you—I hate you" or "You should follow my advice—you need to make your own decisions."

2. *Nonverbal level.* People qualify their communications through many nonverbal modes, including gesture, facial expressions, tone of voice, posture, and intensity of eye contact. Nonverbal messages may reinforce verbal messages ("Thank you" with a smile), contradict or modify a verbal message ("Of course I'm interested," but looks bored), or contradict or modify a nonverbal expression ("I can't stay long," but sits down in a chair).

3. *Contextual level.* The situation in which communication occurs reinforces or disqualifies the verbal and nonverbal expressions of a speaker. For example, a mother leans over to her misbehaving child during church services and threatens, "If you don't stop that, I'm going to punish you *right now!*" The context or situation in which she sends the message inherently disqualifies her verbal expression, as it is unlikely that she will punish the child in church.

Functional communicators identify discrepancies between levels of communication and seek clarification when a person's words and expressions are incongruent. Vital to assessment, then, is the task of ascertaining the extent to which there is *congruence* between the verbal, nonverbal, and contextual levels of messages on the part of individuals in the family system. In addition to considering the congruence of communications, it is important to assess the *clarity* of messages. The term *mystification* (Laing, 1965) describes how some families befuddle or mask communications and obscure the nature and source of disagreements and conflicts in their relationships. Mystification of communications can be accomplished by myriad kinds of maneuvers, including disqualifying another person's experience ("You must be crazy if you think that"), addressing responses to no one in particular even though the intent of the speaker is to convey a message to a certain person, using evasive responses that effectively obscure knowledge of the speaker, or utilizing sarcastic responses that have multiple meanings.

Barriers to Communication

In Chapter 7, we identified a number of barriers to communication that, when utilized by social workers, block client communications and impede therapeutic progress. Likewise, clients often repetitively respond with these and similar responses in their communications with others, thereby preventing meaningful exchanges and creating tension in relationships. Response categories that represent obstacles to open communications, in that they prevent genuine discourse in relationships, are highlighted in Table 10-3.

The assessment of communication barriers also includes nonverbal behaviors—for instance, glaring, turning away from a family member, fidgeting, shifting posture, pointing a finger, raising the voice, having a menacing expression or showing disgust or disdain. Nonverbal behaviors also present obstacles to communication when there are discrepancies between verbal and nonverbal levels of communication.

All families have communication barriers within their conversational repertoires. Members of some families, however, monitor their own communications and adjust their manner of responding when they have had an adverse impact on another person. As you observe the communication styles of families, it is important to assess three issues: (1) the presence of patterned negative communications, (2) the pervasiveness of such negative patterns, and (3) the relative ability of individual members of the system to modify communication styles.

In addition to assessing the preceding factors, it is vital to ascertain the various combinations of communication styles that occur repetitively as individual members of the family system relate and react to one another. For instance, one individual may frequently dominate, criticize, or accuse the

Table 10-3 Communication barriers

Prematurely shifting the subject or avoiding topics

Asking excessive questions, dominating interactions

Sympathizing, excusing, or giving reassurance or advice

Mind reading, diagnosing, interpreting, or overgeneralizing

Dwelling on negative historical events in a relationship

Making negative evaluations, blaming, name-calling, or criticizing

Directing, threatening, admonishing

Using caustic humor, excessive kidding, or teasing

Focusing conversations on oneself

other, whereas the other may defend, apologize, placate, or agree, as illustrated in the following exchange between a couple:

Wife: You never spend time with Jody [*their child*]. It's more important to you to surf the Internet and talk to people you don't even know.

Husband: I do spend time with her [*gives examples*]. You just don't ever notice.

Wife: I do notice. You spend very little time with her, and when you do, it is clear that you can't wait to get back the Internet.

Husband: Last Saturday I spent several hours with her. [*Further elaborates on how he spent the time.*]

In the preceding exchange, the wife continues to attack the husband, who continues to defend his position, thus manifesting a "fault–defend" pattern of marital communication. In such situations, even though the topic of conflict or the content of the discussion may change, the manner in which couples or family members relate to each other and orchestrate their scenario remains unchanged. Further, repetitions of the same type of partner-to-partner interchanges will be manifested across many other areas of the couple's interaction. The thematic configurations that occur in marital communication are limited in number and vary from couple to couple. Your task as the social worker is to assist family members to recognize that their patterned ways of communicating represent a thematic pattern of communicating. For instance, rather than allowing them to follow the fault–defend pattern, you might assist the previously mentioned couple in learning to engage in reciprocal or symmetrical patterns of expressing feelings or complaints, so that issues can be resolved.

It is also useful to help individual family members develop an awareness of how they send and receive messages, as well as the skills needed for sending a receiving messages in a productive manner.

Receiver Skills

A critical dimension of communication is the degree of receptivity or openness of family members to the inner thoughts and feelings of other members in the system. Receptivity is manifested by the use of certain receiving skills, which we will discuss shortly. These skills are decidedly in keeping with Western traditions, and therefore may be inconsistent with the preferences of some racial or ethnic groups. Before considering these skills, however, it should be stressed that a majority of families operate along a continuum with respect to their skills in verbal and nonverbal responses. You may observe response patterns in some families that convey understanding and demonstrate respect for the sender's message. In other families, the reactions of members may take the form of ridicule, negative evaluations, or depreciation of character. Still on other families, members may engage in "dual monologues"; that is, they communicate simultaneously, which to the casual observer might appear to be a free-for-all. Family members may also use words, sayings, or gestures particular to their family or reference group. In general, facilitative receiver skills invite, welcome, and acknowledge the views and perceptions of others. Family members then feel free to express agreement or disagreement, even though doing so may sometimes spark conflict. Facilitative responses that convey understanding and acceptance include the following:

- Physical attending (i.e., direct eye contact, receptive body posture, attentive facial expressions)
- "Listening" or paraphrasing responses by family members that restate in fresh words the essence

of a speaker's message (e.g., "You seem to be saying that . . ." or "I sense you're feeling . . .")

- Responses by receivers of messages that elicit clarification of messages (e.g., "I'm not sure what you meant. Will you tell me again?" or "Am I right in assuming you meant . . .?)
- Brief responses that prompt further elaboration by the speaker (e.g., "Oh," "I see," "Tell me more")

In assessing the communication styles of families, you must gauge the extent to which individual members (and the group as a whole) utilize these facilitative communication skills.

Sender Skills

Another dimension of communication is the extent to which members of families can share their inner thoughts and feelings with others in the system. Becvar and Becvar (2000b, p. 274) refer to this quality as the ability of individual family members to express themselves clearly as feeling, thinking, acting, valuable, and separate individuals and to take responsibility for their thoughts, feelings, and actions. Operationalized, "I" messages are messages phrased in the first person that openly and congruently reveal either pleasant or unpleasant feelings, thoughts, or reactions experienced by the speaker ("I feel . . . ," "I think . . . ," "I want . . ."). For the social worker, an essential task is to help families create a climate in which members can be candid, open, and congruent in their communications.

This climate stands in sharp contrast to the situation in which family communications are characteristically indirect, vague, and guarded and individuals fail to take responsibility for their feelings, thoughts, or participation in events. Rather than "I" messages, these family members are likely to use "you" messages that obscure or deny responsibility, or that attribute responsibility for the feelings to others (e.g., "You've got me so rattled, I forgot"). Such messages are barriers to communication, and are often replete with injunctions ("shoulds" and "oughts") concerning another's behavior or negatively evaluate the receiver of the message (e.g., "You shouldn't feel that way").

Responses That Acknowledge Strength and Achievement and Accredit Growth

Critical to the development of self-confidence in individual family members are messages from others that consistently validate the person's worth and potential. In observing patterns in which the communication repertoires are characterized by constant negative messages (e.g., putdowns, attacks, or criticism) or otherwise humiliate or invalidate the experience of family members, you should intervene to alter these patterns. Family members caught in a cycle can, when given the opportunity, focus on positive attributes of members, rather than on deficiencies. The essential thrust of your work is to increase the family's capacity to acknowledge strengths and achievements, and to create an atmosphere conducive to growth. It is also wise to keep in mind that family transitions or internal and external stressors may, in fact, challenge even previously effective communication skills.

Family Life Cycle

The family life cycle is the final dimension of family assessment. It encompasses the developmental stages through which families as a whole must pass. Based on the seminal work of Duvall (1977) and other theorists, Carter and McGoldrick (1988) developed a conceptual framework of the life cycle of the middle-class American family. This model, which focuses on the entire three- or four-generational system as it moves through time, includes both predictable development events (e.g., birth, marriage, retirement) and unpredictable events that may disrupt the life-cycle process (e.g., untimely death, birth of a developmentally delayed child, divorce, chronic illness, war).

Carter and McGoldrick (1988) identified six stages of family development, all of which address nodal events related to the comings and goings of family members over time:

1. Unattached young adult
2. New couple
3. Family with young children
4. Family with adolescents
5. Family that is launching children
6. Family in later life

To master these stages, families must successfully complete certain tasks. The unattached young adult, for example, must differentiate himself or herself from the family of origin and become a "self" before joining with another person to form a new family system. The new couple and the families of origin must renegotiate their relationships with one another. The family with young children must find the delicate balance between over- and under-parenting. In all of these stages, problems are most likely to appear when an interruption or dislocation in the unfolding family life cycle occurs, signaling that the family is "stuck" and having difficulty moving through the transition to its next phase.

Variations in the life cycle are, of course, highly likely to occur in today's world, particularly in the lives of reconstituted families. As Meyer (1990) notes, the ground rules have changed as far as the timing and sequence of events are concerned. In much of our society, education, work, love, marriage, childbirth, and retirement are now out of synch. Older adults return to school; adult children live with their parents; and childbirth is no longer part of the exclusive realm of the family. As a result, one phase may not necessarily follow the other in linear fashion. In this world, life events are not preordained. Instead, they are more likely to be atomistic, mixed-and-matched responses to self-definition and opportunity (Meyer, 1990, p. 12). Variations also occur in the family life cycle among cultures.

Every culture marks off stages of living, each with its appropriate expectations, defining what it means to be a man or woman, to be young, to grow up and leave home, to get married and have children, and to grow old and die. Exploring the meaning of the life cycle with diverse families is particularly critical to determine important milestones from their perspective. Cultural variants that have a negative connotation in Western society include the legal versus the culturally derived age for marriage, responsibilities and roles for children, and responsibilities to the family. Families from other countries may, therefore, experience adverse reactions to practices that were common in their country of origin. Recall the earlier case example of the young Somali woman, in which the social worker felt that her family obligations prevented her from living independently and thus had the potential to create a disruptive family dynamic. Carter and McGoldrick (1999b) emphasize that culture plays an important role in family progression and life-cycle expectations. Therefore, culture is an essential dimension in the assessment of family functioning at a particular development stage in the life cycle.

Summary

This chapter introduced concepts and dimensions that will facilitate your assessment of family functioning. Families are not made up of equals, nor do they reflect in their totality the preferred norms of functioning. The systems perspective is useful for understanding family context, processes, interaction, and structure. This perspective can help you assess both internal and external factors that impinge on family functioning. As social systems, families influence and are influenced by every member, creating their own implicit rules, power structure, forms of communication, and patterns of negotiating and problem solving. They also influence and are influenced by transactions in the larger social environment.

Irrespective of their configuration, composition, class, race, or ethnicity, families play an essential role in meeting the needs of their constituent members. The task of assessing family functioning has never been more challenging than it is today, because of the changing definition of the family as well as the greater diversity of racial and ethnic groups in the United States. It is vitally important that we as social workers respect family variants and cultural variants in family leadership, hierarchy, decision-making processes, patterns of interactions and communication styles.

As a final note, we want to emphasize that for the most part the dimensions of assessment discussed in this chapter have evolved from a Western perspective with regard to the family system and family functioning. The extent to which all aspects of these dimensions may be observed among diverse groups is not well documented in the literature. As such, family context (i.e., culture) may be a highly salient factor in the assessment process with diverse families, as it may determine to a large extent the family's rules, roles, bounding, or communication patterns as well as the family's experience with other social systems.

Internet Resources

See our companion website for hot links to some helpful URLs. Note that URLs are subject to change. We will endeavor to update the links on the companion website as much as possible.

For additional information on "Putting Families First," send a message to jdickens@che.umn.edu.

Information on the Institute on Domestic Violence in the African American Community may be obtained by visiting *http://www.dvinstitute.org*. Access the website of *Families in Society, The Journal of Contemporary Human Services*, at *http://www.familiesinsociety.org*, and the website of the *Journal of Ethnic and Cultural Diversity in Social Work* at *http://www.haworthpress.com/web/ECDSW*.

Related Online Content

Visit the *Direct Social Work Practice* companion website at *http://socialwork.wadsworth.com/hepworth7* for additional learning tools such as glossary terms, chapter outlines, InfoTrac College Edition keywords, relevant web links, and chapter practice quizzes. Also, be sure to check out the Direct Practice Virtual Reader, where the authors have personally selected articles relevant to this chapter using InfoMarks.

Notes

1. For further reading on family diversity, we recommend the following: Demo, D. D., Allen, K. R., & Fine, M. A. (Eds.). (1996). *The handbook of family diversity*. New York: Oxford University Press.
2. Jordan and Franklin (2003) is an excellence resource for further study on family assessment tools.
3. Although our discussion centers largely on families, the concepts presented are pertinent to couples as well.
4. The social worker in this case was Marilyn Luptak, Ph.D., from the University of Minnesota.
5. The focus group leader was Patience Togo, MSW, a doctoral student at the University of Minnesota. The groups were a part of an agency's initiative to develop responsive services identified by diverse groups.

CHAPTER **11**

Forming and Assessing Social Work Groups

CHAPTER OVERVIEW

Social workers plan and lead groups in a variety of settings and with an array of populations. Chapter 11 describes essential processes in developing the purpose of the group, forming and structuring the group, and conducting appropriate assessments with a variety of group types. Groups can provide a powerful mechanism for change, whether they are used as the only intervention or in conjunction with individual counseling, family work, or other treatments. As Pack-Brown, Whittington-Clark, and Parker (1998) note when discussing Afro-centric women's groups, the forces for change include the capacity of groups to instill hope and encouragement as well as their capacity to universalize experiences, experience unity, break down isolation, experience altruism and the satisfaction of helping others, grapple with existential questions and learn coping skills for life experiences, and experience healing through cohesion and mutuality. These powerful features are common to an array of well-designed and well-executed treatment groups (Reid, 2002).

Social workers frequently practice with groups. Barker defines group work as occurring when "small numbers of people who share similar interests or common problems convene regularly and engage in activities designed to achieve certain objectives" (2003, p. 404). Thus, social work practice with groups is goal directed. It may focus on helping individuals to make changes—for example, through *treatment groups* that attempt

to enhance the socioemotional well-being of members through the provision of social skills, education, and therapy. Group goals may also focus on the group as a whole as a unit of change or the group as a mechanism for influencing the environment. Examples include *task groups*, such as committees, treatment teams, and task forces that seek the completion of a project or development of a product.

Whichever type group the social worker leads, he or she must: (1) create a group that can effectively serve the purpose for which it was designed; (2) accurately assess individual and group dynamics; and (3) intervene effectively to modify processes that are affecting the group's achievement of its goals.

The success or failure of a group frequently rests on the groundwork that takes place before the group even meets. The social worker must thoughtfully and skillfully visualize a group and determine its purpose, structure, and composition. Without careful forethought in creating group structure and atmosphere, all assessment and intervention efforts will be jeopardized by the lack of a firm foundation.

This chapter provides a framework that will enable you to effectively form groups and accurately assess group processes. It lays the foundation for effective group interventions, the subject of Chapter 16. Before focusing on these objectives, we briefly discuss the types of groups that social workers create and lead in their practice settings.

CLASSIFICATION OF GROUPS

Social workers are typically associated with two types of groups: *treatment groups* and *task groups.* Each of these categories, in turn, has several subtypes. Stated broadly, the purpose of treatment groups is to meet members' socioemotional needs. Task groups, by contrast, are established to "accomplish a task, produce a product, or carry out a mandate" (Toseland & Rivas, 2001, p. 15). Treatment and task groups can be distinguished in a number of basic ways. In treatment groups, communications are open and members are encouraged to actively interact. In task groups, communications are more structured and focus on the discussion of a particular issue or agenda item. Member roles in treatment groups evolve as a result of interaction; in task groups, they may be assigned (e.g., facilitator, minutes-taker). Procedures in treatment groups may be flexible or formal, depending on the group; task groups usually follow formal agendas and rules.

In addition, treatment and task groups differ with respect to self-disclosure, confidentiality, and evaluation. In treatment groups, self-disclosure is expected to be high, proceedings are kept within the group, and group success is based on individual members' success in meeting the treatment goals. In task groups, self-disclosure is low, proceedings may be private or open to the public, and the success of the group is based on members' accomplishing a task, fulfilling a particular charge, or producing a product.

Toseland and Rivas (2001) further refine their classification of treatment groups by describing subtypes that are characterized by their unique purposes.

1. *Support groups* help members cope with life stresses by revitalizing coping skills so that they can more effectively adapt to life events (e.g., schoolchildren meeting to discuss the effect of divorce, persons with cancer discussing the effects of the disease and how to cope with it) (Magen & Glajchen, 1999).
2. *Educational groups* have the primary purpose of helping members learn about themselves and their society (e.g., an adolescent sexuality group, a diabetes management group, a heart attack recovery group).
3. *Growth groups* stress self-improvement, offering members opportunities to expand their capabilities and self-awareness and make personal changes (e.g., a communication enhancement group for couples). Growth groups focus on promoting socioemotional health rather than alleviating socioemotional illness.
4. *Therapy groups* help members change their behavior, cope with or ameliorate their personal problems, or rehabilitate themselves after a social or health trauma (e.g., a drug addiction group, an anger management group, a dialectical behavior therapy group for persons diagnosed with personality disorders). While support is emphasized in therapy groups, they primarily focus on remediation and rehabilitation.
5. *Socialization groups* facilitate transitions through developmental stages, from one role or environment to another, through improved interpersonal relationships or social skills. Such groups often employ program activities, structured exercises, role plays, and the like (e.g., a social club for formerly institutionalized persons, a social skills group for children who have difficulty making friends).

These groups meet in a variety of public and private settings serving both voluntary and involuntary clients. For example, today's social workers are exploring connections with clients who cannot meet in the same physical place through the use of telephone and online groups (Carr, 2004; Fingeld, 2000; Meier, 1997; Rounds, Galinsky, & Stevens, 1991; Schopler, Galinsky, & Abell, 1997). Social workers also find that groups are useful for supporting people who may traditionally have been marginalized by society, such as people of color, gay/lesbian/bisexual/transgendered (GLBT) individuals, and those with stigmatizing illnesses (Miller, 1997; Peters, 1997; Saulnier, 1997; Schopler, Galinsky, Davis, & Despard, 1996; Subramian, Hernandez, & Martinez, 1995).

Involuntary clients, such as perpetrators of domestic violence and adolescents in correctional settings, may also benefit from the mutuality found in groups (Rooney & Chovanec, 2004; Goodman, 1997; Thomas & Caplan, 1997). Groups can also be used as a method for increasing intergroup understanding and conflict reduction—for example, between clashing racial and ethnic groups (Bargal, 2004).

Some group types overlap as they are designed to meet multiple purposes. For example, Bradshaw (1996) describes therapy groups for persons with schizophrenia that simultaneously provide therapy, have a major educational component, and provide support. Groups to assist gay men who are acting as caregivers for others with AIDS provide support as well as education and resources exchange (Getzel, 1991). A men's cooking group at a community center is intended to educate members, prepare them with skills, and provide socialization for the members, all of whom are widowed or newly divorced (Northen & Kurland, 2001).

In self-help groups, members have central shared concerns, such as coping with addiction, cancer, or obesity. These groups are distinguished from treatment and task groups by the fact that the self-help group is led by nonprofessionals who are struggling with the same issues as members of the group, even though a social worker or other professional may have aided in the development or sponsorship of the group. Self-help groups emphasize interpersonal support and the creation of an environment in which individuals may retake charge of their lives. Such groups offer resources and support for such shared problems as addictions, aggressive behavior, mental illness, disabilities, the death of a child, gambling, weight control, family violence, sexual orientation, and AIDS, among others. It is the social worker's task to offer support and consultation to such groups without taking them over. For example, in a self-help group for Temporary Aid for Needy Families (TANF) recipients, the social service provider's role was to initiate the group, assist a member to become the group facilitator, and evaluate the group's effectiveness. Other members took active roles on tasks such as advertising, recruitment, supportive contact between meetings, and outreach to inform agencies of the group (Anderson-Butcher, Khairallah, & Race-Bigelow, 2004).

Task groups are generally organized into three different types (Toseland & Rivas, 2001):

- Those that are created to meet client needs (treatment teams, case conferences, staff development committees)
- Those that are intended to meet organizational needs (committees, cabinets, boards)
- Those that address community needs (social action groups, coalitions, delegate assemblies)

While group types may differ, several underlying principles are common to all forms of group work practice. We will begin with the common features of creating and assessing treatment groups before proceeding to task groups.

FORMATION OF TREATMENT GROUPS

The success or failure of a treatment group rests to a large extent on the thoughtful creation of the group and the careful selection and preparation of members for the group experience. In this section, you will learn the steps needed to foster a positive group outcome.

Establishing the Group Purpose

Clarifying the overall purpose of a group is vital, because the group's objectives influence all the processes that follow, including recruiting and selecting members, deciding on the group's duration, identifying its size and content, and determining meeting location and time. Kurland and Salmon (1998) describe several common problems in developing an appropriate group purpose.

1. Group purposes are promoted without adequate consideration of client need. That is, the purpose may make sense to the prospective leaders or the agency, but not to the potential clients. For example, clients may be assembled because they share a status, such

as having a serious and persistent illness and living independently. From the viewpoint of these potential clients, a purpose that relates to a commonly perceived need such as recreation or socializing may be more attractive than grouping by status.

2. The purpose of the group is confused with the content. For example, the group's purpose is described in terms of what the members will do in the group—their activities—rather than the outcome toward which those activities are directed.

3. The purpose of the group is stated too generally, so that it is vague and meaningless to potential members and provides little direction to prospective leaders.

4. Leaders are reluctant to share their perceptions about the purpose, leaving members to wonder why they are there or to grapple with the issue alone.

5. The group is formed with a "public" purpose that conflicts with its actual hidden purpose. For example, prospective members may not know the basis on which they were contacted to become part of a group. Potential clients may be invited to join on the basis of the fact that they overuse prescription drugs, yet this commonality is not shared with them.

6. Group purposes may be understood as static rather than dynamic (adjusting to the evolving desires and needs of the members).

General group purposes may include overarching goals such as the following:

• To provide a forum for discussion and education whereby divorced women with small children who live in a rural area may explore and seek solutions to common problems, such as a sense of alienation, scarcity of resources, and lack of opportunities for adult companionship

• To provide an opportunity for lesbians with problems of alcoholism to explore their marginalization and environmental context as a means for creating coping responses to alcoholism (Saulnier, 1997)

• To participate in decision making that affects the quality of life in a nursing home by establishing a governing council for residents

• "To teach young probationers how to protect their physical safety and avoid rearrest by adopting prosocial thinking and actions" (Goodman, Getzel, & Ford, 1996, p. 375)

• "To enhance the development of personal and racial identity as well as professional advancement" of African American women (Pack-Brown, Whittington-Clark, & Parker, 1998, p. xi)

The overall purpose of a planned group should be established by the social worker in consultation with agency administrators and potential clients prior to forming the group. Goals subsequently negotiated by the group should reflect the perspectives of the agency, the clients, and the social worker.

The Agency's and Social Worker's Perspectives

Because of the agency's key role in determining and perhaps influencing the group's purpose, social workers must ensure that the agency's objectives are reflected in the group's overall purpose and the agency must ensure that the leader selected will be appropriate for the group's purpose and target population (Northen & Kurland, 2001). However, the agency and the social worker may not always share a common perspective regarding desired goals for a new group. Differences between the views of the agency and social worker may arise, for instance, because of the latter's personal or professional orientation or because of preferences of either the agency or the social worker for particular theories, ideologies, or techniques not espoused by the other party. For example, one of the authors of this book was asked to form a group of women in an outpatient mental health setting who were perceived to overuse tranquilizers. Rather than focus on the negative identity of "drug abuser," the author formed a women's growth group. That growth was defined as including reduction of inappropriate use of drugs.

In the pre-formation period, then, social workers must be clear about their own objectives for a proposed group and must engage in dialogue with administrators and staff *and potential clients* to elicit their views concerning group purpose. If the agency's goals differ from the social worker's goals, those involved must negotiate a general group purpose that is agreeable to both parties. Failing to do so may lead to ambiguity in the group and send mixed messages to its members.

The Client's Perspective

The potential member of a group wants some questions answered: "Why should I join this group? What is in it for me? What will it do for me? Will it help me?" (Kurland & Salmon, 1998, pp. 7–8). The potential voluntary group member wants these questions settled before deciding whether to join a group and, later, whether to continue attending. The potential member who is mandated or pressured to attend also wants to know the answers to these questions, even if the consequences of failure to join or attend are more punishing for this individual than they would be for the voluntary client.

At the point of entry into a group, the client's goals may differ considerably from those of either the agency or the social worker. This is particularly true when potential members have been referred by others or are mandated to participate in the group (Rooney, 1992). Schopler and Galinsky (1974) note that the client's goals may be influenced by many internal or external forces, such as the expectations of others and the client's personal comfort, motivation, and past experiences in group settings.

During group formation, the social worker must carefully explore clients' expectations of the group; help them to develop individual and collective goals that are realistically achievable; and negotiate between individual, group, and agency purposes. For example, in an "alternatives to prostitution" group for which potential members make a choice to participate or risk prosecution, it is important to acknowledge members' goal of avoiding prosecution as central while recognizing that exploring alternative lifestyles is a non-negotiable condition for participation in the group (Rooney, 1992). Even in voluntary groups, leaders must not negate clients' goals, because, as

Levinson (1973) notes, groups tend to operate well when the leader's and the members' purposes are compatible or when the purposes of the two diverge but the social worker goes along with the group's purpose. However, when the social worker advocates purposes that are rejected by members, groups may prematurely dissolve.

Deciding on Leadership

Once the group's purpose is established, group planners must consider whether individual or co-leadership will be necessary to assist the group in meeting its aims. Many types of groups benefit from co-leadership. Having two leaders can provide additional eyes and ears for the group, with one leader specifically attending to content and the other taking note of the process and meta-messages by group members. Co-leaders bring different perspectives, backgrounds, and personalities to the group process, which can appeal to a wider array of members than a single leader might. They can also use their interactions to model effective communication and problem solving (Jacobs, Masson, & Harvill, 1998). In addition, two leaders can keep a watchful eye on each other, providing feedback and noting patterns where individual facilitators' needs and motives may impede effective management of the group (Corey, Corey, Callanan, & Russell, 2004).

Sometimes co-leadership is necessary for practical reasons. With two leaders, one can check on a member who has left the room or has been asked to take time out, while the other continues working with the group. Co-leadership can provide continuity if illness or another emergency on the part of one leader might otherwise result in cancellation of a session. With some populations, two leaders may help send a message of authority in an otherwise disruptive group; they may also provide a sense of physical safety and protection from liability by their very presence (Carrell, 2000). In groups such as those for men accused of partner violence, mixed-gender co-leaders can provide "deliberate and strategic modeling of alternative forms of male–female interactions" (Nosko & Wallace, 1997, p. 5).

Of course, co-leadership is sometimes impractical because of the costs involved and the time needed to coordinate roles, plan the group sessions, and debrief together. In managing the cost concern, some agencies utilize volunteers or "program graduates"—consumers who have had group training and can bring personal experiences to the group process.

Co-leaders who work together on a regular basis may find increased efficiencies as they formulate a common "curriculum" for the group and develop comfort and rapport with each other. Such coordination is essential to avoid disruptive rivalries from occurring or to prevent members from pitting the co-leaders against each other (Northen & Kurland, 2001). As Levine and Dang note, "co-therapists constitute an inner group that must work through its own process while facilitating the progress of the larger group" (1979, p. 175). Borrowing from Paulson, Burroughs, and Gelb, Nosko and Wallace suggest three ground rules for effective co-leadership: "establish a common theoretical orientation; agree on the identification and handling of problems; and agree on what constitutes the appropriate quantity and quality of each leader's participation" (1997, p. 7).

Because characteristics such as gender and race affect personal interactions and are reflected in power dynamics and status expectations, co-leaders of different genders or races must deliberately share all group functions and roles (such as confrontation and support). In doing so, they model equality, undo damaging expectations that members may hold, and help the group adopt the same norms of fairness and flexibility outside of members' stereotyped notions.

Establishing Specific Individual and Group Goals

After establishing an overall purpose and convening the group, the social worker engages members in formulating specific goals at both individual and group levels. Individual goals embody the hopes and objectives of members as they enter the group. Group goals, by contrast, "are the emergent product of the interaction of all participants together, the organizer and the members, as they express their ideas and feelings about the reasons for the existence of the group and its anticipated outcomes" (Hartford, 1971, p. 139).

The following list gives examples of specific goals that may be formulated at either individual or group levels:

1. To identify strengths and steps of growth in myself and in others and to give and receive positive feedback in relation to these
2. To expand awareness of my own behavior (or the group's processes)
3. To identify my self-defeating behaviors and replace them with more functional behaviors
4. To develop problem-solving skills that enhance decision making in my personal life and apply them to specific problems
5. To relate to others more honestly and authentically
6. To become free from external imperatives—that is, "shoulds," "oughts," and "musts"
7. To learn employment skills that will assist me in getting a better job
8. To learn how to hear accurately the messages of others and to convey to others that I understand these messages
9. To grow in self-acceptance and to explore hidden potentials and creativity
10. To learn to express thoughts, feelings, needs, and ideas to others
11. To develop trust in my own judgment
12. To learn and practice skills in making friends

Conducting a Preliminary Interview

Before convening a group, social workers often meet individually with potential group members for the purpose of screening members, establishing rapport, exploring relevant concerns, formulating initial contracts with those motivated to join the group, and clarifying limits and options for involuntary clients. Individual interviews are essential to providing effective group composition; they ensure that the members are selected according to predetermined criteria and possess the behavioral or personality attributes needed for them to make effective use of the group experience.

When creating a group of involuntary clients (e.g., court-referred adolescents or parents referred to meet child protective service mandates), these interviews are a vital first step in clarifying options and assisting potential members to identify acknowledged as well as attributed problems. In rural areas, preliminary interviews provide an opportunity to notify potential members that others they know might attend; in doing so, the group leader can address any concerns that this group composition provokes. With groups from diverse ethnic or racial groups, pre-group orientation can use a rationale congruent with cultural beliefs to socialize prospective members to the treatment process, help them understand what to expect, reduce apprehension, and learn how best to participate (Pack-Brown, Whittington-Clark, & Parker, 1998; Subramian, Hernandez, & Martinez, 1995).

Pre-group meetings with potential members also help leaders obtain information that may prove valuable in selecting and directing interventions in early sessions. Without these early meetings, such information might not emerge until several weeks into the group's sessions. Further, conducting preliminary interviews enables social workers to enter the initial group sessions with a previously established relationship with each member—a distinct advantage given that leaders must attend to multiple communication processes at both individual and group levels. In addition, previous knowledge facilitates the leader's understanding of the members' behaviors and enables the leader to focus more fully on group processes and the task of assisting members to develop relationships with one another. For example, the leaders in one bereavement support group knew from initial interviews that two members had lost loved ones in a traumatic fashion through homicide. This information alerted them to these members' unique concerns and needs and fostered a connection between the two participants who shared a common experience. Establishing rapport with the leader is also beneficial for members, in that it enables them to feel more at ease and to open up more readily in the first meeting.

Social workers should focus on the following in preliminary interviews:

1. *Orient potential members to proposed goals and purposes of the group,* its content and structure, the philosophy and style of the leader in managing group processes, and the respective roles of the leader and group members. Now is also a good time to identify ground rules, such as attendance, confidentiality, the appropriateness of relating to members outside the group, and so on (Yalom, 1995). With involuntary groups, you must distinguish between non-negotiable rules and policies, such as attendance expectations and general themes to be discussed, and negotiable norms and procedures, such as arrangements for breaks, food, and selection of particular topics and their order.

In preliminary meetings, you should also elicit each client's reactions and suggestions on ways that the group might better meet his or her unique needs. Orientation should also include a sharing of the time and place of meetings, length of sessions, and the like. In addition, the social worker may wish to emphasize commonalities that the client may share with other persons considering group membership, such as problems, interests, concerns, or objectives.

2. *Elicit information on the client's prior group experiences,* including the nature of the client's relationship with the leader and other members, his or her style of relating in the previous group, the goals that he or she accomplished, and the personal growth that was achieved. Social workers should anticipate negative reactions from involuntary group members, recognize them as being expected, and yet emphasize ways that these clients can make use of their decision to participate in the group to reach both the mandated goals and their own goals.

3. *Elicit, explore, and clarify the clients' problems,* and identify those that are appropriate for the proposed group. In some instances, either because clients are reluctant to participate in the group or because their problems appear to be more appropriately handled through other treatment modalities or community agencies, you may need to refer them to other resources. To determine whether

family treatment may be more appropriate than group work, Garvin suggests using three criteria:

  "a. Is the problem maintained by processes operating in the family as a system?

   b. How will the family respond to changes the individual may choose to make, and will these responses support or retard such changes?

   c. Does the individual wish to involve the family, and is the family amenable to such involvement?" (1981, p. 74)

4. *Explore the client's hopes, aspirations, and expectations* regarding the proposed group (e.g., "What would you like to be different in your life as a result of your attending this group?").

5. *Identify specific goals that the client wishes to accomplish,* discussing whether these goals can be attained through the proposed group, and determining the client's views as to whether the group is an appropriate vehicle for resolving personal problems. With involuntary groups, sharing personal goals that prior members have chosen, in addition to mandated goals, may make the group more attractive to the reluctant member.

6. *Mutually develop a profile of the client's strengths and attributes,* and determine any that the client might like to enhance through work in the group.

7. *Identify and explore potential obstacles* to participation in or benefiting from the group, including reservations the client may have about attending the group. Obstacles may include shyness or discomfort in group situations, opposition from significant others about entering the group, a heavy schedule that might preclude attending all group meetings, or problems in transportation or child care. In addition to exploring these barriers to group membership, the social worker and client may generate possible alternatives or determine whether the obstacles are so difficult to overcome that participation is unwise at this time.

8. *Ensure that screening for the group is a two-way process.* Potential members should have the opportunity to interview the group leader and determine whether the group is appropriate for their problems and interests and whether the relationship with the leader will likely facilitate a successful outcome.

Deciding on Group Composition

Composition refers to the selection of members for the group. On occasion, composition may be predetermined—for example, when the group consists of all residents in a group home, all patients preparing for discharge, or all motorists referred to alcohol treatment due to drunk driving charges. In rural areas or other settings, the leader may work with a naturally formed group, which has already developed around a common problem, rather than recruit and create a new group (Gumpert & Saltman, 1998).

When the leader is responsible for deciding the group composition, the overriding factor in selecting members is whether a candidate is motivated to make changes and is willing to expend the necessary effort to be a productive group member. Another key factor is the likelihood of that person being compatible with other members in the group. Social workers also usually consider the following issues in determining the composition of groups: sex, age, marital status, intellectual ability, education, socioeconomic status, ego strength, and type of problem (Flapan & Fenchal, 1987).

Homogeneity versus heterogeneity of these characteristics is a vital issue in creating a group. Significant homogeneity in personal characteristics and purpose for joining the group is necessary to facilitate communication and group cohesion. Without such homogeneity, members will have little basis for interacting with one another. Toseland and Rivas (2001), for example, identify levels of education, cultural background, degree of expertise relative to the group task, and communication ability as characteristics vital to creating group homogeneity. Sometimes, the group's purpose will influence the decision for homogeneity along certain characteristics. For example, there are advantages to creating female-only groups for women who have chemical dependencies, as their issues often differ from those of men (Nelson-Zlupko, Kauffman, & Dore, 1995). Likewise, a group for those charged with domestic violence might contain members of a single sex due to the nature of the issues involved. In cognitive-behavioral groups for troubled youth, similarity in age and socioemotional development is essential to avoid dominance by older members who are less mature (Rose, 1998).

Conversely, some diversity among members with respect to coping skills, life experience, and levels of expertise fosters learning and introduces members to differing viewpoints, lifestyles, ways of communicating, and problem-solving skills. To attain the desired outcomes of support, learning, and mutual aid, a treatment group, for example, might include members from different cultures, social classes, occupations, or geographic areas. Heterogeneity is also vital in task group membership so that the group has sufficient resources to fulfill its responsibilities and efficiently divide the labor when dealing with complex tasks (Toseland & Rivas, 2001). The challenge is to attain a workable balance between homogeneity and heterogeneity.

Corey (1990) cautions against including members in voluntary groups whose behavior or pathology is extreme, inasmuch as some people reduce the available energy of the group for productive work and interfere significantly in the development of group cohesion.[1] This is particularly true of individuals who have a need to monopolize and dominate, hostile people or aggressive people with a need to act out, and people who are extremely self-centered and who seek a group as an audience. Others who should generally be excluded from most groups are people who are in a state of extreme crisis, who are suicidal, who are highly suspicious, or who are lacking in ego strength and prone to fragmented and bizarre behavior (Milgram & Rubin, 1992, p. 89).

A decision to include or exclude a client has a lot to do with the purposes of the group. For example, a person with alcoholism might be excluded from a personal growth group but appropriately included in a homogeneous group of individuals who suffer from various types of addictions. Oppositional behavior may be a common denominator in some groups, such as those formed to address domestic violence and drug addiction (Milgram & Rubin, 1992); in such cases, this behavior would not be a criterion for exclusion, but rather a central problem for work. An older woman raising her grandchildren might find little benefit in a parenting group where the focus is on education for first-time parents. This does not mean that the grandparent is not in need of group assistance, but rather that it is important for her needs to be congruent with the group purpose and composition.

Garvin warns against including in a treatment group a member who is very different from others, for the danger is that this person "will be perceived as undesirable or, in sociological terms, deviant by the other members" (1987, p. 65). Differences in socioeconomic status, age, race, problem history, or cognitive abilities may lead to the individual's discomfort and difficulty in affiliating with the group. It may also produce member behaviors that isolate or scapegoat the person. "Outliers" should be avoided, both for the satisfaction of the individual and for the health of the group.

When group composition could potentially lead to the isolation of a member, Garvin recommends enrolling another member who "is either similar to the person in question or who is somewhere in the 'middle,' thus creating a continuum of member characteristics" (1987, p. 65) and assisting in establishing the members' affiliation and comfort.

Open versus Closed Groups

Groups may have either an *open* format, in which the group remains open to new members, or a *closed* format, in which no new members are added once the group gets under way. Typically, groups that are open or closed in terms of admitting new members are also open or closed in regard to their duration. Alcoholics Anonymous and Weight Watchers are examples of open-ended and open-membership groups. A 10-week medication management group and a 5-week social skills group would be examples of closed-membership, closed-ended groups.

Open-ended groups are generally used for helping clients cope with transitions and crises, providing support, acting as a means for assessment, and facilitating outreach (Schopler & Galinsky, 1981). Having open-ended groups ensures that a group is immediately available at a time of crisis. An open format itself presents different models (Henry, 1988; Reid, 1991), including the *drop-in* (or *drop-out*) *model* in which members are self-selecting, entry criteria are very broad, and members attend whenever they wish for an indefinite period. In the *replacement model,* the leader immediately identifies someone to fill a group vacancy. In the *re-formed model,* group members contract for a set period of time, during which no new members are added but original members may drop out. At the end of the contract period, a new group is formed consisting of some old and some new members.

The choice of format depends on the purpose of the group, the setting, and the population served. An open format provides the opportunity for new members to bring fresh perspectives to the group and offers immediate support for those in need, who can stay as long as they choose. At the same time, the instability of this format discourages members from developing the trust and confidence to openly share and explore their problems—a strong feature of the closed-ended group. Frequent changes of membership may also disrupt the work of the open-ended group, although the developmental patterns in such groups vary according to how many new members enter and the frequency of turnover (Galinsky & Schopler, 1989). Leaders of open-ended groups need to be attuned to clients being at different places in the group process and to be able to work with core members to carry forward the particular group's traditions (Schopler & Galinsky, 1981).

Advantages associated with a closed group include higher group morale, greater predictability for role behaviors, and an increased sense of cooperation among members. Disadvantages are that the group may not be open to members when potential participants are ready to make use of it and that, if too many members drop out, the group process will be drastically affected by the high rate of attrition.

Determining Group Size and Location

The size of the group depends in large part on its purpose, the age of clients, the type of problems to be explored, and the needs of members. Seven to 10 members is usually an optimal number for a group with an emphasis on close relationships (Reid, 2002). Bertcher and Maple (1985) suggest that the group should be small enough to allow it to achieve its purpose, yet large enough to ensure that members have a satisfying experience. As such, educational and task groups may accommodate larger numbers of members than would therapy and support groups, where cohesion is central to the group progress.

The location of group meetings should be selected with convenience and image in mind. *Image* speaks to the impression that the site makes on members—the message it conveys that may attract them to the group or make them uncomfortable in attending. For example, a parenting group held at a school building may not be attractive to potential members if their own experiences with education or with the particular school system have been unfavorable. A parenting group that meets at a local YMCA/YWCA or community center may be perceived as comfortable to members who are used to going there for their children's sports or other community events.

Convenience refers to the accessibility of the site for those people whom the group chooses to attract. For example, is the site readily accessible to a public transportation line for those who do not own automobiles? Is it safe, with plenty of parking, and easy to find for those who may be uncomfortable venturing out at night? Social workers who are familiar with a community might make note of the "participation patterns" of residents, as these may reveal neutral locations for meetings (Gumpert & Saltman, 1998).

Leaders may have little choice over the meeting location if the sponsoring agency's site must be used. Those planning groups should take the image and accessibility of the location into account, however, when recruiting prospective members or when diagnosing problems in group membership.

Setting the Frequency and Duration of Meetings

Closed groups benefit from having a termination date at the outset, which encourages productive work. Regarding the possible lifespan of a group,

Corey notes: "The duration varies from group to group, depending on the type of group and the population. The group should be long enough to allow for cohesion and productive work yet not so long that the group seems to drag on interminably" (1990, p. 92). For a time-limited therapy group, Reid (1991) recommends approximately 20 sessions, stating that this length provides adequate time for cohesiveness and a sense of trust to develop. Reid recommends the use of time limits, noting that if the leader errs in estimating the length of time needed, "there is an end point in which the group can be reformulated as opposed to it going on indefinitely" (p. 189).

Others might suggest that a 20-session limit is not feasible; that attrition and other obligations may erode participation; and that shortening this length as Reid suggests may lead to an unwarranted sense of failure. Shorter durations, during which attendance can be assured, may leave clients "wanting more" but with a sense of accomplishment and goal achievement at the group's conclusion. In general, short-term groups vary between 1 and 12 sessions, with the shorter-duration groups being targeted at crisis situations, anxiety alleviation, and educational programs (Northen & Kurland, 2001).

Formulating Group Guidelines

Developing consensus concerning guidelines for behavior (e.g., staying on task, adhering to confidentiality) among members is a vital aspect of contracting in the initial phase of the group. Some group guidelines, especially when clients are involuntary, cannot be determined by consensus. Wherever possible, however, voluntary agreement should be sought on as many group guidelines as possible. In formulating guidelines with the group, the social worker takes the first step in shaping the group's evolving processes to create a "working group" capable of achieving specific objectives. Unfortunately, attempts to formulate guidelines often fail to achieve this intended effect for three major reasons.

First, the social worker may establish parameters *for* the group, merely informing members of behavioral expectations to which they are expected to

adhere. While non-negotiable requirements such as attendance are often part of involuntary groups, overemphasis on such control may convey the message, "This is my group, and this is how I expect you to behave in it." Such an emphasis may negate later actions by the social worker to encourage members to assume responsibility for the group. Without consensus among members concerning desirable group guidelines, power struggles and disagreements may ensue. Further, members may not feel bound by what they consider the "leader's rules" and may deliberately test them, creating a counterproductive scenario.

Second, the social worker may discuss group guidelines only superficially and neglect either to identify or to obtain the group's commitment to them. This is unfortunate, because the extent to which members understand what these parameters mean will influence the extent to which they conform to them.

Third, just because the group adopts viable guidelines for behavior does not mean that members will subsequently conform to them. To the contrary, there is often little relationship between contracted behaviors and actual behaviors in a group. Establishing group guidelines merely sets guideposts against which members may measure their current behavior. For negotiated behaviors to become normative, leaders must consistently intervene to assist members in adhering to guidelines and in considering discrepancies between contracted and actual behaviors.

Because formulating guidelines is a critical process that substantially influences the success of a group, we offer the following suggestions to assist you in this aspect of group process:

1. If there are non-negotiable agency rules (e.g., adolescents often are not allowed to smoke in correctional settings), you should present the rules, explain their rationale, and encourage discussion of them (Behroozi, 1992). Confidentiality is often a non-negotiable rule. The rationale for ensuring that issues discussed in the group will not be shared outside the group should be explained.

2. Introduce the group to the concept of *decision by consensus* on all negotiable items

(explained later in this section), and solicit agreement concerning adoption of this method for making decisions *prior* to formulating group guidelines.

3. Ask group members to share their vision of the kind of group they would like to have by responding to the following statement: "I would like this group to be a place where I could . . ." Reach for responses from all members. Once this has been achieved, summarize the collective thinking of the group. Offer your own views of supportive group structure that assists members to work on individual problems or to achieve group objectives.

4. Ask members to identify guidelines for behavior in the group that will assist them to achieve the kind of group structure and atmosphere they desire. You may wish to brainstorm possible guidelines at this point, adding your suggestions. Then, through group consensus, choose those that seem most appropriate.

Depending on the setting and purpose of your group, you may need to develop guidelines that pertain to group concerns such as group format, decision-making processes, and more. Guidelines adopted by many groups regarding these issues have proven conducive to achieving individual and group objectives.

Group Format

In addition to determining the group purpose, goals, composition, duration, and other elements, leaders must attend to the group *structure*, or how the time in the group will be used to most effectively meet the needs of participants. In research on interventions in rural groups, Gumpert and Saltman (1998) found that worker interventions were determined by the group purpose (reported by 98% of respondents), by a recent incident or event in the group (reported by 61%), by agency expectations (46%), and by the group curriculum (28%).

The following activities will assist you and your members to focus your energies so as to achieve therapeutic objectives effectively and efficiently.

Table 11-1 Example of a group format

15 MINUTES	1½ HOURS	15 MINUTES
Check-in Reviewing and monitoring tasks	Focusing on relevant content (presentation and discussion) and formulating tasks Plan for the week	Summarizing plan for the week Evaluating group session

1. Define group and individual goals in behavioral terms and rank them according to priority.

2. Develop an overall plan that organizes the work to be done within the number of sessions allocated by the group to achieve its goals. The leader (or co-leaders) should have done preliminary work on this plan while designing the group.

3. Specify behavioral tasks (homework) to be accomplished outside the group each week that will assist individuals to make the desired changes.

4. Achieve agreement among members concerning the weekly format and agenda—that is, how time will be allocated each week to achieve the group's goals. For instance, a group might allocate its weekly 2 hours to the format shown in Table 11-1. The group leader is responsible for developing the format and presenting it and the rationale to the group. Although input and mutuality are important, group members are often ill equipped, due to their own pain or lack of group experience, to give meaningful input in creating group structure. They may, however, respond with concerns or preferences about the format offered, and may be better able to offer input as the group evolves.

The result should be a clearly conceptualized format that provides the means for evaluating the ongoing process experienced by group members. Regardless of the treatment modality utilized, clients have a right to receive help within a format that provides for accountability in the form of continuing and concrete feedback concerning their progress. The structure adopted by your group should also be flexible enough to accommodate differing group processes and the unique needs of members. To ensure its continued functionality, review the format periodically throughout the life of the group.

Group Decision Making

Effective deliberation and decision making are critical in determining the productivity and success of a group. This is particularly true of task groups. To achieve its objectives, every group ultimately develops methods of making decisions. Left to their own devices, however, groups may evolve counterproductive decision-making processes. Some groups, for example, permit the power for making decisions to be vested in a few members, "counting in" some members and "counting out" others. This pattern perpetuates conflict and intrigue in the group, causing unrest and resentments that divert energies from productive tasks and block developmental progress.

Members of newly formed groups have varying styles of making decisions and typically do not know how to make decisions effectively as a group. As a result, most treatment groups learn problem solving through extended trial-and-error processes, gradually gaining from their mistakes (we hope). In fact, most groups can quickly learn to adopt a model of decision by consensus, given effective leadership in educating the group. Further, equipping groups with an effective decision-making model in the early stages of development can expedite group process and assist groups in more readily achieving an advanced level of group functioning.

The decision-by-consensus method can be taught early in the first group session according to the following sequence:

1. Explain that groups need a decision-making method that gives each person an equal vote and "counts everyone in."

2. Gain group acceptance of this method of making decisions.

3. Explain steps for effective decision making (these steps are discussed in Chapter 13).

4. Identify the leader's function in assisting the group to make decisions that meet the needs of all members.

5. Use the decision-by-consensus approach in setting up the initial contract and focus explicitly on the process to enhance group awareness of the use of this approach.

Additional Group Issues to Address

This section provides guidelines for 10 issues that are pertinent to treatment groups, although each guideline's applicability depends on the specific focus of the group.

Help-Giving/Help-Seeking Roles. Groups formed to assist individuals with personal problems benefit from clarification of what might be termed *help-giving* and *help-seeking* roles. Although the two terms are self-explanatory, you may wish to assist the group to operationalize these roles by considering the behaviors embodied in them. The help-seeking role, for example, incorporates such behaviors as making direct requests for help, authentically sharing one's feelings, being open to feedback, and demonstrating willingness to test new approaches to problems. The help-giving role involves such behaviors as listening attentively, refraining from criticism, clarifying perceptions, summarizing, maintaining focus on the problem, and pinpointing strengths and incremental growth.

The leader should give special attention to the issue of advice in the help-giving role, and emphasize the necessity of carefully exploring fellow members' personal problems before attempting to solve them. Otherwise, groups tend to move quickly to giving advice and offering evaluative suggestions about what a member "ought" or "ought not" to do. You can further help the group to appropriately adopt the two roles by highlighting instances in which members have performed well in either of these helping roles.

Visitors. A group convened for treatment purposes should develop explicit guidelines specifying whether and under what conditions visitors may attend group meetings. Depending on the group purpose or structure (open or closed), visitors can detrimentally affect group processes by causing members to refrain from sharing feelings and problems openly, by threatening the confidentiality of the proceedings, or by creating resentment toward the individual who invited the visitor and thereby violated the integrity of the group. Anticipating with members the possible effects of visitors on the group and establishing procedures and conditions under which visitors may attend sessions can avert group turmoil as well as embarrassment for individual members.

New Members. Procedures for adding and orienting new members may need to be established. In some cases, the group leader may reserve the prerogative of selecting members. In other instances, the leader may permit the group to choose new members, with the understanding that those choices should be based on certain criteria and that the group should achieve consensus regarding potential members. In either case, procedures for adding new members and the importance of the group's role in orienting those entrants should be clarified. As mentioned earlier, adding new members in an open-ended group should occur in a planned way, considering the stage of development of the group.

Individual Contacts with the Social Worker. Whether you encourage or discourage individual contacts with members outside the group depends on the purpose of the group and the anticipated consequences or benefits of such contacts. In some cases, individual contacts serve to promote group objectives. For example, in a correctional setting, planned meetings with an adolescent between sessions may provide opportunities to focus on troubling actions in the group, support strengths, and develop an individual contract with the youth to modify behaviors. In the case of couples' groups, however, individual contacts initiated by one partner may be a bid to form an alliance with the social worker against the other partner (or may be perceived as such by the partner who did not initiate the contact). If you have questions regarding the advisability of having individual contacts outside the group, you should thoroughly

discuss these questions with members and mutually develop guidelines pertaining to this matter.

Care for Space and Cleanup. Making group decisions regarding care of the room (e.g., food, furniture, trash) and cleanup (before having to contend with a messy room) encourages members to assume responsibility for themselves and for the group space. Otherwise, resentments may fester, and subgroups destructive to group cohesiveness may form when some members feel responsible for cleanup and others do not.

Use of Recorder. The social worker should always ask for the group's permission before making audio or video recordings of a group session (NASW, 1999). Before asking for such a decision, you should provide information concerning the manner in which the recording will be utilized outside the session. Reservations regarding recording the session should be thoroughly aired, and the group's wishes should be respected.

The organization sponsoring the group will dictate the written records that should be kept, their format, and the content needed. In any event, you should take care not to record identifying information about other group members in an individual member's record.

Eating, Drinking, and Smoking. Opinions vary among group leaders concerning these activities in groups. Some groups and leaders believe that they distract from group process; others regard them as relaxing and actually beneficial to group operation. You may wish to elicit views from members concerning these activities and develop guidelines with the group that meet member needs and facilitate group progress.

A related issue is the use of profanity in the group. Some social workers believe that group members should be allowed to use whatever language they choose in expressing themselves. However, profanity may be offensive to some participants, and the group may wish to develop guidelines concerning this matter. If it appears that the leader might be the only one offended, he or she needs to be aware that imposing the leader's preferences as a guideline might inhibit the group.

Attendance. Discussing the problems that irregular attendance can pose for a group before the fact and soliciting commitments from members to attend regularly can do much to solidify group attendance in future group sessions. Involuntary groups often have attendance policies that permit a limited number of absences and late arrivals. Late arrivals and early departures by group members can typically be minimized if the group develops norms about this behavior in advance and if the leader starts and ends meetings promptly. Exceptions may be needed, of course, to accommodate crises affecting the schedules of members or to extend the session to complete an urgent item of business if the group concurs. However, individual and group exceptions to time norms should be rare.

Programming. Sometimes, group formats include activities or exercises. For example, domestic violence or substance abuse groups may use psychoeducational programming, children's groups may use activities or field trips (Rose, 1998; Ross, 1997), and cognitive-behavioral groups may use role plays and mnemonic devices to remind members of options for problem solving (Goodman, Getzel, & Ford, 1996). It is essential that the activities selected relate directly to the group's purpose. Any such activities should be prefaced and concluded by discussions or debriefing that relate the programming to the group's goals and evaluate the effectiveness of the experience.

Touching. The sensitive nature of some group topics may lead to expressions of emotion, such as crying or angry outbursts. It is important to have group guidelines that provide physical safety for members (no hitting). It is also important to set a climate of emotional safety, to sanction the appropriate expression of feelings. Some group guidelines prohibit members from touching one another with hugs or other signs of physical comfort. Sometimes these rules are included to protect members from unwanted or uncomfortable advances. Other groups maintain that touch is a "feeling stopper" when one is tearful, and insist that group members can display their empathy in other ways—through words or through eye contact and attention to the other, for example. Whatever the group's policy, it is important to explain the expectation and the rationale, and to address member concerns, rather than impose the guideline unilaterally.

Guidelines are helpful only to the extent that they expedite the development of the group and further the achievement of the group's goals. They should be reviewed periodically to assess their functionality in relationship to the group's stage of development. Outdated guidelines should be discarded or reformulated.

When the group's behavior is incompatible with the group guidelines, the leader would be wise to describe what is happening in the group (or request that members do so) and, after thoroughly reviewing the situation, ask the group to consider whether the guideline in question is still viable. If used judiciously, this strategy not only helps the group to reassess its guidelines but also places responsibility for monitoring adherence to those guidelines with the group, where it belongs. Leaders who unwittingly assume the role of "enforcer" place themselves in an untenable position, because group members tend to struggle against what they perceive as authoritarian control on the leader's part.

ASSESSING GROUP PROCESSES

In group assessment, social workers must attend to processes that occur at both the individual and the group levels, including emerging themes or patterns, in an effort to enhance the functioning of individuals and the group as a whole. This section describes the procedures for accurately assessing the processes for both individuals and groups. A systems framework facilitates the identification and impact of such patterns. Instruments may also help in the identification and quantification of group processes and outcomes. For example, Macgowan (1997) has developed a group work engagement measure (GEM) that combines measures of attendance, satisfaction, perceived group helpfulness, group cohesion, and interaction.

A Systems Framework for Assessing Groups

Like families, groups are social systems characterized by repetitive patterns. All social systems share an important principle—namely, that persons who compose a given system gradually limit their behaviors to a relatively narrow range of patterned responses as they interact with others within that system. Groups thus evolve implicit rules or norms that govern behaviors, shape patterns, and regulate internal operations. Leaders who employ a systems framework in assessing the processes of groups can attend to the patterned interactions of members, infer rules that govern those interactions, and weigh the functionality of those rules and patterns. For example, a group may develop a pattern in which one person's complaints receive a great deal of attention while others' concerns are dismissed. The "rules" leading to such a pattern may be that "if the group didn't attend to Joe, he might drop out or become angry" or "Joe is hurting more than anyone else" or "Joe's issues resonate with those of others, so he deserves the additional attention, whereas the other concerns that are raised aren't shared concerns and don't deserve group time." This pattern may result in the disenfranchisement of the members who feel marginalized. Conversely, the other members may concur that Joe's issues are symptomatic of the group and thus be glad that he is bringing them to the surface for discussion.

Conceptualizing and organizing group processes into response patterns enables leaders to make systematic, ongoing, and relevant assessments. This knowledge can help "make sense" of the process and bring comfort to group leaders, who may otherwise feel that they are floundering in sessions.

As leaders observe groups to determine patterned behaviors, they must concurrently attend to individual and group behaviors. Observing processes at both levels is difficult, however, and leaders sometimes become discouraged when they realize they attended more to individual dynamics than to group dynamics (or the converse), resulting in vague or incomplete assessment formulations. Recognizing this dilemma, we discuss strategies for accurately assessing both individual and group patterns in the remainder of this chapter.

Assessing Individuals' Patterned Behaviors

Some of the patterned behaviors that group members display are *functional*—that is, they enhance the well-being of individual members and the quality of group relationships. Other patterned behaviors are *dysfunctional*—that is, they erode the self-esteem of members and are destructive to relationships and group cohesion. Many members of growth groups, in fact, join such groups because some of their patterned dysfunctional behaviors are currently producing distress in their interpersonal relationships. Often, of course, these members are not aware of the patterned nature of their behavior, nor do they realize that some of these entrenched behaviors cause interpersonal problems. Instead, they may blame others as the source of their difficulties.

A major role of leaders in growth groups, then, is to aid members to become aware of their patterned behavioral responses, to determine the effects of these responses on themselves and others, and to choose whether to change such responses. To carry out this role, leaders must formulate a profile of the recurring responses of each member.

Understanding Content and Process

To formulate accurate assessment of individual behavioral responses, you must apply the concepts of *content* and *process*, which we discussed in Chapter 10. Recall that content refers to verbal statements and related topics that members discuss, whereas process involves the ways members relate or behave as they interact in the group and discuss content. To expand your understanding of the concept of group process, consider the following description of a member's behavior in two initial group sessions.

CASE EXAMPLE

In the first group meeting, John moved his chair close to the leader's chair. Several times when the leader made statements, John expressed agreement. In the second group meeting, John again sat next to the leader and used the pronoun *we* several times, referring to opinions he thought were jointly held by himself and the leader. Later, John tried to initiate a conversation with the leader concerning what he regarded as negative behavior of another group member in front of that member and the rest of the group.

This case example describes how John is behaving and communicating rather than what he is saying, so it deals with process rather than content.

It is at the process level that leaders discover many of the patterned behavioral responses of individuals. The preceding case example revealed John's possible patterned or *thematic behaviors.* For example, we might infer that John is jockeying to establish an exclusive relationship with the leader and bidding for an informal position of co-leader in the group. Viewed alone, none of John's discrete behaviors provides sufficient information to justify drawing a conclusion about a possible response pattern. Viewed collectively, however, the repetitive responses warrant inferring that a pattern does, in fact, exist.

Identifying Roles of Group Members

In identifying patterned responses of individuals, leaders also need to attend to the various roles that members assume in the group. For example, members may assume *leadership roles* that are *formal* (explicitly sanctioned by the group) or *informal* (emerging as a result of group needs). Further, a group may have several leaders who serve different functions or who head rival subgroups.

Some members may assume *task-related* or *instrumental roles* that facilitate the group's efforts to define problems, implement problem-solving strategies, and carry out tasks. These members may propose goals or actions, suggest procedures, request pertinent facts, clarify issues, or offer an alternative or conclusion for the group to consider. Other members may adopt *maintenance* roles that are oriented to altering, maintaining, and strengthening the group's functioning. Members who take on such roles may offer compromises, encourage and support the contributions of others, or suggest group standards. Some members may emerge as spokespersons around concerns

of the group or enact other *expressive* roles. Rather than confront such a person as a negative influence, it is often useful to explore whether, in fact, that person is bringing to the fore issues that have been discussed outside of the group. In short, that person may be acting as an informal group leader who can be joined in seeking to make the group succeed (Breton, 1985). Still other members may assume self-serving roles by seeking to meet their own needs at the expense of the group. Such members may attack the group or its values, stubbornly resist the group's wishes, continually disagree with or interrupt others, assert authority or superiority, display lack of involvement, pursue extraneous subjects, or find various ways to call attention to themselves.

Members may also carry labels assigned by other members, such as "clown," "uncommitted," "lazy," "dumb," "silent one," "rebel," "over-reactor," or "good mother." Such labeling stereotypes members, making it difficult for them to relinquish the set of expected behaviors or to change their way of relating to the group. Hartford elaborates:

> For instance, the person who has become the clown may not be able to make a serious and substantial contribution to the group because, regardless of what he says, everyone laughs. If one person has established a high status as the initiator, others may not be able to initiate for fear of threatening his position. If one has established himself in a dependency role in a pair or subgroup, he may not be able to function freely until he gets cues from his subgroup partner. (1971, p. 218)

One or more members may also be assigned the role of scapegoat, bearing the burden of responsibility for the group's problems and the brunt of consistent negative responses from other members. Such individuals may attract the scapegoating role because they are socially awkward and repeatedly make social blunders in futile attempts to elicit positive responses from others (Balgopal & Vassil, 1983; Klein, 1970). Or they may assume this role because they fail to recognize nonverbal cues that facilitate interaction in the group and thus behave without regard to the subtle nuances that govern the behavior of other members (Balgopal & Vassil, 1983; Beck, 1974). Individuals may also unknowingly perpetuate the scapegoating role they have assumed in their nuclear families, workplaces, schools, or social systems. Although group scapegoats demonstrate repetitive dysfunctional behaviors that attract the hostility of the group, the presence of the scapegoating role signals a group phenomenon (and pattern) whose maintenance requires the tacit cooperation of all members.

Individuals may also assume the role of an isolate, which is characterized by the individual being ignored by the group, not reaching out to others, or doing so but being rejected. Sometimes this lack of affiliation may arise from poor social skills or values, interests, and beliefs that set the individual apart from the other group members (Hartford, 1971). The isolate differs from the scapegoat in that the latter gets attention, even if it is negative.

It is important to identify all of the roles that members assume because those roles profoundly affect the group's capacity to respond to the individual needs of members and its ability to fulfill the treatment objectives. Identifying roles is also vital because members tend to play out in treatment groups the same roles that they assume in other social contexts. Members need to understand the impact of dysfunctional roles on themselves and others.

Some members, of course, assume roles that strengthen relationships and enhance group functioning. By highlighting these positive behaviors, leaders may boost members' self-esteem and place the spotlight on behaviors that other members may fruitfully emulate.

Developing Profiles of Individual Behavior

During assessment, group leaders need to develop accurate behavioral profiles of each individual. To carry out this function, leaders must record functional and dysfunctional responses that members displayed in initial sessions. Operating from a strengths perspective, it is important to record and acknowledge functional behaviors such as the following:

FUNCTIONAL BEHAVIORS

1. Expresses caring for group members or significant others
2. Demonstrates organizational or leadership ability
3. Expresses her/himself clearly
4. Cooperates with and supports others
5. Assists in maintaining focus and helping the group accomplish its purposes
6. Expresses feelings openly and congruently
7. Accurately perceives what others say (beyond surface meanings) and conveys understanding to them
8. Responds openly and positively to constructive feedback
9. Works within guidelines established by the group
10. "Owns" responsibility for behavior
11. Risks and works to change self
12. Counts in others by considering their opinions, including them in decision making, or valuing their differences
13. Participates in discussions and assists others to join in
14. Gives positive feedback to others concerning their strengths and growth
15. Acknowledges his or her own strengths and growth
16. Expresses humor constructively
17. Supports others nonverbally

DYSFUNCTIONAL BEHAVIORS

1. Interrupts, speaks for others, or rejects others' ideas
2. Placates or patronizes
3. Belittles, criticizes, or expresses sarcasm
4. Argues, blames, attacks, or engages in name-calling
5. Verbally dominates group "air time"
6. Gives advice prematurely
7. Expresses disgust and disapproval nonverbally

8. Talks too much, talks too loudly, or whispers

9. Withdraws, assumes the role of spectator, ignores others, or shows disinterest

10. Talks about tangential topics or sidetracks the group in other ways

11. Displays distracting physical movements

12. Is physically aggressive or "horses" around

13. Clowns, mimics, or makes fun of others

14. Aligns with others to form destructive sub-groups

15. Intellectualizes or diagnoses (e.g., "I know what's wrong with you")

16. Avoids focusing on self or withholds feelings and concerns pertinent to personal problems

These behaviors can also be tracked by client self-reports or by peer observation within the group. In either case, the data may be captured through charts, logs, diaries or journals, self-anchored rating scales or observations, which can be naturalistic; through role plays and simulations; or through analysis of videotapes of group process (Toseland & Rivas, 2001).

Table 11-2 is a record of a women's support group that illustrates how leaders can develop accurate behavioral profiles of each member by keeping track of the members' functional and dys-functional behaviors. The profile of behaviors in Table 11-2 identifies specific responses by individuals in the group but does not necessarily identify their *patterned or stylized* behaviors. Recording the specific responses of individuals at each session, however, aids in identifying recurring behaviors and roles members are assuming. For example, a glance at Table 11-2 suggests that Dixie is vulnerable to becoming an isolate in the group.

In addition to direct observation, information about the behavioral styles of members can be obtained from many other sources. In the formation phase of the group, for example, leaders can elicit pertinent data in preliminary interviews with the prospective member or from family members, agency records, or other professionals who have referred members to the group. Within the group, leaders may glean substantial data concerning patterned behavior of members by carefully attending and exploring members' descriptions of their problems and interactions with others.

Identifying Growth of Individuals

Because growth occurs in subtle and diverse forms, a major role of leaders is to document (and to assist the group to document) the incremental growth of each member. To sharpen your ability to observe individuals' growth, we suggest that you develop a record-keeping format that provides a column for notations concerning the growth that members demonstrate from one session to the next or across several sessions. Without such a documentation system, it is easy to overlook significant changes and thus miss vital opportunities to substantiate the direct relationship between member's efforts to change and the positive results they attain.

The Impact of Culture

Assessment of individual functioning, of course, must take group members' cultural backgrounds into account. Tsui and Schultz stress that "the group norms comprising the so-called therapeutic milieu are actually Caucasian group norms that, in themselves, resist intrusion and disruption from minority cultures" (1988, p. 137). Individuals from other cultures living in a majority culture different from their own are influenced by that majority culture in unique ways and may vary in their degree of acculturation. The behavior of a minority group member might be significantly influenced by cultural norms about sharing personal material with strangers, speaking up before others, offering answers, or advising other members. Assessment of group interactions must occur in light of knowledge about each member's culture and his or her individual characteristics within that culture. As with individual practice, group workers must be careful not to discredit behavior they do not understand, behavior that may arise from the member's upbringing, or attempts to cope with the current environment and the stress and strain of adaptation (Chau, 1993; Mason, Benjamin, & Lewis, 1996; Pack-Brown, Whittington-Clark, & Parker, 1998).

Table 11-2 Examples of behavioral profiles of group members

NAME	DESCRIPTIVE ATTRIBUTES	FUNCTIONAL BEHAVIOR	DYSFUNCTIONAL BEHAVIOR
June	35 years old Legal secretary 8-year-old son Divorced 5 years	Gave positive feedback several times Expressed feelings clearly Outgoing and spontaneous Adds energy to group	Ruminated several times about the past Sometimes interruped others and dominated discussion
Raye	29 years old Homemaker Three children	Articulate Sharp at summarizing feelings of group Expressed ambivalence about attending group	Seemed to have self-doubt concerting validity of own opinions
Janet	34 years old Clerical supervisor Divorced 1 year	Initiated group discussion of several topics	Was dogmatic and unyielding about several of her opinions Became angry several times during session; appears to have short fuse
Pam	35 years old Truck driver Six children Divorced 3 years	Joined in discussions Accredited self for several strengths	Responses indicate she labels and puts down her children Twice challenged the comments of others
Dixie	30 years old Homemaker Two children Divorce in progress	Stated she came to group despite considerable apprehension Artist; exhibits paintings	Very quiet in session Acts intimidated by group Sat in chair slightly outside circle
Rachael	30 years old Unmarried	Readily shared problems Responsive to others Able to describe feelings Articulate	Seemed to pull the group toward feeling sorry for her through constant storytelling
Li	31 years old Homemaker Three children Divorced 1 year	Seemed eager to work on problems Talked about self introspectively	Several times appeared to appease others rather than expressing how she really felt about issues
Elaine	45 years old Cafeteria worker Two teenagers Divorce in progress	Listened attentively to others Nodded approvingly when others spoke	Did not speak up in group

Assessing Individuals' Cognitive Patterns

Just as group members develop patterned ways of behaving, so they also develop patterned cognitions—that is, typical or habituated ways of perceiving and thinking about themselves, other persons, and the world around them. Such patterned cognitions are revealed in the form of silent mental speech or internal dialogue that individuals utilize to define the meaning of life events. To use an analogy, it is as though various types of events in a person's life trigger a tape recording in his or her mind that automatically repeats the same messages over and over, coloring the person's perceptions of events and determining his or her reality. Examples of negative internal dialogue that tend to create problems for group members include repeated messages such as "I'm a failure," "No one wants to hear what I have to say," and "Other people are better than I am."

Patterned cognitions and behavior are inextricably related and reciprocally reinforce each other. The following case example of a group member's problem illustrates the marriage between cognitions and behavior and the insidious effect that negative cognitions may have on a client's life.

CASE EXAMPLE

Juanita, a 25-year-old dental assistant, entered an adult support group because of problems at work that were jeopardizing her position. She reported her problems to the group as follows: Juanita was experiencing severe negative reactions toward her employer, Dr. A. An attractive young dentist, Dr. A was the "darling" of the large dental organization for which Juanita worked. Watching Dr. A, who was single, pursue other young women in the office, she concluded that he was disinterested in and "bored" with her and that she was doing an inadequate job. As Juanita worked daily with Dr. A, she made repeated statements to herself such as "He doesn't like me," "He'd rather have someone else as an assistant," and "There's something wrong with me."

Juanita worked at hiding her growing resentment toward Dr. A but ultimately could not contain her feelings. Defensive and easily riled because of what she constantly said to herself, Juanita repeatedly snapped at Dr. A in front of patients. Angered and confused by her irritable behavior, Dr. A began to grow annoyed himself and to relate to Juanita more and more coolly. Juanita interpreted Dr. A's behavior as evidence that she was correct in her conclusion: He did not like her and she was inadequate not only as an assistant but also as a person.

Because patterned behavioral and cognitive responses are inextricably interwoven and perpetuate each other, leaders must be able to intervene in groups to modify dysfunctional cognitions. Prior to intervening, however, leaders must fine-tune their perceptions to identify the thematic cognitions that lie behind members' verbal statements. The following statements, for example, reveal conclusions members have drawn about themselves and others:

Husband [*about wife's behavior*]: She doesn't allow me to smoke in the house. (My wife is in charge of me.)

Teen in group on adjusting to divorce in the family I can't tell how I feel. (If I do, they'll reject me or I will hurt them.)

Member of alcoholics group: If I can't trust my wife, how can I stop drinking? (My recovery rests in the hands of someone else.)

You can record the cognitive themes or patterns of members in the same manner that you observe and record their functional and problematic behavioral responses. Returning to the example of the women's support group profiled in Table 11-2, note the cognitive responses of several members recorded by the leader in the same session, as illustrated in Table 11-3.

Leaders can help group members identify cognitive patterns during problem exploration by asking questions such as "When that happened, what did you say to yourself?", "What conclusions do you draw about others under those circumstances?", or "What kind of self-talk do you remember before your anxiety level rose?" Leaders can also teach groups to recognize symptoms of patterned cognitions. As the group grasps the significance of internal dialogue and attends to cognitive patterns expressed by members, leaders should reinforce the group's growth by giving members descriptive feedback concerning their accomplishments.

Assessing Groups' Patterned Behaviors

Toseland and Rivas (2001) recommend examining group patterns in four areas: communication, cohesion, norms of social control, and group culture. To heighten your awareness of functional and dysfunctional patterned group behaviors, we provide contrasting examples in Table 11-4.

Table 11-3 Examples of cognitive responses made by group members

NAME	FUNCTIONAL COGNITIONS	PROBLEMATIC COGNITIONS
June	It's okay to risk talking about feelings. Other people will usually treat those feelings with respect and be responsive. I can do things to make myself feel better. I can get help from this group.	I've been hurt by the past. I don't think I'll ever get over it. I will always blame myself for what happened. I can't stop myself from talking so much. I always do that when I get anxious.
Raye	I care about other people. I want to help them. I'm willing to risk by staying in this group because I know I need help.	Other people's opinions are more important than mine. If I express my opinion, other people may disagree with me or think I'm not very bright. People in this group may not like me.
Elaine	I have personal strengths. There are some good things about me. I'm a survivor. I can take care of myself.	My ideas, beliefs, positions are right; those of other people are wrong. I have to be right (or others won't respect me). You can't trust other people; they will hurt you if they can. The less you disclose about yourself, the better.

The functional behaviors in the table are characteristic of a mature therapeutic group. These facilitative group behaviors may also emerge in the *initial* stages of development, although their appearance may be fleeting as the group tackles early developmental tasks, such as building trust and defining common interests and goals. Brief or short-lived positive behaviors that are revealed early in the life of a group include the following:

- The group "faces up to" a problem and makes a necessary modification or adjustment.

- The group responds positively the first time a member takes a risk by revealing a personal problem.

- Members of the group are supportive toward other members or demonstrate investment in the group.

- The group works harmoniously for a period of time.

- Members effectively make a decision together.

- Members adhere to specific group guidelines, such as maintaining focus on work to be accomplished.

- Members give positive feedback to another member or observe positive ways the group has worked together.

- The group responsibly confronts a member who is dominating interaction or interfering in some way with the group's accomplishing its task.

- Members pitch in to clean up after a group session.

This list of positive behaviors is by no means exhaustive. Once social workers fine-tune their observational skills to register positive group behavior, they will catch glimpses of many newly developing behaviors that enhance a group's functioning. Social workers can then intervene in a timely fashion to note these positive features and reinforce their continuing use (Larsen, 1980).

The group may also display transitory negative behaviors in initial sessions. Many of these behaviors are to be expected in the early phases of group development. Their appearance may signal evolving group patterns that are not firmly "set" in the group's interactional

Table 11-4 Examples of group behaviors

PROBLEMATIC GROUP BEHAVIOR	FUNCTIONAL GROUP BEHAVIOR
• Members talk on a superficial level and are cautious about revealing their feelings and opinions.	• Members openly communicate personal feelings and attitudes and anticipate that other members will be helpful.
• Members are readily critical and evaluative of each other; they rarely acknowledge or listen to contributions from others.	• Members listen carefully to one another and give all ideas a fair hearing.
• Dominant members count out other members in decision making; members make decisions prematurely without identifying or weighing possible alternatives.	• Decisions are reached through group consensus after considering everyone's views and feelings. Members make efforts to incorporate the views of dissenters rather than to dominate or override these views.
• Members focus heavily on negatives and rarely accredit positive behaviors of others.	• Members recognize and give feedback regarding strengths and growth of other members.
• Members are critical of differences in others, viewing them as a threat.	• Members recognize the uniqueness of each individual and encourage participation in different and complementary ways.
• Members compete for the chance to speak, often interrupting one another.	• Members take turns speaking. Members use "I" messages to speak for themselves, readily owning their own feelings and positions on matters.
• Members do not personalize their messages but rather use indirect forms of communication to express their feelings and positions.	• Members encourage others to speak for themselves.
• Members speak for others.	• Members adhere to guidelines for behavior established in initial sessions.
• Members display disruptive behaviors incompatible with group guidelines. Members resist talking about the here and now or addressing personal or group problems. Examples of distracting behaviors include fidgeting, whispering, or reading while others are talking.	• The group is concerned about its own operations and addresses obstacles that prevent individual members from fully participating or the group from achieving its objectives.
• Members show unwillingness to accept responsibility for themselves or the success of the group and tend to blame the leader when things are not going well.	• Members assume responsibility for the group's functioning and success. Members also express their caring for others.
• Members dwell on past exploits and experiences and talk about issues extraneous to the group's purpose.	• The group shows its commitment by staying on task, assuming group assignments, and working out problems that impair group functioning.
• Members focus on others rather than on themselves.	• Members concentrate on the present and what they can do to change themselves.
• Members show little awareness of the needs and feelings of others; emotional investment in others is limited.	• Members are sensitive to the needs and feelings of others and readily give emotional support.

repertoire. Counterproductive behaviors that may evolve into patterns include any of the examples of dysfunctional behavior listed in Table 11-4.

Just as we have suggested that you employ a written system to record the functional and dysfunctional responses of individual members, so we also recommend using the same type of record-keeping system to track the functional and dysfunctional behaviors of the group itself, adding a column to record the growth or changes that you note in the group's behavior. For example, using the categories that you wish to track, you might develop a chart like the one depicted for individuals in Table 11-2.

Assessing Group Alliances

As members of new groups find other members with compatible attitudes, interests, and responses, they develop patterns of affiliation and relationship with these members. As Hartford (1971) points out, subgroup formations may evolve that include pairs, triads, and foursomes. Foursomes generally divide into two pairs, but sometimes shift to three- and one-member subgroups. Groups as large as five may operate as a total unit, but generally these groups begin to develop subdivisions influencing "who addresses whom, who sits together, who comes and leaves together, and even who may meet or talk together outside of the group" (Hartford, 1971, p. 204).

The subgroupings that invariably develop do not necessarily impair group functioning. Group members, in fact, often derive strength and support from subgroups that enhance their participation and investment in the larger group. Indeed, it is through the process of establishing subgroups, or natural coalitions, that group members achieve true intimacy. Problems may arise in groups, however, when members develop exclusive subgroups that disallow intimate relationships with other group members or inhibit members from supporting the goals of the larger group. Competing factions can often impede or destroy a group.

To work effectively with groups, leaders must be skilled in identifying subdivisions and assessing their impact on the group. To recognize these subdivisions, leaders may wish to construct a sociogram of group alignments. Credited to Moreno and Jennings (Jennings, 1950), a sociogram graphically depicts patterned affiliations and relationships between group members by using symbols for people and interactions.

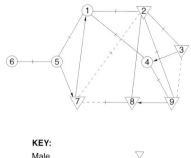

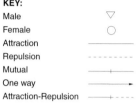

KEY:

Male	▽
Female	○
Attraction	————
Repulsion	- - - -
Mutual	—+—
One way	———▶
Attraction-Repulsion	—+- - -

Figure 11-1 Sociogram Capturing the Attractions and Repulsions among Group Members

Source: *Groups in Social Work* by Margaret Hartford (New York: Columbia University Press, 1971, p. 196). Reprinted by permission of the author.

Hartford (1971, p. 196) illustrates a sociogram that captures the attractions and repulsions among group members (see Figure 11-1).

Sociograms are representations of group alliances *at a given point*, because alliances inevitably shift and change, particularly in the early stages of group development. Charting the transitory bondings that occur early in group life can prove valuable to leaders in deciding where and when to intervene to modify, enhance, or stabilize relationships between members.

We suggest that you construct a sociogram of members' interactions after every session until you are confident that group relationships have stabilized in positive ways that support the group's therapeutic objectives. Be creative with your sociograms. Perhaps you might use different colors to show attractions, repulsions, or strength of relationships or place members closer together or farther apart on the sociogram to convey emotional closeness or distance. Avoid trying to capture in a single sociogram the exact nature of all the relationships each member has with every other member of the group, as the drawing will become overly complicated. Rather, depict only the major subgroupings in the group and identify the relationships in which major attractions or repulsions are occurring.

Assessing Power and Decision-Making Styles

Like families, groups develop ways of distributing power among members. To ensure that their needs are not discounted, some members may make bids for power and disparage other members. Others tend to discount themselves and permit more aggressive members to dominate the group. Still others value power and actively pursue it as an end in itself. When their members are involved in power struggles, groups may initially fail to make decisions on an equitable basis.

Some subgroups may try to eliminate opposing factions from the group or align themselves with other members or subgroups in a bid to increase their power. Groups, in fact, are sometimes torn apart and meet their demise because unresolved power issues prevent the group from meeting the needs of some members (Smokowski, Rose, & Bacallao, 2001).

When social workers assess groups, they need to identify the current capacity of members to share power and resources equally among themselves and to implement problem-solving steps that ensure "win-win" solutions. Leaders must help the group make each member count if the group is to advance through stages of development into maturity. You can accelerate the group's progress through these stages by assuming a facilitative role in teaching and modeling effective decision making and by assisting the group to adopt explicit guidelines for making decisions in the initial sessions.

Assessing Group Norms, Values, and Cohesion

To understand a group, the social worker must assess its norms, values, and cohesion. Imbedded in the norms, or ways of operating, are the members' implicit expectations and beliefs about how they or others should behave under given circumstances. The interplay of these values and the emergence of constructive group norms affect the group's capacity to develop cohesion and mutual aid.

Norms

Norms are regulatory mechanisms that give groups a measure of stability and predictability by letting members know what they can expect from the group and from one another. Norms may define the *specific* behaviors that are appropriate or permissible for individuals, or they may define the *range* of behaviors that are acceptable in the group. Group norms represent the internalization of the guidelines discussed earlier in this chapter.

Just as families have processes for dealing with rule violations, so groups also develop sanctions to reduce behaviors that are considered deviant and to return the system to its prior equilibrium (Lieberman, 1980). For example, an implicit group norm may be that other group members may not challenge the opinions of the informal leader. If a new group member treads on this norm by questioning the opinion of the informal leader, other members may side with the informal leader against the "upstart," pressuring him or her to back away.

People often learn about the norms of particular groups by observing situations in which norms have been violated. Toseland and Rivas (2001) note that, as group members watch the behavior of other members, they reward some behaviors and punish others. Once members realize that sanctions are applied to certain behaviors, they usually attempt to adapt their behavior to avoid disapproval or punishment.

The extent to which members adhere to norms varies. Some norms are flexible, and the psychological "costs" to members of violation are low or nonexistent. In other instances, the group's investment in norms is significant and group reaction is severe when members violate them. The relative status of members—that is, the evaluation or ranking of each member's position in the group relative to the others—also determines the extent to which members adhere to norms. Toseland and Rivas (2001) observe that low-status members are the least likely to conform to group norms because they have little to lose by deviating. Such behavior is less likely if the member has hopes of gaining a higher status. Medium-status group members tend to conform to group norms so that they can retain their status and perhaps gain a higher status. High-status members generally conform to valued group norms when they are establishing their position. At the same time, because of their elevated position, high-status members have more freedom to deviate from accepted norms.

Norms may or may not support the treatment objectives of a group and should be assessed in terms of whether they are beneficial or detrimental to the well-being of members and the overall treatment objectives of the group. Table 11-5 provides examples of both functional and problematic norms.

All groups develop norms, and once certain norms are adopted, they influence the group's response to situations and determine the extent to which the group offers its members therapeutic experiences. A major role for the leader, then, is to identify evolving group norms and influence them in ways that create a positive climate for cohesion and change. Discerning norms is often difficult, however, because they are subtly embedded in the group process and can be inferred only from the behavior occurring in the group. Leaders may be able to identify norms by asking themselves key questions such as the following:

1. What subjects can and cannot be talked about in the group?
2. What kinds of emotional expressions are allowed in the group?
3. What is the group's pattern with regard to working on problems or staying on task?
4. Do group members consider it their own responsibility or the leader's responsibility to make the group's experience successful?
5. What is the group's stance toward the leader?
6. What is the group's attitude toward feedback?
7. How does the group view the contributions of individual members? What kind of labels and roles does the group assign to them?

These questions also enable the leader to improve his or her observations of redundant or patterned behaviors exhibited by members. This is a vital point, because *patterned behaviors are always undergirded by supporting norms.*

Another strategy for identifying norms is to explain the concept of norms to group members and to ask them to identify the guiding "rules" that influence their behavior in the group. This strategy forces members to bring to a conscious level the group norms that are developing and to make choices in favor of those that advance the group's goals.

Table 11-5 Examples of group norms

FUNCTIONAL	PROBLEMATIC
• Take a risk by spontaneously revealing personal content about yourself.	• Keep the discussion centered on superficial topics; avoid taking risks or self-disclosing.
• Treat the leader with respect and seriously consider the leader's input.	• Play the game "Let's get the leader." Harass, criticize, or complain about the leader whenever the opportunity arises.
• Focus on working out personal problems.	• Spend time complaining about problems and don't commit the energy necessary to work them out.
• Allow members equal opportunity to participate in group discussions or to become the focus of the group.	• Let aggressive members dominate the group.
• Talk about any subject pertinent to your problem.	• Don't talk about emotionally charged or delicate subjects.
• Communicate directly to other group members.	• Direct comments to the leader.
• Talk about obstacles that get in the way of achieving the group's goals.	• Ignore obstacles and avoid talking about group problems.

Values

In addition to norms, every treatment group will create a set of values held in common by all or most of the group's members that include ideas, beliefs, ideologies, or theories about the truth, right or wrong, good or bad, and beautiful, ugly, or inappropriate (Hartford, 1971). Examples of such values include the following:

- This is a "good" group and worth our commitment and investment of time. (Alternatively, this is a "dumb" group, and we're not going to get anything out of it.)
- It is "bad" to betray confidences to outsiders.
- People who belong to different groups (e.g., authorities or individuals of a different race, religion, or status) are "bad" or inferior.
- It is undesirable to show feelings in the group.
- It is fun to try to outwit authority figures (particularly applicable to groups of juvenile or adult offenders).

Just as the group's "choice" of norms significantly affects its capacity to offer a therapeutic milieu, so does the group's "choice" of values. Similar to norms, values can be categorized as functional or dysfunctional when viewed in light of the group's therapeutic objectives. Values that encourage work on personal problems or self-disclosure, acceptance of others, and a positive attitude toward the group, for example, are functional to the group's development. By contrast, values that discourage self-disclosure, create barriers in relationships or negative attitudes toward the group, or prevent members from working on problems are obviously dysfunctional.

Cohesion

In the initial phases of the group's life, leaders must also assess and foster the development of cohesion in groups. Defined as the degree to which members are attracted to one another, cohesion is correlated, under certain conditions, to productivity, participation in and out of the group, self-disclosure, risk taking, attendance, and other vital concerns (Rose, 1989; Stokes, 1983). Cohesion in groups positively affects members' satisfaction and personal adjustment. Greater cohesiveness leads to increased self-esteem, more willingness to listen to others, freer expression of feeling, better reality testing, higher self-confidence, and more effective use of other members' evaluations in enhancing a member's own development (Toseland & Rivas, 2001; Yalom, 1985).

Cohesion is inextricably linked to the development of norms in a beginning group. Norms that may potentially interfere with both group formation and cohesion include irregular attendance, frequent tardiness, pairing off, changing membership, excessive interpersonal aggression, excessive dependence on the leader, dominance of interaction by a few members, and general passivity in the interaction (Rose, 1989). Research on negative group experiences indicates that the individuals who are damaged by the group may be those very members who are too timid to help contribute to group rules and thus have little investment in the norms that have been negotiated between the leader and more vocal members (Smokowski, Rose, & Bacallao, 2001). These detrimental norms require the attention of both the leader and the group members, because the failure to address them discourages group development and jeopardizes the group itself.

FORMATION OF TASK GROUPS

We move now from consideration of treatment groups to task groups. Although many of the same issues considered with treatment groups also apply to task groups, this section focuses on planning and beginning task groups. Task groups are organized to meet client, organizational, and community needs (Toseland & Rivas, 2001, p. 29). Among the various types of task groups are teams, treatment conferences, and staff development groups. Task groups may also be formed to meet organizational needs such as committees, cabinets, and boards of directors. Task groups instituted to meet community needs include social action groups, coalitions, and delegate councils (Toseland & Rivas, 2001). All of these groups focus on producing products, developing policies, and making decisions rather than on enhancing the personal growth of members (Ephross & Vassil, 1988).

Important early tasks in forming and assessing task groups are planning for the group and structuring initial sessions to address the purpose of the group.

Planning for Task Groups

Whereas members of treatment groups are recruited for the specific purpose that prompted the group's formation, membership in task groups may be constrained by organizational bylaws or dictated by organizational structure (Toseland & Rivas, 2001). For example, members of a delegate council may be elected by constituents, and an organization may decide who should participate in a treatment conference by the professional role needed (e.g., speech therapist, teacher, social worker, behavior specialist). Task group composition may be voluntary, by appointment, or by election, and should be responsive to the group's purpose and goals. For example, a treatment conference may have the purpose of coordinating the efforts of members of a team involved in serving a particular client or family. An ad hoc committee may be recruited to work on a fundraising event for an agency. A board of directors is appointed or elected to provide guidance and accountability to an organization. A community crime prevention panel may consist of volunteers from the neighborhood who are especially concerned about this issue.

The initiation of a task group and the determination of its purpose may come from many sources. For example, a staff member might propose a delegate council in a halfway house, the director of an agency might propose a committee to develop better agency communications, or residents of a housing development might suggest a social action group to deal with poor housing conditions.

Members of a task group should have the interest, information, skills, and power needed to accomplish the purpose of the group. The specific purpose of the group suggests sources for its membership. For example, a group formed to study how managed care affects service delivery might include consumers, providers, and representatives from insurance groups and regulatory agencies.

Membership should be large enough and sufficiently diverse to represent the major constituencies affected by the problem being targeted by the group, and participants should possess adequate skills and knowledge for addressing the group's purposes. As with treatment groups, organizers should ensure that no individual is an isolate. For example, a special education advisory committee should not consist of a group of professionals plus a token parent. When consumers or those whose personal experience is valuable to the task group's purpose are included, multiple representatives should be recruited for the group and, if possible, should serve as representatives of other consumers. For example, in a committee on mental health reform, multiple consumers and parents might be involved and some should represent groups, such as the National Alliance for the Mentally Ill. Taking these steps will help enhance the comfort, power, and legitimacy of group members.

Quality planning in this stage is reflected by transmitting a clear message about the group's purposes to prospective members. The level of clarity achieved has important implications for whether those prospective members decide to attend and, later, how well they perform the functions of the group.

As with treatment groups, task groups may be open or closed in time and in membership. Formal boards or committees generally are ongoing but have structures that provide for the rotation of membership in and out of the group, allowing for "staggered" changes to assure continuity. Other groups may be time limited and relatively closed in membership (e.g., a task force to review an incident where a resident was injured, a committee to plan an agency's anniversary celebration). Other groups may be ongoing but have closed membership (e.g., an ethics committee that hears different cases each month, as brought to them by members of the hospital staff).

Beginning the Task Group

The agenda for a beginning session of a task group is similar to that for a treatment group. It includes facilitating introductions, clarifying the purpose of the group, discussing ground rules, helping members feel a part of the group, setting goals, and anticipating obstacles (Toseland & Rivas, 2001). An opening statement, including the agency's function and mission as it relates to the group purpose, should be shared so that members will understand why they have been called together. Members can then be assisted to find commonalities in their concerns and experiences and to identify shared goals for group participation. Some members may know one another from previous roles and have positive or negative preconceptions from that past. "Ice breakers" and other introductory activities can be used to facilitate communication and identify experiences and resources that members possess (Dossick & Shea, 1995; Gibbs, 1995).

Developing group rules and concurrence on decision making (e.g., majority rule, consensus) then follows. A common rule involves adherence to confidentiality, as premature or distorted release of information might hinder the work and destroy the cohesion of the group. Other rules in task groups usually include expectations about attendance and preparation, and structural issues such as timing of meetings, submission of agenda items, and timely communications.

Task groups then proceed to goal setting. Such goals always include those mandated by the external purpose of the group, such as reviewing managed care arrangements in the agency, planning a conference, implementing new regulations on confidentiality, or coordinating care. In addition, the group may generate its own goals—for example, generating a list of best practices in achieving its purpose or tailoring its response to the group's purpose based on the specific talents and assets available in the group.

As with treatment groups, task group members may take on or be assigned formal (e.g., secretary, chairperson, treasurer) and informal roles (e.g., timekeeper, devil's advocate, instrumental leader, expressive leader). Whether these roles are constructive depends on how they are enacted and the extent to which they help the group fulfill its purpose. As with other types of groups, assessing the behaviors of individual members and the group as a whole will help identify functional and dysfunctional patterns. Tables 11-4 and 11-5 include many attributes that apply to task groups as well as to treatment groups.

Summary

This chapter presented guidelines for assessing and beginning treatment groups and task groups. We addressed considerations in structuring the group, such as format (open or closed), size, frequency, duration, and composition. We used a systems framework to examine the intersection of individual needs and behaviors and with those of the group as a whole. We discussed common concerns for members at the outset of a group and the strategies for introducing and assessing group guidelines, norms, and values. Chapter 12 turns to considerations of how to build on the social worker's assessment knowledge to construct workable contracts with individuals. We will return to consideration of groups in Chapter 16.

Internet Resources

See our companion website for hot links to some helpful URLs. Note that URLs are subject to change. We will endeavor to update the links on the companion website as much as possible.

You can find many useful group work sources at the website of the Association for the Advancement of Social Work with Groups, *http://www.aaswg.org*. Using InfoTrac College Edition, you can search using keywords such as "group norms," "group cohesion," and "group leadership." You can also find out about online support groups in the care of cancer patients at *http://www.noah.cuny.edu/ illness/cancer/cancercare/services/support_groups/on line.html* and *http://www.noah.cuny.edu/illness/ cancer/*.

Related Online Content

Visit the *Direct Social Work Practice* companion website at *http://socialwork.wadsworth.com/hepworth7* for additional learning tools such as glossary terms, chapter outlines, InfoTrac College Edition keywords, relevant web links, and chapter practice quizzes. Also, be sure to check out the Direct Practice Virtual Reader, where the authors have personally selected articles relevant to this chapter using InfoMarks.

Notes

1. Magen and Glajchen (1999) report that members of 12 different cancer support groups ranked cohesion, hope, and altruism as important factors in their satisfaction with the group process.

Negotiating Goals and Formulating a Contract

CHAPTER OVERVIEW

Chapter 12 elaborates on elements in Phase I, which introduced the preliminary work to be completed between the social worker and the client. The focus of this chapter includes developing goals, establishing procedures for measuring progress, and formulating the contract. It is intended to help you to gain the knowledge and skills essential for developing goals. First, the chapter discusses the purpose, development, and measurement of goals. Then, the remainder of the chapter is devoted to components of the contract and the process of mutually formulating a contract between the social worker and the client. Goals and the contract are products of the assessment process discussed in Chapters 8 and 9.

GOALS

The importance of formulating goals has been emphasized in social work literature for many years. Advances regarding the efficacy of goals in the helping process occurred as a result of research studies that extended from the mid-1960s to the late 1970s. Based on landmark research studies, Reid (1970) and Wood (1978) concluded that social workers tended to be too general in specifying goals, which in turn contributed to a lack of focus and led to unrealistic or vague outcomes. More recently, Dillon (1994), Kazdin, Stolar, and Marciano (1995),

and Ribner and Knei–Paz (2002), citing work with several different client populations, have drawn similar conclusions. In addition, social workers are cautioned against setting goals that seek to transform clients. Likewise, they should avoid establishing goals that are vague or that might unreasonably subject clients to an unproductive experience that might erode their confidence in their own capacities.

The involvement of clients in establishing goals or solutions is also emphasized in the literature (Finn & Jacobson, 2003; Jordan & Franklin, 2003; Lum, 2004; Marsh, 2002; DeJong & Berg, 2001). As Marsh (2002) reminds us, having clients identify changes that they wish to make supports the axiom of "starting where the client is" (p. 341). Another point made in the various discussions linking client involvement to goal development is simply that when goals are set without the clients' participation, clients and social workers may focus their change efforts on different outcomes. Without their participation in developing goals, clients tend to attend sessions sporadically and eventually drop out (Meyer, 2001). In these instances, social workers become frustrated, believing their efforts to be directed in the best interests of decidedly unmotivated clients (Smith & Marsh, 2002; Meyer, 2001; Pardeck, Murphy, & Chung , 1995; Jackson, 1995; Lum, 2004). In summary, clients are more motivated when their concerns and related goals in their contract with the social worker reflect their own experience.

Factors Influencing Goal Development

Goal setting with clients represents an opportunity to empower clients and reinforce their sense of self-efficacy as they cope with a difficult situation. Goal development and negotiation are further facilitated by the social worker's skill and cultural competence in exploring goals in the context of the client's value system and reality. Social workers should also be cognizant of the fact that individuals and families from minority groups are often referred to seek help, under pressure and because of mandates (Rooney, 1992; Tieso & Rooney, in progress). The experience of having both problem and solution externally defined fosters an atmosphere of suspicion that intrudes upon the helping process (Boyd-Franklin, 1989; Lum, 2004). This dynamic may especially be present when goals are constructed around perceived deficits, and assigned on the basis of attributes such as culture, race, or status such as gender, class, sexual orientation, or family form. The ability to define the problem and the solution is a source of power. Therefore, when agencies and social workers have predetermined the concerns and goals for a particular population, irrespective of their benign intent, feelings of oppression are heightened, as is the perception of having limited control.

In essence, exploring and supporting the client's reality is a powerful means of engagement. Finn and Jacobson (2003) refer to the inclusion of the client's reality as the "ethics of participation," emphasizing that clients have a right to their reality, and to having their reality be a part of their service provisions (pp. 128–129). Consequently, you would be prudent to be sensitive to the viewpoints of clients, which is an empowering aspect of the helping process. Empowerment assumes that despite their difficulties, people have the capacity to change, and further that this capacity can be utilized in resolving their problems (Boehm & Staples, 2004). Sensitivity to the perspectives of clients is especially important in cross-cultural practice (Lum, 2004; Al-Krenewa & Graham, 2000; Lee, 2003; Paz, 2002; Weaver, 2004; Jordan & Franklin, 2003). In the social justice framework articulated by Finn and Jacobson (2003), we can conclude that minority persons are within their rights to refrain from engaging in a process that is counterproductive to their interests and that reinforces their previous experiences with prejudice, bias, and discrimination.

Other considerations in developing goals include attention to environmental conditions such as racism, classism, sexism, bigotry, oppression, and discrimination, as they may be barriers to goal achievement. When trying to find housing, for example, a client who is a single-parent, minority female receiving TANF (Temporary Assistance to Needy Families) benefits in a suburban community where there are few minorities is likely to face discrimination, even though this practice is illegal.

Flexibility is also advised in work with minority, immigrant, or refugee group members with regard to who will be involved in the identification of concerns and outcomes. Potocky-Tripodi (2002) stresses the importance of involving family members in the health/mental health treatment plans and goal setting for immigrant and refugees. A study by Saulnier (2002) reinforces this point. This study, which examined the preferences of lesbian women in selecting mental health and health care professionals, found that a deciding factor for many clients was whether their partners could be involved.

Another consideration when developing goals is related to the dynamics of whether a client voluntarily seeks help or becomes involved in the helping process by a mandate or court order.

Finally, ethical practice demands that social workers critically examine their own values; cultural, political, or religious beliefs; and biases, paying careful attention to whether the potential exists for them to become intrusive in the helping process.

The Purpose of Goals

Goals specify what clients wish to accomplish and are instrumental in facilitating achievement of desired outcomes. Goals are formulated around situations, statuses, behaviors, and attitudes that are the target of change. Inherent in goals are desired changes in clients' life situations that correspond to wants and needs identified in the initial contact when problems were explored and assessed.

Program Objectives and Goals

Goals are also found in agency program objectives and mission statements. Such program objectives and mission statements guide the organizations' services and define expected outcomes. Examples of agency program objectives include assisting clients to find affordable housing, assisting clients to achieve a level of functioning or live in the least restrictive setting, providing independent living for elderly or youth clients, providing job training to enhance self-reliance, and developing safe and permanent housing for homeless or runaway youth. Organizations may clarify their missions and program objectives in such a way as to further distinguish themselves from other service providers. For example, an agency might define its mission as providing culturally specific services that strengthen ties to the community. In each of these situations, service objectives are predetermined and their intent is to address a specific concern. Thus, clients generally voluntarily seek out those services provided by the organization, although some may be referred as a result of an identified and agreed-upon need. The fact that agencies have established program objectives and goals should not be confused with the earlier point that goals should not be decided without the client's participation. In instances where clients seek out a particular agency to obtain a particular service, the

dynamic is different—namely, the key element is self-selection. Even so, these clients will want to participate in the assessment of their own unique concerns, decisions about how they achieve their goals, and determine the fit between their needs and the agency's resources.

To distinguish agency program objectives from client goals, it may be useful to think of program objectives as being broad statements that guide program activities and apply to all clients. When incorporating program objectives into clients' case or treatment plans, you will need to develop specific goals and tasks so that clients are able to accomplish these program objectives. For example, "increasing the participant's awareness of individual cues that trigger anger" is a program objective in the treatment plan of a domestic abuse program, but each client would have an individual goal related to this objective. At other times, goals developed between social workers and clients involve utilizing services from other agencies. For example, a goal of obtaining a job for an unemployed individual with limited skills may require obtaining an assessment from a vocational-technical program.

As illustrated in Table 12-1, goals are inextricably connected with and flow directly from the assessment process. Indeed, as you explore clients' wants and needs, you are engaging in preliminary goal selection work. With involuntary clients, some goals may be agreed to as a means to responding to a legal mandate.

In addition to observing the linkage between goals and target concerns as illustrated in Margaret's

---

Table 12-1 Linkage between target concern and goals

ASSESSMENT SUMMARY	TARGET CONCERN	GOALS
Margaret, age 87, feels unable to remain in her home because of concerns for her safety. She has expressed an interest in moving into an assisted living apartment complex and she wants to maintain her independence.	Margaret is concerned about safety in her home.	Maintain maximal safe independence. Explore assisted living options.

case in Table 12-1, goals specified in the helping process serve several other functions:

- They ensure that social workers and clients are in agreement, where possible, about outcomes, to be achieved.
- They provide direction, focus, and continuity to the helping process and prevent wandering.
- They facilitate the development and selection of appropriate strategies and interventions.
- They assist social workers and clients in monitoring their progress.
- They serve as outcome criteria in evaluating the effectiveness of specific interventions and of the helping process.

Utilizing goals to perform the preceding functions requires knowledge of the types of goals, criteria for selecting them, and knowledge of and skill in negotiating goals. These topics are discussed in the following sections.

Types of Goals

The systems or subsystems that will be the focus for change are factors that determine the type of goal developed. With individual clients, this focus typically involves intrapersonal subsystems as well as the client's interaction with the social and physical environment. Goals generally involve changes in both overt and covert behaviors. Common examples include changes in *cognitive functioning* (e.g., increase positive self-talk), changes in *emotional functioning* (e.g., reduce oppositional deviant behaviors), or *behavioral changes* (e.g., reduce frequency of alcohol consumption). Goals may also include changes in interpersonal behavior (e.g., engage others in conversation).

Goals may be further categorized according to both their type and their function. When the target system is a couple, family, or group, goals typically embody changes on the part of all relevant participants in the system. In these larger systems, *shared goals* are held in common by members of the system. In contrast, *reciprocal goals* are agreed-upon exchanges of different behavior.

An example of shared goals is a parent and child agreeing to listen to each other without interrupt-

ing. In family or group situations, members may agree on a shared goal of increasing messages to one another that are positive and emotionally supportive. In the case where both the parents and a child have a goal of on-time school attendance, each individual assumes a role that involves taking action toward this end. The distinguishing feature of shared goals is that participants commit to change their behaviors in essentially the same way.

With reciprocal goals, members of a system seek to solve interactional problems by exchanging different behaviors. Consider this scenario: A wife has complained that her husband seldom talks with her. The husband counters that he stopped talking with her because she did not listen to him, and states that she ridicules his viewpoint. After exploring their problem, the couple agree to a shared goal of communicating their concerns to each other in an effort to reduce conflict in their relationship. They further agree to reciprocal individual subgoals that include attentive verbal and nonverbal listening by the wife and increased verbal sharing by the husband. Thus reciprocal goals tend to be *quid pro quo* in nature; that is, each person agrees to modify his or her personal behavior contingent upon the other person making a corresponding behavioral change.

Guidelines for Selecting and Defining Goals

Because goals serve several vital functions, it is important to select and define them with care. In our discussion of selecting and defining goals, we make a point of distinguishing between goals for voluntary and involuntary clients because the dynamics between the social worker and the client are different in each case.

With the voluntary client, the psychological authority attributed to the social worker is positive. Therefore, the client's perception of the social worker's goodwill positively influences the collaborative nature of the social worker–client relationship.

In contrast, the dynamics of the psychological contract inherent in the explicit authority of the social worker and the involuntary client has a decidedly different texture. Perhaps the most volatile issue relates to the fact that client needs have been predetermined by a mandate or coercion. Most often in these situations, fear, authority, compliance, and paternalism exert the greatest influence on the social worker–involuntary client relationship, rather than the collaboration that is the hallmark of the social worker–voluntary client relationship (DeJong & Berg, 2001; Rooney, 1992) Thus, in developing goals with involuntary clients, your understanding of these dynamics and empathy are critical to reducing client reactance and to ensuring effective engagement.

The following guidelines will assist you in advancing your proficiency in formulating goals.

Goals Must Relate to the Desired Results Sought by Voluntary Clients

To be adequately motivated, voluntary clients must believe that accomplishing the selected goals will enhance their life situations by resolving or diminishing their problems. Clients are thus likely to pursue only those goals in which they are emotionally invested and that respond to their concerns (Marsh, 2002; Lum, 2004; Meyer, 2001) Thus, if you define goals unilaterally or impose goals on clients, you are unlikely to enlist your clients' participation. In this scenario, clients may superficially agree or simply not return to future sessions. Eliciting client participation in negotiating and selecting goals does not mean that you, as a social worker with expertise, should assume a passive role. To the contrary, a majority of clients will seek your guidance, and you have a responsibility to share your expertise in this regard. Your role in negotiating goals is discussed in detail later in this chapter.

Goals for Involuntary Clients Should Include Motivational Congruence

Work on problems on which there is motivational congruence—that is, where action targets goals that are personally meaningful for the client—is more likely to succeed and result in longer-lasting change than in cases where the client's motivation is primarily devoted to escaping punishments or gaining rewards (Rooney, 1992). Consequently, although you should limit involuntary goals to

legal mandates, you can nevertheless include goals perceived as desirable by involuntary clients. Involuntary clients will want to express their own views of problems or situations that resulted in the mandated referral. Typically their views diverge from those of the legal authority or person who mandated the referral.

Like voluntary clients, involuntary clients want to play a role in making decisions related to their lives. The *agreeable mandate* strategy entails a search for common ground that bridges the differing views of the client and the legal mandate (DeJong & Berg, 2001; Rooney, 1992). According to DeJong and Berg (2001), congruence is achieved when social workers enable mandated clients to "take control by allowing them to describe the mandated situation themselves" (p. 364). Pursuing the agreeable mandate may also involve reframing the definition of the problem in such a way that it adequately addresses the concerns of the client as well as the mandate or referral source. Reframing is a useful technique for reducing reactance, facilitating a workable agreement, and increasing the client's motivation.

Bargaining can also be used as part of a "Let's make a deal" strategy in which the private concerns of the involuntary client are combined with the problem that precipitated the referral. For example, a student who is having difficulty getting along with his peers may reject the view that he cannot control his impulses, but have concerns about being angry because he feels awkward in social situations. You may agree to focus on the latter problem if he agrees to explore the former. The efficacy of this strategy derives from the social worker being able to offer a payoff to a client, thus creating an incentive for the client to be involved in problem solving.

With some involuntary clients, none of the preceding strategies are viable. In these cases, the only recourse left is to appeal to clients' desire to be free of the restraints imposed by the mandating referral source. In such a strategy, a goal of *getting rid of the mandate or outside pressure* is included (Rooney, 1992). Again, the technique of reframing is useful. For example, both Rooney (1992) and Jordan and Franklin (2003) use the example of the involuntary clients involved with child protection services. Essentially, the client is motivated to "get child protection out of my hair," to escape what he or she considers an adversarial or invasive presence. If the overall goal is child safety and the return of the children to the home, then incremental steps may be developed with the client that satisfy both the mandate and the client's desire to be rid of oversight from child protective services. In essence, both the social worker and the client have a shared goal—specifically, the return of the children to the home, albeit when certain requirements are met.

Of course, goals may change over time and the client may transition from being involuntary to reaching a level of voluntary status. In other instances, goals may emerge as a result of self-evaluation as a client progresses from the stage of pre-contemplation ("I don't have a problem") to contemplation ("I am willing to look at my behavior") For example, in the pre-contemplation stage, the claim of an abusive partner is that "I had little choice in assaulting my wife; she was in my face. I don't have a problem because she is the only woman that ever got me this upset." Rather than developing an immediate goal of reducing his behavior, you and this client would develop a goal of self-reflection and self-evaluation, and he would commit to gathering information about the effects of his behavior on self and significant others.

Goals Should Be Defined in Explicit and Measurable Terms

To provide direction in the helping process, goals must specifically define the desired end results so that all participants are clear about changes to be accomplished within the problem system. In other words, each actor should be able to specify what she or he will do differently or what environmental factors will be changed. Goals should thus be defined in specific rather than general terms.

When appropriately stated, goals will specify both overt and covert changes to be accomplished and will be measurable. Overt behavioral changes (e.g., "Terrence will get out of bed when he hears the alarm and prepare for getting to school on time") may be observed by others and precise measurement of them is possible. Covert changes (e.g., "increasing positive thoughts about school") may be recorded and are also measurable, albeit only by the client. Measures of covert behavior thus are more subject to error as a result of inconsistent self-monitoring, the effects of self-monitoring on the target behavior, and other factors.

In either case, documenting goals in the case record maintains focus and assists both the client and the social worker to review ongoing progress. This tool may also be used at termination and in the evaluation of outcomes. Although agencies typically have their own forms for recording progress, we provide an example, which is illustrated in Figure 12-1. Note that both strengths and obstacles are recorded, as well as steps or tasks for both the client and the staff.

Goals and General Tasks. Table 12-2 distinguishes between goals and general tasks so as to further assist you in discriminating between global and explicit goals. The table also helps you to conceptualize the relationship that exists between goals and general tasks. General tasks flow from goals and are first steps toward goal attainment. Included in Table 12-2 are goals that involve both overt and covert behaviors. Notice that explicit goals refer to specific behaviors or environmental changes that suggest the nature of corresponding interventions.

Goals can be expressed at various levels of abstraction. Because both clients and social workers tend to define goals generally, you will need to further refine them by increasing their specificity. Goals should be considered the desired end product of a change effort. For example, completing an academic program to obtain a GED is a specific goal. It is important to distinguish a goal, which represents the desired outcome of intervention efforts, from general tasks, which represent the instrumental strategies used to reach those goals (Reid, 1992). In Table 12-2, goals are listed in the left column, and the corresponding general tasks are described in the right column. For example, obtaining a GED is a goal. Securing financial assistance, attending classes on a regular basis,

Client/Family:	Staff:		
Statement of Concern:			
Goal Statement:			Goal # __
General Tasks:			

Identify Strengths/Resources:	Identify Potential Barriers/Obstacles:
Tasks/Steps—Participant:	Tasks/Steps—Staff:

Date:	Progress Notes:	Staff

Goal Status Summary: C __ PC __ NC __ (Need summary explanation)

Figure 12-1 Case Progress Notes

and completing assignment are all general tasks directed toward accomplishing this goal. Attending classes, for example, is not in and of itself a goal, but doing so is a primary way of reaching the goal of obtaining the GED.

General tasks may also be categorized in a broad sense as either *discrete* or *ongoing* (or continuous). Discrete general tasks consist of one-time actions or changes that resolve or ameliorate problems. Examples include obtaining a needed resource

Table 12-2 Goals and general tasks

GOALS	GENERAL TASKS
1. Gain increased control over emotions	1. Reduce frequency of anger outbursts by being aware of cues that elicit anger; increase use of internal dialogue to decrease anger
2. Improve social relations	2. Approach others and initiate and maintain conversation by employing listening skills and furthering responses
3. Enhance interactions with social environment	3. Explore living arrangements in a center for elderly persons that provides outside activities
4. Enhance self-confidence	4. Focus on strengths and positive attributes and qualities; express self-approval
5. Improve parenting skills	5. Demonstrate competence in planning and preparing nutritious meals and maintaining adequate sanitary and hygienic conditions
6. Increase social participation in a group context	6. Resolve fears about fitting in, initiate discussion of personal views, ask questions, and participate in group discussions
7. Improve marital communication	7. Listen without interrupting, check out meaning, and increase frequency of positive messages
8. Resolve conflict when interacting with peers	8. Learn methods of problem-solving skills that contribute to conflict resolution
9. Express anger in a constructive manner	9. Practice alternative productive ways of expressing anger
10. Complete job-training skills assessment	10. Contact vocational-technical program

(e.g., public assistance, housing, or medical care), making a major decision (e.g., deciding whether to keep an unborn infant or place it for adoption), or making a change in one's environment (e.g., moving into an assisted living complex). Ongoing general tasks, in contrast, involve actions that are continuous and repetitive, and progress toward such goals is therefore incremental. Examples of ongoing general tasks include managing conflict effectively, expressing feelings openly, asserting one's rights, setting limits with children, controlling anger, and participating in group discussions. To facilitate goal attainment, general tasks are further broken down into a series of actions or steps to be taken toward achieving a goal. This identification of the subcomponents of goals and specific tasks is discussed at length in Chapter 13.

Another facet of defining a goal explicitly is specifying the essential behavioral changes of all persons in the target system with respect to shared or reciprocal goals. Observing this guideline ensures that all participants are clear about what part they play in accomplishing the overarching goal that relates to the broader system. For example, if a global or *ultimate* goal presented by a family is to reduce conflict and to achieve more harmonious relationships, each member must be clear about his or her individual goals in relationship to the larger system. Specifically, each person must commit to the shared goal of harmonious family relationships. Likewise, each family member would develop a reciprocal goal and general tasks to achieve this outcome. The same principle applies in practice with couples and small groups.

A final facet of defining goals explicitly is to specify whether the degree or extent of change desired by clients is congruent with their situation. With goals that involve ongoing behavior, growth is potentially infinite, so it is desirable to determine the extent of the change or the scope of the solution sought by the client. The advantage of specifying desired levels of change is that you and the client mutually agree to the ends sought by the latter. For example, suppose a group of boys are participating in a social skills group designed to increase their positive social interaction with peers. Within this general group goal, each boy will no doubt aspire to varying levels of goal accomplishment. One boy may be satisfied with engaging in occasional conversations as a participant in a team sport. Another may aspire to become active in a broad array of social situations, including after-school or community activities. Similarly, a family seeking to reduce the frequency of crises may differ in how each member defines what constitutes a crisis and thus differ in their perceptions of an acceptable level of goal attainment. Your role is to assist individuals to develop goals that are consistent with their desired level of attainment.

Goals Must Be Feasible

Selecting unachievable goals sets up clients for failure that may produce discouragement ("Why bother?"), disillusionment ("The situation is hopeless"), or a sense of defeat ("Nothing ever changes"). Therefore, both the capacity of clients for accomplishing goals and environmental constraints that could potentially inhibit goal accomplishment must be taken into consideration. Most clients have the capacity to accomplish the goals they set for themselves, so it is important to affirm their sense of self by reinforcing the validity of those goals. For example, you might say, "Arda, as we discuss your goal of completing the nurse practitioner training program, you clearly have the motivation, skills, and resources to reach this goal." Occasionally, you will encounter clients who have grandiose aspirations or who deny personal limitations that are obvious to you and others. Faced with this dilemma, you can perform a valuable service by sensitively and tactfully assisting them to establish incremental and partialized goals that can realistically be achieved. For example, you might say, "Arda, I appreciate and understand your motivation to finish the nurse

practitioner training program as soon as possible. You have completed almost all of the first-year requirements. Yet, given the remaining requirements, it would appear that completing the program in less than 6 months is not practical. Would it be more useful to think of completing a specific number of courses in 6 months? Then we could review your progress and establish a time frame for completing the remaining coursework that needs to be completed." This statement clarifies what Arda can realistically expect to achieve within a given time period, even as it highlights the incremental progress she has made toward reaching her ultimate goal.

In some situations, especially those involving involuntary clients, you may encounter agencies and judges who have vague and unrealistic expectations about what clients can accomplish in a given time period. Some social workers seeking to satisfy other agencies and court personnel have been inclined to develop "kitchen sink" contracts (i.e., the contracts include "everything but the kitchen sink"). Essentially, these contracts outline changes to be made in almost every aspect of the client's life. In other instances, agency program goals are applied uniformly in the case plan of each client, a strategy known as the "cookie cutter" approach. In other words, program objectives are not selectively applied based on the client's unique situation. On the whole, this approach and the types of goals involved may commit the client to simultaneously become involved with numerous service providers, each of which may unintentionally create difficulties for the client.

Consider this example, which involves a complaint from a client who has been ordered by the court to attend parent education classes, participate in a job-training program and subsequently secure employment, be evaluated for substance abuse, and obtain treatment, thereby providing the court with evidence that she is able to care for her children. When asked about whether she had found a job after completing a job-training program, the client stated, "The majority of my time is devoted to complying with the court-ordered requirement that I attend various groups weekly and attend appointments with a host of helping professionals, including the social worker." Even when she found a job, the client questioned, "How am I supposed to work? As a new employee, no employer is going to let me have time off to go to these various appointments." Also, she asked, "How will I find enough time to take care of my kids and other household duties?" after she met all of the other requirements. This client was frustrated because the plan made it appear as if she were destined to undergo a life of "treatment"; not unreasonably, she wondered when she would be able to get on with her life.

With respect to intrapersonal or environmental resources or constraints and the feasibility of goals, it is important to weigh opportunities and challenges—in relationships, for example, the receptiveness and capacity of significant others to change, in the case of reciprocal goals. Finding employment may be constrained by such environmental factors as the state of the economy, the availability of jobs commensurate with the client's skill level, discrimination, or the geographical location of available jobs. The following case example with an elderly client illustrates the importance of considering environmental resources.

CASE EXAMPLE

An elderly client wishes to move from a short-term rehabilitation facility after receiving medical care for a broken hip. Medical advice is that the client is unable to care for himself, and the client has indicated a desire to live with relatives. Relatives, however, are unwilling or unable to provide the care needed, emphasizing the client's need for special accommodations and personal assistance. To facilitate meeting his goal, the social worker agrees to help the client and relatives to obtain assistance and support from the key outside resources and agents needed to reach goals.

As illustrated in this case example, support is critical to successfully meeting the client's goal. In instances where supportive assistance is unavailable and cannot be obtained, agreeing to a goal that is not feasible would simply be equivalent to setting up the client to fail.

Clearly, it is unethical to set up clients to fail. Although mandates or other pressures may take

the form of "kitchen sink" goals, the client's ability to achieve those goals requires social worker skill and client involvement in prioritizing the goals. Prioritizing goals would involve identifying a definite contract period and focusing on legal mandates and issues of greatest significance to the presenting problem. This process can enable the involuntary client to have a reasonable opportunity to develop and demonstrate the skills and capacities needed to resolve concerns related to the mandate (Rooney, 1992).

As an illustration of how this process works, recall the client who complained about her ability to fully complete the mandate from the court in light of the time commitments required to do so. As the social worker responsible for this mandated case plan, you could help this client to navigate these multiple demands by reporting her progress to the court (i.e., completing the job-training and chemical dependency treatment program), and by requesting that the judge consider the constraints related to other goals and prioritize the remaining requirements.

Goals Should Be Commensurate with the Knowledge and Skill of the Practitioner

You should agree to work with clients toward only those goals for which you already have requisite knowledge and skill or for which you can gain that knowledge and skill through supervision and case consultation. Certain problems and goals require high levels of expertise that you may not yet have attained in particular areas—for example, family therapy, child sexual abuse, sex therapy or behavior modification, emotional disorders, and certain treatment techniques. It is your ethical responsibility to clients, and to the social work profession, not to undertake interventions beyond your scope of practice and competence. Doing so can create a liability issue for both you and your employing agency.

Alternatively, if you have access to supervision from a qualified professional, it may be possible for you to contract for goals beyond your competence under their guidance. Caspi and Reid (2002) refer to this approach as *secondary supervision*. That is, the "supervisor of record" performs the supervisory functions required by the employing organization. The secondary supervisor or consultant provides guidance with regard to a particular area of practice expertise (p. 295). This arrangement can involve a contract between the expert and the agency to provide supervision or, in some instances, a social worker may contract with individuals on his or her own. We strongly recommend that in the latter case, you apprise your agency supervisor of this arrangement, as this individual is ultimately responsible for oversight of your work. Secondary supervisions and consultation are viable options in instances when you lack the competence and skills to effectively assist a client at any stage of the helping process. Nevertheless, you should exercise caution when undertaking such arrangements, as engaging in practice beyond your scope (as defined by legal regulation in your state or province) is potentially risky. In general, it is ethical and legal to engage in practice that is commensurate with your scope and competence, and to refer clients who require service beyond your competence or that of your agency to qualified professionals.

Of course, questions may be raised about what options are possible in situations in which qualified professionals are not readily available, as may occur in some geographical areas. For example, county social services departments in rural areas or small communities often contract with and refer clients to social workers and agencies in suburban or urban cities for specialized services. In some circumstances, the choice may be between providing no services or providing less than optimal service.

In our judgment, social workers are justified in extending services in such cases under two conditions. First, social workers are obligated to explain the limitations of their competence with regard to the goals in question, enabling clients to decide on an informed basis whether to continue with the contact. Second, social workers should be confident that undertaking the goals does not place clients or others at risk. With severely depressed clients, the risk of suicide may necessitate a medical consultation and arranging precautionary measures with the client and significant others. A similar risk may exist when clients have a history of violent behavior that poses a threat to others.

When professional supervision or consultation is unavailable, you may seek this support from a consultant or secondary supervisor by relying on technology resources. One staff group, with the approval of the agency supervisor, arranged for weekly case consultation with a professional located in another city via teleconference. The consultant also met face-to-face with staff at the agency on a quarterly basis. During this time, the staff, supervisor, and the consultant all evaluated the benefits and drawbacks of the teleconferencing arrangement. When using technological resources in this manner, all parties involved must take precautions to protect client confidentiality.

Goals Should Be Stated in Positive Terms That Emphasize Growth

Goals should stress growth, highlighting the benefits or gains to be realized by clients as a result of their attainment. In formulating goal statements, stipulating negative behaviors that must be eliminated tends to draw attention to what clients must give up, thereby emphasizing deficits in their behavior.

Consider this example from a case plan of a father who had been released from prison and regained custody of his children: "Parent will demonstrate understanding of his inability to manage stress and anger, and the resulting tendency to use punishment, resulting in physical abuse of the child." This particular situation is reminiscent of the "kitchen sink" case plan previously discussed. The father in this case wanted help and was distraught over the fact that he had used physical discipline with an older child. He reported that he understood that prison had not prepared him to be a parent. In addition, when he was released from prison, he had regained custody of his own children and had also married his girlfriend. When they moved in together, there were eight children and two adults occupying a two-bedroom apartment. He perceived the case plan as identifying him as a poor parent, when, in fact, he felt that he was "trying to do the right thing."

Even though clients ordinarily welcome assistance to help them resolve problematic situations or behaviors, emphasizing negative aspects of their lives provokes additional psychological stress and anxiety.

Table 12-3 Negative and positive goal statements

NEGATIVE	POSITIVE
Reduce the incidence of criticism among family members	Increase family members' awareness of one another's strengths and increase the frequency of positive messages
Eliminate conflict between marital partners	Communicate specific disagreements promptly and address them in a constructive manner
Prevent formation of coalitions and nonparticipatory behavior by group members	Unite the efforts of the group in working collectively and draw each member into participation
Discontinue the frequency of drinking binges	Achieve ever-increasing periods of sobriety, taking one day at a time
Refrain from running away from home	Identify alternative options to running away from home
Decrease the use of physical punishment	Consistently apply new ways of disciplining children, such as utilizing "time out," and increase positive feedback
Reduce explosive outbursts of anger	Increase use of alternative nonabusive ways of expressing anger

In the preceding example, the case plan statement included multiple goals, which created an additional stressor for the father. These goals were stated as negatives, emphasizing the client's deficits, rather than his strengths. To alleviate the stress experienced by the father, the social worker partialized and reframed the goals so that they were stated positively:

1. Learn ways of managing stress, with a subgoal of keeping a journal of situations that triggered an angry response.
2. Attend parenting classes to learn about parenting, with a subgoal of learning alternative and age-appropriate methods of discipline.

The social worker also developed an interim goal with the father—taking time for himself when he experienced stress.

Psychologically, defining goals in terms of gains rather than losses or deficits tends to enhance client motivation and to mitigate conscious or unconscious opposition to change. Table 12-3 gives additional examples of contrasting negative and positive goal statements.

Avoid Agreeing to Goals about Which You Have Major Reservations

Instances sometimes occur in which it is neither ethical nor legal to enter into agreements to pursue certain goals. The following case example illustrates this point.

CASE EXAMPLE

A mother who had been a victim of political torture in Liberia escaped to a neighboring country with her children and her mother. After living in the refugee camp for 2 years, the mother obtained a permit that allowed her to come to the United States. She was in the process of completing the paperwork so that her children and her mother could immigrate to the United States as well. This process required DNA reports for the children as well as their birth certificates, which the mother was able to provide for two of the children. When asked by the Legal Aid attorney whether the third and youngest child was her child, the mother replied yes. However, the family had actually found the child abandoned and had taken her in. Although not biologically related, in Liberia this child was considered to be the mother's child. The social worker assisting the mother knew the status of this child, and felt uncomfortable with the information that the mother had provided to the attorney. When the attorney left the room, the social worker expressed her concern and the mother became upset, telling the social worker to "remove" herself from the case if she could not be more supportive.

This situation presented both a legal and an ethical dilemma for the social worker. Although feeling somewhat intimidated by the mother's reaction, she explained the legal consequences of providing false information to the attorney and to the Immigration and Naturalization Service (INS) for the family, as well as the ethical and legal implications for the social worker of being a party to the mother's deception. She further explained that while she empathized with the mother's situation and was sensitive to the Liberian culture's definition of "family," she would not be able to continue working with the mother unless she agreed to tell the truth about the younger child. The social worker also proposed helping the mother explain the child's status to the attorney and on the INS forms, in an effort to resolve the matter.

In a review of this case during a peer consultation session, some staff believed this to be primarily a legal issue because the child was not a biological relative of the family. Others including the social worker who presented the case viewed the situation differently. Instead they perceived the situation as an issue of cultural competence, although there were ethical and legal implications. Specifically, they suggested that it was the role of the social worker to assist the attorney representing the mother to understand the cultural context within which this child was considered to be a member of this family. Increasingly, as social workers have contact with diverse clients they are likely to encounter situations that require them to act as cultural interpreters and advocates.

Social workers are also justified in having reservations about clients' goals that appear to be potentially harmful to the physical or emotional well-being of themselves or others. A noncustodial parent may, for example, have a goal that involves using devious means to gain custody of children. In these and similar situations, you have both a legal and an ethical justification for declining to assist clients. In such instances, candidly explaining the basis of your decision while expressing your willingness to consider other goals is appropriate. In particular, when a client's proposed actions pose a threat to another individual, you have an ethical and legal duty to act upon this information.

Clients may have goals that are incompatible with your values or those of your agency. Values, of course, are highly individualized, yet many social workers and agencies have reservations about working with clients whose life philosophies, moral values, sexual practices, customs, language, or stylized dress differs from their own. Because of deeply held religious or moral beliefs, some social workers may not work effectively with people who are considering abortions or who are in a committed same-sex union. For example, a social worker working toward parent–child reunification reported that she had to be careful to avoid assessing the skills of her clients based on her own parental expectations—such as evidence of attachment, and a nurturing and clean home environment.

In situations where your reservations have the potential to intrude upon your fiduciary obligation to the client, ethical practice demands that you refer the client to another professional social worker or agency. It is important to be explicit about your reservations, and to explain your rationale for making a referral. Of course, this action assumes that such a resource is available. In cases in which a referral cannot be made, reservations about the kind of help you may be able to provide should be stated up front, and other goals should be negotiated if possible. Continuing to work with clients in circumstances where you disagree with their goals requires achieving a delicate balance between clients' rights to effective treatment and their rights to self-determination. Attempting to change clients in a manner that is consistent with your own or your agency's beliefs is paternalistic and coercive. Cases in which you have strong reservations about the work to be done or the individuals involved pose an ethical dilemma for which you will need to seek supervision. While we recognize that some situations may tax your ability to work effectively with some clients, you should be aware of the primacy of the client's rights, and the professional nature of the client–social worker relationship. Specifically, this means that your personal values should not dictate how you work with clients.

Goals Must Be Consistent with the Functions of the Agency

Explorations of clients' problems and wants sometimes reveal desired changes that are incompatible with the agency's functions or program objectives. For example, a family services agency does not provide vocational counseling. Similarly, in hospital settings, an assessment of the client's needs may reveal problems that require services beyond the scope of the hospital's function, such as family counseling or financial assistance.

In such instances, it is appropriate to assist the client in securing the needed services through referral to another agency. To facilitate the referral, it is often useful to make the call while the client is with you. Afterward, you will want to follow up to confirm that the client has, indeed, been connected with the needed services and is satisfied with the referral.

The Process of Negotiating Goals

Having considered the rationale of developing goals and delineated criteria for selecting and defining those goals, we are now ready to consider the process of negotiating goals. Goal negotiation includes translating program objectives into goals that are pertinent to the client. The negotiation process consists of several activities that may be implemented in the following sequence, with the sequence being adapted to the unique circumstances of each case.

Determine Clients' Readiness for Goal Negotiation

When you have explored and assessed clients' problems sufficiently, it is appropriate to summarize the goals to determine whether clients agree with them. Summarizing is a communication skill that highlights key content, and assists you and clients to focus on the work to be done. Further summarization (as illustrated in the examples in this section) is a means of checking with clients to facilitate their ongoing engagement in the helping process.

A message similar to the following may be used to assess clients' readiness to begin the negotiation process: "You've provided a good description of your concerns and situation, and I feel I have a good understanding of the changes that you would like to make." Summarizing at this point conveys to the client your understanding of what the client has said—for example, "We've talked about your desire to move from transitional to permanent housing"; "You also indicated a desire for your children to have a more stable and secure future, and you had some ideas about how this could be accomplished." Summarization as used here leads to agreement, which enables you and the client to move to the next step, that of exploring and negotiating goals. A furthering statement to confirm a client's readiness to identify goals such as the one that follows could also be used: "I wonder if you are prepared at this point to identify goals related to each of these issues, or would you like to provide additional information?"

Explain the Purpose and Function of Goals

Many elements of the helping process are educational. That is, the better clients understand the purpose and process, the more likely they are to become and remain engaged and to appreciate the significance of goals in the problem-solving process. In either case, a brief explanation is usually all that is required. This explanation of goals, their functions, and their purposes complements the role socialization process discussed in Chapter 5. It may be particularly critical when working with individuals who are unfamiliar with the Western structure of formal helping systems or procedures (Potocky-Tripodi, 2002 In explaining the purpose of goals to all clients, you will want to emphasize that goals provide direction, focus, and serve as guideposts to "make sure we stay on track." Further, you might state that "with goals, we can evaluate progress and determine how successful we've been in our work together." Your explanation, of course, should emphasize the importance of clients' participation and their ultimate authority in selecting voluntary goals. Finally, you should emphasize that the goals selected represent the changes that are most important to the individual, group, or family—for example, "Although I have some ideas, I'd like to hear which goals you regard as the most important." Eliciting this information assures that both you and your clients are trying to accomplish the same results.

Negotiating Goals with Involuntary Clients

Taking into consideration our earlier discussion of the dynamics involved when working with involuntary clients, educating these clients about the purpose and function of goals may significantly change the tone of the contact and their reaction to mandated goals. You might use statements similar to the following: "We have talked about the problems we are legally mandated to resolve. Your own views of those problems as well as your other concerns that you may have are also important." Review the mandate as well as the client's concern, and specify what is to be accomplished—for example, "As you know, participation in a parent-training group and an assessment of your parenting skills after you complete the program are part of your court order. You can, however, choose among the various programs on an approved list." In addition to reviewing the mandate, you will want to provide clients with an opportunity to explain their understanding of the situation and describe the circumstances from their point of view—for example, "It would be useful for me to hear from you how you came to be involved in the court." In this way, you can respond to the client's viewpoint and explore goals important to the client in addition to those defined by the mandate. In doing so, you create another opportunity to maintain engagement, empower the client and change the tone of the client's reaction.

Because agencies also have objectives that specify requirements for completing their programs, where appropriate these objectives should be clarified and integrated into the case plan. For example, parent-training programs may require participants to "attend and actively participate in a certain number of sessions." In negotiating goals, agency program objectives that are relevant to clients are included as well as mandated timelines imposed by the court.

As mentioned earlier, goals that are included in mandates or court orders are often stated in vague, global, and negative terms. Clients may be confused about what is expected of them, and may feel a sense of defeat, anxiety, and a lack of confidence. Therefore, you should clarify the expected changes, explain the intent of the goals, and reframe them in positive terms. For example, you might say, "The court expects that the parent-training sessions will help you learn to set limits with your children and introduce you to other methods of discipline." Explaining the intent of goals to clients provides specificity and indicates that they will be able to retain some control over their lives. You will also want to clarify the importance of demonstrating progress toward completing the mandate as a way to prevent further action by the court.

With involuntary clients, goal setting may also uncover a goal that is important to the client. While summarizing the goals that emerged during the negotiation, you might begin by focusing attention on this client-identified goal: "In addition to the goals set by the court, you mentioned a desire to return to school. This is not a mandated goal, and we can decide together the best way to approach this goal." Combining a mandated goal with an identified goal of the parent—for example, to talk to your children without yelling"—can also be emphasized as a benefit of the requirement of attending a parenting class. In this respect, both mandated and client goals are congruent.

Jointly Select Appropriate Goals

The social worker can help both voluntary and involuntary clients to identify goals they would like to achieve. The following messages demonstrate effective ways of engaging clients in this process:

- If we succeed in our work together, how will you think and behave differently?
- If your family could be the way you would like it to be, in what ways would each of you behave differently?
- It's been very evident in our session so far that both of you want to improve your relationship. I'd like to hear from each of you about specific improvements you'd like to achieve.
- As you know, the court would like to see changes in your parenting. What kinds of

changes do you want to make on your own, in addition to those the court has ordered?

- When you complete the parent-training program, what would be different in your relationship with your children?

Notice that each message asks clients to identify specific changes desired, which paves the way to the next step of defining goals explicitly.

If clients have difficulty identifying goals, you can prompt them by referring to problems and wants identified during the exploration and assessment process and suggest they consider related changes. To illustrate prompting, we return to the case of the Diaz family. Recall that Mr. Diaz reported that he wanted to maintain some independence in his living arrangements and medical regimen.

Social worker: As you talked about your feeling that your family wanted to infringe on your freedom, you mentioned that you could be capable of administering your own medication with your son's help. I wonder if you might like to work toward getting the kind of assistance necessary that would make this possible?

As with most clients, Mr. Diaz's statement as summarized by the social worker includes emotional content that could have derailed the process of goal selection. The social worker's statement effectively summarized the key issue and helped Mr. Diaz to focus on a particular goal.

With a little encouragement, most clients will identify key goals. As they define goals, you should write them down, explaining that because goals are extremely important, you are keeping a record of them. As clients verbalize goals, you may need to interject comments that seek clarification or to suggest rewording a goal to clarify its meaning and specificity. In recording or paraphrasing, be cautious about taking liberties with what clients have said and obtain their approval of rewordings by reading what you have written. Suppose that Mrs. Lenora Johnson, an elderly African American client who has been referred for depression, states, "I'd like to not feel blue." You would write what she has said, and then seek clarification by asking her to describe

what she means so that you understand "feeling blue" in her terms and determine whether it is consistent with symptoms of depression. Also, unless this client has indicated otherwise, she should be addressed as Mrs. Johnson, rather than her first name. This level of respect is consistent with the norms of other minority communities as well.

Clients often identify most or all of the goals and general tasks that must be accomplished to resolve their problems. Frequently, however, because of your external vantage point, general task strategies will occur to you that clients may have overlooked or omitted. Consequently, you have a responsibility to introduce these methods for reaching goals for clients' consideration. In introducing such general tasks, it is important to offer them as suggestions and to explain your reasoning, referring to related information discussed earlier in the session as necessary. Giving clients a copy of the goals that have developed also encourages their ongoing engagement in the helping process and fosters a more collaborative client–social worker relationship. To further enhance this sense of collaboration, many experienced social workers provide clients with a folder that contains goal statements, tasks, and progress notes, to help them keep track of goals and their progress.

Define Goals Explicitly

After mutually selecting goals, you are ready to refine them by defining them explicitly and determining the extent of change desired by the client or required by legal mandate. If you were successful in the previous steps, this task may require little or no further attention. If the goals were expressed in somewhat general terms, however, you will need to increase their specificity. Examples of messages you can employ to do so were discussed in the preceding section. You may need to supplement these messages with suggestions of your own about pertinent behavioral changes that would further operationalize general goals. With respect to determining the desired extent or level of changes, you can employ messages similar to the following:

- "You say you want to improve your housekeeping. What standards do you want to achieve?"

- "You have set increasing the times when you do not feel anxious as a goal. What would be signs for you that would indicate to you that you are less anxious?"

- "When you say that you would like to not feel blue, tell me what it would be like for you to not have this feeling."

- "You say that you want to maintain your independence in any kind of new living arrangement. What level of independence do you want to assure in a new place?"

- [*To family members*]: "Your goal of wanting to do more things together as a family appears to be a shared goal. What level of family-centered activities would you like to achieve?"

Determine the Feasibility of Goals and Discuss Their Potential Benefits and Risks

Prior to finalizing goals, it is important to assess their feasibility as well as the benefits and risks associated with them. To assist clients in evaluating the feasibility of, and potential obstacles to, achieving goals, you can employ responses similar to the following:

- "Clearly, maintaining a clean house is important to you. What are your thoughts on how this can be accomplished?"

- "What obstacles do you foresee that might prevent you from maintaining your standards for a clean house?"

- "Each of you is involved in a number of individual activities. Is it possible that these activities could interfere with family time?"

- "In maintaining sobriety, are there events or individuals who might cause you to experience a relapse?"

- "Being on time for school every day is a very ambitious goal. Let's think about what could happen that would interfere with you accomplishing this goal."

Reviewing potential obstacles, risks, and benefits is intended to help clients think in advance about events or situations that might influence their ability to attain their goals, ultimately ensuring that goals are feasible and can be achieved. In much the same way, a discussion of the benefits of attaining goals tends to enhance clients' commitment to sustained efforts toward achieving those goals. Responses similar to the following may assist you in identifying such benefits:

- [*To individual client*]: "What benefits do you expect to receive by moving your family to a different community?"

- [*To individual client*]: "In maintaining your sobriety over the next several months, how do you expect that you will feel?"

- [*To parent-child*]: "How will your relationship be improved by the goal of listening to each other? What changes are each of you willing to make?"

- [*To family members*]: "In what ways will your family life improve by doing more activities together?"

- [*To group members*]: "What do you think will be different in your interactions with peers as a result of participating in this social skills group?"

- [*To student*]: "Are you thinking that your grades will improve if you are on time for school?"

Social workers are also obligated to assist clients in assessing the possible risks associated with attaining goals. In particular, changes in behaviors might evoke ambivalent feelings and both positive and negative consequences. Examples of the negative consequences might include losing old and valued friends as a result of maintaining sobriety. Increasing the time spent in family activities, although enjoyable, may mean decreasing the amount of time for oneself. Making a change to listen to each other does not necessarily mean that two people will always agree. Clients generally have ideas about the expected positive results from the changes they wish to make. At the same time, they may be unaware of, overlook, or give superficial attention to risks or negative consequences. By drawing their attention to these potential outcomes and encouraging them to anticipate possible benefits and risks, you will enhance their commitment to the change process and foreshadow frustrations that could potentially lead to their becoming discouraged. Most importantly, prudent practice suggests that the social worker explore both benefits and potential risks with clients as an integral part of ethical practice.

Assist Clients to Make a Choice about Committing Themselves to Specific Goals

After analyzing the consequences, potential outcomes, and benefits and risks of pursuing specific goals, the next step is to reach a decision about making a commitment to strive to attain the goals in question. In most instances, benefits are likely to outweigh risks, and clients will demonstrate adequate readiness to contract to work toward the goals. A simple but effective means to assess clients' willingness to change is to ask them to rate their readiness on a scale from 1 to 10, where 1 represents "extremely uncertain and not at all ready" and 10 represents "optimistic, eager to start, and totally committed." Most clients report their readiness factor to be in the range of 6–8, which usually indicates a sufficient willingness to proceed with the contracting process. In contrast, when clients indicate their readiness level is 5 or lower, they usually are not prepared to proceed. In such a case, it might be useful to ask clients to visualize which of their goals would bring them immediate relief or change.

Occasionally, clients are ambivalent, which suggests that you need to explore their reservations further. In these cases, we recommend that you respect clients' misgivings and refrain from attempting to convince them to immediately sign on to the goals identified. At the same time, it is important to identify the basis for their misgivings (e.g., a teenager may hesitate to pursue a goal of avoiding conflict due to concerns about appearing timid in front of peers, an immigrant family may fear that moving away from their community will result in a loss of cultural ties). In these situations, you should explore the extent to which their concerns are an important dynamic affecting the problem. With the teenager, for example, this might mean exploring with him whether conflict with his peers is the reason for his multiple school suspensions and his

mandate to attend an anger management class. As a next step, you might advise this client that his fear of appearing timid should not be the basis for not accomplishing the goal of decreasing school suspensions. Instead, you and the teenager could agree to resolve his concerns by negotiating an intermediate goal before moving on—perhaps by exploring the importance (i.e., the client's reality) of being bold, rather than timid. Negotiating an intermediate goal in this way reduces the threat to the primary goal of decreasing the number of school suspensions and enhances the client's readiness to enter into a working contract. In this case, negotiating the client's agreement to become involved in a conflict resolution group and learn conflict resolution skills represents an intermediate goal.

With involuntary clients, commitment to mandated goals is not expected to be in the highest range. You should anticipate, respect, and appreciate these clients' reactance to the mandates. In many cases, involuntary clients may want help, but not in the way it is offered or for the reason it is offered, especially if the goal emphasizes deficiencies or behavioral compliance. For example, in the teenager's case, conflict may arise between the mandated goal of attending an anger management class and his belief that not backing down in a confrontation is necessary for survival.

While you may empathize with the feelings and pressures the client experiences when ordered to work on a mandated goal, you can emphasize that the client has the freedom to choose the approach of attaining the goal. A minority client, for example, may choose a culturally specific substance abuse treatment program. The client also has the option to reject working on the goal and to risk the legal consequences of this choice (Rooney, 1992). As professionals, social workers are obligated to advise their clients about the potential consequences of their actions and to ensure that, in fact, they are making an informed choice. Involuntary clients have the same right of self-determination as clients who voluntarily seek help, but it is your ethical responsibility to advise them of the risks associated with their chosen course of action, and to help them work through their concerns related to the mandate.

Encountering reactance as exhibited by some resistance from involuntary clients can be very frustrating. The social worker may become the target of their anger, especially when clients do not perceive the social worker as being separate from the court. In the face of hostility, anger, and sometimes abusive language, it is easy to simply give up on the client, and rely on the old adage that people will only change when they are ready or suffer enough. Instead, we encourage you to depersonalize the experience, and focus on exploring the feelings and frustrations underlying the client's reaction. Moreover, a client's hostile reaction may often be countered by emphasizing the potential benefits and the opportunity for growth as a result of working on goals related to the mandate. With a parent who is ambivalent and angry about attending court-ordered parenting classes, for example, the following response would be appropriate:

Social worker: I understand and respect your claim that you do not need parenting skills. You have said that your mother was a parent, that your grandmother was a parent, and that you learned from them. Yet there seems to be a problem in the way that you discipline your children. Consider that a benefit of attending the parenting class may be that you gain skills in setting limits with your children, and decrease some of the stress that you indicated that you experience in dealing with your children.

Rank Goals According to Clients' Priorities

After clients have established goals and are committed to working toward them, the final step in goal negotiation is to assign priorities to the goals. Usually clients select two to five goals as high priorities. Depending on the nature of the goals, the developmental stage, the resources available to the client, and the time required, settling on no more than three goals is advisable. The purpose of identifying high-priority goals is to ensure that beginning change efforts are directed toward the goals of utmost importance to clients. When mandated goals are included, these can also be prioritized because simultaneous efforts to achieve all goals may not be possible and some goals will necessarily have greater consequences than others. Participating in

a drug treatment program, for example, may take priority over a goal of returning to school or attending a parent support group. This step further ensures maximum responsibility and participation in the process by clients, thereby enhancing their motivation to work on goal attainment.

As a lead-in to the ranking process, we recommend using a summary message similar to the following:

Social worker: When we were exploring your concerns, you indicated that as a single parent you feel socially isolated, that you are exhausted by the demands of caring for four children by yourself, and that you lack sufficient income to move to a larger apartment. In our sessions thus far, we have identified goals related to each of these concerns. Now that you've settled upon these goals, how would you rank them according to priority? Perhaps we should start with the goal most important to you, the one on which you will focus your energy at this point. Then you can rank the others as you see fit. We'll get to all of the goals in time, but we want to start with the most important one.

With involuntary clients, you might use a message like this:

Social worker: While we are coming to agreement about which goals are most important to you, we also need to prioritize those goals that are mandated. Your court order states that you need to complete a chemical dependency evaluation immediately, so that is a top priority. While exploring educational and employment possibilities might be delayed until the evaluation has begun, you can, however, choose whether you want to pursue employment or educational opportunities first.

In some instances, you may be able to work toward achieving a mandated goal and the client's own goals simultaneously.

CASE EXAMPLE

William, 16, has been repeatedly truant from school and recently became involved with a group of other truants who were caught stealing from a local convenience store. Because this crime was a first offense, the judge ordered William to attend school. Failure to attend school would result in his being sent to a juvenile detention center for 90 days. During the initial session with the social worker, William indicated that he was unlikely to attend school because he thought school was stupid and that he was not learning anything that he valued. When asked to explain his assertion, he stated that he would like to learn how to play the guitar and that guitar lessons were not offered by the school. Thus, he did not feel that he needed school. William's goal of learning to play the guitar was, of course, inconsistent with the mandate. The social worker was able to find a music teacher at the school who was willing to give William guitar lessons after school, but William had to be a student at the school to participate in the lessons. The social worker and William negotiated a goal plan that specified that if he attended school on a regular basis, he could also learn to play the guitar. The importance of this intermediary or transitional goal—learning to play the guitar—made William more amenable to attending school.

In developing and negotiating goals, it is important to consider clients' developmental age and stage. William, who is 16 years old, in addition to being an involuntary client, has a strong reaction to authority—not unusual for people in his age group. At this developmental stage, asserting independence is important. Yet one facet of asserting independence is that this age group often experiences conflict with authority. You might question the quid pro quo goal arrangement, instead insisting on the behavioral change—specifically, that William attend school as mandated by the court. You might also attempt to coerce William to attend or persuade him by pointing out that responding to the court mandate is in his best interest. Given his developmental stage, the context that frames his perception of school, and his values, he is unlikely to continue in school if you apply this approach. Thus the quid pro quo arrangement facilitates problem solving and may motivate William to tackle other goals—for example, achieving a certain grade point average.

When the target system involves more than one person, different members may naturally accord different priorities to goals. For the court, attending school is a priority goal for William.

Further, group or family members may have individual goals as well as shared or reciprocal goals. In the case of William, presumably the court, his family, teachers, the social worker, and William have a shared goal of his attending school. His parents, neither of whom completed high school, hope that he will go to college. They are frustrated with him and do not readily see the value of his learning to play the guitar. The social worker in this case met with the parents so that they understood the rationale for the arrangement that he had negotiated with William and the music teacher.

In this scenario, the parents also had a reciprocal role in ensuring that the goal of attending school is accomplished. Similarly, if the target system is a couple, a group, an organization, or a family, it is desirable to have goals that pertain both to individuals and to the larger system. When working with larger systems, for example, you might create lists of goals for both individuals and the systems and then rank the goals for each person and the system. Where differences arise in ranking goals for a system, your help is needed to assist all parties to negotiate the final rankings.

MEASUREMENT AND EVALUATION

Evaluation of the outcomes of treatment with clients is an essential component of direct practice. Once goals have been developed, agreed upon, and explicitly defined, jointly deciding with the client how progress will be measured and recorded is a logical next step in the helping process. Measurement involves the precise definition of what is to be changed, and it clarifies the observations to be made that indicate progress toward the identified goal (Bloom, Fischer, & Orme 2003). For example, William will attend school. Attendance records, parental and self-reports will be used to measure progress toward this goal.

Evaluation, by comparison, assesses the effectiveness of the intervention in relationship to the goal. In the case of William, enabling him to take guitar lessons is the intervention. To assess the effectiveness on this intervention, you could devise a scale that recorded school attendance prior to his taking guitar lessons and then monitor his attendance after the intervention was introduced. Change is often incremental, and clients should be encouraged to identify indicators or levels of desired change. For example, because William has not had a record of attending school on a regular basis, you might establish an incremental change of attending school 4 out of 5 days each week.

Evaluation is an ongoing process, occurring at various levels of the intervention or action taken to rectify a target concern. The process also informs both you and the client of progress (or lack of progress) and indicates whether the intervention is producing the intended results (Berlin & Marsh, 1993). Poulin suggests that the process of evaluation "can help motivate clients, and further their resolve to make progress" (2000, p. 142). He poses several questions that may assist the social worker to "take stock" when monitoring progress: Are we making progress? Are the interventions working? Do we need to try another approach? (p. 142). Evaluation is, of course, an integral element in the termination process, as discussed in Chapter 19.

Measurement and evaluation in the field of human services poses a real challenge because of the environmental complexities of both the organizations involved and the clients they serve. Demands for accountability from funding sources, third-party payers, managed care, and administrators have nonetheless increasingly required service providers to gather evidence proving the efficacy of their work with clients. Both social welfare organizations and social workers have responded to these demands by developing programmatic outcomes for clients, along with information systems that increase their ability to track the impact of services with regard to the desired outcomes (Lewis, Lewis, Packard, & Souflee, 2001). As the field of evaluation has matured, evaluation methods have evolved to include the extent to which practice influences both intermediate and final outcomes (DePoy & Gilson, 2003). Another major improvement in the field of evaluation has been the increasing number of social

work graduates who possess the competency and inclination to employ evaluation procedures.

In the final analysis, evaluation assists practitioners to answer the essential questions related to the effectiveness of intervention strategies and to document changes in client conditions (Corcoran & Gingerich, 1994; Bloom, Fischer & Orme, 2003). This information is critical to the feedback loop so that it can improve both the social worker's and and the program's effectiveness and ensure ethical practice.

Methods of Evaluation and Measuring Progress

This section provides an overview of both quantitative and qualitative methods that may be used to measure progress and to evaluate outcomes. We consider the following components to be fundamental to this process:

- Identification of the specific problem or behavior to be changed
- Specific, measurable, and feasible goals
- Matching goal and measurement procedures
- Maintenance of a systematic record of relevant information
- Evaluation of intermediate and final outcomes

The first three factors were discussed earlier in this chapter. At this point, we want to stress the importance of systematically recording data in the case record. The information on the case progress recording form (see Figure 12-1), as well as other information discussed in this section, will allow both you and your client to track the client's progress over the course of the contract. If progress falls short, then goals should be reviewed or renegotiated as needed.

Available Resources

Numerous computerized information systems are available that can assist you with collecting and evaluating information. A number of standardized instruments are also available, some of which use computers to track progress over time (Hudson, 1990, 1996; Springer & Franklin, 2003). Standardized measures, including those employing computer-assisted technologies, have several advantages. As summarized by Streeter and Franklin (2003) and Bloom, Fischer, and Orme (2003), they are uniform in both administration and scoring procedures and outcome results. In addition, the measures have undergone rigorous research procedures, being tested on a large representative sample (p. 98). You may use these tools either to augment the assessment process or to measure and evaluate change. A number of resources provide extensive information and examples of scales, questionnaires, and information systems, both qualitative and quantitative, that measure, for example, depression, social skills, mental status, and functioning in both children and adults.[1]

Cautions and Strengths

While we do not want to dissuade you from utilizing standardized instruments for evaluation and monitoring progress, a discussion about their limitations is warranted. A notable limitation of standardized instruments is the fact that they focus on problems rather than strengths, resources, or situational factors, thus the kind of information collected is limited (Jordan & Franklin, 2003; Berlin & Marsh, 1993; Vosler, 1990). For example, completing a structured risk assessment may confirm that risks exist. Yet the narrow band of questions in the assessment tends to focus solely on assessing risk factors and ignores ecological, environmental, or other interactions that may contribute to the underlying the situation. Kagle asserts that standardized instruments have the tendency to emphasize the "credibility of science, and the practitioner as the expert" (1994, p. 96). Further, she states that the results may place members of socioeconomic, cultural, and sexual minority groups at greater risk of appearing more "deviant or troubled."

Fortunately, there has been an increased recognition of this limitation in recent years, resulting in new interest in assessing client strengths. The Clinical Assessment Package for Assessing Client Risks and Strengths (CASPARS) developed by Gilgun (1999, 2001) is an example of one of these new instruments. This assessment tool attempts to capture and weigh both risks and strengths, and in doing so provides a more complete picture of the client's situation. In this respect, CASPARS is

consistent with social work practice and the multidimensional assessment process.

Despite the fact that standardized measures may have relied on a representative sample during their development, few evaluation/monitoring instruments take into account differences related to culture, race, ethnicity, or language. For example, the words, symptoms, or expressions used to describe depression as well as the attitudes toward illness are different in different populations. Recall the words of Mrs. Johnson, the elderly African American client mentioned earlier: "I'd like to not feel blue." In immigrant or refugee groups, cultural norms, beliefs, and language may not have an explanation for feelings, so symptoms of depression may be reported as a physical condition (Potocky-Tripodi, 2002; Kagle, 1994). Finally, standardized instruments, even those with established reliability and validity, may not be appropriate for use with certain populations or directly related to the goals of a specific client concern.

These factors should not totally preclude the use of standardized instruments in your practice. Rather, when choosing resources for measuring progress and evaluating outcomes, you should be sure to match the methods selected with the client situation and need. You may also find that a standardized instrument enables you to assess a client's situation and evaluate outcomes in a more complete manner. In deciding whether an instrument is appropriate, Jordan and Franklin suggest that practitioners consider the ethical question of whether the tool provides the means "to assess and serve the clients better" (2003, p. 128).

In instances where an available assessment tool is inappropriate or no tool exists, you and your clients can agree to develop scales or measures tailored to their specific conditions (Jordan & Franklin, 1995, 2003; Collins, Kayser, & Platt, 1994). One example is illustrated in Figure 12-2. This goal and task form is developed jointly by the client and the social worker and allows each to track progress toward the desired outcome. This information, although tailored to the client's unique situation, may be aggregated with other client information to provide social workers with data relevant to their practice as a whole.

Name: _____

Statement of Problem/Condition to Be Changed: _____

_____

Goal
Statement: _____

General
Tasks: _____

_____

Potential
Barriers: _____   _____   _____   _____

Benefits: _____   _____   _____   _____

Specific Tasks (steps to be taken to achieve goal):

	Completion Date	Review Date	Outcome Code
1. _____	_____	_____	_____
2. _____	_____	_____	_____
3. _____	_____	_____	_____

Outcome Codes

Tasks and Goal Status [ ] C (completed) [ ] P (partially completed) [ ] NC (not completed)

Figure 12-2 Sample Goal and Task Form

Quantitative Measurements

The process of evaluation described in this section is essentially a form of single-subject or single-system evaluation. The same approach can also be used for research purposes, including testing the effectiveness of specific interventions and comparing the effectiveness of different interventions. Quantitative evaluation embodies the use of procedures that measure the frequency and/or severity of target problems. Measurements taken before implementing change-oriented interventions are termed *baseline* measures because they provide a baseline against which measures of progress and measures at termination and follow-up can be compared. These comparisons thus provide quantitative data that make it possible to evaluate the efficacy of work with clients.

Solonim-Nevo and Vosler (1991) have explored the benefits and limitations of using single-subject design in systemic problem-solving therapy. They conclude that in a variety of settings, including mental health, family practice, and private practice, this methodology can be adapted so that social workers can integrate evaluation as a key element in their practice.[2]

Measuring Overt Behaviors

Baseline measures can analyze either overt or covert behaviors. Overt behaviors are observable and, as such, lend themselves to frequency counts. For example, if family members have negotiated a shared goal of increasing the frequency of positive messages sent to one another, you might instruct them to keep a daily tally of the number of such messages they convey for a period of 1 week. The daily average would then serve as a baseline against which progress could be measured. Similar baselines can be determined for target behaviors such as reducing the incidence of a child having temper tantrums, increasing the number of times that students raise their hands before speaking in class, speaking up in social situations, and expressing feelings. Such measures quantify problem behaviors and make it possible to ascertain both weekly progress and ultimate outcomes of change efforts. In addition, clients can observe even small incremental changes, a factor that sustains hope and increases motivation.

Clients, observers, or social worker may perform frequency counts. They can also be done when the target behavior occurs in family or group sessions. Social workers often have clients record behaviors that occur outside the therapeutic sessions as well. Baselines obtained through self-monitoring, however, are not true measurements of behavior under "no treatment" conditions, because self-monitoring itself often produces therapeutic effects. For example, monitoring the rate of a desired behavior (i.e., raising one's hand before speaking) may, in fact, act to increase the frequency of that behavior. Similarly, measuring the rate of negative behavior may influence a client to reduce its frequency.

These effects of self-monitoring on the target behavior are termed *reactive effects*. When viewed by a researcher, reactive effects represent a source of contamination that confounds the effects of the interventions being tested. From a clinician's viewpoint, however, self-monitoring may be employed *as an intervention* precisely because reactive effects tend to increase or decrease certain target behaviors. Although desired changes may result from self-monitoring of either positive or negative behaviors, emphasizing positive behaviors is preferable because doing so focuses on strengths related to goals. It may be useful to use multiple measures or observations, of which self-monitoring is just one measure. For example, the teacher in the classroom situation may also serve as

a source of information with respect to the frequency of a student raising his hand prior to speaking in class. Another measure could involve the number of times the student is referred to the "time-out" room for being disruptive in the classroom.

When baseline measures focus on current overt behaviors, repeated frequency counts across specified time intervals are typically used. The time intervals selected should be those during which the highest incidence of behavioral excesses occurs or times at which positive behaviors are desired. It is also important to obtain measures under relatively consistent conditions. Otherwise, the measure may not be representative or reflect the true picture accurately Bloom, Fischer, & Orme, 2003).

Retrospective Estimates of Baseline Behaviors

Baseline measurements are obtained before change-oriented interventions are implemented, either by having clients make retrospective estimates of the incidence of behaviors targeted for change or by obtaining data before the next session. Although it is less accurate, the former method often is preferable because change-oriented efforts need not be deferred pending the gathering of baseline data. This is a key advantage, because acute problems or a crisis may demand immediate attention and delaying the intervention for even 1 week may not be advisable. Conversely, delaying interventions for 1 week while gathering baseline data in general does not create undue difficulty, and the resultant data are likely to be far more reliable than clients' estimates.

When determining the baseline of target behavior by retrospective estimates, it is common practice to ask the client to estimate the incidence of the behavior across a specified time interval, which may range from a few minutes to one day, depending on the usual frequency of the target behaviors. Time intervals selected for frequent behaviors, such as nervous mannerisms (tapping a pencil on a desk), should be relatively short (e.g., 15-minute intervals). For relatively infrequent behaviors, such as a child having a temper tantrum, intervals may consist of several hours or days.

Measuring Covert Behaviors

Baseline data can also be obtained for covert behaviors, such as troubling thoughts or feelings (e.g., irrational fears, depressed states, or self-deprecating thoughts). Clients may make frequency counts of targeted thoughts or rate degrees of emotional states. Where goals involve altering feelings, such as anger, depression, loneliness, or anxiety, it is desirable to construct self-anchoring scales that denote various levels of an internal state. To do so, you and the client would develop a five- or seven-point scale that represents varying levels of internal states, ranging from total absence of the troubling feeling or thought at one extreme to maximal intensity at the other extreme. To "anchor" such scales, ask clients to imagine themselves experiencing the extreme degrees of the given internal state and to describe what they experience. You can then use these descriptions to define at least the extremes and the midpoint of the scale. Developing scales in this manner quantifies internal states in a unique manner for each client. In constructing self-anchoring scales, it is important to avoid mixing different types of internal states: Even though emotions such as "happy" and "sad" appear to belong on the same continuum, they are qualitatively different, and mixing them will result in confusion. Figure 12-3 depicts a seven-point anchored scale.

Clients can use self-anchoring scales to record the extent of troubling internal states across specified time intervals (e.g., three times daily for 7 days) in much the same way that they take frequency counts of overt behaviors. In both instances, clients keep tallies of the target behaviors. A minimum of 10 separate measures is generally

necessary to discern patterns among data, but urgent needs for intervention sometimes require that you settle for fewer readings.

This type of scale is also useful for examining incremental change. In the range of most to least anxious, the practitioner and the client will want to explore events or situations that appear to trigger an anxiety response, providing additional descriptive information.

Guidelines for Obtaining Baseline Measures

When you are using baseline measures, it is vital to maximize the reliability and validity of your measurements (Bloom, Fischer, & Orme, 2003; Berlin & Marsh, 1993). Otherwise, your baseline measures and subsequent comparisons with those measures will be flawed and lead to inappropriate conclusions. Adhering to the following guidelines will assist you in maximizing the reliability and validity of the data collected:

1. *Define the target of measurement in clear and operational terms.* Reliability is enhanced when the behavior (overt or covert) targeted for change is specifically defined. For example, measurements of compliments given to a partner are more reliable than measurements of positive communications, because the client must make fewer inferences when measuring the former than when counting the latter instances.

2. *Be sure your measures relate directly and specifically to the goals targeted for change.* Otherwise, the validity of your measurements both at the baseline and at subsequent points will be highly suspect. For example, when a client's goal is increasing social skills, indicators of social skills should be used as measurement targets. Likewise, if child care and household organization are to be improved, measures should be devised that directly specify observable behavioral changes. Similarly, measures of violent behavior and alcohol abuse should correspond to the frequency of angry outbursts (or control of anger in provocative situations) and consumption of alcohol (or periods of abstinence), respectively.

1	2	3	4	5	6	7
Least anxious (calm, relaxed, serene)		Moderately anxious (tense, uptight, but still functioning with effort)		Most anxious (muscles taut, cannot concentrate or sit still, could climb the wall)		

Figure 12-3 Example of a Self-Anchored Scale

3. *Use multiple measures and instruments when necessary.* Clients typically present with more than one problem, and individual problems may involve several dimensions. For example, flat affect, fatigue, irritability, and anxiety are all frequently indicators of depression. A client may also present with goals related to a lack of self-confidence and limited social skills, which would require the use of multiple measures and instruments to track.

4. *Measures should be obtained under relatively consistent conditions.* Otherwise, changes may reflect differences in conditions or environmental stimuli, rather than variations in goal-related behaviors. For example, if a child's difficulty is that she does not talk while she is at preschool, measuring changes in this behavior while the child is at home, in church, or in other settings may be informative, but it is not as helpful as the indications of change at preschool, where the behavior primarily occurs.

5. *Baseline measures are not relevant when clients present with discrete goals.* Evaluating the efficacy of helping efforts in such instances is clear-cut, because either clients accomplish a goal or they do not. For example, with a goal of getting a job, the job seeker is either successful or not successful. By contrast, progress toward ongoing goals is incremental and not subject to fixed limits as in the case of completing a job application. Employing baseline measures and periodic measures, therefore, effectively enables both practitioners and clients to monitor incremental changes. Consider the following baseline measure for an ongoing goal: "Justin will sit in his seat and keep his hands on his desk during English class." If Justin's baseline indicated that he is out of his seat (off task) 25 times per week, then improvement to 15 times per week would be significant.

Measuring with Self-Administered Scales

Self-administered scales are also useful for obtaining baseline data. Many psychological scales are available, but the WALMYR assessment scales (Hudson, 1992) are especially useful for social workers. Designed by Hudson and fellow social workers, the 22 separate scales (see Chapter 8) tap into many of the dimensions relevant to social worker practice. Their ease of administration, scoring, and interpretation, as well as acceptable reliability and validity, are among the advantages of these scales.

Self-administered scales may also be used to quantify target problems. Although they are somewhat subjective and less precise than behavioral counts, they are particularly useful in measuring covert behavioral states (e.g., anxiety, depression, self-esteem, clinical stress) and clients' perceptions of their interpersonal relationships. Like tools to measure overt behaviors, selected scales can be administered before implementing treatment and thereafter at periodic intervals to monitor progress and to assess outcomes at termination and follow-up. Interestingly, unlike behavioral self-monitoring (i.e., counting behaviors or thoughts), subjective self-reporting through self-administered instruments is less likely to produce reactive effects (Applegate, 1992).

Receptivity of Clients to Measurement

Some social workers hesitate to ask clients to engage in self-monitoring or to complete self-report instruments because they are concerned that clients will resist or react in a negative manner. Research studies by Applegate (1992) and Campbell (1988, 1990) indicate that such concerns are not justified. These researchers found that clients generally were receptive to formal evaluation procedures. In fact, Campbell found that clients preferred being involved in evaluation of their progress. In addition, clients preferred "the use of some type of systematic data collection over the reliance on social worker's opinion as the sole mean of evaluating practice effectiveness" (Campbell, 1988, p. 22). Finally, practitioners were able to accurately assess clients' feelings about different types of evaluation procedures (Campbell, 1990).

After obtaining baseline measures of targets of change, the next step is to transfer the data to a graph on which the horizontal axis denotes time

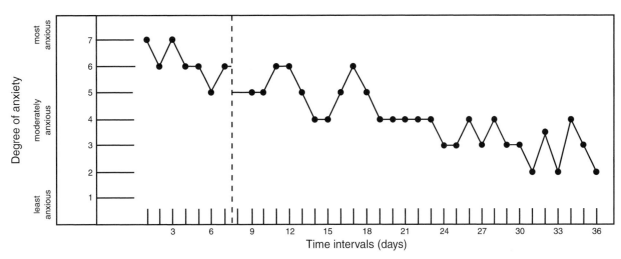

Figure 12-4 Example of a Graph Recording the Extent of Anxiety during Baseline and Intervention Periods

intervals (days or weeks) and the vertical axis denotes the frequency or severity of target behaviors. Simple to construct, such a graph makes it possible to observe the progress of clients and the efficacy of interventions. Figure 12-4 depicts the incidence of anxiety before and during the implementation of change via such a graph.

In Figure 12-4, note that the baseline period was 7 days and the time interval selected for self-monitoring was 1 day. Interventions to reduce anxiety were implemented over a period of 4 weeks. As illustrated in the graph, the client experienced some ups and downs (as usually occurs), but marked progress was nevertheless achieved.

In monitoring progress by taking repeated measures, it is critical to use the same procedures and instruments used in obtaining the baseline measures. Otherwise, meaningful comparisons cannot be made. It is also important to adhere to the guidelines for measurement listed in the preceding section. Repeated measurement of the same behavior at equal intervals enables practitioners not only to assess progress, but also to determine variability in clients' behavior and to assess the effects of changes in the clients' life situation. For example, by charting measures of depression and increased social skills from week

to week, it becomes possible to discern either positive or negative changes that correspond to concurrent stressful or positive life events. In this way, graphs of measured changes enable clients both to view evidence of their progress and to gain awareness of how particular life or environmental events contribute to their emotional states or behaviors.

Monitoring Progress with Quantitative Measurements

Monitoring progress has several other advantages. Measures establish indicators, and monitoring tells both the client and the social worker when goals have been accomplished, the relationship can be terminated, or the court mandate has been satisfied. For example, when observable behaviors of parenting skills have improved to the degree that they conform to explicit indicators, termination is justified. School attendance that has improved beyond the initial baseline measure is yet another indication for termination. Similarly, termination is indicated when measurements of depression decrease to the range of nonclinical depression. Results of monitoring can also substantiate progress and be used to justify continued coverage by third-party payers, and in reports to the court in the case of mandated clients. For clients, monitoring provides evidence of change, assuring them that they are not destined to remain forever involved with the social worker or agency. A final and critical advantage of monitoring is that if interventions are not achieving measurable results after a reasonable period, you can explore the reasons for this lack of progress and negotiate the use of different interventions as necessary.

Qualitative Measurements

Within the last several years, qualitative measurement methods have emerged as a viable option for practice evaluation. Qualitative measures are consistent with practice approaches such as narrative therapy and social constructivism. We believe that qualitative evaluation measures have significant advantages for monitoring progress depending on the information that you are seeking. When combined with quantitative measures, a more complete picture of the intervention and the contextual conditions of the change emerges (Holbrook, 1995; Shamai, 2003). Although the literature on the utilization of qualitative measures remains limited, we nonetheless think that it is important to acquaint you with the information that is available.

Qualitative methods differ in their philosophical, theoretical, and stylistic orientation from quantitative methods (Jordan & Franklin, 1995, 2003; Shamai, 2003). The process of data collection is more open-ended, for example, and allows clients to express their own reality and experience. In the assessment and evaluation process, the goal is to explore the individual's (or family's or group's) experience, frame of reference, beliefs, values, and cultural realities. In essence, the client is considered to be the key informant or expert regarding his or her problem and the desired change (Crabtree & Miller, 1992; Jordan & Franklin, 1995, 2003). Gilgun (1994) has suggested that qualitative measurements' focus on client perception makes for a good fit with social work values emphasizing self-determination.

In evaluating progress or assessing outcomes using qualitative methods, social workers attempt to understand the change from their clients' viewpoint. Information obtained from clients provides the context for and the dimensions of their concerns. In this sense, qualitative measures provide insight into the interaction or combination of factors that contribute to change. This descriptive information may be expressed in words, graphs, pictures, diagrams, or narratives. For example, in the structural approach to family therapy, symbols are used to create a visual map of family relationships and interaction patterns. Narratives provided by the family and individual members at the points of change (even change that is incremental) in patterns of interaction highlight the dynamics or events associated with the change. This information could also be graphically summarized, noting change over time.

Some critics have questioned the reliability and validity of qualitative measurement methods. The aim of qualitative information, however, is to ensure credibility, dependability, and confirmability (Jordan & Franklin, 1995, 2003; Crabtree & Miller, 1992). Like quantitative methods, qualitative measurements require systematic observation and may involve multiple points of observation or triangulation—for example, client self-reports, the observations of the practitioner, and data from other relevant systems. The triangulation of data replication establishes the credibility of information and guards against bias.

Two methods that may be used to measure and monitor change are logical analysis effects and informative events or critical incidences. They are discussed in the next two subsections

Logical Analysis Effects

The case of William, the truant from school discussed earlier in this chapter, will be used to illustrate the use of the logical analysis effects method. Recall that William was ordered by the court to attend school rather than being placed in a juvenile detention center. He thought school was stupid; as a result, William either continued to miss a significant number of days or would go to school but would not attend classes. The social worker working with William arranged for him to begin working on his goal of learning to play the guitar. The music teacher agreed to give William guitar lessons providing that he was a student. After several weeks, William reported that he had missed fewer days in school, and the majority of his absences were excused.

Davis and Reid (1987) describe logical analysis effects as establishing a linkage among context, intervention, and change. In William's case, the intervention was arranging for him to receive guitar lessons. To track this change, we would need to establish that his improved school attendance resulted from this intervention. This information could be obtained by collecting and charting William's pre- and post-intervention attendance, combined with client self-reports, parent reports, and the attendance record. The pertinent question here: Specifically, what was the effect of the guitar lessons on William's school attendance?

Informative Events or Critical Incidences

Clients and social workers are often able to identify a "turning point" or "therapeutic effect" associated with a particular event or intervention that contributed to a reduction in the target problem (Shamai, 2003; Davis & Reid, 1988). Clients may also describe intervention strategies in terms of the most and least helpful. Greater weight may be assigned to those strategies about which the client and the social worker agree. For example, you and a client might agree that the completion of a certain task working toward a particular goal contributed to a change and a particular outcome. This method may also be used for program evaluation purposes. For example, in a focus group conducted by one of the authors of this book, a group of mothers in a family reunification and preservation program were asked to identify the particular intervention that marked a change in their ability to move toward reunification with their child or children. In this particular case, a major turning point was a parent support-group session during which they were able to reflect on and discuss their grief related to their children being removed from the home in an enabling and supportive atmosphere. A similar process may be used in task groups in which members are asked to evaluate meetings and to note an event or discussion that facilitated the group accomplishing its work.

Existing assessment tools may be utilized to measure progress or change in the target problem. Consider the eco-map, an assessment tool that examines the relationship between a family and other social systems. It helps both the client and the social worker identify areas of tension as well as potential resources. For evaluation purposes, the eco-map may be used in a pre- and post-intervention fashion to graphically demonstrate change, assuming that the tension lines were identified as a target problem. In Figure 12-5a, for example, credit card debt was identified as a major stressor in the Strong family. The family identified paying off their debt as a priority, and the social worker referred them to a consumer credit counselor. After the family had worked with this counselor, they and the social worker charted the change. In Figure 12-5b, the tenuous relationship initially reported by the family has changed to a strong resource relationship following the intervention of consumer credit counseling. Of course, this change occurred incrementally. Over time, it might be useful to insert one or more lines to credit card debt to demonstrate the progression or change.

Monitoring Progress with Qualitative Measurements

The aim of qualitative methods in monitoring progress and assessing outcomes is to understand the individual's or family's experience, and the meaning that this experience holds for them (Witkin, 1993). For the Strong family in Figure 12-5, reducing their level of credit card debt meant that they could begin saving to buy a house. In completing the eco-map with the family the social worker learned about the family's desire to buy a home, once they were able to manage their debt. Using qualitative methods in this case along with the narratives of the family provided insight into the interaction or combination of factors that contribute to their desired change. Numbers (i.e., quantitative data) also represent descriptive information and inform us about change or the reduction of symptoms; thus, statistical data fulfill an important function. Statistical data, however,

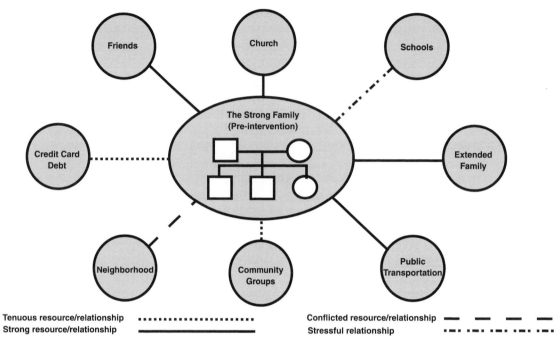

Figure 12-5a Pre-intervention eco-map

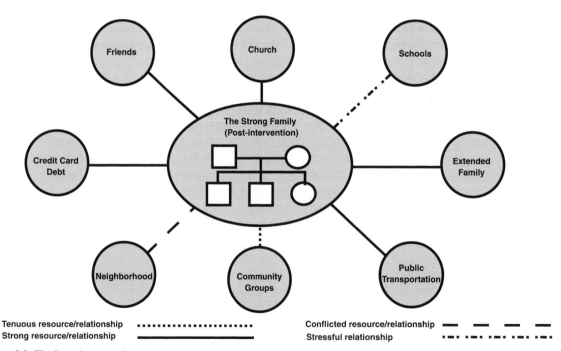

Figure 12-5b Post-intervention eco-map

cannot provide the contextual narratives provided by qualitative data. The most salient characteristic of qualitative evaluation methods is that the data add "a human texture to statistical data," thereby increasing our understanding of progress (Shamai, 2003).

Measurement and monitoring of progress may be accomplished by using either qualitative or quantitative methods, or a combination of the two. Monitoring progress may take the form of notations made in the case record, session reviews and evaluations, rating or behavioral scales, graphs or grids, or reflective methods (e.g., informative events or incidences). In essence, monitoring progress involves tracking in a systematic manner the effectiveness of an intervention strategy and the client's progress toward his or her goals.

One criterion for choosing methods of measurement and monitoring is the extent to which the measure selected is compatible and consistent with the goals related to the target concern and the intervention strategy. Irrespective of the method selected, the client's receptivity to measurement and monitoring is an important factor. Potocky-Tripodi (2002) also notes the importance of choosing measurement and monitoring procedures that are culturally relevant and consistent with clients' values and beliefs. In deciding whether any instrument is appropriate, Jordan and Franklin (2003) suggest that social workers pose the ethical question of whether the tool provides the means to "assess and serve the client better" (p. 128). Jayaratne (1994) and Lum (2004) emphasize involving clients in establishing systematic measures, monitoring, and evaluation procedures, thereby "giving voice" to their perspective as a means of empowerment. Kagle (1994) supports including clients' perspectives as a means to balance the power held by the social worker and the impact of systematic methods, which she believes casts clients' viewpoints as being less scientific (p. 98).

These points of view are consistent with the empowerment and collaborative nature of the social worker–client relationship that are emphasized throughout this book. Irrespective of which methods are used to monitor progress and meas-

ure change, social workers should always attend to the central question: How is change systematically measured and recorded?

CONTRACTING

Contracting with clients is intended as a facilitative tool that enables both client and practitioner to reach agreement about the purpose, focus, and expected outcomes of their work together. Depending on the practice setting, contracts may also be referred to as service agreements. Contracts should not be confused with case plans, although elements of a case plan may be part of the contract; rather, the case plan outlines the concerns upon which the contract is based.

In addition to the example contracts provided at the end of this chapter, other types of contracts can be developed that are more short-term in nature and focus on a particular behavior or situation. For example, in the contract used in a crisis situation, the social worker and the client develop an agreement or safety plan that states the client refrains from harmful behavior and identifies crisis resources the client can use in specific circumstances. Other types of contract used in cognitive-behavioral family therapy are contingency (quid pro quo) and good-faith contracts (Nichols & Schwartz, 2004). In essence, a contingency contract identifies a desired behavior change on the part of all parties involved, and its fulfillment is contingent on each individual's behavior in response to the other parties' behaviors. In a good-faith contract, the parties involved agree to change their behavior independently of one another.

The key ingredients of the various types of contracts are that this tool frames the purpose and focus of the client–social worker relationship, and emphasizes the mutual accountability of each party within the change process.

The Rationale for Contracts

Contracting is the natural culmination of the assessment phase and the introduction of the change-oriented (goal attainment) phase, which is essentially the heart of the helping process. Contracts specify goals to be accomplished and the means of accomplishing them, clarify the roles of the participants, and establish the conditions under which assistance is provided. An initial contract thus is an agreement that guides social workers and clients in their joint efforts to achieve specified goals and objectives. While these tools are most appropriate with voluntary clients, semivoluntary contracts can also be negotiated with involuntary clients (Rooney, 1992).

Research findings attest to the value of social work contracts. Early studies conducted by Wood (1978) and Reid and Hanrahan (1982) emphasized the positive outcomes in practice when contracts were utilized. Conversely, outcome studies of direct practice reviewed by Wood (1978) revealed that negative outcomes were more likely when explicit contracts were not utilized to guide the work of the social worker and the client. Reid and Hanrahan (1982) have suggested that the contracts in the studies with more successful outcomes were characterized by motivational congruence. Motivational congruence encompasses the fit between the client's perceptions of the problem, his or her motivation, and the services that the social worker and agency provide. Clearly, contracts have both historical and contemporary functions in facilitating problem solving and maintaining focus in the client–social worker relationship.

Types of Contracts

Earlier in this chapter, we outlined the purpose and utility of goals and the various components involved in their development. As a general rule of thumb, the social worker and the client are ready to formulate a contract when problems have been explored and assessed, they have reached agreement as to the nature of the problems and the systems involved, and the decision has been made that the social worker and agency are appropriate choices for addressing the problem. When this process is completed, you are ready to formulate a contract.

Social workers construct contracts with varying degrees of formality. Public agencies often require signed service agreements. Such *written contracts* provide space for entering the particular concerns

or problems of a client situation and listing the expected intervention outcomes. The client and the social worker sign the contract, giving it much the same weight as a legal document. Some private agencies prefer *agreements* to contracts, believing that contracts are more appropriate for administrative purposes rather than for client–practitioner relationships. Students often ask whether written or verbal contracts are preferable. For some practitioners, the rationale for using a written contract is that it provides a tangible reference to the commitments to the structural nature of the client–social worker relationship, thereby minimizing the possibility of misunderstandings. Other social workers prefer *verbal contracts* that include all of the same provisions but lack the sterility and finality of a written contract. A third option is to utilize a partially verbal and partially written contract, with the latter including the basics of problems and goals identified, role expectations, time limits, and provisions for revision.

Whatever the final form of the contract, goals and their priority should be recorded in the case record in the form of progress notes, along with any other graphic depictions that document progress—for example, goal attainment scales. This information is then reviewed during each session with the client. Whether the contract is verbal or written, we recommend that, at a minimum, the client receive a copy of the goals to be accomplished.

If a written contract is not used, note that questions related to informed consent may potentially arise later. Although contracts may not be considered legally binding (a fact that should be emphasized to clients), the social worker must commit to outline the work to be done, thereby obtaining informed consent from clients. Otherwise, clients may believe they are justified in filing suit for malpractice if they do not achieve their goals.

Developing Contracts

Contracting is the final discrete activity of Phase I of the helping process. To assist you to use contracts to their maximal advantage, we will focus here on the component parts of the contract and the knowledge and skills required for their systematic negotiation. Thus, the purpose of the following discussion is to assist you to gain knowledge and skill in utilizing contracts effectively.

Generally, contracts should include the following elements:

1. Goals to be accomplished (ranked by priority, and related to identified concerns)
2. Roles of the participants
3. Interventions or techniques to be employed
4. Time frame, frequency, and length of sessions
5. Means of monitoring progress
6. Stipulations for renegotiating the contract
7. Housekeeping items, such as the beginning date, provisions for canceling or changing scheduled sessions, and financial arrangements

Goals to Be Accomplished

First and foremost, the goals to be accomplished in relation to the target concern are ranked by priority. Goals are an integral part of the contract in that they provide a focus for work over the course of ongoing sessions. At the same time, goals are fluid and can be expanded or modified as situations change and new information emerges that has a bearing on the initial goals. Of course, there must be a valid reason for changing goals, as continuous shifting of the target has the potential to alter the initial focus. If these kinds of shifts occur repeatedly, you will want to reassess the client's readiness to pursue the goals that have been identified.

In instances where goals are changed for good reason, the time limits, the types of interventions employed, the frequency of sessions, and the participants in the helping process may be altered to reflect the changing circumstances of the case. It is for these reasons that stipulations for renegotiating contracts are included as an essential element of the contract. Ongoing, explicit understandings between the practitioner and the client are vital. Keeping the contract updated also conveys the social worker's continual respect for the client and facilitates motiva-

tion and participation. The initial contract is only preliminary and must be tailored to fit the changing circumstances of each case.

Roles of Participants

We reviewed the verbal process of socialization to the client and practitioner roles in Chapter 5. Those roles should be reviewed in the contracting process and, in the case of mandated clients or as often required in public agency practice, specified in writing. The contract—whether written, verbal, or some combination of the two—provides an opportunity to identify the mutual accountability of all parties. The social worker should spell out what services he or she and the social worker's agency are committing themselves to providing. For example, the agency may agree to provide child care during sessions or transportation to certain appointments. Similarly, if the client has agreed to participate in a youth diversion group, the client's participation would be specified as well as the expected outcomes.

The contracting process may also require further socialization and education of clients about the purpose and function of contracts. For some clients, trust may be an issue, despite the heretofore positive dynamics of the client–social worker relationship. Involuntary clients may feel particularly vulnerable and ambivalent when asked to sign a contract because they may feel pressured or controlled. Potocky-Tripodi (2002) points out that clients who are immigrants or refugees may have fear and apprehension about contracts related to their perceptions and experiences. For these individuals, the contract may be "perceived as an instrument of authoritarian coercion" (p. 167). In all instances, taking the time to explain the function and purpose of contracts and the client's role will facilitate the client remaining active in the process.

Interventions or Techniques to Be Employed

This aspect of the contract involves specifying the interventions and techniques that will be implemented to accomplish the stated goals. During initial contracting, it is often possible to identify interventions only on a somewhat global level—for example, individual, group, or family sessions or a combination of strategies. You can, however, indicate that you will be discussing problematic situations and considering alternative courses of action, as is common in virtually all problem-solving efforts. In some instances, depending on your assessment, you can discuss interventions with greater specificity—for example, social skills training; identifying and eliminating irrational thoughts, beliefs, and fears (cognitive restructuring); role-playing and behavioral rehearsal; self-management techniques; and developing skills (e.g., communication, assertiveness, problem solving, and conflict resolution). As a case manager, you would also indicate if a referral source would be the primary agent in assisting a client to meet a particular goal (e.g., finding housing). Whenever you consider implementing interventions it is vital to discuss them with clients, providing a brief overview of the intervention, to elicit clients' reactions, and to gain their consent. Bear in mind that contracting is an ongoing process.

Time Frame and Frequency and Length of Sessions

Another integral aspect of the contract involves the duration of the helping process and the frequency and length of sessions. Most people tend to intensify their efforts to accomplish a given goal or task when a deadline exists—just consider the last-minute cramming that students do before an examination. Specifying a time frame in contracts, therefore, counters the human tendency to procrastinate. Yet another argument that supports the development of time-limited contracts is the fact that in therapy, most of the gains are achieved early in the change process. According to Nichols and Schwartz (2004) the duration of family therapy has historically been brief and time-limited, based on the rationale that change occurs quickly, if it occurs at all. Moreover, whatever their intended length, most treatments turn out to be relatively brief; the median duration of treatment is between five and six sessions (Corwin, 2002).

On the whole, clients respond favorably to services that are offered when they need them the most and when they experience relief. Are time-limited

contracts effective with racial and ethnic minority groups? According to some outcome studies, time-limited contracts are preferable with these clients because they focus on immediate, concrete concerns (Egli, 1991). Similarly, Gilliland and James (1993) note that in stressful situations, persons of color respond best to a present- and action-oriented approach. Corwin (2002), citing the work of Koss and Shiang (1994) and Sue and Sue (1990) points out the advantages of time-limited, brief treatment by noting that these approaches are "congruent with how many minority clients understand and utilize mental health and social services" (p. 10). Finally, time-limited contracts are perceived as making a useful distinction between talking and actual change. Some theorists, however, believe that time limits are inconsistent with perspectives of time held by some minority groups (Green, 1999; Devore & Schlesinger, 1999; Logan, Freeman, & McRoy, 1990).

Of course, time-limited contracts are not appropriate for all client populations or situations. Such contracts that involve case management for individuals for whom you have an ongoing responsibility may be impractical, except when circumscribed problems of living or concrete needs are defined as goals. Even in these instances, however, time-limited contracts may be effective when they are divided into multiple short-term contracts related to specific problems and episodes.

Increasingly, time limitations are imposed on the work to be completed between clients and social workers. The demands of the managed care environment (specifically the brevity of the period in which outcomes are expected to be achieved) have dramatically affected both the private and the public sectors of social welfare services. In this environment, public policy, the courts, and third-party payers arbitrarily make decisions with respect to the time frame and the duration of contact. For example, in child welfare, with concurrent planning parents have 12 months in which to regain custody of their children who have been placed outside of the home. For example, concurrent planning does not take into consideration whether services are available to remedy a situation, nor whether the delivery of those services is within the required time frame. These time limits must be included in contracts that you develop with clients. You can assist clients—particularly when imposed time limits represent a race against time—to prioritize and focus their efforts on responding to the concerns indicated.

We recommend the following time frame, which is commonly used in the task-centered social work model, because of its extensive prior use and substantial research supporting its efficacy: 6 to 12 sessions conducted over a time span of 2 to 4 months. Given the flexibility inherent in this time frame, you can negotiate with the client regarding the specific number of sessions to be undertaken. In most agencies, weekly sessions are the norm, although more frequent sessions may be required in cases that need intensive support and monitoring. For example, child welfare/child protective services, job-training programs, outpatient drug treatment, services for the frail elderly, and school truancy or programs that assist homeless or runaway youth may require daily contact. Provisions can also be made in contracts for spacing sessions farther apart during the termination phase of the helping process.

A final time-related factor concerns the length of each session. There are few solid guidelines as to the amount of time for sessions. Agencies generally have established guidelines for the billable hour. Public agency social workers—for example, those in child and family or protective services—may spend considerable time arranging for and monitoring visitations between parents and children, problem solving, and teaching parenting skills. Because some children, adolescents, and elderly clients have difficulty tolerating sessions that last for extended periods of time, shorter and more frequent sessions are common practice when working with these clients. Finally, requirements related to the setting (e.g., school, hospital, correctional facility) may influence the length and duration of sessions. For example, contacts in a hospital setting may last 15 or 20 minutes, depending on the condition of the patient and the goals to be achieved. For groups that meet in schools, the duration and length of sessions depend on a structured time frame, most often related to the concerns of teachers about how much time students spend out of the classroom.

Means of Monitoring Progress

Stipulating in the contract how progress will be monitored serves the vital function of fostering an action-oriented mindset that is conducive to change. Maintaining an expectancy of change enhances motivation and actualizes a positive self-fulfilling prophecy. When baseline measures on target problems have been obtained, the preferred method of monitoring progress is to apply the same measuring devices at specified intervals, as we noted earlier in this chapter. If baseline data are not available, a crude method of quantifying progress is to ask clients to rate their progress on a scale of 1 to 10, where 1 represents no progress and 10 represents complete achievement of a given goal. Comparing their ratings from one session to the next gives a rough estimate of clients' progress.

In addition to the narrative progress review that is a part of each session, progress may be assessed by depicting it graphically. Options include using scales or calibrated drawings of thermometers with a scale from 1 to 10, where a colored marker indicates progress on the chart. Visual methods of monitoring progress are particularly appealing to young children.

The frequency of monitoring may be negotiated with the client. We recommend spending a few minutes every other session to review progress. Of course, you can be flexible, but no more than three sessions should pass between discussions of progress. Less frequent monitoring dilutes the growth and benefits achieved and the focus on desired changes.

Stipulations for Renegotiating the Contract

Because contracting continues during the entire helping process, it is important to clarify for clients that conditions in the contract are subject to renegotiation at any time. Circumstances change, new facts emerge, assessment evolves, and progress occurs (we hope). These and other factors require that the contract be continually updated to maintain its relevance and fit. We therefore recommend that you explain that any participant in the helping process (including you) may request modifications in the contract at any time. Such an explanation highlights and enhances mutuality in the helping process. When contracting with involuntary clients, any circumstances that would cause a unilateral change in the contract (e.g., evidence of new legal violations) should be specified.

Housekeeping Items

The final element involved in formulating a contract is establishing a beginning and ending date for the contact, provisions for canceling or changing scheduled sessions, and an agreement regarding financial responsibility when fees are required.

With respect to changes in appointments, it is important to stress that clients are responsible for time that has been set aside for them. Of course, social workers should observe the same principal. There are, of course, legitimate circumstances that warrant changing or canceling an appointment by either the social worker of the client. Most agencies have policies under which clients are expected to pay the session fee for appointments they fail to keep, inasmuch as the time was allocated for them. If this is the case, explicitly discussing this policy in advance reinforces the expectations that the client will attend sessions, prevents misunderstandings, and may reduce the frequency of changes, cancellations, and failed appointments.

In situations where an agency has a purchase-of-service agreement with a state or county agency to provide services to a client group, the issue of failed appointments and fees may not be as prominent. Nevertheless, it is still advisable to discuss expectations with these clients. Nothing can be more frustrating than waiting on a client or making a home visit only to find that the client is unavailable or unprepared for the visit. At times, some confusion may arise about who the client is. Specifically, is the client the purchase-of-service contract agency or the family or individual client? To minimize such confusion, you should keep in mind that your agency has

an administrative arrangement with the state or county agency that is removed from your relationship with actual clients. Thus, it is important that you inform clients of expectations regarding appointments and cancellations, because the individual or family is ultimately your client.

Discussing financial arrangements may feel awkward. This discomfort is understandable given that the basic instinct of social workers is to help people. Even so, most private agencies have policies that require payment for services, and the majority of clients expect to pay, albeit on a sliding-scale fee arrangement. Moreover, insurance companies have co-payment requirements for mental health services. Currently, the expectation to pay, or at least to engage in work as a requirement for receiving benefits, is a policy that influences services provided by public agencies in the United States. Most notable are the requirements in the United States. for welfare recipients to perform public service in exchange for benefits. In some states individuals are also required to contribute to receive legal representation from public defenders.

Financial arrangements, where required, are a fundamental part of the professional client–social worker relationship. A component of a social worker's competency is being able to effectively discuss financial arrangements, openly and without apology, when payment of services is expected. When clients fail to pay fees according to the contract, you should explore the matter with them promptly. Avoidance and procrastinating just make matters worse, and may result in the social worker developing negative feelings toward the client. Moreover, a failure to pay fees may derive from the client's passive, negative feelings toward the practitioner, financial strains, or irresponsibility in meeting obligations, each of which merits immediate attention.

Sample Contracts

To assist you in developing contracts, we have included sample contracts at the end of this chapter (see pages 350–353). Each contract includes most of the components discussed in preceding sections, although some are emphasized more than others. Elements of the first contract, "Agreement for Professional Services," were adapted from Houston-Vega, Nuehring, and Daguio (1997). This informative resource includes sample contracts for individuals, families, and groups, as well as ethical guidelines for practitioners and managing malpractice risks.

In the "Agreement for Professional Services" contract, note that only a brief reference is made to the client's role in Section I and the practitioner's role has been excluded. These aspects of the contract are excluded because they should be explicated in length as part of the verbal agreement. Delineating roles in a written agreement would result in an excessively long document.

The second contract is used by "the back door" (DeLine, 2000), a program committed to helping homeless and runaway youth get off the streets. It outlines the program objective and the services provided by the agency. In addition, the role of the youth clients is amplified, because the focus is exclusively on how they will use the agency's services to alter their situation. The goal of the contract is to identify priorities and the most manageable tasks. For additional information on the back door, and their use of contracts, you can access the agency's website: *www.infor@buildingdoorways.org.*

The third contract is an example of a behavioral treatment agreement that is used in a county mental health center with men in a domestic violence program. Note that program requirements and objectives are a part of each client's treatment plan.

Summary

This chapter focused on goals, their purpose and function, measurement, and the contract or service agreement as essential elements of the helping process. As you reflect on the chapter, it might be useful to think of goals as global, whereas tasks are akin to the objectives that you as a student would develop in field contracts. General and specific tasks (objectives) are measurable and represent the manner in which an outcome will be achieved. For example, suppose you have designated that you wish to increase your practice skills as a part of your field contract. Your general tasks would include observing your supervisor and other social workers when they interview clients, and then carrying out your own interviews. From that general task, you would develop specific tasks (steps) that are also measurable, which you will complete to accomplish your ultimate goal of increasing your direct practice skills.

Students and even seasoned practitioners often experience difficulty in developing specific, workable goals and have indicated that the ability to do so requires practice. In training sessions related to goal development, we have encouraged participants to develop goals for themselves as a means of refining their skills. This chapter has provided you with that knowledge, emphasized the skills needed for the development of goals, and affirmed the importance of client participation. The negotiation and development of goals must include the context of clients' value systems and their lives' reality and worldview—all perspectives that cannot be obtained without clients' participation. Goal development should also take into account challenges that result from clients' socioeconomic status, race, culture, or other issues related to minority status. Client strengths are also important considerations, as they can be channeled to help clients to reach their goals. Finally, assumptions about the dynamics in the voluntary client–social worker relationship are unlikely to apply when goals are developed with involuntary clients. Nevertheless, as discussed in this chapter, certain strategies can facilitate work with clients for whom participation is mandated.

This chapter also emphasized the criticality of measurement and evaluation, whether quantitative

Agreement for Professional Services

Name(s) of Client(s) _____ Name _____

Address _____ City _____ State/ZIP Code _____

I (we) have discussed my (our) situation with _____ _____ and hereby agree to work collaboratively in achieving certain goals that will enable me (us) to improve my (our) situation. I (we) agree that to achieve these goals I (we) will share my (our) experiences, life events, and reactions to them. I (we) agree that I (we) will participate actively in planning and carrying out activities or behaviors that are for the purpose of achieving these goals.

I. **Problem/Concern:** I (we) have discussed my (our) situation with _____ and have identified and agreed upon the statements of concerns listed below:

   1 _____

   2 _____

   3 _____

II. **Goals:** I (we) hereby agree to work collaboratively in achieving certain goals that will enable me (us) to resolve the statement of concerns listed above to improve my (our) situation. I (we) agree that to achieve these goals I (we) will share our experiences and life events, and will actively participate in the planning and carrying out of actions or steps that are mutually developed for the purpose of achieving goals. The initial goals and general tasks that I (we) have agreed upon in order of priority are as follows:

   Goals   General Tasks

   1 _____   _____

   2 _____   _____

   3 _____   _____

   I (we) understand that I (we) may add to, change, or revise these goals in the course of our work together. I (we) also understand that there may be time limits that may influence the rate at which goals may need to be accomplished or where significant progress toward goals may need to be documented.

III. **Sessions:** I (we) agree to meet with _____ on a _____ basis, for a total of _____ sessions, and that these meetings will last _____ (duration).

   I (we) agree that the format of our sessions will be: _____ Individual _____ Marital or Family _____ Group or Combination.

   I (we) understand that each session will last about _____ beginning on _____ and ending by _____ for a total of _____ sessions.

   I (we) have discussed the fee for professional service and agreed to the fee of _____ per session, which I (we) will pay _____ (specify arrangement).

IV.   Evaluation:

    a)   I (we) agree that I (we) will participate in evaluating my (our) progress each session by reviewing the goal plan and the steps taken to achieve goals (specify procedure).

    b)   I (we) agree to participate in a final evaluation session after we have completed our work together.

    c)   I (we) agree to participate in a follow-up evaluation after we have completed our work together.

V.   Reports and Records:

    a)   I (we) understand and give consent for releases of information or reports about my (our) service plan and progress to others (e.g., court, third-party payer, referral source) with whom _____ is required to share about my family or me.

    b)   I (we) understand that in all other instances, I (we) will be asked to sign a consent form to release information about my family or me.

    c)   I (we) understand that _____ will maintain a confidential case record on me (us) and that I (we) have access to this record.

    d)   I (we) understand that _____ is by law mandated to report abuse or neglect of children or vulnerable adults; and actions by me (us) in instances where I (we) am (are) in danger or pose a threat, or place someone else in danger, or when a court of law orders the disclosure of information.

VI.   Agreement:

    a)   I (we) have discussed and reviewed the above terms of this agreement and on this date agree to abide by them in my (our) work with _____.

    b)   I (we) understand that this agreement can be renegotiated at any time.

Signature (Client/Family/Group Member)

Name   _____   Name   _____   Date   _____

VII.   Social Worker:

    a)   I agree to work collaboratively with _____ to achieve the goals outlined in this service agreement, and others that we may subsequently agree upon.

    b)   I agree to adhere to the conduct that XYZ agency expects of its staff, and to abide by the regulatory laws and ethical codes that govern my professional conduct.

    c)   I have provided a copy of agency information about the rights of clients, available agency services, and information about the agency.

    d)   I have read the above terms of the service agreement, and pledge to do my best to assist the client(s) to achieve the goals listed and others that we may subsequently agree upon.

Professional's Signature: _____

Date: _____

the back door
MAKING CHANGE

Name: _____ Date: _____

File #: _____

❏ Housing   ❏ Planning   ❏ Drugs/Alcohol
❏ Employment   ❏ Volunteering   ❏ Problem Solving
❏ Education   ❏ Finances   ❏ Identification
❏ Personal   ❏ Leadership   ❏ Legal
                                                        ❏ Other

CONTRACT STEP: _____ Step#: _____

WHAT I WANT TO WORK ON TODAY (i.e., WHERE I AM TODAY IN MY LIFE):
_____
_____

WHAT RESULT(S) I WOULD LIKE TO SEE (i.e., WHERE I WOULD LIKE TO BE):
_____
_____

WHAT I NEED TO MAKE IT WORK:
_____
_____

MY STEPS:
1 _____

2 _____

3 _____

4 _____

Contractor: _____ Paid by: _____

The following principles & questions reflect how *the back door* hopes to work. Please take time to think about how they worked for you in THIS contract step.

1. Principle: INTEGRITY/DIGNITY
   How did contracting this step contribute positively to your self esteem?
2. Principle: LIFE IS SUCH THAT THINGS DO NOT ALWAYS WORK
   In attempting the above step how did you find this to be so?
3. Principle: ACCEPTANCE WITHOUT JUDGMENT OR PREJUDICE
   How did contracting this step allow you to experience positive input from another person?
4. Principle: FORGIVENESS: EVERY DAY IS A NEW DAY
   How did contracting this step give you the freedom to learn from the past and try again?
5. Principle: PEOPLE WHO LISTEN TO EACH OTHER LEARN FROM EACH OTHER
   How did planning/working on this step help you to understand another person's point of view?
6. Principle: ALL ACTIONS/CHOICES AFFECT OTHER PEOPLE
   Did your working on this step have any effect on other people in your life?

Source: Used by permission of *the back door* © 2000.

Behavioral Treatment Agreement

Name _____ Client # _____ Date _____ Therapist _____

1. Progress

Summary _____

_____

2. New Treatment Goals

1. Increased awareness of individual cues that trigger getting angry
2. Increased awareness of nonabusive alternative ways of expressing anger
3. Increased use of support networks
4. Accepting responsibility for my past abusive behavior

3. Plan

Attend 18 educational themes/complete 9 tasks

4. Outcomes

1. Side effects of treatment discussed ❐ yes ❐ no
2. Outcomes of treatment discussed ❐ yes ❐ no
3. Treatment options discussed ❐ yes ❐ no
4. Cost of treatment explained to client ❐ yes ❐ no
5. Client and staff rights form provided to client ❐ yes ❐ no
6. Is client considering:
   Chemotherapy ❐ yes ❐ no
   Hospitalization ❐ yes ❐ no
   Other medical treatment ❐ yes ❐ no

If the answer is yes to any of the above, the physician or consulting psychiatrist shall inform the client of the treatment alternatives, the effects of the medical procedures, and the possible side effects.

All clinical services shall be provided according to the individual treatment plan.

5. Expected Duration of Treatment

18 weeks/dependent on task completion. You need to begin completing the required tasks within the first 4 weeks of the program

6. Frequency of Treatment

Weekly

7. Collateral Resources and Referrals

_____

I understand the terms of this treatment agreement as well as my responsibilities in implementing the same. I have received a copy of this treatment plan.

Client _____ Date _____

Therapist _____ Date _____

Clinical Director _____ Date _____

Source: Used by permission. © MHC.

or qualitative. Irrespective of which method is employed, measurement requires systematic and oftentimes multiple points of observation. As noted earlier, goals relate directly and specifically to the target problem or concern. Thus, the measure selected to monitor and evaluate progress must also be consistent with goal-related behaviors or conditions. The essential evaluation question is, Did change occur and, if so, in what way? Be mindful of the fact that in addition to the requirements of funding resources, agencies, and third-party payers, ethical practice demands that we as social workers demonstrate that our work with clients is effective.

The contract examples provided in this chapter are intended as guides that may be adapted to a particular situation or setting. Depending on the age, or stage, or client situation, a certain form may be more appropriate. The contract defines the work to be completed between the practitioner and the client, identifies roles and expectations, and specifies the structured time frame in which the collaborative work is to be completed and evaluated.

Internet Resources

See our companion website for hot links to some helpful URLs. Note that URLs are subject to change. We will endeavor to update the links on the companion website as much as possible.

Additional resources related to this chapter may be accessed by using the following keywords with InfoTrac College Edition: "evidence-based practice," "goals or objectives," "measurement and evaluation," "involuntary clients," and "contracting".

Related Online Content

Visit the *Direct Social Work Practice* companion website at *http:// socialwork. wadsworth.com/hepworth7* for additional learning tools such as glossary terms, chapter outlines, InfoTrac College Edition keywords, relevant web links, and chapter practice quizzes. Also, be sure to check out the Direct Practice Virtual Reader, where the authors have personally selected articles relevant to this chapter using Info-Marks.

Notes

1. In addition to the procedures for measurement and monitoring discussed in this book, we recommend Jordan and Franklin (2003), Bloom, Fischer, and Omre (2003), and Corcoran and Fischer (1999) for more in-depth information on standardized instruments and methods to evaluate practice.

2. For those interested in further study on single-subject research, informative resources are Bloom, Fischer, and Orme (1999, 2003), Corcoran and Fischer (1999), and Thyer (2001). These texts are informative resources and describe a wide variety of methods that may be used to evaluate practice.

PART 3

The Change-Oriented Phase

After formulating a contract or service agreement, the social worker and the client begin Phase II of the helping process—the goal attainment or change-oriented phase. In Phase II, social workers and clients plan and implement strategies to accomplish goals related to the identified problems or concerns. Implementing these strategies involves employing interventions and techniques specified in the contract and contracting to use others as indicated by changing circumstances. Before considering these factors further, however, a preview of Part 3 is in order.

Chapter 13 begins with a discussion of planning goal attainment strategies and includes two brief treatment practice models—the task-centered system and crisis intervention. Crisis intervention is a model that is related to the task-centered system but is applied in somewhat more specific situations. In addition, Chapter 13 delves into cognitive restructuring, a technique used in cognitive-behavioral therapy. It is useful for addressing the cognitive component of diverse problems and may be employed in conjunction with other interventions.

Subsequent chapters of Part 3 explicate a number of widely used interventions, many of them empirically grounded. Given the large number of treatment models in the helping professions and an even larger number of specific interventions, it is not possible to examine all of them in a single volume.[1] In keeping with the focus on brief, time-limited practice in this book, however, we have included a discussion of the solution-focused approach. The tenets and techniques of the solution-focused approach are compatible with the task-centered, crisis intervention, and cognitive restructuring approaches to practice. The latter strategies seek to empower clients through systematic and collaborative problem solving, whereas the solution-focused approach aims to provide empowerment through the construction of solutions.

Chapter 14 focuses on macro practice; its coverage is enriched by case examples from social workers addressing environmental or institutional barriers in which macro-level interventions were indicated. In Chapter 15, the family interventions introduced build on the material from Chapter 10 on family assessment. Similarly, Chapter 16 presents group interventions, which build on Chapter 11's discussion of group formation and assessment. Techniques employed to expand self-awareness and to pave the way to change (additive empathy, interpretation, and confrontation) are considered in Chapter 17. Part 3 concludes with Chapter 18, which introduces skills in managing barriers to change.

CHAPTER 13

Planning and Implementing Change-Oriented Strategies

CHAPTER OVERVIEW

The "helping process" as conceptionalized in this book is divided into three distinct phases. Each of these phases requires skills and knowledge necessary to complete the dimensions and processes of assessment, the development of goals, and the evaluation of progress and outcomes. In this chapter and those that follow, we focus your attention on goal attainment and intervention strategies that may be used to affect the target problem or concern as identified during the assessment process and the development of related goals.

Effective intervention strategies must flow from the assessment of the problem and must be the most relevant and promising means of achieving the goals identified in the contract. As beginning social work practitioners, students have often reported that they have an understanding of models, theories, and practice principles, yet they do not know what they should do next. This chapter introduces four goal attainment strategies that you may use in collaboration with clients to help them achieve their goals: the task-centered system, crisis intervention, cognitive restructuring, and solution-focused treatment.

The four approaches are useful with clients in different situations. They have the advantage of being adaptable to various theories of human behavior, need, and lifestyle, and they recognize the critical social work principle stating that individuals have the capacity to change and grow. Although each approach has certain limitations, each nevertheless lends itself to framing the problem or concern, related goals, and intervention strategies in the reality of an individual's environment and culture. Increasing the power of the client to participate in and influence the change in their lives is perhaps the most salient characteristic of the four approaches. The approaches are also compatible with both qualitative and quantitative methods to monitor and evaluate outcomes.

This chapter begins by discussing goal attainment principles that will assist you in preparing for and selecting the most appropriate strategy. To avoid a mismatch between interventions and problems/goals, it is important that interventions be relevant to the target system or subsystems and to clients' specific problems.

PLANNING GOAL ATTAINMENT STRATEGIES

Goal attainment strategies as presented in this book emphasize mobilizing individuals and families toward positive action that demonstrates that change can occur. Within this context, strengths (rather than deficits) are emphasized, as well as strategies that promote an increased sense of self-efficacy, which is a critical element of empowerment.

Empowerment makes use of resources within the client system and actively encourages clients' participation in taking control over their lives (Gutierrez, Parsons, & Cox, 1998; Saleeby, 1992, 1997). Empowerment as considered by Salzar

357

(1997) and Staples (1990) is both a process and an outcome. The process of empowerment involves the full participation of clients in decision making, which ultimately promotes their ability to exercise control over their lives. Empowerment is important because many clients served by social workers feel or have experienced powerlessness, and they may perceive themselves as merely reactors to personal, family and environmental problems. While the particular client–social worker relationship may reflect an appreciation of the criticality of empowerment, the culture of the organization itself must also demonstrate the same commitment (Linhorst, Hamilton, Young, & Eckert, 2002). That is, social workers must be assured of being able to spend the time required to include clients in treatment planning and evaluation. Thus, empowerment is an interpersonal and structural dynamic in the helping relationship.

Ethical practice ensures that clients are involved in planning the strategies that will be implemented to accomplish their goals. Besides safeguarding clients' rights to self-determination, client involvement, including those who are involuntary, is the heart of collaborative practice and positive engagement. The greater the extent to which clients feel involved in the helping process, the more likely they will remain engaged. Clients who do not understand an intervention or see its relevance to their problems and goals are unlikely to be invested in the change effort and may participate in a half-hearted fashion or not at all. To achieve cooperative participation, interventions must make sense to the client. For example, a client who expresses a need for housing may be puzzled by a focus on resolving interpersonal conflicts—unless, of course, that conflict is pertinent to the housing concern.

Involving clients in planning strategies, of course, does not mean discussing strategies in detail or even identifying all strategies that will be employed. Having established rapport, a level of trust, and heretofore a collaborative alliance, clients are generally satisfied with a brief explanation of the strategies and their rationale. In planning intervention strategies, we emphasize the following criteria to ensure that interventions make sense to both the

social worker and the client, and are relevant to the situation. The operative word that facilitates this process is *matching*. That is, the intervention selected should match each of the following:

- The target system
- The problem
- The developmental phase
- The stressful transition
- The client's racial or ethnocultural group

Matching Interventions to Target Systems

To achieve expected outcomes, interventions must be directed to the systems implicated in problems, as well as be appropriate for those systems. Mismatches tend to lead to negative outcomes, often in the form of premature terminations by clients. To accomplish this coordination is no small task, because the complexities of clients' problems often necessitate having knowledge of an array of interventions and techniques, and being skillful in selecting and using them. Some interventions are appropriate only for individual problems; others are appropriate for modifying harmful interactions in families and groups; still others relate to modifying the environment. It is important, therefore, to select and utilize interventions that match the systems targeted for change.

For example, if the assessment of a client's depression reveals that social isolation associated with an impoverished physical and social environment is significant, then an intervention aimed at enhancing the client's self-awareness (i.e., an insight-oriented strategy) is inappropriate. Similarly, planning separate sessions for partners would be counterproductive if their problems are largely the product of problematic communication patterns, unless there are compelling reasons to do so. Finally, a narrowly focused intervention to assist parents to change their methods of discipline by managing their emotional distress, without also considering stressors such as insufficient income, inadequate housing, or a lack of social support networks is tantamount to prescribing an aspirin for severe bacterial infection. Clearly, selecting the appropriate intervention strategy demands that you recognize the context of the situation or condition presented by the client. That is, you must consider all factors that influence or maintain the problem.

Matching Interventions to Problems

In treatment planning, matching interventions to problems is a task that is facilitated when empirical evidence has demonstrated that a certain intervention is effective treatment for a specified problem. For example, cognitive therapy is known to be effective in treating depression, and certain behavioral problems. Social skills training programs have proven to be effective in treating people whose problems stem from deficiencies in basic interpersonal and problem-solving skills, and educationally focused group interventions have proven effective in treating men who have abused their spouses. Likewise, parent training or support groups have proven to be effective in assisting parents to improve their skills in communication, setting limits, negotiation, and problem solving.

Increasingly research and evaluation studies have provided social workers with comprehensive empirical knowledge they can use to guide treatment selection. The emergence of evidence-based practice represents significant progress in this regard (Corcoran, 2000; Jordan & Franklin, 2003). Another hopeful sign is the increasing number of social workers and other professional practitioners who are engaging in practice evaluation and research. *The Journal of Research on Social Work Practice* has made a significant contribution to evidence-based social work practice, and *The Journal of Evidence-Based Social Work* promises to do the same.

Matching Interventions to Developmental Phases

Because clients vary in terms of their level of cognitive, social, and psychological development as well as stage in life, intervention strategies must also consider these factors. We will not attempt to discuss interventions appropriate for all developmental and life-cycle phases. Instead, we will simply emphasize that you should carefully consider the developmental stages of individuals and families in

planning interventions. Young children, for example, typically lack the capacity to think abstractly, so play therapy, interactive structured group activities, or mutual storytelling can facilitate their development of coping, cognitive, and social skills. When you work with elderly clients, you should be attuned to their functional status (i.e., Is it consistent with the client's age?), their role in the family system and life cycle, and their life experiences and current perspectives on life. When working with clients who are immigrants or refugees, their stage of acculturation and related stress are other important factors to consider.

A substantive issue, such as the stage of development in which the youth is asserting independence, often lies at the center of parent–adolescent child conflicts. This factor, along with acculturation-related stress, is often exaggerated in immigrant families where independence is not a normative value, and particularly when the youth embraces customs that are different from the family's cultural expectations. Selecting strategies appropriate to a child's age and stage emerged as a substantive issue in a situation in which a social worker was assisting a parent to establish a bedtime routine for her children. The mother had been attempting to have each child in bed by 9:00 P.M., even though the children ranged in age from 2 to 12 years. Not surprisingly, her efforts had been ineffective. The intervention suggested by the social worker involved setting a bedtime that was consistent with the age of each child. Further, she suggested that the mother establish facilitative bedtime rituals—for example, reading a story to the youngest children from a book they selected. For the 12-year-old child, bedtime could be established as occurring when he finished playing video games or watching television, where each activity had to be finished at 9:00 P.M.

Matching Interventions to Stressful Transitions

Clients' problems often arise in conjunction with overwhelming stresses precipitated by major life transitions or situational events. Although varying levels of stress are common in everyday life, prolonged stress or dramatic events such as a disaster may diminish coping capacity, affecting both physical and emotional health. The ability to cope depends on a number of factors—for example, adaptability, ego strength, emotional and physical status, and adequacy of social and institutional resources. For families, the ego strengths of members, cohesion, communication patterns, and commitment among members may determine how they cope, as might interactions beyond the family, such as social support networks (Janzen & Harris, 1997).

Transitional events that naturally occur in the various stages of the family life cycle are also sources of stress. These transitions may involve death, marriage, birth, the coming of age of a child, relocating to a new home or new country, or changes in role.

Aging and the accompanying physical changes and limitations may prove stressful for elderly persons. Elderly individuals often experience stress when they perceive their role in the family, their work life, or their community as diminishing. Family events may add to this pressure or serve as a source of generativity for elderly persons. Consider the enormous changes in lifestyle for 67-year-old grandparents who begin caring for the children of their deceased daughter. This situation may represent a welcomed opportunity, but, as one grandparent noted, becoming a parent all over again is "not for sissies" because of the stress and strain of rearing and attending to the needs of young children.

People of color and other minorities often experience situational stress as a result of their interactions with the larger social environment. For example, consider how a Mexican American family looking for an apartment felt when told by the manager, "Cockroaches are not welcome in this apartment complex." Similarly, a gay or lesbian partner can experience stress because he or she is unable to make health care decisions for the partner, because their relationship is not recognized legally. The successful African American actor Danny Glover referred to race as a lifelong stressor: "Every day of my life I walk with the idea that I am black, no matter how successful I am" (Semotan, 2004). In the aftermath of the September 11, 2001, terrorist attacks, Muslims who were citizens of the United States, those who were visitors, and individuals who were perceived to be Muslims experienced enormous stress and distress.

Situational stress should also be considered in a cultural context, and families may play a significant role in this respect. Potocky-Tripodi (2002) points out that immigration-related stress may actually create stronger family ties, even as it increases family dependence. Specifically, immigrants may out of necessity rely on family members for functions that may be burdensome for their U.S.-born relatives. In one case in which care of relatives was not included in an employer's leave policy, a female client had to take unpaid time off so that she could provide support and be an interpreter during the birth and delivery of her sister's child. Immigrants, migrants, and refugees all move from the familiar to the unfamiliar. They leave behind familiar geography, politics, customs, and patterns that shape their way of life. One immigrant couple stressed both the opportunities and the challenges associated with their transition. On the one hand, they were happy with the opportunities, such as public education for their children. On the other hand, they spoke of unlearning ways of thinking—for example, the disciplining of their children, the custom of arranged marriages, and their loss of position in their community. Their young daughter said, "I miss my grandparents."[2]

While encounters by persons of color or minority groups with the larger society may not be as difficult as described in the previous examples, societal presumptions about people do pose challenges for them in everyday life. The simple act of shopping for people of color may mean the humiliation of being categorized as a shoplifter and being observed and followed while they browse in a store. The presumption that a person is a drug dealer based on his or her language, dress, ethnicity, or skin color may bring stress as well.

Other tensions may result from stressful interactions between diverse groups. For example, African Americans may perceive that immigrants compete with them for jobs. African immigrants do not like to be referred to as African Americans. In certain minority communities, gay and lesbian persons of color are stigmatized, and as a consequence they lack support. The point being made here is that minority persons may discriminate against and hold biased perceptions about other minority groups. You should be aware of stressors related to the minority experience and include this contextual knowledge in both your assessment and intervention strategies.

Finally, we note that different cultures may react differently and assign different levels of importance to a crisis of a situational or transitional nature—for example, death. For some groups, death is a time of celebration; for others, it is a time of great mourning and sacred rituals (Hines, Preto, McGoldrick, Almeida, & Weltman, 1999).

Public policy and the extent to which policies support family life and family transitions may also produce stress. Consider the timelines associated with "welfare to work" and child welfare policies that have increased the level of stress in some families, and in particular created stressful transitions for poor women and their children. Welfare reform, for example, was envisioned as an incentive that would empower people to leave welfare because it linked behavioral compliance with economic outcomes. Instead, parents are now held responsible for their children's school attendance, and financial sanctions may be applied to them for educational neglect, with little regard for the underlying reason for a child's poor attendance. Furthermore, no provisions were made in the 60-month welfare time limits for parents with disabled children who could not work, or for individuals who were incapable of working due to mental or physical health limitations. Welfare reform created equally stressful situations for immigrant and refugee families. States were allowed to discriminate against them, by limiting the access of immigrants to food stamps, Supplemental Security Insurance (SSI), and other social welfare benefits to which they had previously been entitled.

Matching Interventions to Racial and Ethnocultural Groups

Accurate assessment of the problems faced by ethnic minority persons requires knowledge of their culture, their degree of acculturation, and the psychosocial and socio-environmental aspects of the problem within the minority experience. The same is true when planning interventions for these individuals. Lum (2004), Hurdle (2002), and Potocky-Tripodi (2002) suggest that intervention planning should take into account strategies that address clients' concerns at the micro, mezzo, and macro levels. Thus, in planning intervention strategies, factors such as race, class, gender, sexual orientation, and the accompanying issues of oppression and powerlessness must be considered. (Lum, 2004; Green, 1999). As an example, Carter and McGoldrick (1999a) cite the case of an African American female who was "depressed as a result of her lack of progress at her job, which "she blamed on herself." An assessment and further questioning by the therapist revealed that the racial attitude of the woman's supervisor was a significant factor in her lack of job advancement. Without the persistence of the therapist, the intervention in this case might have included medication along with "an exploration of her family of origin as the reason for her poor job performance" (p. 21).

Green (1999) informs us that "help-seeking behavior" is embedded in a cultural context as well as influenced by the experience of minorities with helping professionals and society (pp. 50–51). Exploring the client's cultural context may include considering gender relations, position in the family, and community. Helping may, in fact, necessitate a blending of Western and traditional healing systems (Al-Krenawi & Graham 2000). Kung (2003) explored the help-seeking behaviors of Chinese Americans and concluded that the act of asking for help—whether formally or informally—has different meanings in different cultures, although the behavior may be influenced by the degree of acculturation. For Asians, according to Kung (2003), personal or emotional problems may not be perceived as important; but instead are considered as personal thoughts, lack of willpower, or failure of self-control (p. 111). The impetus to solve one's own problem is a common phenomenon in many minority and cultural communities, as is the drive to repress feeling and emotions so as not to be characterized as vulnerable or a cultural anomaly (Green, 1999; Potocky-Tripodi, 2002; Nadler, 1996; Mau & Jepson, 1990). Potocky-Tripodi

(2002) explains that many immigrants and refugees have had limited contact with formal helping systems before their current contact with the social worker and, furthermore, this contact may have been repressive. Reluctance to seek help may also be associated with limited knowledge about available resources and inexperience with the complexities of formal service delivery systems.

Help-seeking behavior is inevitably guided by culture, acculturation, historical experiences, subjective perceptions, and interpersonal deliberations related to the cost-benefit trade-off of seeking help (Nadler, 1996). At this point you might ask, "How am I supposed to help diverse individuals with whom I have contact as a social worker?" Green (1999) refers us to the "discovery procedure" in planning interventions with racial or ethnic minority persons. *Discovery* means to solicit clients' views of the problem at hand; the related symbolic, cultural, and social nuances of their concerns; and their ideas about what should be done to remedy their difficulties. Clients' suggestions will be in harmony with their beliefs, values, and religion or spirituality. Determining clients' worldview through discovery allows social workers to implement interventions that clients will perceive as relevant, and to frame the rationale for selecting them in terms that make sense to clients.

When planning interventions with ethnic minority clients, another consideration is the importance in some cultures of family ties and the extended family. Family ties and relationships have tended to be a source of emotional and concrete support for diverse groups; as such, their inclusion may be critical to goal attainment; (Congress, 2002; Potocky-Tripodi, 2002; Green, 1999). Citing the fact that family is a primary source of support and identity in Mexican American culture, for example, Rothman, Gant, and Hnat (1985) and De Las Fuentes (2000) emphasize that contributions from the family (*familia*) should be routinely considered in the implementation of intervention strategies with Mexican American clients. In addition, the extended family and the church are often sources of resilience and strength. Of course, the inclusion of family members or other resources needs the

agreement of the client. Within some groups, integrating traditional healing practices are important. Because elders hold esteemed positions in some communities, we recommend exploring their involvement and according them due respect.

MODELS OF PRACTICE

The task-centered system and crisis intervention are brief practice models that have general application to problems in living and to problems related to crises and transitions. Each model lends itself to implementing change-oriented strategies in the context of individual experience, culture, and environmental factors that influence or sustain the problem. This section discusses the major tenets and theoretical frameworks of each model, their implications for practice with diverse populations, and their various strengths and limitations. Both models are time limited and action oriented. The section concludes with a discussion of cognitive restructuring, a technique used in cognitive-behavioral therapy and Solution Focused Treatment. Before moving to a discussion of each of these approaches, we briefly summarize the evolution of time-limited treatment.

Evolution of Brief Treatment Models

Brief therapies achieved a strong momentum in the 1960s that has continued to the present. Research studies have consistently shown that brief therapies are as effective as long-term therapies and, in some instances, more effective (Reid & Shyne, 1969; Wells, 1994; Wells & Gianetti, 1990; Corwin, 2002). What in particular led to the emergence of brief (i.e., short-term) treatment strategies during this period? In the 1960s, challenges to the prevailing views of resistance emerged, and advocates suggested that the lengthy time often required for successful treatment could be attributed to the treatment methods employed. In addition, across treatment modalities, a focus on immediate or focused concerns, an active stance by the practitioner, and conscious use of time limits were found to be productive ways of making the best use of available time (Corwin, 2002; Hoyt, 2000).

THE TASK-CENTERED SYSTEM

The task-centered system is a social work model of practice that emphasizes the use of tasks and time limits to reduce or alter the target problem identified by the client. It attempts to "reduce problems in living," including those related to interpersonal conflict, difficulties in social relations or role performance, reactive emotional distress, inadequate resources, or difficulties with organizations (Epstein, 1992). Central themes of this approach are that people are capable of solving their own problems and that it is important to work on problems that are identified by the client. Client identification of priority concerns and the collaborative nature of the client–social worker relationships is an empowering aspect of the model, and the use of tasks to achieve goals increases the client's sense of self-efficacy. In their evaluation of models of practice, Devore and Schlesinger (1999) conclude that the basic principles of the task-centered system are a "major thrust" in ethnic sensitive practice (p. 121). Figure 13-1 presents an overview of this model.

The task-centered approach to attaining goals is both systematic and efficient. It is based on advances in methods that have resulted from the advent of short-term interventions over several decades. The task-centered system emerged when the prevailing view of resistance and open-ended treatment in social work and allied disciplines was the norm. Resistance to change was viewed as a powerful force that required an extensive time commitment to resolve. The development of the task-centered system, a social work method characterized by highly specific tactics of intervention, was a tailor-made solution to this problem. This system has the key advantage of providing a framework that accommodates interventions and techniques from other brief practice models (e.g., cognitive-behavioral and solution-focused therapies).

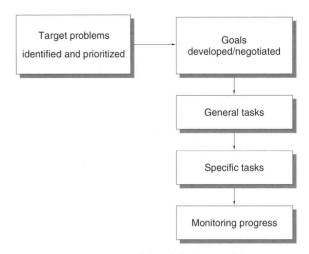

Figure 13-1 Overview of the Task-Centered System

Theoretical Framework

The task-centered model integrates social learning and behavioral theories, as well as techniques and theory from the problem-solving process and crisis intervention. Its intervention approaches have both strengths and weakness when applied in particular circumstances. For example, time limits, which are central to the task-centered system, are not feasible for certain types of clients or groups and in certain problematic situations. Nevertheless, many of the tactics of the system can be employed to increase the efficiency of other types of interventions. Progress can often be accelerated in open-ended interventions, for example, by maintaining sharp focus and continuity—another key aspect of the system. In fact, the major components of task accomplishment—namely, preparation, implementation, and follow-up—undergird all of the more specific change-oriented interventions (Hoyt, 2000).

The task-centered system has been adapted to various settings in which social workers practice, and its efficacy has been empirically established with many different client populations, organizations, and groups (Reid, 1987, 1997a; Tolson, Reid, & Garvin, 1994; Reid & Fortune, 2002). Adaptations of the task-centered approach have been tested in most settings in which social workers practice, including mental health, health care, and family practice (Reid, 1987, 1992, 2000), case management with elderly clients (Neleppa & Reid, 1995), and in schools

(Bailey-Dempsey & Reid, 1996; Kilgore, 1995) Further, the approach has been adapted and tested with groups (Fortune, 1985a; Garvin, 1987; Larsen & Mitchell, 1980) and in supervision and staff development (Caspi & Reid, 2002).

Developing General Tasks

As illustrated in Figure 13-1, when you and the client have identified a target problem and related goals, you are ready to develop general tasks. Recall from the discussion in Chapter 12 that general tasks are those strategies that are planned to reduce target problems and facilitate goal attainment. They consist of discrete actions to be undertaken by the client and, in some instances, by the social worker. Tasks, both general and specific, are a means of partializing plans for achieving goals. Task may be covert acts, such as completing a job application. They could also be covert and cognitive, such as monitoring positive and negative self-talk when preparing for a job interview.

Partializing Goals

Partializing goals is not a new technique in social work practice. Indeed, partialization has long been a basic tenet of social work practice theory (Perlman, 1957, pp. 147–149). This process is consistent with social work values reflecting a commitment to empowerment in facilitating clients' ability to make decisions. Even goals formulated with a high level of specificity often are complex and involve multiple actions that must be completed in a logical sequence. Because of this complexity, many clients feel overwhelmed and intimidated when facing the prospect of tackling goal implementation. For these reasons, it is important that you break their ultimate goals into constituent parts. As goals are dissected into manageable portions, guided by you the practitioner, clients will gain a sense of efficacy and be able to engage in discrete corrective actions (tasks), which will ultimately lead to goal accomplishment.

To illustrate this process, we consider three varied goals and identify general tasks associated with them.

Goal 1. The ultimate goal of the clients (parents) is to regain custody of children removed from their custody because of the condition of their living environment and because of neglect. As the social worker and the parents explore the conditions that must be met to regain custody of the children, they develop the following general tasks.

GENERAL TASKS
1. Improve conditions in the home by developing and following a housekeeping schedule developed in collaboration with the social worker.
2. Develop and implement acceptable hygienic and nutritional standards under the supervision of a public health nurse.
3. Improve parenting effectiveness by participating in a parenting class and a parents' group.
4. Explore and develop support systems that will make child care available, thereby freeing time to socialize in the evenings.

Goal 2. The goal of an 18-year-old homeless youth is to obtain safe and affordable housing. The goal is partialized into the following general tasks.

GENERAL TASKS
1. Obtain information about job opportunities.
2. Work with the youth program's housing coordinator to identify resources for housing options.
3. Explore opportunities to learn independent living skills.

Goal 3. The goal is to influence the landlord to maintain city housing code sanitation standards in an apartment-housing complex. General tasks are described below.

GENERAL TASKS
1. Talk with other tenants and mobilize an action group.
2. Plan meetings of the tenants to enlist leaders and develop strategies.
3. Explore resources for obtaining legal representation.

4. Present a formal grievance to the landlord and express the group's intention of resorting to legal means to force him, if necessary, to make needed improvements.

5. File a complaint with the health department and initiate court action, if necessary.

From these examples, it is apparent that general tasks may involve actions on the part of the client, the social worker, or both. In the first example, the practitioner may assume responsibility for securing a public health nurse. Similarly, the housing coordinator may undertake the task of locating housing options for the youth in the second example. In the third example, the social worker may explore possible legal resources, subsequently involving the client or representatives of the tenants' group in talking with legal counsel.

Partializing Group Goals

The same processes also pertain to a family or a treatment group. In such cases, the family or all members of the group may engage in formulating relevant general tasks to accomplish an identified objective. In the following situation, to achieve a group goal for women preparing to move from a shelter for battered women to transitional housing, the members may decide on the following courses of action:

1. Visit transitional housing programs, inquiring about facets of the program, such as daily schedule, living arrangements, rules concerning behavior, and family or friends visitation.

2. Use group time to discuss members' observations and reactions related to community resources, and reach agreement on preferences.

3. Identify schools in the area.

4. Explore case management and other services that support community living.

After partializing goals into general tasks, the next step is to order the general tasks so that they flow from one to another in a natural sequence, as was done in the earlier example in which the goal was improving the sanitation of the apartment complex.

General tasks sometimes tend to be disconnected, however, and do not fall into a logical sequence, as in the example in which the goal was regaining custody of the couple's children. In such instances, you must determine which general tasks are most significant in moving toward the client's goal and prioritize and focus your beginning change efforts on those general tasks. For example, the social worker might recommend that the parents concentrate on improving hygiene and nutrition standards if they are critical factors in regaining custody. If timing is critical, then the completion of a task such as the development of support systems to make child care available might be tabled. It is important to settle on tasks that have an excellent chance for successful accomplishment by the client. Success with one task engenders confidence and encourages clients to tackle another task; failure produces discouragement and undermines confidence in the helping process.

Developing Specific Tasks

Even general tasks can prove overwhelming to some clients, so the process of partializing continues with the development of specific tasks. The key to the task-centered system is to divide general tasks into specific agreements about which actions the client and the social worker will attempt between one session and the next. A general task such as "seek employment" must be developed into specific tasks such as "develop a resume" and "contact employment services." The parents seeking to regain custody of their children may be unable to begin work on all of the general tasks in the first week. They might agree to draft a housekeeping schedule to share with you in the following week. As the social worker, you might agree to contact the public health nurse to arrange for a first home visit. To facilitate their participation in parenting classes, you could provide descriptions of the classes and groups available for the following session, at which time the clients would decide which ones to contact first.

Specific tasks may consist of either behavioral or cognitive actions that require effort and perhaps discomfort on the client's part. The following lists illustrate both behavioral and cognitive forms of specific tasks.

Behavioral Tasks

- Telephone the employment center for information about available jobs in the metropolitan area.
- Contact a neighbor about providing child care.
- Study the independent skills manual each day for a specified length of time.
- Follow a schedule for completing household tasks.
- Keep other tenants updated on the improvements made related to housing code violations.

Cognitive Tasks

- Reflect on the advantages and disadvantages of each transitional housing facility in preparation for the group discussion.
- Engage in cognitive rehearsal involving talking to a potential employer.
- Review the major food pyramid and include that information in daily meal planning.
- Keep a daily tally of self-demeaning thoughts over three one-hour intervals.
- Recognize manifestations of anger arousal before they become out of control.

Essential tasks are sometimes readily apparent. Further, because clients are experts about their situation, they may themselves be able to propose tasks. As with goals, if such tasks are feasible and realistic, they should be supported. Clients are usually committed to tasks that they identify on their own. In instances, however, when tasks are less readily apparent, it becomes necessary for the social worker to explore alternative ways of accomplishing a general task. The challenge is to select an alternative that optimally fits a particular client.

Brainstorming Task Alternatives

An effective way of identifying a range of task alternatives is to brainstorm with clients. Brainstorming is the creative process of mutually focusing efforts on generating a broad range of possible options from which clients can choose. Although useful in any situation, brainstorming is particularly helpful in eliciting alternatives in work with groups or families. If clients overlook options, it is important to suggest additional ones to ensure a broad range of alternatives. As the social worker, you may need to take the initiative in the brainstorming process, if clients have not had experience dealing with similar issues in the past. Clients are generally receptive to suggested tasks, and research indicates little difference in the rate with which they accomplish tasks suggested by practitioners as compared to those they propose themselves (Reid, 2000; Reid, 1978, p. 251).

When social workers suggest tasks, it is critical to check with the clients to ensure that they agree with and are committed to those tasks. Therefore, you should be sensitive to clients' reactions to proposed tasks. In research studies, "the degree of the client's apparent commitment or expressed willingness to work on the task was positively related to task progress" (Reid, 1978, p. 250). Clients may be just as committed to tasks you introduce. However, if you "assign" tasks, thereby failing to enlist their commitment, it is unlikely that clients will expend their best efforts in implementing the tasks, if they even undertake them at all. Assigning tasks, whether in the form of providing advice or giving a directive, is least likely to result in those tasks being implemented by clients (Reid, 1997a).

Reactance theory suggests that clients are inclined to protect valued freedoms when they perceive that they have limited choices or when choices are imposed on them (Brehm & Brehm, 1981). The same is true in groups and families. Participants in family or group situations may quickly suggest tasks that they think other members should complete. In these situations, the social worker should protect individual members' right to choose, without pressure, which tasks they will undertake and, indeed, whether they will complete any tasks. But don't confuse a healthy assertion of individuality with opposition to change. Group or family members may, however, assist others by brainstorming additional options.

CASE EXAMPLE

This case example demonstrates how specific tasks flow from general tasks by considering the experience of Don and Jean, a couple who have identified a goal of reducing their marital conflict by communicating more effectively. By exploring the specific ways they would communicate differently if they accomplished their goal, the social worker assisted them to partialize the goal of communicating more effectively into several general tasks.

For example, one general task was "We will express ourselves without antagonizing each other." Further exploration of how they antagonized each other revealed that, when discussing various topics, Jean complained that Don demeaned, dismissed, or invalidated her opinion, which "gets my hackles up." Don agreed that her complaint was legitimate and expressed a desire to avoid putting her on the defensive. He explained that he was unhappy with his work situation, that his job held little satisfaction or sense of accomplishment for him. Also, Don felt that he had been supportive of Jean when she experienced challenges at work, and he resented her lack of reciprocal behavior toward him. Jean acknowledged Don's work situation, explaining that, "When he arrives home from work, he is very glum, which dampens the spirit of the entire family." Don agreed with her perception of his mood, adding that he didn't feel very important to anyone: "I need strokes, and to have Jean listen and respond to my concerns about work." He attributed his behavior of putting Jean down to his situation, rather than to anything that she was doing.

In this case example, the social worker observed that each partner was giving the other valuable information that, if acted upon, could assist the couple in achieving their general task of expressing themselves without antagonizing each other. After exploring their feelings and ascertaining that both were receptive to making changes in line with the discussion, the social worker and the couple developed the following reciprocal tasks:

- When Jean expresses her opinions, Don will listen attentively without criticizing or dismissing her.
- Don will take steps to be more positive when he arrives home from work.
- Jean will be more attentive and supportive of Don when he talks about his frustrations with his work.

- The two of them will set aside time on a weekly basis to talk to each other, during which they could identify concerns and engage in problem solving together.

Both Jean and Don agreed to keep daily tallies of the number of times they performed the actions inherent in their respective tasks, committing themselves to increase the frequency of these actions to at least twice daily during the first week.

As another example, consider the general task of talking with other tenants and mobilizing an action group mentioned earlier. This general task can be partialized further by developing plans for contacting specific tenants, establishing a time frame for accomplishing the tasks, and preparing a presentation for a tenants meeting. When the tasks are detailed at this level, both the social worker and tenants group are clear about what must be accomplished before the next session.

Notice that the specific tasks have been formulated in terms of positive behaviors that clients are to perform rather than behaviors from which they are to refrain. Positively framed tasks that specify undertaking desired behaviors highlight growth and gains that clients will achieve. By contrast, tasks that specify eliminating negative behaviors focus exclusively on what clients must give up. Clients tend to be more enthusiastic about tasks oriented to growth and achievement, and accomplishing such tasks often motivates them to undertake even further changes.

Certain situations present opportunities for combining tasks that involve decreasing the frequency of problematic behaviors and increasing the frequency of related functional behaviors. An adolescent, for example, may agree to increase positive thoughts (*cognitive*) about his stepfather, to reduce the frequency with which he complains (*behavioral*) about him to other family members, and to focus more on his stepfather's positive attributes. Still another example might involve devoting less time to brooding over work-related frustrations and increasing time spent in recreational activities with family and friends.

The process of partializing goals into general tasks and ultimately into specific tasks consumes a substantial portion of the time in the early portion of the change-oriented phase. Much time is also spent in preparing to accomplish one or more tasks before the next scheduled session. Although it is often appropriate to identify multiple tasks, it is important to focus on and carefully plan implementation of at least one task before concluding a session. In fact, many clients ask for "homework assignments." Mutually identifying tasks and planning their implementation in each session sharpens the focus on change and facilitates progress by maintaining the action-oriented involvement of clients between sessions. Without such actions, sessions become primarily verbal, and little or no change may occur between them. By contrast, the ongoing focus on task accomplishment concentrates, intensifies, and accelerates the helping process.

Task Implementation Sequence

After agreeing on one or more tasks, the next step is to assist clients in planning and preparing to implement each task. When skillfully executed, this process augments clients' motivation for undertaking tasks and substantially enhances the probability of successful outcomes. The *task implementation sequence* (TIS) has been described by Reid (1975, 2000), who reported research findings to the effect that clients were more successful in accomplishing tasks when TIS was implemented than when it was not. The TIS involves a sequence of discrete steps that encompass major ingredients generally associated with successful change efforts; these steps are summarized in Table 13-1.

Although Reid recommends that the TIS be applied systematically, he cautions practitioners to remain sufficiently flexible to permit its adaptation to the circumstances of each case. TIS can also be modified to fit groups. In addition, this sequence of steps is applicable to case management (Neleppa & Reid, 2000), organizations (Tolson, Reid, & Garvin, 1994), and educational supervision (Caspi & Reid, 2002).

Before considering each step in the TIS, you must recognize that the accomplishment of a task may pose a formidable challenge to clients. It would be simplistic to assume that merely agreeing to carry out a task assures that the client has the knowledge, resources, courage, interpersonal

Table 13-1 Task implementation sequence (TIS)
1. Enhance the client's commitment to carry out tasks.
2. Plan the details of carrying out tasks.
3. Analyze and resolve obstacles.
4. Rehearse or practice behaviors involved in tasks.
5. Summarize the task plan.

skill, and emotional readiness to implement a task successfully. Moreover, careful planning on your part with the client—including reviewing obstacles, reviewing rewards or incentives, and summarizing the planned task—will increase the chances of a successful outcome.

Having provided the rationale for implementing the TIS and the potential challenges to task completion, we now consider the details of each step of the task implementation sequence.

Enhance the Client's Commitment to Carry Out a Task

Directly aimed at enhancing clients' motivation to carry out a task, this step involves clarifying the relevance of tasks to clients' goals and identifying their potential benefits. To follow through with tasks, clients must perceive that the potential gains outweigh the potential costs (including anxiety and fear) associated with risking a new behavior. Because change is difficult, exploring apprehension, discomfort, and uncertainty is especially critical when clients' motivation to carry out a given task is questionable.

In many instances, the potential gains of carrying out a task are obvious, and it would be pointless to dwell on this step. For example, the potential gains from applying for a job or obtaining essential information about eligibility for financial assistance are self-evident. The benefits of other tasks may be less apparent, however, so a discussion of benefits may be essential for the client to grasp the relationship between the task and the goals. For example, the benefits of following a medical regimen may not be clear if the client's physician has not explained the need for the regimen and the consequences of not following the recommendation. Similarly, the benefits of keeping a daily log on self-defeating thoughts may be unclear if the client does not see the connection between this behavioral task and the ultimate goal of achieving increased self-confidence.

It is advisable to begin implementing step 1 of the TIS by asking clients to identify benefits they will gain by successfully accomplishing the task. To illustrate, we return to two earlier cases: Don and Jean and the homeless youth.

Don and Jean were concerned with conflict in their relationship, as expressed in their verbal interactions with each other. Both thought the tasks that they had agreed to undertake would decrease the frequency of their caustic verbal interactions. The obvious benefit for the couple was reduced conflict in their relationship, at least around the issues they identified. The social worker in this case perceived another benefit: When Don made a conscious effort to be more positive when he arrived home from work, it might improve the climate in the family system. Also, both Don and Jean would feel more confident in their ability to deal with difficult situations, without holding each other emotional hostage, and without resorting to counterproductive communications.

In addition to highlighting benefits, you should engage clients in assessing potential risks and barriers to task completion. In work with groups, the social worker can facilitate a discussion of the benefits and risks of individual goals by eliciting suggestions from other group members. Recall that the homeless youth's goal was to achieve independent living. Group members were able to give voice to some of his concerns about being on his own. As peer consultants, group members, who had experienced similar feelings as the youth related to the task of looking for a job, provided insights from their own experiences with regard to risks and benefits. For example, several group members made suggestions about "how he should dress." Preferably, ideas from members should be solicited after the individual considering a potential change has had an opportunity to contemplate the relative benefits and risks in assuming a task.

Rewards and Incentives for Adult Clients. In enhancing clients' motivation to change ingrained behaviors, it is sometimes necessary to create immediate incentives by planning tangible rewards for carrying out planned actions. One client had a long-established pattern of gambling at various casinos, during which time she spent more money than she could afford. Initially, she viewed herself as helpless to control the impulse to play the slot machines, attributing her difficulties to "lack of willpower." Of course, she also had the belief that one day she would hit the "Big One." Assessment of the situation led the social worker in this case to disagree with her explanation, and to explore other ways in which the client did maintain self-control in her life.

To enable this client to experience success in exercising self-control, the social worker suggested that she identify something she wanted to buy. However, to actually make the purchase, she would need to decrease the amount of money she poured into the slot machines at the casino. The client had wanted to purchase a pair of red leather boots for several months. She and the social worker negotiated an agreement whereby she could reward herself by buying the boots if she limited her visits to the casino to once a week, and her spending to $50. Conversely, if she overindulged, she would forfeit the right to purchase the boots for at least 4 months. The client was excited by this challenge and agreed to share it with her husband, whose knowledge of her agreement would be an additional motivating force. If she successfully completed the task, she would realize another incentive—the fact that she had consciously exercised self-control.

Rewarding oneself (self-reinforcement), as illustrated in this example, can increase one's motivation for completing a task. Rewards and incentives are particularly relevant when a change in behavior or cognition is associated with the choice of pain over pleasure, such as relinquishing one's free time to engage in activities that may be perceived as unattractive (e.g., studying, household chores). Possible rewards should be identified by assessing each client's unique situation and should be realistically within reach.

Rewards and Incentives for Children. Rewards can motivate and create incentives for children to

complete tasks, such as finishing homework assignments, minimizing rivalry with siblings, being respectful to teachers, raising a hand and waiting to be called upon in class, or doing household chores. In addition to negotiating tasks with children, social workers can establish complementary tasks with parents or other significant persons for the purpose of assisting children in carrying out their tasks or modifying problematic behavioral patterns that involve home and community behavior.

When you create incentives for children, it is important during the early stages of change to reward them immediately, as soon as they perform desired behaviors. Also, reward small changes. Otherwise, children tend to become discouraged and give up, believing they cannot meet the expected standards. Adults often naively assume that elaborate long-range rewards (e.g., get a bicycle in June, go on a field trip) are sufficient incentives. In reality, time does not hold the same meaning for young children as it does for adults. If it is now September, then getting a bicycle in June probably will not sustain motivation for the child. Even for older children, a smaller reward given soon after the behavior is a far more effective incentive.

In setting up tasks with accompanying rewards for children, follow these guidelines:

- Frame tasks so that what children are to do and when they are to do it are explicitly defined. Also, specify the time frame and the conditions under which the task is to be performed (e.g., every 2 hours, twice daily, each Wednesday, for the next 4 days).

- Designate what can be earned for exhibiting the specified target behaviors, and establish a method for tracking the behavior (e.g., each time the child responds appropriately by raising his or her hand in class before speaking, responding to requests clean his or her room). It is useful to construct this system of tracking methods and rewards in conjunction with the child.

- Invite children to choose the type of reward they wish to earn, because they will choose rewards that have maximal value as incentives.

- Establish rewards for specified periods of time (e.g., if the child raises his or her hand for 4 of the 5 days in a week's class, he or she will be able to read a story and earn points toward something the child values. Whenever possible, it is important to offer *relationship* rewards, rather than monetary or material items. Relationship rewards involve things such as going to the mall or spending time with friends or other significant individuals.

Providing a bonus for consistent achievements of tasks over an extended period of time is recommended. Other motivating factors that encourage task completion are consistent and positive feedback, or developing visual indicators that mark the child's progress on tasks.

Plan the Details of Carrying Out Tasks

This step is vital in assisting clients to prepare themselves for all of the actions inherent in a task. Most tasks consist of a series of actions to be carried out sequentially, and they may involve both cognitive and behavioral subtasks. For example, before carrying out an overt action, such as requesting repairs from a landlord or undergoing a medical examination, clients often benefit by preparing themselves psychologically. This effort may involve you reviewing with them potential benefits, addressing and resolving fears by realistically appraising the situation, reflecting on past successes, or focusing on clients' spirituality. By including cognitive strategies in this step, clients are better able to cope with their ambivalence or apprehension over implementing new actions.

Planning overt actions requires considering the real-life details of the desired behaviors. For example, Don and Jean in planning their weekly time together would need to consider their schedules, the topics they would discuss, the way they would express feelings, and their reactions when either one or both experienced tension during their conversations. If, for example, either of them reacted in the old familiar pattern—specifically, Jean not listening to Don, or Don dismissing Jean's opinion—they would be unlikely to follow through on later steps. Thus, the more detailed the plans, the greater the chance of success. Moreover, by discussing discrete actions with them, the social worker could elicit cues about misgivings, fears, or lack of skill, each of which must be addressed if Don and Jean are to complete their tasks successfully.

The Social Worker's Role in Task Planning. Sometimes task planning may involve tasks to be carried out by the social worker; however, these tasks are coordinated with the client's actions. For example, an unemployed and unskilled young woman may be unsure of her vocational interests. A task for her would be to take a battery of tests that assess her aptitudes and interests. The social worker would telephone testing sites to determine the most appropriate resource and convey the information to the client. The client would arrange to take the tests and then meet with the vocational counselor to interpret the results.

In planning the details of tasks, a social worker's tasks are developed when he or she has ready access to resources or information that will facilitate client work. If the client could benefit from eventually being able to carry out the task on his or her own, it will be useful for the client and the social worker to walk through the steps together. In some instances, social workers may accompany or arrange for someone else to accompany the client during the performance of a task. In a group context, a group or family member might also informally assist a client in planning and carrying out actions.

Conditions for Tasks. Planning the details of tasks also involves specifying the conditions under which each task will be carried out. For example, a sixth-grade student who constantly disturbs his peers, speaks without raising his hand, and irritates his teacher through boisterous teasing behavior may accept the following task: listen attentively when the teacher is speaking during the 1-hour math class and raise his hand three times to answer questions during that time. He agrees to carry out this task each day for the next 5 days. Although he exhibits the problematic behavior in other classes, the math class and time frames identified are the conditions in which the behavioral tasks are to occur. Why specify the conditions and time for implementing tasks in such detail? When these points are left vague, clients (and social workers)

tend to procrastinate, leaving little time to effectively implement the requisite actions. Also, focusing on behaviors in the math class further partializes the change effort for the sixth-grader. In determining a time frame, client input should be elicited regarding the amount of time clients feel is needed to accomplish a specific task.

In selecting and planning tasks pertaining to *ongoing* goals, you should observe an additional caution. Because progress on such goals is incremental, it is vital to begin with tasks that are within the clients' capacity to achieve. In the previous classroom situation, for example, a goal of having the student raise his hand for 5 straight days may be difficult to achieve. However, a goal of raising his hand in math class for 3 out of 5 days may, with positive feedback from the teacher, be more attainable. His chances of later completing tasks (5 out of 5 days) are greater if the child succeeds in implementing the initial task. Conversely, if he experiences failure on initial tasks, his confidence and courage may decline, making him reluctant to assume additional tasks. In this instance, a much more difficult task may be reducing boisterous behavior—in particular, if the behavior benefits the boy by drawing the attention of peers, which he values. It is thus preferable to have the first task be easy—for example, raising his hand before speaking in class.

Analyze and Resolve Obstacles

Based on recognition of the inevitability of barriers that impede change, this step is aimed at acknowledging and addressing these forces. When implementing this step, you and the client deliberately anticipate and analyze obstacles that have the potential to influence task accomplishment. In the classroom situation previously described, for example, it would be useful to explore potential obstacles to attentive listening such as social, physical, and psychological barriers.

With simple tasks, such as telephoning to inquire about available jobs, obstacles are generally minor and can be readily identified by asking clients what difficulties, if any, they expect to encounter. A caveat should be observed, however: What is a simple action for some people may prove difficult for others. Making a telephone call may be an overwhelming task depending on the client's level of confidence, cognitive and social ability, and resources for making the call. Fears or the lack of resources pose formidable barriers to accomplishing a task and require careful exploration so that they do not impede progress.

When tasks are complex, obstacles likewise tend to be complex and difficult to identify and resolve. Tasks that involve changes in patterns of interpersonal relationships tend to be multifaceted, encompassing subsidiary but prerequisite intrapersonal tasks as well as a mastery of certain interpersonal skills. Successfully resisting the impulse to engage in boisterous behavior by the sixth-grade student in the classroom may, for example, involve powerful fears about not being popular, appearing to be a "wimp" in front of peers, or being rejected by a certain group that he considered to be important. Change involves not only mastering new behaviors, but also changing patterns of relating to people. Both of these steps require supplanting old beliefs, behaviors, and interpersonal and intrapersonal skills with new ones.

Identifying Potential Barriers and Obstacles.

Clients vary in their capacity to anticipate obstacles. Overlooking or underestimating the impact of barriers can delay or cause needless difficulties in the accomplishment of tasks and lead to outright failure. With continuous engagement and collaboration, however, you elicit from clients (and from group and family members) possible obstacles to achieving their planned course of action. You can safeguard clients' self-efficacy by explaining that obstacles are common and by sharing observations that you have regarding potential obstacles.

Psychological barriers to accomplishing tasks are often encountered regardless of the nature of the target problem. Applying for a job, changing classroom behavior, talking to a judge, and expressing intimate feelings are all tasks that are charged with strong emotions, and therefore seem threatening to some people. A prerequisite to the successful accomplishment of a task, therefore, may be a subsidiary task of neutralizing emotions. This can be accomplished (often in a brief amount of time) by eliciting and clarifying the client's

apprehension, rationally analyzing it, and modeling and rehearsing the behavior required to implement the task successfully. Any time and effort that are invested in the exploration of obstacles are likely to pay dividends in the form of clients achieving a higher rate of success in accomplishing tasks. Consider the economy involved in this process, as failure to complete tasks further extends the time required for successful problem solving.

Assessing Clients' Readiness to Begin Tasks.

You should be alert to nonverbal behaviors as potential obstacles or as possible indicators of clients' apprehension about undertaking a task. When you detect such reactions, you should further explore the presence of this undisclosed barrier. Assessing clients' readiness to engage in mutually negotiated tasks is also vital to successful task implementation. Their readiness, however, should not be confused with feeling comfortable; it is neither realistic nor desirable to expect clients to feel altogether comfortable with the task. A certain amount of tension and anxiety is to be expected. Tension and anxiety nonetheless can act to positively motivate clients to risk the new behavior embodied in the task. Inordinate anxiety, by contrast, may be a major deterrent to undertaking a task or may impair a client's effectiveness upon attempting that task. Obviously, when clients report that they did not carry out a task, you should consider the possibility that the task was developed prematurely and that unforeseen barriers to its completion emerged. Another possible explanation for failure to complete tasks is that the client was inadequately prepared or not committed to the task. These and other factors are discussed later in this chapter.

Clients' readiness for implementing tasks can be gauged by asking them to rate their readiness on a scale from 1 to 10, where 1 represents a lack of readiness and 10 indicates that the client is ready to go. When clients rate their readiness on the low end of this scale, their reticence must be explored. To ease any lingering concerns, you can assure them that a certain amount of apprehension is natural and that relief may come as a by-product of successful implementation of the task. You can provide support by expressing confidence in the client's ability to successfully implement the task and by conveying an expectation that the planned actions will be carried out.

An explanation and support are important especially when clients are hesitant to the point of postponing taking actions. Clearly, when you have reached the point of developing and planning for tasks, hesitations on the part of clients can be frustrating. But exploring the reasons for a low rating on the readiness scale will often uncover vital information concerning potential obstacles that should be addressed, including reservations about completing the task.

Addressing Barriers and Obstacles. After identifying obstacles to task implementation, you must next assist the client in overcoming them. The barriers encountered most frequently include *deficiencies in social skills* and *misconceptions and irrational fears* associated with performing tasks. The former is a formidable barrier that must be overcome, because the client may lack the skill and experience to know how to carry out a task. Some clients (especially children) are afraid of bungling a task and appearing ridiculous. Undertaking the task thus is perceived as placing the client's self-efficacy in jeopardy. Modeling and behavioral rehearsal in sessions may encourage and teach the skills necessary to carry out interpersonal tasks.

Cognitions—specifically, misconceptions and irrational beliefs about self, stereotypic perceptions of others, and intense apprehensions based on distorted consequences of actions—represent major obstacles to task completion. Cognitive theorists present a compelling case to the effect that the quality and intensity of emotions experienced in a given situation are largely determined by the perceptions and attributions of meaning associated with that situation. Inordinate fear and apprehension, for example, signal that something is amiss in the client's patterns of thought. Your task is to elicit the problematic emotions, to identify their cognitive sources, and to assist clients in aligning their thoughts and feelings with reality. Removing this barrier usually enables clients to move several points higher on the readiness scale.

Rehearse or Practice Behaviors Involved in Tasks

Certain tasks involve skills that clients lack or behaviors with which they have had little or no experience. Step 4 of the TIS is aimed at assisting clients to gain the experience and mastery in performing behaviors essential to task accomplishment. Successful experience, even in simulated situations, fosters belief that the individual has the ability to carry out a task effectively. Having an expectation of success is vital, as Bandura (1977) has indicated: "The strength of people's convictions in their own effectiveness is likely to affect whether they will even try to cope with given situations" (p. 193). Bandura builds a strong case, documented by research evidence, that the degree of positive expectation that clients have in their ability to perform tasks effectively determines how much effort they will expend in attempting tasks and how long they will persist in the face of obstacles or aversive circumstances. It follows that a major goal of the helping process is to enhance clients' sense of self-efficacy, which is accrued through successful task completion.

Research evidence cited by Bandura (1977, p. 195) indicates that, once established, self-efficacy and skills tend to be transferred by clients to other situations that they had previously avoided. According to Bandura, people receive information about self-efficacy from four sources: (1) performance accomplishments, (2) vicarious experience, (3) verbal persuasion, and (4) emotional arousal. Of these four sources, performance accomplishment is especially influential because it is based on personal mastery experience.

Major methods of increasing self-efficacy through performance accomplishment include assisting clients to master essential behaviors through modeling, behavior rehearsal, and guided practice, all of which we discuss at length later in this chapter. An example of performance accomplishment would be assisting family members to master certain communication skills during actual sessions. Vicarious experiences gained by observing others demonstrate target behaviors or perform threatening activities without experiencing adverse consequences can also generate confidence and expectations in clients. Efficacy expectations based on observing the social worker or others model desired behaviors or receiving reassurance from the social worker or others, however, are clearly not as powerful as the sense to self-efficacy that results from the client successfully completing a task. Verbal persuasion raises outcome expectations rather than enhancing self-efficacy per se. Information about one's capabilities based on perceptions and assumptions that one can also perform competently is quite persuasive and provides concrete evidence of self-efficacy.

The fourth source of information about self-efficacy, emotional arousal, is based on the fact that the perceived level of emotional arousal affects how people perform. Clients who are extremely anxious or fearful about performing a new behavior are unlikely to have sufficient confidence that they can perform the behavior competently. Interventions directed toward reducing anxiety or fear or toward persuading clients to *believe* they are not fearful or anxious are generally ineffective. Evidence cited by Bandura indicates that to be effective, reductions in emotional arousal must be genuine and not based on deceptive feedback aimed at assuring clients they are not anxious when, in fact, they are anxious. Emotional arousal obviously is an undependable source of self-efficacy because it is not related to actual evidence of capability. Indeed, perceived self-competence tends to reduce emotional arousal rather than the converse.

Increasing Self-Efficacy through Behavioral Rehearsal, Modeling, and Role-Play. Having defined the sources of information about self-efficacy, we return to the topic of behavioral rehearsal. As employed in actual sessions, *behavioral rehearsal* assists clients to practice new coping patterns under the guidance of the social worker. Indications for using this technique include situations that clients feel inadequately prepared to confront a situation. Behavioral rehearsal is also indicated when clients are uneasy or appear overwhelmed by the prospects of carrying out a given task. This technique is an effective way of assisting clients to develop the requisite skills and diminish the threat posed by the action. Such tasks usually involve interacting with significant other people with whom strain already exists or is expected to develop as a result of the planned actions.

Role-playing is the most common mode of behavioral rehearsal. Before engaging clients in rehearsal of desired behaviors, however, social workers can use role-playing to have clients demonstrate their initial levels of skills, thereby enabling social workers to model skills that build on clients' existing skills. Social workers can *model* behavior that clients are expected to perform before actually having them rehearse the behavior. This approach is particularly effective when the behavior is unfamiliar to the client, or when the client is anxious or concerned about how others will perceive his or her behavior. Modeling through role-play has been amply documented to be an effective means of enabling clients to learn vicariously new modes of behavior and of reducing anxieties or other concerns.

When modeling a particular behavior, ask the client to play the role of the *other* person involved in the real-life difficulty and, in doing so, simulate as accurately as possible the anticipated behavior to be encountered in the actual situation. In the following case example, the social worker successfully assisted a client to overcome perceived obstacles using role-play.

CASE EXAMPLE

The client had lost his job because the chicken processing plant in the small town where he lived relocated its operations out of state. Although he had contact with potential employers, he was anxious about approaching them regarding a job. Both his father and his grandfather had worked at the chicken processing plant, so when he applied to work there after high school, few questions was asked. Now, however, there were issues in his past that the client felt might deter a potential employer from hiring him.

To address his concerns, the social worker acted out the role of the client, with the client assuming the role of a potential employer. In this role, the client was able to pose the questions that he feared he might be asked, as well as explore his qualifications for potential jobs. The role-playing enabled the social worker to model appropriate behavioral responses to questions that might otherwise overwhelm the client. After the role-playing, they discussed what happened, focusing on the client's behavioral and cognitive reactions. The social worker also found it beneficial to explain her rationale for particular responses and to share difficulties she experienced with particular questions. In assuming the role of the client in an interaction with a potential employer, the social worker gained new insights and a fuller appreciation of the difficulties the client expected to encounter.

After completing a modeling exercise, the client and the social worker moved to the next step. They reversed roles, so that the client was able to rehearse the actual target behavior. When the social worker assumed the role of a potential employer, she attempted to approximate the anticipated behavior of an employer, including tone of voice, facial expressions, gestures, choice of words, and provocative behavior as modeled earlier by the client. The client's responses to the simulated behavior provided an opportunity for the social worker to make corrective suggestions, and gave the social worker a chance to provide reinforcement and encouragement.

Role-playing and behavioral rehearsal are techniques that can increase a client's capacity to tackle situations in real life. Indeed, potential barriers or obstacles can best be assessed and resolved by observing behavior rehearsal and role-play. Most importantly, clients' confidence to carry out tasks is enhanced by this technique.

Behavioral rehearsal need not be confined to sessions. It is often productive to encourage clients to continue rehearsing target behaviors outside the interviews by pretending to be involved in real-life encounters. Also, modeling and behavioral rehearsal need not be restricted to social workers and individual clients. Members of a group or family session may be able to model effective and realistic coping for another group member. Indeed, a rule of thumb in conducting group role-playing sessions is to tap into group resources for coping models whenever possible, which enhances the help-giving role of group members.

If modeling proves ineffective, an interim strategy could focus on implementing *coping efforts* rather than achieving *mastery*. Coping emphasizes the struggles that a person might expect to experience in performing the behavior or activity. Emphasizing coping lessens anxiety and, hence, the threat of having to perform without making a mistake.

Modeling need not be limited to overt behaviors. Many clients will benefit from modeling of covert behaviors that seek to overcome cognitive barriers to task accomplishment. Covert modeling involves expressing aloud thoughts and feelings associated with manifest difficulties and restructuring thoughts in a way that is more productive for dealing with or coping with problems. As with modeling of overt behavior, covert modeling could emphasize coping rather than mastery. As clients mobilize the efficacy, energy, and courage gained through behavioral rehearsal, they prepare themselves to confront problematic situations directly with a more realistic perspective.

Guided Practice. Closely related to behavioral rehearsal, *guided practice* is another technique to aid performance accomplishment. It differs from behavioral rehearsal in that it consists of in vivo rather than simulated behavior. Using guided practice as a mode of intervention, you assist clients to gain mastery of target behaviors by coaching them as they actually engage in the target behaviors. For example, in family sessions, you can observe interactions and subsequently assist family members to master problem-solving or conflict resolution skills. As you observe problematic behavior firsthand, you can provide immediate feedback. Such on-the-spot interventions enable you to clarify what is occurring as well as coach clients in engaging in more productive behavior.

Summarize the Task Plan

Implementation of this final step of the TIS involves reviewing the various actions that clients must engage in to accomplish a task. This step, which takes place in the concluding segment of an individual, family, or group session, enables clients to leave the session with a clear understanding of what they are to do, in what sequence, and under what conditions. To enable clients to gain maximum benefit from this step, we recommend that you ask them to review the details of their plan for implementing the task, including strategies for dealing with potential obstacles. By eliciting clients' descriptions of their plans, you can assess whether certain aspects of the plan need to be clarified. It is often useful to begin by describing your own plans to complete the social worker's tasks in a specified time frame: "I have agreed to contact the public health nurse by our meeting next week." Follow this description with a request for a review of client plans: "What are your plans for talking to a neighbor about child care by our next session?"

Many clients find it beneficial to have a written list of agreed-upon tasks. Some clients prefer to write their own lists. In other cases, you can write the assigned tasks down, give the client a copy, and keep a copy for the case record.

After summarizing the plan for task implementation, it is appropriate to terminate the session. An effective way of closing the session is to express support for clients' plans and an expectation that they will implement the assigned tasks. We recommend that you devote the beginning of the next session to task review and progress.

Maintaining Focus and Continuity

The strength of the task-centered system lies in its focus on change through task accomplishment and its systematic format that promotes continuity of change efforts. Individual sessions are sharply focused, and continuity is maintained from one session to the next. Each session begins with a review of clients' experiences in implementing tasks that were agreed upon during the previous session. The task form introduced in Chapter 12 (Figure 12-2 on page 335) enables both social worker and client to monitor progress. Social workers in the case examples included in this section report that the task form is not merely a useful guide for task development, but also a helpful tool for reviewing the status of tasks at the beginning of each session. Copies of this form may be given to clients to help them maintain focus on activities to be implemented between sessions and to serve as a visual reminder that they are making progress.

There are two major objectives (and benefits) when discussing clients' experiences in implementing tasks. First, both clients and social workers can identify ways in which clients can further improve their effectiveness in performing newly developed behaviors. This discussion may enhance clients' comfort in coping with problematic situations and suggest additional activities in the session to refine their skills. Second, social workers can explore clients' perceptions of the tasks' effects on others and clients' feelings as they implemented the tasks. This discussion provides an opportunity to identify additional work to be done and prepares the ground for mutually planning future tasks.

In reviewing task accomplishments, it is critical to elicit the details about the conditions, actions, or behaviors that assisted clients in achieving a task. Even when tasks have been only partially completed, it is important to connect the results achieved to clients' efforts. Highlighting that clients have more control than they had previously realized is a powerful force for increasing their sense of self-efficacy.

After completing a review of task implementation, social workers and clients should mutually plan additional tasks that will enable clients to make more progress toward their final goals. In addition to following the steps previously delineated for defining tasks, it is important in working toward accomplishment of *ongoing goals* to plan tasks that involve incremental changes and build on one another. Planning tasks that are graded in difficulty improves clients' chances of success and tends to increase their motivation to exert greater efforts in the change process. To illustrate the gradual progression in developing tasks, recall the client who was seeking employment after the plant closure. His initial task involved contacting potential employers to find out about available jobs. After talking with potential employers by phone, as a next step he would complete applications at those employers where jobs were available. An additional next step may involve the client following up by phone to determine the status of his applications.

Failure to Complete Tasks

In actual practice, progress may not be as smooth as the preceding example implies. Maintaining focus and continuity can become derailed when tasks are not completed. Clients may fail to carry out tasks for a variety of reasons, some of which are summarized in Figure 13-2. In the figure, the reasons for low task performance are classified into two categories: reasons related to specific tasks and reasons related to the target problem.

Performance Problems Related to the Task

Occasionally, unforeseen circumstances or unanticipated obstacles such as the unavailability of others necessary to complete the task or a crisis may preclude task accomplishment between sessions, necessitating carrying them over to the next week. In other cases, the failure to complete tasks may stem from a lack of commitment, the emergence of more pressing problems, negative reactions to the practitioner or to the group, vague or unspecified tasks, or inadequate preparation. In any event, it is vital to explore the reasons for the failure, and to attempt to resolve factors that have blocked implementation. The caveat, of course, is that both the social worker and the client agree that the specified task remains valid. If the task is not valid, it is important to shift the focus to more relevant tasks.

Occurrence of a Crisis. Although you should be flexible in shifting focus, it is advisable to avoid allowing crises to dominate change efforts. For those clients who live from crisis to crisis, it is beneficial for them in the larger scheme of their lives to maintain focus on tasks through to completion. Certain situations may dictate taking brief detours, of course, especially when the failure to complete tasks in the focal situation is related to overriding problems a client has not yet revealed. Some clients disclose only relatively minor difficulties during initial interviews and defer discussing more thorny problems until they feel more comfortable with the social worker. Hence, the initial tasks may not be valid in that they do not relate to the clients' paramount concerns. In such cases, it is appropriate to shift the focus to more burdensome difficulties and

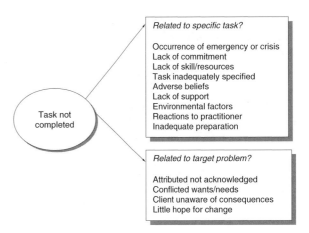

Figure 13-2 Reasons For Low Task Performance

to formulate new goals and tasks accordingly. It is important, however, to assess whether the shift in focus is not reinforcing a pattern of avoidance.

Lack of Commitment. Clients may sometimes fail to complete tasks because of a lack of commitment. Reid (1977, 1997a; 2000) has documented this factor as a statistically significant predictor of task progress on a consistent basis. A lack of commitment should not be confused with a lack of readiness. In the former case, the willingness to change is absent. In the latter case, clients possess the willingness but are blocked from acting by other barriers.

One frequent cause of a lack of commitment to undertake interpersonal tasks is a covert unwillingness to own one's part of a problem. For example, a spouse or parent may pay lip service to carrying out a specific task but subsequently make excuses for not doing so. Inwardly, unwilling clients often blame others for their difficulties and passively wait for those parties to initiate corrective actions. In such instances, it is important to explore further the interactions between clients and others and to clarify which part of the difficulty is owned by each individual. The technique of confrontation may also be employed to help clients recognize their responsibility for maintaining the undesirable status quo when they dawdle and wait for others to change. If clients exhibit a continued hesitancy to work on tasks, it is appropriate to explore their willingness to change.

A lack of commitment to carry out specific tasks is frequently a dynamic in practice with involuntary clients. Their reactions may also reflect the fact that their problem is attributed, rather than acknowledged (e.g., the judge believes that I have a drinking problem). In other instances, clients may not fully appreciate the consequences of failing to address the requirements of a mandated problem. In these instances, it is the social worker's responsibility to engage such clients by acknowledging and respecting their reactions, and by creating an incentive for change. Persistent failure to carry out tasks, however, belies expressed intentions; inaction certainly speaks louder than words, and the benefits of continuing to work with the client should be carefully weighed.

Of course, what may initially appear to be clients' lack of commitment may actually reflect their focus on other, more pressing concerns. Clients with multiple problems and limited coping skills may be beset between sessions with difficulties that supersede the target problem. Such situations require judicious handling, because both social worker and client face a difficult decision. On the one hand, it is important to be flexible and to shift focus when emerging problems demand immediate attention. On the other hand, some clients perpetually live in a crisis state. They should be made aware of the consequences of making minimal progress with any one of the problems that they experience when the slow progress results from constantly shifting from one issue to another.

Unspecified or Vaguely Specified Tasks. Frequently clients fail to complete tasks because those tasks are vague or inadequately specified— that is, the client did not understand what to do. In other cases, failure may result from clients' adverse beliefs. For example, some parents hesitate to utilize reward systems, believing that parents should not barter with children (Rooney, 1992, p. 241). In practice with families or couples, individual members may renege on their commitments to carry out tasks because each party does not trust the other members to carry out their part of the bargain. Further,

individuals may gather "evidence" that others are uncommitted to the agreed-upon task, in an effort to justify their own noncompletion of tasks. Adequate preparation for an initial task with couples thus entails exploration of the trust issue and establishment of a contract stating that each partner will strictly monitor his or her own task performance regardless of whether the other person does or does not.

Lack of Support. When a client's problems involve the family system—and especially when the behaviors of other members impose on identified problems—relevant members of the family should be included in the sessions. Although sometimes families will accommodate change in individual members, at other times family dynamics can conspire to defeat efforts to change or modify behavior, with the family opting instead to maintain a sense of equilibrium. Other families exhibit pervasive interactional patterns that make it extremely difficult for members to change without great cost unless adjustments are made in the entire system. Although involving all family members in such situations is difficult, their participation is essential in sessions to assess individual needs and to garner their support for the individual's goal and task planning.

Stage of group development is a factor that plays a role when the social worker is assisting groups to assume tasks. Group members have difficulty accomplishing significant change-oriented tasks in the first two stages of group development. In these stages, members generally test out the social worker, other group members, and the group itself, while simultaneously attempting to find their own positions. Thus, they sometimes have little psychic energy or commitment to accomplish individual or group tasks. For this reason, tasks should be kept simple, and accomplishing them should not require an inordinate investment of effort by members. For instance, requiring a newly formed group of delinquent adolescents in a correctional facility to change their antagonistic behavior toward staff or peers before they are "emotionally committed" to the purposes of the group is doomed to failure. Conversely, asking members to complete small tasks during the week so that the group might participate in an attractive activity may be more appealing.

Negative Reactions to the Social Worker. Negative reactions to the social worker may also block task accomplishment. Such reactions often result when you arbitrarily assign tasks, ignoring the collaborative nature of the client–social worker relationship. Assigning tasks tends to activate negative feelings in clients akin to those experienced toward a parent or another authority figure.

Negative reaction to a social worker who has failed to complete a task on behalf of the client is another factor that may block task accomplishment. Progress is also impeded when the social worker neglects to review the client's experience in implementing a task, is unorganized or appears unprepared for the session, or changes the focus to other topics before actually seeing previous efforts through to completion. Such shifts disrupt the continuity of change efforts and foster "drift," which dilutes and prolongs the helping process. Clients may also have strong reactions to both verbal and nonverbal cues sent by the social worker, particularly if they perceive a lack of empathy, attentiveness, or positive regard on the practitioner's part.

Inadequate Preparation. A final factor sometimes involved in failures either to attempt or to implement tasks is inadequate preparation. A practitioner may overestimate the skills of clients or may not devote sufficient time and effort to the task implementation sequence. Actually, it is better for clients not to attempt tasks than to attempt them and fail because they are not adequately prepared. In the former instance, the impact on self-confidence is usually minimal, and additional efforts can be made to prepare a client more adequately. Failure, by contrast, may undermine clients' confidence in the helping process.

Even when preparation has been adequate, successful outcomes of task efforts are not guaranteed. Unanticipated reactions of others, ineffectual task performance, panic reactions, inappropriate task selection based on inaccurate assessment, and adverse circumstances may all block goal attainment.

To avoid or minimize undue discouragement of clients when results are negative, you should interpret such results not as failures but as indications of the need for additional information and task planning. Indeed, negative results sometimes serve a constructive purpose by further elucidating the dynamics underlying problems, thereby enabling clients and social workers to sharpen their assessment, goals, and tasks.

Performance Problems Related to the Target Problem

Issues related to low task performance with regard to the target problem can occur when the problem is attributed to, rather than acknowledged by, the client. This situation frequently occurs when clients are mandated (involuntary) or coerced (nonvoluntary) to seek help. Furthermore, if goals and tasks have already been determined by an outside authority, involuntary or nonvoluntary clients may be reluctant to seek help for a problem that they have not acknowledged: "I don't have a drug problem. Sometimes I do a little meth [methamphetamine] with my buddies, but that don't mean that I'm a drug head."

In other instances, failure to perform a required task may stem from the client's lack of understanding about the consequences of, for example, completing a chemical dependency treatment program and providing clean urinalysis tests (UAs) so as to return to work. In some cases, clients may have coped with a problem for so long, and seen their own efforts to resolve the issue fail so many times, that they lack hope. Clients may then agree to undertake certain tasks without having any confidence that they have the capacity to alter their situation (e.g., "I tried to break away from the gang, but they kept coming at me"). Any of these circumstances will require concerted effort on the social worker's part to assist clients to gain the momentum to move forward.

Monitoring and Evaluating Progress

One way of maintaining focus and continuity is to regularly evaluate progress made toward goal attainment. Although we discussed this process in

Chapter 12, here we add the following objectives served by systematically monitoring progress:

1. By eliciting clients' views of their progress or by comparing their latest rates of the target behavior with the baseline, you maintain focus on goals and enhance the continuity of change efforts.

2. Clients gain perspective in determining where they stand in relationship not only to their ultimate goals but also to their pretreatment level of functioning. Discerning incremental progress toward goals tends to sustain motivation and to enhance confidence in the helping process and in the social worker.

3. Eliciting clients' feelings and views regarding their progress enables social workers to detect and to work through feelings of disappointment and discouragement that may impede future progress and lead to premature termination.

4. Social workers can evaluate the efficacy of their interventions and change strategies. If a given approach fails to yield positive results within a reasonable period of time, more of the same is unlikely to produce different results. We recommend you apply the maxim "If what you're doing isn't working, try something different."

5. Indications of marked progress toward goal attainment alert social workers to possible readiness by clients to shift the focus to another goal or to consider planning for termination if all goals have been achieved.

Overall, the methods for assessing and evaluating progress should be consistent with the agreement negotiated in the contracting process. Progress toward goals should be monitored every two to three sessions at a minimum.

CRISIS INTERVENTION

Crisis intervention (CI) is the second general intervention strategy or modality discussed in this book. It shares much in common with, and is considered to be complementary to, the task-centered model. Crisis intervention has the following characteristics:

1. It is time limited.
2. It focuses on problems of living.
3. It is oriented to the here and now.
4. It requires a high level of activity by the practitioner.
5. It employs tasks as a primary tactic of change efforts.
6. It is an eclectic framework that can accommodate various practice theories and interventions.

Because crisis intervention addresses urgent situations precipitated by stressful or traumatic events, maturational crises, and acute transitional situations, its potential applications are somewhat more limited than those of the task-centered model. Intervention methods may also involve cognitive restructuring strategies.

Implications for Diverse Groups

Lum (2004) asserts that crisis intervention as a generalist practice approach has "universal application to people of color" (p. 272). This assertion is based on the fact that people of color "often experience personal and environmental crisis" and in many instances have "exhausted community and family resources" prior to seeking professional help (p. 273). In some instances, patterns of help-seeking behavior and historically based anxieties about helping professionals will mean that problems have reached a chronic state by the time of the initial contact. For this and other reasons, Potocky-Tripodi (2002) suggests that while crisis intervention strategies with immigrants and refugees are appropriate, ideally they should be implemented as preventive measures prior to the resettlement stage. Congress (2002) likewise identifies common precipitants of crisis among immigrants and refugees—namely, intergenerational conflicts, changes in roles, unemployment, and interactions with formal institutions. The Culturalgram (Congress, 2002) is an assessment tool that may be used to identify areas for intervention with such clients.

Ligon (1997) presents a case study of a young adult African American female in which cultural and ecological approaches were integrated and empowerment was included as predominant strategies used in resolving her crisis. Ligon's approach has merit with other populations of color, immigrants, refugees, and individuals with serious health or mental health concerns (Potocky-Tripodi, 2002; Lum, 2004; Poindexter, 1997). Poindexter (1997) makes the point that for HIV-infected individuals, the experience may involve a series of crises. Learning of the disease is a precipitating event; yet as the condition progresses, multiple crises—social, situational, and developmental—can occur simultaneously. Poindexter's work, along with that of Ell (1995) and Potocky-Tripodi (2002), is significant in that it helps us to move beyond certain assumptions about the episodic nature and to understand the evolving stages of certain crisis situations.

Definition and Stages of Crisis

James and Gilliland define a *crisis* as "a perception of an event or situation as an intolerable difficulty, that exceeds the resources or coping mechanism of the person" Prolonged, crisis-related stress without relief has the potential to severely affect cognitive, behavioral, and physical functioning.

A *crisis reaction* may be described as any event or situation that upsets "normal psychic balance" (Lum, 2004, p. 272) to the extent that the individual's sense of equilibrium is severely challenged. Crisis Intervention theory posits that people's reactions to crises typically go through several stages, although theorists differ as to whether three or four stages are involved. Our description involves a synthesis of stages identified by various authors (Okun, 2002; James & Gilliland, 2001; Caplan, 1964).

Stage 1: The initial rise in tension is accompanied by shock and perhaps even denial of the crisis-provoking event.

Stage 2: To reduce the tension, the individual resorts to his or her usual emergency problem-solving skills. When they fail to alleviate the tension, heightened tension ensues.

Stage 3: The individual experiences tension so severe that the person feels confused, overwhelmed, helpless, angry, or perhaps acutely depressed. The length of this phase varies according to the nature of the hazardous event, the strengths and coping capacities of the person, and the degree of responsiveness from social support systems.

Patterns associated with these stages may be characterized as the crisis event, disorganization, recovery, and reorganization (Roberts, 1990; Parad & Parad, 1990; Lum, 2004). As people move from stage 2 to stage 3, they resort to different coping tactics, the outcomes of which depend on whether these tactics are adaptive or maladaptive. If the tactics are maladaptive, tension may continue to escalate and the person may suffer a mental breakdown or, in extreme instances, attempt suicide. If the efforts are adaptive, the person will regain equilibrium and perhaps achieve a higher level of functioning.

Much of the literature has tended to focus on the adverse effects of crises on people. Not surprisingly, then, interventions and strategies, while incorporating strengths and social support, have sought to restore functioning to the pre-crisis level. Some theorists and researchers suggest that negative events may actually promote growth in the aftermath of a crisis (Caplan, 1964; McMillen & Fischer, 1998; McMillen, Zuravin, & Rideout, 1995; McMillen, Smith, & Fischer, 1997; Joseph, Williams, & Yule, 1993). Building on prior research as well as the notion of benefit advanced by Caplan, McMillen and Fisher (1998) explored the perceived harm and perceived benefits with individuals who had experienced a negative event. They found that people did report some benefits from negative events in the form of positive life changes. Among the benefits perceived by the study subjects were self-efficacy, spirituality, faith in people, compassion, and an increase in community closeness. According to McMillen and Fisher, the perceived benefit varied in relationship to the perceived harm, symptoms triggered by the event or situation, and the type of support or assistance received.

This study's results are significant for two reasons, according to McMillen and Fisher:

- The deficit approach to psychosocial consequences appears to influence how human services professionals view their clients and how clients view their experience. Specifically, practitioners may tend to focus on the trauma alone, whereas clients may view the situation or event through multiple lenses.

- In understanding the positive benefits that accrue from crises, practitioners become able to construct interventions that strengthen these factors and increase successful outcomes.

These findings also emphasize aspects of adaptation, cognition, and psychosocial transitions as key elements in crisis intervention. Likewise, they point to a need for practitioners to incorporate client perceptions of benefit into their assessment of the post-crisis experience and client level of functioning.

Crisis Events and Situations

Hazardous or traumatic events or situations can be experienced as a threat, challenge, or loss. A threat (e.g., the possibility of losing employment or a spouse, relocation, disasters, removal of a child from the home by authorities, the potential for harm or valued status) may involve anticipated loss of an individual's sense of integrity or autonomy. A threat thus engenders high anxiety and apprehension about a possible dreaded event—for example, revealing one's sexual orientation to family, friends, or colleagues.

Threats may be experienced at the emotional or cognitive level, and may be grounded in reality. For example, the threats to gay and lesbian individuals in the social environment in the form of hate crimes, brutal beatings, and even death are very real. Intense anxiety and the perception of threats and potential harm are also pervasive in poor minority communities with respect to violence, poverty-related stressors in daily life, neighborhood conditions and resources, and especially encounters with the police. For these communities, crisis dynamics are not closely associated with *the big event*; instead, they are woven into the fabric of everyday life. Ultimately, these factors undermine the individual's sense of self and organization and produce a steady state of disequilibrium. Ell (1995) challenges the assumption that crisis is necessarily time-limited as well the notion of homeostasis—specifically, the ability to achieve equilibrium. According to Ell, these assumptions are not valid for individuals, and perhaps entire communities, that experience chronic and constant stress.

A crisis may also encompass challenges and loss. A challenge may produce anxiety over the possibility of failure in the immediate future—for example, not performing adequately in an area that is perceived as being crucial to one's future. Of course, a challenge may also invoke the motivation to succeed and hope of success. Loss, by contrast, involves an acute sense of deprivation resulting from an event that has already occurred, such as a death, divorce, or leaving one's homeland. It produces a depressed affect associated with the grieving process. Refugees, immigrants, and migrants may simultaneously experience transitional loss, hazards, and threats associated with leaving their homeland, jobs, family, friends, and familiar culture. An additional challenge for them is to become familiar with and (to the extent considered desirable) acculturated to the norms, values, and language of another country. Perceived and real threats may emanate from such challenges as finding a job and interacting with a social environment that often seems both welcoming and hostile.

Crisis can also be characterized by a significant, prolonged event or situation. War is one example. Emotional and psychosocial crisis resulting from the traumatic experience of combat military personnel is well documented in the literature on post-traumatic stress disorder (PTSD). PTSD was classified as a valid mental health disorder in *Diagnostic Manual of Mental Disorders* (DSM-III) in 1980. Traumatic stress-related symptoms may also be observed in human services staff and members of other disciplines, especially those who work in highly stressful, emotionally charged situations (i.e., child sexual abuse, family violence, crisis intervention or critical response teams, hostage negotiators). Schwartz and Berry (1994) have added to the knowledge base for PTSD by focusing on the traumatic response in children and adolescents. Their work integrates neurodevelopmental and psychosocial aspects of trauma, and makes a distinction between the adaptations of adults and those of children.

Over the past two decades, traumatic events have dominated the national and international landscape. Events such as the bombing of the federal office building in Oklahoma City; the September 11, 2001, terrorist attacks on the World Trade Center and the Pentagon; the student-led shootings at Columbine High School; the murders by the Washington, D.C.–area snipers; and more recently the Columbia space shuttle disaster profoundly affected the communities in which they occurred. However, these events may be characterized as involving a significant number of indirect victims because of the constant media coverage that exposed the rest of U.S. society to the trauma (Belkin, 1999). Traumatic experiences of this magnitude are relatively new for the U.S. public.

In the rest of the world, political conflicts embedded in everyday life, ongoing wars, and natural disasters often foster crisis situations and reactions. Examples include ever-present conflicts in the Middle East; political instability and flooding in Haiti; the humanitarian crisis in the Sudan; ongoing conflict between warlords in Somalia; and the December 2004 tsunami, a devastating natural disaster. In each of these circumstances, we might expect to find families and individuals who feel particularly vulnerable and experience anxieties; prolonged physical, emotional, and cognitive distress; and an overall sense of diminished coping capacity.

Crisis Responses

Depending on the nature of the crisis, multiple resources may be available to respond to the needs of individuals, families, and communities. For example, the American Red Cross is a national organization that provides emergency services as part of its mandate. Other services may be devoted entirely to crisis situations—for example, 24/7 assault, health, and mental hotlines; clinics; drop-in centers for homeless youth; and shelters for youth, battered women, and homeless people. Disaster relief and critical incident teams may become mobilized in the aftermath of catastrophic events such as natural disasters, plane or train accidents, school or workplace violence, chemical exposure, and other events that affect a large number of people or broad geographical area.

Critical response or critical incident teams are increasingly involved in workplaces, communities, and schools in instances where people experience trauma following a dramatic event. Following the violence at Columbine High School in Littleton, Colorado, intervention efforts were directed toward responding to the entire community; combined with intervention strategies targeting affected individuals and families. In this instance, the focus was on assisting people to mourn and grieve as well as "adjusting to an environment in which the deceased is missing" (Fast, 2003, p. 484). Social workers and members of other disciplines were immediately deployed after the September 11 attacks in an effort to reduce distress and restore equilibrium. Many of these professionals reported that the swift timing of the response was not necessarily an effective strategy. Indeed, the promptness of the response as a fundamental tenet of crisis work was not useful in this case. Many individuals and families were so traumatized by the September 11 catastrophe that the benefit of any intervention with them was diminished by a sense of denial and numbing similar to that encountered in combat situations.

Responses to a traumatic event, however, may vary based on such factors as age, gender, and cultural differences. Zeira, Astor, and Benbenishty (2003) examined school violence and found that perceived threats were more prominent among younger children. Their fear of violence also affected their school attendance. Crisis situations inevitably have a subjective element, because people's perceptions and coping capacities vary widely. What is severely stressful and overwhelming for one person or family may be stressful but manageable for others. Nevertheless, most people would agree that natural disaster, death of a loved one, disabling or life-threatening illness or injury, cultural dislocation, sexual assault, and other traumatic events usually pose a crisis to those involved. Although members of multiple disciplines play important roles in responding to crisis situations, social workers have traditionally had a leadership role in such circumstances. In addition, they have been responsible for advancing practice methods, theory, and skills and formulating strategies for responding to crises (Fast, 2003; Bell, 1995; Komar, 1994; Roberts, 1990; Parad & Parad, 1990; Lukton, 1982).

Tenets of Crisis Intervention Theory

Crisis intervention (CI) as a brief treatment model is designed to reduce stress, relieve symptoms, restore functioning, and prevent further deterioration within a limited time frame. The assessment in crisis intervention is rapid. In this respect, it differs from the process questions outlined in Chapter 8. Nevertheless, attention to emotional reactions, coping capacity, the conditions that prompted the occurrence of the crisis, and clients' perception of the situation, social supports, and strengths are relevant to the crisis assessment process. Assessment in the crisis situation, as outlined by James and James (2001), involves determining the following:

- The severity of the crisis
- The client's current emotional status and level of mobility/immobility
- Alternatives, coping mechanism, support systems, and other available resources
- The client's level of lethality—specifically, is the client a danger to self or others?

Gilliland and James (2001) cite the Triage Assessment System (TAF) developed by Meyer, Williams, Otten, and Schmidt (1991) as a "fast" and efficient way to assess and "obtain a real time estimate of what is occurring with a client" (pp. 40–42). This three-dimensional assessment scheme allows the professional to assess the client's affective, behavioral, and emotional functioning and the severity of the situation and to plan appropriate intervention strategies.

Basic to CI theory is the concept that when people are beset by a crisis, a potential exists for them to cope in ways that are either adaptive or maladaptive. Stress occurs when an individual or family experiences a situation that is beyond their capacity to handle. Prolonged stress may exceed the ability of the family or individual to effectively handle the stressors, such that the usual ways of coping are unlikely to work. According to CI theorists, most crisis situations are limited to a period of 4 to 8 weeks, during which time people achieve a degree of equilibrium, which may be equivalent to, lower than, or higher than the pre-crisis level of functioning. The amount of time required before a crisis is resolved depends on the stress; the individual's ego strengths, social supports, and resources; and the type of crisis (acute or chronic). Duration of sessions and time are also factors in determining the crisis response, in that interventions may range from a single-session, telephone intervention to an expanded intervention with groups, families, and entire communities (Fast, 2003; James & Gilliland, 2001; Gilbar, 1992; West, Mercer, & Altheimer, 1993). Departures from the traditional weekly 50-minute sessions are common, and some clients may even be seen daily during an acute crisis period.

Promptness of response is a major issue in crisis intervention. In this regard, assessing the nature of the client's problem, identifying priority concerns, and developing limited goals around those concerns are key elements of the model. CI theory emphasizes the importance of intervening immediately to assist clients who are overwhelmed by crises. Timely intervention is critical not only to prevent deterioration in functioning but also to reach people when their defenses are low and their receptiveness to therapeutic interventions is highest, as occurs during acute periods of crisis. An inherent assumption of CI theory is that crisis periods have a limited duration and people achieve a degree of equilibrium, for better or for worse, during this time. Consequently, immediate intervention aims to restore clients to their pre-crisis level of functioning or better.

Duration of Contact

Time limits (generally 6 to 8 weeks) and tasks are both utilized in CI. Some clients may require shorter or longer periods of treatment. Social workers and other professionals assume an active role and deliberately employ their authority and expertise to inspire hope and confidence in clients. The temporal focus of CI is on the here and now, and goals are limited to alleviating distress and enabling clients to regain equilibrium. No attempt is made to deal with either pre-crisis personality dysfunction or intrapsychic conflict, although attention to these symptoms may be required to satisfy two of Okun's (2002) categories.

Another aspect of CI involves delineating tasks that clients can perform to achieve a new state of equilibrium. Although crisis professionals are active and directive in defining tasks, clients are encouraged to participate to the extent that they are capable of doing so, because their active participation fosters autonomy. Obviously, clients' abilities to participate actively are limited during periods of severe emotional distress but may increase as the distress subsides.

After completion of the essential tasks, CI moves into the final major activity, anticipatory guidance. This activity, which has preventive implications, involves assisting clients to anticipate future crisis situations and to plan coping strategies that will prepare them to face future stresses.

Theoretical Framework

Parad (1965), Caplan (1964), and Golan (1981) were early and significant contributors to the crisis intervention literature, delineating the nature of crises, stages, and intervention strategies for crisis resolution. Lukton (1982) further developed practice theory and skills for social workers. Early crisis intervention theory focused on grief and loss reactions, maturational biopsychosocial crisis at various developmental stages, role transitions, or traumatic or accidental life events (Lindemann, 1944; 1956; Rapoport, 1967). Strategies tended to reflect this paradigm, so early tenets and theory were generally psychoanalytic in nature. Therefore, consideration for environmental and situational factors as contributors to crisis and crisis reactions were not as prominent as they are today (Gilliland & James, 1993).

In expanding the tenets of crisis intervention theory, Gilliland and James (1993) and Okun (2002) more broadly defined the context in which a crisis may occur and, in doing so, expanded the underlying theoretical framework of crisis work. According to Gilliland and James (1993, pp. 16–18), this expanded view is influenced by the factors summarized in Table 13-2.

In differentiating the kinds of crises, Okun (2002), has integrated a composite of theoretical frameworks. According to Okun, which as Lum (2004, p. 272) suggests, "helps to differentiate incidents and events more accurately." Okun's (2002, p. 245) six categories of crises are summarized as follows:

1. *Dispositional Crisis:* Occurs when an individual lacks the information needed to make a decision.

2. *Anticipated Life Transition:* Normative life and developmental events such as marriage, divorce, changing jobs or careers, entering into a different stage of life (e.g., midlife or aging).

3. *Traumatic Stress:* Situations that are imposed on an individual by circumstances or events out of his or her control, and that emotionally overwhelms the individual. Examples include unexpected death, sudden loss, rape, receiving health status information, and illness.

4. *Maturational/Developmental Crisis:* Crucial transitions and points in the lifespan process that mark significant developmental changes, such as midlife crisis, leaving home as a young adult, adolescent identity, and independence.

5. *Psychopathological Crisis:* An emotional crisis that is precipitated by a preexisting psychopathology and emerges during a time of distress because of situational or environmental factors related to transitions, trauma, or developmental age.

6. *Psychiatric Emergency:* Occurs when an individual's functioning becomes severely impaired such that he or she is incapable of performing daily living functions, poses a danger to self and others, or sometimes both.

Understanding the nature of the crisis, the perception of threat, the harm to or vulnerability of

Table 13-2 Expanded crisis theory

THEORY	ASSUMPTIONS
Psychoanalytic	The experience of disequilibrium for an individual in a crisis state can be understood by examining unconscious thought patterns and prior emotional experiences, and by assisting clients to "gain insight into the dynamics and causes of their problems."
Systems	Fundamental concepts of systems theory—for example, the interaction and interdependence between individuals and the environment, and "between people and events"—are used to explore interpersonal relationships (e.g., in the family system) as well as social and environmental forces that give rise to a crisis situation or event.
Adaptational	A crisis is stressful and disruptive. It can adversely affect biological, psychological, and social functioning, and it may produce disturbed emotions, impaired functioning, and maladaptive behaviors. This theory is based on the "premise that a person's crisis will recede when maladaptive coping behaviors are changed to adaptive behaviors, therefore moving to a more positive mode of functioning."
Interpersonal	A crisis emerges and persists when individual validation is influenced by the evaluation of others, and is dependent on this evaluation. Referred to as "conferring their locus on control," on an external source, the crisis will continue until the individual gains a sense of self-efficacy over his or her life by taking action.

those involved, and the client's affective, emotional, and behavioral functioning will assist the practitioner to respond and plan appropriate interventions. Otherwise, interventions may have little or no value to the client.

Process and Procedures of Crisis Intervention

Having reviewed the basic tenets, theoretical framework, and essential concepts of crisis intervention, we now turn to the procedures for implementing this treatment modality. For our purpose, we rely on the six-step problem-solving model developed by James and Gilliland (2001, p. 32) for systematically intervening in a crisis situation.[3] Here we briefly discuss these steps (which are illustrated in Figure 13-3) as they apply to a case situation.

Step 1: Define the Problem

Social workers must determine the unique meaning of a crisis situation to each client. Determining the

meaning and significance of precipitating events can be highly therapeutic to clients. Through an exploration of precipitating events, the complex forces involved in the crisis situation, and the client's reactions, the social worker becomes able to view the situation from the client's perspective. Because CI has such a short duration, professionals concurrently assess and alleviate clients' emotional distress. Objectives of the assessment involve determining the nature of the crisis situation, its significance to and effects on the client, factors or events that precipitated the crisis, the client's adaptive capacities, and resources that can be tapped to alleviate the crisis situation. These factors are crucial to formulating tasks that must subsequently be accomplished. The nature of a crisis, of course, provides valuable clues as to the source of the client's distress.

Cultural factors and status are equally essential in assessing clients' problem definitions and reactions to crisis situations as well as in selecting inter-

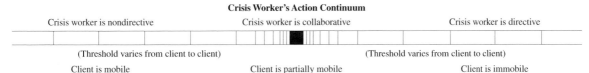

ASSESSING:
Overarching, continuous, and dynamically ongoing throughout the crisis; evaluating the
client's present and past situational crises in terms of the client's ability to cope, personal threat, mobility or immobility,
and making a judgment regarding type of action needed by the crisis worker. (See crisis worker's action continuum, below.)

Listening	Acting
LISTENING: Attending, observing, understanding, and responding with empathy, genuineness, respect, acceptance, nonjudgment, and caring.	ACTING: Becoming involved in the intervention at a nondirective, collaborative, or directive level, according to the assessed needs of the client and the availability of environmental supports.
1. *Define the problem.* Explore and define the problem from the client's point of view. Use active listening, including open-ended questions. Attend to both verbal and nonverbal messages of the client.	4. *Examine alternatives.* Assist client in exploring the choices he or she has available to him or her now. Facilitate a search for immediate situational supports, coping mechanisms, and positive thinking.
2. *Ensure client safety.* Assess lethality, criticality, immobility, or seriousness of threat to the client's physical and psychological safety. Assess both the client's internal events and the situation surrounding the client, and, if necessary, ensure that the client is made aware of alternatives to impulsive, self-destructive actions.	5. *Make plans.* Assist client in developing a realistic short-term plan that identifies additional resources and provides coping mechanisms—definite action steps that the client can own and comprehend.
3. *Provide support.* Communicate to the client that the crisis worker is a valid support person. Demonstrate (by words, voice, and body language) a caring, positive, nonpossessive, nonjudgmental, acceptant, personal involvement with the client.	6. *Obtain commitment.* Help client commit himself or herself to definite, positive action steps that the client can own and realistically accomplish or accept.

Crisis Worker's Action Continuum

Crisis worker is nondirective   Crisis worker is collaborative   Crisis worker is directive

(Threshold varies from client to client)   (Threshold varies from client to client)

Client is mobile   Client is partially mobile   Client is immobile

The crisis worker's level of action/involvement may be anywhere on the continuum according to a valid and realistic assessment of the client's level of mobility/immobility.

Figure 13-3 The six-step model of crisis intervention

Source: From *Crisis Intervention Strategies* 4th ed. by James and Gilliland. Copyright © 2001 Wadsworth, a division of Thomson Learning.

vention strategies. Situations deemed to be crises vary widely from one culture to another, as do the reactions to them. Interventions often work best when they include family, focus on empowerment, and are combined with cultural values or rituals (e.g., spiritual healing, circles of care).

CASE EXAMPLE

Lia is a 17-year-old Southeast Asian pregnant female referred to a community health/mental health center by the teen group leader at her high school. The extremity of the situation, family dynamics, and the stress involved had led her to miss a number of days in school, but she would show up for the group sessions. On the day of the referral, during group Lia became so emotionally distraught that the group leader took her aside to talk with her individually. Lia told her that she was pregnant and that she was in trouble with her family

as a result. The group leader referred her to a social worker at the center.

During the initial interview Lia was crying, had trouble breathing, and expressed concern about whether the social worker could understand her situation. The magnitude of the crisis became even more significant when Lia indicated that she had thought of suicide because she was pregnant, and said that her 12-year-old brother was also involved in her discussion about suicide.

The social worker's task in this initial session was twofold: (1) to assess and alleviate Lia's emotional distress, and (2) to elicit Lia's definition of the problem. The objectives of the assessment entailed determining the nature of the crisis situation, and its significance for and impact on Lia. Assessing the nature of a crisis provides valuable clues about the sources of clients' distress—in this case, the fact that Lia was pregnant and unmarried; which violated a cultural norm She was also despondent because she felt that she had shamed her family. In addition, Lia had concerns about the safety and well-being of both herself and her unborn child. Drawing out clients' emotions and responding empathically to them encourages clients to unburden themselves of painful and sometimes overwhelming emotions. Social workers can also provide needed emotional support when clients ventilate pent-up emotions by reassuring them that their emotions are a natural reaction to an extremely distressing situation. Eliciting Lia's definition of the problem allowed the social worker to gather valuable information about those factors or events that precipitated the crisis, Lia's adaptive capacities, and resources that might be tapped to alleviate the crisis. Clearly, being pregnant and unmarried was worrisome to Lia, but she believed that she could cope with her situation and had some ideas about how to do so. Her family's definition of the problem, however, was grounded in the context of cultural norms and expectations. Unwed pregnancy requires considerable adaptation in most cultures, but may pose an extreme challenge for first-generation immigrant families. From the perspective of her family, the fact that Lia was pregnant and unmarried brought shame to them. Upon learning that she was pregnant, her father had dismissed her from the family and now refused to talk to her or allow other family members to do so. As a result, Lia faced social ostracism, loss of face, and a disconnection from her family and members of the clan.

Step 2: Ensure Client Safety

Ensuring client safety is the first and foremost concern in crisis intervention and, as James and Gilliland (2001) suggest, remains an ongoing consideration. The social worker requested, and Lia agreed to complete, a depression scale. The results of the test prompted a referral for a medical evaluation. Because Lia had spoken of considering suicide, the social worker developed an immediate safety plan contract with her; with each party identifying resources, including a crisis hotline that Lia could call when her feelings reached the level at which she contemplated harming herself.

In the assessment of her affective, cognitive, and behavioral domains, Lia's scores were moderate. In addition, she displayed some coping behaviors—namely, she reported that she often volunteered for the closing shift at work and then walked to her sister's home to spend the night to avoid going home. Furthermore, the fact that she was concerned about the well-being of her unborn child was an indication of her future-oriented thinking, a factor that the social worker focused on to minimize the threat of self harm. An additional safety concern was the fact that Lia was walking to her sister's house late at night after work, so she and the social worker explored other transportation alternatives.

Step 3: Provide Support

Within this step, the objective is to identify clients' social support systems, because mobilizing a helping network can be enormously helpful as part of crisis intervention. Another valuable resource is self-help groups that include people with similar problems. Members can provide mutual support and can assist one another with problem solving. (Chapter 9 also discussed assessment of support systems.) Identifying and assisting clients to connect with social support systems may reduce emotional distress for some clients. Social supports may include friends, relatives, and in some cases institutional programs that care about the client and that can provide comfort and compassion (James & Gilliland, 2001).

As Lia and the social worker explored potential support resources, several were identified: her sister, certain clan members, and an aunt who was sympathetic to her situation. These resources were also included in the safety plan. A school-based group for pregnant teens was identified as a new resource. The social worker was also a support source in that she accompanied Lia to her appointments with the psychiatrist and the prenatal clinic in the center, and arranged a daily check-in schedule.

Step 4: Examine Alternatives

In this step, both the social worker and the client recognize and explore courses of action appropriate to the situation. Of course, some choices are better than others, and it is important to be selective when prioritizing available options. Ideally, the practitioner should think about alternatives and the extent to which they are (1) situational supports, involving people who care about what happens to the client; (2) coping mechanisms, represented by actions, behaviors, or environmental resources that clients may use to get past the crisis situation; and (3) positive and constructive thinking patterns that effectively alter how the client views the problem, lessening his or her level of stress and anxiety.

Lia had actually thought of alternatives, yet was sufficiently immobilized emotionally that she had not acted upon them. For example, in response to the threat from her father to change the locks on the doors, effectively forcing her out of the house, she had considered moving in with her sister or aunt (*situational supports*) until after her child was born, at which time she would be 18 years of age and able to live independently. Instead of acting on this option, however, she planned to wait until her parents were asleep or at work, and appeal to her siblings (*coping mechanism*) to let her in the house. This choice was a short-term solution at best, and posed some risks for both Lia and her siblings.

A more viable alternative explored by Lia and the social worker involved Lia moving into a transitional housing complex for pregnant teens, located near her high school and job (*positive constructive thinking and action*). Program services offered in the housing complex included transportation for prenatal visits, group counseling, individualized independent living skills classes, and assistance in finding permanent housing. Although she was initially reluctant, Lia agreed to consider this option. As Gilliland and James indicate, professionals are better able to plan alternatives with clients and alter their thinking when they understand the client's view of the problem. For example, Lia's qualms about the alternative of the housing program reflected her desire to remain with—or at least near—her family and community.

Step 5: Make Plans

Planning and contracting flow from the previous steps and involve the same elements as were described in Chapter 12. The client and the practitioner agree on specific action steps or tasks as well as time limits relevant to the overall goal of restoring equilibrium. General and specific action steps (tasks) will, of course, vary according to the nature of the crisis situation and the unique characteristics of each person and/or family. In developing and negotiating action steps, it is important to involve clients (thereby increasing their autonomy) by soliciting their views on what they believe will help them return to a pre-crisis state. Gilliland and James caution against professionals "benevolently imposing" a plan on clients, and suggest that they should instead strive to balance control and client autonomy. As with any intervention method, the ideal is to assist the client in problem solving and developing a greater sense of self-efficacy.

In facilitating clients' accomplishments of actions or tasks deemed essential to mastery of crisis situations, practitioners should observe the guidelines of the TIS. Social workers should assume an active and directive role and give advice to a greater extent than when using other approaches. Nevertheless, it is important to foster client autonomy by involving clients in planning for task implementation and by encouraging and reinforcing independent actions whenever feasible.

Lia and the social worker identified her safety as a priority in planning. Additional planning involved exploring alternative living arrangements and obtaining prenatal and maternal health care. Lia's concern about her estrangement from her parents was also a central issue. Thus, she and the social worker agreed that Lia would explore ways in which she could resume some form of contact with her family. The social worker inquired about the cultural appropriateness of a letter of apology. They also planned to involve the aunt and the sister in Lia's attempt to reconnect with her family.

Step 6: Obtain Commitment

The sixth and final step of the CI model involves a commitment on the part of the client and the practitioner to collaboratively engage in specific, intentional, and positive action steps designed to restore the client to a level of pre-crisis functioning. The sequence in which specific actions are undertaken and the time limits for this process may vary from client to client. In making a decision about sequence and time limits, it is important to involve clients (thereby increasing their autonomy) by soliciting their views on both.

After a week, Lia agreed to pursue the alternative plan of moving into the transitional housing program for pregnant teens. In the interim, she would explore living with her sister or her aunt, perhaps dividing her time between the two of them. The plan also included action steps for ensuring her safety. Specific action steps (tasks) involved the following:

LIA

- Call the 24-hour crisis line or other supports when she was feeling despondent
- Talk to her sister or aunt about moving in with one of them
- Visit the transitional housing complex
- Explore ways to have contact with family members
- Continue to attend the school-based group for pregnant teens

SOCIAL WORKER

- Provide Lia with information on the transitional housing program prior to her visit
- Accompany Lia on her visit to the transitional housing program
- Obtain information about financial support for Lia and her unborn child

Anticipatory Guidance

To the intervention steps outlined by Gililand and James, we would add anticipatory guidance, which can be integrated into the terminal phase of any practice model. *Anticipatory guidance* involves assisting clients to anticipate future crises that might develop and to plan effective coping strategies, using knowledge and skills gained during the preceding period of problem solving. Relevant strategies might include analyzing sources of distress, recalling and accrediting successful efforts in coping with past crisis situations, anticipating needs, identifying and utilizing support systems and other potential resources, and formulating and implementing essential tasks. It is important, however, not to convey an expectation that clients will always be able to independently manage all problem situations in the future. Indeed, during the process of termination, you should express continuing support, reassure clients that you are available if they need future help, and plan to contact them to check on their continued progress.

Strengths and Limitations of Crisis Intervention

Crisis intervention involves a structured, time-limited series of steps utilizing techniques that are guided by crisis theory. During the initial intervention phase, the practitioner has three objectives: (1) to relieve the client's emotional distress, (2) to complete an assessment of the client's cognitive, behavioral, and emotional functioning, and (3) to plan the strategy of intervention, focusing on relevant tasks the client must perform. Much of crisis theory assumes that people experience an event or situation that alters their usual patterns of living, so that the goal of interventions is to restore their functioning. When clients in an acute crisis become immobilized by tension and anxiety, other techniques such as deep breathing and progressive muscle relaxation procedures can be helpful in alleviating tension and in assisting clients to regain their composure. Practitioners should also consider the need for antianxiety or antidepressant medications in extreme cases.

Over the last several years, crisis theory has been expanded to include a classification of different kinds of crises. It has also integrated assumptions from other theories—for example, systems and interpersonal theories. Likewise, crisis theory includes trauma and disaster in its definition of a crisis, for which it is necessary to implement strategies that respond to the needs of entire communities and groups. Each of these contributions is significant in that it advances our understanding and ability to differentiate crisis work.

While there is consensus about the definition of a crisis, what actually constitutes a crisis is less well defined. Perceptions of a crisis may vary based on associated threats, individual cognitions, and the significance of the situation, ego strengths, coping capacity, and problem-solving skills. In some instances, people may perceive and be able to articulate positive benefits that emerge as a result of a negative experience. Of course, these perceptions of benefits may be derived from the nature of the crisis, as well as the resources and supports that are available at an opportune time.

Crisis intervention models retain the assumption of an episodic, time-limited event as crisis, responding to the stress and distress of individuals, communities, or groups at this level. Specifically, crisis professionals aim to relieve emotional distress and develop a plan of action that will restore individuals to a pre-crisis level of functioning. Furthermore, there is the assumption that certain behaviors and cognitive tasks must be mastered.

Crisis intervention strategies do not address prolonged crisis exposure such as occurs in war, political conflicts, or living continuously in stressful environments or under inherent structural and socio-environmental threats. Indeed, it is quite possible that individuals and entire communities facing these situations live in a constant state of disequilibrium or vulnerability. In many instances, in poor and minority communities, the crisis intervention point of entry is the hospital emergency room or the police station, and may result in a DSM classification. It is quite possible that not all of the stages of crisis reactions occur in these communities, and people in these situations may lack the power or resources to problem-solve. For example, an individual's initial response to gang or politically motivated violence may be shock or denial. From this point, according to the crisis reaction stages, they become angry, overwhelmed, and hopeless or depressed. In prolonged crisis situations, where normal problem-solving skills are inadequate and in which people lack power to change their situation, there is the potential for

individuals to remain at this stage. Thus, as suggested by Ell (1995), the notion of the time-limited crisis is not always applicable, and the potential to restore equilibrium may be neither feasible nor realistic.

The efficacy of crisis intervention strategies with diverse populations and in diverse settings is not diminished by these observations. These possibilities do suggest, however, that social workers need to include assessment of socio-environmental factors and their impact on cognitive, affective, and behavioral functioning in their work with clients in crisis. In addition, social workers must recognize that even though the potential exists to restore the individual's self-efficacy, the notion of time-limited episodes may not be universally applicable in all crisis situations.

COGNITIVE RESTRUCTURING

Cognitive restructuring is a therapeutic process derived from cognitive-behavioral therapy (CBT). Intervention techniques in CBT are designed to help individuals modify beliefs, faulty thought patterns or perceptions, and destructive verbalizations, thereby leading to changes in behavior. An assumption of cognitive restructuring is that people often manifest cognitive distortions—that is, irrational thoughts derived from negative schemas that lead to unrealistic interpretations of people, events, or circumstances. Frequently, clients report that even though they are aware of their faulty thinking, they lack the emotional strength to alter it. Once clients become aware of their biases, self-thoughts, and patterns, they are in a position to evaluate the accuracy of their validity.

A goal of cognitive therapy intervention strategies is to restructure or change the thoughts, feelings, or overt behaviors that maintain problem behavior. Similar to the strategies associated with the task-centered system, crisis intervention, and other brief therapies, cognitive restructuring focuses on the here and now, and on specific target behaviors and goals (Corwin, 2002). Cognitive restructuring also expects the client to perform behavioral and cognitive tasks between sessions. In general, the aim of cognitive therapy is to increase the client's cognitive and behavioral skills so as to enhance his or her functioning. To be maximally effective, social workers must become proficient in assessing cognitive functioning and in applying appropriate interventions. (We focused on assessing cognitive functioning in Chapters 9 and 11.)[4]

Theoretical Framework

As defined by Ingram and Scott (1990), cognitive-behavioral therapy is "those sets of therapeutic procedures that (1) embody theoretical conceptualizations of change that place primary importance on cognitive process; and (2) procedurally target some therapeutic maneuvers specially at altering aspects of cognition." Much of CBT is derived from social learning theory (Bandura, 1986). This theory suggests that thoughts and emotions are best understood in the context of behaviors associated with cognition or cognitive processes as well as the extent to which individuals adapt and respond to different stimuli and make self-judgments. The primary goal of cognitive restructuring is to alter thoughts, feelings associated with thought processes, and the accompanying self-statements or behaviors.

According to cognitive theorists, most social and behavioral dysfunction results directly from misconceptions that people hold about themselves, other people, and various life situations. Theories and models of social work, counseling, and psychotherapy acknowledge the central role of cognition in human behavior and the problems associated with cognitive dysfunction. The early and historic work of Ellis (1962), Beck (1976), and others in this arena led to cognitive theories and techniques that can be applied directly and systematically to problems of cognitive dysfunction. Ellis's (1962) seminal work, *Reason and Emotion in Psychotherapy,* explicated the theory underlying rational-emotive therapy (RET). Numerous books and articles have since been published delineating the significance of mistaken beliefs and faulty thought patterns in diverse emotional and behavioral problems, ranging from those occurring in childhood and adolescence (Weisz, Weiss, Wasserman,

& Rintoul, 1987) to those appearing in old age (Lam, Brewin, Woods, & Bebbington, 1987). Many of these publications also describe the application of cognitive therapy to widely varying disorders. Perhaps the most significant is *The Cognitive Therapy of Depression* (Beck, Rush, Shaw, & Emery, 1979), which is widely recognized as the definitive work on treatment of depression. Research studies have also documented that CBT is one of the two major psychotherapeutic approaches that yields outcomes equivalent to those produced by antidepressant medication (Elkin, Shea, Watkins, & Collins, 1986).

A significant body of social work literature describes CBT as a major treatment modality and includes cognitive restructuring as a component of the treatment regimen. Cohen (1985) expounds on the use of cognitive therapy with criminals. Barth (1985) and Marshall and Mazie (1987) describe its use in the treatment of depression. Other treatment programs have employed cognitive restructuring to reduce the anger of parents at risk of abusing children (Nugent, 1991), with adolescents (Schrodt & Fitzgerald, 1987), and in cases of spousal abuse (Eisikovits & Edleson, 1989).

Gambrill (1995) summarizes the utilization of CBT in a variety of practice settings and a variety of populations. More recent literature includes studies related to the reduction of school violence (Whitfield, 1999); the treatment of anxiety, panic, and social phobia (Dia, 2001; Feeny, 2004); behavioral groups for relatives caring for family members with dementia (Gendron, Poitras, Dastoor, & Perodeau, 1996); and treatment of post-traumatic stress disorder (Grunert, Smucker, Weis, & Rusch, 2003; Jaycox, Zoellner, & Foa, 2002).

On a more practical level, Friedmann (1997) notes that cognitive therapy—like other brief treatment models—has value in today's managed care environment because it deals with highly specific problems and focuses on concrete problem and symptom reduction as indicators of measurable change. This movement is apparent in both public and private agencies, where scarce resources and time limits are key factors in determining which treatment approaches have relevance (e.g., for child welfare, public assistance, health/mental health care).

Uses of Cognitive Restructuring

Cognitive restructuring is particularly useful in assisting clients to gain awareness of self-defeating thoughts and misconceptions that impair their personal functioning and to replace them with beliefs and behaviors that are aligned with reality and a shift in schema (Ackerman-Engle, 1992). Behavioral tasks are often assigned between sessions so that clients take action in this regard.

Cognitive restructuring techniques are particularly relevant for treating problems associated with low self-esteem; distorted perceptions in interpersonal relations; unrealistic expectations of self, others, and life in general; irrational fears, anxiety, and depression; inadequate control of anger and other impulses; and lack of assertiveness. Social workers and other professionals have found cognitive restructuring to be effective in assisting people with problems of impulse control that are manifested as child abuse, gambling (Sharpe & Tarrier, 1992), and substance abuse and relapse (Steigerwold & Stone, 1999; Bakker, Ward, Cryer, & Hudson, 1997). This technique is often blended with other interventions (e.g., modeling, behavioral rehearsal, imagery, desensitization), because combinations of interventions are often more potent than single interventions in producing change (Corcoran, 2002).

Selected studies that demonstrate the range of cognitive restructuring as a component of treatment have focused on a program to assist women to reframe their thoughts and address cultural messages with regard to ideal body images (Srebnik & Saltzberg, 1994), treatment of social phobia and anxiety (Feeny, 2004), spousal caregiver support groups (Gendron, Poitras, Dastoor, & Perodeau, 1996), and crisis situations following an industrial accident or sexual assault (Jaycox, Zoellner & Foa, 2002).

Cognitive Restructuring with Diverse Groups

Limited information exists in the literature with respect to the efficacy of cognitive restructuring with diverse racial and cultural groups. Potocky-Tripodi (2002) suggests that cognitive restructuring delivered as "supportive" counseling may help immigrants and refugees respond to maladaptive thoughts and increase their coping skills in intercultural situations (pp. 292–293). As shown by Srebnik and Saltzberg (1994) and Brown (1994), cognitive restructuring has helped women gain their sense of power in the face of gender-related behavioral expectations and assisted them to confront images of ideal physical attributes. This literature, while specific to women, nevertheless demonstrates cognitive restructuring's promise as an intervention with racial or cultural minority individuals.

Tenets of Cognitive Therapy

A major tenet of CT is that thinking is a basic determinant of behavior. *Thinking* consists of statements that people say to themselves. This inner dialogue, rather than unconscious forces, is the key to understanding behavior. To fully grasp this first major tenet, practitioners must clearly differentiate thinking from feeling. Clients (and practitioners) often confuse feelings and thoughts, which tends to create confusion in communication and hinders successful implementation of cognitive restructuring techniques. The confusion is manifested in messages such as "I feel our marriage is on the rocks," or "I feel nobody cares about me." Here, the use of the word *feel* does not actually identify feelings, but rather embodies views, thoughts, or beliefs. Thoughts per se are devoid of feelings, although they are often accompanied by and tend to generate feelings or emotions. Feelings consist of emotions, such as sadness, joy, disappointment, and exhilaration (recall the hundreds of feelings listed in the list of affective words and phrases in Chapter 5). In contrast, cognitive processes, according to social learning theory, are manifested in behavioral responses. Behavioral responses are a function of the cognitive processes of attention, retention, production, and motivation, as well as of rewarding or unrewarding consequences (Bandura, 1986). To assist clients to distinguish between feelings and cognitions, you should explain the difference and provide several examples of each. Likewise, you should quickly intervene when clients fail to distinguish between these functions, because self-monitoring of cognitions requires this ability to discriminate between the two.

A second major tenet of cognitive therapy is that the past is important only in identifying the origins of faulty thinking. That is, it is the present faulty thinking—not the past—that motivates behavior. Furthermore, new patterns of thinking can be learned and problems can be resolved without determining the origins of faulty thinking. For these reasons, cognitive therapy concentrates on the present and the future, so that clients are not permitted to use the past as an excuse for their current difficulties.

A third major tenet of cognitive therapy is that to make constructive changes, clients must realize that their misconceptions may produce or contribute to many of their problems, and they must assume responsibility for modifying these misconceptions. The thrust of this tenet is that practitioners must assist clients to assume maximal responsibility for themselves. You should, of course, temper this assumption by recognizing that many factors contribute to the problems of clients, including inadequate resources and adverse environmental conditions. For example, you should not assume that cognitions are always faulty when they stem from interpersonal interactions in which race, gender, or sexual orientation are major issues. With clients whose problems are generally rooted in misconceptions and faulty logic, however, this tenet is valid.

Steps in Cognitive Restructuring

Several discrete steps are involved in cognitive restructuring. Although different authors may vary slightly in how they define these steps, the similarities between their models are far greater than the differences. These steps, as summarized in Table 13-3, have been adapted from those identified by Goldfried (1977) and Cormier and Nurius (2003).

1. *Assist clients in accepting that their self-statements, assumptions, and beliefs largely mediate their*

Table 13-3 Steps in cognitive restructuring

1. Assist clients in accepting that their self-statements determine their emotional reactions to events. (Tool: explanation and treatment rationale)

2. Assist clients in identifying dysfunctional beliefs and thought patterns. (Tool: self-monitoring)

3. Assist clients in identifying situations involving dysfunctional cognitions.

4. Assist clients in replacing dysfunctional cognitions with functional self-statements.

5. Assist clients in identifying rewards and incentives for successful coping efforts.

---

emotional reactions to life's events. Assisting clients to accept this explanation is vital, because clients are unlikely to commit themselves to procedures that they view skeptically or reject outright. We recommend that you provide a rationale for cognitive restructuring and demonstrate its relevance by citing common life experiences that document how cognitions mediate emotions and thinking.

To guide you in assisting clients to understand cognitive restructuring, the following example demonstrates how a practitioner might use self to explain the technique. Here the client is an adolescent who is inhibited in social situations by feelings of inadequacy and social incompetence. The adolescent's goal is to increase his comfort level in expressing himself in social situations with his peers.

Explanation of Cognitive Restructuring

Social worker: For you to achieve your goal of expressing yourself more openly with others, we first need to determine what happens inside you that maintains your fears. That will involve your becoming aware of thoughts you experience in social situations—in other words, what you say to yourself before, during, and after social situations. Generally, such thoughts occur automatically, and you won't be fully aware of many of them. We also want to discover assumptions and beliefs you have about social situations—beliefs you may have had much of your life. Becoming aware of self-defeating thoughts, assumptions, and beliefs is an important first step in replacing them in favor of others that serve you better.

Social Worker's Use of Self

In some instances, as illustrated in the following dialogue, social workers may draw upon their own experiences to illustrate ways of thinking and responding to a situation.

Social worker: What you think determines in large measure what you feel and do. For example, if a friend tells me I'm stupid because I bought a new car instead of a used one, I can make various meanings or self-statements related to that message, each of which results in different feelings and actions. Consider the potential responses that I might have to my friend's comment:

> *Response 1*: He's probably right; he's a bright guy, and I respect his judgment. Why didn't I think of buying a used car? He thinks that I am stupid.

If I think that I am, I'll feel crummy about myself, and I probably won't enjoy my new car as much.

> *Response 2*: Who does he think he is, calling me stupid? He's the one who's stupid. What a jerk!

If I think that, I'll feel angry and defensive and I may get in an argument over the merits of a new car or a used one.

> *Response 3*: It's apparent that my friend and I have different ideas about cars. He's entitled to his opinion, although I certainly don't agree with him and I do feel good about what I did. I don't like his referring to my decision as stupid, though. There's no point in getting bent out of shape over it, but I think I'll let him know I don't feel good about his saying this to me.

If I think these thoughts, I'm least likely to experience negative feelings about myself. I'll feel good about my actions despite the other person's difference of opinion, and I won't be unduly influenced by his insensitivity.

The social worker then adds that other responses could be made, but these three should suffice to make the point. The social worker points out that

the task at hand is to enable the adolescent to master his fears, and to explore together the client's self-statements and how they affect his feelings and behavior. As the social worker explains, after identifying thoughts and beliefs that are causing difficulties, the practitioner and the client will begin working on developing other thoughts that are realistic and consistent with his goal of expressing himself more openly in social situations.

When the rationale is presented in a simple, straightforward manner, the majority of clients will respond positively. Nevertheless, it is important to elicit clients' reactions to your explanation and to invite discussion of it. You should not proceed with cognitive restructuring until clients manifest receptivity and commitment to implementing the intervention. This commitment is necessary because clients tend to resist changing their beliefs when they feel they are being coerced to adopt your beliefs or those of someone else.

2. *Assist clients in identifying dysfunctional beliefs and patterns of thoughts that underlie their problems.* Once clients accept the proposition that thoughts and beliefs mediate emotional reactions, your next task is to assist them to examine those personal thoughts and beliefs that pertain to their difficulties. This step requires detailed exploration of events related to problematic situations and their antecedents, with particular emphasis on cognitions that accompany distressing emotions. For example, some clients may attribute their problems to fate, inherent personal attributes, and other forces beyond their control. In identifying key misconceptions, both the social worker and the client need to agree on the beliefs that will be the focus of change. As with any intervention strategy, ensuring client involvement and active participation is ethical practice.

You can begin the process of exploration by focusing on problematic events that occurred during the preceding week or on events surrounding a problem the client has targeted for change. As you mutually explore these events, you should elicit specific details regarding the client's overt behaviors, cognitions (i.e., self-statements and images), and emotional reactions. Focusing on all three aspects enables both you and the client to see the connections between them and to grasp the role of cognitions in mediating feelings and behaviors. As clients identify their self-statements and beliefs, they will become increasingly aware that automatic thoughts and beliefs they have not subjected to critical analysis act as powerful determinants of their behavior. This, in turn, increases their receptivity and motivation to work on tasks that seek to liberate them from counterproductive thoughts, misconceptions, and beliefs.

As you and the client further explore the situation, you will be able to *identify thoughts and feelings that occur before, during, and after events.* To elicit self-statements, ask the client to recreate the situation just as it unfolded, recalling exactly what he or she thought, felt, and did. For example, with the adolescent in the preceding example, the social worker asked him to describe his thoughts and feelings when he was in a social situation with his peers. If reflection proves difficult for clients, you might ask them to close their eyes and *run a movie* of their thoughts and feelings prior to, during, and after the problematic event.

Through this process, you should be able to pinpoint cognitive sets that predispose clients to experience certain emotions and to behave in predictable ways. To illustrate, consider the self-statements that the social worker elicited from the adolescent about encountering his peers in the school lunchroom:

- "I'm outey [out of here—disappear]. Straight up [the truth is], I'm not sure I want to join the others. If I do, I'll just cool [sit] there and feel that they be [are] hating [left out] on me."
- "If I show, they'll dis me [disrespect] me about something."
- "I'd better show [join in]; otherwise, they will be hollering at me later about some other stuff. I'm outey, straight up."
- "I'm cool" [okay].

Given these self-statements, the adolescent clearly felt uneasy and apprehensive about joining his peers. These thoughts predisposed him to enter the situation programmed for defeat. In addition to

the self-debate, his nonverbal cues—for example, his physical posture—spoke volumes. His self-defeating statements not only dominated his thinking, but also contributed to his presentation of self within the group.

Exploration of self-statements during events often reveals that thoughts maintain self-defeating feelings and behaviors and drastically reduce personal effectiveness. For example, clients who dwell on worries and are hypervigilant to the possible negative reactions of others are unable to *tune in* fully to conversations or to express themselves in positive ways that create favorable impressions. In other words, they find it difficult to be fully present and involved because of their self-consciousness and fears of exposing their imagined personal inadequacies.

To illustrate the destructive impact of such thoughts, let us again consider the self-statements of the adolescent during lunch with his peers:

- "Well, here I am, just like always, I am being dissed [disrespected—left out of the conversation]."
- "I wish I had the low, low [something interesting to say], but my life's ain't about doing anything [uninteresting]. What's up with this? They ain't interested in any low [ideas, information] that I might put out [say]."
- "How you figure, they're wondering why I even show [join them]. I don't add anything to the group. I cool, I out of here [I don't add anything to the group]."

It is apparent from these and other like self-statements that the adolescent dwells on self-defeating thoughts. Because he thinks of himself as having little or nothing to offer, he behaves accordingly, and he feels unwanted and unworthy to actively participate. His preoccupation with these thoughts and assumptions about himself effectively blocks him from engaging with his peers.

Clients' self-statements and feelings following events reveal the impact of earlier thoughts and behaviors on subsequent feelings, highlighting further the mediating function of cognitions. Moreover, the conclusions that clients draw about the outcomes of events indicate whether they are able to focus on positive aspects of their behavior and to identify challenges for further growth or whether they merely perceive an event as the latest in a long series of failures caused by their personal inadequacies. The meanings that clients draw from events, of course, powerfully shape their attitudes and feelings toward future events. Consider the thoughts and feelings of our adolescent client:

- "I out man [blew it again]. I'm too threw [I'm finished; I might as well quit trying]. This ain't real for sure [no use kidding myself; I just can't talk with others]."

- "It ain't like that [they didn't really try to include me]. They be hating on me [it's obvious they could care less about me]. They'd probably be pleased if I didn't join them tomorrow."

- "This is whack [uncomfortable; I won't eat lunch with them anymore]. I don't enjoy it, and I'm sure they don't either. Tomorrow I outey [eat by myself], for shiddley [for sure]."

Clearly, this client's feelings and thoughts have led to a sense of failure. Without intervention into his circular self-defeating thought patterns, he will tend to withdraw even further socially. It can be expected that he would experience further self-demeaning thoughts, perhaps accompanied by depression.

The following techniques can be used to challenge clients to assess the rationality of their beliefs and self-statements:

- Asking them how they reached certain conclusions

- Challenging them to present evidence supporting dysfunctional views or beliefs

- Challenging the logic of beliefs that magnify feared consequences of certain actions

To assist the adolescent to assess the rationality of his conclusions, for example, the social worker responded as follows:

Social worker: So did someone "dis" you when you joined the group? What did they say that made you think that they were "hating" on you?

Through this kind of guided practice, social workers can provide clients with the impetus to critically analyze the validity of their thoughts, and prepare them to engage in a similar process in real situations. As illustrated in the following example with the adolescent, clients may not immediately acknowledge the irrationality of certain beliefs, especially those that are deeply embedded in their belief systems:

Adolescent client: Well, you see, this girl, I got the low [perception, idea], by the way she was looking at me, straight-up, this was whack [not good].

Clients can tenaciously cling to key misconceptions and argue persuasively about their validity. You must therefore be prepared to challenge or "dispute" such irrational beliefs and to persist in assisting clients to recognize the costs or disadvantages associated with not relinquishing these beliefs. At this point, the social worker prompts the adolescent to consider the relationships between his thoughts and his goals.

Social worker: Well, if you continue think that joining in with the group is whack, and you continue to be "outey," how will this affect your goal of becoming comfortable with interacting with your peers?

To further illustrate the applications of these techniques, we have provided three self-statements, or beliefs, followed by practitioner responses that direct clients to analyze their validity.

Student Preparing for Exam

Self-statement:

- "I've got to study every available moment. If I don't get the highest score on that test, it will be just awful."

Social worker responses:

- "Let's just suppose for a moment you really bombed on the test. What would it really mean for you?"

- "So if you're not number one, it will be a catastrophe. I can agree it's nice to get the highest

Table 13-4 Beliefs and self-expectations

BELIEFS	SELF-EXPECTATIONS
Beliefs about oneself	I am usually not very good at anything that I do.
	My accomplishments aren't that significant, anyone could have done it.
Beliefs about others' perceptions and expectations of oneself	My partner dismisses my opinion, because I am not very smart.
	When I compare myself with others, I never quite measure up.
Expectations of oneself	At work, I feel I must perform better than others in my unit.
	I should be able to do lots of things and perform at a high level.
Expectations of others	She should understand how I feel without my having to tell her.
	My children should want to visit me.

score, but why would it be such a disaster to get the second highest score, or even another score for that matter?"

Relative Caring for Children

Self-statement:

- "I don't want to care for her children, but if I don't she'll be furious. I don't want to risk displeasing her and get her angry at me."

Social worker responses:

- "How have you concluded she'd be furious?"

- "Suppose you did risk turning her down and she did become angry. Perhaps a question you should answer is whether you are going to let possible unreasonable reactions on her part dictate your behavior."

Elderly Client Concerned about Visits

Self-statement:

- "There's no point in my asking my daughter to come and visit me more often. She will just see it as my attempting to get attention and trying to embarrass her. If I bring up the topic, we will just end up in an argument. She's busy with her job and her own family."

Social worker responses:

- "What evidence do you have that your daughter will respond to your request in this manner?"

- "Sounds like you've convinced yourself that your daughter would not understand that you would like to see her more often. Have you explained this to her?"

- "So you think that your daughter will not come to visit you more often because she is too busy with her own life?"

Clusters of misconceptions are commonly associated with problematic behavior. Often it is possible to discern such patterns of thoughts within one session by closely following feelings and eliciting accompanying thoughts. Table 13-4 provides our conception of belief clusters typically associated with unreasonable self-expectations.

By identifying clusters or patterns of misconceptions, you can direct your efforts to the theme common to all of them, rather than dealing with each misconception as a separate entity. The cluster identified with the elderly client concerned about her daughter's visiting pattern, for example, is characterized by the theme of setting unrealistic expectations for oneself and others. Focusing on the central theme identified for a particular client allows you to conserve your efforts, because the related misconceptions are often merely derivatives of the central one and lose their potency when the core misconception is resolved.

Self-Monitoring. In cognitive restructuring, self-monitoring *between* sessions is a concrete technique for assisting clients to explore and recognize cognitions related to their difficulties and problematic events. Through this practice, clients become increasingly aware of the pervasive nature of their dysfunctional thoughts and recognize the need to cope actively with them.

Date: Tuesday, September 6, 2005		
Situation or Event	Feelings (Rate intensity from 1 to 10)	Beliefs or Self-Statements (Rate rationality from 1 to 10)
1. Asked boss for a day off	Scared (7)	He'll be annoyed and critical of me (4)
2. Clerk gave me incorrect change; I didn't say anything	Annoyed (4); afraid to tell clerk (8); disgusted with self (7)	I ought to tell clerk (9); she'd be displeased and I'd feel embarrassed (2); it is not worth the hassle (3)

Figure 13-4 Sample Daily Log

Self-monitoring thus expands self-awareness and paves the way for later coping efforts. Moreover, self-monitoring alone often enables clients to nip self-defeating thoughts in the bud as they realize the irrational and destructive nature of these thoughts. To facilitate self-monitoring, we recommend that you ask clients to keep daily logs to record information, as illustrated in Figure 13-4.

Daily self-monitoring logs are valuable because they focus clients' efforts between sessions; clarify the connections between cognitions and feelings; and provide valuable information about the prevalence and intensity of thoughts, images, and feelings. Moreover, they stimulate clients to engage in logical analysis of their thoughts. To prevent clients from feeling overwhelmed by the task of keeping a log, you might suggest they initially limit their recording to events related to those identified during the session and that they record only about three such events each day. Otherwise, clients tend to experience this task as unduly burdensome because they may have a host of troubling thoughts during a given day. As other counterproductive patterns of thoughts emerge during sessions, the focus of self-monitoring can be shifted as necessary.

In addition to situations and events, explorations of cognitions and self-monitoring should include images, as they may also play a key role in mediating emotions. Some clients are immobilized by terrifying images such as those associated with rape, violence, or events that have left a permanent imprint upon their minds. For example, one client found it extremely difficult to engage in sexual relations with her husband because of images and memories associated with a man who had raped her earlier.

3. *Assist clients in identifying situations that engender dysfunctional cognitions.* As you and the client review completed log sheets and continue to identify problematic feelings and cognitions associated with stressful events, it is important to note recurring situations or themes. Pinpointing places where stressful events occur, key persons involved, and situations that involve demeaning oneself in the face of self-expectations enables you and the client to develop tasks and coping strategies that are tailored to those specific situations. For example, a client who has difficulty managing anger may discover that certain situations or individuals consistently trigger an angry response. Other clients may experience depression when their performance at work or at school is evaluated. Still others may feel inadequate and demeaned in response to the slightest hint of criticism by others. Again, awareness of their areas of vulnerability may lower clients' susceptibility to problematic thoughts and feelings.

4. *Assist clients in substituting functional self-statements for self-defeating cognitions.* As clients gain expanded awareness of their dysfunctional thoughts, beliefs, and images, and as they recognize how these produce negative emotional reactions, they generally welcome efforts to learn new coping patterns. These coping strategies typically consist of self-statements that are both realistic and effective in eliminating negative emotional reactions and self-defeating behaviors. Although functional self-statements foster courage and facilitate active coping efforts, they are not completely idealistic. That is, they do not ignore the struggles inherent in shifting from habitual, ingrained patterns of thinking, feeling, and behaving to new patterns. Instead, coping self-statements embody recognition of the difficulties and anxiety inherent in risking

new behavior. To introduce clients to coping self-statements, we recommend an explanation similar to the following:

Social worker: Now that you've identified many of your key self-defeating beliefs and thoughts, we're going to focus on how to replace them with new self-statements. It will take a lot of hard work on your part, but as you practice new coping self-statements, you'll find that they will become more and more natural to you until they finally crowd out the old ones.

After providing such an explanation, you should model coping self-statements that can be substituted for self-defeating thoughts and beliefs. As part of this modeling, explain that you will assume the role of the client and will think aloud as the client might when coping with a target situation. To illustrate the process, we return to the example of the socially inhibited adolescent. Here, the practitioner models coping self-statements he might substitute for self-defeating ones before joining in with his peers.

Adolescent client: I know a part of me wants to avoid being dis [the discomfort of socializing]. I feel whack [scared], but it's not going to get any better by being outey [withdrawing]. "I don't have to low [talk] a lot to be part of the group. If I tune [listen] to the others and get my mind off myself, I can be cool [involve myself more].

Social worker: Yes, you might think: "I can't expect them to draw me into the conversations. It would be nice if they did, but if I'm going to be included I'll have to be responsible for including myself. It's better than withdrawing and feeling out of it."

Notice how the social worker models the struggle going on within the adolescent rather than modeling "mastery" self-statements. This is important because coping self-statements must closely reflect clients' actual experience, whereas mastery self-statements do not. Moreover, the former convey empathy for and understanding of the client's struggle, which in turn inspires greater confidence in the process and in the social worker.

After modeling coping self-statements, it is appropriate to ask whether the client feels ready to practice similar behavior. With a little encouragement, most clients will agree to engage in guided practice. To enhance the effectiveness of this practice, you could suggest that clients close their eyes and picture themselves in the exact situation they will be in before engaging in the targeted behavior. When they report they have succeeded in capturing this situation, ask them to think aloud the thoughts they typically experience when contemplating the targeted behavior. Then ask them to substitute coping thoughts, coaching them as needed. Give positive feedback when they produce functional statements independently, and provide encouragement as they struggle with conflicting thoughts. Expect your clients to express doubt and uncertainty about their ability to master new patterns of thinking. If they do, explain that most people experience misgivings as they experiment with new ways of thinking. Continue to practice with them until they feel relatively comfortable in their ability to generate coping self-statements.

When the client demonstrates increased confidence in employing coping self-statements before entering a target situation, you can shift to a strategy for employing such statements when the client is actually in the target situation. Again, model coping self-statements, as done here with the adolescent client:

Social worker: Okay, so you're feeling anxious. That's to be expected. You can still pay attention and show interest in the others. You can communicate nonverbally, for example, by nodding your head, indicating that you are interested in what is being said. When you feel more comfortable, you can join in by asking for clarification if you want to know more. This is another way to show interest. If you have some take on the subject they're discussing, think that your opinions are worth as much as theirs. Go ahead, take a chance and express them, but look at others as you talk.

Following the modeling exercise, ask how the client is feeling about what has happened so far. If the client is overly anxious, uncomfortable, or skeptical, you must first deal with these feelings before proceeding further. If the client continues to respond positively, you may then ask him or her to rehearse coping self-statements, following essentially the same format as for the preceding phase.

When the client has demonstrated the ability to generate coping self-statements in the *during* phase, he or she is ready to enter the *after* phase. Again, it is important to model coping self-statements. Here are some examples:

- "Well, I did it. I stuck it out and even said a couple of things. That's a step in the right direction."

- "No one ignored me when I expressed myself. They appeared genuinely interested. Maybe I'm not so bad after all."

- "Even though I was anxious, it went pretty well, even better than I expected. I handled it, and that's an accomplishment. I'll join them again tomorrow and maybe do even better."

When modeling such self-statements, you should explore clients' reactions and feelings. If they indicate they are ready, you can proceed to have them rehearse more coping self-statements.

To assist clients to utilizing coping statements in real-life situations, it is beneficial to negotiate tasks that they can tackle between sessions. But don't rush them, because undue pressure may be perceived as threatening or discouraging. Use the readiness scale (defined earlier in this chapter) as a gauge.

Continued self-monitoring by clients is essential as they implement this step of the cognitive restructuring process. Maintaining a daily log, similar to the format suggested in Figure 13-4, is also important. To this log, the client should add a fourth column, titled "Rational or Coping Self-Statements." Filling in this column should facilitate active coping efforts by clients. It requires them to attempt to place situations and events in realistic perspective by identifying coping self-statements that they can substitute for self-defeating ones. Furthermore, maintaining a log and implementing between-session tasks fosters autonomy and independent action by clients.

Substituting coping self-statements for self-defeating thoughts or misconceptions forms the heart of cognitive restructuring. Because they tend to be automatic and deeply embedded, however, dysfunctional thoughts tend to persist. As a result,

clients sometimes become discouraged when they do not achieve quick mastery of this step. It is important to recognize that step 4 extends across a number of weeks. If clients express discouragement with their progress, you can reassure them by explaining that change occurs only gradually and that a satisfactory degree of mastery can be achieved over time. At the same time, stress that clients can hasten the process by planning at the beginning of each day to anticipate situations they will encounter that present opportunities for using their newly discovered coping skills.

Another technique that equips clients to cope with automatic dysfunctional self-statements is to encourage them, upon first awareness of such thoughts, to nip them in the bud. Clients' first awareness of such thoughts is a flashing signal that they need to apply coping techniques immediately. One option involves *having a talk with oneself*, being mindful of the fact that the individual can *make a choice* whether to continue these thought patterns given their predictable outcomes.

5. *Assist clients in rewarding themselves for successful coping efforts.* For clients who attend only to their failures and shortcomings and rarely, if ever, give themselves positive feedback, step 5 in cognitive restructuring is especially important. To reinforce their coping efforts, clients learn to savor their progress in developing yet another new and functional cognitive pattern.

In implementing this step, the social worker should explain the rationale for giving oneself credit for progress. The following is an example of such an explanation:

Social worker: Antonia, now that you've experienced some success in substituting coping self-statements for self-defeating ones, it's important to learn to give yourself credit for your accomplishment. This is also an important way of learning to feel good about yourself, and not feel taken advantage of. I'm going to help you learn to reward yourself by pretending that I am you. I'll say aloud self-statements you might think after successful coping with the experience of talking to your sister about caring for her children.

After providing such an explanation, you then model several laudatory self-statements:

- "You weren't sure you could do it, but you did."
- "You didn't back off. You dismissed those negative thoughts and stayed with your game plan."
- "Talking to her about caring for her children was a big step. Sure, you may feel that you have a long way to go, but you've made a good start, and it feels just great."

During this modeling, the practitioner should observe and elicit clients' reactions. If clients appear receptive, instruct them to recreate a recent success and practice making approving self-statements by expressing them aloud. Because formulating positive self-statements may be difficult for many clients, initially they may feel awkward or self-conscious. Empathic understanding and encouragement on your part will usually prompt them to try this exercise. Indeed, it is vital that you give them consistent, positive feedback, identifying the small and often subtle incremental signs of growth.

To facilitate the transfer of coping skills from client–social worker sessions to real life, it is important to negotiate tasks with clients that involve making positive self-statements about their progress and about other accomplishments in daily living. In addition, self-monitoring using a daily log is a valuable tool for facilitating this process. We recommend that you encourage clients to record their daily successes, including small ones and self-statements that give themselves credit for the achievements. This process acts as a powerful reinforcer, enabling clients to curtail patterns that focus on shortcomings, failures, and negative experiences.

Limitations and Cautions

Cognitive restructuring is an effective technique that has been employed to address a range of problems in which perceptions, beliefs, and thought patterns result in dysfunctional behaviors. As a technique, it is also compatible with crisis intervention, task-centered practice, and solution-focused treatment. The "miracle question" utilized in solution-focused practice may, indeed, motivate clients to address problematic behaviors and encourage them to formulate specific change goals.

In assisting clients to make changes, however, social workers must not mistakenly assume that clients will be able to perform new behaviors solely as a result of changes in their cognitions or beliefs. In reality, they may lack social skills and require instruction and practice before they can effectively perform new behaviors, such as making social overtures, expressing personal feelings, engaging in problem solving, and asserting themselves.

Cognitive restructuring removes cognitive barriers to change and fosters a willingness to risk new behaviors, but it does not always equip clients with the skills required to perform those new behaviors. In addition, as noted by Vodde (2002), simply changing one's story does not ensure a certain outcome, given the presence of very real constraints such as oppression, adverse social forces, and lack of power. Without an acknowledgment of these factors, minority clients, for example, may potentially perceive cognitive restructuring as just another form of social control and ideological domination. Client opposition or reactance to cognitive restructuring may result from a failure on the part of the social worker to account for these externalizing factors.

The worldview and social psychological processes that shape minority perceptions and resulting thoughts or experiences are different from those noted with the majority culture. Hays (1995), as cited in Cormier and Nurius (2003), in critiquing cognitive restructuring with multicultural groups, observes that this approach supports the status quo of mainstream society and suggests that standardized beliefs exist about how people should perceive and react to their world. Thus, according to Hays, cognitive restructuring has the potential to place blame on the individual when, in fact, the client's perceptions, beliefs, and behaviors may accurately reflect injustices experienced by that person. Furthermore, as observed by Bronfenbrenner (1989) and Bandura (1989), the expectations, beliefs, and self-perceptions that give purpose and direction to what people think and feel exist within a cultural and environmental context. For example, in some cultures, a sister's refusal to provide care for her sister's children would be considered highly irregular behavior.

Herein lies a central challenge to using cognitive restructuring with minority group clients. Attempts to reshape thought patterns and perceptions so as to reflect a construction of reality that stands in contrast to their actual experience may potentially turn off involuntary clients who are members of minority groups. Oppositional involuntary clients who are minority adolescents often are encountered in school settings. Despite their style of dress, behavior, language, and choice of music, these clients may respond to interventions based on cognitive and social learning theories of vicarious capability and modeling. Indeed, modeling or observational learning procedures of cognitive restructuring may hold promise when working with such individuals because these strategies may be perceived as less threatening, especially if the focus is on a specific behavior, rather than the perceptions or experiences of the whole person.

Of course, some minority group members have mastered a dual frame of reference that is selectively congruent with dominant views and beliefs. For these individuals, cognitive restructuring may be a useful intervention procedure. Similarly, this approach may be beneficial when thoughts or beliefs are derived from interpersonal relations within groups—for example, the socially inhibited adolescent client in the peer group situation. In either case, use of cognitive restructuring strategies with minorities requires an orientation to the realities of the minority experience.

Finally, although cognitive theorists attribute most dysfunctional emotional and behavioral patterns to mistaken beliefs, these are by no means the only causes. Dysfunctions may be produced by numerous biophysical problems, including brain injury, neurological disorders, thyroid imbalance, blood sugar imbalance, circulatory disorders associated with aging, ingestion of toxic substances, malnutrition, and other forms of chemical imbalance. Consequently, these possibilities should be considered before undertaking cognitive restructuring.

SOLUTION-FOCUSED TREATMENT

Solution-focused treatment embodies the same features that are common to other brief treatment modalities: a focus on the present, and the premise that change can occur over a brief period of time. The approach has emerged over the past 20 years as a strategy for working with individuals, families, and involuntary clients. Similar to the task-centered approach, the solution-focused approach utilizes time limits. Work with clients is also facilitated by the development of specific goals, as formulated and prioritized by the client.

The solution-focused approach differs from other brief practice approaches in that it emphasizes the construction of solutions and deemphasizes problems. In this regard, it is similar to the narrative approach and cognitive restructuring because the professional has an active role in first "helping clients to question self-defeating constructions," and then assisting them to construct "new and more productive perspectives" (Nichols & Schwartz 2004, p. 101).

In the view of de Shazer and Berg, practice has traditionally been saturated with an emphasis on problems (De Jong & Berg, 1998). The solution-focused approach "avoids an assessment of how problems developed," neither tracking nor studying behaviors that perpetuate a problem (Nichols & Schwartz, 2004, p. 317). Although the approach focuses on the generation of solutions, it is in many respects a complaint-based strategy. That is, clients begin with a problem statement, yet are encouraged to move quickly to solutions.

According to proponents of the solution-focused approach, solutions and problems are not necessarily connected. Hence, it is considered preferable to engage clients in developing solutions rather than to involve them in assessing and discovering antecedents (Koob, 2003). Studying the exceptions to problems is often considered more useful.

Further, the solution-focused approach assumes that change can occur when clients are motivated and empowered to construct solutions. Clients and families are considered to be the experts because they have the knowledge, resources, and strengths needed to formulate solutions. Social workers' role is to listen, to absorb information, and to guide clients toward solutions utilizing the "language of change" (De Jong & Berg, 2002, p. 49). Lee (2003) believes that this motivational principle strengthens the viability of solution-focused practice in cross-cultural practice. In summary, the solution-focused approach is based on the present and is oriented to the future.

Theoretical Framework

The solution-focused approach grew out of de Shazer and Berg's work and the work of their associates at the Brief Family Therapy Center in Milwaukee, Wisconsin (Nichols & Schwartz, 2004; Goldenberg & Goldenberg, 1991). It was strongly influenced by the views of Milton Erickson, who believed that people were constrained by the social construction of their problems. According to this view, people have untapped unconscious resources, which can be released by shifting their perspectives.

The solution-focused approach borrows from constructivists the belief that people use language to create their reality (de Shazer & Berg, 1993). In addition, the approach draws from cognitive-behavioral theory the assumption that cognitions guide language and behavior. According to de Shazer and Berg (1993), solutions are facilitated when professionals and clients engage in discussions away from problems and without using the accompanying problem language. The approach also draws upon the constructivist notion that absolutes do not exist. For example, normal family development might be considered a phenomenon that has been imposed on families by professionals (Nichols & Schwartz, 2004).

Solution-Focused Procedures and Techniques

A strength of the solution-focused approach is the development of several practical techniques and procedures that are readily learned by practitioners and are applicable in many situations.

One such procedure is the development of *well-formed goals* (De Jong & Miller, 1995, p. 730) Well-formed goals comprise plans for actions that are important to the client, feasible, and usually the beginning of something (Tohn & Oshlag, 1996, p. 158). They are comparable to tasks in the task-centered approach in that they focus on small feasible actions that clients can undertake outside of sessions. In the task-centered approach, however, goals are outcomes sought rather than actions directed toward achieving outcomes.

An important premise in the development of well-informed goals is that client solutions are sought on the basis of exceptions. Several types of interview questions are employed to enable clients to arrive at specific goals and to think of exceptions to problems—namely, scaling, coping, exception, and miracle questions (Berg, 1994).

Scaling questions solicit the client's assessment of progress or readiness to complete a well-formed goal. For example, asking a client, "On a scale of 1 to 10, how ready do you feel to talk to your mother about moving out?" helps the social worker and the client gauge the client's readiness to attempt a well-formed goal about leaving home. Similarly, a client might be asked to assess progress hazards of an alcohol relapse: "On a scale of 1 to 10, where 1 is 'there is no chance I will relapse' and 10 is 'I feel like having a drink as soon as I leave here,' where would you rate yourself?" Use of such a scale could then be used to determine what kinds of well-formed goals might prove useful in moving the risk to a lower and safer level.

Coping questions capture the resources and strengths that clients have used previously when dealing with issues. For example, the social worker might ask, "In the past, when you were attempting to find affordable housing, what were some of the things that you tried that worked?" Coping questions are intended to uncover and energize clients' strengths and resources. They can also be used to reinforce strengths and focus on positives: "Please tell me how you have managed as a single parent to work full-time and raise three healthy, safe children?"

Another procedure designed to diminish problem focus relies on the use of *exception questions* (Shoham, Rorhbaugh & Patterson, 1995). For example, such questions assist clients to identify when the current concern did not exist. For example, a parent and an adolescent caught in conflict might be asked to think of times in which they interact now or have interacted in the past without conflict, including enjoying each other's presence. Such questions cue clients to explore their past for clues to solutions that they have within their own experience.

Finally, *miracle questions* draw attention to what could be different and what would need to change to reach a desired state (Koob, 2003; Lipchik, 2002). Koob (2003) cites research that concludes that having a positive vision about the future is a motivating force. In responding to miracle questions, clients identify goals related to where they would like to see themselves tomorrow. Their responses also shape the work to be completed between the client and the social worker into a collaborative construction of solution-oriented solutions. The client is asked to imagine how things would look if, by a miracle, the problem disappeared overnight. Typical interview questions that enlarge a client's capacity to think about the future and identify solutions include the following queries adapted from Lipchik (2002) and de Shazer & Berg (1993):

1. How will you know when your problem is solved?
2. What will be different when the problem is solved?
3. What signs will indicate to you that you don't have to see me any longer?
4. Can you describe what will be different in terms of your behavior, thoughts, or feelings?
5. What signs will indicate to you that others involved in this situation are behaving, thinking, or feeling differently?

To accomplish goals identified by the miracle questions in a proactive manner, a *formula task* might be used. For example, a social worker might direct a couple who are experiencing conflict in their relationship to engage in *exceptions,* such as talking more with each other when they are not in conflict. Other formula tasks may require clients to make observations—for example, "Before the next session, observe family interactions, and focus on those interactions that you would like to continue." Clients may also be assigned *prediction tasks,* in which they are asked to predict the status of their problem, for better or for worse, tomorrow (de Shazer, 1988).

The solution-focused approach emphasizes the collaborative nature of work with clients by referring to people who are seeking help as customers, complainants, or visitors (Jordan & Franklin, 2003). The

individual who is willing to make a commitment to change is called a *customer.* Those individuals who identify a concern but do not see themselves as part of the problem or solution are called *complainants.* A person who is willing to be minimally or peripherally involved but is not invested in the change effort is referred to as a *visitor.* In this way, the solution-focused approach identifies where potential clients stand relative to their commitment to change and ownership of concerns.

Uses of Solution-Focused Strategies

Solution-focused strategies have been utilized in a variety of settings and with diverse populations. For example, focusing on the positive attributes of nursing home residents with dementia, rather than their behavioral problems, changed the manner in which aides and nurses interacted with these residents (Ingersoll-Dayton, Schroepfer, & Pryce, 1999). In school settings with children and adolescents, scaling and miracle questions have been employed to explore feelings, develop behavioral goals, and encourage positive behaviors (Springer, Lynch, & Rubin, 2000; Corcoran & Stephenson, 2000). Using an ecological framework, Teal (2000) describes involving teachers, parents, and school counselors as resources and as co-creators of solutions to behavioral problems that occur in the classroom. Similarly, for children who were assigned to social skills training groups, parents have become involved in developing solutions as a means to address behavioral problems (Watkins & Kurtz, 2001). Studies have suggested that this approach has been effective in handling classroom management and school-related behavior problems (Gingerich & Wabeke. 2001; Gingerich & Eisengard, 2000).

In some instances, the change process has combined solution-focused strategies with other approaches such as CBT. For example, one study involving women in abusive relationships combined several different approaches as a means to move away from the "problem-saturated" stories of women and to elicit their participation in solutions. The women's stories were analyzed using techniques derived from psychodynamic and cognitive-behavioral approaches, but solution-focused narratives were used as the basis for changing the clients' emotional state (McQuaide, 1996). The results of this study were similar to those obtained with a treatment group of male domestic violence offenders. In working with these men, Lee, Greene, and Rheinscheld (1999) found that empowering them to engage in identifying solutions to their behavior was more effective than focusing on their violent behavior.

In other studies, exception questions were found to be effective in fostering behavioral changes. These studies involved high-risk youth and the issue of physical abuse. Specifically, Corcoran and Franklin (1998) found that exception-based solutions were more successful in situations where physical abuse was a concern, compared with attempts to stop or change the abusive behavior. Exception and scaling questions used with high-risk, middle and high school students who were referred for academic or behavioral problems were found to be effective means for setting goals and identifying solutions (Corcoran, 1998).

Strengths and Limitations

A positive, strengths-oriented approach is attractive to social work practitioners as a source of practical, readily learned techniques. For example, miracle questions may encourage clients to become invested in a vision of the future. The emphasis on clients' strengths and positive attributes as well as the attention paid to exceptions to the problem also make significant contributions. The solution-focused approach affirms that change—albeit even small gains—can occur over a brief period of time and that rapid change can encourage clients to feel optimistic about their future.

How the solution-focused approach is used in the future will depend in part on the results of studies analyzing when and how the approach is best applied. For example, research by family therapists using the solution-focused approach found discrepancies between clients' experiences related to outcomes and the observations made by their therapists (Metcalf, Thomas, Duncan, Miller, & Hubble, 1996). Storm (1991) and Lipchik (1997) found that the primary focus on adherence to solutions was disconcerting for some clients and that the positive thrust of the approach prevented them

from discussing their real concerns. It is possible that this emphasis leads some clients to avoid talking about problems in sessions with the therapist (Efran & Schenker, 1993).

Some critics have suggested that the very simplicity and practicality of some of the solution-focused techniques may lead in some cases to a simplistic, "cookbook" adoption of techniques, ignoring the relational dynamics between the professional and the client. As noted by Lipchik (1997), collaboration that keeps the "axles turning" as well as the "speed and success of solution construction depend on the therapist's ability to stay connected with the client's reality throughout the course of therapy" (p. 329). In fact, Metcalf et al. (1996) found that therapists had a tendency to focus on techniques, whereas clients were more concerned with the therapist–client relationship.

Both critics and proponents of the solution-focused approach have questioned whether this treatment strategy is, in fact, collaborative as opposed to being more directive in nature (Wylie, 1990, Lipchik, 1997; O'Hanlon, 1996). For example, solution-focused practitioners attempt to influence clients to talk about solutions based on their belief that problem talk has limited value. Similarly, this approach appears to downplay the expertise of professionals, even as professionals take charge of developing well-informed goals as assignments. The assignment of tasks by the practitioner would appear to be more directive than collaborative. For example, the assignment of generic formula tasks raises concerns about the individualization of the task plan. As the solution-focused approach is not a problem-solving model, it does not propose directly to assist clients in future resolution of difficulties. By comparison, the task-centered approach that is most attuned to empowering clients toward resolving future difficulties without professional help emphasizes the collaborative development of tasks such that clients can ultimately develop their own tasks in the future.

The social worker should aim to explain a particular type of formula task in the solution-focused approach to the client, with both practitioner and client then working together to tailor the task to the client's circumstances. We recommend the importation of the obstacle analysis feature of the task-centered approach to address this concern. That is, tailoring a task to the individual and his or her environment seems compatible with the spirit of the collaborative approach and more useful than simply assigning a generic task.

The assumption of client competence that is made in the solution-focused approach is a value consistent with social work's commitment to self-determination. However, having faith in and wishing to support client capacities should not lead us to assume that clients, in fact, have within them the solutions to all difficulties. We believe that social work practice entails mutual assessment of problems in a collaborative fashion as well as mutual formulation of goals. As Chapters 8 and 9 attest, assessments need not focus exclusively on problems and deficits. Rather, an appraisal of strengths and resources is important in developing a realistic view of the situation and systems involved.

We find it laudable that the solution-focused approach specifically addresses involuntary clients, an often-neglected population (De Jong & Berg, 2001). Specifically, motivational congruence can be enhanced by listening to the client's version of the circumstances of the situation that originally led to the mandated contact. For example, if a child has been removed from the home, use of the miracle question may clarify the actions and resources required for reunification rather than focusing exclusively on the events that prompted removal of the child. The approach is relatively silent, however, regarding situations in which the social worker is a public agency employee. For example, the solution-focused approach respects the role of "visitors" to treatment who have not chosen contact and hence has no expectations for their involvement. As a public agency worker, you may have mandated involvement with a client such that, for example, you are charged with carrying out a court order whether or not the "visitor" wishes such contact.

Practitioners have found it challenging to employ the solution-focused approach in an environment that is frequently at least problem-focused, if not pathology-focused (Trotter, 1999). For example, the legal system typically wants to see proof that problems have been resolved or dangers have been reduced. The treatment literature is, on the whole, focused on problem reduction. The solution-focused approach offers much promise for fomenting positive client commitment toward improving their situations and reaching solutions. Indeed, the very utility of the client-empowerment procedures behooves us to conduct more studies of this treatment strategy's effectiveness.

The body of evidence supporting the solution-focused approach is growing but is not yet robust. As a consequence, we encourage the continued study of this treatment option especially in a social work setting, and preferably in comparison with other approaches. For example, comparative studies of the solution-focused and task-centered methods might prove useful, as might exploration and study of blended approaches.

Summary

The goal attainment strategies discussed in this chapter may be used with clients in a variety of settings. The three approaches are empirically based, are time-limited and emphasize clients' capacity to change and grow through autonomous independent action. They also represent systematic processes for achieving desired outcomes through the collaborative action-oriented steps undertaken jointly by the client and the practitioner. As discussed in Chapter 12, structured, time-limited and action-oriented interventions appeal to racial and cultural minority groups. These characteristics, along with the focus on increasing clients' power to influence change in their lives, are perhaps the most salient attractions of each approach. Of course, each approach has limitations, some of which include specific populations. Nevertheless, each has merit in that these interventions are brief, are action-oriented, and focus on specific goals for change.

Any of these interventions begins with a clear description of goals. Goals flow from the problem or concern identified by the client or, in the case of involuntary clients, from the mandate. The criteria for developing goals are that they must be measurable, feasible, and stated in positive terms. Selecting the most suitable intervention strategy requires consideration of developmental stages, racial or cultural beliefs, customs and values, and environmental factors that may influence goal attainment. For the intervention to be effective, the goal attainment strategy must be consistent with the target problem or behavior. It has been our experience as practitioners that people who come in contact with social workers are seeking relief. Often, they are overwhelmed and may be paralyzed when they contemplate the complexity and longevity of their problems. The very act of setting goals, taking action, and being able to see movement is an empowering experience. Clients are invariably energized and motivated when they see incremental progress toward an outcome.

The ease in learning and practical usage of solution-focused procedures such as coping, scaling, exception, and miracle questions make them attractive adjuncts to much social work practice. The emphasis on engaging clients in talk about solutions—not just problems—is an empowering method that should be expanded in social work practice.

Internet Resources

See our companion website for hot links to some helpful URLs. Note that URLs are subject to change. We will endeavor to update the links on the companion website as much as possible.

A series of videotapes is available from Ronald H. Rooney at the University of Minnesota depicting individual and family practice using the task-centered approach. For a list of those videos, contact Dr. Rooney at rrooney@che.umn.edu. To order them, contact insight.media.com.

Information on crisis intervention is available at *http://www.vcun.org/-shabert/433/433crisis.html/ and http://www.cmrg.com/.*

You can also access resources about cognitive therapy, brief therapy, and the task-centered approach at *http://www.cognitivetherpay.com/, http://www.brief-therapy.org/hottips.htm,* and *http://www.task-centered.com/.*

Using InfoTrac College Edition, use the keywords "crisis intervention," "task-centered practice," "cognitive therapy," and "post-traumatic stress disorder" to obtain more information on these topics. You can also enter key words such as "miracle," "exception," and "coping questions" in InfoTrac and can access articles such as that by Lee (2003).

Related Online Content

Visit the *Direct Social Work Practice* companion website at *http://socialwork. wadsworth.com/hepworth7* for additional learning tools such as glossary terms, chapter outlines, InfoTrac College Edition keywords, relevant web links, and chapter practice quizzes. Also, be sure to check out the Direct Practice Virtual Reader, where the authors have personally selected articles relevant to this chapter using InfoMarks.

Notes

1. For additional information on brief treatment models, see Corwin (2002), Roberts and Greene (2002), and Wells and Gianette (1990).
2. Potocky-Tripodi (2002) has written an informative text on "best practices" for social work with immigrants and refugees.
3. For additional information on models of crisis intervention, see Parad and Parad (1990), Roberts (1990, 2000), and Okun (2002). For more extensive information on the definition and early development and critique of crisis intervention strategies, see Aguilera and Messick (1982), Golan (1978), Puryear (1979), Caplan (1964), and Lukton (1982).
4. We strongly recommend Cormier and Nurius (2003) for more comprehensive information on change strategies and skills in cognitive-behavioral therapy and cognitive restructuring. Also Walen, DiGuiseppe, and Wessler (1980) present and illustrate comprehensive strategies for disputing beliefs.

CHAPTER 14

Developing Resources, Planning, and Advocacy as Intervention Strategies

CHAPTER OVERVIEW

Chapter 14 moves from the consideration of intervention strategies for direct practice to the consideration of macro-level change. Macro practice interventions are illustrated by case examples in which social workers are guided by the principle of empowerment. The chapter concludes with a discussion of service coordination and collaboration at the macro level and general guidelines for evaluating outcomes.

Throughout its history, social work has focused on improving the human condition through social reform and striving for social justice and equality. The National Association of Social Workers (NASW) Code of Ethics has consistently included the primary obligation of enhancing the welfare of individuals, improving social conditions through resources development, and planning social action (NASW, 1996). The overarching principles of promoting social and economic justice and improving social conditions also encompass social work practice with populations at risk as outlined in the Educational Policy and Accreditation Standards (EPAS) of the Council on Social Work Education (CSWE), which emphasizes a commitment "to enhancement of human well-being and to the alleviation of oppression" (CSWE, 2003, p. 31).

Additionally, the CSWE stresses that social work programs "prepare social workers to alleviate poverty, oppression, and other forms of social injustice, to include the formulation and influence of social policies, and social work services in diverse political contexts" (2003, p. 32). Similarly, global standards that frame the core purpose of international social work emphasize social action, political action, and advocacy, "to facilitate the inclusion of marginalized, socially excluded, dispossessed, and vulnerable at-risk groups of people" (Global Standards for Social Work Education and Training, 2004, p. 3). Fundamental among the principles of international social work are respect for diverse beliefs, traditions, and cultures as well as regard for human rights and social justice. These principles are also articulated in the NASW Standards for Cultural Competence in Social Work Practice (NASW, 2001).

Macro-level intervention strategies are intended to facilitate achieving these broad goals and objectives. Although interventions with individuals (micro level) or families (mezzo level) also strive to achieve these goals, intervening at a systems level (macro) is equally important. In some instances, and based on multiple levels of need, intervention strategies may involve a combination or all levels (Lum, 2004). The blending of micro and macro strategies deemphasizes the distinction between the two practice arenas, instead suggesting that a more multisystemic approach may be preferable in responding to clients' needs and social conditions. As Netting, Kettner, and McMurtry (1993) note, social workers—regardless of their specializations—will at some time "engage in macro level interventions as the appropriate response to a need or problem" (p. 5).

DEFINING MACRO PRACTICE

By definition, macro practice has as its focus problem solving around situations or problems at the systems rather than the individual level. Parsons, Jorgensen, and Hernandez (1988) frame social problems as targets to be addressed by professional social workers using a range of social work roles (e.g., educator, enabler, mediator, advocate, resource developer, and broker). Netting, Kettner, and McMurtry (2004) identify the professional titles associated with these roles as including supervisor, manager, program coordinator, planner, policy analyst, and community organizer. Problem solving through development of resources, advocacy, and social action is not the exclusive domain of the social work profession, of course. Other professionals who act as change agents and address some or all of the same concerns include clergy, physicians, environmentalists, political activists, and community planners. However, social work—unlike any other profession—has accepted as its mandate a focus on the person-in-the-environment, social justice, oppression, and equality. In addition, the principles of social work mandate intolerance for systems that create and maintain social conditions that result in personal problems.

As characterized by Brueggemann (2002), social work practice on the macro level is the "practice of helping people solve social problems and make social change at the community, organizational, societal and global levels" (p. 3). Similarly, White and Epston (1990) emphasize broad societal concerns and social conditions that create and sustain problems experienced by individuals; according to these authors, the social worker has a duty to assist clients to externalize problems and conditions beyond the individual level.

This point is illustrated by a program initiated by a county health and human services agency. Staff found that their welfare caseloads consisted of a significant number of fathers who did not pay child support. This failure to pay child support, in turn, negatively impacted families who were struggling with limited financial resources. In addition, nonpayment of child support was frequently reported as a source of interpersonal tension between the custodial and noncustodial parents. The county board was adamant about pursuing the fathers for payment of their debts because board members viewed the families affected by this problem as a financial drain on county resources.

Focus groups were convened to explore issues related to the nonpayment of child support. The dominant themes that emerged from the groups included unemployment, underemployment, and a lack of low-skill-level employment opportunities in the county. The focus group participants also identified the metro area's inadequate public transportation as a complicating factor. The county agency's staff used the results from the focus groups sessions to develop a job skills program, thereby enabling the fathers to develop employable skills. The social workers also enlisted the community at large to help in locating jobs, providing transportation, and donating cars that allowed the fathers to pursue jobs outside of the county.

On a policy level, staff made presentations to the county board and the courts, seeking to fully explain the situations faced by the nonpaying fathers. Ultimately, they persuaded the county board and the courts to support a disciplinary approach that was less punitive toward the fathers. Undoubtedly, some fathers were shirking their parental responsibility. Nevertheless, by taking action that empowered those fathers who had the desire but not the means to provide for their children, the county reframed the problem and the problem arena, and developed services accordingly. In pursuing a macro-level strategy, the staff of the health and human services agency were able to achieve the county's goal: The fathers paid child support. This action effectively bridged micro and macro practice strategies by addressing the external social conditions that perpetuated individual problems (Vodde & Gallant, 2002; White & Epston, 1990; Parsons, Jorgenson, & Hernandez, 1994).

As conceptualized by Netting et al. (2004), macro activities are professionally guided interventions, beyond the individual level, that may

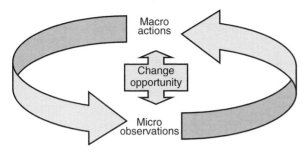

Figure 14-1 Linkage between Micro and Macro Practice

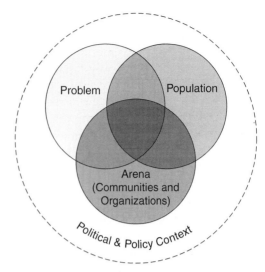

Figure 14-2 Macro Practice Conceptual Framework: Understanding Problem, Population, and Arena

Source: From Netting, Kettner, & McMurtry, *Social Work Macro Practice*, 3rd ed. Published by Allyn & Bacon, Boston, MA. Copyright © 2003 by Pearson Education. Reprinted by permission of the publisher.

emerge in the course of direct practice interaction with clients. Problems faced by individual clients may lead to a broader question: To what extent does the individual's situation reflect a group experience? Sometimes micro-level observations reflect social conditions that are actually shared by groups and communities, which macro strategies are required to rectify. At the same time, macro strategies (e.g., developing resources, organizing, advocacy, or social action) can sometimes improve or alter the problems of individuals. Figure 14-1 provides a perspective on the interrelationship between micro and macro practice.

Macro practice targets system-level change, so its strategies involve larger entities such as groups, organizations, and communities (Rothman, Erlich, & Tropman, 2001; Brueggemann, 2002; Netting et al., 2004). As seen in the previous example of the county agency's response to fathers' nonpayment of child support, organizations can take the lead as change agents equally as well as individual practitioners. When they engage in change, the intervention approach is systematic, as indicated by the framework to macro practice conceptualized by Netting, Kettner, and McMurty (2004). Figure 14-2 provides an overview of the macro-level change episode and the three overlapping focal points: the problem, the population, and the change arena.

Macro-level intervention strategies involve the same basic skills and processes introduced earlier in the helping process: identification and assessment of the condition or situation to be changed; goal development; selection of the intervention strategy; and evaluation. Many different forms of interventions are used to alter conditions, improve

environments, and respond to needs found within organizations, groups, or communities. A full discussion of the various macro-level strategies is beyond the scope of this text. Instead, we will focus our discussion on selected general strategies using case examples that emphasize the following aspects of intervention:

- Developing and supplementing resources
- Utilizing and enhancing support systems
- Advocacy and social action
- Social planning and organizing
- Improving institutional environments
- Collaboration and coordination of services

Why Focus on Empowerment?

Our emphasis throughout this chapter is on macro strategies in the context of empowerment, drawing upon case examples provided by social workers. By *empowerment*, we mean that groups or communities gain or regain the capacity to interact with the environment in ways that expand the resources available to meet their needs, thereby contributing to their well-being, potential, life satisfaction, and, to the extent possible, control over their lives. As social workers, we must respond to the needs and interests identified by groups or communities in ways that will assist them to realize their hopes, dreams, and aspirations and to build on their strengths. In addition, we emphasize ways in which organizations can act to empower people through programs, policies, and practices. We believe that macro-level intervention strategies, when combined with principles of empowerment, support collaborative problem solving.

Constituents of social work may include individuals, groups, and entire communities who lack the power of self-determination. Indeed, the powerless are more likely to have government agencies and public policy exert significant authority in their lives. Public policy examples include welfare programs, child protection services, educational systems, immigration and naturalization services, housing authorities, police protection, and transportation agencies. The empowerment perspective assumes that issues of power (and powerlessness) are inextricably linked to the experiences of oppression, which are most frequently seen in racial and ethnic minority groups and communities. Embedded in the experiences of most minority groups is a history of discrimination, stigma, and oppression. Certain vulnerable groups may exhibit a limited sense of individual or collective self-efficacy coupled with a pervasive sense of powerlessness and hopelessness to alter their circumstances. Moreover, enhancing one's sense of power is closely linked to developing competence, self-efficacy, support systems, and the belief that individual actions or actions in concert with others can alter or improve situations or conditions (White & Epston, 1990). Gutierrez (1994) suggests that in addition to increasing self-efficacy and developing new skills, empowerment includes the development of a critical consciousness about the causes of injustice.

Although these groups or communities may lack power and experience poor congruency between themselves, their needs, and the social environment, these communities nevertheless exhibit some strengths—for example, natural helping networks and support systems. Unfortunately, in some instances, the strengths of groups and communities may become taxed in the face of overwhelming needs and be obscured or eroded by oppressive and discriminatory forces. Even so, valuing the community's or group's definitions of problems and building on their strengths to forge a collaborative helping relationship are critical aspects of the empowerment process (Gutierrez & Lewis, 1999). In essence, the social work role in the empowerment process is to "help individuals develop the capacity to change their situations" (Gutierrez & Ortega, 1991, p. 25). As conceptualized by Gutierrez and Lewis (1999), measurable methods of empowerment are education, participation, and capacity building.

OPPORTUNITIES AND CHALLENGES

The social environment, in which groups and communities interact, also exerts influence over their lives and contains both challenges and opportunities. Most citizens of the United States enjoy a standard of living that provides for safety and protection through regulatory agencies and general welfare services, such as transportation and public education. Demographic characteristics such as immigrant or refugee status, race, sexual orientation, class, or ethnicity may impinge upon certain groups' opportunities, however. Specifically, gaining access to the same opportunities and resources (e.g., transportation and housing) that nonminority citizens enjoy may create challenges for members of certain groups. Minority communities (particularly those in the urban core of many cities) frequently cannot take advantage of job opportunities because city transportation systems do not provide service to the suburban areas where the new jobs are located. In addition, shortage of affordable housing in suburban areas may create tensions. As a consequence, many inner-city families remain below the poverty level despite the fact that many members work multiple jobs. Earned income typically comes through minimum-wage, low-level service jobs that do not allow workers to reach a standard of living beyond the poverty level. Thus, individuals and families continue to live in poverty—and many become homeless—because of the combination of low-income wages, inadequate transportation systems, and lack of affordable housing.

Housing remains a challenge for low-income families. Many depend on Section 8, a government subsidy program that allows low-income families to rent in the private market using vouchers provided under a federal housing program. In April 2004, in seeming contradiction of the George W. Bush administration's proposal to end long-term homelessness, the U.S. Department of Housing and Urban Development announced retroactive budget cuts to the Section 8 Housing Choice program. This action converged with the trend among landlords to discontinue accepting Section 8 vouchers and a resurgence of regentrification in inner cities to effectively lessen the ability of low-income people to obtain affordable housing.

Trends in the global economy, such as the outsourcing of high-paying manufacturing jobs, have resulted in a loss of jobs in the United States, even as they improved economic conditions in other countries. A significant number of jobs were created in the U.S. service sector over the last two decades. For individuals who had the education and experience needed to obtain highly skilled jobs, the emergence of the technology service industry has created numerous opportunities. Conversely, individuals who are employed in low-level jobs in the service sector (e.g., fast food restaurants, retail, cleaning services), many of which are part-time and lack health care benefits, have struggled.

The question of whether the U.S. economy is currently thriving depends on which segment of the population. Congress has continually resisted raising the minimum wage, so the issue of mandating "a living wage" remains unresolved. Adequate income and poverty are challenges faced by immigrants, refugees, and migrants, many of whom are employed in low-level jobs in the service sector or as day laborers. In cities across the United States, men from Mexico and various Central American countries stand on designated street corners every

morning, waiting for potential employers to drive by and offer seasonal construction work or odd jobs, albeit at a much lower wage than the market rate. Not surprisingly, these jobs do not offer any benefits or legal protection.

This issue of unemployment and underemployment for the poor is not unique to the United States. For example, nearly one-tenth of the population of the Philippines works overseas (Mydans, 2004). Among the immigrant or migrant workforce in the United States, many are undocumented, so their vulnerability goes unobserved and their numbers are uncounted for in times of natural disasters or political conflicts (as was the case after the September 11, 2001, disaster, for example). The countries from which these men and women emigrate rely on these workers to fuel their economies by providing ongoing financial support to family members left behind in their homeland. At the same time, neither their home countries nor U.S. laws protect these immigrants and migrants against exploitation.

Opportunities for macro-level intervention strategies also exist in educational systems where significant numbers of children of color are labeled and segregated as underachievers or as oppositional deviants in need of anger management or training in social skills. Such labeling results in "enormous social costs to individuals and society" and "sustains class, economic, and social inequities" (Williams, 1990, p. 236). In 2004, *U.S. News and World Report* reported that, 50 years beyond the landmark *Brown vs. Board of Education* case, equality in public education remains unfinished business in the United States. While *Brown vs. Board of Education* focused on racial inequality in education rather than economic status, race and economic status continue to influence the quality of education available to children. Specifically, a disproportionate percentage of minority children are poor and live in impoverished urban areas where the educational systems are inadequate. As reported by *USA Today* (January, 26, 2003) the failure of minority students to achieve higher test scores is frequently related to the fact that their classroom teachers often lack the educational qualifications and competencies in math and science. Moreover, educational systems are burdened with unfunded mandates such as the No Child Left Behind Act enacted under the George W. Bush administration. Research findings point out that minority and poor parents have the same educational aspirations for their children as nonminority parents, but often find that educational systems are unresponsive to their needs. Instead, parents and indeed entire communities (e.g., the culture of poverty) are blamed for the failure of their children to achieve academic success.

Poverty continues to play a role in social problems—in particular, child development, family stability, health, and mental health status. Being poor means having limited access to the resources that are typically available to other citizens (Ewalt, 1994b; Halpern, 1990; Brooks-Gunn & Duncan, 1997; McLoyd, 1997). Moreover, in some respects, poverty and race are synonymous. A study conducted by Rank and Hirschl (1999) traced poverty over the lifespan and suggested that minorities—in particular, poor African Americans—are likely to remain impoverished throughout their lifetime. Brooks-Gunn and Duncan (1997) discuss the incidence of poverty within third-generation minority and immigrant groups. Poor and minority families struggle with obstacles and challenges that may be institutionalized, further exacerbating their marginal status in society. These challenges affect entire communities, the majority of which are racially or ethnically diverse and female, as well as those groups who are segregated by geographical location and have limited access to alternatives. The term "extra-familial obstacles" denotes the situations faced by families who are regarded differently because of their race, class, or sexual orientation.

Many groups and even entire communities experience chronic stressors in their everyday lives because they lack the minimum resources required to meet their basic needs (Tolan & Gorman-Smith, 1997). In the article "Enough to Make You Sick," Epstein (2003) vividly describes life in "America's rundown urban neighborhoods," noting that illnesses normally associated with old age are showing up in young, inner-city residents.

A parent interviewed for the article described her life as "you wake up stressed, you go to sleep stressed." In his portrayal of the stark ecological realities of inner-city life, *There Are No Children Here,* Alex Kotlowitz (1991) described a situation in which 1,000 new appliances were found waterlogged and infested with rodents in the storage area of a public housing project despite the fact that a majority of the residents did not have adequate appliances. While his story focused on one family, they are representative of groups of families—indeed, entire communities—who live, cope, and survive in circumstances beyond their control.

The harmful effects of prolonged exposure to poverty and stressful life events on child and adolescent development are well documented in the literature (e.g., Mosley & Lex, 1999; Icard, Longres, & Spenser, 1999; McLoyd, 1997; Smith & Carlson, 1997; Freeman & Dyers, 1993; Jose, Caffasso, & D'Anna, 1994). In a study examining the relationship between poverty and psychopathology (specifically, behavioral symptoms identified in DSM-IV), the findings suggested that improved income, rather than the dominant political theme of personal responsibility, had a "major effect on children's psychiatric disorder" (Costello, Compton, Keeler, & Angold, 2003, p. 2023). Similarly, behavioral symptoms such as oppositional defiant behavior decreased significantly in those families whose income improved, effectively moving them out of poverty.

To a large extent, social welfare services continue to be directed primarily toward individual change. This focus has been reinforced over the last two decades by the emphasis on personal responsibility. Because various organizations have their own mission, structure, and service goals for which they receive funding, clients with multiple concerns may experience a service system that is fragmented, is segmented, and lacks coordination. The Personal Responsibility and Work Opportunity Reconciliation Act of 1996 (PRWOR), which reformed the system of public welfare, and the Adoption and Safe Family Act of 1997 (ASFA) are examples of both segmentation and limited coordination. The PRWOR requires the head of the family receiving welfare assistance to become employed within 2 years and sets a 60-month life-time limit on receiving assistance. At the same time, the ASFA emphasized greater scrutiny of poor families' ability to care for their children but did not take into account the removal of some of the safeguards by the PRWOR.

Undoubtedly, there was a need to reexamine both the public welfare and the child welfare systems, but the competing and conflicting demands of these two concurrent pieces of legislation resulted in many families experiencing system-level difficulties in meeting requirements and timelines. Ultimately, the burden of the corrective action undertaken in both welfare reform and child welfare reform fell on individuals. The assumption made in child welfare policy was that neglectful parents' lack of parental responsibility was the primary culprit when they failed to meet the timelines required to achieve family reunification or permanency. However, the review of the delays in permanency and reunification failed to consider the possibility that the excess time that a child remained in care resulted from an over-loaded, underfunded, fragmented system. In much the same manner, a core belief driving welfare reform was that people receiving public assistance lacked motivation to work. In reality, the previous policy disallowed those receiving benefits from being employed. Some research suggests that the welfare reform efforts may be linked to increased reports of child maltreatment and neglect (Courtney, 1999; Hutson, 2001).

Implementation of policy often has had an uneven impact on segments of the population, and in particular on minority communities. Consider AFSA, for example. This legislation was intended to move children to permanent homes. Specific timelines were enacted to ensure that children did not languish within the family services system; for instance, parents were given 12 months to achieve reunification. The implementation of this law disproportionately struck some segments in African American communities and families, as the majority of the children involved in the child welfare system were African American (Morton, 1999). Roberts (2002) likens the child welfare system to apartheid, the effects of which constitute "group

harm" because entire communities experience the impact. In fact, in large urban communities, the intervention of child welfare and child protection services may be traced to specific ZIP codes primarily populated by poor and minority families. In large part, according to Chipungu and Bent-Goodley (2003), the child welfare system has become a "safety net for poor children" funded by Title IV-E (p. 9).

With increasing frequency, the context in which social welfare services are delivered is framed by a series of rules, policies, and procedures (RPPs); legislative and court mandates; and managed care directives. Social workers often experience pressures that demand their compliance, and that of their clients, at the expense of their professional knowledge and discretion. Recognizing this inevitability, social workers should understand and be able to articulate the impact of legislation or court mandates, policies, and "therapeutic jurisprudence" on their constituent groups (Alexander, 2003; Wexler, 1992; Madden & Wayne, 2003). It is important for social workers to remain grounded in the historical roots of their profession, which compel them to promote social and economic justice, advocate for social change, address issues of inadequate resources, and seek to reverse policies that adversely impact their clients' well-being. Such understanding includes cultural competence at the individual, organizational, and policy levels. When initially formulated, policies and legislative mandates may be neutral with respect to race, class, gender, culture, or sexual orientation, only to have a disparate impact on certain groups when they are actually implemented.

Analyzing Social Problems and Conditions

The preceding discussion identified conditions and trends that demand the attention of social work and a focus on problem solving at the macro level. At this point, you might wonder about their importance to you as a direct practice practitioner. In response, we offer the following points. First, micro-level practitioners should understand the reality of the lives of the people that they serve. Moreover, practice at all levels interacts with and is influenced by forces external to the profession, including societal values, laws, and policies. Second, the experiences of people, especially those without power, and the conditions they face should prompt social workers to examine their situation using the lens of social justice, and to assess whether civil and human rights are being violated. Armed with this knowledge, social workers and social welfare organizations should assume proactive roles in providing the leadership for problem solving that address issues beyond the individual level.

The following questions, which are adapted from the work of Finn and Jacobson (2003) can be used in analyzing problems from a macro perspective.

- What are the social justice issues affecting the people with whom I work?
- What are the set of values expressed for groups and communities when resources are distributed in our society?

To these questions, we add a core question from the FrameWorks Institute:

- Who and what is responsible for the problem?

The FrameWorks Institute is a nonprofit organization that provides training for professionals and other advocates in "thinking strategically" about social problems and reframing issues that appeal to basic societal values when communicating with policy-makers or the public. You may obtain additional information about the institute by accessing its website (*www.frameworksinstitute.org*).

Linking Micro and Macro Practice

Understanding the ecological, systems nature of social problems requires you to emphasize macrolevel interventions in concert with other intervention strategies. Before proceeding further, we add a cautionary note: Social workers must be mindful that when client concerns are multidimensional and involve reciprocal interactions among multiple systems, interventions aimed exclusively at one system (e.g., the environment, the individual, or the family) may ignore critical dimensions. Conversely, multiple interventions may overlap and be employed to simultaneously address both the

individual and the social conditions that affect individuals, communities, and groups. Constituents served by social workers benefit from all levels of practice because their concerns and problems are often complex, and involve micro, mezzo, and macro issues. It is possible, however, that macro-level situations may be generalized to the groups to which clients belong and with whom social workers interact on a daily basis. In many instances, opportunities to employ macrolevel strategies evolve from caseloads, as illustrated in the following example:

CASE EXAMPLE

As a member of an interdisciplinary community-based health team, a practitioner works in a neighborhood health clinic that is located in a low-income community. Her caseload consists primarily of young mothers and their children. In reviewing her case records, the social worker notes a common theme: "running out of food near the end of the month" among the families that she sees individually. By tracking the time period of failed appointments, she notes that the mothers and their children are also more likely to miss clinic appointments in the last week of the month. When a team member raises a concern about families missing appointments and suggests implementing more strident measures as a response, the social worker shares her observations. She further suggests exploration of failed appointments as a group issue rather than an individual issue. In response to her suggestion, the team agrees to sponsor a series of focus groups with young mothers to examine this issue in addition to other resource and service needs.

In this situation, the social worker effectively moved from a micro-level focus of a specific problem to a strategy that has the potential to address "running out of food" as a condition that is representative of a larger group issue. The social worker's hypothesis of the linkage between the issue of food shortage and failed appointments was a focal point, but expanding the conversation to include other resource and service needs avoided the potential for humiliation or embarrassment of the participants.

Within the interdisciplinary team's larger purpose—for example, its joint effort to provide individuals or families in the community with health care—the social worker brings a unique systems perspective to the various theoretical and professional orientations represented on the team (Long & Holle, 1997). In this case example, the social worker made a unique contribution by examining system-level factors that might potentially contribute to what was originally perceived as an individual issue. In addition, the social worker's suggestion to use focus groups to study the issue is an example of empowerment because an open-ended discussion among the mothers will allow them to define and prioritize their concerns, using their own frame of reference.

DEVELOPING AND SUPPLEMENTING RESOURCES

Regular, meaningful contact with individuals, families, and groups places you in a strategic position to identify resources and needs of people living in impoverished conditions. Within the context of this work, resource development includes working with policy-makers, civic groups, and administrators of social welfare organizations to educate and create an awareness of social conditions in need of improvement. In augmenting or developing resources for groups and communities, some specific needs of individuals may also be met. However, as noted by Vosler (1990), resource needs often go unnoticed, perhaps in large part due to the structure of social welfare services in which the primary focus tends to be on individual treatment. Because of this emphasis on individual treatment, the need for aggregate information about whole groups or populations may not be as obvious as in the previous case example.

Mobilizing Community Resources

Resources for addressing concrete needs may vary depending on the community. For example, rural communities may have fewer formal resources, and those that do exist are often taxed beyond their limits. We have a tendency to construct an idealized positive image of the rustic rural community, in which informal networks exist and seamlessly meet all needs—in essence, "neighbor helping neighbor." Although this image has some merit, informal networks cannot make up for a shortage of affordable housing, transportation, job opportunities, and adequate health and mental health services. While rural communities tend to be racially homogeneous, significant disparities may exist between income levels. The assumption of affluence in suburban communities often means that low-income individuals in those communities are invisible, remain isolated, and lack access to adequate services.

In each of these situations, resource development may be required to help secure essential services for these individuals. Macro-level practice in these scenarios would focus on the development of programs to address group needs. Thus, developing or supplementing resources is indicated when it is apparent that a significant number of people within given ecological boundaries (e.g., neighborhoods, communities, institutions) or populations who share certain characteristics have needs for which matching resources are unavailable. Moreover, in a world characterized by relentless change—whether in the physical environment, technology, or politics—social workers are constantly confronted with the need to organize resources in response to both existing and evolving needs.

The roles of enabler, broker, and mediator, as supported by the principles of empowerment, may be particularly important for social workers who are involved in mobilizing and developing resources. The earlier case example of young mothers involved with the community-based health clinic illustrates these social work roles and suggests ways to adhere to the principle of empowerment. By eliciting information from the mothers, the social worker assumed the role of enabler, so that resources were developed *with*, rather than *for*, the mothers. Results from the focus group discussions revealed that, among other things, the mothers were reluctant to use the neighborhood park with their children because of drug traffic, police harassment, and men soliciting prostitutes. Community safety was another concern that emerged, along with the need for developing child care options.

Encouraged by the social worker, a number of the mothers began attending meetings of a community organization to discuss their concerns about the park. The community organization also included members of area churches and representatives from local businesses. The social worker and a group of mothers built on this initial contact by visiting several of the large churches in the neighborhood to explore options for evening activities. Although many of the mothers had used the community food pantry provided by the churches, they were generally skeptical of the churches' interest in their situation and reluctant to approach them. In talking to church leaders, the social worker found a vibrant interest in becoming more involved in the community, especially with children, and discovered that the churches also had concerns about community safety. The social worker arranged a meeting (mediator role) between the group of mothers and church leaders. Following a series of meetings between the mother's group, church officials, and area business owners, several churches agreed to open their buildings for a "mother's night out" child care program, staffed by the mothers and volunteers from the churches. In addition, the social worker helped the women to establish a child care cooperative, which provided the mothers with more free time.

While their concerns about the use of the parks were not resolved, the women gained a greater sense of their ability to effect change in their community and in themselves as a result of their involvement with the churches and the community organization. Likewise, the community organization, whose meetings had previously not been well attended, was revitalized. In joining the community effort, the mothers had an opportunity to take charge and become involved in efforts to increase the livability of the community.

This example illustrates the potential for developing and mobilizing community resources by forging partnerships between various groups who may not routinely interact, despite sharing common concerns. In working with the mother's group and contacting the churches, the social worker recognized the need to educate the church members about the community because the majority did not live in the community; she also sought to address their concerns about additional traffic in the building by nonmembers of the church.

What happened to the health center staff's concern about failed appointments, and did the social worker's activities constitute the best use of the health center's resources? Actually, the mothers did talk about food shortages as an issue, especially at the end of the month. During that time their children were apt to be more restless and irritable than usual, and the mothers consequently felt a tremendous amount of stress. For many, the end-of-the-month appointments scheduled at the health clinic conflicted with their visits to the community food pantry. Thus, they made the decision that food was a priority. While understanding this need, the social worker was able to educate the mothers about the importance of respecting the center's resources by keeping appointments, or at least canceling them in advance.

Ultimately, was this the best use of the social worker's time? Consider what she learned, what the staff learned, and how she was able to intervene and resolve other concerns of the mothers and the larger community. Perhaps more importantly, consider the fact that a partnership between the two groups emerged.

Supplementing Existing Resources

Needs for resources vary according to specific concerns and differ substantially from one community to another. In some instances, existing resources may be inadequate for the level of need. Factors such as stigmatization and dominant values and beliefs often clash with the realities of need, however, and may unintentionally reinforce oppression and denial of access to needed resources. An overview of the social condition of homelessness illustrates this point.

Views of the homeless in which individuals are characterized as lazy, immoral, or possessing other attributes of depravity resemble nineteenth-century thought (McChesney, 1995). More recently, the homeless have been characterized as mentally ill, addicts or substance abusers, lacking personal responsibility, and having minimal job skills. Certainly, some individuals among the homeless are in need of health or mental health services, employment or rehabilitation counseling, and social support, but not all of them. The prevailing view of the homeless ignores social and economic conditions as contributing factors to the status of homelessness. The following factors are known to contribute to being or becoming homeless:

- Poverty is a primary factor for families becoming homeless, which extends to the ability to find and maintain affordable housing. Many families have exhausted or overextended informal networks and have few alternatives (McChesney, 1995).
- Limited housing options for low-income families in rural communities.
- Limited and aging housing stock in inner cities.
- Resistance of suburban communities to allow low-income housing.
- The phasing out of governmental subsidy programs that counter the effects of the lack of affordable housing.
- Youth who are unable to live in the parental home.
- Youth who have aged out of the child welfare system.

Although the homeless are a homogenous group in that they share a need for shelter and food, the demographics of the homeless differ in both composition and geography. As reported by the Child Welfare League of America, children account for a large percentage of the homeless in the United States; yet, children do not exist apart from their families. Studies have established that the majority of homeless in urban areas are families rather than individuals, and most are African American. In rural and suburban areas, the issue of homelessness has not been sufficiently acknowledged or discussed, making it difficult to determine the composition of this geographical group (McChesney, 1995; Gershel, Bogard, McConnell, & Schwartz, 1996). Youth leaving their homes for a variety of reasons

increasingly represent yet another significant portion of the homeless population (Nord & Ludloff, 1995). Kurtz, Jarvis, and Kurtz (1991) reported on a regional research study conducted in the southeastern states in which most of the homeless youth lacked stable and supportive families. Homeless youth constitute a highly vulnerable population that presents a wide range of problems and needs. They include runaways, throwaways, youth in conflict with their parents, and youth who have aged out of the child welfare system without essential supports.

Living arrangements for the homeless also vary. Being homeless may mean making frequent moves between shelters and transitional housing facilities. Some individuals may be living on the streets, while others live in shelters or with a series of family or friends. Irrespective of the various entry points to homelessness status, the resources for this population are clearly inadequate and contribute to further problems. For example, homeless families are at risk for intervention by child protective services. Homeless youth are often victimized by violence and may engage in illegal and risky behaviors (e.g., prostitution) to support themselves. Whether a homeless family or youth is able to exit from this status greatly depends on the availability and accessibility to substantial institutional and governmental supports (McChesney, 1995; Piliavin, Wright, Mare, & Westerfelt, 1996).

In response to the needs of this growing population, a group of social workers working with communities and homeless groups have been instrumental in supplementing an existing resource for homeless populations. They have been simultaneously involved in actively influencing legislative and policy initiatives. Unfortunately, while the group achieved their overall goal of augmenting resources for the homeless, an oversight in planning the change effort resulted in difficulties, as seen in the following case example.

CASE EXAMPLE

In response to a growing demand for additional shelter, social workers and residents from a homeless shelter convened with a group of community, religious, and business leaders to explore the possibility of expanding available shelter beds. A proposal to use churches throughout the city for "bed only" space was developed and presented to the Social Justice Committees of the various churches. Several churches agreed to the proposal, and minimal opposition was encountered from the business community, city officials, and neighbors.

However, the social workers had neglected to elicit the views of a key group—the parents served by and staff of the day-care center housed in one of the churches. Believing that they had involved all of the critical stakeholders, the social workers were unprepared for the most vocal opposition that came from these parents. Parental concerns centered on child safety and fears about the presence of homeless men in proximity to their children.

In conceptualizing change, good intentions—no matter how noble and practical—may often prove to be insufficient. In the debriefing and evaluation sessions, the social worker learned a point emphasized by Rothman, Erlich, and Tropman (2001) and Netting, Kettner and McMurtry (1993): It is important to explore potential barriers such as ideological conflicts, fears, and value conflicts that community members may have to any proposed change. In this situation, the day-care center parents and staff were not involved in the initial discussion and, therefore, their concerns were not adequately addressed.

The case example emphasizes how important it is for social workers to work closely with community leaders, civic or religious groups, elected officials, and organized task as well as informal groups that include vulnerable people and their advocates. Managing and coordinating these various groups requires the social worker to fill the roles of broker, mediator, and enabler. In this case, the opportunity to implement long-range solutions also required social planning efforts to be made at the federal, state, and local levels. The social workers recognized that finding the additional shelter space was merely an interim solution, not a permanent solution. Intermediary efforts are by no means a substitute for advocacy, and long-range planning and action are required when a particular issue affects a significant number of people or the community as a whole. Toward this end, the social workers in the shelter lobbied and educated elected officials about the plight of the homeless and

actively sought the involvement of groups that focused on larger systemic issues—for example, advocating for affordable housing, "living wage" jobs, and improved public transportation.

Developing Resources with Diverse Groups

It is critical for social workers to familiarize themselves with the cultural nuances, values, norms, and political structures of various groups while they are developing or supplementing supportive systems or networks within a community. The tendency to generalize information about certain groups may potentially lead to conflicts, because there may actually be status and power differences or clan or religious differences within groups, even among those who may share the same country of origin.

Many non-Western cultures are characterized as valuing interdependence and collectivism over the more Western post-industrial trait of independence (Greenfield, 1994; Ogbu, 1987). This tendency would suggest that resources are more readily available in immigrant or refugee communities. In some cases, this belief leads to a useful framework for understanding cultural influences or pressures and social and economic arrangements. Nevertheless, social workers must recognize that length of stay, extent of acculturation, within-group power structures, and kinship ties may ultimately influence social support systems.

For example, domestic violence may thrive when a code of silence prevails in a particular community. Oliver Williams, Executive Director of the Institute on Domestic Violence in the African American Community, interviewed in the May 2002 issue of *Essence* magazine, asserts "that often abused Black women do not believe that the police are there to protect them," while others suffer for "fear of the consequences their partner may suffer at the hands of the police." In other communities, silence may be related to cultural barriers. For example, a social worker seeking assistance for immigrant women who were abused by their husbands found that the larger community was sympathetic to the issue. At the same time, fear of the husband's status in the community and relationships between clans prevented community members from providing a safe haven for these women. Moreover, perceptions in this community of what constituted an abusive relationship were not the same as those found in Western society. In another situation, a social worker urged a woman to seek assistance from a shelter (rather than relying on the family and clan to help resolve a marital conflict); as a result, the woman became isolated from her community. Intervention strategies must always be informed by and remain sensitive to how particular communities resolve situations and, wherever possible, those strategies should be supported. These types of situations often present ethical and legal dilemmas for social workers, particularly in instances of flagrant harm. (Note that the domestic abuse examples cited in this discussion are not intended to suggest that such violence is more prevalent in communities of color. Rather, they are simply used as examples to emphasize the necessity of understanding the structure and political realities of different communities.)

These examples as well as others provided by Hirayama, Hirayama, and Cetingok (1992) and Green (1999) highlight the fact that diverse groups may differ in their definition of a problem and therefore may not respond to the same resources developed to address a particular concern. As Hirayama et al. (1992) and Potocky-Tripodi (2002) note, although immigrants, migrants, and refugees experience reactive depression, they may not access mental health services because of a negative perception of the "mental illness" label. Similarly, cultural beliefs and perceptions may influence the extent to which some Hispanics access mental health services (Green, 1999). An individual's reluctance to articulate concerns may also be influenced by the threat of stigmatization or the negative perceptions held by his or her community and by the larger society.

UTILIZING AND ENHANCING SUPPORT SYSTEMS

In the assessment phase of the helping process, the whole person is explored along with that individual's concern. This assessment is most comprehensive and inclusive when it examines the ecology of the client's identified problem, systems involved, strengths, resilience and support systems. Social supports or kinship networks exist in almost all groups and communities. Despite suffering from chronic stressors and experiencing both positive and negative life events, many groups demonstrate a tremendous amount of resilience, coping skills, and the capacity to help others in times of need. Relatives, neighbors, and congregations are natural ecological structures, and as such may offer resources needed by a variety of groups. Although support networks were common in pre-industrialization communities, they are virtually an untapped resource in post-industrial Western society, especially with the advent of more formal social welfare systems. In exploring the dynamics of help, Bertha Reynolds (1951) stressed, "people seem to look upon taking and giving help as they do any other activity of life" (p. 16).

In recent years, social workers have increasingly relied on interventions that tap both formal and informal support networks and have developed new resources that provide vitally needed resources to specific populations. The child care cooperative and the "mother's night out" program organized by neighborhood mothers in an earlier case example highlights an informal support network that provided a much-needed respite for overburdened mothers and their children. Relatives, friends, neighbors, and organizations located in communities are all support systems that can be activated in times of adversity. The trend among social workers to identify and utilize natural support systems is both warranted and welcomed by groups and communities. Such support systems are not merely valuable today; they are essential because social workers and other professional helpers are limited in the time they can spend with each client. In contrast, members of support systems can often be available immediately when a crisis occurs and can provide ongoing support.

Community Support Systems and Networks

While modern social welfare services have tended to remove or become a substitute for the natural helping that has sustained people over time, there is a rich history detailing the contributions of Jewish, Catholic, Protestant, fraternal, and civic groups as mutual aid societies in support of individuals and families. Furthermore, reliance on indigenous networks and community support was critical for economic and social survival among historically oppressed groups. In addition, members of minority groups have traditionally been reluctant to seek assistance from resources outside of their communities because they had demeaning, impersonal, or negative experiences with formal social welfare organizations or because services were not available to them as a result of discriminatory practices (Green, 1999; Lum, 2004).

A series of examples can provide a few glimpses into various group traditions and values related to support systems and their resource potential. (Of course, these examples represent general observations that may not be pertinent to all members of the particular group.) Horejsi, Heavy Runner, and Pablo (1992) note that persistent poverty among Native Americans has resulted in a norm of sharing concrete resources. Tribal gaming has energized this tradition, by providing housing, social and mental health services, and educational and economic opportunities for tribal members using profits from the casinos. In African American and Hispanic communities, the strength and survival of families and groups have often been dependent on strong kinship ties, flexibility in family membership, and connections to the church as a social and economic resource. In the African American community, for example, the legacy of helping includes the building of institutions of higher education, care for orphaned children, and establishment of widows' pensions and insurance societies. Other communities of color likewise have a long history of formal and informal human services—witness the Buddhist mutual aid associations and social services in Asian communities (Canda & Phaobtong, 1992). In an interview with a Somali student, one of this book's authors learned that religious teaching prevented the accumulation of personal wealth. The student emphasized the fact that family groups tended to pool their resources to buy a business with the understanding that

it was for the support of a number of families and to benefit the community.

A number of studies have emphasized the efficacy of natural support systems. Indeed, research has shown that feeling lonely and being isolated from support networks are risk factors for neglect and abuse (Beeman, 1993). Mothers in a research group that sought to define "neglect" reported that "sometimes the best thing that you can do for somebody is to be their friend" (Rooney, Neathery, & Suzek, 1997, p. 19). McRoy (2003) describes the action of a church in a small town in Texas, where the minister led the congregation in adopting African American children. The movement, called "Saving a Generation," resulted in more than 50 children being adopted. Kinship care and support systems such as the church and neighborhood group or networks also serve as community-level protective factors (Testa, 2002; Gibson, 1999; Haight, 1998; Tracy & Whittaker, 1990; Jackson, 1998; Brookins, Peterson, & Brooks, 1997). In fact, kinship studies (e.g., the placement of children with kin) found that the utilization of informal resources lasts longer, is more supportive of the child's cultural and ethnic identity, is more supportive of community and familial connections, and is relatively stable as compared to nonkin placements (Hegar, 1999; Danzy & Jackson, 1997).

Informal networks and natural support systems can act as both resources and preventive measures. Wendy Auslander, of Washington University in Saint Louis, investigated the effects of culture on health, using natural support systems (Mays, 2003). The project's goal was to find ways to teach healthy eating habits to African American women who were deemed to be at risk for diabetes. Inner-city women were trained as nutritional counselors, and findings showed that the at-risk women were most receptive to the information about diabetes when peers, neighbors, and friends provided it. Auslander found that the natural support networks were well developed, interconnected at various levels in the community, and very efficient and effective in achieving changes in the eating habits of women in the community.

Similar results were reported in Montgomery County, Maryland, with "Barber's Cuttin Cancer Out." This project was initiated by the Maryland Department of Health and Human Services in partnership with local barbershops, in an effort to remove the barriers that prevented African American men from seeking oncology screening (Mallory, 2004).

Organizations as Support Systems

Organizations can also act as support systems, particularly for people who are in the midst of a transition. The American Red Cross is an example of a formal organization that assists communities in times of disaster. Examples of supportive systems include transitional housing, shelters for battered women, work environments that have responsive policies to family demands, workplaces that provide classes for individuals for whom English is a second language, and programs that promote health and wellness for employees. Other organizations that function as support systems include Habitat for Humanity, an organization devoted to building affordable housing for low-income families; the National Doula Society, which provides indigenous or professional helpers to women during birth and delivery; Alzheimer's disease groups for caretakers; Parents, Family, and Friends of Lesbians and Gays (PFLAG), an organization founded by a parent of a gay man; and the National Alliance for the Mentally Ill (NAMI), which consists of family members and consumers of mental health services.

CASE EXAMPLE

An innovative residential reunification and permanency program for youth in out-of-home placements illustrates how one human services organization built support into its program design. The agency was concerned about the significant numbers of African American males between the ages of 12 and 17 who had multiple stays in its shelter system; these youth seemed destined to remain adrift or cycle through various foster home placements and institutions. The goal of the program was to move the youth in this target population toward permanency, through reunification with the family, living with a relative, or independent living in the community.

During the development of the program, groups of youth in the shelter were interviewed to obtain their views of their situation and to determine the need for resources to support the goal of reunification and permanency. The final program included features such as a residential component to help the youth achieve stability, youth and family counseling to resolve youth and family problems, crisis services, home visits to reintegrate the youth into the family system, and respite care.

Following the first complete year of implementation, evaluation sessions were conducted with youth, parents, and relatives participating in the program. Youth and family members identified home visits and respite care as the most helpful aspects of the program. Home visits facilitated the youth's gradual reentry into the family system as well as their transition into the community. During the development of the program, it was recognized that the transition from institution to a home environment could pose difficulties for families, so respite care was included as a central program feature and regarded as being both supportive and preventive. In addition to residential beds, the agency maintained respite beds that could be used for as long as 72 hours by the youth and family in times of crisis. As an alternative, the youth could reside for a brief period with kin or a member of the community network. During the respite period, kin or community members were involved in the effort to resolve the difficulty and avoid another placement. One parent attending a focus group designed to evaluate the program's effectiveness offered particularly poignant commentary on the support the agency provided: "The staff held our family's hand until we could go it alone."

This innovative program illustrates how support and community networks can be incorporated into and facilitate agency program goals. It is also an example of a macro-level intervention strategy designed to alter the situation of a particular group. The agency determined from its experience as a short-term shelter that a significant number of minority youth continued to cycle throughout the system. The system-level response was intended to reverse the destructive pattern of continuous shelter placements that caused youth to remain disconnected from their families and communities.

In developing this program, the organization perceived its role as supportive. This support was integrated with the work of natural support systems (e.g., relatives, mentors, and community networks), each of which played a critical role in achieving the ultimate program goal of permanency. The shift in the agency's program focus required gathering information about the lack of permanency for youth in the shelter system. Statistical data compiled by the agency included a profile of the youth as well as the number of days spent in the shelter system. This information was then used to advocate for a different approach, which necessitated convincing other organizations, funding sources, county officials, the community, and, in some instances, shelter staff of the program's potential.

Immigrant and Refugee Groups

Immigrant or refugee groups have particular needs for organizational social support and resources. Geographic relocation is, in and of itself, traumatic. While formal organizations and civic, social, and governmental agencies provide assistance to recognized immigrant or refugee groups, these services cannot make up for the cultural isolation, discontinuity, accompanying grief, and guilt or occupational concerns that members of these groups experience. In addition, some groups may be unfamiliar with formal services or assistance from the government and therefore may not seek the services to which they are entitled.

Undocumented individuals are not eligible for government programs and may also be underserved by civic groups or churches. They have needs unique to their status—for example, fear of deportation and exploitation as cheap labor. Consider what happened when a group of hotel employees consisting of both legal and undocumented individuals attempted to join the local union. The hotel's management retaliated by calling immigration authorities. This action mobilized numerous community and professional groups, and the issue was successfully resolved. Increasingly, social workers will be involved in the workplace as organizations seek to respond to their needs for a viable labor force. Social work practice in the workplace may resemble the period at the

beginning of the twentieth century, referred to as welfare capitalism, when social workers played an active role in developing organizational supports and resources while advocating for the needs of a largely immigrant workforce (Brandes, 1976).

Children are often included as undocumented individuals, although some may have been born in the United States and are therefore entitled to services. Unfortunately, many families remain reluctant to seek or utilize services even for children who are entitled to services for fear of calling attention to themselves. A case of a social worker who was asked for consultation illustrates this point. In this case, the social worker was employed in a Hispanic agency that had a purchase-of-service contract to serve the Spanish-speaking population, including child welfare services.

CASE EXAMPLE

This case involved a widowed mother with three children; the two younger children had been born in the United States. The mother and her eldest child were undocumented. The mother and father had originally come to the United States 5 years earlier to work in sugar beet fields in the Midwest. They later moved to a larger city, where the father obtained a job with a roofing company. Two years prior to the referral to the agency, the father died as a result of an accident at a construction site.

The eldest child's teacher reported the family to the agency's child and family services unit for maltreatment because the child appeared to be malnourished. An investigation revealed that the charge of maltreatment was unsubstantiated and that the basis of the child's condition was medical. The mother understood the need for medical care, but was fearful of the family being reported to immigration authorities and subsequently deported. After assuring the mother of confidentiality and receiving her permission to act, the social worker approached the development officer of a local private children's hospital. A pediatrician on staff agreed to evaluate the child and provide the necessary medical care.

In exploring the resources available to this family, the social worker learned that the hospital board viewed outreach to this immigrant community as a part of the hospital's mission. Thus, while the intervention focused primarily on the needs of one family, the social worker developed an additional resource for the larger community. The social worker ultimately became a member of a hospital and community task group charged with making recommendations regarding prenatal and infant care programs and infant loss support groups—needs previously identified by the local Hispanic community.

Cautions and Advice

While social work has long acknowledged the strengths and resources found in chronically impoverished communities, many in the profession believe that we have yet to fully exploit the opportunities for networks and social support systems in these areas. Building on the natural helping systems of communities or groups recognizes strengths and resilience, which may thrive despite the chronic stressors and adverse life events that groups and communities experience. Social supports and relational networks are protective factors that may buffer and extend coping capacity. Agencies may also be included as supportive systems when their programs are responsive in their approach to social conditions and client concerns.

Caution is advised when working with these networks, however. When utilizing or developing social support systems, you should not favor one type over the other. For example, groups or communities may be supplemental resources to more formal services and agency programs to which people may be entitled. Nonetheless, informal resources should not be strained, be exhausted, or cause a hardship to the providers. They cannot provide long-term solutions to social problems. Instead, the preferred approach should focus on coordination between formal and informal resources.

In some segments of society, social support and social network may play a critical role, yet be difficult to develop. For example, persons in controlled therapeutic environments, prison environments, or institutional group placements may be psychologically and sometimes geographically isolated from the larger community. Even in the best of situations, contact with relatives, neighbors, or friends may remain grossly inadequate. Although the objective is for these individuals to eventually return to the community, connections to the community are rarely an integral part of services. These situations provide social workers with opportunities to develop social support and networks through connections with the community for these individuals, as well as to create supportive networks among individuals within institutions

ADVOCACY AND SOCIAL ACTION

The social work profession has a long and proud tradition of advocacy and social action leading to social reform. Indeed, Stuart (1999) characterizes the focus on the person and the environment as "linking of clients and social policy as a distinctive contribution of the social work profession" (p. 335). Haynes and Mickelson (2000) trace the involvement of social workers during the development of some of the more enlightened and humane social policies in both the nineteenth and twentieth centuries. Practice, especially in the African American community, involved advocacy and social action that focused on the "private troubles of individuals and the larger policy issues that affected them" (Carlton-LaNey, 1999). Diverse individuals and groups of social workers have been devoted activists and advocates, often acting in concert with grassroots or minority civic groups. For example, social workers supported the United Farm Workers, the Equal Rights Amendment, the National Welfare Rights Organization, and the Civil Rights Movement, by either joining in the activities of these groups directly or providing expert testimony. More recently, the president of the NASW responded to the Abu Ghraib prison situation in Iraq by sending a letter to the Senate Armed Services Committee, "demanding the U.S. Congress take steps to end the abuse of prisoners of war in Iraq" (Stoesen, 2004). Additional information may be found at the NASW website (*www.socialworkers.org/practice/intl.051404/ Iraqletter.asp*).

Despite this rich history, social work has not always been attentive to the sociopolitical and historical mandates of the profession. In tracing the "cycles of social work practice," Franklin (1990) concluded that social work practice changes to reflect the dominant views and ideologies of the times. At some times, the profession has focused on social action and environmental factors; at other times, the focus has been on the individual. In their book *Unfaithful Angels,* Specht and Courtney (1994) ignited a debate about the profession's goals with regard to the role of social workers as advocates and initiators of change. This argument has roots in the "emergence of two separate and interacting movements" from which the profession evolved—specifically, the Charity Organization Societies and the Settlement Houses. Some have perceived that social work has failed to maintain a leadership role in social efforts over time (Haynes & Mickelson, 2000). Nevertheless, the Council on Social Work Education, the National Association of Social Workers, the International Association of Schools of Social Workers, and the International Federation of Social Workers have all affirmed their support for the prominent inclusion of social action and social advocacy in social work education and professional standards. For a more comprehensive review of the profession's involvement with advocacy and social action, we refer you to the 1999 Centennial Issue of *Social Work.*

Policies and Legislation

Earlier in this chapter, we discussed social conditions and trends that provide both opportunities and challenges for macro-level intervention. Here, we consider the policy and legislative initiatives that influence social work practice, the resources available to clients, and the extent to which they are affected by social conditions. Sometimes social workers, agencies, and funding sources distinguish between direct (micro) and indirect practice, especially when funding decisions identify individuals and families as the targets for change. This distinction is bolstered by an emphasis on "billable hours" for direct client contact. We take the position that this distinction is at best artificial and fails to acknowledge the systemic integration or relationship between clients, the larger social environment, and social work practice.

On a day-to-day basis, social workers confront a vast array of social policies and legislation for which advocacy and social action are indicated. Policies and legislative initiatives during the final decades of the twentieth century have had profound and adverse effects on significant segments of the population, but principally the poor and minorities. Beginning with the Reagan administration, the federal government has increasingly adopted an aggressive stance in working against both the philosophy and funding of social programs. Cuts or reductions in spending for social programs, stemming from political ideology transformed into social policy, have fueled a movement toward personal responsibility, mandated "welfare to work," and an ambiguous notion of family values. Those adversely and disproportionately affected by these trends are women, minorities, and children. The new policies have largely ignored the social and economic supports needed by the working poor. Unfortunately, few opposing voices emerged to counter criticism of the "War on Poverty" when important social and economic programs were replaced by the Contract with America in 1992. As Haynes and Mickelson (2000) note, "blaming the poor took on new meaning" (p. 17) with the Contract with America, reflective of the political negativism and activism of the times. Programs or policies that sought to improve social conditions such as sustainable wages, affordable housing, and health care essentially became peripheral to political agenda, and those affected by these programs were all but forgotten.

During the final decades of the twentieth century, crime became a central focus of legislative policy, as did family structure and values, despite the acknowledged relationship between poverty and the incidence of crime, and despite the documented costs and failures of incarceration. The prison industry grew, as did the incarceration of minority males. Under the Clinton administration, comprehensive legislation such as the Personal Responsibility and Work Opportunity Act of 1996 dramatically changed the welfare system; likewise, drastic changes were implemented in child care, the Food Stamp Program, Supplemental Security Income (SSI), benefits for legal immigrants, nutrition programs, and health, education, and welfare funding to the states (Potocky-Tripodi, 2002; Haynes & Mickelson, 2000; Schneider & Netting, 1999). Human rights and basic dignity—both important to the values of social work—were also eroded by government policies during this time.

Withorn (1998) has questioned the ethics of welfare reform and the lack of discussion among both liberal and conservative politicians about the consequences of the revised mandates in federal entitlement programs. The perception that the primary goal of the new legislation was a reduction in caseload as opposed to a reduction in poverty raised new ethical questions:

- Have people actually left poverty?
- Are children, for whom welfare was actually intended, living healthier lives?

Few truly understood the vague notion of "compassionate conservatism," as championed by the George W. Bush administration, and there was little time to clarify its meaning before the administration shifted its attention to tax cuts for the wealthiest citizens, the war against terrorism, and the war in Iraq. It later became clear that the assaults on social welfare programs begun during the Reagan administration would continue. Believing that welfare recipients simply needed sufficient motivation to lift themselves out of poverty, even more strident welfare measures were added to the Bush administration's domestic agenda, along with reductions in pay for active duty military personnel, reductions in veterans' benefits, and attempts to curtail unemployment benefits and overtime pay for workers. Co-opting the name of a program initiative developed by the Children's Defense Fund, President Bush promoted the No Child Left Behind Act (an educational initiative), while simultaneously cutting funding for public education and promoting school vouchers for private education.

In an unprecedented level of conservative intrusion into family life, marriage was promoted as value added for the poor, even as civil unions for gay and lesbian couples became a source of political debate in the 2004 presidential election campaign. Policies directed toward gay and lesbian couples, when examined in the context of the Clinton administration's military policy of "don't ask, don't tell," further marginalized and stigmatized this group of citizens. In writing for *The New York Times*, Barbara Ehrenreich (2004) questioned how unions between gay and lesbian individuals might affect the institution of marriage as well as the extent to which marriage could hope to alter the situation of poor women. Citing poverty as the number one problem among this group, she suggested that since people tend to marry within their social class, a female Temporary Assistance to Needy Families (TANF) recipient would have to marry 2.3 men to exit poverty. The policy, which has been promoted as low-income marriage education sponsored by the government and financed at the level of $200 million, comes at a time when the Bush administration plans cuts in housing subsidies, more stringent requirements for welfare recipients, and a reduction in welfare programs.

Case and Class Advocacy

The prior review of selected policies and legislation highlights the importance of social workers' roles as advocates and change agents. Although minorities are generally disproportionately affected, social policy actually influences the lives of all people, and it adversely affects those who are poor, who lack power, or who are otherwise disenfranchised. Laws and public policies invariably influence and regulate social work and agency practice, and they determine whether social programs or services remedy the sociopolitical conditions experienced by clients. As a social worker, you may engage in case advocacy at the individual level, but class advocacy is often needed to confront the effects of legislation and policies on groups, including the one to which the individual client belongs. Polls have tended to show that most Americans consider themselves to be centrists. Thus, the opportunity exists for the profession to educate, advocate, and appeal to the basic instincts and values of the public to ensure equality and dignity for the disenfranchised.

We define a*dvocacy and social action* as the process of affecting or initiating change. This process involves working with or on the behalf of clients (1) to obtain services or resources that would not otherwise be provided; (2) to modify or influence policies, procedures, or practices that adversely affect groups or communities; and (3) to promote legislation or policies that will result in the provision of requisite resources or services. "In social work, advocacy involves championing the rights of individuals or communities, through direct intervention or through empowerment" (Barker, 1996). Agency mission statements and program goals strongly influence the amount of job-related advocacy by social workers, and that advocacy tends to be focused on individual cases (Ezell, 1994). Yet social workers are often involved in class advocacy as private individuals and through their membership in professional associations, such as the Child Welfare League of America, Influence, and the National Association of Social Workers' PACE Committee. In addition, some national organizations, such as Family Service of America, have advocacy units that work with citizens' groups at the local level.

Advocacy embodies two separate yet related thrusts. The first facet is *case advocacy*—that is, working with and on behalf of individuals or families to ensure that they receive those benefits and services to which they are entitled and that the services are delivered in ways that safeguard their dignity. Because this aspect of advocacy functions on behalf of an individual or family, it closely corresponds to one dictionary definition of an *advocate* as "one who pleads the cause of another." Individual or case advocates may act with or on behalf of battered women, rape victims, homeless youth, vulnerable children, or the elderly, for example.

The second facet of advocacy is *class advocacy*—that is, acting to promote laws or effect change in policy, practice, or laws that benefit or affect a specific class or group. The Children's Defense Fund (CDF), the American Association of Retired Persons (AARP), the American Civil Liberties Union (ACLU), and the

National Rifle Association (NRA) are all examples of advocacy organizations. Advocacy groups may also be formed in support of particular demographic groups such as the Jewish Defense League, the National Association for the Advancement of Colored People (NAACP), the National Organization for Women (NOW), the National Center for Lesbian Rights, United Farm Workers (UFW), the National Urban League, the Puerto Rican National Defense League, the League of United Latin American Citizens, and the National Asian Pacific American Legal Consortium.

Although this list of organized advocacy groups is by no means inclusive, it does illustrate a common feature of advocacy groups—namely, their ability to advocate on behalf of a specific segment of the population, to engage in social and political action, and to mobilize around concerns that affect a particular group. For example, the ACLU has focused on racial profiling, which entails the indiscriminate stopping and searching of minority males by the police. Advocacy groups may begin in a particular geographical area at a grassroots level, then subsequently expand a model to respond to an issue. Consider the activities of WATCH (Women at the Courthouse), an advocacy organization that uses volunteers who monitor and issue reports on court proceedings, sentencing practices, and judges in court cases related to battered women and abused children. Both judges and attorneys have reported that volunteers with "the red clip boards," are a positive presence in the courtroom. This organization's mission "is to make the justice system more effective and responsive in handling cases of violence, particularly against women and children, and to create a more informed and involved public." The original impetus for organizing WATCH was the failure of laws and court proceedings to provide adequate protection for battered women and children.

The results of research findings can also spur class advocacy. Rice (1998), in integrating research and class advocacy, reports on the use of focus groups in which welfare participants discussed their experiences with welfare reform legislation. Data from the focus groups were provided to the state legislature.

Class advocacy is much broader in scope than case advocacy and may lead to macro-level interventions such as community organizing or influencing legislation. In discussing feminist community intervention strategies, Hyde (1996) refers to a number of examples in which class advocacy and social action were combined to achieve the desired result. A major tenet of feminist organizing and advocacy is that "the personal is political"; as such, organizing and advocacy emerge at the grassroots level focused on the issues that affect the lives on women (Hyde, 1996).

Barker (1996) defines *social action* as "a coordinated effort to achieve institutional change to meet a need, solve a social problem, correct any injustices or enhance the quality of human life" (p. 350). Class advocacy is inherently political. Policy models for political advocacy are defined and discussed by Haynes and Mickelson (2000), who stress that models are important because they guide the intervention and ensure a match between the problem and the strategy employed. We refer you to their book as an informative guide.

Although the two types of advocacy take somewhat different paths, they are nevertheless highly interrelated. Advocacy action on behalf of an individual client or family may result in a precedent that produces change that benefits others in the same position. Class advocacy as illustrated by the following example may be an extension of case advocacy.

CASE EXAMPLE

A social worker in a child protection unit was assigned to complete a child safety assessment in a situation in which a child, age 5 years, had opened the door of her home and walked about two blocks to the home of a relative. The incident occurred while the father, a single parent, was asleep on the couch. Two policemen observed the child walking unsupervised by an adult and placed the child in a temporary shelter. They later spoke to the father. In their police report, they referred to the father as a "drunken Indian" because of his speech pattern.

The assessment of the situation showed no indication that the child was in danger, so the social worker advocated for the child to be returned to the home. Furthermore, that while it was unusual for the child to visit relatives alone, she and her father routinely spent time with these family members. In talking to the father and other family members, the social worker learned that Native Americans often experience encounters with the police and helping professionals who are influenced by the flawed perception held by the police officers in this situation. The speech pattern that caused the police officer to assume that the father was drunk was, in fact, the manner in which he pronounced or enunciated words.

The social worker, with the support of her agency and the permission of the community, organized a meeting between Native Americans in the community and the police. The meeting was intended to educate the police about the experience of the community and in the process curtail discriminatory practices, thereby avoiding further adverse interactions.

This case example demonstrates participatory empowerment practice (Gutierrez & Lewis, 1999), or working collaboratively within a community to confront issues of concern. A key element is using one's own power to develop the power and build the capacity of others. Here, the social worker was instrumental in resolving a much larger issue—the relationship between the police and this community.

Before we leave this case, it is important to acknowledge that the police were justified in their actions, as there was the potential of danger for the child. Both the police and the child protection social worker have a responsibility to ensure safety and their assessment of this situation was clearly warranted. At issue, however, is the insensitive and racially biased statement in the police report. Because this case was representative of much of the experience of the Native American community with police, it could therefore be expanded from the individual level and become a cause for class advocacy.

Indications for Advocacy or Social Action

Class advocacy ands social action may be appropriately employed as illustrated in the preceding case example and in numerous other situations, including the following:

1. When services or benefits to which people are entitled are denied to a group or community

2. When services or practices are dehumanizing, confrontational, or coercive

3. When discriminatory practices or policies occur because of race, gender, sexual orientation, religion, culture, family form, or other factors

4. When gaps in services or benefit cause undue hardship or contribute to dysfunction

5. When people lack representation or participation in decisions that affect their lives

6. When governmental or agency policies and procedures, or community or workplace practices adversely affect or target groups of people

7. When a significant group of people have common needs for which resources are unavailable

8. When clients are denied civil or legal rights

Special circumstances for which advocacy or social action may be indicated include situations in which clients are unable to act effectively on their own behalf. These situations may involve persons who are institutionalized, children in need of protection, or those who have a need for immediate services or benefits because of a crisis situation or cannot act as self-advocates because of their legal status.

Competence and Skills

The overall goal of macro-level advocacy or social action is system change. Targets of advocacy or social action may be individuals, communities, organizations, public officials, policy-making bodies, courts, legislatures, and divisions of government. Approaches to situations vary considerably according to the target system, but all require a through understanding of how organizations or communities are structured, how they function, and how the legislative and rule-making processes work, along with an appreciation for organizational politics (Rothman, 1991; Roberts, 2000; Alexander, 2003). Advocacy can also involve different levels of assertive intensity, ranging from discussion and education to a high level of social action and organizing. Sosin and Callum (1983) have developed a useful typology of advocacy that assists practitioners in planning appropriate advocacy actions. Along with the models discussed by Haynes and Mickelson (2000), this typology can help determine the context of the advocacy action, the opportunities that exist, and the techniques or strategies to be used and at what level.

Skills required in advocacy or social action include policy analysis, group facilitation, interviewing, and the ability to gather and analyze multidimensional and systematic information, similar to the process used with individuals and families. It is prudent to carefully assess the situation and the systems involved, thereby avoiding premature and erroneous conclusions that may lead to undesired or embarrassing consequences. Group facilitation, negotiation, consensus building, and organizing skills are essential in coalition building. Information that documents the problem, as well as the manner and the extent to which groups or communities are affected, is also critical. Recall the earlier case example of the innovative program in which the social work agency compiled statistical information to document the pervasiveness of the problem and outcomes of minority youth remaining in the shelter system; these data were then used as a means to obtain support. Both advocacy and social action assume a wide range of social work roles and skills, each of which utilizes the values and ethics of the profession as guiding principles.

Ethical principles guide social workers in the context of agency practice at both the micro and the mezzo levels. Netting et al. (1993) discuss the principles of autonomy, beneficence, and justice as principles that guide macro practice for social workers who are initiating change. Strengths and empowerment are equally important in macro practice. Focusing on strengths allows for the mobilization of the positive capacities of people, thereby highlighting their resources, hopes, talents, and aspirations as key components of the change process (Weick, 1992, p. 24). Strengths also embody the process and outcome of empowerment as outlined by Gutierrez and Lewis (1999) and Gutierrez (1994), moving from the individual to entire groups or communities.

Advocacy and social action as interventions may constitute a delicate balance between self-determination and beneficence. Ezell (2001) calls our attention to this balance in class advocacy by citing the conflict engendered by deciding "whether to empower clients to advocate for themselves, or to represent them" (p. 45). Another potential dilemma with respect to self-determination is that some clients may not wish to assert their rights in the face of formidable opposition. Social workers are ethically bound to respect their position.

In pursuing an action, social workers must be certain that the proposed action targets what the client has defined as important. The sense of empowerment that people gain through identifying their own concerns and participating in the solutions may be significant and sufficient, without moving on to more global-type actions. Moreover, practitioners should go no further in advocacy or social action activities than the client group wishes to go.

As in direct practice with clients, during advocacy practitioners have the responsibility to explore potential barriers to goal achievement with clients, and possible adversarial or negative consequences to advocacy and social action activities. Weighing the likelihood of success, securing resources, organizing groups and coalitions, and following a strategic plan are important steps in the change process. Yet, implementing advocacy and social action typically creates a certain amount of strain and tension; moreover, a positive outcome cannot be assured. Discussing possible consequences or barriers not only allows for the planning of alternative strategies, but also ensures that clients are well educated about the pros and cons, leaving the final decision in their hands.

Clients should also be made aware of the risks and limitations to advocacy and social action. Rothman (1999) cautions community practitioners about the potential for opposition and obstacles to social action and organizing activities, including "institutions that block needed improvements in education, housing, employment and law enforcement." He further states that "change advocates have to keep in mind that elites will lash out when they perceive that their interests are challenged"; to deal with this resistance, advocates should "calculate" their ability to sustain, remain focused, and defend themselves against counterattacks (p. 10). The example of the innovative agency program to reunify youth with their families and prevent their continuous cycling through the shelter system was, in many respects, a form of social action and advocacy. As such, the agency initially encountered considerable opposition from other agencies that provide shelter placement, and their opposition effectively derailed program planning for an extended period of time.

Techniques of Advocacy and Social Action

Many techniques for advocacy and social action exist, and deciding which ones to employ depends on the nature of the problem, the wishes of the group or community, the nature of the action, the political climate, and the extent to which the social work agency will support advocacy and social action as interventions. As a rule of thumb, you should employ no more techniques than are required to achieve a given objective. Although militant action may be required in some instances, this approach should be utilized with great discretion, because the short-term gains may not outweigh the long-term negative images or fractured relationships. Techniques and methods of advocacy and social action involve building coalitions, organizing client groups, and providing expert testimony. They also include the roles of system analyst, researcher, enabler, mediator, broker, and educator. Administrators, supervisors, social workers, and organizations may all assume these roles.

Effective social action and advocacy require a rational, planned approach incorporating the following steps:

1. Define the problem.
2. Systematically gather information and analyze the people, structure, or system to be changed.

3. Assess both the driving forces that may promote change and the resistance forces that
   may conceivably retard it.

4. Identify specific goals, eliciting a broad range
   of viewpoints.

5. Carefully match techniques or strategies of
   social action and advocacy with a model and
   the goal desired.

6. Make a feasible schedule for implementing
   the plan of action.

7. Incorporate in the plan a feedback process
   for evaluating the changes that the action
   stimulates.

In addition to these steps and the skills and
competence areas discussed previously, three
other ingredients are required to ensure effective
social action and class advocacy: a g*enuine* concern for that cause, the ability to keep the cause
in *focus,* and *tenacity.* Successful advocates have a
thorough understanding of how their government and service systems are organized and
changed. Blind emotion may work a few times,
but maintaining a successful, sustained advocacy
action requires know-how. In many instances,
class advocacy and social action are best
described as a marathon rather than a race.
As noted some years ago by John Gardner, a
leader of the Common Cause organization, "The
first requirement for effective citizen action
is stamina."

Finally, the manner in which an issue is framed
may make a substantial difference. As noted earlier,
the political climate has changed, as have societal
responses to the core concerns of the social work
profession. The FrameWorks Institute suggests
translating messages about what can be done to
address social problems into language that engages
ordinary people and advances their interest in
policy and program solutions. Questions that facilitate formulating a "strategic frame analysis"
include the following:

• What shapes public opinion about issues that
  affect children, families, and poor people?

• What role do the media play?

• How do policy-makers gauge public opinion?

Answering these questions will assist advocates and
social activists to communicate more effectively
about social issues and social conditions.

SOCIAL PLANNING/COMMUNITY ORGANIZATION

As a macro approach to enhancing environments
and improving social conditions, the practice
method of social planning/community organization (SP/CO) goes beyond the typical activities of
direct practice in that the focal units with which
practitioners engage are larger systems such as
neighborhoods, citizens groups, representatives of
organizations, agency executives, and governmental leaders. The joint efforts of the participants are
typically directed to solving social problems ranging in scope from those affecting various resident
groups to international problems. Policies and programs of national scope that have emerged over the
past 30 years as a result of intensive planning aimed
at social problems include the Community Health
Act (1963), the Economic Opportunity Act
(1964), Model Cities Programs (1967), the Housing and Community Development Act (1974), the
Jobs Training Partnership Act (1983), the Title XX
amendments to the Social Security Act (1974),
Volunteers in Service to America (VISTA, under
the direction of a social worker), and the Peace
Corps. More recently, AMERICORP was established as a way to involve youth in some of the
pressing problems facing communities.

Trends in legislation, policy initiatives, and
funding patterns highlighted previously in this
chapter are evidence of an "increasing inequality in
our society" (Gutierrez, 1999, p. 375). They also
provide opportunities for organizing communities
and building broad-based community participation.
Current problems on which planners are or should
be focusing include homelessness, welfare reform,
child welfare legislation, child and partner abuse,
substance abuse, health care, affordable housing,
adolescent runaways, poverty, high rates of unemployment in urban and rural communities, and
transportation and education. In some communities, economic empowerment zones have been

established in an attempt to address the issue of jobs, education, and transportation. However, in an analysis of these empowerment zones, Gutierrez (1999) concludes that they offer more support for corporate projects, but do not create significant numbers of job opportunities in the designated communities. Another trend identified by Gutierrez that has relevance for community organizers is "the increasingly multicultural composition of our society" (p. 375). Social workers must account for this trend in determining whether the community will be defined as a separate locale where services are aimed at a particular segment of the community, or whether they should pursue a more holistic approach that brings resources to people together without regard to race or ethnicity.

Strategies of community practice along with their basic means of influence as described by Rothman, Erlich, and Tropman (2001) include social action, social planning, and policy and locality development. In some instances, these strategies may overlap or be employed simultaneously (Hyde, 1996). In keeping with an empowerment focus, we emphasize locality development as a strategy for social planning and community organizing. Unlike planning and policy development that rely on the technical process of problem solving conducted by expert professionals, locality development aims to involve the community in defining a problem and determining goals. As defined by Cnaan and Rothman (1986), *locality development* seeks to build relationships within the community and enhance community integration. Indeed, funding sources such as the United Way and foundations often expect social services agencies to include citizens and consumers in the development of their programs or services. To satisfy this expectation, both public and private organizations use focus groups as a means to involve communities and clients in the development of services and funding priorities.

Community living rooms are also mechanisms for the building and integration of communities. For example, Farmer and Walsh (1999) report the use of a community living room in a homeless shelter. The community living room, which was founded by a social worker, evolved into a source

for community networks and celebrations as well as being a venue for social action. In this instance, community living room participants organized to call attention to and exert pressure on public officials regarding city services, police brutality, and housing code violations.

In another community, a supportive network of a community living room consisted of women who had been homeless. These women compiled a booklet of tips on locating housing, a checklist and critical questions to ask landlords, and information about properties to avoid. The community social worker assisted the women in their efforts by securing the funds needed to print the booklets and ensuring their distribution to women who were homeless or in transitional housing.

Locality development should not replace other strategies that may be preferable, but rather should be viewed as a viable means for engaging communities and groups. Irrespective of the strategy employed, inclusion of community participants in planning and community organizing is preferable and consistent with the principles of social work practice. An advantage of community living rooms is that they reinforce empowerment in the context of participants' social construction of their reality and experiences. As described by O'Melia and Miley (2002), empowerment is socially constructed, taking into account the individual, social processes, and the reciprocal interaction between the two domains in approaches to problem solving.

STRATEGIES AND SKILLS OF COMMUNITY INTERVENTION

Theorists conceptualize the problem-solving process in SP/CO in different ways, defining different numbers of stages that vary according to the levels of elaboration of relevant tasks. Rothman, Erlich, Tropman, (1995) and Rothman (1999) use a six-phase process to address problem solving:

1. Identification of a need or problem
2. Definition and clarification of the need or problem
3. Systematic process of obtaining information

4. Analysis of the information
5. Development and implementation of a plan of action
6. Terminal actions and evaluation of outcome or effects

You recognize that these steps are similar to those of the problem-solving process. Note that the steps in community intervention, like those in advocacy and social action, are consistent with methods of change. Specifically, the change effort has an initial phase focusing on problem identification and assessment; a middle phase that involves developing and implementing an action plan; and a final phase that consists of termination and evaluation. This process may not be entirely linear, because the emergence of new information may require alternative action, including making a new start or reframing strategies and tactics (Rothman, Erlich, & Tropman, 1999). In any event, maintaining focus is important in the change process, and this schema of activities will assist in this regard.

Implementing these activities requires some of the same skills and competencies employed in direct practice—for example, the ability to establish rapport, empathy, assessment, communication, interviewing skills, group facilitation, and knowledge of interpersonal relationships and group dynamics. Other skills required include those embodied in policy analysis and program evaluation, research methods, management of data, and knowledge of sociopolitical processes. As Homan (1999) points out, we should keep in mind that organizing or planning to promote change "involves more than just fixing a specific problem. Productive organizing includes the intent to increase the capability of people to respond meaningfully and effectively in the face of future challenges" (p. 160). In this regard, the practitioners work collaboratively with communities and facilitate the process by engaging in the roles of enabler, educator, and mediator.

Alternative Approaches

Several innovative approaches hold promise for enhancing the effectiveness of planning community programs. The first approach utilizes the methodology of developmental research (Thomas, 1989). Developmental research is a rigorous, systematic, and distinctive methodology consisting of techniques and methods taken from other fields and disciplines. Its methodology relies on social research and model development. That is, models or program development can be tested, then modified based on the feedback.

To see how this process works, recall the earlier example in which an agency developed a program for youth who had repeated stays in the shelter system. Home visits while the youth were still in the residential phase of the program were identified as a critical factor in moving the youth toward reunification with their families. After a period of time, this program component was examined using qualitative and quantitative data on the number of home visits, resources required, events that had disrupted the visit, and interviews with the youth, parents, and other kin. These data enabled the agency to direct its resources toward achieving the second goal of the program—permanency for the youth. As a result of the feedback, respite care and community intervention were added to the program. Specifically, it was learned that reintegration into the family system required additional support for the families to avoid further placement.

A second approach implemented in Quebec takes advantage of natural helping networks and lay citizens in analyzing problems and planning remedial measures (Gulati & Guest, 1990). Users of services are considered to be partners in the provision of services, rather than client–consumers. They facilitate the integration and coordination of local programs and services and prevention efforts. The flexibility in organizational structure and decentralized administration enable local communities to develop programs that respond to their unique needs.

The *capacity model,* a third approach developed under the auspices of Communities United to Rebuild Neighborhoods (CURN), similarly engages the community in resolving members' concerns. Operationalizing the notion of community strengths, this model relies on the premise that individual talents at all age levels are central and must be identified, energized, and deployed.

The focus of organizing and development efforts is always on community concerns. The capacity-development approach takes exception to the assumption that governmental intervention is a primary solution. Instead, community participants develop their own agenda and work is directed "from the inside out" (Rivera & Erlich, 1998, p. 68).

Organizing and Planning with Diverse Groups

Rivera and Erlich (1998), in analyzing models of community development or organizing, reject the assumption that prevailing models (i.e., locality development, social planning, and social action) are color-blind and therefore applicable in any community. They conclude that additional factors must be included when working with communities of color:

- Racial, ethnic, and cultural aspects of the community

- Implications of this uniqueness in particular communities

- The empowerment process and the development of a critical consciousness

Rivera and Erlich's work is intended to guide our thinking in planning and organizing and,

in fact, represents a significant contribution to macro practice strategies. Heretofore, models have included the implied assumption that good intentions sufficed in community interventions and that, unlike with direct practice strategies, considerations of the race, ethnicity, and culture of the practitioners engaged in this work were secondary. The three levels of contact as conceptualized by Rivera and Erlich (1998) for entry into communities facilitate a greater understanding of work with diverse groups and of the roles beyond those traditionally considered in social work. Table 14-1 outlines these three levels.

This schema provides an opportunity to rethink approaches to communities as well as the classical view of communities. Even the most impoverished communities have strengths, formal helping networks, and informal helping networks, and they are best able to identify their concerns. In instances where communities may lack the know-how for achieving resolution, social work practitioners may fill a role by participating as partners. In addition, agencies may adopt an alternative approach such as the one described by Gulati and Guest (1990) that was initiated in Quebec. By taking this alternative approach, agencies become more flexible in how they deliver services and which services are delivered, because they rely on

Table 14-1 Levels of community contact

ENTRY LEVEL	CHARACTERISTICS
Primary	Requires that an individual has the same racial, cultural, and linguistic background as the community. The community is open to and respects this individual.
Secondary	The individual need not be a member of the same racial, ethnic, or cultural group, but should be closely aligned and sensitive to community needs. He or she may serve as a liaison to the broader community, and facilitate contact with institutions outside the community.
Tertiary	The individual is an "outsider," yet shares the community's concerns. The practitioner's skills and access to power—rather than his or her ethnic, racial, or cultural identity—are valued assets.

Source: Adapted from Rivera and Erlich (1998).

the social construction of unique communities for guidance. This approach has merit in that governmental services to communities are often fragmented and their resources for addressing community needs frequently vary, depending on whether they are rural, urban, or suburban.

In addition to the paradigm advocated by Rivera and Erlich (1998), we propose contact with key informants or individuals who can act as cultural guides as a means to facilitate entry into communities. Values, beliefs, and cultural traditions guide preferences in matters that are assumed to be universal. Home ownership among some immigrants, for example, lags behind the rates seen for other groups. In part, this discrepancy may be attributed to differences in income levels, lending practices of financial institutions, and suspicions about governmental agencies. Lending practices and discrimination are areas in which social workers can assist communities to organize.

In other instances, it is prudent to be aware of the influence of cultural barriers and attitudes. As reported by Serres (2004), language and traditions may prevent home ownership. The Hmong language, for example, lacks words for "mortgage" and "credit." In some cultures, religious beliefs forbid the payment of interest associated with debt. For example, in the Somalian community, there is an aversion to owning property. Somalis, who are predominately nomadic people, are accustomed to being mobile and thus perceive home ownership to be a burden. Moreover, many hope to return to their homeland. Religious views for this group also affect their home ownership rates, as the Koran speaks against paying or receiving interest.

These examples are by no means exclusive, but rather illustrate the complexities of diverse beliefs or value in defining need. In addition to values and beliefs, the accepted ways of doing things in these communities are normative strengths.

In working with communities, Shannon, Kleiniewski, and Cross (2002) caution us against pitting the "rosy picture" of rural communities as close-knit, family-centered enclaves against the view of urban communities as disorganized, chaotic, and impersonal. In fact, rural communities have a number of problems, including poor living conditions, racial and class conflicts, and challenges that are similar to those faced by their urban counterparts (e.g., transportation, unemployment, funding for schools, and affordable housing). According to Shannon et al., traditional urban neighborhoods patterns may have changed, but these residents remain more likely than their rural counterparts to have a broader reach into the outside world—for example, through employment, mass transit ties and relationships between neighborhoods, and friends or family members who live elsewhere.

This assessment suggests that communities have unique patterns and characteristics. Thus, it is incumbent on social workers to take into account each community's particular political, economic, interpersonal, and power relationships, as well as the strengths of community resources. Perceived strengths may be identified by eliciting the views of the community. In the case example in which the mothers joined the community organization in addressing local community concerns, each group had different perceptions of the community. Church members were primarily nonresidents who viewed the urban neighborhood as fragmented, poor, crime-ridden, and unsafe. Conversely, residents described their community as close-knit and they emphasized such positive features as ease of access to public transportation, the various cultural institutions located in the community, and the historical significance of many of the older houses.

As a final point, we stress the fact that although community demographics may constrain local resources, it is the individuals within those communities who are best able to identify the needs of their community. As social workers, we can become involved in their efforts as advocates, change agents, and planners, using our skills, knowledge, and values grounded in principles of social justice and empowerment to help groups and communities to achieve their goals. An ongoing question—and perhaps an ethical dilemma (posed by Ezell, 2001)—for advocates and change agents is when to act on behalf of the community and when to provide the skills and resources that will allow clients to represent themselves.

Much like direct practice interventions, community intervention strategies may combine tasks that the social worker implements with tasks that are performed by individuals in a community or group. You might carry out certain tasks because you have access to needed resources or knowledge or skills that facilitate task completion. For example, you may be able to attend meetings, prepare reports, deal with established and formidable institutions, or make contacts that may be inaccessible to individuals, groups, or communities. These scenarios suggest that you must engage in strategic reflection. Specifically, does the planned action call for joint efforts? By acting alone, will you disempower your clients? Can clients do or speak for themselves? If not, what skills are required to assist them (Ezell, 2001)?

Improving Institutional Environments

Social welfare organizations are organized to provide a service, information, benefits, or goods. They are formal social systems with multiple constituents and dynamic arenas in which client eligibility for services is determined and the resources vital to the organization's existence are distributed. The culture of organizations includes core values and purposes as portrayed in mission statements, leadership styles, and assumptions and rituals. Schein (1985) describes organizational culture as follows:

> A pattern of basic assumptions—invented, discovered, or developed by a given group as it learns to cope with its problems of external adaptation and internal integration—that has worked well enough to be considered valid and therefore to be taught to new members as the correct way to perceive, think and feel in relation to those problems. (p. 9)

Organizational Change

Change strategies in organizations require an understanding and analysis of organizational structure, function, culture, and resource environment. Martin and O'Connor (1989) analyze the social welfare organization using systems theory. They offer a conceptual scheme for understanding social welfare organizations as open systems. This view focuses on (1) the organization's relations with the environment, (2) internal structures and processes, and (3) dilemmas associated with a conflicting—indeed, sometimes hostile—social, cultural, and political-economic environment. Netting, Kettner, and McMurtry (2004) provide guidelines for analyzing change effort in social welfare organizations; we refer you to their work for further elaboration of this process. Similar to the other strategies for macro-level interventions, the process begins with identification of the goal or problem to be changed.

Organizational learning and the learning organization offer yet another approach to organizational change. A *learning organization* is a process that enables the organization to periodically review its performance and make adjustments to improve. It is also considered to be a relevant factor in the quality of staff work life, with respect to job design and performance awards (Lewis, Lewis, Packard, & Souflee, 2001; Morgan, 1997). A learning organization positions itself so that it can continuously review and revise its operations, purposes, and objectives so as to ensure the quality of the organizational experience for clients and staff. Questions that might be posed include "How is work done?" and "What are the outcomes of this work?" The process also provides an opportunity to reflect on the organization's strengths and limitations, so that the organization can develop strategies that enhance the former and address the latter.

While organizational learning and the learning organization are often discussed as a single concept, the learning organization, as characterized by Senge (1990) and Morgan (1997), essentially speaks to the ecology of the organization. That is, it refers to a particular type of organization and its ability to scan, anticipate, and respond to environmental changes. The learning organization develops capacities that enable members to question and challenge operating norms and assumptions, thereby ensuring its stability and promoting its evolution through strategic responses and direction (Morgan, 1997). In contrast, *organizational learning* emphasizes a set of activities pertinent to the organization's inner workings as well as the interdependence among the various units of the organization.

Both organizational learning and the learning organization require a supportive environment, in which the culture of the organization fosters dialogue and promotes feedback. One county human health and human services agency, under the leadership of its director, initiated a series of "community dialogues" among staff to position itself as a learning organization and to facilitate organizational learning. Lewis et al. (2001) encourage the adoption of the learning organization as a way to create opportunities for growth in human service organizations.

ORGANIZATIONAL ENVIRONMENTS

The quality of the organizational environment and the values of the organization as experienced by clients are important aspects of service delivery. In this section we consider ways of enhancing three major facets of institutional environments: staff, policies and practices, and programs.

Staff

The organization's staff form the heart of an organization's environment. The staffing mix of an organization includes professionals who have regular contact with clients; support personnel; and administrative personnel. Administrative personnel—specifically, managers and supervisors—direct, monitor, coordinate, evaluate, and bear the responsibility for the oversight of overall organizational operations. In the organization's highly interdependent environment, each position is key to achieving its mission. To a large extent, staff behavior is governed by a mix of internal and external factors, including professional orientations, ethical codes and standards, licensing or regulatory boards, union contracts, funding sources, the media, and the public.

When staff of an organization are dedicated, caring, and responsive to clients' needs, as well

as congenial with one another, the organization's environment tends to be conducive to the growth and well-being of all concerned. To be optimally effective, an organization's culture should promote staff empowerment and a sense of commitment to deliver high-quality client services. Among the factors that characterize a healthy organizational culture and climate are open communication, a willingness to deal with conflict, flexibility and risk taking, a sense of interdependence and cohesiveness, and respect for boundaries. Although the creation of an organization's environment is within the domain of organizational leadership, it is the responsibility of all staffing levels.

Hackman and Oldham (1976, 1980) have conceptualized the most elaborate and widely accepted theories of job design and motivation as contributing to the overall psychological states of meaningfulness, staff responses, morale, and job satisfaction of staff. They have identified five core characteristics:

- Task identity
- Task significance
- Skill variety
- Job feedback
- Autonomy

Task identity, task significance, and skill variety add to the feeling that work is meaningful. Feedback with regard to one's job performance provides information about the results achieved, thereby acting as both a developmental and a motivating factor. Autonomy inspires a sense of responsibility for one's own work, the outcomes of this work, and the work of the team. Empowerment, which is implicit in autonomy, works in much the same way as self-determination does for clients. Just as clients may terminate social work contact when their interests and needs are ignored, so a lack of staff empowerment may affect job performance, reduce productivity, and contribute to more rapid turnover.

Dynamics within the organization—whether stemming from conflicting professional orientations, competing ideologies, diversity, or controversies over values—may also create tensions that affect job satisfaction, morale, and identity. These dynamics have the potential to spill over into interactions with clients. If these conflicts are left unresolved, staff members may react in ways that are counterproductive to the goals and purpose of the organization. Organizational environments with rigid rules, a lack of autonomy, and resistance to change become "psyche prisons" (Morgan, 1997). In sharp contrast to the growth found in the learning organization, staff in organizations perceived as psyche prisons frequently feel trapped in a construction of reality and a preferred way of thinking.

The extent to which staff feel empowered and are able to participate in work-related decisions makes a significant difference in the extent to which they feel valued. Likewise, these characteristics influence how much they engage in pro-social or extra-role behavior. Problem solving is also impacted by staff-related issues. For example, one social worker recounted how staff attempts to address concerns in his organization resulted in a manager stating, "If staff were involved in decision making, there would be no reason for upper management." When staff input was later solicited about ways to decrease indirect service expenditures, not surprisingly personnel showed little interest in the problem or its resolution. This situation is perhaps unique in that most organizations, having recognized the importance of developing an organizational climate that is conductive to change, encourage staff to identify needed changes. Many organizations also have mechanisms whereby proposals for change can be suggested and initiated. Finally, large human services organizations, in an effort to provide for greater staff participation in decision making and improve services, have become less hierarchical and more decentralized by implementing total quality management teams (Martin, 1993; Lewis et al., 2001).

Clients are affected by organizational environments in much the same way as staff. Clients reap the benefits when staff are motivated and treated as autonomous, yet interdependent, knowledgeable professionals. Conversely, they experience the residual effects when the opposite is true. The experience of clients may also reflect individual staff behaviors (i.e., the impaired professional) or failure to respect their right to be treated with dignity and having worth.

Of course, staff in the best of organizational environments will experience stress and frustrations when their work is constrained by limited resources, skewed funding priorities, and constant exposure to the "magnitude and complexities of client's problems" (Kirk & Koeske, 1995). Does work with families who have multiple needs and are involved with multiple agencies, in a managed care environment, with pressures further exacerbated by public policy, timelines, or compliance issues, sound familiar? For example, social workers and other professionals who work in programs serving youth are often frustrated in this regard. Their frustrations are related to individualized program objectives and funding resources that ignore an ecological or family system perspective, but instead focus on resolving specific problems (e.g., truancy). At the same time, work with the family as a whole is neither considered nor reimbursed.

We raise these points for discussion because funding priorities and organizational environments (i.e., climate and culture) are factors that affect staff morale, performance, and job satisfaction. These factors also affect the experiences of clients, as well as the quality of the services they receive.

Staff as Agents of Change

Although social workers may be very adept in advocating for clients, developing resources or support networks, and organizing, they are often reticent or feel unable to influence or propose changes within their own organizations. In some instances, practitioners may identify organizational concerns in a hierarchical fashion, then conclude that the impetus for change or resolutions resides in the domain of management. In some instances, this view may be valid. For example, staff performance or budgetary problems are ultimately the responsibility of management.

Nonetheless, we encourage you to assess situations, to present your concerns and ideas in a systematic manner, and to actively participate in change efforts. Because of the close interactions that take place between staff and clients, managers and administrators rely on street-level staff to alert them to the dynamics that might affect the work environment and client well-being. Assuming responsibility for and participating in change is the essence of staff empowerment; and participation in change efforts is consistent with the ethical principles of the social work profession. The skills and competencies relevant in interventions with clients, as well as macro practice strategies, are pertinent to organizational change.

Change Strategies

Netting et al. (2004) suggest two types of macro-level changes in organizations: (1) changes to improve resources provided to clients and (2) changes to enhance the organization's working environment so that personnel can perform more efficiently and effectively, thus improving services to clients. Brager and Holloway (1978) have outlined organizational change as focusing on three areas: people-focused change, technological change, and structural change. Changes may take the form of a policy, a program, or the initiation of a project (Kettner, Daley, & Nichols, 1985). Change at the organizational level requires that practitioners act as organizational diagnosticians and facilitators/expediters.

To be effective, you must have the knowledge and skills that will enable you to analyze the organization as well as the risks and benefits of the proposed change. Frey (1990) has developed a useful framework with which direct practitioners can assess organizational opposition. The change strategy requires you to assume various social work roles and begins with the identification of the problem area. In assessing the potential benefits of a proposal, it is important to consider the input of and effects on four groups:

- Clients, including the extent to which the proposed change offers direct benefits to this group and will effectively alter and enhance the services they receive

- Administrators, who ultimately have legitimate authority for accepting the proposal and providing the resources for implementation

- Supervisors or staff, who will have responsibility for planning and/or overseeing implementation

- Staff persons, who ultimately carry out the change or are affected by it, once it is implemented

By considering the impact of the potential change on each group, practitioners can weigh benefits against detrimental effects and can plan strategies to counter reactions and resistance when the former (i.e., the benefits) clearly and substantially outweigh the latter.

Risks and Benefits

Promoting change in organizations is a complex process, and organizational opposition to change is perhaps as common as that found in families, individuals, and groups. Central to the change proposal is the documentation of need and the questions of who is affected, in what way, and who benefits. Frey (1990) identifies high-risks proposals as those with the following characteristics:

- Substantial costs to the organization—for example, purchasing expensive equipment or creating new units

- Actions that must be adopted in their entirety rather than implemented in stages

- Radical ideas that are in conflict with the dominant values of the organization, its members, or the public

In addition, opposition may arise in response to proposals that challenge or exceed the capacity of the organization to implement proposals due to resource constraints or ideological differences. Likewise, proposals that would significantly change the purpose, mission, and goals of the organization may spur resistance. For example, extending an agency's hours of operation may be considered to be a peripheral change, and have little or no effect on organizational goals or mission. In contrast, programmatic changes, which alter a program's objectives, have greater effects on organizational depth. The following case example describes a successful low-risk proposal initiated by a social worker.

CASE EXAMPLE

The primary client group served by the agency were individuals for whom English was their second language (ESL population). The agency provided counseling, educational programs, and services to assist clients in applying for financial assistance benefits. However, a majority of clients had difficulty in completing the applications for financial assistance, despite the fact that the applications had been translated into several different languages. The particular problem documented by the social worker was the amount of time required (which far exceeded the contact hours allowed) for staff to assist individuals or families in completing the forms. The situation was further complicated by the routine need for additional appointments when incomplete eligibility forms resulted in the delay of benefits.

To rectify this situation, the social worker proposed convening instructional groups scheduled at different times during the week instead of staff meeting with individuals or families. She envisioned that using a group format and the services of volunteers would respond to two concerns. First, use of groups would mitigate staff concerns related to scheduling and contact hours. Second, recruiting agency clients who had successfully completed the forms to serve as volunteer helpers would ensure that clients, especially new arrivals, became connected to a social network.

The success of this proposal was attributed to the fact that the change did not require substantial organizational expenditures. Nor did it radically compromise the organization's goals and mission. In fact, rather than taxing organizational resources, it redeployed resources in a more efficient manner. By using a group approach and taking advantage of volunteers, the social worker's proposal augmented the agency's ability to serve this ESL population. Staff working on this program responded favorably, as it effectively addressed their frustrations about the time they spent in assisting individuals and families to complete the financial forms.

In general, proposals that fit with an organization's ideology, resource capacity, and potential are likely to win the support of a significant number of members and, therefore, are more likely to succeed.

Of course, irrespective of its nature, change is often met with skepticism and resistance. Indeed, the social worker's proposal encountered some opposition. In response to this resistance, the social worker documented the cost-benefit ratio to the organization (which satisfied administrators) and clarified the benefits for staff (their time would be freed so that they could accomplish other tasks). In an effort to build support for the proposal, the social worker spoke with co-workers, especially those who were most affected by the need to reschedule appointments for the purpose of completing the eligibility forms. The social worker met with other staff even though they would not be directly affected by the proposal, because she recognized that their support would facilitate acceptance of the proposal. A final point illustrated in this situation is that groups within organizations act favorably to proposals that they perceive either as being benign or as benefiting their position and function.

Policies and Practices

Social workers are in strategic positions in agencies and institutions to evaluate the impact of policies, procedures, and practices on service delivery because of their close contact with clients. When certain organizational practices or policies impede service delivery or block the agency from fulfilling its mission in an optimal fashion, they are well positioned to identify the barriers and proposed changes. In this role, they function as organizational diagnostician/facilitator, mediator, expediter, and advocate.

In this section, we focus on three areas in which organizational policies and practices act as barriers to service delivery: promoting dignity and worth, institutionalized racism or discrimination, and cultural competence at the organizational level. Before beginning the discussion of the factors, we introduce a tool that will assist you in critiquing policies and practices in your organization.

Examining Organizational Policies and Practices

The extent to which organizational policies and practice promote social justice, support client self-determination, and adhere to the principles of empowerment and strengths are lenses through which practitioners may examine agency policies and practices. Rooney (2000) has developed an exercise for students designed to examine the values and ethics reflected in organizational policy decisions and practice. Policies or practices that lend themselves to assessment include criteria for determining eligibility for services, rules that govern clients' behavior in residential or institutional settings, policies related to access to services, and procedures for developing treatment plans. Rooney (2000) outlines the following key points to consider when assessing organizational policies or practices:

1. What are the origins, ideology, and values that appear to have influenced the policy?

2. What are the intended and unintended consequences of the policy's application?

3. To what extent are the policy and its expectations of clients influenced by societal ideology (e.g., the worthy and unworthy poor), social control, or compliance?

4. What is the image of clients and practitioners portrayed by the policy?

5. What does the policy or practice demand of clients and practitioners?

6. How do clients react to the practice or policy?

7. To what extent do the policy and its procedures support or constrain social work values, ethics, and social justice concerns?

Unfortunately, some organizations may have dysfunctional policies or may engage in practices that create barriers to delivering services fully and effectively. The implementation of such policies may, in fact, deny resources to clients to which they are entitled, or certain clients may receive services that are of lesser quality than others receive. For example, in implementing the permanency rules under the Adoption and Safe Family Act of 1997, some states chose to reduce the amount of time that parents had to work toward reunification to less than the 12 months allowed under the federal guidelines. Similarly, with welfare reform, states had discretion in establishing funding priorities and in determining the

components of the services that they provided such as child care subsidies. Sometimes, discretionary decisions reflect a lack of knowledge about resources or the availability of limited resources. At other times, they represent attempts to separate out the worthy from the unworthy. In either case, they have the potential to have deleterious effects on clients, especially when they limit accessibility to services, limit clients' rights, or promote inequality.

The series of questions for assessing organizational policies and practices developed by Rooney is intended to provide social workers with guidelines so that they may critique the effects of policy on clients and service delivery. Many students who have completed this assessment have reported the emergence of insightful questions. For example, in working with involuntary clients, does the policy or practice require clients to be compliant, such that the social worker acts as the enforcer? How do you reconcile unintended consequences of the implementation of rules? For example, rules limiting the number of times a family can access a food bank's resources are intended to preserve resources, thereby ensuring that help will be available to the greatest number of people possible. At the same time, these limits convey the idea that clients may be dishonest or take advantage of the program. When clients have a strong reaction to a policy or practice, are there mechanisms in place so that the organization can respond to their concerns? Do policies and practices provide an image of clients that promotes dignity and worth, and acknowledges strengths as well as problems? How does the policy or practice ensure equal access to and equality of services? In particular, does the policy or practice provide differential treatment for one client group at the expense of another group?

Policies may also exclude some needy persons from obtaining resources. Consider, for example, the requirement that homeless persons have an address to receive benefits. Other examples include instances in which migrants have been denied food stamps because they could not verify their income, or when welfare recipients were ready to work but lacked child care subsidies that would enable them to accept employment. Many times, these policies are intended to help organizations manage limited resources and to ensure their distribution to those in need. Obviously, more flexible policies are needed to remedy these situations, along with advocacy. Policies may be considered to be dysfunctional when they intend to ensure compliance but unduly burden clients, and when procedures are implemented such that the potential for cheating takes precedence over service provisions.

Promoting Dignity and Worth

Human services organizations have the best of intentions when it comes to serving clients. Yet, in many ways, promoting service delivery in ways that enhance clients' dignity remains a challenge. These difficulties may be related to the images portrayed of clients in public policy, the media, or funding resources; organizational practices; and the actions of individual practitioners. In some cases, organizations may strip clients of their dignity by requiring them to go to unreasonable lengths to establish eligibility for concrete aid or services. A vignette entitled "Four Pennies to My Name" is a powerful illustration of one client's perspective of this experience as she attempts to respond to eligibility requirements for financial assistance (Compton & Galaway, 1994)

Clients' dignity may also be compromised if practitioners are habitually tardy for appointments, cancel or frequently change scheduled appointments, or do not extend common courtesies. It is unfortunate when prior negative experiences (e.g., clients have been degraded or humiliated by the actions of staff persons, by breaches of confidentiality, or by demeaning procedures) dissuade individuals from accepting or seeking available services. Even worse, some staff persons may be either openly or subtly judgmental of clients, making remarks about their morality, veracity, character, or worthiness to receive assistance. Still other staff members may be brusque or rude, or they may intrude unjustifiably into deeply personal aspects of clients' lives, needlessly subjecting them to embarrassment and humiliation. These behaviors evolve from bad personal behavior into an organizational issue when supervisors, managers, and staff allow them to go unchallenged. In addition, such behaviors are inhumane and unethical. Beyond the organizational response, social workers who are aware of such behavior by staff members should comply with the ethical standards of social work practice, which require discussion of the concern with the staff member and/or the organization's administration and, if necessary, filing a complaint with the appropriate licensing board and professional organization.

Another organizational issue is inadequate provisions for privacy in the physical space of the organization, such that interviews with clients (either by telephone or in person) are conducted in view of or within earshot of others. Many large public agencies are faced with limited space and increasing numbers of clients and thus struggle to ensure that both staff and clients are comfortable in the organizational environment. Measures initiated by organizations to address this issue include staff visits to clients' homes, locating smaller satellite offices in communities with proximity to target populations, and contracting with community-based agencies to provide services.

Concerns for safety and threats of violence have prompted both public and private organizations to employ private security personnel or off-duty police in an effort to minimize risks. In responding to this very real concern, organizations must be aware of both what sort of image of clients this practice implies and how clients experience the organization. One of this book's authors paid a visit to a Social Security Administration office located in a low-income neighborhood on behalf of a client; this visit illustrated all too well how demeaning an experience can be when a person perceives a lack of power in the face of authority. Entry into the Social Security office required that security personnel examine the content of the author's purse and briefcase. The author then had to pass through a metal detector. The experience was further exacerbated by the impersonal attitudes of the three officers, who asked what the author perceived to be rather personal questions.

While administrators and managers may regard this practice as routine and essential for managing risks and providing a safe work environment, they should be aware of the message it conveys to the clients they serve and its implications for social justice and equality. A first impulse of the author—and one surely experienced by clients—was to argue against the search and demand an explanation for it. She also wondered whether she would have been subjected to the same experience if she had chosen to visit an office in a different part of the city. Broad legal questions have been raised about the legitimacy and authority of security guards. Realistically, although some view their presence as another form of oppression and social control, this practice is unlikely to go away. Nonetheless, social workers in organizations can play a key role in humanizing these situations by providing interpersonal and human relations skills for security personnel, and in developing criteria for the hiring and training of these individuals. When practices such as this result in clients being treated without regard for their dignity, social workers must act as diagnosticians about the policy's effects and as advocates for change.

Institutionalized Racism and Discrimination

Racism and discrimination are embedded in the fabric of our society to such a pervasive extent that many people fail to recognize their many manifestations. Institutional racism often affects service delivery and availability of resources and opportunities in subtle ways. Therefore, it is vital that administrators and practitioners be sensitized to its manifestations so that they can liberate themselves and others from its pernicious effects. The effects of institutional racism range across the entire developmental span, beginning with pre-natal care and continuing through services for the elderly, and beyond—even to burial arrangements. Racism and discrimination pervade our educational, legal, economic, and political institutions; determine employment opportunities; and constrain access to health care services.

Social workers have an ethical responsibility to work toward (1) obliterating institutional racism in organizational policies and practices and (2) enhancing cultural competence. These are worthy goals, of course, but also represent formidable challenges. The first step toward meeting these challenges is developing awareness of possible traces of racist attitudes within oneself. Social workers must also analyze policies, procedures, and practices of their own (as well as those of other social welfare agencies) to ensure that all people are treated equitably. Wolf (1991), for example, describes problems encountered by African Americans in mental health settings in which standardized diagnostic manuals are used to classify and label behaviors. According to Wolf (1991) and Longres and Torrecilha (1992), in most instances a relationship exists between the client's race and the diagnostic or social labels applied to that person. That is, in their encounters with systems, minorities are often labeled without regard to their ecological circumstances or needs. In school settings, subtle institutional racism persists, as evidenced by a disproportionate number of suspensions of minority children and frequent assignments of children to segregated instructional groups. The direct effect of these practices is an assault on the self-efficacy and confidence of minority children (Williams, 1990). These practices have a group effect as well, because the majority of those involved in suspensions and segregated groups are children of color—in particular, African American males.

The failure of child welfare programs to acknowledge the interrelationship between parental neglect related to poverty and minority status has resulted in the out-of-home placement of a disproportionate number of minority children. This continuing trend, which was bolstered by the enactment of the Adoption and Safe Family and Act of 1997, has given rise to the ethical question of whether a larger proportion of minority parents are dysfunctional, or whether they are facing conditions (both personal and environmental) that act as risks rather than protective factors (Halpern, 1990; Roberts, 2002). As Morton (1999) and Chipungu and Bent-Goodley (2003) have emphasized, in comparisons between poor minority and poor nonminority families, children of color are more likely to be placed out-of-home, whereas nonminority families are more likely to receive preservation services. In some instances, these differences can be accounted for by analyzing the problems of the families. Nonminority poor families often present with problems related to parent–child conflicts. Conversely, poor minority families often enter the child welfare system as a result of poverty-related neglect. Rodenborg (2004) refers to this phenomenon as indirect discrimination in that the child welfare agency is unable to provide the resources, such as housing, jobs, or education, needed by these families. At the same time, the child welfare agencies fail to advocate for or educate policy-makers about the plight of these families. In other instances, the disparate placement of children of color may be linked to the use of structure decisions assessment tools. These tools may be inherently biased against poor families, because many of the risk factors assessed are structural family vulnerabilities.

Cultural Competence: A Macro Perspective.
As noted earlier in this book, cultural competence is an issue in the interaction between clients and practitioners who are different, by virtue of their race, language, and culture. Cultural competence is typically discussed at this level in the social work literature. It is not a matter limited to sensitive and aware social workers, practitioners, and staff who work with a particular racial or cultural group, nor is it limited to printed materials and organizational practices. Although cultural competence requires the commitment, competence, and effort of the entire organization, external factors (e.g., public policy) may affect the organization's ability to make a commitment to cultural competence. At the macro level, we discuss two components of cultural competence that go beyond social workers: organizational competence and public policy.

Organizational Competence.
Cultural competence and its assumptions were intended to address issues related to racism, bias, and discrimination by increasing culturally sensitive interventions in recognition of the fact that "traditional forms of practice were often ineffective with and sometimes oppressive to ethnic minority clients" (Rodgers & Potocky, 1997, p. 391). To be effective, organizations must embrace cultural sensitivity and competence and demonstrate their commitment through their policies and practices Chesler, 1994a.; Chesler, 1994b). Both public and private organizations have attempted to accommodate diverse populations by hiring professionals or community staff who represent a target group. Public agencies have also developed purchase-of-service (POS) contracts with ethnic or race-specific community-based agencies. The assumption is that these individuals and agencies are more likely to identify with their clients, and have a greater understanding of the group experience.

This practice initiative, while useful on one level in nonminority agencies, in effect creates an agency within an agency. This practice also raises concerns because, in essence, the ethnic or racial representative becomes solely responsible for same-race or same-culture clients, and therefore may rarely have the opportunity to work with other clients. In some ways, this practice is akin to the child welfare practice wherein white families are recruited as foster or adoptive parents for children of color, but the reverse is rarely the case. In addition, where minority staff serve primarily minority clients, nonminority staff may ignore or limit their exposure to clients who are different. Furthermore, the practice limits the organization's ability to expose nonminority or other clients of color to diverse professionals. A final factor is that the representative staff, whether assigned because of race, culture, or sexual orientation, are often overwhelmed by the volume of work, which includes responding to the demands of representing their community. One Hmong social worker spoke of his frustration with being called each time a South East Asian family was seen at intake and with being assigned only cases for this group.

The NASW Standard for Cultural Competence in Social Work Practice speaks to this issue, asserting that the "special skills and knowledge that bicultural and bilingual staff bring to the profession" should compensated, rather than exploited (2001, p. 26). This issue should be addressed on the systems level, because it has implications related to workload, morale, and unintentional discrimination.

The practice of hiring same-race or same-culture staff in organizations evolved out of a very real need to have a diversity of color, language, and understanding in organizations where the majority of staff members were white. At the same time, this practice is inadequate as a means to achieve cultural competence. Of course, not everyone would agree with this assessment, with many pointing out that same-race or same-culture staffs provide important services to their communities. We agree with this argument. On another level, however, while same-race or same-culture staff members can be empathetic, many express frustration that they are rarely able to alter the policies that affect their clients and their situations. Another matter that has emerged from talks with clients and supervisors is the fact that minority staff often perceive that they need to apply policies more harshly, so as not to appear too lenient or unprofessional when compared to their nonminority counterparts.

Organizations should analyze the public policies that influence their service provisions to ensure that their color-blind nature is not bias and discriminatory. The Child Welfare League of America (1990) has developed a Cultural Competence Self-Assessment Instrument, which enables organizations to assess and develop cultural competence at all levels of the organization. For social workers, Strom-Gottfried and Morrissey (2000) have developed an organizational audit, which assesses agency policies and practices as well as organizational strengths and effectiveness with respect to diversity.

In making their assessments, both organizational leadership and social workers can utilize indicators developed by Cross, Bazron, Dennis, and Issacs (1989), which describe a continuum of cultural competence at the organizational level. At a midpoint on this continuum is the practice of implementing policies that could be described as "color blind" and lacking sensitivity to their effects on minorities. At one extreme of the continuum are agencies that carry out culturally destructive policies. As an example, Cross et al. discuss policies and practices used in boarding schools in the early twentieth century that had the express purpose of eliminating Native American culture. At the other extreme of Cross et al.'s continuum is culturally sensitive and culturally competent practice, which actively seeks to provide services relevant to various minority client populations. In general, the various levels provide a means for organizations to examine their policies and practices so as to determine their differential impact on populations served and to encourage proactive development of culturally sensitive policies.

Public Policy. Cultural competence comprises a set of behaviors and skills that have implications at the level of both the individual social worker practitioner and the organization. In both instances, competence must be supported and reinforced in agency practices. With few exceptions, the literature has emphasized cultural competence in the interactions between clients and practitioners (Weaver, 2004). Unfortunately, few guidelines beyond the standard policy analysis questions (who is affected and in what way) exist for analyzing cultural competence in public policy.

A culturally competent social worker cannot always ensure that clients will not experience racism or bias in public policy. In fact, in the face of public policy, organizations and practitioners are often at a disadvantage, irrespective of the level of cultural competence they have attained. What is the basis of this assertion? Bias is inherent in most policies, even though their intent is to be neutral with respect to race, class, culture, and gender. Yet, as seen in the previous discussion related to racism and inequality in education and child welfare services, policies as implemented often have disparate effects on certain segments of the population.

Public policy has tended to take a narrow view of the culturally or racially determined dynamics that influence how people function. Further, public policy has paid little attention to how family networks and relationships are defined within diverse groups. For example, services for the elderly, mental health services, and child welfare services are structured around the Western concept of the nuclear family, rather than a broad kinship network. Services for the elderly include provisions for assistance either in nursing homes or in-home care, both of which are based on the assumption of nuclear family support. Thus, while resources are available for biological kin to provide care and support, church members, neighbors, and other nonrelatives are deemed ineligible. Informal kinship arrangements, such as those found in many minority communities, also go unrecognized in public policy. In the child welfare situation, for example, relatives as well as non-relatives have often assumed responsibility for children; nevertheless, these individuals are unable to access resources unless they formally adopt the children. The concept of formally adopting a relative, while it has certain legal safeguards, is perceived differently in minority communities.

Van Soest and Garcia (2003) suggest that cultural competence at the public policy level is an issue of social justice. As such, administrators and social workers who are acting as advocates are required to confront aspects of policies that are inherently biased and that have disparate and oppressive effects on various segments of the population. As Weaver (2004) asserts, "the social justice aspect of cultural competence is often obscured by cultural competence conceptualized and highly focused on individual interaction." In effect, this focus means that analyzing the cultural relevance of public policy has been ignored. Conclusions drawn by Voss, Douville, Little Soldier, and Twiss (1999), speaking to policies related to Native Americans, are relevant in this broader context. Specifically, these authors claim that when "social policies and interventions are not inclusive of cultural dynamics, they "rigidly enforce a kind of clinical colonialism" (p. 233).

In light of this discussion, we would add another dimension to the definition of cultural competence for the organization and the social worker. Given that laws and public policy influence service provisions—in particular, who is served—a stronger focus on and analysis of public policy are as crucial to cultural competence as are organizational practices and practitioner–client interaction. This analysis should examine the effects as well as the extent to which public policies and laws are culturally relevant or incompetent, such that they lead to different treatment of different groups or to

discrimination. Organizations should also proactively examine the implementation of policies within their own practices to ensure that they are not, in fact, acting as a party to social injustice. Finally, procedural justice demands that leaders of organizations position themselves so that they are able to articulate the needs of diverse groups to policy-makers, thereby ensuring that public policy is indeed culturally competent. Distributive justice may be compromised without an articulation of the needs of diverse groups. Only through the three-prong efforts of practitioners, organizations, and public policy can the tenets of cultural competence and equality in services ultimately be achieved.

Institutional Programs

Programs are the third facet to be addressed in improving the institutional or organizational environment. The program of an institution is crucial to the effective functioning of its clients. Stimulating, constructive, and growth-promoting programs tend to enhance client functioning, whereas custodial care that fosters idleness produces the opposite effects. Moreover, institutional environments where even the most routine resident behavior is governed by rules constitute unproductive environments that often inspire challenges to the rules and lead to swift punishment of clients.

An important factor in institutional programming is the extent to which residents can exercise choice and control in their daily living and their participation in treatment plans. When people have little control over what happens to them, they tend to become helpless, hopeless, depressed, passive, or even rebellious. To enhance choice and control, progressive institutions foster democratic participation in governance of the institution and allow choice where feasible in how residents spend their time.

CASE EXAMPLE

Social work students involved in a cooperative study experience in Taiwan were housed in a group facility for children and adolescents. While living in the facility and working with the Taiwanese social workers (who also resided in the facility), the U.S. students were surprised to observe the relative unimportance of rules governing the behavior of children and adolescents living in the facility. They found the facility at times chaotic and noisy. Although the children had structured study and quiet periods, after school they engaged in activities of their choosing, with staff joining the children at play. In response to a question posed by one of the students about what was assumed to be a lack of rules (at least by U.S. standards), the Taiwanese social worker explained, "This is the children's home, and therefore they are allowed to behave as if this is so." Both choice and vigorous activity were perceived as essential elements of the program. Among the other positive components of the facility was the fact that the children remained connected to the community by attending and becoming involved in community activities.

Obviously, many other factors come into play in ensuring that programs provide opportunities for social interaction as well as cultivate a sense of mastery and connectedness. Nevertheless, you should be sensitive to your client's needs and should act as an advocate when factors within a program adversely affect the client's well-being.

Empowerment, self-determination, and a sense of self-efficacy are important factors in residential programs. Certain vulnerable groups of clients who have a sense of powerlessness or helplessness are particularly needful of you to act as an advocate and broker. Empowerment and self-efficacy are also achieved in residential programs when residents are able to exercise control over their lives and their environment to the best of their capacity. When this is not the case, both residents and staff may experience the residual effects of discord. For example, a resident complained to the case management social worker that he did not like to have his cigarettes and money rationed to him by staff; he felt that this practice suggested he was incapable of making his own decisions. A common complaint among group home or institutional residents, particularly adolescents, is the point system in which they lose points or privileges for failing to comply with rules (e.g., failing to comply with "lights out" orders, or exhibiting independent behaviors). Many perceive

these systems as further constraining their already limited choices. Often, failure to respond to complaints of this nature escalates in the form of more assertive or aggressive behaviors on the part of clients and leads to discipline by staff members.

Institutional environments are most effective when they empower clients by including them in decisions that affect their lives and that enable them to gain or regain the capacity to interact with the environment. A sense of power is closely linked to competence, self-esteem, and the belief that individual actions or actions in concert with and supported by other systems can lead to improvement in one's life situation. These attributes or factors, in turn, are reciprocally influenced by the quality of the environment.

Empowerment as an aspect of the organization's own culture works in much the same way as for residents, as was described for staff earlier in this chapter. Nutritive environments that produce strong goodness of fit between individuals' needs and corresponding resources foster positive attributes, behaviors, and morale. Conversely, poor goodness of fit caused by major environmental deficiencies, rules, and inflexibility tends to produce powerlessness, reactance, and in some instances depression.

SERVICE COORDINATION AND INTERORGANIZATIONAL COLLABORATION

Social welfare organizations have always interacted through referrals, POS agreements, and sometimes sharing space in a central community service center. Cooperative networks and the content of their relationship may be described as discretionary in that interactions occur on an ad hoc basis, with each organization maintaining its own resources, capabilities, goals, and mission. Cooperation, as defined by Graham and Barter, "facilitates support and assistance for meeting goals that are specific to the individual stakeholders" (1999, p. 7).

Within the last several years, concerns related to service fragmentation, duplication, the complexities

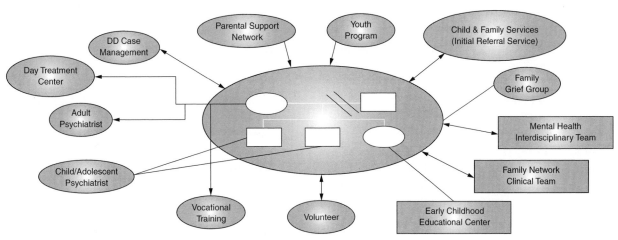

Figure 14-3 Service Fragmentation and Duplication

of social problems, and the managed care environment have influenced more formal interorganizational relationships. In addition, concerns about improving the quality and availability of services have resulted in an increased demand for interdependence between social welfare organizations. Funding initiatives and formal mandates from both local and federal agencies have also served as an impetus for more formal linkages between agencies in the form of coordination or collaborations. Much of the thinking behind this movement has been that effective relationships between organizations are often needed to enhance aspects of the environment of a group of clients who share a common condition.

The experience of clients (see Figure 14-3) is perhaps the most telling with regard to service fragmentation and duplication. In Figure 14-3, the family consists of a mother who is developmentally delayed and her three daughters; the father is deceased. The family was referred for services soon after the father died. This referral led to others, so that eventually the family was involved with 12 service providers.

Each of the service agencies involved with this family had its own goals, many of which were contradictory, conflicting, or competing, and which were responsible for adding stress to the family system. For instance, two agencies provided parent support or parenting services. Parenting support

was also the reason the volunteer became involved with the family as well as family treatment teams from different agencies. Individual family members have their own therapists and are involved with other service providers as a result of referrals. In addition to the overwhelming number of providers, the lack of coordination and duplication of efforts fragmented the family system.

A crisis developed for the family when the condition of their housing required them to relocate. This particular family—which is far more representative than we would like to admit—was spending more than 50 hours per week in appointments with the various agencies involved in their case. When the mother cancelled appointments to look for housing, several of the service agencies reported that she was resistant to change or lacked initiative to make progress; some threatened to withdraw their services. Instead of encouraging the family's problem-solving efforts, the providers' actions inhibited independent thought and action. Both the family and a social worker involved in this situation were extremely frustrated by the service providers' failure to acknowledge the family's housing crisis.

Types of coordination and collaboration between organizations include interdisciplinary or multidisciplinary teams, joint planning or programming, and case management. For example, many school districts are using interdisciplinary teams to address school truancy. These teams consist of staff from a group of organizations that have an interest in this issue. Multidisciplinary teams staffed by mental health and medical professionals are another form of collaborative practice. The use of teams as a form of collaborative practice is beyond the scope of this book, so we refer you to the literature for more on this topic (e.g., Lim & Adleman, 1997; Rothman, 1994; Glisson, 1994). In addition, Congress (1999) and Reamer (1998a) articulate the ethical standards, dilemmas, and principles related to interdisciplinary collaboration for social workers who are functioning as members of interdisciplinary teams.

Interorganizational Service Coordination

Interorganizational service coordination, which includes case management, and interorganizational collaboration are macro practice strategies because they involve the development and coordination of resources and services as system-level interventions to address complex social issues or target groups.

Interorganizational coordination seeks to improve service to clients and to address community or target population concerns by offering a range of services, bridging service gaps, or implementing policies that are too broad for one agency to achieve alone (Alter & Hage, 1992; Beatrice, 1990; Alexander, 1991). Within this context, the collective behavior of the organizations involved is conceptualized as a social action system, in which interdependent processes, tasks, and functions emerge through a division of labor between the members of the coordinated effort. Although the organizations may join together in a coordinated effort and share compatible goals, they remain separate and continue to function independently. At the federal level, coordinated service programs are often designed to effect system change, program development, or service innovations (Alter & Hage, 1992).

Interorganizational coordination provides a range of options for the coordination of services. For example, an individual coordinator, a coordinating unit, or an organization may act as the leader of this effort. The function of this individual, unit, or agency is to "coordinate the decisions, activities of an inter-organizational system with respect to a given area, issue, problem or program" (Alexander, 1991, p. 217). This management of services or resources is meant to provide an effective, integrated mix of services for groups or communities.

A critical issue in service coordination is that the agencies involved should share a common priority—for example, "to strengthen family shelter and transitional housing capacity in the state" (Beatrice, 1990). This arrangement requires that each organization contribute the elements necessary to achieve the joint goal (Rothman, 1994).

Case Management

Case management, a type of interorganizational service coordination, reflects the blending of micro and macro systems, in which the essence of ecological practice comes to life. Case management is not a unitary type of service, and the literature contains varied conceptualizations of micro and macro case management (e.g., Walsh, 2000; Solomon & Draine, 1996; Patterson & Lee, 1998; Rose, 1992; Rothman, 1994; Austin, 1990; Moore, 1990; Roberts-DeGennaro, 1987). In health care settings, case management functions can include utilization review, program management, and locating and coordinating a defined group of services for a specific group of people. Capitman, MacAdam, and Yee (1988) have identified program types and models of case management in health care settings. All models, however, share a basic premise: Case management serves to link clients with essential resources and services.

As a macro strategy, case management functions to locate, organize, coordinate, monitor, and evaluate services at a systems level. Staff in administrative units generally perform these tasks. Large state agencies and managed care providers have units in which staff administer and coordinate services for a target group. At this level, service coordination involves POS contracts, designated care providers, or information and referral services. Rarely are these administrative units directly involved with clients; instead, they have a relationship with the service delivery agency. Although case management may vary in terms of its goals and settings, Rothman (1991), Holt (2002), Naleppa and Reid (2000), and Kane, Penrod, Davidson, Moscovice, and Rich (1991) emphasize that case management always includes the following characteristics:

- Screening
- Multidimensional assessment
- Care planning
- Implementation
- Monitoring the progress and adequacy of services
- Reassessment at fixed intervals
- Outcome evaluation/termination

Case Managers

At the micro level, social workers may perform their case management roles somewhat differently based on the type of setting and role definitions within specific agencies. This role may involve acting as an advocate, broker, and mediator. In some instances, case managers may be involved in direct practice. The case manager role focuses on work at the interface between clients and their environments. In recent practice models, case management has moved to the forefront of direct social work practice as providers have recognized that the needs of increasing numbers of clients with major disabilities (e.g., frail elderly, developmentally and mentally disabled persons) were not being met because these people could not negotiate the complex and often uncoordinated human services delivery systems (Austin, 1990).

Social workers are well qualified to serve as case managers because of their knowledge of community resources, their skills in communication and advocacy, and the purposes and objectives of the profession. Recall from Chapter 1 that their central objectives include (1) helping people to obtain resources, (2) facilitating interactions between individuals and others in their environment, and (3) making organizations and society as a whole responsive to people. Clearly, the case manager role is in harmony with the spirit of social work.

Knowledge of resources, skills in connecting clients with resources (as delineated in Chapter 3), and skills in following up to ensure that clients receive services and resources in a timely fashion thus are common to all case management roles.

Some have asked how case management differs from traditional social work practice. In truth, all social workers engage in case management in varying degrees and, as Moore (1990) has aptly put it, "case management is just old-fashioned social work wearing new clothes" (p. 444). *Case management* in a strict sense entails "generalist" practice. Viewed more broadly, case managers are resource "specialists" who possess knowledge about community resources (in areas of practice defined by the populations they serve) and employ skills in utilizing community resources to benefit their clients.

An Empirically Based Model

In carrying out their roles, case managers do much more than perform the broker role in connecting clients with resources. Indeed, they must be competent in implementing all aspects of the problem-solving process. Recognizing that case management cuts across many human services fields, Rothman (1991), Holt (2002), Walsh (2000), and Naleppa and Reid (2000) have developed and articulated systematic procedures for implementing the case manager role. Rothman developed an empirically grounded model of case management based on a review of 132 pertinent articles and a survey of 48 case managers. Next, we discuss the steps of case management (adapted from the previously mentioned sources).

1. *Access to agency/outreach.* Case managers need to facilitate clients' access to the system by being receptive and by arranging appointments as quickly as possible when people are referred to the organization. Outreach efforts may also be required to encourage people in need of case management services to enter the system (e.g., homeless, mentally disabled, and frail elderly people).

2. *Intake/prescreening.* This step involves exploring clients' problems, needs, and strengths to

determine their eligibility for services and financial resources. Information about the services offered by the organization is provided, and forms are completed as needed. Skills in fostering rapport and eliciting information are employed. Some preliminary planning may be initiated.

3. *Assessment.* Problems are defined more explicitly, and additional collateral information is obtained when needed. Assessment includes existing health, functional, social, psychological, cognitive, environmental, and social supports, as well as supports needed by the client. The family of the client is carefully assessed to determine their capability in coping with a disabled client and their potential as a support system that can be tapped. Clients are assessed in context, but this context should not be generalized to the whole person. Accurate assessment may require collaboration among different professionals or other agencies with which the client may be involved.

4. *Goal setting/case planning.* Objectives are determined by soliciting the client's perceptions of areas needing improvement and the case manager's perceptions. Both short-term and long-term goals are formulated—for example, treating acute physical/mental symptoms and securing housing versus engaging in a rehabilitation program and building self-esteem. Goals must be realistically geared to the capacities of clients, while also respecting their autonomy.

5. *Planning interventions or identifying and indexing resources.* This step is dual in nature, because planning interventions (e.g., counseling or therapy and planning services) and linking clients with resources are inextricably connected. Resources needed may not be available at a given time, new ones may need to be developed, and access to services may have changed based on service demand. Identifying resources may require the case manager to make telephone or personal contacts with agencies. Many case managers establish files on available resources and then use this information in intervention planning with specific clients. As with assessment, clients should be involved in planning interventions to the fullest possible extent.

6. *Linking clients.* Linking clients with resources is both an active process and a facilitative step. To prepare clients for linkage, the case manager provides detailed information, indexes resources, performs advocacy, anticipates difficulties, engages in role-playing, and accompanies clients on the first visit if required.

7. *Monitoring and reassessment.* This vital process aims to determine whether the arrangements implemented are adequately maintaining the client in the community. Monitoring requires a substantial allotment of time to ensure that the provisions of service are appropriate and that they continue to meet the client's needs. Crisis situations are expected, and careful monitoring enables case managers to implement timely remedial measures. In the context of long-term continuing care, ongoing reassessment is essential. During reassessment, the client's status, function, progress, obstacles, and outcomes are reviewed at periodic intervals within a structured time frame. Clients should be actively involved in reassessment. Note that this procedure may revisit instruments employed in the initial assessment phase to obtain baseline measures on specific aspects of the problem situation.

8. *Outcome evaluation/termination.* Where appropriate, outcome evaluation assesses how well goals have been attained (e.g., locating housing, securing medical care, or attaining the capacity to live independently) and whether client needs have been met. When baseline measures were employed during the assessment phase; they will be revisited as part of outcome evaluation. Termination may mean a gradual withdrawal of services as indicated by the situation, or as planned for in brief case management models. The case manager and client may jointly determine whether periodic reviews or contact is appropriate.

Other Case Manager Functions

Embodied in the preceding systematic steps are a number of other common functions performed by case managers. Indirect functions that also benefit clients include interagency coordination and the development of effective working relationships with agencies that will enhance the linkage function. Formulating policies and agreements, either formal or informal, are indirect functions that foster mutual understanding and define procedures for service coordination. Naleppa and Reid (2000) have identified these activities as *parallel intervention functions* to the core case management model. They further identify accountability and outcomes as parallel functions in which the case manager and the agency evaluate performance and outcome of interventions. Finally, Naleppa and Reid (2000) have suggested that class advocacy is a function in which the case manager acts on behalf of clients, and perhaps in collaboration with groups, with a goal of addressing needs or increasing benefits to the client population.

Case advocacy and empowerment are basic elements in case management (Holt, 2000; Walsh, 2000). Case advocacy may be necessary on an intermittent basis to assist a client in obtaining services. Although some critics suggest that case management is not necessarily a form of client empowerment, Cnaan (1994) and Holt (2000) believe that empowerment is not only a valuable goal within the function of the case manager, but also essential to the development of a trusting relationship between the case manager and the client. Guidelines for case management services developed by Naleppa and Reid (2000) articulate a consumer-driven approach that emphasizes empowerment and autonomy as elements of the helping process; these authors also draw a distinction between the "inability to execute a decision" for which clients may need assistance and their "ability to make decisions" (pp. 21–22). Both empowerment and advocacy assist clients with securing needed resources or services, while simultaneously encouraging them to manage their own affairs to the extent of their capabilities. When authority to act is delegated by the client, it is done so within a specified time frame and the decisions made during the period should reflect the client's choices, rather than the case manager's rational expectations.

Interorganizational Collaboration

Although the terms *cooperation, coordination,* and *collaboration* are often used interchangeably to denote formal relationships between organizations, collaboration involves a much more elaborate process and more formal planning. A more recent term used to denote this relationship is "wrap-around services." Reitan (1998) describes three models of interorganizational collaboration as well as a rationale for the formation of an agency relationship within each model. In this discussion, collaboration is both a process and a product of the collaborative arrangement.

Unlike service coordination, in which the goals and missions of the organizations remain separate, collaboration involves creating a shared vision and developing new goals. Thus, the organizational members determine the new venture's mission and authority. Ownership and control of the project are balanced; risks and benefits are shared and mutual. Mattesisch and Monsey (1992) defines interorganizational collaboration as follows:

> a mutually beneficial well defined relationship entered into by two or more organizations to achieve common goals. This relationship includes a commitment to: a definition of mutual relationships and goals; a jointly developed structure and shared responsibility; mutual authority and accountability for success; and sharing of resources and rewards. (p. 7)

Similar to coordination, interorganizational collaboration draws upon the collective strength, knowledge, and expertise of each member organization to achieve through joint effort more than a single organization working alone can accomplish. Other assumptions of collaboration include the delivery of efficient and effective services, a reduction in staff costs, and the ability to address the total needs of a client group. In this respect, interorganizational collaboration is consistent with the trends described earlier in this chapter as well as the emergence of a more holistic framework in human services.

Collaboration can also involve the development of innovative approaches utilizing intervention and practice research (Hasenfeld & Furman, 1994; Galinsky, Turnbull, Meglin, & Wilner, 1993), case management to improve the flow and form of

Table 14-2 Phases of collaboration

1. Problem setting in which stakeholders within a domain are identified with mutual acknowledgment and common definition of issues

2. Agreement on direction and common values that guide individual pursuits and purposes, including expectations of outcome

3. Implementation of the plan and skills—for example, conferring, consulting, cooperation, and understanding the interdependence between the various professional orientations involved

4. Creation of a long-term structure that enables the collaboration to sustain, evaluate, and nurture the collaborative effort over time.

Source: Adapted from Graham and Barter (1999).

services that clients receive (Rothman, 1994), the development of social policy (Beatrice, 1990), and the development of practice knowledge shared by researchers and practitioners (Hess & Mullen, 1995). Graham and Barter (1999, pp. 9–10) have identified four phases of collaboration, which are summarized in Table 14-2.

Several authors have outlined the antecedents, conditions, and factors that facilitate successful interorganizational collaboration (Graham & Barter, 1999; Sandfort, 1999; Reitan, 1998; Brunner, 1991). As Table 14-2 makes clear, collaborative relationships require a blending of resources, a relational system in which joint goals are created, joint decision making, and the creation of a new structure to accomplish the mutually determined goals (Alexander, 1991; Graham & Barter, 1999; Sandfort, 1999; Reitan, 1998). It means that organizations are willing to relinquish their old ways of conducting business and to redefine roles: "Collaboration assumes the inevitability of conflicting ideas and differential power relationships as well as the necessity for compromise, continued advocacy for a position, and the knowledge and skills to differentiate between the two" (Graham & Barter, 1999, p. 10). The dynamics of creating and sustaining the collaborative relationship are illustrated in the following case example.

COLLABORATION: A CASE EXAMPLE[1]

One example of a successful collaborative effort between two organizations involves an initiative that joined staff from a community youth services agency with a group of county probation officers. Both organizations were interested in addressing the recidivism rate of youth offenders. Resources to ensure the development of the newly created organization combined budgetary allocations from both the agency and the county. Staff and managers were responsible for developing the organization's mission and goals, developing joint interventions and strategies, and creating case plans for youth.

Although members of the collaboration had a shared vision, actually coming together posed some difficulties. Concerns centered on issues of trust among staff as well as trust within the community based on community perceptions of probation officers. In particular, staff from the community agency had working relationships with families that tended to be more family and community oriented than the relationships between the families and the probation officers. For example, the agency staff, in their role as advocates for youth, had experienced adversarial relationships with probation officers. Another level of concern had to do with loss of autonomy, decision-making abilities, and communication. Probation officers, for example, were reluctant to relinquish their authority over case plans and decisions about expectations for the youth. Differences in salaries, both actual and perceived, were also complicating factors.

The issues highlighted in this example are among those identified by Mattesisch and Monsey (1992), Meyers (1993), and Sandfort (1999) as influencing the formation of a successful collaboration. Many of the concerns related to this initiative were resolved over time as the two groups worked to refine their vision, develop problem-solving skills, and improve their relationships.

The social and political climate also influences service coordination and interorganizational collaboration. Critical to creating and sustaining interorganizational efforts are the communication and problem-solving processes that participants use to establish goals, objectives, roles, decision-making procedures, and conflict resolution procedures.

Sandfort (1999), in describing the structural impediments that affected the collaboration between a private and a public agency, suggests that the culture and beliefs of each organization as well as the prior relationships that existed between staff play an important part in determining how effectively front-line staff will ultimately be able to work together.

While no one model can ensure coordination or collaboration in all situations, the importance of having a shared vision about service delivery, the outcomes that participants wish to achieve, and the dynamics involved in forging a relationship should not be underestimated. Social workers can play an important role in both the development and implementation process. First, through their contact with client groups, they can identify areas where new initiatives are needed. Second, in the implementation process, social workers can play a valuable role in problem solving and facilitating group processes. They can also ensure that clients' rights and confidentiality are maintained. For example, tensions in coordination and collaborative arrangements often stem from member organizations' struggles over how much information to share. Finally, social workers can use their skills to manage the collective actions and to deal with beliefs that organizations may have about each other. These skills are especially critical when the parties need to resolve philosophical differences about how clients are viewed or treated. In this role, the social worker acts as a mediator and advocate.

Macro Practice Evaluation

Each of the macro-level strategies discussed in this chapter lends itself to a variety of procedures for which outcomes may be assessed. Evaluation seeks to assess the extent to which the change effort and the strategies employed were successful. For example, evaluation of the social worker's efforts to expand the number of beds for the homeless (discussed earlier in this chapter) would measure whether new beds were added through the recruitment of churches and would count the number of beds available. Here, the evaluation focuses on the overall outcome. Because evaluation also examines process, another aspect of the evaluation is to examine how the outcome was achieved—for example, the strategies used to recruit churches. Soliciting feedback from the church groups and participants is one way to obtain this information, such as asking participants to rate the level of appeal of particular recruitment literature. Collecting this information helps to determine which strategies were the most effective, under what conditions, and with which populations.

A pre- and post-intervention rating scale measuring the change in problem status may be applied in situations involving social action and advocacy (e.g., Single Subject Design, scales). Change could be measure on an incremental basis, after a particular action technique, and at the end of the project. You may also decide to collect qualitative information along with statistical data. For example, in an interview format, community members could provide descriptive information regarding improved relationships between the police and a community. The evaluation may be implemented as a summative or formative process and include both qualitative and quantitative data.

Evaluation—whatever its form—requires clearly specified goals and objectives in measurable terms. In general, evaluation is an ongoing process for which it is important to establish indicators at the beginning of the intervention The process involves continuous, systematic monitoring of the intervention's impact, which requires development and implementation of techniques of data management. Systematic analysis of data allows you to determine, for example, if the program activity or intervention is being implemented as planned and whether it is accomplishing the stated program goals. Conducting evaluation requires skills in selecting an appropriate research design, techniques of measurement, and analysis of data. The specific details of the various methods utilized are beyond the scope of this book. The requisite knowledge needed to implement the evaluation process is commonly discussed in research courses.

In keeping with the empowerment theme emphasized throughout this chapter, we stress the importance of including client groups in the evaluation process. They should be involved in establishing success indicators as well as in evaluating the outcomes (Gutierrez, Parsons, & Cox, 1998; Lum, 2004).[2]

Summary

This chapter emphasized the range of roles filled by social workers who are acting as change agents at the macro level. Today's social, economic, demographic, and political trends present numerous opportunities for action and intervention at the macro practice level. In talking to social workers in preparation for writing this chapter, we were impressed with the breadth and depth of macro practice strategies they used. The social workers saw their practice as holistic and were comfortable employing a range of strategies to help people resolve problems or change social conditions. As one social worker stated, "It would be difficult to ask people to change without also addressing the circumstances and conditions that contribute to their situations." The person and environment focus reflected in this statement, in essence, frames the fundamental tenets and foundation of macro practice.

Internet Resources

See our companion website for hot links to some helpful URLs. Note that URLs are subject to change. We will endeavor to update the links on the companion website as much as possible.

Use the following keywords to explore articles through InfoTrac College Edition: "advocacy," "social planning," "cultural competence," "immigration," "migration," "refugees," "grassroots organizing," "case management," "wrap-around services," "service coordination," "social reform," "resource development," "organizational culture," "learning organizations," "organizational learning."

In addition, you may find the following websites useful:

> Mental health outreach for older adults: *www.wiche.edu//MentalHealth/ElderBroch/index.htm*
>
> Community building tools: *http://www.acosa.org*
>
> Community toolbox: *http://www.ctb.ukans.edu*
>
> The FrameWorks Institute: *www.frameworks intstitute.org*
>
> Institute on Domestic Violence in the African American Community: *www.dvinstitue.org*

Also, many of the advocacy groups mentioned in this chapter have websites.

Related Online Content

Visit the *Direct Social Work Practice* companion website at *http://socialwork.wadsworth.com/hepworth7* for additional learning tools such as glossary terms, chapter outlines, InfoTrac College Edition keywords, relevant web links, and chapter practice quizzes. Also, be sure to check out the Direct Practice Virtual Reader, where the authors have personally selected articles relevant to this chapter using InfoMarks.

Notes

1. The authors wish to thank the many social workers and agencies that provided the rich examples of macro-level intervention strategies discussed in this chapter.
2. For additional information, we refer you to Gutierrez, Parsons, and Cox (1998) for examples of facilitating empowerment through evaluation.

CHAPTER  15

Enhancing Family Relationships

CHAPTER OVERVIEW

Chapter 15 builds on the family assessment skills you learned in Chapter 10, by describing skills in enhancing family relationships and interactions. You will learn how to engage families, improve communications, and practice in a culturally sensitive manner.

APPROACHES TO WORK WITH FAMILIES

Social workers are involved with families in a variety of settings and for diverse purposes. Social work practice with families may involve assisting a family to prepare for the discharge of a member from an institution, helping a mother to take action so that her child is returned from foster care, conducting crisis-oriented interviews with distraught parents with an injured child in a hospital emergency room, or mediating a conflict situation with a housing complex manager (Reid, 1985). These examples suggest that social work practice with families encompasses a range of interventions, including therapy, home-based interventions, and community-based services in a variety of settings.

The recurring emphasis in the various approaches taken to work with families has been on the family as a social unit. As conceptualized by Mary Richmond in the late nineteenth century, the family is a social system and thus the focus of intervention (Nichols &

Schwartz, 2004). As a social system, the family is influenced by and interacts with larger social systems in the environment. These other social systems include organizations, communities, and groups; thus some approaches emphasize the family in an ecological or systems context. In the ecological context, Kilpatrick and Cleveland's integrative model assesses and intervenes with families, based on their level of need (Kilpatrick & Holland, 2003). Boyd-Franklin and Bry (2000) recognize the experience of family interactions in a multisystems context, and suggest that effective strategies intervene with the family and other systems that affect family life. The focus of this chapter emphasizes family as a social unit; moreover, we examine the continuous interaction and relationship patterns internal to the family system that influence family functioning.

Family relationships and interactions are often punctuated and strained by numerous factors. Family life transitions, structural arrangements, patterns of communication, and roles (including role definition, overload, and strain) are but a few sources that contribute to family relational dynamics. Therapeutic intervention strategies and goals—whether the focus is on family structure or family processes—have as their primary aim to alter relationship and interaction patterns so as to support growth and development of all family members. Concepts related to family structure are rooted in family transaction patterns, interpersonal boundaries, and arrangements between subsystems. Process-oriented approaches tend to

457

focus on the nature of family dynamics, their patterned interaction, circularity, and cause-and-effect sequences.

Intervening in the family system is intended to "change the family, and in doing so, change the life of each of its members" (Nichols & Schwartz, 1998, p. 6). A variety of approaches are employed to accomplish this goal. For example, cognitive behaviorists seek to help individuals and the family learn new behaviors, thereby altering the process of circular or reciprocal sequences of behavior (Becvar & Becvar, 2000a). Regulating communication and altering communicational styles is another strategy used to promote positive interactions and family relationships. Virginia Satir (1967) was the first social work family therapist to examine and modify faulty communications processes through direct intervention A family systems approach developed by Murray Bowen seeks to reduce anxiety and symptoms by resolving multigenerational issues that intrude upon an individual's ability to balance emotional and intellectual functioning, intimacy and autonomy, and interpersonal relations (Goldenberg & Goldenberg, 2004). Conversely, the goal for structural therapy (Minuchin, 1974) is to strengthen current family relationships, interactions, and transactional patterns. The structural approach emphasizes the "wholeness" of the family—that is, its hierarchical organization and the interdependent functioning of subsystems (Goldberg & Goldberg, 2004, p. 212). Given its primary focus on improving family relationships, structural therapy pays attention to boundaries, alignments in the family system, and power, using the resources and power of families to effect change.

More recently, approaches to work with families have encouraged us to rethink earlier assumptions about what constitutes healthy or normal family development and functioning. Inspired by the feminist critique and loss of faith in truth and objectivity, these approaches give attention to diversity and pluralism and diminish the authority of the family social worker. New approaches include solution-focused therapy. A core assumption of this model is that solutions and exceptions create new narratives and can serve as potent forces that motivate people toward change. In the same vein, narrative or interpretative reality and social construction approaches to the family are collaborative and conversational. All of these approaches have as a goal helping families create new meaning and viewpoints (Nichols & Schwartz, 1998; Hartman, 1993).

This chapter draws upon a cross section of family practice and family therapy approaches and intervention techniques that you can use to enhance family interactions and relationships. These interventions and techniques, of course, flow from the multidimensional assessment and emphasize the assessment dimensions discussed in Chapter 10. Mastering the content of this chapter and practicing relevant skills will advance your competence in the following areas:

- Engaging families (voluntary, referred, or mandated) in the helping process and initial sessions
- Assisting families to enhance their interactions by increasing positive feedback
- Modifying dysfunctional patterns in interactions
- Modifying misconceptions and distorted cognitions that impair interactions
- Modifying dysfunctional family alignments

Although the interventions and techniques discussed in this chapter are applied to couples and families, most are also relevant to work with treatment groups, a topic discussed in Chapter 16.

Families, as defined in Chapter 10, vary in their configuration or form. They may include same-sex or heterosexual couples, blended families, single-parent families, guardians, or second-generation families in which grandparents are caring for their grandchildren. Families also reflect social or cultural arrangements extending to kin, friends, and informal and formal intergenerational relationships. Clearly, there is great flexibility in how each family chooses to define the relevant members of its family system.

The family system functions and is influenced as a system within larger systems. As a consequence, family context and hence family functioning may be influenced by factors that are external to the family system influence. For example, lesbian or gay families or a family consisting of a low-income single parent may encounter difficulties in their interactions with other systems due to discrimination. Discrimination and other socio-environmental factors are capable of influencing family interactions. Family processes and structure may also be embedded in cultural values and norms, so conventional techniques used to intervene with families may not match the needs of diverse families. We highlight some of these issues later in this chapter as well as discuss ecologically based concerns that influence family functioning.

By way of review, you may also want to reread Chapter 10's discussion of family rules, boundaries, and communication styles that frame family interaction patterns. We begin this chapter by setting the stage for the initial contact with families and couples and introducing the skills that will facilitate engaging them in the helping process.

INITIAL CONTACTS

Enhancing the functioning of couples and family systems requires you to be skilled in engaging members and in focusing on the family as a whole. Generally, when seeking help, families or couples do not think from a systems perspective. Instead, they tend to identify a concern, and often target the behavior of another member as primary to their difficulties. Thus, it is important to manage initial contacts in ways that encourage work with relevant members of the family system, rather than settle prematurely on a problem identified in an individual's request for service. This section describes ways of handling the initial contacts that lay the groundwork for implementing the systems-oriented interventions discussed later in this chapter.

Managing Initial Contacts with Couples and Families

Most often, a member of a family initiates the initial request for service. Depending on the practice setting or the nature of a referral, the initial contact may occur in the home, in a school or hospital setting, over the telephone, or in your office.

If the family has previously been screened for a family approach at intake, all that you may need to do in the initial contact is to work out scheduling details. If there has been no previous contact with the caller—for example, if the contact came about because of a referral from a teacher—you may need to accomplish several other objectives. In particular, you may need to determine whether intervening at a family level is appropriate. A family approach is usually indicated when a problem involves other family members or persons living in the same household, such as a relative, friend, or live-in partner. In contrast, when a problem involves persons less intimately involved with the caller, such as an employer or a relative who lives elsewhere, the initial appointment is made with the individual who initiated the contact.

Other critical objectives of the initial contact include reaching an agreement as to who will attend the first session and establishing rapport with the member who initiated the request for service. Wright and Anderson (1998) call our attention to attachment skills, which essentially concern "connecting" to clients and ensuring that they are heard and that their experience is validated. Even so, the initial contact should be kept short and tightly focused on relevant objectives of the session to avoid becoming entangled in the individual's perception of the family's problem. To this end, we recommend that you follow these guidelines:

1. Ask the family member to describe the problem briefly, and empathically respond to their messages. This strategy not only helps establish rapport, but also yields important information. In addition, elicit information that will help you determine who else is involved in the problem. When you believe you have begun to establish rapport and have heard the presenting complaint, summarize the individual's view of the problem, his or her relevant feelings, and emphasize that person's needs or wants.

2. In the instance of referred or mandated contact, you should share the circumstances of the referral, including the source and the expressed purpose and goals included in the referral or mandate. You

should also clarify choices that the potential client may make, including whether to meet at all (in the case of referred contact) or what might be addressed. Also, any mandates that might affect potential client choices should be shared (Rooney, 1992), including applicable time limits.

3. If your exploration reveals that family involvement is appropriate, introduce the client to the family systems approach, using a message such as the following:

Social worker: In helping people with the kinds of problems you've described, it is often helpful to have other family members come for sessions. It has been my experience that when some members of the family have problems, other members are affected, and they also experience stress and discomfort. Equally important, changes in one member may require changes and adjustments in other family members. People accomplish change more frequently when all family members work together. For this reason, it will be important that other family members are involved.

4. Specify which family members you want to see in the initial session. Social workers who espouse a family systems orientation differ in their views as to whether the entire family should be included in the initial session, with some strongly advocating involving all members from the beginning. Because of potential difficulties that may be encountered in managing initial contacts with entire families (which requires advanced skills), we recommend a less ambitious approach. For example, if a parent identifies a child-related problem, request that one or both parents attend the first session *without* the child (or children) unless the parent voices a strong objection ("He needs to be here, too!") or in unusual circumstances (a child threatening suicide). In instances where circumstances dictate excluding other family members from the initial contact, convey the message that you will want to see these individuals in future sessions.

5. When a caller complains of problems involving a spouse or partner, ask that this individual be included in the initial session. Respond, however, to the preference of a caller to be seen alone in a first session. Even though you may agree to see an individual alone at first, you should indicate that a next step would be to schedule an individual interview with the other person, thus giving him or her "equal time." Because people differ in their opinions, seeing each member individually allows you to obtain a balanced view of the problem. Some clients will comply with requests to include specific family members in the initial session, but others may offer explanations such as "My husband works odd hours," "She won't come," or "He's not the one with the problem." These messages often reflect the caller's reluctance to include other members, and perhaps the reluctance of others to engage and participate in resolving difficulties.

When family members emphatically state that they do not want to involve certain or any family members in the initial session their reasoning should be explored. If their position is not subsequently modified, you should begin where they are and arrange to see any family members whom they are willing to bring. When clients maintain that other family members are unwilling or unable to attend the initial session, ask their permission to contact those persons directly. If you gain permission (as will usually happen), you can telephone the individual, using a message similar to the following, after introducing yourself and stating the purpose of the call:

Social worker: As you know, [caller's name] has contacted me concerning problems involving your family. I understand that you are quite busy, but I thought I would give you a call to ask you to join us. Your participation would be extremely helpful, and I am interested in getting your perspective on the problem the family is experiencing as well as your ideas about how this problem can be resolved. Would you available for an appointment, say, at 4:00 P.M. next Wednesday?

In the best-case scenario, the individual will agree to your request. Some people, however, may react less favorably, and you will need to explore this response. Subsequently, you could ask the person to participate in *at least one* session, yet respect his or her decision to not participate. Exerting pressure may alienate the individual, thereby destroying future opportunities to obtain his or her involvement in the helping process. With skillful handling, most often you will be able to dissipate strong opposition. Furthermore, insisting on a recalcitrant individual's participation may introduce dynamics that undermine the helping process; in fact, the first contact may be the last. There may, of course, be instances in which not all family members need to the present. For example, children are generally excluded from family sessions that focus on the relationship between the parents.

Because social work practice with families takes place in a variety of settings, the initial contact may not follow the scenarios we have outlined here. For example, your initial contact may take place in the family's home. This contact may be voluntary or involuntary. In the latter case, you may need to manage problematic client–social worker dynamics. In any event, home visits require making arrangements with families to ensure that sessions will be free of interruptions, especially when the family includes small children. During home visits, you may also encounter other family members or friends, in which case privacy and confidentiality issues need to be resolved. For example, a social worker sought consultation on whether he should proceed with the initial contact session with a family because of the presence of an unidentified elderly man. This individual clearly held an esteemed position in the family. In fact, the father would often look for nonverbal cues from this individual before responding to the social worker. In this case, it was decided that the social worker should ask to be introduced to the elderly man and inquire about his role in the family.

In some situations, a key family member may be unavailable, as occurred in one case in which the mother was incarcerated. Despite her imprisonment, the mother wanted to remain connected to her husband and children, so family sessions had to be arranged at the prison. The social worker had to arrange for transportation to the prison. She also had to navigate the system's rules for visitation,

comply with time limits, and ensure that the mother adhered to certain rules of conduct so that she could participate in the family sessions.

The requirements of other systems involved in this case—namely, child protective services and the probation office—also had to be met. For example, the child protection social worker had to be present during the initial and subsequent family sessions, as the mother was not allowed to have unsupervised visits with her newborn child. Also, child protection was moving to terminate the mother's parental rights for the newborn because she had experienced a relapse while she was on probation for drug use; furthermore, her sentence would exceed the concurrent planning time frame for reunification. The situation was further complicated because the father of the older children was not the father of the newborn, yet he was willing to obtain custody of his stepchild. The management of the initial contact and of subsequent family sessions required the social worker in this case to assist the family to develop specific goals, within a limited time frame, as well as to coordinate services with the other systems involved.

Managing Initial Contacts with Parents

Initial sessions with parents should involve other persons who perform the executive parental function in the household. Children may be included in subsequent sessions. This strategy gives you more time to become acquainted with the problems of the family and, on the basis of known information, to plan strategies for engaging the children in the helping process. By having an initial session with parents, you are able to establish rapport with them and, where indicated, influence their behavior in future sessions that include the children. Some parents, for example, manifest such ingrained and adversarial styles of relating to their children that initial attempts to see parents and children together would prove disastrous. Further, having an initial session with parents alone enables you to clarify the systemic nature of problem.

Interviewing parents first in an initial session also enables you to coach them about how best to bring an identified child into the helping process. For example, in talking to the child, they should clarify that the *family* is having a problem, rather than indicating that the family is having problems *with the child*. In addition, they should provide a general explanation of what the child can expect in the session with you. In doing so, they should be alert to any reservations that the child has about coming to the session.

When meeting with parents or other individuals who perform this role in initial sessions for which a child is the identified problem, you will need to examine the basis of their belief. Depending on how the parents have communicated about the problem in front of the child, you may expect that in parent–child sessions the child will be defensive and perhaps oppose becoming involved in the helping process. You can take some pressure off this individual by engaging all members in a discussion of changes they would like to make and by emphasizing the *family's* problem. This strategy is also appropriate when an adult has been designated as the source of a problem.

When parents bring a child to the initial session, you may need to coach them about how to behave constructively. For example, suggest to parents that they assist you in creating a climate that is conducive to open communication, ask them to refrain from sending blaming messages ("He continues to mess up in school, and hang around the wrong people"), and request that they focus on positive behaviors ("He was a helper this past summer in a program for kids in the park"). Using a technique from solution-focused treatment, you might divert the parent's attention to those instances of exceptions—for example, when "messing up in school does *not* occur."

In the initial session, you should provide an opportunity for the child to tell her or his story. This step allows you to hear directly from the child, without being biased (as the child perceives it) by information provided by the parents. At the same time, you should be careful to avoid subordinating the parent's executive function or giving the impression that you are forming an alliance with the child. In some cultures, inviting children to voice their concerns is unacceptable and perceived to be inappropriate role behavior. In other instances, interviewing a child alone is required— for example, in situations of reported child maltreatment or sexual abuse. If culture permits, and there is no indication of child maltreatment, you can interview the child either with the parents present or alone.

The last part of the session is reserved for seeing all family members together. At this time, you will want to reemphasize the systemic nature of the family problem and assist members to share individual goals with one another and to formulate family goals.

ORCHESTRATING THE INITIAL FAMILY SESSION

The goal of bringing the family together is to identify the problem at hand by eliciting the viewpoints of the various family members. The initial session, whether it occurs in the office or in the home, is referred to as the *social* or *joining stage* (Nichols & Schwartz, 1998; Boyd-Franklin, 1989). In this stage, it is important to establish rapport and build an alliance with the family. It is useful to restate the reason for the voluntary contact ("James contacted our agency because of . . .") to gather information about the family and to listen to their perspectives on the problem. If the family has been referred or mandated for treatment, then you must acknowledge this fact—for example, "Katie's teacher referred the family to our agency because. . . ."

In facilitating the *joining stage,* your tasks are twofold. First, you must ensure that each family member can voice his or her opinion without interruptions from other family members. Second, you must encourage family members to listen so that other members feel understood and accepted. You can further facilitate the joining stage by adopting a stance that emphasizes the question, "What can I learn from and about this family that will help me work with them?"

The initial session with families is crucial. Clients' experiences during this session determine in large measure whether they will join with you and contract to work toward specified goals. Moreover, clients perceive the initial session as a prototype of the helping process. To lay a solid foundation for future work with families, it is important that you accomplish a number of objectives. We briefly discuss each of these objectives in this section, but first we list them so that you may use them as a guide in both planning for and evaluating initial sessions:

1. Establish a personal relationship with individual members and an alliance with the family as a group.

2. Clarify expectations and explore reservations about the helping process.

3. Clarify roles and the nature of the helping process.

4. Clarify choices about participation in the helping process.

5. Elicit the family's perception of the problem(s).

6. Identify needs and wants of family members.

7. Define the problem as a family problem.

8. Emphasize individual and family strengths.

9. Ask questions to elicit information about the patterned behaviors of the family.

10. Draw the family's attention to repetitive communications and discuss whether they wish to change these patterns.

11. Begin assisting members to relate to one another in more positive ways.

12. Establish individual and family goals.

13. Gauge motivation of family members to return for future sessions and negotiate a contract.

14. Negotiate tasks to be accomplished during the week.

15. End the session by summarizing problems discussed, goals formulated, and progress achieved.

Note these objectives are essentially the same as those identified in earlier chapters of this book. In the following sections, however, we explain how to accomplish these objectives in work with families. This discussion will also assist you in consolidating knowledge and skills that have been presented earlier.

1. *Establish a personal relationship with individual members and an alliance with the family as a group.* In working with families (or groups), social workers have a twofold task of establishing personal relationships with each individual while developing a "connectedness" with the family as a unit. To cultivate relationships with family members, you can employ several techniques. The technique of *socializing* involves the use of social chitchat and is used briefly by you at the beginning of the session to reduce tension. Joining or coupling techniques to expedite entry in to the family system must respect culture, family form, family rules, and the current level of functioning. You can further convey your acceptance of the family by highlighting their strengths or offering support to vulnerable members. You will also want to use the family's language and idioms—for example, "He's messing up in school." Appropriate self-disclosure may be used in statements that establish similarities or parallels between you and the family.

Empathic responding can be particularly useful in establishing rapport with reserved or reluctant family members. For instance, when members do not spontaneously participate, you may attempt to draw them into the session: "Tamika, we haven't heard from you about how you felt when you learned you were coming to see a social worker. Would you tell us how you felt?" You can then respond empathically to what that member says or does: "Yes, I can understand why you would feel this way. At your age, I probably would have felt the same." Such an empathic message shows genuine interest that can cause reserved family members to become more active. Conversely, if their lack of involvement is related to family dynamics rather than to their feelings, you will need to be mindful of the potential risks of encouraging reticent members to express their opinions. In either case, you should endeavor to distribute time and attention somewhat equally among members, to highlight individual strengths, and to intervene when one member speaks for another or when one member is the target of blaming or put-down messages.

Finally, effectively connecting with families requires that you demonstrate an understanding and have empathy for the sociopolitical and cultural context of the family, and family members' strengths and competencies. Often, it is positive qualities that have enabled the family to function in spite of their difficulties.

2. *Clarify expectations and explore reservations about the helping process.* Family members have varying and often distorted perceptions of the helping process and may have misgivings about participating in sessions. To identify obstacles to full participation in these areas (which is a prerequisite to establishing a viable contract), you should elicit the responses of all family members to questions such as the following:

- "What were your concerns about meeting with me?"
- "What do you hope might happen in our meetings together?"
- "What were your fears about what might happen in this meeting today?"

Questions of a more general nature are useful to help family members articulate their concerns, as illustrated in the following examples:

- "Are you concerned that your family might be judged?"
- "In your community, how would others deal with this problem?"
- "Does seeking help from someone outside of your family make you feel uncomfortable?"
- "In what way do you think that I can be of help to your family?"

As you elicit reservations, concerns, and even hopes from each family member, you can broaden the focus to the family by asking, "I'm wondering if others share the same or similar concerns as. . . ." As members acknowledge similar feelings, they often begin to realize that despite feeling some degree of alienation from others in the family, they share certain common concerns. This realization tends to identify members as a unit. Exploring reservations about participating in the helping process often

diminishes negative feelings or enables clients to move forward with the process.

As always, you should remain sensitive to cultural norms. For example, you should be cautious about insisting upon expressions of feelings, as some families may be baffled by *feeling* questions. Culture aside, certain family members will continue to have strong reservations about meeting with you. You can address their reluctance by asking them one or both of the following questions and addressing their subsequent responses:

- "What, if anything, would make you feel better about participating?"
- "Given your concerns, are you willing to stay for the remainder of the session and decide at the conclusion whether to continue?"

Your willingness to negotiate the terms under which clients participate and your acknowledgment of their right to make a choice will often reduce their negativism to the point that they will agree to continue. For example, you might ask a person to attend a family session, but emphasize that the individual is not obligated to participate. Further, you may advise the reluctant member that there is no need to talk; the person can read a book or just be physically present in the session. This type of invitation diminishes the pressure on the person to contribute.

The Dynamics of Minority Status and Culture in Exploring Reservations

In general, individuals may be reluctant to join sessions when they are singled out as the problem. In this regard, reluctance acts as a protective function, rather than representing opposition to change. Minority status and culture are additional factors that may cause a family or family member to have reservations about seeking help. Families may fear "what might happen" if their problems are brought out into the open (Nichols & Schwartz, 1998, p. 132). Boyd-Franklin (1989) and Lum (2004) explains that the historical experience of minority families and their being perceived as "unhealthy" may cause these families to hide their problems until they escalate to a point of crisis. Indeed, the experiences of other family members and entire communities may reinforce this silence. Also, in some minority families, there is an unspoken rule of keeping family secrets, a high value placed on privacy, or a sense of shame about involving an outsider in family matters. Flores and Carey (2000) note, for instance, that the comfort level of Hispanic families is increased when they do not feel the need to be defensive about their culture. Lum (2004, p.153) emphasizes the importance of "confianza," the art of establishing mutual trust in the helping relationship as a means to address the concerns of people of color.

Reservations about attending family sessions may be a particular issue among ethnic minority families in which some members are undocumented or residing illegally in the United States (Pierce & Elisme, 1997; Fong, 1997; Falicov, 1996). In addition, immigrant or refugee families may be unfamiliar with formal helping systems (Potocky-Tripodi, 2002). Moreover, poor minority and gay or lesbian families have good reasons for their apprehensions and anxieties about seeking help. Wright and Anderson (1998) suggest that in actively tuning into the family, you might pose the question, "What is it like being with the client [family]?" especially during the initial session (p. 202). In effect, you are evaluating whether your reactions will enter into the helping process. You are also actively attempting to understand the family's frame of reference. We would add two additional questions: "What is it like to be this family?" and "What does it mean to this family to seek professional help?" The answers to these questions will help you show sensitivity in your initial interactions with the family and to understand their experience in seeking help. You are also encouraged to acknowledge the protective function of reluctance, whether in a family member or the family system as a whole, and to create a nonblaming atmosphere where the family and individual members feel safe and affirmed.

3. *Clarify roles and the nature of the helping process.* In exploring misgivings and reservations, you should educate families about the nature of the helping process and clarify both your own and their roles. In educating families about the helping process, you create an atmosphere and structure where problem solving can occur. Role clarification is also addressed toward the end of the initial session in which an initial contract is negotiated.

4. *Clarify choices about participation in the helping process.* In the instance of referred contact, you can reiterate that the family is free to decide whether further contact with you will meet their needs and, if so, what to work on, regardless of the concerns of the referring source. If contact is mandated, it is necessary to clarify what you are required to do (e.g., submit a report to the court) and the parameters of required contact. In addition to mandated concerns, you can advise families that they can choose to deal with other problems of concern to them.

5. *Elicit the family's perception of the problems.* In initiating discussion of problems, social workers ask questions such as "Why did you decide to seek help?"(in the case of voluntary contact), "What changes do you want to achieve?", or "How could things be better in the family?" Eliciting the client's view of the problem is equally important in involuntary or referred contacts. In such cases, the nature of the referral is summarized, but families are encouraged to tell their story: "Your family was referred to our agency by the courts, because Juan was reported to the school truancy officer for missing school. This is the information that I have, but I still need to hear from you why you believe you were referred." Because each person has his or her own viewpoint about both the problem and its solution, your task is to move the family toward reaching a consensus. It is important to elicit the support of each member during the process of achieving consensus.

In the initial session, you will want to be aware of differences in interpretation and the various family roles within the family with respect to issues of gender, power, and boundaries. Rosenblatt (1994) urges us to pay attention to the language and metaphors used by the family as they describe their concerns. In particular, how individual family members express their views reflects their culture, their realities, and the meaning assigned to the family experience. The family experience includes exploring spirituality or religion in the life of the family (Anderson & Worthen, 1997).

6. *Identify needs and wants of family members.* As you engage the family in a discussion of problems, listen for needs that are inherent in their messages as illustrated in the following family session. The social worker begins with a summary explanation of his observations.

Social worker: You're here because some of your wants or needs are not being met in the family. As we discuss the family's problems, I'm going to ask you to help me identify those needs and wants. In turn, we will consider them as we formulate goals and plan our change efforts.

The initial session takes place in a family service agency, and involves Marcos, a 16-year-old youth, and his father, Mr. G. Tensions between father and son are related to the son's choice of friends, his desire to be independent, and the father's concerns for his safety. The mother is not involved because she is in another city taking care of her parents, both of whom are ill.

Marcos [*to father*]: You don't ever let me do anything with my friends. [*Feels resentful, wants more autonomy and freedom.*]

Social worker: It sounds to me, Marcos, as though you want to be more independent. You'd like more freedom to move around and more trust from your parents. Am I hearing your needs correctly?

Sometimes, other family members, perhaps uneasy about where the discussion may lead, may interrupt your message or in some way discount others' opinions. For example, Marcos's father, Mr. G, responds as follows:

Mr. G: Wait a minute, I'm not about to let you run around wherever you want, particularly with that friend who's been coming around lately, because he's nothing but trouble.

The social worker prevents Mr. G's comment from diverting the focus by using the technique of temporarily "putting clients on hold." This technique involves blending an empathic response that addresses the participant's feelings with a focusing response that restructures the interpersonal interaction to achieve the immediate objective. As illustrated in the following excerpt, the social worker works to enable members to listen and acknowledge each other's needs and perceptions:

Social worker: I hear your concerns about your son—you don't want him to just run loose—and I hear your concerns about his new friend. I also know you want to have your views heard and I'd like to hear your views in a minute. But first, I'd like to ask you to hear Marcos's point of view. I would also ask that you listen to him describe what he needs or wants.

In initial discussions of needs, you can correct misperceptions often held by some members that a discussion of the needs of one person means that you will support that person's position. In the following message, for example, the social worker attempts to allay Mr. G's fear that he may support his son's desire for independence and that Marcos's wants take precedence over his concerns as a parent:

Social worker: Identifying needs and the conflict surrounding various viewpoints precedes problem solving. When we get to the point of considering solutions, we'll identify options that might help you and Marcos with problems you've pinpointed and select ones that meet both your needs.

When one person (Marcos) is perceived as the problem, your task is to challenge this linear thinking by asking others about their roles in creating or maintaining the problem. In the family life cycle, Marcos's desire for greater independence is to be expected, and his behavior reflects age-appropriate autonomy and differentiation. Changes in the bonds between an adolescent seeking greater autonomy and his or her parents are consistent with adolescent development; however, they may also require changes in parenting behavior and communication patterns (Baer,

1999). At the same time, Mr. G feels responsible as a parent and is making certain demands consistent with this role. This role often results in parents establishing protective boundaries, which may include anxieties about both peers and the neighborhood, and undertaking intense monitoring. Baer's (1999) study of family relations and parenting styles in three ethnic groups found that while monitoring was "significant" for all ethnic and racial groups as a deterrence to deviance, it was heightened in some families because of real or perceived dangers (p. 282). Low-income African American parents, for example, may initiate intense monitoring of adolescents in an attempt to minimize dangers in neighborhoods and counteract the outright hostility of society toward minority male youth (Jarrett, 1995). In some cultures, Marcos's desire for greater autonomy may signal an attempt to reconcile acculturation and traditional values.

We pick up at the point where the social worker returns to Mr. G's needs. Notice that he moves to a point in which *common* needs are established between father and son:

Social worker: You probably noticed that I kept the discussion focused on Marcos's needs. I did so because it is critical for me to understand what each of you would like to change. I'd like you to help me to identify *your* needs now. You were saying, "I can't go along with Marcos's just running around," indicating that you are worried. What would you like to see change?

Mr. G: I guess I need to know where he's going—after all, I'm responsible for him. And I need to know he's not getting in trouble when he's gone.

Social worker: Marcos, did you hear what your father said?

Marcos: He said that he needs to know where I am and what I'm doing.

Social worker: Good. Now I'm going to try filling in your dad's message. I think he's also saying, "I need to know because I care very much about my son and I am afraid of what might happen to him." Is that accurate, Mr. G? [*Father nods.*]

[*To Mr. G*] I'd like you to talk directly to Marcos.

Mr. G: I do care, and I am anxious about your going around with people that I don't know. [*Hesitates.*] I also feel that we don't do things together anymore. I always listened to my father and did what he said, even though I did not always agree with him.

Marcos: But Dad, things are different now. Besides, you never told me that you wanted to spend time with me. I never heard you say this before.

Mr. G: No, you were too busy running around with that trashy friend of yours.

Social worker [*interrupts this sequence by refocusing on common needs*]: Marcos, tell your dad how you feel when he makes statements about your friends.

Marcos: I feel bad. I'd like to do things with him also, but I can't talk to him. All he does is bad-mouth my friends. He's always critical of what I'm doing. He thinks that I should stay in my own community. I try to tell him that things are different from when he was my age.

Social worker: Talk directly to your dad rather than to me, and tell him what you need from him.

Marcos: I'd like for us to do things together, but I also want to be with my friends. I'd also like to able to talk to you without always ending up in an argument over my friends, my music, and my clothes.

By identifying and highlighting common needs, the social worker was able to focus the intervention on the similarities rather than the differences between father and son and to formulate goals they can mutually work toward to improve their relationship. Both Marcos and his father have expressed a desire to spend time together. The social worker also assisted the two of them to communicate and negotiate their concerns directly, thereby relieving some of the tension in their relationship. Negotiating their concerns included a plan that would allow Marcos the freedom he is seeking, while letting the father function in his parental role.

7. *Define the problem as a family problem.* Earlier in the chapter, we highlighted the type of

messages you can use in clarifying the systemic nature of problems. Continue to maintain that stance throughout the family session, emphasizing that every member's perspective is important; that family members can do much to support the change efforts of other family members; that all members will need to make adjustments to alleviate the family's stress; and that the family can do much to increase the quality of relationships and the support that each member receives from others.

Despite your efforts to define problems as belonging to the family, you will often encounter a persistent tendency of some members to blame others. Your consequent task is twofold. First, you must *monitor* your own performance to ensure that you do not collude with family members in labeling others as problems, and thus holding them responsible for the family's difficulties. Second, you must model the circular orientation to *causality* of behavior and emphasize that family members *reciprocally* influence one another in ways that perpetuate patterns of interaction. In the case of Marcos and his father, the patterned interaction between the two consisted of a statement from Mr. G about Marcos's friends, who he referred to as "trashy," followed by a negative reaction from Marcos. Neither talked about what they really wanted from the other, and their interactions ended up with both being dissatisfied. Both also contributed to the problem.

Delabeling is another strategy that counteracts the tendency of family members to attribute blame to others and highlights the fact that they, too, are contributing to the problem. To illustrate this strategy, consider the example of a mother of a young man with mental illness who has decided to move out of a group home and live independently with his girlfriend. The mother is adamant that this move is a "stupid" decision and insists that the son is incapable of living independently. Rather than turning to the son, the social worker utilized the following questions to focus on the mother's participation in the problematic situation:

- "You've said that your son doesn't listen to you about your concerns related to his plans. When you want to discuss these concerns with him, how do you approach him?"
- "When he says he doesn't want to talk to you, how do you respond? How does his reluctance to talk to you affect you and your relationship with him?"

After first posing questions to the mother, the social worker then divided questions between the mother and the son to explore the son's participation in the identified problem by asking the following questions:

- "How does your mother approach you when she wants to discuss her concerns?"
- "What is your reaction to her approach?"
- "What might she do differently that would make you feel more like talking to her?"

This line of inquiry emphasizes the reciprocal nature of the problem. In addition, the last question enabled the social worker to set the stage for identifying positive behaviors that each participant would like from the other. In this case, both mother and son were receptive, so the social worker helped them formulate a reciprocal task that each could work on during the week to improve their relationship. In subsequent sessions, they were able to focus on the son's goal of living independently and address the mother's concerns. The social worker also helped the mother and son to change the dynamics of their interaction by changing their own behavior or responses to each other.

8. *Emphasize individual and family strengths.* In work with families, you can highlight family strengths on two levels: the strengths of individual members and the strengths of the family as a whole. At the individual level, you may observe the strengths and resources of members during the session, drawing them to the attention of the family (e.g., "Marcos is a good student"). At the family level, you can report on the strengths you have observed in the way members operate as a group. Examples of strengths-oriented statements follow:

- "In your family, it is my sense that even though there are problems, you seem to be very loyal to each other."

- "The way that your family observes traditional ways seems to connect the family."

- "Supporting Shauna to finish high school by taking care of her young child shows that your family is really supportive of each other."

Family strengths may also be utilized to communicate a focus on the future. In particular, the hopes, dreams, talents, or capacities of individual members and the family unit can be means to energize the family to resolve current difficulties. While a goal in the initial session is to move the family toward reaching a consensus on their concerns, it is the strength of the family—rather than the problem itself—that will ultimately enable them to resolve their difficulties. By exploring coping patterns with previous difficulties, experiences with positive episodes or past successes, and hopes and dreams for family life, you can activate family strengths and engender a greater commitment to goals and problem solving (Weick & Saleebey, 1995).

9. *Ask questions to elicit information about the patterned behaviors and structure of the family.* For example, you might ask these questions:

- "What brought the family here? Who made the decision, and what was the process of deciding to seek help?"

- "How are decisions usually made in the family?"

- "Who is most likely to argue in the family? The least likely? With whom?"

- "Who is the most likely to support other family members? The least likely?"

Base your questions about family patterns and structure on the dimensions of the assessment. In cases where your race or culture is different from that of the family, asking questions related to race or culture is appropriate:

- "What are the traditional ways in which families in your culture have approached this issue?"

- "How does your family express anger?"

- "Is expressing anger acceptable in your household?"

- "Are other people in your community involved in making decisions in your family?"

Asking questions such as these will aid you in entering the family's frame of reference and allow the family to articulate the extent to which their culture or race is a critical element in the family's experience.

10. *Draw attention to repetitive communications.* Once these behaviors are identified, you can discuss whether the family wishes to change these patterns. If counterproductive communications occur during the initial session (as they frequently do), you can intervene to counteract their influence—for example, by translating a blaming message into a neutral one and by empathically reflecting the feelings and wants of the sender of the message. Or, when one family member speaks for another, you can intervene to elicit the views of the latter. Assisting families to improve their communication patterns occurs over time, so in the initial session your task is simply to begin this process. As the initial session proceeds, you can begin to draw counterproductive communications to the family's attention through responses such as the following:

- "I observed [*describes behavior and situation*] occurring between family members. How do you see the situation?"

- "Did you notice a reaction from other family members as you talked about . . . ?"

Questions such as these help clients to become aware of potentially dysfunctional communication patterns.

You can also stimulate family members to analyze their behaviors further and to consider whether they wish to modify such communication patterns. This can be accomplished by asking clients questions similar to the following:

- "How would you like to address these concerns?"

- "How would you like to solve these problems?"

- "How would you like to relate differently?"

- "How would behaving differently change your relationship?"
- "Given the problem your behavior creates in the relationship, how important is it to you to change the behavior?"

Utilizing this line of exploration in initial and subsequent sessions, you can assist family members to define for themselves the relative functionality of behavior and to decide whether they wish to change it. If they choose to modify their behavior, you can negotiate relevant goals that will guide their efforts (and yours) in the helping process.

11. *Begin helping members to relate to one another in more positive ways.* To begin, you can highlight counterproductive patterns: "Mr. G, when you referred to Marcos's friends as 'trash,' did you notice his reaction? How might you express your concern to him in a different manner?" Strategies for accomplishing this objective are discussed in greater detail later in this chapter. At the same time, you should communicate hope that the family can change by assisting individual members to see how they can reduce pressures, thereby allowing them to relate to one another in a more positive manner.

12. *Establish individual and family goals based on your earlier exploration of wants and needs.* Goals that flow from this exploration include individual goals, family goals, and goals that pertain to subsystems (e.g., "Mr. G and Marcos, you indicated you wanted to spend time together"). You might also facilitate members to identify family goals by exploring answers to the "miracle question" (De Shazer 1988, p. 5): "Suppose that one night, while you were asleep, a miracle happened and your family became perfect, just the way you wanted. When you woke up in the morning, how would your family be different?" When asked this question, even the most troubled couples or families are able to describe a "new" miracle relationship. This vision and other desired conditions that they identify could then become goal statements, guiding efforts of both the family and the social worker.

13. *Gauge the interest of family members in returning for future sessions and negotiate a contract.* Because family members may not always reveal their feelings openly, never assume that all members want to return for another session (even if you were successful in engaging members and sparking their interest in working on problems). You will also want to assess the difference between the attitudes of participants at the beginning and at the end of the session. Ask about reservations that participants may still have about engaging in the helping process. After exploration of these issues, if reluctant members agree to return for another session, indicate that you will continue in future sessions to check on their concerns about continuing. Note that it may take a number of sessions before a family member decides to participate fully or to commit to making changes. If family members are sufficiently motivated to return for another session, specify the time of the next session, identify who will be involved, and negotiate the rest of the contract (refer to Chapter 12). Other important elements of the contract discussion include any time limits that may be imposed by, for example, a referral source, court mandate, or third-party payer.

In instances where family members are unwilling to attend the initial session or to continue with subsequent sessions, help them to consider ways in which they can support other family members or at least not block their efforts. Paralleling this work, help other family members to identify and modify processes that may discourage the participation of the reluctant member.

14. *Negotiate tasks to be accomplished during the week.* Although tasks were discussed at length in Chapter 13, we reemphasize that tasks should directly relate to goals identified by individual members or by the family system. Assisting the family to explore and decide upon steps that can be taken during the week aids in focusing their attention on problem resolution.

15. *End the session by summarizing the problems discussed and the goals, tasks, and progress achieved.* Wrapping up the session by summarizing major topics, goals, and tasks highlights what has been accomplished in the session and is another means to encourage hope and to increase the momentum of change efforts.

INTERVENING WITH FAMILIES: CULTURAL AND ECOLOGICAL PERSPECTIVES

In intervening with clients of a different ethnicity, social workers must strive to be culturally sensitive in their approach, modifying as necessary the expectations espoused as universal norms for family functioning. They must also be aware of the potential intrusion of their own bias into the helping process. A study by Lavee (1997), for example, revealed "noticeable differences" between how social workers and clients defined a healthy marriage. Professionals tended to focus more on process indicators such as cooperation and communication, whereas clients tended to place greater emphasis on love, understanding, and family cohesion. Different emphases on the quality of family life, marital relationships, or problem definition may be a function of cultural and class differences between social workers and clients.

Your sensitivity to culture and the acquisition of knowledge that will prepare you to be culturally competent are ongoing learning processes. While certain factors may be germane to various cultural or racial groups, it is important that you clarify specific content and its relevance to a family's culture, subculture, or race. Goldenberg and Goldenberg (2000) suggest that learning about specific cultures requires social workers to assess the extent to which families identify with their ethnic or cultural background and to ascertain how much their background plays a role in the presenting family concern. Toward this end, "therapists must try to distinguish family patterns that are universal (common to a wide variety of families), culture-specific (common to a particular group) or idiosyncratic (unique to this particular family)" (p. 52). Patterns in family interactions may vary, of course, and your understanding this fact essentially minimizes a tendency to formulate generalizations about family dynamics. Identification with a particular culture or race may be a peripheral issue for some families. In other instances, it may be useful to help families determine how culturally specific behavior affects the problem at hand (Flores & Carey, 2000).

Note that culture should not be used as an excuse to minimize or overlook family behavior or relationships that are damaging or harmful to the family or individuals. With these words of caution in mind, we highlight factors that may be considerations when initiating interventions with families who are diverse with respect to culture or race.

Differences in Communication Styles

Because there are differences in the speech patterns in non-native English speakers, in many situations it may be more important to focus on process rather than content. In many Native American tribes, for example, there may be a "pause time"—a period signaling when one person has finished and another can begin speaking. Discomfort with this silence may result in your interrupting the Native American speaker. Individuals from some groups may be more demonstrative in both verbal and nonverbal language; others who are unaccustomed to seeking outside help may appear to be passive, because of a sense of shame or suspicion in their encounter with professional helpers (Fong, 1997; Pierce & Elisme, 1997; Berg & Jaya 1993; Boyd-Franklin, 1989).

Studies that examined conflict resolution, emotional expression, and means of coping with stress conducted by Mackey and O'Brien (1998) and Choi (1997) revealed differences in communication styles based on gender and ethnicity. Emotions are complex experiences, expressing reactions to past, present, and future events. The person's worldview frames the emotional experience, as does his or her language. The range of words and language that many of us use daily to describe emotions may, in fact, be unfamiliar to or have a different connotation for diverse groups. Moreover, it is important that you examine your own communication style and assess how it is informed by your own culture preferences.

In facilitating communication styles and differences, techniques and strategies from postmodern family practice models may be used. For example, the narrative and social constructionist approaches emphasize a more conversational, collaborative approach, allowing for a dialogue that is more meaningful to the client, as well as facilitating communication between client and social worker (Laird, 1993).

Hierarchical Considerations

Depending on the age–sex hierarchies in some cultures, you are advised to address questions to, for example, the father, then the mother, then other adults, and finally the older and younger children. Grandparents or other elders in the family may actually be held in greater esteem than parents and figure prominently in the family's hierarchical arrangement. Caution is particularly advised in working with immigrant families where a child who has greater proficiency in the English language and is used as an interpreter in interviews with parents. You should be sensitive to the fact that the child's role in this instance may undermine traditional roles in the family and result in tensions between parents and their children (Ho, 1987; Pierce & Elisme, 1997). Beyond being sensitive, being empathetic and exploring the parents' feelings are means by which you reinforce your understanding of their role. In addition, when clients come from a culture in which chronological age and familial hierarchy play a significant role (e.g., Asian Indian and African American families), open dialogue between parents and children may be viewed as insolent or disrespectful (Segal, 1991; Carter & McGoldrick, 1999a). Also note that what may appear to you to be hierarchically defined roles in the family may instead be complementary. Flores and Carey (2000), in counteracting the popular notion of machismo dominance in Hispanic families, emphasize this point. Specifically, the father functions as the authoritarian, protective figure in the family; the mother's role is complementary to that of the father in that she is expected to be expressive, caring, and nurturing. As you join with the family, it is best to ask questions, seek their preferences, and explore their rules with respect to family order and hierarchy.

Authority of the Social Worker

Many Asian Americans and Pacific Islanders do not understand the social worker's role and may confuse him or her with a physician. Nevertheless, as

observes Ho (1987), members of these groups will perceive you as a knowledgeable expert who will guide them in the proper course of action. Thus, you will need to take a more directive role rather than a more passive role in working with such families. Social workers should not hesitate to discuss their professional background, because these families need assurance that you are more powerful than their illnesses or family problems and will "cure" them with competent know-how. When writing notes, you should be aware that writing and documenting—while necessary for creating case notes—may reinforce perceptions of the unequal power balance between you and the family (Flores & Carey, 2000; Boyd-Franklin, 1989). To alleviate clients' concerns, you will find it helpful to explain the purpose of case notes, standards of confidentiality, and requirements for information that may involve an identified third party.

When working with African American clients, your perceived authority also reflects your use of first names with families and social distance. Robinson (1989) recommends that you use last names until invited by clients to do otherwise: "The racial importance of first names is magnified for the black client because of the historical tradition of calling black people by their first names in situations in which first names would not be permitted if both participants were white" (p. 328). Similarly, Berg and Jaya (1993) note that addressing Asian American elders by their first names may inhibit establishing a positive therapeutic alliance. Similar to African Americans and Asian Americans, the use of last names is appropriate in the introductory stage with Mexicans (Flores & Corey, 2000).

An informal and egalitarian approach, which is second nature to many Americans, is actually considered improper in many cultures. For example, Mexican Americans typically expect their initial encounter with you to be quite formal, polite, and reserved, with the social worker taking the initiative in solving the family's problem (Janzen & Harris, 1997). Passivity among immigrants, for example, may stem from their social and political status in the United States, a distrust of helpers, and a fear about expressing their true feelings to figures of authority (Potocky-Tripodi, 2003; Pierce & Elisme, 1997). While direct questioning, the informal use of language and expectations of full disclosure may diminish trust, Devore & Schlesinger (1999) suggest using empathy as a facilitative means to form an alliance.

Aponte (1982) perhaps summarizes these issues best by stating that power and authority are critical elements of the family and the client–social worker relationship, especially for ethnic or racial groups. Most diverse families perceive the social work practitioner as acting in his or her professional role rather than as fulfilling a social role, and as being a representative of majority society, thereby symbolizing the larger society's power, values, and standards. Because of the authority that is assigned to you as a professional, it is important to explicitly recognize families as decision makers and experts on their situation, and to ensure that you have their informed consent before proceeding further (Palmer & Kaufman, 2003).

Engaging the Family

Techniques for engaging or joining are particularly crucial when working with diverse families. Listening in context—especially allowing the family to present their story in their own way—and being mindful of the communication process are key concerns. For example, you should be aware of differences in communication styles, the cultural context of seeking help outside of the family, and the family's perceptions of your own and your agency's authority. While knowledge of culture is not guaranteed to provide you with an advantage in working with a particular family, exploring the relevance of cultural meanings of particular groups can facilitate the process of engagement (Janzen & Harris, 1997).

Engaging the family may also include accounting for extended family members in the process of joining, whether or not they participate in family sessions. Boyd-Franklin (1989), in stressing the importance of the joining stage with African American families, points to the crucial linkage between engagement and problem solving. The former process enables you to establish credibility and trust with the family, and move to goals and problem solving. In the engagement phase, your entry into the family system is greatly enhanced by your respect for the problem as identified by the family. Finally, in the initial session, be aware that minority families tend to respond more favorably to brief intervention strategies that are directed toward taking action and implementing solutions (Lum, 2004; Corwin, 2002; Berg & Jaya, 1993; Boyd-Franklin, 1989). Subsequent to engagement, then, it would be prudent for you and the family to specify and agree upon a time frame for the treatment.

Families from diverse backgrounds may feel more welcome in agencies where objects and symbols of their culture are visible in offices and waiting rooms. Home visits may be invaluable in the engagement stage with some families, because such visits afford you with an opportunity to observe and assess a family in its natural environment (Berg, 1994). Visits to the home may also allow you to learn about and observe the practices of families and important members of the family network. You will have an opportunity to convey your interest in the family by inquiring about portraits, cultural objects, and other items of interest. In visits to the home, "remember that you are on the client's home turf," caution Boyd-Franklin and Bry (2000), which means that you should remain flexible and show deference to the rules and structure of the family and the order of the household (p. 39). Even so, some family members may resent or resist involvement in the initial session, and they may cite culture as a defense against joining (Flores & Carey, 2000).

In instances where the family has been referred for treatment, members may be angry and resentful of this intrusion. Be mindful of the fact that most minority families are involuntary help-seekers. If you represent an agency that they feel has power and authority over their lives, this "baggage" will affect their reaction to you. In situations where these dynamics have a significant impact, it is suggested that you avoid personalizing this experience and move quickly to acknowledge, accept, and validate clients' feelings (Berg, 1994; Rooney, 1992).

Finally, engaging diverse families is facilitated when you understand the cultural relevance of terminology describing family dynamics and structure. Autonomy and self-differentiation, for example, when considered in a sociopolitical or cultural context, may be neither desired nor expected.

Using an Ecological Approach with Families

Culture and race are merely two factors in the ecological schema of practice with families. Other salient factors include religion, gender, class, family status, and work and family concerns. To demonstrate sensitivity to multisystems influences and elucidate their relationship to family concerns, you must focus on the family and their environmental interactions and assess the extent to which they affect family relationships and interaction patterns. For example, work and family pressures may intrude upon parental ability to fulfill role functions within the family, producing role overload, conflict, and strain (Rooney, 1997; Marlow, 1993).

For poor families, meeting immediate survival and resource needs may take precedence over pursuing more insight-oriented approaches (Kilpatrick & Holland, 2003). The family context–environment interaction may include intervening to address problems of housing, financial assistance, school–child conflicts, and unresponsive social institutions. Social support networks such as the extended family, tribe or clan, or other key people may be included in the discussion to reduce dysfunctional interactions and to increase concrete support for the family. A failure on your part to focus on family–environmental interactions may cause you to have an incomplete understanding of family functioning and hence to develop interventions that emphasize pathology over strengths. For example, dysfunctional interactions may emerge in immigrant families resulting from their attempts to cope with adjustment-related stressors or problems. In emphasizing this possibility, a study by Fong (1997) links spousal or child abuse to the stress-related adjustment problems among Chinese immigrants.

Flores and Carey (2000) note that many well-established approaches to work with families remain "silent" on issues of social justice, oppression, and the marginalization inherent in the minority experience. Until recently, the same was true regarding issues that are important to women. Thanks to the fuller understanding of families produced by feminists' evaluation of family practice approaches, social workers at a minimum should be acutely aware of the need to be sensitive to age, gender, and patriarchy. Goldenberg and Goldenberg (2000) note that gender sensitivity does not mean merely being nonsexist. Instead, they suggest that gender-sensitive practice is proactive and deliberate in helping women move beyond the limitations imposed by social and political barriers (pp. 50–51). For minority women, the combination of gender with race or culture adds yet another series of social and political barriers. For this reason, you should not assume that minority women perceive their gender as the more prominent factor, when compared to race or ethnicity.

Although the ideal of egalitarian roles for men and women is becoming more evident in both rural and urban families as well as in some cultures, women for the most part still manage multiple roles—wife, daughter, mother, parent, employee (Rooney, 1997; Marlow, 1993). Acculturation may mean that gender roles enter into a transition, yet adaptation to the new roles may become a source of tension in much the same way that parent–child conflict intensifies, thereby resulting in stressors within the family system.

Negative societal attitudes and conditions can also pose environmental threats to families and thus influence the family system. For example, society almost always views single-parent families from the perspective of pathology rather than by recognizing their strength as a viable family form. Likewise, lesbian families are largely ignored as a viable family form. In both types of families, internal family stress is a given because of the hostile and indifferent external environment. Concerns voiced among lesbian mothers related to reactions toward their children and the need to protect them from harm represent a case in point. Hare (1994) found that while lesbian families were accepted by their own families, they experienced tensions in their interactions with the larger community.

The preceding examples highlight but a few of the many cultural, ecological, and authority dynamics to which social workers must attend in engaging diverse families and in intervening in family functioning and relational dynamics. Fitting practice and intervention strategies to the ecology of a particular family is a complicated process that requires a multidimensional assessment; this assessment must include examination of the myriad internal and external factors that shape family life. You are urged to use your knowledge of culture, race, gender, sexual orientation, and sociopolitical issues as a lens through which to view families. The considerable diversity encountered among families may mean that some factors have greater relevance than others. For some families, culture or race may be peripheral to their identity, yet they may retain essential attributes that guide their family life. Acquiring sensitivity to gender, sexual orientation, and racial and cultural preferences can be achieved by facilitating the family narratives, taking an active and genuine interest in their story, and collaborating with the family to resolve their concerns.

INTERVENING WITH FAMILIES: FOCUSING ON THE FUTURE

Families are often overwhelmed, frustrated, and perhaps saturated with their problems when you encounter them. You have a responsibility to create a structure and climate that will alleviate their stress and guide the family toward change. One major obstacle to change is the propensity of couples or families to focus on what they do not have or what is not working, rather than on what they would like *in the future*. Solution-focused therapy is a brief treatment approach that addresses problems in the present and inspires a future orientation beginning with the initial contact. Using miracle or scaling questions (two solution-focused techniques), you might ask the family, "What would you like to do about the future?" or "How would you know that your family members have improved their communications with one another?" Scaling questions (e.g., "When you called for an appointment with me, your family was in trouble. Imagine how you might feel on a scale of 1 to 10 after you have achieved your goal.") are also useful in helping families to reframe their problems and feel more in control of their lives.

Focusing on the future can serve as a guiding principle in the helping process for families and social workers when it is used in the following manner:

- A discussion or argument can lead quickly to consideration of what each person is willing to do to prevent a recurrence of that argument *in the future*.
- Complaints or criticisms can be translated into information about how changes in others might affect the family *in the future*. Recipients can also give information: "This is what you could do *in the future* that would help me make the changes you are suggesting."
- Breakdowns in communication can be analyzed from a future-oriented point of view: "What can we learn from what just happened that we can apply *in the future*?"
- Conflicts of interest can alert families to engage in "win-win" problem solving: "How can we resolve this problem right now so we can feel good about each other *in the future*?"

"Opting for the future," when adopted as a philosophy and guideline by families and social workers for how they focus on problems and issues, takes the blame out of relating. The future, not the past, is seen as relevant. The future is fresh, hopeful, and untainted by tensions or stressors. Opting for the future, of course, requires that each family member commit to attending only to what *he or she* will do in the future, rather than monitoring the activities of the other person in that regard. You can increase families' focus on the future by putting problem talk on hold and by always starting sessions with a question regarding what successes they have enjoyed in achieving goals or tasks, and by creating fresh, positive ways of interacting.

Although no relationship completely escapes the accumulation of past hurts, a future orientation enables clients to let go of past slights that have been recycled in relationships and that provided a fertile field for fights and arguments. Dwelling on the past, in fact, is one of the most common and destructive problems families encounter as they attempt to communicate. You can aid the family in giving up the past and learning to focus on the future by declaring a moratorium for a period of time. Complementing this approach, Weiner-Davis (1992) teaches clients to focus on the "exceptional times" to determine what is working and why, and then encourages them to turn productive behaviors into habits. Focusing on exceptions diminishes problems, because identifying what they *can* do is infinitely more hopeful and empowering to clients than noting what they *cannot* do. It also demonstrates to clients that they are changeable and that seemingly fixed traits are fluid. Finally, focusing on exceptions supplies clients with a blueprint for describing exactly what they need to do the next time a particular situation occurs.

GIVING AND RECEIVING FEEDBACK

Communication theorists believe that the patterns that family members employ to communicate with one another are often interpreted in various ways, and are often punctuated by faulty cognitions and perceptions. What the sender believes is the message is not necessarily what the receiver understands the message to be. A dysfunctional relationship between sender and receiver can also strain or distort the message.

Communication approaches to families consist of teaching family members the rules of clear communication. Positive feedback from significant others (i.e., expressions of caring, approval, encouragement, affection, appreciation, and other forms of positive attention) nourish morale, emotional security, confidence, and the feeling of being valued by others. Thus, increasing positive feedback fosters the well-being of individuals and harmonious family relationships. To enable family members to increase positive feedback, social workers must have skills in the following areas:

- Engaging clients in assessing the extent to which they give and receive positive feedback
- Educating clients about the vital role of positive feedback

- Cultivating positive cognitive sets
- Enabling clients to give and receive positive feedback

In the following sections, we focus on each of these skills.

Engaging Clients in Assessing How Well They Give and Receive Positive Feedback

Destructive communication patterns often result from strained relationships, so that the family systems eventually becomes unbalanced. Communication theorists view the family as a functional system that depends on two communication processes: negative and positive feedback. They also believe that all behavior is communication. Thus, they view the social worker's goal as being to help the family change the process of family interactions.

You can assist families and individual members to directly explore dimensions of communication by assessing how often and in what manner they convey positive feedback to significant others. Questions you might ask in couple or family sessions to achieve this end include the following:

- "How do you send messages that let family members [or your partner] know that you care about them?"
- "How frequently do you send such messages?"
- "How often do you give feedback to others concerning their positive actions?"

In instances of severe marital or family breakdown, members may acknowledge that they send positive messages infrequently or not at all. In some instances, they may actually have tepid positive feelings, but they usually experience more than they express. Besides exploring how couples or family members convey positive feedback, you can explore their desires to receive increased feedback from one another. Discussing how family members send positive messages or to what extent they desire increased positive feedback often opens up channels for positive communication and enhances relationships that have been stuck in a cycle of repetitive arguments, criticisms, blaming, and put-down messages.

Educating Clients about the Vital Role of Positive Feedback

As family members communicate about their needs to receive positive feedback, they will begin to appreciate the significance of this dimension in interpersonal relationships. You can further expand their awareness by explaining why positive feedback is crucial to family interactions. The logic behind increasing positive feedback is straightforward. Teaching clients to express their needs involves assisting them to send personalized messages in which they own their feelings and needs. The following are examples of messages that explicitly express a need for positive feedback:

- *Partner:* When we were talking about plans for my mother, I didn't interrupt you. I wish you would notice when I do something different.

- *Adolescent:* I felt discouraged when I showed you my grades yesterday. I really worked hard this term, and the only thing you seemed to note was the one B. It didn't seem to matter that the rest were A's. Sometimes I wonder if I can please you at all.

In each of these statements, the speaker used "I" to personalize his or her messages. Each message also clearly indicates what the speaker is seeking from the other person. When messages are less clear, they may lead to a further breakdown in communications. You can intervene in these situations by using the technique of *on-the-spot interventions*. When using this technique, you coach clients to formulate clear messages that express their feelings and needs as illustrated in the following exchange. It begins with a message from a wife, who is seeking positive feedback from her husband, but what she wants from him is unclear.

Ruth [*to husband*]: I worked really hard at picking up around the house before our guests arrived, but the only thing you noticed was what I had not done—like the comment you made about fingerprints on the bathroom door.

Carl [*to Ruth*]: Well, let's face it, the fact is, the fingerprints were on the door and you admitted it.

Social worker: Carl, Ruth was expressing what is important to her in the relationship, and I don't want this to get lost in an argument. Ruth, think for a moment about what you said. What is it you are asking of Carl?

Ruth [*after pausing*]: Do you mean his not noticing what I do?

Social worker: In a way, yes. Would you like for Carl to let you know you're appreciated for what you had done?

In this scenario, Ruth has shared something that is very important—namely, the need to feel valued. People want to receive positive feedback for what they are and what they do. Interactions that continuously focus on negative results may leave an individual feeling discouraged and insecure, and as a consequence relationships suffer.

In instructing Ruth and Carl about the importance of positive feedback, the social worker used this opportunity to allow them to practice communicating in a different manner.

Social worker: Ruth, I'd like you to start over and express that you want positive feedback from Carl. This time, however, send an "I" message to clarify what you need from him.

Ruth [*somewhat reluctant*]: I hope that I can. Carl, I need to hear from you about the things that I do well and not only about what is wrong.

Initially, clients may feel timid about expressing their feelings clearly. The second part of helping clients to communicate is by assisting them to listen attentively. Asking Carl to repeat what he heard in Ruth's message is one way to emphasize listening for content. Because all individuals may not always express their needs openly and clearly, family members may need to go beyond just listening. That is, they may need to become *attuned* to needs expressed in the form of complaints, questions, and the attitudes of others. *Tuning in* may also involve alerting family members to nonverbal messages and what those messages communicate about feelings.

Because it is difficult for family members to be attuned to the needs inherent in the messages of others, you should take advantage of "teachable moments" to help them to learn this skill, as illustrated in the preceding situation. Specifically, the social worker encouraged Ruth to express her need for positive feedback from Carl. Also, when the social worker focused on Ruth, she played a facilitative role in prompting her to express herself directly to Carl. The social worker likewise had Carl provide feedback to Ruth, thus performing a critical role in *facilitating positive interaction between the couple*. This is a crucial point. Serving as a catalyst, the social worker helped Carl and Ruth learn new communication skills by having them *actually engage in positive interaction*, which is an effective mode of learning.

Cultivating Positive Cognitive Sets

Before family members can provide positive feedback, they must first be able to acknowledge the strengths, positive attributes, and actions of others. Some will be attuned to these qualities, while others will habitually perceive weaknesses and flaws. Cognitive sets can consist of distorted assumptions or automatic thoughts from other relationships—that is, thoughts derived from negative schemas that are not based in reality, yet function to sustain dysfunctional relationships (Collins, Kayser, & Platt, 1994; Berlin & Marsh, 1993). In essence, schemas are problematic when the individual has an unrealistic or faulty view of the world. Thus, their behavior in interacting with others is influenced by their distortions. A key point is recognizing that attitudes, thoughts, and expectations are intertwined with emotions.

Using the cognitive-behavioral approach, the social worker attempts to improve family interactions by helping individual family members alter cognitive distortions and learn new behaviors. The social worker has the responsibility for bringing negative cognitive sets that influence thoughts, feelings, and actions to the attention of family members, ultimately helping them learn to focus on positive behaviors. Strategies for accomplishing these tasks are described next.

Sensitizing Couples to Positive Cognitive Sets

You can set the stage for helping families and couples to develop positive cognitive sets by negotiating

a *contingency contract*. The contingency contract identifies desirable behavior change between two parties and explicit rules for interaction, specifying that they agree to exchange positive rewarding behavior with each other (Becvar & Becvar, 2000a). Based on the theory of social exchange, cognitive behaviorists maintain that behavior exchange adheres to a norm of reciprocity. Specifically, negative or positive behavior from one person will induce reciprocal behavior from others. Using the contingency contract, you can actively intervene in the early stages of the helping process to highlight strengths and growth and to help clients incorporate "attention to positives" as part of their normative behavior. Families can develop their own set of positive indicators for desirable behavior change along with reciprocal goals. Generally, you would review progress on these indicators with the family (or couple) each week.

Reviewing Progress and Accrediting Incremental Growth

Social workers can also increase a family's sensitivity to positives by engaging members in briefly reviewing at the end of each session the work that has been accomplished and by observing incremental growth. To highlight incremental growth, ask members to contrast their current functioning with their functioning at an earlier time, as illustrated in the following message:

Social worker: This is your fourth session. Let's see if you can identify any changes you've made in the way you communicate by contrasting how you relate today with the way you related in the first session. I have some observations about that, but first I would like to hear from you.

Employing Tasks to Enhance Cognitive Sets

Negotiating tasks that family members can implement between sessions can facilitate the development of positive cognitive sets. For example, to further expand family members' or couples' awareness of the frequency with which they provide positive feedback, ask each to keep a daily tally of the number of positive messages they send to one another. They should also note the reciprocal behaviors of other members as a result of their own actions. This practice not only enables family members and the social worker to gain a clear picture of their performance on this dimension, but also establishes baselines that can be used later to assess their progress. Without explicitly planning to do so, clients often begin to increase the frequency of the desired behavior as a result of monitoring. By systematically focusing on the positive attributes of others, clients can gradually achieve more positive cognitive sets. Of course, the ultimate reinforcement derives from improved interactions with others.

Enabling Clients to Give and Receive Positive Feedback

To assist clients in learning to convey positive feedback, you can teach them to personalize their messages and guide them in giving positive feedback to others. Timely use of this educational intervention assists family members in conceptualizing the elements of positive messages and in developing the skills needed to share their positive experiences in an authentic manner. You may also need to help some family members learn how to accept positive feedback.

After completing these activities, family members are ready to work on the ultimate goal—increasing their rates of positive feedback. You can assist them by negotiating tasks that specify providing positive feedback at higher levels. Clients, of course, must consent to such tasks and determine the rate of positive feedback they seek to achieve. We recommend that you have family members review their baseline information (gathered earlier through monitoring), and that you encourage them to set a daily rate that "stretches" beyond their usual level. For example, an adolescent whose mean baseline daily rate in giving positive feedback to his father is 0.8 might select an initial task of giving positive feedback twice daily. He would then gradually increase the number of positive messages until he reached a self-selected optimal rate of five times daily.

As some family members implement the task of increasing positive feedback, they may inappropriately engage in insincere positive expressions. You should caution against this behavior, as such expressions are counterproductive for both the sender and the receiver.

In planning with family members to implement tasks, it is important to adhere to the task implementation sequence (TIS). In part, this exercise involves anticipating obstacles, including the two most common. First, family members who have been inhibited in expressing feelings may initially report discomfort: "It just doesn't come naturally to me." Second, other family members may respond unfavorably to an increased level of positive feedback and question the sender's sincerity, especially if this is a new behavior: "I wonder what she wants from me now?" You can assist family members to deal with others' skepticism by modeling, by having them rehearse appropriate coping behavior (including asserting the sincerity of their efforts), and by emphasizing the necessity of changing their behavior despite the obstacles. As with any tasks, you should plan to review progress in subsequent sessions and to explore favorable reactions and any difficulties that family members encountered.

Many of the strategies previously mentioned as instrumental in helping families give and receive positive feedback are applicable to couples and parents as well. Therefore, we will only briefly identify some additional tasks that may be used with couples and parents. One technique that you can employ to increase positive interactions between couples involves a strategy discussed by Stuart (1980) and Collins, Kayser, and Platt (1994). That is, both partners are asked to identify desired actions or behaviors: "Exactly what would you like your partner to do as a means of showing that he or she cares for you?" After giving each spouse or partner an opportunity to identify desired actions, you can ask each to develop a task directed toward engaging in a specified behavior identified by the other party. It may be useful to have them develop and prioritize a list of desirable positive behaviors. A reinforcing aspect of such tasks occurs when each person gives feedback and expresses appreciation when the other engages in the desired behavior.

Before negotiating tasks with parents to increase positive feedback to their children, you can request that parents list behaviors of each child. You can then ask parents to choose the three behaviors they would most like to change. The next step is to negotiate a task that involves parents giving positive feedback at opportune times during the week when the specified behavior is *not* occurring—for example, when the child is *not* fighting with a sibling. Further, you should instruct parents to give positive feedback when children manifest behaviors that parents would like them to assume *in place of the targeted behaviors*—for example, when the child *has* told the truth. Parents may be understandably reluctant to agree to this strategy, especially if continual nagging or threats of punishment have been their only means for getting the child to engage in desirable behavior. In such instances, you will need to motivate children to comply by establishing with the parents an agreement under which children may earn certain rewards in exchange for specified behavior.

Because parental attention to children's behavior is a potent force for modifying or reinforcing behavior, it is vital that you work with parents so that they master the skill of providing positive feedback. Oftentimes, when children behave as expected, parents unfortunately take their behavior for granted. But children need to know what they are *already* doing that pleases parents. When used consistently by parents, messages such as these have a significant effect in shaping and cultivating desired behavior. If parents want their children to assume particular behaviors, they must give them positive feedback when those behaviors occur. Note the reinforcing property of the following parental messages:

- "I really appreciate your taking the time to visit your grandmother. It really adds joy to her day."
- "I am glad that you made the choice to tell me the truth when I asked if you had tried smoking cigarettes."

Parents must also be aware of their own behavior as it relates to vicarious learning and modeling. Specifically, children learn the consequences of behavior by observing other people and events.

In addition to providing positive messages and tangible rewards that reinforce desired behavior, social workers can help parents and children develop tasks as a means to achieve desired behaviors. Tasks that involve incremental change and subsequent reinforcement are particularly useful with young children. Referred to as *successive approximation,* tasks that involve incremental change act as a shaping process that divides the desired behavior into subparts, providing contingencies and rewards until the whole of the desired behavior is achieved. Thus, if having a child sit quietly at her desk, pay attention to the teacher, raise her hand, and wait to be called upon before speaking are targeted behaviors, parents might initially reward "sitting" as the first subpart of the whole" (Becvar & Becvar, 2000a, p. 262).

INTERVENING WITH FAMILIES: STRATEGIES TO MODIFY DYSFUNCTIONAL INTERACTIONS

Interactional difficulties that families commonly present include repetitive arguments; struggles over power and authority; conflict over issues related to dependence, independence, or interdependence; dissension in making decisions; friction associated with discrepant role perceptions and fulfillments; and other forms of faulty communication. Interpersonal conflicts tend to be redundant; that is, in relations with others, individuals repeat over and over again various types of interactions that predictably lead to the same negative consequences. To assist you in helping families in developing more functional patterns of communication and interaction, we delineate guidelines and techniques that you can use in persuading them to modify their dysfunctional interactions. We draw from techniques used by cognitive-behavioral, structural, family systems, and communication theories as well as task-centered family practice. Note that teaching communication skills to family members is a vital aspect of modifying dysfunctional communications.

Metacommunication

To modify dysfunctional communication, family members must discuss their communication patterns, analyze their behaviors and emotional reactions, and consider the effects of the interaction on their relationship. Such discussions are termed *metacommunication,* because they involve "communication about communication." When you discuss with families a communication that has just occurred, they are also engaging in metacommunication. Indeed, much of couple, family, and group therapy focuses on metacommunication. Likewise, when you discuss relational reactions that occur in the context of the helping relationship, you are clarifying the meanings of messages and actions. Still other examples of metacommunication are messages that clarify intentions (e.g., "I'm teasing you" or "I want to talk with you because I feel bad about the strain between us") or messages that "check out" or seek clarification of others' messages that are vague or ambiguous (e.g., "I'm not sure what you mean by that" or "Let me see if I understood what you were saying"). Metacommunications contain both verbal and nonverbal content. The content of a message is established through the tone of voice and body language, further shaping and defining the intent of the message and the relationship between those involved.

Skills in metacommunications play an important role in effective communications because they avoid needless misunderstandings (by checking out the meanings of messages) and provide feedback that enables others to make choices about modifying offensive or abrasive communication styles. Moreover, conflicts in relationships are kept at a minimum level of antagonism or disruption. A major role for the social worker, therefore, is to assist clients to learn to metacommunicate in a productive manner.

Although skills in assisting people to metacommunicate are important with all client systems, they are especially critical in working with families who manifest dysfunctional patterns of communication, including frequent use of incongruent and double-bind messages. Such families seldom clarify meanings or attend to the effects that their messages have on one another.

The following example illustrates use of metacommunication to enhance communication between Anne, age 14, and her mother, Ms. T, who acts as a spokesperson for Anne and sends disconfirming messages.

Social worker: Anne, could you tell me how you've been doing in your gym class? I know you were having a rough time in gym.

Ms. T: It's been *really* rough for her, having to change clothes and shower in front of all the other girls. She feels like she's a sideshow. I know what it's like because I went through it when I was in junior high. [*Anne lowers her head and looks at the floor.*]

Social worker: Excuse me, Ms. T, I'd like to hear from Anne you what it has been like. [*Intervening to counter Ms. T's acting as Anne's spokesperson.*]

Anne [*looking up slightly*]: Well, it has been going a little better, I think. The gym teacher hasn't been after me. In fact she was pretty friendly this last week. And I . . . [*Ms. T interrupts.*]

Ms. T: But it hasn't been going better, Anne. [*Disconfirming Anne as a separate person.*] When you shower, you just feel everyone's eyes are glued on you.

Social worker [*to mother*]: I'd like to hear from Anne about how she feels about showering with the other girls in gym class.

[*To Anne*] I hear your mother's view, but I don't know what your experience has been.

Anne: Actually, it hasn't been like my mother said. It was bad until the past couple of weeks, but I've made friends with a couple of girls, and we shower together. It isn't nearly as bad now.

Ms. T: But you were saying . . .

Social worker [*interrupts to avert another disconfirming message*]: Anne, when your mother spoke for you the first time, you looked at the floor as if you were distressed. I wonder if you could tell your mother how you feel when she speaks for you. [*Encouraging metacommunication.*]

Anne: I don't mind, sometimes. But, Mother, you don't always know how I feel. You get your feelings mixed up with mine, and it confuses me. I want to speak for myself.

Ms. T: But, darling, I was just trying to help. I know how hard it's been for you. I mean, you understand that, don't you?

Anne: I guess so, but I wish you wouldn't do it so much.

Social worker [*to Ms. T*]: I know you're trying to help, Ms. T. But what do you hear Anne telling you? [*Using metacommunication to check out Ms. T's perception.*]

Ms. T: That she doesn't want me to say how she feels?

Social worker: Yes. I think Anne's saying that she wants to be her own person. Is that right, Anne? [*Using metacommunication to check out meaning attribution.*]

[*To Anne and Ms. T*] What we've been talking about is very important in improving your communication as well as helping Anne to grow up.

[*To Ms. T*] Although you mean to help, your assumptions about Anne's feelings are sometimes inaccurate. If you want to understand Anne, you'll need to ask how she feels rather than assume you know.

[*To Anne*] If you want to help your mother understand, you'll need to remind her that she is speaking for you. And you'll also need to tell her your real feelings rather than just keeping them inside. You did a good job of telling her how you feel just now. I know that was difficult for both of you.

In the preceding exchange, the social worker actively intervened to prevent the interaction from following its usual destructive course. By not permitting Ms. T to act as Anne's spokesperson and by involving the two of them in metacommunicating about how Ms. T's behavior affects Anne, the social worker further clarified how each can modify their pattern of communication, thereby initiating corrective processes. Of course, such interventions must occur over a period of time if they are to produce enduring changes.

Modifying Dysfunctional Family Rules

Family rules govern the range of behavior in the family system and the sequence of interactions or reactions to a particular event. Rules are a means by which the family system maintains its equilibrium. Dysfunctional family rules, however, can severely impair the functioning of family members. Because family rules are often covert, it follows that changes can occur only by bringing them into the open. You can assists family members through metacommunication to acknowledge and consider the effects of rules on family interactions. Openly discussing rules suggests options for replacing them with other processes that might better serve the needs of all family members.

You can prepare families to consider rules by introducing them to the concept, as illustrated in the following message:

Social worker: As we begin to work on problems the family is experiencing, we need to know more about how your family operates. Every family has some rules or understandings about how members are to behave. Sometimes these rules are easy to spot. For example, each person is to clear his or her own plate when leaving the table is a rule that all members of a family might be expected to follow. This is an apparent rule because every member of the family could easily tell me what is expected of them at the end of the meal. But the family's behavior is also governed by other rules that are less easy to identify. Even though members follow these rules, they are often unaware that they exist. I'm going to ask you some questions that will help you to understand these two kinds of rules better and to identify some of the ones that operate in your family.

You can then ask family members to list some apparent rules and coach the family, if needed, by asking questions such as "What are your rules about bedtime?" (or watching television or getting the work done around the house). Once family members have identified some of their common and readily apparent rules, you can then lead them into a discussion of implicit rules by asking them to identify guidelines they follow with regard to any of the dimensions of assessment listed in Chapter 10. For example, you might ask family members to identify family rules about showing anger or positive feelings or to explore facets of decision-making or power (e.g., "Who do the kids go to in the family when they want something?"). Rather than engaging the family in a lengthy exploration of these rules, you should use the discussion to illustrate how hidden rules may significantly influence family behavior or interactions, stressing that certain rules may undermine opportunities for members and hurt family well-being.

Consider the social worker's role in this regard in the following excerpt from a third session with Mr. and Mrs. Johnson and their three daughters, in which the social worker assisted the family to identify how hidden rules influence their patterned interactions:

Martha [*age 14*]: You took the red jersey again, right out of my closet—and you didn't ask. That really gripes me.

Cynthia [*age 15*]: You took the Britney Spears CD last week, and you still have it. What's up with that?

Mr. Johnson: In this family, we share and you girls should know this.

Social worker: This seems to be a family rule. What does that mean in this family?

Mr. Johnson: It means that we have a limited amount of money to spend on extras, so we buy things for the girls to use together and no one person owns the things we buy. Besides, the girls are expected to share because they are so close in age and like similar things.

Social worker: So, what happens when there is a disagreement about a particular item?

Martha: I got mad at Cynthia, and I told her so.

Social worker [*to Cynthia*]: Then what did you do?

Cynthia: I told Martha she didn't have any right to complain because she wasn't sharing things either.

Social worker: Cynthia and Martha, the two of you were engaged in what is referred to as blaming messages; do you see it the same way? [*Girls nod.*]

[*To Mr. Johnson*] I wonder if you remember what you did when your daughters were involved in their argument?

Mr. Johnson: I was trying to get them to stop arguing and blaming each other, and remind them of the family expectation to share.

Social worker [*exploring hidden rule*]: Is everyone in the family aware of the expectation of sharing? Are you willing to explore this further? If so, I'd like to begin by asking a few questions, to see if you can figure out what the rules are in your family.

[*To 13-year-old Jennifer*] You weren't involved in this argument. Do you argue with anyone in the family?

Jennifer [*laughs*]: My mother and my sisters.

Social worker: When you get in an argument with your mother, what happens?

Jennifer: If my dad is home, he tries to stop it. Sometimes he tells my mother to go upstairs, and he'll talk to me.

Social worker [*to Mrs. Johnson*]: When your husband stops an argument between the girls, or you and one of the girls, what do you do?

Mrs. Johnson: Sometimes I let him handle the problem with Jennifer or one of the other girls. But when he gets involved like that, it makes me so furious that sometimes he and I end up in a fight ourselves.

Social worker: We need to do a lot more work to understand what happens in such situations, but for the moment, let's see, Mr. Johnson, if you can put your finger on the rule.

Mr. Johnson: I guess I'm always trying to stop everyone from fighting and arguing in the family. I expect the girls to share and get along with each other, and not cause their mother grief.

Social worker: It does appear that you are the family's mediator. I would think that would be a very difficult role to play.

Mr. Johnson: "Well, there are no rewards for it, I can tell you that!

Social worker: There's more to the rule. Who lets the father be the mediator?

Mrs. Johnson: We all do.

Social worker: That's right. It isn't the father's rule; it's the family's rule. It takes the rest of the family to argue and the father to break up the fights.

Many avenues could be explored in this scenario, but the social worker chose to narrow the focus by assisting the family to identify one of its major rules. Specifically, the father has the role of mediator in disputes. After further exploring specific patterned interactions of the family, the social worker introduced the following questions to help the family to weigh whether they wish to continue relating under the old rule.

To Father

- "How effective are you in actually stopping the girls and their mother from fighting?"
- "What are your worst fears about what might occur in the family if you didn't play that role?'
- "Would you like to free yourself from the role of being the family mediator?"

To Other Family Members

- "Do you want the father to continue to be the third party in your arguments?"
- "What are the risks to your relationship if he discontinued playing the role of mediator?"
- "Do you want to work out your own disputes?"

Questions such as these focus the attention of all members on their patterned interactions and encourage them to determine the *function* of the behavior in the system.

Next, the social worker had the major task of assisting the family to modify their rules, by teaching them new skills for resolving disagreements. The social worker also needed to coach the father in declining the role of mediator and the girls and their mother in requesting that he let them manage their own conflicts.

On-the-Spot Interventions

On-the-spot interventions are a potent way of modifying patterns of interaction by intervening immediately when metacommunications occur between couples or family members. They are appropriate when clients send fuzzy or abrasive messages, when receivers distort meanings of or fail to respond appropriately to important messages or feelings, and when destructive interaction occurs.

In implementing on-the-spot interventions, you would focus on the destructive effects of the preceding communication, labeling the type of communication so that family members can subsequently identify their own dysfunctional behavior. In doing so, you will need to teach and guide them in how to engage in more effective ways of communicating.

In the following example, a social worker intervenes in a "blind alley" argument, one that cannot be resolved because neither party can be proved right or wrong.

Husband: I distinctly remember telling you to buy some deodorant when you went to the store.

Wife: You just think that you did, but you didn't. I'd have remembered if you said anything about it.

Husband: No, you just didn't remember. I told you for sure, and you're shifting the blame.

Wife [*with obvious irritation*]: Like hell you did! You're the one who forgot to tell me, and I don't appreciate your telling me I forgot.

Social worker: Can we stop for a moment and consider what's happening between you? Each of you has a different recollection of what happened, and there's no way of determining who's right and who's wrong. You are involved in what I call a blind alley argument because you can't resolve it. You just end up arguing over who's right and feeling resentful because you're convinced the other person is wrong. That doesn't help you solve your problem; it just creates conflict in your relationship. Let's go back and start over. Are you willing to allow me to show you both a more effective way of dealing with this situation?

Alternatively, after labeling and intervening in the interaction and guiding the couple to communicate constructively, you might challenge the couple (or family members) to identify their challenging behavior and to modify it accordingly. For example, interrupt their interactions with a statement like this: "Wait a minute! Think about what you're doing just now and where it's going to lead you if you continue." In modifying patterns, the intermediate objective is for family members to recognize and decrease their counterproductive behavior, and to substitute newly gained communication skills for the harmful communication style. The ultimate goal, of course, is for family members to *eliminate* the counterproductive processes through concentrated efforts between sessions.

Guidelines for Making On-the-Spot Interventions

1. *Focus on process rather than content.* For you to be infinitely more helpful to family members, you must focus on their interaction processes rather than on the content of their conflicts. Conflicts typically are manifested over content issues, but *how* family members interact in dealing with the focal point of a conflict is far more important. As the "blind alley argument" example illustrated, the issue of who is right in a given dispute is usually trivial when compared to the destructive effects of counterproductive processes. Thus, you should usually ignore topics of disputes and focus instead on assisting family members to listen attentively and respectfully, to own feelings and their responsibility in problems, and to increase positive feedback. Ultimately, you will want to teach them how to compromise, to disengage from competitive interaction, and to engage in effective conflict resolution.

2. *Give feedback that is descriptive and neutral rather than general or evaluative.* As you intervene, it is important that you present feedback in a neutral manner that does not fault family members but rather allows them to pinpoint specific behaviors that produce difficulties. Feedback that evaluates their behavior produces defensiveness; overly general feedback fails to focus on behavior that needs to be changed.

To illustrate, consider a situation in which a man glares at his wife and says, "I've had it with going to your parents' house. You spend all the time there visiting with your mother, and I do not feel included or welcomed in the conversation. You can go by yourself in the future." A *general and evaluative message* would take the following form:

Social worker: Garth, that message was an example of poor communication. Try again to send a better one.

The following message is *neutral and behaviorally specific:*

Social worker: Garth, I noticed that when you just spoke to Barbara, you glared at her and sent a "you" message that focused on what you thought she was doing wrong. I watched Barbara as you spoke, and noticed that she frowned and seemed to be angry. I'd like you to get some feedback from Barbara about how your message affected her. Barbara, would you share with Garth what you experienced as he talked?

In this message, the social worker implies that the client's message was problematic but avoids making an evaluative judgment, as he had done in the first example evaluative response. Moreover, by describing specific behavior and eliciting feedback about its impact, the social worker enhances the possibility that Garth will be receptive to examining his behavior and to modifying it. Note also that this message highlights the interaction of *both* participants, as specified in the following guideline.

3. *Balance interventions to divide responsibility.* When more than one family member is involved in sessions, you must achieve a delicate balance while avoiding the appearance of singling out one person as being the sole cause of interpersonal difficulties. Otherwise, that person may feel that you and other family members are taking sides and blaming. By focusing on all relevant actors, you can distribute responsibility, model fairness, and avoid alienating one person. Moreover, although one person may contribute more to problems than others, all members of a system generally contribute to difficulties in some degree.

The following example illustrates the technique of balancing in a situation in which the husband and wife are at odds with each other over caring for their baby and the amount of time the husband spends at work:

Social worker: Both of you seem to have some feelings and concerns that are legitimate, but for some reason you seem to be stuck and unable to work things out.

[*To wife*] You resent your husband not doing his part in child care so you can go ahead with the plan you agreed to about going back to work part-time.

[*To husband*] You feel that because you are on a new job, now is not the time to ask for time off for child care.

[*To both*] I'd like to explore what the two of you can do to make things better for each other.

In this example, the social worker responds empathically to the feelings of both husband and wife, thereby validating the feelings of each. In so doing, the social worker remains neutral rather than siding with or against either of the participants. The empathic responses also soften the impact of the social worker's messages.

Here are two more guidelines for making on-the-spot interventions into dysfunctional patterns:

1. Balance interventions equally between family members in much the same way as the social worker in the previous example divided responsibility for the couple's interactions. Because diverse interactions occur among family members, you must make choices about intervening in processes until all members have had an opportunity to focus on their concerns.

2. Direct messages from family members to one another, because couples and family members need to learn to communicate effectively with each other. Your role is to facilitate effective communication between them rather than to act as an intermediary. Family members do not learn the essential skills in communicating with one another by talking through you. Therefore, you should redirect messages to the parties whom they concern. For example, use a message such as "Would you tell your son how you feel about his being in trouble with juvenile corrections, please?"

When people are angry, they may express messages that are hostile, blaming, or critical, exacerbating an already difficult situation. Before redirecting messages, therefore, you must consider the likely consequences of the ensuing interaction. As you redirect such messages, you should actively intervene to facilitate positive interaction:

• Coach family members to own their feelings: "I am really angry with you for getting this family involved with juvenile corrections."

• Translate complaints into requests for change: "I wish that you would stay in school and stop hanging around with those kids who are not in school."

• Metacommunicate by clarifying positive intentions: "I want you to stay in school because I want you to have a better life than I have."

Of course, these messages will be more effective when speakers' nonverbal behaviors are consistent with their message. For example, unless there is a cultural imperative observed in the family, when family members are speaking they should face one another and maintain eye contact. You may need to interrupt and direct them as illustrated in the following message:

Social worker: Cassandra, please stop for just a moment. You were talking to me, not to Jamal. Will you please start again, but this time talk and look directly at him.

Assisting Clients to Disengage from Conflict

One of the most common and harmful types of interaction within families involves arguments that quickly escalate, producing anger and resentment between participants. When sustained over time, these interactions may eventually involve other family members and subsystems. More often than not, the family system becomes factionalized, and individual efforts to regain equilibrium may result in further conflict. The content issues involved are generally secondary to the fact that on a process level each participant is struggling to avoid being one-down, which would mean losing face or yielding power to the other participants.

To assist family members to avoid competitive struggles, you can use metacommunication about the dysfunctional process, emphasizing that all participants lose in competitive arguments because of the negative feelings and emotional estrangement that ensue. It is also vital to stress that safeguarding mutual respect is far more important than winning an argument. The concept of disengaging from conflict simply means that family members avoid escalating arguments by declining to participate further. A graceful way in which people can disengage is by making a comment similar to the following: "Listen, it doesn't really matter who's right. If we argue, we just get mad at each other, and I don't want that to happen." Teaching family members to evaluate their behavior and its effects on others is another strategy: "How do the children react when the two of you are having an argument?" You can further assist family members to avoid arguing between sessions by teaching them to develop code words that signal the need to disengage or reframe their message. Sentences or questions such as "When you do . . . ," "How could you think . . . ," "Did you think . . . ," "I know that you won't . . . ," "You never . . . ," "Don't tell me what to do . . . ," and "Why did you . . ." are generally powerful prompts, along with labeling, that set the stage for conflict.

Although the process of disengagement is easy to learn, it is not simple to apply. Many family members have nearly always responded in a reactive competitive pattern. In sessions, you will need to intervene frequently at first, gradually transferring the responsibility for recognizing and disengaging to the family. Take care, however, that one family member does not assume the role of mediator, thereby diminishing the responsibility of the entire family to resolve conflict. Negotiating tasks for applying disengagement in interactions between sessions can help family members transfer these skills to their daily lives. Of course, family members may be incapable of intervening to disengage conflict in some instances—for example, in domestic violence situations where there is a threat or the actuality of physical harm. In these situations, you can teach family members—especially children—to call for help as well as to develop a safety plan.

Conflict resolution strategies may vary based on differences in both gender and ethnicity (Mackey & O'Brien, 1998; Berg & Jaya, 1993). Being aware of these differences will assist you in choosing interventions strategies that recognize how these factors affect the family's behavior. Berg and Jaya (1993) note that in Asian families, concerns are viewed as "our problems," emphasizing the interdependence between family members. This example suggests that you should explore the family narrative regarding how conflict is managed in the family's particular culture as well as the attached meanings or feelings. By doing so, you are able to engage members in formulating an effective intervention strategy.

In fact, accessing the family narrative with respect to conflict may yield benefits with all families, irrespective of their culture or ethnicity. Each family has its own style of communicating. In some families, everyone talks simultaneously and makes outrageous statements; other members may remain passive during this display. Perhaps yelling or name-calling is a norm, as are demonstrative hand gestures, apparent threats, and a hostile or belligerent tone of voice. Be sensitive to the fact that the presence of these interactions in family communication styles are not necessarily evidence of destructive patterns of relating, even if they are not your own style. Observing the family and inquiring about their preferred patterns of relating will enable you to assess family members' communication styles, and avoid drawing conclusions about their functional or dysfunctional status.

Modifying Dysfunctional Complementary Interactions

Relationships, as described by communication theorists and without attributing a value to either descriptor, are either symmetrical or complementary (Becvar & Becvar, 2000a). *Symmetrical relationships* are thought to be more of an egalitarian arrangement. In contrast, the parties in *complementary relationships* have developed an exchange as a means for avoiding conflict, resolving differences, and creating a workable relationship.

Preferences for relationship patterns may be culturally derived and are considered to reflect a practical division of roles and responsibilities. Therefore, it is important that you avoid concluding that these patterns are an issue unless the family has indicated otherwise.

Note, however, that a complementary type of relationship may prove to be a concern to one or both partners. Frustrations may stem from role overload or strain, limitations imposed by role expectations, and disagreements related to decision making. One partner may grow to resent what she or he perceives as dominance. In such a case, the relationship may become *asymmetrical,* and one person may engage in passive resistance behavior or openly challenge the other. Moreover, an individual who is weary of the exchange may devalue the other party, or disengage, ultimately resenting his or her lack of involvement. In either event, harmful interactions are likely to occur, culminating in the participants seeking professional help.

In modifying dysfunctional complementary relationships, it is vital to work with couples and family members to adopt changes that will bring the relationship more into balance, assuming that they have chosen this goal. As part of this work, you may assist members to develop agreements that involve reciprocal changes.

Negotiating Agreements for Reciprocal Changes

In family or couple sessions, you can facilitate changes in specific behaviors by assisting one member to develop an agreement if another person will agree to make a reciprocal change. In this kind of *quid pro quo contract,* a member agrees to disengage from conflict if the other party agrees to avoid using code words that always prompt a negative response. Individuals are receptive to making changes when other parties agree to make reciprocal changes for two reasons. First, people are more prone to give when they know they are getting something in return. Second, when all involved parties agree to make changes, no single person loses face by appearing to be the sole cause of an interactional problem.

Contracting for reciprocal changes can be a powerful means of inducing change. Another advantage of reciprocal contracting is that it counters the tendency to wait for others to initiate changes. Still another benefit is that in working on reciprocal tasks all parties become *mutually*

involved in a change venture. This mutual involvement may spark collaboration in other dimensions of their relationships—an important gain where interactions have been largely dysfunctional rather than collaborative.

Note, however, that family members are unlikely to be able to implement reciprocal contracts if they have not moved beyond competitive bickering and blaming one another for their problems. For this reason, we recommend deferring use of this technique (unless clients spontaneously begin to negotiate) until you have assisted them to listen attentively to one another, and to change the tone of their interactions. It is also essential that participants demonstrate a commitment to improving their relationship. As Becvar and Becvar (2000a) point out, if family members view their own or others' changes as emanating primarily from meeting the stipulations of an agreement, rather than as a way to improve their relationship, they are likely to devalue the changes. Therefore, we strongly recommend you ask family members to explicitly clarify that improving their relationship is the primary factor motivating their willingness to make changes.

The following are examples of reciprocal agreements that could have been utilized in previous examples from this chapter. You may use them as a guide in assisting families to develop their own agreements:

- Garth agrees to visit Barbara's parents if she agrees to talk with her mother about interfering in their affairs.
- Mr. G agrees to refrain from talking about Marcos's friends if Marcos agrees to tell his father where he is going and when he will be home.
- Cynthia and Martha agree not to argue if the other will not keep shared items for an extended period of time.
- Anne agrees to express her feelings to her mother, if Ms. T agrees to listen without interrupting.

In developing reciprocal contracts, it is wise to engage family members in making their own proposals. By so doing, you enhance the investment of clients in proposed changes. Moreover, clients often generate innovative and constructive ideas that might not occur to you. To engage clients in making proposals, you can use a message such as the following: "It's clear that both of you are unhappy with the situation. I'd be interested in hearing each of you make proposals as to what you could do to make it better." You could then prompt them to think about reciprocal actions.

As you mutually consider proposals, it is important to consider potential barriers and guard against encouraging clients to undertake overly ambitious actions. Initial task exchanges in reciprocal agreements should be relatively simple and likely to succeed, especially when intense conflict has marked the participants' interactions. After eliciting or offering one or more feasible proposals for a reciprocal contract and determining that members are willing to carry out the contract, you should assist them to reach an explicit agreement. This agreement specifies the tasks each member agrees to implement prior to the next session. In developing and planning to implement these tasks, follow the steps of the TIS (outlined in Chapter 13).

As you plan task implementation with family members or couples, stress that each person must exercise *good faith* in carrying out his or her part of the contract, as illustrated in the following message:

Social worker: I am pleased that you have agreed to make the changes we've discussed, because the changes can make things better for everyone. To carry out these changes successfully, however, each of you will need to carry out your part—no matter what the other person does. If you wait for the other person to carry out his or her part first, you may both still be waiting for the other to make the first move by the time of our next session. Remember, failure by the other person to honor the contract is no excuse for you to do likewise. If your partner doesn't keep to the agreement, you can take satisfaction in knowing that you did your part.

Emphasizing the individual responsibility of all family members in the helping process to fulfill their respective commitments, as in the preceding message, counters the tendency of clients to justify

their inaction in subsequent sessions by asserting, "He (or she) didn't carry out his part. I knew this would happen, so I didn't do my part either." If one or more family members have not fulfilled their parts of the agreement, you can focus on obstacles that prevented them from doing so. When the results have been favorable, you can focus on this experience to set the stage for exploring additional ways of achieving further positive interaction.

INTERVENING WITH FAMILIES: MODIFYING MISCONCEPTIONS AND DISTORTED PERCEPTIONS

Cognitions are often the basis for erroneous beliefs that produce dissatisfaction in couple and family relationships, and resentment toward others is often the dynamic that results in dysfunctional interactions. Unrealistic expectations of others and myths are two other forms of misconceptions that contribute to interactional problems. As with rules, myths and unrealistic expectations often are not readily apparent, so you may have to infer them by exploring family members' expectations of one another and other family relationships. Myths are also similar to rules in that they govern family operations by shaping beliefs and expectations that can profoundly influence interactions in couple and family relationships.

To eliminate misconceptions and dispel myths, bring them to the awareness of family members, using empathy to assist clients to accept the errors in their misconceptions. Because misconceptions and myths commonly protect people from having to face certain unpleasant realities and to make changes that are perceived as threatening, individuals may not relinquish them without a struggle. Moreover, cognitive dissonance occurs when individuals receive information that is contrary to their beliefs and perceptions. To facilitate clients' making essential changes, you must recognize that the change process entails resolving fears and risking the consequences of learning and implementing new behavior. Responding empathically to an individual's fears and ambivalence and offering emotional support often provide the impetus for people to change their dysfunctional patterns of interaction.

To illustrate this process, we consider a family in which an adolescent, age 17, manifests extreme tension and anxiety. During family sessions, it becomes apparent that the parents have exerted intense pressure on him to perform well academically and have made it clear they expect him to become a doctor. It has also been apparent that they mistakenly believe the following myth: "If you try hard enough, you can become anything you want." In an effort to reduce the pressure on the son, dispel the myth, and modify the parents' expectations, the social worker arranged to meet separately with the parents. The following excerpt is taken from that session.

Social worker: I've been very concerned that Gary has been making an almost superhuman effort to do well in chemistry and physics but is still floundering in these subjects. I get the impression that he believes he has to become a doctor at any price, and that one reason he's so uptight is that he realizes he isn't cutting it despite his efforts. It's terribly important to him to meet your expectations, and he's falling short even though he drives himself.

Father: I know he's working hard, but it will come. He can become a doctor if he really wants to. I could have been a doctor if I had applied myself, but I didn't. I goofed off too much. I don't want Gary to make that mistake. He has opportunities that neither his mother nor I had.

Social worker: I sense your concern and care for Gary. Still, my impression is that both of you convey to your children the belief that they can become anything they want, and that Gary is blaming himself because he's not making it, no matter how hard he tries.

Mother: Don't you think anyone can succeed in anything if they try hard enough?

Social worker: That belief is inconsistent with what I know about differences between people. People have different aptitudes, talents, and learning styles. Some are able to handle types of work that require finger dexterity. Others are able to

visualize spatial relationships. Everyone has certain aptitudes, types of intelligence, and limitations. What's important in career planning is discovering what our own aptitudes are and making choices that match them. I wonder if each of you can identify talents and limitations that you have.

Observe that as the social worker sought to dispel the family myth, he highlighted the adverse impact of the myths on Gary. This tactic switched the focus from the abstract to the concrete and provided the parents with a good opportunity to review and evaluate their beliefs. The social worker then further attempted to invalidate the myth by asking them to apply it to themselves.

No doubt, you will frequently encounter families who have distorted perceptions of one another that contribute to dysfunctional interactions. Recall from Chapter 10 that labeling others is a common source of such perceptual distortions. The effect of labeling is tantamount to that of wearing blinders, because assigning a label obscures others' strengths, feelings, beliefs, interests, goals, and attributes. As a result, perceptions are limited to attributes and behaviors that are inherent in the label.

Myths that distort individual or family perceptions are also linked to discrimination, bigotry, and negative schemas engrained in societal and institutional perceptions and to attitudes held about certain groups. Perceptual distortions may take the form of criticizing the intelligence or performance of children of color on standardized achievement tests; drawing conclusions about youth based on their style of dress or music preferences; insisting that immigrants act, dress, and speak in a certain way that is comfortable for mainstream society; and avoiding or having adverse reactions to people who are different by virtue of their physical attributes, language, or customs. These macro-level perceptions and distortions can influence where families choose to live, how they perceive their safety, and with whom children are allowed to interact.

When you observe myths and distortions about others operating in families, you have a responsibility to address them in the same manner as you would while intervening in family dynamics, because they affect the families toward whom this behavior is directed. They are also a source of stress and strain for those who hold these beliefs, infusing negativity in their interactions. A word of caution is in order, however: In focusing on the impact of labeling, myths, and distorted perceptions, either in interfamilial or extra-familial interactions, take care to label the process and not the client.

INTERVENING WITH FAMILIES: MODIFYING DYSFUNCTIONAL FAMILY ALIGNMENTS

All families develop patterns of affiliation between members that either enhance or impair opportunities for individual growth or the family's ability to carry out operations vital to its survival. The functional structure—that is, the family's invisible or covert set of demands or code of behavior—reflects and regulates family functioning and determines transactional patterns (Minuchin, 1974). In this section, we draw upon structural approach techniques to guide intervention strategies when family functioning is impaired by dysfunctional alignments.

According to the structural approach, well-functioning families are hierarchically organized and feature a cohesive executive parental subsystem and age-appropriate roles, responsibilities, and privileges for children. Interventions to modify alignments are generally indicated in the following circumstances:

- Bonds are weak between spouses, other individuals who form the parental subsystem, or other family members.

- Enmeshed alliances—that is, rigid or overly restrictive boundaries between members—limit appropriate bonds with other members (or outsiders).

- Two members of a family attempt to cope with dissatisfaction or conflict in their relationship by forming a coalition with a third family member, a phenomenon known as *triangulation*.

- Family members are disengaged or alienated from one another, tending to go their own ways, with little reliance on each other for emotional support.

- Members of the family have formed alliances with persons outside the immediate family (e.g., friends and relatives) that interfere with performing appropriate family roles or providing appropriate emotional support to other family members.

In intervening to modify alignments, *structural mapping* may be used to delineate family boundaries and to highlight and modify interactions and transactional patterns. Structural mapping identifies symptoms that may be exhibited by an individual family member as an expression of dysfunction in the family system. The structure of the family is revealed by who talks to whom, and in what way; who is in an unfavorable or favorable position; and how intense the family's transactions are. The goal of the structural approach is to change family structures by altering boundaries and by realigning subsystems to enhance family functioning. Interventions are thus devised to achieve the following goals:

- *Develop alliances, cultivate new alliances, or strengthen underdeveloped relationships.* For example, a social worker might assist a new stepfather and stepson to explore ways that they can develop a relationship or might work with a parent who has been in prison to strengthen emotional bonds to his or her children.

- *Reinforce an alliance,* by acting to maintain the alliance or to amplify its scope and/or strength. For instance, a social worker might assist a single parent to increase his or her ability to operate as an effective executive subsystem.

- *Differentiate individuals and subsystems.* For example, a social worker might help a mother who gives most of her attention to a newborn infant to understand the need for supervision of older children, and to invest some of her emotional energy in them.

- *Increase family interactions* in disengaged families to make boundaries more permeable by changing the way in which members relate to one another.

- *Help family members accommodate changing circumstances or transitions* by decreasing rigid structures or rules that are no longer viable. For example, as a child reaches adolescence, the social worker might help the parents revise their expectations of the child's behavior so as to accommodate this developmental change.

As can be surmised from these examples, structural problems may arise when the family structure is unable to adequately adjust to changing circumstances that result from external environmental forces or from stressful transitions or relationships within the family. Before you intervene, it is important to understand the structural change as unique to the family's situation and to elucidate the nature of the structural dysfunction. Thus, the family should be involved in determining whether and in what ways such changes should take place.

Your first task in this respect is to assist family members to observe the nature of their alignments. This may be accomplished by asking general questions that stimulate family members to consider their alignments:

- "If you had a difficult problem and needed help, whom would you seek out in the family (tribe or clan)?"

- "Sometimes members of a family feel closer to some members than to others and may pair up or group together. Which members of your family, if any, group together?"

- "In most families, members argue to some extent. With whom do you argue? With whom do other members argue?"

- "Is there one person in the family who is considered to be a favorite?"

- [To parents] "When you make a decision, do you feel that your decision is supported by the other parent? Are other people involved in your decisions?"

You can also bring alignments and coalitions to the family's attention as they are manifested in family sessions:

- "Martha, it seems that you're the center of the family. Most of the conversation seems to be directed through you, while other family members, with the exception of Joe, appear to be observers to the discussion."

- "In your description of how you spend your day, it appears that the baby receives a great deal of your attention."

- [To siblings] "When you are upset with your parents, who do you talk to about how you feel?"

- "I noticed that each of you identified the same individual on your map. Can you tell me about this person and his (or her) role in your family?"

As family members become aware of their alignments, you can assist them in considering whether they wish to become closer to others and to identify obstacles that could prevent this movement from happening. Family alignments may, in fact, involve "complex extended patterns or configurations (Boyd-Franklin, 1989, p. 124). Members of the various configurations may include clan or tribal members, extended kin, friends, or individuals from the family's religious or spiritual community, such as a minister, shaman, rabbi, monk, medicine person, or priest. Be mindful of the fact that any of these people (or a combination of them) may be involved in family decisions. As a consequence, it may be necessary to explore relationships and alignments beyond the immediate family system.

Family sculpting is a technique used in experiential family practice models for assisting family members to analyze and observe their alliances and to make decisions concerning possible changes. This technique allows family members to communicate spatial family system relationships in a nonverbal tableau, to discern alignments, and to recognize the need to realign their relationships. A variation of this technique is to have family members draw family relationships using the Genogram.

In family sculpting, family members are instructed to use rectangles in their drawing to represent each person in the family. Rectangles can be of any size and located anywhere on a sheet of paper. You can coach family members to position the rectangles in ways that depict relative closeness and distance among family members as well as perceptions of power. After family members have completed their drawings, you would ask participants to draw family relationships as they would *like* them to be on the other side of the paper. In a subsequent discussion, you would ask members in turn to share their drawings of existing family relationships.

The benefit of the exercise is that family members can observe the nature of their alignments and the emotional closeness and distance that they experience in their relationships with others. Invite family members to comment on their observations:

• "It appears that Martha and I are quite close to each other, but that Jennifer doesn't feel as close to Martha as I do."

• "Jennifer and I seem to have the least conflict with each other."

• "We all seem to be close to our grandmother."

After each family member has an opportunity to make their observations, you can ask them to explain their second drawings, which show how they would like family relationships to be. During this discussion, you can highlight the desired changes, assist individuals to formulate goals that reflect changes they would like to make, and identify "exceptional" times—for example, when Jennifer and Martha are not in conflict with each other.

A family sculpting or structural mapping exercise can also be used with parents to strengthen parental coalitions and mark generational boundaries. For example, does one parent triangulate with a child or children, or permit them to intrude into the parental subsystem? Does the father act as a mediator in family conflicts? Does one parent

have the final say? The hazard associated with this alignment is that children become adept at playing one parent against the other, which fosters parental divisiveness and produces strain between children and the "excluded" parent. In the case of the mother who expends a majority of her emotional energy on a newborn, emotional bonds and loyalty between her and her other children may be lacking.

Developing cohesiveness, unity, and more effective alignments is a challenge that often confronts two families who have joined together—for example, when they are trying to develop a relationship between a new stepfather and his stepson. Because these factors are apt to be present in foster or adoptive families, your attention to alliances and cohesiveness is equally important in such cases, especially when there are biological children in the home.

In situations where two families have joined together, you can assist parents to analyze whether differences or lack of agreement about their parenting styles is a factor in parent–child alignments. Hare (1994) urges us to be mindful of the fact that in lesbian families, issues related to two families joining together and parenting styles are not dissimilar to those problems faced by heterosexual families. Strategies for strengthening parental coalitions may include negotiating "united front" agreements in parent–child transactions requiring decision making and/or disciplinary actions (unless, of course, the other partner is truly hurtful or abusive to the child). Finally, assisting families to realign themselves and forge new alliances is particularly important when a child who has been placed outside of the home returns to the family, or when a parent has been absent from the family's life.

Summary

This chapter focused on intervention techniques and strategies that may be used to strengthen families' or couples' relationships. These strategies are drawn primarily from cognitive-behavioral and task-centered approaches, communication theories, family systems, and structural family therapy. Each approach shares the view of the family as a social system, and thus has the unit of intervention in common. To a beginning social worker, employing these techniques may appear to be a daunting challenge, and we encourage you to seek supervision and consultation in applying them. To further enhance your skills, we recommend that you pursue additional comprehensive knowledge of the various approaches.

In implementing the intervention strategies discussed in this chapter, we caution you against making assumptions about what constitutes "normal" family functioning. You should examine family functioning, communication patterns, and alignments in light of each family's particular culture, race, structure, and social class. Solution-focused family practice reminds us that attempts to identify families as functional or dysfunctional are inherently flawed. Instead, you should concentrate on assisting the family to envision solutions and diminish the focus on problems. Those social workers operating in a framework of social constructionist or narrative therapy also find it unproductive to characterize or label families as functional or dysfunctional, preferring instead to honor the unique story of each family. We further urge that an appraisal of family ethnicity, race, configuration and sexual orientation must be factored into any assessment and intervention strategies.

Any approach that you may utilize in intervening with families requires systematic application of techniques and strategies, ongoing monitoring, and evaluation of the results. Research as summarized by Nichols and Swartz (1998) points to positive outcomes when specific problems are treated in a systematic manner.

Chapter 13 detailed the importance of matching intervention strategies to clients' goals and the client system. This chapter amplified this point here, as well as pointing out the need for matching the intervention with the specific problem, developmental stages, and ethnocultural factors, taking into account internal family functioning and the external factors that may influence the family system.

Internet Resources

See our companion website for hot links to some helpful URLs. Note that URLs are subject to change. We will endeavor to update the links on the companion website as much as possible.

Using InfoTrac College Edition, you can obtain additional information by entering these keywords: "family practice," "family therapy," "cognitive-behavioral therapy with families," "solution-focused practice with families," "task-centered practice with families." You may also use these keywords to find Internet resources.

We also recommend the *Journal of Family Social Work* for more information on family therapies and family practice. Online resources include the following websites:

Psychotherapy Networker: *www.psychotherapynetworker.org*

Families in Society, The Journal of Contemporary Human Services: *www.familiesinsociety.org*

Journal of Ethnic and Cultural Diversity in Social Work: *www.haworthpress.com/web/ECDSW*

Related Online Content

Visit the *Direct Social Work Practice* companion website at *http://socialwork. wadsworth.com/hepworth7* for additional learning tools such as glossary terms, chapter outlines, InfoTrac College Edition keywords, relevant web links, and chapter practice quizzes. Also, be sure to check out the Direct Practice Virtual Reader, where the authors have personally selected articles relevant to this chapter using InfoMarks.

CHAPTER  16

Intervening in Social Work Groups

CHAPTER OVERVIEW

This chapter builds on the skills introduced in Chapter 11 for forming and composing task, treatment, and support groups. This chapter addresses the stages of group development and skills needed to intervene effectively throughout group processes.

In any group with social work goals, it is the task of the leader to intervene facilitatively to enable the group to achieve those goals. In treatment groups, the leader's role is particularly challenging, requiring in-depth, balanced interventions to assist the growth of both individuals and the group as a whole. To add to the complexity of this role, the leader must be astute in sorting through the maze of multilevel communication to bring meaning to the group's experience, to shape the group's therapeutic character, and to provide direction and focus to the group's processes at critical moments. Finally, the leader must formulate all interventions within the context of the stages of development through which a group progresses to reach full maturity. Similarly, in a task group, the leader plays a variety of facilitative roles in assisting the group to meet its objectives. This chapter focuses primarily on treatment groups, but provides additional content on task groups in the final section.

Because the leader's interventions are inextricably related to the group's stage of development, we begin at that point.

STAGES OF GROUP DEVELOPMENT

All groups go through natural stages of development, although the pace and complexity of each stage may vary. Your understanding of these stages is essential in anticipating and addressing the behaviors that characterize each phase, so that the group's objectives can ultimately be met. You are also responsible for removing obstacles that threaten to derail the group's development and hinder the success of individual members. In doing so, you must make strategic, informed choices regarding your actions and input across the lifespan of the group.

Without knowledge of the group's stage of development, you may be prone to making errors, such as expecting group members to begin in-depth explorations in initial sessions or concluding that you have failed if the group exhibits the discord that is typical of early development. Leaders may also overlook positive behaviors that indicate that the group is approaching a more mature stage of development, or they may fail to intervene at critical periods to assist the group's evolution (for example, encouraging them to "stay on task," to "count in" all members in decision making, to foster free expression of feelings, or to adopt many other behaviors that are hallmarks of a seasoned group).

Various models of group development offer frameworks for organizing your observations about the group and its characteristics, themes, and behaviors. All of these models identify progressive steps in group development, although they may organize these steps into four, five, or even six stages. Some theorists have noted variations in group stages based on the gender of group members. For example, Schiller (1997) has noted that groups composed of women may emphasize intimacy for a longer period and come to power and control later in the group's history. Berman-Rossi and Kelly (2000) suggest that stages of group development are influenced by variables such as attendance patterns, worker skills, group content, and gender and other member characteristics. Open-ended groups and those with turbulent changes in membership may not move through these phases in a linear fashion and may require more time at formative stages if cohesion is slow to develop (Galinsky & Schopler, 1989).

In this chapter, we will use the model developed by Garland, Jones, and Kolodny (1965), which delineates five stages. At the same time, we will comment on recent developments that influence the stages of any particular group.[1] The five stages of Garland et al.'s model are as follows:

1. Preaffiliation
2. Power and control
3. Intimacy
4. Differentiation
5. Separation

Stage 1. Preaffiliation: Approach and Avoidance Behavior

The initial stage of group development is characterized by members exhibiting *approach/avoidance* behavior. Their tentativeness toward becoming involved in the group is reflected in their wavering willingness to assume responsibility, to interact with others, and to support program activities and events. Hesitancy to participate is also shown by silence or tentative speech, as when members are occupied by their own problems and the feelings of uneasiness and apprehension that emanate from their first encounter with the group. Often fearful and suspicious, members may be sensitive to the responses of others, fearing possible domination, aggression, isolation, rejection, and hostility.

At this stage, participant behavior is wary, sometimes even provocative, as members assess possible social threats and attempt to discern the kinds of

behaviors the group wants and expects. Members also tend to identify one another in terms of each individual's status and roles and to engage in social rituals, stereotyped introductions, and detailed intellectual discussions rather than in-depth or highly revealing conversation (Berman-Rossi & Kelly, 2000). They may be uncertain about the group's purpose and the benefits it may bring to them.

At times, members may employ testing behaviors to "size up" other members, to test the group's limits, to find out how competent the leader is, and to determine to what extent the leader will safeguard the rights of members and protect them from feared hurt and humiliation. Members may also move tentatively toward the group as they seek to find common ground with other members, search for viable roles, and seek approval, acceptance, and respect. Much of the initial communication in the group is directed toward the leader, and some members may openly demand that the social worker pursue a "take charge" approach, making decisions regarding group issues and structure and issuing prompt directives to control the behavior of members. As noted earlier, Schiller (1997) suggests that groups composed entirely of women experience a longer preaffiliation phase as they explore empathic identification with others and differences.

Stage 2. Power and Control: A Time of Transition

The first stage of group development merges imperceptibly into the second stage as members, having determined that the group experience is potentially safe and rewarding and worth the preliminary emotional investment, shift their concerns to matters related to autonomy, power, and control. The frame of reference for this stage is that of *transition*—that is, members must endure the ambiguity and turmoil of change from a non-intimate to an intimate system of relationships while they try to increase the understandability and predictability.

After dealing with the struggle of whether they "belong" in the group, members now become occupied with how they "rank" in relation to other members. Turning to others like themselves for support and protection, members create subgroups and a hierarchy of statuses, or social pecking order

(Yalom, 1995). Gradually, the processes of the group become stylized as various factions emerge and relationships solidify. Conflicts between opposing subgroups often occur in this stage, and members may team up to express anger toward the leader, other authority figures, or outsiders. Failed competition for favored status with the social worker may also produce hostility toward the group leader (Yalom, 1995).

Disenchantment with the group may reveal itself through hostility, withdrawal, or confusion about the group's purposes. Verbal abuse, attacks, and rejection of lower-status members may occur as well, and isolated members of the group who do not have the protection of a subgroup may discontinue coming to sessions. Attrition in membership may also occur, as individuals find outside pursuits more attractive than the conflicted group experience. In fact, this depleted membership may put the group's very survival in jeopardy.

Stage 3. Intimacy: Developing a Familial Frame of Reference

Having clarified and resolved many of the issues related to personal autonomy, initiative, and power, the group moves from the "pre-intimate" power and control stage to that of intimacy. As the group enters this stage, conflicts fade, personal involvement between members intensifies, and members display a growing recognition of the significance of the group experience. Members also experience an increase in morale and "we-ness," a deepening commitment to the group's purpose, and heightened motivation to carry out plans and tasks that support the group's objectives. Mutual trust increases as members begin to acknowledge one another's uniqueness, spontaneously disclose feelings and problems, and seek the opinion of the group. To achieve this desired intimacy, however, group participants may suppress negative feelings that could produce conflict between themselves and others. In contrast to earlier sessions, they express genuine concern for absent members and may reach out to invite them to return to the group.

During this stage of development, a group "character" emerges as the group evolves its own culture, style, and values. Clear norms are established, based on personal interests, affection, and other positive forces. Roles also take shape as members find ways to contribute to the group and leadership patterns become firmly settled. The frame of reference for members is a familial one, as members liken their group experience to their experience with their own nuclear families, occasionally referring to other members as siblings or to the leader as the "mother" or "father" of the group.

How groups experience this stage depends on factors such as how regularly members attend group sessions, whether the group is open or closed, and how much member turnover occurs (Berman-Rossi & Kelly, 2000; Galinsky & Schopler, 1989). In groups that endure frequent transitions, it is important to develop rituals to help the members achieve a sense of cohesion so that they can move successfully to later stages.

Stage 4. Differentiation: Developing Group Identity and an Internal Frame of Reference

The fourth stage of group development is marked by cohesion and harmony as members come to terms with intimacy and make choices to draw closer to others in the group. In this stage, group-centered operations are achieved and a dynamic balance between individual and group needs evolves. Members, who participate in different and complementary ways, experience greater freedom of personal expression and come to feel genuinely accepted and valued as their feelings and ideas are validated by other members of the group. Gradually, the group becomes a mutual-aid system in which members spontaneously give emotional support in proportion to the needs of each individual.

In experiencing this newfound freedom and intimacy, members begin to perceive the group experience as unique. Indeed, as the group creates its own mores and structure, in a sense it becomes its own frame of reference. Customs and traditional ways of operating emerge, and the group may adopt a "club" name or insignia that reflects its purpose. The group's energy is channeled into working toward purposes and carrying out tasks that are clearly understood and accepted. New roles—more flexible and functional than those originally envisioned—are developed to support the group's activity, and organizational structures (e.g., officers, dues, attendance expectations, rules) may evolve. Status hierarchies also tend to be less rigid, and members may assume leadership roles spontaneously as the need for particular expertise or abilities arises.

By the time the group reaches the differentiation stage, members have accumulated experience in "working through problems" and have gained skill in analyzing their own feelings and the feelings of others, in communicating their needs and positions effectively, in offering support to others, and in grasping the complex interrelationships that have developed in the group. Having become self-conscious about their own operations, members bring conflict out into the open and identify obstacles that impede their progress. All decisions are ultimately the unanimous response of the group and are strictly respected. Disagreements are not suppressed or overridden by premature group action; instead, the group carefully considers the positions of any dissenters and attempts to resolve differences and to achieve consensus among members. New entrants serve as catalysts and may express their amazement at the insight shared by veteran members, who in turn become increasingly convinced of the group experience's value.

Members may now publicize their group meetings among peers, whereas previously membership in the group may have been linked with secret feelings of shame. Secure in their roles and relationships within the group, members may become interested in meeting with other groups or in bringing in outside culture.

Stage 5. Separation: Breaking Away

During the last phase of group development, members begin to separate, loosening the intense bonds often established with other members and with the leader, and searching for new resources and ties to satisfy their needs. Group members are likely to experience a broad range of feelings about leaving the group. Indeed, the approach of group termination may set off a number of reactions, the diversity of which is reminiscent of the approach/avoidance

maneuvers displayed in stage 1. Members may again feel anxiety, this time in relation to moving apart and breaking bonds that have been formed. There may be outbursts of anger against the leader and other members at the thought of the group ending, the reappearance of quarrels that were previously settled, and increased dependence on the leader. Denial of the positive meaning of the group experience is not uncommon. These separation reactions may appear in flashes or clusters as members attempt to reconcile their positive feelings about the group with their subconscious feelings of abandonment, rejection, and apprehension over the group's ending.

Termination is also a time of evaluation, of contemplation of the work achieved, and of consolidation of learning. It is a time of finishing unfinished business, of getting and giving focused feedback, and of savoring the good times and the close relationships gained in the group.[2] Members, who have often begun to pull back their group investments and to put more energy into outside interests, speak of their fears, hopes, and concerns about the future and about one another. There is often discussion of how to apply what has been learned in the group to other situations and talk of reunions or follow-up meetings (Toseland & Rivas, 2001).

THE LEADER'S ROLE IN THE STAGES OF GROUP DEVELOPMENT

As suggested earlier, the role of the leader shifts and changes with the evolution of the group. Referring to earlier work by Lang (1972), Henry (1992) conceptualizes the leader as enacting certain roles and occupying different locations throughout the group's lifespan. The shifting *role* of leader exists along a continuum that ranges from primary to variable to facilitative, depending on the needs, capacities, and characteristics of the group's membership and its stage of development. Likewise, the leader occupies a *location* in the group that may be cast along a continuum ranging from central to pivotal to peripheral, depending again on the same variables. Research on damaging experiences in therapeutic groups indicates that group leaders' behaviors (e.g., confrontation, monopolizing, criticizing) or inaction (e.g., lack of support, lack of structure) play a primary role in group casualties or dropouts (Smokowski, Rose, & Bacallao, 2001).

The leader's role—a primary one at the outset of the group—is to select candidates for the group. Likewise, the leader is in a central location at this phase of group development, in that he or she recruits members and determines the group's purpose, structure, location, and duration. The leader retains this primacy and centrality before the group convenes, as he or she brings structure to the group, plans its content and function, conducts pre-group interviews, and negotiates reciprocal contracts with each prospective member. This set of role and location conditions prevails throughout the beginning phase of the group. During this stage, the leader initiates and directs group discussion, encourages participation, and begins blending the individual contracts with members into a mutual group contract.

As the group evolves to a new level of connectedness, the leader intentionally takes a variable role and occupies a pivotal location with respect to the group. According to Henry (1992):

> As the worker steps back from the central location and primary role, the members begin to supplant some of what the worker has been doing. In the vernacular of cinematography, the worker fades out as the group system comes up. However, because the group's (internal and external) systems are not yet stabilized at full functioning capacity, the worker needs to let the process run at its own speed and sometimes needs to move back in to help keep the system afloat. This is why the worker's role is referred to as variable, and the worker's location as pivotal. This role and location will be part of the mutual contract that is being negotiated at this time. (p. 34)

Henry notes that the leader's variable role and pivotal location continue in the group during the conflict/disequilibrium stage (stage 2, "power and control," in Garland, Jones, and Kolodny's terminology). When the group enters its maintenance or working phase (stages 3 and 4, "intimacy" and "differentiation"), the leader assumes a facilitative role and occupies a peripheral location. Inasmuch as the group has achieved full capacity to govern itself, the leader fulfills a resource role rather than assuming a primary role.

As the group moves into its separation or termination phase (stage 5), the leader once again returns to a primary role and central location to support the divesting of members, who are launching their own independent courses. In this role the leader aids the group in working through any regression to earlier stages of development and assures the successful ending of the group.

Table 16-1 illustrates the evolution of the leader's focus as a group advances through the various stages of development. Information contained in the table comes from a variety of sources, including Garland, Jones, and Kolodny (1965), Rose (1989), Henry (1992), and Corey and Corey (1992).

INTERVENTION INTO STRUCTURAL ELEMENTS OF A GROUP

The primacy of the leader's role and the centrality of the leader's location are related at one level to the ability of members to assume responsibility for the group's treatment functions. At another level, these leader positions are related to the relative need to intervene to shape the group's therapeutic character, thereby creating a vehicle for members' change. In that respect, across the various stages of group development, the leader pays particular attention to shaping the following group elements:

- Cohesion
- Normative structure
- Role structure
- Subgroup structure
- Leadership structure

Table 16-1 Stages, dynamics, and leader focus

STAGE	DYNAMICS	LEADER FOCUS
Preaffiliation	Arm's-length exploration	Observes and assesses
	Approach/avoidance	Clarifies group objectives
	Issues of trust, preliminary commitment	Establishes group guidelines
	Intellectualization of problems	Encourages development of personal goals
	Interaction based on superficialattributes or experiences	Clarifies aspirations and expectations of members
	Protection of self; low-risk behavior	Encourages discussion of fears, ambivalence
	Milling around	Gently invites trust
	Sizing up of leader and other members	Gives support; allows distance
	Formulation of individual and group goals	Facilitates exploration
	Leader viewed as responsible for group	Provides group structure
	Member evaluation as to whether group is safe and meets needs	Contracts for help-seeking, help-giving roles
		Facilitates linkages among members
	Fear of self-disclosure, rejection	Models careful listening
	Uncertainty regarding group purpose	Focuses on resistance
	Little commitment to goals or group	Assures opportunities for participation
Power and control	Rebellion; power struggles	Protects safety of individuals and property
	Political alignments forged to increase power	Clarifies power struggle
	Issues of status, ranking, and influence	Turns issues back to group
	Complaints regarding group structure, process	Encourages expression and acceptance of differences
	Challenges to leader's role	Facilitates clear, direct, nonabrasive communication
	Emergence of informal leadership, factional leaders	Examines nonproductive group processes
	Individual autonomy; everybody for himself/herself	Examines cognitive distortions
	Dysfunctional group roles	Facilitates member evaluation of dissident subgroups
	Normative and membership crisis; drop-out danger high	Holds group accountable for decision by consensus
	Testing of leader; other group members	Clarifies that conflict, power struggles are normal
	Dependence on leader	Encourages norms consistent with therapeutic group
	Group experimentation in managing own affairs	Consistently acknowledges strengths, accomplishments
	Program breakdown at times; low planning	Nondefensively deals with challenges to leadership
	Feedback highly critical	Focuses on the "here and now"
Intimacy	Intensified personal involvement	Encourages leadership
	Sharing of self, materials	Assumes flexible role as group vacillates
	Striving to meet others' needs	Aids sharper focus on individual goals
	Awareness of significance of the group experience	Encourages deeper-level exploration, feedback

STAGE	DYNAMICS	LEADER FOCUS
	Personality growth and change	Encourages acknowledgment, support of
	Mutual revelation, risk taking	differences
	Beginning commitment to decision by	Guides work of group
	consensus	Encourages experimentation with different roles
	Beginning work on cognitive restructuring	Encourages use of new skills inside and
	Importance of goals verbalized	outside group
	Growing ability to govern group	Assists members to assume responsibility
	independently	for change
	Dissipation of emotional turmoil	Gives consistent feedback regarding successes
	Member initiation of topics	Reduces own activity
	Constructive feedback	
Differentiation	Here-and-now focus	Emphasizes achievement of goals,
	High level of trust, cohesion	exchange of skills
	Free expression of feelings	Supports group's self-governance
	Mutual aid	Promotes behaviors that increase cohesion
	Full acceptance of differences	Provides balance between support,
	Group viewed as unique	confrontation
	Clarity of group purpose	Encourages conversion of insight into action
	Feelings of security; belonging; "we" spirit	Interprets; explores common themes
	Differentiated roles	Universalizes themes
	Group self-directed	Encourages deeper-level exploration of
	Intensive work on cognitions	problems
	Goal-oriented behavior	Assures review of goals, task completion
	Work outside of group to achieve	Stimulates individual and group growth
	personal goals	Supports application of new behaviors
	Members feel empowered	outside group
	Communication open, spontaneous	
	Self-confrontation	
Separation	Review and evaluation	Prepares for letting go
	Development of outlets outside group	Facilitates evaluation and feelings about
	Stabilizing and generalizing	termination
	Projecting toward future	Reviews individual and group progress
	Recognition of personal, interpersonal growth	Redirects energy of individuals away from
	Sadness and anxiety over reality of separation	group and toward selfing process
	Expression of fears, hopes, and others'	Enables individuals to disconnect
	anxiety for self	Encourages resolution of unfinished business
	Some denial, regression	Reinforces changes made by individuals
	Moving apart, distancing	Administers evaluation instruments
	Less intense interaction	
	Plans as to how to continue progress	
	outside group	
	Talk of reunions, follow-up	

In fact, the evolution of these structures over time encompasses the phenomenon of group development (Rose, 1989; Yalom, 1995). Because of their importance, these elements are considered successively in the sections that follow.

Cohesion

Cohesion plays a central role in group success, and leaders play a key role in developing this positive force. The leader forges connections among group members and tries to expand the interpersonal networks of subgroup members, so that they relate to other people outside their subgroup. Further, the leader encourages cohesive behaviors by "pointing out who is present and who is absent, by making reference to 'we' and 'us' and 'our,' and by including the groups as a whole in his or her remarks in group sessions" (Henry, 1992, p. 167).

Leaders also encourage the development of cohesion by commenting on and reinforcing positive group-building behaviors as they occur. Henry (1992) identifies signs of cohesiveness that leaders might highlight. For example, attraction to the group is indicated when participants inquire about missing members, return to the group after absences or conflicts, take others' opinions into account in decision making, and seek increased responsibility for the group's operations. Although these indicators of cohesion are earmarks of advanced stages of group development, they may also make fleeting appearances early in a group, and should be explicitly acknowledged when they do.

Leaders also increase the attractiveness and cohesion in groups by facilitating high levels of interaction; by aiding members to successfully achieve goals, fulfill expectations, and meet needs; and by providing opportunities for prestige and access to rewards and resources that individual members alone could not obtain (Toseland & Rivas, 2001).

Ironically, these efforts at developing cohesion may be reversed during the termination phase:

> Members must be helped to become less attracted to the group and, when appropriate, more attracted to alternative relationships. The worker, therefore, also reverses the application of principles for attaining group cohesion. For example, instead of increasing the frequency with which members have contact with one another, this may be reduced by having meetings less often and/or for a shorter time. . . . The worker may place less emphasis on resolving conflicts within the group and may not call attention to commonalities of experiences or attitudes except as those relate to ways of coping with termination. This may not be true in group psychotherapy, when this type of process is maintained until the very end. (Garvin, 1987, p. 222)

Normative Structure

Chapter 11 introduced strategies to facilitate the development of constructive group norms. However, counterproductive norms may also emerge. For example, the group may split into several self-serving factions or subgroups that compete for control. Members may develop a habit of socializing rather than focusing on legitimate group tasks. Some participants may repeatedly cast others as scapegoats, harassing those members and blaming them for various group ills. In these and countless other ways, groups may develop negative behaviors that undermine their ability to coalesce and aid each other in reaching their goals.

As described in Chapter 11, leaders must observe evolving group behavior and determine whether these emerging patterns undermine or support the group's purposes. Once leaders have determined the impact of emerging patterns, they may then intervene to nurture functional group behaviors and to assist participants to modify behaviors that are destructive to individuals or to the group.

The facilitator sets the stage for a therapeutic atmosphere and a "working group" by establishing an explicit contract with members in initial sessions that includes normative "guideposts" for the group. Along the way, the leader helps the group identify and articulate norms they wish the group to follow. Once decided, the guidelines should be recorded and revisited regularly, and the leader should take an active role in helping members consistently adhere to them. Some groups will even list them on a board that is posted in the meeting room. Sample guidelines follow:

- Make group decisions by consensus.
- Personalize communications by using "I statements" (e.g., "I (think) (feel) (want) . . .").

- Keep the group's focus on its task and mission.
- Keep the group's discussion focused primarily on the present rather than the past.
- Avoid "gossiping."
- Take responsibility for concerns about how the group is going by bringing them to others' attention.

In addition to generating structural guidelines that pave the way for the adoption of therapeutic norms, leaders may aid members in adopting the following personal guidelines, adapted from Corey and Corey (2002):

- Help establish trust. Initiate discussions of personal issues rather than waiting for someone else to make the first move.
- Express persistent feelings. Rather than bury feelings of boredom, anger, or disappointment, air your feelings related to the group process.
- Decide how much to disclose. You are in charge of what, how much, and when you share personal issues.
- Be an active participant, not an observer. Share reactions to what others are saying in the group rather than remaining an unknown entity and thus a possible object of others' flawed observations.
- Listen closely and discriminately. Do not accept others' feedback wholesale or reject it outright, but decide for yourself what does and does not apply to you.
- Pay attention to consistent feedback. If a message has been received from a variety of sources, it is likely to have a degree of validity.
- Focus on self. Talk about your role in problems; avoid blaming and focusing on extraneous situations or people outside of the group.

The leader often intervenes to remind people of these individual-level norms or to point out when they are being violated. In established groups, members will also speak up to hold one another accountable. Ultimately, the locus of control for enforcing norms should reside with the group rather than with the leader (Carrell, 2000).

Role Structure

Roles are closely related to norms, as Toseland and Rivas (2001) explain:

> Whereas norms are shared expectations held, to some extent, by everyone in the group, roles are shared expectations about the functions of individuals in the group. Unlike norms, which define behavior in a wide range of situations, roles define behavior in relation to a specific function or task that the group member is expected to perform (p. 68).

Within the group, roles include formal positions (e.g., chairperson or secretary) and informal positions created through group interactions (e.g., mediator, clown, rebel, initiator, or scapegoat). Like norms, roles may help fulfill group functions or meet individual treatment aims. Leaders must be attuned to the development of antitherapeutic roles and address them as they arise. For example, a member who struggles with honesty might make jokes to keep discussion at a superficial level, or a member who struggles to be taken seriously may make distracting or ridiculous comments, thereby reinforcing his destructive role. Yalom discusses the effect of "the monopolist" (1995, p. 369), who, perhaps due to anxiety, talks excessively, taking up airtime and turning the group mood into one of frustration.

The key when facing counterproductive roles is to encourage members to be self-observant, assure that they do not become locked into dysfunctional roles, and empower other participants to confront the member about the role and its impact. As Garvin notes:

> The "clown" may wish to behave more seriously, the "mediator" to take sides, and passive people to function assertively. The worker, being cognizant of roles that are created out of group interactions, will attend to those that impede either the attainment of individual goals or the creation of an effective group. (1986, p. 112)

Dysfunctional role performance is a critical choice point for intervention. One means of intervening is to use a technique developed by Garvin (1986) to identify informal roles occupied by group participants. Leaders administer a questionnaire asking members to "vote" on who, if anyone, fulfills group roles such as referee, humorist, nurturer, spokesperson, and "devil's advocate." The discussion that results from this exercise can powerfully influence both members' awareness and the group process. Another technique is to simply describe a specific role that a member seems to have assumed and to ask that member for observations regarding the accuracy of that assessment. Preface this observation by asking the member if he or she would like group feedback. Doing so reduces defensiveness and gives the member appropriate control over the situation.

Another aspect of role performance involves aiding members in role attainment—that is, enabling them to fulfill the requirements of roles that they aspire to or are already in, such as student, parent, spouse, employee, friend, or retired person. In doing so, the leader helps members assess their own interactions, practice the skills needed for their roles, and apply new ways of approaching and enacting those roles. Groups can assist members in these tasks through role-playing, through giving feedback, and through sharing personal examples. Some groups may be designed to specifically address the development of social skills (LeCroy, 2002). Chapter 13 offers further examples of change through behavioral rehearsal and skill development.

Subgroup Structure

Subgroups inevitably emerge and exist in groups, affecting them in numerous ways. Subgroups may both hinder and enhance group process. Negative subgroups, like cliques, can raise issues of loyalty and exclusion in the group, challenge the leader's authority, and fragment communication as members of a subgroup talk among themselves. The leader can modify the impact of such subgroups by taking these steps:

1. Initiating discussion of the reasons for the formation of the dissident subgroups and their impact on the group as a whole. This discussion may reveal the difficulties that they create for goal setting, communication, interaction, and decision making

2. Neutralizing the effects of negative subgroups through programming or structuring. The leader, for example, might challenge dissident subgroups to work toward a common goal, change seating arrangements, use a "round robin" approach to get feedback from all members, assign members from different subgroups to work on common group tasks, or use programming materials or exercises to separate subgroup members (Carrell, 2000).

3. Creating safe positions or roles for marginal members of the group that require minimal activity but at the same time involve them in a group activity (Balgopal & Vassil, 1983).

4. Helping powerful subgroups or individuals to relinquish power or to use it sparingly in the interest of other members. This may be accomplished by encouraging concern for others in the group and by enabling members to grasp the possibility that domination of others might be destructive to themselves (Garvin, 1987).

5. Appointing powerless members to roles that carry power, such as arranging for group activities, securing resources for the group, or fulfilling significant roles (e.g., observer, chairperson, or secretary).

6. Finding means to "connect" with dissident subgroups and to demonstrate a concern for their wants (Garvin, 1987).

7. Providing ways for subgroups to attain legitimate power by creating useful roles and tasks in the group.

Leadership Structure

The leader's role in a group can be described as a set of behaviors that facilitate the attainment of group and individual goals and ensure the maintenance of the group. Ultimately, the leader "puts him/herself out of business" by gradually distributing leadership functions to members as the group matures, while continuing to attend to the work of the group (Rose, 1989, p. 260).

Helping members to assume leadership behaviors is important for three reasons. First, members develop vital skills that they can transfer to other social groups, where leadership is usually highly valued. Second, the more that members exercise leadership, the more likely they are to become invested in the group. Third, performance of leadership activities enhances the perceived power or self-efficacy of members, who often experience powerlessness in a wide array of social situations (Rose, 1989).

Leaders may expedite the distribution of power by taking four steps (Shulman, 1984):

1. Encouraging member-to-member rather than member-to-leader communications

2. Asking for members' input into the agenda for the meeting and the direction the group should take in future meetings

3. Supporting indigenous leadership when members make their first tentative attempts at exerting their own influence on the group

4. Encouraging attempts at mutual sharing and mutual aid among group members during the first meeting.

Group leadership problems occur when individuals or vying subgroups attempt to usurp the reins of power. Challenges to leadership (or lack of it) are, in fact, an inherent part of the group's struggle over control, division of responsibility, and decision making (Corey & Corey, 2002). It is important not to interpret these efforts as negative, because they may actually help the group succeed by calling attention to issues or roles that are important to individual members (Hurley, 1984). Examples of messages that illustrate control issues follow:

- I don't want to talk just because you want me to talk. I learn just as much by listening and observing.

- There are several people in here who always get the attention. No matter what I do, I just don't seem to get recognized, especially by the leaders.

- You should pay more attention to Paul. He's been crying several times, and you haven't been taking care of him.

The facilitator might respond to such a challenge by empathically exploring the statement, eliciting feedback from other members regarding leadership style, and asking for input (e.g., "What would you have me do differently?"). Corey and Corey also recommend responding authentically. They note that leaders must be self-aware when challenged and avoid focusing on "problem members" or difficult situations, rather than on how they are affected personally when group processes go awry:

> Typically, leaders have a range of feelings: being threatened by what they perceive as a challenge to their leadership role; anger over the members' lack of cooperation and enthusiasm; feelings of inadequacy to the point of wondering if they are qualified to lead groups; resentment toward several of the members, whom they label as some type of problem; and anxiety over the slow pace of the group, with a desire to stir things up so that there is some action. (Corey & Corey, 1992, p. 155)

By ignoring their reactions, leaders leave themselves out of the interactions that occur in the group. Instead, Corey and Corey urge leaders to model

> a "direct" style of dealing with conflict and resistance. . . . Your own thoughts, feelings and observations can be the most powerful resource you have in dealing with defensive behavior. When you share what you are feeling and thinking about what is going on in the group—in such a way as not to blame and criticize the members for deficiencies—you are letting the members experience an honest and constructive interaction with you. (1992, p. 155)

By consistently responding authentically, even when challenged or under attack, the leader encourages the group to adopt this mode of representing self—one that is vital to members dealing effectively with the inevitable differences they encounter among themselves.

LEADER INTERVENTIONS ACROSS STAGES OF GROUP DEVELOPMENT

As previously mentioned, a leader's role must always be pursued within the framework of the group's stages of development. Thomas and Caplan (1999) suggest a wheel metaphor for leadership. That is, the leader takes a particularly active role in getting the "wheel spinning," then gradually provides a "lighter touch," and finally reduces that role as the group gathers its own momentum, while still standing by to assure that events or digressions don't throw the wheel off track. These authors identify three key intervention techniques that leaders must employ over the life of the group:

- *Process,* attending to both individuals' processes in addressing problems and the process for the group as a whole
- *Linking,* or helping members see the common themes in the issues raised, thereby building the reciprocity and mutuality essential to self-worth and group cohesion
- *Inclusion,* or tactics to engage reluctant members with the group

Social workers must also take care not to make errors that inhibit group development and process. Thomas and Caplan (1999) identify some of the most common mistakes. These mistakes include:

- Doing one-on-one work in the context of the group. This practice inhibits the mutual aid that is the hallmark of group work
- Having such a rigid agenda that members cannot pursue emerging themes or otherwise own the group process
- Scapegoating or attacking individual members. This behavior inhibits others' involvement by sending a message that the group is not a safe place
- Overemphasizing content and failing to universalize themes so that all members can benefit from and relate to the experience of other members
- Ridiculing members or discounting some members' need to be heard
- Lecturing the group. This practice disempowers members and inhibits group investment and momentum
- Failing to address offensive comments or colluding with members around inappropriate, anti-authoritarian, racist, or sexist statements

It may be helpful to think of the preceding list as behaviors that stop the spinning wheel or send it veering off course. The following sections detail key aspects of *effective* group work, examining the leader's role across the group phases identified in Garland, Jones, and Kolodny's (1965) model.

Preaffiliation Stage

As discussed in Chapter 11, pre-group individual interviews will serve as orientation for potential members of the group. In initial sessions the leader can prepare members for the experiences to come by explaining the basics of group process—for example, the stages of development through which the group will pass, ways to create a therapeutic working environment, behaviors and attitudes characteristic of an effective group, the importance of establishing and adhering to guidelines that lend structure and purpose to the group, and the importance of committing to "win-win" decisions regarding group matters. Research, in fact, suggests that direct instruction or teaching regarding group processes tends to facilitate a group's development during its early stages (Corey & Corey, 2002; Dies, 1983).

Leaders must also intervene to address the initial concerns of members. In early sessions members will probably be tentative about expressing what they hope to get from the group. Most also experience fear and apprehension regarding the group experience. They worry about many things: how they will be perceived by other members, whether they will be pressured to talk, whether they will be misunderstood or look foolish, whether they will be at risk of verbal attack, and whether they want to go through a change process at all. The leader may address and allay these anxieties by asking all members to share their feelings about coming to the initial group session. For example, the leader might ask members to rate their feelings about being present in the group at that moment on a scale of 1 to 10, where 1 represents "I don't want to be here" and 10 represents "I'm completely at ease with being in the group." The leader could then ask members to explain the reasons for their ratings.

In focusing on members' fears, leaders need to draw out all members' feelings and reactions, validate the importance of their fully disclosing feelings, and emphasize the need for the group to be a safe place in which such issues can be expressed openly. Finally, leaders should elicit suggestions for a group structure that will address member fears, out of which may flow the formulation of relevant group guidelines.

Leaders can measure the progress of a new group in addressing initial member concerns by administering a questionnaire developed by Rose (1989). This instrument contains items to which members can respond by circling a point on a scale. Examples of items include the following:

- How useful was today's session for you?

- Describe your involvement in today's session.

- Rate the extent of your self-disclosure of relevant information about yourself or your problem.

- How important to you were the problems or situations you discussed (or others discussed) in the group today?

- Circle all the words that best describe you at today's session (e.g., excited, bored, depressed, interested, comfortable).

- How satisfied were you with today's session?

In initial sessions, facilitators must repeatedly review basic information regarding the group's purpose, the manner in which the group will be conducted, and its ground rules. Reid (1991) emphasizes that none of this information should surprise members. However, reiteration is necessary because "in the beginning, members are often so preoccupied that they do not comprehend the group's purpose, their particular role, the worker's role, and what will be expected of them" (1991, p. 205). Making sure that all members are "on the same page" helps to prevent these issues from erupting later in the life of the group.

In preliminary interviews, members contract with the leader for general goals they would like to achieve. In the initial group sessions, the leader must then blend these individual goals with the group's collective goals. Along the way, the binding contract expands from a reciprocal one between leader and individuals to a mutual contract between individuals and group. In the first meeting, the leader engages "all persons present in a discussion that establishes a group way of functioning yet allows each person's initial objectives to be addressed" (Henry, 1992, p. 80). Henry, who views finding common ground as "an unfolding process,"

utilizes what she calls a "Goal Questionnaire" to facilitate formulation of the mutual contract. On this questionnaire are two questions to which members respond in writing:

1. Why do you think all of you are here together?

2. What are you going to try to accomplish together?

Discussion of responses gives the group a beginning point from which to proceed (Henry, 1992).

In the contractual process of initial sessions, leaders also aid members to refine their general goals. Corey and Corey (2002, pp. 139–140) provide examples that illustrate the role of the leader in seeking concreteness to clarify global goals:

Member: I want to get in touch with my feelings.

Leader: What kind of feelings are you having difficulty with?

Member: I want to work on my anger.

Leader: With whom in your life are you angry? What do you most want to say?

The leader also keeps accomplishment of goals at the forefront of the group's work. Through bibliotherapy, journaling, and mindfulness, members can read, write, and reflect on the themes they are addressing and the insights they have achieved during and between group sessions (Corey, 1990). Session time may be allocated for discussing these insights, thereby reinforcing the value of continuing work between sessions.

Paying attention to the way each session opens and concludes is important for maximizing member productivity and satisfaction. Corey and Corey (2002) encourage leaders to draw from the following procedures in opening meetings:

1. Give members a brief opportunity to say what they want from the upcoming session.

2. Invite members to share their accomplishments since the last session.

3. Elicit feedback regarding the group's last session and give any reflections you have of the session.

To bring meetings to a close, Corey and Corey (2002) emphasize the need to summarize and integrate the group experience by following these procedures:

1. Ask members what it was like for them to be in the group today.

2. Invite members to identify briefly what they're learning about themselves through their experience in the group. Are they getting what they want? If not, what would they be willing to do to get it?

3. Ask members whether there are any topics, questions, or problems they would like to explore in the next session.

4. Ask members to indicate what they would be willing to do outside of the session to practice new skills.

Incorporating group rituals into the structure of sessions increases the continuity that flows from meeting to meeting. Examples include check-in as a ritual to start each session, structured refreshment breaks, and closing meditations or readings (Subramian, Hernandez, & Martinez, 1995). Such continuity heightens the transfer of insights and new behaviors from the group session into daily life.

Power and Control Stage

In stage 2 of group development, the group enters a period in which its dynamics, tone, and atmosphere are often conflict-ridden, although some groups may need encouragement to address underlying conflicts that threaten the health of the group (Schiller, 1997). Groups may be beset by problems in dealing with divisions among individuals and subgroups; complaints and unrest over group goals, processes, and structure; and challenges to leadership. At the same time, the group is trying out its capacity to manage its own affairs. The leader is responsible for guiding the group through this stormy period so that it remains intact and demonstrates an emerging capacity to cope with individual differences and to manage its own governance. Leaders can employ several strategies in carrying out this responsibility: minimize changes, encourage balanced feedback, increase effective communication, and develop therapeutic group norms.

Minimize Changes

During the "power and control" stage, groups with a closed format are particularly susceptible to inner and outer stressors such as a change of leader, a move to a new meeting place, the addition or loss of members, or a change in the meeting time. Traumatic events such as a runaway, a death, an incidence of physical violence in an institutional setting, or acutely disturbing political or natural events at the community or national level may also significantly affect a group at this stage.

Although such changes or events can be upsetting to a group at any stage of development, they are particularly difficult to manage in stage 2. At this point, members have not yet become invested in the group to an appreciable extent and thus may become easily disenchanted. Adding new members or changing the group's leader is particularly stressful, causing members to raise their defenses because there are risks involved in revealing themselves when either the leader or a member is an unknown entity. The loss of a leader can also prove inordinately traumatic to members who have difficulty investing in relationships, affirming their stance that trusting others just brings disappointment.

In addition, making a significant change in the group structure without group involvement may cause members to conclude that the leader or agency has disregard for the impact of such decisions on the group and that the group is not important. Although changes are sometimes unavoidable, it behooves leaders to keep them to a minimum, to prepare members in advance whenever possible, and to aid them to "work through" their feelings when change is necessary.

Encourage Balanced Feedback

In stage 2 of group development, leaders must ensure that feedback is balanced. As they observe that group members are tentatively moving into their first authentic encounters, leaders should intervene in negative interactions to draw the group's attention to the need to provide balanced feedback. They thus remind members of the provision in the contract for focusing on positives as well as negatives. The following excerpt from an early group session with adult members illustrates this point.

Gary [*to Wayne, in irritated voice*]: Why do you keep grilling me with questions like that? I feel like I'm being interrogated.

Wayne: I didn't know I was coming across like that. Frankly, I just wanted to get to know you better.

Leader [*to Wayne*]: You said in the first session that you'd like to use the group as a way of getting feedback about how you come across to others. I'm wondering if this might be a time for that?

Wayne: Yeah. I don't know what's coming, but I really think I do need to know more about how you all see me. I was really surprised at what Gary said.

Leader [*to Wayne*]: Good. I can understand you may have reservations, but I'm also pleased that you're willing to take a risk this early in the group.

[*To group*] Because this is the group's first experience in giving feedback to members, I'd like to remind you of the contract not only to help members identify problems but also to share positive observations you may have. As you do so, I'd like you to personalize your statements. I'll help you do so.

Group members' first experiences in giving feedback to one another are crucial in setting the tone for all that follows in the group. By guiding members' first cautious efforts to drop their facades and to engage at an intimate level, the leader enables the group to experience success and incorporate attention to positives as a part of its character. As individuals come to trust that the group will attend to positives as well as negatives, they will often increase their level of participation and take the initiative in soliciting group feedback.

In addition to encouraging positive feedback for individuals, leaders can elicit examples of behaviors observed during a session that support the group's work in accomplishing its tasks. Such behaviors may include being willing to participate in discussions, to answer questions, and to risk revealing oneself; showing support to others; speaking in turn; giving full attention to the task at hand; accepting differing values, beliefs, and opinions; and recognizing significant individual and group breakthroughs. The

leader can also highlight the *absence* of destructive behaviors that might have occurred earlier (e.g., whispering, fidgeting, introducing tangential topics, dominating, or verbally and physically pestering other members).

In addition, the leader must assist members to hear, acknowledge, and accept positive feedback, as illustrated in the following example:

Kim [*to Pat*]: I know you get discouraged sometimes, but I admire the fact you can manage four children by yourself and still work. I don't think I could ever manage that in a million years.

Pat: I don't always manage it. Actually, I don't do near enough for my children.

Leader: I hear you saying, Pat, that you feel inadequate as a mother—and I'll ask you in a moment whether you'd like to return to those feelings—but right now would you reflect on what you just did?

Pat: I guess I blew off Kim's compliment. I didn't feel I deserved it.

Leader: I wonder if others of you have experienced the same feeling when someone has told you something positive.

The last response broadens the focus to include the experience of other group members, which may lead into a discussion of the difficulties that individuals sometimes encounter in accepting and internalizing positive feedback. The leader may also wish to help individuals or the entire group to identify dysfunctional cognitive patterns that underlie their discomfort in receiving positive messages (e.g., "I have to do things perfectly" or "If they knew me better, they'd realize I'm no good"). Identifying the disconfirming cognitions represents a first step toward replacing them with more accepting messages ("I do a good job considering all I have responsibility for" or "My group sees another side of me that I don't let myself acknowledge").

Increase Effective Communication

Achieving success during the "power and control" phase requires moment-by-moment interventions to increase the chances of effective communication. Previous chapters have described five basic relationship skills that, when possessed by clients, significantly increase their personal efficacy and ability to create satisfying relationships:

- Positive feedback
- Empathic listening (the receiver skill)
- Authentic responding (the sender skill)
- Problem solving and decision making
- Requesting (a skill for expressing one's needs)

Other facets of communication enable members to relate effectively as a group, such as taking turns in talking; learning how to explore problems before offering solutions; speaking for themselves, not others; and speaking directly to the person for whom the message is intended. In addition, members can learn to distinguish between effective and ineffective ways of responding and can include improving their communication repertoire as one of their individual goals for work.

Leaders increase the probability that members will adopt these effective communication skills by heavily utilizing and modeling these skills themselves. In addition, leaders aid the acquisition of skills by assuming the role of "coach" and intervening to shape the display of communications in the group, as illustrated in the following examples:

- [*Eliminating negative communications*] "I'd like you to shy away from labeling, judging, lecturing, criticism, sarcasm, 'shoulds' and 'oughts,' and the words 'always' and 'never.' As we discussed in our group contract, try to give self-reports rather than indirect messages that put down or judge another person."

- [*Personalizing messages*] "That was an example of a 'you' message. I'd like you to try again, this time by starting out with the pronoun 'I.' Try to identify your feelings, or what you want or need."

- [*Talking in turn*] "Right now, several of you are speaking at the same time. Try to hold to the guideline that we all speak in turn. Your observations are too important to miss."

- [*Speaking directly to each other*] "Right now, you're speaking to the group, but I think your message is meant for Fred. If so, then it would be better to talk directly to him."

- [*Exploratory questions*] "Switching from closed- to open-ended questions right now could help Liz to tell her story in her own way." (The leader explains the difference between these two modes of questioning.)

- [*Listening*] "Try to really hear what she's saying. Help her to let out her feelings and to get to the source of the problem."

- [*Problem exploration versus problem solving*] "When the group offers advice too quickly, folks can't share their deeper-level feelings or reveal a problem in its entirety. We may need to allow Richard five to ten minutes to share his concerns before the group offers any observations. The timing of advice is critical as we try to help members share and solve problems."

- [*Authenticity*] "Could you take a risk and tell the group what you're feeling at this very moment? I can see you choking up, and I think it would be good for the group to know what you're experiencing."

- [*Requesting*] "You've just made a complaint about the group. On the flip side of any complaint is a request. Tell the group what would help. Make a request."

Intervening moment by moment to shape the communications of members, as in the instances illustrated here, increases the therapeutic potential of a group.

Stage 2 of group development may also present a challenge when the group has co-leadership. The presence of two leaders may increase members' defensiveness as they seek to erect boundaries that protect them from the influence presented by two leaders. Members may also attempt to split the leaders by exploiting disagreements or differences between them or by affiliating with one leader and working against the other. Clarity of purpose, preparation for these maneuvers, and strong communication can help co-leaders resist these efforts when they emerge (Nosko & Wallace, 1997).

Create Therapeutic Norms

As mentioned earlier, leaders must be concerned about the nature of the norms that evolve in the group. Many of the group patterns form in the "power and control" stage. The leader can intervene then to shape the power structure, the stylistic communications of the group, and the ways in which the group chooses to negotiate and solve problems.

In shaping the group's therapeutic norms, leaders need to intervene, for example, in the following instances:

- When socializing or distracting behavior substantially interferes with the group's task

- When one or more members monopolize the group's airtime

- When one or more members are "out of step" with the group process and/or experience strong feelings such as hurt, anger, disgust, disappointment, or disapproval

- When several members or the entire group begin to talk about one member

- When a member's behavior is incompatible with the governing guidelines set by the group

- When participants intellectualize about emotion-laden material

- When one or more members display hostility through jokes, sarcasm, or criticism, or when they interrogate, scapegoat, or gang up on a single member

- When the group offers advice or suggestions without first encouraging a member to fully explore a problem

- When there is silence or withdrawal by one or more members or the group itself seems to be "shut down"

- When a member adopts a "co-leader" role

When problems such as these emerge, the leader must focus the group's attention on what is occurring in the "here and now." Leaders may simply document what they see by describing specific behaviors or the progression of events that have occurred and then request group input. Once the group focuses on the problem, the leader should facilitate discussion and problem solving rather than take decisive action on his or her own. Ultimately, the responsibility for resolution needs to rest with the group.

In regard to turning issues back to the group, Henry notes:

> When the members are vying for ownership of the group, the wisest intervention for the worker is to join their struggle and to put issues and decisions back to them. The worker does not wholly give up her or his power, but holds back from what had previously been a more directive and active performance. (1992, p. 148)

However, as Henry notes, at the end of a particularly conflict-filled episode or session, leaders need to intervene with a proposal to process what has occurred and to lead that processing. In such instances, leaders do not simply turn issues back to the group but opt, in the interest of closure and resolution, to "clarify what information people carry away from the confrontation, and to see what level of discomfort people are experiencing" (1992, p. 151).

Although leaders need to avoid reaching premature closure on heated issues in a group, they must intervene immediately to refocus the process when group members criticize, label, or "cut down" others, or when they argue among themselves. Leaders may assume—incorrectly—that letting members verbally "fight it out" when they have conflicts is cathartic or helpful. In fact, ample research indicates that aggression begets aggression and that not intervening in conflict merely encourages members to continue venting their anger in the same fashion. A leader's passive stance could allow conflict to escalate to the point that it turns into physical fighting. In instances of serious disruption, a leader's lack of intervention may "prove" to members who are scrutinizing the leader's behavior that it is dangerous to take risks in the group because the leader will not protect them (Smokowski, Rose, & Bacallao, 2001).

It is vital that leaders intervene assertively when dysfunctional group processes arise. Otherwise, they will be in a "one-down" position in the group and lose their ability to effect change. Leaders must be willing to respond decisively when significant group disruption occurs, using physical and verbal measures as needed, such as clapping their hands loudly, standing up, speaking louder than group members, or putting themselves between members who are arguing.

Interventions should generally focus on group-related matters (rather than on individual attitudes or behaviors), because it is rare that the destructive or self-defeating behavior of an individual or subset will not affect the entire system. In fact, some problematic behaviors may be fostered or reinforced by the group as a whole. Focusing interventions on a pair, a trio, a foursome, or the group also avoids singling out one person or inadvertently "siding" with one segment of clients over others.

Consider, for instance, the following leader intervention in an adolescent group: "Mark and Jeannie, you're whispering again and interrupting the group. We need your attention." This message places the responsibility for the distracting behavior solely upon the two members and does not take into account what is happening with the group. In this instance, the leader's message is more likely to reinforce negative behavior than to encourage positive change for the following reasons:

- It may polarize the group by aligning the leader with members who are irritated by this behavior ("the good guys") and against the two offending members ("the bad guys").

- The leader's solution ("We need your attention") circumvents group handling or problem solving of the matter.

- The leader's blunt intervention fails to attend to the message inherent in the problem behavior: "This group does not meet our needs at the moment." In fact, this view may be shared but not expressed by other members.

A guideline to formulating interventions that confront dysfunctional behavior is that the behavior must be analyzed in the context of the group process, with the leader considering how such behavior affects and is affected by group members. This approach is illustrated by the following message to the same situation:

Leader: I'm concerned about what is happening right now. Several of you are not participating; some of you are whispering; one of you is writing notes; a few of you are involved in the discussion. As individuals, you appear to be at different places with the group, and I'd like to check out what each of you is experiencing right now.

This message focuses on all group members, neutrally describes behavior that is occurring, and encourages the group process. By not imposing a solution on the group, the leader assumes a facilitative rather than an authoritarian role; the latter is the "kiss of death" for productive group discussion.

Intimacy and Differentiation Stages

Stages 3 ("intimacy") and 4 ("differentiation") of group development constitute the group's working phase. In the initial stages of a group's evolution, the critical issues at stake focused on trust versus mistrust, the struggle for power, and self-focus versus focus on others. In the working phase, however, issues shift to those of disclosure versus anonymity, honesty versus game playing, spontaneity versus control, acceptance versus rejection, cohesion versus fragmentation, and responsibility versus blaming (Corey & Corey, 2002).

In the working phase, leaders continue to promote conditions that aid members to make healthy choices in resolving issues by straightforwardly addressing and resolving conflict, openly disclosing personal problems, taking responsibility for their problems, and making pro-group choices. Thanks to the relaxed stance that characterizes this phase, leaders have more opportunities to intensify therapeutic group conditions. They may focus on refining feedback processes—for example, coaching members to give immediate feedback, to make such feedback specific rather than global, to render feedback in nonjudgmental ways, and to give feedback regarding strengths as well as problem behaviors (Corey & Corey, 2002).

Leaders can also enhance individual and group growth by focusing on the universality of underlying issues, feelings, and needs that members seem to share:

> The circumstances leading to hurt and disappointment may be very different from person to person or from culture to culture. But the resulting emotions have a universal quality. Although we may not speak the same language or come from the same society, we are connected through our

feelings of joy and pain. It is when group members no longer get lost in the details of daily experiences and instead share their deeper struggles with these universal human themes that a group is most cohesive. (Corey & Corey, 1992, p. 209)

Common themes identified by Corey and Corey include

fears of rejection, feelings of loneliness and abandonment, feeling of inferiority and failure to live up to others' expectations, painful memories, guilt and remorse over what they have and have not done, discovery that their worst enemy lives within them, need for and fear of intimacy, feelings about sexual identity and sexual performance, and unfinished business with their parents. (1992, p. 210)

This list is not exhaustive, note Corey and Corey, but "merely a sample of the universal human issues that participants recognize and explore with each other as the group progresses" (p. 210).

During these middle phases of group development, group members can participate in a number of activities to work on individual and commonly held goals. Such activities may reduce stress and encourage pleasure and creativity; assist the leader in assessment as members are observed while "doing" rather than "saying"; facilitate communication, problem solving, and rapport among members; and help members develop skills and competence in decision making (Northen & Kurland, 2001). Nevil, Beatty, and Moxley (1997) suggest a variety of structured activities and socialization games that can be employed to improve interpersonal skills, increase social awareness, and enhance pro-social competence. While intended for use with persons with disabilities, many of these exercises can be adapted for use with a variety of populations. Other authors note their effectiveness with diverse populations, such as those of Hispanic heritage (Delgado, 1983) and Native Americans (Edwards, Edwards, Davies, & Eddy, 1987).

One element of a structured program targeting delinquency reduction consists of multifamily group meetings in which 8 to 10 families meet for eight weekly sessions lasting 2-1/2 hours each. In the meetings, family members sit together at designated tables, share a meal, and engage in "structured, fun, interactive" (McDonald, 2002, p. 719)

activities that enhance communication skills, strengthen relationships, and facilitate networking among the families.

While art therapy and other expressive techniques generally require specialized training, reviewing resources such as Ross (1997) and Rose (1998) can acquaint social workers with the principles for applying these techniques in groups to address issues related to aggressive behavior, self-esteem, body image, and awareness of emotions. With all groups, the leader must take the group's purpose, stage of development, and member characteristics into account when selecting and implementing an experiential exercise or activity (Wright, 1999).

In the working phase, leaders also support a continuing trend toward differentiation, in which members establish their uniqueness and separateness from others. Leaders do not create these expressions of differences but rather stimulate or advance them. For example, the leader may note when a member reveals

a heretofore hidden talent, or access to a resource that was previously believed inaccessible, or possession of a needed skill or perspective. A member may articulate a previously unspoken need, or offer an interpretation not thought of by the others, or pose a question that catalyzes or synthesizes a piece of the group's work. (Henry, 1992, p. 183)

The working phase is a time of intensive focus on achieving members' goals. Much of the group's work during this phase is devoted to carrying out contracts developed in the group's initial sessions. Members may have lost sight of their individual goals, so a major leadership role involves confirming goals periodically and promoting organized and systematic efforts to work on them.

The leader assumes the ongoing responsibility of monitoring the time allocated to each member to work on goals. Toseland and Rivas (2001) suggest that the leader help each member to work in turn. If a group spends considerable time aiding one member to achieve his or her individual goals, the leader should generalize the concepts developed in this effort to other members so that everyone benefits. The leader should also encourage participants to share relevant personal experiences with the member receiving help, thus establishing a norm for mutual aid. In addition, he or she should check on the progress of members who did not receive due attention and encourage their participation in the next session.

Finally, the leader should establish a systematic method of monitoring treatment goals and tasks in sessions. Without such procedures, monitoring may be haphazard and focus on only those members who are more assertive and highly involved; members who are less assertive or resistant will not receive the same attention. Without systematic monitoring, tasks to be completed between sessions may not receive the proper follow-up. As Toseland and Rivas (2001) suggest, group members may become frustrated when they have completed a task between sessions and have no opportunity to report on the results. The expectation of a weekly progress report helps increase motivation to work toward goals between sessions, reduces the necessity of reminding members of their contract agreements, and aids them in gaining a sense of independence and accomplishment.

In the working phase, leaders continue to encourage members to analyze the rationality of their thoughts and beliefs that maintain or exacerbate dysfunctional behaviors. According to Toseland and Rivas (2001), group members may

> (1) overgeneralize from an event, (2) selectively focus on portions of an event, (3) take too much responsibility for events that are beyond their control, (4) think of the worst possible consequence of future events, (5) engage in either/or dichotomous thinking, and (6) assume that because certain events have led to particular consequences in the past they will automatically lead to the same consequences if they reoccur in the future. (p. 288)[3]

Termination Stage

Termination is a difficult stage for members who have invested heavily in the group; have experienced intensive support, encouragement, and understanding; and have received effective aid for their problems. Leaders must be sensitive to the mixed feelings engendered by termination and carefully intervene to assist the group to come to an effective close. Chapter 19 identifies significant termination issues and change-maintenance

strategies that may be utilized with clients in facilitating termination and generalizing changes to the outside world. Here, we address aspects of the leader's role that are specific to facilitating planned endings in groups.

Leaders may assist group members in completing their "commencement" proceedings (Mahler, 1969) by adopting strategies such as the following:

- Ensure that the issues and concerns worked on by the group resemble those that members will encounter outside the group. Assure that the group is a place where members get honest feedback about how their behavior is likely to be received outside the group and a setting where they may obtain help in coping with those reactions (Toseland & Rivas, 2001).

- Refer to a variety of situations and settings throughout the group experience to aid members to practice and acquire skills, thereby better preparing them for the multifaceted situations they will inevitably encounter outside the group (Toseland & Rivas, 2001).

- Facilitate members' discussion of how they will respond to possible setbacks in an unsympathetic environment. Build member confidence in existing coping skills and abilities to solve problems independently. Also, teach therapeutic principles that underlie intervention methods, such as those inherent in assertiveness, effective communication, or problem solving (Toseland & Rivas, 2001).

- Share your reactions to endings as a way of helping members to identify their own conflicted feelings and any sense of abandonment, anger, sadness, or loss.

- Reinforce members' positive feelings about themselves and the group, including the potency that comes from realizing that they are capable of accomplishing goals and assuming responsibility for their own lives; the sense of satisfaction, pride, and usefulness in being able to help others; and the sense of growth and of accomplishment that comes from successfully completing the group experience (Lieberman & Borman, 1979; Toseland & Rivas, 2001).

- Increase review and integration of learning by helping members to put into words what has transpired between themselves and the group from the first to the final session and what they have learned about themselves and others. Solicit information about what members were satisfied and unsatisfied with in the group and ways in which sessions could have had greater impact. Ask members to spontaneously recall moments of conflict and pain as well as moments of closeness, warmth, humor, and joy in the group (Corey & Corey, 1992).

- Several sessions before termination, suggest that members consider using the remaining time to complete their own agenda. For example, ask, "If this were the last session, how would you feel about what you have done, and what would you wish you had done differently?" (Corey & Corey, 2002, p. 261).

- Facilitate the completion of unfinished business between members. One technique involves an exercise in which each person, in turn, says in a few short phrases, "What I really liked was the way you . . . (supply a specific behavior exchanged between the persons, such as 'always gave me credit when I could finally say something that was hard for me to say')," and then, "But I wish we . . . (supplying a specific wish for a behavioral exchange between the two persons that did not occur, such as 'had made more opportunities to talk to each other more directly')"(Henry, 1992, p. 124). Note that this and other closure exercises should not be used to generate new issues but rather to bring resolution to the present situation.

- Encourage members to identify areas for future work once the group concludes. Consider asking members to formulate their own individual change contracts, which may be referred to once the group ends, and invite each member to review his or her contract with the group (Corey & Corey, 2002).

- Engage individual members in relating how they have perceived themselves in the group, what the group has meant to them, and how they have grown. Ask the other members to give feedback regarding how they have perceived and felt about each person, including measured feedback that helps members strengthen the perceptions that they gained during the course of the group (e.g., "One of the things I like best about you is . . .," "One way I see you blocking your strengths is . . .," or "A few things that I hope you'll remember are . . .") (Corey, 1990, p. 512).

- Use evaluative measures to determine the effectiveness of the group and the leader's interventions. Such measures have the following benefits: (1) They address the leader's professional concerns about the specific effects of interventions; (2) they help workers improve their leadership skills; (3) they demonstrate the group's efficacy to agencies or funding sources; (4) they help leaders assess individual members' and the group's progress in accomplishing agreed-upon objectives; (5) they allow members to express their satisfactions and dissatisfactions with the group; and (6) they help leaders develop knowledge that can be generalized to future groups and other leaders (Reid, 1991; Toseland & Rivas, 2001).

NEW DEVELOPMENTS IN SOCIAL WORK WITH GROUPS

Contemporary developments in group work include increased attention to evaluating groups' effectiveness, the application of group techniques to new populations and new problem areas, and the use of technology in the delivery of group work services. We will address each in turn.

Like other areas of social work practice, group interventions face increased scrutiny seeking to determine the efficacy of certain processes and the outcomes they can obtain. Tolman and Molidor's (1994) review of research on social work with groups indicates that group work evaluation is growing ever more sophisticated and that multiple measures are being employed to determine group efficacy. For example, in addition to undertaking evaluation at the termination phase, more than one-third of the groups studied by Tolman and Molidor (1994) used follow-up measures to determine whether earlier gains had been maintained. These authors note, however, that while it is important to examine outcomes, the evaluative challenge lies in isolating those elements of group process that actually contributed to those outcomes.

Increasingly, curricula for group interventions include measurement instruments to assist in understanding both baseline and outcome measures. For example, in groups consisting of adolescents and pre-teens, Rose (1998) suggests using a variety of methods and sources of data, including standardized ratings by parents and teachers; self-monitoring or self-reports through checklists, logs, questionnaires, or sentence completion; observation of in-group behavior; performance during role-plays or simulations; sociometric evaluations; goal attainment scaling; and knowledge tests. Anderson-Butcher, Khairallah, and Race-Bigelow (2004) suggest that qualitative interviews may be used to ascertain client outcomes and to identify the characteristics of effective self-help groups. Magen's (2004) review of measurement issues in group evaluation offers guidance for effective selection of outcome and process measures.

At termination, members and the leader may all record their satisfaction with the group and their sense of its effectiveness. Members may respond to open-ended questions or a structured checklist, either of which may inquire about the changes the group brought about in the participant's life or relationships, the techniques used that had the greatest and least impact, perceptions of the leader, and so on (Corey, Corey, Callanan, & Russell, 2004). These authors also recommend that the leader keep a journal to evaluate group progress over time, note his or her reactions at various points, keep track of techniques or materials used and the perceived outcomes, and share self-insights that emerged during the life of the group.

Group services are also being applied to novel populations and problems. For example, building on the success of groups with gay and lesbian adolescents and with middle-aged persons in the coming-out process, Getzel (1998) notes that life review and socialization groups may serve as a promising resource for elder GLBT persons. Others note that groups can be effective in supporting

compliance with other forms of care and reducing treatment dropouts. These goals are met as members share feelings about their illnesses and medications, offer mutual aid, empathize with one another's experiences and side effects, break through isolation and grief, and generate strategies for self-care (Miller & Mason, 2001).

There is also increased interest in the use of social work groups for empowerment. For example, Lewis (1991) notes the influences of feminist theory and liberation theology as resources for empowerment-focused social group work. Feminist theory is egalitarian, is participatory, and validates each person's life experiences in context. By contrast, liberation theology focuses on the participation in economic and political action by those persons who are most vulnerable to injustice (Lewis, 1991). For example, Cox has described how female welfare recipients have begun to advocate for themselves with social services and other agencies through participation in empowerment-oriented groups (1991).

As new theories of change and new treatment modalities emerge, they will also be applied to work with groups. For example, evolving solution-focused interventions have been applied to groups in an array of situations, including recovery from sexual abuse, improving parenting skills, and resolving symptoms of anxiety and depression (Metcalf, 1998). Multifamily groups, composed of family members who share a common concern, have proved useful for addressing severe and persistent psychiatric disorders (McFarlane, 2002) and the risk for child abuse and neglect (Burford & Pennell, 2004; Meezan & O'Keefe, 1998), among other issues (Vakalah & Khajak, 2000).

In applying group work concepts to practice in rural areas, Gumpert and Saltman (1998) identified several challenges that warrant leaders' attention:

- Cultural factors—for example, distrust of confidentiality assurances, strong values of self-reliance, and suspicion of outsiders

- Geographic factors—for example, distance, weather and travel conditions, and difficulty finding a convenient location

- Demographic factors—for example, insufficient numbers of individuals with similar difficulties, resource problems such as the lack of public transportation, insufficient child care, and too few potential group leaders

Attention is also turning to the application of group work concepts to groups that meet only for a single session. For example, in interdisciplinary case meetings, membership shifts based on which professionals are involved with the particular case. In critical incident debriefing groups, professions intervene to assist people affected by a traumatic event—for example, after a workplace shooting (Reynolds & Jones, 1996). Some concepts used in the single-session groups—purpose, contracting, and worker roles—are variations on those used in groups of longer duration. Others—composition, member roles, norms, and group stages—may be less germane to single-session groups.

As described in Chapter 11, social workers are beginning to explore technological advances that could potentially enhance the delivery of service to clients through groups. Persons who are homebound or who find attendance at agency settings difficult may be able to experience the support and benefit of groups through the medium of telephone, e-mail, or the Internet (Harris, 1999; Hollander, 2001). Online group facilitators must assure through informed consent that members understand the risks and benefits of such a model. The nature of typed, asynchronous communication means that members have more control and time for reflection as they craft their responses. In addition, they can participate in the virtual group at their convenience (Fingeld, 2000) and with a high degree of anonymity (Meier, 2002). However, participation may be stymied by Internet provider system problems and by trust issues, especially with "lurkers" (those who read e-mail but do not post to the group) and with participants' actual level of engagement with the process.

Leaders who work with these new technologies must be more active in guiding the process and drawing out implications for feelings and tone that are masked by the communication medium. This effort may require development of conventions or signals for indicating emotions in content (Schopler, Galinsky, & Abell, 1997). As access to such media increases, it behooves social workers to take advantage of the emerging media to reach groups who cannot be reached by conventional means, as well as those individuals who may be reluctant to participate in face-to-face meetings.

WORK WITH TASK GROUPS

As described earlier, a significant aspect of professional social work practice is performance in task and work groups. In contrast to treatment groups, task groups try to accomplish a purpose, produce a product, or develop policies. You are likely to participate in task groups throughout your career, starting with student group projects, continuing as a staff member, and eventually serving as a leader of such groups in your practice. As with treatment groups, task groups may have open or closed membership, and they may be time-limited or open-ended. Members take on formal and informal roles, and the execution of these roles can facilitate or impede the group's success.

Task groups may be composed of professionals, community members, clients, or a mixture of these parties, depending on the group's purpose and the way that members are recruited and assigned. Congress and Lynn (1997) discuss the complexities that can arise in community-based task groups, particularly when the group plans to undertake advocacy initiatives, such as striking against a landlord for better living conditions or mobilizing to address concerns with a school system. They suggest six considerations for ethical practice under these circumstances:

1. Social workers should understand their values and personal biases and the way these interface with the values and biases of the group as a whole.

2. They should explicitly discuss confidentiality expectations and agree to abide by them.

3. They should emphasize the adoption of constructive group norms.

4. They should clearly inform members about the potential risks and benefits of group participation.

5. They should help members differentiate their personal needs from collective, community needs.

6. They should "operationalize values of democracy and self-determination in task group process" (Congress & Lynn, 1997, p. 72).

Effective task groups do not rely solely on the skills of the formal group leader. For example, as members of such groups, social workers are often effective participants in interdisciplinary teams thanks to their knowledge of group processes (Abramson, 2002). They can offer particular assistance in task groups in identifying which needs the group can meet, getting members involved, and paying attention to stages of development (including managing conflict during each stage).

Problem Identification

Leaders can help groups effectively identify problems that the group is capable of solving, that are within the group's domain, and that, among the many problems that could potentially be chosen, would provide a meaningful focus. During this process, the leader should help the group avoid responding prematurely with solutions before the problem is well defined. In defining appropriate problems and goals, the group can employ techniques such as brainstorming and nominal group techniques to consider an array of possibilities before selecting a focus. *Brainstorming* involves generating and expressing a variety of opinions without evaluating them. In the *nominal group* technique, members first privately list potential problems. The group then takes one potential problem from each member until all are listed. Finally, it evaluates and ranks those potential problems as a group (Toseland & Rivas, 2001).

Groups must also determine the strategies that will support effective decision making. Some procedures may be prescribed. For example, the charter of the group may require certain periods for commentary, use of clearly specified rules on who can vote, and adherence to Robert's Rules of Order. Other groups may determine their own norms, such as decision by consensus or majority rule (Toseland & Rivas, 2001).

Getting Members Involved

Task group membership may be voluntary (a neighborhood task force on crime), appointed (a coalition consisting of representatives of homeless shelters), elected (a board of directors), or determined by roles (an interdisciplinary team consisting of all professionals serving a particular family). To the maximum extent possible, the membership should possess the skills and resources needed to accomplish the purpose for which the group was convened. For example, if a committee concerned about crime found that no law enforcement personnel were members, it might seek out someone to fill that niche. As with therapeutic groups, those convening task groups should be alert to the characteristics of potential members and ensure that no member will be an isolate or an outlier. This consideration is particularly important when service consumers or their family members fill representative roles in a group consisting largely of professionals and service providers. Multiple representatives from consumer or family organizations should be included in committee membership, thereby ensuring that they are empowered and that their positions move beyond a token role.

All members of the group need to have a clear understanding of the functions of the group, to have input into the agenda and decision making. Each session or meeting should be carefully planned and designed to take advantage of the time and talents available (Tropman & Morningstar, 1995). Roles can be assigned such that members will have to depend on each other to get the work of the group accomplished (Toseland & Rivas, 2001). Background papers often need to be circulated to get all members to the appropriate level of information. It is often helpful to conduct the brainstorming or ice-breaking exercises in small groups to facilitate member interaction. Recognition of the particular skills, experiences, and perspectives that different members bring can also facilitate more confident sharing by new members.

Enhancing Awareness of Stages of Development

The stages of group development observed in treatment settings will also occur in task groups, albeit not in a linear fashion. Instead, some issues will recur, taking the group back to revisit earlier stages. In the preaffiliation stage, individuals enter with varying hopes for the group because common goals have not yet been established.

Early identity development in the group may be affected by preexisting relationships among group members, who may know or work with each other in other capacities. Depending on the quality of these past experiences, friction may be carried over into the new group, or trust and comfort may facilitate rapid movement into the work of the group. In either case, it is essential that individuals with existing relationships not form subgroups, as these splinter groups may diminish the comfort and cohesion of all members of the group.

The "power and control" phase (stage 2) in task groups often features competition over which programs or ideas the group will adopt. Conflict about ideas is to be expected—indeed, it should be encouraged if options are to be generated and thoroughly explored. All too often, task groups avoid conflict by evading thorny issues, sometimes even tabling an issue despite the availability of enough facts to make a decision. Establishing norms in which differing options are sought and evaluated on their own merits will aid the group in accomplishing its objectives. Leaders should attempt to stimulate idea-related conflict while managing and controlling personality-related conflict. Failure to achieve this balance may result in the marginalization of potential contributors and a less complete product. Without such healthy conflict, there is always the danger of "group-think," a condition in which alternative views or options are not expressed or taken seriously. Leaders (and members) can assist others to express the rationale behind particular opinions, clarifying what information needs to be developed to answer questions raised in the course of the conflict.

Group leaders and members can use the communication skills described earlier in this book to reframe communications, thereby making them understandable to all parties, as well as to reflect, probe, seek concreteness, and summarize what is being heard. Facilitators can contribute to the creation of a productive working atmosphere by conveying that each member has something to contribute and by maintaining civility such that no member—or his or her ideas—is allowed to be degraded (Toseland & Rivas, 2001).

Termination in task groups may occur when individual members leave or when the group disbands. "Commencement" in task groups is often overlooked, as members experience relief at the reduction of the demands on their time and their group-related responsibilities, and perhaps satisfaction in successfully achieving their goal. Nevertheless, it is important to evaluate what worked and what did not work well in the group process, to acknowledge the contributions of time and effort made be group members, and to share gratitude about the roles that facilitated group success.

Summary

This chapter focused on the knowledge and skills you will need to effectively intervene in social work task and treatment groups. We focused on the stages of group development and the common member and group characteristics that arise with each phase, illustrating the leadership roles and skills necessary for an effective group experience. We applied those concepts to novel or emerging areas of group work, including practice in rural settings, online groups, and task groups with mixed membership of consumers and professionals. For groups to be successful, leaders must thoughtfully apply the concepts of group formation, and flexibly use their role and interventions to suit the needs of the individuals and the group as a whole, from inception to termination.

Internet Resources

See our companion website for hot links to some helpful URLs. Note that URLs are subject to change. We will endeavor to update the links on the companion website as much as possible.

You can find useful resources with InfoTrac College Edition by entering the keyword "group problem solving" to access a helpful article by Friedman. Other useful connections and information can be found at the Association for the Advancement of Group Work's website: *http://www.aaswg.org/*.

Related Online Content

Visit the *Direct Social Work Practice* companion website a *http://socialwork.wadsworth.com/hepworth7* for additional learning tools such as glossary terms, chapter outlines, InfoTrac College Edition keywords, relevant web links, and chapter practice quizzes.

Also, be sure to check out the Direct Practice Virtual Reader, where the authors have personally selected articles relevant to this chapter using Info-Marks.

Notes

1. We also refer you to Hartford (1971), Henry (1992), Corey and Corey (2002), Tuckman and Jensen (1977), and Yalom (1995) as sources from which we have drawn information to complement the Garland, Jones, and Kolodny model.

2. Reid (1991) has reviewed procedures for evaluating outcomes in groups, including group testimonials, content analysis of audio- or videotapes, sociometric analysis, self-rating instruments, and other subjective measures. We refer you to Reid (1991) and to Corey (1990) for further discussion of these evaluative measures.

3. Although it is beyond the scope of this chapter to provide details, techniques abound in the literature to address the preceding issues and other self-defeating client attitudes, including those found in Meichenbaum (1977), Mahoney (1974), and Burns (1980). Both Toseland and Rivas (2001) and Rose (1989) offer specific ways of altering cognitions within a group context.

CHAPTER 17

Additive Empathy, Interpretation, and Confrontation

CHAPTER OVERVIEW

Chapter 17 builds on the skills introduced in Chapters 5 and 6 to assist clients in achieving a deeper understanding of their own behavior, the behavior of others, and their options in exploring change. Appropriate timing for and uses of confrontation are presented as a means of gaining greater self-knowledge and assisting clients in making informed decisions about their potential consequences.

THE MEANING AND SIGNIFICANCE OF CLIENT SELF-AWARENESS

Self-awareness is a priceless ingredient generally acknowledged as essential to sound mental health. Humans have long known of the profound importance of self-awareness, as reflected by Socrates, the ancient Greek philosopher, in his often-quoted admonition, "Know thyself." Self-awareness is often sought by voluntary clients and is indispensable to the helping process they seek, particularly during the change-oriented phase. Individuals' efforts to solve problems and to change are effective only if they are properly directed, which in turn depends on accurate awareness of behaviors and circumstances that need to be changed. Indeed, many people experience incessant problems in daily living related to their lack of awareness of the forces that produce these problems.

As we employ the term, *self-awareness* refers largely to awareness of the various forces operating in the present. Social workers assist clients to expand their awareness of their needs or wants, motives, emotions, beliefs, and problematic behaviors, and of these items' impact on other people. We do *not* use self-awareness to refer to insight into the etiology of problems. As we noted in earlier chapters, people can and do change without achieving this type of insight. On occasion, brief excursions into the past may be productive and enlightening—for example, to determine which qualities attracted marital partners to each other, to identify factors that have contributed to sexual dysfunction, to assess the chronicity of problems, or to highlight previous successes. When making such brief excursions, however, it is important to relate the information elicited along the way to *present* work and *present* problems, emphasizing to clients that they can change the present. In other words, they can alter the current effects of history but not history itself.

Social workers have numerous tools at their disposal to assist clients to gain expanded self-awareness. Of these tools, additive empathy, interpretation, and confrontation are probably employed most extensively. This chapter defines these techniques, specifies indications for their use, presents guidelines for employing them effectively, and provides skill development exercises related to these tools.

521

ADDITIVE EMPATHY AND INTERPRETATION

By now, you should be well aware that empathy on the social worker's part is critical to the helping process. Earlier chapters examined uses of empathy in the initial phase of the helping process. During the action-oriented phase, additive levels of empathy serve to expand clients' self-awareness, to cushion the impact of confrontations (discussed later in this chapter), and to explore and resolve relational reactions and other obstacles to change (which is discussed at length in Chapter 18). Of course, social workers also continue to use reciprocal levels of empathy during the goal attainment phase because the purposes for which empathy was employed in the initial phase persist throughout the helping process. The difference is that additive levels of empathy are employed sparingly in the initial phase but occupy a prominent position during the action-oriented phase.

Additive empathic responses go somewhat beyond what clients have expressed and therefore require some degree of inference by social workers. Thus, these responses are moderately interpretive—that is, they interpret forces operating to produce feelings, cognitions, reactions, and behavioral patterns. Indeed, after an exhaustive study of research involving psychoanalysis, Luborsky and Spence (1978) concluded that interpretation, as employed by psychoanalysts, is basically the same as empathic communication.

Insight through *interpretation*, it should be noted, is the "supreme agent" in the hierarchy of therapeutic principles that are basic to psychoanalysis and closely related therapies. Proponents of several other theories (most notably, client-centered, Gestalt, and certain existential theories) have avoided the use of interpretation. Still others (Claiborn, 1982; Levy, 1963) maintain that interpretation is essential to the counseling process, regardless of the social worker's theoretical orientation, and that many behaviors of social workers (whether intentional or not) perform interpretive functions.

Semantic and conceptual confusion have contributed to the divergence in views. Additional writings have sharpened concepts and reduced vagueness and confusion. Based on Levy's (1963) conceptualization, Claiborn (1982) posits that interpretation, whatever the social worker's theoretical orientation, "presents the client with a viewpoint discrepant from the client's own, the function of which is to prepare or induce the client to change in accordance with that viewpoint" (p. 442). Viewed in this light, interpretation assists clients to view their problems from a different perspective, thereby opening up new possibilities for remedial courses of action. This generic view, which emphasizes a *discrepant viewpoint,* is sufficiently broad to encompass many change-oriented techniques identified in different theories, including refraining (Watzlawick, Weakland, & Fisch, 1974), relabeling (Barton & Alexander, 1981), positive connotation (Selvini-Palazzoli, Boscolo, Cecchin, & Prata, 1974), positive reinterpretation (Hammond et al., 1977), additive empathy, and traditional psychoanalytic interpretations. The content of interpretations concerning the same clinical situation thus can be expected to vary according to the theoretical allegiances of social workers. Research (summarized by Claiborn, 1982), however, indicates that "interpretations differing greatly in content seem to have a similar impact on clients" (p. 450).

Levy (1963) classifies interpretations into two categories: *semantic* and *propositional.* Semantic interpretations describe clients' experiences according to the social worker's conceptual vocabulary: "By 'frustrated,' I gather you mean you're feeling hurt and disillusioned." Semantic interpretations thus are closely related to additive empathic responses. Propositional interpretations involve the social worker's notions or explanations that assert causal relationships among factors involved in clients' problem situations: "When you try so hard to avoid displeasing others, you displease yourself and end up resenting others for taking advantage of you."

Social workers should avoid making interpretations or additive empathic responses (we are using the terms interchangeably) that are far removed from the awareness of clients. Research (Speisman, 1959) has indicated that moderate interpretations (those that reflect feelings that lie at the margin of the client's experiences) facilitate self-exploration and self-awareness, whereas deep interpretations engender opposition.[1]

Because the latter are remote from clients' experiences, they appear illogical and irrelevant to clients, who therefore tend to reject them despite the fact that such interpretations may be accurate. The following is an example of such an inept, deep interpretation:

Client: My boss is a real tyrant. He never gives anyone credit, except for Fran. She can do no wrong in his eyes. He just seems to have it in for me. Sometimes I'd like to punch his lights out.

Social worker: Your boss seems to activate the same feelings you had toward your father. You feel he favors Fran, who symbolizes your favored sister. It's your father who you feel was the real tyrant, and you're reliving your resentment toward him. Your boss is merely a symbol of him.

Understandably, the client would likely reject and perhaps resent this interpretation. Although the social worker may be accurate (the determination of which is purely speculative), the client is struggling with feelings toward his boss. To shift the focus to his feelings toward his father misses the mark entirely from the client's perspective.

The following interpretation, made in response to the same client message, would be less likely to create opposition because it is linked to recent experiences of the client:

Social worker: So you really resent your boss because he seems impossible to please and shows partiality toward Fran. [*Reciprocal empathy.*] Those feelings reminded me of similar ones you expressed about 2 weeks ago. You were talking about how, when your parents spent a week with you on their vacation, your father seemed to find fault with everything you did but raved about how well your sister was doing. You'd previously mentioned he'd always seemed to favor your sister and that nothing you did seemed to please him. I'm wondering if those feelings might be connected with the feelings you're experiencing at work.

In the preceding message, notice that the social worker carefully documented the rationale of the interpretation and offered it tentatively, a technique discussed later in the section titled "Guidelines for Employing Interpretation and Additive Empathy." Because we discussed, illustrated, and provided exercises related to additive empathy in Chapter 5, we will not deal with these topics in this chapter. Instead, we limit our discussion here to the uses of interpretation and additive empathy in expanding clients' self-awareness of (1) deeper feelings; (2) underlying meanings of feelings, thoughts, and behavior; (3) wants and goals; (4) hidden purposes of behavior; and (5) unrealized strengths and potentialities.

Deeper Feelings

Clients often have limited awareness of certain emotions, perceiving them only dimly, if at all. Moreover, emotional reactions often involve multiple emotions, but clients may experience only the dominant or surface feelings. Further, some clients experience only negative emotions, such as anger, and are out of touch with more tender feelings, such as hurt, disappointment, compassion, loneliness, fears, and caring. Additive empathic responses (semantic interpretations) may assist clients to become aware of the emotions that lie at the edge of their awareness, thereby enabling them to experience these feelings more sharply and fully, to become more aware of their humanness (including the full spectrum of emotions), and to integrate these emerging emotions into the totality of their experience.

Social workers frequently employ additive empathic responses directed at expanding clients' awareness of feelings for several purposes, which we identify and illustrate in the following examples.

1. To identify feelings that are only implied or hinted at in clients' verbal messages

   Client [*in sixth session*]: I wonder if you feel we're making any progress. [*Clients frequently ask questions that embody feelings.*]

   Social worker: It sounds as though you're not satisfied with your progress. I wonder if you're feeling discouraged about how it's been going.

2. To identify feelings that underlie surface emotions

   Client: I've just felt so bored in the evenings with so little to do. I play video games and channel surf, but that doesn't seem to help. Life's just a drag.

   Social worker: I'm getting the impression you're feeling empty and pretty depressed. I wonder if you're feeling lonely and wishing you had some friends to fill that emptiness.

3. To add intensity to feelings clients have minimized

   Thirty-year-old mildly retarded, socially isolated woman: It was a little disappointing that Jana [*her childhood friend from another state*] couldn't come to visit. She lost her job and had to cancel her plane reservations.

   Social worker: I can see how terribly disappointed you were. In fact, you seem really down even now. You'd looked forward to her visit and made plans. It has been a real blow to you.

4. To clarify the nature of feelings clients experience only vaguely

   Gay male client: When Robert told me he didn't want to be with me any more, I just turned numb. I've been walking around in a daze ever since, telling myself, "This can't be happening."

   Social worker: It has been a crushing blow to you. You were so unprepared. It hurts so much it's hard to admit it's really happening.

5. To identify feelings manifested only nonverbally

   Client: My sister asked me to tend her kids while she's on vacation, and I will, of course.[*Frowns and sighs.*]

   Social worker: But your sigh tells me you don't feel good about it. Right now the message I get from you is that it seems an unfair and heavy burden to you and that you resent it.

Underlying Meanings of Feelings, Thoughts, and Behavior

Used for this purpose, additive empathy or interpretation assists clients to conceptualize or make meaning of feelings, thoughts, and behavior. Social workers thus assist clients in understanding what motivates them to feel, think, and behave as they do; to grasp how their behavior bears on their problems and goals; and to discern themes and patterns in their feelings, thoughts, and behavior. As clients discern similarities, parallels, and themes in their behavior and experiences, their self-awareness gradually expands in much the same way as single pieces of a puzzle fit together, gradually forming discrete entities and eventually coalescing into a coherent whole. The previous interpretation made to the client who resented his boss for favoring a coworker is an example of this type of additive empathic response (it is also a propositional interpretation).

In a more concrete sense, then, social workers may employ this type of interpretation or additive empathy to assist clients to realize that they experience troublesome feelings in the presence of a certain type of person or in certain circumstances. For example, clients may feel depressed in the presence of critical people or feel extremely anxious in situations wherein they must perform (e.g., when expected to give a talk or take a test). Social workers may thus use additive empathy to identify negative perceptual sets and other dysfunctional cognitive patterns that can be modified by employing cognitive restructuring. Clients may attend exclusively to trivial indications of their imperfections and completely overlook abundant evidence of competent and successful performance.

Similarly, a social worker may assist a client to discern a pattern of anticipating negative outcomes of relatively minor events and dreading (and avoiding) the events because of his or her perception of those outcomes as absolute disasters. One client dreaded visiting a lifelong friend who had recently sustained a severe fall, leaving her partially paralyzed. When the social worker explored possible negative events that the client feared might occur if she were to visit the friend, she identified the following:

- "What if I cry when I see her?"
- "What if I stare at her?"
- "What if I say the wrong thing?"

Using an additive empathic response, the social worker replied, "And if you did one of those things, it would be a total disaster?" The client readily agreed. The social worker then employed cognitive restructuring to assist the client to view the situation in a more realistic perspective. The social worker discussed each feared reaction in turn, clarifying that anyone might react as the client feared reacting and that if she were to react in any of these ways it would be uncomfortable but certainly not a disaster. The social worker and client jointly concluded that the client had a certain amount of control over how she reacted rather than being totally at the mercy of circumstances. Following behavioral rehearsal, the client's fears of disaster gradually dwindled to manageable proportions.

Social workers may also employ this type of additive empathy to enhance clients' awareness of perceptual distortions that adversely affect their interpersonal relationships. For example, parents may reject children because they perceive characteristics in them that the parents abhor. Previous exploration, however, may have disclosed that parents identify the same qualities in themselves and project their self-hatred onto their children. By assisting clients to recognize how self-perceptions (which may also be distorted) warp their perceptions of their children, social workers enable such parents to make discriminations and to perceive and accept their children as unique individuals who are different from themselves.

Similar perceptual distortions may occur between marital partners. These problems may cause spouses to perceive and to respond inappropriately to each other as a result of unresolved and troublesome feelings that derive from earlier relationships with parents of the opposite sex.

Wants and Goals

Another important use of additive empathy is to assist clients to become aware of wants and goals that they imply in their messages but do not fully recognize. When beset by difficulties, people often tend to think in terms of problems and ways to obtain relief from them rather than in terms of growth and change—even though the latter two processes are often implied in the former. When they become more aware of the thrust toward growth implied in their messages, clients often welcome the prospect and may even wax enthusiastic about it. This type of additive empathy not only expands self-awareness, but may also enhance motivation.

As is apparent in the following excerpt, additive empathic messages that highlight implied wants and goals often results in the formulation of explicit goals that pave the way to change-oriented actions. Moreover, such messages play a critical role in arousing hope in dispirited clients who feel overwhelmed by their problems and have been unable to discern any positive desires for growth manifested in their struggles. This type of message plays a key role both in the first phase of the helping process and in the change-oriented phase.

Client: I'm so sick of always being imposed upon. All of my family just take me for granted. You know: "Good old Marcie, you can always depend on her." I've taken about all of this that I can take.

Social worker: Just thinking about it gets your hackles up. Marcie, it seems to me that what you're saying adds up to an urgent desire on your part to be your own person—to feel in charge of yourself rather than being at the mercy of others' requests or demands.

Client: I hadn't thought of it that way, but you're right. That's exactly what I want. If I could just be my own person.

Social worker: Maybe that's a goal you'd like to set for yourself. It seems to fit, and accomplishing it would liberate you from the oppressive feelings you've described.

Client: Yes, yes! I'd like very much to set that goal. Do you really think I could accomplish it?

Hidden Purposes of Behavior

Social workers sometimes employ interpretation to help clients become more fully aware of the basic motivations that underlie their concerns. Other people may misinterpret clients' motives, and clients themselves may have only a dim awareness of them because of the obscuring effect of their problematic behaviors.

Prominent among these motives are the following: to protect tenuous self-esteem (e.g., by avoiding situations that involve any risk of failing), to avoid anxiety-producing situations, and to compensate for feelings of impotency or inadequacy. The following are typical examples of surface behaviors and the hidden purposes served by those behaviors:

- Underachieving students may exert little effort in school (1) because they can justify failing on the basis of not having really tried (rather than having to face their fears of being inadequate) or (2) because they are seeking to punish parents who withhold approval and love when they fall short of their expectations.

- Clients may present a facade of bravado to conceal from themselves and others underlying fears and feelings of inadequacy.

- Clients may set themselves up for physical or emotional pain to offset deep-seated feelings of guilt.

- Clients may engage in self-defeating behavior to validate myths that they are destined to be losers or to live out life scripts determined by circumstances beyond their control.

- Clients may avoid relating closely to others to protect against fears of being dominated or controlled.

- Clients may behave aggressively or abrasively to avoid risking rejection by keeping others at a distance.

Interpretations must be based on substantial supporting information that clients have disclosed previously. Without supporting information, interpretations are little more than speculations that clients are unlikely to accept. Indeed, such speculations often emanate from social workers' projections and are typically inaccurate. Clients may regard such interpretations as offensive or may question social workers' competence when they receive such responses.

The following example illustrates appropriate use of interpretation to expand awareness of the motives underlying a client's behavior.

CASE EXAMPLE

The client, Mr. R, age 33, and his wife entered marital therapy largely at his wife's instigation. Mrs. R complained about a lack of closeness in the relationship and felt rejected because her husband seldom initiated affectional overtures. When she initiated overtures, he typically rebuffed her by pulling back. Mr. R had revealed in the exploratory interviews that his mother had been (and still was) extremely dominating and controlling. He felt little warmth toward his mother and saw her no more than was absolutely necessary.

The following excerpt from an individual session with Mr. R focuses on an event that occurred during the week when the couple went to a movie. Mrs. R had reached over to hold her husband's hand. He abruptly withdrew it, and Mrs. R later expressed her feelings of hurt and rejection. Their ensuing discussion was unproductive, and their communication became strained. Mr. R discussed the event that occurred in the theater:

Mr. R: I know Carol was hurt when I didn't hold her hand. I don't know why, but it really turned me off.

Social worker: So you're wondering why you turn off when she reaches for some affectional contact. I wonder what was happening inside of you at that moment. What were you thinking and feeling?

Mr. R: Gee, let me think. I guess I was anticipating she'd do it, and I just wanted to be left alone to enjoy the movie. I guess I resented her taking my hand. That doesn't make sense when I think about it. Why should I resent holding hands with the woman I love?

Social worker: Jim, I think you're asking an awfully good question—one that's a key to many of the difficulties in your marriage. Let me share an idea with you that may shed some light on why you respond as you do. You mentioned you felt resentful when Carol took your hand. Based on the feelings you just expressed, I'm wondering if perhaps you feel you're submitting to her if you respond positively when she takes the initiative and pull back to be sure you're not letting yourself be dominated by her [*the hidden purpose*]. Another reason for suggesting that is that as you were growing up you felt dominated by your mother and resented her for being that way. Even now you avoid seeing her any more than you have to. I'm wondering if, as a result of your relationship with her, you could have developed a supersensitivity to being controlled by a female so that you resent any behavior on Carol's part that even suggests her being in control. [*The latter part of the response provides the rationale for the interpretation.*]

Unrealized Strengths and Potentialities

Another vital purpose served by interpretation and additive empathy is to expand clients' awareness of their strengths and undeveloped potentialities. Clients' strengths are demonstrated in a variety of ways, and social workers need to sensitize themselves to these often subtle manifestations by consciously cultivating a positive perceptual set. This objective is vital, because clients are often preoccupied with their weaknesses. Moreover, becoming aware of strengths tends to arouse clients' hopes and to generate the courage they need to begin making changes.

Drawing clients' awareness to strengths tends to enhance self-esteem and to foster courage to undertake tasks that involve risking new behaviors. With conscious effort, social workers can become increasingly aware of their clients' strengths. For example, when a client faces a child welfare investigation because his or her children were left alone, part of the assessment must necessarily focus on the circumstances of danger that occurred and alternatives that were available to the client. This investigation often provokes defensive behavior from the client. Clients are more likely to respond positively to explorations for other solutions if their own strengths are recognized (De Jong & Miller, 1995; McQuaide & Ehrenreich, 1997). For example, the following response identifies both strengths and problems:

Social worker: You have explained that you did not intend to leave your children alone for any extended period. Your daughter was cooking for her little brother when the grease fire broke out. She knew how to call 911 and get the fire department. We would all want this situation to never have happened. Still, your daughter knew what to do in case of an emergency. She was able to prepare a meal. You have done many things to prepare your children to cope. We will need to plan together so that they are not left alone without adult supervision.

In this case, the supporting of strengths is paired with identification of continuing concerns and the need to plan together to eliminate dangers.

Guidelines for Employing Interpretation and Additive Empathy

Considerable finesse is required to employ interpretation and additive empathy effectively. The following guidelines will assist you in acquiring this skill.

1. *Use additive empathy sparingly until a sound working relationship has evolved.* Because these responses go somewhat beyond clients' current level of self-awareness, clients may misinterpret the motives of a social worker and respond defensively. Hence, when clients have brief contact with a social worker, such as in discharge planning, they are unlikely to develop the kind of relationship in which additive empathy is appropriate. When clients demonstrate that they are confident of a social worker's goodwill, they are able to tolerate and often to benefit from additive empathic and interpretative responses.

The exceptions to this guideline involve messages that identify (1) wants and goals and (2) strengths and potentialities, both of which are also appropriate in the initial phase of the helping process. Social workers must avoid identifying strengths excessively in the initial phase, because some clients will interpret such messages as insincere flattery.

2. *Employ these responses only when clients are engaged in self-exploration or have shown that they are ready to do so.* Clients or groups that are not

ready to engage in self-exploration are likely to resist social workers' interpretive efforts and may perceive them as unwarranted attempts by social workers to impose their formulations upon them. Exceptions to this guideline are the same as those cited in the first guideline.

3. *Pitch these responses to the edge of clients' self-awareness, and avoid attempting to foster awareness that is remote from clients' current awareness or experiences.* Clients generally are receptive to responses that closely relate to their experiences but resist those that emanate from social workers' unfounded conjectures. It is poor practice to attempt to push clients into rapidly acquiring new insights, because many of these deep interpretations will prove to be inaccurate and produce negative effects, including reducing clients' confidence in social workers, conveying lack of understanding, or engendering resistance. Social workers should not employ interpretive responses until they have amassed sufficient information to be reasonably confident their responses are accurate. They should then take care to share the supportive information upon which the interpretation is based.

4. *Avoid making several additive empathic responses in succession.* Because interpretation responses require time to think through, digest, and assimilate, a series of such responses tends to bewilder clients.

5. *Phrase interpretive responses in tentative terms.* Because these responses involve a certain degree of inference, there is always the possibility that the social worker might be wrong. Tentative phrasing openly acknowledges this possibility and invites clients to agree or disagree. If social workers present interpretations in an authoritarian or dogmatic manner, however, clients may not feel free to offer candid feedback and may outwardly agree while covertly rejecting interpretations. Tentative phrases include "I wonder if . . . ," "Could it be that your feelings may be related to . . . ?", and "Perhaps you're feeling this way because . . ." Using additive empathy to explore strengths is, of course, less threatening and can be done with less hesitance.

6. *To determine the accuracy of an interpretive response, carefully note clients' reactions after offering the interpretation.* When responses are on target,

clients affirm their validity, continue self-exploration by bringing up additional relevant material, or respond emotionally in a manner that matches the moment (e.g., ventilate relevant feelings). When interpretations are inaccurate or are premature, clients tend to disconfirm them (verbally or nonverbally), change the subject, withdraw emotionally, argue or become defensive, or simply ignore the interpretation.

7. *If the client responds negatively to an interpretative response, acknowledge your probable error, respond empathically to the client's reaction, and continue your discussion of the topic under consideration.*

To assist you in expanding your skill in formulating interpretive and additive empathic responses, a number of exercises, together with modeled responses, appear at the end of this chapter.

CONFRONTATION

Confrontation is similar to interpretation and additive empathy in that it is a tool to enhance clients' self-awareness and to promote change. Confrontation, however, involves facing clients with some aspect of their thoughts, feelings, or behavior that is contributing to or maintaining their difficulties. Social workers, perhaps more than members of some other helping professions, must struggle to maintain a dual focus on both the individual's rights and social justice. Some claim that the ability to juggle these sometimes conflicting demands is an essential strength of the profession (Regehr & Angle, 1997). Others argue that "there are some activities people can do that put them outside any entitlement to respect . . . some people called clients are not much respected (Ryder & Tepley, 1993, p. 146). For example, individuals who act to harm or endanger others, such as the perpetrators of domestic violence or sexual abuse, challenge this dual commitment and social workers' ethical obligation (described in Chapter 4) to respect the inherent worth and dignity of all individuals regardless of the acts they may have committed.

In this context, when is confrontation appropriate? With whom? And under what conditions? Is confrontation a skill or a style of practice?

In some settings, confrontation has become a style of practice rather than a selective skill. That is, practitioners believe that some clients are so well defended with denial, rationalization, and refusal to accept responsibility that only repeated confrontations will succeed. For example, in work with batterers, some have claimed that "almost every word they [batterers] utter is either victim blaming or justification for their violence. So I have to start confronting all of that stuff right from the beginning and it gets very intense" (Pence & Paymar, 1993, p. 21). It was believed that only when the offender admitted responsibility for the behavior and accepted the label of offender could meaningful change occur. If the clients did not accept the label, and if they defended themselves, they were labeled as being in denial and resistant (Miller & Sovereign, 1989). Hence, confronting them in an authoritarian and aggressive style (Miller & Rollnick, 1991) was considered necessary to achieve an admission of guilt—that is, admission that they had a problem and were not in control of their behavior.

In short, clients were expected to give up their own views and to accept the views of those who had the power to confront them. It was assumed that disempowered persons—who had no motivation owned by them, and were incapable of making their own decisions and controlling their behavior—would then accept and cooperate with the formulation of the problem by the social workers and/or group (Kear-Colwell & Pollock, 1997). If they reacted by showing disagreement and resistance, they were seen as persisting in denial, as lacking motivation, and often as demonstrating pathological personality patterns.

This view too often leads to an interactive cycle of confrontation and denial in which the client acts to protect his or her self-esteem by denying charges (Miller & Sovereign, 1989). Social workers and theorists in fields such as treatment of domestic abuse perpetrators, persons with addictions, and sexual offenders are now questioning whether this style is effective or ethical (Fearing, 1996; Kear-Colwell & Pollock, 1997; Miller & Sovereign, 1989; Murphy & Baxter, 1997). These helping professionals are questioning whether intense confrontation of defenses is beneficial or whether it may unwittingly reinforce the belief that relationships are based on coercive influences (Murphy & Baxter, 1997). They suggest that a supportive and collaborative working alliance is more likely to increase motivation in clients. Motivational interviewing is more likely to create dissonance and encourage offenders to own the process. Even in work with addicted persons, new approaches acknowledge the importance of developing a positive, respectful approach toward the person who is the subject of the intervention (Fearing, 1996).

Instead of all-purpose confrontation delivered at any time, it may be more useful to acknowledge the stage of change the client is at regarding the problematic behavior when using this technique. Prochaska, DiClemente, and Norcross (1992) have proposed a six-stage process of change (see Table 17-1). Their model begins with precontemplation, in which the person has not considered the behavior to be a problem.

In the motivational interviewing approach, the social worker takes responsibility for pursuing a positive atmosphere for change based on accurate empathic understanding, mutual trust, acceptance, and understanding of the world from the offender's perspective (Kear-Colwell & Pollock, 1997). In this exploration, the focus is on the offending behavior and its effects and origins, not on the person of the offender (Kear-Colwell & Pollock, 1997). The effort seeks to be persuasive by creating an awareness that the person's problem behavior is dissonant with his or her personal goals. By engaging in a risk-benefit analysis, the social worker assists the client in deciding whether it makes sense to explore a change so as to better reach those goals. The social worker would then assist the client to make a decision.

Once a client has decided to act, then the form of influence can help him or her decide which action to pursue. For example, after he has decided to deal with a domestic violence problem, a male client can be helped to consider alternatives for how to go about it. When a decision has been made, efforts are aimed at

Table 17-1 Stages of change model

STAGE	CHARACTERISTIC BEHAVIOR	SOCIAL WORKER'S TASK
Precontemplation	Client does not believe that he or she has a problem; is considered unmotivated by others	Raise awareness of concerns held by others: "What does your partner think about the effect of your drinking on your home life?" Stimulate dissonance with risk-benefit analysis: "What are the benefits to you from making your living by selling drugs? What are the costs to you from living by selling drugs?"
Contemplation	Becomes aware of the existence of the problem but is not moved to action Appears ambivalent—shows awareness, then discounts it	Attempt to tip decisional balance by exploring reasons to change: "As you add it up, what do you think the benefits are in relation to the costs? If you get a legal job, then what?" Strengthen confidence in change as a possibility
Preparation	Recognizes problem; asks what can be done to change Appears motivated	Help client plan appropriate course of action
Action	Implements plan of action	Develop plan to implement action Plan details to make it possible (e.g., transportation, child care)
Maintenance	Sustains change through consistent application of strategies	Identify strategies to prevent lapses and relapse: "What have been the triggers to expose you to a dangerous situation?"
Relapse	Slips into problematic behavior and may return to precontemplation stage	Attempt to return to contemplation without being stuck or demoralized Reinforce achievement; treat with respect: "This is a difficult time. You have been at this point before and you overcame it. What do you think about whether you want to overcome it again?"

Source: Adapted from Kear-Colwell & Pollock (1997) and Prochaska, DiClemente, and Norcross (1992).

planning useful action to reach the goal. When a change has occurred, efforts are aimed at exploring in detail the contingencies and triggers that have been associated with the behavior. Armed with such knowledge, alternatives can be planned and practiced to avoid a relapse into the offending behavior.

Confrontation is most likely to be heard when it comes from a source liked and respected by the client. Consequently, confrontations that occur early in contact are often not accurately heard or heeded. Nevertheless, social workers sometimes have responsibilities to confront clients with violations of the law and with dangers to themselves and others before a helping relationship has developed. Such confrontations should occur sparingly, given the likelihood that they will not be heeded so early in contact (Rooney, 1992).

In the middle phase of work, social workers employ confrontation to assist clients to achieve awareness of the forces blocking their progress toward growth and goal attainment and to enhance their motivation to implement efforts toward change. Confrontation is particularly relevant when clients manifest blind spots to discrepancies or inconsistencies in their thoughts, beliefs, emotions, and behavior that produce or perpetuate dysfunctional behavior. Of course, blind spots in self-awareness are universal because all humans suffer from the limitation of being unable to step out of their perceptual fields and look at themselves objectively.

Additive empathy and confrontation have much in common. Skillful confrontations incorporate consideration of clients' feelings that underlie obstacles to change. Because fears are often among these feelings, skill in relating with high levels of empathy is a prerequisite to using confrontation effectively. Indeed, effective confrontation is an extension of empathic communication because the focus on discrepancies and inconsistencies derives from a deep understanding of clients' feelings, experiences, and behavior.

It is important for social workers to possess a range of confrontation skills and not to confront clients primarily to vent their own frustration with clients' lack of progress. Social workers would more appropriately consider confrontation to exist along a continuum that ranges from fostering *self-confrontation* at one extreme to *assertive confrontation* at the other extreme (Rooney, 1992). That is, clients can often be engaged quickly in self-confrontation by asking them questions that cause them to reflect on the relationship between their behaviors and their own values.

Skillfully designed intake forms can serve a similar function, asking potential clients to reflect on concerns and their perceptions of the causes. Such confrontations are subtle and respectful, and they rarely engender strong client opposition. As clients gain expanded awareness of themselves and their problems through self-exploration, they tend to recognize and to confront discrepancies and inconsistencies themselves. Self-confrontation is generally preferable to social worker–initiated confrontation, because the former is less risky and because clients' resistance to integrating insights is not an obstacle when they initiate confrontations themselves.

Clients vary widely in the degree to which they engage in self-confrontation. Emotionally mature, introspective persons may engage in self-confrontations frequently. In contrast, individuals who are out of touch with their emotions, who lack awareness of their effects on others, and who blame others or circumstances for their difficulties are least likely to engage in self-confrontation.

Inductive questioning can be a form of confrontation that is more active on the social worker's part but is still conveyed in a respectful manner. The social worker asks questions that lead the client to consider potential discrepancies between thoughts, values, beliefs, and actions. Also, when the therapist asks a question that relates to facts rather than one that requires the client to label himself or herself, the question is more likely to be effective. For example, asking a client with a chemical dependency problem, "Are you powerless over alcohol?", would require the client to essentially label himself an alcoholic. On the other hand, "Do you ever have blackouts?", "Do you find it easier to bring up a problem with another person when you have had something to drink?", and "Do you ever find that once you begin drinking you can't easily stop?" are questions that, taken together, raise the possibility that drinking is a problem that might need attention (Citron, 1978).

When a danger is imminent, the social worker may not be able to rely on tactful self-confrontation facilitated by inductive questioning. Instead, he or she may have to engage in more assertive confrontation in which the connection between troubling thoughts, plans, values, and beliefs is stated in declarative form, connecting them explicitly for the client. Such assertive confrontation is a more high-risk technique because clients may interpret social workers' statements as criticisms, put-downs, or rejections. Paradoxically, the risk of these reactions is greatest among clients who must be confronted most often because they rarely engage in self-confrontation. These individuals tend to have weak self-concepts and are therefore prone to read criticism into messages when none is intended. Moreover, ill-timed and poorly executed confrontations may be perceived by clients as verbal assaults and may seriously damage helping relationships.

Using confrontation therefore requires keen timing and finesse. Social workers must make special efforts to convey their helpful intent and goodwill as they employ this technique. Otherwise, they may engender hostility or offend and alienate clients.

Effective assertive confrontations embody four elements: (1) expression of concern; (2) a description of the client's purported goal, belief, or commitment; (3) the behavior (or absence of behavior) that is inconsistent or discrepant with the goal, belief, or commitment; and (4) the probable negative outcomes of the discrepant behavior. The format of a confrontive response may be depicted as follows:

$$\text{I am concerned because you} \begin{cases} \text{(want)} \\ \text{(believe)} \\ \text{(are striving to)} \end{cases}$$

_____
(describe desired outcome)

but your _____
          (describe discrepant action, behavior, or inaction)

is likely to produce _____
                     (describe probable negative consequences)

This format is purely illustrative. You may organize these elements in varying ways, and we encourage you to be innovative and to develop your own style. For example, you may challenge clients to analyze the effects of behaviors that are incongruous with their purported goals or values, as illustrated in the following excerpt:

Social worker [_To male on parole_]: Al, I know the last thing you want is to have to return to prison. I want you to stay out, too, and I think you sense that. But I have to level with you. You're starting to hang out with the same bunch you got in trouble with before you went to prison. You're heading in the same direction you were before, and we both know where that leads.

In this confrontation, the social worker begins by referring to the client's purported goal (remaining out of prison) and expresses a like commitment to the goal. The social worker next introduces concern about the client's behavior (hanging out with the same bunch the client got in trouble with before) that is discrepant with that goal. The social worker concludes the confrontation by focusing on the possible negative consequence of the discrepant behavior (getting into trouble and returning to prison).

Notice these same elements in the following examples of confrontive responses:.

- [_To father in family session_]: Mr. D, I'd like you to stop for a moment and examine what you're doing. I know you want the children not to be afraid of you and to talk with you more openly. Right? [_Father agrees._] Okay, let's think about what you just did with Steve. He began to tell you about what he did after the school assembly, and you cut him off and got on his case. Did you notice how he clammed up immediately?

- [_To mother in child welfare system_]: I have a concern I need to share with you. You've expressed your goal of regaining custody of Pete, and we agreed that attending the parents' group was part of the plan to accomplish that goal. This week is the second time in a row you've missed the meeting because you overslept. I'm very concerned that you may be defeating yourself in accomplishing your goal.

Because employing assertive confrontation runs the risk of putting clients on the defensive or alienating them, expressing concern and helpful intent is a critical element because it reduces the possibility that clients will misconstrue the motive behind the confrontation. Tone of voice is also vital in highlighting helpful intent. If the social worker conveys the confrontation in a warm, concerned tone of voice, the client will be much less likely to feel attacked. If the social worker uses a critical tone of voice, any verbal reassurance that criticism was not intended is likely to fall on deaf ears. Keep in mind that people tend to attach more credence to nonverbal aspects of messages than to verbal aspects.

Guidelines for Employing Confrontation

To assist you in employing confrontation effectively, we offer the following guidelines.

1. *When a violation of the law or imminent danger to self or others is involved, a confrontation must occur no matter how early in the working relationship.* Such confrontations may impede the development of the relationship, but the risk of harm to self and others is more important than the immediate effect on the relationship.

2. *Whenever possible, avoid confrontation until an effective working relationship has been established.* This can occur when a client is contemplating action (or inaction) that impedes his or her own goals but is not an imminent danger to self or others. Employing empathic responsiveness in early contacts conveys understanding, fosters rapport, and enhances confidence in the social worker's perceptiveness and expertise. When a foundation of trust and confidence has been established, clients are more receptive to confrontations and, in some instances, even welcome them.

3. *Use confrontation sparingly.* Confrontation is a potent technique that generally should be employed only when clients' blind spots are not responsive to other, less risky intervention methods. Poorly timed and excessive confrontations can inflict psychological damage on clients (Lieberman, Yalom, & Miles, 1973).

   Another reason to employ confrontation judiciously is that some clients may yield to forceful confrontation for counterproductive reasons. Seeking to please social workers (or to avoid displeasing them), they may temporarily modify their behavior. But changing merely to comply with the expectations of a social worker leads to passivity and dependence, both of which are anathema to actual growth. Some clients are already excessively passive, and pressuring them for compliance merely reinforces their passivity.

4. *Deliver confrontations in an atmosphere of warmth, caring, and concern.* If social workers employ confrontations in a cold, impersonal, or critical way, clients are likely to feel that they are being attacked. By contrast, if social workers preface confrontations with genuine empathic concern, clients are more likely to perceive the helpfulness intended in the confrontation.

5. *Whenever possible, encourage self-confrontation.* Recall from the previous discussion that self-confrontation has decided advantages over social worker–initiated confrontation. Learning by self-discovery fosters independence and increases the likelihood that clients will act upon their newly gained self-awareness. Social workers can encourage self-confrontation by drawing clients' attention to issues, behaviors, or inconsistencies that they may have overlooked and by encouraging them to analyze the situation further.

   For example, the social worker may directly intervene into dysfunctional interactions and challenge individuals, couples, families, or groups to identify what they are doing. Responses that encourage self-confrontation in such a context include the following:

- "Let's stop and look at what you just did."
- "What did you just do?"

Other inductive question responses that highlight inconsistencies and foster self-confrontation are as follows:

- "I'm having trouble seeing how what you just said (or did) fits with . . ."
- "I can understand how you felt, but how did (describe behavior) make it better for you?"
- "What you're saying seems inconsistent with what you want to achieve. How do you see it?"

Yet another technique is useful when clients overlook the dynamic significance of their own revealing expressions or when their manifest feelings fail to match their reported feelings. This technique involves asking them to repeat a message, to listen carefully to themselves, and to consider the meaning of the message. Examples of this technique follow:

- "I want to be sure you realize the significance of what you just said. Repeat it, but this time listen carefully to yourself, and tell me what it means to you."
- [*To marital partner in conjoint interview*]: "Joan just told you something terribly important, and

I'm not sure you really grasped it. Could you repeat it, Joan, and I want you to listen very carefully, Bob, and check with Joan as to whether you grasped what she said."

• [*To group member*]: "You just told the group you're feeling better about yourself, but it didn't come through that way. Please say it again, but get in touch with your feelings and listen to yourself."

6. *Avoid using confrontation when clients are experiencing extreme emotional strain.* Confrontation tends to mobilize anxiety. When clients are under heavy strain, supportive techniques rather than confrontation are indicated. Clients who are overwhelmed with anxiety or guilt generally are not receptive to confrontation and will not benefit from it. In fact, confrontation may be detrimental, adding to their already excessive tension.

Conversely, confrontation is appropriate for clients who experience minimal inner conflict or anxiety when such reactions would be appropriate in light of their problematic behavior as perceived by others. Self-satisfied and typically insensitive to the feelings and needs of others (whom they cause to be anxious), such clients—popularly referred to as having "character disorders"—often lack the anxiety needed to engender and maintain adequate motivation. Confrontation, when combined with the facilitative conditions, may mobilize the anxiety they need to examine their own behavior and to consider making constructive changes.

7. *Follow confrontation with emphatic responsiveness.* Because clients may take offense to even skillful confrontation, it is vital to be sensitive to their reactions. Clients often do not express their reactions verbally, so social workers need to be especially attuned to nonverbal cues that suggest hurt, anger, confusion, discomfort, embarrassment, or resentment. If clients manifest these or other unfavorable reactions, it is important to explore their reactions and to respond empathically to their feelings. Discussing such reactions provides opportunities (1) for clients to ventilate their feelings and (2) for social workers to clarify their helpful intent and to assist clients to work through negative feelings. If social workers fail to sense negative feelings or clients withhold expressions of

them, the feelings may fester and adversely affect the helping relationship.

8. *Expect that clients will respond to confrontation with a certain degree of anxiety.* Indeed, confrontation is employed to produce a temporary sense of disequilibrium that is essential to break an impasse. The anxiety or disequilibrium serves a therapeutic purpose in impelling the client to make constructive changes that eliminate the discrepancy that prompted the social worker's confrontation. Empathic responsiveness following confrontation is not aimed at diluting this anxiety, but rather seeks to resolve untoward reactions that may derive from negative interpretations of the social worker's motives for making the confrontation.

9. *Do not expect immediate change after confrontations.* Although awareness paves the way to change, clients rarely succeed in making changes immediately following acquisition of insight. Even when clients fully accept confrontations, corresponding changes ordinarily occur by increments. Known as working through, this change process involves repeatedly reviewing the same conflicts and the client's typical reactions to them, gradually broadening the perspective to encompass increasingly more situations to which the changes are applicable. Unfortunately, some naive social workers press for immediate change, sometimes inflicting psychological damage on their clients.

Indications for Assertive Confrontation

As noted previously, confrontation is appropriate in three circumstances: (1) when violations of the law or imminent threats to the welfare and safety of self or others are involved; (2) when discrepancies, inconsistencies, and dysfunctional behaviors (overt or covert) block progress or create difficulties; and (3) when efforts at self-confrontation and inductive questioning have been ineffective in fostering clients' awareness of these behaviors or attempts to make corresponding changes. Discrepancies may reside in cognitive/perceptual, emotional (affective), or behavioral functions or may involve interactions between these functions.

A comprehensive analysis of types of discrepancies and inconsistencies has been presented elsewhere (Hammond et al., 1977, pp. 286–318); therefore, we merely highlight some of the most commonly encountered.

Cognitive/Perceptual Discrepancies

Many clients have behavioral or perceptual difficulties that are a product of inaccurate, erroneous, or incomplete information, and confrontation may assist them in modifying their problematic behaviors. For example, clients may lack accurate information about indicators of alcoholism, normal sexual functioning, or reasonable expectations of children according to stages of development.

Even more common are misconceptions about the self. The most common of these, in the authors' experience, involve self-demeaning perceptions. Even talented and attractive persons may view themselves as inferior, worthless, inadequate, unattractive, or stupid. Such perceptions are often deeply embedded and do not yield to change without extensive working through. Nevertheless, confronting clients with their strengths or raising their awareness of other areas of competence can prove helpful in challenging such self-deprecating views.

Other cognitive/perceptual discrepancies include interpersonal perceptual distortions, irrational fears, dichotomous or stereotypical thinking, denial of problems, placing responsibility for one's difficulties outside of oneself, failing to discern available alternative solutions to difficulties, and failing to consider consequences of actions.

Affective Discrepancies

Discrepancies in the emotional realm are inextricably linked to cognitive/perceptual processes, because emotions are shaped by the cognitive meanings that clients attribute to situations, events, and memories. For example, a client may experience intense anger that emanates from a conclusion that another person has intentionally insulted, slighted, or betrayed him or her. This conclusion is based on a meaning attribution that may involve a grossly distorted perception of the other person's intentions. In such instances, social workers can assist clients to explore their feelings, to provide

relevant detailed factual information, to consider alternative meanings, and to realign their emotions with reality.

Affective discrepancies that social workers commonly encounter include denying or minimizing actual feelings, being out of touch with painful emotions, expressing feelings that are contrary to purported feelings (e.g., claiming to love a spouse or child but expressing only critical or otherwise negative feelings), and verbally expressing a feeling that contradicts feelings expressed nonverbally (e.g., "No, I'm not disappointed," said with a quivering voice and tears in the eyes). Gentle confrontations aimed at emotional discrepancies often pave the way to ventilation of troubling emotions, and many clients appreciate social workers' sensitivity in recognizing their suppressed or unexpressed emotions.

If a client appears unprepared to face painful emotions, the social worker should proceed cautiously. Indeed, it may be wise to defer further exploration of those hurtful emotions. Confronting the client vigorously may elicit overwhelming emotions and engender consequent resentment toward the social worker.

Behavioral Discrepancies

Clients may experience many behavioral concerns that create difficulties for themselves and for others. Even though these patterns may be conspicuous to others, clients may remain blind to their patterns or to the effects of their behaviors on others. Confrontation may be required to expand their awareness of these patterns and their pernicious effects.

Irresponsible behavior tends to spawn serious interpersonal difficulties for clients as well as problems with broader society. Neglect of children, weak efforts to secure and maintain employment, undependability in fulfilling assignments, failure to maintain property—these and similar derelictions of duty often result in severe financial, legal, and interpersonal entanglements that may culminate in loss of employment; estrangement from others; and loss of property, child custody, self-respect, and even personal freedom.

Irresponsible behavior often pervades the helping process as well, sometimes indicated by clients' tardiness to sessions, unwillingness to acknowledge problems, and failure to keep appointments or pay fees. Effective confrontation with such clients requires employing a firm approach couched in expressions of goodwill and concern about wanting to assist them avoid the adverse consequences of not assuming responsibilities. Social workers do a disservice to their clients when they permit them to evade responsibility for their actions or inaction. Further, social workers must counter clients' tendency to blame others or circumstances for their difficulties by assisting them to recognize that *only they* can reduce the pressures that beset them.

Other common behavioral discrepancies involve repeated actions that are incongruous with purported goals or values. Adolescents may describe ambitious goals that require extensive training or education but make little effort in school, be truant frequently, and otherwise behave in ways that are entirely inconsistent with their stated goals. Spouses or parents may similarly espouse goals of improving their marital or family life but persistently behave in abrasive ways that further erode their relationships.

Confrontation often must be used to assist clients to desist from engaging in self-defeating behaviors. In some instances, therapeutic binds (a special form of confrontation discussed in Chapter 18) may be employed to supply needed leverage to motivate clients to relinquish destructive and unusually persistent patterns of behavior.

Three other common categories of discrepancies or dysfunctional behavior that warrant confrontation are manipulative behavior, dysfunctional communication, and resistance to change. In groups, certain members may attempt to dominate the group, bait group members, play one person against the other, undermine the leader, or engage in other destructive ploys. The price of permitting members to engage in such behaviors may be loss of certain group members, dilution of the group's effectiveness, or premature dissolution of the group. To avert such undesired consequences, the leader may elicit the reactions of other group members to this behavior and assist members to confront manipulators with their destructive tactics. Such confrontations should adhere to the guidelines delineated earlier, and the leader should encourage members to invite offending members to join with them in constructively seeking to accomplish the purposes for which the group was formed.

Because problematic communication frequently occurs in individual, conjoint, and group sessions, social workers encounter abundant opportunities to employ confrontation to good effect. Intervening during or immediately following dysfunctional communication is a powerful means of enabling clients to experience firsthand the negative effects of their dysfunctional behaviors (e.g., interrupting, attacking, claiming, or criticizing). By shifting the focus to the negative reactions of recipients of problematic messages, social workers enable clients to receive direct feedback about how their behavior offends, alienates, or engenders defensiveness in others, thereby producing effects contrary to their purported goals.

Summary

Chapter 17 discussed three vital tools in working through clients' opposition to change and to relating openly in the helping relationship: additive empathy, interpretation, and confrontation. If individual clients are left to struggle alone with negative feelings about the helping process or the social worker, their feelings may mount to the extent that they resolve them by discontinuing their sessions. If family members or groups are permitted to oppose change by engaging in distractive, irrelevant, or otherwise dysfunctional behaviors, they may likewise lose both confidence in the social worker (for valid reasons) and motivation to continue. For these reasons, social workers must accord the highest priority to being helpful to clients who encounter obstacles or who may be opposed to change.

Internet Resources

See our companion website for hot links to some helpful URLs. Note that URLs are subject to change. We will endeavor to update the links on the companion website as much as possible.

Articles related to the content in this chapter can be read and downloaded through InfoTrac College Edition by using keywords such as the following: "interpretation," "empathy," "confrontation," "stages of psychological change." Hanson and Gutheil's (2004) article, which relates to stages of change, can also be accessed through InfoTrac College Edition.

Related Online Content

Visit the *Direct Social Work Practice* companion website at *http://socialwork. wadsworth.com/hepworth7* for additional learning tools such as glossary terms, chapter outlines, InfoTrac College Edition keywords, relevant web links, and chapter practice quizzes. Also, be sure to check out the Direct Practice Virtual Reader, where the authors have personally selected articles relevant to this chapter using InfoMarks.

Skill Development Exercises in Additive Empathy and Interpretation

To assist you to advance your skills in responding with interpretation and additive empathy, we provide the following exercises. Read each client message, determine the type of response required, and formulate a written response that you would employ if you were in an actual session with the client. Keep in mind the guidelines for employing interpretive and additive empathic responses. Compare your responses with the modeled responses provided at the end of the exercises.

Client Statements

1. *White female client* [*to African American male social worker*]: You seem to be accepting of white people—at least you have been of me. But somehow I still feel uneasy with you. I guess it's just me. I haven't really known many black people very well.

2. *Married woman, age 28:* I feel I don't have a life of my own. My life is controlled by *his* work, *his* hours, and *his* demands. It's like I don't have an identity of my own.

3. *Prison inmate, age 31* [*1 week before the date of his scheduled parole, which was canceled the preceding week*]: Man, what the hell's going on with me? Here I've been on good behavior for 3 years and finally got a parole date. You'd think I'd be damned glad to get out of here. So I get all uptight and get in a brawl in the mess hall. I mean I really blew it, man. Who knows when they'll give me another date?

4. *Male, age 18:* What's the point in talking about going to Trade Tech? I didn't make it in high school, and I won't make it there either. You may as well give up on me—I'm just a dropout in life.

5. *Widow, age 54:* It was Mother's Day last Sunday, and neither of my kids did as much as send me a card. You'd think they could at least acknowledge I'm alive.

6. *Female secretary, age 21:* I don't have any trouble typing when I'm working alone. But if the boss or anyone else is looking over my shoulder, it's like I'm all thumbs. I just seem to tighten up.

7. *Female, age 26, in a committed relationship; she is 5 pounds overweight:* When I make a batch of cookies or a cake on the weekend, Terri [her partner] looks at me with that condemning expression, as though I'm not really trying to keep my weight down. I don't think it's fair just because she doesn't like sweets. I like sweets, but the only time I eat any is on the weekend, and I don't eat much then. I feel I deserve to eat dessert on the weekend at least.

8. *Disabled male recipient of public assistance (with a back condition caused by recent industrial accident):* This not being able to work is really getting to me. I see my kids needing things I can't afford to get them, and I just feel—I don't know—kind of useless. There's got to be a way of making a living.

9. *Depressed male, age 53:* Yeah, I know I do all right in my work. But that doesn't amount to much. Anyone could do that. That's how I feel about everything I've ever done. Nothing's really amounted to anything.

10. *Mother, age 29, who has neglected her children:* I don't know. I'm just so confused. I look at

my kids sometimes, and I want to be a better mother. But after they've been fighting, or throwing tantrums, or whining and I lose my cool, I feel like I'd just like to go somewhere—anywhere—and never come back. The kids deserve a better mother.

Modeled Responses for Interpretation and Additive Empathy

1. [*To clarify feelings experienced only vaguely*]: I gather that even though you can't put your finger on why, you're still somewhat uncomfortable with me. You haven't related closely to that many African Americans, and you're still not altogether sure how much you can trust me.

2. [*Implied wants and goals*]: Sounds like you feel you're just an extension of your husband and that part of you is wanting to find yourself and be a person in your own right.

3. [*Hidden purpose of behavior, underlying feelings*]: So you're pretty confused about what's happened. Fighting in the mess hall when you did just doesn't make sense to you. You know, Carl, about your getting uptight—I guess I'm wondering if you were worried about getting out—worried about whether you could make it outside. I'm wondering if you might have fouled up last week to avoid taking that risk.

4. [*Underlying belief about self*]: Sounds like you feel defeated before you give yourself a chance. Like it's hopeless to even try. Jay, that concerns me because when you think that way about yourself, you are defeated—not because you lack ability but because you think of yourself as destined to fail. That belief is your real enemy.

5. [*Deeper feelings*]: You must have felt terribly hurt and resentful they didn't as much as call you. In fact, you seem to be experiencing those feelings now. It just hurts so much.

6. [*Underlying thoughts and feelings*]: I wonder if, in light of your tightening up, you get feeling scared, as though you're afraid you won't measure up to their expectations.

7. [*Unrealized strengths*]: I'm impressed with what you just said. It strikes me you're exercising a lot of control by limiting dessert to weekends and using moderation then. In fact,

your self-control seems greater than that of most people. You and Terri have a legitimate difference concerning sweets. But it's exactly that—a difference. Neither view is right or wrong, and you're entitled to your preference as much as she is entitled to hers.

8. [*Unrealized strength and implied want*]: Steve, I can hear the frustration you're feeling, and I want you to know it reflects some real strength on your part. You want to be self-supporting and be able to provide better for your family. Given that desire, we can explore opportunities for learning new skills that won't require physical strength.

9. [*Underlying pattern of thought*]: Kent, I get the feeling that it wouldn't matter what you did. You could set a world record, and you wouldn't feel it amounted to much. I'm wondering if your difficulty lies more in long-time feelings you've had about yourself, that you somehow just don't measure up. I'd be interested in hearing more about how you've viewed yourself.

10. [*Underlying feelings and implied wants*]: So your feelings tear you and pull you in different directions. You'd like to be a better mother, and you feel bad when you lose your cool. But sometimes you just feel so overwhelmed and inadequate in coping with the children. Part of you would like to learn to manage the children better, but another part would like to get away from your responsibilities.

Skill Development Exercises in Confrontation

The following exercises involve discrepancies and dysfunctional behavior in all three experiential domains—cognitive/perceptual, emotional, and behavioral. After reading the brief summary of the situation involved and the verbatim exchanges between the client(s) and social worker, identify the type of discrepancy involved and formulate your next response (observing the guidelines presented earlier) as though you are the social worker in a real-life situation. Next, compare your response with the modeled one, keeping in mind that the model is only one of many possible appropriate responses. Carefully analyze how your response is similar to or differs from the modeled response and whether you adhered to the guidelines.

Situations and Dialogue

1. You have been working with Mr. Lyon for several weeks, following his referral by the court after being convicted for sexually molesting his teenage daughter. Mr. Lyon has been 15 minutes late for his last two appointments, and today he is 20 minutes late. During his sessions he has explored and worked on problems only superficially.

   Client: Sorry to be late today. Traffic was sure heavy. You know how that goes.

2. The clients are marital partners whom you have seen conjointly five times. One of their goals is to reduce marital conflict by avoiding getting into arguments that create mutual resentments.

   Mrs. J: This week has been just awful. I've tried to look nice and have his meals on time—like he said he wanted—and I've just felt so discouraged. He got on my back Tuesday and . . . [*Husband interrupts.*]

   Mr. J [*angrily*]: Just a minute. You're only telling half the story. You left out what you did Monday. [*She interrupts.*]

   Mrs. J: Oh, forget it. What's the use? He doesn't care about me. He couldn't, the way he treats me. [*Mr. J shakes head in disgust.*]

3. The client is a slightly retarded young adult who was referred by a rehabilitation agency because of social and emotional problems. The client has manifested a strong interest in dating young women and has been vigorously pursuing a clerk (Sue) in a local supermarket. She has registered no interest in him and obviously has attempted to discourage him from further efforts. The following excerpt occurs in the seventh session.

   Client: I went through Sue's check stand this morning. I told her I'd like to take her to see a movie.

   Social worker: Oh, and what did she say?

   Client: She said she was too busy. I'll wait a couple of weeks and ask her again.

4. Tony, age 16, is a member of a therapy group in a youth correctional institution. In the preceding session, he appeared to gain a sense of power and satisfaction from provoking other members to react angrily and defensively, which disrupted the group process. Tony directs the following message to a group member early in the fourth session.

   Tony: I noticed you trying to get next to Meg at the dance Wednesday. You think you're pretty hot stuff, don't you?

5. The client is a mother, age 26, who keeps feelings inside until they mount out of control, at which time she discharges anger explosively.

   Client: I can't believe my neighbor. She sends her kids over to play with Sandra at lunchtime and disappears. It's obvious her kids haven't had lunch, and I end up feeding them, even though she's better off financially than I am.

   Social worker: What do you feel when she does that?

   Client: Oh, not much, I guess. But I think it's a rotten thing to do.

6. You have been working for several weeks with a family that includes the parents and four children ranging in age from 10 to 17. The mother is a domineering person who acts as spokesperson for the family, and the father is passive and soft-spoken. A teenage daughter, Tina, expresses herself in the following dialogue.

   Tina: We always seem to have a hassle when we visit our grandparents. Grandma's so bossy. I don't like going there.

   Mother: Tina, that's not true. You've always enjoyed going to her house. You and your grandmother have always been close.

7. Group members in their fifth session have been intently discussing difficulties of the members in social interaction. One of the members takes the group off on a tangent by describing humorous idiosyncrasies of a person she met while on vacation, and the other group members follow suit by sharing humorous anecdotes about "oddballs" they have encountered.

8. The client is an attractive, personable, and intelligent woman who has been married for

3 years to a self-centered, critical man. In the fourth session (an individual interview), she tearfully makes the following statements:

Client: I've done everything he's asked of me. I've lost 10 pounds. I support him in his work. I golf with him. I even changed my religion to please him. And he's still not happy with me. There's just something wrong with me.

9. The clients are a married couple in their early thirties. The following excerpt occurs in the initial interview.

Wife: We just seem to fight over the smallest things. When he gets really mad, he loses his temper and knocks me around.

Husband: The real problem is that she puts her parents ahead of me. She's the one who needs help, not me. If she'd get straightened out, I wouldn't lose my temper. Tell her where her first responsibility is. I've tried, and she won't listen to me.

10. The clients are a family consisting of the parents and two children. Taylor, age 15, has been truant from school and smoking marijuana. Angie, age 16, is a model student and is obviously her parents' favorite. The family was referred by the school when Taylor was expelled for several days. The father, a highly successful businessman, entered family therapy with obvious reluctance, which has continued to this, the fourth session.

Mother: Things haven't been much different this week. Everyone's been busy, and we really haven't seen much of each other.

Father: I think we'd better plan to skip the next 3 weeks. Things have been going pretty well, and I have an audit in process at the office that's going to put me in a time bind.

Modeled Responses for Confrontation

1. [*Irresponsible behavior by the client*]: Ted, I'm concerned you're late today. This is the third time in a row you've been late, and it shortens the time available to us. But my concerns go beyond that. I know you don't like having to come here and that you'd like to be out from under the court's jurisdiction. But the way

you're going about things won't accomplish that. I can't be helpful to you and can't write a favorable report to the court if you just go through the motions of coming here for help. Apparently it's uncomfortable for you to come. I'd be interested in hearing just what you're feeling about coming.

2. [*Discrepancy between purported goal and behavior, as well as dysfunctional communication*]: Let's stop and look at what you're doing right now. I'm concerned because each of you wants to feel closer to the other, but what you're both doing just makes each other defensive.
   [*To husband*]: Mr. J, she was sharing some important feelings with you, and you cut her off.
   [*To wife*]: And you did the same thing, Mrs. J, when he was talking.
   [*To both*]: I know you may not agree, but it's important to hear each other out and to try to understand. If you keep interrupting and trying to blame each other, as you've both been doing, you're going to stay at square one, and I don't want that to happen. Let's go back and start over, but this time put yourself in the shoes of the other and try to understand. Check out with the other if you really understood. Then you can express your own views.

3. [*Dysfunctional, self-defeating behavior*]: Pete, I know how much you think of Sue and how you'd like to date her. I'm concerned that you keep asking her out, though, because she never accepts and doesn't appear to want to go out with you. My concern is that you're setting yourself up for hurt and disappointment. I'd like to see you get a girlfriend, but your chances of getting a date are probably a lot better with persons other than Sue.

4. [*Abrasive, provocative behavior*]: Hold on a minute, guys. I'm feeling uncomfortable and concerned right now about what Tony just said. It comes across as a real put-down, and we agreed earlier one of our rules was to support and help each other. Tony, would you like some feedback from other members about how you're coming across to the group?

5. [*Discrepancy between expressed and actual feeling*]: I agree. But I'm concerned about

your saying you don't feel much. I should think you'd be ticked off and want to change the situation. Let's see if you can get in touch with your feelings. Picture yourself at home at noon and your neighbor's kids knock on the door while you're fixing lunch. Can you picture it? What are you feeling in your body and thinking just now?

6. [*Dysfunctional communication, disconfirming Tina's feelings and experiences*]: What did you just do, Mrs. Black? Stop and think for a moment about how you responded to Tina's message. It may help you to understand why she doesn't share more with you. [*or*] Tina, could you tell your mother what you're feeling right now about what she just said? I'd like her to get some feedback that could help her communicate better with you.

7. [*Discrepancy between goals and behavior, getting off topic*]: I'm concerned about what the group's doing right now. What do you think is happening?

8. [*Misconception about the self, cognitive/ perceptual discrepancy*]: Jan, I'm concerned about what you just said because you're putting yourself down and leaving no room to feel good about yourself. You're assuming that you own the problem and that you're deficient in some way. I'm not at all sure that's the problem. You're married to a man who seems impossible to please, and that is more likely the problem. As we agreed earlier, you have tasks of feeling good about yourself, standing up for yourself, and letting your husband's problem be his problem. As long as your feelings about

yourself depend on his approval, you're going to feel down on yourself.

9. [*Manipulative behavior*]: I don't know the two of you well enough to presume to know what's causing your problems.

    [*To husband*]: If you're expecting me to tell your wife to shape up, you'll be disappointed. My job is to help each of you to see your part in the difficulties and to make appropriate changes. If I did what you asked, I'd be doing both of you a gross disservice. Things don't get better that way.

10. [*Discrepancy between behavior and purported goals*]: What you do, of course, is up to you. I am concerned, however, because you all agreed you wanted to relate more closely as family members and give one another more support. To accomplish that means you have to work at it steadily, or things aren't likely to change much.

    [*To father*]: My impression is that you're backing off. I know your business is important, but I guess you have to decide whether you're really committed to the goals you set for yourselves.

Notes

1. Claiborn (1982) presents numerous examples of both types of interpretation as well as a comprehensive discussion of this important topic. Other researchers (Beck & Strong, 1982; Claiborn, Crawford, & Hackman, 1983; Dowd & Boroto, 1982; Feldman, Strong, & Danser, 1982; Milne & Dowd, 1983) have also reported findings comparing the effects of different types of interpretations.

Managing Barriers to Change

CHAPTER OVERVIEW

Chapter 18 focuses on potential barriers to change and ways of managing them so that they do not unduly impede progress or precipitate premature termination by clients. Clients who have the best of intentions and who are highly motivated may nevertheless encounter obstacles that intrude upon the helping process and goal attainment. These obstacles may occur within the individual (representing conflicting wants and needs), arise within the environment, or involve a combination of the two. Social workers' behaviors may either contribute to resolution of clients' barriers or inadvertently aggravate them. This chapter includes guidelines for becoming aware of the social worker's role in assisting clients to remove barriers to change.

BARRIERS TO CHANGE

Progress toward goal attainment is rarely smooth. Instead, the change process is characterized by rapid spurts of growth, plateaus and impasses, relapses, and sometimes brief periods of regression. Even getting started can be a formidable challenge with involuntary clients, when the help that is offered has not been solicited. For example, social workers contacting parents who have been reported for abusing their children or individuals who have been charged with domestic assault often face initial hostility. The degree and rate of change vary widely and are affected by many variables—most importantly, variations in the motivation and strengths of clients; the severity and duration of problems; the dynamics of the helping relationship; the environmental forces that support or work against change; and the responsiveness (or lack thereof) of institutions in providing needed resources.

This chapter first addresses the relational reactions and potential barriers that may emerge in cross-racial and cross-cultural relationships. We include sexual attraction toward clients as a barrier, and discuss both the ethical and legal implication of this behavior on the part of the social worker. Next, it focuses on managing opposition to change manifested by individuals, families, or groups. Recall that organizational barriers were discussed in Chapter 14, as they are typically macro practice issues. Chapter 18 concludes by providing skill development exercises related to managing relational reactions.

RELATIONAL REACTIONS

The client–social worker relationship is the vehicle that animates the helping process, especially for voluntary clients. Indeed, the quality of the helping relationship critically determines both the client's moment-to-moment receptiveness to the social worker's influence and intervention and the ultimate outcome of the helping process. Because of the profound importance of the helping relationship, it is critical that you be skilled both in cultivating relationships and in keeping those relationships intact. Feelings that influence the relationship—for better or worse—constantly flow back and forth between the social worker and the client. To maintain positive helping relationships, you must be alert to threats to those relationships and manage them carefully.

Helping relationships that are characterized by reciprocal positive feelings between social workers and clients are conducive to personal growth and successful problem solving. Social workers strive to develop positive helping relationships by relating in a facilitative fashion with high levels of warmth, acceptance, unconditional caring, empathy, genuineness, and a sensitivity to differences. Despite these efforts, however, some clients are unable to respond positively for a number of reasons. Social workers, too, may have difficulty responding positively to clients with certain personality or physical attributes and types of problems. For example, consider the following exchange from a case consultation session:

Social worker, presenting a case: How can you feel empathy for every client? I have this one client, and when I go to her house, she is just sitting there like a big lump. She doesn't seem to understand that she may lose her children. She tells me that the man who abused her children is out of her life, but I don't believe her. She tells lies, she doesn't do anything to help herself, and she sits there in the midst of a cluttered filthy apartment watching television. I am just waiting to catch her in one of her lies. It is hard for me to feel anything for this client or to help her keep custody of her children.

Consultant: Wow, you really don't like this client and she knows it! Perhaps she feels, "Why bother to establish a relationship with you."

Upon reflection, the social worker agreed with the consultant's conclusion. With the help of the consultant, she was able to focus on the work to be done in this case—specifically, ensuring the safety of the children.

Chapter 6 discussed the importance of maintaining psychological contact with clients, and Chapter 8 focused on exploring the nature of the

problem. Both of these issues are relevant in the preceding situation. When we do not like clients for whatever reasons, they are able to sense our feeling toward them.

Another factor in this case was the social worker's preoccupation with whether the client was telling the truth. Obviously, truth telling is a reciprocal expectation in the helping relationship. Yet, is it really necessary to determine whether the client is lying, unless her dishonesty threatens the welfare of her children?

Even when a positive relationship evolves, various events and moment-by-moment transactions may pose risks to the continuing viability of the relationship. Social workers must be vigilant to manifestations that something is going awry in the relationship. Failure to perceive these manifestations and to manage them effectively may result in needless impasses or, even worse, premature termination. Next, we focus on threats to the relationship that emanate from the client, from the social worker, and from dynamic mixes of both.

Under- and Over-Involvement of Social Workers with Clients

Social workers desire to be attuned to clients and relational dynamics in the helping process. However, it is not unusual for contact to be less than facilitative in some circumstances. If clients experience negative emotional reactions during the course of sessions that create a temporary breach in a helping relationship, and if you fail to recognize and respond to those reactions, then they may expand into major obstacles in the helping process. Raines (1996) has suggested that such reactions can be classified as *over-involvement or under-involvement*. Levels of over- or under-involvement can also be classified according to the social worker's general viewpoint or attitude toward the client. Even though you may strive to maintain a balanced attitude, be appreciative of strengths, and be aware of obstacles, sometimes you may be inclined to emphasize one side of the story that is generally favorable or unfavorable to the client. Table 18-1 presents an adaptation of Raines's schema for classifying involvement (Raines, 1996).

Table 18-1 Social worker's under- and over-involvement with clients

	SOCIAL WORKER WITH UNFAVORABLE ATTITUDE TOWARD CLIENT	SOCIAL WORKER WITH FAVORABLE ATTITUDE TOWARD CLIENT
Under-involvement	• Finds it difficult to empathize with the client • Is inattentive to or "tunes out" the client • Has lapses of memory about important information previously revealed by the client • Is drowsy or preoccupied • Dreads sessions or comes late, cancels sessions inappropriately • Is off the mark with interpretations • Client perceives feedback as put-downs • Fails to acknowledge client growth • Never thinks about the client outside of sessions	• Withholds empathy inappropriately due to belief in strength • Refrains from interpretation to promote insight • Reflects or reframes excessively without answering • Never considers self-disclosure • Gives advice or assignments that the client feels incapable of carrying out
Over-involvement	• Has an unreasonable dislike of the client • Is argumentative • Is provocative • Gives excessive advice • Employs inept or poorly timed confrontations • Disapproves of the client's planned course of action inappropriately • Appears to take sides against the client (or subgroup) or actually does so • Dominates discussions or frequently interrupts the client • Uses power with involuntary clients to interfere in lifestyle areas beyond the range of legal mandates • Competes intellectually • Has violent thoughts or dreams about the client	• Is overly emotional or sympathetic • Provides extra time inappropriately • Fantasizes brilliant interpretations • Is unusually sensitive to criticisms • Has sexual thoughts or dreams about the client • Seeks nonprofessional contact with the client

Source: Adapted from Raines (1996).

1. *When the social worker is under-involved and has a negative attitude toward the client,* it can be reflected in lack of attention or empathy, tuning out, having memory lapses, and the like. All (or most) social workers (certainly including the authors of this book) have had bad sessions and even bad days in which their attentiveness was less than desirable. Table 18-1 highlights circumstances in which such under-involvement becomes associated with the social worker's services to a particular client. Such social worker behaviors are a signal that the cause of the behavior must be examined. Hence, part of professional behavior is the capacity for self-observation and correction. Noting one of these patterns and examining its cause in supervision or consultation with peers can assist you in developing plans for rectifying the behavior.

2. *Under-involvement when there is a positive social worker attitude* can occur when the social worker withholds assistance because of an overly optimistic assessment of the client's current capacity and need for help. For example, a client who has been making good progress but encounters a setback might need more support than usual, and a lack of expressed empathy can impede the social worker's ability to address that need. Similarly, settling on assignments or tasks that the client feels incapable of completing can be a sign of positive under-involvement. As in negative under-involvement, such occurrences may happen with particular clients at a particular time. Patterns of repeated positive under-involvement, however, call for examination and correction. Once again, reflection on these patterns with peers and supervisors can assist social workers in finding ways to adjust the involvement level. Hence, while generally focusing on client strengths and having a positive attitude toward clients is consistent with social work values, the possibility of under-involvement alerts us to ways that attention to strengths could be exaggerated and not completely helpful in some circumstances.

3. *Over-involvement with a negative social worker attitude* refers to negative attention such that clients feel punished or in combat with the social worker. Patterns of arguing, acting provocatively in an inappropriate fashion, employing power arbitrarily, and the like can signal negative over-involvement. Note that if the social worker is operating under a legal mandate to provide, for example, services to persons who have mistreated their children, then power and authority could be used appropriately and in an ethical manner. In contrast, in cases of over-involvement with a negative social worker attitude, the use of power becomes personal and punishing rather than appropriate to the circumstances and safety of children. This behavior is contrary to social work values, but it does occur. This behavior is often observed in high-stress settings in which social workers have close contact with clients who have been harmed and with individuals who have either harmed those clients or not acted fully to prevent the harm. Over-involvement with negative attitude may also be evident in court mandated case plans. It may also spill over and take the form of

rigid rules of conduct in educational, residential, and corrections settings. Social workers in such settings and their supervisors should take special precautions to avoid stereotyping clients and ignoring client strengths and values.

Being under- or over-involved with clients may also be related to *burnout*. James and Gilliland (2001) attribute burnout to identifying closely with clients and their problems, as well as to being dedicated and idealistic. A social worker's strong need to be liked may be manifested in such actions as taking calls at home, feeling responsible for clients' mistakes or regressions, and panicking when carefully detailed plans fail to produce the expected results. Cunningham (2003) and Holly (2003) have also recognized the vicarious or indirect effects of stress on practitioners of trauma, especially those who work in family violence, child sexual abuse, and hospital oncology units. In a study of secondary trauma for family violence professionals, Holly found that constant "exposure to clients' stories negatively affects cognitions" (2003, p. 514). Further, the response level of the professional was related to whether the client's situation was similar to his or her own experience.

Over-involvement may also arise as a result of a combination of positive and negative dynamics, as illustrated in the following case example.

CASE EXAMPLE

Marta is a youth worker in a shelter for homeless youth. She is passionate about her work and believes that her relationship with her young clients will help them to become independent, productive adults. She sees herself as an example of a survivor. Her supervisor has approached her several times, because she believes that Marta sometimes crosses professional boundaries with her clients. Marta's primary goal is to prepare homeless youth to become independent. Actually, youth gaining independence is a program goal, so her behavior is consistent with the intended program outcome. Another goal of the program is to assist the youth to resolve conflicts with their parents whenever possible. Marta's work with youth is often in conflict with this goal.

Marta's own youth was marked by constant battles with her parents. At age 17, she left home, lived with friends for a period, and eventually was homeless. Her relationship with the youth on her caseload is generally as a "survivor of the streets," encouraging a dependency by urging her clients to rely on her for support. When a youth raises the issue of reconnecting with his or her parents, Marta routinely rejects this idea as being unhealthy to the youth's progress and refuses to help make contact. The supervisor considers Marta's work with youth to be exemplary, with the exception of her negative attitude toward parents.

4. *Over-involvement with a positive social worker attitude* entails excessive preoccupation with a particular client such that the client dominates the social worker's thoughts and dreams, including sexual fantasies. In the most extreme cases, that positive over-involvement can lead to more serious consequences—for example, boundary violations such as sexual contact with clients. Because of the seriousness of boundary violations, we discuss this issue later in greater detail.

Assessing Potential Barriers and Intervening

Although most of the preceding events or circumstances involve mistakes by social workers, others result from misperceptions by clients. Whatever their source, it is vital to sense and to discuss clients' feelings and thoughts as they are manifested, thereby preventing them from escalating. Often clients will not initiate discussion of their negative reactions. If you are not sensitive to nonverbal cues, these feelings and cognitions will linger and fester. To avert such a development, it is crucial to watch for indicators of negative reactions including the following nonverbal cues: frowning, fidgeting, sighing, appearing startled, grimacing, changing the subject, becoming silent, clearing the throat, blushing, and tightening the muscles. When you observe these or related cues, it is important to shift the focus of the session to the client's here-and-now feelings and cognitions. You should do this tentatively, checking out whether your perception is accurate. If it is accurate, proceed by expressing genuine concern for the client's discomfort and conveying your desire to understand what the client is experiencing at the moment. Examples of responses that facilitate discussion of troubling feelings and thoughts follow:

- "I'm sensing you're reacting to what I just said. Could you share with me what it meant to you and what you're thinking and feeling at this moment?"
- "You appear distressed right now. I'd like to understand exactly what you're experiencing and if I may have said or done something that caused you to feel this way."
- "You are quiet right now, looking away from me. I am wondering if you have some feelings about the draft of the progress report to the court that I just shared with you."

Keep in mind that in view of a real or perceived power differential between you and clients, discussing negative feelings and cognitions toward you may be extremely difficult for many clients. You can reduce the threat that clients experience by being attentive and accepting, even though their thoughts and feelings may be entirely unrealistic. By eliciting their feelings and thoughts, you also have the opportunity to correct any misunderstandings, clarify your intentions, remedy any blunders, or identify adverse beliefs or thought patterns. Indeed, some clients benefit from observing a model who can acknowledge mistakes and apologize without being humiliated. Moreover, they may gain self confidence by realizing that social workers value them sufficiently to be concerned about their thoughts and feelings and to rectify errors of omission or commission. After productive discussions of here-and-now thoughts and feelings, most clients will regain their positive feelings and resume working on their problems.

On some occasions, a client may succeed in concealing negative thoughts and feelings, or you may overlook nonverbal cues. The feelings may fester until it becomes obvious that the client is relating atypically by holding back, being overly formal, responding defensively, or engaging in other forms of opposition. Again, you should give priority to the relationship by shifting focus to what is bothering the client and responding to it. After you have worked through the negative reaction of the client, it is helpful to negotiate a "mini-contract" in which you and the client agree to discuss troublesome feelings and thoughts as they occur. The objective of this contract is to avert similar recurrences in the future. Learning to express negative feelings and thoughts can be a milestone for clients who may have withheld their reactions to the detriment of themselves and others.

The following is an example of a message aimed at *negotiating an appropriate mini-contract:*

Social worker: I'm pleased that you shared your feelings with me today. In doing so, you helped me to understand what you've been thinking and feeling, and it gave me a chance to explain what I really meant last week. For us to work well together, it is important for both of us to put negative reactions on the table so that we can prevent strains from developing between us. I wonder how you'd feel about our developing a mini-contract in which we agree to immediately discuss any troubling thoughts and feelings that might present obstacles in our relationship so that we can deal with them together and work them out.

In developing the mini-contract, you are conveying to the client your willingness to be open to and respectful of his or her reactions.

Pathological or Inept Social Workers

Although all social workers occasionally commit errors, some social workers repeatedly make mistakes, causing irreparable damage to helping relationships and inflicting psychological damage upon their clients. Gottesfeld and Lieberman (1979) refer to such social workers as *pathological,* pointing out that "It is possible to have therapists who suffer from as many unresolved problems as do clients" (p. 388). Ineptness and unethical practices on the part of social workers can be manifested as abrasive, egotistical, controlling, judgmental, demeaning, patronizing, or rigid behavior; being habitually late or unprepared for appointments; and appearing to be detached or disinterested. The ineptness of social workers may also be attributed to anxiety, a lack of skill or experience, dealing with problems beyond their scope of practice, or an inability to build collaborative relationships with clients. According to Meyer (2001), agencies may also contribute to this problem by assigning the most difficult cases to professionals with the least amount of experience. These behaviors and attributes can create additional difficulties for clients and harm the client–social worker relationship. Social workers who behave in this manner described tend to lose clients prematurely or to have clients who miss appointments.

The majority of voluntary clients discern these behaviors or attributes and have the good sense to "vote with their feet" by terminating such contacts. Mandated clients suffer greater consequences for deciding to terminate unilaterally. They are more likely to evade contact or attempt to be transferred to another social worker. Supervisors should be alert when there are several requests for transfer from the same social worker. Pathological social workers are injurious to their clients, their agencies, and the profession as a whole.

Often, other social workers face a difficult situation in deciding which steps to take when they become aware of such situations. As Meyer (2001) notes, both agencies and professionals may ignore these dynamics, instead characterizing clients' behavior as resistant or oppositional. Of course, it is difficult to be an observer in situations where the behavior of a colleague is harmful to client well-being. At the same time, it is difficult to judge or question the behavior or competence of a professional social work colleague. Nonetheless, both you and your agency have a responsibility to protect clients.

The NASW Code of Ethics speaks directly to the "primacy of clients' rights" as well as to your obligation to peers and the employment organization. A caution by Gottesfeld and Lieberman (1979) is timeless in this regard. They assert that, to protect clients' rights, "agencies organized to help clients should not accept employee pathology that defeats the system's purpose" (p. 392). Actions to rectify such situations, however, must safeguard the rights of both social workers and clients. Reports should be based on facts, not judgments or bias. Reviewing information with supervisors or a consultant provides an additional safeguard.

Ultimately, a referral to the local NASW chapter and state licensing or certification board may become necessary. NASW chapters and regulatory boards have committees that investigate complaints of unethical and unprofessional conduct. Information about misconduct is shared between NASW chapters and state boards of social work. Infractions that constitute egregious harm are also reported to the Disciplinary Actions Reporting System (DARS), a national database maintained by the Association of Social Work Boards (ASWB). "This system is a means by which social work regulatory boards can verify the historical disciplinary background of individuals seeking licensure or renewal" (*ASWB Member Policy Manual*).

Cross-Racial and Cross-Cultural Barriers

Clients may experience adverse reactions in cross-racial or cross-cultural relationships with social workers for a variety of reasons. Tensions in social relations that may be grounded in society may present as dynamics in the helping relationship. The fact that a majority of racial minority clients are involuntary or nonvoluntary is another factor, along with clients' perceptions of the authority and power vested in the helping professional. As Rooney (1992) has noted, oppressed groups are disproportionately represented among involuntary clients. These factors may be macro-level, environmental issues, but they nevertheless influence micro-level practice and relationships.

In their most basic form, barriers to the social worker–client relationship may stem from either lack of knowledge of the client's culture or lack of experience in working with members of a given racial or minority group, despite the fact that most social workers strive to be culturally competent. Foster (1988), for example, suggests that goals of treatment often include achieving separation from others and autonomy, and that these goals are bounded by assumptions in certain Western cultures. Persons from cultures in which interdependence and group belonging assume a greater value may not share goals of this nature. In cross-cultural, cross-racial situations, it is therefore important to understand clients from the viewpoint of their lifestyles and the standards for well-being set by their reference group.

Cross-racial and cross-cultural relationships are challenging on many levels. Social workers who are members of ethnic or racial minority groups are perhaps more attuned to the values of majority-group clients. Conversely, as Proctor and Davis (1994) have noted, Caucasian social workers may have limited knowledge or exposure to the realities of other cultures. The same is true of social workers who are members of racial or ethnic minority groups. In U.S. society, social interactions and professional relationships remain configured around assumptions of sameness, including social class. For the most part, however, a certain social distance separates social workers and their clients, the majority of whom are members of racial or cultural groups. A lack of contact and familiarity may cause social workers to fill in any information void with stereotypes, preconceived notions, and media images. There is also the resulting tendency to become overly positive or negative about a particular racial or ethnic group. On the positive side, social workers may over-identify with these clients, losing sight of their individuality as well as the subgroups within a racial or ethnic culture. On the negative side, perceptions or stereotypes may lead them to erroneously generalize clients' problems to the group in which they are members, thereby influencing the social worker's capacity to be empathetic to the individual's situation.

Given the potential obstacles that may emerge in cross-racial and cross-cultural relationships, you might wonder if the solution is to match clients with social workers of the same racial or ethnic group. This solution is, of course, not practical, nor does the evidence suggest that matching always works to the clients' advantage. In addition, some clients will react to and distrust *any* social worker—even those who share their background or heritage. This distrust often arises at a systems level—specifically, at the level of the organization that you represent—yet the dynamics emerge in your relationship with the client.

In any of the situations previously described, it can be expected that dynamics in the client–social worker relationship will reflect a mutual strangeness. In some instances, social workers and agencies emphasize sameness rather than differences in an attempt to minimize potential barriers. Too often, differences of race and culture are ignored in a form of "color-blind" practice designed to avoid conflict (Proctor & Davis, 1994; Davis & Gelsomino, 1994). Davis and Gelsomino also caution both majority and minority practitioners to be aware of their biases related to socioeconomic factors. In addition to the implications that these factors have for racial and ethnic minority groups, these authors suggest that they are equally relevant to the "social realities of low-income white clients." Social workers may perceive that these clients are responsible for their difficulties, and they may assess these individuals at a higher level based on the assumption that they have failed to take advantage of their life opportunities.

What can be done to minimize the dynamics of difference and its role as a barrier in the helping process? Empathy and empathic communication are basic skills that facilitate engagement and bridge the gaps that may be present in cross-racial and cross-cultural client-social worker relationships. Dyche and Zayas (2001) and Parson (1993) emphasize that knowledge of culture is insufficient to evoke empathy. Instead, they refer to *cultural empathy* as a more effective treatment tool. Cultural empathy is expressed by the social worker at the affective level, rather than solely at the cognitive level. Whereas the cognitive level references knowledge about different cultures, at the affective level social workers make an effort to see and hear the world through the client's eyes and experiences and to grasp meaning from the client's perspective. Parson (1993) further characterizes cultural empathy as *ethnotherapeutic,* meaning that it relies on the cross-cultural professional's capacity for introspection and self-disclosure when this information would support the helping process.

Another facilitative measure is demonstrating acceptance and understanding of the client's situation, even though you may not be fully aware of each and every cultural or racial nuance. Assessment skills in determining acculturation levels, including culturally derived behaviors or dysfunctions in the context of culture, are critical. How a problem is perceived and framed by the social worker can be either an inhibiting factor or a facilitative factor. Clients need to be able to trust that you understand their situation. In a study that examined cross-cultural practices, Davis and Gelsomino (1994) found that social workers tended to ignore environmental factors and instead were more inclined to explore internal or personal difficulties as the source of client problems.

Another facilitative measure is actively engaging the client in defining both the problem and the desired solution from his or her perspective. Lee (2003) for example, in applying the solution-focused approach in cross-cultural relationships, emphasizes utilizing the techniques of social constructivism—specifically, including the view of the client. Lee further suggests that empowerment-based practice, which focuses on client strengths, is essential in assisting clients to create solutions for themselves.

Minority clients, because they have had the normative experience of interacting with nonminority social workers, may have a combination of positive and negative feelings. Their negative feelings may be based on relational tensions in the larger society. You should also be aware that clients absorb and react to the negative media images and political messages that are used to describe them. For example, these hurtful messages may suggest that immigrants are taking jobs from Americans; teaching immigrant or refugee children diminishes education for others and contributes to higher costs for education; welfare recipients are adverse to working; certain neighborhoods are dangerous and crime-ridden drug zones; minority children consistently have lower achievement scores on standardized tests; and minority groups do not hold the same values as the rest of society.

When clients have negative feelings, you can neutralize the situation by empathically confronting and responding to their feelings. As a preventive measure, in the initial contact you might inquire about whether the client has concerns on this front. In addition, you might ask how problems are handled in their culture and explore who else should be involved in the problem-solving effort. As one social worker in a mental health setting observed, "It is not unusual for 10 to 15 family members to accompany my client to sessions with me." Also, she noted, "I have to arrange transportation for the entire group." Her statement suggests an additional factor that is crucial in cross-racial and cross-cultural interactions—the need to be sufficiently flexible so as to accommodate cultural preferences and customs.

"Helper attractiveness" is a final interpersonal factor noted by Harper and Lantz (1996) as an attribute that diverse clients are reported to respond to favorably. Essentially, it means that the client perceives that the practitioner has an interest and ability to help. Further, helper attractiveness implies that diverse clients experience respectful, warm, genuine, committed, and ethical behavior on the part of the social worker. Of course, no matter which facilitative measure you use and no matter how much goodwill, warmth, and empathy you convey, some clients will remain guarded or will test you for a period of time before finally engaging in the helping process. A rationale for this behavior is cultural or systems paranoia, both of which frequently overlap with involuntary client status.

Despite what may appear to be the challenging trials and tribulations inherent in cross-cultural and cross-racial relationships, it is quite possible to have productive helping relationships with clients who are different from yourself. Dean (2001), however, challenges the notion of cultural competence as an arrival point, stating that it is based on the "belief that knowledge brings control and effectiveness which is to be achieved above all else" (p. 624). Instead, she suggests, it is equally important for social workers to be aware of their lack of competence, and therefore to understand competence to be a process of evolving and changing.

Earlier, we noted some general measures and conditions that can facilitate a level of competence with diverse groups in an effort to lessen the impact of potential barriers in the helping relationship. In the spirit of an evolving and changing level

of competence, we would add these measures to those previously discussed:

- Being comfortable with differences
- Adopting a posture of discovery with individual clients, and assessing behavior in the context of their reality
- Taking steps to calm vulnerabilities, anxieties, and fears about making mistakes
- Focusing on cultural and racial strengths, including adaptive behaviors
- Understanding that rigid, reactive behavior on the part of clients may not be specific to you
- Continually evaluating your knowledge of differences, and increasing your level of cultural competence
- Understanding that clients' worldviews may be different from your own
- Being prepared to intervene at the micro, mezzo, or macro level, because racial and ethnic minority individuals' problems often involve all three levels
- Understanding macro-level influences in relationships as well as the extent to which macro-level social conditions affect the lives of racial and cultural minority groups

Finally, note that the literature suggests that racial and ethnic minority clients show a preference for time-limited, goal-directed, action-oriented intervention methods, in which they quickly experience change (Corwin, 2002; Al-Krenawi & Graham, 2000; Gelman, 2004).

Difficulties in Establishing Trust

Clients vary widely in their capacity to trust. Some clients have levels of interpersonal functioning that enable them to quickly engage in the helping process, after only a few moments of checking out the social worker. For others, including racial and ethnic minority clients, despite the goodwill, knowledge, and skills that you display, revealing their feelings, gaining their trust and dismantling their defenses may take a longer period of time. Involuntary clients who have not sought a helping relationship should not be expected to readily trust you. In fact, attempting to persuade such clients of your helpful intent is usually counterproductive. Many distrustful clients trust actions before words. That is, they see trust as a product of the relationship that emerges over time. Trust in this regard is a process and is reinforced by attributes and actions, such as your commitment, patience, respect, and completion of the tasks that you agreed to do.

With involuntary clients, pushing for self-disclosure before trust and a positive working relationship are established may alienate them or prolong the period in which you must prove yourself as being trustworthy. Because these clients do not enter helping relationships voluntarily, they may disclose their problems only superficially during early sessions. Involuntary clients often enter the helping relationship in the pre-contemplation stage of change. They may not readily identify or own the problem as prescribed by others or even agree that they have a problem. Time limits—in particular, when a mandate requires certain actions or behavioral changes to take place by a certain date—may further exacerbate the problem.

In seeking to establish trust and a viable working relationship, you may find it necessary to reach out to involuntary clients to engage them in the helping process. When they cancel or miss appointments, you can continue the contact by phoning them, making a home visit (if your agency permits), or writing a letter. You can review the work that needs to be accomplished, empathize with their situations, and reiterate your support for helping them resolve their difficulties. Many involuntary clients urgently need help. A failure to trust and engage or keep appointments on their part may emanate from fear or a pattern of avoidance rather than from a lack of motivation. Your assisting clients to come to terms with their avoidance behavior thus may be therapeutic, whereas allowing them to terminate by default perpetuates their avoidance behavior and has grave consequences. The movies *Antoine Fisher* (with Denzel Washington as therapist) and *Good Will Hunting* (with Robin Williams as therapist) are excellent examples of reaching out to a client and building trust.

Transference Reactions

Unrealistic perceptions of and reactions to a social worker are known as *transference reactions*. In such reactions, the client transfers to the social worker wishes, fears, and other feelings that are rooted in past experiences with others (usually parents, parental substitutes, and siblings). Trauma survivors can experience several stages of transference. For example, they may experience "rage" at the social worker that attributes their behavior to significant others in their lives or project their responses to their grief, frustration, and fears onto the crisis worker (James & Gilliland, 2001). Transference reactions not only impede progress in the helping process, but also create difficulties in other interpersonal relationships. For example, a male may transfer his relationship experience with his mother to all females. If this relationship was overbearing and punitive, he will similarly perceive other females in this context.

Transference can also occur at the group or community level. In minority communities in which youth perceive that they are being harassed police, for example, transference reactions to authority may be manifested in the classroom, in social skills or anger management groups, and in interactions with the social worker. Also, when communities have experienced a high level of oppressive police tactics, members may be reluctant to assist police in solving crimes. Transference then is subject to racial and political overtones, and is often reinforced by the powerful messages of music about injustices and inequalities, which further shapes cognitions and worldviews.

Transference may also occur in treatment groups between clients and in work with couples where one or both partners are having a transference reaction with the other. The latter type of transference is illustrated in the following case example

CASE EXAMPLE

Connie and Kim had been together for more than 20 years. They experienced what they believed to be the usual relationship tensions—disagreements about finances, household chores, and whose turn it was to walk the dog. Their families were supportive of their relationship, so their reactions were not a source of strain for the couple. They were generally able to work through their interpersonal conflicts, although neither was very good at resolving conflicts together. This lack of skill was most apparent when Kim would present solutions for issues over which they had disagreements. In their usual pattern, Connie would avoid dealing with unpleasant situations and brood. Kim would work out a solution on her own and then present it to Connie. Connie's explosive reaction would further escalate the situation, and each would retreat to a more comfortable place.

The situation that finally placed their relationship in crisis was Connie's involvement with another woman. At first she denied any involvement other than friendship, but eventually she admitted her attraction to this individual. The tension, stress, and strain on the couple's relationship escalated to the point that they agreed to seek professional help.

During a session with the social worker, Connie stated that she had no intention of dissolving their relationship, which she valued. She did, however, state that she was attracted to the other woman, because this person was affirming, praising her for her accomplishments, and generally thought her to be a wonderful individual. She felt that Kim rarely behaved in this way toward her; in fact, she thought that Kim did not appreciate her at all.

After further probing by the social worker, Connie admitted that when Kim raised issues and presented solutions, it reminded her of her father, who was always telling her what to do. During her teenage years, he rarely found reasons to praise her, often finding fault with her decisions and anything that she did. Most of all, Connie did not like the fact that he told her what to do and how to do it. Even now, although Connie was a successful professional, he rarely had anything good to say about her. Kim's behavior reminded Connie of her father, and her reactions to him spilled over into her relationship with Kim. When Kim presented solutions, in Connie's mind she was telling her what to do.

Transference reactions involve overgeneralized and distorted perceptions that create difficulties in interpersonal relationships and sometimes in systems relationships. On a system-to-individual or system-to-group level, transference can involve responses to authority in any form. Besides preventing a client from making progress in resolving problems, transference reactions in therapeutic relationships may also create opportunities for growth. The therapeutic relationship is, in effect, a social microcosm wherein clients' interpersonal behavior and conditioned patterns of perceiving and feeling are manifested. In this context, clients can recreate here-and-now interactions that are virtually identical to those that plague and defeat them in other relationships. The consequent challenge for the social worker is to assist them to recognize their distorted perceptions and to develop perceptual sets that help them differentiate between individuals and situations, rather than relying on overgeneralized projections, mental images, beliefs, or attitudes.

The frequency with which transference reactions related to the practitioner occur during the course of the helping process varies considerably. In time-limited, task-focused forms of intervention, the likelihood of transference reactions may be minimal because of a focus on current concerns. When treatment has a focus on the past, and involves in-depth analysis of intrapsychic processes, transference may assume a more prominent role in the helping process. Similarly, working with marital partners conjointly tends to discourage transference reactions involving social workers, whereas working with only one partner may foster transference by the client and over-identification on the social worker's part.

Multiple transference reactions can emerge in groups. They may be invoked by interactions with the social worker who is facilitating the group or by interactions with individual members. An individual can be experienced as a mother by one member, as a father by another member, and as a sibling by still another member. Similarly, that individual can perceive friends, authority figures, and siblings in the group. Usually the leader is experienced as an authority figure or expert. In either case, transference reactions can stall the group's progress. Your role as group facilitator is to assess the impact of this dynamic on the group and intervene appropriately. You can then utilize group process and communication skills to refocus the attention of members on the group's purpose. You may also use this occasion as a teachable moment, emphasizing how distorted perceptions of group members are based on distortions in other interpersonal relationships.

Managing Transference Reactions

Whatever the agency setting and the intervention, you will occasionally encounter transference reactions and must be prepared to cope with them. For example, the authors have encountered the following situations:

- A client who had great difficulty discussing her problems because the social worker resembled her brother in appearance
- A client who wanted the social worker to embrace her because it was important to know he cared for her
- A client to whom it was important to be the social worker's favorite
- A client who was sure the social worker couldn't possibly have a genuine interest in her and saw her only because it was his job
- A client who misinterpreted a message of the social worker and almost terminated as a result of feeling put down
- A client who accused the social worker of colluding with her husband when the social worker, in fact, viewed the husband as the major contributor to their marital difficulties

Clearly, although such reactions originate in the past, they become manifest in the here and now. This raises an interesting question: Are transference reactions best resolved by focusing on the past to enable clients to gain insight into their origins? We maintain that because reactions driven by past experiences are played out in the present, they can be resolved by examining clients' current inaccurate and distorted perceptions. Of course, when clients bring up experiences and circumstances from their past, brief excursions often facilitate productive emotional catharsis and lead to an understanding of the origins of patterns of thinking, feeling, and behaving. Moreover, when clients

have experienced traumatic stresses (e.g., physical or sexual abuse, sexual assault, war, injury, or other crisis events), probing and exploration of these experiences may be vital to gaining understanding of and recovery from the detrimental effects of those experiences (James & Gilliland, 2001; Wartel, 1991; Rosenthal, 1988)

Except for these circumstances, it is counterproductive to focus extensively on the past, because doing so diverts the social work efforts from problem solving in the present. Further, no evidence indicates that focusing on the remote origin of unrealistic feelings, perceptions, and beliefs is more effective in modifying them than scrutinizing their validity in the here and now.

To manage transference reactions, you must first be aware of their manifestations. Here are some typical behaviors symptomatic of transference:

- Relating to the social worker in a clinging, dependent way or excessively seeking praise and reassurance
- Attempting to please the social worker by giving excessive compliments and praise or by ingratiating behavior
- Asking many personal questions about the social worker
- Behaving provocatively by arguing with or baiting the social worker
- Questioning the interest of the social worker
- Attempting to engage the social worker socially by inviting him or her to lunch or parties, offering personal favors, presenting gifts, or seeking special considerations
- Having dreams or fantasies about the social worker
- Responding defensively, feeling rejected, or expecting criticism or punishment without realistic cause
- Behaving seductively by flirting, wearing revealing clothing, or making affectionate gestures
- Regressing or behaving in destructive ways when the social worker must cancel or miss sessions
- Being unusually silent, inattentive, or drowsy in sessions

- Being tardy for appointments or striving to stay beyond the designated ending time
- Dressing or behaving in ways that diverge markedly from the client's usual style

When clients manifest these behaviors or show other possible indications of transference reactions, it is vital to shift the focus to their here-and-now feelings, because such reactions generally cause clients to disengage from productive work and may undermine the helping process. To assist you in managing transference reactions, we offer the following guidelines:

1. *Be open to the possibility that the client's reaction is not unrealistic* and may be a product of your behavior. If discussion and introspection indicate that the client's behavior is realistic, respond authentically by owning responsibility for your behavior.

2. *When clients appear to expect you to respond in antitherapeutic ways, as significant others have in the past, it is important to respond differently,* thereby disconfirming those expectations. Responses that contrast sharply with the client's expectations may produce temporary disequilibrium and force the client to differentiate the social worker from past figures. The client must thus deal with the social worker as a unique and real person, rather than perpetuating fictional expectations based on past experiences.

3. *Assist the client to determine the immediate source of distorted perceptions by exploring how and when the feelings emerged.* Carefully explore antecedents and meaning attributions associated with the feelings. Avoid attempting to correct distorted perceptions by immediately revealing your actual feelings. By first exploring how and when problematic feelings emerged, you can assist clients to expand their awareness of their patterns of overgeneralizing and making both faulty meaning attributions and unwarranted assumptions based on past experience. This awareness can enable them in the future to discriminate between feelings that emanate from conditioned perceptual sets and reality-based feelings and reactions.

4. *After clients have discerned the unrealistic nature of their feelings and manifested awareness of the distortions that produced these feelings, share your actual feelings.* This revelation can be a source of reassurance to clients who have felt offended, hurt, resentful, rejected, or the like.

5. *After you have examined problematic feelings, assist clients to determine whether they have experienced similar reactions in other relationships.* Through this exploration, clients may recognize patterns of distortions that create difficulties in other relationships.

The application of these guidelines is illustrated in the following excerpt taken from the eighth session with a 30-year-old female who had sought help because she was discouraged about her failure to find a marital partner.

Client: Boy, the weeks sure go by fast. [*Long pause.*] I don't have much to talk about today. [*Ambivalence.*]

Social worker [*sensing the client is struggling with something*]: I gather you didn't really feel ready for your appointment today. [*Empathic response.*] How did you feel about coming? [*Open-ended probing response.*]

Client: I didn't want to come, but I thought I should. Actually, it has been an eventful week. But I haven't felt I wanted to tell you about what has been happening. [*Indication of a possible transference reaction.*]

Social worker: Sounds like you've had some misgivings about confiding certain things in me. [*Paraphrasing response.*] Could you share with me some of your thoughts about confiding these things in me? [*Open-ended probing response/polite command.*]

Client: Okay. I've wanted to keep them to myself until I find out how things turn out. I've wanted to wait until it really develops into something. Then I would tell you. [*Testing.*]

Social worker: So you haven't wanted to risk it turning out bad and worrying about how I would feel if it did. [*Additive empathy, interpretation.*]

Client: I guess I've wanted to impress you. I had a date with the fellow we talked about last week. It was wonderful. He's just the opposite of the other creep I told you about. He either has a real line or he's a super guy. I couldn't believe how considerate he was. [*Seeking approval/praise.*]

Social worker: You can't be sure yet what he's really like, and you want to be sure he's for real before you tell me about him? [*Additive empathy/ interpretation.*]

Client [*with an embarrassed smile*]: Yes! And if it really developed into something, then I could tell you.

Social worker: And that way you could be sure I'd be favorably impressed? [*Additive empathy/ interpretation.*]

Client: Yes! I've felt I wanted you to know someone really good could be attracted to me.

Social worker: Hmm. Sounds like you've felt I've doubted you have much to offer a man and wanted to prove to me you do have something to offer. [*Additive empathy/interpretation.*]

Client: Yes, that's true. I have wanted you to think of me as a desirable person.

Social worker: I'd like to explore where those doubts or fears that I don't see you as a desirable person come from. I'm wondering how you've concluded I don't see you as having much to offer a man. Have I done or said something that conveyed that to you? [*Probing, addressing perceptions/feelings.*]

Client [*thinks for a moment*]: Well, no. Nothing that I can think of.

Social worker: Yet I gather those feelings have been very real to you. I wonder when you first became aware of those feelings.

Client [*after a pause*]: Well, I think it was when we began to talk about my feelings that guys are just interested in me for what they can get. I guess I wondered if you thought I was a real dud. I wanted you to know it wasn't so, that a desirable person could be attracted to me.

Social worker: You know, when we were discussing your feelings toward your mother two or three weeks ago, you said essentially the same thing. [*Using summarization to make a connection between separate but related events.*]

Client: I'm not sure what you mean.

Social worker: You had said you felt your mother doubted you would ever marry because you were so cold you couldn't attract a man.

Client [*smiles pensively and nods affirmatively*]: You know I never wanted to elope. I always wanted to marry in my hometown and have a big wedding. When I had my ring on my finger, I would turn to mother and say, "See, you were wrong!"

Social worker: So you've felt you needed to prove to her that someone could love you. And that's also what you wanted to prove to me. [*Additive empathy reflection.*]

Client: Yes. [*Nods affirmatively.*]

Social worker: I'm interested you've thought maybe I, too, didn't see you as lovable. Could you share with me how you reached that conclusion? [*Social worker continues to explore the unrealistic nature of her perception and how it pervades other relationships. Focus on here and now.*]

By sensitively exploring the client's reluctance to attend the session, the social worker not only resolved an emerging obstacle to productive work, but also assisted the client to explore further her doubts about her attractiveness and to expand her awareness of how these doubts distorted her perceptions of how others viewed her—in this instance, the social worker. Through the exploration, she was able to identify a basic misconception that pervaded her relationships with others and to relate more comfortably with the social worker. Note also that the communication and facilitative skills used by the social worker brought the client to a place where she could examine her thoughts and feelings.

Countertransference Reactions

Social workers may also experience adverse relational reactions that can damage helping relationships if they are not recognized and managed effectively. Just as with clients, social workers' feelings may be realistic or unrealistic. The counterpart of transference, such reactions are known as *countertransference*. Like transference, this phenomenon involves feelings, wishes, and unconscious defensive patterns on the part of the social worker. They are derived from past relationships, interfere with objective perception, and block productive interaction with clients. Countertransference further contaminates helping relationships by producing distorted perceptions, blind spots, wishes, and antitherapeutic emotional reactions and behaviors.

Often, social workers have failed to integrate anger or conflict resolution into their repertoire of skills or personalities. For example, when confronted by a client who is angry, a social worker may be unduly uncomfortable and attempt to divert the expression of such feelings. Other social workers have unresolved feelings about rejections by significant others, and thus find it difficult to relate to clients who are cool and aloof. Still others have failed to resolve resentful feelings toward authority and thus may over-identify with the rebellious adolescent. Marital therapists whose spouses have been unfaithful or controlling may also over-identify with clients who have similar problems and be blind to reciprocal behavior in the marital difficulties they describe. Finally, some social workers have excessive needs to be loved and admired and may behave seductively or strive to impress their clients by disclosing personal information inappropriately. Of course, selective self-disclosure in the form of empathic responsiveness can be beneficial (Goldstein, 1997). Raines (1996) suggests that self-disclosure decisions may be considered within a range of over- and under-involvement; therefore, personal sharing should be rational and related to the current relationship.

Countertransference on the part of the practitioner may also signal a stage of burnout, especially in high-stress situations. James and Gilliland (2001) note that crisis professionals may experience "reawakened" unresolved thoughts and feelings as a result of working with clients who have had similar experiences (p. 419). Maintaining a professional distance may be difficult, especially when the countertransference reaction is related to the trauma experiences and "horror stories" of clients

(Potocky-Tripodi, 2002). As a result, a tendency to become over-involved may emerge as professionals experience vicarious or secondary trauma. Neither situation is productive, and both severely impair the ability to work effectively with clients. Your conscious assessment of these dynamics is critical to both you and the client. You may need to seek supervision and consultation and to consider whether taking time off will assist you to refocus and reenergize your professional work.

Before discussing how to manage countertransference reactions, it is first important to identify their typical manifestations (see Table 18-2).

Note the similarity between the list in Table 18-2 and the reactions that were described in Table 18-1

Table 18-2 Typical practitioner countertransference reactions

- Being unduly concerned about or protective of a client
- Having persistent dreams or erotic fantasies about clients
- Dreading or anticipating sessions with clients
- Feeling uncomfortable when discussing certain problems with a client
- Hostility directed toward a client or inability to empathize with a client
- Blaming others exclusively for a client's difficulties
- Feeling bored, being drowsy, or tuning out a client
- Regularly being tardy or forgetting appointments with certain clients
- Consistently ending sessions early or extending them beyond the designated time
- Trying to impress or being unduly impressed by clients
- Being overly concerned about losing a client
- Arguing with or feeling defensive or hurt by a client's criticisms or actions
- Being overly solicitous and performing tasks that clients are capable of performing
- Probing into a client's sex life
- Liking or disliking certain types of clients (may also be reality based)

for over- and under-involvement. Also note that these countertransference behaviors may evidence a lack of professional distance, unprofessional conduct, and burnout. Unrealistic feelings toward a client and reactions such as those in Tables 18-1 and 18-2 are signals that should prompt you to immediately take appropriate corrective measures. Otherwise, the countertransference will limit your capacity to help, create an impasse in therapy, contribute to the client's problem, and ultimately impair the effectiveness of the helping relationship.

Ordinarily, the first step in resolving countertransference (and often all that is needed) is to engage in introspection. *Introspection* comprises analytical dialogue with oneself aimed at discovering sources of feelings, reactions, cognitions, and behavior. Examples of questions that facilitate introspection include the following:

- "Why am I feeling uncomfortable with this client? What is going on inside me that I am not able to relate in a professional manner?"

- "Why do I dislike (or feel bored, impatient, or irritated) with this client? Are my feelings rational, or does this client remind me of someone from the past?"

- "What is happening inside of me that I don't face certain problems with this client? Am I afraid of a negative reaction on the client's part?"

- "What purpose was served by arguing with this client? Was I feeling defensive or threatened?"

- "Why did I talk so much or give so much advice? Did I feel a need to give something to the client?"

- "What's happening with me that I'm fantasizing or dreaming about this client?"

- "Why am I constantly taking sides with Jean? Am I overlooking Don's (or the parent's or child's) feelings because I'm over-identifying with Jean? Could my own experience or feelings block my objectivity?"

Introspection will also assist you to achieve or regain a realistic perspective on your relationships with clients. Discussion of such topics should also be part of consultation with colleagues and supervisors, enabling you to explore your feelings and to obtain their perspective and advice. Just as clients are sometimes too close to their problems to view them objectively and thus benefit from seeing them from the vantage point of a social worker, so you can likewise benefit from viewing the client–social worker relationship from the unbiased perspective of an uninvolved colleague, consultant, or supervisor.

Professionals who repeatedly become enmeshed in countertransference reactions may need professional help beyond mere introspection. Specifically, these ongoing countertransference reactions will limit the range of their effectiveness and create barriers to effective work with clients.

Realistic Practitioner Reactions

Not all negative feelings toward certain clients represent countertransference reactions. Some clients are abrasive, arrogant, or obnoxious; have irritating mannerisms; or are exploitative of and cruel toward others. Even the most accepting social workers may have difficulty developing positive feelings toward such clients. Social workers, after all, are only human; thus they are not immune to disliking others or feeling irritated and impatient at times. Despite their behavior, clients are entitled to service. In fact, often these clients need help precisely because their behavior alienates others, leaving them isolated and confused about what created their difficulties.

When you look beyond the offensive behaviors of certain clients, you will often discover that beneath the facade of arrogance and toughness are desirable—even admirable—qualities and vulnerability. Further, when you gain access to the private worlds of these individuals, you may find that such clients have endured severe emotional deprivation, and perhaps physical or sexual abuse, or have experienced other types of trauma that exceed their coping ability and capacity to trust. In response to these individuals, and in spite of their behavior, you should convey warmth, acceptance, and empathy, providing a corrective emotional experience for these clients.

Abrasive clients need far more than acceptance, however: They need feedback about how certain aspects of their behavior offend you and others. You can also encourage these clients to risk new behaviors and give them opportunities to learn and practice those skills. Feedback can be extremely helpful if it is conveyed sensitively and imparted in the context of goodwill. In providing such feedback, you must be careful to avoid evaluative or blaming comments that tend to elicit defensiveness—for example, "You boast too much and dominate conversations" or "You are insensitive to other people's feelings and say hurtful things." Clients are far more likely to be receptive to messages that describe and document their behavior and that personalize your response. The following descriptive message embodies ownership of feelings: "When you sneered at me just now, I began to feel defensive and resentful. You've done that several times before, and I find myself backing away from you each time. I'm concerned because I suspect that this is how you interact with others." This message, of course, is highly authentic and would not be appropriate until a sound working relationship has been established.

Sexual Attraction toward Clients

Romantic and sexual feelings toward clients can be especially hazardous, although such feelings are by no means uncommon. One survey of 585 psychotherapists (psychologists) revealed that only 77 (13%) had never been attracted to any client (Pope, Keith-Spiegel, & Tabachnick, 1986). The majority (82%), however, had never seriously considered sexual involvement with a client; of the remaining 18%, 87% had considered becoming involved only once or twice. Of the 585 respondents, approximately 6% had actually engaged in sexual intimacies with clients.

In a more recent study, Strom-Gottfried (1999a) found that of the ethics complaints reported to NASW, 29% involved boundary violations. Of this total, almost three-fourths involved some form of sexual violation. As Strom-Gottfried notes, "Even a small incidence warrants the attention of the profession, particularly supervisors and educators, to assure that any measures available to reduce the incidence further are fully pursued" (1999a, p. 448). Social workers need to be informed about appropriate professional behaviors, exposed to good modeling, explore challenging situations, and use

critical thinking skills in such examinations. When the setting, location, or population exposes the social worker to particular risk (e.g., in rural areas; close religious, cultural, and ethnic communities; and substance abuse treatment settings), potential dilemmas and dual relationships must be explored. Raines (1996) suggests that in situations where sexual attraction is evident, self-disclosure decisions must be considered within a range of over- and under-involvement. Likewise, he suggests, personal sharing should be based on rational grounds and related to the current relationship.

As noted earlier, most social workers have at some point in their careers experienced sexual attraction toward a client. Managing such attraction appropriately is critical. Fortunately, data indicate that the majority of therapists handle their attractions successfully. Although 83% believed the attraction to be mutual, others assumed that the client was unaware of their attraction. When the latter was the case, they believed the attraction did not have any harmful effects on the helping process. By contrast, therapists who believed clients were aware of their attraction understood the detrimental impact on the helping process.

Although Strom-Gottfried (1999a) found that only 6% of those surveyed had engaged in sexual activities with clients, this percentage is quite alarming. Sexual involvement has grievous consequences for clients. They often experience confusion and intense guilt, and thereafter have great difficulty trusting professionals. Some social workers have justified engaging in sexual activities with clients on the basis of assisting them to feel loved or helping them to overcome sexual problems. Such explanations are often thinly disguised and feeble rationalizations for exploiting clients. Typically, such attractions or sexual activities involve clients who are attractive and relatively young. In other instances, justifications are based on the client's behavior toward the social worker. Irrespective of circumstance, this behavior is unacceptable. It is a grave disservice to the client and damaging to the public image of the profession.

The consequences of sexual involvement are devastating for social workers as well. When such behaviors are discovered, offending social workers may be sanctioned, sued for unethical practice, and have their license or certification revoked, essentially removing them from the profession. Ethical standards of conduct established by licensing boards and the NASW Code of Ethics are unequivocal in this regard. The NASW Code of Ethics states: "The social worker should under no circumstances engage in sexual activities or sexual contact with current clients, whether such contact is consensual or forced" (Section 1.09a).

Sexual attraction to a client is normal but must be managed, because acting on an attraction is always unethical in the client–social worker professional relationship. Effectively managing sexual attraction requires engaging in the corrective measures identified earlier for unrealistic feelings and reactions—namely, introspection and consulting with a supervisor. In this regard, it is noteworthy that in the Strom-Gottfried study previously cited, 57% of respondents had the good sense to seek consultation or supervision when they were attracted to a client. We cannot state too strongly that you must not allow feelings to go unchecked. Furthermore, you should take measures to prevent and avoid any problematic circumstances, by altering the manner in which you dress or behave so that it will not prompt either a client or you to become sexually attracted to or involved with each other. Social workers who frequently experience erotic fantasies about clients are particularly vulnerable, are considered impaired professionals, and should consider entering treatment.

MANAGING OPPOSITION TO CHANGE

Social workers and other helping professionals have been inclined to label client behaviors that oppose the direction in which the social worker wishes to go as *resistance*. Resistance has been defined as holding back, disengaging, or in some way subverting change efforts, whether knowingly or not, without open discussion (Meyer, 2001; Nichols & Schwartz, 2004), and as any action or attitude that impedes the course of therapeutic work. Resistance as first conceptualized by Freud

was described as a normal, healthy response. More recently, this concept has been used in a fashion that holds the client responsible for the opposition (Meyer, 2001).

In understanding resistance as a normative self-protective function, think about a situation in which you were told that you needed to make certain changes, whether at work (complete your case notes on time), at home (be more helpful around the house), or in a relationship (lose weight). What was your emotional response? Your behavioral response? Now transfer this experience to your clients. To see how resistance arises with involuntary clients, think about your response and emotional reaction when a telemarketer telephones your home at dinnertime and offers you a product for which you have little interest and no desire to have. In this situation, you have the option of disconnecting the call. When we encounter involuntary clients, they are often acting on these same feelings, but may feel that they do not have the option of disconnecting.

There are several factors involved in understanding the dynamic of resistance. Lum (2004) notes, for example, that resistance is prominent in interactions with persons of color. It may take the form of "minimal involvement, reserved or superficially pleasant." (p. 152–153). The basis for resistance on the part of minority individuals, and indeed entire communities is rooted in a lack of trust or confidence in the professional. Establishing trust and reciprocity in relationships is a major thrust in overcoming the reluctance that people of color have about seeking help from agencies "that are controlled and dominated by whites." (Lum, 2004 p. 152) Another factor in avoiding blaming clients for resistance is to recognize opposition to change as a universal phenomenon, as anyone who has attempted to break long-established habits knows all too well. The force of habits is relentless; moreover, making a change often means foregoing gratifications or coping head-on with frightening or aversive situations. In addition, making a change may entail risking new behavior in the face of unknown consequences. Even though the status quo may cause pain and distress, it is familiar, and the consequences of habitual behavior are predictable. Further, it is not uncommon for clients to have mixed feelings about change, both desiring it and being hesitant or ambivalent about implementing it. Opposing feelings generally coexist—that is, part of the client is motivated to change even as another part strives to maintain the familiar status quo.

Recognizing clients' ambivalent feelings about changing enables you to assist them to explore their feelings and to weigh the advantages and disadvantages of making changes. Indeed, as clients think through their feelings and reassess the implications of maintaining the status quo, the scales often tilt in favor of change. In the helping process, by accepting clients in spite of their opposition to change or the fact that they are in the pre-contemplation stage of change ("I am not sure that I have a problem"), and thereby recognizing their right to self-determination, you may be able to use ethical persuasion to engage them in the change effort. Also, when clients feel free to make up their own minds, they are more likely to become engaged. This factor is crucial, because pressure often engenders an opposing force or reactance. Viewed in this light, recognizing and accepting oppositional feelings to change prevent such feelings from going underground, where they might subtly undermine the helping process. Recognizing, openly discussing, and accepting oppositional feelings thus can liberate a desire and willingness to change.

Reactance theory provides a more fruitful perspective for considering opposition to change. Rather than blaming clients for their oppositional behavior, this theory leads the social worker to anticipate objectively the range of responses to be expected when valued freedoms are threatened (Brehm, 1976). First, some clients may try to regain their freedom directly by attempting to take back what has been threatened. Second, a frequent response is to restore freedom by implication or to "find the loophole" by offering up superficial compliance while violating the spirit of requirements. Third, threatened behaviors and beliefs may be more valued than ever before. Finally, the person or source of the threat may be met with hostility or aggression (Rooney, 1992, p. 130).

Reactance theory lends itself to proactive strategies designed to reduce this kind of opposition.

For example, clients who perceive global pressure to change their lifestyle are likely to experience less reactance if those pressures are narrowed in scope and the change effort emphasizes behaviors that remain free. Second, reactance is likely to be reduced if the client perceives that he or she has at least some constrained choices (Rooney, 1992). Understanding the client's perspective on the situation and avoiding labeling can also act to reduce reactance (p. 135).

Preventing Opposition to Change

Opposition to change may emanate from sources other than ambivalence about changing. Clients may misunderstand the nature of service or of a specific intervention and may therefore be reluctant to cooperate fully. Should this occur, it is vital to explain fully the nature of the service or intervention (informed consent), exploring what is required and where there is room for choice. This discussion should also clarify the roles of the participants and permit voluntary clients to feel free to decide whether to proceed with the therapy. The best way of preventing opposition to change is to be thorough in formulating contracts, clarifying roles, developing specific goals, providing a rationale for specific interventions, inviting questions, eliciting and discussing misgivings, and fostering self-determination.

Other sources of opposition to change include apprehension or fear associated with engaging in behavior that is alien to one's usual functioning or cultural beliefs or having to face a situation that appears overwhelming. These feelings are generally so intense that clients resist carrying out essential actions. Their difficulties may then be compounded by embarrassment over failure to implement the actions, which may produce resistance to seeing the social worker or discussing the problematic situation further. This kind of opposition can also be prevented by anticipating and exploring the fears or values and beliefs and by preparing clients through modeling, behavioral rehearsal, and guided practice. These strategies are discussed at length in Chapter 13, along with other factors that may hinder the change process.

Transference Resistance

Some clients become so enmeshed in major transference reactions that their reactions create an obstacle to progress. Some clients may idealize the social worker and attempt to use the helping relationship as a substitute for other relationships, for example. They may then become preoccupied with this dynamic, rather than focusing on goal attainment. Other clients may be disappointed and resentful because a social worker does not meet their unrealistic expectations. Perceiving the social worker as uncaring, withholding, and rejecting (as they likewise perceived their parents), these clients may struggle with angry feelings (negative transference) toward the social worker, which diverts them from working productively on their problems. Unless social workers recognize and assist such clients to resolve these feelings by discussing them, accepting them, and placing them in a realistic perspective, these clients may prematurely terminate the contact, convinced that their perceptions and feelings are accurate.

Manifestations of Opposition to Change

Opposition to change takes many forms, and the frequency with which clients manifest different forms varies according to the type of setting, the client's personality, and the client's ethnicity and socioeconomic level. The following can be common manifestations of opposition:

- Mental blocking (mind going blank)
- Lengthy periods of silence
- Inattention or mind wandering, changing the subject
- Rambling on at length or dwelling on unimportant details
- Restlessness or fidgeting
- Discussing superficialities or irrelevant matters
- Lying or deliberately misrepresenting facts
- Intellectualizing (avoiding feelings and problems by focusing on abstract ideas)
- Forgetting details of distressing events or of content of previous sessions

- Being tardy for or forgetting, changing, or canceling appointments
- Minimizing problems or claiming miraculous improvement
- Bringing up important material at the end of a session
- Not paying fees for service
- Not applying knowledge and skills gained in sessions in daily life
- Assuming a stance of helplessness

Various verbal ploys to justify not engaging in the change process or taking the requisite corrective action may be expressed as follows:

- "I couldn't do that; it just wouldn't be me."
- "I just can't!"
- "I've tried that, and it doesn't work."
- "I understand what you're saying, but . . ."
- "I'm not so different; isn't everyone . . . ?"

Many of the preceding examples do not necessarily indicate opposition to change. Saying that one cannot complete a particular action needs careful exploration. In fact, if the client continues to work productively, then the phenomenon may not warrant special handling. If the client appears to have reached an impasse, however, one can safely conclude that opposition is involved and shift the focus to exploring the factors that underlie this opposition.

Opposition can also emerge in family and group sessions. Individual members may manifest any of the preceding phenomena, for example. In addition, they may form subgroups and ignore the total group process. Other manifestations of resistance in groups and families include scapegoating individual members. In families, one individual may be characterized as the source of the family's difficulties; in groups, a scapegoat may be faulted for poor group processes. In groups, oppositional behavior may take the form of a client or even several members isolating themselves and not participating, attempting to force the leader to assume responsibility that belongs with the group, engaging in social banter, failing to stay on topic, and struggling for power rather than working cooperatively.

Bear in mind that the family or group member who is opposing change may actually be presenting a concern that other members feel as well. As with individuals, when impasses occur, the social worker should shift the focus of group or family members to the dysfunctional processes so that energies are not diverted to counterproductive activities.[1]

Because opposition to change is a universal phenomenon, it is not necessary to become alarmed about every possible manifestation of it. Moreover, focusing on trivial opposition may elicit adverse reactions from clients, who may feel that the social worker is attempting to scrutinize and analyze their most minute behavior. In fact, overreacting to manifestations of opposition may ultimately produce opposition. A rule of thumb is that if opposition is not strong enough to impede progress, then it is best ignored. Nevertheless, when a client's opposition blocks progress, it is imperative to grant the highest priority to its resolution.

The first step in managing potential opposition to change is to bring it into the light of discussion by focusing on the client's underlying here-and-now feelings. Sensitive and skillful handling is essential because personal feelings toward the social worker are commonly associated with such opposition, and clients find it difficult to risk sharing their feelings in this scenario. (Otherwise, they would have shared them already.) Empathy, warmth, and acceptance play a critical role in eliciting clients' feelings because these ingredients of the client–social worker relationship foster a nonthreatening interpersonal climate.

In exploring sources of opposition, the social worker should not focus on the manifestation per se but rather cite it as an indication that the client is experiencing troubling thoughts and feelings toward the social worker or toward what is happening in the helping process. An authentic response that conveys the social worker's goodwill and concern that progress has bogged down reaffirms the social worker's helpful intent and desire to work out whatever difficulties have arisen. Sometimes, the content discussed in an earlier session may yield cues as to the sources of difficulties. For example, the client may have discussed extremely painful material, disclosed personal feelings that involved shame or guilt, or bristled in response to being confronted with personal contributions to a problematic situation. In such instances, the social worker may open up these feelings for discussion: "You appear awfully quiet today, as though you're struggling with some troubling feelings. I know our last session was upsetting to you. Could you share with me what you're feeling about it just now?"

Discussing sources of opposition often reveals fears about where exploring certain personal feelings might lead. Some clients mistakenly fear that they are losing their minds and that the social worker will initiate steps to admit them to a mental hospital if they share certain thoughts and feelings. Other clients fear that the social worker will condemn them if they disclose hostile feelings toward a child or discuss extramarital affairs. Still other clients fear that the social worker will pressure them to obtain a divorce if they reveal their lack of love for a spouse. With respect to their feelings toward the social worker, some clients fear that the social worker will be hurt or offended if they share negative feelings or that the social worker will see them as ridiculous and reject them if they share warm and affectionate feelings.

As you initiate exploration of the source of opposition, some clients may hesitate to reveal relevant feelings. One technique that often proves successful in cutting through such reluctance is to focus empathically on here-and-now fears about disclosing other troublesome feelings. Your sensitivity, empathy, and genuineness may well pave the way for the client to risk opening up more. The following empathic response is one example of this technique:

Social worker: I'm sensing that you're very uncomfortable about discussing your feelings. I may be wrong, but I get the impression you're afraid I would react negatively if you shared those feelings. I can't say for sure how I'd respond, but I want you to know I'd do my best to understand your feelings. Could you share with me what you're feeling at this moment?

When clients do risk sharing their feelings, it is often therapeutic to accredit their strength for their ability to take this risk and to express reassurance. Such positive responses further cultivate a climate that is conducive to reciprocal openness, obliterate the feared consequences, and reinforce the client for disclosing risky feelings. The following is an example of such a response:

Social worker: I'm very pleased you expressed the anger that has been building up inside you. That took some courage on your part. It's a lot safer to keep those feelings inside, but then they eat away at you and create distance in our relationship. I can accept your anger, and your sharing it with me gives both of us an opportunity to talk things out. I'd feel badly if those feelings continued to build and I didn't even know it.

Positive Connotation

Positive connotation is another technique that is useful in reducing the threat level and enabling clients to save face, thereby protecting their self-esteem after risking revealing problematic feelings. In positive connotation, positive intentions are attributed to what would otherwise be regarded as a client's undesirable or negative behavior. In using this technique, the social worker recognizes that the meaning ascribed to behavior can be viewed both positively and negatively, depending on one's vantage point. When viewed as an obstacle to progress, opposition takes on a negative meaning. When viewed from the client's perspective, however, the same behavior may have positive intentions. The following examples clarify this point:

- A client cancels an appointment and holds back in the following session. Exploration reveals that she resented the social worker "pressuring her" to follow a certain course of action. The social worker empathizes with her feelings as evidence of her determination to be her own person.

- A client has been preoccupied with thoughts or fantasies about the social worker and has digressed from working on problems. The social worker interprets this feeling as evidence that he is moving away from his self-imposed isolation and is permitting himself to experience feelings of closeness that he can gradually risk in social relationships.

- After an extended period of silence and exploration of feelings related to it, a spouse launches into a tirade over how the social worker took sides with the partner in the previous session. The social worker labels the client's response as a legitimate effort to be understood and to ensure that the social worker does not make the marriage worse by drawing erroneous conclusions about it.

The goal of positive connotation is not to condone clients' opposition or to reinforce their distorted perceptions. Rather, the objectives are to minimize clients' needs to defend themselves, to safeguard their already precarious sense of self, and to act in a manner that is consistent with a strengths perspective. When using this technique, it is important to assist clients to recognize that their reactions are derived from distorted perceptions (if they are) and to encourage them to express their feelings directly.

Redefining Problems as Opportunities for Growth

The technique of redefining problems as growth opportunities is a close relative of positive connotation because it also involves relabeling or reframing. Both clients and social workers tend to view problems negatively. Moreover, clients often view remedial courses of action as "necessary evils," dwelling on the threat involved in risking new behaviors. Therefore, it is often helpful to reformulate problems and essential tasks as opportunities for growth and means to gain liberation from stifling and self-defeating behaviors. Relabeling or reframing emphasizes the positives—that is, the benefits of change rather than the discomfort, fear, and other costs of modifying one's behavior.

In using this technique, it is important not to convey an unrealistically positive attitude. The fears and threats are very real to clients who risk change, and being unduly optimistic may simply convey a lack of understanding on your part. Neither reframing nor relabeling minimizes clients' problems or ignores fears in risking new behaviors. Both do, however, enable clients to view their difficulties in a fuller perspective that embodies positive as well as negative factors. The following are examples of how problem situations might be relabeled as opportunities for growth:

Relabeling

- A teenage foster child who has run away because the foster parents insisted he adhere to a night-time curfew does not want to return to the foster home because the foster parents "are unreasonable." The social worker describes returning as a challenge to deal with a problem head-on and to work it out rather than running away from it, which has been the client's pattern.

- An elderly female with a family history of breast cancer is reluctant to see a doctor because she fears she has cancer. The social worker empathizes with her fears but describes the checkup as an opportunity to rule out the frightening possibility or to receive treatment before the disease progresses, should she have cancer.

Reframing

- A youth feels embarrassed about taking a battery of vocational tests and attending a vocational-technical school, rather than going to college. The social worker acknowledges his discomfort but emphasizes that taking the tests offers an opportunity to learn more about his aptitudes and to expand his choices in planning his future.

- A woman expresses intense apprehension about leaving her abusive spouse. The social worker empathizes with her fear, but points out that leaving her spouse will allow her to pursue opportunities she envisioned for herself and for her children.

Confronting Patterns of Opposition

In some instances, clients fail to make progress toward their goals because of the persistence of pervasive dysfunctional patterns of behavior. For example, some clients may intellectualize extensively to avoid having to experience painful emotions such as loneliness or depression. Other clients may relate in a distant, aloof manner or in aggressive ways to protect against becoming close to others and risking painful rejection. Still others may consistently hold other people or circumstances responsible for their difficulties, failing to

examine or acknowledge their part in creating the situation. Because such patterns of behavior often create impasses in therapy, social workers must be able to recognize and handle them. Confronting clients with discrepancies between expressed goals and behaviors that defeat accomplishment of those goals is often needed to break such impasses. Because Chapter 17 discussed confrontation at length, we will limit our discussion here to a special type of confrontation: therapeutic binds.

Therapeutic Binds

Occasionally, social workers may encounter clients who stubbornly cling to self-defeating behaviors despite awareness that these behaviors perpetuate their difficulties. In such instances, placing clients in a *therapeutic bind* may provide the impetus needed to modify the problematic behaviors. In using a therapeutic bind, social workers confront clients with their self-defeating behaviors in such a way that they must either modify their behaviors or own responsibility for choosing to perpetuate their difficulties despite their expressed intentions to the contrary (Nichols & Schwartz, 2004; Goldenberg & Goldenberg, 2004) The only way out of a therapeutic bind, unless one chooses to acknowledge no intention of changing, is to make constructive changes.

Following are some examples of situations in which the authors of this book successfully employed therapeutic binds:

- Despite intensive efforts to resolve fears of being rejected in relationships with others, a client continued to decline social invitations and made no effort to reach out to others. The social worker asked her about her apparent choice to perpetuate her social isolation rather than to risk relating to others.

- A supervisor complained to an Employee Assistance Program (EAP) social worker about conflict with other members on his team. In exploring the situation, the supervisor admitted that he consistently made unilateral decisions despite repeated feedback and negative reactions from other team members. The social worker asked the supervisor whether he had decided it was more important to him to be in control than to improve his working relationships.

- An adolescent persisted in being truant from school, violating family rules, and engaging in antisocial behaviors despite his assertion that he wanted to be independent. The social worker countered that the client seemed unprepared to use his freedom wisely, because being a law unto himself would simply result in the juvenile court further constraining his choices until he demonstrated a capacity to set limits on his behavior.

- In marital counseling, a wife constantly harped on her husband's previous infidelity despite expressing a desire to strengthen their marriage. The husband's response to her behavior was to withdraw and disengage from the relationship. The social worker presented the wife with the contradictions in her behavior, stressing that it

appeared to be more important to her to punish her husband than to focus on strengthening the relationship.

In using therapeutic binds, it is vital to observe the guidelines for confrontation, thereby avoiding "clobbering" or alienating the client. In this way, asking a question about the apparent contradiction or conclusion can be experienced as a more respectful form of confrontation leading to self-reflection. A therapeutic bind is a potent but high-risk technique, and social workers should use it sparingly. When it is employed, the social worker should take care to temper its jarring effect with empathy, concern, and sensitive exploration of the dynamics behind the self-defeating patterns. Above all, the social worker should be sure that the technique is being used to assist the client and not to act out the social worker's own frustrations about the client's opposition.

Summary

This chapter described barriers to change with individuals, including relational reactions, over- and under-involvement, and racial and cultural barriers. Relational reactions can occur as a result of social workers' real or imagined perceptions of clients, or they may derive from perceptions that clients formulate about social workers. Other relational dynamics include transference and countertransference. Acting on sexual attraction toward clients is particularly damaging and exploitative and has severe consequences; instead, social workers should recognize these attractions and deal with them appropriately (i.e., ethically).

Relational reactions, including resistance, are normal manifestations of opposition to change. In view of this reality, this chapter discussed at length techniques for recognizing and managing these reactions and opposition to change. Your skillful handling of these dynamics is critical to ensuring that the helping relationship is productive and remains focused on the desired outcome. Be aware, however, that barriers to change can be the

result of environmental factors beyond the control of the client; in such a case, you may need to assume the role of advocate.

Internet Resources

See our companion website for hot links to some helpful URLs. Note that URLs are subject to change. We will endeavor to update the links on the companion website as much as possible.

Using InfoTrac College Edition, you can add to your knowledge and skills related to managing barriers to change by entering the following keywords: "stages of change," "barriers to change," "transference," "countertransference," "therapeutic binds," "working alliance," "client–social worker relationship," "cross-cultural practice," "cross-cultural counseling," "empathy and cultural competence."

You can also read two articles pertinent to this chapter: Bower (1997), Handmaker, Miller, and Manicke (1999), and Bower (1997).

The Journal of Ethnic and Cultural Diversity in Social Work (www.haworthpress.com/web/

ECDSW) and *the Journal of Human Behavior in the Social Environment* are excellent resources that augment the content in this chapter.

For additional information on the legal regulation of social work practice, visit *www.aswb.org* or *www.aswb.org/members_policy_VII_7.htm.*

Related Online Content

Visit the *Direct Social Work Practice* companion website at *http://socialwork. wadsworth.com/hepworth7* for additional learning tools such as glossary terms, chapter outlines, InfoTrac College Edition keywords, relevant web links, and chapter practice quizzes. Also, be sure to check out the Direct Practice Virtual Reader, where the authors have personally selected articles relevant to this chapter using InfoMarks.

Skill Development Exercises in Managing Relational Reactions and Opposition

The following exercises will assist you in expanding your skills in responding appropriately to relational reactions and opposition to change. Study each client message and determine whether a relational reaction or opposition to change might be involved. Then write the response you would give if you were the social worker. Compare your response with the modeled response provided at the end of the exercises. Bear in mind that the modeled response is only one of many possible appropriate responses.

Client Statements

1. *Male client* [*has been discussing feelings of rejection and self-doubt after his partner broke up with him; suddenly he looks down, sighs, then looks up*]: Say, did I tell you I got promoted at work?

2. *Female client, age 23* [*to male social worker, age 25*]: I've been feeling very close to you these past weeks. I was wondering if you could hold me in your arms for just a moment.

3. *Male client, age 27* [*agitated*]: I've been coming to see you for 8 weeks, and things haven't changed a bit. I'm beginning to question your competence.

4. *Delinquent on probation, age 16:* I think it's ridiculous to have to come here every week.

You don't have to worry about me. I'm not getting into any trouble.

5. *Female in welfare-to-work program:* Sure, you say you want to help me. All you social workers are just alike. You don't understand the pressure I have to get a good job in the time I have left on welfare. If you really want to help, you would increase the time I have left.

6. *Client, age 27* [*to male social worker*]: I've just never been able to trust men. My old man was alcoholic, and the only thing you could depend on with him was that he'd be drunk when you needed him most.

7. *Male client* [*to female mental health social worker*]: Sometimes I really felt I was cheated in life, you know, with parents who didn't give a damn what happened to me. I think about you—how warm and caring you are, and—I know it sounds crazy but I wish I'd had you for a mother. Sometimes I even daydream about it.

8. *Client* [*after an emotion-laden previous session, the client yawns, looks out the window, and comments*]: Not much to talk about today. Nothing much has happened this week.

9. *Male client, age 24* [*in fifth session*]: I have this thing where people never measure up to my expectations. I know I expect too much, and I always end up feeling let down.

10. *Middle-aged minority male* [*challenging*]: I suppose you see me in the usual stereotype, you people have for [minority] males. I want you to know that I'm ambitious and want to do right by my family. I just need a job right now.

Modeled Responses

1. "No, but before you do, I'd like to know more about what you were feeling just a moment ago when you were discussing your breakup with your partner. I was sensing that was painful for you to talk about. Could you share what you feel as you think about it?"

2. "I'm flattered that you would want me to hold you and pleased you could share those

feelings with me. I want you to know that I feel close to you, too, but if I were to let myself feel romantically inclined toward you, I'd be letting you down. I couldn't be helpful to you if I were involved in that way. I hope you can understand."

3. "I can see you're anxious to get things worked out, and that's a plus. [*Positive connotation.*] But you're pretty ticked off with me, as though I haven't been doing my job. I'd like to understand those feelings more. What do you feel I should be doing differently? [*Exploring feelings and expectations.*]"

4. "You sound pretty angry about having to report to me each week. I can't blame you for that. Still, the judge ordered it, and neither of us really has any choice. How do you suggest that we make the best of the situation?"

5. "I'm sorry you feel I'm not really interested in helping you. I gather you've had some bad experiences with other caseworkers, and I hope our relationship can be better. I sense your frustration at working under this time pressure and your anxiety about what will occur if you don't succeed in the time available. I will work with you to make the best use of the time to get a job you can feel good about. Sometimes as we come to the end of the time frame there are some possibilities for an extension, but that can't be guaranteed. I wonder if the best use of our time might be to do the best we can to get the kind of job you want in the time available."

6. "I can understand, then, that you might find it difficult to trust me—wondering if I'm really dependable."

7. [*Smiling.*] "Thank you for the compliment. I gather you've been experiencing my care for you and find yourself longing for the love and care you didn't receive as a child. I can sense your feelings keenly and appreciate your sharing them."

8. "Somehow that doesn't fit with what we talked about last week. You expressed some very deep feelings about yourself and your marriage. I'd like to hear what you've been feeling about what we discussed last time."

9. "I wonder if that's what you're feeling just now in our relationship—that I haven't measured up to your expectations in some way. Could you share with me what you've been feeling in that regard?"

10. "I appreciate your sharing those feelings with me. I gather you've wondered how I see you. I see you as an ambitious and responsible person, and I want you to know I appreciate those qualities in you."

Notes

1. In some instances, manifestations of group behaviors that may appear at first to be opposition will actually prove to be adjustment reactions of members to excessive changes (e.g., loss of members, canceled sessions, or a move to another meeting place), which tend to frustrate and discourage group members.

PART 4

The Termination Phase

The third and final phase of the helping process encompasses the final evaluation of progress and the termination of the helping relationship. Although it has received less attention in the literature than the beginning and middle phases of the helping process, the final phase is important because the way social workers bring the helping relationship to a close strongly influences whether clients will maintain the progress they have achieved and continue to grow following termination. For this reason, social workers must understand how to sensitively and skillfully conclude their work with clients, even if the end of the helping process is unplanned.

This chapter introduces you to strategies for evaluating case progress in work with individuals, groups, and families. The bulk of the chapter addresses the varieties of planned and unplanned terminations, the common worker and client reactions to termination, the strategies for maintaining client gains post-termination, and the use of rituals in effectively ending the helping relationship.

The Final Phase: Evaluation and Termination

CHAPTER OVERVIEW

Chapter 19 reviews methods for evaluating case progress, describes various factors that affect the termination process, identifies relevant tasks for both social workers and clients, and discusses skills essential to managing termination effectively.

EVALUATION

Evaluating outcomes of the helping process has assumed ever-increasing significance in direct practice; indeed, the majority of social workers engage in some form of evaluation, as we noted in Chapter 12. If you have systematically obtained baseline measures, clients will be prepared for evaluation at termination. You can further enhance their cooperation by again reviewing the rationale and actively involving them in the process. For example, you can introduce this topic to the client by making any of the following statements:

- "An important part of termination is to assess the results we have achieved and to identify what helped you most and least during our work together."

- "As an agency, we're committed to improving the quality of our services. Your honest feedback will help us to know how we're doing."

- "Our evaluation measures will help you and me see how your symptoms have changed since we began working together."

Several different evaluation methods can be used to determine client progress throughout the helping process and at its conclusion—for example, standardized tests, direct observation, goal attainment scaling, and client self-reports though logs, journals, and surveys. The power of evaluation is strengthened when multiple sources of information are used. Whatever method is used, evaluations focus on three dimensions of service: (1) outcomes, (2) process, and (3) satisfaction.

Outcomes

Outcome evaluation involves assessing the results achieved against the goals that were formulated during the contracting phase of work. As described in Chapters 8 and 12, the methods utilized during the assessment and goal-setting phases will, in part, determine which outcomes you measure. For example, you may measure changes in the *frequency* of difficulties (e.g., getting to work on time, getting detention, binging, experiencing negative cognitions, forgetting to take medications), the *severity* of problems (e.g., self-esteem scores on rapid assessment instruments or anxiety as measured by a self-anchored rating scale), or the *achievement* of goals or tasks (e.g., applying for and getting a job, completing homework, improving parenting and disciplinary practices). These items, when compared with the baseline measures taken when the client first entered service, will help determine the extent of progress and the client's readiness for termination (Epstein & Brown, 2002).

If the initial goals for work were vague or unmeasurable, or if no baseline measures were taken, you will need to use an interview or questionnaire to determine your clients' views so you can then compare their sense of progress against your own observations. The difficulty with these recollections, of course, is that they may be highly selective and may be affected by numerous factors, such as the client's desire to please (or punish) the social worker, the client's interest in concluding service, or the hope that problems *are* resolved and that further services are not necessary. Although it is unwise to challenge clients' perceptions, you can reduce biases by asking clients to provide actual examples of recent events ("critical incidents") that illustrate their attainment of goals. This discussion also provides an opportunity for you to reaffirm the client's accomplishments, which tends to heighten his or her confidence and satisfaction.

In addition to clients' perceptions of their progress, evaluation should include other criteria where feasible. For example, feedback from collateral contacts, such as family members, teachers, other helpers, or fellow clients (in groups or group settings), may provide additional perspectives on client progress.

Process

Another aspect of evaluation relates to clients' perceptions of aspects of the helping process that were useful or detrimental. Feedback about techniques and incidents that enhanced or blocked progress will help you to hone certain skills, eliminate others, and use techniques with greater discrimination. Such "formative evaluation" methods also help organizations to determine which elements of their programs were effective in bringing about the desired change or whether the techniques used were consistent with standardized agency protocols (Royse, Thyer, Padgett, & Logan, 2001). These evaluations capture the nuances of client–social worker interactions that contribute to treatment effectiveness. A technique that is useful with an assertive client, for example, may produce the opposite effect with a depressed client. Likewise, a family intervention may be most

effective if it is structured in a particular way. A social worker may have attributed a positive outcome to a masterfully executed technique, only to find the client was helped far more by the practitioner's willingness to reach out and maintain hope when the client had almost given up (McCollum & Beer, 1995).

With children and other clients who lack high written or verbal ability, the use of expressive techniques, such as collages or painting, may help to tap into evaluative content. For example, the client may be asked to draw or display something to illustrate "what I liked best/least about our work together" or "what helped me during my time here."

Evaluation instruments can also be used to more precisely measure the aspects of the helping process that were instrumental in achieving change. For example, Yalom's Curative Factors Scale (Stone, Lewis, & Beck, 1994) might identify the dimensions of treatment groups and their relative therapeutic effectiveness. You can also construct valid measures of practice effectiveness by combining measures (e.g., records about sessions, client self-reports, observations) to provide an approximate measure of the effectiveness of the intervention processes used (Toseland & Rivas, 2001).

Satisfaction

The outcomes achieved and the means used to achieve them are important measures of client progress. Another measure in the increasingly competitive and consumer-conscious practice environment seeks information about client satisfaction. You may gauge this level of satisfaction in your evaluative discussions with the client. Some settings facilitate gathering formal feedback by sending out written client feedback forms at the termination of service or at a specified follow-up period. Some payers, such as managed care companies, will also evaluate providers by directly seeking client input.

These instruments address satisfaction with the social worker's service by asking questions such as "Would you refer a friend or family member to us for services in the future?" "Were you and the clinician able to meet your goal?", and "Do you believe you needed additional services that were not provided?" (Corcoran & Vandiver, 1996, p. 57). Satisfaction surveys also evaluate structural or operational issues such as appropriateness of the waiting room, convenience of parking, time elapsed between the client's request for service and first appointment, and friendliness of reception staff (Ackley, 1997; Corcoran & Vandiver, 1996).

TERMINATION

Termination refers to the process of formally ending the individual social worker–client relationship. It is a feature of practice with a variety of client systems, from individuals and families to task groups, coalitions, and communities, and it occurs regardless of the duration of the helping relationship.[1] Terminations can occur when goals are met, when clients make a transition to other services, when time-limited services are concluded, and when social workers or clients leave the helping relationship. Even if clients are likely to "come and go" from service over a period of time as their concerns and needs change, it is important to draw closure to each unique episode of care.

The notion of ending is often introduced at the beginning of service, when the social worker notes the likely duration of care, the number of sessions allotted, or the goals that will guide the helping process. In some time-limited treatment models, the fixed length of care is part of informed consent discussions at the outset. For example, the social worker might explain, "We believe that brief treatment is effective and helps both you and me make efficient use of our time together. So we'll begin today by getting an idea of the goals you want to work on, and the best way to use our time over the next 6 to 8 weeks to achieve those goals."

Whether in short- or long-term therapy models, successful termination involves preparing clients adequately for separation from the social worker and/or group and accomplishing other tasks that

facilitate the transition from being a client to being "on one's own":[2]

1. Evaluating the service provided and the extent to which goals were accomplished[3]
2. Determining when to implement termination
3. Mutually resolving emotional reactions experienced during the process of ending
4. Planning to maintain gains achieved and to achieve continued growth

The significance of these tasks and the extent to which they can be successfully accomplished are determined in large measure by the context in which the helping relationship takes place. The intensity of the termination process is affected by factors such as the type of contact (voluntary or involuntary), the size and characteristics of the client system, and the nature of the intervention used. Emotional reactions will vary depending on the nature and length of the helping relationship. That is, involuntary clients and those with more structured and time-limited services will likely experience less of a sense of loss at termination than those who have engaged in longer and more voluntary relationships with the social worker. For example, termination of a time-limited educational group may be less intense and require less preparation of members than would the ending of an ongoing interpersonal support group. Terminations from brief crisis intervention, case management, or discharge planning relationships may differ in intensity depending on the nature of the needs met and the length of service. Termination from family sessions may be less difficult than from individual work, because most of the client system will continue to work and be together, albeit without the social worker's involvement.

Types of Termination

Terminations generally fall into one of two categories: unplanned and planned. *Unplanned terminations* occur when the clients withdraw prematurely from services or when social workers leave the helping relationship due to illness, job change, or other circumstances. *Planned terminations* occur when clients' goals are achieved, when transfer or referral is necessary, or when service is concluded due to the time-limited nature of the setting (such as hospitals or schools) or the treatment modality used (such as brief treatment or fixed-length groups).

Unplanned Terminations

Unplanned terminations can be initiated by the actions of the client, the social worker, or both.

Client-initiated termination can be triggered by dropping out of treatment, by an adverse event that renders the client unavailable for service, or by the client behaving in such a way that services are withdrawn or he or she is ejected from the setting. Examples of adverse events include being arrested, running away, committing suicide, or otherwise dying unexpectedly. The category of "dropouts" from service is similarly broad, including clients who are seeking services involuntarily or are otherwise unmotivated, clients who are dissatisfied with the social worker but are unable to verbalize those concerns, clients who feel they have made satisfactory progress and thus "are done" whether the clinician thinks so or not, and clients who decide to quit for pragmatic reasons, such as a lack of funds or the inconvenience of the service setting. A mixed form of unplanned termination can be characterized as a "pushout," where the social worker and the client have failed to "click" and the client's discontinuation is prompted or reinforced by the practitioner's disinterest or lack of commitment (Hunsley, Aubrey, Vestervelt, & Vito, 1999).

A common theme of all these client-initiated endings is that they are unanticipated and thus allow no opportunity for discussion, processing, or closure, yet the residue of feelings and unfinished business remains. The tasks of termination (reflection on the work together, planning for the future, marking the end of treatment) remain undone and both parties may experience feelings of abandonment, anger, rejection, failure, relief, and shame.

Similar issues can arise from certain forms of practitioner-initiated unplanned endings—for example, when the social worker dies, becomes incapacitated, or is dismissed. Other practitioner-initiated unplanned endings, such as those due to layoffs or job transfers, may elicit negative reactions from the client, but generally allow time for processing and closure. We will discuss managing those feelings and endings in a later section. Other unplanned endings require special measures so that the tasks of termination can be approximated to the extent possible.

Managing Unplanned Terminations. Some estimates suggest that 50% of the overall client population will drop out of service (Kazdin & Wassell, 1998; Sweet & Noones, 1989) and that this figure may be even higher for certain subgroups. Some settings may have their own protocols for dealing with "no shows," and a different mechanism may be needed for the client who fails to reappear after a first session (see Meyer, 2001) compared to one who ceases to appear for service midway through the course of treatment.

A common response to unplanned termination by the client is for the social worker to reach out to him or her by phone or letter. The goal in doing so may be to acknowledge the decision to conclude services, to encourage the client to come in for a closing session, or to achieve the purposes of such a session through the phone call or letter. For example, one client who was arrested could not receive phone calls or return for services. Nevertheless, the social worker was able to write him a letter in which she reviewed the goals he had achieved and the issues with which he continued to struggle. She conveyed her regard for him and informed him of the availability of other services during his incarceration and following his release. A similar technique can be used when a social worker must leave abruptly, when a client quits service, or when a client leaves an institution against medical advice. Such endings are not ideal because they do not allow the client the opportunity to express his or her views or participate in evaluation, but they do help to mark the ending and "clear the air" regarding future services.

When a worker dies or otherwise becomes incapacitated, it is incumbent upon his or her colleagues to intervene for the care or transfer of the clients involved. They must also recognize that these clients' needs and reactions will be shaped by the abruptness and nature of the loss, their personal loss histories, and the nature of the needs for which they were seeking help (Philip & Stevens, 1992; Philip, 1994). Thus, grieving the lost relationship may become a primary task alongside continued work on their treatment goals identified earlier.

Likewise, when a client dies unexpectedly, whether through an accident or a traumatic act such as homicide or suicide, the loss has significant implications for the helping professionals left behind. For reasons of propriety and professional development, supervisory and collegial support should be the primary resource to the mourner, with coworkers offering empathy, permission to grieve, and encouragement to talk about and integrate the feelings that emerge (Chemtob, Hamada, Bauer, Torigoe, & Kinney, 1988; Krueger, Moore, Schmidt, & Wiens 1979).

Formal processes for reviewing the case—referred to as "postvention" by Shneidman (1971)—can take the form of individual or group processing of the case (Pilsecker, 1987), a psychological autopsy (Kleepsies, Penk, & Forsyth, 1993; Chemtob et al., 1988) or critical incident stress debriefing (Farrington, 1995). Each of these mechanisms has a slightly different intent and focus, but each offers the opportunity for the social worker to acknowledge the loss, contemplate the experience with the client, have supportive review, and deepen understanding of what took place.

Unplanned terminations of a member from a group may occur for a number of reasons, both related and unrelated to the group itself, such as poor fit, discomfort with the group, transportation difficulties, or time conflicts (Toseland & Rivas, 2001). In any case, the unplanned departure presents challenges for achieving termination-related tasks. Because cohesion is central to the success of a group, the loss of a member can threaten that bond, make members question their own achievements or appropriateness for the group, and make them reluctant to continue building trusting relationships with the remaining group members. The social worker should try to encourage closure in some form, both for the departing member and for the rest of the group. Even if it derails the group's preexisting agenda or timeline, this effort is time well spent because it supports the future health and success of the group process and the individual members.

CASE EXAMPLE

A cohort of 16 students had spent 18 months taking every class together. At the midpoint of the MSW program, however, one student decided to drop out to spend more time with family members who were aging and ailing. Moira was a respected and successful member of the class, and her decision took her instructor and faculty advisor by surprise. Nevertheless, they were persuaded by her confidence that her decision was the correct one for her at that particular point in time. Still, Moira felt sheepish about her decision. Although she e-mailed her classmates to let them know of her decision, she declined the instructor's suggestion that she come back for one more session to achieve closure for herself and the group. She did, however, give permission for the instructor to discuss her decision with the group and understood that they would be processing it in class the next time they met.

The day of the class, the instructor opened the conversation by noting Moira's empty seat and asking the class to share what they knew about her decision not to return. Because she had contacted many of them individually, it wasn't necessary for the instructor to share what she knew about Moira's decision. Next, the group discussed their reactions to Moira's departure, which included self-doubt ("If she can't do it all, how can we?"), anger and confusion ("She put so much into this—why quit now?"), sorrow ("She brought a lot of important things to this group"), hope ("Maybe this will just be a temporary choice"), and understanding ("I think she's doing what she needs to do for her family").

The instructor then asked, "What did Moira give to the group and how can we acknowledge that?" After discussing what they had learned from and valued in their time with Moira, class members wrote notes to her to share these impressions. The instructor collected the notes and, without reading them, included them with a letter to Moira in which she detailed her view on Moira's achievements, capacities, and options should she decide to return to the program in the future.

Following this, the class discussed the impact of acknowledging and processing her departure. They compared it to other losses that the class had experienced when classmates had earlier dropped out ("Here today, gone tomorrow") and the feelings evoked by the lack of closure on those losses, which included suspicion ("Were they forced out?"), apprehension ("Can I cut it? Am I next?"), guilt ("Was it something I said or did?"), and hurt ("Nobody really matters here"). The process of closure in Moira's case, even in her absence, achieved the goals of termination and sent a powerful message to the class—just as it does with other types of groups who experience such a loss.

Note that "closure," as used here and elsewhere in this chapter, does not mean that the matter is resolved, that the person and the loss are tucked away permanently and are not subject to further consideration. It does not mean, "Okay, I'm done. I can move on." Instead, closure simply means that the experience or episode has been reflected upon and the importance of the transition has been marked. It signifies an end in a way that helps free the participants to move on. Clinically, an ambiguous or mishandled termination may leave the social worker and client with a sense of unfinished business, and it may make it difficult for the client to invest easily or fully in future therapeutic relationships. Closure makes a difference.

Planned Terminations with Unsuccessful Outcomes

Sometimes termination occurs in a planned manner, but the endings are not marked by successful achievement of service goals. This may occur when the social worker or the client is dissatisfied with the helping relationship, when the client is hopelessly stalemated despite vigorous and persistent efforts to overcome his or her difficulties, when the social worker is not competent to address the client's needs, or when the client fails to comply with appropriate treatment requirements. Unlike unplanned terminations, these endings are not accompanied by abrupt disappearance from service and thus afford the social worker and client a chance to achieve the goals of closure. Groups also occasionally end with unsuccessful results, and members may be frustrated, disappointed, or angry with the leader or with other members (Smokowski, Rose, & Bacallao, 2001).

When the helping process ends unsuccessfully, termination should include discussion of (1) factors that prevented achieving more favorable results and (2) clients' feelings about seeking additional help in the future. This effort requires the social worker to create as safe an atmosphere as possible so that both parties can honestly air concerns, with the intention of both achieving closure and keeping open possibilities for future service. It also requires the ability to hear and share feedback in a nondefensive manner. Sometimes, as a result of this termination conversation, the social worker and client may come to agreement on the conditions under which they would reconnect and develop a new contract for future services. At this final session, the social worker should be prepared to offer referrals to other services if the issue for termination has been a poor fit with the individual practitioner or agency.

Planned Terminations with Successful Outcomes

As noted earlier, planned terminations can take many forms. The nature of the setting, intervention method, or funding source can all impose external pressures to terminate within a specific period of time. Other planned endings emerge from the helping relationship itself, as clients achieve their goals and move on to independence from the social worker. This step may not signal that the client has completed all of his or her desired goals or tasks (or that they are "done" in the social worker's eyes), but means only that the client has experienced "at least enough relief so that he no longer wants help *at that point*" (Reid, 1972, p. 199). Related to this development is what Cummings calls "brief intermittent therapy throughout the life cycle" (1991, p. 35). That is, individuals who need social work services may come to use them as they do medical and other services—seeking them out in times of need to address acute problems rather than pursuing single episodes of extended treatment. In these termination situations, the social worker and client may therefore establish contingencies under which they will resume services in the future.

In organizations or agencies whose function involves providing service according to fixed time intervals, termination must be planned accordingly. In school settings, for example, services are generally discontinued at the conclusion of an academic year. In hospitals and other institutional settings, the duration of service is determined by the length of hospitalization, confinement, or insurance coverage.

Some service models, such as time-limited groups or fixed-length residential programs, are clearly designed to pace and conclude services within a specific time frame. For example, some treatment programs are organized such that clients progress from one program (and one set of workers) to another as their needs change. In residential programs or other settings with fixed lengths of stay, the course of treatment will involve a relatively predicable process whereby the client progresses through steps or phases leading to termination. Depending on the context of treatment, services may extend from several days to several months. Temporal factors are also central in termination for social work students, who leave a given practicum setting at the completion of an academic year.

Terminations that are prompted by program structure or preexisting time constraints involve certain factors peculiar to these circumstances. First, the ending of a school year or of a training period for students is a predetermined time for termination, which reduces the possibility that clients will interpret time limits as being arbitrarily imposed or perceive the social worker's leaving as desertion or abandonment. Knowing the termination date well in advance also provides ample time to resolve feelings about separation. Conversely, it also means that in school settings student clients may lose many supports all at one time.

Another factor common to terminations that are determined by temporal constraints or agency function rather than by individual factors is that the client's problems may not have been adequately resolved when termination occurs. The predetermined, untimely ending may lead to intense reactions from the client who is losing service and ending the helping relationship in what feels like midstream (Weiner, 1984). Social workers are therefore confronted with the dual tasks of working through feelings associated with untimely separation and referring clients for additional services when indicated.

Predetermined endings imposed by the close of a school year or a fixed length of service do not necessarily convey the same expectations of a positive outcome as do time limits that are determined by individual client progress. In other words, to say "I will see you until May because that is sufficient time to achieve your goals" conveys a far more positive expectation than "I will see you until May because that is all the time I will have available before leaving the placement." Nevertheless, time-limited work does not necessarily lead to unsatisfactory outcomes. Clients can benefit from the focused nature of this work and may experience a fruitful relationship with the social worker even if termination results in referral for other services.

For example, one of the authors of this book worked with a client with serious, long-term mental health problems. During the time allotted for her field placement, she was able to help the client through a crisis and assist him to build his social supports so that future crises would not inevitably result in rehospitalization. In the termination process, they reviewed the accomplishments made during the year and the client met his new social worker, who would meet with him on a less intensive basis for support and maintenance of the gains made previously.

When terminations are not predetermined by agency setting, client circumstance, or form of service, how do the social worker and client know when to end? When services are highly goal directed, the termination point may be clear: It occurs when goals are reached and changes are sustained. When goals are amorphous or ongoing, however, determining a proper ending point can be more difficult. Theoretically, humans can grow indefinitely, and determining when clients have achieved optimal growth is no simple task. Ordinarily, it is appropriate to introduce the idea of termination when the client has reached the point of diminishing returns—that is, when the gains from sessions taper off to the point of being minor in significance. The client may indicate through words or actions that he or she is ready to discontinue services, or the social worker may initiate such discussion.

Two other variants on planned termination warrant discussion. "Simultaneous termination" occurs when the client and the social worker leave the service or agency at the same time. It offers the advantage of mutually shared, powerful experiences of ending, and it often focuses the time and attention devoted to termination tasks (Joyce, Duncan, Duncan, Kipnes, & Piper, 1996). Simultaneous termination also requires a good deal of self-awareness on the part of the social worker to ensure that his or her personal reactions to termination are not projected on the client. As with other endings involving the social worker's departure from the organization, the conditions and resources for future service should also be addressed.

The second type of planned termination occurs when the client dies, but the death is anticipated and planned for. Some settings, such as hospice care, nursing homes, or hospitals, expose social workers and other caregivers to death on a regular basis. The orientation and supervision offered in such settings must address this crucial aspect of practice, as particular skills are needed to assist clients in such circumstances and effectively manage social worker responses. For example, when the helping relationship is expected to end in conjunction with the patient's death, it may involve life review and reminiscences, plans to address end-of-life concerns, and attention to spiritual matters (Arnold, 2002).[4]

Understanding and Responding to Clients' Termination Reactions

Inherent in termination is separation from the social worker (and other clients, in the case of groups, inpatients, or residential settings). Separation typically involves mixed feelings for both the social worker and the client, which vary in intensity according to the degree of success achieved, the strength of the attachment, the type of termination, the cultural orientation of the client, and his or her previous experiences with separations from significant others (Bembry & Ericson, 1999; Dorfman, 1996). When clients successfully accomplish their goals, they experience a certain degree of pride and satisfaction as the helping process draws to a close. If they have grown in strength and self-esteem, they view the future optimistically as an opportunity for continued growth.

Most clients in individual, conjoint, family, and group therapy experience positive emotions in termination. The benefits from the gains achieved usually far outweigh the impact of the loss of the helping relationship. Clients may reflect on the experience by saying things like "I was such a wreck when I first came to see you—I'm surprised I didn't scare you away," "You helped me get my thinking straight, so I could see the options I had before me," or "Even if things didn't change that much with my son, it helped me a lot to be in the group and know I'm not alone."

As noted earlier, clients and social workers alike commonly experience a sense of loss during the termination process. Indeed, sadness is a common element of many of the endings that are a part of life itself (even positive ones), such as leaving parents to attend school, advancing from one grade to another, graduating, moving into a new community, or changing jobs. The loss in termination may be a deeply moving experience involving the "sweet sorrow" generally associated with parting from a person whom one has grown to value. Adept social workers help clients to give voice to these ambivalent feelings, acknowledging that transitions can be difficult but that successfully handling both good times and difficult ones is a necessary part of growth.

For the social worker, the nature of termination and the comfort with which it occurs appear to be linked to the overall health of the organization in which it takes place and the practitioner's level of job satisfaction (Resnick & Dziegielewski, 1996). In work sites where caseloads are high, where there is a rapid turnover in clients, or where staff support and effective supervision are lacking, sufficient attention may not be paid to the tasks and emotions that accompany clinical endings. Of course, like other elements of practice, the impact of termination on the social worker is also shaped by his or her overall "health," including the ability to maintain a proper balance between the practitioner's personal and professional lives.

Because termination can evoke feelings associated with past losses and endings, clients (and social workers) may respond to it in a variety of ways (and in any of these ways to varying degrees).

1. *Anger.* Clients may experience anger at termination, especially when termination occurs because the social worker leaves the agency. Because the termination is not goal related and occurs with little forewarning, reactions are sometimes similar to those that involve other types of sudden crises. The social worker may need to reach for the feelings evoked by his or her departure, as clients may have difficulty expressing negative emotions while they are simultaneously experiencing sadness or anxiety about the impending loss. It is important to encourage the expression of emotions and respond empathically to them. It is vital, however, not to empathize to the extent of over-identification, thereby losing the capacity to assist the client with negative feelings and to engage in constructive planning.

When the social worker's departure is caused by circumstances outside his or her control (layoffs or firing), it is important that the practitioner not fuel the client's anger to satisfy his or her own indignation or desire for vindication. Not only is this clinically unhelpful to the client, but it is at odds with the NASW Code of Ethics. The Code of Ethics cautions us not to "exploit clients in disputes with colleagues or engage clients in any inappropriate discussion of conflicts between social workers and their colleagues" (NASW, 1999, 2.04b).

2. *Denial.* Clients may contend that they were unaware of the impending termination or time limits on service and behave as if termination is not imminent. They may deny having feelings about the termination or refuse to acknowledge that it affects them. Others may avoid endings by failing to appear for concluding sessions with the social worker (Dorfman, 1996). In other cases, the client may thus respond by shutting off thoughts of the impending loss (denial) and relate as though nothing has happened. It is a mistake to interpret the client's "business as usual" demeanor as an indication that he or she is unaffected by the termination or is taking it in stride, because the unruffled exterior may represent "the calm before the storm."

A client's temporary denial of feelings represents an attempt to ward off the psychic pain associated with a distressing reality that must eventually be faced. To assist clients in getting in touch with their emotions, it is helpful to reintroduce the topic of termination and to express your desire to assist them in formulating plans to continue working toward their goals after your departure. As you bring up the topic of termination, be sensitive to nonverbal cues to clients' emotional reactions. We also recommend employing empathic communication that conveys understanding of and elicits the hurt, resentment, and rejection clients commonly experience when a valued person leaves. The following responses demonstrate this type of communication:

- "I know that being discharged is scary and that makes you wish you didn't have to leave, but not talking about it won't keep it from happening. I want very much to use the time remaining to reflect on our work together so you are prepared to carry all that you've achieved here out into the world."

- "You've worked really hard here, and I know a lot of it wasn't easy for you. It's hard for me to believe you now when you shrug your shoulders and say it means nothing. I think it means a lot."

3. *Avoidance.* Occasionally, clients may express their anger and hurt over a social worker's leaving by rejecting the social worker before the social worker can reject them. Some clients may silently protest by failing to appear for sessions as termination approaches. Others may ignore the social worker or profess that they no longer need him or her—in effect, employing the strategy that "the best defense is a good offense." When clients act in this fashion, it is critical to reach out to them. Otherwise, they may interpret the failure to do so as evidence that the social worker never really cared about them at all. In reaching out, a personal contact by telephone, letter, or home visit is essential, because it creates an opportunity for interaction in which the social worker can reaffirm his or her concern and care and convey empathy and understanding of the client's emotional reaction.

4. *Reporting Recurrence of Old Problems or Generating New Ones.* Some clients tend to panic as treatment approaches closure and experience a return of difficulties that have been under control for some time (Levinson, 1977). In an effort to continue the helping relationship, some may introduce new stresses and problems during the terminal sessions and even during the final scheduled session. Clients who normally communicate minimally may suddenly open up, and other clients may reveal confidential information they have previously withheld. Other clients may display more severe reactions by engaging in self-destructive or suicidal acts.

The severity of the client's revelation, regression, or return of symptoms will dictate how you respond. It is important to acknowledge the anxiety and apprehension that accompany termination. Some clients will benefit from a preemptive discussion of these issues as termination nears. The social worker might say, "Sometimes people worry that problems will reemerge once services end, but I'm confident about how far you've come. I trust that even if there are setbacks, they won't affect our ending." Some theoretical models suggest that the social worker engage the client in an explicit discussion about what it would take to return to the former level of functioning that necessitated treatment. The underlying idea here is that such a discussion creates significant discomfort and paradoxically inoculates the client from setbacks (Walsh, 2003).

At some occasions, it may make sense for you and the client to reconsider a planned ending. Limited "extensions by plan" (Epstein & Brown, 2002, p. 232) can be made to accomplish agreed-upon tasks if it appears that additional time would enable the client to achieve decisive progress. There may be legitimate reasons for recontracting for additional sessions—for example, identifying key problems only late in the helping process, returning to problems that were identified earlier but had to be set aside in favor of work on more pressing problems, or anticipating transitional events that bear on the client's problems (e.g., getting married, being discharged from an institution, regaining custody of a child). In these instances, continuing the working relationships may be warranted, if supported by the agency, especially if the client has achieved substantial progress on other problems during the initial contract period.

Determining whether the emergence of new issues (or the reemergence of old ones) is a ploy to avoid termination or a legitimate cause for developing a new contract can be tricky, but the decision should be based on your sense of the client's progress to date, the degree of dependency, and the significance of the issues being raised (Reid, 1972). If you believe that the problem is worthy of intervention but worry that continuing treatment may foster harmful dependence, you might consider referring the client to another clinician, or continuing work with the client yourself but in a less intensive format—through groups or through less frequent sessions, for example.

5. *Attempting to Prolong Contact.* Sometimes, rather than reveal new or renewed problems, clients may seek continued contact with the social worker more directly by suggesting a social or business relationship with the practitioner following termination. For example, the client may suggest meeting for coffee on occasion or exchanging cards or letters, or may propose joining a training program that will put him or her in regular contact with the social worker. This phenomenon is also evident when groups decide to continue meeting after the agency's involvement has concluded.

Unfortunately, the security brought by such plans is only fleeting and the negative effects of continued contact can be serious. Clearly, some requests for continued contact would be inappropriate, given the profession's ethical proscriptions against dual relationships. Other forms of contact, while not prohibited, may still be unwise in that they may undo the work done in the helping relationship and may undermine the client's confidence in his or her ability to function without the social worker. Further, continued informal involvement may constrain the client from becoming invested in other rewarding relationships (Bostic, Shadid, & Blotcky, 1996).

In the case of groups, it is not usually the social worker's role to discourage the group from continuing to meet, although he or she should be clear about his or her own stance and may share the wisdom of past experience. For example, at the conclusion of one bereavement group, the group members planned a cookout at one member's home. In response to the invitation to join them, the group leader simply said, "I'll be ending with you after our session next week, but I appreciate your offer to include me." In another group with a particularly fragile and more easily disappointed membership, the social worker said, "I'm glad you feel close enough to one another to try to continue meeting after the group has formally ended. It's been my experience that sometimes it's hard to keep that going outside the group. If that happens to you, I hope you won't be discouraged or take it as a reflection on all you've accomplished in your time together."

This is not to say that planned follow-up phone calls, appointments, and "booster sessions" are always inappropriate. To the contrary, such plans are made within the goals of the helping process and have a clear therapeutic purpose, rather than being an attempt to evade the inevitability of ending.

6. *Finding Substitutes for the Social Worker.* Although finding one or more persons to replace the social worker may be a constructive way of developing social resources, it may also represent an attempt to locate a person on whom the client can become dependent, thereby compensating for the loss of the social worker. Group members may also seek to compensate for losses of group support by affiliating with other groups and never actually developing enduring social support systems. This problem is most likely to arise when the client has limited social supports. As such, the need for enhanced socialization should be visible during the helping process and may even be a goal for work. Indeed, plans for sustaining gains should include building networks and resources that can replace professionals as sources of assistance to the client.

Social Workers' Reactions to Termination

Clients are not the only ones who have reactions to termination. Social workers' responses may include guilt (at letting the client down or failing to sufficiently help the client), avoidance (delaying announcement of termination to avoid the feelings or reactions evoked), relief (at ending involvement with a difficult or challenging client), and prolonging service (because of financial or emotional fulfillment experienced by the clinician) (Dorfman, 1996; Joyce et al., 1996; Murphy & Dillon, 2003). In settings where premature terminations are the norm, workers may experience burnout and decreased sensitivity to clients after repeatedly working on cases where closure is not possible and treatment ends before interventions are carried out (Resnick & Dziegielewski, 1996). Self-understanding and good supervision are the essential elements by which even seasoned social workers can recognize the reactions involved in terminations. These reactions negatively affect clients, so identifying and managing them is crucial.

CONSOLIDATING GAINS AND PLANNING MAINTENANCE STRATEGIES

In addition to managing the emotional and behavioral reactions to ending, another task of termination involves summarizing and stabilizing the changes achieved and developing a plan to sustain those changes. A similar aim in work with groups is to assist members to not only interact successfully within the group context but also transfer their newly developed interpersonal skills to the broad arena of social relationships.

Failure to maintain gains has been attributed to a variety of factors:

1. A natural tendency to revert to habitual response patterns (e.g., use of alcohol or drugs, aggressive or withdrawn behavior)

2. Personal and environmental stressors (e.g., family conflicts, pressures from landlords, personal rejection, loss of job, health problems, and deaths of loved ones)

3. Lack of opportunities in the environment for social and leisure activities

4. Absence of positive support systems

5. Inadequate social skills

6. Lack of reinforcement for functional behaviors

7. Inadequate preparation for environmental changes

8. Inability to resist peer pressures

9. Return to dysfunctional family environments

10. Inadequately established new behaviors[5]

In planning maintenance strategies, you must anticipate such forces and prepare clients for coping with them. A monitoring phase may be useful for some clients. In this phase, the number and frequency of sessions decrease while support systems are called on to assist the client with new concerns. This technique, in effect, "weans" the client from the social worker's support, yet allows a transitional period in which the client can try out new skills and supports while gradually concluding the helping relationship.

When working with individuals and families, you may actively encourage clients to consider means for coping with setbacks. One model suggests asking what "would be required of each person to contribute to a resurgence of the problem" and organizing role-plays in which the members engage in old behavioral patterns and describe afterward what thoughts and feelings they experienced in doing so (Walsh, 2003, p. 206). Similar forms of anticipation and practice may help inoculate clients against future relapses.

Social workers may encourage clients to return for additional help if problems appear to be mounting out of control. Although it is important to express confidence in clients' ability to cope independently with their problems, it is equally important to convey your continued interest in them and to invite them to return if they need to do so.

Follow-Up Sessions

Post-termination follow-up sessions are another important technique in ensuring successful termination and change maintenance. These sessions benefit both clients and social workers. Many clients continue to progress after termination, and follow-up sessions provide an opportunity to accredit such gains and encourage clients to continue their efforts.

These sessions also provide the social worker with an opportunity to provide brief additional assistance for residual difficulties. Social workers may assess the durability of changes in these sessions—that is, determine whether clients have maintained gains beyond the immediate influence of the helping relationship. An additional benefit of planned follow-up sessions is that they may soften the blow of termination.

By introducing the notion of the follow-up session as an integral part of the helping process, social workers can avoid the pitfalls of clients later viewing these sessions as an intrusion into their private lives or as an attempt to satisfy the social worker's curiosity. Wells (1994) recommends that in arranging for the follow-up session, social workers not set a specific date but rather explain that they will contact the client after a designated interval. This interval offers the client an opportunity to test out and further consolidate the learning and changes achieved during the formal helping period.

In the follow-up session, the social worker generally relates more informally than during the period of intervention. After observing the appropriate social courtesies, you should guide the discussion to the client's progress and obtain post-intervention measures when appropriate. The follow-up session also provides an excellent opportunity for further evaluation of your efforts during the period of intervention. In retrospect, what was most helpful? What was least helpful? Further efforts can be made to consolidate gains at this point as well. What was gained from treatment that the client can continue to use in coping with life? Finally, at this point you can contract for more formalized help if this step appears necessary. Follow-up sessions thus enable social workers to arrange for timely assistance that may arrest deterioration in functioning.

One caution related to follow-up sessions is warranted: They may not allow the client to make a "clean break" from services. Clients who had difficulty separating during termination may use follow-up sessions as an excuse to prolong contact with the social worker. This continued attachment is detrimental to the change process and inhibits the client from establishing appropriate attachments with social networks and with other helping professionals. Social workers should be alert to this possibility in proposing follow-up sessions and ensure that clients understand the specific purpose and focus of these sessions.

Ending Rituals

In many settings, termination may be concluded by a form of celebration or ritual that symbolically marks the goals achieved and the relationship's conclusion (Murphy & Dillon, 2003). For example, in residential programs and some treatment groups, termination may be acknowledged in "graduation" or "status elevation" ceremonies, during which other residents or members comment on the departing member's growth and offer good wishes for the future. Certificates, cards, or "memory books" (Elbow, 1987) are but a few of the symbolic gifts that terminating clients may receive from staff or fellow clients. In individual and family work, social workers may choose to mark termination with small gifts such as a book, a plant, a framed inspirational quote, or some other token that is representative of the working relationship or the achievements while in service. Groups may conclude by creating a lasting product that is symbolic of the group, such as a collage; in the process of creating this item, participants can reflect on the meaning the group had for them as members (Northen & Kurland, 2001).

The decision to use rituals to mark termination should be based on an understanding of the client, the appropriateness of such actions for the agency or setting, and the meaning that the client may attribute to such actions. For example, giving a personal greeting card may be misinterpreted as a gesture of intimate friendship by some clients; for other clients, such as a child leaving foster care for a permanent placement, it may be a source of comfort and continuity. A gift that is too lavish may cause discomfort if the client feels the need to reciprocate in some way. "Goodbye parties" may reinforce feelings of accomplishment and confidence, or they may obviate the feelings of sadness or ambivalence that must also be addressed as part of closure (Shulman, 1992). Graduation ceremonies may recreate past disappointments and lead to further setbacks if, for example, family members refuse to attend and acknowledge the changes the client has achieved (Jones, 1996).

Dorfman (1996) suggests asking the client how he or she would like to mark the final session and offering options if the client seems unsure what to suggest. Useful and meaningful ending rituals are numerous. For example, at the final session of the "Banana Splits" group for children of families undergoing divorce or separation, participants make and eat banana splits (McGonagle, 1986). A social worker may create a card depicting the "gift" or wish that he or she has for the client's continued success; participants in groups may write poems or rewrite lyrics to popular song melodies to mark the ending of a class or group (Walsh, 2003). Some clients may ask the social worker to create a "diploma" indicating what they have achieved and ask to have a photo taken together (Dorfman, 1996). Graduation ceremonies and other events to mark group terminations can facilitate the tasks of termination and model meaningful rituals in a way that clients might not have experienced previously (Jones, 1996). These endings can be linked symbolically to the goals for work and may help motivate other clients to strive toward the achievements being celebrated by fellow group or residence members.

CASE EXAMPLE

Horizons is a halfway house for youth whose behavioral problems have resulted in hospitalization or incarceration. The program is intended to help teenagers readjust to community life and establish social supports so that they can return to their homes or move successfully into independent living. Given this focus, the length of stay for any individual resident varies considerably. Some youth encounter difficulties or re-offend; they are then returned to jail or to inpatient settings or simply "drop out of sight." These endings can be difficult for staff as they deal with disappointment in the client's failure to "make it" this time around and perhaps question what they might have done to prevent this outcome. It is also disturbing for other clients as they worry about their own challenges and their ability to successfully move on to the next step.

When residents terminate prematurely from the program, they are asked to attend a community meeting, where they can process with the group their experiences in the program and the things they learned that can be of use in the future. Staff and other residents are also invited to share their observations and feelings, with the intention of giving supportive and constructive feedback from a caring community—one to which the resident might someday return. When clients quit the program and drop out of sight, such sessions are still held. In these sessions, the residents and staff who remain process their feelings about the departure and discern lessons they can take away from it.

When residents have met their goals and are ready to move on to a more permanent living situation, staff discuss the plan and timeline for departure and stay alert to the difficulties that can arise at termination. The staff make a point of discussing, in groups and individual sessions, the fears that can arise in moving from some place "comfortable" to the unknown.

Sometimes, alumni of the program will visit to talk about their experiences and offer advice and encouragement. At this time, goals are reviewed, progress is charted, and the client's views are sought on which aspects of the program facilitated change. Clients and staff work together to anticipate the challenges ahead and to put in place the strategies necessary to address them.

During a resident's final days, the Horizons staff and residents create a "graduation" ceremony, and each resident offers the one who is leaving symbolic gifts to take on "the journey." These gifts may consist of inspirational quotes, reminders of inside jokes or shared experiences, and more tangible items, such as towels or pots and pans to help get established in the new setting.

Family members, teachers, and workers from other agencies are encouraged to attend the graduation, and at the ceremony are asked to support the client in the next steps ahead. These ceremonies are often tearful and moving events, where the emphasis is on achievement and on hope for the future.

Summary

Social workers are well aware of the importance of engagement with clients and the skills and attitudes needed to build an effective working relationship. Unfortunately, when this relationship concludes, social workers may not be equally astute about "taking the relationship apart." Effective evaluation and termination leave both the practitioner and the client with a shared sense of the accomplishments achieved in their work together. This process affords the opportunity to model ending a relationship in a way that is not hurtful or damaging to the client. Effective termination equips the client with the skills and knowledge necessary to sustain gains or to seek further help as needed in the future.

Internet Resources

 See our companion website for hot links to some helpful URLs. Note that URLs are subject to change. We will endeavor to

update the links on the companion website as much as possible.

You can access many resources related to evaluation by visiting *http://www.nyu.edu/socialwork/wwwrsw/*, choosing "social work practice," and then clicking on "evaluation." You can also use the keyword "termination" in InfoTrac College Edition to access Medquest Communications (1997), an article on treatment dropouts. You can also access a useful article on evaluation by Gardner (2000) through InfoTrac College Edition.

Related Online Content

Visit the *Direct Social Work Practice* companion website at *http://socialwork.wadsworth.com/hepworth7* for additional learning tools such as glossary terms, chapter outlines, InfoTrac College Edition keywords, relevant web links, and chapter practice quizzes. Also, be sure to check out the Direct Practice Virtual Reader, where the authors have personally selected articles relevant to this chapter using InfoMarks.

Notes

1. For information on the concepts and steps of termination as they apply to macro practice, we suggest an article by Harrigan, Favri, and Netting (1998).
2. For an excellent source on the considerations and strategies in termination across settings or using various theoretical orientations, see Walsh (2003).
3. See Meyer (2001) for a discussion of the dynamics of "no shows" and an effective clinical response.
4. For information on services in end-of-life care, see NASW's Standards of Social Work Practice in Palliative and End of Life Care (*www.naswdc.org*, 2004).
5. Brownell, Marlatt, Lichenstein, and Wilson (1986); Daley (1987, 1991); Marlatt and Gordon (1985); and Catalano, Wells, Jenson, and Hawkins (1989) have authored articles and books that identify various factors that contribute to relapse, discuss beliefs and myths associated with addictions, and delineate models for relapse education and treatment with addicted and impulse-disordered clients.

References

A

Abbott, A. A., & Wood, K. M. (2000). Assessment: Techniques and instruments for data collection. In A. Abbott (Ed.), *Alcohol, tobacco, and other drugs: Challenging myths, assessing theories, individualizing interventions* (pp. 159–186). Washington, DC: NASW Press.

Abramson, J. S. (2002). Interdisciplinary team practice. In A. R. Roberts & G. J. Greene (Eds.), *Social workers' desk reference* (pp. 44–50). New York: Oxford University Press.

Abramson, M. (1985). The autonomy–paternalism dilemma in social work. *Social Work, 27,* 422–427.

Ackerman-Engel, R. (1992). Brief cognitive therapy. In L. Bellak, *Handbook of intensive brief and emergency psychotherapy* (2nd ed., pp. 165–229). Larchmont, NY: C.P.S.

Ackerson, B., & Harrison, D. (2000). *Practitioners' perceptions of empowerment. Families in Society: The Journal of Contemporary Human Services, 81,* 3.

Ackley, D. C. (1997). *Breaking free of managed care.* Orlando, FL: Guilford Publications.

Agbayani-Siewart, P. (2004) Assumptions of Asian-American similarity: The case of Filipino and Chinese American students. *Social Work, 49* (1), 39–51.

Aguilar, I. (1972). Initial contact with Mexican-American families. *Social Work, 20,* 379–382.

Aguilera, D., & Messick, J. *(1982). Crisis intervention: Theory and methodology* (4th ed.). St. Louis: Mosby.

Alcabes, A. A., & Jones, J. A. (1985). Structural determinants of clienthood. *Social Work, 30,* 49–55.

Alexander, E. (1991). Sharing power among organizations: Coordination models to link theory and practice. In J. M. Bryson & R. C. Einsweiler (Eds.), *Shared power: What is it? How does it work? How can we make it work better?* (pp. 213–247). Lanham, MD: University Press of America.

Alexander, R., Jr. (2003). *Understanding legal concepts that influence social welfare policy and practice.* Pacific Grove, CA: Brooks/Cole, Thomson Learning.

Al-Krenawi, A. (1998). Reconciling western treatment and traditional healing: A social worker walks with the wind. *Reflections, 4* (3), 6–21.

Al-Krenawi, A., & Graham, J. (2000). Culturally sensitive social practice with Arab clients in mental health settings. *Health and Social Work, 25,* 9–22.

Alter, K., & Hage, J. (1992). *Organizations working together.* Newbury Park, CA: Sage Publications.

American Psychiatric Association. (2000). *Diagnostic and statistical manual for mental disorders* (4th ed. text revision). Washington, DC: American Psychiatric Association.

Anderson, D. A., & Worthen, D. (1997). Exploring a fourth dimension: Spirituality as a resource for the couple therapist. *Journal of Marital and Family Therapy, 23* (1), 3–12.

Anderson, S., & Grant, J. (1984). Pregnant women and alcohol: Implications for social work. *Social Casework, 65,* 3–10.

Anderson-Butcher, D., Khairallah, A. O., & Race-Bigelow, J. (2004). Mutual support groups for long-term recipients of TANF. *Social Work, 49* (1), 131–140.

Andrews, L. B. (2001). *Future perfect: Confronting decisions about genetics.* New York: Columbia University Press.

Aponte, H. (1982). The person of the therapist: The cornerstone of therapy. *Family Therapy Networker, 21* (46), 19–21.

Applegate, J. S. (1992). The impact of subjective measures on nonbehavioral practice research: Outcome vs. process. *Families in Society, 73* (2), 100–108.

Arnold, E. M. (2002). End-of-life counseling and care: Assessment, interventions and clinical issues. In A. R. Roberts & G. J. Greene (Eds.), *Social workers' desk reference* (pp. 452–457). New York: Oxford University Press.

Arnowitz, E., Brunswick, L., & Kaplan, B. (1983). Group therapy, with patients in the waiting room of an oncology clinic. *Social Work, 28,* 395–397.

Aronson, H., & Overall, B. (1966). Treatment expectations of patients in two social classes. *Social Work, 11,* 35–41.

Atchey, R. C. (1991). *Social forces and aging* (6th ed.). Springfield, IL: Charles G. Thomas.

Austin, C. D. (1990). Case management: Myths and realities. *Families in Society, 71* (7), 398–405.

Austin, K. M., Moline, M. E., & Williams, G. T. (1990). *Confronting malpractice: Legal and ethical dilemmas in psychotherapy.* Newbury Park, CA: Sage Publications.

B

Bakker, L., Ward, T., Cryer, M., & Hudson, S. M. (1997). Out of the rut. A cognitive-behavioral treatment program for driving-while-disqualified offenders. *Behavioral Change, 14,* 29–38.

Baer, J. (1999). Family relationships, parenting behavior, and adolescent deviance in three ethnic groups. *Families in Society, 80* (3), 279–285.

Bailey-Dempsey, C., & Reid, W. J. (1996). Intervention design and development: A case study. *Research on Social Work Practice, 6* (2), 208–228.

Balgopal, P., & Vassil, T. (1983). *Groups in social work: An ecological perspective.* New York: Macmillan.

Bandura, A. (1977). Self-efficacy: Toward a unifying theory of behavioral change. *Psychological Review, 84,* 191–215.

Bandura, A. (1986). *Social foundations of thought and action.* Englewood Cliffs, NJ: Prentice-Hall.

Bandura, A. (1988). Social cognitive theory. In R. Vasta (Ed.), *Annals of child development: Six theories or child development: Revised formulations and current issues* (pp. 1–60). Greenwich, CT: JAI Press.

Bandura, A., & Locke, E. (2003). Negative self-efficacy and goal effects revisited. *Journal of Applied Psychology, 88* (1), 87–99.

Barber, J. G. (1995). Working with resistant drug abusers. *Social Work, 40* (1), 17–23.

Bargal, D. (2004). Groups for reducing intergroup conflicts. In C. D. Garvin, L. M. Gutierrez, & M. J. Galinsky (Eds.), *Handbook of social work with groups* (pp. 292–306). New York: Guilford Press.

Barker, R. L. (1996). *The social work dictionary* (3rd ed.). Washington, DC: NASW Press.

Barker, R. L. (2003). *The social work dictionary* (5th ed.). Washington, DC: NASW Press.

Barth, R. P. (1985). Beating the blues: Cognitive-behavioral treatment for depression in child-maltreating mothers. *Clinical Social Work Journal, 13,* 317–328.

Barth, R., & Schinke, S. (1984). Enhancing the supports of teenage mothers. *Social Casework, 65,* 523–531.

Bartlett, H. (1970). *The common base of social work practice.* New York: National Association of Social Workers.

Barton, C., & Alexander, J. (1981). Functional family therapy. In A. Gurman & D. Kniskern (Eds.), *Handbook of family therapy* (pp. 403–443). New York: Brunner/Mazel.

Beatrice, D. F. (1990). Inter-agency coordination: A practitioner's guide to a strategy for effective social policy. *Administration in Social Work, 14* (4), 45–60.

Beck, A. (1974). Phases in the development of structure in therapy and encounter groups. In D. Wexler & L. Rice (Eds.), *Innovations in client-centered therapy.* New York: Wiley.

Beck, A., Kovacs, M., & Weissman, A. (1979). Assessment of suicidal intention. *Journal of Consulting and Clinical Psychology, 47,* 343–352.

Beck, A., Resnik, H., & Lettieri, D. (Eds.). (1974). *The prediction of suicide.* Bowie, MD: Charles Press.

Beck, A., Rush, A., Shaw, B., & Emery, G. (1979). *Cognitive therapy of depression.* New York: Guilford Press.

Beck, A., Ward, C., Mendelson, M., Mock, J., & Erbaugh, J. (1961). An inventory for measuring depression. *Archives of General Psychiatry, 4,* 561–571.

Beck, J. S. (1995). *Cognitive therapy: Basics and beyond.* New York: Guilford Press.

Beck, J., & Strong, S. (1982). Stimulating therapeutic change with interpretations: A comparison of positive and negative connotation. *Journal of Counseling Psychology, 29,* 551–559.

Becvar, D. S., & Becvar, R. J. (2000a). *Family therapy: A systemic integration* (4th ed.). Boston: Allyn & Bacon.

Becvar, D. S., & Becvar, R. J. (2000b). Family relationships, parenting behavior, and adolescent deviance in three ethnic groups. *Families in Society, 80* (3), 279–285.

Beeman, S. (1993). Social network structure and interaction among neglecting and nonneglecting mothers. Unpublished doctoral dissertation. University of Chicago.

Behroozi, C. S. (1992). A model for work with involuntary applicants in groups. *Social Work with Groups, 15* (2/3), 223–238.

Belkin, L. (1999, October 31). Parents blaming parents. *New York Times Sunday Magazine,* p. F61.

Bell, J. L. (1995). Traumatic event debriefing: Service delivery designs and the role of social work. *Social Work, 40* (1), 36–43.

Bell, L. (2001). Patterns of interaction in multidisciplinary child protection teams in New Jersey. *Child Abuse and Neglect, 25* (1), 65–80.

Bembry, J. X., & Ericson, C. (1999). Therapeutic termination with the early adolescent who has experienced multiple losses. *Child and Adolescent Social Work Journal, 16* (3), 177–189.

Bennett, C. J., Legon, J., & Zilberfein, F. (1989). The significance of empathy in current hospital based practice. *Social Work in Health Care, 14* (2), 27–41.

Berg, I. K. (1994). *Family-based services: A solution-focused approach.* New York: Norton.

Berg, I. K., & de Shazer, S. (1993). Making numbers talk. Language in therapy. In S. Friedman (Ed.), *The new language of change.* New York: Guilford Press

Berg, I. K., & Jaya, A. (1993). Different and same: Family therapy with Asian-American families. *Journal of Marital and Family Therapy, 19* (1), 31–38.

Berg-Weger, M., McGartland, D., & Tebb, S. (2000). Depression as a mediator: Viewing caregiver well-being and strain in a different light. *Families in Society, 81* (2), 162–173.

Berg-Weger, M., Rubio, D. M., & Tebb, S. (2000). Depression as a mediator: Viewing caregiver well-being and strain in a different light. *Families in Society, 81* (2), 162–173.

Berkman, B., Chauncey, S., Holmes, W., Daniels, A., Bonander, E., Sampson, S., & Robinson, M. (1999). Standardized screening of elderly patients' needs for social work assessment in primary care. *Health and Social Work, 24* (1), 9–16.

Berlin, S. B., & Marsh, J. C. (1993). *Informing practice decisions.* New York: Macmillan.

Berman-Rossi, T., & Kelly, T. B. (2000, February). Teaching students to understand and utilize the changing paradigm of stage of group development theory. Paper presented at the 46th annual program meeting of the Council on Social Work Education, New York, NY.

Bernal, G., & Flores-Ortiz, Y. (1982). Latino families in therapy: Engagement and evaluation. *Journal of Marriage and Family Therapy, 8,* 357–365.

Bernhardt, B., & Rauch, J. (1993). Genetic family histories: An aid to social work assessment. *Families in Society, 74,* 195–205.

Bernstein, B. (1977). Privileged social work practice. *Social Casework, 66,* 387–393.

Bertcher, H., & Maple, F. (1985). Elements and issues in group composition. In P. Glasser, R. Sarri, & R. Vinter (Eds.), *Individual change through small groups* (pp. 180–202). New York: Free Press.

Beutler, L. E., & Clarkin, J. (1990). *Systematic treatment selection: Toward targeted therapeutic interventions.* New York: Brunner/Mazel.

Beyer, J. A., & Balster, T. C. (2001). Assessment and classification in institutional corrections. In A. Walsh (Ed.), *Correctional assessment, casework, and counseling* (3rd ed., pp. 137–159). Lanham, MD: American Correctional Association.

Bidgood, B., Holosko, M., & Taylor, L. (2003). A new working definition of social work practice: A turtle's view. *Research on Social Work Practice, 13* (3), 400–408.

Biesteck, F. (1957). *The casework relationship.* Chicago: Loyola University Press.

Bisman, C. D. (1999). Social work assessment: Case theory construction. *Families in Society, 80* (3), 240–246.

Bloom, M., Fischer, J., & Orme, J. G. (1999). *Evaluating practice: Guidelines for the accountable professional* (3rd ed.). Boston: Allyn & Bacon.

Bloom, M., Fischer, J., & Orme, J. G. (2003). *Evaluating practice. Guidelines for the accountable professional.* Boston: Allyn & Bacon.

Boehm, A., & Staples (2004). Empowerment: The point of view of consumers. *Families in Society: The Journal of Contemporary Human Services, 85* (2), 270–280.

Borys, D. S., & Pope, K. S. (1989). Dual relationships between therapist and client: A national study of psychologists, psychiatrists, and social workers. *Professional Psychology: Research and Practice, 20,* 283–293.

Bostic, J. Q., Shadid, L. G., & Blotcky, M. J. (1996). Our time is up: Forced terminations during psychotherapy. *American Journal of Psychotherapy, 50,* 347–359.

Bower, B. (1997). Therapy bonds and the bottle (establishment of therapeutic alliance linked to higher success rate in treatment of alcoholics). *Science News, 152,* 8.

Boyd-Franklin, N. (1989a). *Black families in therapy: A multisystems approach.* New York: Guilford Press.

Boyd-Franklin, N. (1989b). Major family approaches and their relevance to the treatment of black families. In N. Boyd-Franklin, *Black families in therapy: A multisystems approach* (pp. 121–132). New York: Guilford Press.

Boyd-Franklin, N., & Bry, B. H. (2000). *Reaching out in family therapy: Home-based school and community interventions.* New York: Guilford Press.

Bradshaw, W. (1996). Structured group work for individuals with schizophrenia: A coping skills approach. *Research on Social Work Practice, 6*(2), 139–154.

Brager, G., & Holloway, S. (1978). *Changing human service organizations: Politics and practice.* New York: Free Press.

Brager, G., & Holloway, S. (1983). A process model for changing organizations from within. In R. M. Kramer & H. Specht (Eds.), *Readings in community organization practice* (pp. 198–208.) Englewood Cliffs, NJ: Prentice-Hall.

Brandes, S. D. (1976). *American welfare capitalism, 1880–1940.* Chicago: University of Chicago Press.

Brehm, S. S. (1976). *The application of social psychology to clinical practice.* New York: Wiley.

Brehm, S. S., & Brehm, J. W. (1981). *Psychological reactance: A theory of freedom and control.* New York: Academic Press.

Brent, D. A., Johnson, B., Bartle, S., Bridge, J., Rather, C., Matta, J., et al. (1993). Personality disorder tendency to impulsive violence, and suicidal behavior in adolescents. *Journal of the American Academy of Child and Adolescent Psychiatry, 32*(1), 69–75.

Breton, M. (1985). Reaching and engaging people: Issues and practice principles. *Social Work with Groups, 8*(3), 7–21.

Bridges, G. S., & Steen, S. (1998). Racial disparities in official assessments of juvenile offenders: Attributional stereotypes as mediating mechanisms. *American Sociological Review, 63,* 554–570.

Brill, C. K. (1990). *The impact on social work practice of the social injustice content in the NASW Code of Ethics.* Doctoral dissertation, Brandeis University.

Brindis, C., Barth, R. P., & Loomis, A. B. (1987). Continuous counseling: Case management with teenage parents. *Social Casework, 68*(3), 164–172.

Brisette, C. S. (1997). Child protection risk assessment and African American children: Cultural ramifications for families and communities. *Child Welfare, 76,* 45–63.

Bronfenbrenner, U. (1989). Ecological systems theory. In R. Vasta (Ed.), *Annals of child development: Six theories of child development: Revised formulations and current issues* (p. 187–247). Greenwich, CT: JAI Press.

Brookins, G. K., Peterson, A. C., & Brooks, L. M. (1997). Youth and families in the inner city: Influencing positive outcomes. In H. J. Walberg, O. Reyes, & R. P. Weissberg (Eds.), *Children and youth: Interdisciplinary perspectives* (pp. 45–66). Thousand Oaks, CA: Sage Publications.

Brooks-Gunn, J., & Duncan, G. J. (1997). The effects of poverty on children: The future of children. *Children and Poverty, 7*(2), 55–71.

Brown, L. S. (1994). *Subjective dialogues: Theory in feminist therapy.* New York: Basic Books.

Brown, L., & Root, M. (1990). *Diversity and complexity in feminist theory.* New York: Haworth Press.

Brownell, K., Marlatt, G., Lichenstein, E., & Wilson, G. T. (1986). Understanding and preventing relapse. *American Psychologist, 41*(7), 765–782.

Brownlee, K. (1996). Ethics in community mental health care: The ethics of nonsexual relationships: A dilemma for the rural mental health professionals. *Community Mental Health Journal, 32*(5), 497–503.

Brueggemann, W. G. (2002). *The practice of macro social work.* Pacific Grove, CA: Brooks/Cole, Thomson Learning.

Brunner, C., (1991). *Thinking collaboration: Ten questions and answers to help policy makers improve children's services.* Washington, DC: Education and Human Services Consortium.

Burford, G., & Pennell, J. (1996). Family group decision making: Generating indigenous structures for resolving family violence. *Protecting Children, 12*(3), 17–21.

Burford, G., & Pennell, J. (2004). From agency client to community-based consumer: The family group conference as a consumer-led group in child welfare. In C. D. Garvin, L. M. Gutierrez, & M. J. Galinsky (Eds.), *Handbook of social work with groups* (pp. 415–431). New York: Guilford Press.

Burman, S., & Allen-Meares, P. (1991). Criteria for selecting practice theories: Working with alcoholic women. *Families in Society, 72,* 387–393.

Burns, D. (1980). *Feeling good.* New York: Avon Books.

Buss, T. F., & Gillanders, W. R. (1997). Worry about health status among the elderly: Patient management and health policy implications. *Journal of Health and Social Policy, 8*(4), 53–66.

Butz, R. A. (1985). Reporting child abuse and confidentiality in counseling. *Social Casework, 66,* 83–90.

C

Cain, R. (1991a). Relational contexts and information management among gay men. *Families in Society, 72*(6), 344–352.

Cain, R. (1991b). Stigma management and gay identity development. *Social Work, 36*(1), 67–71.

Campbell, J. A. (1988). Client acceptance of single-subject evaluation procedures. *Social Work Research Abstracts, 24,* 21–22.

Campbell, J. A. (1990). Ability of practitioners to estimate client acceptance of single-subject evaluation procedures. *Social Work, 35*(1), 9–14.

Canda, E. (1983). General implications of Shamanism for clinical social work. *International Social Work, 26,* 14–22.

Canda, E. R. (1997). Spirituality. In R. L. Edwards (Ed.), *Encyclopedia of social work 1997 supplement* (19th ed., pp. 299–309). Washington, DC: NASW Press.

Canda, E., & Phaobtong, T. (1992). Buddhism as a support system for Southeast Asian refuges. *Social Work, 37*(1), 61–67.

Capitman, J., MacAdam, M., & Yee, D. (1988). Hospital-based managed care. *Generations, 12*(5), 62–65.

Caplan, G. (1964). *Principles of preventive psychiatry.* New York: Basic Books.

Caplan, T. (1995). Safety and comfort, content and process: Facilitating open group work with men who batter. *Social Work with Groups, 18*(2/3), 33–51.

Caple, F. S., Salcido, R. M., & di Cecco, J. (1995). Engaging effectively with culturally diverse families and children. *Social Work in Education, 17*(3), 159–169.

Carkhuff, R. (1969). *Helping and human relations: Practice and research.* New York: Holt, Rinehart & Winston.

Carlozzi, A., Bull, K., Stein, L., Ray, K., & Barnes., L. (2002). Empathy theory and practice: A survey of psychologists and counselors. *Journal of Psychology, 36* (2), 161–171.

Carlton-LaNey, I. (1999). African American social work pioneers' response to need. *Social Work, 44* (4), 311–321.

Carniol, B. (1992). Structural social work: Maurice Moreau's challenge to social work practice. *Journal of Progressive Human Services, 3* (1), 1–19.

Carr, E. S. (2004). Accessing resources, transforming systems: Group work with poor and homeless people. In C. D. Garvin, L. M. Gutierrez, & M. J. Galinsky (Eds.), *Handbook of social work with groups* (pp. 360–383). New York: Guilford Press.

Carrell, S. (2000). Group therapy with adolescents. In *Group exercises for adolescents: A manual for therapists* (pp. 13–26). Thousand Oaks, CA: Sage Publications.

Carrillo, D. F., Gallant, J., & Thyer, B. (1995). Training MSW students in interviewing skills: An empirical assessment. *Arete, 18,* 12–19.

Carter, B., & McGoldrick, M. (Eds.). (1988). *The changing life cycle: A framework for family therapy* (2nd ed.). New York: Gardner Press.

Carter, B., & McGoldrick, M. (Eds.). (1999a). *The expanded family life cycle: Individual, family, and social perspectives* (3rd ed.). Boston: Allyn & Bacon.

Carter, B., & McGoldrick, M. (1999b). Coaching at various stages of the life cycle. In B. Carter & M. McGoldrick (Eds.), *The expanded family life cycle: Individual, family, and social perspectives* (3rd ed., pp. 436–454). Boston: Allyn & Bacon.

Cascio, T. (1998). Incorporating spirituality into social work practice: A review of what to do. *Families in Society, 79* (5), 523–531.

Caspi, J., & Reid, W. J. (2002*). Educational supervision in social work. A task-centered model for field instruction and staff development.* New York: Columbia University Press.

Catalano, R., Wells, E. A., Jenson, J. M., & Hawkins, J. D. (1989). Aftercare services for drug-using institutionalized delinquents. *Social Service Review, 63* (4), 553–577.

Chandler, S. (1985). Mediation: Conjoint problem solving. *Social Work, 30,* 346–349.

Chau, K. L. (1990). A model for teaching cross-cultural practice in social work. *Journal of Social Work Education, 26* (2), 124–133.

Chau, K. L. (1993). Needs assessment for group work with people of color: A conceptual formulation. *Social Work with Groups, 15* (2/3), 53–66.

Chelune, G. J. (1979). Measuring openness in interpersonal communication. In G. Chelune & Associates (Eds.), *Self-disclosure.* San Francisco: Jossey-Bass.

Chemtob, C. M., Hamada, R. S., Bauer, G., Torigoe, R. Y., & Kinney, B. (1988). Patient suicide: Frequency and impact on psychologists. *Professional Psychology Research and Practice, 19* (4), 416–420.

Chesler, M. (1994a). Strategies for multicultural organizational development. *Diversity Factors, 2* (2), 12–18.

Chesler, M. (1994b). Organizational development is not the same as multicultural organizational development. In E. Y. Cross, J. H. Katz, F. A. Miller, & E. H. Seashore (Eds.), *The promise of diversity* (pp. 240–351). Burr Ridge, IL: Irwin.

Child Welfare League of America. (1990). *Agency self-improvement checklist.* Washington, DC: Child Welfare League of America.

Chipungu, S. S., & Bent-Goodley, T. B. (2003). Race, poverty and child maltreatment. *APSAC Advisor, American Professional Society on the Abuse of Children, 15* (2).

Choi, G. (1997). Acculturative stress, social support, and depression in Korean American families. *Journal of Family Social Work, 2* (1), 81–79.

Cingolani, J. (1984). Social conflict perspective on work with involuntary clients. *Social Work, 29,* 442–446.

Citron, P. (1978). Group work with alcoholic poly-drug involved adolescents with deviant behavior syndrome. *Social Work with Groups, I* (1), 39–52.

Claiborn, C. (1982). Interpretation and change in counseling. *Journal of Counseling Psychology, 29,* 439–453.

Claiborn, C., Crawford, J., & Hackman, H. (1983). Effects of intervention discrepancy in counseling for negative emotions. *Journal of Counseling Psychology, 30,* 164–171.

Clayton, J. M., Glidden, L. M., & Kiphart, M. J. (1994). The Questionnaires on Resources and Stress: What do they measure? *American Journal of Mental Retardation, 99,* 313–316.

Clinical Social Work Federation. (1997). Definition of clinical social work (revised). *http://www.cswf.org/www/info/html*

Cnaan, R. A. (1994). The new American social work gospel: Case management of the chronically mentally ill. *British Journal of Social Work, 24* (5), 533–557.

Cnaan, R. A., & Rothman, J. (1986). Conceptualizing community intervention: An empirical test of three models of community organization. *Administration in Social Work, 10* (3), 41–55.

Cohen, B.-Z. (1985). A cognitive approach to the treatment of offenders. *British Journal of Social Work, 15,* 619–633.

Cohen, E. D., & Cohen, G. S. (1999). *The virtuous therapist: Ethical practice of counseling and psychotherapy.* Belmont, CA: Brooks/Cole.

Collins, P. M., Kayser, K., & Platt, S. (1994). Conjoint marital therapy: A social worker's approach to single-system evaluation. *Families in Society, 71* (8), 461–470.

Compton, B. R., & Galaway, B. (1994). *Social work processes* (6th ed.). Pacific Grove, CA: Brooks/Cole.

Compton, B., Galaway, B., & Cournoyer, B. (2005). *Social work processes.* (7th ed.) Pacific Grove, CA: Brooks/Cole.

Congress, E. P. (1994). The use of culturegrams to assess and empower culturally diverse families. *Families in Society, 75,* 531–540.

Congress, E. P. (1999). Ethical dilemmas in interdisciplinary collaboration. In E. Congress (Ed.), *Social work values and ethics: Identifying and resolving professional dilemmas* (pp. 117–128). Chicago: Nelson Hall.

Congress, E. P. (2002). Using the culturegram with diverse families. In A. R. Roberts & G. J. Green (Eds.), *Social workers' desk reference* (pp. 57–61). New York: Oxford University Press.

Congress, E. P. & Lynn, M. (1997). Group work practice in the community: Navigating the slippery slope of ethical dilemmas. *Social Work with Groups, 20* (3), 61–74.

Constable, R., & Lee, D. B. (2004). Social work with families: Content and process. Chicago: Lyceum Books.

Corcoran, J. (1998). Solution-focused practice with middle and high school at-risk youth. *Social Work in Education, 20,* 232–243.

Corcoran, J. (2000b). *Evidence based practice with families: A lifespan approach.* New York: Springer.

Corcoran, J. (2000b). Evidence based treatment of adolescents with externalizing disorders. In A. R. Roberts & G. J. Greene (Eds.), *Social workers' desk reference* (pp. 112–115). New York: Oxford University Press.

Corcoran, J. (2002). Evidence based treatment of adolescents with externalizing disorders. In A. R. Roberts and G. J. Greene (Eds.), *Social workers' desk reference* (pp. 793–796) New York: Oxford University Press.

Corcoran, J., & Franklin, C. (1998). A solution-focused approach to physical abuse. *Journal of Family Psychotherapy, 9*(1), 69–73.

Corcoran, J., & Stephenson, M. (2000). The effectiveness of solution-focused therapy with child behavior problems: A preliminary report. *Families in Society: The Journal of Contemporary Human Services, 81*(5), 468–474.

Corcoran, K., & Fisher, J. (1999). *Measures for clinical practice* (3rd ed.). New York: Free Press.

Corcoran, K., & Gingerich, W. J. (1994). Practice evaluation in the context of managed care: Case recording methods for quality assurance reviews. *Research on Social Work Practice, 4*(3), 326–337.

Corcoran, K., & Vandiver, V. (1996). *Maneuvering the maze of managed care: Skills for mental health practitioners.* New York: Free Press.

Corcoran, K., & Winslade, W. J. (1994). Eavesdropping on the 50-minute hour: Managed mental health care and confidentiality. *Behavioral Sciences and the Law, 12,* 351–365.

Corey, G. (1990). *Theory and practice of group counseling.* Pacific Grove, CA: Brooks/Cole.

Corey, G., Corey, M. S., & Callanan, P. (2003). *Issues and ethics in the helping professions* (6th ed.) Pacific Grove, CA: Brooks/Cole.

Corey, G., Corey, M. S., Callahan, P. J., & Russell, J. M. (2004). *Group techniques* (3rd ed.). Pacific Grove, CA: Brooks/Cole.

Corey, M. S., & Corey, G. (1992). *Groups: Process and practice* (4th ed.). Pacific Grove, CA: Brooks/Cole.

Corey, M. S., & Corey, G. (2002). *Groups: Process and practice* (6th ed.). Pacific Grove, CA: Brooks/Cole.

Cormier, S., & Nurius, P. S. (2003). *Interviewing and change strategies for helpers: Fundamental skills and cognitive behavioral interventions.* Pacific Grove, CA: Brooks/Cole, Thomson Learning.

Cormier, W., & Cormier, L. (1979). *Interviewing strategies for helpers. A guide to assessment, treatment, and evaluation.* Pacific Grove, CA: Brooks/Cole.

Corwin, M. (2002). *Brief treatment in clinical social work practice.* Pacific Grove, CA: Brooks/Cole.

Costello, E. J., Compton, S. N., Keeler, G., & Angold, A. (2003). Relationship between poverty and psychopathology: A natural experiment. *Journal of the American Medical Association, 290* (15), 2023–2029.

Council on Social Work Education. (1995). *Accreditation standards and self-study guides.* Alexandria, VA: Council on Social Work Education.

Council on Social Work Education (2003). *Educational policy and accreditation standards* (5th ed.). Alexandria, VA: Council on Social Work Education.

Courtney, M. (1999). Challenges and opportunities posed by the reform era. Presented at the "Reconciling welfare reform with child welfare" conference. Center for Advanced Studies in Child Welfare, University of Minnesota, February 26.

Cowger, C. D. (1992). Assessment of client strengths. In D. Saleeby (Ed.), *The strengths perspective in social work practice* (pp. 139–147). New York: Longman.

Cowger, C. D. (1994). Assessing client strengths: Clinical assessment for client empowerment. *Social Work, 39*(3), 262–267.

Cox, E. O. (1991). The critical role of social action in empowerment oriented groups. *Social Work with Groups, 14*(3/4), 77–90.

Crabtree, B. F., & Miller, W. L. (1992). *Doing qualitative research.* Newbury Park, CA: Sage Publications.

Crenshaw, A. B. (2003, October 14). "Middle-class families are richer, study shows." *The Dallas Morning News,* p. 3D.

Cross, T. L., Bazron, B. J., Dennis, K., & Issacs, M. R. (1989). *Toward a culturally competent system of care.* Washington, DC: Georgetown University Child Development Center.

Crosson-Tower, C. (2004). *Exploring child welfare: A practice perspective.* Boston: Allyn & Bacon.

Cull, J. G., & Gill, W. S. (1991). *Suicide Probability Scale (SPS).* Los Angeles: Western Psychological Services.

Cummings, N. A. (1991). Brief intermittent therapy throughout the life cycle. In C. S. Austad & W. H. Berman (Eds.), *Psychotherapy in managed health care: The optimal use of time and resources* (pp. 35–45). Washington, DC: American Psychological Association.

Cunningham, M. (2003). Impact of trauma social work clinicians: Empirical findings. *Social Work, 48*(4), 451–459.

Curriculum Policy Statement. (1996). Educational Policy and Standards (EPAS). Council on Social Work Education.

D

Daley, D. C. (1987). Relapse prevention with substance abusers: Clinical issues and myths. *Social Work, 32,* 138–142.

Daley, D. C. (1991). *Kicking addictive habits once and for all: A relapse prevention guide.* New York: Lexington.

Dane, B. O., & Simon, B. L. (1991). Resident guests: Social workers in host settings. *Social Work, 36*(3), 208–213.

Danish, J., D'Augelli, A., & Hauer, A. (1980). *Helping skills: A basic training program.* New York: Human Sciences Press.

Danny Glover, the fire within. (2004, May/June). *AARP Magazine,* 41–42, 87–88.

Danzy, J., & Jackson, S.M. (1997). Family preservation and support services: A missed opportunity. *Child Welfare, 76*(1), 31.

Davidson, J. R., & Davidson, T. (1996). Confidentiality and managed care: Ethical and legal concerns. *Health and Social Work, 21*(3), 208–215.

Davis, I. P., & Reid, W. J. (1988). Event analysis in clinical practice and process research. *Social Casework, 69*(5), 298–306.

Davis, L. E., & Gelsomino, J. (1994). An assessment of practitioner cross-racial treatment experiences. *Social Work, 39*(1), 116–123.

Deal, K. H. (1999). Clinical social work students' use of self-disclosure: A case for formal training. *Arete, 23*(3), 33–45.

Deal, K., & Brintzenhofeszok, K. (2004). A study of MSW students' interviewing skills over time. *Journal of Teaching in Social Work, 24*(1/2), 181–197.

Dean, R. G. (2001). The myth of cross-cultural competence. *Families in Society: The Journal of Contemporary Human Services, 82*(6), 623–630.

De Anda, D. (1984). Bicultural socialization: Factors affecting the minority experience. *Social Work, 29,* 172–181.

De Anda, D., & Becerra, R. (1984). Support networks for adolescent mothers. *Social Casework, 65,* 172–181.

DeAngelis, D. (2000). Licensing really is about protection. *ASWB Association News, 10*(2), 11.

Deibel-Braun, M. A., Dulmus, C. N., Wodarski, J. S., & Feit, M. D. (1998). Cognitive variables. *Journal of Human Behavior in the Social Environment, 1*(4), 73–102.

De Jong, P. (2001). Solution-focused therapy. In A. R. Roberts & G. J. Greene (Eds.), *Social workers' desk reference* (pp. 112–115). New York: Oxford University Press.

De Jong, P., & Berg, I. K. (1998). *Interviewing for solutions.* Pacific Grove, CA: Brooks/Cole.

De Jong, P., & Berg, I. K. (2001). Co-constructing cooperation with mandated clients. *Social Work, 46*(4), 361–374.

DeJong, P. & Berg, I. K. (2002). Lerner's workbook interviewing for solutions (2nd ed.). Pacific Grove, CA: Brooks/Cole, Thomson Learning

De Jong, P., & Miller, S. D. (1995). How to interview for client strengths. *Social Work, 40* (6), 729–736.

De Las Fuentes, C. (2000). Group psychotherapy: Adolescent Latinos. In M. T. Flores & G. Carey, *Family therapy with Hispanics: Toward approaching diversity* (pp. 151–156). Boston: Allyn & Bacon.

Delgado, M. (1983). Activities and Hispanic groups: Issues and suggestions. *Social Work with Groups, 6* (1), 85–96.

DeLine, C. (2000). *The back door: An experiment or an alternative.* Alberta, Canada: The Back Door.

Denison, M. (2003). The PDR for mental health professionals. *Psychotherapy: Theory, Research, Practice, and Training, 40* (4), 317–318.

DePoy, E., & Gilson, S. F. (2003). *Evaluation practice. Thinking and action principles for social work practice.* Pacific Grove, CA: Brooks/Cole

De Shazer, S. (1988). *Clues: Investigating solutions in brief therapy.* New York: Norton.

De Shazer, S., & Berg, I. K. (1993) Constructing solutions. *Family Therapy Networker, 12,* 42–43.

Devore, W., & Schlesinger, E. G. (1999). *Ethnic-sensitive social work practice* (5th ed.). Boston: Allyn & Bacon.

Dewayne, C. (1978). Humor in therapy. *Social Work, 23* (6), 508–510.

Dia, D. A. (2001). Cognitive-behavioral therapy with a six-year-old boy with separation anxiety disorder: A case study. *Health and Social Work, 26* (2), 125–128.

Dickson, D. T. (1998). *Confidentiality and privacy in social work.* New York: Free Press.

Dies, R. R. (1983). Clinical implications of research on leadership in short-term group psychotherapy. In R. R. Dies & R. McKenzie (Eds.), *Advances in group psychotherapy: Integrating research and practice* (American Group Psychotherapy Association Monograph Series) (pp. 27–28). New York: International Universities Press.

Dillon, D. (1994). Understanding and assessment of intra-group dynamics in foster family care: African American families. *Child Welfare, 73* (2), 129–139.

Dore, M. M. (1993). The practice–teaching parallel in educating the micropractitioner. *Journal of Social Work Education, 29* (2), 181–190.

Dore, M. M., & Durnois, A. O. (1990). Cultural differences in the meaning of adolescent pregnancy. *Families in Society, 71* (2), 93–101.

Dorfman, R. A. (1996). *Clinical social work: Definition, practice, and vision.* New York: Brunner/Mazel.

Dossick, J., & Shea, E. (1995). *Creative therapy III: 52 more exercises for groups.* Sarasota, FL: Professional Resource Press.

Doster, J., & Nesbitt, J. (1979). Psychotherapy and self-disclosure. In G. Chelunc & Associates (Eds.), *Self-disclosure* (pp. 177–224). San Francisco: Jossey-Bass.

Dowd, E., & Boroto, D. (1982). Differential effects of counselor self-disclosure, self-involving statements, and interpretation. *Journal of Counseling Psychology, 29,* 8–13.

DuBray, W. (1985). American Indian values: Critical factors in casework. *Social Casework, 66,* 30–37.

Duehn, W., & Proctor, E. (1977). Initial clinical interactions and premature discontinuance in treatment. *American Journal of Orthopsychiatry, 47,* 284–290.

Duvall, E. M. (1977). *Marriage and family development* (5th ed.). Philadelphia: Lippincott.

Dyche, L., & Zayas, L. H. (2001). Cross-cultural empathy and training the contemporary psychotherapist. *Clinical Social Work Journal, 29* (3), 245–258.

E

Edwards, A. (1982). The consequences of error in selecting treatment for blacks. *Social Casework, 63,* 429–433.

Edwards, E. (1983). Native-American elders: Current issues and social policy implications. In R. McNeely & J. Colen (Eds.), *Aging in minority groups.* Beverly Hills, CA: Sage Publications.

Edwards, E. D., Edwards, M. E., Davies, G. M., & Eddy, F. (1987). Enhancing self-concept and identification of American Indian girls. *Social Work with Groups, 1* (3), 309–318.

Efran, J., & Schenker, M. (1993). A potpourri of solutions: How new and different is solution-focused therapy? *Family Therapy Networker, 17* (3), 71–74.

Ehrenreich, B. (2001). *Nickel and dimed. On (not) getting by in America.* New York: Metropolitan Books.

Ehrenreich, B. (2004, July 11). Let them eat cake. *The New York Times,* p. 3.

Eisikovits, Z. C., & Edleson, J. L. (1989). Intervening with men who batter: A critical review of the literature. *Social Services Review, 63* (3), 384–414.

Elbow, M. (1987). The memory books: Facilitating termination with children. *Social Casework, 68,* 180–183.

Elkin, I., Shea, T., Watkins, J., & Collins, J. (1986). *Comparative treatment outcome findings.* Presentation of the NIMH Treatment of Depression Collaborative Research Program. Paper presented at the annual meeting of the American Psychiatric Association.

Ell, K. (1995). Crisis intervention: Research needs. In E. L. Edwards (Ed.), *Encyclopedia of social work* (19th ed., pp. 660–667). Washington, DC: NASW Press.

Ellis, A. (1962). *Reason and emotion in psychotherapy.* New York: Lyle Stuart.

Ellor, J. W., Netting, F. E., & Thibault, J. M. (1999). *Religious and spiritual aspects of human service practice.* Columbia, SC: University of South Carolina Press.

Ensign, J. (1998). Health issues of homeless youth. *Journal of Social Distress and the Homeless, 7* (3), 159–174.

Ephross, P. H., & Vassil, T. V. (1988). *Groups that work: Structure and process.* New York: Columbia University Press.

Epstein, H. (2003, October 12). Enough to make you sick. *The New York Times Magazine,* pp. 76–86.

Epstein, L. (1985). *Talking and listening: A guide to interviewing.* Columbus, OH: Merrill.

Epstein, L. (1988). *Brief treatment: A task-centered approach.* New York: McGraw-Hill.

Epstein, L. (1992). *Brief treatment and a new look at the task-centered approach* (3rd ed.). Boston: Allyn & Bacon.

Epstein, L., & Brown, L. B. (2002). *Brief treatment and a new look at the task-centered approach* (4th ed.). Boston: Allyn & Bacon.

Epstein, R. S., Simon, R. I., & Kay, G. G. (1992). Assessing boundary violations in psychotherapy: Survey results with the Exploitation Index. *Bulletin of the Menninger Foundation, 56* (2), 150–166.

Erickson, S. H. (2001). Multiple relationships in rural counseling. *The Family Journal: Counseling and Therapy for Couples and Families, 9* (3), 302–304.

Ewalt, P. L. (1994a). Welfare: How much reform? *Social Work, 39* (5), 485–486.

Ewalt, P. (1994b). Poverty matters. *Social Work, 39* (2), 149–151.

Ewalt, P. L., & Mokuau, N. (1996). Self-determination from a Pacific perspective. In P. L. Ewalt, E. M. Freeman, S. A. Kirk, & D. L. Poole (Eds.), *Multicultural issues in social work* (pp. 255–268). Washington, DC: NASW Press.

Ezell, M. (1994). Advocacy practice of social workers. *Families in Society, 75* (1), 36–46.

Ezell, M. (2001). *Advocacy in the human services.* Thousand Oaks, CA: Brooks/Cole, Thomson Learning.

F

Falicov, C. (1996). Mexican families. In M. McGoldrick, J. Giordano, & J. Pearce (Eds.), *Ethnicity and family therapy* (2nd ed.) (pp. 169–182). New York: Gullford Press.

Farina, A., Burns, G. L., Austad, C., Bugglin, C., & Fischer, E. H. (1986). The role of physical attractiveness in the readjustment of discharged psychiatric patients. *Journal of Abnormal Psychology, 95,* 139–143.

Farmer, R., & Walsh, J. (1999). Living room assessment. *Journal of Community Practice, 6* (4), 79–94.

Farrington, A. (1995). Suicide and psychological debriefing. *British Journal of Nursing, 4* (4), 209–211.

Fast, J. D. (2003). After Columbine: How people mourn sudden death. *Social Work, 48* (4), 484–491.

Fauri, D. P., & Bradford, J. B. (1986). Practice with the frail elderly in the private sector. *Social Casework, 67,* 259–265.

Fearing, J. (1996). The changing face of intervention. *Behavioral Health Management, 16,* 35–37.

Feeny, S. L. (2004). The cognitive behavioral treatment of social phobia. *Clinical Case Studies, 3* (2), 124–146.

Feldman, D., Strong, S., & Danser, D. (1982). A comparison of paradoxical and nonparadoxical interpretations and directives. *Journal of Counseling Psychology, 29,* 572–579.

Finn, J. L., & Jacobson, M. (2003a). Just practice: Steps toward a new social work paradigm. *Journal of Social Work Education, 39* (1), 57–78.

Finn, J. L., & Jacobson, M. (2003b). *Just practice: A social justice approach to social work.* Peosta, IA: Eddie Bowers.

Fischer, J. (1978). *Effective casework practice: An eclectic approach.* New York: McGraw-Hill.

Flaherty, J. A., Gaviria, F. M., & Pathak, D. S. (1983). The measurement of social support: The Social Support Network Inventory. *Comprehensive Psychiatry, 24,* 521–529.

Flapan, D., & Fenchal, G. (1987). *The developing ego and the emerging self in group therapy.* Northvale, NJ: Aronson.

Flores, M. T., & Carey, G. (2000). *Family therapy with Hispanics: Toward appreciating diversity.* Boston: Allyn & Bacon.

Fong, R. (1997). Child welfare practice with Chinese families: Assessment issues for immigrants from the People's Republic China. *Journal of Family Social Work, 2* (1), 33–47.

Fortune, A. E. (1985a). Treatment groups. In A. E. Fortune (Ed.), *Task-centered practice with families and groups* (pp. 33–44). New York: Springer.

Fortune, A., Pearlingi, B., & Rochelle, C. D. (1992). Reactions to termination of individual treatment. *Social Work, 37* (2), 171–178.

Fowler, R. C., Rich, C. L., & Young, D. C. (1986). San Diego suicide study, II: Substance abuse in young cases. *Archives of General Psychiatry, 43,* 962–965.

Frager, S. (2000). *Managing managed care: Secrets from a former case manager.* New York: Wiley.

Franklin, C. (2002). Developing effective practice competencies in managed behavioral health care. In Roberts, A.R. &

Greene, G.J. (Eds.) *Social workers desk reference,* (pp. 3–10). New York: Oxford.

Franklin, D.L. (1990). The cycles of social work practice: Social action vs. individual interest. *Journal of Progressive Human Services, 1* (2), 59–80.

Freed, A. (1988). Interviewing through an interpreter. *Social Work, 33,* 315–319.

Freeman, E. M., & Dyers, L. (1993). High risk children and adolescents: Families and community environments. *Families in Society, 74* (7), 422–431.

Frey, G. A. (1990). Framework for promoting organizational change. *Families in Society, 7* (3), 142–147.

Friedman, M. J. (1996). Facilitating productive meetings, *Training & Development, 50* (10), 11–13.

Friedmann, S. (1997). *Time effective psychotherapy: Maximizing outcomes in an era of managed resources.* Needham Heights, MA: Allyn & Bacon.

G

Gabbard, G. O. (1996). Lessons to be learned from the study of sexual boundary violations. *American Journal of Psychotherapy, 50* (3), 311–322.

Galinsky, M. J., & Schopler, J. H. (1989). Developmental patterns in open-ended groups. *Social Work with Groups, 12* (2), 99–114.

Galinsky, M. J., Turnbull, J. E., Meglin, D. E., & Wilner, M. E. (1993). Confronting the reality of collaborative practice research: Issues of practice, design, measurement, and team development. *Social Work, 38* (4), 440–449.

Gallo, J. J., Fulmer, T., Paveza, G. J., & Reichel, W. (2000). Mental status assessment. In *Handbook of geriatric assessment* (3rd ed., pp. 29–99). Gaithersburg, MD: Aspen.

Gambrill, E. (1995). Behavioral social work: Past, present and future. *Research on Social Work Practice, 5* (4), 466–484.

Gambrill, E., & Barth, R. (1980). Single-case study designs revisited. *Social Work Research and Abstracts, 16,* 15–20.

Gardner, R.A. (1971). *Therapeutic communication with children.* New York: Science House Press.

Gardner, F. (2000). Design Evaluation: Illuminating social work practice for better outcomes. *Social Work, 45* (2), 176–182.

Garland, J., Jones, H., & Kolodny, R. (1965). A model for stages in the development of social work groups. In S. Bernstein (Ed.), *Explorations in group work.* Boston: Milford House.

Gartrell, N. K. (1992). Boundaries in lesbian therapy relationships. *Women & Therapy, 12* (3), 29–50.

Garvin, C. (1981). *Contemporary group work.* Englewood Cliffs, NJ: Prentice-Hall.

Garvin, C. (1987). *Contemporary group work* (2nd ed.). Englewood Cliffs, NJ: Prentice-Hall.

Gelman, C. R. (2004). Empirically-based principles for culturally competent practice with Latinos. *Journal of Ethnic and Cultural Diversity in Social Work, 13* (1), 83–108.

Gelman, S. R., Pollack, D., & Weiner, A. (1999). Confidentiality of social work records in the computer age. *Social Work, 44* (3), 243–252.

Gendlin, E. (1974). Client-centered and experiential psychotherapy. In D. Wexler & L. Rice (Eds.), *Innovations in client-centered therapy.* New York: Wiley.

Gendron, C., Poitras, L., Dastoor, D. P., & Perodeau, G. (1996). Cognitive-behavioral group intervention for spousal caregivers: Findings and clinical observations. *Clinical Gerontologist, 17* (1), 3–19.

George, L., & Fillenbaum, G. (1990). OARS methodology: A decade of experience in geriatric assessment. *Journal of the American Geriatrics Society, 33,* 607–615.

Germain, C. (1979). Ecology and social work. In C. Germain (Ed.), *Social work practice: People and environments* (pp. 1–2). New York: Columbia University Press.

Germain, C. (1981). The ecological approach to people–environmental transactions. *Social Case-Work, 62,* 323–331.

Gerstel, N., Bogard, C. J., McConnell, J. J., & Schwartz, M. (1996). The therapeutic incarceration of homeless families. *Social Service Review, 70* (4), 542–572.

Getzel, G. S. (1991). Survival modes for people with AIDS in groups. *Social Work, 36* (1), 7–11.

Getzel, G. S. (1998). Group work practice with gay men and lesbians. In G. P. Mallon (Ed.), *Foundations of social work practice with lesbian and gay persons* (pp. 131–144). Binghamton, NY: Haworth Press.

Giannandrea, V., & Murphy, K. (1973). Similarity of self-disclosure and return for a second interview. *Journal of Counseling Psychology, 20,* 545–548.

Gibbs, J. (1995). *Tribes: A new way of learning and being together.* Sausalito, CA: Center Source Systems.

Gibson, P. A. (1999). African American grandmothers: New mothers again. *Affilia, 14* (3), 329–343.

Gilbar, O. (1992). Workers' sick fund (kupat holim) hotline therapeutic first intervention: A model developed in the Gulf War. *Social Work in Health Care, 17* (4), 45–57.

Gilbert, D. J. (2003). Multicultural assessment. In C. Jordan & C. Franklin (Eds.), *Clinical assessment for social workers: Quantitative and qualitative methods* (2nd ed., pp. 351–383). Chicago: Lyceum Books.

Gilbert, N. (1977). The search for professional identity. *Social Work, 22,* 401–406.

Gilgun, J. F. (1994). Hand to glove: The grounded theory approach and social work practice research. In L. Sherman & W. J. Reid (Eds.), *Qualitative research in social work* (pp. 115–125). New York: Columbia University Press.

Gilgun, J. F. (1999). CASPARS: New tools for assessing client risks and strengths. *Families in Society, 80* (5), 450–458.

Gilgun, J. F. (2001). CASPARS: New tools for assessing client risks and strengths. *Families and Society: The Journal of Contemporary Human Services, 82,* 450–459.

Gilliland, B. E., & James, R. K. (1993). *Crisis intervention strategies* (2nd ed.). Pacific Grove, CA: Brooks/Cole.

Gingerich, W. J., & Eisengart, S. (2000). Solution-focused brief treatment. A review of outcome research. *Family Process, 39,* 477–498.

Gingerich, W. J., & Wabeke, T. (2001). A solution-focused approach to mental health interventions in school settings. *Children in Schools, 23* (1), 33–47.

Gitterman, A. (1996). Ecological perspectives: Response to Professor Jerry Wakefield. *Social Service Review, 70* (3), 472–483.

Giunta, C. T., & Streissguth, A. P. (1988). Patients with fetal alcohol syndrome and their caretakers. *Social Casework, 69* (7), 453–459.

Glisson, C. (1994). The effects of service coordination teams on outcomes for children in state custody. *Administration in Social Work, 18* (4), 1–25.

Global standards for social work education and training. (2004). International Association of Schools of Social Work and International Federation of Social Workers. Final document for discussion and adoption at the General Assemblies, Adelaide, Australia.

Golan, N. (1978). *Treatment in crisis situations.* New York: Free Press.

Golan, N. (1981). *Passing through transitions: A guide for the practitioners.* New York: Free Press.

Gold, M. (1986, November). (As quoted by Earl Ubell.) Is that child bad or depressed? *Parade Magazine, 2,* 10.

Gold, N. (1990). Motivation: The crucial but unexplored component of social work practice. *Social Work, 35,* 49–56.

Goldenberg, I., & Goldenberg, H. (1991). *Family therapy: An overview* (3rd ed.). Pacific Grove, CA: Brooks/Cole.

Goldenberg, I., & Goldenberg, H. (2000). *Family therapy: An overview* (5th ed.). Pacific Grove, CA: Brooks/Cole.

Goldfried, M. (1977). The use of relaxation and cognitive re-labeling as coping skills. In R. Stuart (Ed.), *Behavioral self-management* (pp. 82–116). New York: Brunner/Mazel.

Goldstein, E. G. (1997). To tell or not to tell: The disclosure of events in the therapist's life to the patient. *Clinical Social Work Journal, 25* (1), 41–58.

Goodman, H. (1997). Social group work in community corrections. *Social Work with Groups, 20* (1), 51–64.

Goodman, H., Getzel, G. S., & Ford, W. (1996). Group work with high-risk urban youths on probation. *Social Work, 41* (4), 375–381.

Goodwin, D. W., & Gabrielli, W. F. (1997). Alcohol: Clinical aspects. In J. H. Lowinson, P. Ruiz, R. B. Millman, & J. G. Langrod (Eds.), *Substance abuse: A comparative textbook* (3rd ed., pp. 142–148). Baltimore, MD: Williams & Wilkins.

Gordon, T. (1970). *Parent effectiveness training.* New York: P. H. Wyclen.

Gordon, W. (1965). Toward a social work frame of reference. *Journal of Education for Social Work, 1,* 19–26.

Gottesfeld, M., & Lieberman, F. (1979). The pathological therapist. *Social Casework, 60,* 387–393.

Graham, J. R., & Barter, K. (1999). Collaboration: A social work practice method. *Families in Society, 80* (1), 6–13.

Grame, C., Tortorici, J., Healey, B., Dillingham, J., & Wilklebaur, P. (1999). Addressing spiritual and religious issues of clients with a history of psychological trauma. *Bulletin of the Menninger Clinic, 63* (2), 223–239.

Grant, G. B., & Grobman, L. M.(1998). *The social worker's Internet handbook.* Harrisburg, PA: White Hat Communications.

Green, J. W. (1999). *Cultural awareness in the human services: A multi-ethnic approach.* Boston: Allyn & Bacon.

Greenfield, P. M. (1994). Independence and interdependence as developmental scripts: Implications for theory, research and practice. In P. M. Greenfield & R. R. Cocking (Eds.), *Cross-cultural roots of minority child development* (pp. 1–24). Hillsdale, NJ: Lawrence Erlbaum Associates.

Gross, E. (1995). Deconstructing politically correct practice literature: The American Indian case. *Social Work, 40* (2), 206–213.

Grunert, B. K., Smucker, M. R., Weis, J. M., & Rusch, M. D. (2003). When prolonged exposure fails: Adding an imagery-based cognitive restructuring component in the treatment of industrial accident victims suffering from PTSD. *Cognitive and Behavior Practice, 10* (4), 333–346.

Guierrez, L., & Lewis, E. (1999). *Empowering women of color.* New York: Columbia University Press.

Gulati, P., & Guest, G. (1990). The community-centered model: A garden variety approach or a radical transformation of community practice? *Social Work, 35* (1), 63–68.

Gumpert, J., & Saltman, J. E. (1998). Social group work practice in rural areas: The practitioners speak. *Social Work with Groups, 21* (3), 19–34.

Gurman, A. (1977). The patient's perception of the therapeutic relationship. In A. Gutman & A. Razin (Eds.), *Effective psychotherapy: A handbook of research*. New York: Pergamon Press.

Gutierrez, L.M. (1994). Beyond coping: an empowerment perspective on stressful life events. *Journal of Sociology and Social Welfare, 21* (3), 201–219.

Gutierrez, L. M., & Lewis, E. A. (1999). Strengthening communities through groups: A multicultural perspective. In H. Bertcher, L. F. Kurtz, & A. Lamont (Eds.), *Rebuilding communities: Challenges for group work* (pp. 5–16). New York: Haworth Press.

Gutierrez, L. M., & Ortega, R. (1991). Developing methods to empower Latinos: The importance of groups. *Social Work with Groups, 14* (2), 23–43.

Gutierrez, L. M., Parsons, R. J., & Cox, E. O. (1998). *Empowerment in social work practice: A sourcebook*. Pacific Grove, CA: Brooks/Cole.

H

Hackman, J. R., & Oldham, G. R. (1976). Motivation through the design of work: Test of a theory. *Organizational Behavior and Human Performance, 16,* 250–279.

Hackman, J. R., & Oldham, G. R. (1980). *Work design*. Reading, MA: Addison-Wesley.

Hackney, H., & Cormier, L. (1979). *Counseling strategies and objectives* (2nd ed.), Englewood Cliffs, NJ: Prentice-Hall.

Hage, D. (2004). *Reforming welfare by rewarding work*. Minneapolis: University of Minnesota Press.

Hagen, J. L. (1998). The new welfare law: "Tough on work." *Families in Society, 79* (6), 596–605.

Haight, W. L. (1998). Gathering the spirit at First Baptist Church: Spirituality as a protective factor in the lives of African American children. *Social Work, 43* (3), 213–221.

Halpern, R. (1990). Poverty and early childhood parenting: Toward a framework for intervention. *American Journal of Orthopsychiatry, 60* (1), 6–18.

Hammond, D., Hepworth, D., & Smith, V. (1977). *Improving therapeutic communication*. San Francisco: Jossey-Bass.

Handmaker, N. S., Miller, W. R., & Manicke, M. (1999). Findings of a pilot study of motivational interviewing with pregnant drinkers. *Journal of Studies on Alcohol, 60* (2), 285–287.

Hanson, M., & Gutheil, I. (2004). *Motivational strategies with alcohol-involved older adults: Implications for social work practice. Social Work, 49,* 3.

Hardy, K. (1993). War of the worlds. *The Family Therapy Networker*, 51–57.

Hardy, K. V. (1997). Steps toward becoming culturally competent. *Family Therapy News, 28* (2), 13–19.

Hare, J. (1994). Concerns and issues faced by families headed by a lesbian couple. *Families in Society, 75* (1), 27–35.

Hargrove, D. S. (1986). Ethical issues in rural mental health practice. *Professional Psychology: Research and Practice, 17* (1), 20–23.

Harper, K.V., & Lantz, J. (1996). *Cross-cultural practice*. Chicago: Lyceum Books.

Harrigan, M. P., Favri, D. P., & Netting, F. E. (1998). Termination: Extending the concept for macro social work practice. *Journal of Sociology and Social Welfare, 25* (4), 61–80.

Hartford, M. (1971). *Groups in social work*. New York: Columbia University Press.

Hartman, A. (1981). The family: A central focus for practice. *Social Work, 26,* 7–13.

Hartman, A. (1993). The professional is political. *Social Work, 38* (4), 365, 366, 504.

Hartman, A. (1994). Diagrammatic assessment of family relationships. In B. R. Compton & B. Galaway (Eds.), *Social work processes* (5th ed., pp. 153–165). Pacific Grove, CA: Brooks/Cole.

Hartman, A., & Laird, J. *(1983). Family centered social work practice*. New York: Free Press.

Hasenfeld, Y., & Furman, W. M. (1994). Intervention research as an interorganizational exchange. In J. Rothman & E. Thomas (Eds.), *Intervention research: Design for human services* (pp. 297–313). New York: Haworth Press.

Haynes, K. S., & Mickelson, J. S. (2000). *Affecting change: Social workers in the political arena* (4th ed.). Boston: Allyn & Bacon.

Hegar, R. (1999). The cultural roots of kinship care. In R. Hegar & M. Scannapieco (Eds.), *Kinship foster care, policy, practice, and research* (pp. 17–27). New York: Oxford University Press.

Henderson, S., Duncan-Jones, P., Byrne, D., & Scott, R. (1980). Measuring social relationships: The interview schedule for social interaction. *Psychological Medicine, 10,* 723–734.

Henry, M. (1988). Revisiting open groups. *Group Work, 1,* 215–228.

Henry, S. (1992). *Group skills in four-dimensional approach* (2nd ed.). Pacific Grove, CA: Brooks/Cole.

Hernandez, M., & McGoldrick, M. (1999). Migration and the life cycle. In B. Carter & M. McGoldrick (Eds.), *The expanded family life cycle: Individual, family, and social perspectives* (3rd ed., pp. 169–184). Boston: Allyn & Bacon.

Hess, P. M., & Mullen, E. J. (1995). Bridging the gap. Collaborative considerations in practitioner–researcher knowledge-building partnerships. In P. M. Hess & E. J. Mullen (Eds.), *Practitioner–researcher partnerships* (pp. 1–30). Washington, DC: NASW Press.

Hill, B., Rotegard, L., & Bruininks, R. (1984). The quality of life of mentally retarded people in residential care. *Social Work, 29,* 275–281.

Hines, P., & Boyd-Franklin, N. (1996). African American families. In M. McGoldrick, J. Giordana, & J. Pearce (Eds.), *Ethnicity and family therapy* (2nd ed., pp. 68–84). New York: Guilford Press.

Hines, P. M., Garcia-Preto, N., McGoldrick, M., Almeida, R., & Weltman, S. (1992). Intergenerational relationships across cultures. *Families in Society, 73* (3), 323–338.

Hines, P. H., Preto, N. G., McGoldrick, M., Almeida, R., & Weltman, S. (1999). Culture and the family life cycle. In B. Carter & M. McGoldrick (Eds.), *The expanded family life cycle. Individual, family and social perspectives* (3rd ed.). Needham Heights, Boston: Allyn & Bacon.

HIPAA medical privacy rule. (2003). Retrieved May 1, 2004, from *http://www.socialworkers.org/hipaa/medical.asp#*

Hirayama, K. K., Hirayama, H., & Cetingok, M. (1993). Mental health promotion for South East Asian refugees in the USA. *International Social Work, 36* (2), 119–129.

Hoehn-Saric, R., Frank, J., Imber, S., Nash, E., Stone, A., & Battle, C. (1964). Systematic preparation of patients for psychotherapy—I. Effects on therapy behavior and outcome. *Journal of Psychiatric Research, 2,* 267–281. *Social Casework, 62,* 30–39.

Holbrook, T. L. (1995). Finding subjugated knowledge: Personal document research. *Social Work, 40* (6), 746–750.

Hollander, E. M. (2001). Cyber community in the valley of the shadow of death. *Journal of Loss and Trauma, 6,* 136–146.

Holly, B. (2003). Strengths and secondary trauma in family violence work. *Social Work, 48* (4), 513–522.

Holman, W. D. (1997). Who would find you? A question for working with suicidal children and adolescents. *Child and Adolescent Social Work Journal, 14* (2), 129–137.

Holt, B. J. (2000). *The practice of generalist case management.* Boston: Allyn & Bacon.

Homan, M. S. (1999). *Promoting community change: Making it happen in the real world* (2nd ed.). Brooks/Cole.

Horesji, C., Heavy Runner, B., & Pablo, C. J. (1992). Reactions by Native American parents to child protection agencies: Cultural and community factors. *Child Welfare, 71* (4), 329–342.

Houston-Vega, M. K., Nuehring, E. M., & Daguio, E. R. (1997). *Prudent practice: A guide for managing malpractice risk.* Washington, DC: NASW Press.

Hoyt, M. F. (2000). *Some stories are better than others: Doing what works in brief therapy and managed care.* Philadelphia, PA.: Brunner/Mazel.

Hudson, W. W. (1990). Computer-based clinical practice: Present status and future possibilities. In L. Videka-Sherman, & W. H. Reid (Eds.), *Advances in clinical social work research* (pp. 105–117). Silver Springs, MD: NASW Press.

Hudson, W. (1992). *The WALMYR assessment scales scoring manual.* Tempe, AZ: WALMYR.

Hudson, W. W. (1996). Computer assessment package. Tallahassee, FL: WALMYR.

Hulewat, P. (1996). Resettlement: A cultural and psychological crisis. *Social Work, 41* (2), 129–135.

Hull, G. Jr. (1982). Child welfare services to Native Americans. *Social Casework, 63,* 340–347.

Hunsley, J., Aubrey, T., Vestervelt, C. M., & Vito, D. (1999). Comparing therapist and client perspectives on reasons for psychotherapy termination. *Psychotherapy, 36* (4), 380–388.

Hurdle, D. E. (2002). Native Hawaiian traditional healing. *Social Work, 47* (2), 183–192.

Hurley, D. J. (1984). Resistance and work in adolescent groups. *Social Work with Groups, 1,* 71–81.

Hurvitz, N. (1975). Interactions hypothesis in marriage counseling. In A. Gutman & D. Rice (Eds.), *Couples in conflict* (pp. 225–240). New York: Jason Aronson.

Hutson, R. Q. (2001). *Red flags: Research raises concerns about the impact of "welfare reform" on child maltreatment.* Washington, DC: Center for Law and Social Policy.

Hyde, C. (1996). A feminist's response to Rothman's "The interweaving of community intervention approaches." *Journal of Community Practice, 3* (3/4), 127–145.

I

Icard, L. D., Longres, J. F., & Spenser, M. (1999). Racial minority status and distress among children and adolescents. *Journal of Social Service Research, 25* (1/2), 19–40.

Imbrogno, A. R., & Imbrogno, S. (2000). Mediation in court cases of domestic violence. *Families in Society, 81* (4), 392–401.

Indyk, D., Belville, R., Lachapelle, S. S., Gordon, G., & Dewart, T. (1993). A community-based approach to HIV case management: Systematizing the unmanageable. *Social Work, 38* (4), 380–387.

Ingersoll-Dayton, B., Schroepfer, T., & Pryce, J. (1999). The effectiveness of a solution-focused approach for problem behaviors among nursing home residents. *Journal of Gerontological Social Work, 32* (3), 49–64.

Ingram, R. E., & Scott, W. D. (1990). Cognitive behavioral therapy. In A. S. Bellack, M. Hersen, & A. E. Kazden (Eds.), *International handbook of behavior modification and behavioral therapy* (2nd ed.). New York: Plenum Press.

International Federation of Social Workers (2000). New definition of social work. Berne: International Federation of Social Workers.

Ivanoff, A. M., Blythe, B. J., & Tripodi, T. (1994). *Involuntary clients in social work practice: A research-based approach.* New York: Aldine de Gruyter.

J

Jackson, A. (1995). Diversity and oppression. In C. H. Meyer & M. A. Mattani (Eds.), *The foundation of social work practice* (pp. 42–58). Washington, DC: NASW Press.

Jackson, A. P. (1998). The role of social support in parenting for low-income, single, black mothers. *Social Service Review, 72* (3), 365–378.

Jacobs, E. E., Masson, R. L., & Harvill, R. L. (1998). *Group counseling strategies and skills.* Pacific Grove, CA: Brooks/Cole.

Jacobson, W. (2001). Beyond therapy: Bringing social work back to human services reform. *Social Work, 46* (1), 51–61.

James, R. K., & Gilliland, B. E. (2001). *Crisis intervention strategies.* Pacific Grove, CA: Brooks/Cole, Thomson Learning.

Jang, M., Lee, K., & Woo, K. (1998). Income, language, and citizenship status: Factors affecting the health care access and utilization of Chinese Americans. *Health and Social Work, 23* (2), 136–145.

Janzen, C., & Harris, O. (1997). *Family treatment in social work practice* (3rd ed.). Itasca, IL: F. E. Peacock.

Jarrett, R. L. (1995). Growing up poor: The family experience of socially mobile youth in low-income African American neighborhoods. *Journal of Adolescent Research, 10* (1), 111–135.

Jayaratne, S. (1994). Should systematic assessement, monitoring and evaluation tools be used as empowerment aids for clients? In W. W. Hudson & P. S. Nurius (Eds.), *Controversial issues in social work research* (pp. 88–92). Needham Heights, MA: Allyn and Bacon.

Jayaratne, S., Croxton, T., & Mattison, D. (1997). Social work professional standards: An exploratory study. *Social Work, 42* (2), 187–199.

Jaycox, L. H., Zoellner, L., & Foa, E. B. (2002). Cognitive behavioral therapy for PTSD in rape survivor. *Journal of Clinical Psychology, 58* (8), 891–907.

Jennings, H. (1950). *Leadership and isolation.* New York: Longmans Green.

Jilek, W. (1982). *Indian healing: Shamanic ceremonialism in the Pacific Northwest today.* Laine, WA: Hancock House.

Johnson, H. C. (1989). Disruptive children: Biological factors in attention deficit disorder and antisocial disorders. *Social Work, 34* (2), 137–144.

Jones, D. M. (1996). Termination from drug treatment: Dangers and opportunities for clients of the graduation ceremony. *Social Work with Groups, 19* (3/4), 105–115.

Jordan, C., & Franklin, C. (1995). *Clinical assessment for social workers: Quantitative and qualitative methods.* Chicago: Lyceum Books.

Jordan, C., & Franklin, C. (2003). *Clinical assessment for social workers. Quantitative and qualitative methods* (2nd ed.). Chicago: Lyceum Books.

Jordan, C., & Hickerson, J. (2003). Children and adolescents. In C. Jordan & C. Franklin (Eds.), *Clinical assessment for social workers: Quantitative and qualitative methods* (pp. 179–213). Chicago: Lyceum Books.

Jose, P. E., Cafasso, L. L., & D'Anna, C. A. (1994). Ethnic group differences in children's coping strategies. *Sociological Studies of Children, 6,* 25–53.

Joseph, S., Williams, R., & Yule, W. (1993). Changes in outlook following disaster: Preliminary development of measures to assess positive and negative responses. *Journal of Traumatic Stress, 6,* 271–279.

Joshi, P. T., Capozzoli, J. A., & Coyle, J. T. (1990). The Johns Hopkins Depression Scale: Normative data and validation in child psychiatry patients. *Journal of the American Academy of Child and Adolescent Psychiatry, 29*(2), 283–288.

Joyce, A. S., Duncan, S. C., Duncan, A., Kipnes, D., & Piper, W. E. (1996). Limiting time-unlimited group therapy. *International Journal of Group Psychotherapy, 46*(6), 61–79.

Julia, M. C. (1996). *Multicultural Awareness in the health care professions.* Needham Heights, MA: Allyn & Bacon.

K

Kaduchin, A. (1977). *Consultation in social work.* New York: Columbia University Press.

Kadushin, G., & Kulys, R. (1993). Discharge planning revisited: What do social workers actually do in discharge planning? *Social Work, 38*(6), 713–726.

Kagle, J. D. (1991). *Social work records* (2nd ed.). Chicago: Waveland Press.

Kagle, J. D. (1994). Should systematic assessment, monitoring and evaluation tools be used as empowerment aids for clients? Rejoiner to Dr. Jayaratne. In W. W. Hudson P. S. Nurius (Eds.) *Controversial issues in social work research* (pp. 88–92). Needham Heights, MA: Allyn aand Bacon.

Kagle, J. D. (2002). Record-keeping. In A. R. Roberts & G. J. Greene (Eds.), *Social workers' desk reference* (pp. 28–33). New York: Oxford University Press.

Kane, N. (1995). Looking at the lite side. "I feed more cats, than I have T-cells." *Reflections, 1*(2), 26–36.

Kane, R. A., Penrod, J. D., Davidson, G., Moscovice, I., & Rich, E. (1991). What cost case management in long-term care? *Social Service Review, 65*(2), 281–303.

Kardas, E. (1999). *Psychology resources on the World Wide Web.* Pacific Grove, CA: Brooks/Cole.

Kauffman, J. M. (1997). *Characteristics of emotional and behavioral disorders of children and youth* (6th ed.). Upper Saddle River, NJ: Prentice-Hall.

Kazdin, A. E., Stolar, M. J., & Marciano, P. L. (1995). Risk factors for dropping out of treatment among white and black families. *Journal of Family Psychology, 9*(4), 402–419.

Kazdin, A. E., & Wassell, G. (1998). Treatment completion and therapeutic change among children referred for outpatient therapy. *Professional Psychology: Research and Practice, 29*(4), 332–340.

Kear-Colwell, J., & Pollock, P. (1997). Motivation or confrontation: Which approach to the child sex offender? *Criminal Justice and Behavior, 24,* 20–33.

Keefe, T. (1978). The economic context of empathy. *Social Work, 23*(6), 460–465.

Kettner, P. M., Daley, J. M., & Nichols, A. W. (1985). *Initiating change in organizations and communities.* Monterey, CA: Brooks/Cole.

Kilpatrick, A. C., & Holland, T. (1999). *Working with families: An integrative model by level of need* (2nd ed.). Boston: Allyn & Bacon.

Kilpatrick, A. C., & Holland, T. (2003). *Working with families: An integrative model by level of need.* Boston: Allyn & Bacon.

Kirk, S. A., & Koeske, G. F. (1995). The fate of optimism: A longitudinal study of case managers' hopefulness and subsequent morale. *Research on Social Work Practice, 5*(1), 47–61.

Kleespies, P. M., Penk, W. E., & Forsyth, J. P. (1993). The stress of patient suicidal behavior during clinical training: Incidence, impact, and recovery. *Professional Psychology: Research and Practice, 24*(3), 293–303.

Klein, A. (1970). *Social work through group process.* Albany, NY: School of Social Welfare, State University of New York at Albany.

Komar, A. A. (1994). Adolescent school crises: Structures, issues and techniques for postventions. *International Journal of Adolescence and Youth, 5*(1/2), 35–46.

Koob, J. J. (2003). Solution-focused family interventions. In A. C. Kilpatrick & T. P. Holland. *Working with families: An integrative model by level of need* (3rd ed., pp. 131–150). Boston: Allyn & Bacon.

Kooden, H. (1994). The gay male therapist as an agent of socialization. *Journal of Gay and Lesbian Psychotherapy, 2*(2), 39–64,

Kopp, J. (1989). Self-observation: An empowerment strategy in assessment. *Social Casework, 70*(5), 276–284.

Kopp, J., & Butterfield, W. (1985). Changes in graduate students' use of interviewing skills from the classroom to the field. *Journal of Social Service Research, 9*(1), 65–89.

Koss, M. P., & Shiang, J. (1994). Research on brief psychotherapy. In A. E. Bergin & S. L. Garfield (Eds.), *Handbook of psychotherapy and behavioral change* (3rd ed., pp. 664–700). New York: Wiley.

Kotlowitz, A. (1991). *There are no children here.* New York: Doubleday.

Kovacs, M. (1992). *Children's depression inventory manual.* Los Angeles: Western Psychological Services.

Kruger, L., Moore, D., Schmidt, P., & Wiens, R. (1979). Group work with abusive parents. *Social Work, 24,* 337–338.

Kumabe, K., Nishada, C., & Hepworth, D. (1985). *Bridging ethnocultural diversity in social work and health.* Honolulu: University of Hawaii Press.

Kung, W. W. (2003). Chinese Americans' help seeking behavior for emotional distress. *Social Service Review, 77*(1), 110–134.

Kurland, R., & Salmon, R. (1998). Purpose: A misunderstood and misused keystone of group work practice. *Social Work with Groups, 21*(3), 5–17.

Kurtz, P. D., Jarvis, S. V., & Kurtz, G. L. (1991). Problems of homeless youths: Empirical findings and human services issues. *Social Work, 36*(4), 309–314.

L

Laing, R. (1965). Mystification, confusion and conflict. In I. Boszormenyi-Nagy & J. Framo (Eds.), *Intensive family therapy: Theoretical and practical aspects.* New York: Harper & Row.

Laird, J. (1993). Family-centered practice: Cultural and constructionist reflections. *Journal of Teaching in Social Work, 8*(1/2), 77–109.

Lam, D. H., Brewin, C. R., Woods, R. T., & Bebbington, P. E. (1987). Cognition and social adversity in the depressed elderly. *Journal of Abnormal Psychology, 96,* 23–26.

Lambert, M. J., Bergin, A. E., & Garfield, S. L. (2004). Introduction and historical overview. In M. J. Lambert (Ed.), *Handbook of psychotherapy and behavioral change* (5th ed., pp. 3–15). New York: Wiley.

Lambert, M. J., & Ogles, B. M. (2004). The efficacy and effectiveness of psychotherapy. In M. J. Lambert (Ed.), *Handbook of psychotherapy and behavioral change* (5th ed., pp. 139–193). New York: John Wiley.

Land, H. (1988). The impact of licensing on social work practice: Values, ethics and choices. *Journal of Independent Social Work, 2*(4), 87–96.

Lane, F. E. (1986). Utilizing physician empathy with violent patients. *American Journal of Psychotherapy, 40,* 448–456.

Lang, N. (1972). A broad range model of practice in the social work group. *Social Service Review, 46,* 76–89.

Lantz, J. (1996). Cognitive theory in social work treatment. In F. Turner (Ed.), *Social work treatment: Interlocking theoretical approaches* (4th ed., pp. 94–115). New York: Free Press.

Larsen, J. (1975). *A comparative study of traditional and competency-based methods of teaching interpersonal skills in social work education.* Unpublished doctoral dissertation, University of Utah, Salt Lake City.

Larsen, J. (1980). Accelerating group development and productivity: An effective leader approach. *Social Work with Groups, 3,* 25–39.

Larsen, J. (1982). Remedying dysfunctional marital communication. *Social Casework, 63,* 15–23.

Larsen, J. (1991). *I'm a day late and a dollar short and it's okay: A woman's survival guide for the 90's.* Salt Lake City, UT: Deseret Books.

Larsen, J., & Hepworth, D. (1978). Skill development through competency-based education. *Journal of Education for Social Work, 14,* 73–81.

Larsen, J., & Mitchell, C. (1980). Task-centered, strength-oriented group work with delinquents. *Social Casework, 61,* 154–163.

Lavee, Y. (1997). The components of healthy marriages: Perceptions of Israeli social workers and their clients. *Journal of Family Social Work, 2* (1), 1–14.

Lazarus, A. A. (1994). How certain boundaries and ethics diminish therapeutic effectiveness. *Ethics and Behavior, 4* (3), 255–261.

LeCroy, C. W. (2002). Child therapy and social skills. In A. R. Roberts & G. J. Greene (Eds.), *Social workers' desk reference* (pp. 406–412). New York: Oxford University Press.

Lee, M. Y. (2003). A solution-focused approach to cross-cultural clinical social work practice: Utilizing cultural strengths. *Families in Society: The Journal of Contemporary Human Services, 84* (3), 385–395.

Lee, M. Y., Greene, G. J., & Rheinscheld, J. (1999). A model for short-term solution-focused group treatment of male domestic violence offenders. *Journal of Family Social Work, 3* (2), 39–57.

Lehman, A. F. (1996). Heterogeneity of person and place: Assessing co-occurring addictive and mental disorders. *American Journal of Orthopsychiatry, 66* (1), 32–41.

Levick, K. (1981). Privileged communication: Does it really exist? *Social Casework, 62,* 235–239.

Levine, C. O., & Dang, J. (1979). The group within the group: The dilemma of cotherapy. *International Journal of Group Psychotherapy, 29* (2), 175–184.

Levinson, H. (1973). Use and misuse of groups. *Social Work, 18,* 66–73.

Levinson, H. (1977). Termination of psychotherapy: Some salient issues. *Social Casework, 58,* 480–489.

Levy, C. (1973). The value base of social work. *Journal of Education for Social Work, 9,* 34–42.

Levy, L. (1963). *Psychological interpretation.* New York: Holt, Rinehart & Winston.

Lewis, E. (1991). Social change and citizen action: A philosophical exploration for modern social group work. *Social Work with Groups, 14* (3/4), 23–34.

Lewis, E. A., Skyles, A., & Crosbie-Burnett, M. (2000). Public policy and families of color in the new millennium. National Council on Family Relations Annual Program Meeting, Minneapolis, MN, November 12, 2000.

Lewis, J. A., Lewis, M. D., Packard, T., & Souflee, F. (2001). *Management of human service programs* (3rd ed.). Pacific Grove, CA: Wadsworth/Brooks/Cole.

Lieberman, M. (1980). Group methods. In F. Kanfer & A. Goldstein (Eds.), *Helping people change* (pp. 470–536). New York: Pergamon Press.

Lieberman, M., & Borman, L. (Eds.) (1979). *Self-help groups for coping with crisis.* San Francisco, CA: Jossey-Bass.

Lieberman, M., & Videka-Sherman, L. (1986). The impact of self-help groups on the mental health of widows and widowers. *American Journal of Orthopsychiatry, 56,* 435–449.

Lieberman, M., Yalom, I., & Miles, M. (1973). *Encounter groups: Firstfacts.* New York: Basic Books.

Ligon, J. (1997). Brief crisis stabilization of an African American woman. Integrating cultural and ecological approaches. *Journal of Multicultural Social Work, 6* (3/4), 111–123.

Lim, C., & Adelman, H. S. (1997). Establishing a school-based collaborative team to coordinate resources: A case study. *Journal of Social Work in Education, 19* (4), 266–277.

Lindemann, E. (1944). Symptomatology and management of acute grief. *American Journal of Psychiatry, 101,* 141–148.

Lindemann, E. (1956). The meaning of crisis in individual and family. *Teachers College Record, 57,* 310.

Linhorst, D. M., Hamilton, J., Young, E., & Eckert, A. (2002). Opportunities and barriers to empowering people with severe mental illness through participation in treatment planning. *Social Work, 47* (4), 425–234.

Linzer, N. (1999). *Resolving ethical dilemmas in social work practice.* Boston: Allyn & Bacon.

Lipchik, E. (2002). *Beyond technique in solution-focused therapy: Working with emotions and the therapeutic relationship.* New York: Guilford Press.

Lipchik, E. (1997). My story about solution-focused brief therapist/client relationships. *Journal of Systemic Therapies, 16,* 159–172.

Lister, L. (1987). Contemporary direct practice roles. *Social Work, 32,* 384–391.

Long, D. D., & Holle, M. C. (1997). *Macro systems in the social environment.* Itasca, IL: F. E. Peacock.

Long, K. A. (1986). Cultural considerations in the assessment and treatment of intrafamilial abuse. *American Journal of Orthopsychiatry, 56,* 131–136.

Longres, J. F. (1991). Toward a status model of ethnic sensitive practice. *Journal of Multi-cultural Social Work, 1* (1), 41–56.

Longres, J. F. (1995). *Human behavior in the social environment.* Itasca, IL: F. E. Peacock.

Longres, J. F., & Torrecilha, R. S. (1992). Race and the diagnosis, placement and exit status of children and youth in a mental health and disability system. *Journal of Social Service Research, 15* (3/4), 43–63.

Lowinson, J. H., Ruiz, P., Millman, R. B., & Langrod, J. G. (Eds.). (1997). *Substance abuse: A comprehensive textbook* (3rd ed.). Baltimore, MD: Williams & Wilkins.

Luborsky, L., & Spence, D. (1978). Quantitative research on psychoanalytic therapy. In S. Garfield & A. Bergin (Eds.), *Handbook of psychotherapy and behavior change* (pp. 331–368). New York: Wiley.

Lukas, S. (1993). *Where to start and what to ask: An assessment handbook.* New York: Norton.

Lukton, R. (1982). Myths and realities of crisis intervention. *Social Casework, 63,* 275–285.

Lum, D. (1996). *Social work practice and people of color: A process-stage approach* (3rd ed.). Pacific Grove, CA: Brooks/Cole.

Lum, D. (2004). *Social work practice and people of color. A process-stage approach* (5th ed.). Pacific Grove, CA: Brooks/Cole.

M

Macgowan, M. J. (1997). A measure of engagement for social group work: The group work engagement measure (GEM). *Journal of Social Service Research, 23* (2), 17–37.

Mackelprang, R., & Hepworth, D. H. (1987). Ecological factors in rehabilitation of patients with severe spinal cord injuries. *Social Work in Health Care, 13,* 23–38.

Mackey, R. A., & O'Brian, B. A. (1998). Marital conflict management: Gender and ethnic differences. *Social Work, 43* (2), 128–141.

Madden, R. G., & Wayne, R. H. (2003) Social work and the law: A therapeutic jurisprudence perspective. *Social Work, 48* (3), 338–349.

Magen, R. (2004). Measurement issues. In C. D. Garvin, L. M. Gutierrez, & M. J. Galinsky (Eds.), *Handbook of social work with groups.* New York: Guilford Press.

Magen, R. H., & Glajchen, M. (1999). Cancer support groups: Client outcome and the context of group process. Research on Social Work Practice, 9 (5), 541–554.

Mahler, C. (1969). *Group counseling in the schools.* Boston: Houghton Mifflin.

Mahoney, M. J. (1974). *Cognition and behavior modification.* Cambridge, MA: Ballinger.

Mailick, M. D., & Vigilante, F. W. (1997). The family assessment wheel: A social constructionist perspective. Families in Society, 80 (1), 361–369.

Mallory, K. (2004, May 8). Barbers cutting cancer out in Montgomery County. *The Washington Afro American, 112,* 39.

Maluccio, A. (1979). Perspectives of social workers and clients on treatment outcome. *Social Casework, 60,* 394–401.

Mann, B., & Murphy, K. (1975). Timing of self disclosure, reciprocity of self-disclosure, and reactions to an initial interview. *Journal of Counseling Psychology, 22,* 304–308.

Marlatt, G. A., & Gordon, J. R. (1985). *Relapse prevention: Maintenance strategies in the treatment of addictive behaviors.* New York: Guilford Press.

Marlow, C. (1993). Coping with multiple roles: Family configuration and the need for workplace services. *Affilia, 8* (1), 40–55.

Marsh, J. C. (2002). Learning from clients. *Social Work, 47* (4), 341–342.

Marshall, T. K., & Mazie, A. S. (1987). A cognitive approach to treating depression. *Social Casework, 68,* 540–545.

Martin, L. L. (1993). *Total quality management in human service organizations.* Thousand Oaks, CA: Sage Publications.

Martin, P. Y., & O'Connor, G. G. (1989). *The social environment: Open systems applications.* Upper Saddle River, NJ: Longman.

Mason, J. L., Benjamin, M. P., & Lewis, S. A. (1996). The cultural competence model: Implications for child and family mental health services. In C. A. Heflinger & C. T. Nixon (Eds.), *Families and the mental health system for children and adolescents: Policy, services, and research* (pp. 165–190). Thousand Oaks, CA: Sage Publications.

Mattesisch, P. W., & Monsey, B. R. (1992). *Collaboration: What makes it work.* Saint Paul, MN: Amherst Wilder Research Center.

Mau, W., & Jepsen, D. A. (1990). Help seeking perceptions behaviors: A comparison of Chinese and American graduate students. *Journal of Multicultural Counseling and Development, 18* (2), 95–104.

May, P., Hymbaugh, K., Aasc, J., & Samct, J. (1983). The epidemiology of fetal alcohol syndrome among American Indians of the Southwest. *Social Biology, 30,* 374–387.

Mayadas, N., Ramanathan, C., & Suarez, Z. (1998–1999). Mental health, social context, refugees and immigrants: A cultural interface. *Journal of Intergroup Relations, 25,* 3–14.

Mayer, J., & Timms, N. (1969). Clash in perspective between worker and client. *Social Casework, 50,* 32–40.

Mays, N. (2003, Fall). Investigating how culture impacts health. *Washington University in Saint Louis Magazine.*

McAdoo, J. L. (1993). Decision making and marital satisfaction in African American families. In H. P. McAdoo (Ed.), *Family ethnicity: Strength in diversity* (pp. 109–118). Thousand Oaks, CA: Sage Publications.

McChesney, K. Y. (1995). Urban homeless families. *Social Service Review, 69* (3), 428–460.

McCollum, E. E., & Beer, J. (1995). The view from the other chair. *Family Therapy Networker, 19* (2), 59–62.

McConaughy, S. H., & Auchenbach, T. M. (1994). *Manual for the semistructured clinical interview with children and adolescents.* Burlington, VT: University of Vermont, Department of Psychiatry.

McDonald, L. (2002). Evidence-based, family-strengthening strategies to reduce delinquency: FAST: Families and Schools Together. In A. R. Roberts & G. J. Greene (Eds.), *Social workers' desk reference* (pp. 717–722). New York: Oxford University Press.

McFarlane, W. R. (2002). *Multifamily groups in the treatment of severe psychiatric disorders.* New York: Guilford Press.

McGoldrick, M. (1998). Belonging and liberation: Finding a place called "home." In M. McGoldrick (Ed.), *Revisioning family therapy: Culture, class, race, and gender* (pp. 215–228). New York: Guilford Press.

McGoldrick, M., & Gerson, R. (1985). *Genograms in family assessment.* New York: Norton.

McGoldrick, M., Giordano, J., & Pearce, J. K. (Eds.) (1996). *Ethnicity and family therapy.* New York: Guilford Press.

McGonagle, E. (1986). *Banana splits: A peer support group for children of transitional families.* Ballston Spa, NY: Author.

McIntosh, J. L. (2003). Suicide survivors: The aftermath of suicide and suicidal behavior. In C. D. Bryant (Ed.), *The handbook of death and dying* (pp. 339–350). Thousand Oaks, CA: Sage Publications.

McLoyd, V. (1997). The impact of poverty and low socioeconomic status on the socioemotional functioning of African-American children and adolescents. In R. W. Taylor & M. C. Wang (Eds.), *Social and emotional adjustment and family relations in ethnic minority families* (pp. 2–34). Mahwah, NJ: Lawrence Erlbaum Associates.

McMillen, J. C., Smith, E. M., & Fisher, R. (1997). Perceived benefit and mental health after three types of disaster. *Journal of Consulting and Clinical Psychology, 63,* 1037–1043.

McMillen, J. E., & Fischer, R. (1998). The perceived benefit scale: Measuring perceived positive life changes after negative events. *Social Work Research, 22* (3), 173–187.

McNeely, R., & Badami, M. (1984). Interracial communication in school social work. *Social Work, 29,* 22–25.

McPhatter, A. (1991). Assessment revisited: A comprehensive approach to understanding family dynamics. *Families in Society, 72,* 11–21.

McQuaide, S. (1999). Using psychodynamic, cognitive behavioral, and solution-focused questioning to construct a new narrative. *Clinical Social Work Journal, 27* (4), 339–353.

McQuaide, S., & Ehrenreich, J. H. (1997). Assessing client strengths. *Families in Society, 78* (2), 201–212.

McRoy, R. G. (2003, June 6). *Impact of systems on adoption in the African American community.* Keynote address presented at the meeting of the Institute on Domestic Violence in the African American Community, Minneapolis, MN.

Medquest Communications. (1997). Treatment drop-outs explained. *Behavioral Health Management, 17,* 3.

Meenaghan, T. M. (1987). Macro practice: Current trends and issues. In *Encyclopedia of social work* (18th ed., pp. 82–89). Silver Spring, MD: National Association of Social Workers.

Meezan, W., & O'Keefe, M. (1998). Evaluating the effectiveness of multifamily group therapy in child abuse and neglect. *Research on Social Work Practice, 8* (3), 330–353.

Meichenbaum, D. (1977). *Cognitive-behavior modification.* New York: Plenum Press.

Meier, A. (1997). Inventing new models of social support groups: A feasibility study of an online stress management support group for social workers. *Social Work with Groups, 20* (4), 35–53.

Meier, A. (2002). An online stress management support group for social workers. *Journal of Technology in Human Services, 20* (1/2), 107–132.

Metcalf, L. (1998). *Solution focused group therapy: Ideas for groups in private practice, schools, agencies, and treatment programs.* New York: Free Press.

Metcalf, L., Thomas, F., Duncan, B., Miller, S., & Hubble, M. (1996). What works in solution-focused brief therapy: A qualitative analysis of client and therapist's perceptions. In S. Miller, M. Hubble, & B. Duncan (Eds.), *Handbook of solution-focused brief therapy.* San Francisco: Jossey-Bass.

Meyer, C. (Ed.). (1983). *Clinical social work in the eco-systems perspective.* New York: Columbia University Press.

Meyer, C. (1990, April 1). *Can social work keep up with the changing family?* [Monograph]. The fifth annual Robert J. O'Leary Memorial Lecture. Columbus, OH: The Ohio State University College of Social Work, 1–24.

Meyer, W. (2001). Why they don't come back: A clinical perspective on the no-show client. *Clinical Social Work, 29* (4), 325–339.

Meyers, J. E., & Newton, W. M. (1986). Cognitive strategies and expectations as components of social competence in young adolescents. *Adolescence, 21* (2), 291–303.

Meyers, M. K. (1993). Organizational factors in the integration of services for children. *Social Service Review, 67* (4), 547–571.

Meystedt, D. M. (1984). Religion and the rural population: Implications for social work. *Social Casework, 65* (4), 219–226.

Milgram, D., & Rubin, J. S. (1992). Resisting resistance: Involuntary substance abuse group therapy. *Social Work with Groups, 15* (1), 95–110.

Miller, D. B. (1997). Parenting against the odds: African-American parents in the child welfare system—a group approach. *Social Work with Groups, 20* (1), 5–18.

Miller, J. A. (1994). A family's sense of power in their community: Theoretical and research issues. *Smith College Studies in Social Work, 64* (3), 221–241.

Miller, R., & Mason, S. E. (2001). Using group therapy to enhance treatment compliance in first episode schizophrenia. *Social Work with Groups, 24* (1), 37–52.

Miller, W. R., & Rollnick, S. (1991). *Motivational interviewing: Preparing people to change addictive behavior.* New York: Guilford Press.

Miller, W. R., & Rollnick, S. (2002). *Motivational interviewing: preparing people to change addictive behavior* (2nd ed.). New York: Guilford Press.

Miller, W. R., & Sovereign, R. G. (1989). The check-up: A model for early intervention in addictive behaviors. In T. Loberg, W. R. Miller, P. E. Nathan, & G. A. Marlatt (Eds.), *Addictive behaviors: Prevention and early intervention* (pp. 219–231). Amsterdam: Swets and Zeitlinger.

Milne, C., & Dowd, E. (1983). Effect of interpretation style and counselor social influence. *Journal of Counseling Psychology, 30,* 603–606.

Minuchin, S. (1974). *Families and family therapy.* Cambridge, MA: Harvard University Press.

Mitchell, C. G. (1998). Perceptions of empathy and client satisfaction with managed behavioral health care. *Social Work, 43* (5), 404–411.

Mokuau, N., & Fong, R. (1994). Assessing the responsiveness of health services to ethnic minorities of color. *Social Work in Health Care, 28* (1), 23–34.

Moore, S. T. (1990). A social work practice model of case management: The case management grid. *Social Work, 35* (5), 444–448.

Morgan, G. (1997). *Images of organizations.* Thousand Oaks, CA: Sage Publications.

Morrison, J. (1995). *The first interview: Revised for DSM-IV.* New York: Guilford Press.

Morrow, D. F. (1993). Social work with gay and lesbian adolescents. *Social Work, 38* (6), 655–660.

Morton, T. (1999). The increasing colorization of America's child welfare system. The overrepresentation of African American children. *Policy and Practice, 12,* 21–30.

Mosley, J. C., & Lex, A. (1990). Identification of potentially stressful life events experienced by a population of urban minority youth. *Journal of Multicultural Counseling and Development, 18* (3), 118–125.

Moyers, T., & Rollnick, S. (2002). A motivational interviewing perspective on resistance in psychotherapy. *Journal of Clinical Psychology, 58* (2), 185–193.

Munson, C. E. (2002). The techniques and process of supervisory practice. In A. R. Roberts & G. J. Greene (Eds.) *Social workers' desk reference* (pp. 38–44). New York: Oxford University Press.

Murdach, A. D. (1996). Beneficence re-examined: Protective intervention in mental health. *Social Work, 41,* 26–32.

Murphy, B. C., & Dillon, C. (2003). *Interviewing in action: Relationship, process, and change* (2nd ed.). Pacific Grove, CA: Brooks/Cole.

Murphy, C. M., & Baxter, V. A. (1997). Motivating batterers to change in the treatment context. *Journal of Interpersonal Violence, 12* (4), 607–619.

Mwanza (1990). *Afrikan naturalism.* Columbus, OH: Pan Afrikan Publications.

Mydans, S. (2004, August, 1). Looking out for the many, saving the one. *The New York Times,* p. WR3.

Myers, L. I., & Thyer, B. A. (1997). Should social work clients have the right to effective treatment? *Social Work, 42* (3), 288–298.

N

Nadler, A. (1996). Help seeking behavior as a coping resource. In M. Rosen (Ed.), *Learning resourcefulness: On coping skills, self control and adaptive behavior* (pp. 127–162). New York: Springer Publishing.

Naleppa, M. J. (1999). Late adulthood. In E. D. Hutchison (Ed.). *Dimensions of human behavior: The changing life course.* Thousand Oaks, CA: Pine Forge Press.

Naleppa, M. J., & Reid, W. J. (2000). Integrating case management and brief-treatment strategies: A hospital-based geriatric program. *Social Work in Health Care,* 31 (4), 1–23.

National Association of Social Workers (NASW). (1996). *Code of ethics.* Washington, DC: NASW Press.

National Association of Social Workers (NASW). (1999). *Code of ethics.* Washington, DC: NASW Press. *http://www.naswdc.org/publs/code/code.asp*

National Association of Social Workers (NASW). (2001). *NASW standard for cultural competence for social work practice.* Washington, DC: NASW Press.

National Association of Social Workers (NASW). (2004). *NASW standards for palliative and end of life care.* Retrieved March 25, 2005, from *http://www.socialworkers.org/practice/ bereavement/ standards/standards0504New.pdf*

National parent advisory survey. (2002, Spring). Minneapolis, MN: Search Institute.

Nelson, T., & Trepper, T. S. (1992). *101 interventions in family therapy.* Binghamton, NY: Haworth Press.

Nelson-Zlupko, L., Kauffman, E., & Dore, M. M. (1995). Gender differences in drug addiction and treatment: Implications for social work intervention with substance abusing women. *Social Work,* 40 (1), 45–54.

Netting, F., Kettner, P., & McMurtry, S. (1993). *Social work macro practice.* New York: Longman.

Netting, F. E., Kettner, P. M., & McMurtry, S. L. (2004). *Social work macro practice.* (3rd ed.) Boston: Allyn & Bacon.

Nevil, N., Beatty, M. L., & Moxley, D. P. (1997). *Socialization games for persons with disabilities: Structured group activities for social and interpersonal development.* Springfield, IL: C. C. Thomas.

Nichols, M. P., & Schwartz, R. C. (1998). *Family therapy: Concepts and methods* (4th ed.). Boston: Allyn & Bacon.

Nichols, M. P., & Schwartz, R. C. (2004). *Family therapy: Concepts and methods.* (6th ed.) Boston: Allyn & Bacon.

Nord, M., & Luloff, A. E. (1995). Homeless children and their families in New Hampshire: A rural perspective. *Social Service Review,* 69 (3), 461–478.

Northen, H., & Kurland, R. (2001). The use of activity. In *Social work with groups* (3rd ed., pp. 258–287). New York: Columbia University Press.

Northey, W. F. (2002) Characteristics of clinical practice of marriage and family therapist: A national survey. *Journal of Marital and Family Therapy,* 28 (4), 487–494.

Norton, D. G. (1978). *The dual perspective: Inclusion of ethnic minority content in the social work curriculum.* New York: Council on Social Work Education.

Nosko, A., & Wallace, R. (1997). Female/male co-leadership in groups. *Social Work with Groups,* 20 (2), 3–16.

Nugent, W. (1991). An experimental and qualitative analysis of a cognitive-behavioral intervention for anger. *Social Work Research and Abstracts,* 27 (3), 3–8.

Nugent, W. (1992). The effective impact of a clinical social worker's interviewing style: A series of single-case experiments. *Research on Social Work Practice,* 2 (1), 6–27.

Nugent, W. R., & Halvorson, H. (1995). Testing the effects of active listening. *Research on Social Work Practice,* 5 (2), 152–175.

Nurius, P. S., & Hudson. W. W. (1988). Computer-based practice: Future dream or current technology. *Social Work,* 33, 357–362.

Nurius, P. S., & Hudson, W. (1993a). *Computer assisted practice: Theory, methods, and software.* Belmont, CA: Wadsworth.

Nurius, P. S., & Hudson, W. (1993b). *Human services practice, evaluation, and computers: A practical guide for today and beyond.* Pacific Grove, CA: Brooks/Cole.

O

Ogbu, J. U. (1994). From cultural differences to cultural frame of reference. In P. M. Greenfield & R. R. Cocking (Eds.), *Cross-cultural roots of minority child development* (pp. 365–391). Hilldale, NJ: Lawrence Erlbaum Assoiciates.

O'Hanlon, W. (1996). Case commentary. *Family Therapy Networker,* January/February, 84–85.

Okun, B. (2002). *Effective helping: Interviewing and counseling techniques.* Pacific Grove, CA: Brooks/Cole.

O'Melia, M., & Miley, K. K. (Eds.) (2002). *Pathways to power. Readings in contextual social work practice.* Boston: Allyn & Bacon.

Oritt, E., Paul, S., & Behrman, J. (1985). The perceived Support Network Inventory. *American Journal of Community Psychology,* 13 (5), 565–582.

Ostroff, C., & Atwater, L. E. (2003). Does whom you work with matter? Effects of referent group gender and age composition on managers' compensation. *Journal of Applied Psychology,* 88 (4), 725–740.

Othmer, E., & Othmer, S. C. (1989). *The clinical interview using DSM-III-R.* Washington, DC: American Psychiatric Press.

P

Pack-Brown, J. P., Whittington-Clark, L. E., & Parker, W. M. (1998). *Images of me: A guide to group work with African-American women.* Boston: Allyn & Bacon.

Palmer, B., & Pablo, S. (1978). Community development possibilities for effective Indian reservation child abuse and neglect efforts. In M. Lauderdale, R. Anderson, & S. Cramer (Eds.), *Child abuse and neglect. Issues on innovation and implementation* (pp. 98–116). Washington, DC: U.S. Department of Health, Education and Welfare.

Parad, H. J. (1965). *Crisis intervention: Selected readings.* New York: Family Service Association of America.

Parad, H. J., & Parad, L. G. (Eds.). (1990). *Crisis intervention: Book 2.* Milwaukee, WI: Family Service America.

Pardeck, J. T., Murphy, J. W., & Chung, W. S. (1995). An exploration of factors associated with clients prematurely exiting psychiatric treatment: Implication for the community mental health center act. *Journal of Health Social Policy,* 7 (1), 87–96.

Parlec, M. (1979). Conversational politics. *Psychology Today, 12,* 48–56.

Parloff, M., Waskow, I., & Wolfe, B. (1978). Research on therapist variables in relation to process and outcome. In S. Garfield & A. Bergin (Eds.), *Handbook of psychotherapy and behavior change* (pp. 233–282). New York: Wiley.

Parson, E. R. (1993). Ethnotherapeutic empathy—Part II: Techniques for interpersonal cognition and vicarious experiencing across cultures. *Journal of Contemporary Psychotherapy, 23,* 171–182.

Parsons, R. J., Jorgensen, J. D., & Hernandez, S. H. (1994). *The integration of social work practice.* Pacific Grove, CA: Brooks/Cole.

Parsons, R. J. (2002). Guidelines for empowerment-based social work practice. In A. R. Roberts & G. J. Greene (Eds.), *Social workers' desk reference* (pp. 396–401). New York: Oxford University Press.

Patten, S. B., Gatz, Y. K., Jones, B., & Thomas, D. L. (1989). Posttraumatic stress disorder and the treatment of sexual abuse. *Social Work, 34* (3), 197–202.

Patterson, D. A., & Lee, M. (1998). Intensive case managemtnt and rehospitalization: A survival analysis. *Research on Social Work Practice, 8* (2), 152–171.

Paz, J. (2002). Culturally competent substance abuse treatment with Latinos. *Journal of Human Behavior in the Social Environment, 5* (3/4), 123–136.

Pelton, L. H. (2003). Social justice and social work. *Journal of Social Work Education,* 433–439.

Pence, E., & Paymar, M. (1993). *Education groups for men who batter: The Duluth model.* New York: Springer.

Perlman, H. (1957) *Social casework: A problem-solving process.* Chicago: University of Chicago Press.

Peters, A. J. (1997). Themes in group work with lesbian and gay adolescents. *Social Work with Groups,* 20 (2), 51–69.

Pfeffer, R. C. (1986). *The suicidal child.* New York: Guilford Press.

Philip, C. E. (1994). Letting go: Problems with termination when a therapist is seriously ill or dying. *Smith College Studies in Social Work, 64* (2), 169–179.

Philip, C. E., & Stevens, E. V. (1992). Countertransference issues for the consultant when a colleague is critically ill (or dying). *Clinical Social Work Journal, 20* (4), 411–419.

Pierce, W. J., & Elisme, E. (1997). Understanding and working with Haitian immigrant families. *Journal of Family Social Work, 2* (1), 49–65.

Piliavin, I., Wright, B. R. W., Mare, R. D., & Westerfelt, A. H. (1996). Exits from and returns to homelessness. *Social Service Review, 70* (1), 33–57.

Pilsecker, C. (1987). A patient dies—A social worker reviews his work. *Social Work in Health Care, 13* (2), 35–45.

Pincus, A., & Minahan, A. (1973). *Social work practice: Model and method.* Itasca, IL: F. E. Peacock.

Poindexter, C. C. (1997). In the aftermath: Serial crisis intervention for people with HIV. *Health and Social Work,* 22 (2), 125–132.

Pollio, D. E. (1995). Use of humor in crisis intervention. *Families in Society, 76* (6), 376–384.

Polowy, C. I., & Gilbertson, J. (1997). *Social workers and subpoenas: Office of General Counsel Law Notes.* Washington, DC: NASW Press.

Ponce, D. (1980). The Filipinos: The Philippine background. In J. McDermott, Jr., W. Tseng, & T. Maretski (Eds.), *People and cultures of Hawaii* (pp. 155–163). Honolulu: University of Hawaii Press.

Pope, K. S., Keith-Spiegel, P., & Tabachnick, B. G. (1986). Sexual attraction to clients. *American Psychologist, 41,* 147–158.

Potocky-Tripodi, M. (2002). *Best practices for social work with refugees and immigrants.* New York: Columbia University Press.

Potter-Efron, R., & Potter-Efron, P. (1992). *Anger, alcoholism and addiction: Treating anger in a chemical dependency setting.* New York: Norton.

Poulin, J. (2000). *Collaborative social work. Strengths-based generalist practice.* Itasca, IL: F. E. Peacock.

Presley, J. H. (1987). The clinical dropout: A view from the client's perspective. *Social Casework, 68,* 603–608.

Prochaska, J. O., & DiClemente, C. C. (1986). Towards a comprehensive model of change. In W. R. Miller & N. Heather (Eds.), *Treating addictive behaviors: Processes of change* (pp. 3–28). New York: Pergamon Press.

Prochaska, J., DiClemente, C. C., & Norcross, J. C. (1992). Transtheoretical therapy: Toward a more integrative model of change. *Psychotherapy: Theory, Research, and Practice, 19,* 276–288.

Protecting the privacy of patients' health information. (2003). Retrieved May 1, 2004, from *http://www.hhs.gov/news/facts/privacy.html*

Proctor, E. (1990). Evaluating clinical practice: Issues of purpose and design. *Social Work Research and Abstracts, 26* (1), 32–40.

Proctor, E. K., & and Davis, L. E. (1994). The challenge of racial difference: Skills for clinical practice. *Social Work, 39* (3), 314–323.

Puryear, D. (1979). *Helping people in crisis.* San Francisco: Jossey-Bass.

Q

Queralt, M. (1984). Understanding Cuban immigrants: A cultural perspective. *Social Work, 29,* 115–121.

R

Raines, J. C. (1996). Self-disclosure in clinical social work. *Clinical Social Work Journal, 24* (4), 357–375.

Range, L. M., & Knott, E. C. (1997). Twenty suicide assessment instruments: Evaluation and recommendations. *Death Studies, 21,* 25–58.

Rapoport, L. (1967). Crisis-oriented short-term casework. *Social Service Review, 41* (1), 31–43.

Rapp, C. A. (1998). *The strengths model: Case management with people suffering from severe and persistent mental illness.* New York: Oxford University Press.

Ratliff, S. S. (1996). The multicultural challenge to health care. In M. C. Julia, *Multicultural awareness in the health care professions.* Needham Heights, MA: Allyn & Bacon.

Rauch, J. B. (1993). *Assessment: A sourcebook for social work practice.* Milwaukee, WI: Families International.

Raymond, G. T., Teare, R. J., & Atherton, C. R. (1996). Is "field of practice" a relevant organizing principle for the MSW curriculum? *Journal of Social Work Education, 32* (1), 19–30.

Reamer, F. G. (1994). *Social work malpractice and liability: Strategies for prevention.* New York: Columbia University Press.

Reamer, F. G. (1998a). *Ethical standards in social work: A critical review of the NASW code of ethics.* Washington, DC: NASW Press.

Reamer, F. G. (1998b). The evolution of social work ethics. *Social Work, 43* (6), 488–500.

Reamer, F. (1989). *Ethical dilemmas in social service* (2nd ed.). New York: Columbia University Press.

Reamer, F. G. (1995). Malpractice claims against social workers: First facts. *Social Work, 40* (5), 595–601.

Reamer, F. G. (1999). *Social work values and ethics* (2nd ed.). New York: Columbia University Press.

Reamer, F. G. (2001). *Tangled relationships: Managing boundary issues in the human services.* New York: Columbia University Press.

Red Horse, J., Lewis, R., Feit, M., & Decker, J. (1978). Family behavior of urban American Indians. *Social Casework, 59,* 67–72.

Regehr, C., & Angle, B. (1997). Coercive influences: Informed consent in court-mandated social work practice. *Social Work, 42* (3), 300–306.

Reid, K. E. (1991). *Social work practice with groups: A clinical perspective.* Pacific Grove, CA: Brooks/Cole.

Reid, K. E. (2002). Clinical social work with groups. In A. R. Roberts & G. J. Greene (Eds.), *Social workers' desk reference* (pp. 432–436). New York: Oxford University Press.

Reid, W. (1970). Implications of research for goals of casework. *Smith College Studies in Social Work, 40,* 140–154.

Reid, W. J. (1972). *Task-centered casework.* New York: Columbia University Press.

Reid, W. J. (1975). A test of the task-centered approach. *Social Work, 22,* 3–9.

Reid, W. J. (1977). Process and outcome in the treatment of family problems. In W. Reid & L. Epstein (Eds.), *Task centered practice. Self-help groups and human service agencies: How they work together.* Milwaukee: Family Service of America.

Reid, W. J. (1978). *The task-centered system.* New York: Columbia University Press.

Reid, W. J. (1985). *Family problem solving.* New York: Columbia University Press.

Reid, W. J. (1987). Task-centered research. In *Encyclopedia of social work* (vol. 2, pp. 757–764). Silver Spring, MD: NASW Press.

Reid, W. J. (1992). *Task strategies.* New York: Columbia University Press.

Reid, W. J. (1994). The empirical practice movement. *Social Service Review, 68* (2), 165–184.

Reid, W. J. (1997a). Research on task-centered practice. *Social Work, 21* (3), 131–137.

Reid, W. J. (1997b). Long term trends in clinical social work. *Social Service Review, 71* (2), 200–213.

Reid, W. J. (2000). *The task planner.* New York: Columbia University Press.

Reid, W. J., & Fortune, A. E. (2002). The task-centered model. In A. R. Roberts & G. J. Greene (Eds.), *Social workers' desk reference* (pp. 101–104). New York: Oxford University Press.

Reid, W., & Hanrahan, P. (1982). Recent evaluations of social work: Grounds for optimism. *Social Work, 27,* 328–340.

Reid, W., & Shyne, A. (1969). *Brief and extended casework.* New York: Columbia University Press.

Reisch, M. (2002). *Defining social justice in a socially unjust world. Families in Society, 83,* 4.

Reitan, T. C. (1998). Theories of interorganizational relations in the human services. *Social Service Review, 72* (3), 285–309.

Resnick, C., & Dziegielewski, S. F. (1996). The relationship between therapeutic termination and job satisfaction among medical social workers. *Social Work in Health Care, 23* (3), 17–33.

Reynolds, B. C. (1951). Must it hurt to be helped? In B. C. Reynolds, *Social work and social living: Explorations philosophy and practice.* New York: Citadel Press.

Reynolds, T., & Jones, G. (1996). Trauma debriefings: A one-session group model. In B. L. Stempler, M. Glass, & C. M. Savinelli (Eds.), *Social group work today and tomorrow: Moving to advanced training and practice* (pp. 129–139). Binghamton, NY: Haworth Press.

Ribner, D. S., & Knei-Paz, C. (2002). Client's view of a successful helping relationship. *Social Work, 47* (4), 379–387.

Rice, A. H. (1998). *Focusing on strengths: Focus group research on the impact of welfare reform.* A paper presented for the XX Symposium Association for the Advancement of Social Work with Groups, October 1998, Miami, FL.

Richmond, M. (1917). *Social diagnosis.* New York: Russell Sage Foundation.

Rivera, F. G., & Erlich, J. L. (1998). *Community organizing in a diverse society* (3rd ed.). Boston: Allyn & Bacon.

Roberts, A. R. (1990). *Crisis intervention handbook: Assessment, treatment, and research.* Belmont, CA: Wadsworth.

Roberts, A. R. (2000). *An overview of crisis theory and crisis intervention.* In A. R. Roberts (Ed.), *Crisis interviewing handbook: Assessment, treatment, and research.* Belmont, CA: Wadsworth.

Roberts, A. R., & Greene, G. J. (Eds.) (2002). *Social workers' desk reference* (pp. 112–115). New York: Oxford University Press.

Roberts, D. (2002). *Shattered bonds. The color of child welfare.* New York: Basic Books.

Roberts-DeGennaro, M. (1987). *Developing case.* New York: Columbia University Press.

Robinson, J. B. (1989). Clinical treatment of black families: Issues and strategies. *Social Work, 34,* 323–329.

Robinson, V. (1930). *A changing psychology in social work.* Chapel Hill: University of North Carolina Press.

Rodenborg, N. (2004, November). Services to African American children in poverty: Institutional discrimination in child welfare. *Journal of Poverty: Innovations on Social, Political and Economic Inequalities, 3* (3).

Rodgers, A. Y., & Potocky, M. (1997). Evaluating culturally sensitive practice through single-system design: Methodological issues and strategies. *Research on Social Work Practice, 7* (3), 391–401.

Rogers, C. (1957). The necessary and sufficient conditions of therapeutic personality change. *Journal of Consulting Psychology, 22,* 95–103.

Ronnau, J. P., & Marlow, C. R. (1995). Family preservation: Poverty and the value of diversity. *Families in Society, 74* (9), 538–544.

Rooney, G. D. (1997). Concerns of employed women: Issues for employee assistance programs. In A. Daly (Ed.), *Work force diversity: Issues and perspectives in the world of work* (pp. 314–330). Washington, DC: NASW Press.

Rooney, G. D. (2000). Examining the values and ethics reflected in policy decisions. In K. Strom-Gottfried (Ed.), *Social work practice: Cases, activities and exercises* (pp. 50–54). Thousand Oaks, CA: Pine Forge Press.

Rooney, G. D., Neathery, K., & Suzek, M. (1997). *Defining child neglect: A community perspective.* Minneapolis, MN: Minneapolis Human Services Network Research Report.

Rooney, R. H. (1992). *Strategies for work with involuntary clients.* New York: Columbia University Press.

Rooney, R. H., & Bibus, A. A. (1996). Multiple lenses: Ethnically sensitive practice with involuntary clients who are having difficulties with drugs or alcohol. *Journal of Multicultural Social Work, 4* (2), 59–73.

Rooney, R. H., & Chovanec, M. (2004). Involuntary groups. In C. Garvin, L. Gutirrez, & M. Galinsky (Eds.), *Handbook of social work with groups.* New York: Guilford Press.

Rose, S. D. (1989). *Working with adults in groups: Integrating cognitive-behavioral and small group strategies.* San Francisco: Jossey-Bass.

Rose, S. D. (1998). *Group therapy with troubled youth: A cognitive behavioral interactive approach.* Thousand Oaks, CA: Sage Publications.

Rose, S. M. (1992). *Case management and social work practice.* Menlo Park, CA: Longman Press.

Rose, S. (2000). *Reflections on empowerment-based practice. Social Work, 45,* 5.

Rosen, A. (1972). The treatment relationship: A conceptualization. *Journal of Clinical Psychology, 38,* 329–337.

Rosen, A. & Proctor, E. (2001). Standards for evidence-based social work practice. The role of replicable and appropriate interventions, outcomes and practice guidelines. In A. R. Roberts &

G. J. Greene (Eds.), *Social workers' desk reference* (pp. 743–747). New York: Oxford University Press.

Rosenblatt, E. (1994). *Metaphor of family systems theory.* New York: Guilford Press.

Rosenfeld, J. (1983). The domain and expertise of social work: A conceptualization. *Social Work, 28,* 186–191.

Rosenstein, P. (1978). Family outreach: A program for the prevention of child neglect and abuse. *Child Welfare, 57,* 519–525.

Rosenthal, K. (1988). The inanimate self in adult victims of child abuse and neglect. *Social Casework, 69* (8), 505–510.

Ross, C. (1997). *Something to draw on: Activities and interventions using an art therapy approach.* London: Jessica Kingsley.

Roth, W. (1987). Disabilities: Physical. In *Encyclopedia of social work* (vol. 1, pp. 434–438). Silver Spring, MD: NASW Press.

Rothman, J. (1991). A model of case management: Toward empirically based practice. *Social Work, 36* (6), 521–528.

Rothman, J. (1994). *Practice with highly vulnerable clients: Case management and community-based service.* Englewood Cliffs, NJ: Prentice-Hall.

Rothman, J. (1999). Intent and consent. In J. Rothman (Ed.), *Reflections on community organizations: Enduring themes and critical issues* (pp. 3–26). Itasca, IL: F. E. Peacock.

Rothman, J., Erlich, J. L., & Tropman, J. (1995). *Strategies of community intervention* (5th ed.). Itasca, IL: F. E. Peacock.

Rothman, J., Erlich, J. L., & Tropman, J. E. (2001). *Strategies of community interventions* (6th ed.). Itasca, IL: F. E. Peacock.

Rothman, J., Gant, L. M., & Hnat, S. A. (1985). Mexican American family culture. *Social Service Review, 59,* 197–215.

Rotunno, M., & McGoldrick, M. (1982). Italian families. In M. McGoldrick, J. Pearce, & J. Giordano (Eds.), *Ethnicity and family therapy* (pp. 340–363). New York: Guilford Press.

Rounds, K. A., Galinsky, M. J., & Stevens, L. S. (1991). Linking people with AIDS in rural communities: The telephone group. *Social Work, 36* (1), 13–18.

Rowe, R., Maughan, B., Worthman, C. M., Costello, E. J., & Angold, A. (2004). Testosterone, antisocial behavior, and social dominance in boys: Pubertal development and biosocial interaction. *Biological Psychiatry, 55* (5), 546–552.

Royse, D., Thyer, B. A., Padgett, D. K., & Logan, T. K. (2001). *Program evaluation: An introduction* (3rd ed.). Belmont, CA: Brooks/Cole.

Ryder, R., & Tepley, R. (1993). No more Mr. Nice Guy: Informed consent and benevolence in marital family therapy. *Family Relations, 42,* 145–147.

Rzepnicki, T. L. (1991). Enhancing the durability of intervention gains: A challenge for the 1990s. *Social Service Review, 65* (1), 92–111.

S

Saleebey, D. (Ed.) (1992). *The strengths perspective in social work practice.* New York: Longman.

Saleebey, D. (Ed.) (1997). *The strengths perspective in social work practice* (2nd ed.). Needham Heights, MA: Allyn & Bacon.

Salzar, M. S. (1997). Consumer empowerment in mental health organizations: Concepts, benefits and impediments. *Administration and Policy in Mental Health, 24,* 425–434.

Sandfort, J. (1999). The structural impediments to human services collaboration: Examining welfare reform at the front lines. *Social Service Review, 73* (3), 314–339.

Sands, R. G. (1989). The social worker joins the team: A look at the socialization process. *Social Work in Health Care, 14* (2), 1–14.

Sands, R. G., Stafford, J., & McClelland, M. (1990). "I beg to differ": Conflict in the interdisciplinary team. *Social Work in Health Care, 14* (3), 55–72.

Sanita, J., & Franklin, C. (1998). Assessing post-traumatic stress disorder in children: Diagnostic and measurement strategies. *Research on Social Work Practice, 8* (3), 251–270.

Santos, D. (1995). Deafness. In *Encyclopedia of social work* (vol. 19, pp. 685–703). Washington, DC: NASW Press.

Sarri, R. (1987). Administration in social welfare. In *Encyclopedia of social work* (vol. 1, pp. 27–40). Silver Spring, MD: NASW Press.

Satir, V. (1967). *Conjoint family therapy.* Palo Alto, CA: Science & Behavior Books.

Saulnier, C. F. (1997). Alcohol problems and marginalization: Social group work with lesbians. *Social Work with Groups, 20* (3), 37–59.

Saulnier, C. F. (2002). Deciding who to see: Lesbians discuss their preferences in health and mental health care providers. *Social Work, 47* (4), 355–365.

Schaffer, D. (1992). *NIHM diagnostic interview schedule for children, version 2.3.* New York: Columbia University, Division of Child and Adolescent Psychiatry.

Schein, E. H. (1985). *Organizational culture and leadership.* San Francisco: Jossey-Bass.

Schiller, L. Y. (1997). Rethinking stages of development in women's groups: Implications for practice. *Social Work with Groups, 20* (3), 3–19.

Schneider, R. L., & Netting, F. E. (1999). Influencing social policy in a time of devolution: Upholding social work's great tradition. *Social Work, 44* (4), 349–357.

Schopler, J., & Galinsky, M. (1974). Goals in social group work practice: Formulation, implementation and evaluation. In P. Glasser, R. Sarri, & R. Vinter (Eds.), *Individual change through small groups.* New York: Free Press.

Schopler, J. H., & Galinsky, M. J. (1981). Meeting practice needs: Conceptualizing the open-ended group. *Social Work with Groups, 7* (2), 3–21.

Schopler, J. H., Galinsky, M. J., & Abell, M. (1997). Creating community through telephone and computer groups: Theoretical and practice perspectives. *Social Work with Groups, 20* (4), 19–34.

Schopler, J. H., Galinsky, M. J., Davis, L. E., & Despard, M. (1996). The RAP model: Assessing a framework for leading multicultural groups. *Social Work with Groups, 19* (3/4), 21–39.

Schrier, C. (1980). Guidelines for record-keeping under privacy and open-access laws. *Social Work, 25,* 452–457.

Schrodt, G. R., & Fitzgerald, B. A. (1987). Cognitive therapy with adolescents. *American Journal of Psychotherapy, 41,* 402–408.

Schwartz, G. (1989). Confidentiality revisited. *Social Work, 34* (3), 223–226.

Segal, U. A. (1991). Cultural variables in Asian Indian families. *Families in Society, 72,* 233–244.

Selvini-Palazzoli, M., Boscolo, L., Cecchin, G., & Prata, G. (1974). The treatment of children through brief therapy of their parents. *Family Process, 13,* 429–442.

Senge, P. (1990). *The fifth discipline: The art and practice of learning organization.* New York: Doubleday Currency.

Serres, C. (2004, June 6). House of hurdles. *Minneapolis Star Tribune,* pp. A1, A21.

Shamai, M. (2003). Therapeutic effects of qualitative research: Reconstructing the experience of treatment as a by-product of qualitative evaluation. *Social Service Review, 77* (3), 454–467.

Shannon, T. R., Kleniewski, N., & Cross, W. M. (2002). Urban problems in sociological perspective. In *Nature of urban life* (4th ed., pp. 63–89). Long Grove, IL: Waveland Press.

Sharpe, L., & Tarrier, M. (1992). A cognitive-behavioral treatment approach for problem gambling. *Journal of Cognitive Psychotherapy, 5,* 119–127.

Sheafor, B., Horejsi, C. R., & Horejsi, G. A. (1994). *Techniques and guidelines for social work practice* (3rd ed.). Boston: Allyn & Bacon.

Sherwood, D. A. (1998). Spiritual assessment as a normal part of social work practice: Power to help and power to harm. *Social Work and Christianity, 25* (2), 80–90.

Shneidman, E. S. (1971). The management of the presuicidal, suicidal and postsuicidal patient. *Annals of Internal Medicine, 75,* 441–458.

Shoham, V., Rorhbaugh, M., & Patterson, J. (1995). Problem and solution-focused couples therapies: The MRI and Milwaukee modes. In N. S. Jacobson & A. S. Gurman (Eds.), *Clinical handbook for couple therapy.* New York: Guildford Press.

Shulman, L. (1984). *The skills of helping individuals and groups* (2nd ed.). Itasca, IL: F. E. Peacock.

Shulman, L. (1992). *The skills of helping individuals and groups* (3rd ed.). Itasca, IL: F. E. Peacock.

Simonson, N. (1976). The impact of therapist disclosure on patient disclosure. *Journal of Transpersonal Psychology, 23,* 3–6.

Siporin, M. (1975). *Introduction to social work practice.* New York: Macmillan.

Siporin, M. (1979). Practice theory for clinical social work. *Clinical Social Work Journal, 7,* 75–89.

Siporin, M. (1980). Ecological systems theory in social work. *Journal of Sociology and Social Welfare, 7,* 507–532.

Slater, S. (1995). *The lesbian lifecycle.* New York: Free Press.

Slonim-Nevo, V., & Vosler, N. R. (1991). The use of single-system design with systemic grief problem-solving therapy. *Families in Society: The Journal of Contemporary Human Services, 72,* 38–44.

Smith, B. D., & Marsh, J. C. (2002). Client–service matching in substance abuse treatment for women with children. *Journal of Substance Abuse Treatment, 22,* 161–168.

Smith, C., & Carlson, B. E. (1997). Stress, coping and resilience in children and youth. *Social Service Review, 71* (2), 231–256.

Smith, T. B. (2004). *Practicing multiculturalism: Affirming diversity in counseling and psychology.* Boston: Pearson.

Smokowski, P. R., Rose, S. D., & Bacallao, M. L. (2001). Damaging therapeutic groups: How vulnerable consumers become group casualties. *Small Group Research, 32* (2), 223–251.

Smyth, N. J. (1996). Motivating others with dual disorders: A stage approach. *Families in Society, 77* (10), 605–614.

Social workers and psychotherapist–patient privilege: *Jaffee v. Redmond* revisited. (n.d.) Retrieved March 2, 2005, from *http://www.socialworkers.org/ldf/legal_issue/200503*

Solis, D., & Corchado, A. (2002, January 25). "Recession may hurt Hispanics the most." *The Dallas Morning News,* pp. 2D, 11D.

Solomon, P., & Draine, J. (1996). Service delivery differences between consumer and nonconsumer case managers in mental health. *Research on Social Work Practice, 6* (2), 193–207.

Sosin, M., & Callum, S. (1983). Advocacy: A conceptualization for social work practice. *Social Work, 28,* 12–17.

Sotomayor, M. (1991). Introduction. In M. Sotomayor (Ed.), *Empowering Hispanic families: A critical issue for the 90s* (pp. xi–xxiii). Milwaukee, WI: Family Service America.

Sowers-Hoag, K., & Thyer, B. (1985). Teaching social work practice: A review and analysis of empirical research. *Journal of Social Work Education, 21* (3), 5–15.

Specht, H., & Courtney, M. E. (1994). *Unfaithful angels: How social work abandoned its mission.* Toronto: Maxwell Macmillan Canada.

Specht, H., & Specht, R. (1986a). Social work assessment: Route to clienthood (Part 1). *Social Casework, 67,* 525–532.

Specht, H., & Specht, R. (1986b). Social work assessment: Route to clienthood (Part 11). *Social Casework, 67,* 587–593.

Speisman, J. (1959). Depth of interpretation and verbal resistance in psychotherapy. *Journal of Consulting Psychology, 23,* 93–99.

Spitzer, R., Williams, J., Kroenke, K., Linzer, M., DeGruy, F. III, Hahn, S., Brody, D., & Johnson, J. (1994). Utility of a new procedure for diagnosing mental disorders in primary care: The PRIME-MD 1000 study. *Journal of the American Medical Association, 272,* 1749–1756.

Springer, D. W., Courtney, L., & Rubin. Effects of a soution-focused mutual aid group for Hispanic children of incarcerated parents. *Children and Adolescent Social Work Journal, 17* (5), 431–442.

Springer, D., & Franklin, C. (2003). Standardized assessment measures and computer-assisted assessment technologies. In C. Jordan & C. Franklin (Eds.), *Clinical assessment for social workers. Quantitative and qualitative methods* (2nd ed., pp. 97–137). Chicago: Lyceum Books.

Srebnik, D. S., & Saltzberg, E. A. (1994). Feminist cognitive-behavioral therapy for negative body image. *Women and Therapy, 15* (2), 117–133.

Stalker, C. A., Levene, J. F., & Coady, N. F. (1999). Solution-focused brief treatment: One model fits all? *Families in Society: The Journal of Contemporary Human Services, 80* (5), 468–477.

Staples, L. H. (1990). Powerful ideas about empowerment. *Administration in Social Work, 14* (2), 29–42.

Steigerwald, F., & Stone, D. (1999). Cognitive restructuring and the 12-step program of Alcoholics Anonymous. *Journal of Substance Abuse, 16,* 321–327.

Steinmetz, G. (1992). Fetal alcohol syndrome. *National Geographic, 181* (2), 36–39.

Stoesen, L. (2004). End to Iraq prisoner abuse demanded. *NASW News, 49* (7), 1.

Stokes, J. P. (1983). Components of group cohesion: Intermember attraction, instrumental value, and risk taking. *Small Group Behavior, 14,* 163–173.

Stone, M., Lewis, C., & Beck, A. (1994). The structure of Yalom's Curative Factors Scale. *International Journal of Group Psychotherapy, 23* (2), 155–168.

Storm, C. (1991). The remaining thread: Matching change and stability signals. *Journal of Strategic and Systemic Therapies, 10,* 114–117.

Strean, H. (1997). Comment on James C. Raines' "Self disclosure in clinical social work" *Clinical Social Work Journal, 25* (3), 365–366.

Strom-Gottfried, K. (1998a). Applying a conflict resolution framework in managed care. *Social Work, 43* (5), 393–401.

Strom-Gottfried, K. J. (1998b). Informed consent meets managed care. *Health and Social Work, 23* (1), 25–33.

Strom-Gottfried, K. J. (1999a). Professional boundaries: An analysis of violations by social workers. *Families in Society, 80,* 439–448.

Strom-Gottfried, K. J. (1999b). *Social work practice: Cases, activities and exercises.* Thousand Oaks, CA: Pine Forge Press.

Strom-Gottfried, K., & Morrissey, M. (2000). The organizational diversity audit. In K. Strom-Gottfried (Ed.), *Social work practice: Cases, activities, and exercises* (pp. 168–172). Thousand Oaks, CA: Pine Forge Press.

Stuart, P. H. (1999). Linking clients and policy: Social work's distinctive contribution. *Social Work, 44* (4), 335–347.

Stuart, R. (1980). *Helping couples change.* New York: Guilford Press.

Suarez, Z. E., & Siefert, H. (1998). Latinas and sexually transmitted diseases: Implications of recent research for prevention. *Social Work in Health Care, 28* (1), 1–19.

Subramanian, K., Hernandez, S., & Martinez, A. (1995). Psychoeducational group work for low-income Latina mothers with HIV infection. *Social Work in Groups, 18* (2/3), 53–64.

Sue, D. (1981). *Counseling the culturally different: Theory and practice.* New York: Wiley.

Sue, D. W., & Sue, S. (1990). *Counseling the culturally different: Theory and practice* (2nd ed.). New York: Wiley.

Sunley, R. (1997). Advocacy in the new world of managed care. *Families in Society, 78* (1), 84–94.

Sweet, C., & Noones, J. (1989). Factors associated with premature termination from outpatient treatment. *Hospital and Community Psychiatry, 40* (9), 947–951.

Swenson, C. (1995). Clinical social work. *Encyclopedia of social work* (19th ed.). Washington, DC: NASW Press, 502–513.

Swenson, C. (1998). Clinical social work's contribution to a social justice perspective. *Social Work, 43* (6), 527–537.

T

Tafoya, T. (1989). Circles and cedar: Native Americans and family therapy. In G. A. Saba, B. M. Kerrer, & K. Hardy (Eds.), *Minorities and family therapy* (pp. 71–94). New York: Hawthorne Press.

Taft, J. (1937). The relation of function to process in social casework. *Journal of Social Work Process, I* (1), 1–18.

Teall, B. (2000). Using solution-oriented intervention in an ecological frame: A case illustration. *Social Work in Education, 22* (1), 54–61.

Testa, M. (2002). Subsidized guardianship: Testing an idea whose time has finally come. *Social Work Research, 26* (3), 145–158.

Thibault, J., Ellor, J., & Netting, F. (1991). A conceptual framework for assessing the spiritual functioning and fulfillment of older adults in long-term care settings. *Journal of Religious Gerontology, 7* (4), 29–46.

Thomas, E. (1977). *Marital communication and decision making: Analysis, assessment, and change.* New York: Free Press.

Thomas, E. (1978). Research and service in single-case experimentation: Conflicts and choices. *Social Work Research and Abstracts, 14,* 20–31.

Thomas, E. (1989). Advances in developmental research. *Social Service Review, 63,* 578–597.

Thomas, H., & Caplan, T. (1997). Client, therapist and context: Addressing resistance in group work. *The Social Worker, 65* (3), 27–36.

Thomas, H., & Caplan, T. (1999). Spinning the group process wheel: Effective facilitation techniques for motivating involuntary clients. *Social Work with Groups, 21* (4), 3–21.

Thyer, B. A. (2002). Principles of evidence-based practice and treatment development. In A. R. Roberts & G. J. Greene (Eds.), *Social workers' desk reference* (pp. 739–742). New York: Oxford University Press.

Thyer, B. A., & Wodarski, J. S. (1998). *Handbook of empirical social work practice, volume 1.* New York: Wiley.

Thyer, B., & Wodarski, J. (2004). *Handbook of empirical social work practice.* New York: Wiley.

Tieso, T., & Rooney, G. D. (In press). Involuntary status and oppression. In R. H. Rooney (Ed.), *Social work practice with involuntary clients.* New York: Columbia University Press.

Tohn, S. L., & Oshlag, J. A. (1996). Solution-focused therapy with mandated clients: Cooperating with the uncooperative. In S. D. Miller, M. A. Hubble, & B. L. Duncan (Eds.), *Handbook of solution-focused brief therapy* (pp. 152–183). San Francisco: Jossey-Bass.

Tolan, P. H., & Gorman-Smith, D. (1997). Families and the development of urban children. In H. J. Walberg, O. Reyes, & R. P. Weissberg (Eds.), *Children and youth: Interdisciplinary perspectives* (pp. 67–91). Thousand Oaks, CA: Sage Publications.

Tolman, R. M., & Molidor, C. E. (1994). A decade of social group work research: Trends in methodology, theory and program development. *Research on Social Work Practice, 4* (2), 142–159.

Tolson, E. R., Reid, W. J., & Garvin, C. D. (1994). *Generalist practice. A task-centered approach.* New York: Columbia University Press.

Toseland, R. (1987). Treatment discontinuance: Grounds for optimism. *Social Casework, 68,* 195–204.

Toseland, R. W., & Rivas, R. S. (2001). *An introduction to group work practice* (3rd ed.). Boston: Allyn & Bacon.

Tracy, E. M., & Whittaker, J. K. (1990). The social network map: Assessing social support in clinical practice. *Families in Society, 71* (8), 461–470.

Tropman, J. E., & Morningstar, G. (1995). The effective meeting: How to achieve high-quality decisions. In J. E. Tropman, J. L. Erlich, & J. Rothman (Eds.), *Tactics and techniques of community intervention* (3rd ed., pp. 412–426). Itasca, IL: F. E. Peacock.

Trotter, C. (1999). *Working with Involuntary Clients.* London: Sage

Truax, C., & Carkhuff, R. (1964). For better or for worse: The process of psychotherapeutic personality change. In *Recent advances in the study of behavior change* (pp. 118–163). Montreal: McGill University Press.

Truax, C., & Carkhuff, R. (1967). *Toward effective counseling and psychotherapy: Training and practice.* Chicago: Aldine-Atherton.

Truax, C., & Mitchell, K. (1971). Research on certain therapist interpersonal skills in relation to process and outcome. In A. Bergin & S. Garfield (Eds.), *Handbook of psychotherapy and behavior change* (pp. 299–344). New York: Wiley.

Tsui, P., & Schultz, G. L. (1985). Failure of rapport: Why psychotherapeutic engagement fails in the treatment of Asian clients. *American Journal of Orthopsychiatry, 55,* 561–569.

Tsui, P., & Schultz, G. L. (1988). Ethnic factors in group process: Cultural dynamics in multi-ethnic therapy groups. *American Journal of Orthopsychiatry, 58,* 136–142.

Tuckman, B. W., & Jenson, M. A. (1977). Stages of small group development revisited. *Group and Organization Studies, 2,* 419–427.

Turner, F. J. (Ed.) (1996). *Social work treatment: Interlocking theoretical approaches* (4th ed.). New York: Free Press.

U

Umbreit, M. S. (1993). Crime victims and offenders in mediation: An emerging area of social work practice. *Social Work, 38* (1), 69–73.

U.S. Department of Health and Human Services. (2003). *Office for Civil Rights: HIPAA.* Retrieved August 4, 2003, from *http://www.hhs.gov/ocr/hipaa/*

U.S. News & World Report. (2004, March 22–29). 50 years after Brown, Special Report. *136* (10), 65–95.

V

Vakalah, H. F., & Khajak, K. (2000). Parent to parent and family to family: Innovative self-help and mutual support. In A. Sallee, H. Lawson, & K. Briar-Lawson (Eds.), *Innovative practices with children and families* (pp. 271–290). Dubuque, IA: Eddie Bowers.

VandeCreek, L., Knapp, S., & Herzog, C. (1988). Privileged communication for social workers. *Social Casework, 69,* 28–34.

Van Hook, M. P., Berkman, B., & Dunkle, R. (1996). Assessment tools for general health care settings: PRIME-MD, OARS and SF-36. *Health and Social Work, 21* (3), 230–235.

Van Souest, D., & Garcia, B. (2003). *Diversity education for social justice.* Alexandria, VA: Council on Social Work Education.

Van Wormer, K. (2002). Our social work imagination: How social work has not abandoned its mission. *Journal of Teaching in Social Work, 22* (3/4), 21–37.

Van Wormer, K. (2003). Restorative justice: A model for social work practice with families. *Families in Society 84,* i3.

Van Wormer, K., & Boes (1997). Humor in the emergency room: A social work perspective. *Health and Social Work, 22* (2), 87–92.

Vernon, R., & Lynch, D. (2000). *Social work and the Web.* Belmont, CA: Wadsworth.

Videka-Sherman, L. (1988). Meta-analysis of research on social work practice in mental health. *Social Work, 33* (4), 325–338.

Vodde, R., & Gallant, J. P. (2002). Bridging the gap between micro and macro practice: Larger scale change and a unified model of narrative-deconstructive practice. *Journal of Social Work Education, 38* (3), 439–458.

Vosler, N. R. (1990). Assessing family access to basis resources: An essential component of social work practice. *Social Work, 35* (5), 434–441.

Voss, R. W., Douville, V., Little Soldier, A., & Twiss, G. (1999). Tribal and shamanic-based social work practice. A Lakota perspective. *Social Work, 44* (3), 228–241.

W

Wakefield, J. C. (1996a). Does social work need the ecosystems perspective? Part 1. Is the perspective clinically useful? *Social Service Review, 70* (1), 1–32.

Wakefield, J. C. (1996b). Does social work need the ecosystems perspective? Part 2. Does the perspective save social work from incoherence? *Social Service Review, 70* (2), 183–213.

Waldfogel, D., & Rosenblatt, A. (1983). Introduction: Clinical social work. In A. Rosenblatt & D. Waldfogel (Eds.), *Handbook of clinical social work* (pp. xxv–xxxii). San Francisco: Jossey-Bass.

Walen, S., DiGiuseppe, R., & Wessler, R. (1980). *A practitioner's guide to RET.* New York: Oxford University Press.

Walsh, J. (2000). *Clinical case management with persons having mental illness: A relationship-based approach.* Pacific Grove, CA: Brooks/Cole.

Walsh, J. (2003). *Endings in clinical practice: Effective closure in diverse settings.* Chicago: Lyceum Books.

Walsh, J., & Bentley, K. J. (2002). Psychopharmacology basics. In A. R. Roberts & G. J. Greene (Eds.), *Social workers' desk reference* (pp. 646–651). New York: Oxford University Press.

Waltman, G. H. (1996). Amish health care beliefs and practices. In M. C. Julia, *Multicultural awareness in the health care professions.* Needham Heights, MA: Allyn & Bacon.

Warren, K., Franklin, C., & Streeter, C. L. (1998). New directions in systems theory: Chaos and complexity. *Social Work, 43* (4), 357–372.

Wartel, S. (1991). Clinical considerations for adults abused as children. *Families in Society, 72* (3), 157–163.

Washington, O., & Moxley, D. (2003). Promising group practices to empower low income minority women coping with chemical dependency. *American Journal of Orthopsychiatry, 73* (1), 109–116.

Watkins, A. M. & Kurtz, P. D. (2001). Using solution-focused intervention to address African American male overrepresentation in special education: A case study. *Children & Schools, 23* (4), 223–234.

Watzlawick, P., Weakland, J., & Fisch, R. (1974). *Change: Principles of problem formulation.* New York: Norton.

Weaver, H. N. (2004). The elements of cultural competence: Application with Native American clients. *Journal of Ethics & Cultural Diversity in Social Work, 13* (1), 19–35.

Webb, N. B. (1996). The biopsychosocial assessment of the child. In *Social work practice with children* (pp. 57–98). New York: Guilford Press.

Webber, H. S. (1995). The failure of health-care reform: An essay review. *Social Service Review, 69* (2), 309–322.

Weick, A. (1992). Building a strengths perspective for social work. In D. Saleeby, *The strengths perspective in social work practice* (pp. 18–26). Menlo Park, CA: Longman.

Weick, A., & Saleebey, D. (1995). Supporting family strengths: Orienting policy and practice in the 21st century. *Families in Society, 76,* 141–149.

Weiner, M. F. (1984). *Techniques of group psychotherapy.* Washington, DC: American Psychiatric Press.

Weiner-Davis (1992). *Divorce-busting.* New York: Summit Books.

Weisz, J. R., Weiss, B., Wasserman, A. A., & Rintoul, B. (1987). Control-related beliefs and depression among clinic-referred children and adolescents. *Journal of Abnormal Psychology, 96,* 58–63.

Wells, R. (1975). Training in facilitative skills. *Social Work, 20,* 242–243.

Wells, R. A. (1994). *Planned short-term treatment* (2nd ed.). New York: Free Press.

Wells, R. A., & Gianetti. V. J. (Eds.). (1990). *Handbook of the brief psychotherapies.* New York: Plenum Press.

Wenar, C. (1994). *Developmental psychopathology from infancy through adolescence* (3rd ed.). New York: McGraw-Hill.

West, L., Mercer, S. O., & Altheimer, E. (1993). Operation Desert Storm: The response of a social work outreach team. *Social Work in Health Care, 19* (2), 81–98.

Westermeyer, J. J. (1993). Cross-cultural psychiatric assessment. In A. C. Gaw (Ed.), *Culture, ethnicity and mental illness* (pp. 125–146). Washington, DC: American Psychiatric Press.

Weston, K. (1991). *Families we choose: Lesbians, gays, and kinship.* New York: Columbia University Press.

Wexler, D. (1992). Putting mental health into mental health law: Therapeutic jurisprudence. *Law and Human Behavior, 16,* 27–38.

White, M., & Epston, D. (1990). *Narrative means to therapeutic ends.* New York: Norton.

Whiteman, M., Fanshel, D., & Grundy, J. (1987). Cognitive-behavioral interventions aimed at anger of parents at risk of child abuse. *Social Work, 32* (6), 469–474.

Whitfield, G. W. (1999). Validating school social work: An evaluation of a cognitive-behavioral approach to reduce school violence. *Research of Social Work Practice, 9* (4), 392–426.

Whittaker, J. K., & Tracy, E. M. (1989). *Social treatment: An introduction to interpersonal helping in social work practice.* New York: Aldine de Gruyter.

Williams, L. F. (1990). The challenge of education to social work: The case for minority children. *Social Work, 35* (3), 236–242.

Withorn, A. (1998). No win . . . facing the ethical perils of welfare reform. *Families in Society, 79* (3), 277–287.

Witkin, S. (1993). A human rights approach to social work research and evaluation. In J. Laird (Ed.), *Revisioning social work education: A social constructionist approach.* Binghamton, NY: Haworth Press.

Witkin, S. L. (1998). The right to effective treatment and the effective treatment of rights: Rhetorical empiricism and the politics of research. *Social Work, 43* (1), 75–80.

Wodarski, J. S., & Thyer, B. A. (1998). *Handbook of empirical social work practice. Volume 2: Social problems and practice issues.* New York: Wiley.

Wolf, K. T. (1991). The diagnostic and statistical manual and the misdiagnosis of African-Americans: An historical perspective. *Social Work Perspectives, 10* (1), 33–38.

Wood, K. (1978). Casework effectiveness: A new look at the research evidence. *Social Work, 23,* 437–458.

Worden, J. W. (1991). *Grief counseling and grief therapy: A handbook for the mental health practitioner.* New York: Springer.

Wright, O. L. Jr., & Anderson, J. P. (1998). Clinical social work practice with urban African American families. *Families in Society, 79* (2), 197–205.

Wright, W. (1999). The use of purpose in on-going activity groups: A framework for maximizing the therapeutic impact. *Social Work with Groups, 22* (2/3), 33–57.

Wylie, M. S. (1990). Brief therapy on the couch. *Family Therapy Networker, 14,* 26–34, 66.

Y

Yaffe, J., Jenson, J. M., & Howard, M. O. (1995). Women and substance abuse: Implications for treatment. *Alcoholism-Treatment Quarterly, 13* (2), 1–15.

Yalom, I. D. (1985). *The theory and practice of group psychotherapy* (2nd ed.). New York: Basic Books.

Yalom, I. D. (1995). *The theory and practice of group psychotherapy.* (4th ed.) New York: Basic Books.

Yalom, I. D., & Lieberman, M. (1971). A study of encounter group casualties. *Archives of General Psychiatry, 25,* 16–30.

Yamamoto, J., Silva, J. A., Justice, L. R., Chang, C. Y., & Leong, G. B. (1993). Cross-cultural psychotherapy. In A. C. Gaw (Ed.), *Culture, ethnicity and mental illness* (pp. 101–124). Washington, DC: American Psychiatric Press.

Yamashiro, G., & Matsuoka, J. (1997). *Help seeking among Asian and Pacific Americans: A multi-perspective analysis.* Washington, DC: NASW Press.

Z

Zastrow, C., & Kirst-Ashman, K. (1990). *Understanding human behavior and the social environment* (2nd ed.). Chicago: Nelson-Hall.

Zechetmayr, M. (1997). Native Americans: A neglected health care crisis and a solution. *Journal of Health and Social Policy, 9* (2), 29–47.

Zeira, A., Astor, R. A., & Benbenishty, R. (2003). School violence in Israel: Findings of a national survey. *Social Work, 48* (4), 471–483.

Zimmerman, S. L. (1995). *Understanding family policy: Theories and applications* (2nd ed.). Thousand Oaks, CA: Sage Publications.

Zipple, M., & Spaniol, L. (1987). Current educational and supportive models of family intervention. In A. B. Hatfield & H. P. Lefley (Eds.), *Families of the mentally ill.* New York: Guilford Press.

Zuckerman, E. L. (1997). *The paper office: Forms, guidelines, and resources* (2nd ed.). New York: Guilford Press.

Zung, W. (1965). A self-rating depression scale. *Archives of General Psychiatry, 12,* 63–70.

Author Index

Subject Index